Mastering Psychology

Mastering Psychology

Third Edition

Lester A. Lefton
University of South Carolina

Laura Valvatne

ALLYN AND BACON, INC. Boston London Sydney Toronto

Managing Editor: Mylan Jaixen
Series Editor: John-Paul Lenney
Developmental Editor: Wendy Ritger
Production Editor: Peter Petraitis
Senior Editorial Assistant: Leslie Galton
Text Designer/art coordinator: Karen Mason
Photo Research: Laurel Anderson
Cover Coordinator: Linda Dickinson
Composition Buyer: Linda Cox
Manufacturing Buyer: Bill Alberti

Library of Congress Cataloging-in-Publication Data

Lefton, Lester A., 1946–
    Mastering psychology.

    Bibliography: p. 649
    Includes indexes.
    1. Psychology.   I. Valvatne, Laura.   II. Title.
BF121.L423 1988   150   87-14429
    ISBN 0-205-10626-9

Printed in the United States of America
10 9 8 7 6 5 4 3 2   92 91 90 89 88

Credits

Photo Credits:

CHAPTER ONE Opener—Lee Boltin. p. 6—E. Herwig (The Picture Cube).
p. 8—J. Goell (The Picture Cube). p. 11—K. Buck (The Picture Cube). p. 17, left
to right—Historical Picture Service; The Library of Congress; Granger Collection,
Historical Picture Service. p. 18, left to right—Archives of the History of Ameri-
can Psychology; Larry Murphy (Courtesy, The Univ. of Texas at Austin; Courtesy
Dr. E. Loftus; Courtesy Dr. J. Rodin. p. 21—D. Strickler (The Picture Cube). p. 27
—Courtesy, Dr. Goodale. p. 29—S. Takatsuno (The Picture Cube). **CHAPTER
TWO** Opener—Russ Schleipman. p. 36—E. Roth (The Picture Cube). p. 41—
D. Strickler (The Picture Cube). p. 49—Courtesy, B. F. Skinner. p. 50—J. Albert-
son (The Picture Cube). p. 55—S. Johnson (The Picture Cube). p. 57—S. Lewis
(The Picture Cube). p. 62—D. Strickler (The Picture Cube). p. 67—F. Siteman
(The Picture Cube). **CHAPTER THREE** Opener—John Curtis (Styling by Photo-
synthesis). p. 76—F. Bodin. p. 77—Historical Picture Services. p. 78—S. Takat-
suno (The Picture Cube). p. 80—T. Cordingley. p. 83—F. Siteman (The Picture
Cube). p. 89—J. DeMaio (The Picture Cube). p. 94—T. Cordingley. **CHAPTER
FOUR** Opener—Greg Louganis (Stock, Boston). p. 103—D. Strickler (The Pic-
ture Cube). p. 117—F. Bodin. p. 127—K. Buck (The Picture Cube). p. 139—E.
Hoffman (Archive). **CHAPTER FIVE** Opener—Ellis Herwig (The Picture Cube).
p. 148—D. Phillips (The Picture Cube). p. 150—Courtesy, Dr. Neal Miller. p. 154
—E. Herwig (The Picture Cube). p. 156—Dennis Stock (Magnum Photo). p. 162
—Courtesy, Harvard University Press. p. 166—F. Bodin. p. 173—Courtesy,
Dr. Harlow. **CHAPTER SIX** Opener—Stanley Rowan (The Picture Cube). p. 189
—Phaneuf-Gurdzier (The Picture Cube). p. 207—F. Bodin. p. 222—F. Bodin.
p. 227—E. Herwig (The Picture Cube). **Color Insert**—Seurat painting (3 Lions);
Parachute interior (B. Kliewe/Picture Cube); Potter (G. Roberts/Picture Cube);
Skiier (D. Lissy/Picture Cube). Brain (D. Mollerstuen); Football (M. Godfrey/Ar-
chive). **CHAPTER SEVEN** Opener—David Dempster. p. 241—M. Feinberg (The
Picture Cube). p. 244--Courtesy, Dr. David Linton. The Image Works. p. 250
—S. Takatsuno (The Picture Cube). p. 257—C. Palmer (The Picture Cube). p. 264
—B. Griffith (The Picture Cube). p. 267—C. Palmer (The Picture Cube). **Color
Insert**—Fetal series (Dr. Lennart Nilsson; from A CHILD IS BORN); Infant
(D. Dempster); Infant & toys (S. Ries/Picture Cube). Boy & bear (S. Weigand/
Picture Cube). **CHAPTER EIGHT** Opener John Curtis. p. 281—P. Chandoha.

p. 283—D. Schaeffer (The Picture Cube). p. 294—P. Chandoha. p. 296—M. Vin-
toniv (The Picture Cube). p. 304—D. Strickler (The Picture Cube). p. 311—R. Wood
(The Picture Cube). p. 318—J. D. Sloane (The Picture Cube). p. 320—National
Library of Medicine. **CHAPTER NINE** Opener—John Fogle (The Picture Cube).
p. 327—F. Bodin. p. 333—Courtesy, The Gorilla Foundation. p. 337—D. Strickler
(The Picture Cube). p. 348—Courtesy, N. and D. Kaufman. p. 352L—D. Strickler
(The Picture Cube). p. 352R—G. Cassidy (The Picture Cube). p. 359—P. Price
(The Picture Cube). p. 363—H. Ellis (The Picture Cube). **CHAPTER TEN** Opener
—David Dempster. p. 374—A. Brilliant (The Picture Cube). p. 376—E. Herwig
(The Picture Cube). p. 381—F. Siteman (The Picture Cube). p. 386—S. Stone
(The Picture Cube). p. 394—M. McGovern (The Picture Cube). p. 397—J. Walker
(The Picture Cube). p. 398T—P. Lerner (The Picture Cube). p. 398B—Cour-
tesy Alexandra Milgrim. p. 403—F. Siteman (The Picture Cube). **CHAPTER
ELEVEN** Opener—David Dempster. p. 417—S. Lapides. p. 419L—E. Herwig
(The Picture Cube). p. 419R—D. Grossman (Photo-Researchers Inc.). p. 422—
Bettmann Newsphotos. p. 425—T. Cordingley. p. 429—S. Lapides. p. 431—
Courtesy, Masters & Johnson Institute. p. 440—S. Lapides. p. 442—E. Kroll
(Taurus). p. 445—T. Cordingley. **CHAPTER TWELVE** Opener—George Cassidy
(The Picture Cube). p. 458—S. Lapides. p. 459—E. Kroll (Taurus). p. 467—
E. Stone (Photo-Researchers, Inc.). p. 473T—The Bettmann Archive. p. 473B
—Wide World Photos. p. 475—E. Saloman (Magnum). p. 479—L. Freed (Mag-
num). p. 485—R. Wood (The Picture Cube). p. 493—D. Schaeffer (The Picture
Cube). **CHAPTER THIRTEEN** Opener—Bobbi Carrey (The Picture Cube). p. 504
—R. Frerck (Odyssey Productions). p. 507—A. Kandell (Photo Researchers,
Inc.). p. 513—H. Schafes (Peter Arnold, Inc.). p. 518—A. Tress (Photo Research-
ers, Inc.). p. 523—A. Menashe (Photo Researchers, Inc.). p. 528—E. Bishop
(The Picture Cube). p. 537—S. Lapides. **CHAPTER FOURTEEN** Opener—
Arnold Kaplan (The Picture Cube). p. 552—The Memory Shop. p. 553—S. Rosen-
berg (Photo Researchers, Inc.) p. 558—Bettmann Newsphotos. p. 560—E. Kroll
(Taurus). p. 565—M. Heitner (Taurus). p. 572—B. Freer (Photo Researchers,
Inc.). p. 575—Dr. Jay Weissberg (Photo Researchers, Inc.). **CHAPTER FIFTEEN**

Credits continue on page 699, which constitutes an extension of the copyright page.

Contents

3 **Memory** *73*

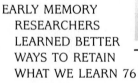

4 **Biology of
Behavior and
Consciousness**
99

5 **Motivation
and
Emotion** *145*

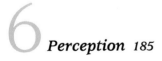

8 *Adolescence and Adulthood* 277

9 *Language and Intelligence* 323

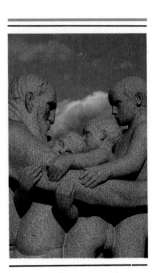

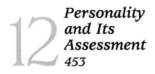

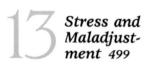

15 *Psycho-therapy* 585

Appendix

Scientific and Statistical Methods 625

Preface

Writing this third edition of *Mastering Psychology* was an exciting undertaking. We did it with the help of dozens of reviewers and students and the results show that a team effort can produce dynamic results. This edition is clearly our best effort. This new edition marks both continuation and departure. We have continued to focus on teaching the science of psychology, and on showing how psychology applies to every day decision making. We have refined this focus by updating content and the format of the text and we have also emphasized key themes. In addition, we have continued to use the *SQ3R* learning system that has made this text so popular. We have departed from previous editions by deleting outdated references, sharpening the writing, and by placing considerably more emphasis on applications. Our goal was to present a refreshing, intellectually accurate view of psychology, but also one which stresses applications. We feel that the outcome is a bright and fresh approach to the teaching, science, and application of psychology.

CONTENT

In this edition we give increased emphasis to several important themes. These themes are often highlighted in newly written panel inserts which occur in each chapter. One such theme is the growing dominance of a cognitive approach to psychology. The chapters on Memory, Personality, Therapy, and Maladjustment especially highlight the role of cognitive decision-making in shaping behavior, though these chapters also stress the traditionally recognized role of biology and learning through reinforcement.

Another closely related and clearly highlighted theme is the complex interaction among biology, learning, and thought processes. While avoiding simplistic evaluations, the text shows clearly where biology may play a more important role than learning—in schizophrenia, for example. In the same manner, learning and environment may play a greater role than any biological predisposition in disorders such as Anorexia Nervosa. We stress the relative importance of nature and nurture, and how extreme care is necessary when laboratory research is generalized to whole populations.

This text has been extensively rewritten and many new, important topics have been included. The Personality chapter, for example, now includes trait and type theory and behavioral assessment. We show behavioral assessment as an adjunct to traditional assessment techniques—this is an example of our attempt to give contemporary formulations to traditional psychological ideas. There is new material on procrastination and what to do about it. There is now coverage of loneliness, rape, and bipolar disorders. The clinically-oriented chapters recognize the new *DSM-III-R* that was published in 1987. There is new coverage of sociobiology and pheremones; there is also coverage of parenthood after age thirty. Every chapter reflects new, expanded, and exciting topical coverage. The following list includes some of the new and expanded topics:

mid-life crisis	eyewitness testimony
brief intermittent therapy	compulsive gambling

women in psychology   job opportunities
sleepiness   single parenting
latchkey children   shyness
ageism   Alzheimer's disease
language disorders   psychoendocrinology
Stress vulnerability   Bulimia Nervosa

STYLE AND ORGANIZATION

Even the best conceived ideas need to be presented in a way which is carefully organized so that those ideas are accessible to students. The format of *Mastering Psychology* has been changed to reflect a more contemporary look which is easier for students to follow. New photographs have been chosen and art redrawn. The text is still 15 chapters in length, plus an Appendix. We have broken interesting and complicated topics such as Learning, Development, and Maladjustment into two chapter units. Some new topical reorganization allows us to show applications more clearly.

PEDAGOGY

The *SQ3R* system provides an organizational framework for learning the material in each chapter. The main **learning objectives** are spelled out at the beginning of each chapter. Each numbered learning objective is then highlighted in the margin adjacent to the text that describes its content. These learning objectives serve as helpful reference points in the *SQ3R* learning system. Students have the opportunity to pause and review their progress through **progress checks,** at convenient division points within each chapter. **Application exercises** at the end of each chapter help students apply generalized knowledge in real life examples. **Self tests,** which occur at the end of each chapter, provide a mini-examination for students to measure their mastery of concepts and their readiness for a real-life examination. The answers to all of these study guide elements are provided for the students with the self-test answers at the end of the text.

This book was written for students; its *SQ3R* method and pedagogical aids help accomplish the goals of providing a vehicle by which students can take an active and participatory role in learning. We have tried to use the very principles we teach in preparing this book. Students are provided immediate feedback, which facilitates learning and performance.

ACKNOWLEDGEMENTS

Writing a textbook is like building a house, it involves many individuals to help in its construction. Students and professors from throughout this country helped us review sections, chapters, and then the entire manuscript. They provided advice, comments, criticisms, and ideas for new topics. Others helped in the planning of this edition by responding to a detailed questionaire, providing advice on how to improve the book. We are especially grateful to all of them. Space limitations do not allow an exhaustive list, however, we feel compelled to single out some of the individuals who went beyond the call of duty and who were especially helpful in preparing this book.

Ronald Murdoff
San Joaquin Delta College

Faye Dumbrot
University of Akron

Donald M. Stanley
North Harris County College

Phil Lau
DeAnza Community College

Carole A. Kendig
Seton Hall University

Velton Lacefield
Prairie State College

Dirk D. Steiner
Louisiana State University

James R. Counsil
North Dakota State University

Henry L. Moreland
Florida Community College at Jacksonville

Dale H. Melton
Manatee Community College

Bobby J. Poe
Belleville Area College

Paula M. Popovich
Ohio University

Rosemary Reed
Seattle Community College

Hal Kiess
Framingham State College

Richard J. McCarbery
Lorain County Community College

David Griese
SUNY-Farmingdale

James M. Knight
Humboldt State University

Allen R. Branum
South Dakota State University

Randy P. Quevillon
University of South Dakota

K. W. Steere
Manchester Community College

Robert T. Wiater
Bergen Community College

Wayne A. Lenko
Marymount University

George Kaluger
Shippensburg University

Tirzah Schutzengel
Bergen Community College

Janice L. Hartgrove-Freile
North Harris County College

Linda L. Lamwers
St. Cloud State University

Gene Cunningham
Henry Ford Community College

Edgar E. Hawkes
Virginia Commonwealth University

Steven G. Cole
Texas Christian University

Jack A. Kapchan
University of Miami

Louis Tharp
Long Beach City College

Dick Eglsae
Sam Houston State

Ray V. Coleman
Mt. Washusett Community College

Harve E. Rawson
Hanover College

Thomas D. Graves
Mesa College

Rosemary Reed
Seattle Community College

Garvin Chastain
Boise State University

Bonnie M. Wright
Gardner-Webb College

Lynn McCutcheon
Northern Virginia Community College

Jerry J. Wisner
FCCJ-North Campus

Linden Nelson
Cal Poly, San Luis Obispo

George C. Rogers
Massachusetts Bay Community College

Lawrence I. Rosenkoetter
Bethany College

Donald M. Stanley
North Harris County College

Kurt F. Geisinger
Fordham University

Ann McNeer
Polk Community College

Paul F. Cunningham
Rivier College

Judith Bridges
University of Connecticut at Hartford

Judith L. Gibbons
St. Louis University

Michael J. Ross
St. Louis University

Irwin Kahn
Ferris State College

Richard J. McCarbery
Lorain County Community College

Dirk D. Steiner
Louisiana State University

John S. Childers
East Carolina University

Velton Lacefield
Prairie State College

Roger L. Terry
Hanover College

Elizabeth A. Andrews
Westbrook College

Peter Flynn
Northern Essex Community College

Charles A. Graessle
Olivet College

Cheryl B. Bradley
Central Virginia Community College

Richard A. Kribs III
Motlow State Community College

Roger G. Gaddis
Gardner-Webb College

Mike Aamodt
Radford University

Benjamin Wallace
Cleveland State University

Writing a textbook essentially becomes a group effort; it takes a whole team of dedicated and talented people to execute a final product. The production and editorial staff at Allyn & Bacon are the best in the industry. Karen Mason and Leslie Galton did superb work designing the book and choosing tasteful photographs. Production administrator Peter Petraitis managed the complex details of the production process with accuracy, skill, and good humor. Working with Peter on a daily basis was a pleasure and this text reflects his fine book-making skills.

Long before production, it was the skilled and clear thinking efforts of developmental editor Wendy Ritger who helped shape *Mastering Psychology;* Wendy worked on previous editions of this text but her imprint is clearly stamped through the pages of this book. We extend our special thanks to John-Paul Lenney whose vision for this project guided our day-to-day activities. His insights into the needs of the introductory psychology instructors are astute; John-Paul's understanding of the intricacies of the balance between scholarship, application, and good writing guided our routine and not so routine decision making processes. We are grateful for his guidance.

We dedicate this book to our spouses, Linda Lefton and Larry Wayne Skeels.

To the Student

Study and Learning Tips
for Keeping Pace with This Book

AFTER SEVEN YEARS OF working as a carpenter, Martin decided he wanted to go back to college and complete his business degree; he ultimately wanted to start his own construction company. Judy, Martin's wife, also wanted to return to college. She had a strong drive to become a child psychologist so she could help children, including her own, become successful, loving, and emotionally stable citizens. The idea of going back to college together thrilled Martin and Judy; but, it scared them too. Could they do it? Martin and Judy were busy people. They could not afford to leave their jobs, they had two children who needed a lot of attention, and they had an important network of friends and relatives.

As Judy and Martin discussed their desires and goals for the future, they realized that they had to give themselves this opportunity—they wanted their degrees and they wanted to learn from their classes. They knew that life would not be the same as it had been seven years ago, when they had few responsibilities, their parents paid for tuition and books, and they were full-time students with plenty of time to study.

On their way home from registering for two classes each, Martin said, "Jude, do you remember how to study?" Judy replied, "I think so, but I've never felt very good at it. I always felt slow and that somehow I was missing something." Martin realized that they may have just jumped in over their heads with school work and said "We have to find some study methods that work and we are going to have to be tigers about managing our time. Let's call Josh; I think he can give us some tips."

Josh was delighted to hear from Martin and Judy; he was proud of their decision to return to college; and because he had struggled with the art of studying, he could empathize with their concerns. Judy and Martin were intrigued as Josh told them about the SQ3R study method he had learned when he took his first psychology class. He said, "This study method is great! It gets you involved in studying chapters in a book, and by being involved you learn what you need to know." Josh promised he would drop by the next day to explain the SQ3R method and that he would loan them his book so they could read about it themselves. Judy and Martin went to sleep that night with images of their future and a sense of hope.

WHAT DOES IT TAKE TO LEARN?

The next day, Josh spent several hours talking to Judy and Martin about SQ3R, memory, time management, motivation, and other techniques that could make their study time worthwhile time. "Psychologists know about these techniques," Josh said; "they have been studying what people need in order to learn and remember for years." As he left, he handed Martin his psychology book and said, "You and Judy read the 'To The Student' section in this book. It will explain all that I've told you and, if you do what it says, you'll get good grades in all of your classes."

Josh had learned well from his psychology course. Not only had he developed skills that allowed him to increase Martin's and Judy's confidence and level of motivation, but he also was accurate in telling them that psychologists know a great deal about how learning occurs and how people remember what they learn. Based on many research studies, psychologists know that you will be more successful if (1) *you organize the material you want to learn; (2) focus your attention on the information you are studying; (3) actively participate by asking and answering questions as you read and listen; (4) study small amounts of material at a time; (5) rehearse the information you are trying to learn; and (6) receive immediate feedback concerning your progress.* This book not only discusses these research studies, but it also puts the knowledge gained from them to work for you. The popular study method based on these principles of learning, known as the SQ3R approach, is used throughout this book to help you learn psychology and the study method itself. If you carefully follow the SQ3R study sequence, you will fulfill each of the activities italicized above. These activities are essential to learning and to remembering what you learn; and many students, like Josh, have found the SQ3R study method to be necessary to their academic success. This is the right time—before you begin studying—to take a closer look at each step involved in the SQ3R study method and at how it is used in this book.

SQ3R: AN ACTIVE READING AND STUDY METHOD

Judy and Martin had looked bewildered when Josh first named his foolproof study method, SQ3R; but, their lost looks quickly disappeared as Josh explained that SQ3R is an acronym for *survey, question, read, recite,* and *review.* If you have never used this five-step strategy, you will discover, as many other students have, that it is an easy-to-follow, effective, and efficient method for studying and learning textbook material. SQ3R works because it takes you away from passive attempts at learning into the realm of actively participating with the reading material. The importance of this has been demonstrated in a number of studies of learning and memory; *being involved with what you are trying to learn is the critical ingredient in learning!* With this in mind, take some time now to explore the steps involved in the SQ3R strategy and how you can use them to keep pace with this text.

Survey

First, observe the title of the chapter, and in this text, read the *learning objectives* listed at the chapter opening. Next, skim over the pages within the chapter assigned for reading. While surveying the chapter, focus your attention on topic headings and subheadings, the captions that accompany pictures, tables, and graphs, and any special features such as boxed material and learning aids. *Your purpose in surveying the chapter is to (1) see how the chapter is organized, (2) form an idea of what is to be learned, and (3) set goals for the amount of material you realistically would like to cover in one study session.* Before reading on, take some time to survey one chapter in this text so you can get an idea about its organization and special features.

To help survey what is to be learned, each chapter in *Mastering Psychology* provides you with a complete survey system, beginning with the numbered **learning objectives** at the chapter openings. These objectives are formal statements of what you must do to show mastery of key concepts in psychology, and you should consider them carefully and refer to them frequently as you study. To help you spot where the text will start discussing each concept, a colored "callout" in the margin provides the reference number for each **learning objective** where it applies. This **margin learning objective number** will direct you back to the chapter-opening statement of objectives, and later, after you have checked your Progress Check and Self-Test answers, you can use the margin learning objective numbers to locate the appropriate text pages for restudying and reviewing the material.

Setting a goal for the amount of material you want to cover in a study session can be done while you survey the chapter. Consider using the Progress Check sections as a point to take a break or end your study session for the day.

Question

Second, while surveying and later when you are reading the chapter, ask some original questions about the information being presented. While surveying, you can turn chapter subheadings into questions. For instance, you might turn the subheading "Sleep Deprivation" on page 136 into a question like, "Why do psychologists care about sleep deprivation? or you could turn the caption, "Schedules of Reinforcement" that accompanies Figure 2.12 on page 56, into the question, "What is a schedule of reinforcement?" While you are reading, ask yourself questions about material you do not understand or understand but want to know more about, and then go to appropriate resources to find answers.

Asking your own questions before you begin to read will increase your interest, involvement, and concentration while you read because, with each question, you will have the goal of finding an answer. The question stage of SQ3R will prove even more effective if you take the time to *write down* your questions and, later as you are reading, their answers.

In addition, a look ahead at the **Progress Check** sections will help alert you to some of the questions you can answer by a careful reading of the text.

Read

After you have surveyed the chapter and formulated some initial questions about the text material, begin reading. As you read, (1) answer your initial questions; (2) refer to the chapter opening **learning objectives** each time you come across a **margin learning objective number** so you can focus on what to learn in the section you are reading; and (3) continue asking and answering your own questions concerning the information you are reading. *Focusing on* *what you are supposed to learn and continually asking and answering your own questions as you read will help you be an active participant and a successful learner.*

Recite

To recite means to repeat something from memory. *This fourth step of SQ3R suggests that you call on your memory to rehearse the information you have read.* With *Mastering Psychology,* there are three ways in which you can approach the recitation step; using all three approaches will prove to be most effective. The first, and standard, SQ3R approach to reciting is to refer to the questions *you* asked and to answer them again from memory.

This method of course, will work if you took the time to write down your questions as you asked them. A second approach is to turn to the chapter opening **learning objectives** and recite everything you can remember in support of them. The third approach is to rely on your memory to answer all of the matching and sentence completion items in the **Progress Check** exercises. As you complete each one, check your answers (in the answer section at the chapter end) and restudy any information you have forgotten—using the **learning objective** numbers for reference—before you read any further in the text.

Review

The review step of SQ3R encourages you to double check your understanding and memory of the chapter information; you try to pull together individual concepts and subtopics within the chapter so you have a complete, organized understanding about the chapter topic. *During this stage of learning, you will want to set everything you have studied into long-term memory.* Review the chapter in the following four ways:

- ☐ Restudy your own questions and answers and compare them with the text.
- ☐ Check the **margin definition** terms to see if you can provide definitions without looking.
- ☐ Restudy **Progress Checks** to be sure you understand the correct answers and the **learning objective,** with its text coverage, to which the questions refer.
- ☐ To insure meaningful learning and better long-term memory of the concepts in the text, test your comprehension and ability to apply your knowledge by completing the **Applying Principles** sections at the end of each chapter.

After thoroughly reviewing, take the **Self-Test** as if it were a graded test given in class. The test results will give you *immediate feedback* about how well you have learned the chapter material. If you miss any questions on the **Self-Test,** use the learning objective reference number to trace back to the **margin learning objective** number where you will find the appropriate discussion of any concepts you need to restudy and review. (See Table 1.)

TIME MANAGEMENT: SCHEDULING YOUR STUDY TIME

Martin and Judy, the students preparing to return to college who opened this section, knew that time management was going to be essential if they were going to keep up with their work, have time for their family and friends, and

TABLE 1: LEARNING AIDS IN MASTERING PSYCHOLOGY

Learning Aid	When to Use	How to Use
Learning Objectives (at the chapter opening)	When surveying, reading, reciting, and reviewing text material	To form an idea of what is to be learned from reading
		To organize information read in the text in a meaningful way
		To recall topics that should be studied and learned
		To practice for exams
Margin Learning Objective Numbers	When reading and reviewing the text	To identify the location of information that supports the Chapter Learning Objectives
Progress Checks (at the end of each subsection)	When reciting and reviewing the text information	To break the chapter into small amounts of study material
		To rehearse text information and set it into memory
		To check your understanding about what you have read
Applying Principles (at chapter end)	When reciting and reviewing the text information	To make the concepts you have read about meaningful
Self-Test (at chapter end)	When reciting and reviewing	To double-check your understanding of what you have read and studied in the text
Study Guide Answers (at end of text)	When reciting and reviewing	To identify your weak areas and know what information needs more study
		To receive immediate feedback about how well you have learned

succeed in their courses. One thing that will help Martin and Judy, and yourself, to focus in on priorities and be efficient with time is to develop a time schedule that can be followed. Once you have attended the first session of each of your classes, plan a weekly study schedule for this and other courses based on the workload you expect to have for each class, your personal needs, your family's needs, and any other obligations you may have. People are often not realistic about their time and think they can do more in a given period than they actually can. When planning your schedule, try very hard to be reasonable; allow time for the unexpected and remember that you have obligations other than school. The study units marked out by the **Progress Checks** may help you plan reasonable study sessions for this course.

BECOMING MOTIVATED: REVIEW YOUR EDUCATIONAL AND PROFESSIONAL GOALS

Martin and Judy have goals that will help them succeed with their studies. Martin wants to become a successful businessman so he can provide his family with some luxuries they currently cannot afford. Judy is determined to become an outstanding child psychologist. Because they have clear goals, Martin and Judy are one step ahead of some students entering college but even they may have trouble feeling motivated when they find themselves enrolled in certain classes. Sometimes students have not decided what their long-term goals are, or they have a professional goal but do not understand how a particular class is going to contribute to their eventual success on the job. When the importance of a class is not clear, putting a lot of effort into learning can seem like a waste of time. Each time you begin a new class, you will find it useful to think about why you are taking the class and decide how it fits in with your long-term educational and professional goals. For example, you are currently enrolled in introductory psychology. How will this class help you with your professional goals? With your personal life? Is it a class required for you major? Knowing why a class is of value to you will help you feel motivated to study and master the material presented. If you cannot think of a meaningful reason for taking the class, perhaps you should talk to your teacher or an advisor. Almost every class has value, but pinpointing the value for yourself may require some careful consideration. In any case, a lack of interest in the class from the outset will probably lead you to struggle through, feel frustrated, and continually wish the term would end. This attitude is not conductive to good study skills.

TWO MEMORY TOOLS: MNEMONICS AND IMAGERY

In Chapter 3, you will read about some techniques described by psychologist Laird Cermak that you can use to increase your memory of new material. One technique is called *mnemonics.* Mnemonics allows you to organize seemingly meaningless material into meaningful stories, words, or phrases. SQ3R is a mnemonic that makes it easy to remember the five-step study method: survey, question, read, recite, review. The first letter of each word was used to make an easy-to-remember phrase. Here is another example. If you wanted to remember the words Skinner, reinforcement, behaviorism, schedule, and conditioning, you could create a story like this:

> A fur *Skinner* received his *reinforcement* of supplies when the helpful *behaviorism* tribe arrived on *schedule* bringing the oils needed for *conditioning* the rabbit skins.

Or, if you wanted to remember the names Sabrina, Ulysses, Romeo, Pandora, Raina, Isis, Sebastian, and Exekiel, you could create one word, the word SURPRISE, to help remember them. Mnemonics provides you with cues for recalling necessary information.

Another aid to memory about which you will read in Chapter 6 is imagery. This technique encourages you to use all of your senses and create images in your mind's eye as you study. By doing so, you will be more likely to remember what you are learning because you are calling on an increased number of memory connections in your brain. For example, if you are studying about a psychologist who conducted an experiment with college students and as a part of the experiment the students were asked to drink cherry, lime, or coconut juice, visualize yourself as one of those students; visualize the movements you would make and the emotions you would feel, in your mind see the colors of the juices, imagine the different tastes and smells, and imagine how the different juices might feel on your tongue. This is just one example; as you study use your imagination and see how well you can visualize even the most seemingly stagnant and boring information. Keep in mind that your images can be very personal; there are no right or wrong images. The important thing is that they help you remember the facts.

MEMORIZATION VERSUS UNDERSTANDING

Meaningful learning is much more permanent than simple memorization. To make the things you are learning about meaningful, try to apply the concepts you are studying to your own experiences, look up unfamiliar words, pay attention to examples given in your textbook, and make good use of the **Applying Principles** exercises at the end of each chapter in *Mastering Psychology*. These special exercises allow you to test your understanding by applying the text's psychology concepts to real-life situations. If you can transfer your textbook knowledge successfully into these examples from everyday life, you will truly have shown a mastery of psychology.

CLASSROOM BEHAVIORS

Active Listening

Although entertainment, socializing with your peers, and conforming to your teacher's expectations may be among your reasons for attending classroom lectures, your primary reasons are probably to listen and learn. As with reading, to be a successful learner through listening you must be an active participant. Here are five tips that might help:

- ☐ Exercise control over your thoughts by consciously directing your attention toward what is being said.
- ☐ Allow the speaker's lead-in statements to act as cues that important information is about to be given. Lead-in statements will begin with such phrases as "The main idea . . . ," "There are four approaches . . . ," "Another viewpoint . . . ," "In conclusion . . . ," and so on.
- ☐ Silently ask yourself questions about what is being said, and, as the lecture proceeds, try to answer them.
- ☐ Ask questions out loud in class, when the lecturer is ready for them, to clarify anything you missed or did not understand.
- ☐ Try to make connections between what is being said now and what you recall from previous lectures or text material.

Taking Notes

Listening and writing at the same time can be somewhat distracting. If you are listening actively and intently, you may find it difficult to write down as much as you would like; if you are writing a lot down, you may find yourself falling behind and missing parts of the lecture. For these reasons, it is important to give some thought toward your listening/notetaking approach, and during the first few lectures of a course adapt your listening and notetaking skills to the style and pace of the lecturer.

As with reading and listening, notetaking can become merely a passive activity. If your approach to notetaking involves trying to write down, word-for-word, just about everything that the lecturer says, you will be more involved in getting words on paper than in focusing your attention and asking questions about what points are important. An effective approach for successful classroom learning is to be an active listener and take well-organized and brief yet explicit notes, making them complete enough to provide you with an overview of the entire lecture. Here are three ideas that may help you take good class lecture notes.

☐ Use an 8½″ × 11″ three-ring binder that allows you to add and remove pages. This will allow you to keep all of your notes in one place and in order.
☐ Develop an outlining system that works well for you. Your outline of what is said in the lecture should reflect major ideas, minor points that follow those ideas, and the relationships among ideas. Complete sentences take time to write and, for the most part, are unnecessary. Try to catch the lecture ideas in short phrases that include key words.
☐ Make some notation of all ideas brought out in the lecture, even those you have read about in the text or already know, so you can be reminded of all of the ideas the lecturer felt were important to the main lecture topic.

Facing Exams

The key to achieving top scores on exams given in class is feeling relaxed and confident while you take the test. These feelings will come about if you are well prepared.

Preparing for Exams

Preparing for exams should be an ongoing process. As you read your text, listen in class and take lecture notes; keep in mind—an exam is coming. Then, about one week before an exam, begin your "cram" sessions. Don't wait until the day before because time pressure, low energy states, and unexpected events are too likely to arise and interfere with your ability to prepare well. About a week before the exam, you should take the following five steps:

☐ Ask your instructor what the exam will cover, what material will be omitted, and what kinds of questions will be used.
☐ Make a list of things you must know and rank them according to their importance. You will want to give the most important and difficult concepts more preparation time.
☐ Spend some time predicting test questions. How might they be worded? How general or detailed might they be? How might two or more concepts be combined into one question?
☐ Begin reviewing. Your text, lecture notes, SQ3R questions and answers, the chapter **learning objectives,** the **Progress Checks,** and the **Self-Test** will become extremely useful tools at this time.
☐ Schedule group study sessions with other students. Sharing ideas about what might be covered on the test and talking out loud about the things you have learned will help clarify and solidify your understanding.

Answering Essay Test Questions

Essay test questions require that you know the material well enough to be able to recall from memory, in an organized way, both major and minor points that will provide an answer. When presented with an essay test, keep these five steps in mind.

☐ Before you begin to answer any test questions, read all of the questions and make some quick notes about the major and minor points you will want to cover when answering them.

☐ Estimate how much time you should give to each question and try to stick to your schedule. You will want to allow more time for difficult questions and questions that carry more points toward scoring of the test. If possible, plan to have some time in the last minutes of the class session to review and polish your answers.

☐ Answer the easier questions first.

☐ Answer each question as directly as possible and avoid wandering and writing too much or too little.

☐ Leave a few blank lines between answers so you can go back and add ideas if time allows.

Answering Objective Test Questions

Objective test questions include multiple-choice, true-false, and matching questions. These questions require you to recognize and discriminate among correct and incorrect answers; the **Progress Checks** and **Self-Tests** should give you good practice for this. When taking an objective test keep the following in mind.

☐ Read each question carefully and completely; do not jump to conclusions and assume you have the correct answer until you have read and considered the entire question.

☐ Give careful thought to questions that include words such as *always, never, all, tendency,* or *sometimes.* The first three terms may indicate that the statement is too extreme and perhaps false; the last two terms show more qualified conditions, suggesting that the statement may be true; however, these rules are not absolute.

☐ Treat each alternative in a multiple-choice test question as a true-false statement. Eliminate alternatives that are definitely false, and if more than one answer seems to be true, choose the one that most thoroughly and directly answers the question.

☐ Do not spend too much time on any one question. If you are unsure of an answer, put a check mark in the margin next to the question and go back to it later.

☐ The rule of thumb about changing answers is to stick with your original answer unless you have *strong* second thoughts about it. If you feel reasonably sure that your second thoughts are correct, then go ahead and change the answer.

SOME FINAL COMMENTS

A student who does well in college plans a study schedule, studies as an active participant, makes use of organized study methods such as SQ3R, and feels confident and at ease with the learning process.

Being a good student does not come naturally or easily for most people. It takes self-discipline, realistic scheduling, and a true desire to succeed. The important thing to remember is that almost anyone who wants to be a good student can be. We sincerely hope you enjoy your experience with *Mastering Psychology* and that it helps you achieve your goals of being a successful student.

Mastering
Psychology

1

What Is Psychology?

1

Learning Objectives

When you have mastered the material in this chapter, you will be able to:

1. Define the terms *psychology* and *behavior,* describe the field of psychology, and make a distinction between applied science and basic research science. (p. 4)

2. Explain how the training and specialized interests of psychologists, psychiatrists, and psychoanalysts are similar and how they are different. (p. 5)

3. State the number of psychologists working in the various subfields of psychology and discuss the potential for becoming employed as a psychologist in the 1990s. (p. 7)

4. Describe clinical psychology, counseling psychology, community psychology, and school psychology—four subfields of human services. (p. 8)

5. Discuss some things a person should keep in mind when selecting a psychotherapist and state several ways a person can locate a qualified therapist. (p. 10)

6. Describe the field of experimental psychology and explain why experimental psychologists often use animals as subjects. (p. 11)

7. Briefly describe the specialized interests of developmental psychologists, social psychologists, educational psychologists, and industrial/organizational psychologists. (p. 12)

8. Give some examples that illustrate the wide variety of research interests found among psychologists. (p. 12)

9. Describe structuralism, functionalism, Gestalt psychology, the psychoanalytic approach, and behaviorism and also several ways that modern psychology differs from early psychology. (p. 16)

10. Make a distinction between causal relationships and correlations and identify the conditions that must be met when determining causation. (p. 20)

11. Cite one strength and one weakness of controlled experiments, describe a typical controlled experiment, and discuss some things a good experimenter will consider when designing an experiment. (p. 23)

12. Describe four research techniques that psychologists use to gather information about noncausal relationships among variables. (p. 26)

13. Explain why the application of research findings requires time and caution. (p. 28)

BEFORE YOU READ ON, take time to **SURVEY** the chapter, form an idea of what is to be learned (from margin Learning Objective numbers), and set goals for your study time. Then, ask yourself **QUESTIONS** about the material as you **READ,** seeking help for any sections you do not understand.

Phil Marshall liked to think back to his teenage years. At that time, Phil had thought his family life unbearable. He had had the usual teenage squabbles about grades and curfews, and his father used to chase him out of the house and down the street. His mother was constantly complaining about the disaster he called his room. His bad complexion, uncoordinated movements, and slouching posture added to his isolation. But all that was behind him; those difficult adolescent years seemed sweet compared to his current troubles.

At age twenty-nine and two years into marriage, Phil Marshall was facing a drinking problem. Phil was a district manager of a supermarket chain and traveled from store to store through his territory in the Midwest. He traveled four days a week and never spent much time in any one town. No one knew something was going awry in Phil's life.

Weekends used to be exciting for Phil and his wife after a long week of separation. Now, Friday afternoons were turning into battle grounds, and Marjorie never really knew why. Phil started drinking at Friday afternoon happy hours at the local tavern. During the last year, those Friday afternoons were extended into Saturdays and Sundays. At first, Marjorie was concerned but not alarmed. Later, she saw Phil's good humor deteriorating. Now, she found that she and Phil battled all weekend while Phil drank. Marjorie did not know that Phil was drinking while he was on the road. She also did not know that he had been in a hit-and-run accident, that he had been arrested for driving under the influence, and that he had a court date pending at which he might lose his driver's license.

Phil's job was in jeopardy, and his marriage was growing very shaky. With all of these problems, Phil Marshall had not yet faced the fact that he was an alcoholic even though the stark reality of his drinking was confronting him regularly. He further chose to deny seeking, accepting, or even considering getting help. As he drank, he often thought back to his teenage years, sometimes blaming current problems on his youthful exuberance, at other times feeling nostalgia for the simplicity of youth.

PHIL MARSHALL IS ONE of approximately twenty-two million Americans who has a drinking problem. Everyone has problems to solve, but for an alcoholic the problems are especially acute. Alcoholism impairs judgment, interferes with a person's livelihood, and often breaks up families. Phil was at a juncture; he could choose the road to therapy, treatment, and self-discovery, or he could let his life and family become consumed by alcoholism.

Whether a person is having an adjustment problem in school, a family crisis, trouble with a child, is seriously depressed, or is an alcoholic, it is not always easy to solve the problems of living. A troubled individual sometimes finds it easier to block out uncomfortable feelings, thoughts, or ideas than to face them. As human beings, however, we have an amazing capacity for self-reflection. We have a large memory for past events and the ability to think about the future. We can reason, think about our problems, and hopefully grow wiser. We can change. Even though Phil Marshall was not yet ready to make changes, he had the capacity to do so. Phil Marshall needed someone to help him cope with today and to give him the tools to make it through tomorrow without alcohol. The process of self-discovery and change is never easy. But with the help of a trained professional—such as a licensed clinical psychologist—the process is possible. Helping people make changes in their lives is one of the many areas in which psychologists work.

This book introduces you to these and other aspects of psychology. We show you how basic principles of psychology, often learned in the research laboratory, have application to the everyday life of people like Phil Marshall.

To help people better understand themselves, psychologists study behavior to discover facts and underlying patterns and to infer principles of behavior. **Psychology** is the science of behavior. **Behavior** refers to every aspect of an organism's functioning—overt actions, mental, emotional, and physiological functioning. Human behavior is complex; no single rule, theory, or explanation can account for everything a person feels, thinks, or does. However, having some basic principles of behavior to go by can help people understand themselves better and thus exert some control over their lives, making their lives happier and more productive. Later chapters show how these principles of behavior have been put to practical use in everyday life. For example, treatment procedures for tension headaches, devised by clinical psychologists in the laboratory, are widely used (as discussed in Chapters 4 and 15); and research in laboratories and hospital settings has shown that a special bond formed between parents and newborns can promote healthy emotional growth in children (as discussed in Chapters 5 and 7).

Many psychologists consider their field to be an applied discipline. They see psychology as a problem-solving science. Some people have problems with their behavior and they need help; others would like to manage their life-styles better through changes in behavior. In either case, these psychologists view psychology as an applied science, a problem-solving science. For other psychologists, psychology is a research discipline—one that aims through research to uncover scientific principles of behavior. There is no question that, to understand behavior, the discipline of psychology has become heavily research oriented. The aims of researchers are to uncover, explore, and understand principles of behavior. Psychologists try to measure and describe behavior in a scientific way, using verifiable observations and carefully controlled research methods. Because behavior is not always directly observable, they must sometimes infer the thinking processes, emotions, and motivations behind the behavior they observe, using both human and animal subjects to obtain controlled observations. From their research, psychologists have developed many theories and models to explain various aspects of behavior. As you study these theories, try to evaluate them: do they help people understand behavior and cope with life and its demands?

From a student's point of view, psychology is fun and can help you understand the world around you. Psychology has serious goals, and professionals take their work and responsibilities seriously. Psychologists also will be the first to tell you that they enjoy their work because it helps people in direct and indirect ways. Whether employed in private practice, in a university, in industry, or in a mental health facility, psychologists are studying the most interesting part of people—their behavior. Whether they view psychology as an applied science or as a basic research science, psychologists study behavior. In doing so, they gain information about basic behavior processes and about behaviors that will help practitioners solve day-to-day problems. In many ways,

---

Learning Objective 1.1

Psychology
The science of behavior.

Behavior
Every aspect of an organism's functioning, including overt behavior, thought, emotion, and physiological activity. These functions may or may not be directly observable.

you can consider psychology a problem-solving science rooted in research and scientific principles.

WHAT IS A PSYCHOLOGIST?

Few children in the third grade really know what they want to be when they grow up. They often respond to queries with stereotyped answers: doctor, lawyer, police officer, or nurse. But Ellen Kittle knew since the sixth grade that she wanted to be a physician. She was sure of it. In high school, she concentrated on getting good grades so she could get into the best college possible. Math and chemistry were her favorite subjects. As a first-year premed student, Ellen studied biology, chemistry, math, English, and psychology. At the end of her freshman year, she worked as an aide in the local hospital. The work was tedious, but Ellen loved talking with the patients; it was the best part of her day. She prided herself on her ability to listen to the patients and make them feel better. She felt she had insight into some of their fears and anxieties and found herself thinking a great deal about them and their problems. In her sophomore year, her roommate, a psychology major, discussed psychological theories with Ellen and took her to a couple of evening lectures sponsored by the psychology department. At those lectures, Ellen realized that her interest in people and their behavior was greater than her interest in treating their physical diseases. She took some psychology courses the next semester, then changed her major to psychology. Throughout her junior and senior years, Ellen worked with a psychologist on the faculty who was studying the effects of day-care centers on preschool children. Her exposure to research confirmed her choice of a career: after four years of graduate study, Ellen obtained a Ph.D. in psychology.

Many people, when they think of psychology, think of Sigmund Freud, black leather couches, and therapy. But, although therapy is an important part of many psychologists' work, emotional disturbances represent only a small part of the world psychology attempts to explore and explain. Psychology involves the study of all aspects of behavior, including thought processes, attitudes, and sexual behavior.

Learning Objective **1.2**

Psychologist One who studies behavior and uses behavioral principles in scientific research or in applied settings such as for the treatment of emotional problems.

Psychologists use behavioral principles in scientific research or in settings in which they can apply their knowledge. Like Ellen, many of them have advanced degrees, usually a Ph.D. Many psychologists also train for an additional year or two in a specialized area and confine their research and applied interests to that area. Many, like Ellen, specialize in mental health. Others research specific areas such as perception, physiology, dreams, or learning. Still others teach.

Regardless of the area in which they specialize, psychologists generally consider research one of their most important activities (Nelson & Stapp, 1983). As trained researchers, they provide the scientific and larger community with reliable data concerning behavior, and they constantly incorporate their own and others' research findings to update their concept of behavior. Their dual aim in all these activities is to be able to predict human behavior and to help people manage it. For a psychologist, prediction and management go hand in hand. Psychologists seek to manage constructive behaviors—such as the rate at which people learn new information; they also seek to help people handle their aggressive impulses and destructive behaviors, such as the behavior of individuals who have emotional problems or who are severely disturbed. Being able to predict the circumstances in which certain behaviors will occur allows

Psychologists have years of training and may work in very specialized fields, such as counseling former prison inmates in residential rehabilitation programs.

Psychiatrist ══════

A medical doctor who has done a residency specializing in the study of behavior and the treatment of patients with emotional and physical disorders.

Psychoanalyst ══════

A person (usually a psychiatrist) who has studied the technique of psychoanalysis and uses it in treating people with emotional problems.

psychologists to help people anticipate and deal with behavior and learn how to express their feelings in manageable and reasonable ways.

Many psychologists have extensive experience with testing, evaluating, and treating emotional disorders. But not all people who treat disturbed individuals are psychologists. **Psychiatrists** are physicians, medical doctors, specializing in the treatment of disturbed behavior. Often, their patients have physical as well as emotional problems. Because of their medical training, psychiatrists can prescribe drugs in treating a problem. A psychologist treating such patients would instead focus primarily on their psychological problems. Even though psychiatrists and psychologists often work well together as part of a mental health team, a friendly rivalry exists between the two disciplines (Berg, 1986) and most practitioners support collaborative efforts. **Psychoanalysts** are usually psychiatrists who have additional training in a very specific method of treating emotional problems. This method, called psychoanalysis, uses special techniques, including the study of unconscious motivation and dream analysis, and often requires a course of daily or weekly therapy sessions that may last several years. Only people who have been trained to use this technique are called psychoanalysts. In mental hospitals, psychiatrists, psychologists, and other mental health practitioners such as psychiatric nurses and psychiatric social workers commonly work side by side, helping one another.

For a person seeking therapy, the choice between a psychiatrist or psychologist is usually determined by availability and by the type of problem needing attention. Most people think of a psychiatrist when they need help with an emotional problem, yet the practitioner of choice should perhaps be a licensed psychologist. Research shows that the mix of clients for both types of practitioner is often very similar (Knesper, Pagnucco, & Wheeler, 1985). Psychologists generally have more extensive training than psychiatrists in the research and treatment of emotional problems. Both psychologists and psychiatrists are mental health practitioners, but they look at behavior differently; the medical approach psychiatrists use involves certain assumptions about behavior that psychologists do not necessarily accept (Kingsbury, 1987). Chapters 13, 14, and 15 discuss this issue in more detail.

PROGRESS CHECK 1.1

1. Complete each of the following sentences with one of the options provided.

Learning Objective 1.1

A. Psychologists use the word *behavior* to describe activities such as _____
_____.
(walking, but not for activities like sleeping : heart beat, thinking, talking, and swimming)

Learning Objective 1.1

B. A psychologist who considers his or her field as an applied discipline tries to _____ behavior.
(solve problems by changing : uncover scientific principles of)

Learning Objective 1.1

C. Behavior _____ always directly observable.
(is : is not)

Learning Objective 1.2

D. A _____ has a graduate degree, usually a Ph.D.
(psychiatrist : psychologist)

Learning Objective 1.2

E. A _____ has extensive training in the methods of scientific research, psychological testing, and the evaluation and treatment of emotional disturbances.
(psychoanalyst : psychiatrist : psychologist)

Learning Objective 1.2

F. Psychiatrists are _____ who specialize in the treatment of disturbed behavior.
(medical doctors : well-trained psychologists)

Learning Objective 1.2

G. A professional who treats emotional problems with a very specific method that takes several years and includes dream analysis and the exploration of unconscious motives is a _____.
(psychologist : psychiatrist : psychoanalyst)

Learning Objective 1.2

H. When comparing the type of clients helped by psychiatrists to those helped by psychologists, there _____ in the types of problems needing attention.
(is a big difference : are often similarities)

PSYCHOLOGISTS WORK IN A VARIETY OF SETTINGS

Learning Objective **1.3**

Contrary to what most people believe, not all psychologists are involved in the treatment of emotional disturbances. A survey of members of the American Psychological Association found that psychologists are working in an increasing variety of settings and that employment opportunities are likely to increase further in the next few years (Stapp & Fulcher, 1983).

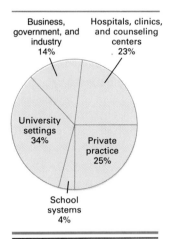

FIGURE 1.1 : The percentage of psychologists with Ph.D.'s working in different areas of psychology.

Psychologists often find employment opportunities in business and industry, where their expertise in human behavior can be helpful in making important business decisions.

If you are considering becoming a psychologist or entering a related field, here is some good news. The employment picture for psychologists is good. Unemployment among psychologists is low, and new psychologists continue to find employment in areas related to their graduate training. Several clear trends appeared in the 1980s. A steady number of new psychologists have entered the field each year, including an increased number of women. Further, many new psychologists have a more applied emphasis and are seeking nonacademic careers in health-care settings, industry, and government. Most experts agree that employment opportunities will improve in the 1990s (Stapp, Fulcher, & Wicherski, 1984). (See Figure 1.1)

Psychologists in Human Service Fields: Helping People Solve Day-to-Day Problems

Learning Objective 1.4

Helping people solve day-to-day problems is the focus of many psychological practitioners. Many psychologists work in settings in which they can apply behavior principles to teach people to cope more effectively with their lives. These human service areas help people with problems and also promote well-being. They generally include the subfields of clinical, counseling, community and school psychology.

Clinical Psychology.   Clinical psychologists specialize in helping clients with behavior problems and with the promotion of human well-being (see L. H.

Levy, 1984). The clients may be experiencing anxiety or fear or may be having trouble adjusting to stresses at home or at work. Clinical psychologists work either in private practice or at a hospital, mental institution, social service agency or university. They administer psychological tests, interview potential clients, and use psychological methods to treat emotional problems. Many universities employ psychologists to help students and staff adjust to the pressures of academic life. In this setting, clinical psychologists often are able to continue their research into the causes of normal and abnormal behavior. More job opportunities exist in clinical psychology than in any other area of psychology.

Counseling Psychology. Counseling psychologists, like clinical psychologists, work with people who have emotional problems, but their clients' problems have traditionally been less serious. For example, a person might ask a counseling psychologist for information about vocational rehabilitation programs or for help in making a job choice or in adjusting to a new life-style. Counseling psychologists tend to work for public agencies, such as mental health centers, hospitals, and universities. Many work in college or university counseling bureaus to help students adjust to a university atmosphere and to provide vocational and educational guidance. Like clinical psychologists, many counseling psychologists use the setting in which they work to continue to explore the causes and treatment of maladjustment.

In the last decade, counseling psychologists have increasingly become engaged in psychotherapy and other activities once the domain of clinical psychologists. According to many practitioners and researchers, counseling and clinical psychology may be converging (Fitzgerald & Osipow, 1986). For some psychologists, this is a controversial idea; for others, it is an idea whose time has come (L. H. Levy, 1984).

Community Psychology. Community psychology is a relatively new field that focuses on community mental health. Community psychologists work for mental health agencies, state governments, and private organizations. They help the community and its institutions adjust to problems. In a rural community, they might work to establish an outpatient mental health treatment center; in an urban community, they might analyze the misuse of drugs and design a drug rehabilitation program. Many community psychologists focus on special populations, such as the elderly or the handicapped. In addition to the redirection and evaluation of current programs and plans, prevention is a major interest.

School Psychology. School psychology has a lengthy history; it started in 1896 at the University of Pennsylvania in a clinic founded to study and treat children who were considered morally or mentally defective (J. L. French, 1984). As school psychology has matured, it has taken on great stature. Currently, there are more than 30,000 school psychologists, most of whom work in educational systems. Their roles vary with their level of training. Those with bachelor's degrees usually only administer tests. Those with master's degrees administer and interpret tests and help teachers with classroom-related problems. Psychologists with Ph.D.s perform those tasks and are also involved in influencing school policies and procedures (Bardon, 1983). Ph.D.-level practitioners comprise nearly half of all newly trained school psychologists (Brown & Mincke, 1986). They establish communication among parents, teachers, ad-

Psychologists at Work: Getting a Job

Many college students like the idea of working with people and consider becoming a psychologist. Psychology is an exciting field with dozens of job opportunities. Most people who receive doctorates in psychology work in psychology-related jobs. In fact, every year there are approximately 3,000 new holders of doctorate degrees, the Ph.D., and nearly all of them get jobs close to their training (Stapp, Fulcher, & Wicherski, 1984). In total, there are slightly more than 100,000 psychologists in the United States (Stapp, Tucker, & VandenBos, 1985).

The employment opportunities for psychologists are diverse. A person's training is the key to job opportunities. If you obtain a Ph.D. from an accredited program in clinical psychology, do an internship in a state hospital, and become licensed, you have a wide variety of opportunities available in both the private and the public sector. For example, 51 percent of the doctoral membership of the American Psychological Association (APA) work in the delivery of human services. The 51 percent is broken down as follows: 25 percent of the APA membership work in clinics, community mental health centers, health maintenance organizations, Veterans hospitals, public hospitals, and both public and private mental health hospitals. An additional 22 percent of the APA are private practitioners who maintain offices, and 4 percent are school psychologists working in public and private school systems (Howard et al., 1986; Stapp, Tucker, & VandenBos, 1985).

Business, government, and universities employ psychologists. For example, 34 percent of the APA are employed by universities in various settings—with nearly half of those in psychology departments. University employees spend most of their time on research and teaching. About 14 percent of psychologists are employed by business, government, and industry. Among those employed by hospital and private practice, most spend their time in the direct delivery of human services, including individual and group therapy. Doctoral-level psychologists provide more than 50 million hours of care on an annual basis to about 4 to 10 million people (Howard et al., 1986; Stapp, Tucker, & VandenBos, 1985).

An interesting finding is that among doctoral-level psychologists, the number of women in training programs has doubled in the last twenty years. Proportionately, more women than men are entering psychology, although women in psychology are more likely than men to be employed on a part-time basis (Stapp, Fulcher, & Wicherski, 1984).

Becoming a psychologist is not easy but the rewards are worthwhile. People pursuing a doctorate have several years of study ahead of them. With a Ph.D., a person can enter many fields of endeavor. Even though individuals with bachelor's level and master's level training are more limited in the types of activities in which they can engage, many opportunities are available. School systems often hire master's level school psychologists to administer tests and to work with school children. State hospitals employ both bachelor's level and master's level individuals to work with groups of impaired individuals.

Unlike many other disciplines, holders of doctorate degrees are finding jobs commensurate with their experience; unemployment is low and the job market for doctoral recipients has stabilized. You may consider entering psychology or a related field because of the opportunities it affords you personally and professionally; it is a field that continues to grow and provide thousands of individuals with a rewarding career.

---

ministrators, and other psychologists at the school. They also provide information to teachers and parents about a student's progress and advise them how to help students and faculty do a better job. Many school psychologists see their primary job as helping students, teachers, parents, and others understand each other (Bardon, 1982; Trachtman, 1981).

Learning Objective $\underline{1.5}$ *Choosing a Therapist.* Among the various practitioners who work in the human service subfields, each one has unique qualifications. But the public often is unaware of those qualifications. Many people experience emotional problems but are hesitant to seek help, perhaps owing to misconceptions or lack of knowledge about therapists. They may think of a therapist as a forbidding figure who dissects and diagnoses a client's personality. Understandably, someone with this conception might try to avoid such an experience. However, a variety of people provide psychotherapy. Counselors, psychologists, and psychiatrists all treat and counsel individuals like Phil Marshall, who opened this chapter.

Sallie Adams, a member of Ralph Nader's health research group, has written a consumers' guide to therapy called *Through the Mental Health Maze.* In addition to reporting on the types of mental health services available, the book provides guidelines for finding a therapist and for determining whether a therapist is competent and has received training at an accredited educational or professional institution.

College students can usually find a therapist through the psychological service center located on campus or through a counseling bureau. If these centers do not have appropriate facilities, the staff there can usually provide references to appropriate qualified mental health professionals in the general community. In larger cities, an individual can usually find a therapist through the outpatient branch of a hospital. Many of today's best mental health centers are outpatient divisions of the psychiatry department of a medical center. The telephone directory also lists people who provide therapy services, usually under the headings of psychologists, psychiatrists, or counselors.

It is a good idea to be relatively cautious even after choosing a therapist. A client should feel free to ask what goals the therapist hopes to achieve in therapy, and how he or she hopes to achieve them. Therapies vary significantly in approach, and someone who does not like the way treatment is proceeding should speak up. As mental health consumers, people have the right to evaluate and perhaps discontinue therapy, just as they have the right to evaluate the services of a tutor, carpenter, or physician.

Experimental Psychology: Research and Teaching

Learning Objective 1.6

As a psychologist, if you are not going to be involved in the delivery of human services, you might seek a career in experimental psychology. Experimental psychology, the other major subfield of psychology, is concerned with identifying and understanding the basic processes involved in behavior. Many experimental psychologists teach in university settings and also do research. Experimental psychology covers many areas of interest, some of which overlap with fields outside psychology. An experimental psychologist may be interested in

By using animals in their research, psychologists have gathered much information about learning and other principles of behavior that can then be generalized to human beings.

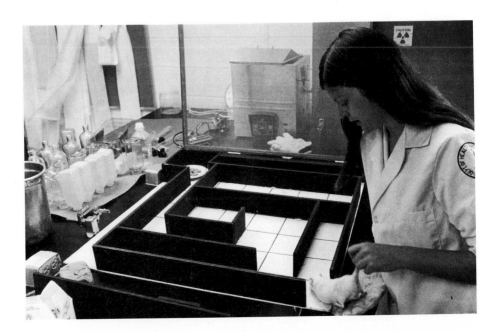

visual perception, in how individuals learn language or solve problems, or in how the activity of hormones influences behavior.

Even casual observation shows that human behavior is exceedingly complex; accordingly, some psychologists study simple elements of behavior by observing them first in animals and then try to generalize those principles to human behavior. They may be concerned with how physiological processes, such as the nervous system, relate to behavior, or with the learning processes of rats or pigeons. Using animals in research studies allows experimenters to isolate simple aspects of behavior and to eliminate the complex distractions and variables that arise in studies involving human beings. It also allows researchers to control the life history of the organism being studied, to perform autopsies in an effort to obtain important information after the animals die, and—since most animals have shorter life spans than human beings—to study several generations of animals in a relatively short time. Many people object to any and all use of animals in research. Unfortunately, there are no viable alternatives to using animals in much behavioral research (Gallup & Suarez, 1985). However, as distinguished psychologist Neal Miller (1985) points out, research on animals is a small part (only about 7 percent) of the research published in psychosocial journals. Psychologists who apply data from animal studies to human beings, however, must do so with caution.

Psychologists more often work with human participants, traditionally called **subjects.** They may study the same processes they do with animals, or they may design experiments that require the performance of more complex tasks. Whether they work with animals or human beings, psychologists' aims are the same: to find the basic components of behavior, understand them, and potentially manage them. By studying how both animals *and* human beings react under different circumstances, psychologists learn more about the basic principles of behavior.

Subject
An individual who participates in an experiment and from whose behavior data are collected.

Learning Objective 1.7

Other nonclinical subfields exist in psychology. Some are directly concerned with discovering general principles of behavior; others have more practical applications. *Developmental psychologists* study the changes that take place over the life span of organisms. *Social psychologists* are concerned with attitude formation, the behavior of groups, and aggression. *Educational psychologists* are interested in how learning proceeds in the classroom. *Industrial* and *organizational psychologists* often focus on applying psychological research and theory to organizational problems, including productivity and management-labor relations.

Research: Solving Important Day-to-Day Problems

Learning Objective 1.8

When you think about research, you may think about test tubes, lab coats, and computers silently chugging through heaps of data. Some psychological researchers do use test tubes, and many researchers who work with animals do wear lab coats, and others use computers; but these are just a few of the tools used by experimental psychologists. You will see that psychological research is extremely diverse. The first psychologists studied the mind, but psychology has broadened its scope as a science, as a technology, and in day-to-day practice. Psychologists have recognized the importance of the many factors that influence behavior, often at the same time (Crawford, 1985). As it has grown, psychology has specialized and, as you have already read, developed several subareas and specialties. Although these areas are diverse, each uses scientific methods to examine behavior. Psychologists conduct research in order to understand behavior and to explain why and under what circumstances particular behaviors occur. They also try to solve a number of real problems. The problems described below illustrate the wide range of behaviors psychologists observe, as well as some of the research methods they use.

Problem 1.   One major cause of heart disease and stroke for many Americans is obesity. Owing partly to internal physiological and emotional factors, overweight individuals eat too much and too often.

Because eating behavior involves both physiological and psychological variables, it is ideally suited to psychological investigation. Some psychologists have focused on the psychological components and have monitored eating behavior to see how often and how much the obese eat compared with people of normal weight. These studies have shown that the obese not only eat more often but they also eat more at each individual eating session.

Stanley Schachter (1971) reported a series of studies in which he manipulated cues for eating behavior. In one study, subjects were placed in a room with food. A clock on the wall was made to work faster so that it seemed as if more time had passed than had really elapsed. For example, if one hour had passed, the clock showed two hours passing. Obese subjects in the room with the fast clock ate more and sooner than obese subjects exposed to a normal clock or than normal subjects. These results suggest that obese people eat in response to external cues (such as a clock on the wall) rather than in response to internal physiological cues (such as hunger). Physiological variables can be shown to be especially important. As you see in Chapter 5, however, they are just one component in the problem of obesity. (Chapter 5 describes in detail a man with a problem controlling his eating behavior.)

Problem 2.   A bank teller arrested in New York City for murdering his wife, two children, and a neighbor is referred by the court for psychological testing. The court asks a psychologist (or team of psychologists) to determine if the teller understood what he was doing at the time of the crime and is therefore legally responsible for his behavior.

Psychologists make decisions regarding legal insanity only after a long process of psychological evaluation. Typically, a psychologist interviews the person for an hour or two each day for two or three weeks. Next, the person takes a battery of tests designed to evaluate personality, intelligence, achievement, motivation, and the ability to perceive reality. The psychologist collects, analyzes, and interprets all these data before delivering an opinion to the court. Using these results, the psychologist tries to report with some degree of accuracy whether the person on trial was aware at the time of the crime of the difference between right and wrong, and to what extent the crime is a direct consequence of emotional disturbance. (Chapter 13 discusses the legal view of maladjustment.)

Problem 3.   What people eat may cause certain behavioral and learning problems. For example, children whose classroom behavior is disruptive may suffer from a behavioral problem called hyperactivity. The symptoms include restlessness, inability to concentrate, inattention, and seemingly unbounded energy. Psychologists at first thought these children were emotionally disturbed, but subsequent investigations have shown that at least some hyperactive children respond to treatment with controlled diets and drugs. Some researchers claim that the intake of certain substances in excessive amounts may account for hyperactivity. For example, a diet too high in sugar and too low in protein may play a contributing role. (Chapter 7 discusses how a change in diet can bring about a change in behavior; Chapter 2 discusses techniques that help control specific outbursts of hyperactivity in a classroom.)

Problem 4. Psychologists specializing in learning theory study how behaviors are learned; more important, they study how antisocial behaviors can be unlearned. For example, many children learn at an early age that their parents are easy to manipulate. Sometimes just a short bout of crying produces the desired results; sometimes it takes yelling, screaming, kicking, and throwing a tantrum to get what they want. Children often use such manipulations quite successfully.

Early research attempts to help children eliminate tantrumlike behavior came from laboratory studies of animals. Psychologists found that when animals were not rewarded for certain behaviors, they stopped exhibiting them. If the researchers started to reward the behaviors again, the behaviors recurred. The researchers reasoned that if tantrum behavior is rewarded, the tantrums will continue. In contrast, if parents stop rewarding the behavior and refuse to give in, the tantrums will eventually decrease in intensity and disappear. In this instance, data from the laboratory were successfully applied directly to the home environment. (Chapters 2 and 15 describe other psychological techniques to help control and manage children's behavior.)

These brief examples demonstrate the wide variety of research interests among psychologists. Understanding the circumstances and causes of specific behaviors (such as overeating or tantrums) helps psychologists help individuals to control their behavior and lead happier, more productive lives.

PROGRESS CHECK 1.2

1. Match the following types of psychologists with the appropriate descriptions.

clinical psychologist	developmental psychologist	counseling psychologist
social psychologist	community psychologist	educational psychologist
school psychologist	industrial/organizational	
experimental psychologist	psychologist	

Learning Objective 1.4   A. _____ A psychologist who provides consultation to help students and teachers to help them improve their work, who works with students, teachers, and parents to improve communications, and who administers and interprets intelligence, personality, and achievement tests.

Learning Objective 1.4   B. _____ A psychologist who might establish an outpatient mental health treatment center, propose a drug rehabilitation program, or circulate information concerning steps children can take to avoid being abducted by strangers.

Learning Objective 1.4   C. _____ A psychologist who works for a mental health agency, hospital, or university, provides vocational or educational guidance, and helps people adjust to changes in life-styles.

Learning Objective 1.4   D. _____ A psychologist who specializes in treating people who have behavior problems and emotional disturbances.

Learning Objective 1.6   E. _____ A psychologist who is primarily concerned with identifying and understanding the basic principles of behavior.

Learning Objective 1.7   F. _____ A psychologist who focuses on the changes that take place as a person proceeds through life from conception to death.

Learning Objective 1.7   G. _____ A psychologist who is concerned with how learning occurs in classrooms.

Learning Objective 1.7   H. _____ A psychologist who helps an employer increase production and who provides consultation concerning good management-labor relations.

Learning Objective 1.7   I. _____ A psychologist who focuses on attitude formation, group behavior, and such topics as aggression.

2. Complete each of the following sentences with one of the options provided.

Learning Objective 1.3   A. Employment opportunities for psychologists were good in the 1980s, _____ in the 1990s.
(and experts expect them to be even better : but experts expect a decline)

Learning Objective 1.4   B. Clinical, counseling, community, and school psychology are considered _____, and the psychologists who work in these areas are applied psychologists.
(human services : experimental fields)

Learning Objective 1.4   C. More job opportunities exist in _____ psychology than in any other area of psychology.
(clinical : experimental : school)

Learning Objective 1.4   D. Recent reports suggest that clinical psychology and counseling psychology _____.
(may be converging : are moving towards opposing therapeutic perspectives)

Learning Objective 1.4   E. A major interest of community psychologists is _____.
(research : prevention : social psychology)

Learning Objective 1.5   F. When choosing a therapist, a client should _____.
(assume the therapist is an authority : ask questions about the therapeutic approach)

Learning Objective 1.6   G. A psychologist who wanted to study the development of a behavior in several generations would probably observe _____.
(animals : an extended family : a nuclear family)

Learning Objective 1.7   H. Developmental, social, educational, and industrial/organizational psychologists are working in _____ subfields of psychology.
(clinical : nonclinical)

Learning Objective 1.8   I. In one of his studies on obesity, Stanley Schachter used _____ to determine certain variables that motivate eating in overweight people.
(monkeys : diet soda : a fast clock)

Learning Objective 1.8   J. Psychologists using data based on animal research have taught parents to _____ in order to end temper tantrums.
(withhold rewards : compromise with children)

PSYCHOLOGY YESTERDAY AND TODAY

At the beginning of this chapter, we saw that Marjorie Marshall was slow to recognize that her husband Phil had developed a serious drinking problem. By contrast, Karl Minsky knew from the beginning that his daughter was feeling the "storm and stress" of adolescence. In college, he had taken several courses in child behavior and adolescence. He knew his daughter's moodiness and short temper were signs that she was having difficulty coping with her new, adult emotions and with new, complex situations. Prompted by a desire to help his adolescent, by his generally curious nature, and by his training, he consulted a psychologist who specialized in treating adolescent problems. He also began reading articles in psychological journals that dealt with adolescence. After two weeks, Karl knew a lot more about adolescent behavior and was better able to understand some of what his daughter might be going through.

Psychology has undergone many changes in the last century. Those developments have resulted in the use of scientific methods to evaluate behavior and behavior disorders. Early psychologists had not developed some of the tools, concepts, techniques, or insights that contemporary psychologists use to understand behavior. A thorough examination of a person's background was not always considered necessary or appropriate. Today, a good psychologist evaluates the full range of biological and environmental factors that might be affecting an individual's current situation.

Modern Psychology: Several Schools of Psychological Thought

Today, it is difficult to imagine a college or university without a psychology department. However, psychology as a formal discipline did not exist until the late 1880s. Before that, psychological questions were considered to be within the domain of philosophy, medicine, or theology. But as scientists developed an understanding of how the body operates, the special importance of the brain in controlling behavior became evident.

Structuralism

A school of psychology founded by Wilhelm Wundt (1832–1920), who believed that the proper subject matter of psychology was the study of the contents of consciousness. Structuralists developed and used the technique called introspection.

Learning Objective 1.9

Psychologists at the turn of the century adopted specific approaches to the study of behavior. The first widely accepted approach was that of Wilhelm Wundt (1832–1920). Wundt founded the **structuralist** school and the first psychological laboratory in Leipzig, Germany, in 1879. Wundt and his followers considered the proper subject matter of psychology to be the contents of consciousness. Instead of looking at the broad range of behavior that modern psychologists consider today, Wundt tried to "look inside" a person by studying the contents of the mind. He used a technique called **introspection** or self-examination, the description and analysis of what a person is thinking and feeling. By today's standards, the structuralists' focus was very limited, and they made little headway in describing the nature of behavior.

Introspection

The technique of examining the contents of the mind through self-report and the careful examination of thoughts and feelings.

Before long, a new school of thought, a new way of thinking about behavior, began to develop. **Functionalism,** an outgrowth of structuralism, tried to discover how and why the brain works and its relation to consciousness and behavior. Functionalism also used such techniques as introspection, but it was closer than structuralism to modern psychology because it not only described but also tried to understand what determines behavior. One of the better known functionalists was William James (1842–1910), an American.

Functionalism

A school of psychology that grew out of structuralism and was concerned with how and why the conscious mind works.

Other approaches to psychology were developing in Europe and the United States. Pracititioners of **Gestalt psychology** analyzed the world in terms of perceptual frameworks. For example, they suggested that conscious experience is more than simply the sum of its parts. Accordingly, they argued that it is necessary to study a person's total experience—not just parts of the mind or behavior. Eventually, Gestalt psychology became a major influence in the field of sensation and perception.

Gestalt psychology

A school of psychology that argues that behavior cannot be studied in parts but must be viewed as a whole.

Unlike psychologists today, most early psychologists were not concerned with a person's emotional troubles. One of the first persons to develop a psy-

Wilhem Wundt (1832-1920).

William James (1842-1910).

Sigmund Freud (1856-1939).

John B. Watson (1878-1958).

Psychoanalytic approach

The theory developed by Sigmund Freud (1856–1939), who was interested in how personality develops. He focused on the unconscious and on how it directed day-to-day behavior.

chological theory about emotional disturbance was Sigmund Freud (1856–1939). Freud was a medical doctor who tried to help people overcome anxiety. He worked from the premise that unconscious processes direct daily behavior. He concerned himself more with the treatment of emotional disturbance than with the functioning of the brain; ultimately he developed techniques, such as free association and dream interpretation, to explore unconscious experiences. Freud's approach was called the **psychoanalytic** approach. Although contemporary psychoanalysis differs from Freud's, the focus remains very similar. Chapter 12 discusses Freud's theory of personality, and Chapter 15 discusses psychoanalysis, the therapeutic technique derived from his theory.

Despite their differences in focus, the structuralists, Gestaltists, and psychoanalysts were all concerned with the functioning of the brain or, as they called it, the mind. All were interested in private perception and conscious or unconscious activity. Modern American psychology has moved away from dealing with the mind and into the study of behavior. At the forefront of this movement was John B. Watson (1878–1958), who founded behaviorism. Watson argued that observable behavior, not the private contents of consciousness, is the proper subject matter of psychology. In his research, Watson observed types of stimuli that brought about different behaviors. He argued that psychologists should study only activities that can be objectively observed and measured. Since Watson, American researchers have further extended and developed **behaviorism.** Behaviorists such as Harvard psychologist B. F. Skinner, for example, have attempted to explain the causes of behavior by cataloging and describing the relations among stimuli and responses. By the 1940s, a distinct division had arisen between behaviorists and nonbehaviorists. In many ways, that division persists today (J. A. Fodor, 1981), although some psychologists, including Skinner, now consider it possible to take a more unified approach to the study of behavior.

Behaviorism

A school of psychology that rejects the notion that the proper subject of psychology is the contents of consciousness. It maintains instead that psychology can describe and measure only what is observable, either directly or through the use of instruments.

Modern American psychology remains undeniably rooted in the principles of behaviorism, although these principles have undergone some modification. In its newer forms, Watson's behaviorism is used both in the laboratory and with patients in need of psychotherapy. Cognitive psychology, which emphasizes the role of thought in behavior, has become increasingly influential in behavioral therapies (see, for example, Bandura, 1983; Sampson, 1981). Philosophical questions and techniques, excluded by strict behaviorists such as

Eclecticism ══════
The practice of combining theories, facts, or techniques. In clinical psychology, this term usually describes the practice of using whatever therapy techniques are appropriate for an individual client rather than relying exclusively on the techniques of one school of psychology.

Skinner, in the 1980s, are being raised again. Today, most American psychologists are **eclectic.** Instead of studying only one aspect of behavior or using only one approach in treatment, they use a variety of approaches in evaluating data, theory, and therapy. Psychologists today recognize that many variables and theories must be considered when human behavior is examined.

Psychologists have sought to understand why people act in characteristic ways and what factors lead to individual similarities and differences. Some psychologists have favored learning and environmental experiences as the principal determinants of behavior. Others have been sensitive to the role of heredity and biological variables in determining behavior. As the study of behavior has grown more sophisticated, psychologists have realized that a complex relation exists between biological and environmental influences. A person's biological heritage provides the foundation for future learning experiences, but you can easily see that many situations from birth onward may modify a developing or already developed set of behaviors.

Women Psychologists

As a discipline, psychology has had some dominating figures. Like many other disciplines, women have often been overlooked when the history of a field is written. But women have always been an important part of psychology. The first women psychologists received training similar to their more numerous male colleagues, but, as Furumoto and Scarborough (1986) point out, they were much less likely to achieve a professional status equivalent to men. Today, women are not only prevalent in psychological circles, but also some of the best and brightest in the discipline are women. Women are presidents of national, regional, and local organizations, and their thinking and work often dominates the psychological journals. It took almost one hundred years, but women are now on the front lines of psychological research and practice. The research of such women as Janet Taylor Spence, Elizabeth Loftus, and Sandra Scarr has been and continues to be on the forefront of scientific inquiry.

Margaret Floy Washburn (1871-1939) was one of the early women psychologists. She served as president of the American Psychological Association in 1921.

Janet Taylor Spence (1923-) became well known due to her development of a test of anxiety. She served as president of the American Psychological Association in 1984.

Elizabeth Loftus (1944-) has an active career as a perception and memory researcher. She is an expert in the area of eyewitness testimony.

Judith Rodin (1944-) received an award from the American Psychological Association as a distinguished scientist for early career contributions.

Psychology and You: Rewarding Learning

Psychologists know that immediate feedback helps people learn. This is one of the principles around which this textbook is written. After every few pages of text and every few behavioral objectives, you are given a chance to check your progress and assess your learning.

The scheme of this textbook uses psychological principles to help you master psychology—hence the book's title. The plan is relatively simple—material is presented in the SQ3R format. We ask you to use the following steps when you study: *Survey, Question, Read, Recite, and Review.* By doing experiments in the laboratory, psychologists have learned that *surveying* text to be learned will help you set goals. They have found that asking yourself *questions* about what is to be learned and then answering them help you probe the material to be learned effectively. A key step in learning any textbook information is actually *reading* the text carefully. *Reciting* and rehearsing newly read information help you remember key points. Last, *reviewing* what you have just learned helps you master the material.

Has SQ3R worked effectively for you? To help you master psychology, we have made it possible for you to receive immediate feedback. The progress checks that follow after every few pages allow you to be rewarded with good news if you do well, or they tell which behavioral objectives you have not yet mastered. To make your task more manageable, we have written the progress checks after just a few behavioral objectives. This arrangement keeps your reading and exercises in manageable units. In the 1920s, psychologists learned that managing a few, small units is easier than conquering one big one. Last, to give you overall feedback and to help you simulate what a real test will be like, we have provided you with a chapter self-test. Again, quickly gaining knowledge about your progress rewards your hard work and points out your deficiencies.

This textbook is an example of how psychologists put their knowledge to work. We have taken principles learned in the laboratory and applied them to make learning easier. The SQ3R model is only one example of how researchers gain information in that laboratory and then apply it in the real world. This text provides hundreds of examples of how you can use psychology to manage your lives better and to help other people do the same.

PROGRESS CHECK 1.3

1. Match each of the following schools of psychological thought with the appropriate definition.

structuralism   psychoanalytic approach   functionalism
behaviorism   Gestalt psychology   eclecticism

Learning Objective 1.9   A. _____ This term describes the theory Sigmund Freud developed in his attempt to understand how personality develops and how unconscious experiences affect one's emotional state.

Learning Objective 1.9   B. _____ This early approach to psychology studied the contents of the mind by using introspection to determine what a person was thinking and feeling.

Learning Objective 1.9   C. _____ This approach became a major influence in the field of sensation and perception and argues that behavior cannot be studied in parts, but instead must be viewed as an interdependent whole.

Learning Objective 1.9   D. _____ This term is used to describe the practice of combining theories, facts, and techniques when studying behavior or providing treatment.

Learning Objective 1.9   E. _____ This approach was concerned with how and why the brain works as it does and its relation to consciousness and behavior.

Learning Objective 1.9   F. _____ This approach argues that the proper subject matter for psychology includes only overt behaviors that can be objectively observed and measured.

2. Complete each of the following sentences with one of the options provided.

Learning Objective 1.9
A. The first psychological laboratory was founded by Wilhelm Wundt, a structuralist, in Germany, in _____.
(1798 : 1879 : 1931)

Learning Objective 1.9
B. One of the better known functionalist psychologists was _____ _____.
(John B. Watson : William James)

Learning Objective 1.9
C. Structuralists, Gestaltists, and psychoanalysts were all concerned with _____.
(observable behavior : private contents of consciousness)

Learning Objective 1.9
D. Behaviorists attempt to explain the causes of behavior by cataloging and describing the relations among _____.
(stimuli and responses : conscious and unconscious thought)

Learning Objective 1.9
E. Modern psychology is strongly rooted in the principles of _____.
(psychoanalysis : behaviorism : structuralism)

Learning Objective 1.9
F. Cognitive psychology, which emphasizes the role of _____ _____ in behavior, has become increasingly influential in therapies based on the principles of behaviorism.
(enigmas : thought : genetics)

Learning Objective 1.9
G. Most modern psychologists use _____ approach.
(an eclectic : a psychoanalytic)

Learning Objective 1.9
H. Modern psychologists have learned that a complex relationship between _____ work together to shape individuals' daily behavior.
(the mind and inherited traits : biological and environmental influences)

Learning Objective 1.9
I. In modern psychology, women _____ a professional status equivalent to men in the profession.
(remain less likely to achieve : have achieved)

PSYCHOLOGISTS: USING A WIDE RANGE OF TECHNIQUES TO STUDY BEHAVIOR

If you ever have the opportunity to tour a psychologist's laboratory, take the tour. Even better, if you have an opportunity to assist a psychologist in research, take it. Psychological research is fascinating to observe and do. It is unique research because it involves behavior—and everybody recognizes that behavior can sometimes be unpredictable. Psychologists use the same techniques as other scientists, but they have had to refine those techniques to deal with the uncertainties of human behavior.

Learning Objective 1.10
Psychologists do research in both laboratory settings and the real world. The majority try to place their research findings and interpretations in a framework of real-world problems and perspectives. Over the years, psychologists have developed an arsenal of techniques and methods for investigating patterns of behavior. Some methods are unique to psychology. It was psychologists who invented techniques to examine how learning occurs, to study the language of chimps, and to measure emotional responses. Their ultimate aims are to understand and make reliable predictions about the complexities of human behavior. Being able to help someone like Phil Marshall, who opened this chapter, depends on knowing what to do and say in similar cases. By knowing the things that bring about a certain behavior, a psychologist is better

able to help people manage their lives. Knowing the causes of behavior thus becomes a focus for psychological inquiry.

Causality and the Process of Discovery

If you were to trace the way the answers to psychological questions come about, you might think that psychologists are constantly searching through mazes. Many scientific phenomena have been discovered almost by accident, sometimes by a young researcher pursuing the cause of a specific behavior that leads unexpectedly to an understanding of a deeper question. This was the case with well-known psychologist Harry Harlow (1905–1981). Part of Harlow's research, in a long and distinguished career, explored the relationship between mothers and infants. Harlow's research began in a curious way. He had been breeding a colony of rhesus monkeys, the first of which were imported from India. In order to keep the monkeys from transmitting Indian diseases to their offspring, Harlow kept the newborns in "splendidly germ free isolation from their mothers" (Sears, 1982, p. 1281). The infants thrived but seemed to have "emotional" problems—for example, as adults, they would not mate. Harlow noted that the infant monkeys clung to blankets that were placed in their cages and became agitated if the blankets were removed. Harlow's good intuitive sense told him that this behavior might be important.

Harlow had an idea—a hypothesis—that the blankets had become surrogate mothers. To test his idea, he designed wire mesh "mothers" with nipples that could convey milk; some of the mothers were covered in terry cloth and some were left bare. He found that infant monkeys exposed to the surrogate mothers became attached to them, and that they became more attached to the cloth-covered mothers. These results stimulated Harlow and other researchers

Mother-infant bonding was first studied by psychologist Harry Harlow in his research on infant monkeys.

to seek the causes of this behavior and to explore in general the nature of early human infant attachment. (Harlow's experiments are discussed in more detail in Chapter 5.) His early experimental work, his search for causes, led him and other researchers to explore more fully and discover the nature of early childhood attachment.

When psychologists study behavior, they try to do so systematically; they try to consider all the aspects of a situation that might cause an organism to behave as it does. Simply observing behavior is not enough. Observation may show that two sets of behaviors happen frequently together, but this occurrence does not necessarily mean that one causes the other. For example, a college student observed in the library taking notes in deep concentration might be writing a term paper or preparing for an exam, collecting background information for a faculty member, or researching a hobby, such as antique furniture. It is impossible to know from a simple observation all the factors that motivate the student's behavior. The only obvious fact is that the note-taker is actively studying and taking notes; little else can be inferred.

Here is an important point to remember: correlated events are not necessarily causally related. Two events are said to be correlated when the presence of a high value of one variable or situation is regularly associated with a high (or low) value of another. For example, if a researcher finds that children from broken homes have more emotional problems than other children, she can state this as a fact; she can compute a correlation. But these data do not permit her to make any causal statements. Although a correlation indicates a relationship, that relationship may result from a common cause (both variables are affected by a third variable, not by each other) or from the method used to gather the data. Psychological researchers are careful to distinguish between events that are causally related and those that are only correlated. Even though it is likely that broken homes do provide an atmosphere conducive to emotional stress and turbulence in children, too many other variables may influence the data for the researcher to state with certainty that broken homes cause emotional disturbance later in life. The topic of correlations is discussed in the Appendix.

You can use correlations to make predictions such as that studying behavior will be found in libraries. But, researchers are much more interested in knowing whether an event or situation *causes* a specific behavior. When psychologists suggest that one situation causes another, they have to be sure that certain conditions are met. They pay close attention to how the data have been collected and to whether the results of the study are repeatable. Researchers try to be sure that the differences they find among people or behaviors are significant differences. For psychologists, a *significant difference* is the statistically determined likelihood that a behavior has not occurred because of chance alone. One aim of psychological research is to gather systematic, reliable knowledge about behavior that shows strong, regular causal relationships. Doing this is usually difficult. So many possible explanations (social, political, economic, and personal) exist for human behavior that finding a single cause for one of them is sometimes impossible. The Appendix describes the many techniques and statistical methods psychologists have devised to help sort through these problems.

Only within the carefully controlled conditions of an experiment can a researcher make either causal inferences or statements about the probability that a result will occur by chance. Using these carefully formulated statements, psychologists interpret the results of an experiment and cautiously extend them to other (sometimes therapeutic) situations (Berkowitz & Donnerstein, 1982; Mook, 1983). The next section and the Appendix describe how psychologists try to create situations in which they can limit the likelihood of obtaining a result that is simply a chance occurrence.

Controlled Experiments

Learning Objective ___1.11___

A technique psychologists use more than any other is the experiment. To explore cause-and-effect relationships, psychologists use controlled experimental conditions. The strengths of controlled experiments are that they allow researchers to make direct observations and infer cause-and-effect relationships. The weakness of controlled experiments is that the researchers, by manipulating the experimental situation, may unintentionally influence the results. The experimental method is also limited by ethical considerations; certain types of research cannot or should not be done with human beings.

Variables. If you want to determine the relationship between a person's eating behavior and his weight gains or losses, you would systematically vary how much he ate, and each day weigh the individual. This situation describes some of the elements of an experiment. An **experiment** is a procedure in which a researcher systematically manipulates variables in order to describe and discover the relation between an independent and dependent variable. A **variable** is a characteristic of a situation or person that is subject to change. Psychological researchers manipulate variables in order to measure how those changes affect behavior. The variable directly and purposely manipulated by the experimenter in a controlled experiment is called the **independent variable.** The behavior (or change) in the organism being measured is called the **dependent variable.** A good experiment tests some of the experimenter's expectations and provides direct and conclusive evidence as to whether those expectations have been met.

Imagine a simple experiment to determine the effects of caffeine, a drug contained in coffee, on behavior. In a simple experiment, the variable manipulated (the independent variable) would probably be the amount of caffeine in the bloodstream. The dependent variable might be running speed. The subjects in the study might be a large group of high school students who have been tested and are observed to run the mile at about the same speed. Half the students are given injections of neutral saltwater (shown to have no effect on behavior); the other half are given injections of caffeine equivalent to the amount in three cups of coffee. The tentative idea, or working hypothesis, of the experiment might be that the students given caffeine, which is a stimulant, will run the mile faster than those who have not. If all other factors are held equal, any observed differences in running speed between the two groups can be assumed to be caused only by the independent variable (the amount of caffeine in the bloodstream). The independent variable will produce changes in the dependent variable (running speed). Therefore, if the results show that students given the injections of caffeine are able to run the mile twenty-five seconds faster than those given the saltwater injections, a researcher could feel justified in concluding that caffeine acts as a stimulant for someone running the mile.

Experiment ═══
A procedure in which a researcher systematically manipulates certain variables in order to describe objectively the relation between the variables of concern and the resulting behavior. Well-designed experiments permit inferences about cause and effect.

Variables ═══
Conditions or characteristics of a situation (or experiment) that can change.

Independent variable ═══
The variable in an experiment that is directly and purposefully manipulated by the experimenter.

Dependent variable ═══
The behavior measured by an experimenter in order to assess whether changes in the independent variable affect the behavior under study.

A similar experiment might test the effects of lack of sleep on a subject's response time. The subject's task might be to push a button as quickly as possible when a light is flashed. Imagine that the subject sleeps in the laboratory on four successive nights, and each morning he is tested in a reaction time task. He is allowed to sleep eight hours on each of the first three nights, but only four hours on the fourth. If the response times after the first three nights have been constant, the researcher can infer that any slowing of reaction time on the fourth test morning is the result of sleep deprivation. (See Figure 1.2.)

Many psychological publications called *journals* are devoted solely to reporting experimental studies in which certain elements or variables like those just described have been manipulated.

Control groups. If you were to conduct an experiment, how would you know if the variable you manipulated actually had an effect? How would you be sure that chance factors did not cause a change? The way researchers insure that they have done a good experiment is to use control groups.

A controlled experiment requires comparisons between at least two groups of subjects, all of whom are alike with regard to important variables before the experiment begins. There must be a control group for comparison purposes. A **control group** is a group of subjects who are tested in the same way as the **experimental group,** but who do not have the treatment under study applied to them. Once the subjects are known to be identical with regard to important variables that may affect results, they are assigned to either the experimental

Control group ══════
In an experiment, the group of subjects that does not receive the treatment under investigation. The control group is used for comparison purposes.

Experimental group ══════
In an experiment, the group of subjects that receives the treatment under investigation.

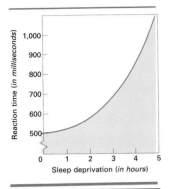

TABLE 1.1 : Design of a Simple Experiment

Number of Subjects	Condition	Independent Variable	Dependent Variable
10	Experimental	Caffeine	Running speed
10	Control	Saltwater	Running speed

FIGURE 1.2 : An experimenter can manipulate the number of hours of sleep deprivation among several groups of subjects. The independent variable in this experiment is the number of hours of sleep deprivation in each of several groups. The behavior being observed and measured (the dependent variable) is the subject's average reaction time in responding to a light after sleep deprivation. By using several groups of subjects, a researcher can observe whether changes in the independent variable cause changes in the dependent variable. In this case, a researcher can observe whether each additional hour of sleep deprivation brings about a corresponding increase in reaction time. In this hypothetical example, each additional hour of sleep deprivation affected reaction time to an increasing extent; short amounts of sleep deprivation produced minimal changes; many hours of deprivation produced significantly greater increases.

or control group by some arbitrary or chance process. In the mile-running experiment, the students who receive shots of neutral saltwater are the control group. Those given injections of caffeine are the experimental group. The independent variable is whether the drug was administered; the dependent variable is running speed. Only the knowledge that all subjects have run the mile at about the same speed before the experiment—that the two groups are truly comparable—allows the experimenter to conclude that the presence of caffeine (and not the previous condition of the runners) is the cause of the second group's improved performance. Without control groups, the importance of the independent variable is not clear and few real conclusions can be drawn from data. (see Table 1.1.)

Sample Size.   It is fairly easy to see that one important factor in an experiment is the size of the sample or group tested—the number of subjects in the group. Suppose there is a ten-second difference between the running times of the control and experimental groups in the running study. An experimenter who has tested only 34 students cannot be certain that the ten-second difference in running time is significant. An experimenter who has tested 2,000 students in both the control and experimental groups can be more certain that the difference is real. The larger the number of subjects observed, the more confident a researcher can be that the results of an experiment are repeatable and accurate. The assumption is that a large sample better represents the population to which the researcher wishes to generalize his or her results. The Appendix discusses these issues in more detail.

Choosing Variables Carefully.   Good experiments usually involve several experimental groups, each tested under different conditions—say, with different dosage levels or different treatment procedures applied. For example, the study of the effects of sleep deprivation on reaction time might involve a control group and four or five experimental groups, with each deprived of sleep for a different length of time. Using several experimental groups allows the researcher to examine the effects of several different periods of sleep deprivation on reaction time.

A good experimenter also looks closely at the nature of the independent variable when designing an experiment. Are there actual values of the independent variable above or below which results will differ markedly? In the experiment on sleep deprivation and reaction time, for example, the researcher might find that a short period of sleep deprivation has no effect on a subject's reaction time and a slightly longer period of deprivation has only a modest effect, but that with more than two hours of sleep deprivation, each additional hour markedly slows reaction time. Thus, sleep deprivation is especially dependent on the duration of the deprivation (look at Figure 1.2 again). Using several groups yields better understanding of how the independent variable (sleep deprivation) affects reaction time (dependent variable).

Few people would debate the importance of careful experimentation to scientific research. But experiments are not the only way to collect data about human behavior. Other techniques, showing other than cause-and-effect relations, also are important. These techniques include questionnaires, interviews, naturalistic observation, and case studies.

Questionnaires

Learning Objective 1.12

Questionnaire
A printed form with questions. Usually given to a large group of people, questionnaires are a means of gathering a substantial amount of data in a short time.

It is very likely that you have filled out surveys before. A survey—or, as it is sometimes called, a **questionnaire**—allows a researcher to gather a large amount of information from a large number of people in a relatively short time. If a survey were sent to all the students taking introductory psychology this year, the results would yield considerable information about the typical student of psychology. The questionnaire might ask each student to list his or her age, sex, height, weight, previous courses taken, grades in high school, SAT scores, number of brothers and sisters, and parents' financial status. There might also be questions regarding sexual relations, career goals, and personal preferences on a number of topics.

One aim of surveys and questionnaires is to discover relationships among traits. For example, surveys often show that family background or socioeconomic status is related to marital status, employment, and number of children desired. By examining the responses on questionnaires, investigators can learn how individual traits group themselves.

The strength of a questionnaire is that it gathers a large amount of information in a relatively short time. Its weaknesses are that it is impersonal and gathers only the information asked in the questions. Because the subjects' range of responses is limited, correlation may be observed, but no cause-and-effect relationships can be inferred.

Interviews

Interview
A series of open-ended questions used to gather basic, detailed information about a person. Though time consuming, this technique allows the interviewer to probe potentially important issues or problems in depth.

You have probably gone through an interview at some time in your life. An **interview** is a face-to-face meeting in which the interviewer asks an individual a series of standardized questions. The subject's responses are usually recorded on tape or written down. The advantage of an interview over a questionnaire is that it allows the interviewer to ask additional questions when appropriate. If the interviewer notes an exaggerated response, instead of recording a simple answer, he or she may decide to ask other related questions, to explore more fully an area that seems to be important to the subject. Although interviews have the advantage of providing detailed information on specific subjects, they also have disadvantages: they take a considerable amount of time and provide a relatively small amount of data. The following list contains typical questions that might be asked in an interview. The questions usually are open-ended—that is, they allow respondents to answer in almost any way they choose.

Describe yourself briefly.
What do you like most about yourself?
What do you like least about yourself?
Have you ever been in trouble?
What was your favorite childhood story?
What would "heaven on earth" be for you?
If by magic you could change anything about yourself, what would you change?

Naturalistic Observation

Probably the simplest way to find out about behavior is to observe it. However, people who are told they are going to be observed tend to become self-conscious and tend to alter their behavior. A psychologist using the technique of **naturalistic observation** tries to observe how people and animals behave in their natural settings, the way birdwatchers watch birds—at a distance, to minimize the effects of their presence on the behavior observed. In fact, many scientists spend a large part of their lives observing the behavior of animals at a distance. Dr. Jane Goodall has spent years in the forests of East Africa observing the behavior of chimps. Slowly, almost imperceptibly, she became a part of the chimps' environment, observing their behavior and taking notes on everything they did. Eventually, she was approached by the chimps. In her naturalistic observation studies, Goodall did not try to interact with the animals, nor did she try to affect their behavior. Her purpose was to gain information about the way these animals behaved naturally.

Goodall's work is neither unique nor exotic. She had to accommodate a bureaucracy that initially would not allow her into the chimpanzee reserve without a European escort; she had to overcome the suspicions of the natives; she suffered from malaria; she had to wait nearly four years to get close enough to her subjects to observe them unobtrusively. She could not be a factor in their behavior.

Good research is often lonely, time consuming, detailed, slow, and expensive. (The National Geographic Society has been a major sponsor of Goodall's projects.) The work is hardly glamorous. Seldom does a researcher get wealthy.

Naturalistic observation ══════
Careful and objective observation of events as they occur in nature, without any intervention by the observer.

Jane Goodall used the technique of naturalistic observation in her study of chimpanzees in Africa.

But work such as Goodall's enables researchers in such fields as zoology, ethology, anthropology, ecology, psychiatry, and psychology to build on her findings to gain new insights in their fields. This cross-pollination of data results in new theories, among them theories on how people behave. Thanks to Jane Goodall, we know more about ourselves.

Naturalistic observers have to take their data where and how they find them. They cannot manipulate the environment, because they might alter the behavior they are observing. Naturalistic observation is an important way to collect data. Its strength is that the data collected are largely free of contamination by the observation situation. Its weakness is that the behavior the psychologist might wish to examine is not always exhibited: sometimes, for example, the animals do not show mating behavior, or groups of people or animals do not migrate. Because variables cannot be manipulated, the data from naturalistic observation, like the data from questionnaires and interviews, do not permit cause-and-effect statements.

Case Studies

Case study

A method of interviewing subjects to gain information about their background, including data on such things as childhood, family, education, and social and sexual interactions.

Perhaps the most exhaustive method of collecting data about a behavior is the **case study.** This method has its roots in other disciplines. When a patient walks into a physician's office, one of the first things the physician typically does is ask for a medical history. Likewise, a psychologist taking a case history tries to find out as much as possible about a person's life. He or she asks about the history of symptoms and about current problems. Like a physician, the psychologist might then diagnose the person's problems and suggest a course of treatment.

A case study is an important research tool; it describes in detail a specific person's responses to the world and can suggest a method of treatment. No two people have exactly the same problems or cope with them in precisely the same way. One person may become jittery and nervous in front of other people; another may laugh or drink excessively. Still, case studies allow researchers to see common behavior patterns or symptoms among people with similar emotional problems.

A case history usually discusses a client's complaints, background, treatment, and other complicating factors. The strength of a case history is that the information it provides is unusually complete. However, that information describes only one individual and his or her unique problem. A researcher cannot generalize from one individual to an entire population. The behavior of one person may be like others', or it may be unique. Psychologists must be cautious even when generalizing from a large number of case histories.

Applying Research Findings

Learning Objective 1.13

Researchers use the five techniques described above—experiments, questionnaires, interviews, naturalistic observation, and case studies—to gather information about behavior. Applying the resulting data and research reports to other settings, such as hospitals or classrooms, however, requires time and caution. For one thing, psychologists do not have all the answers to questions about human behavior. In fact, they have not yet defined all the questions that need to be asked. Psychology is an evolving science; each decade produces new findings and theories, which in turn lead to reevaluations of older theories and results.

With their knowledge and understanding of the complex interactions involved in human behavior, psychologists can help people to lead happy, fulfilled, well-adjusted lives.

For another thing, before actual problems can be solved in meaningful ways, much research and experimentation are necessary. Observing and measuring behavior carefully are themselves time-consuming processes. Then researchers must repeat their successful experiments to ensure that their findings are reliable. In their eagerness to test their theories, researchers sometimes wish that direct applications of their theories could be tested (and validated) sooner in the real world. But even after research has been published and reviewed by professionals, possible applications should be used cautiously at first and with small numbers of people.

Psychologists are both scientists and practitioners. They seek both to gather basic information about behavior and to apply that knowledge in meaningful ways. Often, those applications have direct consequences for people on a day-by-day basis. Psychologists apply their research findings to help people better manage weight loss programs. They develop therapy techniques that help people develop successful coping strategies when under stress. Some psychologists apply behavior principles to classroom management, others to motivational techniques in the workplace. Some work at helping people like Phil Marshall solve problems. In each case, basic science is being used as the foundation on which to build applications.

PROGRESS CHECK   1.4

1. Match each of the following key concepts and terms with the appropriate definition.

variable   independent variable   dependent variable   correlation

Learning Objective 1.10

A. _____ A measure of relationships, expressing how changes in one event are related to changes in another event. Such measures do not permit researchers to make cause-and-effect statements.

Learning Objective 1.11

B. _____ A characteristic of a situation or person that is subject to change in an experiment.

Learning Objective 1.11   C. _____ The part of an experiment that is directly and purposefully manipulated by the experimenter.

Learning Objective 1.11   D. _____ The behavior measured in an experiment to assess whether changes in the variable being manipulated had an effect on the behavior.

2. Complete each of the following sentences with one of the options provided.

Learning Objective 1.10   A. The research methods used by psychologists include the same techniques used by other scientists, are sometimes refinements of those techniques, and, in some cases, are _____.
(more difficult to understand : unique to psychology)

Learning Objective 1.10   B. The description of Harry Harlow's research with monkeys is presented in this chapter to provide an example of how researchers _____.
(sometimes discover things almost by accident : determine significant differences)

Learning Objective 1.10   C. A researcher has found _____ when it is unlikely that the behavioral event under investigation could have occurred by chance alone.
(a significant difference : an independent variable : a correlation)

Learning Objective 1.11   D. One weakness of controlled experiments is that researchers may unintentionally _____.
(investigate a simplistic hypothesis : influence the results)

Learning Objective 1.11   E. A(n) _____ group is used for comparison purposes in an experiment, and the subjects in this group do not receive the treatment under investigation.
(independent : control : experimental)

Learning Objective 1.11   F. The _____ the number of subjects in the control and experimental groups, the more confident we can be that the results of the experiment are repeatable and accurate.
(smaller : larger)

Learning Objective 1.12   G. The advantage of an interview over a questionnaire as a means for collecting data is that the interview allows the researcher to _____.
(save time : ask additional questions : detect lying)

Learning Objective 1.12   H. The disadvantage of the naturalistic observation approach to collecting data is _____.
(the researcher's presence : that the target behavior may not be exhibited)

Learning Objective 1.12   I. Questionnaires, interviews, and naturalistic observation allow researchers to discover _____.
(cause-and-effect relationships : correlations)

Learning Objective 1.13   J. Psychology is _____ science.
(an evolving : a mature)

Keeping Pace with Chapter 1

Applying Principles

Identify the independent and dependent variables in each of the following experiments.

1. A researcher conducts a study in which she measures academic performance among students who do and others who do not eat breakfast regularly.
   A. independent variable _____
   B. dependent variable _____

2. Children in a second-grade classroom are rewarded for cooperative behaviors, and a school psychologist observes to see if their rate of being cooperative increases as a result.
   A. independent variable _____
   B. dependent variable _____

3. A psychologist investigates the effects that alcohol consumption has on the number of dreams subjects have while sleeping.
   A. independent variable _____
   B. dependent variable _____

Self-Test

Before proceeding to the Self-Test, REVIEW the Learning Objectives listed at the chapter opening and RECITE from memory everything you can remember in support of them. Then, take this Self-Test as if it were to be graded by your teacher. Use the Learning Objective numbers in the Answer Section as a reference to restudy the corresponding text pages and Progress Checks for any incorrectly answered questions.

1. Modern psychologists define psychology as the science of

   A. the mind.
   B. behavior.
   C. emotional disturbance.
   D. life-style.

2. Which of the following statements is *false?*

   A. Psychologists tend to consider research one of their most important activities.
   B. Psychoanalysts are usually psychiatrists.
   C. Psychologists, psychiatrists, and psychoanalysts use such different approaches that they seldom are found working together.
   D. Psychiatrists can prescribe medications when treating emotional disturbances.

3. Currently, among psychologists who hold doctoral degrees, _____ work for the government, business, or industry.

   A. 4 percent
   B. 14 percent
   C. 25 percent
   D. 34 percent

4. The main difference between clinical and counseling psychologists is

   A. their ability to conduct research within the job setting.
   B. their ability to work for public agencies.
   C. that counseling psychologists have traditionally worked with less serious behavior problems, but this may be changing.
   D. their interest in helping people adjust to new or stressful situations.

5. People who choose to see a psychotherapist to get help with some personal problem should

   A. determine whether the therapist is competent and has received proper training.
   B. feel comfortable with the therapist's goals and approach to treatment.
   C. consider himself or herself a mental health "consumer."
   D. all of the above

6. In which of the following situations would you be *least* likely to find an experimental psychologist?

    A. Teaching psychology to college freshmen.
    B. Studying how noise affects chimpanzees.
    C. Investigating the variables that lead to attraction.
    D. Working with juvenile delinquents in a detention center.

7. Developmental, social, educational, and industrial/organizational psychologists

    A. may be research psychologists or applied psychologists.
    B. are applied psychologists.
    C. are research psychologists.
    D. make up the field of human services in psychology.

8. Which of the following would be considered a research method? A psychologist

    A. gives a suspected criminal a battery of tests and analyzes and interprets the data.
    B. explains to the parents of hyperactive children why their children might benefit from a low sugar, high protein diet.
    C. writes a child guidance book to help parents raise emotionally stable children.
    D. teaches preschool teachers about children's reading readiness age.

9. The examination of the contents of the mind through self-reports of what one is thinking and feeling is called

    A. interpretation.
    B. introspection.
    C. perception.
    D. free association.

10. Correlations

    A. indicate that the presence of one variable causes a change in a second variable.
    B. allow a researcher to make causal inferences concerning behavior.
    C. tell us that the presence of one variable is regularly associated with the presence of another variable.
    D. provide enough information about relationships that a researcher is able to make statements concerning significant differences.

11. The differences observed among experimental and control groups in a carefully controlled experiment are the result of

    A. the dependent variable.
    B. the independent variable.
    C. the sample size.
    D. A and C.

12. Data gathered from case studies

    A. allow researchers to see common behavior patterns among individuals with similar emotional problems.
    B. do not provide very complete information.
    C. can be used to generalize causes of behavior from one individual to an entire population.
    D. allow the researcher to minimize the effects of his or her presence.

13. Basic information gathered through scientific research should be applied

    A. only when medical treatment is ineffective.
    B. with caution and, in the beginning, to small numbers of people.
    C. as soon as an experiment has been completed so that people in need can benefit from the new knowledge.
    D. to mentally ill patients and then to the normal population.

Learning

2

2

Learning Objectives

When you have mastered the material in this chapter, you will be able to:

1. Define *conditioning* and *learning* and list the three important components found in the definition of learning. (p. 36)

2. Explain how psychologists determine when learning has occurred and state two situations in which the differences between human and animal learning processes become apparent and important. (p. 37)

3. Explain how classically conditioned responses are like and unlike reflexes. (p. 38)

4. Describe the three stages of classical conditioning, identify the various stimuli and responses involved, and state some human reflexes that can be tied to neutral stimuli through conditioning. (p. 38)

5. Explain how emotional responses are learned through classical conditioning, describe higher-order conditioning, and briefly explain how classical conditioning can be used to help people with behavior problems. (p. 40)

6. Identify the reinforcers involved in classical and higher-order conditioning and explain how the strength, timing, and frequency of pairings of the unconditioned stimulus affect the classical conditioning process. (p. 42)

7. Define *extinction* and *spontaneous recovery* and give an example of how these phenomena occur with classically conditioned responses. (p. 44)

8. Describe how stimulus generalization and stimulus discrimination occur in classical conditioning. (p. 44)

9. Explain why active involvement on the part of the organism is not involved in classical conditioning and discuss the extent to which classical conditioning can be used to explain the development of learned behaviors. (p. 47)

10. Describe instrumental conditioning and discuss the efforts and views of Skinner and Thorndike, two American psychologists who clarified this type of conditioning. (p. 49)

11. Name and describe two devices psychologists use to conduct research on instrumental conditioning. (p. 50)

12. Describe shaping and superstitious behavior. (p. 51)

13. Make distinctions between positive and negative reinforcement, primary and secondary reinforcers, and escape and avoidance behavior. (p. 52)

14. Identify and describe the types of punishers that are involved in instrumental conditioning; discuss why punishment works best when combined with reinforcement. (p. 54)

15. Explain how the strength and timing of consequences affect instrumental conditioning. (p. 55)

16. Describe four schedules of consequences. (p. 56)

17. Explain how stimulus generalization, stimulus discrimination, extinction, and spontaneous recovery occur in instrumental conditioning. (p. 58)

18. Give an example of how problem behaviors can be controlled by making practical use of instrumental conditioning and describe how learning theories contributed to the development of computer-aided instructional systems. (p. 61)

19. Compare and contrast classical and instrumental conditioning. (p. 64)

20. Describe observational learning and discuss some of the difficulties involved in studying how it occurs. (p. 66)

BEFORE YOU READ ON, take time to **SURVEY** the chapter, form an idea of what is to be learned (from margin Learning Objective numbers), and set goals for your study time. Then, ask yourself **QUESTIONS** about the material as you **READ**, seeking help for any sections you do not understand.

Lisa and Susan had been friends and co-workers in the middle school office for nine years. As secretaries, they had worked through three principals, two dozen new teachers, and several part-time secretaries. Their hard work, dedication, and years of experience were appreciated by everyone, except, seemingly, the school board.

Both women justifiably felt it was time for a significant salary increase. They felt that they had held the school together during several personnel changes. The school board claimed, however, that the district did not have the money. Lisa and Susan did their jobs in an atmosphere of growing frustration and anger. Late in the school year, there was a significant break—a new paper mill announced it was going to expand its plant. This meant more tax money to the county; it quickly followed that the school board funded new bleachers for the high school gym, three new teacher positions, and an upgrade of one secretary to the position of administrative assistant.

Susan was given the job of administrative assistant. Delighted with a 20 percent increase in salary and new responsibilities, she went about her new job eagerly. She felt rewarded after years of hard work. Lisa was not pleased; she felt that she was deserving, too. After nine years of long hours and dedicated service, Lisa felt put upon. Her work suffered; she was coming into the office late; she was taking her full lunch break and a few extra minutes; she was making mistakes on tasks she had done dozens of times. Her typing, which had always been flawless, now showed careless errors. Her quick smile and enthusiastic responses to teachers and parents were disappearing.

Lisa reasoned that she should not work so hard. From time to time, she thought, "Let Susan do it—she's getting paid the big bucks." Her attitude suffered, and her productivity had clearly dropped. The fact that she was not paid what she felt she was worth made her unhappy. She was angry with the school board, and she thought about looking for other positions. The smiles and appreciation, which had acted as rewards for her work before, were no longer satisfactory. Her anger toward the school board spilled over to Susan, and their relationship suffered.

LISA SHOWED A PHENOMENON well-known to psychologists. People need to feel that their work is worthwhile and that it is appropriately recognized and rewarded. As long as Lisa and Susan were earning the same wage, Lisa felt comfortable in an underpaid position. But as soon as Susan was given more money for what Lisa felt was the same work, she became discouraged, angry, and unproductive. Lisa was thoroughly capable of performing her job duties with skill and enthusiasm; she had shown that for years. She had learned all the tasks and had all the necessary skills. However, her wealth of knowledge about her job was no longer evident.

We all know that learning goes on throughout life. People learn new, productive behaviors like computer programming as well as socially nonproductive behaviors like stealing and drug abuse. Learning is an ongoing process for most of us. Of course, not everything we learn is remembered, nor does it necessarily show in our day-to-day behavior. Many of our learned responses are seen only on certain occasions in response to a specific event. We have come to think of puppets as amusing, blood as frightening, and of the flag as a symbol of honor and patriotism. These responses are learned responses.

Learning to respond in a certain way is often the result of conditioning. Psychologists use the term *conditioning* in a very specific way. **Conditioning** is a systematic procedure through which new responses are learned. This chapter explores several types of conditioning and some of the basic processes of learning and how Lisa's behavior may have been a direct result of these processes. In fact, most of us exhibit behaviors we have learned, and the frequency with which we show them is often determined by some of these same processes that affected Lisa. Let us examine this term *learning* more closely because it has a special meaning for psychologists.

Learning is a relatively permanent change in behavior that occurs as a result of experience. This definition has three important parts: behavior change, experience in the environment, and permanence. Let us consider these three parts of the definition.

Some measurable *behavior change* must be evident for learning to occur. For example, do you remember learning how to whistle? The change in your behavior when you were first asked to whistle is a change anyone could observe: initially, you puckered your lips and blew a silent stream of air; later, you came to pucker your lips, blow air, and produce a tune.

Learning occurs because of an *experience in the environment;* an event or stimulus causes a change in an organism and initiates learning. In the case of

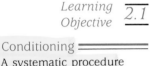

Learning 2.1
Objective

Conditioning ═══════
A systematic procedure through which new responses are learned.

Learning ═══════
A relatively permanent change in behavior that occurs as a result of experiences in the environment.

Through practice and experience, these children will learn to swim, undergoing a change in their behavior that they are not likely to forget.

learning to whistle, the experiences that led you to learn to whistle were probably watching and listening to other people whistle and then practicing until you got it right.

The third component of the definition of learning is *permanence.* To be considered a learned behavior, the learning must be relatively permanent. Before you learned to whistle, you may, perhaps, by chance, have pursed your lips and blown with just the right pressure and surprised yourself by whistling. But, when asked to repeat the whistle, you were unable to do it. In that case, you had not learned to whistle. After you had learned the procedure well, you could whistle successfully at every attempt—without even thinking about how to do it. And, if months were to pass without whistling, you would probably still be able to whistle again at a moment's notice with no relearning required. In that case, your new behavior is said to be permanent—you have learned through experience. Thus, through experience, you have learned to whistle—a relatively permanent behavior change.

Learning 2.2
Objective

Reflex
An involuntary behavior that occurs without prior learning, in response to stimuli.

In contrast to learned responses, **reflexes** are involuntary responses, such as flinching when an object nearly strikes your face. Reflexes are not learned, and they occur without prior experiences. When psychologists study learning, they are curious about how experiences result in relatively permanent changes in the organism. Because the internal processes of learning cannot be seen, psychologists study changes in behavior or performance that are the result of learning. They make inferences about the learning process by observing overt behavior and measuring physiological changes. Psychologists can easily observe such overt behaviors as an eye blink or throwing a ball, and they can measure less obvious, internal changes by monitoring such responses as brain-wave activity, heartbeat, and temperature. An animal or human being may or may not display a change in overt behavior, but once it has learned something, a relatively permanent or stable modification has occurred (Lachman, 1983).

Many inferences that psychologists make about the learning process come from studies of animal behavior. Although some psychologists claim that different processes underlie animal and human learning, this distinction tends to be an arbitrary one. Numerous experiments have shown that similar processes underlie both animal and human behavior. The differences become apparent—and important—only when more complex behaviors are being evaluated and when an experiment requires the use of language.

This chapter discusses the three basic learning processes: classical conditioning, instrumental conditioning, and observational learning. As you read about the principles underlying these processes, try to think how they have helped or hindered your learning a new skill and how they influence your habits.

CLASSICAL CONDITIONING

You will see that many important discoveries in psychology have happened by chance—scientists say that such findings are serendipitous. Serendipity is the ability to find useful things by chance. One of the earliest psychological findings was a serendipitous one: classical conditioning.

Before considering some basics of this conditioning process, let us look at some elements basic to any type of conditioning. Most of us have certain responses to certain stimuli or events in the environment. For example, many people react with a set of learned fear responses when asked to sit in a dentist's chair—they have learned to associate the chair with drilling and subsequent pain. In some cases, even the smell of a dentist's office can elicit these fear responses. A chair by itself does not elicit fear, but when associated with pain it comes to be a stimulus that can elicit a set of fear responses. Conditioning in classical conditioning thus refers to the procedure by which a new response (such as fear) is learned to a stimulus (such as a dentist's chair).

Learning
Objective 2.3

You probably have learned to respond with a feeling of suspense, apprehension, or fear whenever you hear sinister-sounding music during a movie. You may have learned the response of desire on seeing a red hunk of metal crafted into a sleek shape, when it has a t-top, four wheels, leather interior, and a 3.5 liter turbo engine. Our responses to dentists, music, and automobiles have been conditioned over the years. Psychologists call such learned responses *conditioned responses.*

When psychologists first began to study learning, they focused on simple behaviors that seemed related—on behaviors in which specific stimuli seemed to be associated with specific responses. In doing so, they realized that both animals and human beings exhibit reflexive behaviors; that is, like reflexes, the behaviors occur involuntarily. Reflexive behaviors are *elicited,* or brought about, by a stimulus; each time the stimulus occurs, so does the reflexive response: food in the mouth leads to salivation; a tap on the knee leads to a knee jerk; a bright light in the eye leads to pupil contraction. A person's fear responses to a dentist's chair or office may also occur so automatically that they appear to be reflexive. Like reflexes, conditioned responses are involuntary; unlike reflexes, however, they are learned.

Pavlov's Famous Experiment

Learning
Objective 2.4

With the basic idea that a stimulus usually leads to a response of some sort, let us examine the process so closely associated with Pavlov—classical conditioning.

In 1927, Ivan Pavlov, a Russian physiologist turned psychologist, reported a now-famous series of experiments that used conditioning procedures. Pavlov knew it was normal for dogs to salivate when they ate; salivation is a reflexive behavior that aids feeding and digestion. However, he noticed that salivation occurred even *before* the dogs tasted their food. He thought perhaps this happened because the dogs had learned to associate the trainers who brought them food with the food itself. This insight led Pavlov to wonder if he could condition or teach dogs to salivate to a new and neutral stimulus, a bell.

Unconditioned stimulus
A stimulus that normally produces an involuntary, measurable response.

Unconditioned response
The unlearned or involuntary response to an unconditioned stimulus.

Food is a natural (unlearned) stimulus that produces salivation; Pavlov called it an **unconditioned stimulus.** He called salivation an **unconditioned response** because it is a natural (unlearned, involuntary) response to food in the mouth. Pavlov knew that the unconditioned stimulus (food) generally brought about the unconditioned response (salivation). He attached tubes to the inside of the dogs' mouths to measure the amounts of saliva produced by food. Then he introduced a new stimulus, a bell (see Figure 2.1). Because the sound of a bell normally has no relation to salivation, Pavlov called it a *neutral stimulus.* Pavlov measured the amount of saliva the dogs produced when a bell was rung by itself and found it negligible. He then began the conditioning process: he rang the bell and *immediately* placed food in the dogs' mouths. After several pairings in which the sound of the bell was presented along with the food, the dogs salivated normally in response to the sound of the bell alone.

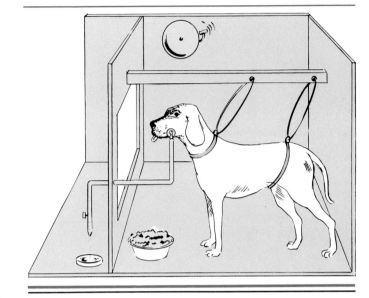

*Ivan Pavlov (1849-1936)
watching an experiment in his
laboratory in 1934.*

FIGURE 2.1 : Pavlov attached a tube to a dog's cheek
and measured the number of drops of saliva produced
in response to food paired with the sound of a bell and
to the sound of a bell alone. The dog learned to associate the ringing of the bell with the presentation of food. This kind of
association is a fundamental component of classical conditioning.

Conditioned stimulus ══
A neutral stimulus that,
through repeated
association with an
unconditioned stimulus,
becomes capable of
eliciting a conditioned
response.

Conditioned response ══
The response elicited by a
conditioned stimulus.

Classical conditioning ══
A conditioning process in
which an originally neutral
stimulus, by repeated
pairing with a stimulus
that naturally elicits a
response, comes to elicit a
similar or even identical
response; sometimes called
Pavlovian conditioning.

At this point, the dogs had learned a new response—of salivating to the sound
of a bell. Pavlov called the bell a **conditioned stimulus** because it elicited
salivation as a result of learning.

The learned response, salivation to the sound of the bell, Pavlov called a
conditioned response. Pavlov discovered that the conditioned stimulus (the
bell) brought about a similar but somewhat weaker response than the unconditioned stimulus (the food). This entire process is called **classical conditioning**
or *Pavlovian conditioning.* Figure 2.2 outlines the three basic stages; Figure 2.3
on the next page shows a typical learning or acquisition curve.

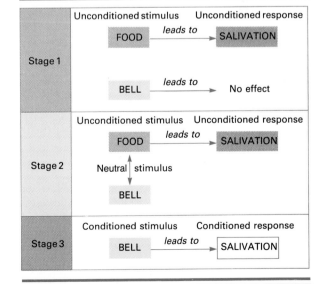

FIGURE 2.2 : In classical
conditioning, there are three
basic stages by which a
neutral stimulus eventually
leads to a conditioned
response, such as salivating.

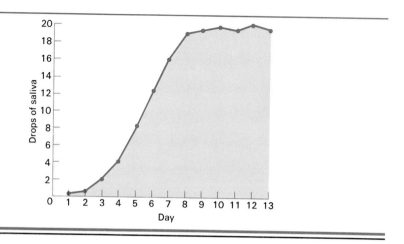

The key characteristic of classical conditioning is the use of an originally neutral stimulus (such as a bell) to elicit a response (such as salivation) through repeated pairing of the neutral stimulus with an unconditioned stimulus (such as food) that elicits the response naturally. In this way, the formerly neutral stimulus comes to elicit a reflexlike response.

Classical conditioning can also be seen in human beings. For example, when an object touches an infant's lips, the infant immediately starts sucking; this occurs because usually the object is the nipple of a breast or bottle, which the infant sucks to get milk. The nipple (an unconditioned stimulus) elicits an unconditioned response, sucking. Repeated pairing of a sound or light with the nipple can condition infants to suck at the mere introduction of the sound or light. D. P. Marquis (1931) obtained this effect in infants after only nine days of conditioning.

Sucking is only one of many reflexive behaviors in human beings. Newborns show reflexive responses to loud noises, pain, falling, and even strange people or surroundings. A loud noise, for example, naturally elicits a startle response—an outstretching of the arms and legs associated with changes in heart rate, blood pressure, and respiration. Psychologists have learned that whenever a stimulus naturally elicits a response, other neutral stimuli can also be used, through conditioning, to elicit the same response. Thus, a person's heart rate, breathing, blood pressure, and sweating can be tied to a neutral stimulus during conditioning.

Psychologists Have Learned about Conditioning Emotional Responses

Some psychologists believe that many emotional responses, such as the fear response to a dentist's chair, are classically conditioned. If you experience pain every time you sit in a dentist's chair, you will eventually become conditioned to feel afraid each time you see it. Consider another example of this process: a child who is repeatedly frightened by a sudden loud noise while playing with a favorite pet will become conditioned to be afraid each time he or she sees the pet. Table 2.1 lists several examples of classical conditioning.

Once a formerly neutral stimulus takes on conditioning value, it is likely to elicit the conditioned response whenever it is presented. Furthermore, through

TABLE 2.1: Examples of Classical Conditioning

Organism	Conditioned Stimulus	Unconditioned Stimulus	Response
Animals			
Dog	Bell	Food	Salivation
Sheep	Buzzer	Electric shock to foot	Flexing of leg
Rat	Tone	Electric shock	Fear, as measured by stopping eating
Rat	Taste of saccharin	Nausea from poison	Avoidance of saccharin
Human beings			
Adult	Buzzer	Electric shock	Fear, as measured by sweating of the hand
Infant	Sight of hot radiator	Burn from radiator	Fear, as measured by crying
Patient	Sound or sight of dentist's drill	Pain in tooth	Fear, as measured by increased heart rate
Coffee drinker	Taste of coffee	Stimulation from caffeine	Arousal (even when drinking decaffeinated coffee)

Source: Adapted from W. F. Hill, 1981.

Higher-order conditioning
The process by which a neutral stimulus takes on conditioned properties through pairing with a conditioned stimulus.

a process known as **higher-order conditioning,** a neutral stimulus that has been associated with a well-established conditioned stimulus can itself take on conditioning properties. Suppose a light is paired with electric shocks so that, on seeing the light, a dog exhibits fear; the light has become a conditioned stimulus that elicits a set of fear responses. After repeated sessions pairing the light and shock, a bell is occasionally presented with or before the light, and the shock omitted. This new stimulus, the bell, has the potential to take on conditioned stimulus properties. After repeated pairings, the dog will learn to associate the two events, and the bell by itself will elicit a fear response. Now suppose a third stimulus is introduced—an experimenter in a white lab coat. The dog may then learn to associate the experimenter in the white lab coat with the bell or light. After enough trials through a chain of associations, the dog may make conditioned fear responses to each of the three stimuli—the light, the bell, and people in white lab coats (Pavlov, 1927; Rescorla, 1977).

Everyday life furnishes many additional examples of conditioning. Letter carriers often experience the pain and fright of being bitten by dogs. Because dogs deliver the unconditioned stimulus (the bite) that elicits the unconditioned response (pain), through this repeated pairing dogs can become conditioned stimuli. At that point, the mere sight or sound of a dog will elicit a series of defensive reactions associated with fear and pain: increased heart rate, respiration, and sweating. Other originally neutral stimuli, such as children, cars, or social gatherings, are equally capable of becoming conditioned stimuli that elicit defensive reactions.

The association of events through the process of classical conditioning is easily seen. For example, a person who once associated pleasant feelings with someone who was dark-haired or chubby may later find other dark-haired or chubby people especially attractive. The producers of television commercials use the same principle by commonly featuring attractive models and settings.

Through repeated exposure, we become conditioned to respond to many common, everyday stimuli.

They hope that by associating their product (a neutral stimulus) with an unconditioned stimulus that naturally elicits a positive emotional response, viewers will be conditioned to experience feelings of pleasure or anticipation whenever they see or think of the product. Similarly, television and movies condition people to associate different types of characters or events in a story with certain types of music. An audience can be cued to respond to a character or scene before either appears on the screen by their mere introduction of appropriate sinister-sounding or romantic music.

Researchers who have studied conditioning, especially such phenomena as higher-order conditioning, have argued that principles derived in the laboratory can be applied to help people with behavior problems. Classical conditioning has been used to treat alcoholics (for example, Lemere & Voegtlin, 1950). By pairing alcohol with a drug that induces nausea and vomiting, the psychologist attempts to condition the subject to avoid alcohol. Researchers reason that conditioning procedures may also be useful to therapists in teaching their clients new, more adaptive behaviors. For example, therapists have used a technique called systematic desensitization (discussed fully in Chapter 15) to teach fearful and tense people new and different responses (such as relaxation) to situations or stimuli that make them fearful.

Classical Conditioning Is Affected by Several Important Variables

Learning Objective 2.6

You may have reasoned that classical conditioning is not as simple a process as it first appears. Being conditioned to lights, buzzers, music, and television commercials has associated with it many important variables that affect conditioning. How loud does the buzzer have to be? How long does the bell have to ring? How sinister must sinister music be? Does soft sinister music act as a conditioned stimulus? As with many other psychological phenomena, situation variables affect when, if, and under what conditions classical conditioning will occur.

One of the most important variables is the reinforcer or reward. In classical conditioning, a *reinforcer* is any event that increases the likelihood that a conditioned response will recur. In higher-order conditioning, the reinforcer can be any well-established conditioned stimulus; but in basic classical conditioning, the reinforcer is always an unconditioned stimulus. For example, in Pavlov's experiment, food acted as a reinforcer: it increased the likelihood that salivation would occur when a bell or light was presented just before it. Similarly, a puff of air acts as a reinforcer by increasing the likelihood that a light or tone presented along with it will elicit a conditioned response, the eyeblink. Some of the most important variables in classical conditioning are the strength, timing, and frequency of the unconditioned stimulus.

Strength of the Unconditioned Stimulus. A puff of air delivered to an organism's eye elicits a conditioned reflex easily, but only if the air puff is sufficiently strong. Research has shown that when the unconditioned stimulus is strong and elicits a quick and regular reflexive unconditioned response, then conditioning of the neutral stimulus is likely. When the unconditioned stimulus is very weak, it is unlikely to elicit an unconditioned response; pairing a neutral stimulus with a weak unconditioned stimulus will not lead to conditioning.

Timing.   For conditioning to occur, an unconditioned stimulus must be paired with a conditioned stimulus closely enough in time that the two become associated. In Pavlov's experiment, conditioning would probably not have occurred if the bell and food had been presented an hour apart. The two stimuli may be presented simultaneously or separated by a short interval. The actual time between the onset of the two stimuli varies from study to study and depends on a number of variables, including the type of conditioned response, the type of unconditioned stimulus, and its duration (Holder & Roberts, 1985). A general guideline for strong conditioned responses, however, is that the conditioned stimulus should occur about 0.5 second before the unconditioned stimulus and overlap with it, particularly for such reflexes as the eyeblink (see Figure 2.4).

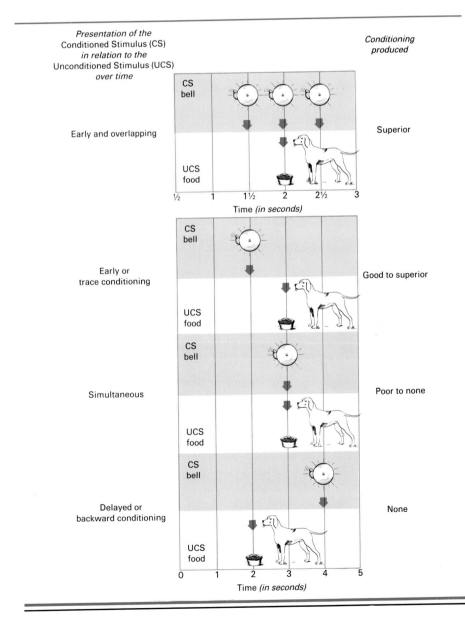

FIGURE 2.4 : The conditioned stimulus (such as a bell) can be presented before, during, or even after the unconditioned stimulus (such as food). The most effective conditioning, however, occurs when the conditioned stimulus precedes and overlaps with the unconditioned stimulus.

Frequency of Pairings.   Merely pairing a neutral stimulus with an unconditioned stimulus does not by itself result in conditioning. Frequent pairings are usually necessary; for example, if food and the sound of a bell are paired on every trial, a dog is conditioned much more quickly than if the stimuli are paired only on every other trial. Once the conditioned response has reached its maximum strength, further pairings of the stimuli do not increase the response.

Are Conditioned Responses Forgotten? Extinction and Spontaneous Recovery

Learning Objective 2.7

Anybody who has played a sport like baseball, tennis, racketball, or golf will tell you that unless you practice, you are likely to forget some of the maneuvers you used two months before. Many things we learn in life are forgotten, including many responses that have been conditioned.

What would have happened to Pavlov's dogs if he had rung his bell each day but never had followed it with food? What would happen if you went to the dentist each day for two months, but the dentist, instead of drilling, always served lunch? Such ideas have been rigorously explored in the laboratory. Let us assume that in a situation such as Pavlov and his dog after conditioning occurred, a researcher continues to present the conditioned stimulus (bell) but no longer presents the unconditioned stimulus (food). With every such trial, the likelihood of a conditioned response decreases.

In classical conditioning, **extinction** is the process by which the withholding of the unconditioned stimulus (the reinforcer) reduces the probability and often the strength of a conditioned response. Imagine an eyeblink study in which a puff of air has been associated with a buzzer that consistently elicits the conditioned eyeblink response. If the unconditioned stimulus (the puff of air) is no longer delivered, the likelihood that the buzzer will continue to elicit the eyeblink response decreases over time (see Figure 2.5). When presentation of the buzzer alone no longer elicits the conditioned response, the conditioned response has undergone extinction. If the sight of a dentist had usually elicited fear, but during office visits for the last sixty days no pain has occurred, the likelihood of a fear response is diminished—it has undergone extinction.

In a phenomenon known as **spontaneous recovery** a conditioned response that has undergone extinction will recur after a rest period. Suppose a dog has been conditioned to salivate to the sound of a bell. After a long series of trials in which food is no longer paired with the bell, the dog will show few or no responses to the bell—the behavior will have undergone extinction. However, if the dog is placed in the experimental situation again after a rest period of twenty minutes, its salivary response will recur briefly (though less strongly than before). This phenomenon shows that the effects of extinction are not permanent and that the learned response is not totally forgotten (see Figure 2.6). Spontaneous recovery is fairly common. Many veterans of combat, for example, show sharp autonomic nervous system responses whenever they hear a siren, even long after returning from war.

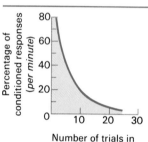

FIGURE 2.5 : In the process of extinction, the percentage of times an organism will display a conditioned response decreases when the unconditioned stimulus (such as food) is no longer presented.

Extinction
In classical conditioning, the process of reducing the likelihood of a conditioned response to a conditioned stimulus by withholding the unconditioned stimulus (the reinforcer).

Spontaneous recovery
The recurrence of a conditioned response following a rest period after extinction.

Is That My Child? Stimulus Generalization and Discrimination

Learning Objective 2.8

Imagine that you had been bitten by a cat when you were three years old. You were being playful but had frightened the cat and she scratched your hand and

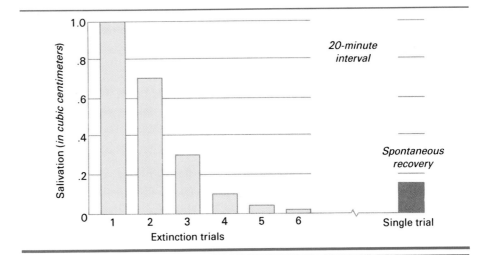

FIGURE 2.6 : In a series of trials at 3-minute intervals, Pavlov extinguished a conditioned salivary response by omitting presentation of the unconditioned stimulus (food). After a rest interval of 20 minutes, the salivary response recurred, but it was not as strong as in previous trials. (Data from Pavlov, 1927, p. 58)

bit your finger. It would not be surprising if you developed a fear of that cat, or other cats. Do you think you might have developed a fear of dogs, or other four-legged animals? If after a bad experience with a kitten you developed a fear of cats or small animals in general, most adults would not be surprised. Everyday experience teaches us that we generalize from one situation to another. In the same way, it is not uncommon for a person who has had a bad experience with a person from out of town to come to dislike all out-of-towners. When people respond in the same way to a similar stimulus, psychologists call this **stimulus generalization.** More formally, when an organism responds to a stimulus that is similar but not identical to a training stimulus, stimulus generalization has occurred. The extent to which an organism responds to a stimulus depends on how similar that stimulus is to the training stimulus. For example, if a loud tone serves as a conditioned stimulus to an eyeblink response, other tones of similar intensity will produce the same conditioned response, less similar tones will produce the response to a lesser extent, and totally dissimilar tones will produce little or no response at all (see Figure 2.7).

Human beings and animals can, however, learn stimulus discrimination—to respond only to a conditioned stimulus rather than to any stimulus that is

Stimulus generalization
Responding to stimuli similar to, but not the same as, the training stimulus.

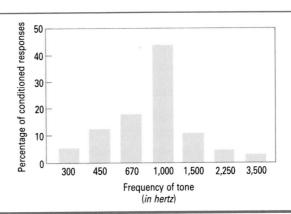

FIGURE 2.7 : *Stimulus generalization* occurs when an organism emits a conditioned response to stimuli similar but not identical to the conditioned stimulus. The bar graph shows the responses of an organism trained with a 1,000-Hertz tone. When the organism was later presented with tones of different frequencies, its percentage of responses decreased as the tone's frequency became increasingly different. (Data from Jenkins & Harrison, 1960)

Stimulus discrimination ═══════
The process by which an organism learns to respond only to a specific reinforced stimulus; the complementary process to stimulus generalization.

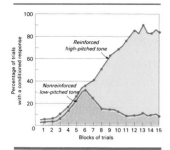

FIGURE 2.8 : In *stimulus discrimination,* two tones initially elicit a conditioned response from an organism. When one stimulus continues to be reinforced and the other is not, stimulus discrimination occurs. In this case, we see conditioned responses being produced for the proper conditioned stimulus but decreasing in frequency for the nonreinforced one.

similar to it. To make organisms better at conditioned **stimulus discrimination,** researchers pair only the exact conditioned stimulus with the unconditioned stimulus (see Figure 2.8). Thus, an organism learns to respond only to the conditioned neutral stimulus. Furthermore, the unconditioned stimulus (for example, food) is never presented along with even slightly dissimilar neutral stimuli. Table 2.2 highlights the four important properties of classical conditioning.

Animals that have learned to differentiate between pairs of stimuli display frustration or even aggression when discrimination is subsequently made difficult or impossible. In a series of experiments, Pavlov (1927) first trained an animal to discriminate between a circle and an ellipse. He then changed the shape of the ellipse on successive trials to look more and more like the circle next to it. Eventually, the animal was unable to discriminate between the shapes and randomly chose one or the other. In other similar studies, animals have become agitated and upset and acted fearful and aggressive. Human beings may exhibit the same sort of behavior when placed in situations in which they feel forced to make a response but do not know how to respond correctly. A football player who is outwitted by a clever opponent may lose his usual agility and stand on the field unsure of which way to go, furious with his own inability to respond. In such situations, behavior may become stereotyped and limited in scope; people may choose either not to respond to the stimuli at all or respond always in the same way (Lundin, 1961; Maier & Klee, 1941).

TABLE 2.2 : Four Important Properties of Classical Conditioning

Property	Definition	Example
Extinction	The process of reducing the probability of a conditioned response by withholding the unconditioned stimulus (the reinforcer)	An infant conditioned to suck in response to a light is no longer given the unconditioned stimulus of stroking the lips; the infant stops sucking in response to the conditioned stimulus.
Spontaneous recovery	The recurrence of a conditioned response following a rest period after extinction	A dog's conditioned salivary response has undergone extinction; after a rest period, the dog again salivates in response to the conditioned stimulus, though less than it did before.
Stimulus generalization	The process by which an organism learns to respond to stimuli similar but not identical to the training stimulus	A dog conditioned to salivate in response to a high-pitched tone also salivates to a lower-pitched tone.
Stimulus discrimination	The process by which an organism learns to respond to a reinforced stimulus and then to no other similar stimulus; the complementary process to stimulus generalization	A goat is conditioned to salivate only in response to lights of high intensity and not to lights of low intensity.

TABLE 2.3 : Types of Learning: Classical Conditioning

Type of Learning	Procedure	Result	Example
Classical conditioning	A neutral stimulus (such as a bell) is paired with an unconditioned stimulus (such as food).	The neutral stimulus becomes a conditioned stimulus—it elicits the conditioned response.	A bell elicits a salivary response in a dog.

Summary of Key Concepts

Learning Objective 2.9

In classical conditioning, neutral stimuli are paired with unconditioned stimuli and take on the properties necessary to elicit conditioned responses. The response may be salivating, sweating, increased heart rate, increased blood pressure or combinations of these behaviors. The organism does not actively participate in this process; a stimulus elicits a response automatically, reflexively, and involuntarily (see Table 2.3).

Classical conditioning involves the following six essential features: (1) an unconditioned stimulus, (2) an unconditioned response, (3) a neutral (or conditioning) stimulus, (4) close timing in the presentation of the neutral stimulus and the unconditioned stimulus, (5) formation of a conditioned stimulus, and (6) acquisition of a conditioned response.

Classical conditioning explains well a limited range of phenomena including emotional responses. It cannot, however, explain nonreflexive, more complex behaviors—such as why a clerk will work forty hours a week in a store, or why a pigeon will press a lever hundreds of times an hour to receive food. These behaviors involve another type of conditioning, called instrumental conditioning (discussed in detail in the next section), in which the organism's own activity is particularly important.

PROGRESS CHECK 2.1

1. Match each of the following key concepts and terms with the appropriate definition.

conditioning   classical conditioning   learning
higher-order conditioning

Learning Objective 2.1   A. _____ A systematic procedure through which new responses are learned.

Learning Objective 2.1   B. _____ A relatively permanent change in behavior that occurs as a result of experiences in the environment.

Learning Objective 2.4   C. _____ A conditioning process where, by being paired with a stimulus that naturally elicits a response, an originally neutral stimulus comes to elicit a similar or even identical response.

Learning Objective 2.5   D. _____ The process by which a neutral stimulus that is paired with a well-established conditioned stimulus takes on conditioned stimulus properties.

2. Complete each of the following sentences with one of the options provided.

Learning Objective 2.2
A. Many scientific studies have shown that _____ processes lead to both animal and human learning and behavior.
(similar : different)

Learning Objective 2.2
B. Psychologists determine whether learning has occurred by observing _____ _____ .
(the learning process : changes in behavior)

Learning Objective 2.3
C. Classically conditioned responses and reflexes are similar because they both occur _____ .
(involuntarily : without prior experience : as a result of learning)

Learning Objective 2.4
D. An unconditioned response is a natural, _____, involuntary response that is brought about by the unconditioned stimulus.
(unlearned : learned)

Learning Objective 2.4
E. Unconditioned and conditioned responses differ in that the conditioned response is learned and slightly _____ than the unconditioned response.
(stronger : weaker)

Learning Objective 2.4
F. A key characteristic of classical conditioning is that through repeated pairings of the unconditioned stimulus and the neutral stimulus, a conditioned stimulus that is able to _____ a conditioned response develops.
(suppress : elicit)

Learning Objective 2.5
G. Higher-order conditioning is the result of _____ associations.
(intellectual : verbal : a chain of)

Learning Objective 2.6
H. In basic classical conditioning, _____ acts as the reinforcer.
(any well-established conditioned stimulus : the unconditioned stimulus)

Learning Objective 2.6
I. If the strength of the _____ stimulus is strong, conditioning is much more likely to occur than if the strength is weak.
(neutral : unconditioned : conditioned)

Learning Objective 2.6
J. Presenting the neutral stimulus simultaneously with, or about a half second before, the unconditioned stimulus follows the rule of _____ and allows strong conditioned responses to be established.
(magnitude : timing : frequency)

Learning Objective 2.7
K. In classical conditioning, extinction is the process in which the probability of the organism's responding with a conditioned response decreases because the unconditioned stimulus is _____ .
(aversive : withheld : too familiar)

Learning Objective 2.7
L. The reoccurrence of a conditioned response following a rest period after extinction is called _____ .
(Pavlovian conditioning : spontaneous recovery : relearning)

Learning Objective 2.8
M. Stimulus _____ is the process by which an organism learns to make a particular response to a specific stimulus and to no other stimulus.
(generalization : discrimination)

Learning Objective 2.9
N. Classical conditioning explains a _____ range of learned responses.
(limited : wide)

INSTRUMENTAL CONDITIONING

Lisa, who opened this chapter, showed a change in productivity when she felt that she was underpaid. Most of us would probably predict that if she were given a raise in her salary, then her attitude, behavior in general, and especially

The renowned psychologist B.F. Skinner (1904–) focused his research on an organism's observable behavior, and refined techniques of instrumental conditioning.

Learning Objective 2.10

Instrumental conditioning
A conditioning procedure in which the probability that an organism will emit a response is increased or decreased by the subsequent delivery of a reinforcer or punisher; sometimes called *operant conditioning.*

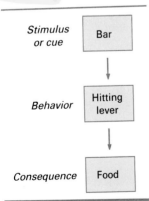

FIGURE 2.9 : In instrumental conditioning—unlike classical conditioning—the behavior to be conditioned (such as hitting a lever) is reinforced or punished *after* it occurs.

her productivity would probably improve; her behavior is to some degree related to her pay. Of course, people work for many reasons, of which pay is only one. For Lisa, however, pay had become very important.

Common sense tells us that performance on the job is at least in part related to pay. If you were able to ask Pavlov to account for Lisa's change in productivity, he would be hard pressed to make a classical conditioning explanation work.

The conditioning procedures used by Pavlov and dozens of other researchers explained a number of important learning phenomena. Classical conditioning, as defined by these learning theorists, explained learned emotional responses especially well; but the explanation was not broad enough. Classical conditioning seemed too limited to some theorists, and they began to challenge the way researchers thought about conditioning and learning. Among these challengers was the noted American psychologist B. F. Skinner. Skinner focused on an organism's *observable* behavior. He questioned whether Pavlovian (classical) conditioning should be studied at all. Skinner and his behavioral colleagues broke new ground by providing a carefully developed framework for the formal study of instrumental conditioning. Although Skinner has since modified some of his most extreme positions, his 1938 book, *The Behavior of Organisms,* continues to have an impact on studies of conditioning.

As Skinner suggested, many behaviors are acquired and maintained not through Pavlovian classical conditioning but through instrumental conditioning. In general, instrumental conditioning is a procedure in which a behavior, such as work, bedmaking, cooking dinner, or writing a story, is followed by a consequence, such as pay, a kiss, verbal praise, or congratulations from a teacher. In **instrumental conditioning** an increase or decrease in the likelihood that a behavior will recur is affected by delivery of a rewarding or punishing event *after* the behavior occurs, as a consequence of the behavior. Further, the conditioned behavior is usually voluntary, not reflexlike as in classical conditioning (see Figure 2.9).

From an instrumental conditioning point of view, Lisa's behavior, her slackened productivity on the job, can be explained by a lack of rewards—or, in Skinner's words, by a lack of an appropriate reinforcer to maintain her behavior. In studying these principles, see if you can observe in your own day-to-day behavior and attitudes elements being maintained by reinforcers (rewards) that come *after* you have performed some behavior. You'll be surprised.

Rewarding Desired Behavior: The Basic Process of Operant Conditioning

Let us say that your child makes his bed, your husband cleans a closet, or your mother buys you a stylish designer sweater. You follow that behavior with a huge hug, great excitement, and endless talk about your wonderful child, husband, or mother. Your relative has exhibited a behavior, and you have followed it with a rousing response. Researchers have studied the same sequence of events in the laboratory. Among the most famous of such experiments in rewarding behavior were those by American psychologist E. L. Thorndike, who pioneered the study of instrumental (or operant) conditioning with several experiments in 1932. Thorndike placed hungry cats in boxes. The cats could escape from the boxes to get food by hitting a lever that opened a door in the box. The cats quickly performed the behavior Thorndike was trying to condition

(hitting the lever) because hitting the lever (at first usually by accident) produced food. Because the response or behavior of hitting the lever was important (instrumental) in obtaining the reward, Thorndike called such behaviors *instrumental behavior.*

Although the two terms are not identical, *instrumental conditioning* is sometimes called *operant conditioning.* This text uses the terms interchangeably. Thorndike talked about instrumental conditioning because the organism's responses were instrumental, or crucial, in obtaining the reward. Skinner, by contrast, spoke of the operant conditioning because, from his view, the organism operates on the environment (perhaps by pressing a lever) and then the behavior is followed by some consequence, perhaps a reward. Both psychologists acknowledged that the behavior is first emitted and then it is followed by a consequence. It is important to realize that this is unlike classical conditioning. In classical (Pavlovian) conditioning, bells and food are paired together and the behavior that is being conditioned is then *elicited.* In direct contrast, operant or instrumental conditioning requires that the behavior be first *emitted;* it is then followed with a consequence, such as a reward.

In instrumental conditioning, as in Thorndike's experiment, an organism emits or displays a behavior, which is followed by a consequence. The kind of consequence applied is a crucial component of the conditioning, for it determines whether the behavior is likely to recur. The consequence is usually either a reinforcer or a punisher. As in classical conditioning, the reward acts as a reinforcer, increasing the likelihood that the behavior targeted for conditioning will recur. In Thorndike's experiment, food was the reinforcer for hitting the lever. A punisher, on the other hand, decreases the likelihood that the targeted behavior will recur. As in classical conditioning, the amount, delay, and type of consequences determine the extent of conditioning. Both reinforcement and punishment are discussed in more detail later in this chapter.

Much of the research on instrumental conditioning has used an apparatus called a **Skinner box,** named for its developer, B. F. Skinner. A Skinner box usually contains a mechanism for delivering a consequence whenever the animal in the box makes a readily identifiable response that the experimenter has decided to reinforce or punish. In studies that involve rewards, the delivery mechanism is often a small lever or bar in the side of the box; whenever the animal inside presses it, the response is rewarded (B. F. Skinner, 1938, 1956).

In a traditional instrumental conditioning experiment, a rat deprived of food is placed in a one-cubic-foot box. The rat moves around the box, often seeking escape; eventually, it stumbles on the lever and depresses it. That action delivers a pellet of food into a cup. The rat moves about some more and

Learning Objective 2.11

Skinner box
Named for its developer, B. F. Skinner, a box containing a responding mechanism (usually a lever) capable of delivering a reinforcer (often food or water) to an organism.

happens to press the lever again; another pellet of food is delivered. After a few trials, the rat learns that pressing the lever brings food. A hungry rat will learn to press the lever many times in rapid succession to obtain the reinforcer. In using instrumental conditioning procedures with human beings, psychologists consider classrooms, workplaces, and homes to be appropriate environments for selective reinforcement of desired behaviors.

Counting lever presses or measuring salivary responses is a tedious but necessary part of studying conditioning. Psychologists have developed a practical and simple device called a *cumulative recorder* to measure animal behavior. The use of such devices largely accounts for the considerable early progress made in animal learning laboratories. Today, computers and devices that act like cumulative recorders continue to help psychologists quantify behavior.

Shaping: Teaching New Behaviors Step-By-Step

Teaching new behaviors, especially if they are complex ones, is time-consuming and often requires several stages. For example, when a parent wants a young child to learn to eat with a knife and a fork, he usually begins teaching the child in small steps; he may teach the child first to use a spoon, then a fork, then a knife. Similarly, when researchers train an animal to press a lever or bar, to jump through a hoop, or to control its bowel movements, they usually do so in stages.

Learning Objective <u>2.12</u>

Shaping
The gradual training of an organism to give the proper responses, by selectively reinforcing behaviors as they approach the desired response.

The process of reinforcing behavior that approximates a desired response is called **shaping.** For example, to teach a hungry rat to press a bar in a Skinner box, a researcher must first give the animal a pellet of food each time it enters the half of the box in which the bar is located. Once this behavior is established, the rat receives food only when it touches the wall on which the bar is located, then only when it approaches the lever, and so on until it actually presses the bar in order to receive the food. At each stage, the reinforced behavior more closely approximates the desired behavior (in this case, pressing the lever).

Shaping is a very effective technique for teaching animals new tricks. It is also helpful in teaching human beings new behaviors. For example, a parent who wants a child to make his bed neatly will at first reinforce *all* attempts at bedmaking, even if the result is sloppy. Over successive weeks, only the better attempts are reinforced, until finally only neat bedmaking is reinforced. Similarly, most adults must learn in small steps how to stand up for themselves and present their views to employers. Psychologists also use shaping in the treatment of emotional disturbances to teach people new, realistic, acceptable behaviors. Therapy for anxious individuals often involves relaxation training, which usually proceeds in small steps. Patience is an important aspect of all shaping procedures. Reinforcing all steps, no matter how small, toward the desired behavior is essential (Fischer & Gochros, 1975).

Superstitious Behavior Can Happen
When Behavior Is Unintentionally Rewarded

We have seen that reinforcement plays a key role in learning new behaviors. Parents and educators try to reinforce their children and students on a regular basis. But what happens when a person or animal is unintentionally rewarded for a behavior? What happens when a reward has nothing to do with the behavior that immediately preceded it? When this happens, people may develop superstitious behaviors. When writing, they may always play a certain record; or when going out on a first date, they may always wear a certain pair of shoes. Some of these behaviors, including fear responses to the number *thirteen,* black cats, and walking under ladders, are centuries old and have strong cultural associations. These **superstitious behaviors** generally arise from a purely random reinforcement immediately after the behavior. Thus, a person who happens to wear the same shoes on two dates and has a good time on both may come to believe in a causal relation between wearing that pair of shoes and having a successful date.

Animals can also learn superstitious behaviors while being trained in Skinner boxes. On trials in which it was learning the bar-pressing response, a rat may have turned its head to the right before pressing the bar and receiving reinforcement. Although reinforcement was contingent only on pressing the bar, to the rat, it may have seemed that both the head turning and bar pressing were necessary (Skinner, 1948). Therefore, the rat will continue to turn its head to the right before pressing the bar.

Reinforcement Is the Key to Establishing New Behaviors

The basic behavior principles that apply to the process of reinforcement have been known for centuries. Two kinds of reinforcers exist: positive and negative. Most people have used positive reinforcers at some time. A person teaching a dog new tricks may give it a bone or a pat on the head when it completes the task. When toilet training a two-year-old, a parent often applauds when the child has successfully completed a bowel movement. The applause is intended as a reinforcer. These behaviors are carried out because they are rewarded; if the reward is important and desired, an organism will continue to behave in a similar manner for the same reward. **Positive reinforcement** increases the probability of a response by the delivery of a reward; behavior is established or maintained because a reinforcer is delivered.

Of course, what is considered a reinforcer for one person may not have reinforcing value for another. Praise from an approving parent may be a powerful reinforcer for a two-year-old, but money, position, or status may be the most effective reinforcer for an adult. In general, psychologists call a **reinforcer** any event that increases the probability of the recurrence of a response that preceded it.

The delivery of food pellets to a hungry rat who has just pressed a lever increased the likelihood that the rat will do so again. But the delivery of these reinforcers works only if the rat is hungry; a rat who has just eaten does not find food pellets reinforcing. An organism must need or want the consequence if the consequence is to act as a reinforcer. In studying learning and conditioning, psychologists create the conditions for reinforcement by depriving animals of food or water before an experiment. In doing so, they motivate the animals and allow the delivery of food to take on reinforcing properties. In most experiments, the organism is motivated in some way. Chapter 5 discusses the role an organism's needs, desires, and physiological state play in determining what can be used as a reinforcer.

Primary reinforcers have survival value for the organism, such as food, water, or the termination of pain; they do not have to be taught. Food serves as a primary reinforcer for a hungry rat, water for a thirsty one. **Secondary reinforcers** are neutral stimuli (such as money) that initially have no intrinsic value

Superstitious behavior Behavior learned through coincidental association with reinforcement.

Learning Objective 2.13

Positive reinforcement Presentation of a rewarding or pleasant stimulus in order to increase the likelihood that a response will recur.

Reinforcer Any event that increases the probability of the reoccurrence of a response that precedes it.

Primary reinforcer Any stimulus or event that by its mere delivery or removal acts naturally (without learning) to increase the likelihood that a response will recur.

Secondary reinforcer A neutral stimulus with no intrinsic value to the organism that acquires reinforcement value through repeated pairing with a reinforcing stimulus.

for the organism. Through pairing with a primary reinforcer, the neutral stimulus becomes a reward. Many human pleasures are secondary reinforcers that have acquired value, such as leather coats that keep us no warmer than cloth ones and racy sports cars that take us from one place to another no faster than four-door sedans. Secondary reinforcers are used more often than primary ones to modify human behavior. A pat on the back, an approving nod, an unlimited use of the family car are all secondary reinforcers that act in powerful ways to establish and maintain a wide spectrum of behaviors.

Many forms of human activity show that the delivery of reinforcers helps establish and maintain behaviors. People will work long hours when the rewards are significant; successful salespeople may work seventy-hour weeks to reach their sales objectives. Managers sometimes offer their salespeople a bonus for increasing their sales by a certain percentage during a slow month. These managers use basic psychology; they reason that by increasing the amount of reinforcer (money), they may be able to get better performance (higher sales) from their salespeople. In fact, research has shown that changing the amount of a reinforcer can alter an organism's behavior significantly (see Figure 2.10).

Whereas positive reinforcement increases the probability of a response through delivery of a reward, **negative reinforcement** increases the probability of a response through *removal* of an aversive stimulus. Suppose a rat is placed in a Skinner box with an electrified grid that delivers a shock every fifty seconds. The rat can escape the shock by pressing the bar. The behavior being conditioned is bar pressing. The reinforcement is the termination of the painful stimulus. Negative reinforcement increases the probability of bar pressing because that is the way to avoid the shock.

Noxious or unpleasant stimuli are often used in animal studies of escape and avoidance. Both of these behaviors are learned through negative reinforcement. In a typical study of escape conditioning, a rat is placed in a Skinner box with an electrified floor. When the electricity is turned on, the rat receives a mild shock that causes it to thrash about the box until it bumps against the bar—stopping the shock. In just a few trials, the rat quickly learns to press the bar to escape being shocked. Studies of avoidance conditioning typically use the same apparatus, but a buzzer precedes the shock by a few seconds. The rat learns that on hearing the buzzer, it should press the bar; pressing the bar allows it to avoid the shock. Avoidance conditioning of this type usually involves some kind of escape conditioning—the animal first learns how to escape the shock by pressing the bar. Then, when a buzzer is introduced to signal the oncoming shock, avoidance behavior is learned easily. In escape conditioning, the organism is exposed to the aversive stimulus but learns to escape it. In avoidance conditioning, an organism learns to respond so that the aversive stimulus is never delivered.

Most children master both escape and avoidance conditioning at an early age. Appropriate signals from a disapproving parent often elicit an avoidance response so that punishment does not follow—a child decides not to eat some candy when he sees his father frown. Similarly, merely knowing the possible effects of an accident can establish safe driving behavior in most adults.

Both positive and negative reinforcement act to increase the likelihood that an organism will repeat a behavior. If they are strong enough, delivered often enough, and important enough to the organism involved, such reinforcements can help maintain behaviors for long periods. Positive reinforcements achieve

Negative reinforcement Removal of an aversive stimulus in order to *increase* the likelihood that a response will recur.

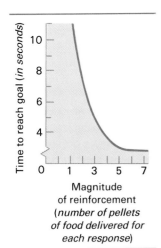

FIGURE 2.10: As the amount of the reinforcer (such as food) increases, an organism's time to reach a goal usually decreases.

their effect by adding pleasant stimuli and rewards; negative reinforcements achieve their effect by removing (subtracting) aversive stimuli.

Remember that Lisa's work productivity decreased when she felt she was no longer being paid an appropriate wage. The reinforcer used to maintain her behavior was no longer satisfactory. You might even argue that when her co-worker, Susan, got a salary raise, this acted in some important ways to punish or hurt Lisa. As you will see in the next section, when people are punished for a behavior, the likelihood that they will continue to show the behavior decreases.

Punishment Is Often Used to Change Behavior

Learning
Objective 2.14

Punishment
Presentation of an undesirable or noxious stimulus in order to *decrease* the probability that a previous response will recur.

Primary punisher
Any stimulus or event that by its delivery or removal acts naturally (without learning) to decrease the likelihood that a response will recur.

Secondary punisher
A neutral stimulus with no intrinsic value to the organism that acquires punishment value through repeated pairing with a punishing stimulus.

Unlike reinforcement, **punishment** acts to *decrease* the probability of a response. Punishment is one of the most commonly used techniques in teaching children and pets to control their behavior. When a pet is nasty to strangers, its owner slaps it; when a child is found writing on the walls with crayons, her parent spanks her. In both cases, people try to indicate their displeasure in order to suppress a behavior. Researchers use the same technique to *decrease* the probability that a behavior will recur: they deliver a noxious or unpleasant stimulus when an organism displays an undesirable behavior. If an animal is punished each time for a specific behavior, the probability that it will continue to perform that behavior decreases.

Punishment techniques have been used to control the behavior of people who are self-destructive, profoundly retarded, or too young to understand the consequences of potentially dangerous behaviors. A **primary punisher** is a stimulus that is naturally painful to an organism, such as an electric shock to an animal or a spanking to a child. A **secondary punisher** is a neutral stimulus that takes on punishing qualities, such as a verbal "no," a frown, or indifference. Secondary punishers can be effective means of controlling behavior, especially when used in combination with reinforcers.

Other forms of punishment involve the removal of a pleasant stimulus. If a child enjoys watching television, removal of the privilege can be used as a punishment each time the child misbehaves. One common punishment procedure that has proven very effective is *time-out*. In time-out, a person is removed from an environment containing potential positive events or reinforcers. For example, a child who hits and kicks is placed in a room in which there are no

The removal of basic freedoms is one form of punishment that will, hopefully, lead to a decrease in criminal behavior.

TABLE 2.4 : Effects of Reinforcement and Punishment

Addition of a Stimulus	Subtraction or Withholding of a Stimulus	Effect
Positive reinforcement *Delivery of food, money, or some other reward*	Negative reinforcement *Removal of shock or some other aversive stimulus*	*Establishes or increases a specific behavior*
Punishment *Delivery of electric shock, a slap on the hand, or some other aversive stimulus*	Punishment *Removal of automobile, television, or some other pleasant stimulus*	*Suppresses or decreases a specific behavior*

toys, television, or people. This strategy helps suppress the hitting and kicking behavior. Punishment, then, may involve adding a noxious event, such as a slap, or subtracting a positive event, such as television watching. In both cases, the aim is to decrease the likelihood of a behavior (see Table 2.4)

As with reinforcement, the strength and timing of the punishing stimulus directly influence the suppression of a behavior. Punishment can suppress simple behavior patterns. Once punishment ceases, however, animals often return to their previous behavior (Appel & Peterson, 1965). Appel and Peterson argue that punishment by itself is not an effective way to control or eliminate behavior. Used in combination with positive reinforcement for correct behavior, however, punishment can be an effective and lasting way of modifying behavior.

Instrumental Conditioning Is Affected by Several Important Variables

The effectiveness of instrumental conditioning depends heavily on the strength, timing, and frequency of consequences.

Learning Objective 2.15

Strength of Consequences. Studies comparing productivity when the amount of reinforcement varies show that as the amount of reward increases, the harder, longer, or faster a subject will work to complete a task. The more food pellets a hungry animal receives, the more frequently it will press a bar, or the more quickly it will run to its goal; the more money workers receive for assembling a piece of machinery, the more pieces they will produce.

The magnitude of a punishment can be manipulated in similar ways. The more intense the punishment, the more quickly and longer the behavior will be suppressed. The length of a child's stay in a time-out room, removing him from positive reinforcements, affects the suppression of his unacceptable behavior: a two-minute stay is not as effective as a ten-minute stay. Similarly, a slap on the wrist is not as effective as a swift hard slap to the rear end.

Punishment, whatever its form, is best delivered in moderation—too much punishment may be as ineffective as too little. If too much punishment is delivered, it may make the person stop responding. It may bring about panic, or it may decrease the likelihood that a person will try to respond in other ways. Punishment has to be delivered forcefully, but carefully. Changing behavior is usually best accomplished by a combination of reinforcement for prosocial behavior and punishment or extinction for antisocial behavior.

Timing of Consequences.   Just as in classical conditioning the length of the interval between presentation of the conditioning stimulus (the bell) and the unconditioned stimulus (the food) is important, so in instrumental conditioning the length of the interval between the occurrence of the behavior (pressing the bar) and the delivery of the consequence is critical. If a hungry rat works and is not given a reinforcer for an hour, it is unlikely to learn the task or perform the behavior again; the shorter the interval between the behavior and the reinforcer, the better the chances that the animal will learn the behavior (see Figure 2.11).

Learning Objective **2.16**

Schedules of Consequences.   In the studies discussed so far, it has generally been assumed that each response is followed by a consequence. However, an organism does not have to be reinforced or punished each time it performs a behavior.

How often do people need to be reinforced? Is a paycheck once a month sufficient to keep someone working regularly? Will people work better if they receive reinforcement regularly or if they receive it at unpredictable times? Most people in most situations are not reinforced continually. For example, a teenager operating a summer lawn-mowing service might charge by the job. This method rewards getting a job done quickly: the more jobs completed, the greater the take-home pay for the week. Another approach would be to charge by the hour. Using this method, the lawn mower would earn more money by working slowly. Both of these arrangements are *schedules of reinforcement:* the first is based on frequency of response; the second on time. Researchers have devised four *basic* schedules of reinforcement: two are interval schedules, which deal with time periods; two are ratio schedules, which deal with work output.

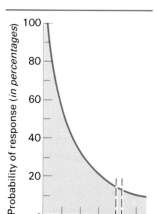

FIGURE 2.11 **:** A delay between a response and reinforcement reduces the probability that the behavior will recur. Short delays (or no delays) between a response and reinforcement maximize the chances that the behavior will recur.

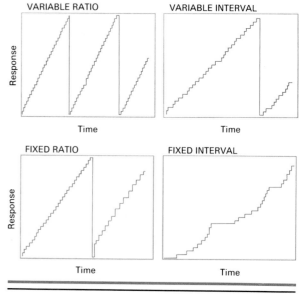

FIGURE 2.12 **:** The four basic types of reinforcement schedules. The fixed-interval schedule produces a scalloping pattern of responses; the variable-ratio schedule produces high performance rates. Each mark on the graph represents another response and so a steep slope represents high work rates.

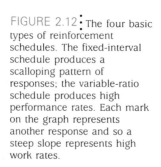

Fixed interval
A reinforcement schedule in which a reinforcer is delivered after a specified interval of time, provided that the required response has occurred at least once after the interval has elapsed.

Imagine a rat in a Skinner box at work pressing a bar and being reinforced with food. If it is on a **fixed-interval** schedule, the rat is rewarded for the first response that occurs after some specified interval of time. That is, regardless of whether it works a great deal or just a little, the rat will be given a reinforcer if it has pressed the bar at least once after a specified interval. The reinforcement schedule is fixed, because the animal's behavior does not determine how often it will be reinforced. As Figure 2.12 shows, output on a fixed-interval schedule follows a scalloping pattern: animals and human beings typically respond slowly just after reinforcement, with an increase in performance just before the reinforcer is due. For human beings, a fixed-interval schedule is likely to generate clock-watching behavior. A lawn mower who is paid by the hour is likely to make sure he is doing some cutting just before another hour or quarter hour of work is completed. In the same way, bored workers often watch the clock until quitting time because as long as they do some work during the day they will be paid.

Variable interval
A reinforcement schedule in which a reinforcer is delivered after a predetermined but varying interval of time, provided that the required response has occurred at least once after the interval.

A reinforcing interval need not be fixed. With a **variable-interval** schedule, an animal is reinforced after varying amounts of time, provided it makes an appropriate response after the variable interval has elapsed. For example, it may be reinforced for responses occurring after forty seconds, after sixty seconds, and then after twenty-five seconds. Rats on this type of work schedule work at a relatively slow, steady rate and do not show the scalloping effect present in a fixed-interval schedule. Because delivery of a reinforcer is tied to time interval more than to work output, their work rate is slow. Nevertheless, rats on a variable-interval schedule have a greater overall rate of response than those on a fixed-interval schedule.

Fixed ratio
A reinforcement schedule in which a reinforcer is delivered after a predetermined number of responses have occurred.

Ratio schedules deal with output instead of with time. In a **fixed-ratio** schedule, the subject is reinforced for a specific amount of work. Thus, a rat who is reinforced for every tenth bar press in a Skinner box will work at a fast, steady, regular rate because it has learned that hard work brings the delivery of a reinforcer on a regular basis. Figure 2.12 shows that the work rate of a rat on a fixed-ratio schedule is much higher than that of a rat on an interval schedule.

If she received her pay for a specific number of flashlights assembled, this factory worker would be on a fixed ratio schedule.

TABLE 2.5 : Schedules of Reinforcement

Schedule	Description	Effect
Fixed interval	Reinforcement is given for the first response after a fixed time.	Response rate drops right after reinforcement but increases near the end of the interval.
Variable interval	Reinforcement is given for the first response after a predetermined but variable interval.	Response rate is steady.
Fixed ratio	Reinforcement is given after a fixed number of responses.	Response rate is rapid.
Variable ratio	Reinforcement is given after a predetermined but variable number of responses.	Response rate is high and steady.

In the same way, a lawn mower who is paid by the job (for the amount of work completed) will probably mow more lawns than will somebody paid by the hour. Knowing that a person's work rate is usually lower if reinforced or paid by time rather than by work output, you might prefer to hire a lawn mower who wants to be paid by the job rather than by the hour.

Variable-ratio schedules can achieve very high rates of responding, up to a point. Unlike a fixed-ratio schedule, in a variable-ratio system the amount of work required before a reinforcer is given varies. Thus, the rat learns that hard work produces a reinforcer, but it cannot predict when the reinforcer will be delivered. Therefore, the rat's best bet is to work at an even, steady, high rate. As a consequence, the variable-rate schedule produces the highest available rate of response. People who work as sales agents for insurance companies know that the more individuals they approach about insurance, the more insurance they will sell. They may not know exactly which individuals will buy, but they do know that a greater number of selling opportunities is bound to result in more sales.

A variable-ratio schedule is not the answer to work productivity for all people at all times. A variable-ratio schedule is introduced usually after an organism has learned a response properly. For example, if you want a rat to work on a variable-ratio schedule, you might first reinforce the rat on every trial. In this way, the rat will quickly learn the proper response. You might then reinforce the rat on every other trial; later, on every fifth trial. Still later, you might make the number of trials before reinforcement a variable number. Once the rat has learned the response, very high rates of lever pressing (or whatever the response might be) can be obtained with an infrequent reinforcer. Table 2.5 highlights the four schedules of reinforcement.

Which Tone Has a Reward?:
Stimulus Generalization and Discrimination

Stimulus generalization and **discrimination** occur in instrumental conditioning much as they do in classical conditioning. A pigeon trained to press a bar when it hears a high-pitched tone (see Hovland 1937) is also likely to respond to a tone just slightly lower in pitch than the training stimulus, though it will not

Variable ratio ═══════
A reinforcement schedule in which a reinforcer is delivered after a predetermined but variable number of responses have occurred.

Stimulus generalization ═══════
Responding to stimuli similar to, but not the same as, the training stimulus.

Stimulus discrimination ═══════
The process by which an organism learns to respond to a reinforced stimulus and then to no other similar stimulus.

Learning Objective 2.17

respond as frequently as it would to the original tone. The greater the difference in pitch, the greater the decrease in the response rate (Honig, 1966; Pavlov, 1927; Stebbins, 1970). Teaching a rat or pigeon to discriminate between two stimuli, such as a vertical and a horizontal line, a square and a circle, or high-and low-pitched tones, usually involves repeated presentation of the stimuli coupled with reinforcements. In instrumental conditioning, however, the reinforcement is delivered *only* when the animal correctly discriminates between the stimuli. Suppose an animal is presented with a vertical or a horizontal line and with two keys: one key is to be pressed if the line is vertical, the other if the line is horizontal. The animal is reinforced only for correct responses. The animal will usually make errors at first; but after repeated presentations of the vertical and horizontal lines, with reinforcements given only for correct responses, discrimination learning will occur. Stimulus discrimination can also be established with colors, tones, and more complex stimuli.

The process of stimulus discrimination and generalization are evident daily. Parents see that babies and children often make mistakes by overgeneralizing. For example, baby Jesse knows that cats have four legs and a tail. Jesse calls all four-legged animals cats. With experience, and with help, guidance, and reinforcement from her parents, Jesse eventually learns to discriminate dogs from cats, using the sounds they make in addition to such characteristics as body size, shape, and fur.

When the Reinforcer Is Removed: Extinction and Spontaneous Recovery

If an instrumentally conditioned behavior is not followed by a consequence, it ultimately undergoes extinction (see Figure 2.13). Suppose a pigeon is trained to peck a key whenever it hears a high-pitched tone (pecking to the high-pitched tone brings reinforcement, but pecking to a low-pitched tone does not). If reinforcement ceases, the pigeon eventually stops working. If the pigeon is on a variable-ratio schedule, and thus expects to work for long periods before reinforcement occurs, it will probably work for a very long time without stopping; if it has been trained on a fixed-interval schedule, and thus expects reinforcement in a relatively brief time, it will stop pecking after just a few nonreinforced trials. Simple, repetitive actions that have generally been reinforced are resistant to extinction, even over long periods of time (Schwartz & Reilly, 1985).

In instrumental conditioning, **extinction** involves withholding a reinforcer, to reduce the probability that an organism will respond with a conditioned response. Thus, one way to measure the extent of conditioning is to measure how long it takes, or how many trials are necessary, to achieve extinction. An animal on a schedule of reinforcement after every trial will quickly extinguish when reinforcers are no longer delivered. One way to eliminate behavior that is normally reinforced is to provide a long series of nonreinforced trials; human beings and animals quickly stop responding if the reinforcers for their work are withheld (see Figure 2.14 on the next page). Few people will continue to work at their jobs if they no longer receive some type of reinforcer.

Suppose a pigeon who pecks when it hears a high-pitched tone is rewarded each time it pecks correctly and is tested daily for thirty minutes over a period of sixty days. On the sixty-first day, the pigeon is placed in the Skinner box and is not reinforced for its correct behavior. For the first few minutes, the pigeon continues to work normally. After a few minutes, its work rate decreases; by the end of a half-hour session, it is not pecking at all. The next day, when the

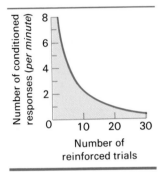

FIGURE 2.13 : When an animal's conditioned behavior is not reinforced over several trials, the likelihood of the conditioned response decreases. After many such trials, the behavior undergoes extinction.

Extinction

In instrumental conditioning, the process of reducing the likelihood of a conditioned response to a conditioned stimulus by withholding the reinforcer.

pigeon is placed in the Skinner box and presented with a tone, it again responds with pecking, but again no reinforcer is delivered. Within a relatively short time, the pigeon's behavior shows extinction, although the eventual decrease in response is not always immediately apparent: when a reinforcer is withheld, organisms sometimes work harder and show an initial increase in performance! In such cases, the curve depicting the extinction process shows a small initial increase in performance, followed by a decrease (Allen, Turner, and Everett, 1970).

Extinction in instrumental conditioning follows principles similar to those of classical conditioning, so it is not surprising that spontaneous recovery occurs in instrumental conditioning, too. If an organism whose conditioned behavior has undergone extinction is given a rest period and tested again, it will show **spontaneous recovery.** If it is brought through this sequence several times with several rest periods, its work rate in each spontaneous recovery session decreases. After one rest period, the organism's work rate almost equals what it was when the conditioned response was reinforced; but after a dozen or so rest periods (with no reinforcements), the organism may make only one or two responses; the level of spontaneous recovery will have decreased markedly. Eventually, the behavior will disappear almost completely.

Human beings also show spontaneous recovery. When students speak up in class and offer answers to questions, reinforcement usually follows: the instructor comments on the adequacy of the response. If the instructor does not reinforce correct answers or does not call on students to answer, their hand-raising behavior decreases (extinction). Generally, after a few classes of not being called on, students stop raising their hands. After a vacation, however, the same hand-raising behavior typically recurs (spontaneous recovery). Of course, extinction will occur again if the hand-raising behavior is not reinforced. (Table 2.6 highlights the four important properties of instrumental conditioning.)

Spontaneous recovery
The recurrence of a conditioned response following a rest period after extinction.

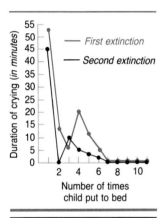

FIGURE 2.14 : A child emitted tantrums at bedtime to gain attention. Williams counted the number of minutes the child cried and instructed the parents not to pay attention to the tantrums. After several days, the number of minutes the child cried decreased to zero. A week later, an aunt put the child to bed; when the child made a fuss (spontaneous recovery), the aunt reinforced the child with attention. The child then had to go through a second series of extinction trials. (Data from C. D. Williams, 1959, p. 269)

TABLE 2.6 : Four Important Properties of Instrumental Conditioning

Property	Definition	Example
Extinction	The process of reducing the probability of a conditioned response by withholding the reinforcer	A rat trained to press a bar stops pressing when it is no longer reinforced after each response.
Spontaneous recovery	The recurrence of a conditioned response following a rest period after extinction	A rat's conditioned bar-pressing behavior has undergone extinction; after a rest interval, the rat again presses the bar.
Stimulus generalization	The process by which an organism learns to respond to stimuli similar but not identical to the training stimulus	A cat presses a bar when presented with either an ellipse or a circle.
Stimulus discrimination	The process by which an organism learns to respond to a reinforced stimulus and then to no other similar stimulus; the complementary process to stimulus generalization	A pigeon presses a key only in response to red lights, not to blue ones or green ones.

Psychologists at Work: Conditioning Behavior

How do I change my little brother's rotten attitude? How can I get more work from my employees? How do I learn to say "no" to my employer's requests? How do I get my dog to stop biting my ankles? These are all questions frequently asked of psychologists. At this point, you may have guessed that the answers lie in some principles of conditioning.

It is important to recall a truism of psychology—*reinforced behaviors tend to occur again.* With this in mind, how do you get your brother to shape up his attitude? You shape him. Each time he acts in the slightest way that you like, you reward him with something—most likely praise or affection. When he acts rotten, you use an extinction procedure—do not let him bait you, withhold attention or rewards, and ignore him. Continue this pattern for a few days or a few weeks, and as he becomes more pleasant, show him even more attention and good will. Remember, reinforced behaviors tend to occur again.

What about getting increased productivity from workers? Most workers get paid a fixed amount each week. They are on a *fixed-interval* schedule; regardless of their specific work output, they get their paycheck. One way (but not the only way) to increase their productivity is to place them on a *fixed ratio* schedule of reinforcement. A worker who is paid by the piece, by the report, by the page, or by the widget is going to produce more pieces, pages, or widgets than one whose productivity does not

matter at the end of the week. Insurance salespeople are well-known for their stick-to-itiveness and their ability to keep calling back to get a sale. They work on commission, and their pay is tied to their ability to close a sale. Research in the laboratory and in the business world shows that when peoples' pay is tied to their work output, they work harder—at least most of the time.

Psychologists like to focus on increasing productivity and prosocial behaviors. From time to time, however, a person needs to decrease someone's annoying or antisocial behaviors. How do you get a dog to stop biting your ankles? Slap him firmly as soon as he does it. How do you get a child to stop writing on walls? Admonish her loudly after she does it. How do you get a teenager to stop using the family car and leaving no gas in it? Do not let the teen use the car for a week following an empty gas tank. Psychologists use punishment—the delivery of a painful or noxious stimulus—after an event has occurred. Punishment acts to decrease the likelihood a behavior will recur. Teenagers learn quickly that their forgetfulness about the gas tank leads to a noxious event—a car-free week.

Through principles of conditioning, psychologists can help people better manage their own behaviors and also help them increase the positive behaviors of the people around them. But, be careful; antisocial behaviors can be conditioned, too.

Managing Behavior: Here Is Some Practical Advice

*Learning
Objective* 2.18
You need not be a psychologist to put to work some of the ideas of learning principles. Learning principles are often the key to self-help, growth, and more effective coping. Using principles of instrumental conditioning, people can manage others' productivity more effectively. Certainly the school board could have handled Lisa and Susan better had they thought about the principles of learning. They might have offered Susan less money and given Lisa some additional compensation. Or, they might have given Susan her raise and also promised Lisa a salary boost in six months. Most parents understand these principles when rearing children. Consider, however, Vicki and Steve Bates.

Vicki and Steve Bates were at their wits' end with their daughter Rochelle. They did not realize the extent of her reign of terror. Rochelle was a nice girl. She was well behaved in school. She played well with the children in the neighborhood. Her parents, however, were afraid to say "no" to her. They were fearful of damaging her psychological life, so Rochelle was given the run of the house. She was rapidly becoming a spoiled brat. She had her parents doing and fetching for her. They fed, washed, and clothed her. Instead of becoming more independent like most school children, Rochelle was becoming more dependent. She had taught her parents to jump at her slightest whim. They had learned that when their daughter did not get her way, she had a temper tantrum. To avoid it, they acquiesced to her every wish.

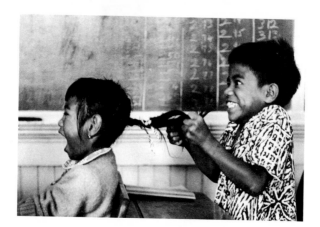

What forms of reinforcement and punishment could be used to control this boy's unruly behavior?

Rochelle's reign of terror was reaching a peak. Vicki and Steve were beginning to realize that all of their education, reading about childhood upbringing, and adult common sense were doing them no good. They had a lovely daughter who was impossible to deal with. She knew how to behave well, but rarely did for them.

What would a psychologist suggest the Bates family do with their problem child? What psychological principles could help them better manage Rochelle's behavior?

Assume that one of Rochelle's especially annoying sets of behaviors focuses around her morning routine. Rochelle refuses to dress herself and dawdles over breakfast. She is generally unpleasant and difficult, and the entire household morning routine seems to center around getting her off to school. Psychological theory suggests that Rochelle's behavior could be changed if she were reinforced for bedmaking, dressing herself, eating breakfast at a reasonable rate, *and* were punished for not making her bed, not getting dressed, and dawdling over breakfast. What should Rochelle's parents do? First, they should decide on a reinforcer. Knowing that Rochelle loves chocolate, they might make a candy bar the reinforcer. Next, they should decide on a punisher. Rochelle hates being sent to sit in a "thinking chair" in a corner of the family den. Rochelle's parents now have the tools to implement change; all they need to do is use them.

Rochelle's parents tell her that if she makes her bed, dresses herself, and eats breakfast in ten minutes, she will find a candy bar waiting for her when she comes home from school. This is clearly a special treat; Rochelle usually gets an apple when she comes home from school. In addition, Rochelle's parents tell her that if she fails to make her bed, dress herself, and finish breakfast within ten minutes, she will be sent immediately to the thinking chair—even if it means being late for school. The procedure is to start the following day.

The next morning, Rochelle rises quickly, makes her bed, and dresses herself, but breakfast is a half-hour ordeal. Her parents send her to sit in the chair and think about things. Rochelle cries, berates her parents, and laments her life; an apple greets her when she gets home from school. The next day, breakfast is quick but Rochelle does not make her bed—more chair, no chocolate. On the third day, Rochelle goes through the morning routine without incident. She arrives home to find a candy bar and lots of praise and hugs from her parents. In a few weeks, Rochelle decides for herself that she prefers chocolate bars to the chair, and that bedmaking, after all, takes only a minute and a half.

From a psychologist's point of view, controlling how and when behaviors are reinforced can easily establish and maintain prosocial behavior. Sometimes the difficult part of the process is identifying the reinforcers in a situation. For example, Rochelle got a lot of attention by acting up each morning. Once her parents stopped reinforcing that behavior and concentrated on tangible reinforcement of behaviors they did want, it was easy for Rochelle to learn to behave in acceptable ways. Thus, behavioral conditioning techniques developed in the laboratory with rats and pigeons can be used successfully to help children and adults learn new, more adaptive, behaviors. We consider in more detail some of these behavioral techniques when we examine various therapeutic techniques in Chapter 15.

Managing the Learning Process with Computers

It is relatively easy to see how Rochelle's behavior might be easily managed through the application of reinforcement and punishment techniques. In the same way, it is probably obvious what it would take to get Lisa the secretary back on the productivity track. But does learning theory have anything to say about helping people learn?

Learning psychologists have tried to put their theories and data to work in the educational system. Beginning with a simple programmed learning procedure using a rather crude teaching machine, their work has evolved into sophisticated computer-aided instruction (CAI) systems that offer choices and interactions as fascinating as those in the computerized games at the video arcades. The first teaching machine was a device that allowed a student to look at a series of frames, presented as windows in the teaching machine. Through the window, a student was presented with a paragraph of text describing a concept. After marking his or her answer, the student turned a knob, and the machine displayed the correct response and the next paragraph or concept. At the end of a series of frames, the student would have been introduced to a complete series of ideas, one step at a time.

In the late 1960s and early 1970s, many psychologists were involved in writing programs for computers that acted as teaching machines. Perhaps the most significant recent event in the development of CAI has been the growing availability of personal computers. Computers such as the APPLE and IBM PC have brought CAI into the home in the form of courseware (courses made into software). To be good, courseware should be highly interactive and not just rote drill. Good courseware optimizes the power of a computer by letting the machine keep track of and help evaluate a student's progress. Good courseware also takes advantage of a computer's color, sound, and graphic display capabilities. Today's $2,000 microcomputers are extraordinarily sophisticated; they can help keep a student's interest and motivation high through the innovative and pleasing presentation of material.

The huge influx of personal computers into homes and schools is making educators rethink the role of CAI in their educational programs. Psychologists know that CAI is not the answer to every learning problem, but it has been of significant help to some teachers and students in some schools. Clearly, the research that psychologists do in the laboratory has practical implications.

Summary of Key Concepts

The essential feature of instrumental conditioning is the delivery of consequences following behavior. Instrumental conditioning stresses *contingency*—consequences are not delivered unless and until the behavior is shown. Behavior followed by a reinforcer tends to recur; behavior followed by a punisher generally is suppressed. As in classical conditioning, stimulus generalization and discrimination occur, and several variables are involved. The consequence must be clearly defined, of sufficient magnitude, and properly timed to establish the conditioned response. If the reinforcer is not delivered over a series of trials, extinction will occur. Although consistent reinforcement is not necessary once a conditioned response is established, certain schedules of reinforcement produce higher rates of conditioned response than do others.

Comparison of Classical and Instrumental Conditioning

Learning Objective 2.19

Both classical and instrumental conditioning are considered basic learning procedures. Some researchers contend that common processes underlie both and that both should be able to produce most conditioned behaviors (St. Claire-Smith & MacLaren, 1983). Most psychologists, however, focus on the differences between classical and instrumental procedures. One basic distinction is that in classical conditioning, the unconditioned stimulus (such as food) is presented *along with* the neutral or conditioning stimulus (such as a bell) regardless of the organism's behavior. In instrumental conditioning, delivery of the consequence (such as food) is *contingent* on the organism's behavior; an animal will get food only *if* it displays the correct behavior (Skinner, 1937, 1938). Many learning theorists distinguish between classical and instrumental conditioning in terms of their different use of reinforcers, but almost all agree that reinforcement is important to almost all learning situations. A second important distinction between classical and instrumental conditioning is the type of behavior with which each is concerned. Classically conditioned behaviors are usually reflexive and involuntary, such as salivation and eyeblinks, whereas instrumentally conditioned behaviors are usually voluntary behaviors, such as pressing a bar or working in a store. Table 2.7 highlights classical and instrumental conditioning.

TABLE 2.7 :Types of Learning: Classical Conditioning and Instrumental Conditioning

Type of Learning	Procedure	Result	Example
Classical conditioning	A neutral stimulus (such as a bell) is paired with an unconditioned stimulus (such as food).	The neutral stimulus becomes a conditioned stimulus—it elicits the conditioned response.	A bell elicits a salivary response in a dog.
Instrumental conditioning	A behavior is followed by a consequence of reinforcement or punishment.	The behavior increases or decreases in frequency.	A pigeon will peck on a key 20 times per hour to achieve a reward or avoid punishment.

PROGRESS CHECK 2.2

1. Match each of the following key concepts and terms with the appropriate definition.

reinforcer	primary reinforcer or punisher
negative reinforcement	secondary reinforcer or punisher
shaping	punishment

Learning Objective 2.12   A. _____ The process of selectively reinforcing behaviors that approximates the desired response, in a step-by-step fashion, until the new, target response has been established.

Learning Objective 2.13   B. _____ A consequence that increases the probability that a response will occur again because the response itself effectively terminates an aversive stimulus before *or* after it is delivered.

Learning Objective 2.13   C. _____ Any event that increases the probability of the recurrence of a response that preceded it.

Learning Objectives 2.13 and 2.14   D. _____ A neutral stimulus with no intrinsic value to the organism that, through repeated pairings with a stimulus that naturally and directly affects the organism's physiological state, becomes a learned, conditioned stimulus with reinforcing or punishing qualities.

Learning Objectives 2.13 and 2.14   E. _____ Any stimulus that has naturally reinforcing or punishing effects on behavior because it either contributes directly to the organism's physiological survival or destruction.

Learning Objective 2.14   F. _____ A process by which a response is suppressed and the probability of it recurring decreases because it has been followed by an undesired consequence.

2. Complete each of the following sentences with one of the options provided.

Learning Objective 2.10   A. Behavior learned through instrumental conditioning is usually considered _____ .
(voluntary : involuntary)

Learning Objective 2.10   B. In contrast to Thorndike, Skinner focused on the idea that _____ _____ .
(responses are "instrumental" in obtaining rewards : an organism "operates" on the environment)

Learning Objective 2.11   C. A _____ is a device that charts responses in a series of steps and allows psychologists to measure animal behavior.
(Skinner box : cumulative recorder)

Learning Objective 2.12   D. The random or coincidental association of reinforcement with a response leads to _____ behavior.
(ambivalent : superstitious : stereotyped)

Learning Objective 2.13   E. In order that a consequence will act as a reward, the organism to whom it is delivered must _____ .
(need it : know it is available : deserve it)

Learning Objective 2.13   F. An organism that is exposed to an unpleasant stimulus and responds in a manner that terminates the stimulus has made an _____ response.
(avoidance : escape)

Learning Objective 2.14   G. Research studies have shown that once punishment is discontinued, animals _____ the behavior exhibited before punishment was delivered.
(show an absence of : often return to)

Learning Objective 2.16

H. The number of responses an organism makes is of little importance in determining when a reinforcer will be delivered in _____ schedule of reinforcement.
(a ratio : an interval)

Learning Objective 2.16

I. Among all schedules of reinforcement, the highest overall response rate is produced by a _____ schedule of reinforcement.
(fixed-interval : variable-interval : fixed-ratio : variable-ratio)

Learning Objective 2.17

J. Stimulus _____ means that an organism responds to stimuli similar to, but not the same as, the training stimulus.
(generalization : discrimination)

Learning Objective 2.17

K. In instrumental conditioning, if a reinforcer is withheld from a behavior that at one time was followed by that reinforcer, and as a result the behavior decreases, we would say _____ is occurring.
(time-out : extinction : negative reinforcement)

Learning Objective 2.17

L. Behavior that is described by the phenomenon known as spontaneous recovery _____ if it is no longer followed by reinforcers.
(strengthens on its own : eventually disappears)

Learning Objective 2.19

M. Classical and instrumental conditioning differ in that in instrumental conditioning the consequence that affects the response _____ the response, whereas in classical conditioning, the opposite is true.
(precedes : follows)

OBSERVATIONAL LEARNING

Important breakthroughs have occurred in psychologists' thinking about learning. Much of what they have learned about learning has taken place in the laboratory, often with animals. Each year for the last few decades, researchers have learned more about reinforcement and punishment and how they operate in altering people's day-to-day behaviors. However, the principles of classical and instrumental conditioning are just two ways that people learn; this was the contention of Albert Bandura, who studied people, often children, in real-world settings.

Learning 2.20
Objective

In 1963, Stanford University psychologist Albert Bandura and his colleagues conducted important research to confirm their idea that people can learn by observing and then imitating the behavior of others (Bandura, Ross, & Ross, 1963c). Today, that research still influences psychologists' thinking about how behaviors are learned.

Bandura and his colleagues argued that Pavlov's ideas explain only a limited range of behaviors. Instrumental conditioning represented a major conceptual breakthrough, generating new theories that explain a much wider range of phenomena. In the last twenty years, **observational learning theory,** sometimes called *social learning theory,* has further expanded the range of behaviors explainable by learning theory (Woodward, 1982). The study of observational learning is not new; its history goes back to the early 1900s. However, Bandura studied it in new ways and suggested its profound implications. Observational learning theory has been especially important to personality theorists; you see later when we study personality in Chapter 12 that many important theories are based on data from studies of observational learning.

Observational learning The process by which organisms learn new responses by observing the behavior of a model and then imitating it; also called social learning theory.

Bandura (1969, 1977b) suggested that people can learn simply by observing the behavior of others and imitating it themselves. In his early studies, Bandura and his colleagues showed children films with aggressive content,

Albert Bandura is one of the leading researchers in the field of observational learning.

then compared play behavior with that of children who had been shown films that were neither aggressive nor nonaggressive in content. The researchers found that the children who had viewed aggressive, violent films tended to be aggressive and violent afterward (Bandura, Ross, & Ross, 1963a; Bandura & Walters, 1963).

Everyday experience shows that people imitate the behavior of others, especially those whom they hold in high esteem. The situations that provide opportunities to observe and learn new behaviors are almost unlimited. For example, when people who have never been exposed to death are faced with the loss of someone close to them, they may not know what to say or how to act. Although most people feel that grieving is a natural (or unlearned) response to such situations, the experience of seeing others grieve provides models for expressing grief.

Lisa the underpaid secretary exhibited a lot of careless behavior after her co-worker, Susan, received a promotion and raise. Although much of Lisa's behavior change can be explained by conditioning principles, some of it is best explained by observational learning. Lisa's sloppy work, negative attitudes, and anger toward the school board and Susan can be explained, at least in part, by realizing that throughout her life, Lisa probably observed other people behaving haphazardly and carelessly when they were unhappy with not being recognized for their efforts.

Laboratory studies of observational learning have shown that people can learn new behaviors by merely observing, and without being reinforced. For example, Bernal and Berger (1976) found that people can learn a classically conditioned response by merely observing it. In their study, subjects watched a film of other subjects being conditioned to an eyeblink response. A tone was paired with delivery of a puff of air to the eyelids of the filmed subjects. After a number of trials, the subjects in the film showed an eyeblink response to the tone alone. The subjects who watched the film also developed an eyeblink in response to a tone. Other studies have obtained similar findings with instrumental conditioning: through observing a reinforced behavior, subjects also learned the behavior. In one study, children observing models who were reinforced for aggressive behavior later tended to show aggressive behavior, too (Bandura, Ross, & Ross, 1963a). Other studies have shown that cats also learn by observing; John, Chester, Bartlett, and Victor (1968) found that cats learned to avoid receiving a shock through a grid floor by watching other cats successfully avoid the shocks by performing a task. A 1984 study showed that monkeys learn to be fearful of snakes when watching their parents exhibit behavior showing fear of snakes. This learned fear persisted for months (Mineka, Deniosm, Cook, and Keir, 1984). Manipulations of verbal learning show that college students can be conditioned to certain kinds of responses (Kanfer & Marston, 1963) and that stutterers can decrease their stuttering by watching others do so (Martin & Haroldson, 1977). Even children who are afraid of animals can learn to become less afraid by watching other children interact with animals (Bandura & Menlove, 1968).

Psychologists have been slow to explain behavior patterns in terms of observational learning. One reason may be that explaining observational learning as a process is more complicated than explaining and describing classical conditioning (Bandura, 1971). For example, people do not always act out the events they observe. Sometimes they have no opportunity to display what they have learned. Another reason may be that early attempts to examine observa-

Many of our everyday activities are learned by watching others and then practicing what we have observed.

tional learning in the laboratory were not initially successful. Finally, and perhaps most important, the study of observational learning requires psychologists to study thinking itself.

The fact that people do not replicate in their own behavior all the behaviors they observe raises two questions. First, do people need to be actively engaged in a behavior to learn it? Can they learn by merely observing? Second, can people learn new behaviors without being reinforced? Research has answered both questions in the affirmative. New behaviors can be learned merely by watching the behavior of others. Reinforcement is not absolutely necessary for new behavior to be established.

Bandura's explanation of learning through observation (1977b) has filled a large gap in psychologists' understanding of how learning occurs. It has also raised new questions: psychologists now need to identify the variables involved in observational learning. Because observational learning involves more than just simple stimuli and responses, in order to understand how people might learn an observed behavior psychologists need to understand what people think about the events they observe. Bandura suggests that observational learning may occur because people rehearse observed behavior; but such rehearsal may not be directly observable and it is therefore difficult to investigate. Increasingly, however, many psychologists suggest that observational learning, in combination with classical and instrumental conditioning, can account for nearly all learned behavior (see Table 2.8). Bandura's observational learning approach does not discount reinforcement, but instead it suggests that reinforcement in combination with observational learning can account for most behaviors. Chapters 12 and 15 further discuss the importance of Bandura's research in helping psychologists discover how people learn.

TABLE 2.8 : Types of Learning: Classical Conditioning, Instrumental Conditioning, and Observational Learning

Type of Learning	Procedure	Result	Example
Classical conditioning	A neutral stimulus (such as a bell) is paired with an unconditioned stimulus (such as food).	The neutral stimulus becomes a conditioned stimulus—it elicits the conditioned response.	A bell elicits salivation in a dog.
Instrumental conditioning	A behavior is followed by a consequence of reinforcement or punishment.	The behavior increases or decreases in frequency.	A pigeon pecks on a key 20 times per hour to obtain a reward or to avoid punishment.
Observational learning	An observer attends to a model to learn a behavior.	The observer learns the sequence of behaviors and becomes able to perform it at will.	After watching television violence, children are more likely to show aggressive behaviors.

PROGRESS CHECK   2.3

1. Complete each of the following sentences with one of the options provided.

Learning Objective 2.20
A. People tend to imitate the behavior of others, especially those whom they
_____.
(see as authority figures ⋮ hold in high esteem ⋮ fear)

Learning Objective 2.20
B. Bandura found that children who viewed aggressive, violent films tended to
_____ afterward.
(withdraw from others ⋮ be aggressive and violent ⋮ be frightened)

Learning Objective 2.20
C. Laboratory studies have shown that classically and instrumentally conditioned responses can be learned _____.
(only when reinforcement is delivered ⋮ by observing such responses)

Learning Objective 2.20
D. One reason psychologists have been slow to accept observational learning is that it requires that they study the influence that _____ has on learning.
(role modeling ⋮ thinking ⋮ group behavior)

Learning Objective 2.20
E. Bandura suggests that observational learning occurs because people _____
_____ observed behavior.
(rehearse ⋮ are reinforced by ⋮ can share)

Keeping Pace with Chapter 2

Applying Principles

2.1 Identify the stimuli and responses that are involved in each of the following examples of classically conditioned behavior.

unconditioned stimulus (UCS)   unconditioned response (UCR)
neutral stimulus that becomes   conditioned response (CR)
  the conditioned stimulus (NS/CS)

A. On several occasions during lightning storms, when Terry switched on the kitchen light she received a shock that caused severe pain and aroused physiological reactions. Now, even when the sky is clear, when she must turn on the light controlled by that particular switch her heart begins to pound and she feels very apprehensive.
1. UCS _____   2. UCR _____
3. NS/CS _____   4. CR _____

B. When Jake first adopted his pet cat, Tiger, he was able to use his electric can opener without any interference. However, after having used the can opener many times just before feeding Tiger his canned food, Jake has found that he can no longer open even a can of peas with the appliance without the nuisance of having Tiger standing underfoot, showing signs of anticipation for eating.
1. UCS _____   2. UCR _____
3. NS/CS _____   4. CR _____

2.2 Identify the schedule of reinforcement that maintains the behaviors illustrated in each of the following situations.

fixed-ratio   variable-ratio   fixed-interval   variable-interval

A. Patsy earns two cents for each envelope she addresses.

B. Doreen calls people at their homes and offers them a "special deal" on magazine subscriptions. She earns a bonus for each subscription she gets. Some people hang up on her, but others think the deal sounds pretty good and they subscribe. Doreen knows the more calls she can make in an hour, the more subscriptions and bonus money she will get.

C. Because Stephan's psychology teacher tends to give unannounced pop quizzes, Stephan studies more frequently and consistently for his psychology class than he does for any other class.

D. Wayne's psychology teacher gives a test every Friday. Because Wayne knows when he will be tested, he procrastinates all week and finally gets around to studying psychology on Thursday evening.

Self-Test

Before proceeding to the Self-Test, REVIEW the Learning Objectives listed at the chapter opening and RECITE from memory everything you can remember in support of them. Then, take this Self-Test as if it were to be graded by your teacher. Use the Learning Objective numbers in the Answer Section as a reference to restudy the corresponding text pages and Progress Checks for any incorrectly answered questions.

1. Which of the following phrases is *not* an important component of the definition of learning?

   A. behavior change
   B. behavior exhibited
   C. experience in the environment
   D. relatively permanent

2. The differences between how animals learn and how human beings learn becomes apparent when an experiment

   A. investigates simple reflexive behaviors.
   B. evaluates complex behaviors and requires the use of language.
   C. requires the researcher to make inferences about learning from observable results.
   D. examines behaviors learned through instrumental conditioning.

3. When comparing reflexive behaviors to classically conditioned behaviors, the main difference between the two is that reflexive behaviors are

   A. elicited.
   B. emitted.
   C. unlearned.
   D. tied to specific stimuli.

4. In Pavlov's famous experiment, the conditioned stimulus was

   A. food.
   B. salivation.
   C. a bell.
   D. a dog's mouth.

5. Which of the following is *not* a response that could be tied to a neutral/conditioned stimulus through classical conditioning?

   A. breathing
   B. sweating
   C. walking
   D. blood pressure

6. In higher-order conditioning,

   A. an unconditioned stimulus is paired with an existing conditioned stimulus.
   B. an unconditioned stimulus is paired with a neutral stimulus.
   C. a neutral stimulus is associated with a well-established conditioned stimulus.
   D. an unconditioned response takes on the properties of a conditioned stimulus.

7. A researcher conducts a conditioning experiment in which he consistently introduces the sound of a chime and immediately follows the sound with the flash of a
   dim blue light located five feet away from the subject. His goal, to establish a
   conditioned eye-blink response in the subject, is not achieved. We can assume that
   the conditioned response failed to occur because

   A. the strength of the unconditioned stimulus was too weak.
   B. the researcher neglected to use a neutral stimulus.
   C. the light should have been presented before the chime.
   D. conditioned stimulus discrimination had occurred.

8. When an organism is placed in the training situation after a rest period following
   extinction, and extinction procedures are still employed, the conditioned response

   A. occurs less frequently and extinguishes more rapidly.
   B. can be stronger than it was in the *classical* conditioning trials.
   C. occurs at irregular intervals.
   D. does not occur.

9. In *classical* conditioning, discrimination is learned when the researcher

   A. delivers a reinforcer when an organism discriminates correctly between stimuli.
   B. reinforces responses that are close to but not quite the same as the target re-
      sponse.
   C. pairs only the exact conditioned stimulus with the unconditioned stimulus.
   D. pairs slightly dissimilar neutral stimuli with the unconditioned stimulus.

10. Responses learned through classical conditioning

   A. are those responses we frequently refer to as emotions.
   B. occur automatically, in a reflexive manner.
   C. are controlled by stimuli rather than by the organism making the response.
   D. all of the above

11. E. L. Thorndike pioneered instrumental conditioning research by

   A. conditioning infants to suck in response to a sound.
   B. teaching pigeons to discriminate between a circle and an elipse.
   C. making food available to cats who hit a lever.
   D. toilet training his two-year-old.

12. A device that allows researchers to control when an organism will receive reinforcement or punishment is called a

   A. cumulative recorder.
   B. Skinner box.
   C. conditioning maze.
   D. differential apparatus.

13. Bobby's dad is teaching him to play baseball. Each time Bobby makes progress
   toward perfecting his swing, his dad tells him he did a good job. When Bobby does
   not show an improved swing, his dad says nothing. Bobby's dad is using
   _____ to teach his son how to swing the bat.

   A. a variable-interval schedule
   B. *primary* reinforcement
   C. shaping
   D. all of the above

14. Before a conditioning experiment begins, a researcher will deprive an animal of food

    A. if the experiment is designed to study negative reinforcement.

    B. to ensure that food has reinforcing properties while the study is being conducted.

    C. to determine whether the animal has enough physical stamina to be a successful subject in the experiment.

    D. to discover what kind of stimuli will act as secondary reinforcers.

15. Ratio schedules of consequences are based on

    A. time passing between responses.

    B. time passing between a response and a consequence.

    C. the number of consequences that are given for one response.

    D. work output, which is determined by the number of responses made.

16. Classical and instrumental conditioning procedures differ when it comes to generalization and discrimination training in that in instrumental conditioning

    A. the behaviors are emitted and then reinforced.

    B. the behaviors are elicited by a stimulus.

    C. lights are used rather than tones.

    D. people, rather than animals, are used as subjects.

17. In the behavior management plan used on the problem child discussed in the text, Rochelle's parents did all of the following *except:*

    A. They let Rochelle decide if she had performed tasks well enough to earn a reinforcer.

    B. They selected a reward they knew would have reinforcing properties for Rochelle.

    C. They stopped giving Rochelle attention when she misbehaved.

    D. They reinforced desirable behaviors and used time-out to punish undesirable behaviors.

18. Studies investigating the effectiveness of computer-aided instruction have found that the most effective courseware

    A. encourages rote drill.

    B. is highly interactive.

    C. presents material in a predetermined order.

    D. should take a serious approach to teaching rather than a fun approach.

19. The difference(s) between classical and instrumental conditioning are apparent when we consider

    A. the type of responses learned from each conditioning procedure.

    B. the way reinforcers are used.

    C. the effort or involvement of the organism who is learning.

    D. all of the above

20. Observational learning is sometimes called

    A. social learning.

    B. operant learning.

    C. Pavlovian conditioning.

    D. watchful learning.

3

Memory

3

Learning
Objectives

When you have mastered the material in this chapter, you will be able to:

1. Discuss the relationship between learning and memory. (p. 76)

2. Describe Ebbinghaus's early memory experiments and discuss how distributed practice and cues affect memory. (p. 76)

3. Describe how psychologists study recall and recognition and make a distinction between free-recall and serial-recall tasks. (p. 78)

4. Discuss several research studies concerning the reliability of eyewitness testimony. (p. 79)

5. Explain how memory is lost through decay and interference. (p. 82)

6. Describe how repression and two forms of amnesia affect memory. (p. 84)

7. Explain what is meant by state-dependent learning and give examples of physiological states that contribute to its occurrence. (p. 84)

8. Explain how the human brain differs from a computer; describe, according to the information processing approach, the three stages of memory; and define the important terms associated with each stage. (p. 86)

9. Describe two basic steps and three techniques that Cermak recommends for improving memory and review the steps involved in the SQ3R approach to learning and remembering. (p. 92)

10. Define *consolidation* and discuss evidence that shows there is a physiological basis to memory. (p. 94)

BEFORE YOU READ ON, take time to **SURVEY** the chapter, form an idea of what is to be learned (from margin Learning Objective numbers), and set goals for your study time. Then, ask yourself **QUESTIONS** about the material as you **READ,** seeking help for any sections you do not understand.

When Dennis Hilton took exams, everything seemed to go blank. He had been complaining about his ability to take tests since he was in the third grade. But now it was time for "the big one"; Dennis was about to take the SAT.

Dennis knew that the SAT is a key element in the total picture he would present to a college admissions committee. He knew that his grades, extracurricular activities, and letters of recommendation also count heavily. But in his case, his grades were not that good—he did poorly on most tests. He claimed he just was not test-wise. So, the SAT, the so-called great leveler, was going to be both difficult and important.

In preparation for the SAT, Dennis took an SAT prep course that focused heavily on memory techniques. The course instructors argued strongly that if people used good memory techniques, they would be better able to focus on the test, not be so nervous, and ultimately perform better. The course was extremely intensive—three two-hour sessions each day for four weeks, during which Dennis learned all about mnemonics, SQ3R, recall, recognition, and reading for memory.

At the end of the course, he told his parents he had sharpened his skills and that he wished he had taken such a course years ago. His reading speed had increased and his comprehension tests showed dramatic improvement. The data said Dennis was going to do well on the SAT. Privately, however, he had doubts. He questioned whether his improved memory and studying techniques would ultimately help him. He knew that the verbal portion of the SAT would have comprehension sections that would be killers. He still had nagging doubts about his ability to retain information. Could a four-week course really make a difference?

DENNIS HILTON HAD REASON to be concerned. He knew that a four-week course on memory techniques was not going to turn him into a memory expert. He also recognized that the comprehension section of the SAT would require more than just memory skills. Dennis's doubts were not unfounded. The memory skills course would not guarantee a high SAT score. However, often students who do poorly on tests have difficulty concentrating, staying focused on a task, and picking out key points. His memory skills course was likely to help in tasks on which he could use those skills, such as the verbal comprehension tests. You have to pay attention to the main idea and the subideas and also filter out the trivial details. You have to stay focused on your task, even when the story is difficult, paying attention and regularly questioning yourself about the key elements. Doing all of this makes answering questions easier. Using his newfound skills, Dennis was likely to do better; it is easy to see that memory is a key element to the process.

Dennis's problem is not unusual. All of us have faulty memories from time to time. We cannot remember who gave us a present, or the telephone number of an old friend. Students vividly recall situations in which an answer to a multiple-choice test item eluded them. You may remember a test for which you prepared well yet forgot answers. You had learned the information but were unable to demonstrate your learning. You had a memory failure.

Learning $\underline{3.1}$
Objective

Memory ═══════
The ability to recall or
remember past events or
previously learned
information or skills.

*A concert musician must not
only learn the notes in order to
play a symphony; she must
also practice them during
rehearsals so that she can
remember them without
mistakes.*

Learning $\underline{3.2}$
Objective

Psychologists have long recognized that recalling even well-learned information can be difficult. Dennis Hilton's instructors focused on elements that would aid his ability to recall information. A number of variables affect your memory. For one thing, you may not have learned the information as well as you thought. For another, your state of concentration may not be at its best. In the same manner, you may be tired, or even unmotivated. Learning information and then being able to remember it are different processes, but they depend on one another.

Memory is the ability to remember past events or previously learned information or skills. This chapter discusses that process and shows that learning and memory are closely related. An organism must learn something before it can remember it. As we saw in Chapter 2, psychologists studying learning and memory usually use performance (such as on an SAT test) to infer that an organism (such as a student) can maintain previously learned information or skills. Organisms that display this ability are said to remember. Most human beings and many animals can remember things for long periods. In animals, physical performance is the only indication of memory. Human beings, however, can also demonstrate memory in verbal performance. This makes it possible for us to study the more complex learning found in human beings.

Early memory studies focused on how quickly people could learn lists of nonsense words and how quickly such lists were remembered or forgotten. Later studies focused on variables that affected retention or forgetting, including the organization of the material to be learned. More recent research has focused on how people code information and then retrieve it from memory, especially over long periods of time. This chapter follows a semihistorical approach. We start with the early studies and show how psychologists' conceptions of memory have developed and how thinking has shifted to coding and retrieval processes.

The study of memory has been important for psychologists and educators. Studying memory has helped psychologists understand basic learning and memory processes, it has helped educators better shape curriculum design, and it has helped students recall previously learned information. It has also helped psychologists who focus on basic brain research who have attempted to study the organization of the brain and its coding mechanisms.

EARLY MEMORY RESEARCHERS LEARNED BETTER WAYS TO RETAIN WHAT WE LEARN

Some of the first psychologists were memory researchers. Hermann Ebbinghaus (1850–1909) was the first person to investigate memory seriously and scientifically. He began studying memory in 1885. In his early studies, he was both the researcher and the subject. His self-assigned task was to learn lists of letters in order of presentation. First, he strung together groups of three letters to make *nonsense syllables* (such as *nak, dib, mip,* and *daf*). He then recorded how many times he had to present the lists to himself before he could remember them perfectly. He found that, when the lists were short, learning was nearly perfect in one or two trials. But when the lists contained more than seven items, they had to be presented repeatedly for accurate recall. Everyday experience confirms Ebbinghaus's finding; many people have trouble remembering more than the seven digits in a phone number.

Hermann Ebbinghaus (1850–1909) was a pioneer in the research of memory.

To study how well people had learned the information stored in their memory, Ebbinghaus measured subjects' difficulty in relearning a list of nonsense syllables, recording how many trials or repetitions of the list were necessary. Ebbinghaus had subjects learn a list of nonsense syllables. He then let them engage in some other activity—sometimes doing other learning tasks. His subjects would forget the list they had initially learned. After varying amounts of time and activity, he measured how quickly the subjects relearned the original list. If a subject relearned the list quickly, Ebbinghaus concluded that he or she still had some memory of it. Ebbinghaus called this learning technique the *savings method.* By using the savings method, Ebbinghaus was able to show that what was initially learned was not totally forgotten—his subjects forgot the material but it was relearned more quickly than it had originally been learned. Ebbinghaus's technique was as important as his findings. He systematically, scientifically, and with some insight did experiments into memory. Some of his early ideas are still used today in modern conceptions of how memory operates.

From the 1930s through the 1960s, many researchers investigated the best ways to teach human beings new material. For example, they studied whether intensive practice at a task or practice over various intervals resulted in optimal learning. One such study, conducted by Baddeley and Longman in 1966, involved teaching postmen to touch-type. The subjects were divided into four groups: one group practiced typing for one hour a day, a second for two hours once a day, a third for one hour twice a day, and a fourth for two hours twice a day. Subjects in this study either used concentrated or mass practice or they distributed their practice over a period of days. The dependent variable was how well they typed—the number of accurate keystrokes per minute. On a typing test, the results showed that distributed practice was best.

Research on mass compared with distributed practice was typical of research of the 1950s and 1960s. In the typing task just described, distributed practice helps most. In exploring the general issues of mass versus distributed practice, researchers learned that the effectiveness of distributed practice depends on a number of variables—particularly the difficulty of the task. Most research confirm the adage that practice makes perfect; research shows that for many tasks, continued practice improves performance.

After studying practice effects, researchers of the 1970s often went on to study the best way to present information to be learned. This then led to investigation of how the information was ultimately stored in memory, and still later, of how it would be retrieved from memory.

Research on memory provides useful information for teachers concerned with helping students to learn and remember. It has been found that if one item in a list differs from the others (for example, if all but one item in a list are animal names), that one item is learned more easily. This phenomenon is called the *von Restorff effect.* In a typical learning experiment, Samuels (1970) presented twenty stimuli on flash cards and required subjects to learn an appropriate response to each. On one trial, the key response stimulus was printed in red and all other stimuli were printed in black. This cue helped subjects learn the correct response, but Samuels also demonstrated and cautioned that any gain in learning would probably be lost when the relevant cues were removed.

*When these two people meet
again, they will probably
recognize each other and also
be able to recall each other's
names.*

IT IS EASIER TO RECOGNIZE SOMETHING
YOU HAVE LEARNED THAN TO RECALL IT

*Learning
Objective* 3.3

No rodent has ever taken a 100-item multiple-choice test; but many human beings do so all the time. Unlike rats, people can remember facts and events, discuss them, place them in new contexts, and choose correct answers. Not only do human beings have very good memories, but they also have several different kinds of memory: memory for faces, memory for names, memory for story lines from old movies. Psychologists commonly divide memory into two classes: *recognition* and *recall.* Recognition involves remembering whether one has seen a stimulus before; that is, whether the stimulus is familiar. Recall involves remembering the details of a situation or idea and placing the details together in a meaningful framework (usually without any cues or aids). Thus, more information is required to recall than in recognition. Asking a college student to say whether William Shakespeare wrote "O Romeo, Romeo! where-fore art thou . . . " would be a test of recognition; asking the student to recite Juliet's balcony soliloquy would be a test of recall.

In recall tasks, subjects have to remember previously presented information, often strings of digits or letters. A typical study might ask subjects to

TABLE 3.1: Two Types of Traditional List-Learning Tasks, Materials, and Requirements

Type of task	Material	Example	Requirement
Serial recall	Nonsense syllables	GIP MAG DEC LIC DEL VEH	Subject learns the items in the order in which they were presented.
Free recall	Words	Ghoul Vanquish Painless Telephone Burp	Subject learns the items in any order.

Source: Based on J. F. Hall, 1982, p. 153.

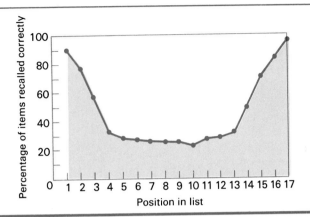

FIGURE 3.1 : This serial-position curve shows the percentage of accuracy of subjects' recall for each item in a serial-recall test.

remember ten nonsense syllables, each of which was presented on a screen every half second. Thus, the subjects would have to repeat the list at the end of five seconds. Two of the most widely used techniques are *free-recall* and *serial-recall* tasks. In free-recall tasks, subjects may recall the items in a list in any order; in a serial-recall task, they must recall the items in the order in which they were presented. Items repeated out of order receive no credit. Clearly, serial-recall tasks are more difficult. Table 3.1 lists typical items and requirements used in the major kinds of recall tasks.

Subjects tested for serial recall usually perform better on the first and last few items in the list than on those in the middle. Figure 3.1 shows some typical results of a serial-recall task for a seventeen-item list, presented in a *serial-position curve*. Notice that the last item is nearly always remembered.

When testing recognition—that is, using recognition accuracy as the dependent variable—researchers generally present more complicated tasks than when they test recall. Their results show that people are amazingly good at recognizing pictures they have been shown previously. Researcher Ralph Haber (1969, 1979) has found that subjects can recognize hundreds or even thousands of pictures with almost 100 percent accuracy. In 1970, Standing, Conezio, and Haber showed subjects thousands of slides, each for a few seconds, then presented pairs of slides containing one that the subjects had seen before, asking subjects to identify which of the pair of slides they had previously seen. The subjects recognized the previously seen slides with better than 95 percent accuracy. Other studies, presenting as many as 10,000 different pictures (Standing 1973) and presenting pictures very quickly (Intraub, 1980), have repeated these results and from them have developed theories of picture memory (Intraub & Nicklos, 1985).

Learning 3.4
Objective

You might think that the findings of research in picture memory would allow psychologists to infer that most people would make reliable eyewitnesses. However, studies of eyewitnesses have found that they often identify the wrong people and recall events incorrectly (Bekerian & Bowers, 1983; Loftus, 1979). Sometimes, people's reports are accurate and detailed; but at other times, important misrepresentations occur. Eyewitnesses of the same event often report seeing different things. To complicate the matter, eyewitnesses often enhance their memories over time. Harvard law professor Alan Dershowitz asserts that the memories of witnesses—particularly those of witnesses with a stake in the eventual outcome—tend to get better with the passage of time. Dershowitz calls this process *memory enhancement* and argues that it occurs when people fit their hazy memories into a coherent theory and pattern of other results. Their initial recollections of an event may be vague, but as a trial approaches, witnesses are coached and rehearsed. They tend to remember "better," with more clarity and less ambiguity. As Dershowitz says, "what began as a hazy recollection becomes frozen into crystalline clarity." The result in the courtroom, however, may be inaccurate, biased, or, at worst, untrue testimony (Dershowitz, 1986).

H. B. Brown conducted an early experiment on eyewitness identification at Dartmouth College in 1935. Students observed an individual and then saw him again in a group and were asked to indicate the person they had seen earlier; only 83 percent picked the correct man. More surprisingly, 29 percent of students who had never seen any of the men in the group before "recalled" having seen one of them. In other words, people reported that they recognized an individual they had never seen before.

Although researchers have demonstrated numerous errors in eyewitness testimony, such testimony continues to be used to convict both the innocent and the guilty (Loftus, 1974; Loftus & Loftus, 1976; Loftus & Palmer, 1974). Langman and Cockburn (1975) recorded the eyewitness testimony of people who reported having seen Sirhan Sirhan shoot Senator Robert F. Kennedy. Eyewitnesses to this event (many of whom had been standing next to each other) reported having seen different things. In a study in which an assault on a professor was staged in a classroom of students, seven weeks after the attack more than 60 percent of the eyewitness students incorrectly identified an innocent man as the assailant from a set of four photographs (Buckhour, Figueroa, & Hoff, 1974). Eyewitness testimony is often far from accurate, and eyewitness judgment is far from reliable (Wells & Murray, 1983). The passage of time, the interference of intervening events, and other more subtle processes may affect a subject's ability to give accurate and reliable eyewitness testimony.

The police line-up is frequently used to identify criminals, even though eyewitnesses often do not accurately recall what they have seen.

Psychologists at Work: New Findings in Eyewitness Testimony

If you see an accident or crime, are you able to report accurately to the police the facts of the situation? The answer to this question is both "yes" and "no." The police and the courts have generally accepted eyewitness testimony as some of the best evidence that can be presented. Here are people who saw the crime; they have no bias, no grudge, and are sworn to tell the "truth, the whole truth, and nothing but the truth." But do they?

In the 1970s, there was a great interest in the memory of witnesses for previously seen events. Research showed that eyewitnesses often do not remember events correctly, they sometimes supplemented their memory with false information, and they can be led astray to assume that certain events happened when they did not (Loftus & Burns, 1982; Wells and Loftus, 1984). Practicing attorneys support the literature by asserting that they know eyewitnesses make serious errors (Dershowitz, 1986). Common sense tells people that as an individual gets closer to a trial, an eyewitness's memory may have faded or been distorted.

However, two researchers from the University of British Columbia assert that eyewitness testimony is accurate and that *laboratory* studies of eyewitness testimony may be inaccurate. Yuille and Cutshall (1986) argue that laboratory studies generally use simulated events, films of events, television presentation, and slide shows to study eyewitness testimony and that they are not the same as actually having seen a *real* crime or accident. Yuille and Cutshall argue that real events are well remembered and that researchers who have studied eyewitness testimony have to do some field work before they make further claims.

Yuille and Cutshall reported a study in which twenty-one witnesses observed a shooting at a major thoroughfare in midafternoon. One person was killed and another was seriously wounded. All twenty-one witnesses were interviewed by the police, and thirteen agreed to participate in a research study that would take place four or five months later. An analysis was then made of the witnesses' reports at the time of the accident and several months later. The eyewitnesses were very accurate in the recall of the events, and there was little change in accuracy over a five-month period. Furthermore, the eyewitness resisted answering leading questions.

The eyewitnesses of Yuille and Cutshall forgot little except some relatively minor details (for example, the color of some people's clothing). The general picture of eyewitness testimony that has been painted in the psychological literature is negative. It has assumed that people are extremely fallible in their memories of past events, especially in recalling actions, personal descriptions, and verbalizations. For centuries, lawyers and juries have relied on eyewitness testimony; only recently has it been called into question. Law students are cautioned in their case books as to the accuracy of such testimony. However, now the research of Yuille and Cutshall shows that, in real situations, eyewitness testimony is accurate.

Do researchers throw out the old studies that claim that eyewitness testimony is fallible? No. Yuille and Cutshall's work is important because it questions laboratory research on eyewitness testimony. Before the issue is resolved, however, more field-based research is needed and simulation studies of the same situation have to be performed in the laboratory for comparison purposes. Actual eyewitness behavior does need to be accurately described. The next few years of research may resolve the issue (see also Shapiro & Penrod, 1986).

You can see that what has recently been interpreted as a weakness in the criminal justice system may not be a weakness. From our view in exploring psychology, you can also see that for every new piece of data, there always seems to be another new piece of research that elaborates and refines the situation. Psychology is a dynamic science, one that is constantly looking for new data, new answers, and the real causes of day-to-day behavior.

PROGRESS CHECK 3.1

1. Complete each of the following sentences with one of the options provided.

Learning Objective 3.1

A. Memory and learning are _____ processes.
   (similar yet independent : different but dependent)

Learning Objective 3.2

B. Ebbinghaus studied how well subjects had initially learned a list of words by measuring how quickly the subjects _____ the words.
   (forgot : could relearn)

Learning Objective 3.2

C. Distributed practice increases performance when learning _____ tasks.
   (easy : difficult)

D. The _____ is the term used to describe a phenomenon by which people find it easier to remember the one item in a group that differs from all other items.
(von Restorff effect : savings method)

E. When recall and recognition are compared, we find that _____ requires more information to be remembered by an individual.
(recall : recognition)

F. _____ is the most difficult recall task.
(Serial-recall : Free-recall)

G. Recognition studies have shown that people are _____ when it comes to identifying pictures they have seen before.
(amazingly accurate : not very accurate)

H. Dershowitz says that witnesses tend to give inaccurate or even untrue accounts in the courtroom because of a process called _____.
(eyewitness anxiety : memory enhancement : forgetting)

FORGETTING: THE LOSS OF MEMORY

How many times have you tried to remember a person's name but were unable to? How many times have you forgotten where you saw an interesting article, or the name of a book you wanted to recommend? How often have you had to look up a telephone number you thought you should remember? In each case, you forgot—you had a memory failure. Yet, most of us remember information for long periods of time. We remember the names of our first-grade teachers and our parents' friends. We remember Social Security numbers, telephone numbers, and dates and places. We have amazingly good memories, but there are things we forget, and sometimes this is frustrating.

There are potentially many causes of forgetting. A person may never have learned the information in the first place—you cannot forget what you never learned. You might forget because of a lack of rehearsal, disuse, or because the information has decayed from memory. Much forgetting occurs because of interference from newly learned information. Some researchers feel you forget unpleasant memories; others assert that people retain some information only when in certain physiological states. Let us examine some of these causes of forgetting.

Decay

Learning Objective 3.5

Decay
The loss of information from memory as a result of the passage of time and/or disuse.

As time passes, unimportant events seem to fade from memory through disuse; details become lost, confused, or fuzzy. The hypothesis that forgetting is caused by the passage of time is known as **decay** theory. According to decay theory, each memory exists in the brain in a physiological form known as a memory trace. With the passage of time and a lack of active use, the trace fades and is lost.

The decay hypothesis was popular for years, but it is not widely accepted today. Although the passage of time has an effect on memory, most researchers believe that many other factors are involved and that probably most of what we forget is not actually lost from our memory stores.

An interruption during studying to discuss tomorrow evening's plans can cause us to forget what we have just learned.

Interference

If your friend tells you a telephone number and then starts to give you another, you are likely to say, "Wait a minute—I am getting confused. The second number is interfering with the first."

The concept of **interference** suggests that when additional competing information is stored in memory, the resulting crowding will affect a person's memory for particular items. Research shows that when long lists of digits are presented, the number of items in the list seems to affect recall more than how quickly the items are presented. Interference in memory is likely to occur when a person is presented with a great deal of new information.

In contrast with notions of decay, research on interference theory shows that the extent and nature of a person's experiences both before and after learning are important. For example, a subject given a list of nonsense syllables, called a *target list,* may recall 75 percent of the items correctly. However, if the subject is given twenty similar lists to learn before the target list, the number of items correctly recalled from the target list will be lower; the previous lists interfere with recall. If the subject is given additional lists to learn after the target list, recall of the target list will be even lower. Psychologists call these effects proactive and retroactive inhibition. *Proactive inhibition* is the decrease in accurate recall of a target list as a result of previous events. *Retroactive inhibition* is the decrease in accurate recall of a target list as a result of subsequent presentation of material. Both effects have been studied extensively, and both have been found to be important in recall (Keppel & Underwood, 1962; Underwood, 1957).

Suppose you were to hear a whole series of lectures, each five minutes long, about some topic. According to psychological research, the proactive and retroactive effects mean that you would most likely remember the earliest and latest speeches you hear. Most of the speeches, for example, number six, would have a speech just before it (number five) and one just after it (number seven). However, there would be nothing to interfere with the first speech on hearing it (except the second speech); similarly, there would be no speech to interfere with the last one you heard (except the one just before it.) So, proactive and retroactive inhibition are important influences on our ability to remember.

Interference
The suppression or confusion of one bit of information with another received either earlier or later.

Can You Forget Unpleasant Memories? Motivated Forgetting and Amnesia

Learning Objective 3.6

Have you ever tried to forget an unpleasant memory? Have you ever tried to push away thoughts of an impending examination, a meeting with an unpleasant relative, or the thought of balancing your checkbook? Everyone tries to push aside uncomfortable thoughts at one time or another.

Freud (1933) was the first psychologist to suggest formally that unwanted or unpleasant events might be lost in memory simply because people wanted to forget them. According to Freud, this loss occurs through repression, the burying of unpleasant ideas in the unconscious, where they remain inaccessible. His formal theory of behavior (discussed in Chapter 12) is based in part on the idea that repressed memories motivate subsequent behavior. Freud's idea is supported by accounts from therapists about how people often choose to forget important and painful events in their lives. Although most researchers agree that motivated forgetting probably exists in some form, they have found it difficult to measure and have thus far been unsuccessful in proving it.

Television soap operas frequently portray people with amnesia, but in fact the condition is relatively rare. Unlike motivated forgetting, *amnesia* is the inability to remember events from the past, usually because of physiological trauma (such as an auto accident, a blow to the head, or a fall from a height). Typically, it involves loss of memory for all events within a specific period. Two basic kinds of amnesia are recognized: retrograde and anterograde. *Retrograde amnesia* is the inability to remember events that preceded the traumatizing event (what might be called "soap-opera loss"). Loss of memory may cover only the period just before the accident, or it may cover several years. Retrograde amnesia may be caused by injuries to the head; it is also associated with carbon monoxide poisoning and certain kinds of shock therapy in patients with depressive problems. Recovery is generally gradual, with older events remembered first (see McGaugh & Herz, 1970).

Anterograde amnesia is the inability to remember events since the time of the injury or brain damage. In studying patients with brain damage or patients who have undergone surgery for major epileptic attacks, researchers have found that the region of the brain called the *hippocampus* may be responsible for the transfer of new information to permanent memory. Milner (1966) suggested that if certain regions of the brain are damaged or removed, people can remember old information but not new information. (Milner, Corkin, & Teuber, 1968). Chronic alcoholics sometimes show anterograde amnesia in a disease called Korsakoff's syndrome. It is assumed that the large amounts of alcohol affect the brain, and that Korsakoff's syndrome and anterograde amnesia that is not a result of Korsakoff's may have a common cause.

The problems of amnesiacs and of people trying to forget an unpleasant childhood experience are different from those of someone trying to remember a list of nonsense syllables. Research in all aspects of how we remember and how we forget helps psychologists piece together a limited but growing understanding of memory (for example, Zola-Morgan, Cohen, & Squire, 1983).

State-Dependent Learning

Learning Objective 3.7

Distinguished psychologist Gordon Bower used the following example to describe the phenomenon known as state-dependent learning, in which information learned in one state is remembered better when the individual is again in that state (Bower, 1981):

> When I was a kid I saw the movie *City Lights* in which Charlie Chaplin plays the little tramp. In one very funny sequence, Charlie saves a drunk from leaping to his death. The drunk turns out to be a millionaire who befriends Charlie, and the two spend the evening together drinking and carousing. The next day, when sober, the millionaire does not recognize Charlie and even snubs him. Later the millionaire gets drunk again, and when he spots Charlie treats him as his long-lost companion. So the two of them spend another evening together carousing and drinking and then stagger back to the millionaire's mansion to sleep. In the morning, of course, the sober millionaire again does not recognize Charlie, treats him as an intruder, and has the butler kick him out by the seat of his pants. The scene ends with the little tramp telling the camera his opinion of high society and the evils of drunkenness.

The millionaire in this story remembers Charlie only when he is intoxicated—the same state in which he originally met him. Psychologists have found that information learned while a person is in a particular physiological state is recalled better when the subject is again in that physiological state. This phenomenon, known as **state-dependent learning,** is associated with drugs, time of day (Holloway, 1977), mental illness (Weingartner, 1977), and electroconvulsive shock (Robbins & Meyer, 1970). State-dependent learning is a fairly rare phenomenon, and its effects depend on several variables (Swanson & Kinsbourne, 1979). For example, in studies using drugs, the occurrence of state-dependent effects depends on the type of drug used, its dosage, and the task involved. Moderate doses of drugs help produce state-dependent effects, and so does repeated occurrence of the information to be learned during the learning phase of study.

State-dependent learning allows psychologists to examine the contexts in which people acquire and retain information. Several theories attempt to explain state-dependent learning. One widely accepted explanation focuses on how altered or drugged states affect the storage of memory. According to this view, part of learning involves the coding of stimuli in specific ways at the time of learning; to access the stored information, a person must evoke the same context in which the coding occurred (see, for example, Bower, 1972; Tulving & Pearlstone, 1966).

State-dependent learning
The tendency to recall information learned in a particular physiological state more accurately when one is again in that physiological state.

PROGRESS CHECK   3.2

1. Complete each of the following sentences with one of the options provided.

Learning Objective 3.5

A. The term _____ is used to describe the idea that each memory exists in the brain in a physiological form.
   (neuron : memory trace : icon)

Learning Objective 3.5

B. Decay theory, as an explanation for why we forget, _____ widely accepted today.
   (is : is not)

Learning Objective 3.5

C. The concept of interference suggests that we forget because of _____.
   (a fading memory trace : crowding of information)

D. _____ is the decrease in accurate recall of information because additional information was presented prior to the target list of information.
(Proactive inhibition : Retroactive inhibition)

E. According to Freud, people bury unpleasant thoughts in their unconscious minds and thus forget them through a defense mechanism known as _____.
(repression : memory bagging : reaction formation)

F. _____ amnesia is the inability to remember events that occurred after a traumatizing event.
(Retrograde : Anterograde)

G. If a region of the brain, such as the hippocampus, is damaged or removed, a person will probably have trouble remembering _____ information.
(old : new)

H. State-dependent learning is a fairly _____ phenomenon.
(common : rare)

I. Altered states appear to affect the _____ memory.
(coding, storage, and retrieval of : intensity of : plasticity of)

STAGES IN MEMORY: THE INFORMATION PROCESSING APPROACH

Dennis Hilton, who opened this chapter, had memory problems. He claimed he just could not remember the critical items on tests. Had Dennis not been able to remember items from just seconds before, an astute psychologist might have suggested that his was a case of retrograde amnesia; but this was not Dennis's problem. Dennis had a good memory for sports trivia, automobile prices, and phone numbers. His memory failed him only on tests. Researchers today know that people have different types of memory and that memory losses often reflect different types of trauma or biological processes that may be taking place.

Learning Objective **3.8**

In the last two decades, researchers have studied memory as if human beings process information the way a computer does, through sequences of coding, storage, and retrieval. Human brains, however, do not work exactly the way computers do. Unlike computers, human beings make mistakes and are affected by biological, environmental, and interpersonal events. Yet enough similarities exist between human brains and computers for psychologists to discuss learning and memory in terms of information processing. Even though people are much more complex than machines, these comparisons have helped psychologists understand memory. This approach assumes that each stage of learning and memory is related but separate. Some psychologists do not agree with this overall approach; however, most do agree that, as a way of thinking about human memory, this approach is useful. It generates research and stimulates thinking. Recognizing that not all researchers agree about their existence or the way they function, let us now examine three stages of memory: the sensory register, short-term memory, and long-term memory.

Stage 1: The Sensory Register

Sensory register _____
The mechanism that performs initial coding and brief storage of stimuli (for about 0.25 second in the visual system).

For learning and memory to occur, a stimulus must exist. The first stage in the process is the representation of the stimulus by a mechanism called the **sensory register,** which performs initial coding and brief storage. This initial cod-

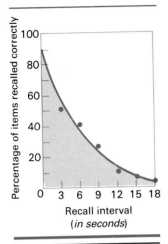

FIGURE 3.2 • Peterson and Peterson found that when they delayed the report of a three-consonant sequence by having subjects count backward, accuracy of recall decreased over the first eighteen seconds. They interpreted these results as evidence for the existence of short-term memory.

Short-term memory
The memory process that temporarily stores information for immediate or short-term use. The duration of short-term memory is about thirty seconds; its capacity is limited to five to nine items.

ing usually contains information in a picture-like representation. In the visual system, for example, the sensory register establishes the stimulus in an electrical or neural form and stores it for 0.25 second with little interpretation, in an almost photographic manner. This visual sensory register is sometimes called the *icon.* Once information is established in the sensory register, it must be transferred elsewhere for additional coding or it will be lost. For example, when you look up a phone number in a telephone book, you probably either repeat the number over and over to yourself or you forget it before you can use it.

A series of studies by George Sperling in the early 1960s demonstrated the existence of a visual sensory register. He visually presented letters to subjects for very brief durations and found they were able to recall a great deal from presentations as short as 1 or 2 milliseconds (one or two thousandths of a second). From his studies and others that followed, researchers have claimed the existence of a brief (250 millisecond), rapidly decaying sensory store. Although some researchers challenged the existence of the sensory register and its physiological basis (Sakitt & Long, 1979), the research literature still holds that it is the first stage of coding. How this storage is used is still controversial. One of the first researchers to explore it in depth has now suggested that its importance is minimal (Haber, 1983), but this notion has been hotly debated (Haber, 1985; Loftus, 1985; Loftus, Shimamura, & Johnson, 1985). Loftus and his colleagues argue that the first part of the icon, perhaps the first 100 milliseconds, may be important. This debate is continuing; but for our purposes, the key facts are that the icon or sensory register is the first stage of information processing and its duration is 250 milliseconds.

Stage 2: Short-Term Memory

After the sensory register, psychologists believe that stimuli either decay and are lost or are transferred to a second stage, called short-term memory. In **short-term memory** information is maintained for about thirty seconds; during this time, a great deal of coding and organization can take place. For example, if you were a waiter in a restaurant and were given a lengthy and complex order to remember, you might say the order over and over to yourself, rehearsing it, until you could write it down or tell it to the chef. Because of the limitations of short-term memory, two minutes later it is unlikely that you could remember with any accuracy all details of the food order.

It is easy to see that short-term memory has a limited duration; this was shown in an important study conducted in 1959 by Margaret and Lloyd Peterson, who changed the course of memory research. The Petersons asked subjects to recall a three-consonant sequence, such as *xbd,* after three-second intervals ranging from no delay to eighteen seconds, during which the subjects were required to count backward by threes. Counting backward would prevent the subjects from rehearsing, or saying to themselves, the sequence they were supposed to remember. The Petersons' aim was to examine recall when rehearsal is not possible. Figure 3.2 presents the results. As the delay interval increased, accuracy of recall decreased. The Petersons interpreted these results as evidence for a decaying short-term memory.

Short-term memory differs from other stages of memory in five ways: duration, capacity, rehearsal, coding, and retrieval. First and most important is *duration.* Psychologists distinguish between short-term memory and long-term memory on the basis of how long information can be stored. The Petersons' experiment showed that information contained in short-term memory is available for only a few seconds; after that, it must either be stored permanently in long-term memory or be lost.

A second important characteristic of short-term memory is its limited *capacity.* In 1956, George Miller argued convincingly that human beings can retain about seven (plus or minus two) items in short-term memory. Subsequent research confirms this claim: subjects given long lists to learn can remember only seven, plus or minus two, items depending on the type of material. Of course, some items are remembered more easily and in greater numbers than others, particularly if they are organized in some meaningful way (such as alphabetically). Another important variable related to capacity has recently been discovered. A person's memory capacity may be affected by the length of time it initially takes to store the material (Schweickert and Boruff, 1986). This idea is not totally new, and the long-standing ideas of Miller regularly face alternative interpretations.

A third distinguishing aspect of short-term memory is *rehearsal.* Rehearsal is the process of actively repeating the items to be remembered. Subjects will quickly forget a list of letters (such as *xbdfmpg*) unless they try to maintain the list in short-term memory by rehearsal. Actively rehearsed items can be maintained in short-term memory almost indefinitely. Usually, however, the information entered in short-term memory is either transferred to long-term memory or lost. Researchers such as Bauer (1977, 1979) suggest that poor rehearsal abilities may account for the deficient short-term memory of some children with learning disabilities.

A fourth characteristic of short-term memory is *coding.* Coding is the initial organization of information in memory. Before being transferred into long-term memory, most items in short-term memory go through some type of visual or acoustic coding. When a series of stimuli are presented visually, the subject must transfer them out of the sensory register into short-term memory. However, it is unlikely that the stimuli are represented in short-term memory exactly as they were in the sensory register. Psychologists know that some information is stored visually in short-term memory and that other information appears to be stored acoustically. For example, after consulting a telephone book for a phone number, you generally repeat the number to yourself while maintaining a visual representation of the digits. In a recall task, a subject might be presented with the letters *COS* but might respond with *QUB.* In this case, the subject is confusing the shapes of the letters (Conrad & Hull, 1964). At other times, visually presented stimuli are coded acoustically. That is why, if a subject makes errors when reporting back a string of letters, the errors are often letters that sound like the correct ones. If the letters to be reported are *x, b, d, p,* and *f,* for example, the subject might say *s, e, d, b,* and *f.*

Retrieval

The process of making available previously learned or experienced events.

Psychologists have found that one of the best ways to identify and study short-term memory is through the study of retrieval processes. **Retrieval** is the use of memory to recall or recognize something previously learned. Modern information-processing theorists use the traditional concepts of decay and interference to explain retrieval problems or the loss of data from short-term memory (see Figure 3.3). According to the decay explanation, information is lost simply due to the passage of time through *disuse.* According to the interference explanation, the limited capacity of short-term memory makes the items in it susceptible to interference or confusion with other learned items. For example, if you look up one telephone number and then are given another to remember, the presence of the second number will probably interfere with

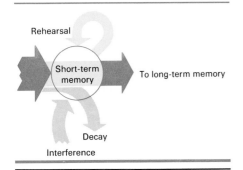

FIGURE 3.3 : When information enters short-term memory, it is subject to decay, interference, rehearsal, or transfer into long-term memory.

Our long-term memory allows us to retain information we consider important, such as the names, faces, and birthdates of our close family members.

FIGURE 3.4 : Information maintained in short-term memory can be transferred into more permanent long-term memory. Long-term memory is subject to both decay and interference.

Long-term memory ═══
The mechanism that keeps a relatively permanent record of information.

your ability to remember the first one. In this case, interference or confusion, not decay, will have affected your recall.

Many researchers think of short-term memory as a series of different subsystems. For example, Baddeley and Hitch (1974) think of short-term memory as a working memory in which several substructures operate in a temporary way. One subsystem may code auditory information; another subsystem may be a visual-spatial scratch pad for temporary use. Baddeley and Hitch's conception of working memory has been well received; the idea of short-term memory as working memory is not inconsistent with previous conceptions of short-term memory research.

In summary, four things may happen to information that has entered short-term memory: (1) it may decay (be lost over time) and be forgotten; (2) it may be confused with other information of a similar nature (interference) and be partially forgotten; (3) it may be rehearsed and used; or (4) it may be rehearsed and transferred to long-term memory (see Figure 3.4).

Stage 3: Long-Term Memory

If Dennis Hilton, who opened this chapter, could have taken a test dealing with computers, he might have done well. Dennis was very conversant with computer hardware and software. He had thousands of facts stored away and available for easy retrieval. Some of his friends told him he was a walking computer encyclopedia. However, the SAT measures reasoning ability, not long-term storage of facts.

Information stored in **long-term memory** is coded in a relatively permanent form. This information may include names, faces, dates, places, smells, and important and trivial events. People who have been required to memorize certain poems or literary passages can often remember much of the material after many years. For example, almost everyone can remember the first few lines of Mark Antony's speech from *Julius Caesar:* "Friends, Romans, countrymen, lend me your ears. . . . "

Even information stored in long-term memory, however, is subject to loss. Most people are able to recite all of Mark Antony's speech just after learning it; a few years later, however, they probably can remember only a few lines. This loss of information from long-term memory may be due either to decay or to interference. People have many bits of information to remember, and learning new ones may interfere with their ability to remember old ones. Most people are aware that their long-term memories are fallible; they take notes during a lecture to help themselves recall the information later. As we mentioned earlier in this chapter, **retrieval** is the process by which a person uses his or her memory to recall something previously learned. In most cases, problems in retrieval involve information stored in long-term memory.

The information stored in long-term memory is either information that an individual considers important or information that must be used frequently. An item such as the price of bananas will probably not be entered in long-term memory, but a person's Social Security number may be, if it must be used often. Information in long-term memory is retained because it is salient and/or because it has been actively rehearsed. Important items that are used often are the most likely to be retained.

Generally, psychologists researching long-term memory have studied people of normal intelligence and behavior, such as students. In a typical experiment, a subject may be asked to study a list of thirty or forty words, one word presented every two seconds. A few minutes later, the subject is asked to recall the list. Such experiments typically show an overall recall of 20 percent. However, recall is higher for words at the beginning of a list than for those at the middle, and highest for those at the end (look again at Figure 3.1). The latter tendency is called the **recency effect** and is due to the active rehearsal of the information in short-term memory. In contrast, the tendency to remember information given at the beginning of a list, called the **primacy effect,** occurs when no information is currently stored in short-term memory at the moment a new task is assigned; the subject's attention to stimuli at this point is at its peak. In everyday life, people are rarely called on to remember long lists of items. However, they are often presented with a large amount of information and later asked to recall certain parts of it. Plays, symphonies, art exhibits, and political speeches often seem to take the recency and primacy effects into account by presenting their most important, most emphatic elements at the beginning and end.

Like short-term memory, long-term memory may have its subdivisions, each with its particular function and content (Collins & Quillan, 1972). In 1972, Tulving suggested that there are two kinds of long-term memory: episodic and semantic. *Episodic* memory covers specific events, objects, and situations such as what a person had for breakfast, the movie he saw last night, or what he did on vacation last summer. Studies of memory for events long past show that people remember them well, especially information about themselves (Barclay & Wellman, 1986). *Semantic* memory covers ideas, rules, and general concepts about the world. It develops after episodic memory.

The results of semantic memory studies indicate that information is stored at particular levels of memory; a person needing more information must go to different levels to access this information. For example, a person presented with the sentence "A canary is a bird that has feathers and can sing" and then asked if the sentence is true or false might need to access different levels of information concerning animals, birds, and canaries. Response time will de-

---

Retrieval
The process of making available previously learned or experienced events.

Recency effect
The more accurate recall of items presented at the end of a list.

Primacy effect
The more accurate recall of items presented first in a list.

FIGURE 3.5: The information-processing approach stresses analysis by stages in which each level can be examined separately. When the information enters the memory processing system, it proceeds from the sensory register to short-term memory and then to long-term memory. At each stage, there is a loss of information owing to decay or interference.

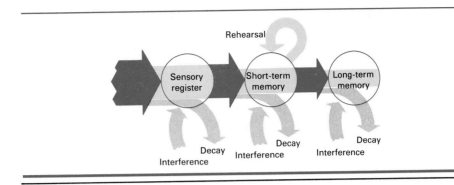

pend on the number of levels that must be examined in order to verify the accuracy of the sentence and on a number of other important variables (Tilley & Warren, 1983).

Summary

The *information-processing* view of memory divides it into a series of stages, thus allowing researchers to consider how each stage works and how it might relate to other stages (see Figure 3.5). There are different theories about how memory works and different terms to describe each process. Some psychologists do not make a distinction between short- and long-term memory, and some attribute different aspects of learning to different memory systems. However, almost all agree that (1) the sensory register is a brief representation of the original stimulus and performs minimal neural coding; (2) short-term memory is a storage mechanism, acoustic in nature (although it may have visual components), that lasts for less than thirty seconds; (3) rehearsal helps maintain information in short-term memory; (4) decay or interference accounts for the major loss of information from short-term memory; and (5) long-term memory is the final coding mechanism in the memory system and is sensitive to an item's importance, salience, and the degree of rehearsal.

PROGRESS CHECK   3.3

1. Match each of the following key concepts and terms with the appropriate definition.

icon   long-term memory   sensory register
episodic memory   short-term memory   semantic memory

Learning Objective 3.8

A. _____ Memory that includes ideas, rules, and general concepts about the world.

Learning Objective 3.8

B. _____ This mechanism performs the initial coding and briefly stores a neural representation of a stimulus.

Learning Objective 3.8

C. _____ A term used to describe the visual sensory register. It converts lightwaves into electrical form and stores the information for 250 milliseconds with little interpretation, in an almost photographic manner.

Learning Objective 3.8

D. _____ The information stored in this stage of memory is relatively permanent. It resists information loss, but, even at this stage, memory is subject to forgetting. Information stored by this mechanism must be retrieved to be of any use.

Learning Objective 3.8

E. _____ The memory process that temporarily stores information for immediate use. The duration is limited in this state to about thirty seconds and the capacity is limited to five to nine items. A great deal of neurological coding takes place.

Learning Objective 3.8

F. _____ Memory that includes specific events, objects, and situations that have occurred in our lives.

2. Complete each of the following sentences with one of the options provided.

Learning Objective 3.8

A. The existence of the sensory register _____.
   (was just recently discovered : is under debate)

Learning Objective 3.8

B. If information stored in short-term memory is not transferred into long-term memory, it _____.
   (decays and is forgotten : returns to the sensory register)

Learning Objective 3.8

C. If you look up the spelling of a word in your dictionary, you probably will remember the proper spelling until you can write down the word by _____ coding it in short-term memory through rehearsal.
   (visually : acoustically)

Learning Objective 3.8

D. Many researchers see short-term memory as a working memory in which _____.
   (previous conceptions are sorted out : subsystems operate in a temporary way)

Learning Objective 3.8

E. One factor that determines whether information will be transferred into long-term memory is its _____.
   (level of difficulty : importance)

Learning Objective 3.8

F. The primacy effect occurs because a person can _____ the incoming information.
   (give full attention to : actively rehearse)

Learning Objective 3.8

G. Episodic and semantic memory are two kinds of _____ memory.
   (short-term : long-term)

Improving Your Memory: Some Practical Advice

When Dennis Hilton took a memory course, he tried to use organizational schemes, mnemonics, and attention tasks to help him learn better. He was on the right track.

Learning Objective 3.9

People usually try to organize information in some way to help themselves remember it later. Sometimes they simply repeat the initial letters of important words. For example, to remember the three major stages of memory, they might repeat the letters, *ssl,* for sensory register, short-term memory, and long-term memory. Or they might try to make *ssl* more meaningful (and more likely to be remembered) by recoding the letters as the words *silly skipping lambs.* In both cases, the aim is to remember the letters and let the letters act as cues for memory.

Coding words through letters is an example of using a *mnemonic.* A mnemonic is a device that helps improve one's memory without expensive or time-consuming memory aids. Laird Cermak, a noted learning psychologist, has outlined a how-to-do-it approach in his book *Improving Your Memory.*

The Cermak method involves two basic steps and three techniques. First, pay close attention to what you want to remember. Second, organize your thoughts. After attending to the material and organizing it, use three techniques to help yourself remember it: mediation, imagery, and mnemonics. *Mediation* is a bridging technique: it associates two items to be remembered by using a third that ties them together. Cermak uses the names John and Tillie as an example. John reminds you of *bathroom,* which can be associated with *tiles,* which sounds and looks like *Tillie.* Remembering a tiled bathroom should help you remember the two names John and Tillie.

Cermak's second technique, *imagery,* involves making mental pictures of events or things you want to remember. Try to form images that involve you in them. For example, you might imagine yourself standing in a tiled bathroom with John and Tillie.

Cermak's third technique, *mnemonics,* combines items into an established format, rhyme, or jingle containing the information to be remembered. For example, most children learn the notes of the musical scale, EGBDF, by using a mnemonic jingle, such as "Every good boy does fine." Mnemonics is the most creative of Cermak's suggestions for organizing material, and it is very effective. All three techniques require practice and repeated use.

As a college student, one of your most important jobs is to learn new facts and details as well as important broad concepts. Mnemonics can be helpful, but most successful students approach a learning situation in logical steps. This is the approach this textbook takes. We recommend in Chapter 1 that you first try to separate the task into small units, reading one or two sections of a chapter each day. Within each chapter, quickly *survey* the material and *question* yourself about the most important aspects of what you have just surveyed. Then, *read* the material carefully. After reading the material, *recite* the important points out loud. Finally, *review* all material covered. The *SQ3R* method—survey, question, read, recite, and review—is a systematic way to improve your ability to learn and remember new material. By reading and studying a few chapter sections each day, you can create a beneficial distributed practice study schedule. Many students use the SQ3R method consistently with every kind of material they have to learn.

Mnemonics can help our memory.

THE PHYSIOLOGY OF MEMORY

People remember only those things that are important to them. This was the argument that the famous psychologist, E. B. Titchener, made in 1898. Psychologists today are still making the same argument. Titchener asserted that, in order to remember, people first must forget a great deal of irrelevant information. However, some psychologists who have studied the biological bases of behavior now believe that most, if not all, memories are retained—even information that has been learned through massed practice. These psychologists believe that a permanent neurological structure develops when something is remembered; and if it appears that a memory has been forgotten, retrieval, rather than memory loss, is the problem.

Learning Objective <u>3.10</u>

Studying memory has been examined in this chapter largely from an information-processing approach. But another especially important approach is a physiological one. In 1949, Canadian psychologist Donald Hebb (1904–1985) presented a major psychological and physiological theory of memory. Hebb suggested that when groups of neurons are stimulated, they form patterns of activity. If a pattern of neural activity fires frequently, a reverberating and regular neural circuit is established. This evolution of a temporary neural circuit into a more permanent structure is called **consolidation.** According to Hebb, consolidation serves as the basis of short-term memory and permits information to be coded into long-term memory. If Hebb is correct, when people first see or hear a new stimulus, only temporary changes in neurons take place; with repetition, consolidation occurs and the temporary circuit becomes a permanent structure.

Consolidation
The evolution of a temporary neural circuit into a more permanent circuit.

Although we may not remember much about a movie the first time we see it, with repeated viewings we can recall many details about the plot.

Many psychologists feel that the consolidation process provides the key to understanding learning and memory—that differences among individuals in the ability to learn or remember may be due to different abilities to consolidate new information properly. Studies using electroconvulsive shock to disrupt consolidation have resulted in impaired memory in both human beings and animals. Additional information has come from studies of accident victims and from people who have undergone brain surgery for specific disorders.

Most studies of the physiology of memory have supported a distinction between short-term and long-term memory. For example, Baddeley and Warrington (1970) conducted several memory experiments comparing normal subjects with amnesiac subjects who had various types of brain damage. Their results showed that amnesiac patients had intact short-term memories but grossly defective long-term memories. Milner (1966) reported the case of a brain-damaged adult whose short-term memory was intact but who was unable to form new long-term memories. As long as the subject was able to rehearse information and keep it in short-term memory, his recall performance was normal; but as soon as he could no longer rehearse and had to use long-term memory, his recall was very poor. Although Milner's data continue to be challenged, they provide neurological support for a distinction between short- and long-term memory (see, for example, Drachman & Arbit, 1966).

Other researchers have used a wide variety of techniques to investigate the physiological basis of memory in both human beings and animals. McGaugh (1983), for example, contends that even hormones may affect the way memories are stored. McGaugh correctly points out that newly established memories are particularly sensitive to chemical and electrical stimulation of the brain.

It is important to remember that memories are not a physical thing but are made up of unique groupings of neurons in the brain. The basis of all memories is ultimately biochemical in nature. Researchers who have tried to study the biochemistry and the pathways of memory have met many roadblocks because the makeup of the brain is so complex. There have been advances, however. For example, if rats are trained to make a response, such as avoiding one half of an electrified cage, learning can be transmitted to other rats by chemical infusion. Proteins from the brains of rats that had learned a response were removed and placed surgically into other rats; the second group showed the same learning. The chemicals transmitted the learning! These results helped isolate the proteins and later the neuropeptides that may be responsible for memory (Tate, Galvan & Ungar, 1976).

More recent research has precisely located some types of memory in rabbits. Researchers found that when a specific area of the rabbit brain was destroyed, previously learned associations were also destroyed. In this case, a classically conditioned response was established (eye blinks in response to tones); the rabbits still gave eye blinks to puffs of air and they still heard tones, but the tones no longer elicited blinks after a precise portion of the cerebellum had been destroyed (McCormick & Thompson, 1984).

The physiological basis of memory is real, biochemical in nature, and is being discovered. The search is exceedingly complex, and the biochemical processes and locations are difficult to find. But we are beginning to ask the right questions. How does consolidation take place? Do changes take place at the cellular level? Are the proteins, neuropeptides, or combinations of these elements the key to memory? We have hints and promising leads, but we are just beginning to discover the biochemical basis of memory.

PROGRESS CHECK 3.4

1. Complete each of the following sentences with one of the options provided.

Learning Objective 3.9

A. Paying close attention to what you want to learn and _____ are the two basic steps in Cermak's memory improvement method.
(memorizing all you can : organizing your thoughts)

Learning Objective 3.9

B. Associating two items to be remembered with a third item is an organizing technique called _____.
(mediation : imagery : mnemonics)

Learning Objective 3.10

C. The evolution of a temporary neural circuit into a more permanent neural structure is called _____.
(memory span : cell assembly : consolidation)

Learning Objective 3.10

D. Most studies investigating the physiology of memory support the idea that there _____ apparent neurological distinction between short-term and long-term memory.
(is no : is an)

Learning Objective 3.10

E. McGaugh has suggested that _____ may affect the way memories are stored.
(hormones : blood pressure : friendships)

Learning Objective 3.10

F. One study with rats provided information concerning the proteins and neuro-peptides that appear to be involved in memory by _____.
(placing proteins into the brains of naïve rats : feeding rats a high protein diet)

Learning Objective 3.10

G. Research with rabbits indicates that at least some types of memory are associated with _____.
(the spinal cord : precise locations in the brain : chemicals)

Keeping Pace with Chapter 3

Applying Principles

Identify the concept that explains why remembering or forgetting occurs in each of the following situations.

decay   retrograde amnesia   retroactive inhibition
anterograde amnesia   proactive inhibition   primacy effect
motivated forgetting   recency effect

_____ A. Neurosurgeons operated on Bettye's brain in an attempt to control her epileptic seizures. After the surgery, Bettye could remember such things as her name, where she grew up, and what she was doing before the surgery, but she could not remember who her doctor is, what she had for breakfast, or that her mother visited her yesterday.

_____ B. On the way to the lumberyard, Clay lost his list of things needed. He had read over the list just before leaving his house, but as he began to shop for what he needed, he realized he could only remember the last few items on the list.

_____ C. Norma forgot her grandfather's version of the family's traditional Thanksgiving blessing after having recited a different one at a church social gathering.

_____ D. Diane dialed her friend Lena's phone number from memory several times a day when they were high school friends. Ten years later, while visiting her hometown she decided to call the old number to see if Lena's parents could make arrangements for the two of them to have a reunion. To her surprise, when Diane went to dial, she realized she could not remember the number.

_____   E. Curtis studied marketing plan "A" and then marketing plan "B." Compared to marketing plan "A," his accuracy of recall on marketing plan "B" was poor.

_____   F. When Janie arrived at the company party, she was immediately introduced to ten people. Janie can remember the names of only the first three people she met, and she is awkwardly wondering what to do since she is talking with the person she met last—a person who happens to be an attractive and important business contact.

_____   G. Frank fell out of his white river raft and received a serious blow to his head. When he regained consciousness, he did not know who he was, where he came from, or when he had been born.

_____   H. When Joel was a child, his sister Susan drank a poisonous household chemical and died. Joel was with her when the accident happened and deep inside has always felt responsible. Years later, while chatting with his parents, memories of Susan's life and death came up. Joel's parents were astonished when Joel indicated it was unfortunate that Susan had died from a serious yet common cold. They figured the true memory must be so painful that Joel could not remember it.

Self-Test

Before proceeding to the Self-Test, REVIEW the Learning Objectives listed at the chapter opening and RECITE from memory everything you can remember in support of them. Then, take this Self-Test as if it were to be graded by your teacher. Use the Learning Objective numbers in the Answer Section as a reference to restudy the corresponding text pages and Progress Checks for any incorrectly answered questions.

1. This text defines memory as
    A. a relatively permanent change in behavior that occurs as a result of experience.
    B. the ability to associate two or more events.
    C. the ability to recall past events or previously learned information.
    D. the ability to discriminate among concepts and to synthesize ideas.

2. Based on research concerning mass versus distributed practice, the most effective study schedule you could follow when studying for your next psychology test would be to study
    A. one hour a day, every day before the test.
    B. three hours a day, starting three days before the test.
    C. for as long as you need to, the day before the test.
    D. in a cram session right before the test.

3. In serial-recall tasks, subjects
    A. tend to remember the first items on a list but, not the last items.
    B. tend to remember the items listed in the middle of a list.
    C. tend to remember the last items on a list but, not the first items.
    D. nearly always remember the last item on a list.

4. Research concerning eyewitness testimony suggests all of the following *except*
    A. Eyewitness testimony is some of the best evidence that can be presented in a court of law.
    B. Eyewitnesses, especially those with a stake in the eventual outcome of the case, often enhance their memories over time of what actually took place.
    C. People sometimes report recognizing individuals they have never seen before.
    D. The passage of time, interference of intervening events, and other subtle processes may affect the accuracy of eyewitness testimony.

5. The crowding or confusion in memory of one bit of information with another is called

   A. amnesia.
   B. interference.
   C. hippocampus.
   D. decay.

6. People with Korsakoff's syndrome

   A. have retrograde and anterograde amnesia.
   B. experience amnesia because a part of their brain was surgically removed.
   C. remember new information but are unable to remember past events.
   D. recover gradually, with older events being remembered first.

7. State-dependent learning has been associated with all of the following *except*

   A. tasks requiring motor skills, such as kicking a ball.
   B. mental illness and electroconvulsive shock.
   C. the time of day.
   D. drugs in moderate doses.

8. Four distinguishing characteristics of short-term memory are

   A. permanence, recall, savings, and recency.
   B. duration, capacity, coding, and rehearsal.
   C. photographic, resistant, complete, and efficient.
   D. acoustical, partial, sequential, and retrieval.

9. If you rehearse a poem on Sunday night for a speech you must give on Monday morning, you are relying on _____ to enable you to recite the poem with no errors.

   A. short-term memory
   B. long-term memory
   C. a recency effect
   D. A and C

10. A student who reads and studies one or two sections of a chapter reading assignment each day instead of reading the entire chapter in one study session

   A. will probably learn definitions well but may have difficulty grasping broader concepts.
   B. is following a distributed practice study schedule, and this could be beneficial to his or her learning.
   C. is making use of a technique called mediation.
   D. is depending on short-term memory abilities.

11. A mnemonic is best described as

   A. a bridging technique.
   B. making mental pictures of the things you want to remember.
   C. creating a rhyme or jingle that contains the information to be remembered.
   D. a complete, systematic, and effective approach to studying an entire chapter in a textbook.

12. The physiological basis of memory

   A. is well understood by most researchers.
   B. is not really all that important to our understanding of memory.
   C. shows us that there is really no difference between learning and memory.
   D. is biochemical in nature.

4

Biology of Behavior and Consciousness

4

Learning Objectives

When you have mastered the material in this chapter, you will be able to:

1. Explain why psychologists study biology. (p. 102)

2. Make a distinction between the terms *nature* and *nurture.* (p. 103)

3. Describe the debate psychologists have about the relative contributions of biological and environmental variables on behavior and state three factors concerning nature and nurture that must be taken into account. (p. 104)

4. Define *heredity* and explain how physical and basic behavioral traits are genetically transmitted from parents to their children. (p. 105)

5. Make a distinction between biological and genetic causes of behavior problems and describe two types of mental retardation that have a genetic cause. (p. 106)

6. Explain how twins develop and why twin studies are important to psychologists. (p. 106)

7. Describe how our genetic heritage and experiences in the environment interact to produce our day-to-day behavior. (p. 107)

8. Discuss some of the effects that the hormones secreted by endocrine glands have on physiological functioning and behavior. (p. 109)

9. Describe some of the ways researchers go about studying the brain and discuss the mutual dependency between the brain and other physiological systems. (p. 114)

10. Identify the parts of a neuron and explain how neurons transfer signals throughout the body. (p. 115)

11. Describe some of the effects neurotransmitters have on physiological functioning and behavior. (p. 116)

12. Identify and describe the structures that make up the central nervous system and the two types of electrochemical signals involved in the transmission of information. (p. 118)

13. Discuss what researchers know about hemispheric specialization and explain how understanding brain lateralization is helping psychologists understand intelligence and learning disabilities. (p. 121)

14. Describe the function of the peripheral nervous system and its subsystems. (p. 123)

15. Describe two techniques used to study the electrical activity of the nervous system and describe some of the brain-wave patterns that have been identified. (p. 125)

16. Explain how people learn to control body functions through biofeedback training and discuss the effectiveness of this therapeutic technique. (p. 126)

17. Define *consciousness* and *altered states of consciousness* and make a distinction between levels and states of consciousness. (p. 128)

18. Describe four theories of consciousness and cite data that support and challenge Ornstein's theory. (p. 129)

19. Discuss what psychologists know about sleep and describe REM and NREM sleep. (p. 131)

20. Describe the effects sleep deprivation can have on behavior and subsequent sleep patterns. (p. 136)

21. Discuss psychologist's interest in dreams, describe the eye movement patterns that accompany dreams, and explain how children's dreams differ from adult's dreams. (p. 137)

22. Explain why sleep is an important aid to memory. (p. 139)

BEFORE YOU READ ON, take time to **SURVEY** the chapter, form an idea of what is to be learned (from margin Learning Objective numbers), and set goals for your study time. Then, ask yourself **QUESTIONS** about the material as you **READ,** seeking help for any sections you do not understand.

Larry Denton felt like a fool with wires attached to his head. He also had an intense headache, and he was feeling pressured—he had other things to do than sit in a recliner and relax.

Three years before, Larry began having anxiety attacks over his business affairs. He was a retailer of nuts, bolts, and screws. Even though most people saw such a business as pretty straightforward, Larry knew better. He was undercapitalized, in debt, running behind last year's sales, and facing payments to the bank he knew he could not meet. It was not surprising that he was having hot flashes and feelings of fear. He had made it through that year by borrowing from one bank to pay another. The next year, things stayed about the same—perhaps with a glimmer of hope. Now, he was faced with another big bank payment. This time, he was not going to be able to borrow from Peter to pay Paul. This time, he was not having hot flashes, but he was developing severe, incapacitating migraine headaches.

Larry quickly realized that his migraines were a reaction to his stressful job and financial problems. In fact, he was able to predict when his migraine headaches would appear. They occurred whenever he prepared to sit down with his monthly financial books. Lately, he was pouring over his finances every three or four days. The headaches were predictably coming every three or four days. To top things off, every telephone call from his lead salesman (often with bad news) was followed by a migraine.

On the advice of his physician, Larry saw a psychologist who had treated many cases of stress-related migraine headaches. The clinician placed Larry on a threefold program. First, he would undergo psychotherapy to explore issues related to his striving for success. Second, he would work on a series of coping exercises for stress-related symptoms. Third, he would undergo a series of six biofeedback sessions to help him relax and control his migraines.

The first day of biofeedback was somewhat discomforting. It started with a brief explanation by the technician about the nature of biofeedback and how it might help his headaches. Wires were attached to Larry's forehead and behind his ears. Larry felt uncomfortable, but relieving his migraines was worth the inconvenience and a few hours away from his business. He would give it a shot.

MOST PEOPLE HAVE DEVELOPED ways of coping with problems. Some people take the attitude that "when the going gets tough, the tough get going." Other people talk about turning obstacles into opportunities. Some people laugh off day-to-day problems. Others analyze and think them through. Most people learn ways to deal with life's difficulties. When people do not have the appropriate coping strategies to deal with their day-to-day problems, however, their problems sometimes show themselves in physical ailments. Larry Denton's migraines were a direct consequence of his financial dealings. His stress and lack of coping mechanisms evidenced themselves in intense headaches. Larry's physician was wise to refer him to a psychologist for help. You will see later in this chapter that biofeedback, one of the treatments prescribed by Larry's psychologist, is a technique in which people learn to control activities in their own bodies. For symptoms like migraines, it has often been successful.

Learning Objective 4.1

Understanding the role of biology in behavior has important advantages. People can be taught to optimize their potential by understanding the behaviors they can manage. Our bodies put limits on our behavior, but at the same time our inherited characteristics give us opportunities to change our behavior. By understanding both our limitations and our potentialities, psychologists can help us better manage our lives. When there is a behavior problem, a physical symptom that affects behavior, or a physical symptom that does not appear to have a physical cause, knowledge of the biological basis of behavior becomes crucial. Psychologists and physicians have long known that many behavioral and physical disorders stem from psychological as well as physical factors. For example, sometimes a physical symptom initiates a behavior problem, and family situations and emotional reactions later complicate matters.

Recognizing the importance of biological factors, psychologists have studied them to discover if the biological bases of behavior can be manipulated or controlled. Can people intentionally control their own physiological processes? Can they alter or manage biologically based behaviors? Consider the role of hormones. The hormone adrenalin is a chemical that increases physiological arousal when released into the bloodstream; among other effects, it gives a runner newfound energy for sprinting. Other hormones affect the menstrual cycle, eating, drinking, and sexual behavior. Psychologists study hormones so that they can teach people how their bodies and certain behaviors are influenced by hormones and so that they can help if the body's hormones are found out of balance. Doctors often prescribe drugs and hormones to help manage some people's behavior on a day-by-day basis. The management of diabetics' hormone levels, for example, is crucial both to their health and to their ability to function normally in society. Drugs have also been used to manage the

This child's inborn musical abilities could not be expressed without access to a piano.

Learning 4.2
Objective

Nurture
An individual's experiences in his or her environment.

Nature
An individual's genetically inherited characteristics.

behavior of alcoholics, depressed individuals, hyperactive children, and schizophrenics.

Recent research has shown that people can learn to monitor and even alter their physiological functioning without drugs, through such techniques as biofeedback. Larry Denton is a prime example of a person whose symptoms were a physical complaint caused by psychological stress. In this chapter, you see that an intimate interplay exists between biological mechanisms and psychological mechanisms. Both elements affect a person's day-to-day behavior.

NATURE VERSUS NURTURE: THE CLASSIC DEBATE

You do not need to be a psychologist to recognize that Larry Denton's migraines were a physical reaction to the stress he was experiencing because of his difficult financial situation. We all know people who complain of physical aches and pains when it is clear to us that the problems have a psychological origin. We sometimes refer to these people as being hypochondriacs. However, the biological–psychological interaction is complex, and it is not always easy to recognize what is causing what. A psychological origin does not lessen the severity of the physical complaint—Larry Denton's migraines were real. Before he saw a psychologist, Larry perceived his headaches as interfering with his ability to think well about finances. Afterwards, he realized that thinking so hard and worrying about finances was causing the headaches. Psychologists know that behavior and many physical complaints are affected by biology, the environment, and a person's ability to cope with day-to-day events.

People's moods and thoughts are often the result of genetic factors and biochemical processes interacting with the environment. A complex interplay exists between experience and biology, between conscious voluntary decision making and inherited traits—between **nurture** and **nature.** Nurture refers to a person's experiences in the environment. Nature refers to a person's inherited characteristics, determined by genetics.

A person can spend years working in a gym to build up physical strength; but that person's body structure still limits his or her capabilities. Even the strongest 170-pound man cannot lift a 2,000-pound weight without help. Similarly, people can try to maximize their intellectual gifts through training and education, yet there is a limit to each person's intellectual ability. Psychologists have also learned that inherited traits do not become evident in behavior unless a person's environment supports and encourages them. Thus, a child who has inherited some special talent must be given opportunities to express and develop it; for example, a child with a musical talent might be given an instrument and lessons. The talented do not express their abilities at birth. Instead, these special abilities unfold as people mature and interact with the environment.

A clear cause-and-effect relation seldom exists between specific biological or environmental variables and specific behavioral patterns. In some cases, biology and genetics predominate; in other cases, environment exerts the greater influence. Usually a combination of environmental and biological causes is responsible. For example, some people might explain a child's misbehavior in the classroom primarily as the result of little supervision at home, or a person's migraine headaches as the result of job-related anxiety. But because many behavioral disorders have a biological, genetic, or even nutritional basis, few psychologists would accept a purely environmental explanation of those conditions. Many behavior disorders are caused (at least in part) by genetic and/or biochemical abnormalities, and many biological diseases are the result of psychological stresses in the environment.

A current controversy highlights the complex interplay between inborn and developed potentialities. A great deal of research has shown that some minority groups in the United States score consistently lower on standardized tests of intelligence than do members of the general population. Some people suggest that this difference stems from a difference in biological endowment—that minorities are born with less intellectual capacity than the middle-class majority. Other researchers argue that the test questions relate to middle-class experiences seldom available to members of minority groups. Thus, a person without those experiences will be unable to give the "correct" answers. Although inborn characteristics clearly affect behavior, so, too, does the opportunity to express and develop one's abilities and talents.

Learning Objective 4.3

Much of psychologists' interest in biology lies in the relation between people's basic physical and intellectual capacities and the extent to which these shape (or even determine) daily behavior. The debate about what determines our day-to-day behavior is really a debate about the relative contributions of biological and environmental variables. Certainly biological makeup affects intelligence. The overall question is, to what extent can the environment modify inherited ability? Can the environment interact with and modify our biological makeup, or are the respective nature and nurture components of behavior fixed? A detailed discussion of intelligence and the role of nature and nurture is presented later in Chapter 9. However, valid answers to these questions must take into account three factors: (1) both nature *and* nurture affect the expression of a trait such as intelligence, (2) the surrounding environment must make it possible for an inherited trait to be expressed in behavior, and (3) the complex and constantly changing relationship between biology and environment affects behavior. Clearly, biological and genetic traits provide the framework for behavior, and experiences shape it further. Inherited abilities along with experience and learned skills ultimately shape everything a person feels, thinks, and does.

This chapter presents an overview of the way psychologists look at the biological basis of behavior. We pay special attention to the potential role of biology in the nature-versus-nurture issue. As we explore the biological underpinnings of behavior, notice the many examples that deal with day-to-day behavior. Watch how our explanations of heredity, the nervous system, and studies of consciousness and sleep show the relationship of basic biological mechanisms to our everyday behavior. You will see that our physiology and the way it works affects us greatly.

HEREDITY: THE GENETIC SIDE

Larry Denton, who opened this chapter, suffered from a physical problem caused by stressors in his life. Chapter 13 discusses stress more fully and how it affects behavior. Obviously, however, not all physical problems are psychological in origin. Consider the case of Karen and Miguel. Their son, three-year-old Jonathan, had been moody and lately had been having temper tantrums. Three-year-olds are known to do that, and Miguel thought Jonathan needed more discipline. One afternoon, however, Jonathan started shaking, fell to the floor, and seemed to pass out. The emergency room staff and later their pediatrician found nothing wrong. Perhaps it was the heat. But when the same thing happened two weeks later, Karen and Miguel were frightened. Both of them were healthy and had been healthy as children. Still, they both feared that Jonathan had a genetic disease such as those they had learned about in childbirth classes. The pediatrician arranged an appointment with a neurologist at the Medical Center, and, in the following weeks, Jonathan had a series of blood tests, X rays, CAT scans, and EEGs. Nothing showed up on the tests. Then, while on the examining table in the doctor's office, Jonathan started shaking. His EEG went wild. The doctor suspected several possibilities, and high on the list was epilepsy. Further testing showed that Jonathan did indeed have epilepsy.

Although their physician reassured her that Jonathan's disorder was treatable, Karen became overly anxious about Jonathan's health. Miguel responded with irritability. Neither of them knew what to do. They were extremely distraught. At first they were convinced that Jonathan had somehow inherited the disorder from one of them. Later, they learned that it was unlikely that Jonathan's disorder had been passed to him genetically or that he would pass it on to his children.

Learning Objective 4.4

Jonathan had a neurological disorder that was accompanied by behavioral symptoms. When such disorders are evident, psychologists often look to the role of genetics, as did Jonathan's parents. Researchers know that behaviors not only have a biological base but also can be genetically transmitted from parents to children. Some disorders may not be modifiable; others can be treated with drugs. Although epilepsy is not a genetically transmitted disorder, Miguel and Karen—and parents like them—often worry about the genetic heritage they pass on to their children. They want to be able to rule out this variable when understanding a disorder. For all of these reasons, psychologists study a person's biological potential.

Heredity

The potential transmitted from parents to offspring, through genes.

Chromosomes

Strands in the nuclei of cells that carry genes. Composed of a DNA core, they are responsible for the hereditary transmission of traits. Found in pairs, they represent the genetic contribution of both parents.

Gene

The unit of heredity transmission carried in chromosomes and consisting of deoxyribonucleic acid (DNA) and protein.

Heredity is the potential each person receives from his or her parents through the transmission of genes. With rare exceptions, discussed later in this chapter, every human being is genetically unique; each of us shares traits with brothers, sisters, and parents, but none of us is identical to them or to anyone else. **Chromosomes,** which consist of strands of deoxyribonucleic acid (DNA), carry genetic information in their basic functional units, the **genes.** Genes are lined up on the chromosomes in the nucleus (or center) of a cell. Each human cell normally contains twenty-three pairs of chromosomes, and each gene or combination of genes on the chromosomes control some aspect of a person's body structure or behavior, such as eye color, hair color, height, and basic intellectual traits.

At the moment of conception, a sperm and an ovum, each containing half of each pair of the parents' chromosomes, combine to form a new individual, and the chromosomes join to form new pairs. There are 8,388,608 possible recombinations of the twenty-three pairs of chromosomes, with a colossal 70,368,744,000,000 possible combinations of genes. Thus, although many people look alike and share common characteristics, except for identical twins no two individuals are exactly alike genetically.

Only one pair of chromosomes determines the sex of a newborn. The first twenty-two pairs are the same in both males and females. The twenty-third pair, however, differs in men and women: in women, it contains two X type chromosomes; in men, one X and one Y type. When sperm are formed, the pairs of chromosomes divide and the twenty-third pair produces one X type and one Y type sperm cell. In females, the twenty-third cell produces an X type chromosome in each cell. If an X sperm fertilizes an ovum, the resulting fetus is female—XX; if a Y sperm combines with an ovum, the result is a male—XY.

Genetic Defects

Learning Objective 4.5

What could happen if we could control the genetics of human beings? Scientists who do genetic research attempt to crack the genetic code, manipulate cell structure, and control the transmission of genetic traits. Most of this research has a medical purpose and is aimed at improving the lives of people who are in need. The primary goal is to control genetically transmitted diseases or behavioral abnormalities. Ultimately, scientists will probably be able to control some aspects of behavior through genetic manipulation. Psychological research has shown, for example, that schizophrenia has at least a partial genetic basis: some people's genetic inheritance makes them more likely than other people to develop schizophrenia. Through genetic research, psychologists may eventually be able to understand and manage severe disorders such as schizophrenia. Some behavioral problems are completely determined by biological characteristics: for example, there are many causes of mental retardation. Sometimes the cause is a prenatal complication, such as oxygen deprivation or a viral infection. At other times, the cause is genetic—a defect in an entire chromosome or in a specific gene.

Down's syndrome ━━━━
A genetic defect in human beings in which three twenty-first chromosomes are present. Most individuals with Down's syndrome exhibit characteristic physical abnormalities and are mentally retarded. Also known as *mongolism*.

Phenylketonuria (PKU)
━━━━━━━━━━━━━━━
A genetic defect that prevents an individual from metabolizing the amino acid phenylalanine. If not detected and treated shortly after birth, PKU usually results in mental retardation. The condition can be treated successfully by a diet low in phenylalanine (an amino acid present in milk).

When a person is born with too few or too many chromosomes, the result is usually dramatic. **Down's syndrome,** or mongolism, occurs when there are three twenty-first chromosomes instead of two. Most children afflicted with Down's syndrome exhibit characteristic physical abnormalities and are mentally retarded. Another disorder, **phenylketonuria (PKU),** is sometimes caused by the presence of a recessive gene that prevents the individual from processing the amino acid phenylalanine. Unless the disorder is detected shortly after birth and the newborn is put on a diet containing low levels of phenylalanine, PKU can cause irreparable mental retardation (Scriver & Clow, 1980). Accordingly, in the United States all newborns are given a PKU test. In this case, manipulating the physical environment (through diet) can help control the harmful consequences of a genetic disorder.

Twins

Learning Objective 4.6

In trying to assess the contributions of nature and nurture to a person's behavior, psychologists often rely on studies of twins. Psychologists are particularly interested in twins because they begin life in the same uterine environment, sharing the same nutrition and other prenatal influences. Thus, twins have potentially much more similar inherited abilities and early experiences than brothers and sisters.

Fraternal twins ━━━━
Double births resulting from the release of two ova in the female that are then fertilized by two sperm. Fraternal twins are no more or less genetically similar than nontwin siblings.

Fraternal twins occur when two sperm fertilize two ova. The two zygotes (fertilized eggs) then implant in the uterus and grow alongside each other. Fraternal twins may be both male, both female, or one male and one female. They are genetically as similar as other brothers and sisters; their genes are not identical. Only about 12 sets of fraternal twins occur in every 1,000 births. **Identical twins** occur when one zygote separates into two identical cells that do not stay together as they normally do and thus become two genetically

Identical twins ══════
Double births resulting
from the splitting of a
zygote into two identical
cells, which then separate
and develop independently.
Identical twins have exactly
the same genetic makeup.

Learning $\underline{4.7}$
Objective

identical organisms. The multiplication of cells then proceeds normally. If
these two cells should also split, the result would be identical quadruplets!
Identical twins are more rare than fraternal twins: only 4 sets occur in every
1,000 births.

Studies of twins have helped researchers determine the role of heredity in
abnormal behavior, such as schizophrenia. When schizophrenia occurs in an
identical twin, both twins are likely to show the disorder, whereas only one
member of fraternal twins may show the disorder. This finding suggests that
heredity is an important factor in schizophrenia; if experience were the only
cause, the disorder would be no more common in pairs of identical twins than
in pairs of fraternal twins. We explore the role of biology in schizophrenia in
Chapter 14.

Many other studies have examined identical and fraternal twins to try to
unravel the nature-nurture puzzle. Studies of both twin and nontwin siblings
who have been adopted into different families have also been useful. When
psychological characteristics of identical twins who have been reared apart are
compared, a researcher can assess the extent to which environment affects
behavior. Remember, the genetic factor is fixed. However, twins who are reared
apart have different homes and situations throughout their lives. If the identical
twins show significant psychological similarities, they must be due to biological variables. If they are very different, this must be due to environmental
variables. The research on twins provides a complex picture of inherited abilities and family environment interacting to affect intellectual development.
Such research continues because many important questions remain unan-
swered. Indeed, researchers are still learning which questions are appropriate.
Our genetic heritage is unaffected by day-to-day experiences. However, over
tens of thousands of years, human beings have evolved a highly organized
brain that allows learning to affect their behavior. Our brains act as libraries
of information. Each new enriching experience affects our later behavior
(Rosenzweig, 1984). Some proponents of the nurture position suggest that people are not limited by their genetic heritage, because experience, training, and
a little hard work can stretch their potential to amazing lengths. (See Figure
4.1.)

FIGURE 4.1 : How closely
matched (correlated) are
intelligence measurements?
The rectangles indicate the
range of correlation over
several studies, with triangles
pointing to the average. There
is little or no correlation
between measurements for
unrelated people, but identical
twins show high correlations.
The data suggest that
intelligence is in part
genetically determined. (Data
from Erlenmeyer-Kimling &
Jarvik, 1963).

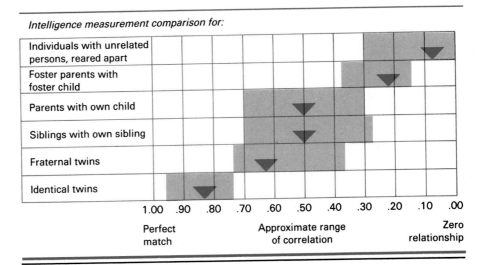

Psychologists at Work: Debating the Sociobiologists

Comedian Flip Wilson has a classic routine in which he dresses up as a woman, the likeable Geraldine. Geraldine tells her husband that the reason she bought a new dress was because of the devil. Flip Wilson appeals to the argument that children use so often, "I just couldn't control myself—something inside me made me do it." At one time or another, most of us think we may be genetically predisposed toward something—obesity, athletic prowess, singing ability, or perhaps buying new and expensive dresses. Is genetics determining our behavior?

When we feel this way, we are expressing a view that Harvard University zoologist Edward Wilson espoused in his 1975 book, *Sociobiology: A New Synthesis.* Wilson presented a hotly debated view that has challenged psychologists' thinking about the causes of behavior. This new view was called sociobiology. Sociobiology argues that biological, genetic factors underlie behavior. Wilson asserts that human beings are the product of evolution—this is not surprising because it is a tenet of most modern science. Wilson goes one step further—he asserts that even day-to-day behaviors are determined by the process of natural selection. In other words, social behaviors that contribute to the survival of our species are passed on through the genes from one generation to the next. For the sociobiologist, genetics, not learning is the key to day-to-day behavior.

At the center of the controversy of sociobiology is the issue of altruism. Altruistic acts are unselfish acts, often involving heroism. When a person sacrifices his or her life for the life of another person this is considered an act of altruism. Sociobiologists account for altruism by saying that when a person lays down his life for another, he is passing on the likelihood that the other person's genes will be passed on to another generation. They point out that people are much more likely to be altruistic toward brothers, sisters, and cousins than to strangers. From a sociobiologist's view, this is because people are instinctively driven to pass on their family's gene pool to another generation. It follows from the same viewpoint (which places little emphasis on learning) that people develop ethnic pride because of shared genetics, a distrust of strangers (people who do not share genetic properties), and again a desire to perpetuate their genes.

Sociobiological theory is hotly debated by psychologists. It places genetics in a position of primary importance and essentially downplays or minimizes the role of learning. For example, it suggests that women are less likely than men to succeed in business and politics because of their built up gene pool of nonaggressive behavior. Most psychologists find these ideas unacceptable. Psychologists feel strongly that learning plays a key role in the day-to-day activities of human beings and that people, men and women alike, can become just about anything they want to become. We learn to love, to become angry, to appreciate fine music, to become business leaders, and to create new technology. It is those special abilities that psychologists consider uniquely human—to conceive of new ways of living. The suggestion that our social interactions, our ability to make peace with our neighbors, and our ability to appreciate beauty may be almost completely genetically determined seems impossible. Sociobiology is too fixed and rigid for most psychologists.

Sociobiology raises our consciousness about the role of biology and genetics in behavior. Some of its ideas may play a key role in a comprehensive model of the role of nature in behavior (Wozniak, 1984). Sociobiology is not met with enthusiasm by the psychological community, which is so deeply committed to a learning perspective or at least a perspective that actively combines learning and biological factors in explaining day-to-day behaviors.

Endowed with a fixed genetic heritage, a biology sensitive to change, and a brain sensitive to experience, human beings have the capacity to experience the world in unique ways, to develop new technologies, and, with each new generation, to better the general human condition. Because of the evolution of their brains, human beings have become more than reflexive organisms whose lives are heavily shaped by genetics. Love for other people, desire to do good, and ability to develop high levels of creativity, communication, and technology all reflect the human genetic endowment and years of learning. Especially important are the abilities to remember, think, combine, recall, and invent new ways of thinking. Genetic makeup may limit potential, but it also contributes to our ability to think about the future and to respond to environmental changes in adaptive ways. A person's genetic makeup is the foundation on which all his or her behaviors are built. Experiences in the environment act in collaboration with this inheritance to shape day-to-day behavior.

PROGRESS CHECK 4.1

1. Complete each of the following sentences with one of the options provided.

Learning Objective 4.1

A. Psychologists study biology because there is _____ between biological and psychological mechanisms.
(very little difference : an intimate interplay)

Learning Objective 4.2

B. Psychologists _____ find a clear cause-effect relation between specific biological or environmental variables and specific behavior patterns.
(can seldom : can usually)

Learning Objective 4.2

C. The terms *inborn, genetic, inherited potential, heredity,* and *biological influences* refer to _____.
(nature : nurture)

Learning Objective 4.2

D. The terms *experience, learned,* and *environmental influences* refer to _____.
(nature : nurture)

Learning Objective 4.3

E. Inherited abilities are expressed in behavior _____.
(early in life : only if the environment encourages them)

Learning Objective 4.4

F. A _____ consists of strands of DNA.
(gene : chromosome)

Learning Objective 4.4

G. In human beings, each cell in the body normally contains _____ pairs of chromosomes.
(23 : 8,388,608 : 70,368,744,000,000)

Learning Objective 4.5

H. Phenylketonuria (PKU) involves the inability to process an amino acid, can cause mental retardation, and is sometimes caused by _____.
(an extra chromosome : a recessive gene : a dominant gene)

Learning Objective 4.6

I. When two sperm fertilize two ova, _____ twins will develop.
(fraternal : identical)

Learning Objective 4.6

J. The behavior of twins is of interest to psychologists because it helps them determine _____.
(genetic probabilities : the relative contributions of nature and nurture)

Learning Objective 4.7

K. Our _____ sensitive to change.
(genetic heritage is : biological states and brain are)

HORMONES AND GLANDS

Learning Objective 4.8

Almost all aspects of a person's behavior are determined by a combination of inherited characteristics and learning experiences. Eating is a behavior dramatically affected by both bodily state and past experiences with food. When people overeat and become fat, they often try to diet to cope with their problem. But dieting is difficult and, for some people, close to impossible or apparently useless. Consider the case of Rhonda.

During most of Rhonda's adult life, people have commented on her pretty face; they avoid mentioning the obvious: Rhonda is five feet two inches tall and weighs 220 pounds. She is fat. Whenever friends talk about Rhonda's weight, they comment that everyone in her family is overweight. They imply that perhaps there is some physiological or genetic reason for her weight problem—perhaps she has a glandular problem. Glandular deficiencies, or metabolic disorders, can help cause obesity. Rhonda may have such a disorder, or her weight problem may be one of self-control. She may eat too often and too much. Research on obesity (discussed in Chapter 5) has shown that it has both psychological and physiological causes. Some obese people eat whenever food is presented, whether or not they are hungry. Other results suggest that people are born with different metabolic rates and that some people may be meant to be obese. More often than not, a combination of factors causes obesity. In Rhonda's case, both a biological predisposition to obesity and the sight of delicious food may cause her to overeat.

Some people are overweight because of glandular deficiencies in their *thyroid.* The thyroid gland is responsible for producing thyroxin, a chemical that partly controls metabolism. Too much thyroxin makes people high-strung, nervous, and thin; too little thyroxin produces loss of appetite, lethargy, limited potential growth, and sometimes obesity. Rhonda's physician might look at her thyroxin production, her eating behavior, and her family's history of obesity.

There are two types of glands in the human body: glands with ducts (such as the tear and sweat glands) and glands without ducts. Psychologists are interested primarily in the ductless glands, or **endocrine glands.** These glands secrete chemicals called **hormones** directly into the bloodstream and can influence a person's behavior dramatically. Table 4.1 lists the endocrine glands, the substances they secrete, and their effects.

The most important endocrine gland is the *pituitary,* the body's master gland. Growth hormones are controlled by the pituitary. Thus, when teenagers have height and weight problems, the pituitary is often suspected. Recently it has been suggested that the endocrine system in general, and the pituitary system in particular, may be crucially involved in depression. Depressed patients (discussed in more detail in Chapter 14) often show abnormalities in their hormonal levels, particularly in those controlled by the pituitary (Van Praag, 1978). Because the pituitary is controlled by the brain, changes in a person's emotional state often affect the pituitary. The pituitary in turn affects other glands and, ultimately, behavior (see Color Plate 4.1).

Another gland, the *pancreas,* is involved in regulating sugar levels. Sugar substances in the blood determine energy level. When blood sugar is high, people have energy; when it is low, they feel weak and tired. The islets of Langerhans cells in the pancreas control the production of **insulin,** which facilitates the transportation of sugar into body cells, where it is metabolized. When an insufficient amount of insulin is produced, resulting in the presence of too much sugar in the blood, **diabetes mellitus** occurs. This condition of excess sugar in the blood is known as **hyperglycemia,** and if untreated it can lead to coma and death. Nearly 10 million Americans have diabetes. They must take daily doses of insulin to ensure that the sugar in their blood can be metabolized properly. If the pancreas errs in the opposite direction and produces too much insulin, the result is **hypoglycemia,** or very low blood sugar. Hypoglycemic patients have no energy and often feel faint. This condition can usually be controlled through a diet that carefully monitors the daily consumption of calories and types of food. Clearly, the pancreas plays an important part in controlling the body's functions. People's performance is greatly affected by their energy level, by their ability and desire to interact with others. A person with low blood sugar may be labeled as lazy and perceived as lacking motivation.

People's emotional responses to these physiological malfunctions, their level of stress, and their willingness to monitor their eating and energy expenditures greatly affect the course and outcome of their treatment. As three

Endocrine glands ══════
Ductless glands that secrete hormones directly into the bloodstream.

Hormone ══════════
A chemical that regulates the activities of specific organs or cells. Hormones are produced by the endocrine glands and are transported by the bloodstream to their site of action.

Insulin ════════════
A hormone produced by the pancreas, necessary for the transport of sugar from the blood into body cells so that it can be metabolized.

Diabetes mellitus ══════
A condition in which too little insulin is present in the blood, with the result that insufficient quantities of sugar are transported into body cells.

Hyperglycemia ═══════
A condition in which too much sugar is present in the blood.

Hypoglycemia ═══════
A condition resulting from the overproduction of insulin, causing very low blood sugar levels. It is usually characterized by a lack of energy, and often by faintness and dizziness.

TABLE 4.1 : The Endocrine Glands, Substances Secreted, and Effects

Gland	Substance Secreted	Effect

Pituitary
  Adenohypophysis
  (anterior pituitary)
	Somatotrophic hormone	Controls rate of protein synthesis; promotes release of fat from fat stores

	Adrenocorticotrophic hormone (ACTH)	Regulates cortex of adrenal gland
	Thyrotrophin	Regulates thyroid gland
	Follicle stimulating hormone	Regulates sex organs
	Luteinizing hormone	Promotes secretion of sex hormones
	Prolactin	Controls milk production

Neurohypophysis
  (posterior
  pituitary)
	Antidiuretic hormone
	Oxytocin
		Controls retention of fluids
		Stimulates uterine contractions; stimulates lactation

Pancreas	Insulin	Regulates use of sugar
		Regulates storage of carbohydrates
	Glucagon	Acts synergistically with insulin
Thyroid	Thyroxin	Regulates metabolic rate
Parathyroid	Parathyroid hormone	Regulates calcium levels
Pineal	Melatonin	Regulates reproduction and growth
Adrenal Cortex	Steroids	Controls resistance to stress
		Regulates carbohydrate metabolism
Medulla	Adrenalin (epinephrine)	Changes metabolic activity
	Noradrenalin (norepinephrine)	Generally inhibits central nervous system
Reproductive Glands Female	Estrogens	Controls menstrual cycle
	Progestins	Maintains pregnancy
Male	Androgens	Promotes male sex characteristics and growth

researchers from Duke University Medical Center have argued, psychology can do much to help solve the problems of effective diabetes care (Surwit, Feinglos, & Scovern, 1983). Psychology offers techniques and strategies for increasing patients' adherence to treatment regimens. Such techniques include self-monitoring, charting of eating behavior, and using thought restructuring techniques (see Chapter 15). They often have a significant effect on patients' ultimate management of their diabetic condition (Fisher, Delamater, Bertelson, & Kirkley, 1982).

One of the most important glands that controls behavior is the *adrenal gland,* which produces adrenalin (epinephrine), a substance that dramatically

TABLE 4.2 : Effects of Adrenalin on the Organs and
         : Systems of the Body

Organ or System	Effect
Heart rate	Increase
Cardiac output	Increase
Blood pressure	Increase
Respiration	Stimulation
Skin vessels	Constriction
Muscle vessels	Dilation
Metabolism	Increase
Oxygen consumption	Increase
Blood sugar	Increase
Central nervous system	Arousal
Uterus in late pregnancy	Inhibition
Kidney	Vasoconstriction

alters energy levels. As Table 4.2 shows, adrenalin production can greatly affect both physiology and behavior.

Researchers still do not know the exact extent to which hormones control human behavior, but there is no doubt that the glandular system is interactive. Each hormone affects behavior *and* eventually other glands. For example, a disorder in the thyroid will affect not only metabolic rate but also the pituitary, which in turn will affect other behavior. Thus, although Rhonda should go to a physician to see whether there are physiological causes for her obesity before embarking on a serious weight-reduction program, her problem is probably not glandular. A serious glandular disorder would affect many areas of her behavior, besides eating. On the other hand, including psychological techniques in a weight-reduction program may help Rhonda improve her self-image and her ability to cope with both physiological and environmental conditions.

Premenstrual syndrome (PMS), a condition some women experience, provides an example of how hormones can affect a person's physical state and behavior. PMS is a recurrent, cyclic condition characterized by one or more symptoms that develop during the seven to fourteen days before the onset of menstruation, subside when menstruation occurs, and are then absent for two weeks. The absence of symptoms during the two weeks following menstruation is essential to a diagnosis of PMS. (The technical term for PMS is Late Luteal Phase Dysphoric Disorder. We will stick with PMS for simplicity.)

About one-third of all premenopausal women, primarily those between twenty-five and forty years of age, may have PMS. During some months, the symptoms may become severe for about 10 percent of these women (Krump, Chatton, & Tierney, 1986).

PMS causes physical discomfort and/or unwanted behavior changes that markedly impair social and occupational functioning. A woman with PMS may experience physical symptoms such as water retention, weight gain, breast tenderness, dizziness, headaches, skin problems, food cravings, fatigue, and swollen hands, feet, and ankles. She may notice behavior changes including depression, anger, irritability, anxiety, mood swings, insomnia, an inability to concentrate, and confusion. Most women who have PMS experience a mild to moderate degree of distress and only a few of the symptoms associated with the syndrome. Some women have only physical symptoms; others have only behavioral symptoms; and still others have a unique combination of both. The severity of discomfort caused by PMS varies from woman to woman and from month to month. During some months, the symptoms may not appear at all.

When the symptoms are present, a woman may experience a lower level of energy, motivation, or enthusiasm. If she does not know that the symptoms are the result of PMS, she may also worry that there is something abnormal about how she is feeling and behaving. In reality, the symptoms are a normal response to physical changes occurring in the body. Understanding that the symptoms are real and a result of PMS enables a woman to reduce some of the discomfort—she can get help from her physician, she can pay special attention to diet and exercise, and she can get emotional support by communicating her needs more clearly with other people. When people who associate closely with a woman who is noticeably affected by PMS understand that the symptoms are both real and temporary, much of the interpersonal tension that can be triggered by the cyclic behavior changes disappears. It is important to recognize that although PMS can be physically and emotionally bothersome, most women who experience the symptoms are able to function effectively, performing their normal activities, in spite of their discomfort.

Researchers are not certain about what causes PMS. According to the American College of Obstetricians and Gynecologists (1985), women who have PMS appear to have normal hormone levels. That is, PMS does not seem to be caused by excesses or deficiencies of a particular hormone but rather by a change in the way the hormones work. Estrogen and progesterone, two hormones produced by the ovaries, appear to be involved. Currently, researchers are investigating a number of possible causes, including the possibility that estrogen and progesterone may act in combination with neurotransmitters in the brain in some unique way before menses and cause some of the symptoms associated with PMS.

The body's system of glands and hormones is only one of many mechanisms regulated by the nervous system. Psychologists study the components of the nervous system to gain insight into *how* we do what we do.

PROGRESS CHECK 4.2

1. Match each of the following key concepts and terms with the appropriate definition.

thyroid gland   pancreas gland   pituitary gland   adrenal gland

Learning Objective 4.8

A. _____ This endocrine gland affects the functioning of other glands and is affected by emotional states. It is frequently referred to as the body's master gland.

Learning Objective 4.8

B. _____ This endocrine gland controls the production of insulin and has a direct effect on one's general energy level.

Learning Objective 4.8

C. _____ This endocrine gland produces thyroxin, is involved in controlling metabolism, and affects appetite, energy levels, growth, and weight.

Learning Objective 4.8

D. _____ This endocrine gland produces epinephrine, a hormone that dramatically increases such physiological responses as heart rate, blood pressure, breathing, and metabolism and also alters energy levels.

2. Complete each of the following sentences with one of the options provided.

Learning Objective 4.8   A. Endocrine glands secrete hormones _____.
(directly into the blood system : into the blood system via ducts)

Learning Objective 4.8   B. Depression has been linked to hormones produced by the _____ _____ and endocrine system in general.
(pancreas : pituitary gland)

Learning Objective 4.8   C. Insulin, which aids the body by transporting sugar to the cells, is produced by the _____ in the pancreas.
(ventricles : islets of Langerhans)

Learning Objective 4.8   D. When a pancreas produces too much insulin, the person will have very low blood sugar, feel weak, and be diagnosed as having _____.
(diabetes mellitus : hyperglycemia : hypoglycemia)

Learning Objective 4.8   E. Hypoglycemia is treated by _____.
(taking daily doses of insulin : managing one's diet)

Learning Objective 4.8   F. If a person is overweight and has no other physical or behavioral abnormalities, we can assume that being overweight is primarily a _____ problem.
(glandular : learned)

Learning Objective 4.8   G. An essential factor for diagnosing premenstrual syndrome is the _____ _____ symptoms during the postmenstrual phase.
(absence of : presence of both physical and behavioral)

THE NERVOUS SYSTEM

Learning Objective 4.9   All activities involved in our day-to-day behavior are under the control of our nervous system. The nervous system is a group of cells that connects the muscle, glands, and other organs together to produce behavior and allow the organism to coordinate activities. When a portion of the nervous system goes awry, the effects are usually evidenced fairly quickly in behavior. By knowing how the nervous system operates, we gain a greater understanding of the foundations of behavior. The techniques devised to study the nervous system are diverse: surgical, chemical, and electrophysiological. You will see how these techniques are used in the next few pages.

Remember three-year-old Jonathan, whom we discussed earlier. He had epilepsy; understanding a disorder like epilepsy is crucial to both psychologists and physicians. Epilepsy is a brain disorder, and the brain plays the central role in controlling behavior. As often happens in science, researchers learn about one phenomenon by studying another. In treating patients with disorders like epilepsy, researchers have learned a great deal about brain organization and behavior.

Over the years, researchers have studied the brains of people who have died of tumors, diseases of the brain, or trauma (injury) to the brain and have tried to correlate the type of brain damage with the loss of specific abilities such as vision or the ability to read or write. Using such information, researchers continue to make inferences about how the brain is organized and operates. Other studies have involved the ablating (damaging) of various areas of an animal's brain with electricity or chemicals, followed by observation of the animal to assess resulting changes in behavior. The aim of both kinds of studies is the same: to understand the complex organization of the brain and its role in directing human behavior. Psychologists have tried to apply each gain in understanding to the interactive effects of nature and nurture.

Although our understanding of the brain is by no means complete, we do know it operates through many mutually dependent systems and subsystems to affect and control behavior. Thousands of brain cells are involved in the performance of even simple activities. When we walk, for example, the visual areas of the brain are activated so that our sight can guide us, motor areas help make our legs move, and the cerebellum helps us keep our balance. Similarly, the endocrine system, which controls the secretion and release of hormones, is dependent on the brain, and the brain is affected by mood alterations caused by changes in the endocrine system. It is the nervous system that allows all these things to happen. Under the control of the brain, a system of nerves communicates with the muscles and glands throughout the body.

The Neuron

Learning Objective 4.10

Neuron
The basic unit of the nervous system. It is a single cell composed of *dendrites,* which receive neural signals; a *cell body,* which generates electrical signals; and an *axon,* which transmits neural signals.

The basic unit of the nervous system is the nerve cell, or **neuron.** Neurons differ in shape, size, and function and are found throughout the body. The human brain, for example, consists of one hundred billion neurons; the covering of the brain, the cortex, itself contains approximately ten billion (Hubel & Wiesel, 1979).

The billions of neurons that comprise the nervous system are all alive and active. They may not all be firing at once, or very actively, but in a real way they are all on alert, ready to convey information and signals to some other part of the nervous system. Typically, a neuron is composed of dendrites, a cell body which contains the nucleus, an axon, and axon terminals. The *dendrites* receive information from neighboring neurons and carry it to the *cell body.* The cell body generates electrical signals that pass along the long, slim *axon* to the *axon terminals* and on to the next neuron (see Figure 4.2). In almost all neurons, the axon terminals are very close to (and sometimes touch) the dendrites or cell body of another neuron. The space between, called a **synapse,** is so small that it cannot be seen without an electron microscope. Figure 4.3 on the next page shows these spatial relationships (Hubel 1979; Stevens 1979).

Synapse
The small space between the axon terminals of one neuron and the receptive site (dendrite, cell body, or axon) of another neuron.

To visualize this space, think of many neurons in a long chain, strung together as a relay team sending signals, conveying information, or initiating some action in a cell, muscle, or gland. As you will see, information flows two ways—to the brain from the senses and muscles, and from the brain to the sense organs and muscles with decisions and actions to initiate new behaviors.

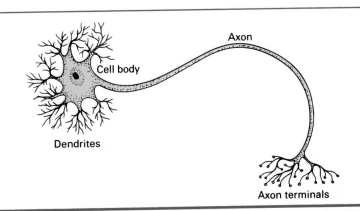

FIGURE 4.2 : The basic components of neuron with dendrites, cell body, and a long, slim axon.

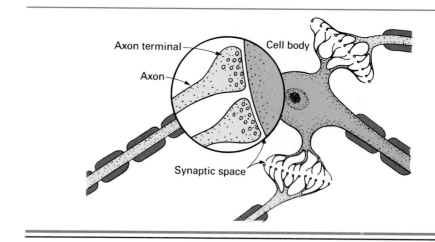

FIGURE 4.3 ⦂ The synapse is very small. Chemicals released by the axon terminal cross the synapse to stimulate the cell body or dendrites of another neuron.

Action potential ══════
An electrical current sent down the axon of a neuron, initiated by a rapid reversal of membrane potential. Also called a *spike discharge.*

All-or-none ══════
The principle by which a neuron will fire either at full strength or not at all.

Refractory period ══════
The recovery period of a neuron after it fires, during which time it cannot fire again. This period allows the neuron to reestablish electrical balance with its surroundings.

Learning ═══ *4.11*
Objective ═══

Neurotransmitter ══════
A chemical substance released from the synaptic vesicles that crosses the synaptic space.

Action Potentials.   Each year, scientists learn more about the nature of the neural impulse and how information is transmitted from cell to cell, across synapses. The process involves both electrical and chemical changes. This is why we sometimes refer to *electrochemical* processes in the brain or nervous system. The process involves chemicals being released from the axons of one cell and transferred to the cell body or dendrites of another cell. Scientists do not completely understand this process. The most reliable and widely accepted explanation is that every cell is surrounded by a semipermeable membrane. Electrically charged fluids and small particles in and around the cell pass through the membrane. Normally, there is a difference in electrical charge on either side of the membrane. When the cell is in its resting state, this balance continues to exist between the inside of the cell (which is negatively charged) and the outside (which is positively charged). The arrival of messages from another neuron at the membrane creates a disturbance in the usual, or resting level. This electrical balance is altered when electrically charged sodium ions move through the membrane into the cell and potassium ions almost simultaneously leave the cell. The rapid reversal of membrane potential is referred to as an **action potential,** or, as it is sometimes called, a *spike discharge.* Action potentials are of constant strength as they move or are propagated along the axon. Cells generate spikes (action potentials) in an **all-or-none** fashion—that is, firing occurs at full strength or not at all. As a rule, neurons cannot fire more than 1,000 times a second. Following each firing is a recovery period of a few thousandths of a second, called a **refractory period.** During this period, the chemical balance between the axon and the area around it is reestablished.

Neurotransmitters.   When an action potential moves down an axon, it stimulates chemicals that reside in the axon terminal and in small packagelike storage structures called synaptic vesicles, located in the axon terminal (Dunant & Israël, 1985). Once released, these chemicals, called **neurotransmitters,** move across the synaptic space conveying information to the next neuron by attaching themselves to receptor sites on the dendrites of the next cell. Sometimes the neurotransmitters affect the cell indirectly. At other times, they cause the receptor sites to make the cell more easily penetrable.

How much of this boy's reaction to the shot is based on neuronal firing, and how much on other influences from his environment?

Understanding neural transmission can help psychologists explain how the brain relays information about a variety of bodily states. Some neurotransmitters appear to be involved in blocking pain; others seem to facilitate sensory experiences. More than thirty substances are known or suspected to be neurotransmitters. Some, such as acetylcholine, norepinephrine, dopamine, and epinephrine, have been well studied; others have only recently been discovered. Each neurotransmitter acts in a different way, depending on where it is released. Sometimes these neurotransmitters are excitatory in nature and cause the next cell to fire; other times, they act in an inhibitory fashion, decreasing the likelihood that a cell will fire.

Scientists have known about the existence of neurotransmitters for a long time, but only recently have they realized their potential significance for the study of human behavior. For example, people with Parkinson's disease, whose symptoms include weakness and uncontrollable shaking, have been found to have low dopamine levels. Treatment with drugs that have the same effects as dopamine (such as L-dopa) alleviates many of their symptoms. Researchers have also found that norepinephrine is involved in changes in motivation and mood. This discovery is important because schizophrenia is thought to be associated with increased levels of neurotransmitter substances. Although it is unlikely that a neurotransmitter alone can cause schizophrenia or depression, it may play an important part in the onset of maintenance or an illness (Freedman & Glass, 1982; for a review, see Cooper, Bloom, & Roth, 1982).

The firing of neurons transfers information from the sense organs to the brain and from the brain to the muscular system and the glands. If psychologists knew precisely how this transfer occurred, they could more successfully predict and manage the behavior of people with neurological damage. They might be able to alleviate or treat differently learning disabilities caused by neural dysfunction. Finally, a complete understanding of this process could help the blind and deaf to see and hear.

The firing of neurons and the release of neurotransmitters, however, do not in themselves explain the biological bases of human behavior. Whether genetic or environmental causes are involved, the nervous system, and especially the brain, control behavior on a minute-by-minute basis. Psychologists must therefore understand the organization and functions of the nervous system and its mutually dependent systems and subsystems. Even then, psychologists still need to understand how the nervous system interacts with a person's heredity, disease states, glandular system, and, most important, learned behaviors. You can see that understanding the nervous system, which is discussed next, is just a first step in the process of understanding human behavior.

The Central Nervous System

Learning Objective 4.12

Central nervous system (CNS)
One of the two major parts of the nervous system, consisting of the brain and spinal cord.

Afferent
Pathways and signals to the central nervous system.

Efferent
Pathways and signals from the central nervous system to other structures in the body.

The **central nervous system (CNS)** is one of the two major components of the nervous system and consists of the brain and the spinal cord (see Figure 4.4). The complex structures in the brain function together to coordinate the receiving and sending of two types of electrochemical signals: **afferent** signals, which go *to* the spinal cord and brain; and **efferent** signals, which go *from* the brain and spinal cord to other structures in the body (see Figure 4.5).

The brain is composed of two halves, two large *cerebral hemispheres,* one on the left side and one on the right side. At first glance, they look alike, in size, shape, and texture. But they are actually somewhat different in their physical makeup, and each controls different functions. You probably know that the left hemisphere controls many aspects of the right side of the body in most people, and the right hemisphere controls the left side (e.g., Milner & Kolb, 1985).

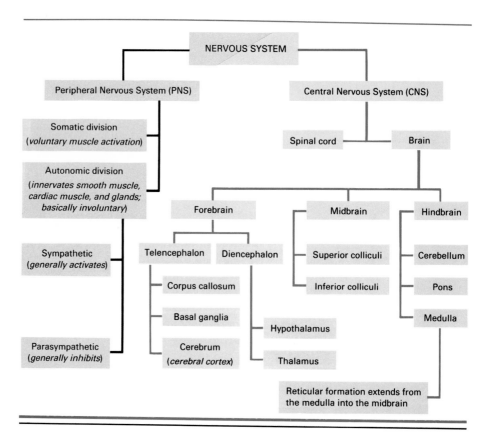

FIGURE 4.4 : The basic divisions of the nervous system and their major subdivisions.

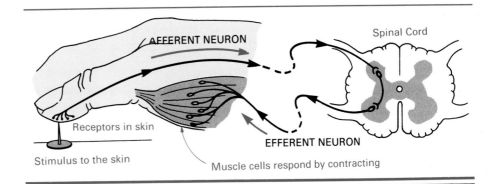

FIGURE 4.5 : *Afferent* neurons carry signals from the muscles and glands to the spinal cord and brain; *efferent* neurons carry signals from the brain and spinal cord to the muscles and the glands.

Convolutions

Folds in tissues that are characteristic of the cerebral hemispheres and overlying cortex in human beings.

The exterior covering of the brain hemispheres is called the *cortex*. The cortex is two millimeters thick and consists of several thin layers of cells that are **convoluted,** folded or crumpled, to accommodate a large surface area in a much smaller space. A large, thick structure called the *corpus callosum* connects the two cerebral hemispheres and permits the transfer of information between them. (See Figure 4.6.) The corpus callosum allows the two sides of the brain to "talk" to one another. Later in this chapter, you can see that the two sides of the brain actively communicate.

Besides being divided into right and left halves, the brain is divided into areas with special functions. Some parts are specialized for visual activities; others are involved in hearing, sleeping, breathing, or eating. Some brain activities are localized; speech and language activity, for example, can be pinpointed to a specific area usually in the left side of the brain. Other activities may occur at several locations; visual activity, for example, occurs in the visual cortex, which occupies both sides of the brain. Psychologists disagree on the extent to which functions are localized in the brain.

A traditional way to divide the brain and its cortex is to consider it as a series of lobes or areas. Characteristic structures help divide the brain's cortex in logical ways. The most prominent structures are the two deep fissures that divide the hemispheres. These easily recognizable fissures are like deep ravines that run among the convolutions; they separate the various lobes. The

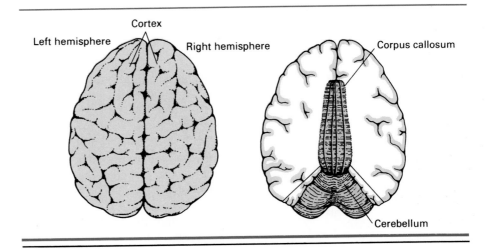

FIGURE 4.6 : Two views of the human brain. Left: A top surface view showing the left and right hemispheres and the cerebral cortex. Right: A schematic cross section showing the cerebellum and corpus callosum.

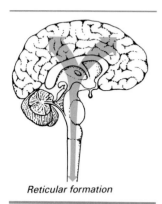

Reticular formation

FIGURE 4.7 **:** Many afferent and efferent signals pass through the reticular formation.

two fissures are the *lateral fissure* and the *central fissure.* As you can see in Color Plate 4.2, in front of the central fissure is the *frontal lobe,* behind it is the *parietal lobe.* Part of the frontal area is concerned with movement; it is sometimes called the *motor cortex.* A lower portion of the left frontal lobe called *Broca's area* is involved in speech and language perception and production.

The *parietal lobe,* located behind the central fissure, has associated with it many activities involved in the sense of touch and of body position. Below the lateral fissure and the parietal lobe are the temporal lobes; the left *temporal lobe* is involved in speech, hearing, and the processing of some visual information. At the back of the head, adjacent to the parietal and temporal lobes, is the *occipital lobe,* which has as its principal responsibility the visual sense.

The cortex covers only the cerebral hemispheres. The central core of the brain is often described as being made up of three sections: *hindbrain, midbrain,* and *forebrain* (see Color Plate 4.3).

Hindbrain. The *hindbrain* consists of three main structures: the medulla, the pons, and the cerebellum. The *medulla,* through which many afferent and efferent signals pass, lies just above the spinal cord and controls heartbeat and breathing. Within the medulla is a latticelike network of nerve cells called the *reticular formation,* which directly controls a person's state of arousal, waking, sleeping, and other bodily functions; damage to it can result in coma and death. The reticular formation extends into and through the pons and the midbrain. Portions of the *pons* are also involved in sleep and dreaming, which we discuss later in this chapter. The *cerebellum* influences balance, coordination, and movement. It has recently been linked to some mental skills beyond movement (Leiner, Leiner, & Dow, 1986).

Midbrain. The *midbrain* is composed of a number of nuclei (collections of cell bodies) that accept afferent signals, interpret them, and either relay this information to a more complex part of the brain or cause the body to act at once. The midbrain continues the reticular formation system (see Figure 4.7).

Forebrain. The *forebrain* comprises two main structures, one of which is the *diencephalon.* The diencephalon is itself composed of two structures, the thalamus and the hypothalamus. The *thalamus* acts mainly to send information to other parts of the brain, although it probably also performs interpretative functions (see Figure 4.8). The *hypothalamus* is involved in many complex behaviors, including motivation, emotion, eating and drinking, and sexual appetite.

The other portion of the forebrain, the *telencephalon,* comprises three main structures: the basal ganglia, the corpus callosum, and the cortex. The *basal ganglia,* a series of nuclei located deep in the brain, control movement and posture and have been shown to be involved in Parkinson's disease (see Figure 4.9). The *corpus callosum* connects and conveys information between the cerebral hemispheres. Damage to this structure results in two essentially separate brains. The cerebral *cortex,* the covering of the cerebral hemisphere, which is involved in movement, perception, and complex cognitive processes, as discussed earlier, is also a part of the forebrain.

As mentioned earlier, the cortex, the thick covering of the cerebral hemispheres, is itself divided into several areas. The *motor cortex* of the frontal lobes

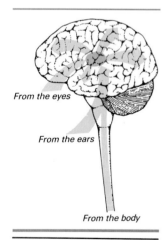

From the eyes

From the ears

From the body

FIGURE 4.8 **:** The thalamus acts as a relay station for sensory information and sends afferent input to the higher centers.

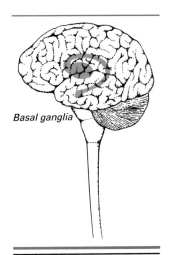

Basal ganglia

FIGURE 4.9 : As shown, the basal ganglia, found deep within the brain, is involved in the regulation and control of gross movement. Damage to this important neurological center can have severe behavioral consequences.

*Learning
Objective* 4.13

Split-brain patients ═══
Term applied to people whose corpus callosum—which normally connects the two cerebral hemispheres—has been surgically severed.

is associated with movement. When portions are damaged, a person loses the ability to make fine motor movements, such as manipulation of the fingers. The *sensory cortex* of the temporal and occipital lobes receives information from lower structures about sensory systems. The visual and auditory systems convey information to the visual and auditory cortices, respectively. Other areas of the cortex have less specific functions. For example, the *association cortex* is believed to be involved in complex behaviors that involve thinking and sensory processes. These activities may not be strictly visual, auditory, or motor: instead, they involve the interaction of many different systems, or association areas.

Probably one of the most complex and least understood areas of the brain is the *limbic system.* This system is an interconnected group of structures (including parts of the cortex, thalamus, and hypothalamus) involved in emotional behavior, memory, alcoholism, and even such brain disorders as epilepsy. Within the limbic system are the hippocampus and the amygdala. In human beings, the *hippocampus* is intimately involved in memory functions. The *amygdala* is thought to be involved in the control of emotional behavior. Stimulation of the amygdala in animals produces attack responses, and surgical removal of the amygdala in human beings has been one way of treating extremely violent behavior. Olds and Milner (1954) discovered that stimulation of several areas of the limbic system in rats produced extremely pleasurable sensations. Rats that were given small doses of electric current as a reward for bar pressing chose bar pressing over eating, even if they had been deprived of food for long periods. Olds and Milner called these areas of the brain "pleasure centers." Their work generated much research into the role of brain organization in emotional behavior.

Localization of Functions.   During the past twenty years, people with uncontrollable epilepsy have undergone operations severing the corpus callosum (see Color Plate 4.4). These operations have proved generally successful and have also shown that the human brain is, in a sense, two brains, each capable of different functions and largely independent of the other. By studying the brain as two separate hemispheres, in such **split-brain patients,** researchers have been able to discover the characteristic functions of each.

Studies by researchers like Michael Gazzaniga (1983) have shown that in most human beings, one cerebral hemisphere—usually the left—is specialized for processing speech and language; the other hemisphere—usually the right—appears better organized to process spatial tasks, musical and artistic talent, and perhaps other creative abilities (see Figure 4.10 on the next page). Some of this evidence comes from studies monitoring brain-wave activity in normal subjects while they are exposed to different kinds of stimuli. When subjects are asked to look at or think about letters or rehearse a speech, certain characteristic brain-wave activity is produced on the left side of the brain; when creative tasks are demanded or the subjects are told to reorganize some spatial pattern, brain-wave activity is apparent on the right side of the brain.

Other evidence of *brain lateralization* comes from studies of people whose corpus callosum has been surgically severed (Gazzaniga, 1967). This operation in effect yields two brains that cannot communicate with each other. As a result, split-brain subjects are unable to use the speech and language capabilities of the left cerebral hemisphere to describe activities carried out by the right one. When stimulus information is presented exclusively to the left hemi-

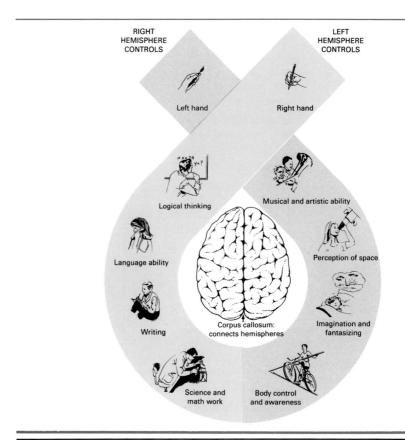

RIGHT HEMISPHERE CONTROLS

LEFT HEMISPHERE CONTROLS

Left hand

Right hand

Logical thinking

Musical and artistic ability

Language ability

Perception of space

Writing

Corpus callosum: connects hemispheres

Imagination and fantasizing

Science and math work

Body control and awareness

FIGURE 4.10 **:** In most people, lateralization of brain functioning occurs by about age thirteen. The left hemisphere controls language and verbal abilities, and the right hemisphere controls spatial, holistic abilities.

sphere, split-brain patients are able to describe the stimulus, match it, and deal with it in essentially normal ways. When the same stimulation is presented exclusively to the right cerebral hemisphere, subjects are able to perform the matching tasks but are unable to describe the stimuli verbally.

In studies of this kind, Gazzaniga and other researchers have also used the fact that each cerebral hemisphere is neurologically connected to the opposite side of the body. Using simple tests, investigators have shown that a split-brain subject holding a pencil in the left hand behind a screen cannot describe it but performs the task easily if the pencil is switched to the right hand.

Although all this evidence suggests that highly specialized brain functions are organized by hemisphere, it is still unclear how permanently isolated these functions are. Electrophysical studies show that before a person reaches age four, the left and right hemisphere seem equally proficient at language processing. Each year thereafter, the left cerebral hemisphere becomes increasingly involved in processing language. By the time their brains have matured at age thirteen, most individuals have a distinctly dominant hemisphere that is responsible for speech and language (B. Jones, 1983) and for verbal processing (Hellige & Wong, 1983).

Notwithstanding the evidence on differences in left- and right-hemisphere functioning, some researchers contend that much of the learning people refer to when they talk about intelligence actually takes place in both hemispheres. If this is so, tests of intelligence should examine both left-hemisphere (logical, verbal, and language skills) and right-hemisphere (spatial and creative abili-

Peripheral nervous system ━━━━
The second major part of the nervous system; it carries information to and from the central nervous system through a system of spinal and cranial nerves. It has two functional subdivisions, the somatic and autonomic nervous systems.

Learning Objective $\underline{4.14}$

Somatic nervous system ━━━━
The part of the peripheral nervous system that controls skeletal muscles and, in turn, bodily movements.

Autonomic nervous system ━━━━
The part of the peripheral nervous system that controls the vital processes of the body, such as heart rate, digestive processes, and blood pressure. Its two main subdivisions are the *sympathetic* and *parasympathetic* systems.

Parasympathetic nervous system ━━━━
The part of the autonomic nervous system that is generally conservatory, storing up bodily resources when they are not needed. Its activities are balanced by those of the sympathetic nervous system.

Sympathetic nervous system ━━━━
The part of the autonomic nervous system that responds to emergency situations. Active only occasionally, sympathetic activity calls up bodily resources as needed.

ties) processing. (Currently, most intelligence tests examine primarily left-hemisphere functioning.)

Not every behavior can be traced to a single structure in the central nervous system. Researchers know that certain structures (such as the visual cortex and the cerebellum) are strongly involved in certain behaviors, but most behaviors involve the combined working of several areas. Because the brain is so complex and its subsystems work so harmoniously, it is often difficult to isolate the effects of a single variable.

The Peripheral Nervous System

The **peripheral nervous system** carries information to and from the spinal cord and the brain via spinal nerves attached to the spinal cord and by a system of twelve cranial nerves that carry signals directly to and from the brain (see Color Plate 4.5).

The peripheral nervous system contains two major systems: the **somatic nervous system** and the **autonomic nervous system.** The somatic nervous system is generally thought to be under voluntary control and consists of both sensory and motor neurons. It carries information from the sense organs to the brain, and from the brain and spinal cord to and from the muscles. Thus, it is involved in perceptual processing and the control of movement and muscles. The somatic system is often thought of as the system that responds to and acts on the outside world. This system interacts with people, things, and stimulation on a minute-by-minute basis. In contrast, the autonomic nervous system is believed to operate involuntarily and generally deals with internal conditions, such as heart rate and blood pressure.

The autonomic nervous system is made up of two parts: the parasympathetic nervous system and the sympathetic nervous system (see Color Plate 4.6). The **parasympathetic nervous system** is active most of the time and controls the normal operation of such functions as digestion, blood pressure, and heart rate. Parasympathetic activity is not easily observable or measurable. In contrast, activation of the **sympathetic nervous system** results in an increase in heart rate and blood pressure, slowing of the digestive processes, dilation of the pupils, and general preparation for emergency—sometimes called the fight-or-flight reflex—usually accompanied by an increased flow of adrenalin. Its activities are easily observed and measured. We saw in Chapter 2, "Learning," that many human behaviors are conditioned. Many of these conditioned responses are autonomic nervous system responses—for example, increased heart rate, increased blood pressure, or dilation of the pupils. So, learning is in part dependent on the biology of behavior, and important interrelationships exist.

Changes in the autonomic nervous system produce rapid changes in the somatic system. When the sympathetic nervous system is activated and the organism is in a fight-or-flight posture, the somatic nervous system is also activated. When a runner's adrenal glands are stimulated, for example, the burst of energy produced by adrenalin affects the somatic system, making the runner's muscles respond strongly and rapidly.

The peripheral and central nervous systems work in harmony. The central nervous system acts on information provided by the peripheral nervous system and sends out efferent signals that either modify the somatic system or leave it unchanged.

PROGRESS CHECK 4.3

1. Match each of the following key concepts and terms with the appropriate definitions.

synapse   all-or-none   refractory period
action potential   neurotransmitter

Learning Objective 4.10   A. _____ When a neuron generates a spike, it either fires at full strength or it does not fire at all.

Learning Objective 4.10   B. _____ The small space between the axon terminal of one neuron and the receptor site of a nearby neuron.

Learning Objective 4.10   C. _____ A neuron cannot fire during this time because a chemical balance is being reestablished.

Learning Objective 4.10   D. _____ An alteration in the electrical balance of a neuron caused by the rapid reversal of sodium ions from the outside to the inside and potassium ions inside to the outside of the neuron.

Learning Objective 4.11   E. _____ Chemicals that reside in small, packagelike structures called synaptic vesicles that convey information from one neuron to the next by crossing the synapse and attaching themselves to receptor sites on nearby dendrites.

2. Complete each of the following sentences with one of the options provided.

Learning Objective 4.9   A. To study how the brain affects behavior, researchers often examine _____ _____.
(how brain damage affects behavior : the size of human brains)

Learning Objective 4.10   B. The long, slim part of the neuron that carries electrical signals to nearby neurons is called _____.
(a dendrite : an axon : the cell body)

Learning Objective 4.10   C. The inside of the cell is _____ charged when the neuron is in a resting state.
(positively : negatively)

Learning Objective 4.10   D. The rapid reversal of potassium and sodium ions in and around the neuron is called an action potential or _____.
(a reverberating loop : a spike discharge)

Learning Objective 4.11   E. Parkinson's disease is accompanied by low levels of _____.
(acetylcholine : epinephrine : dopamine)

Learning Objective 4.12   F. Information is transferred from one cerebral hemisphere to the other via the _____.
(pons : corpus callosum : reticular formation)

Learning Objective 4.12   G. The diencephalon and telencephalon are two main structures that make up the _____.
(forebrain : midbrain : hindbrain)

Learning Objective 4.12   H. An interconnected group of structures throughout the brain that is involved in emotional behavior, memory, epilepsy, and alcoholism is called the _____.
(association cortex : limbic system : basal ganglia)

Learning Objective 4.12   I. The _____ controls emotional behavior and has been the target for psychosurgery in some extremely violent patients.
(hippocampus : amygdala)

Learning Objective 4.13   J. The dominant, left hemisphere of the brain specializes in processing _____.
(language and speech : spatial tasks and creativity)

The pituitary is a small gland that directly affects behavior both through the control of other glands and through the release of hormones into the bloodstream.

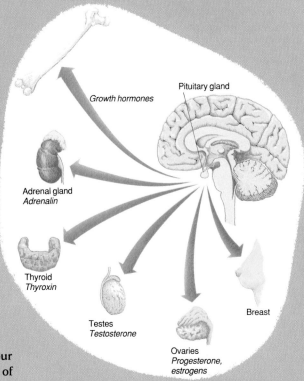

Growth hormones

Pituitary gland

Adrenal gland
Adrenalin

Thyroid
Thyroxin

Testes
Testosterone

Ovaries
*Progesterone,
estrogens*

Breast

Adrenalin dramatically affects energy levels and reduces our sense of pain and fatigue. During strenuous activity, levels of adrenalin increase; thus athletes are able to endure the strain of a long, demanding game.

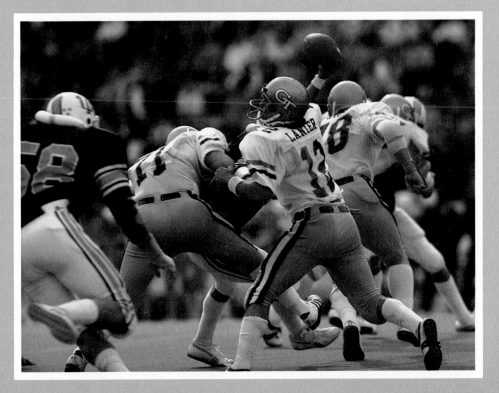

The four lobes of the
cerebral cortex. (Adapted
from Carlson, N. R., *Physiology
of Behavior,* 2nd ed.
Boston: Allyn and
Bacon, 1981.)

The three major
sections of the brain:
the hindbrain,
midbrain, and
forebrain.

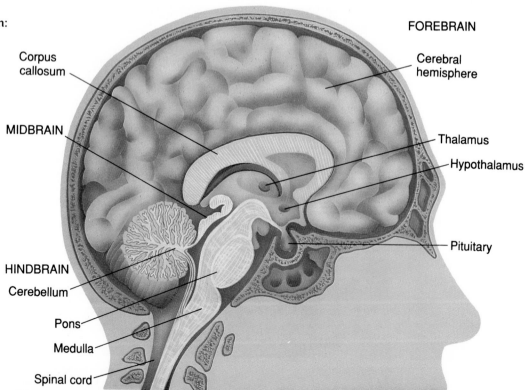

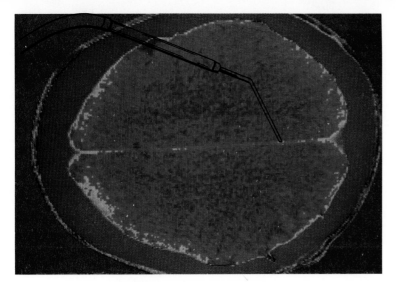

The human brain is divided into two hemispheres of approximately equal size, as shown in this CAT scan photograph. When the corpus callosum is surgically divided, the two hemispheres are permanently separated and no further information can be directly exchanged between them.

Each of the twelve cranial nerves sends information directly to its appropriate location in the brain.

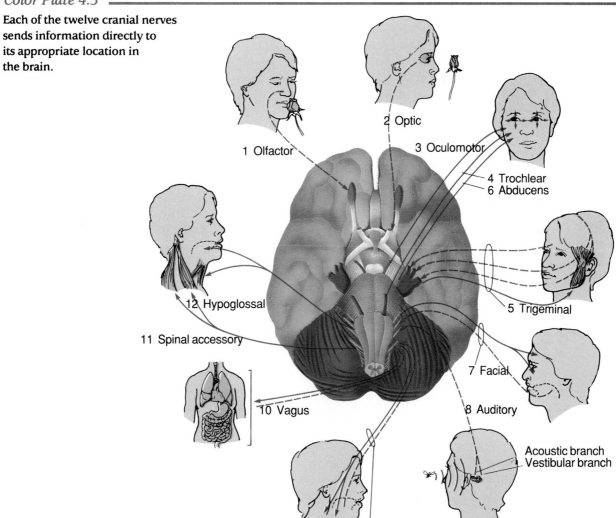

1 Olfactor
2 Optic
3 Oculomotor
4 Trochlear
6 Abducens
5 Trigeminal
12 Hypoglossal
11 Spinal accessory
10 Vagus
7 Facial
8 Auditory
Acoustic branch
Vestibular branch
9 Glossopharyngeal

In the autonomic nervous system, the parasympathetic and sympathetic subsystems control different aspects of bodily functions.

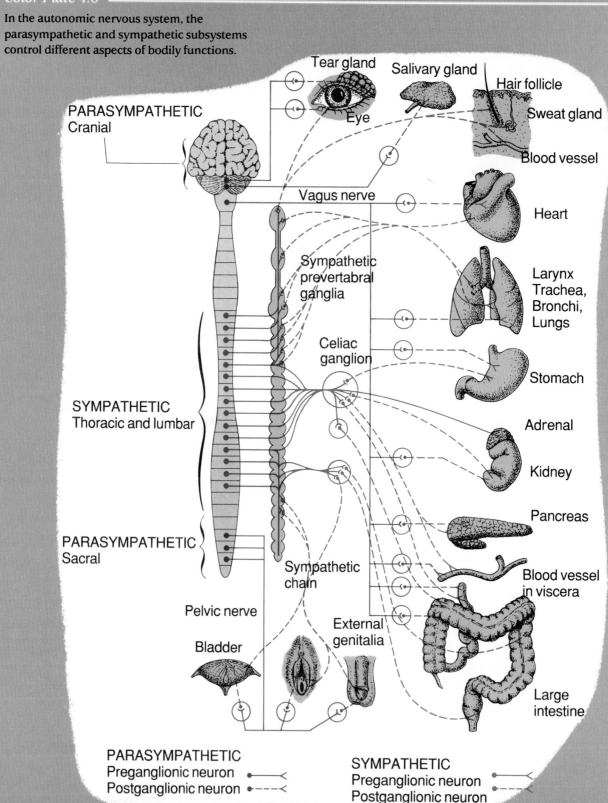

PARASYMPATHETIC
Cranial

Tear gland

Salivary gland

Hair follicle

Sweat gland

Eye

Blood vessel

Vagus nerve

Heart

Sympathetic prevertabral ganglia

Larynx
Trachea,
Bronchi,
Lungs

Celiac ganglion

Stomach

SYMPATHETIC
Thoracic and lumbar

Adrenal

Kidney

Pancreas

PARASYMPATHETIC
Sacral

Sympathetic chain

Blood vessel in viscera

Pelvic nerve

External genitalia

Bladder

Large intestine

PARASYMPATHETIC
Preganglionic neuron
Postganglionic neuron

SYMPATHETIC
Preganglionic neuron
Postganglionic neuron

Learning Objective 4.14
K. The somatic and autonomic nervous systems are subsystems of the
    _____ nervous system.
    (central : peripheral : parasympathetic)

Learning Objective 4.14
L. The activation of the _____ nervous system is sometimes
    called the fight-or-flight reflex.
    (somatic : sympathetic : parasympathetic)

MONITORING NEURAL ACTIVITY

Larry Denton, who opened this chapter, hoped he could be helped through a technique called biofeedback. By understanding how the brain operates and how stress affects biological mechanisms, psychologists devised this technique to help people reduce anxiety and their subsequent physical symptoms, such as migraine headaches. However, as you will see, biofeedback is a controversial technique; some practitioners argue that it does not work. Perhaps it was the therapy or the stress exercises that eventually helped Larry.

Over the years, many psychologists have argued that ultimately a complete description (and therefore explanation) of behavior will rely on biologically based facts. Physiological explanations recognize fully that the nervous system is constantly active; our neurons continue to fire whether we are awake or not, consciously thinking or not. Much of what scientists now know about electrical activity in the nervous system has come from studies of abnormalities in brain structure and function conducted in hospitals and laboratories. For example, some knowledge about epilepsy that helped Karen and Miguel's son Jonathan comes from studies of electrical activity in the brain.

Techniques for Measurement

Learning Objective 4.15

There are two basic procedures for measuring the activity of the nervous system. *Single unit recording* is usually performed on animals such as cats, rats, or monkeys. This technique involves placing a thin wire or needle in or next to a single cell. Long wires attached to the recording needle transmit its record of the cell's electrical activity to an amplifier. The data are then followed on an oscilloscope, a device used for recording changes in electrical voltage. Because neurons fire extremely rapidly, it is often necessary to feed the data into a computer, which averages the number of times the cell fires in a single second or a single minute. The other technique, *electroencephalography,* is widely used for measuring electrical activity in the nervous systems of both human beings and animals. This technique produces a record of brain-wave activity called an **electroencephalogram,** or **EEG,** obtained from a small electrode placed on a subject's scalp. The electrode is usually less than a quarter of an inch in diameter and records the activity of thousands of cells. EEGs are used for a variety of purposes, including the assessment of brain damage, epilepsy, tumors, and other abnormalities. (See Figure 4.11 on the next page.)

In normal, healthy human beings, EEGs show a variety of characteristic brain-wave patterns, depending on the subject's level and kind of mental activity. If people are awake, relaxed, and not engaged in directed thinking, their EEGs show *alpha waves,* which occur at a rate of eight to twelve cycles a second. When people are excited, their brain waves change dramatically from alpha waves to waves of high frequency and low amplitude, called *beta* and *gamma waves.* During sleep, people show patterns of high-frequency, low-amplitude

Electroencephalogram (EEG)
The record of an organism's electrical brain patterns, obtained through electrodes placed on a subject's scalp.

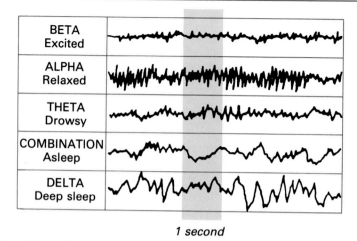

FIGURE 4.11 : Characteristic electrical activity patterns in the EEGs of healthy human beings in different states of excitation. High frequency is indicated by the occurrence of a large number of waves within a single unit or period of time.

bursts and of low-frequency waves at different times during their sleep cycle. We discuss brain-wave activity further later on in this chapter.

Biofeedback: Can You Manage Day-to-Day Activity?

Learning Objective 4.16

In his therapy sessions, Larry Denton began to come in touch with his feelings. In his stress exercises, Larry was learning new thought-coping mechanisms; and in biofeedback training, Larry found he could gain control over his body. It is generally assumed that the human body operates on its own, creating new cells, growing and developing—electrochemical changes taking place without direction or control.

But human beings can be aware of their bodies' responses to various environmental and internal changes. Can such knowledge of internal bodily functions help people better manage their lives? Researchers have traditionally assumed that most basic biological functions, especially those involving the autonomic nervous system, are inaccessible to manipulation except through drugs or surgery. In the last few years, however, studies in a rather new area of psychological interest called **biofeedback** have explored the extent to which subjects can control body functions—and thus behavior—not previously considered susceptible to conscious control, by monitoring their brain-wave activity and other physiological responses.

Neal Miller (1969) was the first researcher to train rats to control certain glandular responses and to then suggest that the same techniques could be used to help people manage their bodies and behavior. Since then, studies have shown that human beings can manipulate the electrical activity of their brains by changing their level of excitation. For example, a relaxed person seeing alpha waves on an oscilloscope can change those alpha waves to high-frequency waves by becoming more alert and paying attention. Similarly, a subject whose heart rate is displayed on an oscilloscope can see her heart rate decreasing as she relaxes. By watching her body's responses, she can learn what kind of physiological states allow her body to work easily and efficiently. She can learn which behaviors relax her heart muscles and lower her blood

Biofeedback ══════
The general technique by which individuals can monitor and learn to control the involuntary activity of certain organs and bodily functions.

FIGURE 4.12 : By providing feedback of internal bodily functions, biofeedback can be useful in training people to reduce the physical symptoms of anxiety.

pressure. In time, she can learn to control her heart rate and blood pressure by reproducing behaviors she has learned are associated with reduced heart rate.

Biofeedback depends on the idea that people can repeat or recall behavior or bodily states they find pleasurable or reinforcing. (Chapter 2 discusses the central role of reinforcing events in psychologists' conceptions of behavior.) People with tension headaches, of whom there are millions, learn to repeat the states that reduce their muscle tension and thus reduce their headaches (see Abramowitz & Bell, 1985; Adams, Feuerstein, & Fowler, 1980; Blanchard et al., 1982) (See Figure 4.12). Dietvorst (1978) successfully used biofeedback training with people who had recently had heart attacks to help them reduce their anxiety and fear of the future, which can impede physical recovery. Dietvorst trained subjects to decrease their level of arousal, and thus their level of anxiety, by monitoring a measure of their autonomic activity, hand temperature.

The results of biofeedback experiments are necessarily complicated by the number of variables involved, and biofeedback training is not always effective (Simkins, 1982). Nevertheless, so far biofeedback has been successfully used to treat hyperactivity (Hampstead, 1977; Whitmer, 1978) and learning disabilities in children (Omizo & Williams, 1982), and depression (Delk, 1977). Researchers have also applied biofeedback techniques to the treatment of other speech disorders (Davis & Drichta, 1980), the acquisition of fine motor movements (French, 1980), the control of sexual arousal (Hatch, 1981; Hoon, 1980), and painful menstrual symptoms (Balick, Elfner, & May, 1982). Some researchers believe that the most effective use of biofeedback is in combination with psychotherapy or other relaxation techniques (M. R. Ford, 1982). Another potential though still controversial application (see, for example, Raskin, Bali, & Peeke, 1980; Surwit & Keefe, 1978) is the use of biofeedback for the treatment of various disorders at home after training by a qualified professional (for example, Pardine, Dytell, & Napoli, 1981). (See Figure 4.12)

Not all studies have found biofeedback to be effective (for example, Drennen & Holden, 1984). However, results such as those described above provide strong support for the effective use of biofeedback in the reduction of stress-related symptoms. (Chapter 15 discusses the potential uses of biofeedback to treat behavior disorders.) As yet, few physicians or psychologists regularly use biofeedback in their practices (Weinman, Mathew, & Claghorn, 1982; (Roberts, 1985). Although many laboratory studies have demonstrated its effectiveness in helping people manage a wide range of problems, only carefully controlled research will ultimately answer persistent questions about its long-term effects. Biofeedback may offer practitioners opportunities as yet unrealized. As some researchers have suggested, biofeedback might be incorporated into mental health plans, despite the lack of support.

PROGRESS CHECK 4.4

1. Complete each of the following sentences with one of the options provided.

Learning Objective 4.15

A. Research that records activity in the brain by placing a small electrode on the scalp is called _____ .
(single unit recording : electroencephalography)

Learning Objective 4.15   B.   EEGs are used to detect _____ .
                       (the number of times a neuron fires per minute : brain disorders)

Learning Objective 4.15   C.   When a person is awake, relaxed, and not engaged in direct thinking, his or her brain-wave pattern will show _____ waves.
                       (alpha : beta : gamma)

Learning Objective 4.16   D.   Biofeedback is a technique that is allowing psychologists to explore the extent to which people can learn to control _____ bodily functions.
                       (involuntary : voluntary)

Learning Objective 4.16   E.   Biofeedback is based on the idea that people can repeat behavior or bodily states that they find _____ .
                       (reinforcing : on their own)

Learning Objective 4.16   F.   Biofeedback has been used to treat _____ disorders.
                       (only heart related : a variety of)

CONSCIOUSNESS

Learning Objective 4.17

All of us know when we are conscious, and we understand that consciousness has a biological base. Consider what happens when you attempt to alter your consciousness. If you have had a couple of glasses of wine, a couple of beers, or a martini or two, you may know that feeling of lightheadedness that accompanies intoxication. It may be for that reason that you drank the wine or liquor. Most people are aware that when they consume various substances, these substances alter the way they think and feel—they alter behavior by altering a person's biological functioning. It is not surprising that psychologists have studied such biological functioning and how it is altered under various states.

Awake and aware human beings are conscious. Their thought is rational. However, people can alter this ordinary state of functioning in several ways. A junkie who is physiologically dependent on heroin is an extreme example. A corporate executive developing a dependence on alcohol is another. Drugs are not the only means of altering normal thinking states. People under hypnosis may be willing to think, say, and do things they might otherwise not do. Sleep also changes people's consciousness, perhaps with dreams and bizarre thoughts. Hypnosis, sleep, meditation, and drug states alter individuals' normal thought processes and normal patterns of behavior.

Psychologists study altered states of consciousness in order to understand normal consciousness. One of the biggest problems in this regard is defining consciousness. Some researchers view normal consciousness and altered states of consciousness as two sides of the same coin. Others argue that normal and altered states of consciousness are separate and significantly different.

Researchers have problems sorting out many aspects of normal and altered consciousness and behavior. They especially need to consider how altered states are affected by biological and environmental variables. For example, biology dictates that people have physiological needs for eating and sleeping; yet social interactions affect the way people eat and to some extent the way they sleep. This is typical of the complex interplay between biology and environment that affects both normal and altered states of behavior.

Even though studying altered states of consciousness does not answer all the questions scientists have about how and why people think and behave as they do, psychologists argue that it provides insight into how consciousness works. Although the task of understanding consciousness is by no means complete, progress has been made.

Consciousness ═══════
The general state of being aware of and responsive to stimuli and events in the environment.

Altered state of consciousness ═══════
A pattern of functioning that is dramatically different from that of ordinary awareness and responsiveness.

Learning 4.18
Objective

In meditation, deep concentration is used to achieve an altered state of consciousness.

Consciousness is the general state of being aware of and responsive to stimuli and events in the environment. An **altered state of consciousness** is a pattern of functioning dramatically different from that of ordinary awareness and responsiveness. These definitions stress the importance of environmental factors. Natsoulas (1978) has listed seven definitions of consciousness. But for some researchers, a complete and accurate definition of consciousness is not so easily obtained (for example, Ornstein, 1977; Shapiro, 1977).

A range of conscious states exists from alert awareness to total unresponsiveness. For example, as you move through the day, your general awareness—responsiveness, thought processes, and physiological responses—changes. In the morning on first waking, you may not be fully aware and responsive. Later, on the job or in a class, you may be very alert. As the day wears on, you may find awareness decreasing. In the evening, you may take a short nap. The idea of a continuum guides many practitioners. Some researchers believe that consciousness is comprised of several layers or levels of awareness. Others believe that distinctly different conscious states explain specific behaviors and attention patterns. Researchers who favor the first view suggest that a person who is, for example, drinking heavily temporarily enters a lower (or deeper) *level* among his range of conscious levels—that of intoxication. Researchers who favor the second interpretation believe that a heavy drinker has entered a totally different *state* of consciousness. A definitive answer to the levels versus states issue has not yet been found.

In the study of consciousness, as in other areas of psychology, theory has guided research. Several researchers have proposed biologically based theories. Julian Jaynes (1976) suggests that understanding the evolution of the human brain holds the key to altered states. He believes that consciousness originates in differences in function and physiology of the two hemispheres of the brain. Weil (1972, 1977), on the other hand, suggests that human beings have an inborn drive to experience altered states of consciousness; he acknowledges that consciousness can be altered by a range of techniques from drugs to meditation, but he claims that it is really people's ideas and concentration that change their functioning. Tart (1972, 1977) makes a similar argument but with a somewhat more systematic approach. He distinguishes normal from altered states and suggests that altered states show radically different patterns of brain activity and behavior than normal states. These diverse approaches remain extremely controversial.

Robert Ornstein (1977) has suggested that two modes of consciousness exist, each controlled by one side of the brain: the active-verbal-rational mode (sometimes called the active mode) and the receptive-spatial-intuitive-holistic mode (sometimes called the receptive mode) (see also Deikman, 1976). In Ornstein's view, evolution has made the active mode automatic; human beings limit their awareness automatically in order to shut out experiences, events, and stimuli that do not directly relate to their ability to act for survival. The active mode focuses attention; the receptive mode is holistic, intuitive, and open. When people need to gain perspective and judgment about what they are doing, they expand their normal awareness by using the receptive mode. Ornstein believes that such techniques as meditation, biofeedback, hypnosis, and even the use of certain drugs can help people learn to use the receptive mode of their consciousness to balance the more active mode.

Ornstein and his collaborator David Galin support many of their ideas with laboratory data showing that the brain is divided and specialized in significant ways and that the left and right hemispheres of the brain function differently (Galin, 1974; Ornstein, 1976). As we learned earlier in the chapter, the brain is divided into two hemispheres. Sperry and others suggest that in both hemispheres learning and memory operate independently, each with its own conscious sphere of activities (Kinsbourne, 1982; Sperry, 1968). Although they are separated and have unique functions, the two hemispheres interact with each other in important ways—especially in matters of attention (Gazzaniga, 1983). We know from everyday experience that in some tasks we use only our right or only our left hand; the choice is principally determined by hemispheric specialization. Most people have a dominant left hemisphere and use their right hand for most specialized tasks—they are right-handed.

No one doubts that the brain is specialized in its operation; but exactly how is a subject of much debate. Max Allen (1983) suggests that the functioning of the brain is even more complicated than previously believed. He believes that smaller processing units within and between each hemisphere perform specific "subprocesses." These subprocesses vary in function and distribution. Although Allen's theory is relatively new, it suggests that the term *hemispheric specialization* may be too loose; it may not really be an accurate description of how the brain works.

A lot of interesting data support the general idea that the left and right sides of the brain are specialized for different functions. (Remember, the left side of the body is controlled to a great extent by the right hemisphere of the brain, and the right side of the body is largely controlled by the left hemisphere.) Galin has concluded that "there appear to be two separate, conscious minds in one head" (1974, p. 31). The existence of two physiological modes of operation in the brain lends support to Ornstein's ideas, but other researchers are skeptical (Levy, 1983; Zaidel, 1983).

Ornstein and Galin suggest that the left-dominated and right-dominated modes of consciousness operate in a complementary and alternating fashion, one working while the other is inhibited. In Ornstein's model (1977), intellectual activities take place in the active, or left-dominated mode, and "intuitive" activities in the receptive or right-dominated mode; the integration of these two modes underlies the highest human accomplishments.

Theories such as Ornstein's are difficult to subject to scientific scrutiny. Many researchers examining the relation between brain structure and behavior or between drugs and behavior are uncomfortable with vague concepts of consciousness and refuse to discuss their findings in terms of consciousness.

Psychologists still do not agree whether separate and distinct stages of consciousness actually exist. Well-known psychologists such as Ornstein (1977) argue that because people's consciousness is constantly changing, the idea of discrete states may be misleading; others, such as Tart (1977), draw fundamental distinctions between normal and altered states. Further research into how altered states of consciousness affect behavior may help resolve this issue.

PROGRESS CHECK   4.5

1. Match each of the following theorists' names with the statements that best describe each one's theory of consciousness.

Jaynes   Tart   Weil   Ornstein

Learning Objective 4.18   A. _____ Human beings have an inborn drive to experience altered states of consciousness. When a person's ideas or concentration changes, consciousness changes. Consciousness can also be altered by such techniques as taking drugs or meditating.

Learning Objective 4.18   B. _____ A distinction can be made between normal and altered states. Altered states show more radically different patterns of brain activity and behavior than do normal states.

Learning Objective 4.18   C. _____ Evolution of the human brain holds the key to understanding altered states. Differences in function and physiology between the two hemispheres of the brain influence consciousness.

Learning Objective 4.18   D. _____ There are two modes of consciousness, active and receptive, that are controlled by the specialized functions of the two brain hemispheres.

2. Complete each of the following sentences with one of the options provided.

Learning Objective 4.17   A. Consciousness and altered states of consciousness are _____
_____ .
(purely cognitive conditions : affected by biological and environmental factors)

Learning Objective 4.17   B. The _____ interpretation of consciousness suggests that there are layers of consciousness that allow for a continuum of normal to altered experiences.
(states : levels : general)

Learning Objective 4.18   C. Ornstein suggests that as human beings evolved and struggled to survive, they shut out the _____ mode of consciousness, and as a result human awareness is automatically limited.
(active : receptive)

Learning Objective 4.18   D. _____ characterizes the active mode of consciousness.
(Focused attention : Holistic, intuitive, and open)

Learning Objective 4.18   E. Meditation, hypnosis, biofeedback, and the use of certain drugs are techniques people use to gain access to their _____ mode of consciousness.
(active : receptive)

Learning Objective 4.18   F. Learning and memory seem to operate _____ in both hemispheres, according to Sperry.
(in unison : independently : rhythmically)

Learning Objective 4.18   G. The two hemispheres have separate and unique functions, and they _____ with one another.
(interact : do not interact)

Learning Objective 4.18   H. Ornstein has argued that because people's consciousness is constantly changing, the idea of discrete states of consciousness _____ .
(seems very accurate : may be misleading)

Learning Objective 4.18   I. Movement and body functions on the left side of the body are controlled by the _____ hemisphere.
(right : left)

Learning Objective 4.18   J. According to Ornstein and Galin, while one hemisphere is working the other is
_____ .
(inhibited : storing information in memory : maintaining body functions)

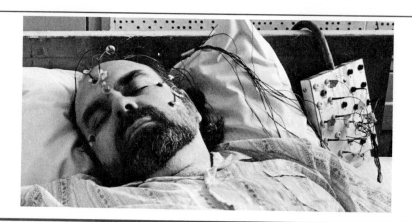

FIGURE 4.13 : In sleep labs, subjects are connected electrically to equipment that monitors their brain waves while they sleep.

SLEEP

Learning Objective 4.19

If Larry Denton, who opened this chapter, were to tell you he was having sleep problems, you probably would not be surprised. People under stress, having migraine headaches, and being treated for stress-related symptoms are likely to have difficulties in sleep. You will see when we study depression and some other maladjustments that sleep disorders are common physiological ailments.

Not everyone who suffers from headaches, backaches, or other disorders seeks the help of physicians or psychologists. Not everyone has such disorders; but a common ailment that most everyone has at one time or another is an inability to sleep. Sleep is an altered state of consciousness; it has a biological basis; and psychologists consider it a behavior. Because lack of sleep so directly affects other behaviors, psychologists study it intensely. Although a great deal is known about what happens physiologically when we sleep, we do not yet understand fully why we sleep or how sleep helps us to recuperate.

Researchers know that, although individuals need different amounts of sleep, everyone sleeps at some time during the day or night (Osterberg, 1973). Sleep is thus a normal everyday behavior. However, it also represents a changed state of awareness. By studying sleep, psychologists learn more about human consciousness. (See Figure 4.13.)

Most people require about eight hours of sleep, but some can function with four or five hours and others need as many as nine or ten (Meddis, Pearson, & Langford, 1973; Tune, 1969). Teenagers tend to sleep longer than do college students, and old people tend to sleep less than young people. Most young adults sleep between six and a half and eight and a half hours a night (Tune, 1969). Although people who are active and expend a lot of energy would logically require more sleep than those who are less active, this is not always the case. For example, bedridden hospital patients sleep about the same amount of time as people who are on their feet all day.

Sleep
A nonwaking state of consciousness characterized by general unresponsiveness to the environment and general physical immobility.

REM and NREM Sleep

Beginning in the late 1950s, studies in sleep laboratories of the electrical activity of the brain during sleep have revealed two basic types of **sleep** and several distinct sleep stages. By attaching electrodes to a subject's forehead, experimenters can monitor the subject's electroencephalogram (EEG)—the record of

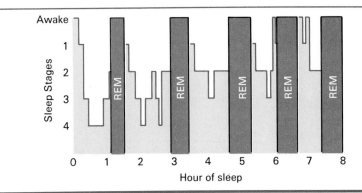

FIGURE 4.14 : Most people complete about five sleep cycles per night. With each cycle, they spend progressively more time in REM sleep.

NREM sleep ═══════
Four distinct stages of sleep during which no rapid eye movements occur.

REM sleep ═══════
A stage of sleep characterized by high-frequency, low-voltage brain-wave activity, rapid and systematic eye movements, and dreams.

brain-wave patterns—throughout the night. Long wires attached to the electrodes allow the subject full mobility. The subject can sleep easily and comfortably. In addition, an electrooculogram can record eye movements and an electromyogram can record muscle tension in the face.

Recordings of sleeping subjects EEGs have revealed five distinct patterns of electrical activity. Four are designated as **NREM sleep** stages (NREM stands for "no rapid eye movements"); the other pattern is called **REM sleep,** because rapid (and systematic) eye movements occur during this period. REM sleep is not designated as a stage, even though it is part of the sleep cycle. Figure 4.14 shows a typical progression through five full cycles of sleep in an eight-hour period. When people first fall asleep, their sleep is rather light, and they can easily be wakened (stage 1). Within the next thirty to forty minutes, they pass through stages 2, 3, and 4 (Langford, Meddis, & Pearson, 1974; Levere, Morlock, Thomas, & Hart, 1974). Considerably more time is spent in stage 4 sleep in the early part of the night than later in the night. After subjects leave stage 4 sleep and pass again through stages 3 and 2, they enter REM sleep for the first time. With each sleep cycle, subjects spend progressively more time in REM sleep. A full sleep cycle lasts approximately ninety minutes. The longer the sleep time (with more sleep cycles), the more REM sleep people experience (Agnew & Webb, 1973). (See Figure 4.14.)

Figure 4.15 on the next page shows the distinctive brain-wave patterns of wakefulness, the four stages of NREM sleep, and REM sleep in a normal adult. The waking pattern exhibits a fast, regular rhythm. In stage 1 sleep, the brain waves are of lower amplitude (height) but remain relatively fast with mixed frequencies. Stage 2 sleep shows low-amplitude, nonrhythmic activity combined with special patterns called *sleep spindles* and *K complexes*. A sleep spindle is a rhythmic burst of waves that wax and wane over a period of one or two seconds. A K complex is the higher-amplitude burst of activity seen in the last third of the stage 2 tracing in Figure 4.15. Sleep spindles and K complexes appear only during NREM sleep. Stage 3 sleep is a transitional stage between stages 2 and 4, with slower but higher-amplitude activity. Stage 4 sleep, the deepest sleep stage, has even higher-amplitude brain-wave traces called delta waves. The bottom pattern in Figure 4.15 shows an EEG transition from NREM stage 2 to REM sleep. The first part of the tracing shows a clear K complex, indicating stage 2 sleep; the last part shows waves characteristic of REM sleep. During periods of sleep in which high frequency, low-amplitude waves are apparent, subjects experience rapid eye movements and typically report dreaming.

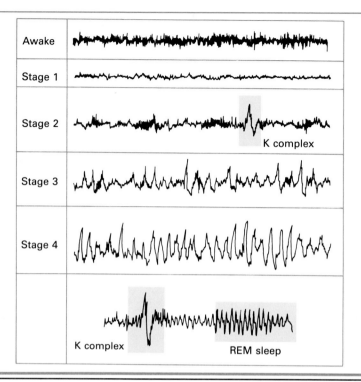

FIGURE 4.15 • EEGs show distinctive characteristic patterns for a wakeful state, REM sleep, and each of the four NREM sleep stages.

Researchers can identify the stage of sleep an individual is in by watching an EEG recording. For example, if delta waves are present, the subject is in stage 4 sleep. To confirm this finding, an experimenter may wake the subject and ask if he or she was dreaming. Stage 4 sleep has two well-documented behavioral characteristics. First, subjects are very difficult to wake. Stage 4 sleep is deep sleep, and wakened subjects often appear confused, disturbed, and take several seconds to rouse themselves fully. Second, when subjects are in stage 4 sleep, they generally do not dream, although they may report some vague notion of mental activity. In contrast, subjects in REM sleep can report in great detail the imagery and activity characteristic of a dream state. Because REM sleep is considered necessary to normal physiological functioning and

TABLE 4.3 • Minutes of REM Sleep, Ages 3 to 15

REM Period	3–5 Yrs.	6–9 Yrs.	10–15 Yrs.	13–15 Yrs.
1	18	18	18	20
2	24	26	29	29
3	27	32	35	30
4	35	35	37	35
5	31	34	32	27
6	29	34	32	27
7	28	58		
8	25			
9	38			

Source: Williams, Karacan, & Hursch, 1974.

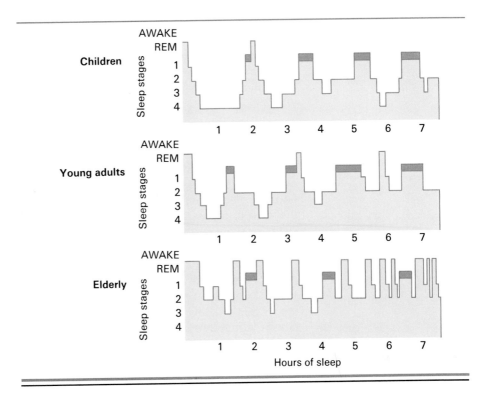

FIGURE 4.16 : REM sleep (darker area) occurs cyclically throughout the night at about ninety-minute intervals in all age groups. However, stage 4 sleep decreases with age. In addition, elderly people awaken more often and spend more time awake.

behavior, it might be expected to be a deep sleep; however, it is an active sleep during which the EEG resembles that of an aware person. For this reason, REM sleep is often called paradoxical sleep. In REM sleep, the deep breathing, slowed heart rate, and lowered blood pressure of stage 4 sleep are absent. Instead of appearing rested, subjects seem agitated. Their eyes move and their heart rate and breathing are much more variable. Subjects are more difficult to awaken during REM sleep.

Sleep cycles develop from before birth into adulthood. Initially, fetuses show no eye movements. Later, they show eye, facial, and body movements. Newborns spend about 50 percent of their sleep time in REM sleep. From age one on, the proportion of REM sleep to stage 4 sleep decreases dramatically (Ellingson, 1975; Kleitman & Englemann, 1953; Parmelee & Stern, 1972) (see Table 4.3 and Figure 4.16).

Telling Time while You Are Asleep

Some people will tell you that they can awaken punctually every morning at a predetermined time. The typical response on the part of psychologists is that some *external* cue usually helps wake people. In a new research study by Zepelin (1986), electroencephalographic readings were made of sleeping subjects and their ability to wake themselves at a predetermined time was assessed. Being able to wake themselves up was easiest when subjects were in REM sleep. Being in REM sleep probably facilitated the subjects' ability to recall the intention to wake, and perhaps the act of wakening itself. Furthermore, the cyclical occurrence of REM sleep probably is another aid. However, no subject was consistently able to wake at a predetermined time, although some subjects could wake up at the proper time some of the time. Most of the time, people who wake up at a predetermined time are doing so because of the birds chirping, heating systems making noise, and their own sleep cycle providing them hints that the time has come to face the new day. People do not have biological alarm clocks.

Sleep Deprivation: Doing without REM

Learning Objective 4.20

That everyone needs sleep becomes painfully obvious to people who are deprived of it. When people who normally sleep eight hours are deprived of a few hours of sleep on a particular night, they may be tired the following day, but they can function quite normally. But when people lose a couple of hours of sleep for several nights in a row, they usually look tired, feel lethargic, and are irritable.

Several researchers have studied subjects who were totally or partially deprived of sleep for various amounts of time (for example, Webb & Agnew, 1974). Subjects in these studies generally sleep in a sleep laboratory, where their EEGs and eye movements are recorded for several nights. Recordings taken the first three or four nights provide baseline data. Once these norms are established, the subjects are deprived of sleep. Some studies deprive subjects of all REM sleep, waking them every time their EEGs and eye movements show REM sleep patterns; others deprive subjects only partially of REM sleep, waking them after a specific period (based on an estimation of how much REM sleep the subjects normally have each night). In studies of total sleep deprivation, subjects are not allowed to sleep at all. A study that deprived subjects of all sleep for 205 hours (eight and a half days) found that on the nights immediately following the experiment subjects spent a greater-than-normal amount of time in REM sleep and stage 4 sleep and the least amount of time in stage 1 and stage 2 sleep—the lightest stages of sleep (Kales et al., 1970; see also Webb & Agnew, 1975). Similarly, subjects in a study that partially deprived them of REM sleep reported feeling sleepy and spent more time in REM sleep on a subsequent night (Dement, Greenberg, & Klein, 1966).

These and other studies show clearly that after sleep deprivation, people catch up on their REM sleep. They also show that deprivation of REM sleep alters people's behavior. Subjects regularly deprived of REM sleep become anxious and irritable and report difficulty concentrating. As soon as they are allowed to have REM sleep again, the psychological changes disappear (see McGrath & Cohen, 1978). Dement (1960) has suggested that a certain amount of dreaming each night is necessary to psychological well-being. He believes that serious disruptions of personality may occur as a result of dream deprivation because of prolonged REM suppression. Other researchers deny that REM sleep deprivation produces serious psychological changes (Albert, 1975; Bonnet, 1980; D. B. Cohen, 1979; Vogel, 1975).

Some sleep researchers have investigated the extent to which people can alter their normal sleep–wakefulness behavior yet maintain a normal sleep-stage pattern. Webb and Agnew (1977) maintained subjects on five different sleep-wakefulness regimens: 3 hours of sleep and 6 hours of wakefulness; 4 hours of sleep and 8 of wakefulness; 6 hours of sleep and 12 of wakefulness; 10 hours of sleep and 20 of wakefulness; and 12 hours of sleep and 24 of wakefulness. They found that after an initial adaptation period, the basic structure of

There is nothing like a good sleep. Everyone knows the feeling of fogginess, when you begin to lose interest in remaining awake, when you would prefer to be lying down, when you feel woozy, when you begin to lose the struggle to remain awake. Everybody sleeps, and everybody has had a time in life when they wanted to sleep more than anything else.

Human beings spend about 35 percent of each day sleeping. The principal determinant of whether you want to go to sleep is whether you are sleepy. This seems simple enough, but psychologists have studied it intensely. Sleepiness is the condition in which, if you were allowed to, you would go to sleep. Sleepiness is not fatigue, not a lack of get-up-and-go, nor lack of interest. Rather, sleepiness is a physiological state a person develops because of an imbalance in his or her body. People become sleepy because they *need* sleep.

One principal way sleepiness has been studied has been to introduce sleep loss. When people are deprived of sleep, they easily become sleepy. The amount of time since you last slept is a principal determinant of your level of sleepiness. Deprive a college student of a night's sleep and the student desperately wants to sleep the next day. If she then gets only five hours sleep, the student's need for sleep on the third day is exceedingly high.

Both psychological and physical factors affect sleepiness. According to sleep researcher Richard Allen of the Johns Hopkins Sleep Center, strenuous exercise may increase the need for sleep slightly, but so will the intake of large amounts of food, particularly carbohydrates. Sleep is facilitated by dark, warm rooms and comfortable environments. Sleepiness is decreased by hunger, fear, work, talking, and novel, unexpected stimulation.

Insomnia, the inability to sleep, is a common sleep disorder. Other sleep disorders are relatively rare, difficult to treat, and have profound effects on the sufferers.

If you snore nearly all the time, if you fall asleep at inappropriate times (while driving a car, for example), you may have a sleep disorder. If you had *narcolepsy,* you would fall asleep suddenly or have profound muscle weakness during the day. Narcolepsy is probably caused because of an autonomic nervous system disturbance and lowered arousal (Levander & Sachs, 1985).

If, while you sleep, you became unable to breathe because of air flow resistance, you might have *sleep apnea.* Sleep apnea creates a stopping of airflow for at least fifteen seconds. People with this disorder often have as many as 100 apnea episodes in a night, and during the day are exceedingly sleepy and sometimes have memory losses. People with severe apnea may have work-related accidents and severe headaches and may fall asleep during the day. Drug therapy and some minor surgical techniques for creating better airflow have been used to treat sleep apnea. Monitoring equipment for prolonged breathing pauses has also been used (Sheridan, 1985). Males are much more likely than females to have sleep apnea (Ingbar & Gee, 1985).

Psychological and work conditions also can cause excessive sleepiness. People who suffer from depressive disorders usually report excessive sleepiness. People who do shift work and are asked to change schedules every few days often have trouble sleeping. Jet lag is experienced by people who travel great east-to-west distances in airplanes.

If your need to sleep is suddenly different—if you fall asleep at inappropriate times, suddenly snore loudly, or have muscle weakness—you may want to see your physician. Both behavioral and medical treatments may be necessary for people who suffer from a sleep disorder. In special cases, referral to a sleep center may be necessary. But for most of us, after the alarm goes off in the morning, catching an extra twenty winks is one of life's simple pleasures.

---

sleep persisted regardless of the regimen, although the proportion of stage 4 sleep decreased in the short regimens, and REM sleep was more likely in some of the sleep conditions than in others. The results suggest that human beings are remarkably adaptable in their sleep patterns and can maintain a basic overall pattern of sleep stages regardless of their sleep–wakefulness regimen, as long as the pattern of sleep stays stable over time. Changing your sleep pattern daily will bring about sleepiness and behavior changes (see the box on sleepiness).

. . . Perchance to Dream

Learning Objective 4.21

Dreams have long occupied an important place in psychology. Freudian psychoanalysts use dream analysis as a therapeutic tool in the treatment of emotional disturbance. Contemporary therapists use patients' dreams in various

REM Sleep   Stage 2   Stage 1

Dream activity occurs
principally during REM sleep.

ways to understand current or past problems. Therapists who use dreams *assume* that they express desires and thoughts that may be unacceptable to the conscious mind. Theoreticians like Freud believed that dreams were *caused* by unconscious impulses and desires. Freud and many practitioners who followed him believe that sexual and aggressive impulses are expressed in dreams because they cannot be expressed in day-to-day behavior due to societal sanctions.

Dreaming =====================
An altered state of
consciousness that occurs
primarily during REM sleep
and is usually
accompanied by vivid
visual, tactile, and auditory
experiences.

Dreaming is an altered state of consciousness that occurs largely during REM sleep and is usually accompanied by vivid visual experiences. With the beginning of active research into sleep and dreaming thirty years ago, experimenters discovered that dreaming occurs principally during REM sleep. Dement and Kleitman (1957) monitored the eye movements of subjects to determine when they were in REM sleep. Each time subjects reached REM sleep, the researchers woke them and asked them if they had been dreaming. They also woke subjects during NREM sleep. Seventy-nine percent of subjects in REM sleep reported dreams, in contrast to only 7 percent of subjects in NREM sleep. The researchers concluded that dreaming is accompanied by rapid eye movements and a characteristic EEG, and that this cycle occurs approximately five times a night. Dement and Kleitman also noted that subjects' patterns of rapid eye movements related to the visual imagery of their dreams. When a subject dreamed about climbing a series of ladders, eye movements were vertical; when a subject dreamed about two people throwing tomatoes at each other, eye movements were horizontal. The content of dreams often parallels the cognitive development of the person dreaming (Foulkes, 1962). Young children's dreams tend to be self-centered, whereas the dreams of older children and adults are more abstract and symbolic.

Two researchers from Harvard Medical School, Allan Hobson and Robert McCarley, believe dreams have a physiological basis (1977). They argue that during periods of REM sleep, the parts of the brain responsible for long-term memory, vision, audition, and perhaps even emotion are spontaneously stimulated. Because this activity is not organized by any coherent external stimuli, the resulting dream is often fragmented and incoherent. Dreamers may experience strange and bizarre scenes, as in nightmares (Hobson, 1983).

Most people dream four or five times a night, although they may recall only one or none. Usually, people recall a dream because they woke in the middle of it (Webb & Kersey, 1967). One study asked 762 subjects whether they recalled dreaming during the previous night. Thirty-seven percent reported having dreamed.

Other kinds of cognitive activity take place even during NREM sleep. However, reports of this activity are vague. In contrast, reports of thoughts during REM sleep are often lengthy, vivid in visual and auditory imagery, and detailed (Foulkes, 1962). Researchers still do not know exactly what functions dreams serve or what they mean.

Sleep and Memory

Learning Objective 4.22

Lack of sleep can lead to impaired performance and feelings of exhaustion.

Can people learn a foreign language while they sleep? Magazines often run ads for "learn while you sleep" programs. Most research shows that claims for real, long-lasting learning occurring during sleep are false at worst and exaggerated at best (Aarons, 1976). However, sleep can aid memory and learning in a different way.

Research in the 1920s showed that sleeping before a test is better than being involved in other kinds of activities. In a now classic study, Jenkins and Dallenbach (1924) had two subjects learn lists of nonsense syllables and recall them either immediately after presentation or up to eight hours later. During the period between learning and recall, the subjects either slept or engaged in normal waking activities. The performance of the subject who slept during the delay period was better than that of the subject who had stayed awake; the waking subject's intervening activity had had deleterious effects on recall ability.

Jenkins and Dallenbach's findings have been confirmed by researchers using more subjects. For example, Lovatt and Warr (1968) using forty subjects, tested paired-associate learning after an eight-hour interval and found that recall after sleep was superior to recall after waking activity. Even more interesting are the results of a study by Benson and Feinberg (1977), who had subjects learn lists of paired associates either in the morning just after sleep or at night before sleep. Subjects were tested on their recall after eight, sixteen, or twenty-four hours. Those who had learned the lists in the morning and were tested at night did worse than those who had learned the material at night and were tested in the morning. Furthermore, after twenty-four hours, when all subjects had had an equal amount of sleep and waking activity, subjects who had learned the paired associates just before sleeping still showed better recall. Benson and Feinberg concluded that sleep not only insulates subjects from interfering activity but also provides a period during which information can be consolidated. This is an exciting and potentially very important finding.

Research has shown that the first half of a normal night of sleep contains little REM sleep, the second half a great deal. Fowler, Sullivan, and Ekstrand (1973) conducted a study to see whether different parts of the sleep cycle affected recall differently. Subjects were brought into a sleep laboratory. One group was given a learning task, allowed to sleep for three hours, and then wakened and given a test requiring the use of memory. Another group was allowed to sleep for three hours, wakened and taught the same material as the first group, then sent back to sleep and wakened again three hours later for testing. Subjects in the second group, who were tested after an interval during which they exhibited large amounts of REM sleep, did not perform as well as subjects in the first group, whose memories were tested after a period during which they exhibited large amounts of stage 4 sleep. The researchers concluded that REM sleep does not facilitate memory, whereas stage 4 sleep may.

Studies such as these show clearly that sleep is an important aid to memory, although psychologists do not yet know exactly how sleep affects memory. A night's sleep will not guarantee learning or excellent memory, but lack of it surely will impair performance.

PROGRESS CHECK 4.6

1. Complete each of the following sentences with one of the options provided.

Learning Objective 4.19

A. People who expend a lot of energy during the day _____ more sleep than people who rest most of the day.
(need : do not necessarily need)

Learning Objective 4.19

B. Researchers measure _____ that are typical of sleep with an electrooculogram.
(brain waves : eye movements : muscle tensions)

Learning Objective 4.19

C. There are _____ stages of NREM sleep.
(three : four : five)

Learning Objective 4.19

D. The transition from NREM sleep to REM sleep generally occurs after a period of _____ sleep.
(stage 2 : stage 3 : stage 4)

Learning Objective 4.19

E. A full sleep cycle lasts approximately _____.
(90 minutes : 2 1/2 hours : 8 hours)

Learning Objective 4.19

F. Special patterns of EEG activity called sleep spindles and K complexes occur only during _____ sleep.
(REM : NREM)

Learning Objective 4.19

G. REM sleep is _____ sleep.
(a deep : an active, almost paradoxical)

Learning Objective 4.20

H. After sleep deprivation, people _____ sleep.
(cannot catch up on lost : catch up on REM and stage 4)

Learning Objective 4.20

I. When people are deprived of REM sleep on a regular basis, they _____.
(daydream more often : become anxious and irritable)

Learning Objective 4.21

J. Eye movements that occur during REM sleep are related to the _____ of a dream.
(length : visual imagery : vividness)

Learning Objective 4.21

K. Hobson and McCarley have suggested that bizarre dreams and nightmares may be the result of _____.
(unacceptable thoughts : unorganized, spontaneous brain stimulation)

Learning Objective 4.21

L. Based on one extensive study, although most people dream four or five times each night, only _____ remember one of their dreams from the previous night.
(7 percent : 37 percent : 79 percent)

Learning Objective 4.22

M. Most research shows that we _____ while we are sleeping.
(can learn a lot : cannot learn much)

Learning Objective 4.22 N. According to several studies, if you sleep right after you have studied, the information you studied has an increased probability of being ――――――――――
――――――――――.

(forgotten : consolidated in memory)

Keeping Pace with Chapter 4

Applying Principles

4.1 Identify the nervous system that is most specifically illustrated by each of the following situations.

central   parasympathetic   somatic   sympathetic

―――――――――――

―――――――――――

―――――――――――

―――――――――――

A. Without really thinking about it, Mary does several yoga stretches to relieve lower-back tension.

B. Immediately after a close-call car collision, Dayton's heart beat and breathing increased to a level faster than usual and, because of a release of adrenalin secretions, he felt very aroused.

C. Lindy encounters a multiple-choice question on her psychology test that is particularly difficult. She carefully analyzes the question, considers each alternative, and, through a process of elimination, narrows her choices to the one answer she considers most accurate.

D. An increase in the secretion of digestive juices and blood flowing to the gastrointestinal system causes the meal Simon just ate to break down into protein and carbohydrate molecules; nutrients are eventually absorbed by his blood system.

Self-Test

Before proceeding to the Self-Test, REVIEW the Learning Objectives listed at the chapter opening and RECITE from memory everything you can remember in support of them. Then, take this Self-Test as if it were to be graded by your teacher. Use the Learning Objective numbers in the Answer Section as a reference to restudy the corresponding text pages and Progress Checks for any incorrectly answered questions.

1. The *primary* issue of concern in the nature versus nurture debate is
   A. which research method to use when studying genetic influences.
   B. which contributes more to behavior patterns—biological determinants or the environment?
   C. the assertion that inherited traits will not become evident unless the environment encourages them.
   D. the assertion that inherited traits provide a foundation for behavior and experiences shape it further.

2. Which of the following statements concerning heredity is *false?*
   A. Sperm cells determine the sex of offspring.
   B. Chromosomes are lined up on the genes in the nucleus of a cell.
   C. The *most basic* determinant of an inherited trait is a gene.
   D. Genes determine such things as hair color, body structure, and intellectual potential.

3. Down's syndrome provides a good example of

    A. what can happen if there are too many chromosomes present.
    B. a genetic disorder that can be controlled by careful management of the physical environment.
    C. how viral infections can modify inherited traits.
    D. an inherited trait that causes schizophrenic behavior.

4. Psychologists believe that heredity is an important factor in determining if a particular person will get schizophrenia because

    A. the eighteenth chromosome is missing in most schizophrenics.
    B. twin studies have shown that if one identical twin has the disorder, the other twin is also likely to have it.
    C. the environment cannot affect behavior in such a dramatic way.
    D. schizophrenia appears shortly after birth.

5. The DNA structure of our genetic heritage

    A. is fixed.
    B. has evolved to provide human beings with a highly organized brain that allows learning to affect behavior.
    C. can be stretched to amazing lengths when combined with enriching environmental experiences.
    D. all of the above

6. A condition known as hyperglycemia

    A. occurs when the pancreas does not produce enough insulin.
    B. occurs when there is too much sugar in the blood.
    C. can lead to coma or death.
    D. all of the above

7. It appears that women who have PMS have

    A. normal hormone levels.
    B. an excess of estrogen.
    C. an estrogen deficiency.
    D. an imbalance of estrogen and progesterone.

8. The brain controls and affects behavior

    A. by means of a matrix system.
    B. through many mutually dependent systems and subsystems.
    C. in an all-or-none fashion.
    D. when the conscious mind directs it to do so.

9. The part of a neuron that receives neural signals is the

    A. cell body.
    B. synapse.
    C. axon.
    D. dendrite.

10. During the refractory period, a neuron

    A. will fire 1,000 times per second.
    B. does not fire because an electrochemical balance is being reestablished.
    C. transmits a relatively weak neural signal.
    D. generates a new spike discharge.

11. Whether a neurotransmitter acts in an excitatory or inhibitory way depends on

    A. the person's mood.
    B. its chemical structure.

C. where it is released.

D. the structure of the neuron that releases it.

12. When catching a ball, your hand knows when to grasp because

A. your parasympathetic nervous system is active.

B. alpha waves are being generated by your brain.

C. participating muscles receive efferent signals from the brain.

D. afferent signals inform your hand that the ball is about to make contact.

13. A portion of the brain that is very much responsible for ability to perceive and produce language is

A. the occipital lobe.

B. the parietal lobe.

C. Broca's area.

D. the central fissure.

14. The midbrain

A. either relays information to a more complex part of the brain or causes the body to respond at once.

B. is where the thalamus and hypothalamus can be found.

C. regulates complex behaviors such as eating, drinking, and sex.

D. has the sole function of transferring information from one cerebral hemisphere to the other.

15. Brain lateralization

A. is apparent at birth.

B. seems to occur sometime after the age of four.

C. occurs only in left-handed individuals.

D. increases a person's chances of having a learning disability.

16. The autonomic nervous system

A. generally deals with involuntary, internal conditions.

B. is considered a major subsystem of the central nervous system.

C. consists of both sensory and motor neurons, allowing it to respond to and act on the outside world.

D. all of the above

17. Biofeedback seems to be especially effective when used to treat

A. self-esteem problems.

B. schizophrenia.

C. stress-related symptoms.

D. memory problems.

18. Based on his theory that small processing units within and between each hemisphere perform specific "subprocesses," Allen has suggested that the term *hemispheric specialization*

A. is accurate.

B. may be too loose and an inaccurate description of how the brain works.

C. should be changed to *hemispheric sublimation.*

D. B and C

19. Which of the following describes the sequence of the first sleep cycle?

A. Stage 1, stage 2, stage 3, stage 4, REM

B. Stage 4, stage 3, stage 2, stage 1, REM

C. Stage 1, stage 2, REM, stage 3, stage 4

D. Stage 1, stage 2, stage 3, stage 4, stage 3, stage 2, REM

20. REM sleep

    A. occurs more frequently in infants than in adults.
    B. increases in amount the longer a person sleeps.
    C. may be very important since some research shows that dreaming is important to one's psychological well-being.
    D. all of the above

21. People can adapt to changes in their sleep–wakefulness regimen without having substantial behavior changes

    A. as long as they get an average of four hours of sleep per day.
    B. under almost any circumstances.
    C. as long as they have a fairly stable sleep regimen.
    D. none of the above; it is very difficult to change sleep–wakefulness

22. The content of young children's dreams tends to be more _____ than the content of adult dreams.

    A. action oriented
    B. abstract
    C. self-centered
    D. colorful

23. Based on research concerning memory, one of the most effective things you can do after checking your answers to this self-test and reviewing any questions you have missed is to fall asleep because

    A. sleep insulates new information from the interference of other information.
    B. REM sleep facilitates memory.
    C. studying is stressful and REM sleep is restful.
    D. it is your second best choice since playing a tape recording of the information while you are asleep would keep you awake.

5

Motivation and Emotion

5

Learning Objectives

When you have mastered the material in this chapter, you will be able to:

1. Define the terms *motivation, motive, need,* and *drive.* (p. 148)

2. Name and describe four theories of motivation and explain what is meant by a mechanistic analysis of behavior. (p. 148)

3. Identify some of the physiological and psychological causes of obesity and describe the hunger drive. (p. 150)

4. Using thirst, sex, and sensory stimulation as examples, explain why the exact causes of human motivation are sometimes difficult to determine. (p. 153)

5. Define *instincts* and *imprinting* and explain how they relate to human behavior. (p. 156)

6. Describe the Yerkes-Dodson law and optimal level of arousal theory. (p. 157)

7. Explain what happens when people are faced with competing goals or needs and list three criteria that can be used to predict how people will respond to conflict situations. (p. 157)

8. Define *social needs* and *social motives* and tell how they differ from physiological needs and motives. (p. 160)

9. Describe the behavior of people with high achievement needs and tell how they differ from people with low achievement needs. (p. 161)

10. Describe Type A and Type B personality styles and discuss the achievement needs of Type A personalities. (p. 163)

11. State a difference in how achievement and cognitive theories interpret behavior and discuss the significance of Lazarus and Alfert's study. (p. 164)

12. Define *intrinsic motivation* and explain how self-esteem affects intrinsically motivated behavior. (p. 166)

13. Contrast procrastination with motivated behavior and explain some of the consequences of procrastination. (p. 168)

14. Explain Abraham Maslow's theory of motivation and personality. (p. 169)

15. Define *emotion* and identify the aspects of emotion that are studied by psychologists. (p. 172)

16. Define *bonding* and discuss Klaus and Kennell's and Harlow's findings concerning the early environmental conditions that are necessary for healthy emotional development. (p. 173)

17. Identify some of the behavioral responses and physiological changes that accompany emotions and explain why facial expressions are not always accurate indicators of emotion. (p. 175)

18. Describe the electrodermal response and explain why the use of lie detector test results may not be valid. (p. 175)

19. Describe the cognitive self-regulation view of emotional expression. (p. 176)

20. Name and describe four subfields in psychology that are investigating the relationship between psychological processes and health. (p. 177)

21. Describe the James-Lange, Cannon, and Schachter-Singer theories of emotion. (p. 178)

22. Explain why it is unlikely that psychologists will find one simple explanation for how and why we experience emotional responses. (p. 180)

BEFORE YOU READ ON, take time to **SURVEY** the chapter, form an idea of what is to be learned (from margin Learning Objective numbers), and set goals for your study time. Then, ask yourself **QUESTIONS** about the material as you **READ,** seeking help for any sections you do not understand.

Beverly Stanton was married when she was eighteen, had a child when she was nineteen, and was divorced at age twenty. Now, at twenty-five, she is trying to survive. Her job as an advertising copywriter has flexible hours, and her boss gave her the job that usually goes to college graduates. Beverly is now completing her third year of college. Her life is difficult: she works during the day, goes to school at night, and plays with her child during the in-between times. She does not have much time for herself, or for friends, social causes, or fashion.

Beverly says she is just doing what she has to. Many of her friends and family, however, question her reasons. Her wealthy parents have volunteered to help her financially. She could go to school full-time and not work. She could live in a nicer apartment, have help with her daughter, and thus have some time to herself each week.

But Beverly Stanton is an individualist and she refuses help. Her mother argues that she is trying to prove something, her father calls her a fool, and her friends cannot figure out why she is wearing herself out. But Beverly vehemently argues that if she is to survive, she needs a sense of accomplishment and independence. She makes fun of the well-heeled ladies who would "do lunch," spend hours at the beauty salons, and complain about their tennis games. She has important things to do and is going to do them on her own with much hard work. Beverly does not have time to think about why she is so determined, nor does she have great psychological insight into "what makes Beverly run." She has the energy, drive, and skills to manage, and she does not really care from where she got her physical and psychological energy.

THE DRIVE AND DETERMINATION Beverly drew on were deep within her. She had always been single-minded and driven as a child. It should not have surprised her parents that she would carry the same approach to her adult life. Her

Sometimes our behavior appears to have no specific goal and it is difficult to assess the motivation behind it.

mother should have realized that she had been instrumental in teaching Beverly to be independent. As a child, Beverly had been encouraged to walk early, talk early, and ride a bicycle before other children. With her parents' encouragement, she was always the first one done with science fair projects. Why should her mother wonder why Beverly was so eager to do it her way, and independently?

The whys of peoples' behavior are not always easily understood, and the ability to look back into our childhood does not always yield a clear picture. People act as they do for many complex reasons. Sometimes their motivation is biological, at other times it is learned in childhood, and at other times behaviors are acquired as adults. An example of a behavior generated by a complex range of motives is eating. Eating has a biological base, is established from birth, and is practiced daily. We know why people eat, but what makes some people overeat? Is it a learned behavior? Can they unlearn it, or is twenty-five years of practice at overeating too much to overcome? In studying the whys of behavior, psychologists attempt to explain both the biological and learned factors, and the effect of years of experience that come into play in adult behavior.

MOTIVATION: AN OVERVIEW

Learning Objective 5.1

People often ask themselves why they did something—perhaps why they went out on Saturday night instead of studying. Sometimes they can answer the question by thinking about the internal conditions that prompted their behavior. But it is not so easy to assess the causes of behavior in other people; observation alone seldom provides an explanation. A person who is a compulsive eater must infer what is directing him or her toward food. **Motivation** is any general condition internal to an organism that appears (by inference) to produce goal-directed behavior. Motivation, or motivated behavior, may develop from physiological needs and drives or from more complex desires. Psychologists know that people are motivated; they also know that people are directed to specific goals by specific **motives.** For example, if you observe someone who has not eaten in a long time, you may see him eat quickly, in large bites, and with little conversation to his lunch partner. From his goal-directed behavior, you might logically infer that his fast eating had arisen due to a physiological imbalance. Most psychologists call a state of physiological imbalance a **need** state.

Motivation
An internal condition initiated by drives, needs, or desires and producing goal-directed behavior.

Motive
A specific internal condition directing an organism's behavior toward a goal.

Need
A physiological condition arising from an imbalance and usually accompanied by arousal.

Drive
An internal aroused condition that initiates behavior to satisfy physiological needs. Drives are inferred from behavior.

An organism that develops a need usually displays it in behavior. Psychologists describe an organism motivated by a need as being in a "drive state." A **drive** is an internal condition of arousal that directs an organism to satisfy physiological needs. Under conditions of drive, both animals and human beings will show goal-directed behavior. As seen in the example just mentioned, an organism that develops a need for food will usually seek out food. Other drives can also initiate and direct behavior; some of these drives, however, may be learned. People want to feel safe and confident. They may also want to feel that they have achieved something in life or that they are loved by their family and friends.

Learning Objective 5.2

In seeking the fundamental causes of people's behavior, psychologists have developed many theories of motivation. Some of the most influential and best-researched theories are forms of **drive theory.** Drive theories have been used to explain many behaviors, but all assume that an organism is motivated to act because of a need to reestablish balance or attain or maintain some goal.

Drive theory ══════
An explanation of behavior that emphasizes internal factors that energize organisms to seek, attain, or maintain some goal. Often the goal is to reestablish a state of physiological balance.

Expectancy theory ══════
An explanation of behavior that emphasizes a person's expectation of success and need for achievement as the energizing factors.

Cognitive theory ══════
An explanation of behavior that emphasizes the role of thought and individual choice regarding life goals and the means of achieving them.

Humanistic theory ══════
An explanation of behavior that emphasizes the role of human qualities, such as dignity, individual choice, self-concept, and self-achievement.

Self-actualization ══════
The process of realizing one's uniquely human potential for good; the process of achieving everything that one is capable of achieving.

Because physiological drives determine behavior in very direct ways, we say they are mechanistic; a mechanistic analysis of behavior views the organism as being pushed, pulled, and energized almost like a machine. Stimuli such as hunger pangs create, energize, and initiate behavior. A hungry organism deprived of food for twenty-four hours spends most of its time looking for food; it is driven to seek food.

Another major class of motivation theory is **expectancy theory.** These theories suggest that a person's expectation of success and the value he or she places on success direct behavior. The most notable expectancy theories are those focusing on achievement. According to achievement theories, people engage in behaviors that satisfy their desires for success, mastery, and fulfillment. Expectancy theory would probably help explain Beverly Stanton's need to do things on her own. Tasks not oriented toward these goals are not motivating and are either not engaged in or are undertaken with a lack of energy and commitment. Clearly, expectancy theories move away from biologically based drive theories and focus on acquired or *learned* social drives.

Another theory of motivation, **cognitive theory,** asserts that people are actively and regularly involved in deciding what their goals are and how they will achieve them. Cognitive theory emphasizes the role of decision making in all areas of life. For example, people decide how they will react to an insult. They decide how emotional they will become at the loss of a friend. They decide how involved they will become with a new weight-loss program. Even more than expectancy theory, cognitive theory focuses on thoughts as initiators and determiners of behavior.

Finally, **humanistic theory** asserts that people's behavior is motivated by desires for creativity, choice, and **self-actualization.** Humanistic psychologists focus both on the dignity of individual choice and freedom and on the individual's feelings of self-worth. Humanistic theory emphasizes the "entirety of life" rather than the components of behavior. Its adherents insist that individuals' behavior must be viewed within the framework of their environment and values.

Regardless of their view of motivation, most psychologists assume that a combination of motivation and learning causes people to behave in certain ways. For most behaviors, even those motivated by basic needs, some learning is necessary for behavior to occur. Behavior is thus often thought of as the product of learning and motivation. Without motivation, it is likely that there would be no behavior. But even if there is motivation, without some knowledge about how to do things, there will be little behavior. Some of our theories consider learning more important to motivation than do others. No one theory is adequate to explain all behavior. This chapter looks closely at the major theories. The first theories considered focus more on biological needs and deemphasize learning and thought. The later theories progress away from the mechanistic views to more cognitive and humanistic views of behavior.

PHYSIOLOGICAL NEEDS: DRIVE REDUCTION

From what you know about Beverly Stanton, do you think she would be likely to have a weight problem? People who are extremely busy with their lives, who are tied into a tight schedule, and who have a great deal of purpose may be motivated to overeat. You might reason that people who are as busy as Beverly might eat junk food that lacks nutrition. You might logically assume that such a busy person eats on-the-run and more often than she needs to. On the other hand, you might argue that a determined person like Beverly would not allow herself to become fat; you might think she was too busy to eat and too goal-directed to let eating slow her down. Beverly Stanton is no more or less prone to obesity than any one of us. She has factors in her life that might lead to overeating, but she has other factors that may lead her to undereating.

The causes of eating are not as simple as you might think. People eat because they are hungry. They also eat for other reasons. In examining the whys of behavior, psychologists have sought to understand as simple a behavior as eating and why we do it when we do it. Eating, drinking, obesity, and eating disorders are all part of the study of motivation. Let's take a closer look at hunger and its origins.

Causes of Obesity

Learning Objective 5.3

Many people in western society are significantly overweight. A majority are 10 or 20 pounds overweight, but an increasing percentage are 30, 50, and 100 pounds overweight. The simple cause of obesity is obvious: People consume more energy than they expend. However, the causes of obesity are usually more complex than a simple analysis suggests. Usually, obese people overeat for both physiological and psychological reasons. For many obese people, eating not only decreases hunger pangs, but also becomes a primary source of pleasure.

One principal physiological cause of hunger is the low blood-sugar level that accompanies food deprivation, creating a chemical imbalance. Because sugar is crucial to cellular activity, the body sends signals to the brain warning of a low blood-sugar level, and the brain immediately responds by generating hunger pangs in the stomach. Experiments with animals whose nerves between the stomach and brain have been severed show that the animals continue to eat at appropriate times—that is, when their blood sugar is low. The amount of food human beings eat does not alone determine how hungry they feel. A hungry adult who eats for five minutes may still feel hungry when he or she stops eating. The type of food eaten determines, in part, how soon the feeling of hunger disappears. A candy bar loaded with easily converted sugar will take away hunger faster than foods high in protein, such as meat, cheese, and milk, because it takes more time to digest and convert complex protein into sugar.

Much of psychologists' understanding of hunger and eating behavior comes from studies of the brain, particularly the region of the forebrain called the hypothalamus (see p. 120). Complex experiments have shown that two distinct areas there are involved in eating behavior. Using weak electrical currents, researchers have stimulated the lateral and ventromedial hypothalamus in animals. Stimulation of the lateral hypothalamus causes the animals to start eating, and stimulation of the ventromedial hypothalamus causes them to stop, *regardless* of their blood-sugar level or the extent of food deprivation (Ball, 1972; Peters, Luttmers, Gunion, & Wellman, 1978). These results indicate that the ventromedial hypothalamus is a "stop eating" center: When the stomach becomes full and/or when the blood-sugar level is high, the ventromedial hypothalamus is activated and the organism stops eating. When the lateral hypothalamus, the "start eating" center, is activated, the organism starts eating. Other researchers have found that the ventromedial hypothalamus may influ-

Rats with surgical damage to the ventromedial hypothalamus will overeat and become extremely obese.

ence eating indirectly, via the hormonal and metabolic systems (Kent & Peters, 1973; Powley, 1977).

Studies since the 1950s and 1960s indicate other areas of the brain and other processes may also be involved in eating behaviors (Alheid et al., 1977; Grossman & Grossman, 1977). For example, people of normal weight take in just about the right amount of food each day to maintain their weight even though most people vary the amount and type of food they eat from day to day. As little as one extra candy bar a day would, at the end of a year, produce approximately eighteen pounds of fat!

A Physiological Explanation.   Richard Nisbett (1972), a psychologist at the University of Michigan, has proposed that the number of fat cells people are born with, which differ with each person, determine their eating behavior. Thus, two people of equal height and body frame but with different numbers of fat cells will not have the same "normal" weight. In other words, some people are genetically programmed to be fat (Keesey, 1980). (As you will learn, however, the social environment also plays an important role.)

Body fat is stored in fat cells, and studies have found that some obese people have three times as many fat cells as normal-weight people. The number of fat cells is genetically determined, but the size is also affected by nutritional experience early in life. People who are born with many fat cells are more likely to be obese than are people born with few fat cells, for two reasons. One is that dieting decreases only the *size,* but not the *number,* of their fat cells. Second, because the body tends to maintain the size of fat cells at a constant level, people who have shrunk the normal size of their fat cells by dieting will experience a constant state of food deprivation. With each significant weight gain, the person may be adding new fat cells. A diet may bring about weight loss, but the person never reduces the number of fat cells. Thus, permanent weight loss becomes extremely difficult. Nisbett argues that many people who are perceived as being overweight may actually be underweight relative to their bodies' ideal weights. This physiological explanation of eating behavior and obesity is compelling because many formerly obese people readily admit that they constantly battle to maintain their lower weight (Brownell, 1982).

Other physiological theories of obesity also abound (Keesey, 1980). Some theories incorporate fat cell theory, others focus on genetics. Some show that the prenatal period contributes to whether a person will be obese (Burdi et al. 1985); and others focus on dietary habits throughout life (E. M. Berry et al. 1986). All of these explanations may play a role. As Stunkard (1980) has suggested, however, the social environment in which a person lives and works strongly influences the development and maintenance of obesity. For this reason, psychological explanations of obesity have had a profound impact on researchers' thinking.

A Psychological Explanation. According to psychologist Stanley Schachter of Columbia University (1971), human beings eat for reasons other than hunger. In a series of experiments, Schachter has shown that obese adults tend to eat not only when they are hungry but also whenever food is present. They also tend to eat if time has passed since they last ate, regardless of whether they are hungry. Whereas subjects of normal weight might eat 50 percent of the time that food is presented, obese subjects nearly always eat food when it is offered (see also Herman & Polivy, 1975).

Psychologists at Work: Understanding Bulimia

Judith Rodin is a psychologist who has a great interest in eating, obesity, and eating disorders. She is one of a large group of psychologists facing a new kind of patient and disorder and seeking causes and cures. The perplexing disorder is Bulimia Nervosa, often called Bulimia, in which a person (usually a woman) experiences compulsive urges to eat enormous quantities of food. This eating binge is then followed by episodes of purging the body of the excess, unwanted calories. Methods of purging include vomiting, laxatives, diuretics, compulsive exercising, and weight-reduction drugs (see Muuss, 1985).

What motivates people to get involved in the binge–purge cycle of Bulimia? Why would a thin person eat excessively, throw up, and then engage in the same behavior again? In their comprehensive review of Bulimia, Rodin and two other researchers from Yale University delineated three important questions around which some answers appear (Striegel-Moore, Silberstein, & Rodin, 1986): Why is Bulimia a woman's problem? Why are weight control and dieting so exceedingly pervasive, especially among women? Why is the disorder so prevalent now?

Is Bulimia a woman's problem? Bulimia is generally considered a woman's problem because the ratio of female to male Bulimics is 10:1; that is, 90 percent of all Bulimics are women. Researchers theorize that women (more than men) have accepted the ideas that fat is bad and thin is beautiful. Women who accept this view are at greater risk for Bulimia because they feel if they did not purge, they would get fat. Women of higher socioeconomic classes are at greater risk, as are members of groups in which weight coupled with high standards for achievement is of a key concern—for example, dancers, athletes, and models. The data also show that Bulimic women have disturbed views of thinness and body image (for example, see Williamson et al. 1985). Along with a low self-esteem and a high need for achievement, Bulimic women often involve themselves in the binge–purge cycle to maintain control over their bodies.

Why are women so concerned with weight control? Psychologists see a developmental progression in which women foster attitudes that put them at risk for Bulimia. In our society, girls as children learn that appearance is central to pursuing overall attractiveness; they also are often taught that pursuing attractiveness can be a full-time activity. Early developing girls are often unhappy with their weight; they, too, are more likely to develop Bulimia.

Bulimia does not appear in children, but groundwork for its later appearance seems to be laid there and is fostered in adolescence. As a pubescent girl's body changes, she often becomes self-conscious about being liked and seeks to avoid negative reactions. In adulthood, self-concept continues to emerge as the importance of body image is continuously reaffirmed for many women. Women often have an ideal body image to which they aspire (Fallon & Rodin, 1985). Older adult women also continue to be especially aware of their appearance.

Bulimia also may have a genetic component. Some women may have a genetic predisposition to obesity, and some women may have a harder time losing weight than others. Family interactions, including preoccupations with dieting, may also play role in Bulimia. As Striegel-Moore, Silberstein, and Rodin observe, "women's battle with weight . . . lasts a lifetime" (1986, 252).

A big question for the three Yale researchers is Why is Bulimia so prevalent now? Bulimia was first formally recognized as a disorder in 1980; with its introduction, attention was called to it. In addition, there has been a shift toward an increasingly "thin" standard in western society. Further, the mass media focuses on dieting, fitness, and the pursuit of "the" look.

What are the causes of Bulimia? At present, there is no single answer. However, our society's preoccupation with thinness, with idealizing a certain look, and with an emphasis on femininity from a thin vantage point, and possibly genetics are all obvious elements that put many women at risk. We see in Chapter 14 that Bulimia Nervosa is only one of several eating disorders, the whys of which researchers are still exploring.

Research in bulimia is difficult to conduct because the disorder often presents itself only when an individual has become extremely sick, dehydrated, and malnourished. On her way to becoming ill, friends and relatives often unwittingly encourage the thin look of the Bulimic patient. Psychologists and physicians usually attempt to find the antecedents of the disorder after the fact. This makes untangling the knot of the binge–purge cycle difficult.

Because people often distort their behavior when told they are being watched by a scientist, Stanley Schachter disguised the true purpose of his experiments when he investigated the eating patterns of obese people. In one such study, Schachter and his fellow researchers told obese and normal-weight subjects that they were investigating accuracy of taste. When some of the subjects arrived, they were given roast beef sandwiches, then seated in front of bowls of crackers and presented with rating scales. They were told to eat as

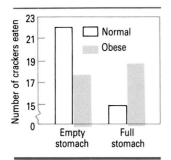

FIGURE 5.1 : In an experiment involving normal-weight and obese subjects, normal-weight subjects ate fewer crackers when their stomachs were full, whereas the obese subjects ate *more* when their stomachs were full.

many of the crackers as necessary to judge whether each cracker was salty, cheesy, or garlicky. The real object of the experiment was to see how many crackers the subjects ate in making their judgments. As Figure 5.1 shows, the normal-weight subjects ate far fewer crackers than they would have if they had not been full from the roast beef sandwiches. In contrast, the obese subjects ate even more than they would have if they had not eaten. The experimenters concluded that the eating behavior of the obese subjects had little to do with the actual state of their stomachs but was determined principally by external factors (Schachter, Goldman, & Gordon, 1968).

What people will eat depends in part on what they have just eaten. It also depends on the general type of eater they are. People who are constant dieters tend to respond differently to food than do nondieters; other factors, such as what they ate earlier in the day, may affect both groups in their later eating behaviors. Thoughts and expectations about later meals affect people differently. Obese eaters tend to have more trouble modifying their eating behavior than do the nonobese, but this is not always the case (Tomarken & Kirchenbaum, 1984).

Little doubt exists that both internal physiological cues and externally learned cues motivate people to seek food. Researchers continue to explore contending claims and possibilities; but whatever the ultimate explanation proves to be, the fact remains that obese people seem to respond to food differently from normal-weight people (Rodin, 1979), particularly in their ability to control themselves when attempting to watch what they eat (Ruderman, 1986).

Other Needs: Thirst, Sex, and Sensory Stimulation

Learning Objective 5.4

People face many types of physiological needs in addition to hunger. One primary physiological need is for water and other fluids. Like hunger, thirst serves a strong drive mechanism in both animals and human beings. But although people can live for weeks without eating, they can live only a few days without replenishing their supply of fluid. A delicate balance of fluid intake is necessary for proper physiological functioning; any imbalance is reflected in a drive to restore the balance. When people experience fluid deprivation, their mouths and throats become dry, cueing them to drink. As with eating, drinking activates receptors in the mouth and throat that signal to the hypothalamus that fluid has been consumed, and people decrease their intake of fluid and resume their normal activities.

Sexual drive as an initiator of behavior in human beings is no longer considered solely or even primarily under physiological control, but to a much greater extent under voluntary control. In contrast, the sexual behavior of lower organisms is controlled largely by their physiological and hormonal systems. (See Chapter 4 for a review of hormones.) If the hormone-generating testes of male rats are removed, the animals show a marked decrease in sexual activity. In human beings (depending on the age at removal), removal of hormone-generating organs may not affect sexual behavior at all. Similarly, most female lower organisms are sexually responsive only when hormones are released into the bloodstream (Beach, 1983). Human beings, and some other primates, on the other hand, can choose whether to respond sexually to encounters at any given time (Hoon, Bruce, & Kinchloe, 1982). Chapter 11 discusses human sexual behavior in more detail.

Learning, cultural influence, and early experience play a greater role in humans' sexual behavior than does physiological drive.

Generally, the higher the organism on the phylogenetic ladder, the more important early sexual experience is to normal sexual behavior later in life. In rats, for example, previous experience is not necessary, but if dogs, cats, and monkeys are isolated from sexual experiences early in life, they later show a lack of sexual responsiveness. Experience and learning play an even greater role in human sexual response. As you will see in Chapter 7, human beings learn about sexual behavior from peers, parents, and the media. In most cultures, the very young are initiated slowly to sexual knowledge and experience. Sexual experiences among adults, however, show great cultural variations. Some cultures initiate sexual activity at adolescence and encourage it throughout life. More restrictive societies inhibit sexual activity until marriage and expect it to diminish with old age. Because human beings have great freedom of choice in their sexual responses, their sexual behavior is varied and subject to change. In western society, many formerly taboo topics, attitudes, and behaviors are accepted and discussed widely today. As attitudes change, so does behavior. Chapter 10 on social psychology discusses further the crucial role attitudes play in determining our day-to-day behavior.

In studying motivation, psychologists seek explanations of both physiological and learned aspects of behavior. Clearly, in most people, behaviors associated with hunger and thirst are physiologically initiated. Other behaviors such as sexual behavior are responsive to hormonal control, cognitive control, and learned behavior. Still more complex are the needs people develop for sensory stimulation and for love and affection. When deprived of a normal amount of visual, auditory, or tactile stimulation, adults may become irritable and consider their situation or environment intolerable. Lack of sensory experience does not result in physiological imbalance, yet both human beings and animals seek sensory stimulation. Kittens like to explore their environment, and young monkeys will investigate mechanica devices and play with puzzles. Indeed, studies have shown that monkeys will work in order to play with puzzles and manipulate locks. Animals and human beings alike appear to have an innate desire to explore, manipulate, and experience the world. (Sensory stimulation is discussed in more detail in Chapter 6.)

PROGRESS CHECK 5.1

1. Match each of the following theories of motivation with the appropriate description.

drive theory   cognitive theory   expectancy theory
humanistic theory

Learning Objective 5.2   A. _____ Behavior is motivated by thinking, decision making, and choice.

Learning Objective 5.2   B. _____ Internal conditions energize people and animals to seek, attain, and maintain a goal and to reestablish a physiological state of balance.

Learning Objective 5.2   C. _____ Individuals are motivated by the desire to achieve everything they are capable of achieving.

Learning Objective 5.2   D. _____ The value a person places on success, mastery, and fulfillment determines the individual's level of motivation for certain behaviors.

2. Complete each of the following sentences with one of the options provided.

Learning Objective 5.1   A. A _____ is a physiological condition that is usually accompanied by arousal and that is the result of a physiological imbalance.
(drive : need)

Learning Objective 5.2   B. A _____ analysis of behavior views the organism as being pushed, pulled, and energized by internal and external forces.
(cognitive : mechanistic)

Learning Objective 5.2   C. _____ theory emphasizes the entirety of life.
(Expectancy : Humanistic)

Learning Objective 5.3   D. Hunger pangs occur because _____ .
(the stomach is empty : the brain detects low blood-sugar)

Learning Objective 5.3   E. The _____ of food we eat determines how soon the feeling of hunger disappears.
(amount : type : amount and type)

Learning Objective 5.3   F. When the stomach is full and/or when the blood-sugar level is high, the _____ hypothalamus is activated and the organism stops eating.
(ventromedial : lateral)

Learning Objective 5.3   G. Dieting decreases the _____ of fat cells.
(size : number)

Learning Objective 5.3   H. According to Schachter, obese people eat primarily because _____ .
(they are hungry : of a variety of external factors)

Learning Objective 5.4   I. In human beings, the sex drive is primarily under _____ control.
(physiological : voluntary)

Learning Objective 5.4   J. Both human beings and animals seek sensory stimulation _____ _____ by a physiological imbalance.
(even though it is not caused : because they are motivated)

Konrad Lorenz's research with ducklings led to the understanding of imprinting behavior in animals.

Instincts as a Need?

Learning Objective $\overline{\underline{5.5}}$

Instincts ════
Inherited, inborn, unlearned, predetermined behavior patterns.

Imprinting ════
The process by which animals form species-specific behaviors during a critical period early in life. These behaviors are not easily modified.

Early researchers considered **instincts,** or inborn unlearned behavior patterns, to be the prime motivators for all organisms. This view stressed heredity, genetics, and predetermined behavior patterns. Early in this century, however, the instinct explanation was abandoned in favor of learning theories, at least for human behavior. Today, most psychologists believe that human beings have few or perhaps no instincts.

Instinctive behavior is more apparent in animals than in human beings. One example is **imprinting,** the process by which a behavior pattern specific to one species is established in a member of that species through exposure to appropriate stimuli during a critical period early in life. Early research showed that ducks (and other species), if imprinted with a moving object other than their mother during the critical period, would follow that object as if it were their mother. Such behavior is clearly biologically determined and instinctive. To date, however, no such process has been shown conclusively to exist in human beings. The best evidence to suggest a biologically determined instinct such as imprinting in human beings comes from studies by Klaus and Kennell (1983), discussed in Chapter 7. These researchers suggest that such behaviors as the desire for love have their origin in a sensitive period in the first few minutes of an infant's life. They vigorously assert that every parent and infant should be given at least thirty to sixty minutes of early contact, in private, in order to enhance the process of bonding. They claim that these and other early experiences determine a person's later ability to feel and express warmth and affection.

The idea that there exist certain key or important periods or stages in a child's life is accepted widely by many psychologists. You see later in Chapter 7 that stage theories of development are very prominent in contemporary formulations of how human beings mature. A fundamental idea of these stage theories is that certain important developmental landmarks regularly occur at certain ages in all people.

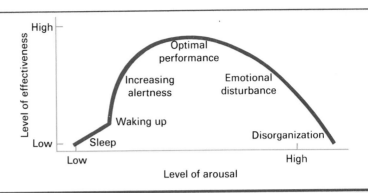

FIGURE 5.2 : In accordance with contemporary interpretations of the Yerkes-Dodson law, increases in motivation and arousal often bring increases in emotional feelings. Most important, according to Hebb, these increases in arousal change the effectiveness of a person's behavior.

How Does Arousal Affect Your Drive States?

Learning Objective 5.6

All of us have at some time experienced the vague discomfort that accompanies fear of the unknown or fear of failure. Clinical psychologists refer to those feelings as anxiety. In 1908, R. M. Yerkes and J. D. Dodson described a relationship (called the Yerkes-Dodson law) between avoidance learning and task difficulty in mice. This relationship was extended by contemporary researchers to suggest that when a person's anxiety and level of arousal are too high or too low, performance will be poor. For easy tasks, optimum performance occurs at higher levels of arousal (Bregman & McAllister, 1982). Thus, people who do not care about what they are doing have little anxiety but also usually perform poorly in both work and play. People who show moderate anxiety (and its accompanying arousal) tend to produce and do best.

Many traditional motivation and learning theorists have assumed that an increase in drive (and an associated arousal level) will result in increased effectiveness of behavior. Later, researchers suggested that drive and ability will predict behavior. According to this simple formulation, as an organism's drive level increases, its performance will improve: the hungrier the rat, the faster it will run down the alley to its food. Researchers who explain motivation in terms of an optimal level of arousal theory assume that individuals seek an optimal level of arousal. Thus, behavior varies from disorganized to effective, depending on a person's level of arousal. The inverted U-shaped curve in Figure 5.2 shows the relationship between level of arousal and effectiveness of behavior.

Fundamental to all arousal theories is the notion that it is not the stimulus but the organism's internal response to the stimulus that determines how an organism behaves. Optimal arousal theory as described by many psychologists is still a mechanistic drive theory: Arousal energizes behavior but does not direct it. An organism's performance is related to its state of receptiveness to the stimulus. However, by locating the cause of behavior in the internal responses of an organism, optimal arousal theory anticipated the development of more cognitive theories.

What Happens When You Have Competing Needs?

Learning Objective 5.7

When Jessica Coopersmith was offered a teaching position at a small Midwestern college, she was pleased. When the following day brought an offer of a lucrative job as a systems analyst in industry, she was undecided what to do.

Both jobs were desirable. The teaching job would give her a flexible schedule for meeting the needs of her family, but it required moving, and the salary was low. The job in industry would give her a chance both to use her skills as a programmer and to make a lot of money, but she would have to commute and her schedule would be much less flexible. She also would be subject to the pressures of corporate politics. At this point, Jessica had conflicting and competing goals (between time and money); whatever her choice, she probably could not satisfy both.

Jessica was facing a real-life problem, one similar to those you are likely to face from time to time. What happens when your goals and needs conflict—for example, if you must choose between two equally desirable jobs or two equally difficult courses? Over the years, psychologists have tried to describe and quantify such conflict situations. One of the first to do this was Neal Miller (1944, 1959). Miller developed some hypotheses about how animals and human beings behave in situations that have both positive and negative aspects. For example, if a hungry rat must run down an electrified alley to get food, its activity has both positive and negative aspects. Similarly, hungry human beings may seek out junk food yet want to avoid its calories.

Let us look at three types of situations involving competing demands. **Approach-approach conflicts** arise when a person must choose one of two equally pleasant goals or choices, such as two desserts or two movies. This conflict generates discomfort, but usually people can tolerate the conflict because either alternative is pleasant. An **avoidance-avoidance conflict** occurs when a choice involves two equally distasteful goals or choices, such as mowing the lawn or painting the garage. Perhaps the most discomfort, however, arises from an **approach-avoidance conflict,** when a particular situation has both appealing and repellant aspects. Studying for an exam is an approach-avoidance situation. Studying can lead to good grades but it can also be both boring and difficult. A student both approaches and avoids this goal by deciding whether or not (or how hard) to study. Miller would characterize Jessica's real-life problem as a *double approach-avoidance conflict*—both job offers had appealing and negative consequences associated with them.

Miller developed a series of descriptions to predict behavior in conflict situations, particularly in approach-avoidance situations. For example, (1) the closer a subject is to a goal (such as dessert), the stronger the tendency is to

Approach-approach conflict ══════
The result of having to choose between two equally attractive alternatives or goals.

Avoidance-avoidance conflicts ══════
The result of having to choose between two equally distasteful or negative alternatives or goals.

Approach-avoidance conflict ══════
The result of having to choose a goal that has both attractive and repellent aspects.

Approach-approach conflict   Avoidance-avoidance conflict   Approach-avoidance conflict

Decisions, decisions, decisions . . .

approach the goal; (2) when two incompatible responses are available, the stronger one will be expressed; (3) the strength of the tendency to approach or avoid is correlated with the strength of the motivating drive (thus, a child who is both hungry and thirsty will seek food if she is more hungry than thirsty). Later studies of approach-avoidance conflicts have yielded data that support Miller's descriptions (for example, Mehrabian, 1980; Murray & Berkun, 1955). Miller's formulations have been used successfully in predicting animal behavior and many human behaviors.

What if you were taking part in an experiment in which you had to endure a painful stimulus but you were being paid for your efforts? How much pain would you take? Money was offered to students to endure muscle pain—the longer they endured the pain, the more money they received. In this study by Cabanac (1986), a French researcher, students were placed in a sitting position against a wall but without a seat. This position is uncomfortable at first and painful after twenty seconds or more. The subjects were informed that for each twenty-second interval that they could stay in the position, they would be given a certain number of French francs. They participated in the study for six days; on each day, they received a different number of francs for the twenty-second intervals. Cabanac found that the more money he offered, the longer his student volunteers were willing to remain in the painful seated position. This experiment is an approach-avoidance situation wherein money and pain are offered together. As Cabanac suggested, "the subjects terminated the sessions when the discomfort associated with the pain exceeded the effect of the monetary reward . . . " (1986, 43). This experimental situation closely mirrors some work situations in which a person's boredom is overcome only by his or her quest for cash.

Much evidence indicates that people are placed in conflict situations regularly. Coping with competing needs can produce serious conflicts. In such situations, people may become anxious and upset. If people's conflicts affect their day-to-day behavior, they may exhibit symptoms of maladjustment. (Chapter 13 discusses how anxiety can affect a person's ability to cope with the world.)

Summary

Any physiological imbalance impels an organism to act to restore a balance. But if physiological drives alone could account for human behavior, everyone would behave in exactly the same way. Responses such as hunger and thirst

TABLE 5.1 Drive Theories of Motivation

Theory	Theorist	Principally Explains	Key Idea	View of Behavior
Drive	Nisbett	Obesity	Number of fat cells determines obesity.	Mechanistic: obesity is biologically determined.
	Schachter	Hunger and obesity	External cues energize eating behavior.	Partially mechanistic but recognizes the role of learning.

are also affected by people's learned experiences with eating and drinking. People initially eat and drink in order to live. When they learn that eating and drinking are pleasurable, problems such as obesity may result. The development of optimal arousal theories has helped psychologists explain the variety in people's responses to situations in terms of a state of internal receptivity, rather than solely in terms of the stimuli encountered. (see Table 5.1.) This shift in emphasis marked a subtle but important transition from solely mechanistic drive-reduction theory toward learning and more cognitive theories. The next section discusses learned motives.

PROGRESS CHECK 5.2

1. Complete each of the following sentences with one of the options provided.

Learning Objective 5.5

A. _____ is defined as a particular behavior pattern specific to one species that is established in a member of that species through exposure to appropriate stimuli during a critical period early in life.
(An instinct : Imprinting)

Learning Objective 5.5

B. Evidence for a biologically determined instinct such as imprinting in human beings is _____ .
(inconclusive : provided by a number of studies)

Learning Objective 5.6

C. According to the Yerkes-Dodson law, people will produce and show their best performance when they are experiencing _____ levels of anxiety.
(low : moderate : high)

Learning Objective 5.6

D. Arousal theories suggest that an organism's behavior is determined by _____ .
(a stimulus : its internal response to a stimulus)

Learning Objective 5.6

E. Optimal arousal theory is a(n) _____ theory.
(cognitive : expectancy : mechanistic)

Learning Objective 5.7

F. Approach-approach, avoidance-avoidance, and approach-avoidance conflicts arise when a person _____ .
(has competing needs or goals : imprints on inappropriate stimuli)

Learning Objective 5.7

G. According to Miller, when two incompatible responses are available, the _____ one will be expressed.
(easier : stronger : most appropriate)

LEARNED MOTIVES: EXPECTANCY THEORY

Learning Objective 5.8

Beverly Stanton, who opened this chapter, did not have a physiological drive that impelled her to action. She had something inside her that drove her—she expected to succeed and to do it on her own. Expectancy theory focuses on people's needs for achievement and success; the theory suggests that people's expectations for success direct their behavior. A key element of expectancy theory is that a person's thoughts and perceptions of the world guide behavior. The social motives and needs a person develops are not physiological in origin; they are not initiated because of some physiological imbalance. Rather, a person learns through personal interactions in the environment to have needs for mastery and/or affiliation, or to be competitive. These needs lead to expectations about the future and about how various efforts will lead to various outcomes.

Beverly Stanton was energetic and determined. She was going to run her life her way, without help. What makes a person like Beverly so goal-directed? A physiological drive state does not motivate her. In the same way, many people are goal-directed to be runners. You may be a jogger yourself. What makes people run around a track for hours each day? Psychologists want to know what urges them on; why, for some people, is jogging a passion? The idea of running five or ten miles through city streets raises many people's hopes, lifts their spirits, and encourages them to complete their work so that they can run before dark. Some avid runners often put themselves through long, physically punishing training in order to compete successfully in a marathon, jogging or running twenty-six miles. Such individuals develop motives to run. Unlike a drive, which has a physiological origin, a motive does not have to have a physiological explanation. A **motive** is a specific internal condition that usually involves some form of arousal directing or impelling a person (or animal) toward a goal. When people are motivated to seek help, to run the mile, or to "do it their way," they are driven, impelled, or aroused to reach some end.

Let us consider a group of motives that are distinctly not physiological. For example, **social motives** are internal conditions that direct people to establish and maintain relationships with other people and to establish feelings about themselves and others. These social motives emerge from a gradual convergence of learned social needs. Earlier, a need was defined as an aroused physiological condition involving imbalance; *social* needs do not involve physiological imbalance. A **social need** is an aroused condition involving feelings about self, others, and relationships. People have social needs for order, achievement, and nurturance. Social needs for affiliation lead people to seek friends, to desire approval, to do favors for others, and to participate in activities that will create friendly relations. Some researchers claim that people also have social needs for aggression, which are fulfilled when they fight, belittle, or curse. These needs for achievement, affiliation, and good feelings about one's self are affected by many factors, including socioeconomic status and race (Littig & Williams, 1978) and experiences from birth onward. Klaus and Kennell (1983) have cited data on the failure of newborns to thrive both physiologically and socially when separated from their mothers at birth. These data suggest that lifelong patterns of behavior, including social needs and motives, may be established very early in life.

Conquering the World: The Social Need for Mastery and Achievement

Motive
A specific internal condition directing an organism's behavior toward a goal.

Social motive
An internal condition directing a person to establish and maintain relationships with other people and to establish feelings about themselves.

Social need
An aroused condition involving feelings about self, others, and relationships.

Learning Objective 5.9

Need for achievement
A social need that directs a person to strive constantly for excellence and success.

Beverly Stanton had a strong need to run her own life, to make her own way. She had developed this sense of purpose early in her life, and it continued to provide her motivation and determination. You might say that Beverly had an exceedingly strong need for achievement. Most psychologists agree that people's need for achievement gives rise to some of the strongest social motives. The **need for achievement** causes people to strive for bigger and better accomplishments.

Even a casual observation of behavior reveals that some people are driven by ambition and the need to get ahead in life. Research indicates that achievement motivation is learned, and that a person's home environment during childhood is important in establishing these needs. Adults with high needs for achievement generally walked early, talked early, had high needs for achievement even on entering grammar school, and had parents who stressed excellence and provided physical affection and emotional rewards in the form of praise for high achievement (see, for example, Teevan & McGhee, 1972). High achievement needs are most pronounced in firstborn children, perhaps because parents typically have more time to give them direction and praise.

Early studies of people's need for achievement used the Thematic Apperception Test, or TAT. In the TAT, subjects are shown pictures with no captions and with vague themes. Thus, the scenes are open to interpretation (see Figure 5.3). Subjects are instructed not to think in terms of right or wrong answers, but to answer four basic questions for each picture:

What is happening?
What has led up to this situation?
What is being thought?
What will happen?

Using a complex scoring system, researchers analyze subjects' descriptions of each scene. Subjects with high needs for achievement often tell stories that stress success, getting ahead, and competition.

High-achievement and low-achievement subjects perform differently in many ways. For example, Lowell (1952) asked subjects to rearrange groups of scrambled letters (such as *wtse*) to construct a meaningful word (such as *west*). Subjects with low need for achievement did not improve much over successive testing periods. In contrast, subjects who scored high in need for achievement showed regular improvement in performance over several periods of testing. When presented with a complex task, subjects with high needs for achievement find new and better ways of performing the task as they practice it, whereas subjects with low needs for achievement try no new methods. High-

FIGURE 5.3 : An item from the Thematic Apperception Test. (From Murry, H. A. *Thematic Apperception Test.* Cambridge, Mass.: Harvard University Press. Copyright 1943 by the President and Fellows of Harvard College, copyright 1971 by H. A. Murray.)

need achievers are constantly striving toward excellence and better performance (Atkinson, 1964; McClelland, 1961, 1975; McClelland, Atkinson, Clark, & Lowell, 1953).

Personality Factors: The Type A Personality

Learning Objective 5.10

Personality studies (discussed in Chapter 12) have provided a wealth of information about why people behave the way they do and especially about how individuals approach other people, problems, and life in general. But the role of personality in motivation is complex, and no single theory has proved adequate to explain it. Two physicians, Friedman and Rosenman (1974), proposed classifying people according to two distinct personality styles or behavior patterns that can be used to predict the likelihood of their suffering a heart attack. They designated people who have a great sense of urgency about all things, are impatient, aggressive, easily aroused to anger, and extremely achievement oriented as Type A, and all other people as Type B. Their purpose was to help Type A individuals, who are at greater risk for heart attacks, become Type B people (Kahn et al. 1982)

Research has confirmed that there are differences between Type A and Type B individuals, although not everyone fits neatly into either category (for example, Glass, 1977; Lovallo & Pishkin, 1980). In the presence of other people, Type A people become more competitive and achieve more, whereas Type B people show only small changes in performance (Gastorf, Suls, & Sanders, 1980). When challenged, Type A individuals show more physiological arousal than do Type B individuals (Dembroski, McDougall, & Shields, 1977). Type A individuals are more likely to compare themselves with other people (Dembroski & McDougall, 1978) and to exhibit an exaggerated need for achievement (Burnam, Pennebaker, & Glass, 1975). This heightened need for achievement is an important characteristic of people who exhibit Type A coronary-prone behavior. It is possible that early needs to achieve may develop into a general behavior pattern that puts these people at risk for serious heart disease.

The development of a Type A behavior pattern can probably be traced to childhood relationships with parents and peers. From the existence of such behavior patterns, psychologists can infer a great deal about individuals' motivations and how they will respond to various situations. For example, Type A people have an intense desire to control their environment (Carver & Glass, 1978) and become irritated when others slow down their rapid pace (Glass, Snyder, & Hollis, 1974). Strong emotional reactions are typical among Type A individuals (see DeGregorio & Carver, 1980). Furthermore, Type A individuals find it very difficult to develop new motives and new behaviors to help them slow down and relax. (Chapter 15 discusses methods for changing behavior.)

PROGRESS CHECK 5.3

1. Complete each of the following sentences with one of the options provided.

Learning Objective 5.8

A. Expectancy theory focuses on _____
    (mechanistic behaviors : learned motives)

Learning Objective 5.8
B. Motives differ from drives in that motives do not always _____ .
    (reflect an internal condition : have a physiological origin)

Learning Objective 5.8
C. A social motive is an aroused condition involving feelings about _____
    (self, others, and relationships : food and safety needs)

Learning Objective 5.8
D. A need for _____ would *not* be considered a social need.
    (order : aggression : sleep)

Learning Objective 5.9
E. High achievement needs are most pronounced in adults who were _____ .
    (late developers : firstborn children : ignored for early achievements)

Learning Objective 5.9
F. When presented with a complex task, subjects with a *low* need for achievement try _____ performing the task.
    (no new methods for : new and better ways of)

Learning Objective 5.10
G. _____ people show only small changes in performance when they are asked to do a task in the presence of others.
    (Type A : Type B)

Learning Objective 5.10
H. _____ people are at a greater risk for having heart attacks.
    (Type A : Type B)

Learning Objective 5.10
I. Type A people have an intense desire to _____ their environment.
    (control : let others control)

COGNITIVE THEORY

At 327 pounds, Dan Workman had entered a never-ending cycle of eating. He seemed unable to control his desire for food. His repeated efforts at dieting did no good: After each 10-pound loss, he would go on an eating binge, putting back the 10 pounds and adding another 10. Dan wanted to lose weight, but he felt uncontrollable urges to eat. He could not explain his behavior, though it was a constant question in his mind. Four weeks earlier, Dan had sought the help of a clinical psychologist. Together, they were exploring the reasons for Dan's over-eating. They both knew that Dan's eating was dangerous to his health, both physical and psychological. They both knew that Dan had to get his eating under control—and soon.

Learning Objective 5.11
Every time Dan thought about his eating problem, it brought him slightly closer to confronting his difficulty and doing something about it. For years, Dan had just eaten his way through mounds of food. Now, he began to think about why he ate and under what conditions he ate. This increased the likelihood that he could help bring his eating under control.

An achievement theorist would assert that the situations in which Dan found himself would determine his expectations and ultimately his behavior; a cognitive theorist, however, would assert that human beings have cognitive (thought) control over day-to-day behavior. From a cognitive theorist's point of view, Dan's thinking about his own behavior was the key to helping him change it. Cognitive theory places the emphasis on the causal role of thought in behavior.

Cognitive Controls

Dan Workman really had two problems: First, he had to learn to deal with food; in addition, he had to learn to control his feelings about himself. He would never get his eating under control until he learned to manage or control his self-perception.

People's motivation to achieve, to go to school, to be successful at what they do is closely related to how they feel about themselves and their situation. Research over the past two decades indicates that by thinking about their behavior and emotions, people can largely control their motivation and subsequent behavior. In what is now regarded as a classic study, Lazarus and Alfert (1964) monitored subjects' levels of arousal under conditions capable of inducing great stress. Subjects watched a film showing a primitive ritual called subincision (which involves deeply cutting the penises of adolescents). During the film, which showed five operations, one group of subjects heard a commentary denying that any pain and harm were associated with the operation. Presented in a detached way, the *denial commentary* allowed viewers to build up psychological defenses against the content of the film. Another group of subjects, the *denial orientation* group, heard the same commentary before the film. A third group saw the film without any commentary. One measure of arousal used was the electrodermal response (EDR), which usually shows increases in skin conductance during stress. Figure 5.4 shows the results, plotted over time. In subjects who saw the film with no commentary, EDR increased at once. More important, the increase in EDR was smaller for the group of subjects who heard the denial commentary during the film. The group that heard the denial before the film began (the denial orientation group) showed the lowest overall EDR increases. These results show that people have some degree of cognitive control over their physiological reactions.

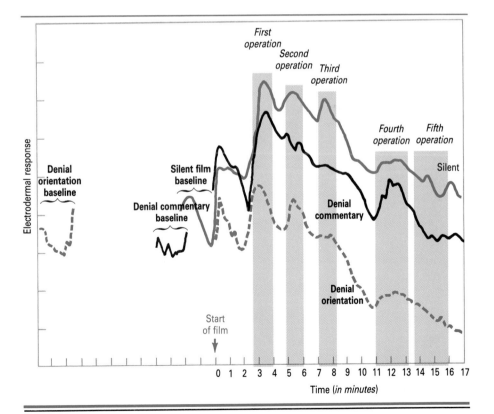

FIGURE 5.4 : Lazarus and Alfert measured the electrodermal response (EDR) of subjects viewing a film of stress-inducing operations. The baseline indicates the level of EDR before the film was shown with the start of the film. EDR increased in all groups. The increase was greatest in subjects who did not hear a commentary denying the pain. (Lazarus & Alfert, 1964, p. 199)

Dan Workman could learn to control his behaviors that dealt with food and, in addition, his feelings about himself. Through thought processes, people like Dan have been able to adjust their arousal levels and later their behavior. Psychologists have used this knowledge to help in a variety of circumstances. For example, they have used it to help people who suffer from erectile dysfunction during sex, and to help people reduce their anxiety before a test, first date, or job interview. Through instruction and self-help techniques, people can alter their behavior by changing their thoughts.

Intrinsic and Extrinsic Motivation

Learning 5.12
Objective

Intrinsically motivated behaviors
Behaviors that a person performs in order to feel more competent and self-determined.

Human beings engage in a wide range of activities that bring no tangible rewards. They do crossword and jigsaw puzzles; they play solitaire and Pac-Man; they build cities with erector sets—then take them down again. Even very young infants are observed to seek out stimulation. Psychologists call behaviors performed for no apparent reward except the pleasure of the activity itself **intrinsically motivated behaviors.** University of Rochester psychologist Edward Deci (1975) has suggested that people perform intrinsically motivated behaviors for two reasons: to achieve stimulation, and to achieve a sense of accomplishment, competence, and mastery over their environment.

In a series of studies, Deci compared two groups of subjects engaged in puzzle solving: One group received no rewards; the other group received rewards. He found that subjects who had been rewarded generally spent less time solving puzzles once the rewards were no longer given, whereas those who were never rewarded spent the same amount of time solving puzzles on all trials (Deci, 1971, 1972). Studies of young children have yielded similar results (Lepper, Greene, & Nisbett, 1973); and if rewards are expected before the activity is performed, the effect of not giving them is even greater (Ryan, Mims, & Koestner, 1983). Research in a variety of settings (e.g. McGraw & Fiala, 1982)

Feelings of accomplishment and mastery over our environment often maintain intrinsically motivated behaviors.

TABLE 5.2 : Drive, Expectancy, and Cognitive Theories of Motivation

Theory	Theorist	Principally Explains	Key Idea	View of Behavior
Drive	Nisbett	Obesity	Number of fat cells determine obesity.	Mechanistic: obesity is biologically determined.
	Schachter	Hunger and obesity	External cues energize eating behavior.	Partially mechanistic but recognizes the role of learning.
Expectancy	McClelland	Achievement motivation	Humans learn the need to achieve.	Partly cognitive, partly mechanistic: achievement is a learned behavior; once established it energizes humans in many ways.
	Friedman & Rosenman	The behavior of Type A people prone to coronary heart attack	Time urgency leads to a competitive, unending search for mastery and success, and to heart disease.	Partly cognitive, partly mechanistic: Type A behavior is initiated early in life through reinforcement and punishment; once established it is difficult to change.
Cognitive	Deci	Intrinsic motivation	Intrinsic motivation is self-rewarding because it makes people feel competent.	Cognitive: motivation is inborn, but extrinsic rewards often decrease it; decision making is crucial.

has shown that offering rewards for engaging in an already attractive task results in a lower level of involvement and often in permanent disengagement (McGraw & Fiala, 1982). Lepper and Greene (1978) refer to this phenomenon as the "hidden cost of reward." (See Table 5.2.)

The delivery of an extrinsic reward does not always decrease intrinsically motivated behavior (Condry, 1977) or suppress it permanently (Morgan, 1983). An **extrinsic reward** is a reward that comes from the external environment; for example, praise, a grade, or money is given to reward a person for a particular behavior. These rewards can strengthen existing behaviors, provide people with information about their performance, and increase feelings of self-worth and competence. It has been shown that verbal extrinsic rewards (like praise) are less likely than tangible rewards (like money) to interfere with intrinsic motivation (Anderson, Manoogian, & Reznick, 1976; see also C. D. Fisher, 1978). Ultimately, if a person truly loves doing something, he or she will probably continue to do it even if extrinsic rewards are given. An athlete who loves a sport will most likely continue to play either with or without extrinsic rewards because of being intrinsically rewarded by the pleasure derived from the game.

A number of important variables affect intrinsic motivation. For example, is a person with a high sense of self-esteem likely to continue pursuing a task after being given extrinsic rewards? Similarly, what if the extrinsic rewards are given to a person with low self-esteem? Baumeister and Tice (1985) have shown that people with high self-esteem aspire to excel and seek opportunities to do so when they are rewarded for intrinsically motivated behaviors. But people with low self-esteem, however, aspire to be only adequate or satisfactory when given rewards for intrinsically motivated behavior. It is not surpris-

Extrinsic reward ═══
A reward that comes from the external environment.

ing, then, that intrinsic motivation is at least in part tied up with a person's past experiences and current level of self-esteem. Other variables, such as the type of task a person is engaged in and the type of reward a person receives, can influence the person's level of intrinsic motivation.

Procrastination—Putting Off until Tomorrow . . .

Learning Objective 5.13

Because everyone procrastinates on occasion, this behavior pattern is frequently dismissed as not being very serious. We sometimes joke about procrastination, letting ourselves off the hook with such words as, "I'm procrastinating," or teasing a friend, "Joe, are you procrastinating again?" After all, if something is not done today, it can be done tomorrow. What's the problem?

When procrastinating, people are avoiding reaching a goal—their motivation is often to avoid doing something that needs to be done. Motivated behavior is behavior that is goal directed and in which an organism feels impelled or driven to do something. **Procrastination** is the behavior of putting off doing something that could and should be done in the present until a future time.

Procrastinators tend to rationalize the reasons something did not get done or did not get done well. For example, a student procrastinates until the night before a term paper is due, hurriedly writes something to turn in, receives an average grade for the work, and rationalizes the grade by saying, "I could have done better but I didn't have time." This rationalization takes the responsibility for not having achieved full potential away from the student and puts it on the clock.

Procrastinators also tend to operate under a "magical system," according to behavioral therapist Kirk Peffer, believing that something outside of themselves will come through and things will get done, problems will get solved, or the need for something to get done will disappear. Sometimes the magical system works; the problem goes away, the procrastinator is able to sneak through without doing something or without doing it well, or someone (a family member, friend, or colleague) gets the job done before negative consequences result. When the magical system works, Peffer refers to the procrastinator as a "successful procrastinator." But, he warns that this is setting up a dangerous life-style because eventually the behavior of procrastinating will catch up with a person. When the magical system does not work, the consequences can be quite costly. Library books not yet returned bring fines; oil not yet added to the car leads to a destroyed engine; failing to confront the issues in a troubled marriage leads to divorce; tasks not completed on the job result in being fired.

When negative consequences occur because of procrastination, self-recriminating thoughts may also occur. A cycle begins in which procrastination leads to self-punishment and decreased self-esteem. These thoughts cause a person to retreat even further from taking action with important matters. The likelihood that the person will procrastinate again and for a longer period of time increases. If the cycle continues, procrastination can become a life-style; the person can be left with a powerful rationalization system, very low self-esteem, and an inability to accomplish much. Although everyone procrastinates to some degree, for people who get caught in this cycle, procrastination becomes maladaptive.

Procrastination
The behavior of putting off doing something that could or should be done in the present.

Psychology and You: Getting Things Done

Kirk Peffer, whose ideas about procrastination are elaborated on in the text, has some specific advice for procrastinators (1986). He has outlined some behaviors that need to change in order for a person to break away from the pattern of ongoing procrastination.

1. Procrastinators tend to do nonconsequential, fun, and easy things first; they let important or more difficult things slide. A procrastinator will benefit from learning to prioritize tasks and responsibilities according to their importance rather than the ease with which they are accomplished.

2. Procrastinators frequently look at a task or a number of tasks that need to be done and feel overwhelmed. They lack the ability to understand how much can be accomplished in a certain amount of time and they do nothing because they feel like they cannot get it all done right now. They will benefit by learning how much can reasonably be accomplished in a day and by establishing small, manageable goals. Rather than looking at a chapter of reading as being three hours of reading, the procrastinator needs to establish a goal of reading for a half hour, taking a short break, and returning to the reading or to some other important-to-get-

done task for a half hour. Half-hour stretches lead to getting things done.

3. Procrastinators need to recognize that failure is a normal component in life. The expectancy of succeeding or failing at something often keeps a procrastinator from doing anything. By recognizing that everyone makes mistakes and that the biggest failure of all is not to try, a procrastinator can achieve the desire to succeed and become motivated to get things done.

4. Procrastinators need to accomplish things in a structured manner. They need a structure tailored to their abilities. They need to start at a point at which they can succeed and to progress toward taking more and more responsibility. A person who procrastinates when making decisions or confronting life problems will benefit by learning how to analyze problems, how to break them into small stages, and how to deal with them one step at a time. Successful experiences generalize and increase self-esteem.

5. Ultimately, says Peffer, procrastinators need to internalize a sense of being in control of their own lives and good feelings about their self-worth.

HUMANISTIC THEORY

Learning Objective 5.14

Some people think that psychologists are too rigid in their conceptions of the whys of human behavior. They assert that mechanistic explanations of stimuli, responses, and even expectations are too formal and limiting and do not account for the wide range of human experiences. Abraham Maslow was a psychologist who agreed with some of these criticisms. Maslow felt strongly that no single theory could account for human behavior. Both the physiological and learned aspects of behavior usually work together to control a person's behavior. Food and water needs must be satisfied before needs for power or glory, yet all these aspects must be considered when seeking the causes of behavior. One appealing aspect of Maslow's humanistic theory is that it incorporates some of the best elements of the drive, expectancy, and cognitive approaches.

Self-actualization
The process of realizing one's uniquely human potential for good; the process of achieving everything one is capable of achieving.

Humanistic theory
An explanation of behavior that emphasizes the role of thought and human qualities, such as dignity, individual choice, self-concept, and self-achievement.

As a humanistic psychologist, Abraham Maslow (1908–1970) assumed that people are essentially good—that they have an innate inclination to develop their potential and seek beauty, truth, and goodness. In other words, they are innately motivated toward **self-actualization,** or self-fulfillment. Like other **humanistic theorists,** Maslow believed that people are innately open and trusting and can experience the world in healthy ways. Maslow was one of many humanistic theorists to develop such notions. For example, Carl Rogers, whom we consider in more detail in Chapter 12, also adopted similar views. For both Rogers and Maslow, self-actualized people are people who have achieved their true natures and fulfilled their potential.

Maslow's influential theory conceived of people's motives as forming a pyramid-shaped structure, with physiological needs at the base and needs for

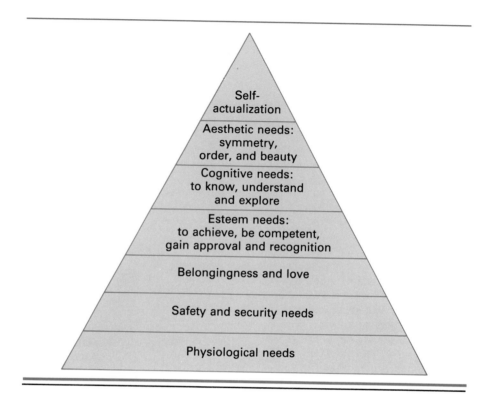

Self-
actualization

Aesthetic needs:
symmetry,
order, and beauty

Cognitive needs:
to know, understand
and explore

Esteem needs:
to achieve, be competent,
gain approval and recognition

Belongingness and love

Safety and security needs

Physiological needs

FIGURE 5.5 : Maslow's
pyramid of needs. Physiological needs are at the base.
Each successive layer is to a
greater extent a learned social
need.

*Abraham Maslow (1908–1970)
was one of the founders of
humanistic psychology.*

love, achievement, and understanding at higher levels (see Figure 5.5). As
low-level needs are satisfied, people strive for the next higher level, culminat-
ing in self-actualization. Unless these lower-level needs are met, people can
never self-actualize. Thus, Maslow's theory of motivation and personality takes
into account not only humanistic, aesthetic, and achievement motives but also
physiological needs and their resulting drives (which direct behavior on an
hour-to-hour basis). Maslow did not claim that a person's basic physiological
needs have to be completely satisfied before he or she can achieve a higher
level of fulfillment. He did claim, however, that once someone's basic physiological needs are met, that person is in a better position to satisfy emotional
needs. This approach takes into account that even a malnourished and starving
child has emotional requirements that need attention.

Maslow's theory provides an interesting way to organize aspects of behavior and their relative importance, but its global nature makes it very difficult to
verify experimentally. Furthermore, his theory may not be valid in all cultures;
his levels of motivation seem closely tied to middle-class cultural experience.
Nevertheless, Maslow's theory does address the fundamental importance of
physiological drives in motivating behavior. Unless people's basic physiological
needs are met, they are unlikely to be able to grow and develop physically, or
to develop or acquire social and aesthetic motives that might direct behavior.
Only if one's needs for food, shelter, and physical safety are met can people
attend to developing a sense of self-respect or sense of beauty. (See Table 5.3)

TABLE 5.3: Drive, Expectancy, Cognitive, and Humanistic Theories of Motivation

Theory	Theorist	Principally Explains	Key Idea	View of Behavior
Drive	Nisbett	Obesity	Number of fat cells determine obesity.	Mechanistic: obesity is biologically determined.
	Schachter	Hunger and obesity	External cues energize eating behavior.	Partially mechanistic but recognizes the role of learning.
Expectancy	McClelland	Achievement motivation	Humans learn the need to achieve.	Partly cognitive, partly mechanistic: achievement is a learned behavior; once established it energizes humans in many ways.
	Friedman & Rosenman	The behavior of Type A coronary heart attack-prone people	Time urgency leads to a competitive, unending search for mastery and success, and to heart disease.	Partly cognitive, partly mechanistic: Type A behavior is initiated early in life through reinforcement and punishment; once established it is difficult to change.
Cognitive	Deci	Intrinsic motivation	Intrinsic motivation is self-rewarding because it makes people feel competent.	Cognitive: motivation is inborn, but extrinsic rewards often decrease it; decision making is crucial.
Humanistic	Maslow	Learned needs for fulfillment and feelings of self-actualization	Self-actualization	Cognitive: humans seek to self-actualize after they have fulfilled basic needs for food and security; conscious decisions determine all higher goals.

PROGRESS CHECK 5.4

1. Complete each of the following sentences with one of the options provided.

Learning Objective 5.11   A. A cognitive psychologist would say that motives, emotions, and behaviors can be managed or changed by making use of _____ .
(tangible rewards : environmental opportunities : one's own thoughts)

Learning Objective 5.11   B. In the classic study conducted by Lazarus and Alfert, the _____ _____ viewers heard the commentary denying pain before the film and showed the lowest overall electrodermal response while viewing the film.
(denial commentary : denial orientation)

Learning Objective 5.12   C. Intrinsically motivated behaviors are maintained by _____ .
(primary reinforcers : the internal pleasures derived from the activity)

Learning Objective 5.12   D. The hidden cost of reward refers to a decline or discontinuation of intrinsically motivated behavior because the behavior _____ .
(receives extrinsic rewards : becomes boring : becomes too easy)

Learning Objective 5.13   E. Procrastination frequently leads to _____ .
(an eventual high-drive state : unhealthy thought patterns)

Learning Objective 5.14

F. According to Maslow, the motive to seek self-actualization is _____

    _____ .

    (innate : learned)

Learning Objective 5.14

G. A self-actualized person is a person who _____ .
    (no longer has any problems : achieves his or her true nature)

Learning Objective 5.14

H. Maslow suggested that it is easier for a person to satisfy emotional and achievement needs if _____ needs are being fulfilled.
    (physiological : aesthetic : humanistic)

Learning Objective 5.14

I. Maslow's theory appears to be _____ .
    (valid in all cultures : tied to middle-class cultural experiences)

EMOTION

Learning Objective 5.15

The pain that an obese person like Dan Workman might feel is difficult to imagine. Few people can understand what it means to carry around with them so blatantly a symbol of their weakness. The causes of Dan's behavior are complex, but the results of it, both physically and emotionally, are easy to see. Still, we human beings have an amazing array of responses to various situations: Some of us would be much better adjusted than Dan; others of us might not cope as well. People can develop great control over their emotional responses, and many individuals have elaborate self-management schemes carefully devised to alter their emotional reactions when they begin to feel out of control.

We all know that, when placed in similar situations, each of us may have different feelings. Almost everyone would agree that crying is a strong emotional reaction; but, people cry when they are happy and when they are sad. When researchers began to study emotional behavior, they realized that a wide range of emotions, including love, joy, fear, disgust, and anger, have motivating properties: They can impel and direct people's behavior.

Emotion

A subjective feeling or response generally accompanied by a physiological change and usually associated with a change in behavior.

An **emotion** is a subjective response usually accompanied by a physiological change and associated with a change in behavior. People tend to cry when they are sad and to find increased energy when they are excited. Fear is often associated with an increase in breathing rate, sweating, dryness in the mouth, and sometimes nausea (see Kleinginna & Kleinginna, 1981). Sometimes a physiological change precedes an emotional response. People often report that their bodies responded to a difficult ordeal even before they grasped the situation. Just before a collision in an automobile accident, for example, people show physiological arousal, muscle tension, and avoidance responses—they brace themselves. Other physiological changes are not evident until after an emotion-causing event. Only after an auto accident do people realize the danger they have been in and start to shake with fear, disbelief, or rage.

People often respond to physiological changes by altering their behavior. Feeling afraid, they scream. Recognizing a tragedy, they may be unable to work. Feeling anger, they may seek revenge or retribution. When in love, they may act especially tenderly toward others. In some situations, people may think about acting out such behaviors but may not express them in directly observable ways.

Most people experience the same kinds of emotions, but the intensity or quality of those emotions may vary among individuals. One person's sense of joy may be different from another's. Thus, emotions have a private, personal, and unique or *subjective,* component. It is this unquantifiable element that we call feeling. Psychologists have long acknowledged that emotion consists of three elements: feeling, physiological response, and behavior. Because the behavioral view so permeates experimental investigation, most researchers who have studied emotion have considered subjective feelings too esoteric to be measurable and have focused on the other two aspects of emotion—physiological response and behavior—which are measurable and observable.

Learning Objective 5.16

According to Marshall Klaus and John Kennell, professors of pediatrics, the first minutes and hours of an infant's life constitute a sensitive period for emotional development. During this time, close contact between the parents and infant allows a specific kind of parental response to occur. The resulting attachment between mother and child is called *bonding.* Although it is unclear what physiological mechanisms may influence bonding, Klaus and Kennell support their claim for its existence in human beings by citing considerable evidence of innate maternal behavior patterns in all organisms. Lower animals show regular stereotyped patterns of attachment in caring for their newborns. Human newborns respond to their mothers through body and eye movements. Such responses may strengthen the mother's attachment bond to her child—a bond already affected by hormonal changes, prevailing cultural biases, and the mother's personal experiences. This early opportunity to form a strong parent-infant attachment may significantly influence both the parent's ability to care effectively for the child and the infant's ability to give and receive affection and love.

Recall from Chapter 1 Harry Harlow's observation that infant monkeys, raised in isolation from their mothers, clung to blankets placed in their cages. This observation led him to try to discover whether infant monkeys had an inborn desire for love or warmth that might be satisfied by soft, warm objects such as terry cloth. In what is now considered a classic experiment, he placed infant monkeys in cages along with two wire-covered shapes resembling adult

FIGURE 5.6: In Harlow's experiment, infant rhesus monkeys clung to terry-cloth mothers.

Harry F. Harlow's (1905–1981) early research with infant monkeys continues to have an impact on studies of attachments.

monkeys. One figure was covered with terry cloth; the other was left bare (see Figure 5.6). Both could be fitted with bottles to provide milk. In some cases, the wire mother surrogate was fitted with a bottle; in other cases the terry-cloth mother surrogate provided milk. The infant monkeys clung to the terry-cloth mother surrogates whether or not they provided milk. They also clung to the terry-cloth mother surrogate in new, fearful situations. The wire mother surrogate, even with a bottle of milk, could not provide the comfort that a terry-cloth-covered mother surrogate could (Harlow & Zimmerman, 1958). Terry cloth is hardly a critical developmental variable in the growth and development of monkeys; yet, its introduction into a wire cage made the difference between life and death for a number of monkeys. Harlow inferred from this that the terry cloth provided some measure of security or warmth for the monkeys. Neither group of Harlow's monkeys, however, were totally normal. Harlow's infant monkeys were more aggressive and fearful than normally raised monkeys. They were also unable to engage in normal sexual relations. Some of the infants raised with wire mother surrogates engaged in self-destructive behaviors (Harlow, 1962).

Although it is a broad leap from Harlow's monkeys to human infants, it is reasonable to assume that infants, like monkeys, have an inborn need for social stimulation. According to Klaus and Kennell (1976), without such periods, infants will not develop as well emotionally as infants who go through social bonding.

On the practical side, Klaus and Kennell claim that traditional hospital arrangements give mothers too little time to care for their newborns and to create a supportive environment. As a result, many mothers describe the first days after their discharge from the hospital as hellish or as the most difficult days of their lives. Klaus and Kennell advocate changing traditional arrangements in United States medical facilities to create the best possible conditions for development of the parent-infant bond and a smooth transition to life at home after discharge from the hospital (Klaus and Kennell, 1976, 1983; see also Ainsworth, 1979).

Emotions: Expressed Behaviorally and Physically

Learning Objective <u>5.17</u>

Since 1898, psychologists have recognized that facial expressions provide reliable cues to how people feel. This behavioral measure is easily observed, captured on film or tape, and interpreted by others. Most important, research has shown that facial expression can be an accurate index of a person's emotional state. Cartoonists, political satirists, actors, opera stars, and children exaggerate facial expressions in order to convey meaning more clearly (Buck, 1980).

Facial expressions can be important indicators of emotion, but they do not have to be (Whissell, 1985). The data show that facial expressions of other people can influence our emotional experience but do not have to determine it. Facial expressions, our own and other people's, can be modified and changed due to a number of factors. Facial features are good indicators of emotion, but they are only indicators; real emotions may be masked by a happy face or by a turned-down mouth.

People may also display emotion through a range of other behavioral responses—such as gestures, body language, and voice, tone, and volume—all of which human beings are expert at interpreting (Cunningham, 1977). Obvious examples are head bowing, fist shaking, and laughter; less obvious examples are clenched teeth, limpness, and loss of energy. Some researchers have studied the smiling responses of infants, children, and adults (Carlson, Gantz, & Masters, 1983). Others have observed animals and human beings when they are placed in situations that might induce stress and emotional responses.

Unlike facial expressions and other observable behavioral responses, the physiological changes that accompany an emotion are hard to mask and are measurable. Many such changes are due to an increase in autonomic nervous system activity. Fear, for example, brings some or all of the following physiological changes: digestion slows or stops; blood pressure and heart rate increase; breathing becomes deeper; pupils dilate; salivation decreases (causing a dry mouth); and muscles often become more tense.

Learning Objective <u>5.18</u>

Much theorizing about emotions is based on measures of known physiological responses. Researchers have recognized that the autonomic nervous system provides direct, observable, measurable responses that can be quantified in a systematic manner. As mentioned earlier, one reliable measure of autonomic nervous system activation is the electrodermal response (EDR) (still often referred to as the *galvanic skin response*). The EDR is recorded by a small electrode placed on the skin (often the palm of the hand) to measure the skin's conductance. Skin conductance increases dramatically with arousal (see, for example, Duffy & Lacey, 1946).

A lie detector is perhaps the most widely recognized recorder of emotion. This device records changes in the autonomic nervous system activity of subjects who are attached to it. It is important to remember that most autonomic nervous system activity is involuntary. Lying is usually associated with an increase in autonomic activity. After monitoring a person's autonomic responses to a series of relatively neutral questions, a trained researcher can compare them with the person's responses to questions about the issue being explored. During noncontroversial questions (such as requests for the person's name or address), autonomic activity remains at what is considered baseline level. During critical questions (such as whether the person used a knife as a holdup weapon), however, a person with something to hide usually shows a dramatic increase in autonomic nervous system activity.

Not all people show marked autonomic nervous system changes when emotionally aroused. Habitual liars show little or no change in autonomic activity when they lie; they seem to be able to lie without becoming emotionally aroused. Recent research has shown that some autonomic responses can be brought under voluntary control through biofeedback. People can also alter the baseline conditions. A lie detector test can be useful in indicating if a person is lying. However, it is subject to significant error, particularly with a habitual liar or someone who deliberately responds so as to confuse the results (Szucko & Kleinmuntz, 1981). Accordingly, most states do not accept the lie detector as valid evidence in court, especially in criminal cases.

Sixteen states have forbidden employers to use lie detectors. Twenty-one states required that examiners be licensed. In many criminal courts, both sides must agree to the use of lie detector test results; and in some states, not even mutual agreement is good enough to make the results admissible as evidence in court. The American Psychological Association has expressed great reservations about the use of polygraph tests; the APA asserts that polygraph tests bring about the possibility of great psychological damage to innocent persons.

PROGRESS CHECK   5.5

1. Complete each of the following sentences with one of the options provided.

Learning Objective 5.15

A. The private, unique, and personal component of an emotion is _____ _____.
(fairly easy to observe and measure : subjective : called a behavior)

Learning Objective 5.15

B. Researchers who investigate emotions tend to study physiological responses and accompanying behaviors rather than subjective feelings because feelings are difficult _____.
(for most people to share : to observe and measure)

Learning Objective 5.16

C. Klaus and Kennell have suggested that the first minutes and hours of an infant's life _____ emotional development.
(is a sensitive period for healthy : are relatively unimportant in)

Learning Objective 5.16

D. In Harlow's classic experiment, some of the infant monkeys raised with wire surrogate mothers _____.
(were comforted if a bottle was attached : engaged in self-destructive behaviors)

Learning Objective 5.16

E. Based on Harlow's studies with monkeys, we can assume that human infants _____.
(have an inborn need for social stimulation : will smile soon after birth)

Learning Objective 5.17

F. _____ is a behavior that accompanies an emotion.
(Sadness : Depression : Crying)

Learning Objective 5.18

G. Most emotions are accompanied by an increase in _____ _____ nervous system activity.
(somatic : autonomic)

Learning Objective 5.18

H. When psychologists study the electrodermal response (EDR) to examine physiological changes that accompany emotions, they measure changes in _____.
(skin conductance : pupil size)

Controlling Emotions

Learning Objective 5.19

Events in our complicated world can bring about a wide range of emotions. We experience happy, jubilant periods and times of despair, sadness, and depression. Researchers have shown that people can use cognitive means to control their arousal level and even their body's biochemistry. Arousal is an essential component in emotion. In the study by Lazarus and Alfert (1964) discussed earlier, subjects were able to manipulate their EDRs when told in advance about a subincision ritual shown in a film.

We also know that people control their emotions because of strong cultural expectations—many people have come to expect certain emotions to be displayed only at so-called appropriate times; for example, in our culture we are expected not to show strong emotions in public places. By using conscious and directed thought, people can control their behavior and wait until the so-called proper time and place before expressing certain emotions. People can also step away from oncoming depression and feel joyful about being alive by focusing on good thoughts and more positive aspects of their lives and by recognizing that they cannot control all of life's disrupting events. People can consciously hold tears back, and many people, especially men, do. Many cultural expectations dictate who can cry and when and where they can do it. In our society, children and women have greater permission to cry than men do. We can control emotion and emotional expression through thought but it may not always be beneficial to do so.

The self-regulation view of emotional expression is another aspect of cognitive theory. It stresses that people are not passive, that they do not respond automatically to environmental or internal stimuli. They manage or determine their emotional state in purposeful ways by constantly evaluating their environment and feelings. Rather than assuming that the obese eat simply because they see food, cognitive theorists claim that these people have decided how they will respond long before food is presented. For example, obese people often prepare themselves for food-oriented vacations, such as ocean-liner cruises, and respond accordingly whenever food is presented. (Lazarus, 1974). Environmental stimuli can determine emotions; from a cognitive psychologist's viewpoint, however, stimuli are only part of the picture.

The Effect of Emotions on Health

By taking herself so seriously, Beverly, the independent young woman who opened this chapter, may have been putting her physical and emotional health at risk. Beverly, determined to carry the full load of raising her daughter, going to school, working, and financially supporting her own endeavors had little time for sharing good times with friends or watching a movie, or even laughing.

Learning 5.20
Objective

We can admire Beverly for her determination and perseverance and at the same time know that her mother and friends had reason to be concerned. Beverly's need to conquer it all put her under tremendous stress. She frequently felt overwhelmed and anxious by all she had to do, angry when things got in her way, and depressed when she did not get things done or did not do them as well as she thought she could. To make matters worse, she contained many of her stressful emotions because she did not have time to deal with them; she had to get things done. Even when her life became very difficult, she did not dare cry, especially in front of her mother; she had to maintain her image of strength and independence. Psychologists, like other health professionals, are learning that prolonged stress and negative emotions like those Beverly was experiencing can put people at risk for illness and serious health problems.

In the last decade, psychologists have joined forces with researchers in other fields to investigate the effects that stress, emotions, and attitudes have on physical health. Their cooperative work has led to the emergence of several new fields. *Behavioral medicine* examines how psychological, biological, and sociocultural factors are related to illness and wellness. *Psychoneuroimmunology* focuses on how psychological processes and the nervous system affect the body's natural defense system—the **immune system**—and how, in turn, the immune system influences psychological processes. *Psychoneuroendrocrinology* investigates the interrelationship of stress, emotions, and attitudes and the body's **endocrine system** and balance of hormones. These new fields focus on the role that psychological factors, such as stress, emotion, thought, and attitude, play in the occurrence, maintenance, treatment, and prevention of physical illness (Ader, 1981). Another related and rapidly growing field, *health psychology,* focuses on prevention of disease and the maintenance of health by teaching people how to regulate emotions, stress levels, thought patterns, and life-styles that may interfere with good health. These four new fields all exchange research findings.

Immune system The network of organs and specialized glands, white blood cells, and proteins that defend the body against disease.

Endocrine system A system of ductless hormone-producing glands that secrete hormones directly into the blood stream.

Theories of Emotion

Learning Objective 5.21

Over the years, three major approaches to the study of emotion have developed. The first two focused on the physiology of emotions and on whether physiological change or emotional feelings occur first in the process. In the last twenty years, researchers have investigated a cognitive theory that claims a role for interpretation as well as for physiology.

The James-Lange Theory. According to a theory proposed by William James (1842–1910) and developed with Carl Lange (1834–1900), people experience physiological changes and then interpret them as emotional states (see Figure 5.7). People do not cry because they feel sad; they feel sad because they cry. People do not perspire because they are afraid; they feel afraid after they have perspired. Simply stated, the James-Lange theory says that people do not experience an emotion until *after* their bodies become aroused and respond with physiological changes. Feedback from the body produces feelings or emotions (James, 1884; Lange, 1885/1922).

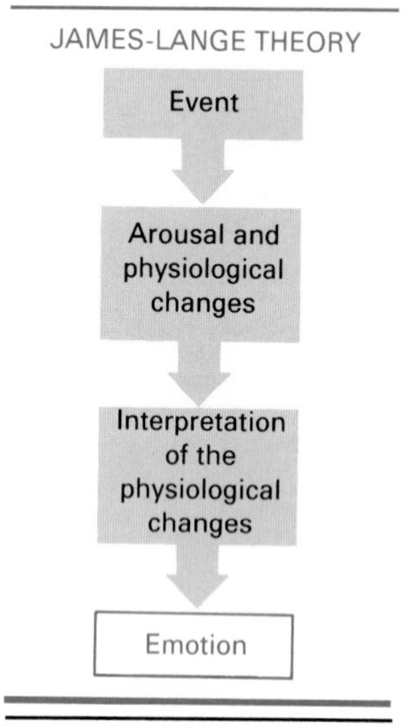

FIGURE 5.7 : According to the James-Lange theory, arousal occurs first, the person interprets the internal changes and then experiences some emotion.

The Cannon Theory. Physiologists such as Walter Cannon (1871–1945) were very critical of the James-Lange theory. Cannon showed that the physiological changes in many emotional states were identical. If increases in blood

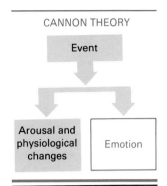

CANNON THEORY

Event

Arousal and
physiological
changes

Emotion

FIGURE 5.8 : According to
Cannon's theory, arousal and
emotion occur simultaneously.

pressure and heart rate accompany feelings of both anger and joy, how can people determine their emotional state simply from their physiological state? Cannon argued that when a person is emotional, two areas of the brain, the thalamus and the cerebral cortex, are stimulated simultaneously. Stimulation of the cortex produces the emotional component of the experience; stimulation of the thalamus produces physiological changes in the sympathetic nervous system. According to Cannon (1927), emotional feelings *accompany* physiological changes (see Figure 5.8).

The Schachter-Singer Theory.   A relatively new cognitive theory of emotion incorporates elements of both the James-Lange and Cannon theories. Stanley Schachter and Jerome Singer observed that people do indeed interpret their emotions, but not solely from bodily changes. Schachter and Singer argued that people interpret physical sensations within a specific context (see Figure 5.9). Observers cannot interpret what a person's crying means unless they know the situation in which that behavior occurs. If a man cries at a funeral, we suspect he is sad; if he cries at his daughter's wedding, we expect he is joyful.

To prove their contention, Schachter and Singer (1962) injected volunteer subjects with adrenalin, a powerful stimulant. The subjects were unaware of the actual effects of their injection. Injections of adrenalin will increase signs of arousal, such as heart rate, excitement, energy, and even sensations of butterflies in the stomach. To see if they could affect how subjects interpreted their aroused state, Schachter and Singer tried to manipulate the setting in which the subjects experienced their arousal. They hired undergraduates and paid them to act either happy and relaxed or sad, depressed, and angry. These hired subjects (called stooges) pretended that they, too, were volunteers in the drug study, but they were given injections of salt-water, not adrenalin. Their emotional behavior was strictly an act. The happy stooges shot wads of paper into a wastepaper basket and flew airplanes around the room. The unhappy stooges complained about the questionnaire they had to fill out and generally voiced their dissatisfaction with the experiment.

All the experimental subjects showed increased physiological arousal. Those who were with the happy stooges reported that the drug made them feel good, and those who were with the angry stooges reported feeling anger. Schachter and Singer reasoned that when people have no immediate explanation for their physiological arousal, they will label their feelings in terms of the thoughts available to them. The physiological feelings that accompany both joy and anger are the same, but the label attached to the emotion depends on the person's situation (see also Manstead, 1979).

Schachter and Singer's theory has modified the way psychologists think about emotional behavior. The cognitive view receives support not only from their own experiments but also from anecdotal data. For example, when people first smoke marijuana (or take other psychoactive drugs) they tend to approach the experience with definite expectations. If told the drug will produce feelings of hunger, new users will report feeling hunger; when a drug is described as a "downer," users often interpret the bodily sensations that accompany the drug as depressive.

In Schachter's and Singer's view, people experience internal arousal, become aware of the arousal, seek an explanation for it, identify an external cue, and finally label the arousal. This labeling determines the emotion felt. Schachter's and Singer's view is not universally accepted (for example, see Reisenzein,

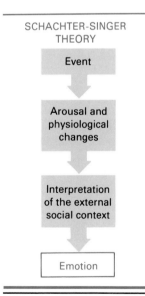

SCHACHTER-SINGER
THEORY

Event

Arousal and
physiological
changes

Interpretation
of the external
social context

Emotion

FIGURE 5.9 : According to the Schachter-Singer theory, people's interpretation of arousal depends on the specific situation in which they find themselves.

1983; Valins, 1966), but it did modify the way psychologists thought about emotion and its expression and continues to exert a strong influence on contemporary psychological thought.

Finding a Single Explanation for Emotions Is Unlikely

Learning Objective 5.22

The complex relationship among emotion, arousal, and behavior has been under study for six decades. Everyday experience shows that emotion is accompanied by changes in arousal and its accompanying physical excitement; as arousal increases, so do emotional feelings. Thoughts can alter emotions. Thus, a direct link exists among arousal, emotion, thoughts, and motivation. Emotions often motivate people to act; sometimes they are displayed only as physiological states, and sometimes they are displayed in behavior. Many researchers have investigated the sources of emotions. Some have argued that they arise from purely physiological states. James and Lange, for example, believed that people infer their emotional states directly from their physiological ones. Others believe the relation between physiology and emotion is more subtle and complex. For example, Cannon argued that the only way to distinguish between two similar physiological states was to postulate the simultaneous experience of both a physiological condition and an emotional condition. Schachter and Singer attempted to prove that emotional states are simply physiological states interpreted in a social context. Valins argues that context alone is sufficient to generate the experience of an emotion. Newer theories of emotion stress increasingly larger roles for thought processes. All of these theorists have contributed to our understanding of emotions and how they motivate behavior.

PROGRESS CHECK 5.6

1. Match the following theorists with the appropriate statement describing a theory of emotion or emotional development.

   Cannon   James-Lange   Schachter-Singer

Learning Objective 5.21   A. _____ Emotional feelings *accompany* physiological changes and, although emotions may vary, the physiological changes are often identical.

Learning Objective 5.21   B. _____ Emotions are determined by the interpretation of physical sensations within a specific environment or social context.

Learning Objective 5.21   C. _____ People experience physiological changes and then interpret these physical feelings as particular emotions.

2. Complete each of the following sentences with one of the options provided.

Learning Objective 5.19   A. A cognitive psychologist would emphasize the role that _____ _____ in the expression of emotions.
   (environmental stimuli play : self-regulation plays)

Learning Objective 5.20   B. _____ is a subfield in psychology that focuses on the prevention of disease by educating people to manage their psychological processes and life-styles.
   (Behavioral medicine : Health psychology)

Learning Objective 5.20   C. The network of specialized organs and glands, white blood cells, and proteins that defends against disease is the _____ system.
(endocrine : immune : cardiovascular)

Learning Objective 5.20   D. Emotional states _____ an individual's physical health.
(can influence : have little or no effects on)

Learning Objective 5.21   E. According to Cannon, the two areas of the brain that are involved in an emotional response are the _____ .
(cortex and thalamus : limbic system and cerebellum)

Learning Objective 5.21   F. Schachter and Singer have suggested that _____ determine whether a person feels joy or anger.
(physiological changes : external cues)

Learning Objective 5.22   G. The complex relationship among arousal, motivation, thought, behavior, and emotion _____ one theory will adequately explain how and why human beings experience emotions.
(indicates that eventually : makes it unlikely that)

Keeping Pace with Chapter 5

Applying Principles

Identify the type of conflict described in each of the following situations.

approach-approach   avoidance-avoidance   approach-avoidance
no conflict exists

A. Glenn has a problem with math anxiety, and the thought of taking Introductory Statistics distresses him. However, Glenn wants to earn his B.A. in Psychology, and to do so he must complete the Intro Stat course. Because his goal of becoming a psychologist is so important to him, Glenn enrolls in the statistics class and also seeks help through the developmental labs on campus so he can overcome his anxiety and succeed in the course.

B. Cathy wants to take both Abnormal Psychology and Child Development during the spring term. When the course schedule arrives, she discovers that only one section of each course has been offered and they both meet on the same day at the same time. Cathy finds it difficult to decide which course to take because she was eager to take them both.

C. Fred knows that his study skills are not as strong as they could be. He wants to be able to study as efficiently and effectively as he possibly can; so, to strengthen his skills, Fred enrolls in a study skills course.

D. Ellen needs to take a Social Psychology course in order to complete her Psychology degree. Two sections have been offered, one at 7:45 in the morning the other by the professor who has a reputation of giving confusing, boring lectures. Ellen is a "night owl" and likes to sleep in the morning. She also is an enthusiastic student and likes to get the most from her classes. Ellen has difficulty selecting a social psychology course because neither quite meets her needs.

Self-Test

Before proceeding to the Self-Test, REVIEW the Learning Objectives listed at the chapter opening and RECITE from memory everything you can remember in support of them. Then, take this Self-Test as if it were to be graded by your teacher. Use the Learning Objective numbers in the Answer Section as a reference to restudy the corresponding text pages and Progress Checks for any incorrectly answered questions.

1. An internal condition of arousal that directs an organism to satisfy a physiological imbalance is called

    A. a need.
    B. a drive.
    C. expectancy.
    D. motivation.

2. Self-actualization refers to

    A. making a conscious choice about how to behave.
    B. the process of reaching one's full human potential for the good.
    C. having expectations for achievement and success.
    D. the ability to resist drive states that are nonproductive.

3. When the nerves between the stomach and the brain have been severed in experimental animals, the animals

    A. do not get hungry and eventually starve.
    B. eat all the time and become obese.
    C. show appropriate behavior by eating when their blood-sugar level is low.
    D. are unable to digest the food that they eat.

4. The human sex drive

    A. is completely controlled by the amount of hormones released into the bloodstream.
    B. is determined to a great extent by early sexual experiences and cultural traditions.
    C. like the human hunger and thirst drives, must be satisfied.
    D. is very similar to the sex drive found in lower organisms.

5. The best evidence to suggest that human beings have instincts and imprint behavior patterns during a critical period is based on

    A. Klaus and Kennell's bonding studies.
    B. the Yerkes-Dodson law.
    C. the human need to explore, manipulate, and experience the world.
    D. the voluntary nature of the human sex drive.

6. Optimal arousal theories have suggested all of the following *except:*

    A. Behavior varies from disorganized to effective, depending on a person's level of arousal.
    B. Optimal performance occurs at higher levels of arousal if a person is performing an easy task.
    C. Arousal directs behavior.
    D. Arousal energizes behavior.

7. Trooper gets a terrific part-time job, but because of this, must drop one of his classes. He has completed two-thirds of the required assignments in his computer programming course and only a quarter of the work in his behavior medicine law course. Trooper is a behavior medicine major, but he needs and likes both classes. Miller would predict that in this approach-avoidance situation, Trooper will

    A. not take the job even though he needs the income.
    B. drop computer programming, even though he likes it and it is required.
    C. drop the behavior medicine law course, because he is further away from completing the course requirements.
    D. drop both computer programming and behavior medicine, because choosing one will cause too much distress.

8. Social motives

    A. direct people to establish and maintain relationships.
    B. direct people to establish feelings about themselves and others.

   C. emerge from a gradual convergence of learned social needs.

   D. all of the above

9. The Thematic Apperception Test (TAT) involves

   A. showing an individual pictures and analyzing his or her responses to see if achievement motives are revealed.

   B. asking a person to complete a complex task and watching to see what level of arousal is induced.

   C. observing how a subject interprets his or her physiological changes in an emotional situation.

   D. showing a subject a stress-inducing movie and playing denial tapes while it is being watched.

10. According to Friedman and Roseman, people in the Type B personality category

   A. are more likely than Type A people to compare themselves to others.

   B. exhibit an exaggerated need for achievement.

   C. tend to be impatient and easily angered.

   D. include all people other than those who have Type A personalities.

11. The results of Lazarus and Alfert's study in which subjects watched a film showing a primitive ritual indicate that people

   A. do not enjoy watching subject matter that is difficult to understand.

   B. will find ways to deny what they have seen.

   C. believe what they see and hear.

   D. have some degree of cognitive control over their physiological reactions.

12. Intrinsically motivated behaviors

   A. allow people to achieve stimulation and a sense of accomplishment, competence, and mastery over their environment.

   B. will weaken if they are not rewarded by someone in the person's environment.

   C. are sometimes called the "hidden cost of reward."

   D. A and C

13. According to Peffer, a "successful procrastinator" is a person who

   A. avoids doing something and does not personally suffer any negative consequences for doing so.

   B. is setting up a dangerous life-style that will eventually catch up with him or her.

   C. schedules time well and can watch a football game today and clean the garage tomorrow.

   D. is not really a procrastinator, but rather is a person who takes personal time.

14. Abraham Maslow's humanistic theory

   A. rejects drive theories.

   B. is an expectancy theory.

   C. suggests that people will be happier if they focus on social needs instead of on physiological needs.

   D. incorporates the best elements of drive, expectancy, and cognitive theories.

15. The subjective component of an emotion is

   A. an unquantifiable component we call a *feeling.*

   B. how others describe the way someone is feeling.

   C. an action or overt response that accompanies a feeling.

   D. always expressed in overt behavior.

16. Klaus and Kennell support the idea that

   A. human beings do not have stereotyped patterns of behavior.

   B. a newborn's body and eye movements strengthen the mother's attachment to the child.

C. bonding at birth increases the parent's and the infant's ability to give and receive affection and love.

D. B and C

17. When it comes to interpreting the behavioral responses that accompany emotions, people

   A. are seldom, if ever, misled by facial expressions.
   B. constantly get confused because we all react differently.
   C. can understand facial expressions but not body language.
   D. are experts.

18. Lie detectors are most effective in measuring the emotions of a person who

   A. is a habitual liar.
   B. deliberately alters baseline questions.
   C. has had extensive biofeedback training.
   D. shows distinct autonomic changes when emotionally aroused.

19. Health psychology focuses on

   A. How athletes can increase their endurance level.
   B. Teaching people how to prevent disease and maintain health.
   C. How the immune system influences psychological processes.
   D. The relationship between sociocultural factors and illness and wellness.

20. Schachter and Singer have suggested that

   A. the physiological changes that accompany joy and anger are quite different.
   B. an emotion is determined by the label a person attaches to physiological feelings.
   C. emotional feelings determine the physiological feelings a person will experience.
   D. emotional feelings accompany physiological changes.

21. "I am frightened because my heart is beating quickly" is characteristic of _____ theory of emotion.

   A. the James-Lange
   B. Walter Cannon's
   C. the Schachter-Singer
   D. Lazarus and Alfert's

22. Which of the following is a *false* statement?

   A. As arousal increases, emotional feelings increase.
   B. Emotions are physiological reactions and nothing more.
   C. Thoughts can alter emotions.
   D. Emotions can motivate people.

6

Perception

Learning
Objectives

When you have mastered the material in this chapter you will be able to:

1. Define *perception* and discuss the impact Gibson's ideas had on the field of perceptual psychology. (p. 188)

2. Name two factors that are necessary for normal perceptual development and describe some of the research that has identified these factors. (p. 190)

3. Describe the results of sensory deprivation studies with human beings and animals. (p. 191)

4. Describe the stimulus that initiates visual perception and explain how various parts of the eye function to code visual stimuli. (p. 193)

5. Define *duplicity theory* and explain how the structure of the retina and dark adaptation studies support this theory. (p. 195)

6. Describe the path that electrical impulses take once they leave the eye and enter the brain. (p. 196)

7. Explain how receptive fields allow us to see form, shape, and color. (p. 197)

8. Describe the relationship between the psychological and physical properties of color. (p. 201)

9. Explain how our visual perceptual system codes color according to the trichromatic and opponent process theories. (p. 201)

10. Describe three types of color blindness and discuss what it means to say color blindness is a gender-linked trait. (p. 204)

11. Explain how we perceive form and what is meant by size and shape constancy. (p. 204)

12. Discuss depth perception and describe a variety of monocular and binocular depth cues. (p. 206)

13. Define *illusion,* give examples of three visual illusions, and explain, based on what researchers know about them, why they occur. (p. 208)

14. Explain how Gestalt psychologists contributed to our understanding of form perception, define Law of Prägnanz, and describe five other Gestalt laws of organization. (p. 210)

15. Identify perceptual processes that affect reading speed and explain how listening and seeing are affected by selective attention. (p. 214)

16. Explain how imagery is an important part of the perception process. (p. 216)

17. Describe subliminal perception and discuss what psychologists know about it. (p. 218)

18. State three reasons this chapter deals primarily with visual perception and describe how our auditory perceptual system works. (p. 220)

19. Make a distinction between conduction deafness and nerve deafness and tell how they are diagnosed. (p. 221)

20. Describe the senses of taste and smell and explain their similarities. (p. 223)

21. Define *kinesthesis* and describe the vestibular sense. (p. 225)

22. Describe the skin senses, the Melzack-Wall gate control theory of pain perception, and how endorphins affect pain. (p. 226)

23. Describe some of the psychological techniques used to help people who experience chronic pain. (p. 228)

24. Define *telepathy, clairvoyance,* and *precognition;* explain why many psychologists maintain a healthy skepticism about many claims concerning extrasensory perception. (p. 229)

BEFORE YOU READ ON, take time to **SURVEY** the chapter, form an idea of what is to be learned (from margin Learning Objective numbers), and set goals for your study time. Then, ask yourself **QUESTIONS** about the material as you **READ,** seeking help for any sections you do not understand.

With weights hanging from her feet, Ruth Lerner was feeling somewhat better, but the pain was still with her. Ruth had never had more than a cold, and at age sixty-three this was her first hospitalization (except for childbirth). She always said she was as healthy as a horse, but during the past two years, she had developed a serious back problem.

Initially, Ruth had felt some lower back pain after walking through shopping malls. A few months later, she began to feel pain most of the time. Aspirin and a heating pad seemed to take care of her discomfort. Then, on a trip to Europe, during which she did a lot of walking, Ruth started to feel numbness in her feet. At that point, she told her doctors, things started to go downhill. The pain became worse, the numbness was constant, and her condition seemed to get worse each week. Even though she had a high threshold of pain, she was suffering. She took heavy doses of pain killers every four hours and could not sleep. Finally, she wound up in the hospital in traction—the pain was so bad, she could not walk.

Her doctors were in disagreement over her disorder. She saw a series of different renowned specialists. She saw an internist, a neurosurgeon, an orthopedic specialist, a chiropractor, and a neurologist. Their diagnoses varied—one claimed a slipped disk, another claimed damaged cartilage. A third said it was both a misaligned disk and damaged cartilage. The fourth said she would have to live with a degenerating nervous system, and the fifth said he had no idea. Her latest physician, Dr. Sullivan, wanted her to enter a pain clinic. At his clinic, he claimed he would help her lose weight, learn appropriate exercises to strengthen her back muscles, and teach her to live with her discomfort. Dr. Sullivan wanted to avoid surgery, especially with an overweight sixty-three year-old otherwise healthy woman.

Dr. Sullivan claimed his pain clinic would help treat Ruth's symptoms, teach her psychological techniques to deal with her pain, and help her to get her body to become stronger than it had been in years. He joked with her that she would become "a lean, mean fighting machine" who could deal with her situation and, most important, could avoid surgical intervention. Part of his treatment involved teaching her about pain, about how people perceive pain, and how the human body deals with pain and medications. In addition, Dr. Sullivan used biofeedback, meditation, and self-hypnosis to help people learn to cope with pain. Dr. Sullivan was as much a psychologist as he was physician. Ruth Lerner agreed with his view. She made her decision while lying in a hospital bed, arguing that she wanted to use every nonsurgical technique possible before "going under the knife." Learning to live with her pain did not seem like an exciting idea, but studying pain physiology and pain perception seemed to her a better alternative than traction. She would be transferred to Dr. Sullivan's clinic the next day.

MANY TIMES, peoples' pain is intensified because of the situation in which they find themselves. A headache seems worse if you are in a stressful situation; a toothache intensifies when the children misbehave. Psychological factors play an important role in our perception of pain. As with emotions and many other human responses, pain is not solely a physical phenomenon. All of our perceptual systems are affected by a number of different variables. For example, our ability to see, hear, and concentrate, as well as the way we perceive pain, are affected by the situation in which we find ourselves. Not only was Ruth Lerner aware of her back pain, but her perceptual systems also were at work interpreting her psychological distress, her environmental and physical stresses, and the visual and auditory world around her. We do these tasks in concert, easily, and with accuracy. We read and sing at the same time. We walk, talk, eat, and experience pleasure and /or pain simultaneously.

Learning $\overline{6.1}$
Objective

The functions of our perceptual systems is extremely complex. Psychologists study perception because what we perceive through our senses forms the basis of our understanding and interpretation of the world—we need to perceive before we can reason, learn, respond, communicate, and remember. Through the complex process of perception, our brains gather information about our world. How is this accomplished? We tend to take perception for granted since most of it is not learned and because it usually comes to people so naturally. However, you need only to think of people with perceptual difficulties to realize how dependent all people are on their senses. Think about Helen Keller, or a perceptually handicapped reader, or even Ruth Lerner, who was living with constant pain.

To appreciate the process involved in perception, imagine trying to locate a friend in a darkened theater. Even in a lighted room, you must sort out many visual cues—faces, clothes, seats, lights, signs—to find what you are looking for. In a dark theater, many of these cues—such as colors, spatial relationships, and fine details—are unavailable, at least temporarily. In a few minutes, the task becomes easier because your eyes have adapted to the dark. The auditory system is similarly complex. To appreciate a symphony orchestra, you must

This rider's vision, balance, and touch all interact as she executes a difficult jump.

make use of your perceptual abilities and distinguish among the sounds of different instruments. However, it is impossible to listen to two lectures or two conversations at the same time. You can only shift your attention between speakers.

Perception is the process by which an organism interprets and evaluates sensory input so that it acquires meaning. This complex process involves several levels of analysis in the nervous system and several sensory systems. Impairment of one or more systems affects the others. Blindness, for example, reduces a person's ability to move around, read, and learn. Deafness reduces a person's ability to speak clearly. This chapter discusses perception in human beings. The visual system receives the most attention because it has been the most thoroughly researched. As you will see, although the sensory systems (vision, hearing, taste, smell, and touch) operate differently, there are many similarities among them.

Perception ═══════
The complex process by which an organism interprets and evaluates sensory input so that it acquires meaning.

SENSORY EXPERIENCE

If you try to touch the tip of your nose with your index finger you will probably find that the task is easier with both eyes open. That is because, with both eyes open, your depth perception tells you where your finger is relative to your nose. If you have trouble completing this task, you may have some type of perceptual problem.

In 1950, Cornell University psychologist James J. Gibson (1904–1979) contended in *The Perception of the Visual World* (1950) that sensation and perception are essentially the same process. Most perceptual psychologists found the idea revolutionary. At that time, it was widely believed that sensation provided a stimulus and that the mind interpreted the stimulus through the process of perception. Today, most perceptual psychologists acknowledge that a distinction between sensation and perception is probably unnecessary.

Gibson's ideas eventually led psychologists to think in terms of perceptual systems—in terms of the structures, functions, and operations by which people perceive the world. Perception is now seen as a process by which the world is analyzed and interpreted. Human beings' various perceptual systems have many similarities in structure and function, but they operate differently and involve different parts of the body and brain.

Interacting Systems

Learning ⎯⎯
Objective 6.2
⎯⎯

The ball is snapped. The quarterback waits for a split second, then turns to his left and throws the ball laterally to his receiver. It all happens in a fraction of a second. Professional athletes have quick reflexes; they also seem to have a special ability to coordinate various perceptual systems to access situations and make decisions regarding how to act. A football player coordinates his visual and motor systems and his sense of balance and posture all at once. Researchers have studied this active integration of the perceptual systems extensively. They have found that, to develop fully, perceptual systems need more than just varied experiences; they need to interact with each other. When a child reaches out to grasp an object, he or she has to coordinate the visual and the touch systems. The two systems must learn to interact properly.

Held and Hein (1963) demonstrated this necessity in a study of visual-motor coordination in kittens. The kittens were placed in a circular enclosure. Some were equipped with a harness and collar that allowed active movement as they explored the visual environment. Each of these kittens was paired with another kitten whose physical movements were restrained so it could move only if the first kitten moved (see Figure 6.1). Active movement initiated by the first kitten caused identical, but involuntary, movement of the second kitten. Only the kittens that were allowed to initiate voluntary movements were later able to make good visually guided motor movements (see also Melamed, Haley, & Gildrow, 1973).

Studies of human beings also show that both varied sensory experiences and interaction among the systems are necessary when a sensory or perceptual system is developing. Von Senden (1932) reported case histories of people who had had cataracts from birth and had them removed in adulthood. These people, who saw for the first time as adults, had deficiencies in several skills. For

FIGURE 6.1 : Held and Hein (1963) raised kittens in a circular enclosure. One kitten was allowed self-locomoting self-initiated movement; the other received visual input that had nothing to do with its own transported movement. Both kittens saw the same view of the world but showed dramatically different types of responses when tested for sensory-motor coordination.

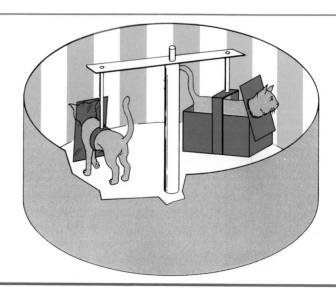

example, they had difficulty recognizing simple forms when they were presented in a different color or in a different situation. These data suggest that sensory experience is critical to the efficient functioning of our perceptual systems. Supporting evidence comes from the findings of sensory deprivation studies, discussed in the next section.

Although many organisms are prepared to perceive the world at birth, many aspects of perception are immature and very sensitive to experience. For example, in rabbits, neurons in the cortex have immature organization; for the thirty days after birth, their visual experiences will affect if and when certain perceptual abilities will develop (Murphy, 1985). This is not always the case: deprivation of light in rabbits has less severe effects than in cats. In human beings and animals, determining which factors of perception are ready at birth, which are affected by deprivation or experience, and how all these factors interact is still years away. We will discuss this further in Chapter 7.

Sensory Deprivation: Restricted Environments

Learning Objective 6.3

Imagine that you are a prisoner confined in a correctional facility. You have received a prison term, which, even after good behavior, requires that you will spend ten years in a cell. You will be deprived of your freedom and have limited access to friends and relatives. Your normal outlets for self-expression will be sharply curtailed. What happens when you are deprived of these outlets?

Studies of sensory deprivation, or as it is now called studies of restricted environmental stimulation, answer some of these questions. In a sensory deprivation experiment, an animal is usually deprived of some sort of sensory stimulant, such as light, from birth to age six months and is later tested on skills involving that sense. If the animal performs at the same skill level as animals who have not been deprived, the experimenters conclude that the equipment necessary for that sensory experience is inborn. If the animal is unable to perform as well as normal animals, the experimenters conclude that experience plays an important role in the normal development of that system. Sensory deprivation studies of kittens and other animals show that experiences with their environment must occur at certain crucial periods if organisms' inborn structures are to develop, and develop properly (Blakemore, 1978; Ganz, 1978). For example, if a newborn animal is deprived of light or patterned vision, its visual apparatus does not develop properly.

Heron (1957) assessed the effects of sensory deprivation on human beings. His subjects were college students who were paid twenty dollars a day (a handsome amount in 1957) to participate in the experiment. The subjects were confined in a comfortable but dull room and heard only the continuous hum of an air conditioner. They wore translucent plastic visors and tubes lined with cotton over their hands and arms (see Figure 6.2).

The results were dramatic. Within a few hours, the subjects' performance on tests of mental ability was impaired. The students became bored and irritable and after long isolation many began to see "images." These images were sometimes simple in form, like animated movie cartoons, and were generally not under the subjects' active control. As described by researchers:

Later they slept, became bored, and appeared eager for stimulation. They would sing, whistle, talk to themselves, tap the cuffs together, or explore the cubicle with

FIGURE 6.2 : In a study by Heron (1957), paid volunteers were confined in a room and deprived of all sensory experiences. Within a few hours, the subjects became agitated and asked to end the experiment.

them. This boredom seemed to be partly due to deterioration in the capacity to think systematically and productively. . . . The subjects also became very restless, displaying constant random movement, and they described the restlessness as unpleasant. Hence it was difficult to keep subjects for more than two or three days. . . . (Bexton, Heron, & Scott, 1954, p. 71)

In this experiment the students' brain-wave patterns also changed. Other studies have placed subjects in identical conditions, but the subjects have been told that their deprivation is an aid to meditation. These subjects did not hallucinate or become irritable; in fact, their mental ability improved (Lilly, 1956; Zuckerman, 1969). When given the opportunity to relax in a quiet place for extended periods of time, many people use that time to meditate and deeply relax—they find such "deprivation" relaxing. Some researchers suggest people in such circumstances are more open to new information and may even have better concentration (Suedfeld and Kristaller, 1982). Such findings indicate the need for caution in interpreting data from deprivation studies involving human beings.

Altogether, it seems clear that the absence of regular and active sensory stimulation changes the behavior patterns of human beings. As Hebb (1972) indicated, *boredom* is too mild a word to describe the effect on human beings of lack of sensory stimulation. In Hebb's view, the need for normal and varied stimulation is fundamental. College students are rarely placed in situations in which they are deprived of sensory stimulation; but after a few hours of studying, most will report they need to talk to a roommate, listen to music, or seek out some kind of stimulation. People's need for affiliation may be physiological as well as social, but the benefits of restricted environment may be underestimated—the research continues.

PROGRESS CHECK 6.1

1. Complete each of the following sentences with one of the options provided.

Learning Objective 6.1

A. Gibson's work changed the way psychologists think about perception, and now most perceptual psychologists _____ a distinction between sensation and perception.
   (*make* : *feel it is unnecessary to make*)

Learning Objective 6.2

B. Perceptual systems must _____ one another for normal perceptual development to take place.
   (*interact with* : *function independently of*)

Learning Objective 6.2

C. Von Senden's research with cataract patients suggested that _____ _____ is necessary for normal perceptual development to take place.
   (*focused attention* : *varied sensory experience*)

Learning Objective 6.3

D. Normal perceptual development depends on experience with the environment _____.
   (*and on passive feedback* : *during critical periods*)

Learning Objective 6.3

E. In Heron's sensory deprivation study with college students, the subjects became _____ and frequently began to see cartoon images.
   (*bored and irritable* : *amused*)

Learning Objective 6.3

F. When subjects are told that they are being deprived of sensory stimulation in order to encourage meditation, their mental ability _____.
   (*shows temporary deterioration* : *improves*)

THE VISUAL SYSTEM

Ruth Lerner's world was dominated by signals that her pain system was sending. Normally, when there is no damage to a person's nervous system, no pain signals are sent. In every perceptual system, the initiation of the perceptual process begins with a stimulus. In Ruth Lerner's case, a slipped or misaligned disk in her spine was probably pressing on a nerve. Pain had become a big part of her world.

Learning 6.4
Objective

For sighted people, the visual sense generally predominates. We pick up so much information through our visual sense and depend on it so greatly that perceptual psychologists have focused much of their research on vision. All sensory systems, vision included, respond to many different kinds of stimuli. For example, you can stimulate the visual system by applying pressure to an eye. However, the appropriate stimulus for vision is light, or electromagnetic radiation. **Electromagnetic radiation** includes visible light, cosmic rays, X rays, and ultraviolet, infrared, and radar waves. **Light** is the small portion of these wavelengths that is visible to the eye, ranging from 400 to 750 nanometers (a nanometer is one billionth of a meter). Light may come directly from a source or be reflected from some other object.

Electromagnetic
radiation
The entire spectrum of waves initiated by charged particles, including visible light gamma rays, X rays, and ultraviolet, infrared, and radar waves.

Light
The portion of the electromagnetic spectrum (ranging from 400 to 750 nanometers) that is visible to the eye.

Structure

In the late 1800s and early 1900s, a studio photographer had to bend over a bellows camera and adjust its length, focal depth, lens opening, and film. The human eye works in much the same way. Color Plate 6.1A shows its main parts. Light first passes through the *cornea,* a small transparent bulge that covers the pigmented *iris.* The iris constricts or dilates to make the *pupil* smaller or larger. Behind the pupil is the *crystalline lens.* Together, the cornea and the lens help form images in much the same way a camera lens does. Constriction of the iris makes the pupil smaller, improving the quality of the image on the retina by increasing the depth of focus; this action also controls light levels. The *retina,* which lines the back of the eye, acts much like film by recording the image. Without the retina, sight would be impossible (see Color Plate 6.1B). (See also Figure 6.3.)

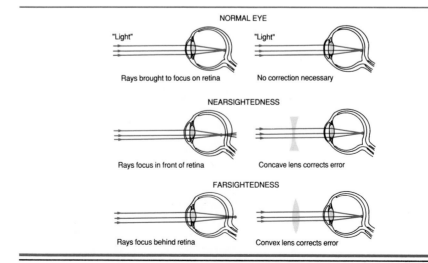

FIGURE 6.3 : The lens focuses light rays directly on the retina in the normal eye. In nearsightedness and farsightedness, the shape of the lens causes the light rays to focus either in front of or behind the retina. Concave or convex lenses correct such visual problems.

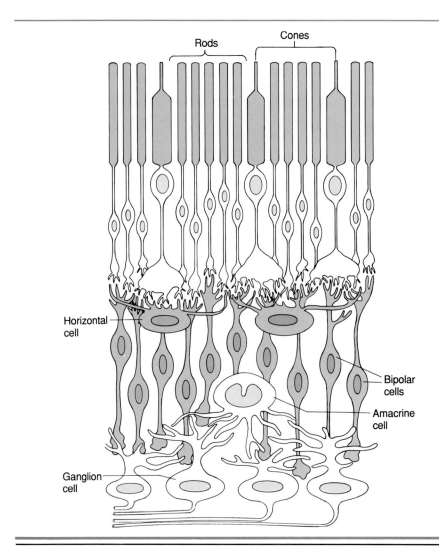

Rods

Cones

Horizontal cell

Bipolar cells

Amacrine cell

Ganglion cell

FIGURE 6.4 : The three major layers of a primate retina. The first layer consists of photoreceptors, either rods or cones; the second, of bipolar cells, connecting cells (called amacrine cells), and horizontal cells; the third, of ganglion cells. The axons of the ganglion cells form the optic nerve. (Redrawn from Dowling & Boycott, 1966).

Photoreceptors
The light-sensitive cells in the retina: rods and cones.

The process by which the visual system analyzes stimuli and converts them into electrical impulses is generally known as *coding*. The first stage of coding happens at the retina. The retina consists of ten layers of cells, three of which are especially important (see Figure 6.4). The first is the layer of **photoreceptors** (light receivers) themselves, consisting of *rods* and *cones*. When light strikes these photoreceptors, in the first step of the visual process, it causes an electrochemical change in the rods and cones, and the electrical energy is transferred to the next major layer.

Each eye contains 120 million rods and 6 million cones. These 126 million photoreceptors do not have individual pathways to the higher visual centers in the brain. By the process of convergence, light energy travels from many rods onto one, single *bipolar cell*. At the same time, several, even dozens, of cones similarly all synapse onto other bipolar cells. There are fewer bipolar cells than there are rods and cones. Further, a number of bipolar cells converge and synapse onto single *ganglion cell*. There are only 1 million ganglion cells connected to the 126 million rods and cones. The axons of the ganglion cells make up the *optic nerve.* The ganglion cell axons, the optic nerve, carry information that was initiated in the rods and cones to higher pathways in the nervous system, where more convergence and still further coding takes place. The coding process is often interrupted by injury to the eye. For example, often people's retinas are detached from the back of the eye as the result of sharp impact to the head in an automobile accident. Without surgery, people with detached retinas are generally unable to form clear visual images.

Learning Objective 6.5

Duplicity Theory.   For more than a century, researchers have known much about the functions of the rods and cones. The *duplicity theory,* which was formulated without the data collected in modern laboratories, correctly suggested that vision is controlled by two classes of receptors with different functions.

Support for the duplicity theory comes from the structure of the eye itself. Rods and cones are not evenly distributed across the retina. The *fovea,* in the center of the retina, contains only tightly packed cones. Other portions of the retina contain mainly rods with a relatively small number of cones (see Figure 6.5). Rods and cones accomplish different tasks. Cones are responsible for day vision, color vision, and fine discrimination. Rods, which lack these capabilities, are used predominantly for night vision.

Other support for the duplicity theory comes from studies of dark adaptation. When people first enter a darkened theater, they have difficulty locating

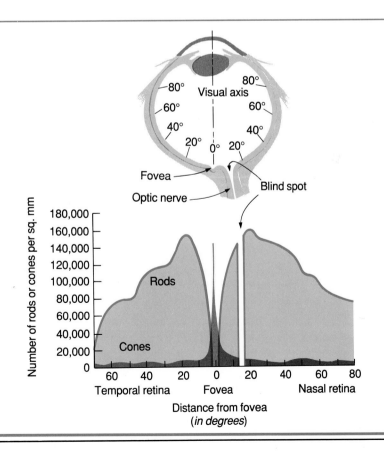

FIGURE 6.5 : Top view of the left eye, with the corresponding densities of rods and cones across the retina. (Pirenne, 1967, p. 32)

and identifying another person, because their eyes have not yet adapted to the dark. Once this adaptation occurs, their ability to discern other objects in the dark increases. People brought into a darkened room and shown a spotlight for a brief period have low sensitivity to the light. Yet, within thirty minutes, they are fully adapted to the dark and much more sensitive to light. **Dark adaptation is the process by which chemicals in the photoreceptors regenerate and return to their inactive pre-light-adapted state. The result is an increase in sensitivity.** Figure 6.6 shows a dark-adaptation curve, which has two parts. Studies in which only cones have been stimulated have shown that the first part of the curve is determined by cones, the second part by rods. The speed at which the photochemicals in the rods and cones regenerate determines the shape of the two parts of the curve. That is why at night, on a dark street, you may have trouble seeing for a few minutes after a car with bright headlights has passed and temporarily blinded you: the photo-chemicals in the rods of your eyes take some time to regenerate fully to their dark-adapted state.

Higher Pathways. A stroke victim who is left with poor vision in half of his or her visual field may have a blood clot obstructing the circulation in the right hemisphere of the brain. A physician is able to make such a diagnosis because of what is known about the way visual structures are connected to the brain. As electrical impulses leave the retina through the optic tract, they proceed via complicated routes to higher centers of analysis (see Figure 6.7). Each

Dark adaptation The process by which chemicals in the photoreceptors regenerate and return to their inactive pre-light-adapted state; this results in an increase in sensitivity.

Learning Objective 6.6

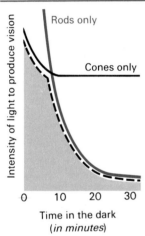

FIGURE 6.6 : The dashed line represents a typical overall dark adaptation curve. The two solid lines represent separate dark adaptation for the rods and cones. The process of light and dark adaptation occurs continually as people's eyes are exposed to different light intensities. The majority of dark adaptation takes place in the first ten minutes after being in a darkened place.

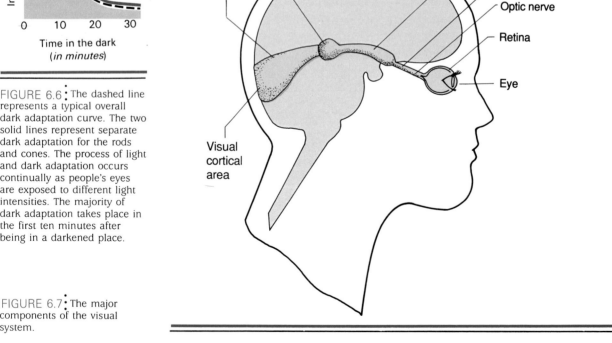

FIGURE 6.7 : The major components of the visual system.

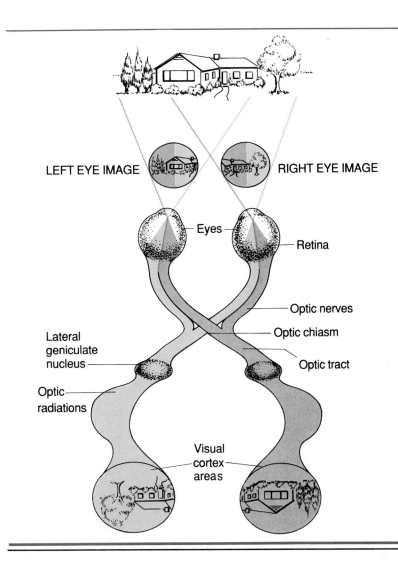

LEFT EYE IMAGE   RIGHT EYE IMAGE

Eyes

Retina

Optic nerves

Optic chiasm

Lateral
geniculate
nucleus

Optic tract

Optic
radiations

Visual
cortex
areas

FIGURE 6.8 : As this
overhead view shows, some
information from each eye
crosses at the optic chiasm.

eye is connected to both sides of the brain. Some impulses go to the same side of the brain, and others cross over to the opposite side. The point at which the crossover occurs is called the *optic chiasm* (see Figure 6.8). This crossing over allows the brain to process two sets of signals about an image and helps us perceive form and depth. Severing the optic nerves at the optic chiasm results in significantly altered vision. Normally, however, impulses proceed along to higher brain structures, including the *lateral geniculate nucleus,* and still further to the *striate cortex.* Each structure performs a specialized task in the total perceptual process (Wolfe, 1983); human beings, however, are seldom actively aware of the processes involved in perceiving depth, color, or shape. (See also Figure 6.9 on the next page.)

The Electrical Connection

Learning
Objective 6.7

Our perceptual processes are electrochemical. When receptors in our perceptual systems are stimulated, the electrochemical processes code information

FIGURE 6.9 : As shown in Figure 6.5, the center of the retina (the fovea) contains only cones. At about 18° of visual angle (a measure of the size of images on the retina), there are no receptors at all. This is the place at which the optic nerve leaves the eye, called the blind spot. Because the blind spot for each eye is on the nasal side of the eyeball there is no loss of vision—the two blind spots do not overlap. To demonstrate that you have a blind spot, close one eye and move the page in and out while staring at the fixation point. The black spot on the opposite side will disappear. If you switch eyes, the blind spot for the other eye will be apparent. Once you have located the correct distance, move the tip of a pencil across the page until it reaches the blind spot and watch the tip disappear.

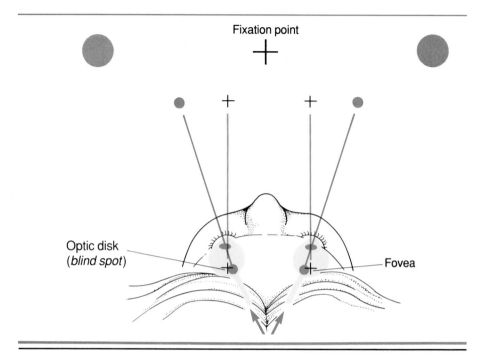

Fixation point

Optic disk
(*blind spot*)

Fovea

Receptive field
An area of the retina that, when stimulated, affects the firing of a single cell in the visual system.

and send it to the brain for interpretation and further analysis. To understand the electrochemical process, consider a simple task—the visual acuity test you probably took when you received your driver's license. A simple vision test may involve reading a chart with letters. A more refined acuity test might present a series of charts consisting of closely spaced lines. The task in such tests is to decide whether the lines are vertical or horizontal in orientation. When the lines are spaced so closely that the observer can no longer tell whether they are horizontal or vertical, that person's limits of acuity have been reached. Psychologists have examined how the visual system analyzes such stimuli by measuring its electrical activity when it is stimulated with horizontal, vertical, and slanted lines. Understanding how electrical activity in the nervous system is transmitted and coded helps psychologists understand electrical coding, form perception, and coding development—it helps them to make a careful analysis of how the human visual system operates.

Stimulation of the photoreceptors with light causes a change in electrical activity at all levels in the visual system. Many researchers have measured this change in activity by means of single-unit recording. By placing an electrode in or next to a single cell and recording its activity in response to stimuli of different sizes and shapes, psychologists have identified specific receptive fields involved in the perception of form, shape, and color. A **receptive field** is any one of many areas on the retina that, when stimulated, produces changes in the firing of cells in the visual system. For example, certain cells will fire if a vertical line is presented at the retina, but not if a horizontal line is presented. Hubel and Wiesel (1962) found cells in the visual system that are sensitive to the position, length, movement, color, and intensity of a line (see Figure 6.10). Their work earned them a Nobel prize in 1981. Of particular importance is their discovery that coding becomes more complex as information proceeds through the visual system.

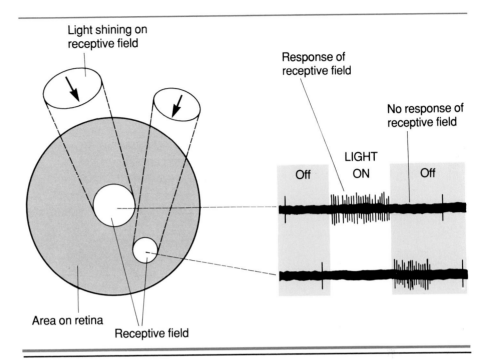

FIGURE 6.10 : Hubel and Wiesel found cells that fire when stimulated in the center of their receptive field but do not fire (and instead produce suppression) when stimulated outside that center area. (Hubel & Wiesel, 1962)

Normally, most organisms experience vertical, horizontal, and slanted visual orientations in their environment. Hirsch and Spinelli (1971) explored how the visual system is organized and developed by raising newborn kittens under conditions that controlled the kittens' visual experiences. Each kitten wore goggles that allowed one eye to perceive only vertical lines and the other to perceive only horizontal lines. Hirsch and Spinelli found that after a few weeks, the kittens' receptive fields were oriented either horizontally or vertically. Cells in the eye presented with only vertical lines fired almost exclusively to vertical lines, with little response to horizontal lines. Cells presented with only horizontal lines showed a similar tendency toward specialization. Studies of the behaviors of such kittens found that those raised with horizontal experiences bumped into chair legs (vertical) but could leap into a chair seat (horizontal), whereas those raised with vertical experiences had problems with horizontal surfaces (see, for example, Blakemore & Cooper, 1970). The data from such studies show that, although the visual system is largely built in, with most of its connections available to the newborn, its organization is sensitive to experience.

PROGRESS CHECK 6.2

1. Match each of the following key concepts and terms with the appropriate definitions.

cornea	rods	iris	cones	pupil
retina	crystalline lens	receptive fields	photoreceptors	fovea

Learning Objective 6.4

A. _____ Ten layers of cells lining the back of the eye; the three major layers are the photoreceptors, the bipolar layer, and the ganglion cells.

Learning Objective 6.4   B. _____ The transparent bulge on the outer portion of the eye that covers the iris and is involved in focusing images on the retina.

Learning Objective 6.4   C. _____ The small, dark opening located in front of the crystalline lens that allows light to enter the inner portion of the eye.

Learning Objective 6.4   D. _____ The pigmented part of the eye that constricts or dilates, making the pupil smaller or larger. It regulates the amount of light that can enter the eye and controls depth of focus.

Learning Objective 6.4   E. _____ A transparent disk located directly behind the iris that expands and contracts and as a result is able to focus images of near or distant objects on the retina.

Learning Objective 6.4   F. _____ The first layer of the cells making up the retina. Composed of rods and cones, these cells start the process of visual perception by transforming light into electrical energy through an electrochemical process.

Learning Objective 6.4   G. _____ The photoreceptors that are responsible for day vision, color vision, and fine discriminations.

Learning Objective 6.4   H. _____ The photoreceptors that are responsible for night vision.

Learning Objective 6.4   I. _____ The center portion of the retina, containing only tightly packed cones.

Learning Objective 6.6   J. _____ Areas on the retina that, when stimulated by light, produce changes in the firing of cells in the visual system and, as a result, allow us to see position, shape, size, and movement.

2. Complete each of the following sentences with one of the options provided.

Learning Objective 6.4   A. Each perceptual system is responsive to _____ of stimuli.
(only one specific type : many types)

Learning Objective 6.4   B. We see because our visual perceptual system is stimulated by _____
_____.
(ultraviolet rays : wavelengths ranging from 400 to 750 nanometers)

Learning Objective 6.4   C. When the iris constricts and the pupil is made smaller, the quality of the image on the retina _____.
(deteriorates : improves)

Learning Objective 6.4   D. There are more _____ in the human eye.
(rods than cones : cones than rods)

Learning Objective 6.4   E. Electrical impulses are transferred from 126 million photoreceptors, to fewer bipolar cells, then to only 1 million ganglion cells, and, finally, to the optic nerve through a process called _____.
(perception : convergence : coding)

Learning Objective 6.5   F. _____ theory suggests that vision is controlled by two classes of receptors whose functions are different.
(Bipolar : Duplicity : Electromagnetic)

Learning Objective 6.5   G. _____ are responsible for day vision, color vision, and fine visual discrimination.
(Rods : Cones)

Learning Objective 6.5   H. The process of dark adaptation allows the photoreceptors to become _____
_____ sensitive to available light.
(less : more)

Learning Objective 6.6   I. Our ability to perceive form and depth is in part the result of electrochemical impulses from our two eyes crossing over to opposite sides of the brain at the _____.
(lateral geniculate nucleus : optic chiasm : striate cortex)

Learning Objective 6.7

J. Researchers use _____ to identify receptive fields in the visual perceptual system.
(a variety of optic lenses : single-unit recording : verbal reports)

Learning Objective 6.7

K. Through their research, Hubel and Wiesel found that neurological coding becomes _____ complex as it proceeds through the visual system.
(less : more)

Learning Objective 6.7

L. Hirsch and Spinnelli found that the organization of receptive fields is _____.
(biologically determined : sensitive to experience)

Color the Sky Blue

When two people gaze at the blue sky, are they seeing the same color? Can psychologists find out? Unlike many animals, most human beings can see color in the world. Color has three main properties: hue, brightness, and saturation. These psychological terms describe, respectively, the physical properties of the wavelength, intensity, and purity of light.

Learning Objective 6.8

Hue
The psychological property of light referred to as color, determined by the wavelength reflected from an object.

When people speak of the color of something, they are referring to its **hue**—that is, to whether the light reflected from the object looks red, blue, or orange. Hue is determined by the wavelengths of the light an object reflects. As shown in Color Plate 6.2, the visible spectrum has different hues associated with specific wavelengths; light with a wavelength of 400 nanometers looks blue, and light with a wavelength of 700 nanometers looks red. Different surfaces reflect wavelengths selectively. Surfaces that reflect primarily blue light will appear blue in color because their reflected light is limited to blue wavelengths (Nassau, 1980). *Hue* is a psychological term because objects do not themselves possess color. People's perception of color is determined by how their eyes and brain interpret reflected wavelengths. An object seen through rose-colored glasses is not really reflecting long (red) wavelengths; instead, the glasses have changed the wavelength mixture that falls on the retina.

Brightness
The lightness or darkness of reflected light that is determined in large part by a light's intensity.

The second major aspect of people's perception of color is **brightness,** which refers to the lightness or darkness of reflected light. Brightness is affected by three variables: (1) the energy or intensity of reflected light may be increased, thus increasing its brightness; (2) reflected light of long wavelengths is less bright because long wavelengths reflect less energy than do short wavelengths; and (3) the photoreceptors in the eye are not equally sensitive or responsive to all wavelengths. As Figure 6.11 on the next page shows, the photoreceptors are most sensitive to wavelengths from 500 to 600 nanometers.

Saturation
The "depth" of hue of reflected light, as determined by the purity (homogeneity) of the wavelengths contained in the light.

The third property of color is **saturation,** or purity. Few objects in the natural world reflect light that is totally pure. Most often, they reflect a mixture of wavelengths. Saturated light has a narrow band of wavelengths. A saturated red light looks very deep and only red; it has no blue or yellow components. An unsaturated red may look either pink or "muddy" because it contains a wider range of wavelengths that make it appear less pure. A mixture of a great many wavelengths produces gray.

Learning Objective 6.9

Color Coding.   Light of various wavelengths proceeds through the optics of the eye and stimulates its photoreceptors, the rods and cones. The rods are not differentially sensitive to wavelength differences, but there are three

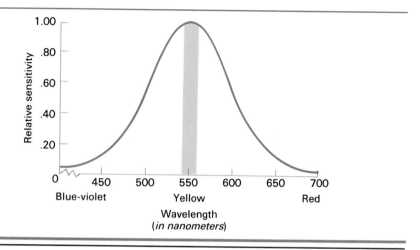

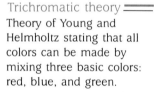

FIGURE 6.11 : The average observer's sensitivity to visible light reaches a peak at 555 nanometers. Thus, the normal human eye is more sensitive to yellow wavelengths than to red or blue. Such a curve is called a *spectral sensitivity curve.*

classes of cones, each of which is maximally sensitive to different wavelengths—short, medium, or long (see Figures 6.12, 6.13). When a cone is stimulated by a light to which it is not maximally sensitive, it will fire, but not as frequently.

Two nineteenth-century scientists, Thomas Young and Herman Von Helmholtz, proposed independently that these different types of cones may provide the basis for color coding in the nervous system. After their deaths, their theories were combined and named the Young-Helmholtz theory. According to this theory, also called the **trichromatic theory,** all colors can be made by mixing three basic colors: red, green, and blue. (*Trichromatic* means "three colors.")

All cones are assumed to respond to all wavelengths that stimulate them, but each type of cone—red, blue, green—responds maximally to the red, blue, or green wavelength. The combined neural output of all three type of cones provides the information that distinguishes color. If the neural output of one type of cone is sufficiently greater than that of the others, a person's perception of color will be determined mainly by that type of color receptor. Some colors like yellow require a certain combination of firing from each of the three cone

Trichromatic theory ══

Theory of Young and Helmholtz stating that all colors can be made by mixing three basic colors: red, blue, and green.

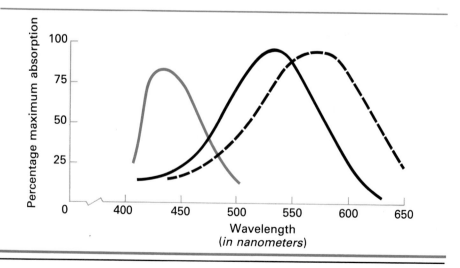

FIGURE 6.12 : Each of the three types of cones in the primate eye has a peak sensitivity in a different area of the visible spectrum. Thus, certain cells are more responsive to some wavelengths than to others. (MacNichol, 1964)

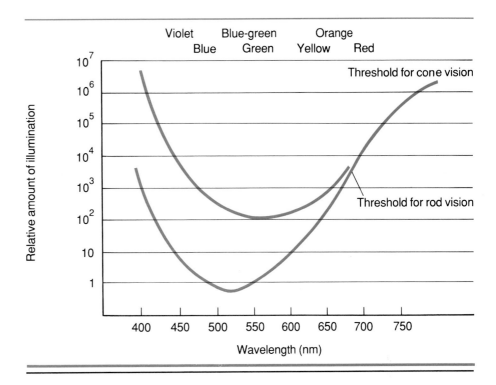

FIGURE 6.13 : The threshold for cone and rod vision according to the wavelength.

types to be seen as yellow. Because each person and his or her neurons are unique, it is likely that each of us see color *somewhat* differently.

Unlike the trichromatic theory, with its three types of receptors, each of which is maximally sensitive to different wavelengths, is the **opponent process theory** of color vision. The opponent process theory assumes that there are three types of receptors, but that each type responds positively when stimulated with one wavelength and negatively when stimulated with another. Initially proposed by Edwald Herring around 1887, the theory assumes that there are red-green, blue-yellow, and black-white receptor types. Every receptor fires to all wavelengths, but each pair fires maximally to one wavelength—for example, firing maximally to red and producing inhibition or lowered firing rates to green.

The trichromatic and opponent process theories are not incompatible. Both have received support from research (for example, Hurvich & Jameson, 1974). Studies of the chemistry and absorption properties of the retina do show three different classes of cones. Thus, the trichromatic theory best describes how information is coded at the retina (Marks, Dobell, & MacNichol, 1964). Support for the opponent process theory comes from microelectrode studies of the lateral geniculate nucleus in monkeys. (The lateral geniculate nucleus is one of the important pathways in the visual system of both humans and monkeys.) These studies show that cells at the lateral geniculate nucleus respond differently to input from different wavelengths. As Figure 6.14 on the next page indicates, when the eye is stimulated with a light of 400 to 500 nanometers, cells in the lateral geniculate nucleus show rate decreases; when stimulated with lights of longer wavelengths, firing frequency increases (Devalois & Jacobs, 1968). Thus, the opponent process theory best describes how information

Opponent process theory

Theory of Hering stating that color is coded by a series of receptors responding positively or negatively to different wavelengths of light.

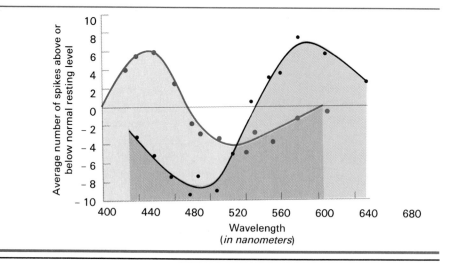

FIGURE 6.14 : This graph
shows how two cells in the
lateral geniculate nucleus
respond to different
wavelengths. The activity of
each wavelength either
increases or decreases above
or below normal resting level
when not stimulated,
depending on the wavelength
presented.

is coded at the lateral geniculate nucleus. Exactly how color information is transferred from the retina to the lateral geniculate nucleus remains to be discovered. (See also Color Plate 6.3.)

Learning   6.10
Objective

Color blindness ═══
The inability to perceive
different hues.

Monochromats ═══
People whose retinas
contain only rods and who
therefore cannot perceive
hue.

**Anomalous
trichromats** ═══
People whose color
perception is deficient at
various wavelengths and to
various extents.

Dichromats ═══
People who can distinguish
only two of the three basic
hues.

Color Blindness.   **Color blindness** is the inability to discriminate among wavelengths. Only a very few people are truly color blind. These **monochromats** have only rods in their retinas and cannot distinguish at all among different wavelengths (hues). About 6 percent of men and 0.5 percent of women are somewhat color deficient (Wyszecki & Stiles, 1967). In these **anomalous trichromats,** the extent of the weakness varies, as do the wavelengths affected. **Dichromats** have deficiencies in either the red or the blue area. About 2 percent of males are dichromats who cannot discriminate between reds and greens (Wyszecki & Stiles, 1967). The red-green deficiencies affect different regions of the visible spectrum in different people. In most cases of color blindness, lack of a specific color-absorbing pigment or chemical in the cones makes accurate color discriminations impossible. Some data suggest that when one cone pigment is missing, one of the other pigments is substituted for it.

Many color-blind people have a distorted response in several areas of the visible spectrum (see, for example, Graham, Sperling, Hsia, & Coulson, 1961). For example, a person with a red-green deficiency not only has trouble distinguishing between red and green, but both colors look yellow. This effect poses obvious difficulties for such a person who must drive where there are traffic lights.

Although the precise role of genetics in color blindness is not yet clear, researchers know that it is a gender-linked trait—that is, it is transmitted genetically, in this case through females (who are unlikely to be afflicted by it) to male offspring.

Form Perception

Learning   6.11
Objective

Everyday experience demonstrates that people tend to "fill in" information that is lacking. For example, even if a woman wears a large hat that conceals most of her face, her friends may recognize enough features to say with certainty that it is she. Artists make use of people's tendency to perceive form inferentially; the subjects of many impressionist paintings are inferred from dots of paint on the canvas. Architects and environmental psychologists also know that perceptions of space and form are influenced by numerous variables, some of them learned and some perhaps inborn. Understanding how people perceive form and space helps designers create pleasant and useful objects and spaces, such as buildings, chairs, and clothes. It also helps psychologists understand how to help people learn and remember what they see and read. (See Color Plate 6.4.)

The perception of form involves more than cortical firing in response to a collection of lines or shapes; it involves interpreting stimuli of different sizes, shapes, and depths as a unity. Two important activities in form perception are recognizing forms at a distance and recognizing forms that appear to have changed size or shape.

Perceptual Constancy. People are fairly accurate when judging the size of an object even if the size of the image on the retina is constantly changing. If they observe a man at a distance of five feet, they may judge his height to be about six feet. The size of his image on their retina is fairly large. If they see the same man at a distance of fifty feet, the size of his image on the retina is smaller, yet they will still estimate that he is about six feet tall. **Size constancy** is the ability of the perceptual system to recognize that an object remains constant in size regardless of its distance or the size of its image on the retina. (See Figure 6.15.)

Because experience is important in establishing and maintaining size constancy, researchers have studied this perceptual phenomenon in infants and other people with little experience. Professor T. G. R. Bower (1966) trained

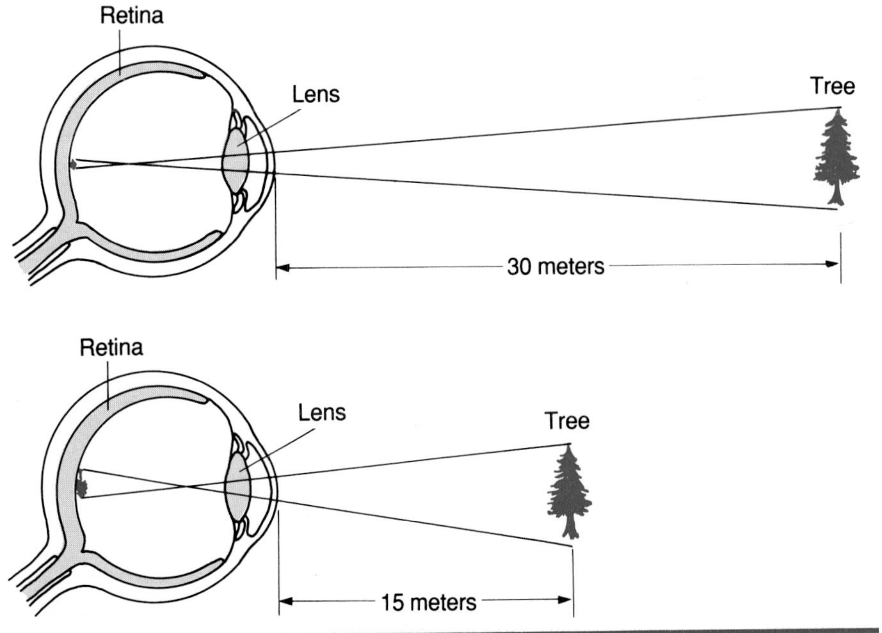

Size constancy
The ability of the perceptual system to know that an object remains constant in size regardless of its distance or the size of its image on the retina.

FIGURE 6.15 : The size of the image on the retina gets larger or smaller as you move closer to or farther away from an object. Due to *size constancy*, people still perceive the object as being the same size, however.

infants who were fifty to sixty days old to look toward an object. Every time they looked at the object, they were reinforced by someone saying "peek-a-boo." Bower then took other objects of varying sizes and placed them at the same distance, closer to, or farther from the infants, so that the size of the image cast on the retina varied. Finally, he arranged the objects so that the small ones were close to the infants and the large ones were farther away and all produced the same size retinal image. The infants showed size constancy, turning their heads only to the original reinforced object, and not to the other objects that produced the same size image on the retina. Infants definitely have size constancy by six months of age and probably as early as four months (Luger, Bower, & Wishart, 1983; McKenzie, Tootell, & Day, 1980).

Colin Turnbull (1961) has described the inability of one group of people to maintain size constancy. The BaMbuti Pygmies live in the dense Ituri forest in Zaire. In this environment, they rarely see distances greater than a matter of yards. One day, Turnbull took a BaMbuti man out of the forest into open space. When the man saw some buffalo on a ridge, he asked what kind of insect they were. Turnbull replied that they were buffalo on a ridge, whereupon the man laughed and, according to Turnbull, talked to himself for want of more intelligent company. As Turnbull and his companion approached the buffalo and watched the "insects" getting larger, the Pygmy realized that the animals were indeed buffalo and wondered why they had looked so small. According to Turnbull, the BaMbuti are unable to maintain size constancy because their environment limits their experience with visual distance; as a result, these people do not develop size constancy. Other isolated but similar examples support the notion that experience is a critical variable in the development of size constancy.

Shape constancy =====
The ability to recognize a shape despite changes in its orientation.

Shape constancy is the ability to recognize a shape despite changes in its orientation. For example, trees are usually standing perpendicular to the ground when people see them, yet even when a tree is leaning at a 45-degree angle people still recognize it as a tree, because they recognize that its orientation is different. Even though retinal image may be somewhat distorted, the perceived shape remains essentially the same. Similarly, doorways appear rectangular regardless of the angle from which they are viewed, even if the observer's head is tilted and the actual retinal image of a door is trapezoidal. Likewise, a round clock viewed from an angle casts an oval retinal image. Although the clock's perceived shape does not change with the position from which we view it. The development of size and shape constancy provides people with a uniform perceptual experience of discrepant and varied visual stimuli.

Learning Objective 6.12

Depth.   Most people take their ability to see three-dimensionally (in terms of height, width, and depth) for granted, yet when they are asked for the first time to draw a picture showing depth, they have to stop and think about how to do it. A drawing has only two dimensions. How can someone portray and perceive three dimensions using only two?

To perceive depth, people use both monocular and binocular cues. Because most observers have the use of two eyes, binocular cues predominate. Monocular cues are used mainly for a two-dimensional field such as a painting and in other cases when binocular cues are not available.

Monocular depth cues =====
Depth cues that do not require the use of two eyes.

Monocular Depth Cues.   Depth cues that do not depend on the use of two eyes are called **monocular depth cues.** At least six monocular depth cues

Depth cues such as linear perspective, interposition, and texture act together so that we are able to perceive distances.

are available to observers. One is *linear perspective:* objects located close to each other are judged to be situated farther away from the observer than are objects located farther apart from each other. For example, railroad tracks in the distance appear very close together, but the same tracks nearer the observer look farther apart. Another cue for depth is *interposition:* when one object blocks out part of another, the first appears closer to the observer. A third cue is *texture.* Surfaces that have little texture or detail give the impression of being in the distance. Two cues artists often use are *clearness* and *shadowing.* Clear objects appear closer; shadowed, dark objects appear farther away. Wavelengths themselves serve as monocular depth cues. For example, mountains seen at a distance generally look blue. This is because long (red) wavelengths are more easily scattered as they pass through the air, leaving more of the short (blue) wavelengths to reach our eyes. Leonardo da Vinci recognized this phenomenon and used it in his paintings. He even developed an equation for how much blue pigment should be mixed with the normal color of an object, depending on how far away he wanted the object to appear.

Another important monocular depth cue, *motion parallax,* is available only when the observer is in motion. When a moving observer stares at a fixed point, objects behind that point appear to move in the same direction as the observer; objects in front of that point appear to move in the opposite direction. For example, if you stare at a fence while riding in a moving car, the trees behind the fence rails will appear to move in the same direction as the car (forward), but the bushes in front of the rails will appear to move in the opposite direction (backward). Motion parallax also affects the speed at which objects appear to move. Distant objects will appear to move more slowly than objects close to the moving observer.

An important monocular depth cue not derived from the stimulus itself is accommodation. **Accommodation** is the change in shape of the eye's lens in order to keep an object in focus on the retina when the object is moved closer to

Accommodation
The change in shape of the lens of the eye to keep an object in focus on the retina when the object moves closer to or farther away from the observer.

or farther away from the observer. Accommodation is controlled by a series of muscles attached to the lens. These muscles provide active, regular feedback about the shape of the lens to higher processing systems in the brain. If a person looks from one object to another one at a different distance, the lenses of his or her eyes will change shape. Accommodation occurs even in young infants (Aslin & Jackson, 1979).

Binocular Depth Cues.   Most people use binocular depth cues as well as monocular ones. Even infants appear to use binocular depth cues. One study (Fox, Aslin, Shea, & Dumais, 1980) has found depth perception in infants as young as three and a half months.

One important binocular depth cue is **retinal disparity,** a slight difference in the image projected on each retina. Retinal disparity occurs because people's eyes are separated by the bulge of their nose and thus are viewing images from slightly different angles. Each eye sees a slightly different view of the world. You can easily demonstrate this to yourself by holding a finger up in front of some distant object. First, examine the object with one eye; then, keeping your finger in the same place, examine the object with your other eye. Your finger will appear displaced relative to the object. The closer two objects are to the eyes, the farther apart their images are on the retina and the greater the retinal disparity. Objects at a great distance produce little retinal disparity.

As an object moves closer, the viewer's eyes move toward each other, or converge, to keep information on corresponding points on the retina. This **convergence** is another important binocular depth cue. Like accommodation, convergence is controlled by a series of muscles in the eye sockets that convey information to the brain regarding the amount of convergence occurring.

Illusions.   When a person's normal visual processes and depth cues seem to break down, an optical illusion is said to occur. An **illusion** is a perception of a stimulus that differs from the commonly expected way the physical stimulus appears. A common example is the *Müller-Lyer illusion,* in which two lines of equal length appear to be of different lengths when angled lines are attached to their ends (see Figure 6.16). In the *Ponzo illusion,* two horizontal lines of the same length appear different in length when enclosed by slanted lines (see Figure 6.16). A natural illusion is the *moon illusion.* The moon appears larger over the horizon than it does overhead, yet the actual size of the moon does not change, nor does the size of its image on the retina. Such illusions have been discussed for many years, yet satisfactory explanations remain to be made.

Recent theories have generally accounted for these illusions in terms of the backgrounds against which they are seen. For example, the moon illusion is explained by the fact that the moon seen overhead has a background of only sky, whereas the moon seen at the horizon has a background of sky and land. Objects in the landscape provide cues about the moon's distance from the observer, and these distance cues change the observer's perception of the size of the moon (Restle, 1970). To demonstrate to yourself how the moon illusion depends on these cues, bend over and look between your legs at the moon on the horizon. The magnitude of the illusion will be reduced by this screening out of some of the horizon cues. Similarly, the Ponzo illusion is accounted for by the linear perspective provided by the background lines in the figure. The Müller-Lyer illusion is explained with reference to the angle and shape of the arrows that are attached to the ends of the lines. Inward-angled lines are often interpreted by observers as far corners—corners far away from the observer;

Retinal disparity ════
The slight difference in the visual image cast on each eye; a principal binocular cue.

Convergence ════
The movement of the eyes toward each other to keep information on corresponding points on the retina as an object moves closer to the observer; a binocular depth cue.

Learning Objective 6.13

Illusion ════
A perception of a stimulus that differs from normal expectations about its appearance.

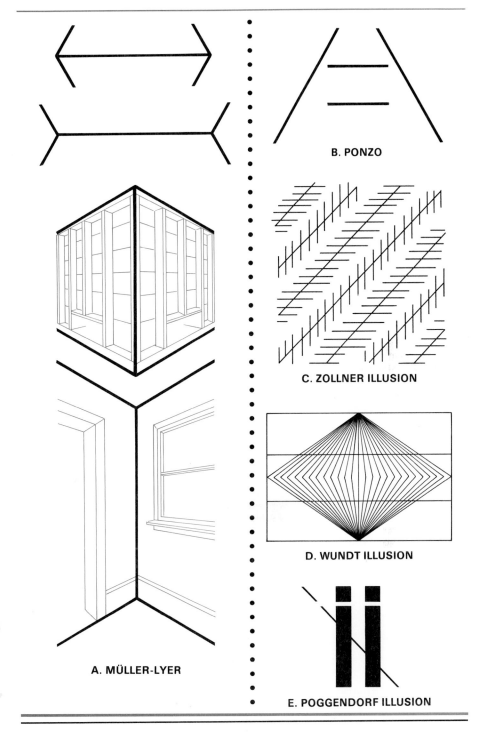

FIGURE 6.16: In the Müller-Lyer and Ponzo illusions at the top, lines of equal length appear different in length. The center and bottom Müller-Lyer illusions show how the arrows in the Müller-Lyer illusion usually represent "near corners" and "far corners." In the Zollner illusion, the short lines make the longer ones seem not parallel, even though they are. In the Wundt illusion, the center horizontal lines are parallel, even though they appear to be bent. In the Poggendorf illusion, the slanted line disappears behind the solids and reappears in positions that seem wrong.

outward-angled lines are commonly interpreted as near corners—corners nearer to the observer (see Figure 6.16). Therefore, in pairs of lines of equal length, those with "far corner" angles attached to them will appear longer because their length will be judged in a context of "distance." They will be "seen" as longer than the same-size "nearer" line.

These explanations of illusions are based on an observer's previous experiences and well-developed perceptual constancies. Researchers like Donald Hoffman (1983) argue that vision is an active process and that the visual system organizes ambiguous retinal images according to rules of inference consistent with often-experienced regularities. Some psychologists, for example, explain both the moon and the Müller-Lyer illusions in terms of perceptual constancy cues and previous experiences with distance and corners. Hershenson (1982) argues that the analysis of stimulation, of electrical impulses, no matter how complex, by itself is insufficient to explain such illusions. Needless to say, psychologists do not know all they would like to know about illusions or constancy. Form perceptions are among the most complex that people have to make and will be understood fully only after much more research into complex perceptual processes has taken place.

Learning Objective 6.14

Gestalt Laws of Organization. No description of form perception is complete without a discussion of the important contributions of Gestalt psychologists. Although few perception researchers today classify themselves as Gestalt psychologists, Gestalt thinking has greatly influenced current theories of form perception. Gestalt psychologists such as Wertheimer, Koffka, and Kohler studied *form* because they assumed that human perceptual processes reflect brain organization. Thus, by studying perception, they hoped to learn about the workings of the brain.

A guiding principle of the early Gestaltists was that "the whole is greater than the sum of its parts." They believed that people organize a complex visual field into a coherent whole rather than see individual, unrelated elements. Early Gestalt psychologists argued that people try to impose organization on any units that are perceived as complete or, as the early Gestaltists called them, "good." They argued that at each level of organization, an individual tends to interpret his or her perceptual field as being made up of wholes rather than parts. According to this principle, called a Law of Prägnanz, items or stimuli that can be grouped together and seen as a whole, or form, will be seen that way. Figure 6.17 shows a series of sixteen dots that people tend to organize into a form—that of a square.

Using the Law of Prägnanz, Gestalt psychologists developed principles of organization for the perception of figures. They especially focused on the nature of figure-ground relationships, arguing that figures are perceived as dis-

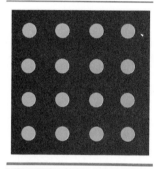

FIGURE 6.17 : The Law of Prägnanz is a Gestalt principle stating that items or stimuli that can be grouped together and seen as a whole will be.

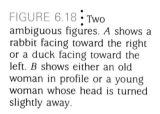

FIGURE 6.18 : Two ambiguous figures. *A* shows a rabbit facing toward the right or a duck facing toward the left. *B* shows either an old woman in profile or a young woman whose head is turned slightly away.

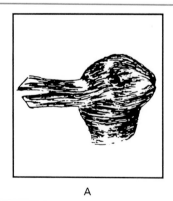

A   B

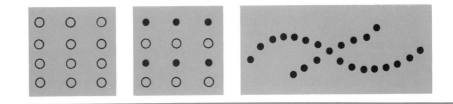

tinct from the background (or grounds) on which they are presented. To handle cases in which the relation of figures to grounds is complicated or subtle, Gestalt psychologists developed a series of laws or rules for predicting which areas of an ambiguous pattern would be seen as the figure (or foreground) and which as the background (Hochberg, 1974, 1979) (see Figure 6.18). The *law of proximity* states that elements close to one another in space or time will be perceived as groups. The *law of similarity* states that similar items will tend to be perceived in groups. The *law of continuity* states that a string of items will indicate where the next item in the string will be found (see Figure 6.19). The *common fate* principle states that items that move or change together will be seen as a whole. The *law of closure* states that parts of a figure not presented will be filled in by the perceptual system.

One of the best known modern attempts to examine Gestalt principles is that of J. Beck (1966). Beck asked subjects to divide patterns such as those shown in Figure 6.20 into regions along the most likely boundary. Although there are two places in the figure where such a boundary might reasonably be placed, subjects tended to place the boundary between regions that differed in orientation rather than between regions that differed in shape. Subjects were more likely to place a boundary between the upright Ts and the diagonally slanted Ts than between the backward Ls and the upright Ts. Similarity in shape and orientation took precedence over shared shape but different orientation. Beck's work thus verified the Gestalt laws, which predict that people will group together the elements they see as being alike.

Gestalt laws of organization suggest that visual perception is the process of grouping items visually into organized, meaningful units. Gestalt ideas have

been used to explain many perceptual phenomena. However, they do not explain several major aspects of perception, including certain perceptual constancies and illusions (Hochberg, 1974). For example, Gestalt laws do not explain why orientation rather than shape predominated in Beck's study. Either orientation or shape could have been used to break up the figure. Thus, although the basic Gestalt principles, formulated more than fifty years ago, continue to exert a powerful influence on perceptual theorists, they do not constitute a complete theory of perception.

PROGRESS CHECK 6.3

1. Match each of the following psychological terms of color with the appropriate physical description.

    hue   brightness   saturation

Learning Objective 6.8   A. _____ The lightness or darkness of a color; its *intensity*.

Learning Objective 6.8   B. _____ Because of the *wavelength* of the light reflected from their surfaces, objects appear to be red, yellow, blue, or one of the many other colors.

Learning Objective 6.8   C. _____ The depth of reflected light as determined by the *purity* or homogeneity of the different wavelengths comprising the color.

2. Complete each of the following sentences with one of the options provided.

Learning Objective 6.8   A. Objects _____ hue—what we usually call *color*.
                              (possess : do not possess)

Learning Objective 6.8   B. Short wavelengths are perceived as being _____ than long wavelengths.
                              (brighter : duller)

Learning Objective 6.8   C. A color like gray is the result of a _____ band of wavelengths.
                              (narrow : wide)

Learning Objective 6.9   D. When a cone is stimulated by a light to which it is not maximally sensitive, it will _____.
                              (not fire : fire, but not as often)

Learning Objective 6.9   E. The trichromatic (Young-Helmholtz) theory of color vision best describes how visual information is coded at the _____.
                              (retina : lateral geniculate nucleus)

Learning Objective 6.9   F. The trichromatic and opponent process theories of color coding _____.
                              (provide contradictory evidence : are different, but compatible)

Learning Objective 6.10   G. _____ have rods, but no cones, in their retinas and cannot perceive the hue of objects.
                              (Monochromats : Anomalous trichromats : Dichromats)

Learning Objective 6.10   H. Anomalous trichromats and dichromats _____.
                              (have fewer cones than normal : lack specific color-absorbing pigments)

Learning Objective 6.10   I. Because color blindness is transmitted genetically to male offspring by females who are themselves unlikely to be color blind, it is called a _____ trait.
                              (hit-and-miss : gender-linked : female-suppressed)

Learning Objective 6.11   J.   Size constancy _____.
(is an inborn perceptual ability : develops with experience)

Learning Objective 6.12   K.   People use monocular depth cues when _____ cues are unavailable.
(linear perspective : interposition : binocular depth)

Learning Objective 6.12   L.   A monocular depth cue that allows us to perceive an object as being far away, because its surface appears to be smooth, with little detail, is known as _____.
(texture : clearness : proximity)

Learning Objective 6.12   M.   _____ differs from other monocular depth cues because it occurs as a result of the physical structure of the eye and is not specifically the result of cues provided by an external stimulus.
(Motion parallax : Accommodation)

Learning Objective 6.12   N.   When an object is far away from the observer, _____ retinal disparity occurs.
(a great deal of : very little)

Learning Objective 6.12   O.   A binocular depth cue called _____ is available because, as an object moves closer to us, our eyes move toward each other, and this keeps the image of the object on corresponding points of the retina of each eye.
(retinal disparity : convergence)

Learning Objective 6.13   P.   When two horizontal lines of the same length are enclosed by two slanted lines and are perceived as different in length, an individual is experiencing the _____ illusion.
(Ponzo : Müller-Lyer)

Learning Objective 6.14   Q.   The law of _____ states that a string of items indicates where the next item in the string will be found.
(closure : common fate : continuity)

Learning Objective 6.14   R.   A guiding principle of Gestalt psychology maintains that "the whole is greater than the sum of its parts" and is called the _____.
(figure-ground principle : Law of Prägnanz : law of organizing)

COMPLEX PERCEPTUAL PROCESSES

The process of perception involves many different elements, each of which is exceedingly complex. Not surprisingly, when a person is having some type of perceptual problem, all factors need to be considered. Consider the case of Brian.

Everything seemed jumbled for Brian Cragmuller. Brian had always had problems with his coordination, and he never understood directions very well. Few people were concerned; but after Brian started school, things became increasingly confusing for him. He had trouble reading, and the regimentation at school made his coordination problems seem more acute. His parents feared he might be dyslexic. His reading teacher thought he might have a behavior problem stemming from too short an attention span. His pediatrician suggested that Brian's inattention might be due to allergies.

Brian's parents decided to visit the school psychologist. Much to their surprise, she recommended that Brian see an ophthalmologist before she made any evaluation. The psychologist had seen cases in which a child's behavior problems in the classroom were caused by poor vision. Poor vision led to inattention, and inattention led to poor behavior and to learning difficulties. The school psychologist might be on the right track because many learning and behavior problems have causes not easily or directly understood.

Brian Cragmuller's problem was ultimately diagnosed. The ophthalmologist who examined him said that Brian's eyes were not working together. He was seeing two images, and the image from the left eye was inverted but the one from the right eye was not. Brian's problems in reading and coordination were due to a mixed-up perception of the world. Had his serious vision problem been diagnosed in infancy, surgery might have helped. For an eight-year-old, however, vision retraining and special glasses were in order.

Brian's difficulties understanding the visual world illustrate some of the complexities of perception. His inverted vision of the world not only made reading—and therefore learning—very difficult, but it also affected his attention span, his coordination, and his ability to move through space.

Reading

Learning Objective 6.15

Brian Cragmuller's inability to form single images made reading and coordination difficult for him. Brian and his parents soon became acutely aware that reading involves several perceptual processes. To read, people have to be able to make fine visual discriminations, and the duration, frequency, and direction of eye movements across the page must be appropriate. When people read English, their eyes move from left to right. People who understand the language can identify and understand the words, whether they are written in typescript or cursive script or are printed. Variables such as the case of the letters can affect reading speed but generally have little or no effect on comprehension.

Of the many variables that affect reading speed, most important is the number of visual fixations. The minimum duration of a visual fixation is 250 milliseconds, or 0.25 second. If you read a thousand-word essay and fixate on each word for 250 milliseconds, it will take you a total of 250 seconds (250,000 milliseconds, or a little more than 4 minutes) to read the essay. You can reduce this time by half—to 125 seconds—if you fixate on every other word rather than on every single word, and by two-thirds—to 83 seconds—if you fixate on only every third word. If each line contains ten words and you fixate only once per line, your reading time decreases to 25 seconds. Thus, one way to increase your reading speed is to fixate fewer times, by examining more words in a single glance. People's reading rate is considerably faster when they are reading feature articles in a magazine than when they are reading a chemistry textbook in part because they look at more words in a single glance. A chemistry text is more detailed and contains specialized words and terms that must be examined carefully. Generally, more eye movements are necessary as the material becomes more complicated. On the other hand, it will be fairly easy for you to increase your speed when you are reading novels or material that is fairly predictable (see Just & Carpenter, 1980; O'Regan, 1979).

Attention

Teachers are concerned that students pay attention. Football players must concentrate their attention on the opposing team. Students believe they will perform better if they pay close attention to their studying. *Attention* is a term frequently used by experimental psychologists, clinical psychologists, and nonpsychologists. Although many psychologists speak about attention in terms of activation or arousal, perceptual psychologists are concerned with the complex process of selective attention and the extracting of information from the environment.

People constantly attempt to extract signals from the world around them. Although they can receive many different messages at once (as at a cocktail party), they can listen to only one message at a time. For this reason, selective attention is often called the "cocktail party problem."

Which stimuli do people decide to listen to? This question has been the focus of several kinds of research. In selective listening experiments, subjects wear a pair of headphones and receive different messages simultaneously in each ear (see Figure 6.21). Typically, subjects report that they are able to listen to either the left or the right ear, and they are able to provide information about the content and quality of that speaker's voice. The task of following one message and not the other is easier if the voice in one ear is male and the voice in the other is female, if the pitch of two male voices is different, or if the content of each message is different. If voice, pitch, intensity, quality, and content are similar in both ears, subjects often shift their attention from one ear to the other.

There are several theories about how people are able to attend selectively. One theory suggests that human beings have a limited capacity to process information and that some type of mechanism or filter must choose between information presented to the left and right ears. An alternative to this filter theory is attenuation theory. Attenuation theorists argue that all information proceeds from early analysis toward higher processing centers but is tuned and selected like a radio signal, to clarify the message. According to attenuation theory, all information is analyzed, but only selected information reaches the highest centers of processing.

Whether or not people filter or attenuate information, selective-attention studies show that they must select some of the available stimuli (Duncan,

FIGURE 6.21 Selective-listening experiments test subjects' ability to attend to one series of signals while ignoring another. Typically, a subject wears a pair of headphones with different signals presented to each ear. The subject is instructed to repeat the message from one ear as it is delivered. Response time and errors are often dependent variables.

1980). People have a limited capacity to process such information. It is impossible to listen to four lectures at once. The listener is forced to extract information from only one speaker at a time.

Both psychological and physiological data suggest that feature extraction or selective attention is one of the tasks constantly performed in the process of perceiving. Selective attention is not confined to hearing. Scanning or searching through a list of letters for a target is a visual selective-attention task. In reading, or in just casting their gaze about the world, people attend selectively to the features that will provide useful information. Psychologists know that the visual system contains single cells that selectively attend to features of the visual environment. Both the auditory and visual systems have limited capacities, and people also have a limited capacity to divide their attention between them (Massaro & Warner, 1977).

Imagery

Learning Objective 6.16

People use perceptual imagery every day, recalling a past event or something they have seen or read to invoke a visual image of some past, present, or future event. People's imagery systems can be activated by visual, auditory, or olfactory stimuli or by other images. As discussed earlier, even lack of sensory stimulation can produce vivid imagery.

Stephen Kosslyn of Harvard University, asked subjects to imagine an animal such as a rabbit next to either an elephant or a fly. In a 1975 study, subjects reported that when they imagined a fly, plenty of room remained in their mental image for an appropriately scaled rabbit, but when they imagined an elephant, the elephant took up most of the space. One particularly interesting result was that the subjects required more time and found it harder to "see" the nose of the rabbit when it was next to an elephant than when it was next to a fly (see Figure 6.22).

FIGURE 6.22 : Kosslyn had subjects imagine elephants and flies; a rabbit that was subsequently imagined appear small in size next to the elephant and large in relation to a fly. (Kosslyn, 1975; after Solso, 1979)

Carrying his research a step further, Kosslyn (1978) tried to measure mental images. In a series of experiments, he asked subjects to imagine an object at a distance, then to imagine that they were moving toward the object. The subjects were next asked if the object now seemed larger to them than before, and if it "overflowed" their mental visual field so they could no longer see all of it. The subjects were instructed to stop "mentally walking" at the point at which the object seemed to overflow. By having the subjects estimate the size of the object and the distance at which the images seemed to overflow the mental image frame, Kosslyn was able to estimate the size of visual image that people can imagine. Using this "mental walk" technique, Kosslyn found a limited "image space": larger objects tended to overflow at greater imagined distances. In addition, images overflowed in all directions at about the same size. Perhaps the most important finding from Kosslyn's research is that images have spatial properties. Although images are mental rather than physical phenomena, they have edges—points beyond which visual information ceases to be represented. Kosslyn made one of the first attempts to measure the size of the mind's eye.

Imagery as a Memory Aid.   Imagery is an important perceptual memory aid. According to Paivio (1971), a person presented with two words to remember is likely to form an image combining those words. For example, a person told to remember the words *house* and *hamburger* might form an image of a house made of hamburgers or of a hamburger on top of a house. Presented later with the word *house,* the person quickly evokes the word *hamburger.* Paivio suggests that words paired in this way are conceptually linked and that the mediation factor is the image. If Paivio is correct, words that evoke high imagery should serve as better links between pairs of words to be learned than words that evoke little imagery.

Eidetic Imagery.   In the 1960s, while Paivio was trying to make the study of imagery respectable, other researchers were investigating a different kind of imagery: photographlike imagery. If everyone could maintain a photographlike image of each glimpse of the world, how easy learning would be. Everyone would have a large memory bank containing each page of text ever read, as well as even the most casually observed objects and scenes. Although many people report they have such memories, none report that they maintain an image of everything they have ever seen. Most reports of photographic memory can be considered normal vivid imagery. However, Ralph Haber (1969, 1979) of the University of Illinois, Chicago Circle, has shown that some children possess a special kind of imagery called *eidetic imagery.*

Eidetic imagery is vivid, long-lasting, and complete. It occurs in less than 4 percent of school-age children. After some initial cross-screening for normal imagery, Haber's basic procedure was to place a picture on an easel for about thirty seconds, instruct the subjects to move their eyes so that they would see all the details in the picture, and then remove the picture. The subjects continued to look at the blank white easel and were questioned as to the nature of their imagery. Children who were eventually termed *eidetic* reported that their images lasted from a half minute to a full minute. Their imagery was so vivid that they could report even minute details of the pictures. For example, if the picture showed a cat with a striped tail, they could report how many stripes were on the tail. Those who could not remember parts of a picture reported that they had not looked at those parts long enough. When asked to move their images from the easel to another surface, they reported that when the image was moved, it fell off the edge of the easel. A few eidetic children were even able to develop three-dimensional images. Children with normal vivid imagery may be able to report the number of stripes on the cat's tail, but their eyes wander while remembering. Eidetic children's eyes look at the point at which the cat's tail was, as if it could still be seen.

Both adults and children use imagery daily as a memory aid, in fantasy, and in solving spatial problems. Research such as Haber's has shown that at least two kinds of imagery exist: normal and eidetic. Each serves a different function and operates differently.

CAN YOU PERCEIVE SOMETHING YOU CANNOT SEE? SUBLIMINAL PERCEPTION

If a visual or auditory stimulus is presented to you so quickly or at such a low volume that you cannot describe it, can it have an effect on your subsequent behavior? Although not fully understood and still controversial, it seems that some types of unconscious or subliminal perception may take place.

Subliminal means below the awareness threshold. Modern studies of **subliminal perception** began in the 1950s, when some innovative advertising agents claimed that moviegoers could be influenced to buy popcorn if an advertising message was flashed on the screen so quickly that it could not be consciously observed. Many psychologists dismissed as nonsense the prospect of such a tool of persuasion.

At the time, however, the popcorn experiment created a sensation, and some advertisers rushed to try subliminal advertising. However, the experiment had been conducted without controls and its results could not be repeated. Advertisers found that subliminal advertising did not work and for a while lost interest in its potential.

Because of the public concern over mind control that began with the popcorn experiment, a debate among psychologists about the existence of subliminal perception was reopened and research resumed. In the past twenty years, research concerning subliminal perception has been extensive (Dixon, 1981). Daniel Goleman (1985) reports that "by 1971, a comprehensive review of the literature concluded that subliminal perception, is indeed possible . . . and by 1977, although some holdouts remained, many cognitive scientists took unconscious perception for granted."

Recent findings by advertisers have found subliminal perception in advertising may have some effect in influencing subject's preference of products (Cuperfain & Clarke, 1985) and on how subjects evaluate ads for certain products (Kilbourne, Painton, & Ridley, 1985). Still, most research concerning the effects of subliminal stimuli in advertising report negative results or only marginal effects.

Some researchers have suggested that the unconscious or some other personality variable acts as a censor of information. They suggest that a stage beyond the sensory or perceptual stages affects the perceptual process and maintain that subliminal perception can best be explained in terms of such nonperceptual variables as motivation, previous experience, and unconscious or critical sensoring processes that influence perceptual thresholds.

Do we need to be concerned about our minds being controlled by advertisers or other unsolicited outside stimuli? The answer is probably no. However,

Subliminal perception
Perception of a stimulus that occurs below some level of duration or luminance with the result that subjects are unaware of the presentation 50 percent of the time. Perception of a stimulus below the awareness threshold.

research needs to continue before we will know exactly what is taking place when subliminal perception effects are shown to occur and before we can understand just how much influence subliminal stimuli can have on us. At this point, it appears that in some controlled situations, for example, in controlled advertising studies or controlled clinical settings in which subjects are relaxed, subliminal stimuli probably can influence behavior. In the real world, however, life is much different. We are constantly faced with many competing sensory stimuli, and what we pay attention to is based on many variables, such as importance, prominence, and interest. Based on all that psychologists know about perception, learning, and behavior, it appears that the stimuli we consciously perceive have a much higher chance of being stored in memory and thus of influencing our subsequent behavior than do stimuli not consciously perceived.

PROGRESS CHECK 6.4

1. Complete each of the following sentences with one of the options provided.

Learning Objective 6.15

A. The minimum duration of a visual fixation is _____ second.
(one-sixteenth of a : one-quarter of a : one-half of a : one)

Learning Objective 6.15

B. When looking up the spelling of a word in a dictionary, you are reading

_____.
(and focusing conservatively : and conducting a visual search : vertically

Learning Objective 6.15

C. When subjects listen to two conversations at once, they find it easier to follow one of the conversations if the voices, pitches, intensity, quality, and content are

_____.
(of interest : different : similar)

Learning Objective 6.15

D. The _____ suggests that people attend selectively because information is tuned and selected as it proceeds toward higher processing centers in the brain.
("cocktail party problem" : filter theory : attenuation theory)

Learning Objective 6.15

E. Selective attention studies have shown that people have a _____ _____ within and between the visual and auditory perceptual systems.
(limited capacity : variated process : repetitious processing cycle)

Learning Objective 6.16

F. By using a "mental walk" technique, Kosslyn was able to determine that our mental images have _____.
(no boundaries : a limited image space)

Learning Objective 6.16

G. Eidetic imagery is _____ imagery.
(mediating : photographlike : vague)

Learning Objective 6.17

H. Some research investigating subliminal perception suggests that experimental results may be influenced by _____.
(a sensory blocking system : nonperceptual variables)

OTHER PERCEPTUAL SYSTEMS

Learning Objective 6.18

When we watch a baby of about a year begin to walk, we see that the baby initially holds on, falls, gets up, looks about, takes a step or two, and begins the process over again. Slowly, over a matter of a few days or weeks, the baby grows stronger and seems to put the whole task together. Learning to walk is as much a perceptual task as a motor task. Walking is a complicated activity that involves perceptual systems.

Perception does not involve simply the independent action of the eyes, ears, or motor systems. It represents the coordination of many different processes acting together. So far, this chapter has examined only visual perception. This was done for several reasons: (1) more data and theories dealing with vision are available than for the other senses; (2) vision often takes precedence over the other senses; and (3) in human beings, vision is typical of the other sense and perceptual systems. However, in discussing perception, more than just visual perception must be considered.

Hearing

Listening to a symphony by Beethoven is delightful, intriguing, and difficult, because so much is going on at once. With more than twenty instruments playing, the listener must process many sounds, rhythms, and intensities simultaneously. To a music enthusiast, this complexity is precisely what makes Beethoven so exhilarating. In hearing as in seeing, converting physical stimuli into a psychological experience is a complex process.

Structure. The physical stimulus for hearing is a pressure change through a medium. The medium may be gaseous, liquid, or solid, but usually the change involves air. The pressure change is experienced as **sound.** When a tuning fork is struck, the prongs of the fork vibrate, displacing air. When their ears respond to the changes in air pressure, human beings experience the perception of sound.

Sound is often discussed in terms of two psychological aspects—*pitch* and *loudness*—which correspond to the physical attributes frequency and amplitude. The pitch of a tone or sound is determined by its frequency. **Frequency** is the number of times a complete change in air pressure occurs during a given unit of time. Thus, within one second there may be 50 complete changes (50 cycles per second) or 10,000 complete changes (10,000 cycles per second). High-pitched tones have high frequencies, and low-pitched tones have low frequencies. Frequency is usually measured in hertz (Hz); one hertz is equal to one cycle per second.

The **amplitude,** or intensity, of a sound wave determines its loudness. A low-frequency tone can be very loud or very soft—of either high or low amplitude. Amplitude is usually measured in decibels. Every increase of 20 decibels refers to a tenfold increase in intensity. As shown in Table 6.1, normal speech occurs at about 60 decibels, painful sounds at about 120 decibels.

The ear acts as the receptive organ for audition, or hearing. Like the eye, the ear is complex, with many important structural features. Only the most important are discussed here. The ear has three major parts: the outer ear, middle ear, and inner ear. The tissue on the outside of the head is part of the outer ear. The eardrum *(tympanic membrane)* serves as the boundary between the outer and middle ear. When sound waves enter the ear, they produce pressure changes on the eardrum. These vibrations start a sequence of events that includes the movement of tiny bones in the middle ear. Eventually, these bones stimulate the *basilar membrane* in the cochlea. The *cochlea,* in the inner ear, plays a central role in hearing. In this tube, shaped like a snail's shell, different frequency sound waves stimulate different areas of the basilar membrane; these areas, in turn, stimulate hair cells that bring about the initial

---

Sound ══════

A psychological term describing changes in pressure through a medium; the medium may be gaseous, liquid, or solid.

Frequency ══════

A measure of the number of complete pressure waves per unit of time, expressed in hertz (Hz), or cycles per second.

Amplitude ══════

The intensity or total energy of a sound wave that determines the loudness of a sound; usually measured in decibels.

TABLE 6.1: Psychological Responses to Various Intensities and Kinds of Sound

Psychological Response	Decibel Scale	Examples
Threshold of severe pain	140	Rock band at 15 ft
Painfully loud	120	Jet takeoff at 200 ft; Riveting machine
Very annoying	100	Subway train at 15 ft
Prolonged exposure produces damage to hearing	90	Water at foot of Niagara Falls
Quiet	80	Inside automobile at 55 mph; Freeway traffic at 50 ft
Very quiet	60	Normal conversation at 3 ft; Quiet restaurant
Just audible	40	Quiet office
Very quiet	20	Library Whisper at 3 ft Normal breathing
Threshold of hearing	0	

electrical coding of sound waves. These hair cells are remarkably sensitive. For example, Hudspeth (1983) found that hair cells respond when they are displaced as little as 100 picometers (trillionths of a meter). Color Plate 6.5 shows the most important structures in the middle and inner ear.

Many theories of hearing have been developed in the past century, most of which fall into two major classes. *Place theories* claim that the analysis of sound takes place on the basilar membrane, with different frequencies and intensities affecting different parts of the membrane. *Frequency theories* maintain that the analysis of pitch and intensity occurs at higher levels of processing (perhaps in the auditory area of the cortex) and that the basilar membrane merely transfers frequency information to those higher centers. Both kinds of theories present problems. To get around these difficulties, modern researchers have developed more complex theories of auditory information processing. These theories attempt to explain hearing both in terms of specific action in parts of the cochlea and in terms of complex frequency analyses at higher levels. No one has yet been conclusively shown to be correct.

Hearing Impairment. A person exposed constantly to loud noise may develop hearing losses. Even a brief exposure may result in temporary loss of hearing. The two main causes of hearing impairment are conduction deafness and nerve deafness.

Conduction deafness arises from interference in the conduction of sound to the neural mechanism of the inner ear. A variety of causes may prevent air waves from reaching the inner ear. Some causes are as simple as a severe head cold or a buildup of wax in the outer ear canal. Other causes include hardening of the tympanic membrane and the destruction of the tiny bones within the ear. Diseases that create middle-ear pressure can also damage portions of the hearing mechanism.

Nerve deafness arises from damage to the cochlea or the auditory nerve. The most common cause is exposure to high levels of sound intensity (Heffler,

Conduction deafness Deafness resulting from interference with the conduction of sound to the neural mechanism of the inner ear.

Learning Objective 6.19

Nerve deafness Impairment in hearing as a result of damage to the cochlea or the auditory nerve.

Repeated exposure to very high levels of noise can result in nerve deafness.

1978; Henry, 1984). If a high amplitude loud noise is presented repeatedly or for a long period, the person's sound threshold may increase permanently; that is, a higher amplitude (louder) sound will be required to achieve the same effect as a lower-amplitude (softer) sound in a normally hearing person. Older people are more susceptible than others to hearing impairments, particularly for sounds in the high-frequency range. Because normal speech involves primarily the lower frequencies (between 1,000 to 5,000 Hz), in most cases such impairment causes few difficulties. However, loss of ability to hear high frequencies would significantly reduce an older person's enjoyment of a flute concerto.

Too many school children have been diagnosed as having low intelligence and labeled as stupid by their classmates because they suffer from hearing losses. Sometimes children with partial hearing do not realize that they are missing much of what is said to them. The same is true of elderly people with hearing losses (Lowell & Pararella, 1977). A hearing impairment is not itself a behavior problem, but the unhappiness that may result from unfair labeling by family and friends can create behavior problems.

The standard clinical tool used for measuring hearing capacity is an audiometer. An audiometer presents different sound frequencies to a patient through a headphone and records how much air pressure is necessary for the person to hear sound. For an older person suffering from nerve deafness, significantly higher-than-normal frequencies must be presented for the sound to be heard. The results of an audiometer testing are presented as an audiogram—a graph showing hearing sensitivity at selected frequencies. The audiogram is compared with an audiogram for an adult with no known hearing loss.

Once hearing loss has been established, several different tests can be used to determine the location and cause of the impairment. These tests include bone-conduction tests and tests to measure damage to the tiny bones in the middle ear. One of the simplest ways of assessing and diagnosing hearing impairment is to test a person's recognition of spoken words. Typically, the person listens to a tape recording of speech sounds that are standardized in terms of loudness and pitch. Performance is based on the number of words the

Color Plate 6.1

When light enters the eye through the cornea and pupil, it is focused by the lens, and then reaches the retina. When the light strikes the retina, chemical processes in rods and cones lead to the firing of neurons, which carry the message to the brain.

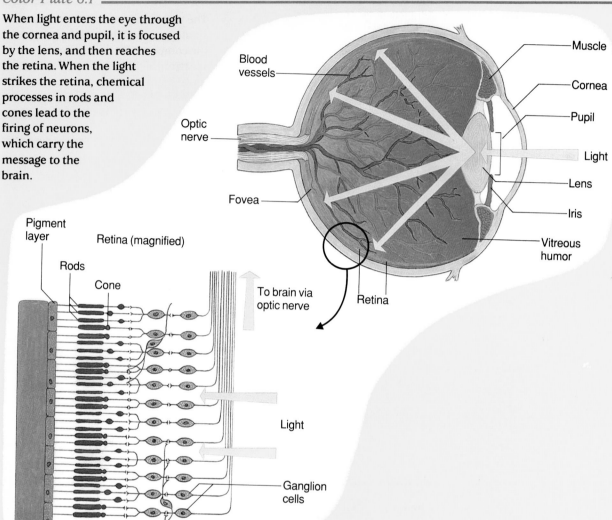

Blood vessels

Optic nerve

Fovea

Muscle

Cornea

Pupil

Light

Lens

Iris

Vitreous humor

Pigment layer

Rods

Cone

Retina (magnified)

To brain via optic nerve

Retina

Light

Ganglion cells

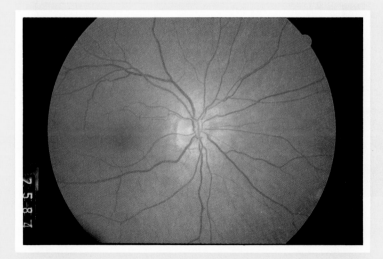

A view of the back side of the eye showing the retina, fovea, optic disk, and blood vessels.

Wavelength in nanometers

400   500   600   700

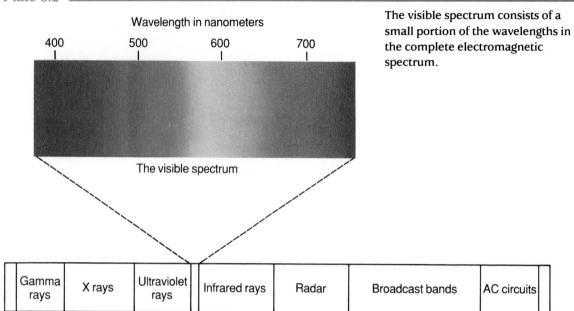

The visible spectrum

The visible spectrum consists of a small portion of the wavelengths in the complete electromagnetic spectrum.

| Gamma rays | X rays | Ultraviolet rays | Infrared rays | Radar | Broadcast bands | AC circuits |

Evidence in support of various theories of color vision has come from studies of afterimages and negative afterimages. Stare for several seconds at the center of the flag; then transfer your gaze to the dot in the center of the grey rectangle. You will see the colors that are complementary (opposite) to the originals.

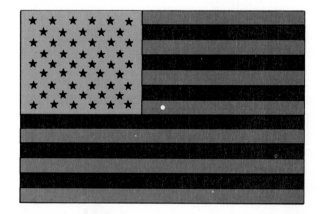

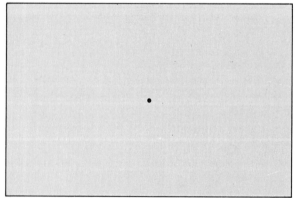

Our impressions of figure–ground relationships are often made up of many smaller elements in the visual world. Impressionist artists utilize this knowledge by juxtaposing small bits of color and form to create an overall painting.

The senses of vision and touch interact to create beauty.

The inside of this 115-foot, hand-made kite provides a dramatic example of linear perspective, an important cue to depth perception.

The major components of the middle and inner ear.

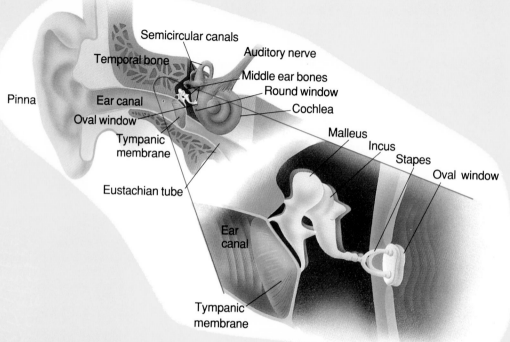

Semicircular canals

Auditory nerve

Temporal bone

Middle ear bones

Round window

Pinna

Ear canal

Cochlea

Oval window

Malleus

Incus

Tympanic membrane

Stapes

Oval window

Eustachian tube

Ear canal

Tympanic membrane

This skier's vestibular sense is dramatically affected by an aerial flip. Structures in the inner ear must accommodate for the rapid change in body orientation.

subject can repeat correctly at various intensity levels. This simple test can be administered by nonmedical personnel, who then refer potential patients to physicians.

Taste and Smell

Learning 6.20
Objective

For many people, one of the great delights of life is eating. For the gourmet, eating provides pleasures for both the palate and the nose. Food contains numerous substances that act as stimuli for both taste and smell.

When food is placed in the mouth, the food is partially dissolved in saliva and stimulates the primary receptors for taste stimuli, the taste buds. On the tongue are thousands of little papillae, shaped like little bumps. Each papilla is separated from the next by a "moat," and on the walls of these moats are the taste buds. Each taste bud consists of several taste cells. Individual taste cells have a relatively short life and are constantly being renewed.

Although psychologists do not yet know exactly how many tastes there are, most accept the idea that there are four basic tastes: sweet, sour, salty, and bitter. Most foods contain more than one primary taste; veal parmigiana, for example, is obviously a complicated stimulus to the tongue. Taste cells are sensitive to all taste stimuli, but certain cells are more sensitive to some stimuli than to others. In this regard, they are much like the cones in the retina: all the cones are sensitive to all wavelengths but each is especially sensitive to a specific wavelength. By isolating stimuli that initiate only one taste sensation, psychologists have also found that certain regions of the tongue seem more sensitive to particular taste stimuli than others. The tip of the tongue is more sensitive than the back of the tongue to sweet tastes, and the back of the tongue is more sensitive than the tip to bitter tastes (see Figure 6.23).

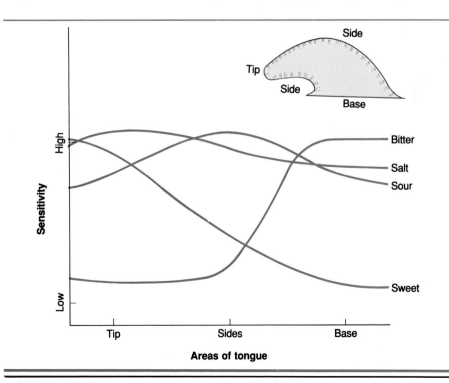

FIGURE 6.23 : Variations in gustatory sensitivity along the edge of the tongue; some areas of the tongue are more sensitive to certain tastes than are other areas.

Psychologists at Work: Smell and Communication

You probably have strong dislikes for certain smells—rotting fish, limburger cheese, and ammonia, for example. The smell of a favorite perfume, roasted chicken, or your grandfather's pipe may evoke a more pleasant response. Human beings have a very good sense of smell; it is not as good as in some animals, however. For example, human beings have only one hundredth as many receptors for smell as do dogs; dogs thus rely much more on their sense of smell than do human beings.

Human beings can detect odors well and often rely on their sense of smell. Unlike other animals, however, they usually do not use smells to communicate with one another. Smell has been found to be an important way that animals communicate with members of their own species. Pheromones (pronounced *fer'-uh-moans*) are substances secreted by animals that act to cause specific reactions among members of the same species. Pheromones act as communicating agents.

The two major kinds of pheromones are primary and releaser. Primary pheromones alter an organism's physiology by releasing hormones that change the way the organism responds in the future. Releaser pheromones usually trigger a more or less immediate behavioral response. Pheromones are widely recognized as initiators of sexual activity. For example, female silkworms release a pheromone that can attract a male silkworm from miles away. Female hamsters, when they are sexually receptive, emit a highly odorous substance that attracts males. Pregnant mice will abort their fetuses rather than let them be attacked if the odor of a strange mouse is around them early in their pregnancies.

Are there pheromones in human beings? Can we communicate with one another by emitting odors? Do women or men emit odors that attract members of the opposite sex? The answer to these questions are riddled with speculations. Some psychologists would like to believe that human beings are affected by pheromones—they argue that human beings would be the exception in the animal kingdom if we were not affected by pheromones. People are affected by smells of other people—for example, perfumes or body odors—but these smells do not trigger specific behaviors. Some data suggest that the smell of other human beings affects physiological processes in women. Because of pheromones, some women who live with other women are thought to develop menstrual cycles that are synchronous. Recent data also suggest that the pheromones a man emits may alter a woman's menstrual cycle. These data suggest that a woman who lives with a man (and has access to his pheromones through such close contact as sex) may have fewer infertility problems and even a milder menopause as well (See Cutler et al, 1986; Preti et al, 1986).

Human beings have too many experiences in the environment that affect their day-to-day behaviors for pheromones to have a direct effect on behavior. The sense of smell does not have a direct route to our emotional life as it does in lower organisms. Other people's physiological processes may affect us (McClintock, 1971), but the evidence that what we smell affects our behavior is only suggestive, at best.

Human beings have a delicate sense of smell. Their olfactory epithelium is well suited for helping people taste and smell the world about them. However, the pheromones that affect animals so greatly are probably not operative in human beings. We can stop to smell the roses, but this smell does not initiate any direct activity—even in the spring.

Like the sense of taste, smell (or, as it is technically called, *olfaction*) is a chemical sense, but the stimulus for smell is a chemical in the air. Much less research has been done on the olfactory system than on the visual or auditory system. One reason may be its relatively inaccessible location. Another may be that there are too many stimuli to classify; there are thousands of possible types of smell to investigate. Typical categories include flowery, foul, fruity, resinous, spicy, and burnt. Perhaps the most likely reason is that human beings do not rely on olfaction as much as they do on vision or hearing, so the motivation to understand it is not as great.

It is not clearly understood how odors affect the receptor cells of the olfactory epithelium. The *olfactory epithelium* contains the olfactory rods, the nerve fibers that transmit information about smell to the brain. There may be as many as 30 million olfactory rods in each nostril. When a chemical substance in the air moves past the receptor cells, it must be partially absorbed into the mucus that covers the cells. When absorbed, it initiates the process of smell (see Figure 6.24). The olfactory system is thousands of times more sensitive than the taste system. It can recognize a smell from as few as forty to fifty molecules of a chemical.

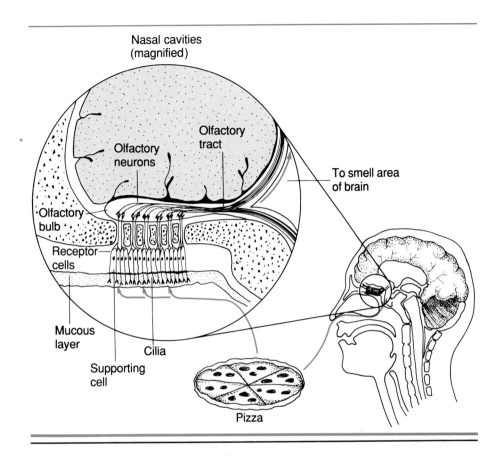

FIGURE 6.24 : Molecules from an object we smell trigger a chemical reaction in receptor cells located in the nasal cavities. Neural signals are then transmitted along olfactory neurons to the olfactory bulbs, and to still higher levels in the brain.

Kinesthesis and Vestibular Sensitivity

Learning Objective 6.21

Kinesthesis refers to feelings aroused by movements of the muscles, tendons, and joints. The study of kinesthesis provides information about bodily movements and internal sensations. For example, as mentioned earlier in this chapter, the movements of muscles around the eye provide information concerning the distance of objects through cues associated with accommodation and convergence. Similar coordination systems are constantly at work throughout the body. When you touch your finger to your nose, play baseball or tennis, or dance, kinesthesis is in part responsible for your ability to do so easily and with few mistakes.

The *vestibular* sense is the sense of bodily orientation and postural adjustment. The structures essential to these functions are located in the ear. Vestibular sacs and semicircular canals, associated with the body wall of the cochlea, act together to provide a person with information about the orientations of the head and body relative to the eye-movement system and the posture system (Parker, 1980). Rapid movements of the head bring about changes in the semicircular canals. These changes produce compensatory eye movements and sometimes changes in body orientation. They may also be accompanied by physical sensations that vary greatly in individuals and with the strength of the stimulus—from pleasant dizziness to almost unbearable motion sickness. Studies of the vestibular sense have recently become important because of its role in space travel. When people move at enormous speeds through weightless space, the workings of the system that bring about dizziness when a person is spun about are important concerns to psychologists and other scientists.

Perceptions of Pain

Learning
Objective   6.22

Ruth Lerner, who opened this chapter, was in extreme pain. In Dr. Sullivan's clinic, Ruth was learning some theories and facts about pain. She first learned that pain, touch, and temperature (warmth and cold) are considered *skin senses.* Particular receptors are responsible for the initial relaying of information about each skin sense. The receptors for different senses vary in shape, size, number, and distribution. For example, the body has many more cold receptors than heat receptors and has more pain receptors behind the knee than on the top of the nose.

The skin sense receptors appear to interact with one another, and sometimes one sensation will seem to combine with, or change to, another. When does pressure become pain? When does a cold stimulus lead to pain? How do you distinguish an itch from a tickle? An itch seems to be produced by a low level of irritation of nerve endings in the skin—this feeling can be produced mechanically; a tickle can be caused by the same stimulus and produce a reflexlike response. Tickles are complex and depend on who does the tickling, the location on the body, and other factors.

Studying pain has traditionally been considered especially difficult. One problem is that pain can be elicited in many ways. Stomach pains are brought about by hunger, toothache by a cavity or abscess, headaches by a wide variety of causes. Many kinds of pain exist, including postoperative pain, pain from terminal cancer, labor pains, frostbite, and even pain in a nonexisting limb lost by trauma or surgery (see Melzack & Loeser, 1978; Omura, 1977).

Certain areas of the body are more sensitive to pain than others. For example, the sole of the foot and the ball of the thumb are less sensitive than the back of the knee and the neck region. Individuals also have different sensitivities to pain. Some people have a low threshold for pain; they will report a comparatively low-level stimulus as painful. Others have fairly high thresholds (Sternbach, 1968, 1975; Woodrow, Friedman, Siegelaub, & Collen, 1972).

Ronald Melzack and Patrick Wall (1965, 1970) developed a theory of how pain is processed based on certain well-established principles of the nervous system. Called the Melzack-Wall gate control theory, it is the most widely accepted explanation for how the body processes pain. The basic idea of gate control theory is that the pattern of nervous system activity established in an individual's body determines the extent to which he or she will feel pain. When a signal is sent to the brain that might normally indicate a painful stimulus, it goes through a series of "gates." These gates can be open or closed (or even partially open or partially closed). How far these gates are open determines how much of the original pain signal gets through.

A chemical called substance-P, released by the sensory nerve fibers, transmits pain impulses across the gates. A brain opiate called *enkephalin* can block this pain signal (Snyder, 1980). Enkephalin is one of a group of naturally produced *endorphins,* which are pain killers produced naturally in the brain and pituitary gland. (*Endorphin* is a contraction of *endogenous,* meaning naturally occurring, and *morphine,* a pain killer.)

Even though pain is an adaptive and important aspect of people's perceptual lives, there has been less research into pain receptors and the nature of pain than into vision and audition (see Weisenberg, 1977). Recently, however, there has been a series of exciting breakthroughs on *endorphins* (Olson, Olson, Kastin, & Coy, 1979). They are implicated in the regulation of several bodily functions, including the control of blood pressure and body temperature (Bloom, 1981). They can produce euphoria and a sense of well-being much as morphine does, but to an even greater extent (Loh et al., 1976). Stress, anticipated pain, and activities such as running bring about an increased endorphin level (Kimball, 1982). Runners often report feeling "high," which many researchers believe is directly related to their endorphin level. Enkephalin increases tolerance to pain, and other endorphins reduce pain. The human body thus has many natural mechanisms that help people cope with physical pain.

Certain drugs, electrical stimulation and even acupuncture needles (Omura, 1976) are thought to close the gates, partially or fully, and thus make the original painful stimulus less potent. The actual Melzack-Wall theory is more complicated and takes into account both the sizes of nerve fibers and their level of development.

It has long been known that some synapses in the body are excitatory and others inhibitory. The Melzack-Wall theory relies heavily on the idea that this interplay of excitatory and inhibitory cells can establish patterns of activity that diminish (inhibit) excitatory or painful sensations. Although gate control theory is popular, it is by no means universally accepted.

Many people who are afflicted with chronic, unrelieved pain have sought help from acupuncture. Initially developed in China, acupuncture is the technique of inserting long, fine needles into various sites of the body in order to relieve pain. These needle insertions are often not near the site of pain, and different practitioners may use different sites. Controlled studies of acupuncture have shown various results. Some have provided support (Lee, Andersen, Modell, & Saga, 1975); others have found weak or nonexistent effects (Day et al., 1975).

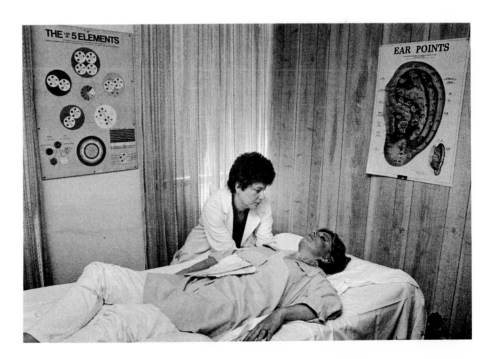

In acupuncture specific body sites are stimulated with needles in order to relieve pain.

Psychologists at Work: Block That Pain

The puzzle of how pain is transmitted to the brain is being pieced together gradually through research. All answers are not in, but the search has led to some startling discoveries. For example, when you stub your toe, a chain of nerve impulses begin at your toe and make their way to the spinal cord and ultimately to your brain. The nerve impulses make this long journey through special pain pathways. The pathways for acute sharp pain end in the cortex; those for chronic, long-lasting pain end in the limbic system.

The study of pain and pain killers led to research on endorphins. Researchers know that endorphins are naturally produced in the body and block pain. They also know that endorphins bind themselves to receptor sites and in doing so do not let pain signals through to higher levels of the nervous system.

You can block pain so that it is not felt; a physician can prescribe to a person in pain endorphins or endorphinlike substances—morphine is one substance very good at killing intense pain because it binds itself to, or occupies, the receptor site (on the spinal cord or in the brain).

New technologies are emerging to kill pain. One leader in pain research, Solomon Snyder, reasoned that some-thing must happen at the site of an injury to initiate or trigger endorphin production. Remember, endorphins work at receptor sites in the spinal cord and brain; what if a drug could stop the whole pain perception process at the actual place an injury starts? Colleagues of Solomon, Innis, and Manning have been studying the receptor sites in skin tissue and observing how chemicals bind to them (Bishop, 1986). They have been searching for compounds that will bind to skin receptors in order to stop the entire pain perception process even before endorphin production starts. The compounds that they discover may themselves not be total pain relievers, but in combination with other analgesics, such as aspirin, they may be very effective. Such compounds might also be used as rub-ons that penetrate the skin and relieve the pain of joint disorders or muscle aches.

By tracing the pain pathways, the sites that receive pain signals, and the substances that the body produces when pain is initiated, researchers are finding new ways to block the pain that pierces, pinches, and paralyzes. Pain blockers at the initial site of an injury may prove to be the most effective pain killer yet.

Relief of Pain

Learning Objective 6.23

Usually pain from a headache, toothache, or small cut can be alleviated with a simple analgesic medication, such as aspirin. For millions of people like Ruth Lerner, however, aspirin is not enough. For the many who suffer from constant pain caused by back injury, arthritis, or illness such as cancer, drug treatment either is not effective or is dangerous because a very high dosage is required. People who suffer chronic pain are not simply uncomfortable; their family and work situations may be disrupted, and their overall level of satisfaction with life may decrease. To meet this problem, pain clinics, like the one Ruth found have been established to treat pain that cannot be ameliorated by the use of simple drugs. Usually, the staff consists of both medical and psychological practitioners. Treatment at a pain clinic combines several methods, such as exercise, diet, relaxation training, education classes, and general psychological support.

Practitioners who deal with pain recognize that pain can have both physical and psychological sources. Although initially the pain may arise from physical complaints, sometimes the attention given pain sufferers is reinforcing, or the pain may provide a distraction from other problems or worries. At a pain clinic, treatment focuses on helping people cope with pain regardless of its origins. For example, a patient may be hypnotized and told that after the hypnotic session her pain will be more bearable. She may be instructed to focus on other aspects of her life.

Anxiety and worry can make pain worse. For example, people who suffer from migraine headaches often make their condition worse by becoming fearful—and thus tense—when they feel a headache coming on. Researchers have found that biofeedback training (discussed in Chapter 4) can help some people suffering from chronic pain and from migraine headaches to achieve some relief (Nuechterlein & Holroyd, 1980).

Especially in pain management, psychological and physiological factors interact in complicated ways. A poor or hopeless attitude can make the pain worse. Cognitive coping strategies (discussed in Chapter 5) are closely related to biofeedback training. They involve teaching patients to have a better attitude about their pain. Patients may learn to talk to themselves in positive ways and divert their attention to pleasant images or to take an active role in managing their pain.

Learning to live with pain is easier said than done, but sometimes recognizing the limits of modern medicine and psychology can help pain sufferers learn to cope with their situation. Initial research suggests that psychological methods for treating pain—such as cognitive coping strategies, biofeedback, and relaxation techniques (discussed in Chapters 4 and 15)—can help people cope more effectively with a life in which pain plays a major role (Turk, Meichenbaum, & Genest, 1983).

Extrasensory Perception

Learning Objective 6.24   People are fascinated by the possibility of extrasensory perception, or ESP. The British Society for the Study of Psychic Phenomena, with Nobel laureates serving as presidents, has critically investigated reports of ESP since the nineteenth century. The term *ESP* is used to describe several different phenomena, including telepathy, clairvoyance, and precognition. *Telepathy* is the transfer of thought processes from one person to another. *Clairvoyance* is the ability to recognize objects or events that are not present to normal sensory receptors, such as the contents of a message in a sealed envelope. *Precognition* is the unexplained knowledge of future events.

Until recently, the psychological community did not take ESP seriously. The resurgence of scientific interest was due largely to articles published in respected scientific journals. The first, appearing in *Nature,* reported some seemingly incredible results of experiments at the Stanford Research Institute with Israeli magician Uri Geller, suggesting that Geller possessed ESP. In the same week, an article in the British magazine *New Scientist* dramatically undermined many findings presented in the Stanford Research Institute report. The evidence in support of ESP is very weak and has not been repeated. Most scientists consider Geller a fraud. Furthermore, when visible, ESP phenomena are not affected by certain experimental conditions the way normal perceptual events are. None of these criticisms means that ESP does not exist, but they do prompt most perceptual psychologists to maintain a healthy skepticism. Active research using scientific methods to investigate these unusual phenomena continues, but, as Child (1985) suggests, psychologists have seen so much trickery and falsification of data and so many design errors in experiments that they remain very skeptical.

PROGRESS CHECK 6.5

1. Match each of the following psychological terms with the appropriate physical description.

sound   pitch   loudness

Learning Objective 6.18   A. _____ The number of times a complete change in air pressure occurs during a given unit of time is called *frequency.*

Learning Objective 6.18 B. _____ The intensity, or *amplitude*, of a sound is measured in decibles. Speech occurs at about 60 decibles and painful sounds at about 120 decibles.

Learning Objective 6.18 C. _____ This is a psychological experience we have when the auditory perception system responds to *changes in air pressure* or sometimes to gaseous, liquid, or solid, pressure changes.

2. Complete each of the following sentences with one of the options provided.

Learning Objective 6.18 A. The _____ sense frequently takes precedence over the other senses.
(*visual : auditory : kinesthetic*)

Learning Objective 6.18 B. The eardrum serves as a boundary between the outer and _____ _____ ear.
(*middle : inner*)

Learning Objective 6.18 C. The initial electrical coding of sound waves takes place when _____ _____ stimulated.
(*the eardrum is : hair cells in the inner ear are*)

Learning Objective 6.18 D. Place theories suggest that the _____ in the inner ear is the location for analysis of sound.
(*tympanic membrane : cochlea*)

Learning Objective 6.19 E. Damage to the cochlea or auditory nerve can lead to _____ _____ deafness.
(*nerve : conduction : interference*)

Learning Objective 6.19 F. An audiometer is a tool used for measuring a person's capacity to hear various _____.
(*amplitudes : frequencies*)

Learning Objective 6.20 G. The tip of the tongue is more sensitive to _____ tastes than is the back of the tongue.
(*sweet : bitter*)

Learning Objective 6.20 H. Smell receptor cells are called _____.
(*the olfactory epithelium : rods : hairs*)

Learning Objective 6.20 I. When taste and smell are compared, the _____ system is thousands of times more sensitive to chemical stimuli.
(*taste : olfactory*)

Learning Objective 6.21 J. Research of the vestibular sense has become important recently because of the role it plays in _____.
(*radiology : military strategies : space travel : pain management*)

Learning Objective 6.22 K. Certain areas of the body are more sensitive to pain than are others; the sole of the foot is relatively _____ compared to the back of the knee.
(*insensitive : sensitive*)

Learning Objective 6.22 L. Melzack and Wall have suggested that pain is determined by the amount of the original pain stimulus that passes through a series of _____ _____ in the nervous system.
(*canals : tunnels : gates : moats*)

Learning Objective 6.22 M. _____ is an innate brain opiate that blocks pain impulses in the nervous.
(*Substance-P : An endorphin called enkephalin*)

Learning Objective 6.23 N. For people who experience chronic pain, pain management techniques are frequently used to reduce the pain because _____.
(*their pain is purely psychological : it is safer than drugs*)

Learning Objective 6.24   O. The process by which thoughts are transferred _____ person to the next without the use of verbal communication skills is _____

(telepathy : clairvoyance : precognition)

Keeping Pace with Chapter 6

Applying Principles

New knowledge becomes more meaningful when you can relate it to actual life experiences. Here, you have an opportunity to think more deeply about some of the concepts discussed in this chapter and to practice applying them. The exercise will contribute to your learning whether it is done before or after the Self-Test. So, whenever you feel prepared, try applying your new knowledge to these situations and to your own life experiences.

6.1 Identify the perceptual process that best explains why each of the following situations is perceived by the observer as described.

monocular depth cue   illusion   binocular depth cue
Gestalt laws of organization

_____   A. Looking off into the distance, an observer sees a barn and a windmill. Because the windmill blocks part of the image of the barn, the observer perceives the windmill as being closer to him.

_____   B. As you move your new record album closer to your face so you can read the song titles, a series of muscles attached to the crystalline lenses in your eyes change the shape of the lenses and keep the image on your retinas in focus.

_____   C. You watch your friends as they get out of their car and walk up the sidewalk to your front door. As they get closer, your eyes converge, moving toward one another and providing you with necessary depth cues so you can focus clearly on their faces as you greet them.

_____   D. At a football game, the people in several sections of the audience participate in holding up blue or gold cardboard rectangles when told to do so. People on the other side of the field are able to read cheer messages because the gold cards are perceived as a figure against the blue background.

_____   E. A billboard clown advertising the new roller coaster ride at the amusement park appears to be waving at you because light bulbs that light up the sign blink in a synchronized manner.

_____   F. As you look at your favorite painting, you notice that darker objects seem to be farther away than the lighter objects.

_____   G. You look at two lines, one of which appears to be longer. When you measure the two lines you find they are the same length. Yet, when you look at them again, one line still appears to be longer.

Self-Test

Before proceeding to the Self-Test, REVIEW the Learning Objectives listed at the chapter opening and RECITE from memory everything you can remember in support of them. Then, take this Self-Test as if it were to be graded by your teacher. Use the Learning Objective numbers in the Answer Section as a reference to restudy the corresponding text pages and Progress Checks for any incorrectly answered questions.

1. The process by which an organism interprets and evaluates sensory input so that it acquires meaning is called

   A. sensation.
   B. feature extraction.
   C. perception.
   D. selective attention.

2. In their study of visual-motor coordination with kittens, Held and Hein found that _____ in the kittens that were prevented from experiencing normal interaction of perceptual systems.

   A. visually guided motor movements lacked coordination
   B. visual perception was distorted, but motor coordination was normal
   C. one system became the dominant system and the others showed impairment
   D. visual and motor systems developed separately

3. In describing the effect that sensory deprivation has on human beings, Hebb said,

   A. it is pleasurable.
   B. fatigue results.
   C. boredom is too mild a word to describe the effects.
   D. it elicits an involuntary meditative state.

4. The part of the eye that contains the rods and cones is called the

   A. retina.
   B. iris.
   C. cornea.
   D. bipolar layer.

5. Dark adaptation is the process by which chemicals in the photoreceptors _____ and return to their inactive pre-light-adapted state.

   A. stimulate rods
   B. regenerate
   C. condense
   D. converge

6. Our visual perceptual system can distinguish between an oval and a square because the image produced by each shape

   A. is clearly different from any other shape.
   B. stimulates the cells of different receptive fields.
   C. passes through a different portion of the crystalline lens.
   D. is recognized by the primary visual center.

7. The brightness of a color is determined by

   A. the homogeneity of wavelengths being reflected by an object.
   B. the intensity of the light being reflected from an object.
   C. whether the reflected wavelengths are long or short.
   D. B and C

8. The opponent process theory assumes that

   A. there are three types of receptors, each maximally sensitive to one group of wavelengths.
   B. three sets of receptors respond positively or negatively to different wavelengths.
   C. color coding occurs at the lateral geniculate nucleus.
   D. B and C

9. A person with a red-green deficiency would

   A. be considered an anomalous trichromat.
   B. be considered a monochromat.

C. perceive both red and green as having a yellow hue.

D. A and C

10. Because the dense forest in which they live limits the BaMbuti Pygmies' visual experience, they

A. lack the ability to make use of binocular depth cues.

B. are unable to maintain size constancy.

C. are unable to maintain shape constancy.

D. perceive vertical forms with ease but have difficulty perceiving horizontal forms.

11. Muscles convey information to the brain concerning the visual stimulus and provide us with the

A. motion parallax depth cue.

B. interposition depth cue.

C. accommodation and convergence depth cues.

D. retinal disparity and linear perspective depth cues.

12. Psychologists account for illusions in terms of

A. the unusual position of the visual stimulus.

B. backgrounds and previous experience with distance and corners.

C. Gestalt laws of organization.

D. extrasensory awareness.

13. Which of the following statements concerning Gestalt principles is *false*?

A. People will group together the elements of visual stimulus that they see as being alike.

B. At each level of organization, people try to interpret the perceptual field as being made up of wholes rather than parts.

C. People try to impose organization on any units that are perceived as complete or "good."

D. Gestalt principles provide a sound explanation about why we are able to perceive perceptual constancies.

14. Although many variables affect reading speed, the most important is the

A. difficulty of the subject.

B. print size.

C. number of fixations made.

D. ability to conduct visual searches.

15. A perceptual psychologist's primary interest in attention focuses on

A. activation.

B. arousal.

C. feature extraction or selective attention.

D. visual versus auditory communications.

16. Eidetic imagery

A. is so vivid that children who have it can report, from memory, even minute details about something they have seen.

B. interferes with a person's ability to see the smaller details of the whole image.

C. is available to most people if they use Kosslyn's technique of "mental walking."

D. begins once an image has "overflowed" the mental visual field.

17. Subliminal perception refers to

A. sensory receptors that have a very high threshold.

B. perceiving stimuli that are presented below the awareness threshold.

C. images that have never been seen before.

D. perception that is slower than normal because it involves the interpretation of confusing stimuli.

18. A low-frequency tone sounds either loud or soft depending on its

    A. frequency.
    B. amplitude.
    C. pitch.
    D. hertz, or cycles per second.

19. Frequency theories maintain that the analysis of sound takes place

    A. in the auditory area of the cortex.
    B. in the basilar membrane of the inner ear.
    C. when air pressure changes stimulate the eardrum.
    D. when tiny bones in the middle ear move.

20. Conduction deafness is caused by all of the following *except*

    A. a buildup of wax in the outer ear canal.
    B. the hardening of the tympanic membrane and damage to tiny bones within the ear.
    C. a severe head cold.
    D. damage to the cochlea or auditory nerve.

21. Taste receptors are

    A. the "moats" that separate the papillae that cover the tongue.
    B. olfactory rods.
    C. taste cells that make up the taste buds.
    D. in the saliva.

22. Sensations aroused by the movement of muscles, tendons, joints, and other internal processes provide us with cues and are called

    A. kinesthesis.
    B. the vestibular sense.
    C. pheromones.
    D. physical exercise.

23. The Melzack-Wall gate control theory suggests that pain is experienced when

    A. the chemical enkephalin is secreted in large doses.
    B. endorphine in the brain are at a high level.
    C. substance-P, released by sensory nerve fibers, transmits impulses across gates.
    D. "gates" are closed.

24. Chronic pain can be the result of

    A. having high pain thresholds.
    B. an interaction of physiological and psychological variables.
    C. avoiding other problems or worries in one's life.
    D. B and C

25. The extrasensory perception phenomenon known as _____ occurs when a person, for some unexplained reason, has knowledge about events before they occur.

    A. precognition
    B. telepathy
    C. transference
    D. clairvoyance

Child Development

7

Learning Objectives

When you have mastered the material in this chapter, you will be able to:

1. Describe the stages of prenatal development beginning with conception. (p. 238)

2. Explain how a mother's health, use of drugs, emotions, and attitude affect the unborn child. (p. 240)

3. Describe the birth process, including the three stages of labor. (p. 241)

4. Discuss reasons many people are against the use of heavy medications during childbirth. (p. 242)

5. Describe the research done by Fantz, Walker-Andrews, Walk and Gibson, and others who have shown that the perceptual abilities in newborns are well formed and sensitive to experience. (p. 244)

6. Discuss one study that shows how a mother's facial expressions can influence the behavior of her baby. (p. 246)

7. Describe five primary reflexes found in human infants and explain what happens to the reflexes as the infant matures. (p. 247)

8. Give Kagan's current view concerning the roles nature and nurture play in development and describe some of the major physical changes that occur during the first two years of life. (p. 248)

9. Discuss the importance of early parent-child attachments and how such attachments can be formed. (p. 251)

10. Using shyness as an example, discuss factors that determine personality differences in the early months and years of life. (p. 252)

11. Discuss some of the things parents can consider when making decisions about breast versus bottle feeding, feeding schedules, and whether a child is spoiled. (p. 252)

12. Explain why understanding stages of development can be helpful to parents, describe the basic premises of Piaget's theory of intellectual development, and define *accommodation* and *assimilation.* (p. 254)

13. Describe Piaget's four stages of intellectual development and define the terms that describe behavioral changes occurring during these stages. (p. 255)

14. Describe the kind of stimulation children need to progress intellectually and socially. (p. 260)

15. Discuss why some psychologists feel that Piaget's theory limits the way we think about children (p. 261)

16. Describe some of the changes that can be observed as children develop language. (p. 261)

17. Discuss the role parents play in their children's personal and social development and discuss some of the changes that can be observed as children learn to interact with others. (p. 263)

18. Describe the extent to which fathers in our society are participating in childrearing. (p. 266)

19. Characterize single-parent families and discuss some techniques single parents can use to assure a quality environment for their children. (p. 267)

20. Describe the affects day-care centers have on emotional, intellectual, and social development of children and discuss some considerations parents should make when selecting a day-care arrangement. (p. 268)

21. Describe the psychological impact of being brought up as a latchkey child and give the results of one study that investigated how self-care affects children. (p. 270)

22. Describe the symptoms of hyperactivity and explain how diet may influence these symptoms. (p. 271)

BEFORE YOU READ ON, take time to **SURVEY** the chapter, form an idea of what is to be learned (from margin Learning Objective numbers), and set goals for your study time. Then, ask yourself **QUESTIONS** about the material as you **READ,** seeking help for any sections you do not understand.

Ron Clement had never been a conformist. As he matured into adulthood, he found it rewarding to do the less obvious, even the shocking. Now, he was about to take on something bigger than he had ever done before: Ron was going to become a father and a house-husband. He had decided he would assume the daytime childcare responsibilities for his soon-to-be-born child while his wife continued working. His wife, Leah, was thrilled.

The decision process began years before. Ron and Leah Clement were both professionals when they married. He was an aspiring accountant and she, a new lawyer. They had decided not to have children. However, like many other people at thirty years of age, they changed their minds. They decided that having a family was important, and if they were to establish a family, it was now or never. They talked endlessly about schedules, babysitters, and daycare. They considered every possibility—but none was satisfactory. The only thing that they had decided was the baby's name—Sarah or Josh. They did not want to leave Sarah or Josh with someone who did not care about their baby the way they did. Sarah or Josh was going to be too special to be left in day care. Their families lived in another state. None of the options seemed inviting.

Then, in characteristic style, Ron announced he would become "father of the year" and stay home for the next few years—until Sarah or Josh was launched into a school setting. He argued that their child would have to be brought up properly and that to optimize his or her development he was going to stay home with the baby. Their friends thought it was a great idea, but that Ron was nuts—giving up his job would have serious economic consequences. Ron's mother argued that he did not know how to take care of a child. He responded that he knew as much as Leah did. Leah's mother was in a frenzy and could not even discuss the idea.

In an eloquent speech to his employer, he announced his intentions. With all of the passion and perhaps naïveté of a new father, Ron Clement declared that his and Leah's child would be brought up in a loving, caring, intellectually stimulating home. He, like many parents before him, was going to optimize this child's development. He asserted, to anyone who might listen, that nobody would be able to do it the way he could. He had taken courses in child and developmental psychology in college and felt he could meet the challenge. If it took being a house-husband, so be it.

THERE ARE NOT MANY MEN like Ron Clement. Few men (and increasingly fewer women) are willing to give up active careers to pursue child-care activities. But Ron and Leah recognized that for optimum development, a child needs a great deal of loving care, attention, and thought. They sought to give their new child every opportunity, every chance to become anything that it might. They hoped their baby would be born healthy. They knew that Sarah or Josh was going to be the product of their genes and would need a good environment in which to grow—and a little luck.

Leah and Ron Clement will have quite a story to tell their child when he or she is grown about their house-husband dad. They will recount how few men were as actively involved in raising their children. They will also probably tell their son or daughter stories they hope will help shape and mold their developing child. Many stories will be about their own childhoods. Development, however, begins long before most people can remember. Some very important events occur even before birth. This chapter and the next discuss how people's basic characteristics, their genetics, interact with the environment to produce individuals who are unique in both heredity and experience.

THE FIRST NINE MONTHS OF LIFE

Learning Objective 7.1

Zygote
A fertilized egg.

Embryo
The term used to refer to the human organism from the fifth through the forty-ninth day after conception.

Fetus
The term used to refer to the human organism from the fiftieth day after the conception until birth.

Leah and Ron Clement knew that Sarah or Josh's developmental history had already begun. They knew that a person's growth starts at the moment of conception, when an ovum and sperm join in the Fallopian tube to form a **zygote,** or fertilized egg. During the next five to seven days, the zygote descends through the Fallopian tube and implants itself in the blood-lined walls of the uterus. From this time until the forty-ninth day after conception, the organism is referred to as an **embryo.** Growth during the embryonic stage has lifelong consequences for the organism. From the eighth week until birth, the organism is called a **fetus.**

Geraldine Flanagan describes the in utero growth of a human being in detail in her excellent book, *The First Nine Months of Life* (1962). On the average, the process of maturation and development for an unborn child takes 266 days. These nine months are divided into trimesters, three periods of three months each.

The First Trimester

The First Day.   Within minutes of formation of the zygote, an individual's basic characteristics—hair, skin, and eye color, sex, likelihood of being tall or short, fat or lean, and perhaps also basic intellectual gifts—are established. Within ten hours, the fertilized egg has divided into four cells.

The First Week   Within a few days, about a dozen cells descend the Fallopian tube to the inner lining of the uterus. There, they begin the process of differentiation that allows formation of the organs and parts of the body. Some of the cells form the umbilical cord, a group of blood vessels and tissues connecting the zygote to the placenta. The **placenta** serves as a mechanism for the exchange of nutrients and waste products between the mother and developing zygote. By the end of the first week, as many as 100 developing cells are attached to the wall of the uterus, and the developing organism is officially an embryo.

Placenta ══════
A group of blood vessels and membranes connected to a fetus by the umbilical cord and serving as the mechanism for the exchange of nutrients and waste products.

The First Month   During the first month, the embryo begins to take shape. Hundreds of cells grow to 10,000, and the arms and legs begin to form. Though only half an inch long, the embryo has the rudiments of eyes, ears, mouth, and brain, By the twenty-fifth day, a primitive version of the heart is beating. At the end of the first month, the embryo is 10,000 times larger than the fertilized egg.

The Second Month   During the second month, the embryo begins to resemble a human being. Each day, it grows approximately a millimeter, and new parts begin to take shape. The nose begins to form on the thirty-third day and seems complete by the thirty-seventh. Around the forty-seventh day, the first true bone cells appear. This development brings the embryonic period to a close. From this point until birth, the growing organism is called a fetus.

The Third Month   In the third month, growth continues, features become more defined, and sex characteristics begin to show. The digestive, breathing, and musculature systems become stronger. At the end of the third month, the fetus is about three inches long and weighs an ounce. It can kick its legs, turn its feet, and swallow, although the mother cannot yet feel the movement of the fetus.

The Second Trimester

During the second three months, the fetus increases in weight and strength, consuming a good deal of food, oxygen, and water through the placenta. In the fourth month, it grows to as much as ten inches in length. Its heartbeat is stronger and can be heard with a stethoscope. Its muscles become significantly stronger. In the early part of the fifth month, the mother begins to feel the movement of the fetus. In the fifth and sixth months, the fetus grows about two inches per month. At the end of the sixth month, it is about fourteen inches long. At the end of the second trimester (about twenty-eight weeks), the respiratory system is mature enough that the fetus receives enough oxygen to continue living outside the uterus.

The Third Trimester

In the last trimester, the fetus gains weight rapidly—usually a pound in the seventh month, two pounds in the eighth, and a pound a week in the ninth

TABLE 7.1 : GENERAL STAGES AND AGE SPANS OF
         : HUMAN DEVELOPMENT

Life Stage	Approximate Age
Prenatal period	
Zygote	Conception to day 5 or 6
Embryo	Day 5 to week 8
Fetus	Week 8 to birth
Postnatal period	
Infancy	Birth to age 2
Toddlerhood	Age 2 to 3
Early childhood	Age 3 to about 6
Middle childhood	Age 6 to 12
Adolescence	Age 13 to 19
Young adulthood	Age 20 to 40
Middle adulthood	Age 40 to 65
Late adulthood	Age 65 onward

month. Its respiratory system and internal organs continue to develop. Its musculature matures significantly. Mothers report feeling strong kicking and movement at this time.

If the fetus is born much earlier than nine months, its lungs and other organs may not be developed enough to sustain life without the help of advanced medical technology. Infants weighing less than five pounds often have difficulty maintaining a constant body temperature and may have trouble breathing. Although medical technology can help premature babies maintain normal temperature until they have matured sufficiently to regulate these functions themselves, the prospects for health and development are best in a full-term baby. (See Table 7.1.)

PREGNANCY AND BIRTH

Learning Objective 7.2

You probably would not be surprised to find that Ron and Leah Clement felt strongly that special care even before the baby is born is important. A person need not be a health-care specialist to realize that the weeks and months of development before birth are crucial. The process of growth and development begins at the moment of conception, when an ovum and sperm join to create what will ultimately be that multicellular wonder called a human baby. This development proceeds with little active involvement from the mother. Yet the mother's nurturing of the growing organism within her, through proper care of her own body, is extremely important. The environment and life-support systems provided by the mother affect an unborn child's future life, though sometimes these influences are not directly observable.

Environmental factors affecting the mother (such as diet, infection, radiation, or drugs) will affect the infant she carries. Throughout pregnancy, the mother's diet is important because oxygen and nutrients are delivered to the child only through the mother's bloodstream. Absence of vitamin E in the diet can create hypoxia, an oxygen deficiency in the unborn child. Babies born to women on low-protein diets are more vulnerable to serious diseases. Alcohol use in early and mid-pregnancy is significantly related to newborn behavior, health (Streissguth, Barr, & Martin, 1983), and to later learning disorders (Shaywitz, Cohen, & Shaywitz, 1980).

Increasingly, scientific studies have shown that drugs of any kind, even aspirin, affect development. The influence of drugs is especially important during the embryonic stage of development, the first two months of which the mother may not realize she is pregnant. During pregnancy, nature and nurture are clearly interacting to affect development and growth.

Maternal Emotions and Attitudes

Do a woman's emotions during pregnancy affect her developing child? Because an unborn child receives its oxygen and nutrients from the mother's bloodstream, changes in the composition of the mother's blood will affect the development of the embryo and fetus. If a woman is angry or upset about her pregnancy, she may not eat properly. Strong emotions such as anxiety or fear can also produce hormonal imbalances that affect both fetal development and behavior at birth. A child born with a hormonal imbalance may be easily distracted, easily upset, and difficult to soothe.

Research has explored the effects of emotional stress during pregnancy on a child's later development. There is little evidence to indicate, however, that maternal emotions directly affect a newborn's subsequent physical development. Data suggest that a pregnant woman's attitude toward her unborn child affects her later attitude toward the child. These complex feelings may influence her ability to nurse the baby successfully and to give it the warmth and love that will foster good emotional growth and development.

The Birth Process

Learning Objective 7.3

Since the urbanization of American society, fathers have tended to be excluded from the birth process, and women have been taught to dread it. In some societies, however, and increasingly in our own, the birth of a baby is an exciting, shared experience that has a marked effect on both parents and consequently on the baby. An expectant father like Ron Clement would not miss the emotional experience of witnessing the birth of his own child and of helping his wife deliver their child.

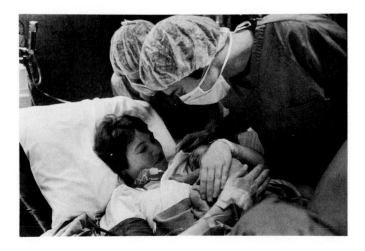

The birth of a baby is a shared, emotional experience for both parents.

Labor ══════════
The process in which the uterus contracts to open the cervix so the fetus can descend through the birth canal to the outside world.

When it is time for a baby to be born, the mother goes into labor. **Labor** is the process in which the uterus contracts to open the cervix and allow the fetus to descend through the birth canal to the outside world. Labor can be divided into three stages: early labor, active labor, and transition. The amount of time women spend in each stage varies dramatically. For women having their first child, labor typically lasts nine to twelve hours; for second- and third-time mothers, labor may be as short as three or four hours. Typically, labor is uncomfortable, but it does not have to be painful. Every woman's labor is different, but all women experience certain characteristic sensations during the three stages.

Early labor is characterized by infrequent contractions of the uterus, sometimes called "labor pains." To allow the fetus to descend through the birth canal, the cervix has to open, or dilate, to about ten centimeters. In early labor, the cervix dilates to about three centimeters. At this stage, the contractions of the uterine muscles occur at fairly regular intervals anywhere from five to thirty minutes apart and last approximately thirty seconds.

In the second stage, *active labor,* the woman's cervix dilates to seven centimeters. Contractions come approximately every three to five minutes and are somewhat more intense. During this stage, a woman usually goes to a hospital or a birthing center if she is not giving birth at home.

Major discomfort to the mother is most likely to occur in the third stage of labor, called *transition.* During transition, the cervix dilates to a full ten centimeters. Contractions are much stronger and last longer.

The baby is now ready to be born. For anywhere from five minutes to two hours, the mother will bear down with her abdominal muscles, pushing the baby from the uterus through the birth canal. This slow descent through the birth canal is what people typically think of when they speak about the birth of a baby. As it emerges from the birth canal, the baby is still attached to its mother by the umbilical cord. Within a few minutes, the placenta at the other end of the cord detaches from the wall of the uterus and is also delivered. This is sometimes called the afterbirth.

Generally, a woman's feelings and behavior in early labor are very different from those in active labor or transition. In early labor, she is very aware of her surroundings and feels good emotionally and physically. During active labor and transition, she becomes tired, less comfortable, and less tolerant of intrusions. In recent years, psychologists and physicians have studied how physical changes during labor affect a woman's emotions and her eventual relationship with her child. Increasingly, researchers are finding that the birth experience, including its discomfort, plays an important role. As you see later in this chapter, the relationship a mother forms with her child, even in its first hours of life, can have long-lasting behavioral consequences for the child.

Childbirth: A Natural Process

Learning Objective 7.4

For most of human history, women have delivered babies without the aid of doctors, nurses, or medication. In developed countries during the past seventy years, women have tended to give birth in hospitals, where personnel can respond quickly to complications that require medical attention. In such settings, few babies and mothers die in childbirth.

Since the 1960s, however, there has been a growing movement to keep medical intervention to a minimum during childbirth. Many women and men now feel that heavily medicated births are unnecessary and potentially harmful. Their belief has received considerable support from researchers. Yvonne Brackbill (1979) has presented a strong case against the use of medication during uncomplicated labors and deliveries. Because the human brain continues to develop to such a great extent for eighteen months after birth, Brackbill contends that potent drugs should not be used during labor unless there is a medical necessity for them. Such drugs, passing through the mother's bloodstream to the unborn child, have long-lasting effects on cognitive and gross motor behavior. Many parents today therefore opt for minimum medication during childbirth (Wideman & Singer, 1984).

PROGRESS CHECK 7.1

1. Match each of the following key concepts and terms with the appropriate definitions.

zygote   fetus   embryo   placenta

Learning Objective 7.1   A. _____ This term describes the developing organism from the fifth to seventh day after conception, when it has implanted itself in the uterine wall and until it has developed its first bone cells, around the fortieth day after conception.

Learning Objective 7.1   B. _____ A fertilized egg that is formed when the female ovum and male sperm join.

Learning Objective 7.1   C. _____ Allows for the exchange of nutrients and waste products and is connected to the developing organism by the umbilical cord.

Learning Objective 7.1   D. _____ The unborn organism from its eighth week until it is born.

2. Complete the following sentences with one of the options provided.

Learning Objective 7.1   A. In human beings, conception occurs in _____ .
(the uterus : a Fallopian tube)

Learning Objective 7.1   B. An average human pregnancy lasts about _____ days.
(177 : 266 : 275)

Learning Objective 7.1   C. Basic characteristics such as hair color, height, and sex are established when the zygote _____ .
(is formed : becomes an embryo)

Learning Objective 7.1   D. In human beings, a primitive heart begins to beat around the twenty-fifth day after conception; it can be heard with a stethoscope for the first time _____ .
(at that time : in the third month : during the second trimester)

Learning Objective 7.1   E. Most human mothers first feel their babies moving in the _____ month.
(third : fifth : seventh)

Learning Objective 7.1   F. The respiratory system of a fetus is mature enough by the end of the _____ that the child can continue living outside the uterus.
(first trimester : second trimester : twentieth week)

Learning Objective 7.2   G. Scientific studies have shown that _____, if consumed during pregnancy, can affect the development and growth of an unborn human organism.
(drugs of any kind : alcohol, but not aspirin)

Learning Objective 7.2   H.   Studies indicate that a mother's emotions during pregnancy have a direct effect on _____ after birth.
(the child's physical development : how the mother responds to the child)

Learning Objective 7.3   I.   Each woman's experience with labor is _____.
(very painful : different)

Learning Objective 7.3   J.   During _____, the cervix dilates to seven centimeters and the mother usually goes to the hospital or a birthing center.
(early labor : active labor : the transition stage)

Learning Objective 7.3   K.   A baby is born _____ the transition stage of labor.
(during : immediately after : within two hours after)

Learning Objective 7.4   L.   People who are against the use of heavy medications during normal child delivery take this position because medications at this time can effect the child's _____.
(subsequent susceptibility to drug abuse : cognitive and motor development)

THE NEWBORN

Learning Objective 7.5

When Josh or Sarah Clement is born, it is likely that he or she will be a happy healthy baby, most newborns are. At birth, they can hear, see, smell, and respond to the environment in adaptive ways—they have good perceptual systems.

To help children optimize their development, psychologists want to know what goes on in the minds of children. They want to know what they think, what they perceive, and how they react generally to the world. Psychologists have devised techniques to "ask" newborns questions about their perceptual worlds. A great deal of study has been devoted to the perceptual and reflexive abilities of newborns to discover whether those abilities are determined by nature from the start, or whether nurture (experience) plays a greater role.

FIGURE 7.1

Using a viewing box to observe newborns' eye movements, Fantz recorded the total time they spent looking at various patterns. He found that they looked at faces or patterned material much more often than at homogeneous fields. (Fantz, 1961; photo by David Linton)

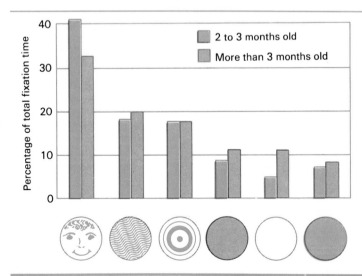

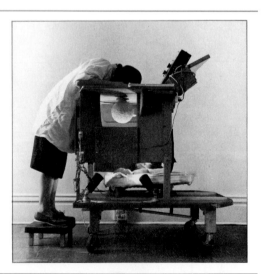

Infants Are Born with Well-Developed Perceptual Systems

To study visual perception in infants, Fantz (1961) designed an apparatus called a viewing box (see Figure 7.1). When an infant is placed in the bottom of a box, an observer or camera can record its responses to stimuli without being seen. Fantz recorded the eye movements of infants two to three months old and of infants more than three months old to discover their visual preferences for various pictures of faces and patterns. The exciting part of Fantz's work for psychologists was not only that he asked interesting questions, but that he also designed a technique to help answer the question of what an infant sees. After recording how long and how often the infants fixated or looked at each picture, Fantz calculated the total time spent viewing each kind of picture (Figure 7.1). If the infants had spent no more time looking at a picture of a face than at a series of random squiggles, he concluded that faces were no more meaningful to them than squiggles. He found that newborns could see patterns and that they preferred to look at faces rather than at squiggles.

Fantz's work touched off an avalanche of research into infant perception. Using techniques similar to Fantz's researchers have learned much about the perceptual capabilities of newborns. Results from studies like Fantz's have shown that newborns have amazingly good perceptual systems. They prefer complex visual fields to simple ones, curved patterns to straight ones (Fantz & Miranda, 1975), and human faces to random patterns or to faces with the features mixed up (see Haaf, Smith, & Smitley, 1983). Newborns look at pictures of their mothers more than at pictures of strangers, and they look at the eyes more often than at any other feature (Mauer & Salapatek, 1976). By two months, they are clearly abstracting information about the patterns they see (Bahrick, Walker, & Neisser, 1981; Nelson & Horowitz, 1983). They have shape constancy (Caron, Caron, Carlson, & Cobb, 1979) and may have size constancy (Day & McKenzie, 1977). Infants will follow moving lights with their eyes. Their pupils dilate and constrict with changes in the light level in a room.

Walk and Gibson (1961) used the visual cliff method to determine the extent of infants' depth perception. Infants are placed on a glass surface, half of which is covered with a checkerboard pattern; the same pattern is placed several feet below the transparent half of the glass surface and also at right angles down from the edge of the top pattern (see Figure 7.2). The infants are allowed to crawl from the patterned area onto the transparent area. If infants have no depth perception, they should be willing to crawl onto the transparent side as often as onto the patterned side. If they do have depth perception, they should refuse to crawl or avoid crawling onto the transparent side, even with a mother's encouragement. Walk and Gibson found that infants who can crawl will show avoidance behavior. Other studies have confirmed and extended their results (Rader, Bausano, & Richards, 1980; Richards & Rader, 1983).

Research on infant perception has grown more complex than in the early days of Fantz's or Walk and Gibson's work. For example, Walker-Andrews (1986) assessed five- and seven-month-old infants when they were simultaneously presented with angry or happy facial expressions and an angry or happy sound. The lower third of each face was obscured so that the infants could not match the sound to the lips. Seven-month-old children could tell when the sound and the facial expression did not match, but five-month-olds were unable to do so. These infants showed no preferences for a particular face or sound.

FIGURE 7.2 : The visual cliff method used by Walk and Gibson (1961).

The research of Walker-Andrews supports the idea of a timetable by which infants' ability to discriminate facial expressions develops (see, for example, Klinnert, Campos, Sorce, Emde, & Svejda, 1983). Similar ideas have been put forth about infant sensitivity to size information. Five-and-one-half-month old infants are sensitive to size differences to which five-month-olds are not sensitive (Yonas, Granrud, & Petersen, 1985.) Clearly, newborns enter the world with an ability to experience and perceive the environment (Lewis & Maurer, 1980). Having already developed for nine months, they know the difference between warmth and cold, between light and darkness. Their taste perception and sense of smell are already well along in development (Crook, 1979), they can experience pain, and they can hear. Even their attentional systems may be ready to make judgments (Linn, Reznick, Kagan, & Hans, 1982). The taste system becomes fully functional within a short time after birth. The nervous system is still sensitive to experience. After birth, new dendrites proliferate, peripheral nerves mature further, and the capacity to use the sensory systems increases. In sum perceptual systems of newborns are well formed.

Throughout this chapter, we see that a healthy pregnancy is crucial to a child's later development and behaviors. From a psychologist's point of view, a baby comes into the world ready to experience the environment. Although biological and genetic factors have already laid the foundations for subsequent behavior, the infant's experiences during the first two years shape both its intellect and outlook of the world.

Keep an Eye on Mom

Learning Objective 7.6

Babies pay close attention to their mother's facial expressions. Most of us think of people's facial expressions as a response. People smile after something pleasant or funny has happened. We see a grimace on a person's face after they have tasted something unpleasant. Facial expressions are generally thought of as external indicators of internal states. But for babies, their mother or caregiver's facial expressions may determine their actions.

An interesting research study was conducted to determine if babies confronted with an ambiguous situation relied on their mothers' facial expressions. To create an ambiguous circumstance, twelve-month-old babies were placed on a visual cliff, like that in the Walk and Gibson study. In this study, the babies were placed on the shallow side and an attractive toy was placed on the deep side. The mothers positioned themselves on the deep side near the toy and each encouraged her baby to approach the toy with smiles. But when the babies got near the point at which they could see the depth change, some mothers changed their smile to a fearful or angry look; other mothers continued to smile (Sorce, Emde, Campos, & Klinnert, 1985).

The researchers were trying to determine if the mother's facial expressions would influence whether the babies would cross the plexiglass table when there was uncertainty about what to do. It has long been known that twelve-month-old-babies recognize the depth change. Generally, the babies in this experiment recognized it and were unsure whether to cross to the other side. The results showed that if the mother posed a fearful or angry response, few babies crossed. By contrast, when the mothers smiled, most babies crossed the visual cliff. When they were uncertain what to do at the visual cliff, the babies used their mothers' emotional state to help them decide.

Sorce and his colleagues argued that a mother's facial expression is a key source of information; there may also be others. Posture, hand position, head turning, and even leg positions might all be ways in which babies pick up information in ambiguous situations. The research continues to show that babies are good at picking up cues in their environment to help them decide how to respond to the world.

Reflexes

Learning Objective 7.7

Rooting
A reflex in which an infant turns its head toward a stimulus applied to its lips or cheeks.

Sucking
A reflex in which an infant makes sucking motions when presented with a stimulus to the lips, such as a nipple.

Grasping
A reflex in which an infant grasps vigorously any object touching or placed in its hand.

Babinski reflex
A reflex in which an infant projects its toes outward and up when the soles of its feet are touched.

Moro reflex
A reflex in which an infant outstretches its arms and legs and cries when there is a loud noise or abrupt change in the environment.

The unlearned responses to stimuli with which infants are born are called *primary reflexes*. These reflexes are innate, like the unconditioned responses discussed in Chapter 2. One primary reflex is **rooting,** in which an infant turns its head toward a stimulus to its lips or cheeks, such as a breast, nipple, or hand. Another reflex is **sucking,** the motions made with the mouth in response to a stimulus to the lips, such as a nipple. The **grasping** response occurs when an object touches or is placed in an infant's hands. The **Babinski reflex** describes an infant's response to a touch to the soles of its feet, projecting its toes outward and up. Another reaction, the **Moro reflex,** is characterized by an outstretching of arms and legs and crying in response to a loud noise or change in the environment. The presence or absence of these primary reflexes can be used to assess neurological damage and to evaluate an infant's rate of development. Table 7.2 summarizes these and other primary reflexes, including the age at which they normally disappear.

Many of an infant's abilities and reflexes are biologically determined through genetic transmission; although biological variables continue to change and affect development, from birth onward, new experiences with the environment become more important in determining an infant's behavior. Gradually an infant's learned responses replace reflex reactions. These complex interactions between nature and nurture continue throughout an individual's life.

TABLE 7.2: HUMAN REFLEX BEHAVIORS

Reflex	Stimulus	Behavior	Age at Disappearance of Reflex
Placing	Backs of feet drawn against edge of flat surface	Withdraws foot	1 month
Tonic neck	Laid down on back	Head turns to one side	2–3 months
Moro	Sudden stimulus, such as loud noise or being dropped	Extends legs, arms, and fingers; arches back; draws back head	3 months
Sucking	Place object in mouth	Sucking	1–4 months
Swimming	Put in water face down	Well-coordinated swimming movements	6 months
Babinski	Sole of foot stroked	Toes fan out, foot twists in	6–9 months
Rooting	Cheek stroked with finger or nipple	Head turns; mouth opens; sucking movements begin	9 months

PROGRESS CHECK 7.2

1. Complete each of the following sentences with one of the options provided.

Learning Objective 7.5

A. Newborns prefer to gaze at _____ visual fields.
(simple : complex)

Learning Objective 7.5

B. Walker-Andrews's research demonstrated that when it comes to recognizing facial expressions, there is a developmental _____, by which the ability to match happy or angry facial expressions with appropriate sound can be measured.
(lag time between vision and hearing : timetable)

Learning Objective 7.5

C. By using the _____ method, Walk and Gibson demonstrated that infants have depth perception at least by the time they have learned to crawl.
(viewing box : pasted face : visual cliff)

Learning Objective 7.6

D. Twelve-month-old babies _____ their caretaker's facial expressions.
(do not understand : can behave according to)

Learning Objective 7.7

E. When the soles of a newborn's feet are touched or scratched, the baby projects its toes outward, this is the _____ reflex.
(rooting : Babinski)

Learning Objective 7.7

F. Babies turn their heads toward the direction of stimulation when their lips or cheeks are stimulated. This _____ reflex has an adaptive value that helps both the mother and child during feeding.
(rooting : sucking)

Learning Objective 7.7

G. The _____ reflex occurs when there is an intense noise or change in the environment; the newborn stretches out its arms and legs and begins to cry.
(Moro : Babinski : grasping)

Learning Objective 7.7

H. All of the primary reflexes with which infants are born usually disappear by the age of _____ months and are replaced by learned behaviors.
(six : nine : twelve)

INFANCY AND CHILDHOOD

Ron Clement thought of himself as a dedicated father-to-be. He was going to make sure that his baby would have an optimum development. Like many psychologists, Ron firmly believed that people's behavior is largely shaped by the influences around them. Like Ron, many people assume that parental influences are the main determinants of children's behavior. Many psychologists consider this the foundation of their research. Not surprisingly, they try to find those characteristics of a child's upbringing that will optimize a child's experiences and consequently the child's development.

Learning Objective **7.8**

In recent years, major proponents of this theory like Jerome Kagan of Harvard University, have modified their positions. They now assert that perhaps there may be more biologically based elements to personality and development than psychologists previously suspected. For example, Kagan, a longtime supporter of the environmental view, is recognizing the important role biology plays in development. Kagan's change in thinking represents a general

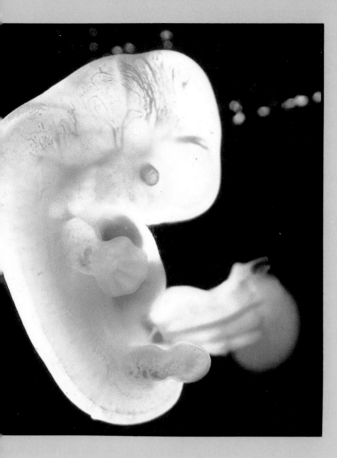

From conception to adulthood, human development is an intriguing process.

In the first five weeks after conception, a zygote has formed the beginnings of hands, feet, face, and spinal cord.

By the third month, the fetus takes on many human characteristics. Fingers and toes develop, and later survival reflexes, such as sucking, are exhibited. ▶

In the second and third trimesters, the fetus continues to receive nourishment from the placenta and to grow. Through maturation and development, the fetus prepares to sustain life on its own.

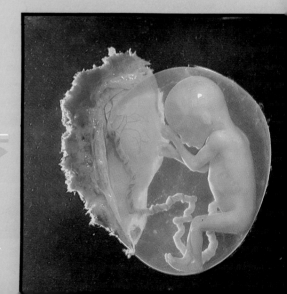

After birth, the infant develops rapidly. Motor skills improve, cognitive skills begin to evolve, and an infant's fascination with environmental stimulation further helps development.

Within a year, the young child becomes more independent. With new-found mobility and curiousity, the toddler begins to discover the world and broaden intellectual abilities.

Once the child reaches school age, most motor skills are fully developed and intellectual capacities are blossoming. At this stage, the child learns to question the world and begins to establish an individual identity that will become deeply rooted in adulthood.

shift in the thinking of mainstream psychology from almost exclusively environmental explanations of child development to integrated biology/experience explanations.

In a growing child's development, there are physical changes that are affected little by a parent's wishes. By contrast, emotional changes can be affected greatly by a parent's behavior. In the infancy and childhood years, profound changes are taking place. As you see in this section and the next on intellectual development, there is a complex interplay of nature and nurture, of biology and environment in the development of children.

Physical Changes

By the age of one year, a typical seven-and-a-half-pound newborn may weigh as much as twenty or twenty-five pounds. At eighteen months, it usually is walking and beginning to talk. For psychologists, infancy ends when a child can begin to represent the world abstractly through language. Thus, *infancy* generally refers to the period from birth to eighteen months, *childhood* to the period from eighteen months to age twelve or thirteen.

The rooting, grasping, and Babinski reflexes disappear in the early weeks and months, and new behaviors appear. At around four to eight weeks, infants begin to sleep for longer periods. When awake, they smile at the sight of their mother, stare at mobiles or other moving objects for long periods, and are enchanted by human speech. Often, they reach out to touch other objects. Figure 7.3 shows the major achievements in motor development for the first fifteen months.

As infants grow older, the amount of time spent focusing on mother increases significantly, and so does a sense of attachment between infant and mother. Dialogues in the form of gestures, smiles, and vocalizations become

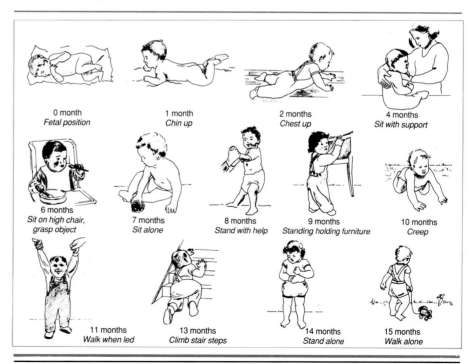

0 month
Fetal position

1 month
Chin up

2 months
Chest up

4 months
Sit with support

6 months
Sit on high chair, grasp object

7 months
Sit alone

8 months
Stand with help

9 months
Standing holding furniture

10 months
Creep

11 months
Walk when led

13 months
Climb stair steps

14 months
Stand alone

15 months
Walk alone

FIGURE 7.3 : Each month an infant's motor abilities increase dramatically; walking is possible within about one year.

By 12 months of age, infants are learning to walk and express strong attachments to their caretakers.

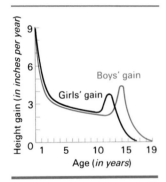

FIGURE 7.4 : Average growth curves in height gain for boys and girls to age eighteen. (Data from Tanner, Whitehouse, & Takaishi, 1966)

Separation anxiety ═══
The fear response in children from eight to fifteen months, displayed when a parent is absent.

Stranger anxiety ═══
The fear response in children from age eight to fifteen months, displayed in the presence of strangers.

more common (L. J. Kaplan, 1978). Newborns, even those less than three days old, imitate adult facial expressions, opening their mouths and sticking out their tongues (Meltzoff & Moore, 1983). Mothers initiate these interactions as often as the infants, and researchers have found these interactions to be important. When mothers in one experimental study remained still and expressionless, their infants became wary and engaged in self-comforting behaviors. Such babies develop hopeless expressions and turn away from their mothers (Cohen & Tronick, 1983; Tronick et al., 1978). The mere presence of the mother is not enough—she needs to interact physically and vocally with her infant (Source & Emde, 1981).

At four months, infants have greater control over head movements and posture and can sit with support, play with toys for long periods, recognize parents, and be soothed by parental voices more easily than before. By this age, most babies have been introduced to solid food. At six or seven months, children learn to sit without support and can turn themselves over. They grasp objects in both hands, manipulate them, and often put them in their mouths. They can be left in a playpen or crib for longer periods and are generally much more independent.

At around the seventh month, infants begin to display further changes in behavior. The newfound ability to crawl gives them freedom to seek out favorite objects and people and to avoid situations that seem potentially threatening. This ability to approach or avoid situations is often demonstrated in a strong preference for their caretaker, usually the mother. From age eight to fifteen months, attachment to the mother may become very strong; her departure from the room may arouse anxiety or fear responses, called **separation anxiety.** Similar behavior at the sight of strangers is called **stranger anxiety.** Many infants who show such strong attachments at this age tend later to be more curious and self-directed than infants showing weaker attachments (Ainsworth, 1979; Bowlby, 1973). In the second year of life, children can walk, climb, and manipulate their environment. Their bodies become wider and taller. This body growth continues throughout adolescence (see Figure 7.4).

Emotional Changes: Attachment

If you take the position that parental influences are the main determinant of children's behavior, you might wonder if day-care experiences would contribute in a negative way to development. Ron Clement reasoned this way. But he was not necessarily correct. You see later in this chapter that day-care centers do not have to have a negative effect, especially if a close attachment between parent and child already exists.

Learning Objective 7.9

Attachments play an important role in developmental processes. Some psychologists consider the establishment of a close and warm mother-child relationship to be one of the major accomplishments in the first year of life. Such a relationship makes subsequent cognitive and emotional development easier (Sroufe & Waters, 1977). Although not all researchers agree, experimental studies have shown that the quality and nature of the attachment formed between newborns and their parents result in real and long-lasting differences (Joffe, 1980; Schwartz, 1983). Children who have not formed warm, close attachments early in life may lack a sense of security and become anxious and overly dependent (Bowlby, 1977).

Bonding
A special process of emotional attachment occurring between parent and child in the minutes and hours immediately after birth.

The attachment process called **bonding,** which occurs between parent and child in the first few minutes and hours of life, seems to be inborn (see Chapter 5). Researchers such as Marshall Klaus and his colleagues believe that a mother experiences a heightened sensitivity to her child immediately after delivery. If allowed to interact with the baby during this time, she begins to form unique, specific attachments to it. Infants who are isolated from their parents at birth will not necessarily lack intelligence or become maladjusted, but infants who have experienced bonding are calmer and quieter, eat better, and sleep better (Klaus & Kennell, 1983). Given these findings, Klaus and his colleagues argue that babies should have as much physical and emotional contact with their mothers (and fathers) as possible and that keeping parents and infant together should be the rule, not the exception (Kennell, Voos, & Klaus, 1979). Providing this contact, of course, involves changes in most hospital routines (Kennell et al., 1979; see also Svejda, Campos, & Emde, 1980).

Early research showed that prolonged sensory deprivation is not good for children (Bowlby, 1958; A. Freud, 1965; Spitz, 1945). Later research shows that it is disastrous (Kennell et al., 1979). Harlow's studies of infant monkeys (discussed in Chapter 5) found that newborn monkeys deprived of their real mothers would cling to terry-cloth-covered wire figures as if seeking love. This seemingly inborn need for love and affection is important in understanding the relationship between a newborn's instincts and peoples' universal need for love and affection. Once established, this early attachment seems to be fairly permanent. Brief separations from the parents (for example, in day-care centers) do not affect it.

Research on attachment and its subsequent effects is intriguing. One study examined how children at three years of age with different histories of attachment responded to visiting strangers (Lutkenhaus, Grossmann, & Grossmann, 1985). The researchers hypothesized that a child with secure, close attachment to its parents would more readily interact with a visiting stranger than would a child with a less secure attachment. Parents and children's attachment was assessed, strangers were introduced, and the strangers attempted to play a competitive game with the children. Children who had developed close attachments were more willing to interact with the stranger and to express feelings about a "loss" in the competitive game. Consistent with previous findings, the researchers claimed that early close attachments affect later development.

Can adoptive parents form the same type of warm, secure close attachment as biological mothers and fathers? Even without the initial postdelivery bonding that Klaus and Kennell describe, adoptive parents form supportive, healthy family relationships. A caretaking atmosphere that is warm, consistent, and governed by the infant's needs is crucial in any family. Adoptive and biological parents can both provide such an atmosphere, and adoptive and natural children can form strong parent-infant attachments (Singer, Brodzinsky, Ramsay, Steir, & Waters, 1985). Any incidence of psychological problems among adoptees cannot be readily explained in terms of insecure attachments during the infancy years.

Shyness

Learning Objective 7.10

During the first months of life, you may notice that an infant seems shy. Some infants smile or reach out to a new face and accept being held, cuddled, or talked to by a stranger. Other babies are more inhibited but will warm up after a while. Still other babies exhibit extreme reticence, even distress. Daniels and Plomin (1985) conducted a study in which adopted infants were tested for shyness at ages one and two years. Information about the adoptive and biological parents was gathered. The researchers also collected data from homes with children who lived with their biological parents.

The researchers found that in biological homes, parental ratings of the infant's shyness were related to the mother's self-reports of her own shyness. This relationship was also observed in adoptive families. These findings led the researchers to conclude that the environment plays a central role in the development of shyness in infants. But they also found an important correlation between the biological mothers' shyness and their adopted-away infants' shyness at two years of age. This finding implicates the role of genetics.

The importance of this study goes beyond shyness. Using a complicated experimental design that involved infants, biological parents, adoptive parents, and unrelated families, the researchers showed scientifically that an element of personality is in part genetically determined. Although personality is affected by both nature and nurture throughout one's life, some of its components, such as a tendency toward shyness, can be seen in infancy.

Childrearing Techniques: Some Practical Advice

Learning Objective 7.11

Most people have ideas about the best way to raise children. Hundreds of articles discuss such issues as breast versus bottle feeding, scheduled versus on-demand feeding, and spoiling. These issues, however, are less important than the emotional climate provided in childrearing. A mother can provide warmth, love, and closeness for her infant by either breast feeding or bottle feeding. Although breast milk contains certain substances not found in cow's milk or in specially prepared formula, all contain most of the nutrients and vitamins necessary for healthy growth. Although disputed by some researchers (Adler & Cox, 1983), feeding by breast or bottle is less important than making the experience a pleasurable, relaxed one for both parent and child.

The same rule applies to feeding schedules. Some parents have felt it was important to follow a relatively rigid schedule so babies would learn a routine of eating, sleeping, and playing. Now, however, there is a growing trend toward self-demand schedules; babies are fed as often as they are hungry. Babies on self-demand schedules generally eat somewhat more often than those on a strict schedule, but parents have become more relaxed about the quantity of food eaten and the frequency of feeding. A more relaxed attitude and willingness to work around the individual baby can produce a warm, satisfying emotional climate for the child.

Self-demand and breast feeding have often been cited as the first steps on the short road to spoiling a child. A five-year-old who makes demands with little tolerance for the feelings of others shows a lack of socialization skills and can be said to be spoiled. However, describing an infant as spoiled makes no sense. Infants are largely self-centered; they demand attention and have no frustration tolerance. Infants are not sufficiently mature, either physically or intellectually, to delay gratification of their needs or to differentiate their desires from the desires of others. Only after age one should infants be expected to develop social skills that require greater social interaction and less self-concern.

PROGRESS CHECK 7.3

1. Complete each of the following sentences with one of the options provided.

Learning Objective 7.8

A. Jerome Kagan, a well-known and respected developmental psychologist, has changed his position concerning the relative contributions of nature and nurture and is now recognizing _____ factors much more than he did in the past.
(biological : environmental)

Learning Objective 7.8

B. Psychologists say that for most children, the transition from infancy to childhood takes place around the age of _____ months.
(twelve : eighteen : twenty-four)

Learning Objective 7.8

C. Babies can imitate adult facial expressions as early as the age of _____ _____.
(three days or less : three weeks : three months)

Learning Objective 7.8

D. Most babies have learned to sit without support by the age of _____ _____ months.
(two to three : four to five : six to seven)

Learning Objective 7.8

E. Separation anxiety and stranger anxiety occur when an infant _____ _____ an attachment with his or her primary caretaker.
(lacks : has developed)

Learning Objective 7.9

F. According to Klaus and Kennell, the unique and specific parent-child attachment that occurs through the bonding process _____ after birth.
(takes place immediately : can occur several days : can occur anytime)

Learning Objective 7.9

G. Several studies have shown that newborns who experience bonding _____ _____ than newborns who are separated from their mothers.
(eat and sleep better : will be more intelligent)

Learning Objective 7.9

H. Parent-child attachments are most likely to occur in a family in which the atmosphere is warm, consistent, and governed by the needs of the _____ _____.
(infant : older children : parents)

Learning Objective 7.10

I.   As a personality trait, shyness seems to be determined by _____
     _____.
     (parental strictness : genetic factors : genetic and environmental factors)

Learning Objective 7.11

J.   When deciding whether to breast feed or bottle feed her newborn, a mother's
     most important consideration should be _____.
     (nutrition : the potential emotional climate : social expectations)

Learning Objective 7.11

K.   _____ feeding is more likely to produce a warm and emo-
     tionally satisfying climate for a newborn.
     (Scheduled : Self-demand)

Learning Objective 7.11

L.   Since infants have no tolerance for frustrating conditions, demand attention, are
     self-centered, and are not mature enough to delay needs for gratification during
     their first year of life, they _____ spoiled.
     (can be easily : should not be thought of as being)

INTELLECTUAL DEVELOPMENT

Both Ron and Leah Clement had their child's best interests at heart when they decided to alter their life-style. Ron was especially concerned about creating the best environment to allow his child to grow intellectually. He knew that parts of his child's intellect, personality, and day-to-day behavior would be determined by genetics—biologically determined—but he wanted to make the most of his child's environment. He felt that during the early stages of his child's life, the environment might exert an especially strong effect. He was going to read to his child, make sure his child heard music, saw colorful books, and experienced taste treats. A multifaceted world would be presented to Ron Clement's child to help intellectual growth.

Learning Objective 7.12

Understanding the stages a child goes through in the course of intellectual development can be a key to understanding childhood behavior. For example, knowing about attachment processes can tell both a researcher and parent a great deal about proper parenting and the likely results of faulty attachment. In the same manner, knowing the stage at which intellectual development is most likely to occur can tell both researcher and parent about the most effective interventions or activities for children at various ages.

Intellectual growth in particular seems to follow a distinct developmental pattern. At birth, infants seem to have few capabilities, responding only with reflexes and random movements; but the infants change dramatically each day. Changes in older children are generally less apparent; they are often intellectual changes, involving the ability to cope with their expanding world. Jean Piaget(1896–1980), the noted Swiss psychologist, believed that the fundamental development of all intellectual abilities takes place during the first two years of life; many psychologists and educators agree. Like Robert Fantz in his studies of perception in newborns, Piaget devised new experimental procedures for examining the intellectual development of young children. A sensitive and careful observer of children, he outlined stages of intellectual development while watching his own three children grow.

Piaget's theory of intellectual development covers a wide range of activities and has had considerable influence on psychology. Although psychologists were initially skeptical of his ideas and some disagreement about them persists (T. G. R. Bower, 1976), other researchers have shown that his assumptions are generally correct (for example, Uzgiris, 1972). Because it focuses on how people think (thought processes) instead of on what they think (content), Piaget's the-

Jean Piaget (1896–1980) formulated the stage theory of cognitive development.

ory applies to all societies and cultures. Perhaps its greatest strength is that it describes how a person's inherited capabilities interact with the environment to produce an intellectually functioning child and adult. As such, Piaget's theory takes into account both nature and nurture. Theories like Piaget's that emphasize the interaction between biology and experience are softening the earlier, more behaviorally oriented theories that once dominated mainstream psychology.

Central to Piaget's theory is the concept of stages. Piaget maintained that just as standing must precede walking, so certain stages of intellectual development must precede others. An individual must successfully complete each stage before embarking on the next. The kind of intellectual achievement possible depends on the child's current stage of development. Thus, if a parent presents a concept that is too advanced, the child will not understand the new concept and no real learning will take place. Piaget's stages are fixed only to approximate ages, allowing for the fairly large differences that exist among children.

Everyone is faced with new concepts and experiences. According to Piaget, people use two processes to deal with new concepts and to advance from one stage to the next. **Assimilation** is the process of absorbing new concepts and experiences, incorporating them into existing cognitive structures and behaviors, and using them in subsequent, similar situations. **Accommodation** is the process of modifying previously developed cognitive structures (thought processes) and behaviors to adapt to a new concept or experience. For example, a child who has learned to grasp a spoon demonstrates assimilation by later grasping similar long, slim objects such as forks, crayons, and sticks. This assimilated behavior then serves as a building block for further accommodation. In learning the new, more complex behavior of grasping a sphere (such as a ball), the child must modify the earlier response by widening his or her grasp. People accommodate to new information and then assimilate it, only to be confronted with more new information. The two processes alternate in a never-ending cycle of intellectual and behavioral growth.

Piaget's Four Stages

Assimilation and accommodation occur throughout all of Piaget's four stages of development, enabling a child to pass from one stage to the next. Figure 7.5 on page 256 shows activities typical of each stage.

The Sensory-Motor Stage.   Piaget considered the **sensory-motor stage,** from birth to age two, as the most important. During this period, the foundation for all intellectual development is established. Consider the enormous changes that take place during the first two years of life. Infants are born uncoordinated, reflexlike organisms, unable to respond to the demands of a complex world. Within a few weeks, they have learned some simple habits: they smile at the sight of mother; they seek out the stimulation of a mobile hanging overhead; they reach out and anticipate events in the environment. When they see mother's breast or a bottle, they know food is coming. At two months, they are developing memory for past visual and auditory events. According to Piaget, this acquisition of memory is a crucial foundation for further intellectual development because it involves learning to use some basic facts in one's environment.

Assimilation
According to Jean Piaget, the process by which new concepts and experiences are incorporated into existing ones so as to be used in a meaningful way.

Accommodation
According to Jean Piaget, the process by which new concepts and experiences modify existing cognitive structures and behaviors.

*Learning 7.13
Objective*

Sensory-motor stage
The first of Piaget's four major stages of intellectual development, covering roughly the first two years of life. During this period, the child begins to interact with the environment, and the rudiments of intelligence are established.

FIGURE 7.5 : Piaget's stages
of intellectual development.

Sensory motor stage
The child begins to interact with the environment

Preoperational thought
The child begins to represent the world symbolically although he or she is not fully logical

Concrete operations
A child learns rules such as conservation

7–11

Formal operations
In this phase adolescents can transcend the concrete situation and think about the future.

12–Adult

FIGURE 7.5 : Piaget's stages
of intellectual development.

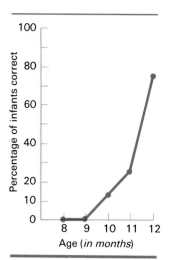

FIGURE 7.6 : *Object
permanence* is the ability to
know that an object continues
to exist even when out of
view. Research shows that the
ability to remember the
location of an object that is
subsequently hidden improves
over time. Most one-year-olds
can remember where an object
has been hidden even after a
delay of seven seconds. (After
Fox, Kagan, & Weiskopf, 1979)

Egocentrism
The inability to perceive a
situation or event except in
relation to oneself; a
characteristic of the
sensory-motor stage. In
infancy, it is the attitude
that directs all concerns
and behaviors to personal
interests and needs.

By the age of six or eight months, children are seeking out new and more interesting kinds of stimulation and are sitting up and crawling. No longer willing just to watch a mobile spin, they manipulate the environment, attempting what Piaget calls "making interesting sights last." At about eight months, they begin to develop a sense of their own intentions; they overcome obstacles in order to reach goals. They crawl to the other side of the room in order to reach an object. From about nine months on, children develop *object permanence,* the ability to realize that objects continue to exist even when they are out of sight. Different aspects of object permanence evolve gradually throughout the rest of the sensory-motor stage (see Figure 7.6).

In the second half of the sensory-motor stage (from about twelve to twenty-four months), children begin to walk, talk, and use rudimentary forms of logic. Object permanence is now much better developed. Children will now follow a ball that has rolled away and will search for a mother who has left the room. Children begin to use language to represent the world. Use of language frees them from the concrete world of visual imagery. By age two, they talk about parents, friends, television programs, and other events. No longer uncoordinated, reflex-oriented organisms, they are thinking, walking, talking human beings.

Throughout the sensory-motor stage, demands on children are minimal. Self-centeredness, or **egocentrism,** shapes all behavior; they are unable to understand that the world does not exist solely to satisfy their interests and needs. For the next few years, they will be unable to see the world or specific situations from the point of view of another person. As Elkind (1981a) points out, this intellectual immaturity makes young children continue to pester mother even after being told she has a headache and wishes to be left alone. Children are unable to put themselves in mother's position.

At the end of Piaget's first stage, children are just beginning to realize the difference between their interests and the world's interests—that they are not the sole event in their parents' world. This **decentration** continues for several years (see Ford, 1979). At the same time, now that their language and thought processes have begun to develop, they may also become manipulative, difficult to deal with, and belligerent. These annoying new habits are signs of normal development and mark the beginning of the stage of preoperational thought.

The Preoperational Stage. In the **preoperational stage,** from about age two to age six or seven, children are beginning to be able to represent the world symbolically and are becoming more socialized. As preschoolers, they play with objects in novel ways and try, often in play, to represent reality. However, they remain somewhat egocentric, still think relatively concretely, and cannot deal with abstract thoughts that are not easily represented. They cannot think about the world the way older persons do or consider how other people might feel. They make little attempt to adapt their speech to that of other people or to justify their reasoning. Behavior problems often arise during this stage; accordingly a major task of adults is to teach children how to interact with others (Flavell, 1963). Major social and intellectual changes will not become fully apparent until the next stage of development.

Decentration The process, beginning at about age two, of changing from a totally self-oriented point of view to one that recognizes other people's feelings, ideas, and viewpoints.

Preoperational stage Piaget's second major stage of intellectual development, lasting from about age two to age seven, when initial symbolic thought is developed.

In the preoperational stage, children begin to imitate reality in their play.

Stage of concrete operations ═══
Piaget's third stage of development, lasting from approximately ages seven to eleven. During this stage, the child develops the ability to understand constant factors in the environment, rules, and higher-order symbolism (such as arithmetic and geography).

Conservation ═══
The ability to recognize that something that has been changed in some way (such as the "shape" of liquid in a container) is still the same thing with the same weight, substance, or volume.

The Stage of Concrete Operations. The **stage of concrete operations** lasts from approximately age seven to age eleven. Children are now actively involved in school, have friends, are able to take care of themselves, and may also have assumed many responsibilities. At this point, they can look at a situation from more than one viewpoint and evaluate different aspects of it. This decentration allows more complicated ways of thinking about situations and objects.

During this stage, children are involved in discovering constancy in the world—in discovering rules and understanding the reasons for them. The hallmark of this stage is **conservation,** the ability to recognize that objects that have been transformed remain the same objects and represent the same amount of weight and/or volume.

Psychologists have studied conservation extensively. In a typical conservation task, a child is shown two beakers: one short, squat, and half full of water, the other tall, thin, and empty (see Figure 7.7). The experimenter pours the water from the short, squat beaker into the tall, narrow beaker and asks the child, "Which beaker had more water, the first or the second?" A child who does not understand the principles of conservation will claim that the taller beaker has more water. In contrast, a child who is able to conserve volume will recognize that the same water was in both beakers, and that therefore the amount of water in both beakers is equal (see, for example, Perret-Clermont, 1980). Each of various conservation abilities seems to occur independently. A child who has mastered one type of conservation (for example, of volume) often cannot transfer that knowledge to other conservation tasks (for example, of weight). The development of conservation is a necessary prelude to the final stage of intellectual development (see also Figure 7.8).

Development of conservation allows a researcher to conclude that children have realized that certain facts are true not just because they are observed, but because they logically follow. Children who have developed conservation fully will tell a researcher that an event they just observed *must* be true. Abundant research supports this claim (see, for example, S. A. Miller, 1986).

Consider the work of distinguished psychologist John H. Flavell on the stage of concrete operations. Flavell and his colleagues have been studying a phenomenon closely associated with conservation—the ability of older versus younger children to distinguish between appearance and reality. Quoting Flavell, "Suppose someone shows a three-year-old and a six-year-old a red toy car covered by a green filter that makes the car look black, hands the car to the

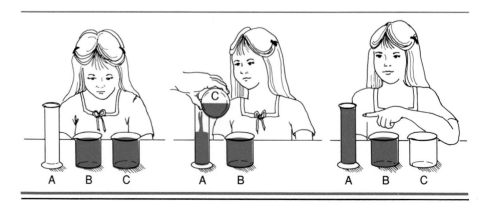

FIGURE 7.7 : *Conservation* is the ability to recognize that an object remains the same object regardless of any changes it has undergone, such as a change in shape. When the water in C is poured into A, young children who have not learned the principle of conservation will indicate that there is more water in A than in B.

A   B   C   A   B   A   B   C

CONSERVATION OF SUBSTANCE

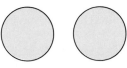

Child is shown two equal balls of clay.   Experimenter flattens one ball of clay.

CONSERVATION OF NUMBER

Child is shown two rows of buttons.   Experimenter moves buttons in one row.

FIGURE 7.8 : Two types of conservation designed to measure children's developmental stage of thinking.

children to inspect, puts it behind the filter again, and asks, What color is this car? Is it red or is it black? The three-year-old is likely to say 'black,' the six-year-old, "red" (1986, p. 418). Flavell asserts and has shown that six-year-olds possess some knowledge about the distinction between appearance and reality and can sense what the task is all about.

Such abilities continue to develop as a child matures. From a Piagetian perspective, a child has moved from the preoperational stage to the stage of concrete operations when an appearance-reality distinction becomes apparent. This development continues throughout the stage of concrete operations because at six or seven years of age, all abilities of appearance-reality distinctions are not yet formed. Even though at age six many components of conservation and other logically necessary truths are beginning to be understood, the process takes several years (S. A. Miller, 1986).

The Stage of Formal Operations.   Piaget's final stage of development, which starts at about age twelve, is the **stage of formal operations.** Unlike concrete operational children, whose thought is still tied to immediate situations, adolescents can transcend an actual situation and think about the future. They do this by forming hypotheses that allow them to think of different ways to represent situations, organizing them into all possible relations and outcomes. Adolescents' intellectual world is full of informal theories of logic and ideas about themselves and life (Flavell, 1963). The egocentrism of the sensory-motor and preoperational stages has, for the most part, disappeared, but a new kind of egocentrism, based on a naïve concept of the world, has developed. According to Piaget, "The adolescent goes through a phase in which he attributes an unlimited power to his own thoughts so that the dream of a glorious future or of transforming the world through ideas (even if this idealism takes a materialistic form) seems to be not only fantasy, but also an effective action which in itself modifies the empirical world" (Inhelder & Piaget, 1958, pp. 345–346). Adolescents' egocentrism and naïve hopes eventually disappear as they face and deal with the challenges of life.

Let us review some of the most important points about Piaget's theory. *First,* Piaget suggests that cognitive development is a process in which each

Stage of formal operations ━━━━━

Piaget's fourth and final stage of intellectual development, beginning at about age twelve, when the individual can think hypothetically, consider all future possibilities, and is capable of deductive logic.

stage builds on the previous one. It has as its base a complex sensory-motor period. *Second,* egocentrism is a critical aspect of development that must be changed through the process of decentration. *Third,* the exact age at which the same stages of development appear is less important than the fact that all children in all societies go through these stages of development. *Fourth,* the actual content of a child's thoughts in the United States compared to the thought content of children in France or India is less important to Piaget's theory than is the nature of their thinking. Piaget was concerned with how people think, not what they think. Knowing the way children think, psychologists can learn how to facilitate thinking.

Learning 7.14
Objective

Implications of Piaget's Theory. Knowing how cognitive abilities develop helps educators and psychologists suggest ways to facilitate children's intellectual development. Piaget recognized that parental love and interaction, though always important to children's development, are essential in the first two years. He also stressed the importance of providing great amounts of stimulation, both physical and intellectual. The stimuli should move and change color, shape, and form. Research confirms that children and animals who are provided with sensory stimulation from birth through the early months develop better intellectually and socially than do individuals deprived of the same kinds of stimulation. However, though acknowledging that it is possible to accelerate children's development, Piaget also stressed that children should not be pushed too fast. Noted psychologist David Elkind (1981b) supports this view in his book, *The Hurried Child,* in which he argues that overacceleration ultimately has deleterious effects. Parents serve their children best by providing intellectual stimulation appropriate to their current developmental level. To ask them to perform tasks beyond that stage is a waste of time.

According to Piaget's theory, a child's development includes the following sequence: Initially (1), "egocentrism . . . directs all concerns and behaviors to personal interests and needs"; thereafter, the child (2) "realizes that there is difference between himself and the world," (3) "represents the world symbolically," (4) "discovers certain facts about the environment which remain constant," (5) "can conceive of different ways to represent situations," and in adolescence (6) "attributes an unlimited power to his own thoughts so that the dream of a glorious future or of transforming the world through ideas . . . seems to be not only fantasy, but also effective action which in itself modifies the empirical world."

Learning *Objective* 7.15   Although Piaget's ideas have had enormous influence on the ways psychologists think about children's development, some researchers claim that his conceptions tend to limit the way people think about children. For example, many studies of young children measure their development by giving the same task to children of various ages. Children who cannot do the task are viewed as cognitively deficient in some way. Psychologist Rochel Gelman argues that in measuring older children's abilities against those of younger children, researchers tend to underestimate the latter. Studies by Gelman and others show that to understand cognitive development fully, psychologists should ask children of different ages different questions (for example, Gelman, 1981; Lancy & Goldstein, 1982). For example, Gelman found that two-year-olds change the length of their sentences depending on whom they are talking to, using shorter sentences when speaking to younger children. Other researchers claim that Piaget may have overestimated the extent of egocentrism in young children. Lempers, Flavell, and Flavell (1977) found that two-year-olds rotated books they were reading in order to show their mothers the illustrations. Like Gelman, these researchers feel that psychologists have sometimes not asked the most appropriate experimental questions. Piaget's work is a landmark, but new research continues to qualify and refine his findings.

Language Development

One of the most important accomplishments in a person's development is the use of language to communicate. Young children have methods of communicating their desires and needs nonverbally, but effective communication begins with the acquisition of language. The ability to use language marks a dramatic step forward in cognitive development and produces dramatic changes in children's lives, allowing them to interact on a more mature level with other people to represent the world in complex ways.

Learning *Objective* 7.16   In the first few months of life, babies coo and babble. By six months, the sounds may become differentiated. Very often, babies of six to eight months repeat the same sounds for hours or days at a time. At the end of a year, most have learned a few simple words: perhaps "mama," "dada," or some other combination of sounds that represents an object. From this naming stage, the child develops simple two- and three-word sentences.

Young children using two-word sentences can convey an amazingly large number of thoughts, although their communication system may be too specialized for individuals outside the family to understand. More important than the individual utterances themselves is the way those utterances evolve into more complex statements as children learn grammar.

Grammar, the rules for generating sentences in a language, is learned at an early age. Although five- and six-year-olds have not learned all the rules of their language, their speech consists of nouns, verbs, and adjectives in essentially correct order. Chapter 9 discusses language and the relative contributions of nature and nurture to language development. Chapter 9 also discusses studies of language development with babies that have examined the complex interactions of parents with children. Such research often looks at the verbalizations of parents, their children's response, and the subsequent response of the parent (e.g. Keller & Schölmerich, 1987). By such tracking of minute-by-minute exchanges, researchers have come to conceptualize how children learn language and how parents influence that learning process.

PROGRESS CHECK 7.4

1. Match each of the following key concepts and terms with the appropriate definitions.

sensory-motor   concrete operations   preoperations
formal operations

Learning Objective 7.13   A. _____ During this stage, thought processes develop that enable the child to understand constant factors in the environment (such as conservation), rules, and higher-order symbolism (such as arithmetic).

Learning Objective 7.13   B. _____ Piaget thought this was the most important stage because as the child learns to perceive and interact with the environment the foundation for all future intellectual development is established.

Learning Objective 7.13   C. _____ Symbolic thought begins to develop during this stage, but the child remains somewhat egocentric, cannot deal with many abstract thoughts, and seldom tries to justify his or her reasoning.

Learning Objective 7.13   D. _____ During this stage, children become adolescents and can use deductive reasoning and hypothetical thought.

2. Complete each of the following sentences with one of the options provided.

Learning Objective 7.12   A. Piaget's theory applies to all societies and cultures because it focuses on _____ people think.
(how : what)

Learning Objective 7.12   B. Piaget's theory is _____ theory.
(strictly a biological : a pure environmental : a stage)

Learning Objective 7.12   C. A behavior or the understanding of a concept becomes a part of an individual's collection of skills or knowledge and can be easily applied to familiar situations when the behavior or concept has been _____.
(assimilated : accommodated)

Learning Objective 7.13   D. _____ begins to develop when an infant in the sensory-motor stage is able to overcome an obstacle in order to achieve a goal.
(Intentionality : Object permanence : "Making interesting sights last")

Learning Objective 7.13   E. The process that begins around the age of two, allowing children to move away from a totally self-oriented viewpoint to one that recognizes other people's feelings and ideas, is called _____.
(egocentrism : decentration)

Learning Objective 7.13   F. A child moves from preoperations to concrete operations when he or she begins to _____.
(form hypotheses : make appearance-reality distinctions)

Learning Objective 7.13   G. Egocentricism based on a naïve concept about how the world operates is typical of the _____ stage.
(preoperations : concrete operations : formal operations)

Learning Objective 7.14   H. Piaget believed that parents could help their children's intellectual development by _____ their current intellectual stage.
(pushing them to accelerate beyond : recognizing and providing stimuli for)

Learning Objective 7.15   I. Gelman challenges Piaget's theory, arguing that to understand cognitive development, psychologists should _____ of younger and older children.
(compare the abilities : ask different questions)

Learning Objective 7.16   J. A dramatic step forward in cognitive development occurs when a child _____.
(plays with other children : acquires language)

PERSONAL AND SOCIAL DEVELOPMENT

Learning $\underline{7.17}$
Objective

Leah and Ron wonder about what growing up will be like for their child if she is working full time and he is parenting full time. Leah has not had experience with such a family, although it seems as if it should work. A generation ago, when Leah was growing up, mothers took care of the children and parents encouraged masculine traits in their sons and feminine traits in their daughters. They accepted and promoted a gender-based social environment.

In recent times, by deemphasizing gender-based interests in their children, many parents seek to reduce and perhaps eliminate society's tendency to stereotype people and their occupations on the basis of sex. Leah knew that Ron would do a good job at parenting and that perhaps because of reversing roles for a few years, their child would not have to ask so many questions about roles when he or she became a parent. Like Ron, a growing number of fathers are taking a greater part in child care, influencing their children's social development more directly than in the past. In this more sustained, more nurturing role, they have more importance than ever before in their children's development and thus may lessen the emphasis on gender-based activities.

With today's higher divorce rates and more diverse adult life styles, children's social development takes place in a wider variety of family settings than ever before. Some children experience a lot of family interaction (Willerman, 1979); others may spend a lot of time alone, perhaps watching television (White, 1978). As their world enlarges, usually at least when they start school, the influence of family (and especially of parents) lessens. Nevertheless, parents play a primary and continuing role in helping children develop social interaction skills.

Social development begins at birth, ideally with the bonding process. The nature of the child's early interactions with parents is a crucial part of personality development. Infants have a great need to be hugged and cuddled, to be nurtured and made to feel good. Children need lots of love and attention. Parenting involves more than giving love, however. As psychoanalyst Bruno Bettelheim has said, "Love is not enough." Eventually, parents have to teach their children to become independent. Social interactions in the first year are limited because in the early months of life children are largely egocentric. They seldom distinguish their needs and desires from those of the world at large. They spend much of their time sleeping and have not yet learned to consider themselves as separate from their parents (See Table 7.3 on page 264).

Around the end of the first year, when they begin to realize they are separate beings, children exhibit strong attachments and a fear of strangers. At eighteen to twenty-four months, children can be extraordinarily difficult and exasperating. Eighteen-month-old children want what they want—and *now*. They have matured sufficiently to have specific desires and needs, but they lack the necessary language skills to make those needs clearly known. For example, they cannot yet tell someone that they want the green bib, not the blue one (Ames, Gillespie, Haines, & Ilg, 1979). By the end of the second year, children tell their parents, "No, this," or "No peas," or "No go." They have learned to differentiate themselves from others, to manipulate the world, and to interact with other people.

During the preoperational stage, egocentrism gives way to increased social interaction. Two-year-olds generally play alone or alongside other children with relatively little interaction, but they are better at controlling their emotional response than they were at eighteen months old. Gradually, they are forced to socialize with their peers. From age two until they begin school, children vacillate between quiet conformity and happy sharing to stubborn negative demands and egocentric behavior (Ames et al., 1979). In nursery school or kindergarten, they must learn to accept responsibility and to share. Sharing is a behavior that is learned, can be taught, and is socially desirable. Very young children seem to be unaware of the notion of sharing. They especially seem unaware of the idea that if you share with another child, he or she is more likely to share with you.

In a laboratory study of sharing, researchers observed groups of two children who were separated by a gate. Initially, one child was given toys and the other was given no toys; the situation was then reversed. The deprivation of the toy to one child was clearly apparent. The researchers found that none of the children shared spontaneously, but 65 percent of the children shared a toy when asked to do so by their mother. After sharing a toy, when they were later deprived of a toy, they often approached the child with the toy; one child even said, "I gave you a toy, why don't you give me one?" Children do not initiate sharing at a young age, but once they share they seem to exhibit knowledge about reciprocal arrangements (Levitt, Weber, Clark, & McDonnell, 1985). Even children with behavior problems can be taught to share (Bryant & Budd, 1984). In addition, the expectations encountered in school necessitate learning a variety of new behaviors, including learning to understand a situation from another's point of view. Being in kindergarten precipitates a breakdown of egocentrism.

Research has shown that many factors in a child's life can either promote or retard the breakdown of egocentrism. One variable is the kind of toys provided. Quilitch and Risley (1973) provided young children with two kinds of toys—those generally played with by one child at a time (isolate toys), and those designed for use by two or more children at a time (social toys). The children were allowed to play with both kinds of toys, but some children were presented with social toys first, and others first received isolate toys. After the initial play period, more children who had been given social toys chose to play with other

TABLE 7.3 MAJOR MOTOR, COGNITIVE, AND EMOTIONAL DEVELOPMENTAL CHANGES

Area	0–2	3–4	5–6	7–8	9–10	11–12
Motor	Turns head; lifts chin when lying on stomach	Lifts chest; holds head erect	Holds head steady; transfers objects from one hand to another	Sits with support	Stands with help	Pulls self to standing position; walks little with support
Cognitive		Recognition of the past	Selected imitation	Object permanence	Language comprehension	Symbolic play; first real words
Emotion		Distress to discrepancy; smiles	Relies on mother for cues as to safety	Stranger and separation anxiety; facial signs of anger		Sadness to loss of attachment figures

Age in Months

Psychologists at Work: Toddlers' Self-Control

How do you keep a toddler from destroying your furniture or getting burned on a hot stove? A child learning to walk suddenly can reach many dangers in the home and thus needs constant supervision. Still egocentric, still dependent on the caregiver, the toddler needs to be taught self-control. To examine how self-control is taught to toddlers, two researchers from the University of Houston, Power and Chapieski (1986), observed fourteen-month-old children and their mothers in the children's own homes.

The methods generally used to help a child develop a sense of self-control are coaxing, verbal commands, threats, and physical punishment. Power and Chapieski knew that the role of physical punishment in the development of self-control had not been studied with younger children. They also knew that every home has certain items, rooms, or objects considered "off limits" for children. They studied toddlers from middle-class homes to observe how these toddlers learned self-restraint. Power and Chapieski used the willingness of the children to "not touch" breakable or dangerous objects in the home as a measure of self-control.

Child-rearing practices were examined by interviews with the mothers and by observing mother-child interactions. The interviews assessed how much physical punishment mothers thought they used to get children to control themselves. The naturalistic observation helped the researchers assess how mothers actually behaved.

The mothers and toddlers were observed in their homes on two separate occasions. The mothers were unaware of the specific purposes of the observation and were told to go about their daily routine and to ignore the observers. The observers noted the arrangement of the homes, the presence of safe objects to play with, and the amount of baby-proofing that had been done. The experimenters recorded the number and type of restrictions mothers placed on their children. Mothers restricted their children an average of about five times per forty-five-minute session—about once every nine minutes. The restrictions were about equally likely to involve unsafe and breakable objects. In nearly half of the cases in which mothers intervened, the infants did not comply on their first request. With a second or third restatement of a restriction, infants generally complied.

Mothers who used physical punishment were compared with mothers who did not use it. The middle-class mothers of this study placed demands on their children to comply and show self-restraint or self-control. These demands were normal and appropriate and were rather strictly enforced. Infants of physically punishing mothers showed the lowest level of compliance and were most likely to manipulate breakable "off limits" objects. The data show that in the long-term, physical punishment is ineffective as a disciplinary strategy. Further, in the homes of mothers who used physical discipline there was more baby proofing and fewer safe, unbreakable objects for the children to play with. This arrangement may have had the unintended effect of limiting opportunities for exploration and play and thus might interfere with the development of self-restraint and even cognitive development.

This study has implications for future researchers and for parents. First, mothers who use punishment to teach self-control are probably the least effective at their task. Second, baby proofing a home too much may limit opportunities for play, exploration, and opportunities to learn self-control. Third, mothers who use firm verbal commands in teaching children what objects are breakable, what situations are dangerous, and generally what is "off limits" are helping their children develop impulse control.

---

children. The researchers concluded that the kinds of toys children were provided with altered the egocentrism of their play.

As children who have successfully passed through the preoperational stage, seven-year-olds dress themselves, have friends and many kinds of social interactions, and are curious and eager to learn in school. Although they seem to be maturing socially very rapidly, they remain attached to their parents and suffer conflicts; a seven-year-old often reverts to babylike behavior to avoid accepting responsibility. School, however, gives children little choice. There, they are required to socialize and to interact with peers and teachers. Preadolescents learn sex-role stereotypes, how to behave "like a boy" or "like a girl," and are otherwise preparing themselves for adolescence, the stage of formal operations. Adolescence, discussed in detail in the next chapter, is a time of transition both intellectually and socially. It is a time when new ways of thinking give way to new views of the world.

The Father's Role in Childrearing

Learning Objective 7.18 Ron Clement decided he was going to have a positive impact on his child's life. He knew the child's development would depend on having quality interactions

School-age children develop social interactions with their peers and this can facilitate learning.

in the environment. Not so long ago, however, it was generally assumed that fathers affected their children only indirectly through the mother (Lewis & Weinraub, 1976). Recent evidence indicates that fathers influence their children directly (Parke, 1979), but few are sufficiently involved to have a lot of influence, especially during an infant's early months. The reason is that in traditional households, the mother assumes primary responsibility for child care, especially in feeding. Consequently, fathers generally spend less time than mothers with their children. Today, some men like Ron Clement are taking on more responsibilities. In a 1976 sample of middle-class parents, only 7.5 percent of fathers shared infant caretaking responsibilities equally with mothers, only 25 percent had a regular caretaking responsibility, and 43 percent reported that they had never changed diapers (Kotelchuck, 1976).

Has the father's role changed? Research indicated that the actual change in fathers' involvement is slow for the population in general. The amount of time men spent in housework and child care time was assessed for a ten-year period from the mid-1960s to the mid-1970s (Coverman & Sheley, 1986.) This was a period of women's increased participation to approximately 45 percent of the work force. During this decade, women began to do less housework, opting to hire people instead. Even though men's participation in child care may be increasing, it is lagging behind women's entry into the work force.

With an ever-increasing number of women entering the work force, and with many younger couples consciously deciding to eliminate gender-based roles, many men have become increasingly involved in childrearing. Research has shown that many more fathers are interested in their newborns (Greenberg & Morris, 1974) and are affectionate and responsive caretakers (Parke &

O'Leary, 1976). Their involvement can begin as early as the bonding process, in the first moments of a child's life.

Although the amount of time many fathers spend with their infants is still limited, the quality of their attention is as high as that of mothers (Booth & Edwards, 1980; Parke, 1979). However, research also indicates that children perceive fathers as playmates, mothers as caretakers. If children want to play, they choose their fathers; if they want to be consoled, they seek out their mothers (Clarke-Stewart, 1978). Children may also engage in different kinds of activities with each parent—in rough-and-tumble play with fathers (DiPietro, 1981), in vocal games with mothers (Yogman, et al., 1977). Like mothers, fathers can engage in a variety of nurturing roles, and a husband and wife's relationship is often a critical determinant of the quality of fathering (Feldman, Nash, & Aschewbrenner, 1983).

The father's role in a child's social development is very important. The absence of a father may produce a variety of negative effects unless the mother is aware of them and takes steps to avert them (Lamb, 1979). Research shows that whether the mother is working, the father is working, or both are working, quality care and interactions are the key. According to Easterbrooks and Goldberg (1985), young children and parents are able to adapt to a variety of life styles that include maternal employment and day care.

Single Parents Raising Children

Learning Objective 7.19

Before this century, one-parent families were more likely to be headed by fathers than by mothers. This was due to high maternal mortality rates at birth and also to men's higher social and financial status. Mothers rarely had the financial means to support children after divorce or being widowed. The work of the early psychologists began to have its impact in the early twentieth century. Sigmund Freud introduced the psychological idea that a child's interactions with the caretaker would affect later development. Freud's ideas about the importance of the maternal role in childrearing came to be widely accepted; mothers were viewed as the most fit parent. Today, the pendulum is

Today, many single fathers are taking on the role of caretaker for their children.

swinging again—fathers and mothers are increasingly seen as equal in their ability to rear and care for children (Greif, 1985).

Although the reasons for divorce and single parenthood are diverse, both men and women are raising children alone, and today single fathers are raising children in greater numbers than before (Greif, 1985). According to the U.S. Department of Commerce, in the decade between 1970 and 1980 the number of single parents raising children increased by at least 28 percent. The data are clear: An increasing number of children in the United States are being raised in single-parent households. For the millions of divorced, widowed, or never-married parents rearing children alone, many of the traditional supports provided for parents are unavailable. Not only do single parents tend to work longer hours than married parents (Weinraub & Wolf, 1983), but their own parents and other relatives seldom live in the same community. Single parents often bear the burden of parenthood alone. In his book *A Single Parent's Survival Guide: How to Raise the Children,* psychologist Leroy Baruth addresses some problems of being a single parent. The following list summarizes his ten specific techniques for optimal child care (Baruth, 1979); Baruth's remarks are a reminder that even in nontraditional or difficult circumstances, it is possible to parent with an awareness of children's needs.

1. Be honest with your children about the situation that caused you to become a single parent.
2. If the situation involves a separation or divorce, assure the children that they are not responsible for the decision to discontinue the relationship.
3. Be honest about your own feelings. This will demonstrate to the children that it is all right for them to express how they feel.
4. Try to maintain as much of the same routine and surroundings as possible. This will provide the children with a feeling of security that not everything has changed.
5. Do not try to be both mother and father to your children. Establish a family atmosphere of team work in which responsibilities are shared.
6. In the case of separation or divorce, realize that the relationship is over and do not encourage the children to hope for a reconciliation.
7. Reassure the children by your words, attitude, and behavior that they will continue to be loved, cared for, and supported.
8. Do not use the children in an effort to gain bargaining power with your separated or divorced spouse.
9. Make use of grandparents and other relatives so the children maintain a sense of belonging to a continuing family.
10. Try to seek the companionship and counsel of other single parents. They can be a source of advice and support that will help immeasurably in childrearing.

Day Care and Development

Learning Objective 7.20

For proper childhood development to take place, a nurturing environment is necessary. Today, day care is one of the principal means through which children are being nurtured. For the single parent or for families in which both parents work, some kind of day care, either a child-care center or in the home of a caring adult (such as a grandfather or babysitter), may be a necessity. More than 42 percent of mothers of preschool children (or about 6 million mothers) are currently in the work force. However, most Americans feel that when children are reared by people other than their parents, their development is less than optimal. As Kagan has described, the parent "is reluctant to let that responsibility slip into the hands of others" (Kagan, Kearsley, & Zelazo, 1980, p. 173). These beliefs have support from early psychological studies, which suggested that the effects of nonparental care could be devastating if the environments were not adequate (Bowlby, 1958; A. Freud, 1965; Spitz, 1945). In the last decade, intensive research has examined the effects of nonparental care on infants and children and their subsequent development. These studies have focused especially on the effects of group day-care centers in three major areas: attachment, intellectual development, and social development (for example, Rutter, 1982).

Attachment is a topic for study because psychologists believe that children's emotional security depends on a strong, loving bond with a parent or primary caretaker (Bowlby, 1973; Kagan et al., 1980; Klaus & Kennell, 1976). Researchers have found that nonparental care does not reduce a child's emotional attachment to the mother (Etaugh, 1980; Portnoy & Simmons, 1978). Furthermore, no firm evidence exists to suggest that separations such as those involved in day care create later psychological trauma.

Considerable research indicates that a stimulating, varied environment is necessary for optimal intellectual development. Parents are concerned that nonparental care will inhibit cognitive growth. The data show, however, that high-quality group day-care centers provide sufficiently stimulating environments; no differences in intellectual functioning have been found between middle-class children in such day-care centers and those reared exclusively at home (Belsky & Steinberg, 1978). Furthermore, high-quality group day care can help prevent the decline in intellectual functioning that is sometimes apparent in children from lower income families (see, for example, Golden et al., 1978).

Socially, children reared at home and those in good group day-care programs are remarkably alike. Although some studies have reported more aggression in day-care children (Largemen, 1976), other studies have found negligible or opposite effects (for example, Macrae & Herbert-Jackson, 1976). Day-care centers increase both positive and negative interactions with peers (Belsky & Steinberg, 1978). The effects of group day-care centers are not the same as home rearing unless the day-care center has an experienced and highly qualified staff, a low staff-child ratio, and a low staff turnover (Farber & Egeland, 1982). The child's age of entry into a day-care program, the extent of the child's previous day-care experience, and the child's family background are also important variables (Etaugh, 1980; Kagan et al., 1980; Wandersman, 1981).

Increasingly, psychologists have suggested that government and industry should support measures to protect or increase the equality of day care and make it affordable (Zigler & Muenchow, 1983). Some companies have responded, but very few. Unfortunately, there is no firm national policy regarding day care, and high-quality day care remains beyond the reach of many families. Parents considering day care as either an option or a necessity for their child should first establish goals for both themselves and their child. If those goals require day-care centers, they should find the highest quality, most nurturing day-care situation they can afford at a reasonable distance between work and home. At the same time, they must provide a psychologically supportive environment at home. Finally, parents must use common sense and do what feels right for them and their children.

An important variable in the issue of development and day care is how often parents switch day-care arrangements. Floge (1985) conducted a four-year study of day-care arrangements of more than 400 children. The findings indicated most parents change day-care arrangements frequently. In addition, R. P. Klein (1985) has reported that with children less than one year of age, the least favored and least used source of day-care were group day-care centers. Relatives, friends, fathers, ex-spouses, and grandparents were used much more frequently to care for infant children than were group day-care centers. Clearly, the duration and place of day-care arrangements are other important variables in the long-term analysis of day care as a means of bringing up children.

Under optimal conditions, children raised in group day-care centers and at home develop similar psychological profiles. However, studies attempting such comparisons must use children from the same social class, similar backgrounds, and intact and psychologically supportive families (Kagan, 1979), and the day-care program involved must be nurturing and cognitively challenging (Kagan et al., 1980). Few day-care centers meet these criteria, and when they do, often the families of the children involved turn out not to be sufficiently supportive. Increasingly, some researchers are questioning the wisdom of day-care centers. Researchers such as Jay Belsky of Pennsylvania State University are suggesting that day-care centers may have some negative effects on social development for children who spend more than twenty hours per week there. Long-term studies of the effects of day care on children's later development are in the process of being conducted.

Latchkey Children: A Recent Trend

Learning Objective 7.21 Who cares for the children who are not in day-care? Millions of children come home from school to empty houses, where they take care of themselves. These are the so-called "latchkey" children. According to Rodman, Pratto, & Nelson (1985), more children are involved in self-care than are in day-care centers, but virtually no research has been done on self-care children. Are there behavioral consequences for children left to care for themselves? Most parents who leave children in self-care arrangements have rules for their children to follow, maintain daily telephone contact, and try to supervise them even while they are not present in the home. Do these arrangements work?

To investigate how self-care children compare with children who are given adult supervision at home, Rodman and his colleagues found children who were alike with respect to age, sex, grade in school, family composition, and mother's and father's occupation. They matched the children so there were an equal number of children within each groups of self-care children (the latchkey group) and children who received supervision by adults. Psychologists say that they matched the two samples of subjects to make them especially comparable. When fourth and seventh graders were compared on measures of psychological and social functioning no important differences were found. The researchers concluded that ". . . the growing public and professional concern about the negative effects of self-care arrangements is premature and may not be warranted" (Rodman, Pratto, & Nelson, 1985, p. 417). Steinberg's research (1986) confirms this conclusion.

Not all children are affected by the day-care or self-care experience in identical ways. For example, Steinberg (1986) found that latchkey adolescents are more susceptible to peer pressure to engage in antisocial activities. This trend depended on whether parents were authoritative—latchkey adolescents of authoritative parents were less likely to get into trouble. Steinberg makes an important point: not all self-care situations and children are the same. The differences among self-care children and their respective situations may be greater than the similarities.

Psychologists are interested in day-care and self-care issues because of the potential behavioral effects on the child. The research on the effects of day-care has shown that the day-care experience does not have to be negative. So, too, with latchkey children; the results do not show deleterious effects—at least in the short-term. Whether there are long-term effects is yet to be seen.

As with day-care, the behavioral effects on the child are the measure of whether day care or self care makes a difference. Many of these effects will have to be examined a generation from now. For now, however, the effects of self-care for children seem nonexistent and for day-care, minimal. Like other areas of research in psychology, many of the effects, or lack of effects, depend on a variety of other circumstances—such as whether the child's parents are authoritative in their general dealings with the child. Caution in interpreting latchkey data is especially necessary given the large variability in the situations wherein latchkey children are being studied.

The Role of Diet

Learning Objective 7.22

Hyperactivity
A component of an attention-deficit hyperactivity disorder whose symptoms include overactivity, distractibility, restlessness, and short attention span.

Given the close links between biology and behavior, the control of diet may be an important variable in shaping children's development. This possibility first emerged in the 1970s, when parents, educators, psychologists, and physicians began seeking new and better ways to treat **hyperactivity,** and *attention-deficit hyperactivity disorders* which affect 3 to 15 percent of school-age children. The symptoms of these disorders (discussed in detail in Chapter 14) include overactivity, distractibility, restlessness, and short attention span. In the late 1970s, one possibility considered as a cause of hyperactivity was the food consumed by children (Williams & Cram, 1978).

Attention-deficit hyperactivity disorders directly affect children's cognitive, social, and emotional development. Children who are restless, inattentive, and easily distracted from work and play tend to do poorly in school (cognitive) and to have trouble establishing and maintaining friendships (social). They also sometimes develop other adjustment problems (emotional). Both nature and nurture are involved in the development, maintenance, and treatment of the disorder (Lahey, Green, & Forehand, 1980; Zentall, 1980).

Because researchers initially thought hyperactivity was caused by brain damage, stimulants became the common method for controlling hyperactivity in children. Paradoxically, stimulants seem to calm hyperactive children and to help them control their classroom behavior and performance (for example, Weingartner et al., 1980). But because stimulants are potent and potentially addictive, parents and physicians sought other treatments. Many settled on a diet developed in the mid-1970s by Benjamin Feingold, a physician. From clinical observations of his own patients, Feingold (1975a, 1975b, 1976) argues that salicylates, artificial food colors, and artificial food flavors trigger hyperactive symptoms in children born with a predisposition to hyperactivity. He devised a diet free of these substances and found that 30 to 50 percent of the children on the diet showed marked improvement.

Some scientists are skeptical about Feingold's diet because it is not based on a formal biochemical theory. Some studies have found modest support for the Feingold diet; others have found none. Many parents using it for their hyperactive children continue to claim that it works.

Feingold's approach has prompted much research into the role of other food substances in hyperactivity. A study at the University of South Carolina has shown that sugar and sugar products are involved in destructive-aggressive and restless behavior in the free play of hyperactive children. Prinz, Roberts, and Hantman (1980) report that when hyperactive children are on a diet low in these substances, hyperactive behaviors are less apparent. Prinz and his colleagues do not claim that removing sugar will decrease all hyperactive behavior, only that sugar plays a potentially important role in such behavior.

Several problems are inherent in the studies of diet and behavior. It is nearly impossible to control totally what a child eats and what the food contains. It is also difficult to assess a child's behavior, because parents and teachers focus on different behaviors and also because children often behave differently at home and in school. Better methods for examining these variables are being developed as research into the role of diet in the management of hyperactivity continues (for example, Pelham, Schendler, Bologna, & Contreras, 1980). So far, it seems clear that for about 10 to 25 percent of younger hyperactive children, a diet free of artificial additives is beneficial.

People's development does not end at age twelve, but their progress in adolescence and throughout adulthood rests on foundations laid by nature and nurture in early childhood. The next chapter discusses the stages of development associated with adolescence and adulthood.

PROGRESS CHECK   7.5

1. Complete each of the following sentences with one of the options provided.

Learning Objective 7.17   A.   Children begin to realize they are separate beings around the age of _____ _____ months.
(six : twelve : eighteen)

Learning Objective 7.17   B.   Two-year-olds tend to play _____ other children.
(alone or alongside : with)

Learning Objective 7.17   C.   Children usually begin to learn responsibility and to share with others when they _____.
(can say "yes" and "no" : enter nursery school or kindergarten)

Learning Objective 7.17   D.   Quilitch and Risley have suggested that the _____ young children play with will promote or retard the breakdown of egocentrism.
(number of children : type of toys)

Learning Objective 7.18   E.   Several studies have shown that the _____ fathers give to their children is as high as what mothers give.
(amount of time : quality of attention)

Learning Objective 7.19   F.   Baruth suggests that single parents _____ to be both mother and father to their children.
(must try : should not try)

Learning Objective 7.20   G. Research suggests that the brief separation that occurs when children are left in day-care centers _____ the childrens' emotional attachments to their mothers.
(does not reduce : has a slight negative effect on : increases)

Learning Objective 7.20   H. Parents who choose day-care arrangements for their babies under one-year of age are most likely to select _____ to care for the child.
(a day-care center : relatives or friends)

Learning Objective 7.20   I. The day-care center environment seems to increase a child's _____ _____ interactions with peers.
(negative : positive : negative and positive)

Learning Objective 7.21   J. Latchkey children are children who _____.
(run away from home : care for themselves when parents are not home)

Learning Objective 7.22   K. Benjamin Feingold argues that the most successful treatment for hyperactivity requires that the child _____.
(take stimulants : take depressants : follow a special diet)

Keeping Pace with Chapter 7

Applying Principles

7.1 Identify the concept of intellectual development that is illustrated in each of the following situations.

assimilation	intentionality	accommodation	object permanence
egocentrism	conservation	decentration	appearance-reality distinction

_____

A. At age ten, Robin grins while watching his excited little sister place her recently lost tooth under her pillow for a surprise from the tooth fairy. The last time the tooth fairy left a surprise for Robin, he put the clues together and realized the "tooth fairy" was really mom and dad. Robin no longer believes in the tooth fairy because he has developed what ability?

_____

B. After playing with her cousin Mary's doll all afternoon, Tammy became very upset when her mother reminded her that the doll was Mary's and that she would have to leave it at Mary's house. Tammy was upset because she was unable to understand why she could not keep the doll.

_____

C. Billy's parents gave him a bicycle for his birthday. Billy had mastered the skills of riding a tricycle, but when he got on his new bike it was apparent that his previously learned skills would have to be modified before he could ride the bicycle with ease.

_____

D. Several weeks after receiving his bicycle, Billy had incorporated the skills necessary into his behavioral repertoire and was able to ride the bike easily.

_____

E. Sara's mother moves her teddy bear and Sara scans the room until she finds its new location.

_____

F. Sally gives her sons, Jason and Kirk, equal-sized balls of modeling clay. Jason takes a few moments thinking about what to do with his clay, while Kirk quickly rolls his out into a long snakelike shape. When Jason saw Kirk's snake he began to fuss, saying Kirk got more clay than he did. From this, we can conclude that Jason lacks what ability?

G. Although Jody would like the red balloon rather than the yellow one, she relinquishes her wishes to her younger brother because she knows he would be disappointed if he could not have the red balloon. Jody is able to recognize her brother's feelings because she has gone through what process?

H. One-year-old Rickie sees his pet kitten sleeping in a chair and wants to touch it. Rather than waiting for the kitten to wake up and stroll by, Rickie craws over to the chair and touches his pet. Rickie is beginning to develop what ability?

Self-Test

Before proceeding to the Self-Test, REVIEW the Learning Objectives listed at the chapter opening and RECITE from memory everything you can remember in support of them. Then, take this Self-Test as if it were to be graded by your teacher. Use the Learning Objective numbers in the Answer Section as a reference to restudy the corresponding text pages and Progress Checks for any incorrectly answered questions.

1. A zygote becomes an embryo when the

   A. second cell division occurs—about ten hours after conception.
   B. fertilized egg has firmly implanted itself in the uterine lining.
   C. first bone cells are formed.
   D. heart begins to beat.

2. Which of the following is a *false* statement?

   A. The use of alcohol during pregnancy can lead to learning disorders
   B. Drugs have their strongest effect on the developing child during the embryonic stage.
   C. Vitamin deficiencies weaken the mother but do not seem to affect the developing child.
   D. Environmental factors affecting a pregnant woman can also affect the unborn child.

3. Contractions that are experienced by the mother during labor occur because

   A. the baby is kicking.
   B. the umbilical cord is swelling.
   C. the cervix is dilating.
   D. the placenta is breaking.

4. Researchers like Yvonne Brackbill take a position against the use of heavy medications by mothers during normal child delivery because

   A. Medications at this time could cause abnormalities.
   B. The child will be more prone to addiction.
   C. Medications cause mothers to be more hostile to their newborns.
   D. The medications can have long-lasting effects on the child's cognitive and motor abilities.

5. The perceptual systems in newborns

   A. are underdeveloped, allowing infants to experience a calm environment.
   B. are well-developed, giving infants amazingly good perceptual abilities.
   C. are fully developed but sensitive to experience.
   D. are fully developed and are not sensitive to experience

6. After studying how babies respond to their mothers' facial expressions, Sorce and his colleagues concluded that

   A. facial expression is a key source of information for babies.

B. babies respond a little to facial expression but much more to hand and body position.

C. babies are unable to detect cues from their mother's emotional state.

D. babies respond to facial expressions but they do not seem to discriminate between expressions of approval and disapproval.

7. Two adaptive reflexes that contribute to a newborn's eating behavior are

A. sucking and rooting.

B. sucking and the Babinski reflex.

C. grasping and rooting.

D. rooting and the Moro reflex.

8. Infancy is defined as ending and childhood as beginning when the child

A. has his or her second birthday.

B. can stand without support.

C. begins to use language to describe experiences.

D. drops the rooting reflex and uses learned behaviors in its place.

9. Separation anxiety and stranger anxiety are often observed in infants who

A. lack attachments to a significant caretaker.

B. have developed the ability to approach and avoid various situations.

C. are curious and self-directed when they get older.

D. B and C

10. Children who *do not* form close attachments early in life are more likely than children who do form close attachments to

A. become anxious and overly dependent.

B. sleep through the night.

C. have serious behavior disorders.

D. become mentally retarded.

11. Daniels and Plomin's study on infant shyness is important because it showed that

A. all babies under age two are shy.

B. human beings do not show signs of shyness until after age two.

C. adopted babies are more likely to show signs of shyness.

D. personality is determined, in part, by genetics.

12. Perhaps the greatest strength of Piaget's theory of intellectual development is that it

A. originated from asking children of different ages reliable questions.

B. focuses on the wealth of human knowledge.

C. describes how inherited potentials interact with the environment to produce intellectual behaviors.

D. provides a model for teaching advanced concepts to young children.

13. The process of _____ takes place when a person must modify previously developed cognitive structures and behaviors in order to adapt to a new concept or experience.

A. conservation

B. decentration

C. accommodation

D. assimilation

14. Children acquire the ability to remember things during the _____ _____ stage.

A. sensory-motor

B. preoperations

C. concrete operations

D. formal operations

15. Psychologists would say that conservation abilities are developing when a child can recognize that
    A. two objects of the same size, shape, and weight are equal.
    B. the number of pennies in a roll of coins is equal to the number of scattered pennies after the roll of coins has been opened.
    C. all four-legged animals are not dogs.
    D. things can still exist even if they are not in sight.

16. Research findings such as those showing that two-year-olds rotate their books for their mothers to see have caused some psychologists to question
    A. Piaget's emphasis on egocentrism in young children.
    B. the validity of the experimental questions Piaget asked in developing his theory.
    C. why infants are giving at times and selfish at other times.
    D. A and B

17. Young children
    A. almost instinctively initiate sharing if another youngster is nearby.
    B. do not share, even when asked to do so by their mothers.
    C. share food but not toys.
    D. develop a sense of reciprocal arrangements once they have learned to share.

18. Children tend to approach their fathers rather than their mothers when they want to
    A. be consoled.
    B. engage in vocal games.
    C. engage in active play, especially rough-and-tumble play.
    D. skip a day of school or get help with homework.

19. Single parents
    A. are provided with more social support than most married parents.
    B. usually live near or with relatives.
    C. are raising an increasing number of children in the United States.
    D. all of the above

20. When parents place their children in day-care centers, it is important that they
    A. find a high-quality, nurturing situation.
    B. provide a psychologically supportive environment at home.
    C. establish goals for themselves and their children.
    D. all of the above

21. Some of the first research conducted in 1985 on latchkey children concluded that
    A. these children are being woefully neglected.
    B. public concerns over self-care arrangements may be premature.
    C. a locked door erodes parent-child attachments.
    D. life is not easy at any age.

22. According to Benjamin Feingold, artificial food additives trigger hyperactivity in
    A. most children.
    B. children who have hyperactive parents.
    C. children who are born with a predisposition toward the disorder.
    D. children who receive insufficient amounts of protein.

23. Prinz, Roberts, and Hantman have shown that
    A. removing sugar from a child's diet will eliminate hyperactive behavior.
    B. sugar is involved in destructive-aggressive and restless behavior.
    C. observational learning is the primary determinant of hyperactive behavior.
    D. hyperactive children are also curious children, and this contributes to their intellectual and social development.

Adolescence and Adulthood

8

Learning Objectives

When you have mastered the material in this chapter, you will be able to:

1. Discuss how psychologists view the process of growing older. (p. 280)

2. Discuss adolescence in regard to the society in which a teenager is raised and identify several factors that cause adolescents in modern Western society to experience conflict. (p. 281)

3. Make a distinction between puberty and adolescence and discuss some of the physical changes that occur as an adolescent goes through puberty. (p. 282)

4. Explain how peers, television, sex roles, and attitudes about sexuality influence social development during adolescence. (p. 282)

5. Explain why teenage pregnancies are likely to occur among sexually active adolescents. (p. 284)

6. Describe some of the special problems that occur during adolescence, including emotional conflict, suicide, drugs, and the search for identity. (p. 285)

7. Identify and describe the eight stages in Erik Erikson's psychosocial stage theory of development. (p. 286)

8. Describe some variables that influence moral development, describe Kohlberg's theory of moral development, and compare and contrast Piaget's ideas about moral development with Kohlberg's ideas. (p. 290)

9. Discuss how the field of developmental psychology has changed in the past two decades and describe Levinson's concept of changing life structures. (p. 296)

10. Identify and describe four basic eras discussed by Levinson in his stage theory of adult development. (p. 297)

11. Discuss the sexual, fitness, and sensory changes that occur during adulthood. (p. 299)

12. Discuss what psychologists know about personality development during the adult years. (p. 300)

13. Identify some major statistics concerning people over age sixty-five and discuss some social conditions that can make life during late adulthood difficult. (p. 302)

14. Define ageism and describe how stereotyping influences the occurrence of this type of discrimination. (p. 304)

15. Identify and describe several theories of aging. (p. 305)

16. Explain how chronic brain disorders, sensory abilities, neurological changes, and a general condition of health affect some aging people. (p. 306)

17. Describe how intelligence changes for some elderly people and give some reasons that these changes seem to occur. (p. 309)

18. Discuss how aging can both enhance and lessen an employee's ability to perform at work. (p. 310)

19. Explain how and why the attitudes toward death held by people in Western society differ from those of people in other societies; also, describe Kübler-Ross's stage theory of death and dying. (p. 315)

20. Explain how hospice care differs from the care provided by traditional hospitals. (p. 317)

BEFORE YOU READ ON, take time to **SURVEY** the chapter, form an idea of what is to be learned (from margin Learning Objective numbers), and set goals for your study time. Then, ask yourself **QUESTIONS** about the material as you **READ,** seeking help for any sections you do not understand.

Teenager Betty Gerson was facing a double whammy. She was going through a difficult time in her own adolescence—her parents called it an adolescent crisis. In addition, she had taken on the emotional burden of her grandfather's well-being.

Betty's own crisis was fairly predictable by psychological standards. She knew she wanted more freedom than her parents would give her at age sixteen. She knew she was sometimes irresponsible, but at other times she behaved more responsibly than her parents (especially when it came to her grandfather). Among other things, Betty wanted more freedom to spend money, a more flexible curfew, and unlimited use of the car. Regularly feeling misunderstood and unloved, Betty had tantrums, door slamming episodes, and, most of all, a desire to control her own life. In addition to all of this, she wanted to help her grandfather, George Gerson.

Grandfather George Gerson was losing his memory. It took him a long time to realize that this was his problem. First, he forgot simple things, like his car keys or his checkbook. These episodes were easy to dismiss. Later, he found himself in situations and did not know why he was there. He went to the supermarket and did not know what to buy. He was able to shake that off, too. Now, his memory lapses were becoming more severe. He would leave his home to go to the bank and not know where the bank was. On three occasions, he could not remember his address. When talking to one of his children, he could not remember his wife's name. To make matters worse, he was arrested for driving too fast and without his license and was unable to tell the police where he lived or the name of his insurance agent.

Betty remembered her granddad talking about his carefree retirement. But she knew that although in otherwise good health, he was forgetting too much, too often. He was scared, tired, and did not know what to do. Even though he had children and grandchildren who loved him, he was embarrassed and felt alone. He became afraid to drive his car and avoided social contacts that might show his confusion. He found himself watching television game shows for hours, sometimes skipping meals.

Betty's parents avoided the difficult questions: Was he becoming senile? Were the next years going to become more difficult? Would he have to go to a nursing home? Did his advancing age mean that he could no longer function as an alert, aware adult? But Betty asked questions. She forced the issue and argued with her parents about her grandfather's future. She took on the emotional burden of her grandfather's situation. Of course, this added to her adolescent problems. She had trouble managing her own emotions, her changing ideas about the world, her love-hate feeling about her parents. Now, she was adding to all of this the responsibility of worrying about her aging grandfather.

BETTY AND GEORGE GERSON shared a bond of love and affection, as most grandparents have with their grandchildren. Betty's love for her granddad caused her to worry about issues that her parents and aunts and uncles should have handled. Betty had reason to be concerned; her grandfather is one of 23 million Americans over the age of sixty-five. Most people recognize that older people are going to experience certain changes. Older people generally have less agility, strength, and stamina. But growing older does not necessarily mean memory losses and old age homes.

Learning   8.1
Objective

Psychologists look at growing older and the process of development as a process of growth, not of deterioration. Both Betty and her grandfather were going through developmental changes. Betty had gone through puberty and was making adolescent changes and facing adult problems and responsibilities. Her grandfather's memory was deteriorating faster than that of many older individuals. Psychologists recognize that at all times of life, people's biological inheritance, life experiences, and thought processes affect their development. People do not follow predetermined paths to emotional turmoil or to mental or physical dependence on others.

For people like Betty, the transition is difficult from the protected world of childhood to the freedom and responsibility of adulthood. Generally, this transition occurs in the years between twelve and eighteen, known as adolescence. Adolescence is a time of dramatic intellectual, social, emotional, and physical changes. Intellectual changes, in particular, affect the way people perceive the world and how they judge situations and behavior. Together with socialization, these changes affect moral development. Although moral development begins early in life and continues throughout adulthood, adolescence is usually a crucial period of transition, a time of learning and growth.

In Betty's case, her sense of morality and her devotion and love forced her to consider the plight and future of her grandfather. Betty was probably less well equipped than she thought to deal with her granddad's situation.

This chapter looks at the issues Betty faced as an adolescent. We also examine the process of growing older by looking at the stages of adulthood and growing old. You will see that growth and development is a process that begins at birth and continues through the life span. You will see that Betty's concern for her grandfather was well-founded, and she could probably thank her parents for her strong sense of responsibility. They helped develop that sense of morality in Betty when she was a child.

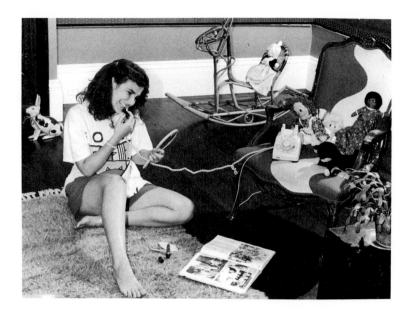

Although adolescents often try to act like adults, they still feel emotional ties to their childhood.

ADOLESCENCE

Betty Gerson was typical of other sixteen-year-old girls. She wanted expanded freedoms, new responsibilities, and the ability to make up her own mind about decisions affecting her life. Betty also worried about other adult issues, especially her grandfather. Most adolescents like Betty face pressure to grow up, become sophisticated, and experience life's pleasures and responsibilities. Betty Gerson was getting her share of pressure fast and furiously.

Learning Objective 8.2

Adolescents like Betty are physically adults; their mental capabilities are mature or nearly mature; their moral development tends to be fairly advanced. Their emotional development, however, often is still far from complete. The conflicts that adolescents experience result in part from this lack of congruity in their physical, intellectual, social, and emotional development. Often, these conflicts are aggravated by the paradoxical demands of adults, who, on the one hand, tell adolescents it is time to behave like an adult, and on the other treat them like children, restricting their income, spending, and social life (Melton, 1983). Adolescence was not seen as a "problem" period in the eighteenth century, nor is it visible today (in the form we know it) in nonindustrial societies. Adolescent problems seem tied to the society and time in which they occur. Today, the pressures on adolescents in Western society are great.

Betty Gerson was dealing with issues that her parents and most adolescents usually avoid. Of course, affecting any adolescent's development is his or her cognitive stage of development. According to Piaget, who we studied in the last chapter, most adolescents have entered the stage of formal operations (see p. 259). Adults may thus expect them to think logically and rationally and to behave like adults. However, developing the ability to cope with the complexities and restrictions of a technological society is a difficult, gradual process. Some adolescents acquire this ability by age thirteen; others take a few more years; some never attain it. Simultaneous changes in intellectual ability, body proportions, and sexual urges (coupled with parental expectations for more adult behavior) create the classic adolescent identity crisis of Western society.

Physical Development

Many people use the words *adolescence* and *puberty* as synonyms, but in fact these words mean different things. Puberty is the time when the reproductive system matures; adolescence is the time following the onset of puberty (see Chumlea, 1982). Thus, puberty occurs at (and signals) the end of childhood; adolescence marks the period afterward.

The onset of puberty varies widely. Although the average age is thirteen, plus or minus a year or two, some girls begin to mature physically as early as age eight, some boys at nine or ten (Marshall & Tanner, 1969). Just before the onset of puberty, both boys and girls experience significant growth spurts, perhaps as much as four to five inches in a single year. Usually at the end of the first or second year of this growth spurt, body proportions change, the hormonal system produces secondary sex characteristics (Villee, 1975), and fat distribution, muscles, bones, physical strength, and agility change (Roche, Wainer, & Thissen, 1975). In boys, the secondary sex characteristics are an increase in the size of the testes, scrotum, and penis and the growth of pubic, underarm, and facial hair. In girls, they are an increase in the size of the breasts, widening of the hips, and the growth of underarm and pubic hair. Puberty ends with maturation of the reproductive organs: boys are able to produce sperm, and girls begin to menstruate, because their ovaries can now produce ova for fertilization. These physical changes almost always take several years to complete, and the individuals experiencing them generally find them both exciting and disturbing, for they lead to both new opportunities and new responsibilities.

Social Development

In addition to biological changes, environmental factors shape adolescents' social development in ways that influence later behavior in adulthood.

Peer Group.   The two most important influences on the social behavior of adolescents are peers and parents. *Peers* are people of the same age with whom individuals identify and compare themselves. Peer groups tend to consist of people of the same age, sex, and race, although adolescents can change peer groups and belong to more than one. As adolescents spend more time away from parents and home, they experience increasing pressure to conform to their peer groups. Peer groups can be a source of information about society, drug use, educational aspirations, and peer group activities (P. R. Newman, 1982). Studies disagree on whether peers or parents have a greater influence on adolescents. Most studies indicate that adolescents' social attitudes tend to fall somewhere between those of parents and peers (for example, Kelly & Goodwin, 1983; Lerner, Karson, Meisels, & Knapp, 1975).

In the classroom, peers often serve as powerful sources of reinforcement in increasing or maintaining positive and negative behaviors of classmates. Peers can serve to correct antisocial behaviors or to reinforce more desired behaviors (Smith & Fowler, 1984). Peer groups on television also can influence an adolescent's developing self-concept. Studies indicate that teenagers watch television on the average of more than seventeen hours per week (Lawrence, Tasker, Daly, Orhiel, & Wozniak, 1986). It thus is not surprising that it affects adolescents' behavior. Many of the hours spent watching television are observing teenagers and young people whom many teenagers see as role models and peers. The "peers" presented on television thus indirectly act as an extended peer reference group to whom teenagers can compare themselves.

During adolescence, males become concerned with their physique and masculinity.

Sex roles. A key point about adolescence is that the teenager is in a period of transition and change. Teenagers know who they are as far as being a male or female—early in childhood they established either boy- or girl-like behaviors. But in adolescence, they are forming an identity, a sense of themselves as independent, mature individuals. It is not surprising that adolescents have some degree of confusion about their self-image and identity. Their bodies change in appearance very rapidly during this time, sometimes in unpredictable ways. During their transition to adulthood, adolescents are often expected by adults to try out various types of behaviors and sometimes to become extreme in their orientations about maleness or femaleness. Males may try out becoming loud and boisterous; females may become overly concerned with their looks and attractiveness. The exaggeration of traditional male or female behaviors is usually short-lived.

Sometimes mistakenly linked with sexual behavior is the process by which people learn attitudes and behaviors characteristic of gender, or *sex-role stereotyping.* Although people's attitudes about sex roles are not always evident in their behavior (Lerner & Shea, 1982), sex role stereotyping exerts strong influences on both adolescent and adult behavior. Sex roles help people establish who they are. Because gender-based behavior tends to be reinforced by society, it is not surprising that sexual attitudes and behavior tend to be perpetuated and maintained.

Asserting a gender identity in adolescence has always been a part of making the transition to adulthood. Today, this task is more complicated, especially for women. In past decades, women often spent a significant portion of their time and energy preparing for marriage and rearing a family. Now women are heavily represented in the workforce. A young woman's aspirations for her future may be different today than they would have been twenty or thirty years ago. In the 1950s, few women were committed to a full-time career. Today, the most common plan for a woman's future is a career that will probably be interrupted for childbearing.

Since the 1970s, men and women (and adolescents) have begun rethinking sex roles. Many have begun to feel that possessing both some traditionally masculine and some traditionally feminine characteristics might be a good thing. These people deliberately adopt *androgynous* behaviors—behaviors shared by both sexes. Thus, both men and women perform such chores as car maintenance, washing dishes, and helping with child care. Some studies have found that subjects who rate high in androgynous characteristics tend to be more fulfilled and more competent in dealing with social and personal issues (S. L. Bem, 1975; Worell, 1978). This finding makes sense, because people with androgynous characteristics have a greater variety of "acceptable" behaviors available to them in which they can seek satisfaction. Reasoning that "anatomy is not destiny" (Lerner & Shea, 1982, p. 516), psychologists in the 1980s increasingly argued in favor of flexibility and creativity in sex roles.

Sexual Behavior. The study of the sexual behavior of both adolescents and adults has been very controversial. There has been much talk and much unscientific research, and psychologists still know less about the nature of human sexuality than they would like. Like any other kind of behavior, sexual behavior is a product of both nature and nurture. In lower animals, reproductive behavior is largely a function of hormone concentrations in the bloodstream. In human beings, learned attitudes have greater influence than do biological factors in determining sexual behavior.

Much sexual behavior is tied to intimate relationships, and people first learn about such relationships at home. Parents teach their children about sexual identity and direct their initial sexual responses (Worell, 1978) through classical conditioning, instrumental conditioning, and especially observational learning. Children watch their parents interact. They notice if their parents hug, kiss, seem ashamed of their bodies, or talk openly about sexual matters. Generally, the more open or permissive parents are, the more open or permissive the child will be.

It is not surprising that a parent's attempts at discipline and control affect a teenager's sexual attitudes and behavior. In an attempt to assess how those two factors were related, Miller, McCoy, Olson, and Wallace (1986) surveyed more than 2,000 teenagers from age fifteen to age eighteen and their parents about parental discipline and teenage sexual behavior. The results showed that sexual permissiveness and intercourse was highest among adolescents who viewed their parents as not having rules or as not being strict at all. Sexual behaviors were lowest among teenagers who reported parents that were moderately strict.

Their rapid sexual maturation makes sex an important part of adolescents' lives. Premarital heterosexual activity has become increasingly common among adolescents, especially among thirteen- to seventeen-year-olds, in the past two decades, accompanied by marked shifts in attitudes about sexuality. Greater numbers of American adolescents view sexual intimacy as an important and normal part of growing up (see Newcomer, Udry, & Cameron, 1983). Although sexual activities have generally increased, so have fears of diseases like AIDS; in spite of AIDS, sexual activities are increasingly common at younger and younger ages. Dreyer (1982) suggests several possible reasons for this: (1) adolescents are maturing sexually earlier, (2) knowledge and use of contraception are becoming more widespread, (3) adult society is changing its sexual attitudes and behavior, and (4) though not totally sure about their behavior, adolescents are considering sexual behaviors "normal" in intimate relationships.

Learning $\underline{\underline{8.5}}$
Objective

There is no doubt that attitudes about adolescent sexual behavior have changed in the last three decades. Along with those changes has been increased awareness among people generally about contraception, the problems of teenage pregnancy, and AIDS.

Not using contraception is the principal reason for teenage pregnancy. Only about 20 percent of sexually active adolescents report using contraception on any regular basis (Dreyer, 1982). According to D. M. Morrison (1985), teenagers are largely uninformed or ill-informed about reproductive physiology and the many methods of contraception and also underestimate the likelihood of pregnancy. Generally, they have negative attitudes about contraception and do not want to use it, although they have trouble articulating why. Frequency of use of contraception increases as teenagers grow older and as they become more sexually active. Contraception norms can change rapidly, but to date, even though widely available, contraception is used by too few too infrequently. Chapter 11 considers sexual behavior in more detail.

Special Problems

Learning $\overline{8.6}$
Objective
Some psychologists view the transition from childhood to adulthood as a time of "storm and stress" (Erikson, 1968). Often, well-meaning friends and relatives warn parents that this is going to be a period of trouble and turmoil. However, the naturally occurring changes of adolescence do not necessarily cause turmoil (Frank & Cohen, 1979). Many adolescents make the transition to adulthood smoothly (Bandura, 1964; Lerner & Shea, 1982). As at any other life stage, individuals vary in their ability to cope with new demands. Unquestionably, physical and behavioral changes create stress in adolescence, and some teenagers are unable to understand or manage it effectively (Siegel, 1982). When this is the case, real problems can develop. Although problems involving emotional conflicts, suicide, drugs, and the search for identity affect people of almost all ages, they tend to be associated especially closely with adolescence.

Emotional Conflicts.   Learning to manage their new feelings of independence, sexuality, and intellectual and physical growth sometimes produces emotional conflicts in adolescents. Faced with moral decisions (discussed later) and peer and family pressures, adolescents often exhibit extremes in emotions, especially right after puberty. Breaking into tears and slamming doors are quite common behaviors. In extreme cases, teenagers may feel so misunderstood that they view running away as the only solution. Typical runaways are thirteen- or fourteen-year-olds seeking escape from the responsibilities, emotions, and difficulties of home. Bored, confused about life, and seeking to defy adult society, they are often victimized and become prostitutes and drug pushers. Though at first considered a purely legal problem, runaway behavior is increasingly seen as a sociological and psychological problem that can be treated with family therapy.

Suicide.   Among adolescents in the United States, suicide is the third most common cause of death after accidents and homicides. One out of every 1,000 adolescents attempts suicide (Walker & Mehr, 1983), and actual suicides among fifteen- to twenty-four-year-olds have reached epidemic proportions—nearly 7,000 a year. This is about the same suicide rate as that among older adults, up from less than one-third that of older adults (Eisenberg, 1980).

From a psychologist's point of view, adolescent suicide is particularly disheartening, because proper counseling or therapy can help adolescents deal with depression and alienation by altering false ideas (discussed in Chapter 15) and by alleviating stress (discussed in Chaper 13). Although little research has been done on suicide among adolescents, psychologists are becoming increasingly involved in research and preventive efforts among this population group (Emery, 1983).

Drugs.   Almost by definition, adolescence is a time of experimentation with the trappings of adulthood. Two drugs, alcohol and tobacco, have been the traditional substances for experimentation. Since the late 1960s, adolescents have also begun using a wide variety of more potent drugs. The use of marijuana, LSD, amphetamines, barbiturates, crack, angel dust, and cocaine is widespread among all segments of the United States population, but particularly among adolescents. The rate of drug addiction and drug-related deaths among teenagers is high. Despite numerous treatment programs and halfway houses, drug-related problems remain acute for adolescents and their families.

Adults use alcohol and other drugs for relaxation. Most adolescents use them to gain social acceptance among peers by imitating older (sometimes parental) role models (see, for example, Brook, Whiteman, & Gordon, 1983). Some use them to produce euphoria and to escape aspects of life that seem complex, demanding, or overwhelming. Many drugs are dangerous in any amount. Other drugs, such as alcohol, may not be dangerous in small or moderate amounts for most people. However, limited experience, poor judgment, or an overriding desire to challenge authority may cause adolescents to indulge too much, too often, and with the wrong substances.

The Search for Identity

Our society makes it difficult for adolescents to form an image of who they are and what they want in life. After years of being allowed to behave like children, suddenly, it seems, adolescents are expected to behave like adults. Yearning for both the freedom and responsibilities of adulthood and the security of childhood creates stress. Society increases this stress by demanding that youngsters begin making career decisions as early as eighth grade. Many thirteen- and fourteen-year-olds are forced to choose among a college-bound curriculum, a business curriculum, or technical training. These decisions affect how they will spend a large part of the rest of their lives. Often, adolescents find this decision so confusing that their parents make it for them.

Perhaps no one has been more closely associated with the problems of adolescents than the noted developmental psychologist Erik H. Erikson (1902–1972). Erikson's well-known theory is a stage theory of development that covers the full life span. It has achieved a great deal of acceptance, and many psychologists have focused on the stages that deal with adolescence. In Erikson's view, the growth and turmoil of adolescence create an "identity crisis," and the major task for adolescents is to resolve this crisis successfully through the formation of an identity. Failure to complete this process leaves the adolescent confused about roles and unable to cope with the demands of adulthood, including the development of mature relationships with members of the opposite sex (Erikson, 1963, 1968).

Erikson believed that the search for identity grows logically from sociocultural pressures and the tasks they impose on development. The process (discussed in more detail in Chapters 10 and 12) is complex because social pressures are complex. People form self-images not only from their own self-perceptions but also from other people's perceptions of them (expressed through behavior). People also tend to attribute characteristics to themselves that derive from their situation. Membership in political, religious, or ideological groups helps adolescents discover what they believe in and what satisfies their needs. The adolescent years are years of social growth, of growth toward a personal sense of becoming a mature adult.

Erik Erikson (1902–1972) developed one of the most influential psychosocial theories.

Learning Objective 8.7

Erikson's theory, like Piaget's theory, describes a series of stages—in this case, "crises"—through which all individuals pass; each crisis has both positive and negative outcomes. Ideally, the positive experiences or outcomes outnumber the negative ones. Erikson's psychosocial stages of development parallel Freud's (discussed in Chapter 12), particularly with reference to the early years. Like Freud, Erikson assumed that a problem at any one stage leads to conflict

TABLE 8.1: Erikson's Eight Stages of Psychosocial Development

Stages	Approximate Age	Important Event	Description
1. Basic trust vs. basic mistrust	Birth to 12–18 months	Feeding	The infant must form a first, loving, trusting, relationship with the caregiver, or develop a sense of mistrust.
2. Autonomy vs. shame/doubt	18 months to 3 years	Toilet training	The child's energies are directed toward the development of physical skills, including walking, grasping, and sphincter control. The child learns control but may develop shame and doubt if not handled well.
3. Initiative vs. guilt	3 to 6 years	Independence	The child continues to become more assertive and to take more initiative, but may be too forceful, leading to guilt feelings.
4. Industry vs. inferiority	6 to 12 years	School	The child must deal with the demands to learn new skills, or risk a sense of inferiority, failure, and incompetence.
5. Identity vs. role confusion	Adolescence	Peer relationships	The teenager must achieve a sense of identity in occupation, sex roles, politics, and religion.
6. Intimacy vs. isolation	Young adulthood	Love relationships	The young adult must develop intimate relationships, or suffer feelings of isolation.
7. Generativity vs. stagnation	Middle adulthood	Parenting	Each adult must find some way to satisfy and support the next generation.
8. Ego integrity vs. despair	Late adulthood	Reflection on and acceptance of one's life	The culmination is a sense of acceptance of oneself as one is and of feeling fulfilled.

and to difficulty passing through later stages. Unlike other theorists, however, Erikson maintained that personality development continues throughout life. Although Erikson presented each stage as a series of polar opposites, it must be stressed that an individual does not "pass" or "fail"; rather, successful resolution of a stage must be viewed as a continuum. As we examine Erikson's stages, it is important to remember that he saw each stage as presenting dilemmas to people. They could face those dilemmas positively, seeing them as opportunities, or they could see those dilemmas as catastrophes that bring with them negative outcomes. Each crisis or dilemma emerges as a person grows older and faces new responsibilities, new tasks, and new social relationships. To emerge as a fully mature, stable adult, a person has to pass through each stage victoriously. Erikson's views have had a particularly strong influence on how psychologists think about adolescence. Table 8.1 lists Erikson's stages and the important events, crises, and opportunities associated with them.

Stages 1 through 4 cover birth through age twelve. Stage 1 involves the development of *basic trust* versus *basic mistrust*. During the first months of life, infants make distinctions about the world and decide accordingly whether it is a comfortable, loving place in which they can place basic trust. In essence, at this stage, infants develop beliefs about the essential truthfulness of other people. As toddlers, children pass through stage 2, the stage of *autonomy* versus *shame and doubt*. Success in toilet training and other tasks involving control leads to a sense of autonomy and to more mature behavior. Difficulties during this stage result in fears and a sense of shame and doubt.

The third stage is that of *initiative* versus *guilt.* At ages four and five, children develop the abilities to use their initiative and to identify with their parents. During this stage, children either develop a sense of independence and good feelings about themselves, or a sense of guilt, lack of acceptance, and negative feelings about their sexuality. In stage 4, the stage of *industry* versus *inferiority,* children either develop feelings of competence and confidence in their own abilities or they experience failure, inferiority, and feelings of incompetence.

Stage 5 marks the beginning of adolescence. During the stage of *identity* versus *role confusion,* adolescents must decide who they are and what they want to do in life. If they do not, they will become confused and often rebellious. Stage 6, *intimacy* versus *isolation,* is the time when young adults begin to select other people whom they can love, identify with, and be intimate with. During this stage, they either learn to relate on a warm, social basis with members of the opposite sex, or they become isolated. Erikson says of this stage:

> It is only after a reasonable sense of identity has been established that a real intimacy with the other sex (or, for that matter, with any other person or even with oneself) is possible. Sexual intimacy is only part of what I have in mind. . . . The youth who is not sure of his identity shies away from interpersonal intimacy; but the surer he becomes of himself, the more he seeks it in the form of friendship, combat, leadership, love and inspiration. (1959, p. 101)

In stage 7, *generativity* versus *stagnation,* people seek more than just intimacy: they also hope to convey information, love, and warmth to others, particularly to their children. In adulthood, people either hope to influence their own family or the world at large, or they stagnate, feeling that life has been boring and unexciting. Erikson's final stage is *ego integrity* versus *despair.* In this stage of development, people decide whether their existence has been meaningful, happy, and cohesive or wasteful and lacking in productivity. Many individuals never complete stage 8; those who do, feel fulfilled, with a sense that they understand at least partly what life is about.

A key point of Erikson's theory is that people go through each stage, resolving the crises of that stage as best they can. Whether you are ready for the next stage, as you grow older, some problems or opportunities of that next stage are on you. You may still have unresolved conflicts, opportunities, and dilemmas from the previous stage. This can cause anxiety, discomfort and can also make resolution of more advanced stages more difficult.

PROGRESS CHECK 8.1

1. Match the Erik Erikson's stages of development with the appropriate definitions.

industry vs. inferiority	identity vs. role confusion	generativity vs. stagnation
ego integrity vs. despair	basic trust vs. mistrust	autonomy vs. shame
initiative vs. guilt	intimacy vs. isolation	and doubt

Learning Objective 8.7   A. _____ Stage 1: During this stage, an infant learns that the environment is either comfortable and loving or hostile and unloving.

Learning Objective 8.7   B. _____ Stage 2: During this stage, the toddler is faced with toilet training and other responsibilities. If the child is successful, a sense of independence and freedom develops; if not, fears and negative feelings about self develop.

Learning Objective 8.7   C. _____ Stage 3: During this stage, four- to five-year-old children learn to do things on their own and to identify with their parents, or they develop a sense of wrongness and negative feelings about their own sexuality.

Learning Objective 8.7   D. _____ Stage 4: During this stage, seven- to eleven-year-old children develop feelings of confidence in their abilities, or they experience failure and develop feelings of incompetence.

Learning Objective 8.7   E. _____ Stage 5: During this stage, adolescents decide who they are and what they want out of life, or they become confused and sometimes rebellious.

Learning Objective 8.7   F. _____ Stage 6: During this stage, the young adult learns to identify with, relate on a warm social basis to, and love others, or the individual feels alone and separated from others.

Learning Objective 8.7   G. _____ Stage 7: During this stage, adults hope to convey information, love, and warmth to others, or they feel life is boring and unexciting.

Learning Objective 8.7   H. _____ Stage 8: During this stage, the aging adult begins to understand what life is about and decides it has been meaningful, happy, and cohesive, or a waste and unproductive.

2. Complete each of the following sentences with one of the options provided.

Learning Objective 8.1   A. Psychologists look at the process of growing older and the process of development as a process of _____ .
(deterioration : growth : crisis and dilemma)

Learning Objective 8.2   B. The conflicts and problems so common to the adolescent stage of development _____ .
(can be observed in all cultures : must be considered in a cultural context)

Learning Objective 8.3   C. _____ is the time during which the reproductive system matures.
(Puberty : Adolescence)

Learning Objective 8.3   D. Boys and girls experience significant growth spurts _____ _____ the onset of puberty.
(just before : soon after)

Learning Objective 8.4   E. Androgynous behaviors are behaviors that are shared _____ _____ .
(exclusively with peers : by both sexes)

Learning Objective 8.4   F. Based on a study that measured the effects of parental discipline on teenage sexual behavior, it appears that sexual permissiveness is lowest among teenagers who have _____ parents.
(permissive : moderately strict : very strict)

Learning Objective 8.4   G. Dreyer has suggested that one reason premarital sexual behavior has become increasingly common among American adolescents is that adolescents today perceive sex as _____ .
(a recreational activity : a normal part of intimate relationships)

Learning Objective 8.5   H. In a study reported in 1982, about _____ of adolescents who were sexually active reported using contraceptives on a regular basis.
(20 percent : 33 percent : 69 percent)

Learning Objective 8.6   I. In the last few years, the actual rate of suicides among fifteen- to twenty-four-year-olds has _____ .
(declined significantly : dropped a little : reached epidemic proportions)

Learning Objective 8.6

J. Erikson believed that an adolescent would remain confused and be unable to cope with the demands of adulthood if he or she _____ _____ identity crisis during adolescence.
(experienced an : failed to resolve his or her)

Learning Objective 8.7

K. Erik Erikson's stage theory of development differs from all other developmental stage theories because it focuses on _____ .
(a full life span : intermittent stages of development : achievement)

Learning Objective 8.7

L. Resolution of conflict during Erikson's stages of development should be viewed _____ .
(in terms of "passing" or "failing" : on a continuum of doing one's best)

MORAL DEVELOPMENT

Adolescence was going to be difficult for Hilary Wang and her parents. Hilary had matured late physically and early intellectually. Her behavior vacillated between childishness and adultlike behaviors, sometimes seeming chaotic. One event, however, would mark the end of those years of vacillation. Hilary's parents were getting a divorce.

Hilary was going to be called as a witness at the custody trial. Both parents were claiming custody and wanted child support and alimony. Hilary commented to a close friend that the whole ordeal seemed like the movie script from a bad movie.

During the trial, Hilary matured a great deal. She was forced to confront her feelings about her parents and their relationship. She was forced to take sides. In addition, after listening to five days of charges and countercharges, Hilary began to see that her parent's marriage was over and had been in trouble for years. She saw that both of her parents were responsible for their marriage failure. Although she developed some strong ideas about who was "right" and who was "wrong" in the custody case, she recognized that her views were subjective; they were based largely on her own life experiences and values. The trial forced Hilary to consider, on a mature level, the nature of human relationships and behavior. Her thoughtful considerations of a complicated issue were evidence of years of careful nurturing by her parents. Hilary knew that she had grown from the experience.

From childhood on, people develop new abilities to conceive of the world in realistic ways. At the same time, they develop a set of values. Children, adolescents, and adults make decisions about morality—about what is right or wrong, good or bad. By the time they are adolescents, people like Hilary Wang may be capable of making moral decisions at the most complex level.

Learning Objective 8.8

Morality is a system of learned personal beliefs about right and wrong that people use to evaluate situations or behavior. Attitudes about morality develop throughout life. From a very early age, children learn from their parents the behaviors, attitudes, and values that their parents consider appropriate and correct. As children mature, these attitudes change to accommodate an increasingly complex view of the world and of what constitutes reality.

In examining children's ability to analyze questions of morality, Piaget found results consistent with his ideas about intellectual development. Young children's ideas about morality are rigid and rule bound. In playing a game, a young child will not allow the rules to be modified for a younger child who does not understand them. Older children recognize that rules are established by

Morality ══════
A system of learned attitudes about social practices, institutions, and individual behavior, used to evaluate events as right or wrong.

social convention and sometimes need to be altered depending on the situation. They have developed a sense of conceptual relativity. Like conservation, this sense allows them to recognize that situations alter the way things are perceived (Piaget, 1932). For example, young children, when questioned about lying, respond that lying is always and under any circumstances bad—a person should never lie. Sometime between the ages of five and twelve, however, children recognize that rules are based on particular circumstances that may not always be pertinent; in some circumstances, lying may be permissible. Piaget believed that as they mature, children move from inflexibility toward relativity in their moral judgments as they develop new cognitive structures and assimilate and accommodate new ideas.

Piaget's theory of intellectual development was based on descriptions of how children respond to certain kinds of questions and at what age they switch and use other forms of answers. The research of Harvard psychologist Lawrence Kohlberg (1969) grew out of Piaget's work. Kohlberg believed that moral development also proceeds through a series of stages. The central concept in Kohlberg's theory is *justice*. Kohlberg presented different types of stories to people and asked what the story meant to them and how they felt about it. In one story, a poor man stole a drug for his wife who would have died without the drug. Here is the story:

Psychologist Lawrence Kohlberg established an influential stage theory of moral development.

> In Europe a woman was near death from a special kind of cancer. There was one drug that doctors thought might save her. It was a form of radium that a druggist in the same town recently discovered. The drug was expensive to make, but the druggist was charging ten times what the drug cost him to make. He paid $200 for the radium and charged $2,000 for a small dose of the drug. The sick woman's husband, Heinz, went to everyone he knew to borrow the money, but he could only get together $1,000, which is half of what it cost. He told the druggist that his wife was dying, and asked him to sell it cheaper or let him pay later. But the druggist said, "No, I discovered the drug, and I'm going to make money from it." So Heinz got desperate and broke into the man's store to steal the drug for his wife. (Kohlberg, 1969, p. 379)

Kohlberg questioned his subjects about the morality of Heinz. "Would a good husband steal for his wife?" "Was it actually wrong—and why?" Adults' interpretations of the man's plight differed from those of adolescents and five-year-olds. Children had difficulty seeing that the man's circumstances might affect the way the morality of his action could be judged (Kohlberg, 1976).

According to Kohlberg's theory, young children initially base decisions about right or wrong largely on the likelihood of avoiding punishment and obtaining rewards. This is level 1 morality. At level 2, school-age children adopt conventional ideas about morality. They conform in order to avoid disapproval by other people and censure by authorities. Level 2 judgments are governed by a process that considers the implications of a person's behavior. Why did he do it? What will be the consequences for him and for others? Level 3 morality is concerned with contracts and laws. In the first part of level 3 morality, people make judgments based on their perception of the needs of society, with an end to maintaining community welfare and order. The second part of level 3 is morality of conscience. At this stage, people make judgments based on their personal values rather than on those of society. Most adults reach at least the first part of level 3.

Kohlberg found that people's judgments of behavior vary with their level of moral development. Behavior can be justified or condemned at each level of

Stage One: Premoral

"I didn't steal the pumpkin because if I did and my dad found out he'd give me a spanking."

"I didn't steal the pumpkin because my big brother told me he'd like me better if I didn't."

Obedience to avoid punishment

Obedience to satisfy needs and gain reward

Stage Two: Conventional role conformity

"I don't steal because my parents wouldn't think much of me if I did."

"I don't steal because it's against the law and I'd feel guilty if I broke the law."

Obedience to avoid disapproval

Obedience to authority

Stage Three: Morality of conscience

"I want people to respect my property and, in turn, I respect theirs. Therefore, I don't steal."

"Normally I wouldn't steal because if I did I'd really look down upon myself. But, if a life depended upon my stealing something, I'd do it."

Obedience to laws that meet the needs of society

Obedience to one's own conscience

Kohlberg suggested a three-stage model of moral development.

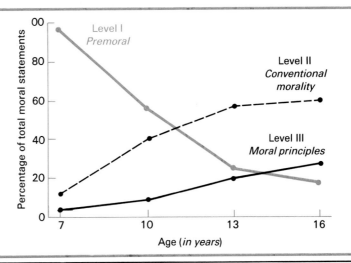

FIGURE 8.1 : In Kohlberg's theory of moral development, there is a distinct progression from one stage of morality to another as age increases. Thus, level I morality decreases with age and maturity, and levels II and III continue to increase. (Data from Kohlberg, 1963)

moral development, but the reasoning behind the justification or condemnation varies significantly. Level 1 children see morality in terms of punishment and reward. Presented with the story of Heinz, who stole a drug he could not afford in order to help his sick wife, level 1 children either condemn Heinz's behavior, explaining he should be punished because he stole, or justify it, explaining that Heinz was good because he tried to save his wife's life. Level 2 individuals judge behavior in terms of rules and the law: Heinz broke the law by stealing, and he should go to jail. Only at level 3 can people make moral judgments based on their own conscience and the needs of other people—for example, that a person's life is more important than the law regarding stealing. By this reasoning, Heinz is justified in his action. (See Figure 8.1)

The Heinz-and-the-druggist dilemma is a frequently used example of how Kohlberg went about developing his theory. Today, Kohlberg's theory still stands as the landmark explanation of moral reasoning. Like Piaget, Kohlberg studied moral reasoning, not moral behavior. Both theorists focused on how people make decisions rather than on the behavior that might result from those decisions (Rothman, 1980).

The theorists who conceptualize moral development do not always agree on the exact nature of moral reasoning. For example, Piaget thought of the stages of moral development as discrete, whereas Kohlberg viewed them as overlapping. From Kohlberg's view, a child might use earlier levels of moral reasoning from time to time. This finding has been substantiated in the work of De Vries and Walker (1986). They asked university students to fill out an attitudes questionnaire and to write an essay on capital punishment. The results showed that the subjects had achieved high levels of moral reasoning but often did not use that same level to substantiate their positions on capital punishment. The researchers found that 24 percent of their subjects used a distinctly different level of moral reasoning to support their views on capital punishment, usually a full stage lower. Interestingly, they found that they used higher levels of reasoning to oppose capital punishment than to support it. This finding makes a researcher wonder if the type of stories or dilemmas used by Kohlberg and other researchers is affecting the nature of the results! Time and another decade of research will tell.

Some people have moral reasoning ability, but they do not always use it; at other times, people develop moral reasoning and become extremely judgmental. For example, many adolescents suddenly develop a sense of morality. When put into a situation such as the one in which Betty Gerson was placed, they may become very critical, moral, and harsh. Their judgments of right and wrong have not been tempered with adult years of experience and understanding. Perhaps this is why Betty Gerson was so angry with her parents over their lack of concern for her grandfather. In Betty's situation, her views of "proper" behavior have yet to be tempered with adult maturity.

No one would argue that Kohlberg's theory has set the stage for psychologists' understanding of morality, but his work has not gone unchallenged. For example, Yussen (1977) has shown that adolescents consider other moral issues in their lives more important than the Heinz-and-the-druggist dilemma. This criticism does not make Kohlberg's work any less important, but it does raise the issue of the generalizability of Kohlberg's work to today's youth.

Kohlberg suggests that many other people besides parents can help promote the development of morality and conscience in children. (Windmiller, 1980). For one thing, he recommends that teachers as well as parents discuss moral issues—such as war, death, education, and even cheating on taxes—with youngsters. Such discussions are especially worthwhile if the adults involved are aware of the stages of moral development (Damon, 1980). Another worthwhile strategy is to provide children and adolescents with opportunities for role playing (Kohlberg, 1971). Role playing is the process of adopting perspectives different from one's own. According to Kohlberg, children who have opportunities to consider moral dilemmas from another person's point of view are more likely to develop a mature sense of morality (see Moran & Jennings, 1983).

Values for children have to be searched for, tried out, and scrutinized for both normal and special children. Unfortunately, special children are often

Charitable volunteer activities can help adolescents develop a sense of morality.

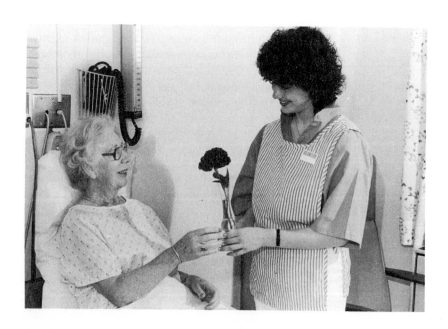

sheltered from moral dilemmas. Israely (1985) found that mentally retarded children can be taught moral reasoning. In the same way, children diagnosed as mildly educationally subnormal have been taught moral reasoning (Hanks, 1985). Learning disabled adolescents have been taught moral values although they are less able to view the moral dilemmas from a societal perspective (Derr, 1986).

A variety of methods for teaching morality are available to parents, teachers, and religious educators. In a classroom, teachers can often detour to deal with moral dilemmas presented. This can help teachers not only teach reasoning and analytical skills, but also shape children's moral thinking (Krogh & Lamme, 1985). Teaching morality to children and adolescents helps them learn society's values and how to think independently, and thus influences day-to-day behavior in important ways.

PROGRESS CHECK 8.2

1. Complete each of the following sentences with one of the options provided.

Learning Objective 8.8   A. Piaget found that young children have ideas about morality that are _____
_____ .
(rigid and rule bound : flexible : relative)

Learning Objective 8.8   B. Piaget suggested that conceptual relativity _____ .
(interferes with moral development : allows a person to be flexible)

Learning Objective 8.8   C. The central concept in Kohlberg's theory of morality is _____
_____ .
(conceptual relativity : justice : social acceptance)

Learning Objective 8.8   D. Kohlberg found that young children make moral decisions based on _____
_____ .
(their egocentric belief system : reward and punishment)

Learning Objective 8.8   E. The second part of Kohlberg's level 3 morality is called morality of _____
_____ .
(laws and contracts : conscience)

Learning Objective 8.8   F. Both Piaget and Kohlberg focused their studies of morality on _____
_____ .
(accepted cultural values : its behavioral content : how reasoning develops)

Learning Objective 8.8   G. A study that investigates moral reasoning abilities and attitudes toward capital punishment found that subjects used _____ reasoning abilities depending on their position.
(discrete : consistent : stage specific : higher or lower)

Learning Objective 8.8   H. According to Kohlberg, children will be more likely to develop a mature sense of morality if they are provided with _____ .
(opportunities for role playing : clear definitions of right and wrong)

ADULTHOOD

At the beginning of this chapter, we met Betty Gerson's grandfather, George Gerson. George had led a good life; he had been healthy, had prospered economically, and was a good family man and citizen. George Gerson had hoped to be facing carefree days of relaxation, catching up on reading, and enjoying family and friends. George was planning on maintaining a life-style that he had established for forty years. He was projecting his life in the future by looking back to the past. Because he had been healthy and led a productive life, he planned to continue to live this way.

Betty Gerson and her grandfather were both in the midst of major transitions. Betty was going through some of the storm and stress that can accompany adolescence. She was moving from one stage of life to another and having a bumpy time in the process. Simultaneously, as her grandfather was entering retirement, he was suffering memory losses. He felt afraid and isolated, and he worried that he might have a disorder, such as Alzheimer's disease (discussed later in this chapter). His family had not yet questioned the causes of those memory lapses. Betty urged facing the problem, but her parents were reluctant.

Learning **8.9**
Objective

Until the 1970s, developmental psychologists focused most of their attention on the development of children, especially on infant or early childhood development. Since then, partly as a result of the number of adults seeking therapy to help them cope with their problems and partly as a result of research, psychologists have begun to realize that adults must develop more complex strategies to deal with a greater complexity of problems. Adults must learn to develop and sustain a sense of well-being in relation to their jobs, children and other family members, and the demands of a constantly changing society. Researchers are now aware that development and maturation continue throughout life. In recent years, psychologists have begun to focus on studying the entire life span of development, not just the years until adulthood.

Levinson's Stage Theory

Some people, such as Erikson, think of life as a journey on which people pass through life's stages almost like acts in a play. You start with Act I, birth, and move on to Act III, death. If you think back to Erik Erikson's stage theory, you will remember that he proposed that people move through a series of stages during which they resolve crises or dilemmas. At the end of each stage, they either have a positive or a negative outcome, and they move on to the next stage. The early stages start at birth and move on toward adulthood and the end of the life span, thus implying that there is a direction a person follows toward that end.

Noted theorist Daniel Levinson of Yale University developed such a stage theory of adult development. Levinson agrees that people go through stages and that at certain points in peoples' lives there are commonalities. Like other psychologists, he would argue that studying those commonalities allows psychologists to help people better manage their lives. But Levinson's stage theory does not envision life as a journey toward some specific goal or objective.

In his theory, Levinson describes four basic eras in the adult life cycle. It is important to remember that each era has its own distinctive qualities that focus on the character of an individual's life. It is not a time when the person moves from one stage to a better or more advanced stage, but rather to a different stage. Each era presents different life problems, tasks, and situations, and each brings with it different life structures. A period ends when new tasks emerge. A new era is preceeded by a transition when people reassess, reappraise, and search for new ways of coping. A move from one era to the next often takes years because it requires a change in the quality of a person's life.

The knowledge of a baby on the way will lead to a period of transition from one life structure to another.

Levinson suggests that as people grow older, they adapt to the demands and tasks life has put before them (Levinson, 1978). No two people have the same life situation, and no two people adapt the same way. Each person develops what Levinson calls a *life structure* to deal with that period. For example, a person in his or her early thirties may become involved in religious work and learn how groups function to achieve common goals; those skills may be less necessary during a person's forties, when the individual focuses on a career. The life structures a person adopts are unique patterns of behaviors and ways of interacting with the world during a specific era. People develop stable life structures that get them successfully through a stage of life. They then enter a new stage of life with new life conditions, challenges, and dilemmas. The old life structures no longer work. This brings about a period of transition wherein a person adjusts. Sometimes that period is a difficult time involving a crisis, anxiety, and even depression. But people pass through that transition time to the next era of their life, and they develop new life structures. In some ways, you can think of a person's life as alternating between stable periods, transition periods, and stable periods, again.

Learning Objective 8.10

Levinson stresses that a valid theory of development is not a mold or blueprint that everyone must follow. People should not and cannot follow a single, "normal" course of development. Rather, a theory of development should lay out the stages or periods during which individuals work out the varied developmental tasks each person faces.

Levinson developed his theory by studying in detail forty men over a period of several years. His subjects were interviewed weekly for several months and they were then interviewed again after two years. Spouses were interviewed, and extensive biographical data were collected. As is shown in Figure 8.2 on the next page, Levinson's four eras are each made up of several stages. The ages of the four basic eras are:

Ages 11–17   Adolescence
Ages 18–45   Early adulthood
Ages 46–65   Middle adulthood
Ages 65–   Late adulthood

During *adolescence,* young people enter the adult world but are still immature and vulnerable. *Early adulthood* involves the first major life choices regarding family, occupation, and style of living. Throughout this period, adults move toward greater independence and toward senior positions in the community. They raise their children, strive to advance their careers, and begin to see their offspring leave home. Early adulthood is a period of striving, gaining, and accepting responsibility. By the end of this era, at about age forty-five, people are removed from childcare activities and are often assuming the responsibility of caring for their parents.

The much-discussed "mid-life crisis" occurs in early adulthood. During this era, many people realize that their life is now half over—that if they are to change their life, they must do so now. Some resign themselves to their original chosen course; others decide to change, grow, and renew their efforts toward excellence. This era is equivalent to Erikson's generativity-versus-stagnation stage.

Middle adulthood spans the years from forty-six to sixty-five. Adults who have gone through a mid-life crisis are now living with decisions they made during early adulthood. Career and families are usually well established.

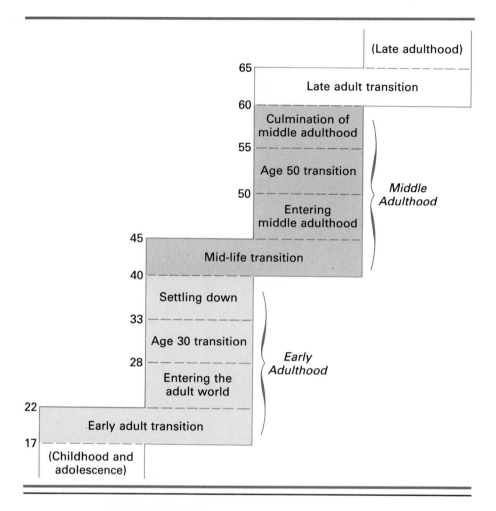

FIGURE 8.2 : Levinson's model of adult development. Note the alternating periods of stable life structures and periods of transition. (Source: *The Seasons of a Man's Life,* by Daniel J. Levinson. Copyright © 1978 by Daniel J. Levinson. Reprinted by permission of Alfred A. Knopf, Inc.)

People are experiencing either a sense of satisfaction and self-worth or a feeling that much of their life has been wasted. In the middle of this period, some people go through a crisis similar to that of early adulthood. Sometimes, this crisis is a continuation of the earlier one; at other times, it is a new one. People approaching their sixties begin to prepare themselves for late adulthood, making what few major decisions remain before retirement. Depending on how well people come to terms with who they are, the next decade may be one of greater fulfillment or even greater despair.

The years after age fifty are years of mellowing. Particularly in their early sixties, people learn to assess their lives, not in terms of money or day-to-day successes, but according to whether their lives have been meaningful, happy, and cohesive. At this point, people stop blaming others for their problems. They are less concerned about disputes with other people. They try to get everything they can from life because they know that two-thirds of life has passed and they wish to make the most of the years remaining. Having achieved perspective, people put aside ambitions for glory, fame, and fortune and either learn to live with who they are or despair and become bitter.

Levinson's fourth and final era, *late adulthood,* typically covers the years from age sixty-five on. During retirement, many people relax and enjoy the fruits of their lives. Children, grandchildren, and even great-grandchildren can become the focus of an older person's life.

Levinson's stage theory was developed by studying men. He also maintains that the theory applies to women. As Levinson says:

> we change in different ways, according to different timetables. Yet, I believe that everyone lives through the same developmental periods in adulthood . . . though people go through them in their own ways. . . . Our theory of life structure does not specify a single, "normal" course that everyone must follow. Its function, instead, is to indicate the developmental tasks that everyone must work on in successive periods, and the infinitely varied forms that such work can take in different individuals living under different conditions. (1980, p. 289)

Levinson's theory of adult development has achieved wide acclaim; it also has not gone unchallenged. Psychologists point out that it is based on information gathered from a few middle-class men. Social class differences exist, and, despite Levinson's claims, women do not necessarily follow the same life stages or changes as men. The next decade will probably see more research that focuses on women and various social classes.

Physical Development

Learning Objective 8.11

Fifteen-year-olds often notice that their "aging" parents have less speed, agility, and energy and more aches and pains than themselves. But human beings are sufficiently complicated and are affected by a sufficient number of variables that growing older does not have to involve a loss of mental and physical functions. People can grow wiser as a result of their experiences. For many individuals, turning thirty may mean a new commitment to physical health through exercise.

Physical changes in adulthood are slower, less dramatic, and sometimes less visible than those of childhood and adolescence. The following discussion is based on an excellent article by Barbara Newman (1982) that traces some of the changes in adulthood: sexual, fitness, and sensory changes.

Sexual changes in adult women are more easily identified than those in men. For example, changes in the hormone cycle at mid-life ultimately lead to cessation of ovulation and menstruation at about age fifty. This process is called menopause. At about the same age, men's testosterone levels decrease, their ejaculations are weaker and briefer, and their desire for sexual intercourse decreases from adolescent levels.

Fitness involves both a psychological and a physical sense of well-being. Physically, human beings are at their peak of agility, speed, and strength between ages eighteen and thirty. From thirty to forty, there is some loss of agility and speed. Much greater losses occur between forty and sixty. Lung capacity and physical strength in a fifty-year-old man are significantly reduced. Sixty-year olds see themselves as less agile and often refrain from physical activities that demand endurance. Although it does not have to be the case, generally speaking, a deterioration in body strength, muscle tone, and overall fitness occurs from age thirty. Disease becomes more probable; respiratory, circulatory, and blood pressure problems are more apparent. Such changes are often the price of lifelong inattention to staying fit.

Adults must also contend with inevitable sensory losses. Reaction time slows, visual acuity lessens, and the risks of glaucoma and retinal detachment

Psychology and You: The Mid-Life Crisis

In about twenty years or so, you probably will have a crisis in your life—so goes the popular idea that people pass through predictable life crises. A life crisis is seen as a time during which you will reevaluate your choices, change your life, reorient, become depressed in the process, and perhaps throw over your spouse for another. The idea that people between thirty-five and forty-five years old will have a life crisis is widely believed and considered almost inevitable. It sounds depressing.

But are crises unavoidable? Does everyone go through a mid-life crisis? At times in people's lives, they go through transitions. At certain junctures, new decisions need to be made and people need to reassess who they are, where they are going, and how they want to get there. But does this have to be a time of crisis? Chapter 15 talks about crises in people's lives, and indicates that a crisis is a point at which things will never be the same. Crises are sharp points of demarcation.

We suggest that a distinction should be drawn between the idea of a *transition* and a *crisis*. A transition suggests that a person has reached a time in life when old ways of coping no longer work, old tasks have been accomplished, and new methods of living are forthcoming. A person in a transition must face new dilemmas, challenges, and tasks, which often require reassessment, reappraisal, and developing new skills and abilities. Transitions can sometimes be stressful and difficult, but they do not have to be. A crisis, by contrast, occurs when old ways of coping become overwhelmed and a person is in a state of helplessness, not knowing what to do, and needs new, radically different coping strategies. Crises are often perceived as painful turning points and catastrophes in a person's life.

We think that most people experience a mid-life transition, sometimes two, or three or even more transitions.

Often, a transition occurs at the beginning of adulthood—people have to give up adolescent ways. Sometimes at around age thirty, another transition occurs when career and relationships begun in a person's twenties are reevaluated and sometimes rejected. In the transitions of early and middle adulthood, people reorient career and family choices—the famous mid-life crisis at about age forty. Often, people experience a transition when children leave the home—sometimes called the empty nest syndrome. Transitions occur at retirement.

The content of these transitions is often similar: people face decisions about careers, family, and the future. As people grow older, they experience transitions that focus on their changing health, family structure, and their own mortality. But these transitions do not have to be experienced as crises.

People who experience mid-life transitions show no evidence of increased maladjustment, or increased suicides or alcoholism. For some groups of people, however, mid-life transitions can be a difficult time. We suggest that the mid-life transition has to be examined within each individual, rather than across all individuals. Like the "storm and stress" of adolescence, some adults face crises in their lives, others merely go through transitions that do not have to be perceived as difficult or painful. Adults, like adolescents, face new experiences, new task demands, and new dilemmas as they grow older. Their unique personalities and ways of coping with the world shape whether they will have a crisis or whether they will move from stage to stage in a relatively smooth manner. We suggest that the term *mid-life crisis* may be a misnomer, and, like Levinson, suggest it should more properly be called a *mid-life transition*—a transition that may be difficult for some individuals.

---

increase (M. E. Smith, 1976). Hearing also decreases. By age sixty, most people can no longer hear high-frequency sounds, and some people are unable to hear ordinary speech. For example, during his presidency, Ronald Reagan suffered from a serious hearing loss despite otherwise generally good health.

Personality Development

Learning Objective 8.12

People recognize that as they go through life's stages, they maintain a certain sense of individuality. They work at maintaining their distinctive personalities and life-styles. George Gerson was certainly concerned with maintaining his independence, which had been established even as a youth. So, while people go through changes, development, and maturation, they also have certain stable characteristics that are unlikely to change. During life's psychological stages, people can grow and move on to new and better things, but it is usually unlikely that they will become someone totally new.

Everyday experience clearly shows that individuals differ dramatically. No one theory of adult development can predict the course of a person's life: too many variables—friends, family, and situation—are involved; even luck, in the form of unfortunate accidents, new job opportunities, or "striking it rich," plays a role. People's self-concept, the relationships they maintain with others, and the societal group to which they belong all affect how individuals cope with specific issues (Levinson, 1978).

The time-honored idea in personality theory is that personality, regardless of the shifts one sees on a day-to-day basis, remains stable. Recent research has shown, however, that some aspects of personality may be particularly sensitive to each individual's experience. According to Haan, Millsap, and Hartka (1986), childhood and adolescence show stability in personality development, but the adult years are times of greater personality change. They collected data from a longitudinal sample of subjects asked to describe themselves on such variables as self-confidence, assertiveness, dependability, and warmth. The researchers found important shifts on many variables once the subjects were adults. They argue that the adult years are the years of greatest personal challenges, opportunities for experiences, and facing new dilemmas. Accordingly, they are also the years in which people can be innovative, flexible, and adaptive. Most psychologists argue that personality is relatively enduring and stable over a person's lifetime. The new data from Haan, Millsap, and Hartka suggest, however, that some elements of personality may be less stable than researchers originally thought. We discuss more about personality development in Chapter 12, devoted solely to personality.

PROGRESS CHECK 8.3

Learning Objective 8.9

A. Developmental psychologists began to put more emphasis into studies concerning adult development during the early _____ .
(part of this century : 1950s : 1970s)

Learning Objective 8.9

B. According to Daniel Levinson, transitions from one era of life to another _____ .
(occur chronologically according to age : can take years)

Learning Objective 8.9

C. Levinson's concept of life structure refers to one's _____ .
(family, friends, and work : unique patterns of interacting with life events)

Learning Objective 8.10

D. According to Levinson, the _____ years are spent striving, gaining, and accepting responsibility.
(adolescent : early adulthood : middle adulthood)

Learning Objective 8.10

E. The mid-life crisis that people experience when they realize that their life is half over occurs during the _____ adulthood years.
(early : middle : late)

Learning Objective 8.10

F. People achieve perspective on the meaning of their lives and put aside ambitions for glory, fame, and fortune during the _____ adulthood years.
(early : middle : late)

Learning Objective 8.11

G. _____ experience changes in the hormone cycle at mid-life.
(Women : Men : Both men and women)

Learning Objective 8.11

H. Deterioration in body strength, muscle tone, and overall fitness generally begins to occur around age _____ .
(eighteen : thirty : forty-five)

Learning Objective 8.11

I.   By age sixty, most people can no longer hear _____ sounds.
     (low-frequency : high-frequency)

Learning Objective 8.12

J.   Research conducted by Haan, Millsap, and Hartka suggests that adult personality traits _____ .
     (remain fairly stable : change as people face new challenges)

AGING

Betty Gerson, who opened this chapter, had a lot to deal with as she faced her own adolescent transition to adulthood. Worrying about her grandfather made this time more stressful. Her grandfather was also facing a transition. He was retiring from his career and was potentially facing a changing health situation.

Betty's parents were not dealing with George Gerson's memory losses because they were afraid that these losses were a symptom of something extremely serious. They knew that older people sometimes have memory losses and other medical problems. But Betty's parents were not particularly knowledgeable about growing older. Because they had not known their own grandparents and were rarely around elderly people, they had only preconceived ideas and stereotypes about growing older.

Most older adults face aging with a mature vantage point, good health, many more years to live, and a prospect of a retirement that will be a continuation of a life-style established over many years. Older adults tend to be realistic; they know they may have some health problems and no longer have the stamina of their earlier years. However, most face the retirement years with enthusiasm and a realistic appraisal of their lives.

Betty's parents were not enthusiastic about the next decade in George's life. They had recently heard about a disease they thought George Gerson might have, and it scared them. Their fear that George had Alzheimer's disease paralyzed them; they did not want to find out and thus put off facing George's problem. Their view of growing older was negative—they assumed the worst for George. But they should not have—there are many medical, as well as psychological, reasons that George could have had memory problems. One likely possibility is that George's various medications—high blood pressure, arthritis pills, heart medication, and special vitamins—might have been interacting. Sometimes people's medications do not mix well and produce adverse effects—one common side effect is memory loss. George Gerson's problems may merely be due to wrong doses or changing needs in his medications. George may have had something more serious to deal with, but putting off finding out was a counterproductive response.

You can see that the challenges for older adults are many. Sometimes failing health complicates life; sometimes the negative stereotypes people have about older Americans complicate it further. Being over sixty-five, like being over twenty-one, brings with it new challenges, dilemmas, and tasks. From Levinson's view, it is a new era of life requiring different coping mechanisms.

Who Are the Elderly?

Learning Objective 8.13

George Gerson is one of about 25 million Americans over the age of 65. In the late 1980s, approximately 12 percent of the population is 65 or over. This percentage is expected to increase to 20 percent by the year 2030 (Eisdorfer,

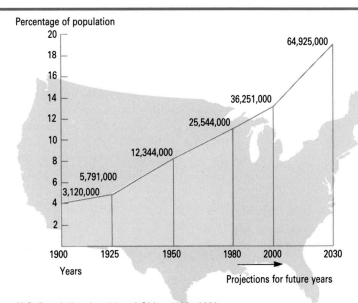

FIGURE 8.3 : This graph shows actual past increases and projected future increases in the percentage of the United States population over age sixty-five. This increase in the average age of United States citizens is sometimes called the graying of America. (Data from Bureau of the Census, Social Security Administration, 1983)

U.S. Population Age 65 and Older, 1900–2030
1985–2030 figures are projections

1983), bringing the total number of people over the age of 65 to over 60 million individuals (see Figure 8.3). The median age is expected to increase from 31 to 41 years. This means that half of our population will be over the age of 41. Medical science is continuing to prolong life and has dramatically increased a person's chances of living to an old age. Today, men's and women's life expectancies are different; women live about four years longer than men on the average, but the average life expectancy at birth in the United States of people is about 74.7 years (see Figure 8.4).

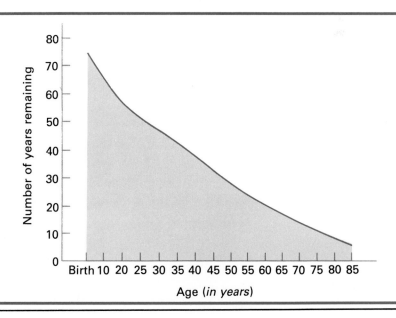

FIGURE 8.4 : Average years of life remaining at various ages. (Source: National Center for Health Statistics, 1983)

For many individuals, the years after age sixty are the best years of their lives. People do not necessarily lose important functions and abilities as they age (see J. L. Horn, 1982). As in childhood and adolescence, individuals show marked variability as they age. Most older people cope well with their advancing age. They maintain close friendships and stay in touch with family. Some, however, experience a financial crisis and become frightened or destitute. Others experience a sense of loneliness and isolation because many of their friends and family have died. Others feel isolated because family has moved far away or become uninterested in them. Today, in the United States, there are as many people over the age of sixty as there are under the age of seven—yet, funding for programs involving the health and psychological well-being of older people is relatively limited.

Aging: Myths, Stereotypes, and Realities

Learning Objective   8.14

Here is the myth: Older people are senile, lacking in common sense, unable to take care of themselves, financially insecure, inflexible, and unhealthy. Even though the people who hold such views are in the minority, these ideas have fostered a widely believed set of negative stereotypes. A *stereotype* is an attitude, it is a combination of traits or attributes about a group of people. Often, stereotypes are rigid, biased, and derogatory. The stereotypes about older individuals usually portray them in negative, pejorative ways.

Here are some of the realities: Stereotypes about the elderly have unhealthy influences on children, adults, and older people themselves. Grandparents often have a special relationship with their grandchildren. Children see older people as grey-haired grandparents, often calm buffers between children and parents, wise advice givers, and a link to the past. Children have trouble understanding why older people are viewed so negatively.

Grandparents and grandchildren often have special relationships that provide mutual warmth and happiness.

Adults who view their parents negatively denigrate their own worth and their own view of their future. An older person's relationship with grown children may be volatile and include unresolved conflicts from childhood. This relationship becomes especially difficult when the parent becomes somewhat dependent on a formerly dependent child. There is sometimes a difficult role reversal.

Negative stereotypes about older individuals hurt older people most of all. Many older Americans may begin to behave as they are expected to behave. Because they are expected to be insecure and inflexible, they adopt those characteristics.

Stereotypes have given way to ageism. *Ageism* is deep prejudice against the elderly and the discrimination that follows from it. Ageism is prevalent in the job market, where older people are not given equal opportunity. Ageism is evident in housing. Ageism also shows itself in the health professions, where some physicians tend to focus their energies on everyone but the aged. People in the clergy, health professions, law, and accounting often prefer to work with younger clients (Geiger, 1978).

Ageism is exceptionally prevalent on television, in newspapers, cartoons, and magazines; it is apparent in every day language. By understanding ageism and the truths about growing older, we have a better likelihood of understanding the full range of human behavior and eliminating the many negative myths about older people.

Theories of Aging

Learning Objective 8.15

Only in the last two decades have psychologists and physicians examined the behavioral and physiological changes that accompany aging. Three basic types of theories have developed, each emphasizing a different likely cause (Kimmel, 1980). Aging probably results from a combination of these factors: heredity, external factors, and physiology.

Heredity. Because genes determine so much of a person's physical makeup, it is possible that heredity determines to some extent how long a person will live. This idea suggests the intuitive notion that if characteristics of physical makeup and behavior may be inherited, then life's duration may also be inherited. For some researchers, this notion makes sense on logical grounds; however, data to support the ideas are controversial because environment plays such an important role in aging (see, for example, Palmore, 1982).

External Factors. Kimmel (1980) suggests that external factors also affect how long a person will live. For example, people who reside on a farm live longer than those living in a city; overweight people live fewer years than people of normal weight; people who smoke cigarettes, who are continually under great tension, or who expose themselves to disease or radiation die sooner than those who do not. The data on external factors are often obtained from correlational studies; therefore, cause-and-effect statements are not possible. But it is reasonable to assume that such external factors might affect a person's life span.

Physiology. A person's physiological processes depend on both hereditary and environmental factors. Changes in an individual's biological life-maintaining processes may be especially important. Physiological factors can determine how aging proceeds and the person's actual life span. Several theories use physiological explanations to account for aging and use both hereditary and environmental concepts.

The *wear-and-tear* theory of aging claims that the human organism simply wears out from overuse, much like the parts of a machine (Rowland, 1977). *Homeostatic* theory suggests that the body's ability to adjust to varying situations decreases with age. Homeostasis is the normal physiological state of the body; deviations from homeostasis may cause aging (although aging may be the cause of deviations from homeostasis). For example, as the ability to maintain constant body temperature decreases, cellular and tissue damage occur, and aging results. Similarly, when the body can no longer control the use of sugar through the output of insulin, signs of aging appear (see Eisdorfer & Wilkie, 1977).

According to another view, aging occurs because of an *accumulation of metabolic waste*. As people grow older, their bodies are less able to deal with waste products. As a result, their cells are slowly poisoned or hampered in their functioning. This view has not received much support (Shock, 1977); the inability to deal with waste products is probably a symptom of aging rather than a cause. *Autoimmunity* theory suggests that aging people generate antibodies that attack their own cells and ultimately destroy life-cycle functions. This theory, too, has received little support. But it is true that older people cannot fight off disease as well as they could when younger (Shock, 1977). Finally, the *cellular aging* theory states that as cells grow older, they lose the ability to replicate themselves. In fact, some data indicate that cells have a finite life and can replicate themselves only a certain number of times (for example, Rockstein & Sussman, 1979).

Many of these physiologically oriented theories of aging are difficult to prove, and all may contain some elements of heredity and environment. Some people may be predisposed to cellular aging or to a failing autoimmune system; other people may be more affected by their environment More research is necessary for a thorough understanding of the aging process. Reliable studies will do much to dispel the many misconceptions that persist, such as that the aged have no feelings, are unable to cope at all, and are generally deficient. So far, investigators have found that several definite physiological and intellectual changes do take place as people grow old.

Physiological Changes: The Biobehavioral Approach

Learning Objective 8.16

Many elderly people must contend with significant physiological changes. These changes include alterations in calcium metabolism, which make the bones more brittle; a greater likelihood of diseases of the joints, such as arthritis, and of gum diseases, which cause the teeth to fall out; and decreased elasticity in the skin, creating folds and wrinkles. Some of these biological changes interact with behavioral ones. For example, people who live alone and lack companionship may become inattentive to eating and as a result suffer vitamin deficiencies. These are often called biobehavioral changes.

Brain Disorders.   Many people assume that senility accompanies aging. *Senility* is an outdated and inappropriate term. When people list the symptoms of a person who might be classified as senile, they are usually listing the symp-

toms descriptive of cognitive change. These disorders usually develop gradually, often starting off with anxiety, confusion, depression, and memory loss.
Brain disorders can occur in old and in young individuals, although typically
the onset is not until age seventy-five. Older people suffer from disorders of
intellectual functions primarily due to degeneration of some parts of the brain.

There are two main types of brain disorders, sometimes called *dementias.*
Dementias involve losses of cognitive functioning. *Reversible dementias* usually
affect younger people and are often due to malnutrition, alcoholism, or toxins
(poisons). *Irreversible dementias* come in two major types—multiple infarcts
and Alzheimer's disease. Multiple infarct dementia is usually the result of
small strokes (ruptures of small blood vessels in the brain). Multiple infarct
dementia is less common than Alzheimer's disease, which is a slow degeneration of the brain itself. We discuss Alzheimer's disease later in this chapter.

Brain disorders like Alzheimer's are not a direct consequence of aging.
Research shows that only 4.4 percent of people over sixty-five have some kind
of serious intellectual impairment. Disorders that often appear in older people
can be apparent at any developmental stage. When these physical disorders
appear at around the same time in an older person, diagnosis becomes difficult, and the problems are dismissed as aspects of senility. Often this misdiag-
nosis of real diseases leads to serious and irreversible damage.

Sensory Abilities.   Older people are much more likely than young ones
to show decreased sensory abilities. Older people's vision, hearing, taste, and
smell require a higher level of stimulation to respond the way younger people's
senses do. For example, older people are usually unable to make fine visual
discriminations without the aid of glasses, and their eyes adapt much less
effectively to the dark (see Figure 8.5). Hearing losses are especially marked in
the high-frequency ranges.

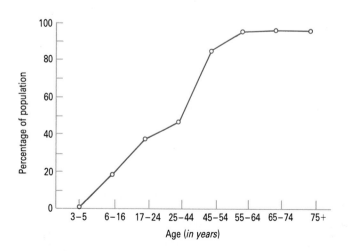

FIGURE 8.5 : Percentage of
persons requiring glasses or
contact lenses for visual
defects. (Source: National
Center for Health Statistics,
1983)

Changes in the Nervous System. The importance of the central nervous system in human behavior becomes clearer than ever when aging affects its functioning. CAT (computerized axial tomography) scans, which permit detailed examination of brain tissue, and other sophisticated new techniques are providing more information about the kind of changes that occur in the brain as people age and about the significance of those changes for other functioning (LaRue & Jarvik, 1982). Such technology has revealed that with aging, the neurons themselves degenerate more rapidly. However, degeneration in the brain cells does not necessarily lead to degeneration in behavior, intelligence, or cognitive abilities. Other changes include alterations in brainwave activity, as measured by an EEG, and in autonomic nervous system activity. Some researchers have suggested that older individuals are "under-aroused." However, studies of autonomic nervous system responsiveness in old and young adults show little support for this once-popular idea (for example, Powell, Milligan, & Furchtgott, 1980).

The greatest changes in the central nervous systems of older individuals are shown in tests of reaction time. The slowing and changing of responses are particularly apparent in sensory-motor functions—the ability of the body to respond to the senses. Although the sensory systems themselves may not be impaired, the ability to respond to changes sensed in the environment is poorer than when people were younger. For example, in an emergency, an elderly driver may be unable to stop a car as quickly as a younger driver under similar

TABLE 8.2 : Summary of Age Changes in the Physical Body and in Health

Age 20–40	Age 40–65	Age 65 and Older
The head grows and changes shape	Height is lost slowly Skin and other tissues begin to lose elasticity	Height continues to be lost Continuation of loss of elasticity in tissues
Peak of sensory acuity in all senses	Senses begin to be less acute starting at about age 50, but these changes are still small enough to make little difference in daily life	More rapid loss of sensory acuity, including vision, hearing, taste, smell. Loss of taste, smell, and hearing are particularly noticeable, and may have significant effects on daily living
Peak of physical strength, stamina, aerobic fitness	Beginning decline in strength, in heart capacity, and equivalent, but wide individual differences and little effect on daily life Loss of brain cells and slowing of nerve conductance speed	Continued loss of strength, stamina, and aerobic fitness, although this is less in physically active adults. Loss begins to have effect on daily life Continued and more rapid loss of brain cells and speed
Deaths mostly from accidents or suicide	Deaths most commonly from heart disease or cancer	Cancer and heart disease continue to be the leading causes of death, with stroke, diabetes, and other diseases also occurring
Highest risk period for acute illness; lowest risk for chronic illness	Medium-level risk for both chronic and acute illness	Lowest risk for acute, and highest risk for chronic illness
Possibly highest risk for depression	No clear data on mental illness rates	
Peak of sexual activity	Sexual activity declines but is maintained by most	Sexual activity declines further, but is maintained by a majority

Source: Bee, H. L. (1987). *The journey of adulthood.* New York: Macmillan Publishing Company.

circumstances. Many explanations for decreased response time have been suggested, but none has been conclusively proved. Whatever their cause, these changes bring about a characteristic slowing of activity with advancing age.

Overall Health. It is common knowledge that people's overall health deteriorates as they age, but the impact of this deterioration on aging individuals' psychological functioning has received very little attention from psychologists (LaRue & Jarvik, 1982). Yet facts such as the following are bound to affect older people's outlook. For men, for example, the likelihood of dying doubles in each decade after mid-life. Generally, blood pressure rises, cardiac output decreases, and the likelihood of stroke increases. Furthermore, cardiovascular disease has been shown to influence intellectual functioning (Hertzog, Schaie, & Gribbin, 1978) (see Table 8.2). A related finding, as yet unexplained, is that some individuals show a rapid decline in intellectual functioning in the year before death. This is known as the *terminal drop*. Some researchers attribute this change to cardiac and vascular disease. They claim that the decreased blood flow (and resulting decrease in oxygen) to the brain results in declining mental ability and, ultimately, in failing health. These researchers contend that health, more than any other variable, accounts for changes in cognitive functioning. Even minor changes in health can have severe consequences (for example, Botwinick, 1973). Furthermore, other types of tests that measure neurological functioning also show evidence of predicting survival. When a person does show evidence of the terminal drop, this decrease is not necessarily within a one-year period. One problem with this type of research is that the researcher never knows when someone is going to die and thus must be able to look backward in time to examine a deceased person's intellectual behavior. Evidence exists for the terminal drop, but according to noted aging authority Jack Botwinick (1984), there has not yet been a satisfactory explanation for this predictability of shortened survival based on poor performance on intelligence or neuropsychological tests.

Intellectual Changes

Learning Objective 8.17

Perhaps the most distressing change that occurs with aging is the decline in intellectual ability. For example, Arenberg (1978) has shown that memory decreases with age. Even researchers who maintain that general intellectual functioning remains stable over a person's life span now acknowledge that certain aspects deteriorate with age (Craik, 1977; Craik & Byrd, 1981). But debate continues about what changes occur and how extensive they are. A major problem is defining intellectual functioning. Aged persons are likely to do poorly on a standardized intelligence test, not because their intelligence is lower but because such tests tend to require the manipulation of objects during a timed interval. Thus, older people's slowed reaction time or decreased manual dexterity (often due to arthritis) may affect their measured IQ even though their intellectual abilities might be as good as ever. Some research indicates that older people learn more slowly and have more difficulty integrating new ideas than they did in their youth (see Table 8.3 on the next page).

Researchers have several ways of measuring intelligence. There is more than one kind of IQ test, and IQ tests measure several types of abilities—for example, verbal abilities and spatial abilities. Furthermore, researchers have several methodologies for measuring intelligence across ages, comparing

TABLE 8.3 : Summary of Age Changes in Intellectual Skills

Age 20–40	Age 40–65	Age 65 and Older
Peak intellectual ability between about 20 and 35.	Maintenance of skill on measures of verbal, unspeeded intelligence; some decline of skill on measures of performance or speeded IQ; decline is usually not functionally significant till age 60 or older	Some loss of verbal IQ; most noticeable in adults with poorer health, lower levels of activity, and less education
Optimal performance on memory tasks	Little change in performance on memory tasks, except, perhaps some slowing later in this period	Slowing of retrieval processes and other memory processes; less skillful use of coding strategies for new memories
Peak performance on laboratory tests of problem solving	Peak performance on real-life problem-solving tasks	Decline in problem-solving performance on both laboratory and real-life tests

Source: Bee, H. L. (1987). *The journey of adulthood.* New York: Macmillan Publishing Company.

young people to older people. If you compare a group of young people to older people, you will see lower IQ test scores for the older adults. By contrast, if you take one group of individuals and you trace them for five, ten, or forty years, you will see less of a change, or no change, in IQ test scores.

A key point is: For the majority of healthy people, intelligence remains essentially stable across the life span. Some older people even increase their intelligence test scores as they grow older. Some people, however, show lower IQ test scores when they are older than age sixty-five, perhaps due to normal biological deterioration. They may show evidence of terminal drop, slowed reaction time, or early stages of brain disorders. These people represent a minority of older adults. For healthy individuals, changes in intelligence should not be evident.

Whatever their causes, deficits in intellectual functioning often do occur with aging, and they usually affect behavior and functioning (for a review, see Denny, 1982). However, they are seldom devastating. The aging adult does lose some ability to learn quickly and to integrate new ideas that characterize a younger person. However, a healthy, motivated person over the age of sixty-five can learn, think, and operate in the complex world of the 1980s in adaptive, flexible, and competent ways.

Getting Older and Better: The Worker

Learning Objective 8.18 Unlike George Gerson, who opened this chapter, you probably have a long way to go before you face old age. You are looking forward to a productive life that may span several decades in the work force. What happens, however, when you or your working spouse grow older? Are you going to be forced into retirement? Will you be able to work as long as you want to? Will you be able to work when you are in your sixties or seventies? Will you face memory losses as George Gerson did? According to Ross Stagner (1985), a retired psychology professor at Wayne State University, the workplace has a great concern about the supposed inefficiency of older adults. Much of the following discussion is based on Stagner's analysis.

Stereotypes. Many employers believe that early retirement of older employees is necessary and beneficial to their companies. They assume that older individuals are less competent, and that early retirement allows promotion of younger (and presumably more competent) workers.

Employers not only seek to retire older workers but they also refrain from hiring individuals over the age of fifty. Employers are reluctant to provide retraining to new technology for older workers. They are also involved in a variety of other discriminatory practices.

Job Performance. Stagner asserts that the overall work output and quality of older workers is as good as younger workers. However, many research reports allege that older workers do not do as well, are less flexible, and are slower to learn new technologies. According to Stagner, however, these reports tend to be biased because many of the individuals who evaluated the older workers had stereotyped ideas about older workers. They evaluated the older workers negatively, regardless of their actual work performance. Researchers still face the question, "Does job performance of older workers suffer?" Surprisingly, they do not have a conclusive answer.

Some individual older workers show declining performance. Some jobs require excellent hearing, excellent vision, or especially good motor abilities. As discussed, older individuals have sensory losses (for example, people over age fifty-five lose hearing ability). In noisy environments in which verbal instructions are given, this loss can have important implications. On the other hand, even though older adults may be losing visual motor coordination in complex tasks, drill operators over age sixty are shown to be more accurate than their younger counterparts. Their years of training and perceptual skills may make up for lost visual-motor coordination.

Job Satisfaction. Older adults tend to be more satisfied with their jobs than are younger workers. Older workers pay more attention to their job's intrinsic job-related characteristics than to its extrinsic values, like pay or work

Older adults can be proficient at and satisfied with their jobs long after they reach the age of retirement.

Psychologists at Work: Alzheimer's Disease

When middle-aged adults socialize, a topic of conversation is often that someone's mother or father has been diagnosed as having Alzheimer's disease.

Alzheimer's disease is a disorder of the brain that may ultimately be called the most widespread neurological disorder of all time (Bloom, Lazerson, & Hofstadter, 1985). It represents a threat of enormous proportion to the health and psychological care communities of the United States (Crook & Miller, 1985). Each year, due to our improving medical care, our population grows older. Accompanying this graying of America is an increase in the number of cases of Alzheimer's.

The causes of Alzheimer's disease are unclear. Tangled neurons is the typical explanation given to relatives. Brain scans usually confirm the finding; the patient's neurons seem twisted, gnarled, and tangled and are coated with placque. Neurotransmitter substances are usually lowered in level. The disease tends to run in families; this fact suggests a genetic basis, or at least a predisposition, that may be inherited. Some research posits a depletion of enzymes; other research suggests an accumulation of such toxins as aluminum (Neustatler, 1982), other research has focused on neurotransmitters (Gibson, Logue, & Growdon, 1985). Vascular problems, autoimmune factors, and viruses have been implicated in Alzheimer's. Unfortunately, all of the research efforts are only a beginning and by themselves are all inconclusive. Researchers do not know the causes of Alzheimer's disease.

Alzheimer's disease diminishes the quality of life of those whom it strikes because of its profound effects. Patients lose their memory. They forget simple things like the time and date and increasingly forget how to do the daily things in life: They forget where they were going, where they have been, what they were going to do next. Hemshorn (1985) reports how her husband, an Alzheimer's patient, forgot how to operate the electric blanket. Eventually, the Alzheimer's patient loses control even of simple bodily functions. Personality changes also become abrupt; the patient often becomes abusive and hostile to family members. The disease is irreversible and ultimately ends in death.

Currently, there are about 1.5 million Alzheimer's patients in the United States. Alzheimer's disease may ultimately affect 10 to 15 percent of the population over the age of eighty. According to the United States Department of Health and Human Services (1984), the projected number of persons over age sixty-five may be as high as 55 million people by the year 2030. Ten to fifteen percent of that population is as many as eight million patients.

The effects on an Alzheimer's patient's family are extensive. Caring for the patient imposes extensive physical, emotional, and financial hardships (Aronson, Levin, & Lipkowitz, 1984).

Hospitalization or providing day care for a deteriorating Alzheimer's patient is often necessary. Families today usually do not have the ability to care for their relatives. Patients are often incontinent, and an aging wife or husband often does not have the strength to help. The total cost of nursing home care for Alzheimer's patients is estimated at $13 billion per year. According to Heckler (1985), the cost may be as high as $41 billion per year in the early 1990s.

The human cost is enormous. Patients are not necessarily stripped of their usual vigor or strength, but they slowly become confused and helpless. The loved one of the patient "walks a tightrope between meeting the patient's needs and preserving their own well-being . . ." (Heckler, 1985, p. 1241).

A new issue for physicians is the over- or underdiagnosis of the disease. Are physicians attributing normal symptoms of aging to Alzheimer's when they should not? According to Filinson (1984), because the symptoms of the disease vary so widely and because the early stages of the disease are often undetectable, some physicians may be overdiagnosing the disease and others may be underdiagnosing. Unfortunately, some physicians dismiss symptoms of Alzheimer's as "old age" setting in.

Alzheimer's is likely to continue to be a health and psychological concern for the patients and for families of patients with the disease. With the graying of America and with the baby-boom generation now approaching middle age, it is likely that more research and less speculation about Alzheimer's will appear. According to Khachaturian of the National Institute of Aging (1985), researchers have just begun the battle, but they have the tools with which to explore the causes and potential treatments for Alzheimer's disease. Recently, experimental drugs that halt the progress of Alzheimer's have been found. The drug called THA apparently blocks the action of enzymes that limit the production of acetylcholine, which is thought to be crucial for normal brain functioning.

Today, researchers are beginning to think that there are many types of Alzheimer's diseases, some of which may be hereditary (St. George-Hyslop et al., 1987). From a psychologist's point of view, this type of research and others to follow are crucial because the behavioral effects for the patient and family are profound.

---

environment. Older workers may find more job satisfaction because they have had more time to find a niche in the right job for them. Furthermore, older workers tend to have fewer mental health problems than their younger co-workers.

TABLE 8.4: A Summary of Changes in Important Domains of Adult Functioning

	Young Adulthood 18–25	Early Adulthood 25–40	Middle Adulthood 40–65	Late Adulthood 65–75	Late, Late Adulthood 75+
Physical Change	Peak functioning in most physical skills; optimum time for childbearing	Still good physical functioning in most areas; health habits during this time establish later risks	Beginning signs of physical decline in some areas—strength, elasticity of tissues, height, cardiovascular function	Significant physical decline on most measures	Marked physical decline on virtually any measure, including speed, strength, work capacity, elasticity, system functioning
Cognitive Change	Cognitive skill high on most measures	Peak period of cognitive skill on most measures	Some signs of loss of cognitive skill on timed, unexercised skills	Small declines for virtually all adults on exercised skills	Often significant loss in many areas, including memory
Work Roles	Choose career, which may involve several job changes; low work satisfaction is common	Rising work satisfaction; major emphasis on career or work success; most career progress steps made	Plateau on career steps, but higher work satisfaction	Retirement	Work roles now unimportant
Personality Development	Conformist; task of intimacy	Task of generativity	Increase in self-confidence, openness; lower use of immature defenses	Perhaps integrated level; perhaps more inferiority; perhaps self-actualized; task of ego integrity	Perhaps integrated or self-actualized
Major Tasks	Separate from family; form partnership; begin family; find job; create individual life pattern	Rear family; establish personal work pattern and strive for success	Launch family; redefine life goals; redefine self outside of family and work roles; care for aging parents	Cope with retirement; cope with declining body and mind; redefine life goals and sense of self	Come to terms with death

Source: Bee, H. L. (1987). *The journey of adulthood.* New York: Macmillan Publishing Company.

Aging in Industry. Considerable ageism and discrimination against older workers exist in industry. The discrimination exists because of the erroneous perception that all older workers are less capable, less efficient, and less productive than their younger counterparts. It is interesting to note that these judgments are often made by a senior executive who may be older than the employees against whom he or she discriminates!

Older workers are in an era of their life in which they can be happy, productive, fulfilled, and as mentally sound as at any era in their lives. They often have fewer stressors that might cause problems. Their children are usually grown, their satisfaction in marriage is often higher than during their younger childbearing years, and they are likely to be skilled at their jobs.

Today, more individuals retire in their late fifties or early sixties than at any other period. Many workers are opting for leisure time and recreation. People who work into their middle or late sixties are likely to be the targets of discrimination. Psychologists need to do much research to prove conclusively what aspects of an older individual's functioning deteriorates and thus would affect job performance (see Table 8.4).

PROGRESS CHECK 8.4

1. Complete each of the following sentences with one of the options provided.

Learning Objective 8.13

A. In the United States, the overall life expectancy for both men and women is _____ years.
(69.3 : 74.7 : 77.6)

Learning Objective 8.13

B. Considering that there are as many people over the age of sixty as there are under the age of seven, funding for programs needed by the elderly is relatively _____.
(limited : high)

Learning Objective 8.14

C. Ageism refers to _____ the elderly.
(the mental health of : a prejudice against : helping)

Learning Objective 8.14

D. The elderly are often treated _____.
(as individuals : according to negative stereotypes)

Learning Objective 8.15

E. The physiological theory of aging that suggests that a person's ability to adjust to varying conditions, maintain constant body temperature, and keep sugar levels in balance selects _____ as its foundation.
(cellular aging : homeostasis)

Learning Objective 8.15

F. The physiological theory of aging that suggests that people generate antibodies which attack their own cells and ultimately destroy the life-cycle functions is based on _____.
(wear-and-tear : cellular aging : autoimmunity)

Learning Objective 8.16

G. Psychologists use the term _____ to describe the anxiety, confusion, depression, and memory loss that can accompany old age.
(senility : chronic brain disorders)

Learning Objective 8.16

H. Studies investigating the hypothesis that older people have slower reaction times because their brain-wave and autonomic nervous system activity is under-aroused have provided _____ support for the idea.
(little : mixed : overwhelming)

Learning Objective 8.16

I. Researchers have concluded that _____ more than any other variable accounts for changes in cognitive functioning in aged people.
(external factors : health : the degeneration of neurons)

Learning Objective 8.16

J. The term *terminal drop* is used to describe _____ found in some elderly people.
(slower reflexive actions : clumsiness : a decline in intellectual functioning)

Learning Objective 8.17

K. Older people are likely to perform poorly on intelligence tests because _____.
(of lost intellectual abilities : the tests are timed)

Learning Objective 8.18

L. Researchers _____ older workers have poorer job performance than younger workers.
(have strong evidence showing that : are not certain about whether)

Learning Objective 8.18

M. Older workers tend to be _____ satisfied with their jobs than are younger workers.
(less : more)

DYING AND DEATH: THE END OF THE LIFE SPAN

As a teenager, Betty Gerson, who opened this chapter, was looking forward to a future that could easily span another sixty years or more. She also knew that her grandfather had fewer decades in his future. At age sixty-five, he could live another ten to twenty years or even longer; but, if his memory losses were symptoms of a serious problem, he might die sooner.

Learning 8.19
Objective

Everybody recognizes that dying is inevitable, but in modern day America few people see other people die. Before this century, people were more likely to see other people die because most people died at home in bed. With the advent of modern technology and modern medicine, however, almost 80 percent of deaths take place in hospitals and nursing homes. Today, although everyone recognizes that death is inevitable, a personally witnessed death has become a relatively rare event (Aiken, 1985).

Widespread differences abound in people's attitudes about death and dying. From a psychologist's point of view, the process of dying is complicated because people do not like to talk or think about death. People fear dying, although they are more fearful of death in middle age than at any other time in the life cycle. Religious people fear it less than others; older women fear it less than men. More positive attitudes are found among the financially stable than among the poor.

Kübler-Ross's Stage Theory of Death and Dying

As people age, many grow sick and develop illnesses from which they know they will not recover. The stress that they often experience characterizes another one of life's stages. Elisabeth Kübler-Ross has studied extensively the way people respond psychologically to death and to those people who are dying. She was one of the first researchers to use a stage theory to discuss the fear people have of their own death or the death of loved ones. Since first interviewing a dying patient for a paper on "Crisis in Human Life," she has interviewed hundreds of dying individuals, established seminars on the process of death and dying, and written several books.

Some people, and some societies, cope with death better than others. Kübler-Ross believes that people in Western society fear death because it is unfamiliar, hidden away in hospitals behind closed doors. She suggests that one way to reduce this fear is to involve members of a dying person's family more closely in what is, in fact, a very natural process. As a person at the forefront of the "natural dying" revolution, Kübler-Ross contends that it is better for people to die at home among people they love than in hospitals, attached to machines and tubes.

Kübler-Ross's ideas about death and dying are not yet fully accepted in the scientific community because some of them rely more on intuition than on facts established through scientific methods. However, her theory that people go through a series of stages in preparing for death has prompted other researchers to investigate some of the psychological and physiological complexities of death. Further research will be necessary to systematize Kübler-Ross's ideas, but her work has helped reshape the way medical and psychological practitioners deal with dying individuals. Many of her ideas are used widely in facilities that care for the terminally ill.

According to Kübler-Ross, people who learn they are terminally ill typically go through five stages: denial, anger, bargaining, depression, and acceptance. On the basis of her own observations, Kübler-Ross suggests that hope persists throughout all these stages: "We were always impressed that even the most accepting, the most realistic patients left the possibility open for some cure, or the discovery of a new drug, or the 'last minute success' in a research project" (1969, p.139).

Denial.   When people are first told they are going to die, their typical response is disbelief. A mistake has been made, the tests are wrong, or perhaps the doctor is incompetent. Kübler-Ross notes that denial serves as a buffer against shocking news at all stages of life. Usually, denial eventually gives way to partial acceptance.

Anger.   Feelings of anger, rage, envy, and resentment follow denial. Once people realize they are going to die, they ask "Why me?" Their anger may be directed toward family, doctors, the hospital, or everyone with whom they come in contact. It may be expressed on a variety of topics, ranging from trivial to important. A woman may find herself criticizing small habits of her family that have never bothered her before. Or, she may experience rage over unresolved issues of real importance, such as the fact that her husband is unable to make her feel loved. Family members, tired of being abused, may begin to react angrily to the patient, making a difficult situation worse, by avoiding the patient or shortening their visits, forgetting the reason for the patient's anger and the need to be loved and reassured.

Bargaining.   Bargaining helps the patient cope, if only for a brief time. In bargaining, the patient makes deals with God, with self, or even with the doctors. The bargaining usually takes the form of "I'll be good if you'll give me some more time, a special treatment, or (most important) an extension of life." Like the opera star who wants to perform "just one more time," the terminally ill bargain to postpone the inevitable. According to Kübler-Ross, most bargains are made with God and are kept secret.

Depression.   For any of a variety of reasons, depression soon sets in. Tests and medication are often painful, and treatments and hospitalization often impose financial burdens. The terminally ill often lose their jobs once they can no longer function normally. Many feel guilty about the inconvenience they are causing their families. Hardest of all is the prospect of losing everything and everyone they love. According to Kübler-Ross, "If the patient is allowed to express his sorrow he will find the final acceptance much easier, and he will be grateful to those who can sit with him during this stage of depression without constantly telling him not to be sad" (1969, p. 87).

Acceptance.   If patients have had time to work through previous stages, they can reach the stage at which they are neither angry nor depressed about their fate. At this point, most patients are tired and weak and have resigned themselves to death. With this acceptance comes some peace of mind. Patients may wish to be left alone without visitors. They may make a gesture or hold someone's hand while sitting in silence. Although some patients fight to the end, most finally admit that they are tired of fighting. This is a time of resignation and surrender.

Coping with Death

Whether or not one accepts Kübler-Ross's stages as typical, it is clear that, as in all other stages of life, people approach death with different patterns of behaviors. Many people who have the chance to anticipate their death have already experienced the stresses of childhood, adolescence, adulthood, and old age and dealt with them well or badly. Many have already dealt with the death of their own parents or with the death of children or other loved ones. Most psychologists believe that the ways in which people have dealt with previous stresses in their lives largely predict how they will deal with death.

Criticisms of Kübler-Ross's Theory.   Many practitioners and theoreticians alike have criticized the Kübler-Ross stage theory as an inadequate description of death and dying. They argue that the sequence Kübler-Ross outlined does not fit with all people and that the stages are not necessarily experienced in the order Kübler-Ross suggested. But Kübler-Ross never meant for her stage theory or its sequence to be taken so literally.

Kübler-Ross has also been criticized for her research technique—her interviews were not very systematic and she offers few statistics. Schaie and Willis (1986) suggest that Kübler-Ross's ideas not be considered so much a stage theory but rather "an insightful discussion of some of the attitudes that are often displayed by people who are dying (p. 483)."

Kübler-Ross's ideas about death and dying are not necessarily the truth, but they have met with a great deal of interest and many practitioners find the theory useful in guiding new medical staff through the difficult task of helping the sick and dying. As Shneidman (1976) suggests, however, there is a great deal of individuality in the way people face death. Reactions to impending death are often a reflection of a person's total personality and the life that individual has lived. Kübler-Ross's ideas have met with criticism, skepticism, and controversy. Her theory has done what any good theory should do: it has raised our awareness and helped researchers and practitioners put into perspective a set of data to make sense out of it. The task is not yet complete.

Hospices.   Kübler-Ross was among the first to acknowledge that the prospect of death imposes severe emotional stresses not only on terminally ill patients but also on their families. As a physician, she is particularly sensitive to the additional stresses created by interactions with doctors, especially in traditional impersonal hospital settings. These factors necessarily affect the family's last memories of the dying person, among other things. Kübler-Ross and many other physicians and psychologists believe that a more homelike setting can help both patients and their families deal better with death. One alternative setting is the hospice.

Learning Objective 8.20

Hospices are special facilities established specifically to provide both efficient and humane care to terminally ill patients and their families. They try to address emotional, social, and spiritual needs in addition to physical ones. They also try to combine humane treatment with sensitivity to the economic side of patient care (Butterfield-Picard & Magno, 1982; Klagsbrun, 1982; Smyser, 1982). Hospices evaluate both the patient and the family before admitting a patient. The first hospice, St. Christopher's, was established in London under the direction of a British physician, Cicely Saunders.

In the United States today, there are more than 440 hospices, with another 360 under construction. Forty-six percent are hospital based; 23 percent are independent home health agencies. Hospices employ nurses, psychologists, physicians, social workers, and chaplains. Most of the patients have terminal cancer, and many of them are in great pain. Most hospices in the United States require that a family member or close friend be available to live with the patient for most of the time (Butterfield-Picard & Magno, 1982; Smyser, 1982).

Hospices offer alternative, home-like care for terminally-ill patients.

Hospice care is not appropriate for every dying person. It requires several specific kinds of commitment from the patient and his or her family. Hospices operate under a different set of guidelines than traditional hospitals and nursing homes that care for the terminally ill. First, control of decisions concerning the patient's care rests with the patient and the family. Second, many aspects of traditional care, such as life-support procedures made possible by advanced technology, are discontinued when the patient no longer desires them. Third, pain is kept to a minimum so that the patient can experience life fully until death. Fourth, an integrated team of professionals provides care around the clock. Fifth, surroundings are homelike rather than clinical. Sixth, when possible, family members and the hospice team are the caregivers. Finally, family members receive counseling before and after a patient dies (Butterfield-Picard & Magno, 1982).

Even though the number of hospices is growing, relatively few of the terminally ill receive hospice care. For those who do, there are ethical and practical questions about care and costs, life-support systems, and medications that families, friends, and practitioners have to answer. Researchers are continuing to explore such issues as exactly when death occurs, how the dying should be treated, and how families might cope better with the process (for example, Dawson, 1981). With time, still other and better alternatives may be found to help patients and their families.

PROGRESS CHECK 8.5

1. Complete each of the following sentences with one of the options provided.

Learning Objective 8.19   A. People tend to fear death most during _____.
(childhood : mid-life : late adulthood)

Learning Objective 8.19   B. Elisabeth Kübler-Ross has suggested that death _____.
(is not inevitable : is a natural process : should be private)

Learning Objective 8.19   C. Denial, the first stage of dying, is experienced _____.
(only by younger people : as a temporary defense)

Learning Objective 8.19   D. Most dying people experience partial acceptance of their condition after the _____ stage of dying.
(denial : bargaining : depression)

Learning Objective 8.19   E. Kübler-Ross has suggested that if dying people are allowed to express their sorrows, they will _____.
(get even more depressed : find the acceptance stage easier)

Learning Objective 8.19   F. Kübler-Ross has noted that although dying people frequently reach a stage at which they resign and surrender to death, they never _____
_____.
(give up hope for a cure : overcome feelings of depression and anger)

Learning Objective 8.19   G. Taking critics' concerns into consideration, Kübler-Ross's work might best be described as _____.
(a stage theory : an insightful discussion of feelings shared by dying people)

Learning Objective 8.20   H. A patient in a hospice typically would be there because _____
_____.
(of a terminal disease : routine meals are provided)

Learning Objective 8.20   I. Hospice care requires the patient and family members to _____
_____.
(make difficult decisions : depersonalize death)

Keeping Pace with Chapter 8

Applying Principles

8.1 Identify Kohlberg's level of morality as illustrated in each of the following situations.
Level 1—decisions about right and wrong
Level 2—conventional ideas about morality
Level 3: Part 1—morality of laws and contracts
Level 3: Part 2—morality of conscience

_____

A. A cashier gives Angie $5.00 more change than she should receive. Angie returns the money because she feels it could hurt the store's chances of staying in business if she kept the money and did not pay for all of her purchases.

_____

B. Timmy does not sneak a chocolate chip cookie from the cookie jar because he fears if his mother noticed one was missing she would punish him.

C. Knowing that he is risking arrest and his family's disapproval, Patrick participates in a peaceful, yet illegal, demonstration, to help make a group statement that supports his own beliefs.

D. Rhonda does what she is told and follows well-established social rules because she wants other people to approve of her and enjoys being thought of as a well-behaved child.

Before proceeding to the Self-Test, REVIEW the Learning Objectives listed at the chapter opening and RECITE from memory everything you can remember in support of them. Then, take this Self-Test as if it were to be graded by your teacher. Use the Learning Objective numbers in the Answer Section as a reference to restudy the corresponding text pages and Progress Checks for any incorrectly answered questions.

1. The classic Western society adolescent identity crisis occurs because
   A. many adolescents have not achieved the level of emotional development necessary to cope with the demands of adolescence.
   B. adults frequently place paradoxical demands on adolescents.
   C. changes in intellectual ability, body proportions, and sexual urges give rise to new, unresolved conflicts.
   D. all of the above

2. When studying physical changes that occur in adolescence, we find that
   A. adolescence begins and puberty follows.
   B. *adolescence* and *puberty* are really synonymous terms.
   C. it takes several years for these physical changes to occur completely.
   D. all of the above

3. Studies investigating the influence that peer groups have on adolescents have *not* been able to agree on whether they do or do not
   A. influence an adolescent's self-concept.
   B. exert a greater influence than the influence of parents.
   C. act as a source of information for their members.
   D. create an atmosphere that pressures members to conform to the group.

4. Sexually active teenagers
   A. use contraceptives about 50 percent of the time.
   B. are generally well-informed about reproduction and contraception.
   C. seem to understand contraception but not reproduction.
   D. underestimate the likelihood of pregnancy.

5. Perhaps one reason that drug use and abuse becomes a problem for some people during adolescence is that
   A. adolescents are so busy they need to take time to relax and choose drugs as their means for doing so.
   B. decriminalization has led to lenient state and local laws.
   C. adolescents tend to have plenty of money to spend on entertainment.
   D. adolescence is a time for experimentation.

6. According to Erikson's theory of development, to emerge as a fully mature, stable adult, toward the end of one's life a person must
   A. pass through each stage victoriously and develop integrity.
   B. keep working, playing, and praying.
   C. have children and grandchildren to take pride in.
   D. do his or her best at each stage in life.

7. Toilet training and other behaviors involving control create a crisis to be resolved by a child during Erikson's _____ stage.

   A. basic trust versus mistrust
   B. autonomy versus shame and doubt
   C. initiative versus guilt
   D. industry versus inferiority

8. Level 2 moral judgments are governed by a process that considers

   A. good and bad or right and wrong.
   B. the needs of society and ways of maintaining order.
   C. the implications of a person's behavior.
   D. a person's personal values.

9. Studies investigating the relationship between moral reasoning and moral behavior have found

   A. a direct relationship between moral reasoning and moral behavior.
   B. that people sometimes use two or three levels of moral reasoning at the same time.
   C. that people do not always use moral reasoning abilities in a consistent way.
   D. all of the above.

10. When studying adult development, developmental psychologists are primarily interested in discovering

    A. childhood conflicts that were never resolved.
    B. teaching strategies from which adults can learn.
    C. physiological changes that lead to aging.
    D. variables that lead to stability and a sense of accomplishment.

11. Daniel Levinson suggests that when people enter a new era of life,

    A. crisis is inevitable.
    B. old life structures no longer work.
    C. they have matured to a more advanced stage.
    D. psychological growth subsides for a few years.

12. According to Levinson, early adulthood ends at about age

    A. twenty-five.
    B. thirty-five.
    C. forty-five.
    D. fifty-five.

13. As a person ages, it is almost inevitable that

    A. sensory abilities will decline.
    B. the risk of disease and illness will increase.
    C. problems with blood circulation and respiration will occur.
    D. all of the above

14. The way an adult copes with particular life events is influenced by

    A. luck.
    B. self-concept.
    C. relationships and social group.
    D. all of the above.

15. The percentage of people over age sixty-five is expected to _____ by the year 2030.

    A. decrease
    B. stabilize
    C. increase by twenty percent
    D. triple

16. Ageism is the result of

    A. having an increased number of older people in our society.
    B. the rising cost of hospital care.
    C. personality characteristics commonly found in aging people.
    D. negative stereotyping.

17. The theory of aging that suggests that cells have finite life and gradually lose their ability to replicate is called

    A. cellular aging.
    B. wear-and-tear.
    C. genetic determination.
    D. accumulation of metabolic waste.

18. Researchers are fairly confident that the greatest changes in the central nervous systems of older people can be observed in

    A. the body's slower response time to the senses.
    B. alterations in brain-wave activity.
    C. brain cells that degenerate.
    D. the responsiveness of the automatic nervous system.

19. Which of the following is a *false* statement?

    A. The work environment is one of the few environments that shows little or no ageism.
    B. Employers tend to resist hiring individuals over the age of fifty.
    C. Employers are reluctant to provide retraining to new technology for older workers.
    D. Older workers pay more attention to a job's intrinsic characteristics.

20. Elisabeth Kübler-Ross believes that terminally ill people should

    A. never be left alone in the final stages of dying.
    B. be ignored or avoided when they become angry.
    C. be encouraged to cheer up when they become depressed.
    D. be allowed to die at home among the people they love.

21. During the bargaining stage, most bargains are made with

    A. God.
    B. doctors.
    C. oneself.
    D. family members.

22. A hospice

    A. is a traditional hospital that admits only terminally ill patients.
    B. attempts to care for a patient's emotional, spiritual, social, and physical needs.
    C. focuses on prevention of death rather than dying.
    D. makes use of traditional clinical jargon when interacting with the patient and family.

Language and Intelligence

9

9

When you have mastered the material in this chapter, you will be able to:

1. Discuss the relation between language and thought and cite some data that show the importance of verbal stimulation during the early years of life. (p. 326)

2. Define *psycholinguistics;* describe grammar and the three major components of language: phonology, syntax, and semantics. (p. 327)

3. Explain how transformational grammar allows human beings to generate an infinite number of sentences, according to Chomsky. (p. 329)

4. Discuss the case of Genie and explain how such cases help researchers determine the relative contributions of nature and nurture on language acquisition. (p. 330)

5. Explain how human beings acquire language according to learning and biological theorists. (p. 332)

6. Discuss the value to psychology of the language research done with chimpanzees. (p. 333)

7. Identify the important components of David Wechsler's definition of intelligence. (p. 337)

8. Explain how psychologists gather data concerning various aspects of a person to make predictions concerning his or her future behavior and discuss why the first intelligence test was originally developed (p. 338)

9. Describe how psychologists go about developing a standardized test that can be used to assess where any one individual stands when compared to a specific population of other individuals. (p. 339)

10. Define *reliability* and *validity* and explain how psychologists ensure that diagnostic tests are reliable and valid. (p. 341)

11. Discuss four theories that attempt to describe the nature of intelligence. (p. 344)

12. Describe the Stanford-Binet Intelligence Test, Wechsler Intelligence Scales, and Kaufman Assessment Battery for Children and identify some of the abilities that these tests measure. (p. 346)

13. Discuss five criticisms concerning the validity of intelligence testing. (p. 350)

14. Discuss the controversy concerning cultural biases in intelligence tests and explain why the interpretation of test scores is the key to the appropriate use of tests and testing. (p. 351)

15. Discuss the controversial research put forth by Arthur Jensen concerning the role genetic heritage plays in the development of intelligence. (p. 353)

16. Explain what psychologists have learned by studying adopted children and other environmental factors about the role the environment plays in the development of intelligence. (p. 354)

17. Discuss the effects that family size and birth order can have on intellectual development. (p. 357)

18. Discuss what it means for a person to be gifted, describe how the gifted are treated in the United States, and identify the populations that are considered exceptional. (p. 359)

19. Identify the criteria used to diagnose mental retardation and discuss the four levels used to categorize the mentally retarded. (p. 360)

20. Describe some of the biological and environmental causes of mental retardation. (p. 361)

21. Explain how the rights of physically and mentally handicapped people are protected, describe the concept of mainstreaming in educational settings, and discuss the potential of mentally retarded people as employees in the workplace. (p. 362)

BEFORE YOU READ ON, take time to **SURVEY** the chapter, form an idea of what is to be learned (from margin Learning Objective numbers), and set goals for your study time. Then, ask yourself **QUESTIONS** about the material as you READ, seeking help for any sections you do not understand.

Rachel Assad was caught between the cracks in her new fourth-grade classroom. She was much too bright to be in an average classroom; but based on her achievement test scores from her previous school, she did not qualify for the gifted and talented program. She was bored in her regular classes but not allowed to be with whom her parents called the "fast trackers."

Even though they were new to the school system, Rachel's parents knew the system should have put her in the appropriate class months ago; but it had not. The school was going to retest Rachel because most of her test scores were exceptionally high, but one score was exceptionally low. She had scored in the 98 or 99th percentile in all of the other achievement tests, but had scored only in the 35th percentile in Reading Comprehension. Rachel's parents and the school psychologist agreed that something was wrong.

However, four months had passed and Rachel had not been retested. Her parents argued to the director of the gifted program that the school was not meeting its obligations. Two weeks later, they made the same case to the superintendent. During that interval, they did a great deal of reading, learning everything they could about testing, achievement tests, and especially intelligence tests. Rachel's IQ test score was exceptionally high. They felt that this score alone was strong enough to qualify her for the gifted program. They argued to the superintendent that the error on achievement tests scores could be significant and that they wanted the school district to provide proper educational services.

Another two weeks passed and no action was taken. Out of frustration and anger, her parents called an attorney who specialized in school-related issues. He advised them about the school's obligations under the law. Their next contact with the school was in writing, informing the system that they had hired an attorney to advise them of their rights. Four days later Rachel was retested. Three days after the testing, the Assads received a letter informing them that

Rachel's test scores qualified her for the gifted and talented program and that she would be transferred to a new teacher and class the following week.

UNFORTUNATELY, SITUATIONS LIKE RACHEL'S are quite common. Children who are gifted or children who are mentally retarded are too often neglected. As the Assads found out, however, the law mandates that a child's educational needs be met, and met promptly.

Learning Objective 9.1

Sometimes school systems are slow to recognize special children. With thirty children in a classroom, it is often difficult to "see" one child's unique qualities. Sometimes quiet children are assumed to be less intelligent, or highly verbal children are assumed to be more intelligent. In some individuals a clear relationship exists between speech and intelligence—many highly verbal individuals are also intelligent. In many other people, however, high verbal abilities seem unrelated to their ability to cope with the demands of the world. An interesting developmental relationship exists between language and thought processes. As children develop, both thought and language mature simultaneously, although often not at the same rate. A mature vocabulary does not necessarily mean mature thoughts. However, because thinking is often expressed in language, psychologists often examine those processes together.

Research has shown that language, thought, and intelligence are sensitive to experience and to genetic factors. As in other areas of human behavior, debate continues about the relative contribution of each. The nature versus nurture issue, as elsewhere in psychology, is central to the study of language behavior, and it has dominated the study of intelligence. For example, caregivers who are attentive and provide a great deal of verbal stimulation can enhance children's cognitive development (Bradley & Caldwell, 1976). White found that well-developing one- and two-year-olds had considerably more talk directed at them than infants who were developing less well (S. H. White et al., 1973). F. F. Schachter (1979) correctly suggests that the quality of verbal stimulation is even more important than the quantity. At the very least, some language exchange between caregiver and child is necessary for normal language development to occur (Curtiss, 1977).

This chapter examines the development of language. It then explores how psychologists think about intelligence and its development. We point out some genetic and environmental factors operating in both language and intelligence that help people communicate and understand each other and the world about them.

LANGUAGE

When Rachel Assad started in her new school, some teachers were undoubtedly surprised at her prodigious vocabulary and use of language. She seemed bright, but she was not in with the more advanced children. The teachers made inferences about her intelligence from her language development. Advanced language development is often, but not necessarily, an indicator of intelligence.

Environmental factors such as parental encouragement facilitate language development.

What could Rachel's teachers infer from her language development? Perhaps a child with language like Rachel's was fostered through special attention at home? Are there ways in which people can facilitate language development? Is language development so universal and fixed in the human species that the environment exerts little influence? Is language a uniquely human quality? It will not surprise you that the answers to these questions are found in the research that psychologists do.

Many psychologists assert that human beings have an innate, unique capacity to acquire and develop language. Although they do not exclude experience as a factor in shaping children's language, they claim that it is human nature itself that allows children to pay attention to language in their environment and ultimately to use it. Language develops so naturally that it does seem as if certain aspects of language are inborn. For example, although individuals begin using words and sentences at different ages, once language emerges, it proceeds at about the same rate and through the same stages for everyone. However, it is also clear that environmental factors affect language development in important ways.

Psycholinguistics: The Study of Language from a Psychologist's Viewpoint

Learning Objective 9.2

Psycholinguistics
The study of how language is acquired, perceived, comprehended, and produced.

Grammar
The linguistic description of how a language functions.

Much of the interaction between nature and nurture has become clear from developmental studies performed by psychologists who specialize in **psycholinguistics**—the study of how language is acquired, perceived, understood, and produced. Psycholinguists have found that children acquire the simplest elements of language first, followed by progressively more complex elements and capabilities.

Grammar is the linguistic description of a language. It contains the rules for how a language works. Knowing how and when children develop a set of grammatical rules can help psycholinguists assess the relative contributions of nature and nurture. If language is based in biology, two things should be true: (1) many aspects of language ability should be evident early in life, and (2) all children, regardless of their culture or language, should develop a grammar in a similar way. On the other hand, if environmental factors account for language acquisition, the role of learning should be preeminent.

The "miracle" of language acquisition in children has long puzzled linguists and psycholinguists. How can a child, with rudimentary cognitive abilities, learn the complicated rules that allow him or her to speak correct English? This section examines three major components of language: *phonology,* the study of the sounds of language; *semantics,* the study of the meanings of words and sentences; and *syntax,* the study of the relationships among words and how they combine to form sentences.

Phonology.   The gurgling, spitting, and burping noises infants make are caused by air passing through the vocal apparatus. At about six weeks, infants begin to make speechlike sound in the form of cooing. During the first twelve months, their vocalizations become more varied and frequent. Eventually, they combine sounds into pronounceable units.

The basic units of sound that compose the words in a language are called **phonemes.** Examples of phonemes in English are the sounds of the letters *b, p, f,* and *v.* Other phonemes in English combine more than one sound to make a more complex basic unit. For example, the sound that results from combining the *w* and *h* sounds in *wheeze* is a single phoneme, the phoneme *wh.* Forty-five phonemes express all the sounds in the English language.

At about one year of age, children utter the first sounds that psychologists classify as real speech. Initially, they may utter only one word, but within a short period they are saying as many as four or five words. Words consist of morphemes. **Morphemes** are basic units of meaning in a language. A morpheme consists of one or more phonemes combined into a meaningful unit. The morpheme *do* is composed of two phonemes, the sounds of the letters *d* and *o.* Other words can be formed by the addition of prefixes and suffixes to existing morphemes. For example, adding *ing* or *er* to the morpheme *do* produces *doing* or *doer.* Often, one of the first utterances that parents worldwide can distinguish as a meaningful unit is the morpheme *ma.* This particular utterance happens to be a word in the English language. Other frequently heard words are *bye-bye, mama,* and *bebe.* These first words often refer to a specific object or person. Nelson (1973) showed that children's first words often referred to food, toys, and animals. In the next year, children's vocabulary increases to about 50 words, and by age three to as many as 1,000 (see Figure 9.1).

Semantics.   Infants do not fully understand the meaning of their parents' utterances. As more words take on meaning, children develop semantic capability. **Semantics** is the analysis of the meaning of individual words, of the relationships among words, and of the placement of words in a context that generates thought.

Consider the sentence, *Now, this guy is fast!* What are the possible meanings of this sentence? It might mean that the man is smart, that he is sneaky, that he is moving quickly, or even that he is stupid. Single words can convey a variety of meanings. In trying to understand the meaning of utterances, a psycholinguist is faced with understanding not only the meanings of single words, but also their relationship to other words. Meaning is more than just referring to or imagining an object or event. The meaning of a sentence is not the same

Phonemes
The basic units of sound in a language.

Morphemes
The basic units of meaning in a language.

Semantics
The study of the meaning of the components of language.

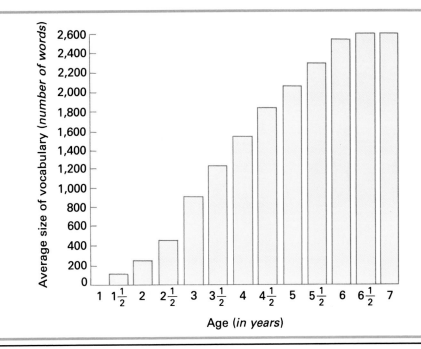

as the definitions of the individual words added together. A word can mean different things depending on its sentence context. Therefore, in studying meaning, psychologists study both individual word meaning and sentence meaning.

Syntax. Once children can use words that have distinct meanings for them, they begin to combine these words into basic two-word sentences, such as *mama look* or *bye-bye mama*. They develop a syntactic capability. **Syntax** is the study of how words and groups of words combine to form phrases, clauses, or sentences. This syntactic capability allows children to convey much more meaning. Initial studies of these short sentences suggested that a description of the order or position of the words and their types could completely characterize early speech (for example, Braine, 1963). Later analyses showed these descriptions to be inadequate (Bowerman, 1973). Other investigations have suggested that young children possess an innate grammar and that they use grammatical relationships in much the same ways that adults do (for example, McNeill, 1970). However, children's speech at this stage does not seem to follow a simple, orderly pattern. Sometimes children use words in incorrect order. The two-word utterances of a two-year-old are not systematic or grammatical in an adult sense. Although children begin to use sentences at different ages, once they begin they tend to develop at similar rates (R. Brown, 1970). As Figure 9.2 on the next page shows, the average length of utterances increases at a fairly regular rate as children grow older.

Syntax
The relation between words and groups of words and how those words are arranged in phrases and sentences.

Learning Objective 9.3

Transformational Grammar. In 1957, linguist Noam Chomsky described a radical approach to grammar that changed many psychologists' view of language development. Chomsky claimed that each person is born with the ability to transform an underlying basic "kernel" of meaning into an infinite

Noam Chomsky developed the theory of transformational grammar.

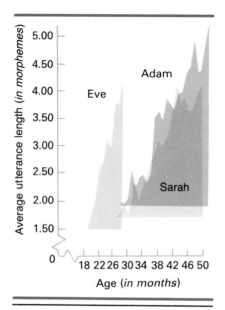

FIGURE 9.2 : The length of children's utterances increases as they get older.

Transformational grammar ═══
Developed by Chomsky, an approach to the study of language that assumes that each surface structure of a sentence has associated with it a deep structure. This grammar includes transformational rules for generating surface structures from deep structures.

Surface structure ═══
The organization of a sentence that is closest to its written or spoken form.

Deep structure ═══
The organization of a sentence that is closest to its underlying meaning.

Learning 9.4
Objective

number of meaningful sentences. Although many other types of grammars have been suggested since then, Chomsky's concept (1972, 1975) has continued to dominate thinking about language.

The fundamental idea of Chomsky's **transformational grammar** is that each sentence has both a surface structure and a deep structure. The **surface structure** is the actual sentence—such as, *Alex gave Mary a dog.* The **deep structure** is the underlying structure or pattern that helps convey meaning. Thus, the sentences *Alex gave Mary a dog* and *Alex gave a dog to Mary* have different surface structures but the same deep structure. Transformational grammar attempts to relate the surface structure of a sentence to its deep structure.

Transformational grammar as presented by Chomsky (1957, 1972, 1975) and tested by others is not the only approach to grammar; that is, it is not the only way linguists describe language. However, we present it here because it has been so widely used, tested, and written about. It is clearly the principal way many linguists and psychologists think about grammar.

How Do We Acquire Language? Nature Versus Nurture

Because it would be unethical to manipulate the language experiences of human infants, psychologists have investigated language development through observational studies of infants and children, case histories of sensory-deprived infants, studies of reading-disabled or brain-damaged individuals, and experiments with chimpanzees.

From time to time, researchers discover children who have been deprived of nearly all forms of stimulation. By studying how these children subsequently acquire language, psycholinguists can learn a great deal about language development in human beings. Curtiss (1977) reported a case involving a girl called Genie. Genie was discovered confined in a small back bedroom, harnessed to an infant's potty seat, unable to move. Restrained either in a harness or a

Parents await their children's first words with great anticipation. After nine months of pregnancy and another many months of childcare, the baby is going to communicate. Fathers and mothers want their children to reach out and say "daddy" or "mommy." This desire is natural, and around one year of age, when children generally utter their first words; parents are often noticeably anxious.

Language development is a central element in child's emotional, thought, and personality development. Children who lag behind others by more than two years are likely to have significant problems later in life. What happens when a child's language is slow to develop? When should parents become concerned that their child's vocabulary is too small or their child's pronunciation of words is too difficult to understand? When does a child have a language disorder?

Parents, relatives, and alert psychology students who often observe children and take note of language development usually see a series of developmental phenomena. Significant deviations from the norm are a source of concern.

The following stages of language development are taken from Linda Smolak's (1986) excellent book on infancy.

1. *Vocabulary size.* The normal vocabulary for an eighteen-month-old child is 10 to 20 words. By twenty-four months, vocabulary increases to about 50 to 250 words. There is considerable variation; a child with a 60-word vocabulary at two years is still within normal ranges.
2. *Sentence use.* By the time they are two years of age, most children begin to combine words into short two-word sentences. By two-and-a-half years of age, sentences are typically three words in length (Valian, 1986). Sentences of the two-and-a-half-year-old are limited—toddlers do not use plurals or the past tense, and they do not carry on "conversations." However, they make themselves known and can clearly get across to parents what they want and do not want.
3. *Pronounciation.* Children under two years of age normally have pronounciation problems. They drop endings off the ends of words. *Pencil* becomes *pe–; cookie* becomes *cook–*. Vowels are not totally intelligible until about two-and-a-half years of age. Even seven-year-olds have trouble with some consonants. Thus, it is normal for a two-year-old to be difficult to understand.
4. *Stuttering.* Children under the age of three often stutter. Stuttering during the preschool years is common, especially when a child is upset or excited. Stuttering often continues, but it should disappear by age five. A child of five years of age who stutters should be referred to a specialist for a consultation.

Normal children will eventually talk, and no special methods are necessary to bring about language in a typical home environment. Parents can speed some aspects of language development, however, by talking a great deal to their children, reading to them, asking them questions, and reinforcing them for verbal utterances.

If you observe a child who is a slow talker the child may be this way because the child does not want to talk or does not have to talk. Sometimes older siblings talk for them, or they make their wants known by whining. But if children are having problems with speech and language or if their speech and language are delayed by a year or two, they should be referred to specialists for evaluation.

When a language problem is suspected, a hearing evaluation is usually done first. Hearing has a great impact on language development. A child who cannot hear well will have severely impaired language development. If hearing is normal, other tests of language, cognitive, and emotional development will usually be administered. Delayed language development can be a sign of important developmental problems, and it thus should not be ignored; for most children, however, a delay is insignificant.

straitjacket, Genie had heard no sounds and seen no daylight for years. Force-fed and deprived of all types of stimulation, Genie grew up malnourished and underdeveloped. When she was discovered at age thirteen, Genie's language consisted of a few words (*rattle, bunny, red, blue, green,* and *brown*) to which she always responded in the same way. Psychologists have followed Genie's language acquisition with particular interest because she has been taught in specific precise ways after the usual developmental period. She now has some language and can develop new sentences of her own design, but her language is constrained and rule-governed. She has not developed what psychologists consider normal language.

Such a case shows the importance of both biological and environmental influences on language acquisition. If a child at a normal biological stage of readiness is environmentally deprived, then no amount of subsequent environmental compensation will overcome completely what only biological readiness could furnish at that crucial earlier growth stage. For most researchers, the issues are not whether nature or nurture is the sole influence on language development, but how much each contributes and how they interact.

Learning   9.5
Objective

Learning Theories.   Learning theories stress the role of environmental influences in language acquisition. According to one learning theory, the *conditioning approach,* both reinforcement (in the form of parental approval) and self-reinforcement (in the form of speech) increase the probability that children will emit words and sentences. Staats and Staats (1963) claim that parents provide specific reinforcement to infants by becoming excited and by poking, touching, patting, and feeding them on hearing vocalization. Similar reinforcement of words in combination leads to the production of sentences. Once the child is able to ask questions and communicate, the acquisition of language is itself reinforcing. A mother asks, *Is daddy going outside?* The child responds, *Allgone daddy.* The mother reinforces the child by responding, *That's right, daddy is allgone, daddy allgone.* Even studies with chimps show that through instrumental training procedures, chimps can be taught to communicate. The conditioning approach stresses the importance of language experiences during the formative years.

Another learning theory claims that children acquire language through *imitation,* by copying adult speech. Through this imitation, they learn to use the proper forms of language. Although reinforcement may occur, it is not a necessary feature of learning. Clearly, children do learn certain rules and speech patterns from parents by imitation. Regional dialects are an example; children from Brooklyn rarely use the expression *Y'all come back, now.* However, imitation is probably not the only way children learn language. If it were, even young children's speech would be fairly grammatical.

Although both conditioning and imitation undoubtedly play a role in language acquisition, learning approaches in general have two serious weaknesses. First, they do not explain why speakers can generate an infinite number of sentences—not only new sentences, but also a wide variety of syntactic combinations that they may never have encountered or used before. Second, learning approaches do not take into account biological or maturational readiness. For example, children generally begin reading sometime between ages four and six. Although some children show reading readiness earlier than others, readiness implies that specific appropriate development must take place before a child can learn. Reading readiness must be to some extent biologically determined. If it were not, theoretically parents could teach a child to read soon after birth.

Biological Theories.   Although the impact of learning theories on the study of language has been great, two major sources of evidence support the biological side of the nature versus nurture debate—studies of brain lateralization and language acquisition in children and chimpanzees.

Norman Geschwind's early work (1972) studying the speech and language disorders of brain-damaged patients has led to many different types of research on brain organization. Considerable evidence suggests that the left and right sides of the brain (normally connected by the corpus callosum) handle distinctly different functions. As you remember from Chapter 4, the left side appears to be specially organized for speech and language activities, the right side for processing music and spatial tasks. Biological theories of language rely heavily on this idea of **lateralization.**

Lateralization

The concentration of a particular brain function in one hemisphere.

The evidence for lateralization of speech and language functions is impressive. Geschwind found that in 97 percent of cases of language impairment resulting from a head injury, the injury involved the left hemisphere. Other studies show that when the corpus callosum is surgically severed, the left and right hemispheres function independently; information transmitted to only one hemisphere is unavailable to the other. Thus, any new language information conveyed only to the right hemisphere will not be appropriately processed.

Some linguists acknowledge the role of learning experiences but attribute greater importance to innate linguistic capacities. Overall, the biological approach assumes that a child's capacity to learn language depends on maturation of certain neurological capacities. Thus, lack of maturity in these structures limits infants' ability to speak in the first months of life; maturation at about eighteen to twenty-four months permits the acquisition of a grammar—the series of rules that allow people to generate sentences and to interact linguistically with others. This view derives in part from observations that most children learn the rules of grammar at a very early age.

Studies with Chimpanzees

Learning Objective 9.6

You know that your dog understands simple commands—come, sit, fetch. But does an animal have the ability to communicate with its owner in a more complete and meaningful way? Do animals have language? If animals have language, is that language the same as, similar to, or totally different from that of human beings? What can human beings learn about language from animals?

Using sign language, the gorilla Koko was able to give her pet kitten a name.

The biological approach to language suggests that human beings are born with a capacity for language. Experience is the key that unlocks this already-existing framework and makes it available for expression. Additional support for the biological approach to language acquisition comes from studies showing that chimps naturally develop some language abilities. In these studies, researchers have been able to control and shape the environment in which language learning occurs—something that cannot be done in studies involving human subjects.

All attempts to teach animals to speak have failed (Kellogg, 1968). These failures led most psycholinguists to conclude that nonhumans do not have the capacity to acquire language. However, research has shown that even though chimpanzees lack the necessary vocal apparatus to speak, they can learn to use different methods of communication (Rumbaugh & Savage-Rumbaugh, 1978), just as deaf people who cannot speak use a different language system. After a lot of training, chimps acquire language on a much smaller scale than children do almost effortlessly.

Research studies have shown that apes also are able to acquire certain specific languagelike abilities. They can learn to attach meanings to symbols and to combine the symbols into meaningful patterns. However, they have not demonstrated a grammatical capability—the ability to generate alternative ways of expressing the same idea. Their language is usually tied to specific word order.

A Columbia University psychologist, H. S. Terrace (1979, 1980), claims that even these results have been greatly overvalued. He suggests not only that apes do not have language abilities, but also that most (or all) of the data reported so far show only that the chimps were mirroring their teachers' signs. If Terrace is correct, this is a devastating criticism.

Terrace has reported significant differences between chimp language and that of young children. For example, in raising his chimp, Nim, he found that Nim's utterances did not increase in length as young children's do. Nim acquired many words, but she did not use them in longer and longer sentences as time passed. In addition, only 12 percent of Nim's utterances were spontaneous. The remaining 88 percent were responses to her teacher. Terrace points out that a significantly greater percentage of children's utterances are spontaneous. Terrace also found no evidence of grammatical competence either in his own data or in those of other researchers.

Terrace's work (1979) challenged the work of previous investigators and made them think about chimp language in new ways. Susan Savage-Rumbaugh and her colleagues at the Yerkes Regional Primate Center at Emory University have brought forth still further challenges (Savage-Rumbaugh, Pate, Lawson, Smith, & Rosenbaum, 1983). They claim that not only is chimp language different from that of human beings, but that the purpose of chimp language is different as well. Unlike young children, who understand that a symbol stands for, refers to, or replaces another object, chimps do not spontaneously develop communication skills such as pointing and naming. For Savage-Rumbaugh and her colleagues, the process of spontaneous naming and pointing is a crucial component of human language. The ability to name is a basic part of human consciousness, according to Terrace (1985). He argues that as part of our socialization, we learn to refer to our various inner states: our feelings, thoughts, and emotions. Although chimps can be taught some naming skills, the procedure is long and tedious; human children, however, develop this skill easily, spontaneously, and at a young age. Accordingly, researchers like Sanders (1985) assert that chimps do not interpret the symbols they use in the manner human children do, and question the comparability of human and chimp language.

Since the beginning of work with chimps there has been controversy. Though few psychologists have been completely convinced about the role of language in chimps, their criticisms do not diminish the chimps' accomplishments. The debate continues (see, for example, Drumm, Gardner, & Gardner, 1986; Sugarman, 1983).

Summary

Like many other areas of psychology, the acquisition of language is not fully understood. Psychologists know that reinforcement helps children learn language and that children imitate the language of their peers and parents. Yet it is also clear that certain aspects of language behavior must be innate. Every few years, researchers make discoveries that require a reevaluation of the relative contributions of nature and nurture by opening up new aspects of the question. Further research will doubtless modify psychologists' understanding of the environmental and biological bases of language.

PROGRESS CHECK 9.1

1. Match each of the following key concepts and terms with the appropriate definition.

psycholinguistics   phonemes   grammar   morpheme
phonology   semantics   syntax   transformational grammar

Learning Objective 9.2   A. _____ The basic unit of meaning in a language—a word or meaningful part of a word.

Learning Objective 9.2   B. _____ The relationships among words and groups of words and how they are combined to form phrases, clauses, and sentences.

Learning Objective 9.2   C. _____ The linguistic description and rules for how a language functions.

Learning Objective 9.2   D. _____ The study of how a language is acquired, perceived, understood, and produced.

Learning Objective 9.2   E. _____ The study of the sounds of language.

Learning Objective 9.2   F. _____ The basic units of sound in a language; for example, the sounds made for *p, f,* and *ch.*

Learning Objective 9.2   G. _____ The study of the meaning of words, their relationship to other words in a sentence, and the meaning of the sentence.

Learning Objective 9.3   H. _____ An approach that assumes each surface structure is accompanied by a deep structure and specific rules are followed when surface structure sentences are generated from deep structure meanings.

2. Complete each of the following sentences with one of the options provided.

Learning Objective 9.1   A. Thought and language _____ at the same rate.
                              (mature : do not necessarily mature)

Learning Objective 9.1

B. Even though the quality and quantity of verbal stimulation are both important to normal language and cognitive development, Schachter has noted that the _____ is more important.
(quality : quantity)

Learning Objective 9.2

C. All of the words in the English language are composed of _____ _____ phonemes.
(twenty-two : forty-five : eighty-seven)

Learning Objective 9.2

D. _____ is a morpheme.
("The dog is big" : To : "Th")

Learning Objective 9.2

E. The meaning of a sentence _____ the same as the definitions of the individual words in the sentence added together.
(is : is not)

Learning Objective 9.3

F. Noam Chomsky suggested that people _____ to transform an underlying basic kernel of meaning into an infinite number of sentences.
(are born with the ability : learn how)

Learning Objective 9.3

G. *"That is an enormous turkey"* and *"That turkey is enormous"* are two sentences that have a different _____ structure.
(surface : deep)

Learning Objective 9.4

H. Genie, the child who was deprived of normal stimulation, _____ _____ language skills.
(was never able to develop : developed constrained and rule-governed)

Learning Objective 9.5

I. The conditioning approach to language acquisition argues that children learn words and sentences by _____.
(imitating adults : being reinforced by parents and their own words)

Learning Objective 9.5

J. Learning theories of language acquisition fail to explain _____ _____.
(regional dialects : the generation of infinite numbers of sentences)

Learning Objective 9.5

K. Biological theorists rely heavily on the idea of brain _____ _____ when explaining language acquisition.
(holograms : syntactical combinations : lateralization)

Learning Objective 9.6

L. Terrace has suggested that chimps _____.
(can acquire true language skills : simply mirror teacher responses)

Learning Objective 9.6

M. Two words that describe the difference between how human beings and chimpanzees learn naming skills are _____.
(spontaneity and effort : meaning and symbols)

INTELLIGENCE AND INTELLIGENCE TESTING

When a child like Rachel—who opened this chapter—is suspected of having exceptional abilities, a parent, teacher, or counselor almost always desires to have a test of intelligence administered. Most people are not psychologists and cannot easily estimate the intellectual capabilities of others. Quiet people are sometimes assumed to be slow-witted, and talkative ones to be bright. Yet the extent to which people talk and communicate ideas, their effectiveness in coping with life, and their ability to demonstrate intelligent behavior are often unrelated. People can demonstrate effective and intelligent behavior in many ways, but they do not necessarily show it in all areas. For example, a student might be able to write a good computer program yet not know much about English poetry. Often, intelligence must be defined in terms of the situation in which people find themselves; intelligent behavior for a dancer can be very different from intelligent behavior for a scientist. Thus, a test of verbal ability in

People demonstrate intelligence in many ways; this mechanic shows an exceptional ability to fix automobiles.

English literature, or any other subject, is not a definitive measure of intelligence, especially for someone whose verbal skills are poor.

What Is Intelligence?

Learning Objective 9.7

This question has plagued psychologists for decades, and the answer for one psychologist often does not satisfy another. In order to examine tests, testing, and intelligence tests, it is important to have a general definition of intelligence with which most psychologists agree. Perhaps the most widely accepted definition of intelligence is that of well-known test constructor David Wechsler (1896– 1981). Wechsler (1975) suggested that intelligence is reflected in a person's ability to cope effectively with the world. Wechsler maintained that **"intelligence is the aggregate or global capacity of the individual to act purposefully, to think rationally, and to deal effectively with the environment"** (1958, p. 7). In Wechsler's definition, intelligence is expressed behaviorally— intelligence is the way people act. Wechsler's definition refers implicitly to people's ability to learn and to use knowledge learned previously. Most important from Wechsler's view, intelligence deals with people's ability to adapt to the environment. Although other definitions are perhaps just as correct, Wechsler's has had far-reaching effects on how test developers devise IQ tests and on how they have investigated the nature of intelligence itself. Specific intelligence tests and theories of intelligence are examined later in this chapter.

Intelligence tests, and tests in general, are carefully constructed to accomplish specific purposes. If Rachel were referred to a psychologist for a complete psychological assessment, the psychologist would give her a battery of tests

David Wechsler (1896–1981) developed a widely-accepted, behavioral definition of intelligence.

and conduct several interviews to evaluate her strengths and weaknesses and to understand her background. Intelligence tests *do not* measure people's innate ability, or their ability in nonacademic skills. Furthermore, some intelligence tests do not give credit for unconventional but highly creative answers. Thus, an intelligence test alone would not provide enough information for a complete assessment of someone's abilities.

Learning   9.8
Objective

A variety of achievement tests would probably reveal more about an individual's abilities, than does a single intelligence test. Achievement tests are designed to measure how much information a person has about a specific topic (such as French) or how well he or she has learned a specific skill (such as car repair). A wide range of such tests is available. The psychologist might also administer a personality test to look for any psychological abnormalities. Personality tests characterize the way people respond to situations, for example, the Minnesota Multiphasic Personality Inventory, or MMPI, (discussed in detail in Chapter 12) when interpreted carefully, accurately indicates the presence of psychological disturbances that might interfere with a person's daily functioning.

Using the results of a variety of tests and other data, psychologists can evaluate any individual's current situation, make predictions about future performance or behavior, and offer suggestions for remedial work or therapy. Although psychologists' predictions do not always come true, some tests do have strong predictive value. For example, intelligence tests generally predict academic achievement very well. Similarly, achievement tests can predict whether an individual will profit from further training in a specific area. The predictive value of tests is a result of careful test construction and standardization. Psychologists are able to make predictions about individuals because they know how others of the same age, sex, socioeconomic status, and academic achievement level have performed previously on the same tests.

At some point in your schooling, you probably took an intelligence test of one type or another. Intelligence testing is a routine procedure in most school systems, although schools do not always give information to parents about the results. Schools use test information, intelligence tests, and other tests, to track students—to place them in classes in which they will get the most from their education.

When a child like Rachel Assad, who opened this chapter, is referred to a psychologist for testing, one of the first of a battery of tests she might be given is an intelligence test. The idea of testing children has a long history. In 1905, the goal of two of the founders of the testing movement, Alfred Binet and Theodore Simon, was to separate children of normal intelligence from those of subnormal intelligence. Binet and Simon were concerned only with measuring general intelligence in children, not with why some children were retarded in intellectual development or what their future might be. One of the most influential IQ tests in use today (the Stanford-Binet), which we discuss later in the chapter, is a direct result of their early tests. As Binet and Simon's interests broadened and their conception of intelligence matured, their tests became more sophisticated. More than eighty years later, psychologists are still following some of their recommendations about how tests should be constructed and administered. However, the tests that psychologists use today—especially intelligence tests—are designed more carefully than Binet and Simon would have thought possible.

Alfred Binet (1857–1911) worked with Theodore Simon to develop the first intelligence test.

Principles of Test Development

Learning Objective 9.9

Developing a test is not a simple procedure. A psychologist does not just write down twenty multiple-choice items and publish a test. An elaborate set of guidelines and procedures must be followed to make a test worthwhile. Understanding this procedure is important.

A test is a standardized device for examining a person's responses to specific stimuli, usually questions or problems. Most people are familiar with tests, especially in school. The results of school tests can be important; they often influence decisions about a student's future. Psychologists use a large number of tests in diagnosing people's strengths and difficulties. Well-constructed tests diagnose specific problems and have good predictive value about future performance.

Developing a well-constructed test involves many steps. The first step is to decide what the test is to measure. Next, specific items must be constructed and evaluated and a uniform procedure clearly established for administering and scoring the test. Without uniform time limits and instruction and demonstration procedures, there is no basis for comparison of individuals' test results with those of a standard reference group.

Standardization is the process of developing a uniform procedure for administering and scoring a test—it also involves establishing norms. **Norms** are the scores and corresponding percentile ranks of a large and representative sample of subjects from the population for whom the test has been designed. A **representative sample** is a group of individuals who match the target population with whom they are to be compared, with regard to important variables, such as socioeconomic status and age. Thus, a test designed for college freshmen might be given to 2,000 freshmen who were chosen in such a way that they were representative of all freshmen who would eventually take the test. There might be an equal number of men and women from large and small schools and from different areas of the country. Their ages would also be representative. Thus, the scores of a sample of forty- to fifty-year-old women returning to college after their children had grown should not serve as a norm for the test results of sixteen- to twenty-year-olds.

After the test has been administered to a representative sample, the results are examined to establish what a normal score is for different segments of the test population. Proper interpretation of future results depends on knowing how most people in the representative sample have done; only then can their scores serve as a reference point for comparison of individual scores. Usually a large representative sample produces a wide spectrum of scores.

Test developers generally plot such data on a graph that shows how frequently specific scores occur. The curve rises at any point at which many people have obtained the same score. On most tests, some people do very well and some do very poorly, but most people do about average. When test scores are distributed this way, psychologists say that the data are normally distributed, or that they fall on a normal curve. A **normal curve** is a bell-shaped graphic representation of data arranged so that a certain percentage of the population falls under each part of the curve. The higher the curve, the more people are represented by a specific score. As Figure 9.3 shows, most people are in the middle range, with a few at both extremes.

The normal curve is divided into standard deviations (discussed more fully in the Appendix). In the context of testing, a standard deviation represents a

Standardization
The process of developing a uniform procedure for the administration and scoring of a test, including the development of norms from a large, representative sample.

Norms
A list of the scores and corresponding percentile ranks or standard scores of the group on whom the test was standardized.

Representative sample
A sample of individuals who match the population with whom they are to be compared, with regard to important variables such as socioeconomic status and age.

Normal curve
A bell-shaped curve arranged so that a certain percentage of the population falls under each part of the curve.

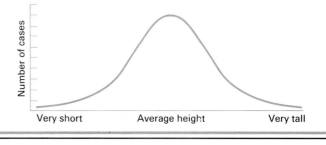

FIGURE 9.3 : This bell-shaped curve shows the normal distribution of height in the general population. As with normal distributions of weight or even intelligence, very few people are represented at the extremes.

Raw score ═══════
An examinee's unconverted score on a test (such as the number of correct answers).

Standard score ═══════
A score that expresses an individual's position relative to the mean based on the standard deviation; it is often derived by converting a raw score to one that can be interpreted on the basis of a population variable (such as age or grade).

FIGURE 9.4 : A normal curve can be divided into standard deviations. Each standard deviation above or below the mean (average) score accounts for a different percentage of the population. The first standard deviation either above or below the mean accounts for 34.13 percent of all individuals who might be measured; the second accounts for 13.59 percent. The next two standard deviations together account for only 2.27 percent. Only 0.13 percent of all people who take a standardized test obtain a score higher than three standard deviations above the mean.

certain number of points on a test that tells how much the scores spread out or vary. Each standard deviation segment accounts for a different number or percentage of the population tested. So, in Figure 9.4, 68.26 percent of all people who took the test scored within one standard deviation (plus or minus) of the mean, whereas only 0.26 percent scored more than three standard deviations above or below.

Many tests are devised to permit comparisons of individual scores against a normal distribution. For example, many intelligence tests are arranged so that the mean score (the average score) is 100 and the standard deviation is 15 or 16 points (see Figure 9.5). On such a test, 34.13 percent of the population will score from 100 to 115, and 0.13 percent will score higher than three standard deviations above the mean, or higher than 145.

Most tests contain many items, sometimes hundreds. Some tests consist of a series of subtests, each of which examines a different aspect of knowledge or intellectual functioning. The **raw score,** or simple number of correct answers, on a subtest is seldom a true indicator of a person's ability. On many tests, particularly intelligence tests, raw scores must be adjusted to take into account a person's age, sex, or grade level. These results are commonly expressed in terms of some kind of **standard score** or percentile, which indicates an individual's position relative to others. For example, suppose a 100-item intelligence test is administered to students in the third and eleventh grades. You would expect students in the eleventh grade to answer more items correctly than students in the third grade. After the test, you compare each student's score to the score typically achieved by other students at the same grade level. If eleventh-graders typically answer 70 questions correctly, then an eleventh-grader who answers 90 questions correctly will have done better than most other

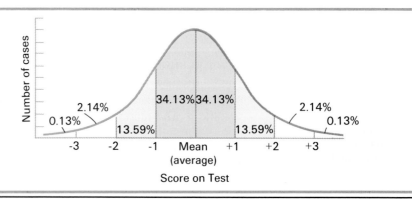

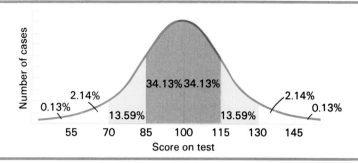

FIGURE 9.5 : On a standardized IQ test with a mean of 100 and a standard deviation of 15 points, 68.26 percent of the population will score between one standard deviation below and one standard deviation above the mean—from 85 to 115. Only 0.13 percent will score higher than 145 or lower than 55.

Percentile score ═══════
A score indicating what percentage of the test population would obtain a lower score.

students at that grade level. Similarly, if third-graders usually answer 25 questions correctly, then a third-grader who answers 15 questions correctly will have performed worse than most other students at that grade level. A **percentile score** is a standard score that indicates what percentage of other students taking the test would obtain a lower score. For example, if someone's percentile score is 84, then 84 percent of people taking the test would obtain a lower score than that person's.

Perhaps the most widely recognized test is the intelligence test. In the early 1900s, intelligence was measured by a simple formula. People's intelligence quotient (IQ) was calculated by dividing their "mental age"—a figure obtained by testing—by their chronological age, then multiplying the result by 100. Thus IQ = (mental age ÷ chronological age) × 100. Children's mental ages were calculated from their number of correct answers on a series of test items: the higher the number answered correctly, the higher their mental age. Children with a mental age of 8 years who also happened to be 8 years old would have an IQ of 100 [(8 ÷ 8) × 100]. Fifteen-year-olds with a mental age of 18 would have an IQ of 120 [(18 ÷ 15) × 100].

Deviation IQ ═══════
A standard IQ test score that has the same mean and standard deviation at all ages.

At each age, an IQ test shows different variability. To simplify measures of IQ, the deviation IQ replaced the traditional mental age/chronological age formula. A **deviation IQ** is a standard score whose mean and standard deviation remain constant at all ages. Thus, a child of nine and a child of sixteen, each with an IQ of 115, occupy the same position relative to other individuals who have taken the same IQ test: both are in the eighty-fourth percentile; that is, both have scored better than 84 percent of all other individuals their age who took the same IQ test.

Making Tests Reliable and Valid

Reliability ═══════
The ability of a test to yield the same score for the same individual through repeated testings.

Of all the achievements by psychologists in making tests useful, perhaps the most important has been to ensure that tests are both reliable and valid. If a student obtains different scores on two versions (or forms) of the same test, which score is the one to believe? **Reliability** is the consistency or stability of test scores. A test is reliable if it yields the same score for the same individual in repeated testing, or if different versions of the test yield the same score for the same individual. If a test's results are not consistent from one testing session to another or for two comparable groups of people, meaningful comparisons are impossible.

TABLE 9.1 : Types of Validity Used to Assess Tests

Validity	Aspect Measured
Content validity	The extent to which a test reflects a sample of the actual behavior to be measured
Face validity	The extent to which a test "looks" appropriate just from a reading of the items
Predictive validity	The extent to which a test can predict a person's behavior in some other setting
Construct validity	The extent to which a test actually measures a particular trait (such as intelligence, anxiety, or musical ability)

Test-retest
A method of assessing reliability by administering a test to the same group of examinees on two different occasions and computing the similarity between the scores.

Alternative-form
A method of assessing reliability by administering two forms of a test and computing the similarity between the scores.

Split-half
A method of assessing reliability by splitting a test into comparable halves and correlating the scores from each half.

Standard error of measurement
Based on statistical formulas, the number of points a score may vary because of imperfect reliability.

Validity
The ability of a test to measure only what it is supposed to measure.

There are several ways to determine whether a test is reliable. The simplest, called **test-retest,** is to administer the same test to the same individual on two or more occasions. If the person achieves a score of 90 one day and 135 another, the test is not reliable. There is also the possibility that the person remembered some of the test items from one occasion to the next. The **alternative-form** method, which involves giving two different versions of the same test, avoids this problem. If the two forms do indeed test the same characteristic and differ only in the items they present, both should yield the same result. Finally, the **split-half** method involves splitting a test into halves. The scores from each half should yield similar, if not identical, results.

A test is considered reliable if it (1) consistently gives the same results and (2) has a relatively small standard error of measurement. The **standard error of measurement** is the number of points a score may vary because of imperfect reliability. If, for example, an individual scores 115 on an IQ test whose standard error of measurement is 3 points, a practitioner can state with a high degree of confidence that the individual's real score is between 112 and 118—3 points above or below the obtained score.

The other crucial feature of a test's usefulness is its **validity**—its ability to measure what it is supposed to measure, and *only* that. A test designed to measure mechanical aptitude must measure that and not musical aptitude or personality characteristics. Similarly, an intelligence test should measure intelligence, not cultural experiences or socioeconomic status (see Table 9.1).

PROGRESS CHECK 9.2

1. Match each of the following key concepts and terms with the appropriate definition.

norms   deviation IQ   raw score   reliability
standard score   validity   percentile score   representative sample

Learning Objective 9.9

A. _____ A standard score indicating what percentage of the population under consideration would obtain a lower score.

Learning Objective 9.9   B. _____ A group of individuals who match the target population with whom they are to be compared with regard to important variables, such as socioeconomic status and age.

Learning Objective 9.9   C. _____ The scores and corresponding percentile ranks of a large and representative sample of subjects. Once the test is made available for general use, these scores serve as a reference point for comparison of the scores individuals achieve on the test.

Learning Objective 9.9   D. _____ A standard IQ test score that has the same mean and standard deviation at all ages.

Learning Objective 9.9   E. _____ The number of correct answers given on a test before the score is converted into a meaningful score.

Learning Objective 9.9   F. _____ A score that expresses an individual's relative position to the mean based on the standard deviation.

Learning Objective 9.10   G. _____ The ability of a test to give the same score for a single individual when testing is repeated or if different versions of the test are given.

Learning Objective 9.10   H. _____ A term used to describe a test that measures what it is designed to measure.

2. Complete each of the following sentences with one of the options provided.

Learning Objective 9.7   A. Wechsler's definition of intelligence is expressed _____.
(with regard to inherited abilities : behaviorally)

Learning Objective 9.7   B. The most important aspect of Wechsler's definition of intelligence is its reference to people's ability to _____.
(remember significant facts : adapt to the environment)

Learning Objective 9.8   C. If a psychologist wanted to base his or her predictions about the future performance of an individual on a complete psychological assessment of the individual, the psychologist would probably administer _____ and conduct several interviews.
(a battery of tests : the MMPI : an intelligence test)

Learning Objective 9.8   D. A test that measures knowledge of a specific topic or specific skill abilities is _____ test.
(an intelligence : an achievement : a verbal skills)

Learning Objective 9.9   E. When norms and a uniform procedure for administering and scoring a test have been established, the test is said to be _____.
(valid : standardized : unbiased)

Learning Objective 9.9   F. Norms for assessment tests are established by giving the test to _____ _____.
(talented individuals : a representative sample of the population)

Learning Objective 9.9   G. A _____ accounts for a percentage of the population that will fall within a predetermined range on a normal curve.
(standard deviation : percentile score)

Learning Objective 9.9   H. On a standardized test that compares individual scores to a normal distribution, _____ of the people who take the test will achieve a score within one standard deviation above (or below) the mean.
(0.13 percent : 34.13 percent : 50 percent)

Learning Objective 9.10   I. A standard error of measurement refers to the number of points a test score may vary from the real score because _____.
(of imperfect reliability : an alternate form of the test was used)

Learning Objective 9.10   J. To be a valid test, an intelligence test should measure intelligence _____ _____.
(as well as cultural experience and socioeconomic status : only)

THEORIES AND TESTS OF INTELLIGENCE

At one time or another, you may have met someone who you knew was a great deal smarter than anyone you had met in a long time. The individual did not necessarily have an extensive vocabulary or may not have been particularly articulate. Yet their use of facts, logical ability, and reasoning power seemed to transcend that of other individuals.

Why do two individuals who study the same amount of time for an examination achieve different scores? Why do some students succeed in medical school while others have difficulty finishing high school? Our response to these questions might be that high intelligence leads to success.

Being intellectually gifted in some cases may be obvious. A four-year-old who takes apart toasters has mechanical ability; a sixteen-year-old who understands advanced mathematics has mathematical ability; and Wolfgang Mozart was a genius musically. Intellectual ability is not easily understood, but it usually is evident.

Theories of Intelligence

Learning Objective 9.11

Different intelligence tests measure different types of intellectual functioning. Each test has its own approach to measuring intelligence. The development of today's intelligence tests followed a logical progression. First there were data, then there was a theory, and then there was a test. In the early 1900s, a large body of data emerged that described the characteristics thought to be involved in intelligence. The data included information on age, race, sex, socioeconomic status, and environmental factors. From these data, researchers developed theories to describe the nature of intelligence and how it is formed. Currently, the most influential approaches to the study of intelligence are the theories of Piaget and Wechsler, factor theories, and Jensen's two-level theory.

Piaget. As discussed in Chapter 7, Jean Piaget's theory of development centers largely on intellectual growth in children. Piaget suggested that (1) intelligence is the process of adaptation to the environment and (2) intellectual development consists of changes in the way an individual accomplishes that adaptation. According to Piaget, every child goes through an invariant series of stages in intellectual development. At each stage, different types of cognitive processes determine the types of intellectual tasks the child can accomplish. According to Piaget, three-year-olds cannot learn calculus because they are not yet ready to perform the mental operations needed to grasp the necessary concepts.

Wechsler. Wechsler argued that IQ tests involving spatial relations and verbal comprehension reveal little about an individual's overall capacity to deal with the world. He developed a test containing several subtests, each of which measures a different aspect of a person's resourcefulness. However, no one aspect measured by a subtest is identical with intelligence; it is their combination in unique ways that allows for intelligent behavior.

Wechsler tried to place test scores in a meaningful context. He contended that test scores do not measure intelligence directly but instead provide information about aspects of a person's functioning and resourcefulness. In

Wechsler's view, psychologists should remember that intelligence is more than simply mathematical or problem-solving ability; intelligence is a broader ability to deal with the world.

Factor Theories.   Factor theories use a correlation technique known as factor analysis to discover what the elements of intelligence really are. In **factor analysis,** large numbers of tasks are given to a subject, scores are derived on each task, and correlations are computed among the different tasks. The assumption is that tasks with high correlations probably test similar aspects of intellectual functioning. For example, verbal comprehension, spelling, and reading speed usually correlate highly. This fact suggests that some underlying attribute of verbal abilities determines an individual's score on all three of these tests. The **factor-theory approach to intelligence** culminated in a theory by J. P. Guilford (1967). According to Guilford, human intellectual abilities and activities can be described in terms of three major dimensions: operations, products, and contents. As Figure 9.6 shows, Guilford's three-dimensional model produces 120 factors, 80 of which Guilford says have already been demonstrated experimentally. Guilford's approach suggests that intelligence must be evaluated in terms of many different dimensions and that several scores are necessary to provide a correct assessment of an individual's abilities. Current research supports the multifactor approach to intelligence testing, and Guilford has refined and extended his model (see also Guilford, 1980, 1982).

Factor analysis
A statistical procedure designed to discover the mutually independent elements (factors) in any set of data.

Factor-theory approach to intelligence
Theories of intelligence based on factor analysis.

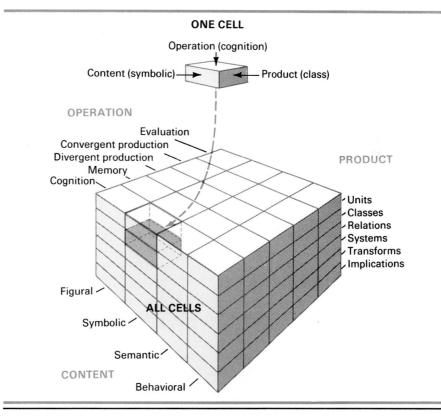

FIGURE 9.6 : Each of Guilford's three dimensions of intellectual abilities—operations, products, and content—has many attributes. Through various combinations, these dimensions and their attributes produce 120 separate factors.

Jensen's Two-Level Theory.   Arthur Jensen (1969, 1970) has suggested that intellectual functioning consists of associative abilities and cognitive abilities, both largely hereditary. Associative abilities are those that associate certain stimuli and events. The short-term memory and information tasks on IQ tests, for example, are associative. Cognitive abilities are those that deal with reasoning and problem solving. Word problems or defining a new word or concept are examples of cognitive ability tasks. This idea is not new; even the founders of the testing movement suggested that different kinds of intellectual functioning are involved in intelligence. But Jensen's claim that these abilities are inherited has prolonged and complicated the controversy (discussed in a later section in this chapter) over the relative contributions of nature and nurture to intelligence.

Three Important Intelligence Tests

Learning Objective 9.12

The Stanford-Binet Intelligence Scale.   The people most often associated with the beginning of IQ testing are Alfred Binet and Theodore Simon. Binet was commissioned in 1904 to identify procedures for the education of retarded children in Paris. Binet collaborated with Simon to develop the Binet-Simon Scale in 1905. Their original test consisted of thirty short tests, arranged in order of difficulty. These tests involved recognizing food from nonfood or pointing to objects and naming them. A child's mental age or ability was divided by chronological age; the resultant ratio was multiplied by 100 to yield an intelligence quotient, or IQ. The test was heavily biased toward verbal questions and was not standardized well. In 1916, Lewis M. Terman in the United States revised the Binet-Simon Scale and developed an intelligence test now

ZIGGY

5-8   Tom Wilson

known as the Stanford-Binet. The Stanford-Binet yields an overall IQ score. The mean is 100; the standard deviation is 16 points. Tests in the Stanford-Binet vary greatly in content. Some require perceptual discrimination; others require following directions. Some require practical considerations and the use of judgment. There are many memory tests, requiring the recall of pictures, digits, or designs. There are also tasks involving maze tracing, paper folding, and rearranging of geometric figures. Some verbal skills are required at all levels of the test and become increasingly important at the upper levels as the age being measured gets higher. A new version of the Stanford-Binet, the Stanford-Binet-Revised, was published in 1986. It provides several scores and attempts to present items that minimize gender and racial characteristics.

The Stanford-Binet has traditionally been shown to be a good predictor of academic performance. Many of its simplest tests correlate highly with one another. The Stanford-Binet Revised also correlates well with the old Stanford-Binet and also with the WISC-R and the K-ABC, discussed next. The most common underlying factors are verbal fluency and verbal reasoning ability. The new version of the Stanford-Binet may be a significant improvement because the tests' authors took great pains to develop careful standardization procedures, which may make the test especially good. However, the results are not in yet.

The Wechsler Scales.   Thanks to the efforts of David Wechsler, a psychologist who was then at the Bellevue Psychiatric Hospital in New York City, psychologists now know that IQ tests can be designed to test both verbal and nonverbal intelligence. In the 1930s, Wechsler recognized that existing versions of the Stanford-Binet were inadequate to test the IQ of adults. He also maintained that some of the Stanford-Binet items lacked validity. In 1939, Wechsler developed the Wechsler-Bellevue Intelligence Scale, standardized on a large representative sample, to test the IQ of adults. The Wechsler Adult Intelligence Scale (WAIS), published in 1955, contained fewer of the technical difficulties of the Wechsler-Bellevue. The 1981 revision is called the WAIS–R. Wechsler also developed the Wechsler Intelligence Scale for Children (WISC); revised in 1974, the WISC–R is an IQ test for children ages six through sixteen. In 1967, the Wechsler Preschool and Primary Scale of Intelligence (WPPSI) was developed for children ages four to six and a half.

The administration of the three Wechsler scales is very similar, but the content differs for adults and preschoolers. On all the tests, verbal tasks determine the verbal IQ, and performance (nonverbal) tasks determine the performance IQ. Verbal tests involve the use of language to respond to questions that require specific information, as well as the ability to describe how things are similar. The performance tests involve the manipulation of pictures, blocks, and objects in logical ways. Most performance tasks require no overt verbal responses.

The Wechsler tests provide three different IQ scores and several different subtest scores, such as vocabulary (verbal) and coding (performance). By referring to appropriate tables, an examiner can determine verbal, performance, and full-scale IQ scores. Each has a mean of 100 and a standard deviation of 15 points. Some psychologists believe that a discrepancy between the verbal and performance scores on the WISC–R can be an important diagnostic indicator (Grossman, 1983; Sattler, 1982). Particularly well researched, the Wechsler scales have been found to be valid cross-culturally (for example, Insua, 1983), with special education students (Covin & Sattler, 1985), and with learning disabled students (Clarizio & Veres, 1984).

The Kaufman Assessment Battery for Children. Psychologists Alan and Nadeen Kaufman have developed a test that they believe eliminates the biases present in other popular IQ tests. In their view, the Kaufman Assessment Battery for Children (K–ABC) uses tasks that tap the experience of all people, regardless of their background. For example, a memory task in the K–ABC might have a subject look at a picture of a face and then, moments later, identify it among pictures of other faces.

The K–ABC is an individually administered measure of intelligence and achievement that assesses styles of information processing and problem solving. It was designed especially for assessment, intervention, and remediation and was standardized on a large representative sample of both normal and exceptional children, ages two and a half through twelve and a half. This sample was derived from 1980 census data and therefore has the advantage of being current. The mean on the K–ABC is 100; the standard deviation is 15 points.

Kaufman and Kaufman (1983) define intelligence in terms of an individual's level of mental processing. Accordingly, on the K–ABC, intelligence is measured in terms of an individual's ability to process information effectively in solving novel problems (Kaufman, 1983). The K–ABC is comprised of four global scales: three measure mental processing abilities (sequential processing, simultaneous processing, and a composite of the two); the fourth assesses achievement.

The Kaufmans believe that the sequential and simultaneous processing scales measure abilities synonymous with intelligence—the ability to process information and solve problems (Kaufman, 1983). This idea is based on research and theory about brain organization. A sequential task requires the manipulation of stimuli in sequential order. For example, the child might have to perform a series of hand movements or repeat a series of digits in the same order as the examiner presented them. A simultaneous processing task involves organizing and integrating many stimuli at the same time. For example,

Nadeen and Alan Kaufman are co-authors of the Kaufman Assessment Battery for Children.

the child might have to recall the placement of pictures on a page that was presented only briefly. The K–ABC assesses the level and style of an individual's problem-solving ability on each task, minimizing the role of language and acquired facts and skills. A separate part of the test, the achievement scale, involves the demonstration of such skills as reading comprehension, letter and word identification, and computation. These tasks resemble those that typically appear on IQ tests; they are heavily influenced by language experience and verbal ability.

Early research on the K–ABC shows it to be a promising IQ test (German, 1983; Zins & Barnett, 1983), but the K–ABC is not without critics. Jensen (1984) has been critical, and Sternberg (1984) has been especially critical. Kaufman (1984) has responded, arguing that his test is valid, reliable, and an evolving test that will continue to get better. He wants it to be an alternative to the standard WISC–R and the Stanford-Binet-Revised. Many practitioners consider it child-oriented and easy to administer. The final evaluations about the K–ABC are still probably a decade away.

PROGRESS CHECK 9.3

1. Complete each of the following sentences with one of the options provided.

Learning Objective 9.11
A. According to Piaget, _____ are the primary determinants of the type of intellectual tasks a child can accomplish.
(environmental opportunities : cognitive developmental stages)

Learning Objective 9.11
B. Wechsler contended that intelligence tests provide _____ measures of intelligence.
(direct : indirect)

Learning Objective 9.11
C. Factor theories of intelligence assume that tasks that yield high correlations probably test _____ of intellectual functioning.
(some underlying attribute : different aspects)

Learning Objective 9.11
D. According to Jensen, _____ abilities are those that deal with reasoning and problem-solving skills.
(associative : cognitive)

Learning Objective 9.12
E. The most common underlying factors measured by the Stanford-Binet Intelligence Scale tests are _____ and verbal reasoning ability.
(verbal fluency : perceptual discrimination : mathematical skills)

Learning Objective 9.12
F. The Wechsler Intelligence Scale called the WPPSI was developed for _____.
(children ages four to six and a half : children ages six to sixteen : adults)

Learning Objective 9.12
G. The Wechsler Scales measure _____ intelligence.
(verbal and nonverbal : cultural : technical)

Learning Objective 9.12
H. The Kaufman Assessment Battery for Children measures an individual's ability to _____.
(solve novel problems : ask original questions : speak fluently)

Learning Objective 9.12
I. The K–ABC minimizes the effects of _____.
(inherited ability and focuses on achievement : environmental background)

Learning Objective 9.12
J. Three of the four global scales used in the K–ABC measure _____.
(achievement : mental processing abilities)

TESTS AND TESTING: CONTROVERSY

When the Assads were insisting that their daughter Rachel be tested, they made a fundamental assumption about testing itself. They trusted the tests as valid predictors of something. They assumed that achievement tests would measure Rachel's past achievement and that IQ tests might accurately predict Rachel's ability to succeed academically. However, not everyone agrees. Many psychologists and educators debate what intelligence tests actually measure. This debate reached a peak in the 1970s, when various minority groups joined psychologists and educators in challenging the usefulness of testing in general and of intelligence testing in particular. The controversy has focused on two major issues. One issue is the validity of intelligence tests. Some psychologists and educators claim that what intelligence tests measure is not really intelligence but some other characteristic. The other issue is testing bias.

Test Validity

Learning Objective 9.13

There are five basic criticisms of the validity of tests and testing. One is that there is no way to measure intelligence because no clear, uniformly agreed-on definition of intelligence exists. Mercer (1977) and other researchers respond that although different IQ tests seem to measure different abilities, as a whole, the major tests have face validity. They generally contain items requiring problem solving and rational thinking, and in Anglo-American society such a standard is considered appropriate. A second criticism is that because IQ test items usually consist of learned information, they reflect the quality of a child's schooling rather than the child's actual intelligence. The usual response to this challenge is that most vocabulary items in IQ tests are learned from the general environment, not in school; moreover, the learning of vocabulary and facts seems to depend on the ability to reason verbally. A third criticism is that school settings may adversely affect IQ and other test scores, not only because tests are often administered inexpertly in such settings, but also because halo effects are more likely there (for example, Crowl & MacGinitie, 1974). A **halo effect** is the tendency to allow preconceived attitudes about an individual to influence an evaluation of that person. People who try to defend testing against this charge acknowledge that incorrectly administered tests given in large groups are likely to result in inaccurate IQ test scores, but they claim that these effects are often exaggerated.

Halo effect
The tendency to let one of an individual's characteristics influence the evaluation of other characteristics.

Two other criticisms are less directly related to the issue of validity. One is that practice in taking tests improves some people's performance. These testwise individuals can make better use of their time than others, guess the tester's intentions, and find clues in the test (Anastasi, 1981; Millman, Bishop, & Ebel, 1965). The usual responses are that the items on IQ tests are unfamiliar even to experienced test-takers and that the effects of previous practice are seldom or never evident on IQ tests. The final criticism is that individuals' scores often depend on their motivation to succeed rather than on actual intelligence. Defenders of IQ tests agree that examinees' attitudes toward a test and their motivation are important, but they deny that the IQ tests themselves influence motivation or are greatly affected by it.

As this summary shows, critics of IQ tests are concerned mainly with the interpretations of scores. They note that test scores provided without interpretation can foster narrow conceptions in both the student and the teacher regarding the student's ability. One possible result is the neglect of talents and abilities unmeasured by such tests, perhaps leading to the inappropriate choice of a career (Rudman, 1977) or placement in school, as in Rachel Assad's case.

Cultural Biases

Learning Objective 9.14

A second major argument against testing, and specifically against IQ testing, is that tests are culturally biased and thus have been used to discriminate against individuals who do not come from, and therefore have not experienced, certain environments. A test item or subscale is considered culturally biased when, with all other factors being held constant, its content is more difficult for members of one group than for those of another (Kaufman, 1982).

Based on experiments indicating that some tests are culturally or racially biased (Shimberg, 1929; Williams, 1970), many people have suggested banning testing, especially IQ testing. They argue that certain groups of individuals who are not exposed to the same education and experiences as the white middle-class individuals for whom the tests are designed are bound to perform less well. Clearly, people who interpret IQ tests must be particularly sensitive to any potential biases in them (see Loehlin, Lindzey, & Spuhler, 1975). But although researchers have found differences among the IQ test scores of various racial and cultural groups, they have found no conclusive evidence of bias in the tests themselves. For example, one factor thought to be a potential source of test bias is the tests' use of standard English, because members of various American minority groups may have less experience with it. Yet research has shown that differences in language alone do not account for IQ differences. Hall and Turner (1974) found that whites and blacks have similar verbal comprehension, and Labov (1970) concluded that even ghetto children are "bathed in verbal stimulation from morning to night" (p. 136). Although they recognize that the quality of verbal stimulation is probably more important than the quantity (Schoggen & Schoggen, 1976), many researchers believe that, by itself, the dialect or language spoken at home has little effect on an individual's performance at school (F. F. Schachter, 1979).

Jensen (1976) examined the WISC–R scores of a random sample of 600 white and 600 black California schoolchildren in grades five through twelve. Although he found that whites scored an average of 12 points higher, he also found an average 12-point difference between siblings. After also examining a number of important variables in several widely used standardized tests of intelligence, Jensen concluded that "the notion that IQ tests discriminate largely in terms of race or social class is a myth" (p. 340). Jensen does not claim that biases cannot exist—only that they do not on tests like the WISC–R. Other well-respected psychologists support his view (Sattler, 1982; Vernon, 1979). Critics argue that IQ tests are culturally biased because they contain some items based on white middle-class experiences, which are not part of the experience of most members of minority groups (see Bersoff, 1981). Sattler has concluded that

> the evidence, gathered from many studies and with a variety of intelligence and ethnic minority groups, points to one conclusion: Intelligence tests are not culturally biased. They have the same properties for ethnic minorities as they do for white children. While there are some limited exceptions . . . this conclusion . . . appears to be warranted from an impartial assessment of the data. (1982, p. 360)

These two children may score differently on an IQ test because of their exposure to different environments.

Many of the arguments against IQ testing are based on emotional readings of the tests by biased, uninformed individuals and do not hold up to scientific scrutiny (Rudman, 1977). When IQ tests are shown truly to be biased or invalid, responsible psychologists will eliminate their use as diagnostic devices (see, for example, N. S. Cole, 1981).

IQ tests cannot predict or explain all types of intellectual behavior. They are measures derived from a small sample of a restricted range of cognitive activities. As Sattler has noted (1982), intelligence can be demonstrated in many ways; an IQ test tells little about someone's ability to be flexible in new situations and to function in mature and responsible ways (see Table 9.2). The IQ

TABLE 9.2 : Some Misconceptions about Intelligence Tests and Testing

Misconception	Reality
Intelligence tests measure innate intelligence.	*IQ scores measure some of an individual's interactions with the environment; they never solely measure innate intelligence.*
IQs are fixed and never change.	*People's IQs change throughout life, but especially from birth through age six. Even after this age, significant changes can occur.*
Intelligence tests provide perfectly reliable scores.	*Test scores are only estimates. Every test score should be reported as a statement of probability, such as: "There is a 90 percent chance that the child's IQ falls between X and Y."*
Intelligence tests measure all we need to know about a person's intelligence.	*Most intelligence tests do not measure the entire spectrum of abilities related to intellectual behavior. Some stress verbal and nonverbal intelligence but do not adequately measure other areas, such as mechanical skills, creativity, and social intelligence.*
A battery of tests can tell us everything we need to know in making judgments about a person's competence.	*No battery of tests can give a complete picture of any person. A battery can only illuminate various areas of functioning.*

Source: Adapted from Sattler, 1982, p. 64.

test score is not without use; the professional and the client must understand the meaning of the IQ test score and the insights it might provide (Tallent, 1985).

In the last two decades, the public, educators, and psychologists have scrutinized some of the weaknesses of IQ tests (Kamin, 1974). Even the courts have acknowledged the complexity of the issues involved in tests and testing. Critics have been vocal and persuasive (for example, R. L. Williams, 1970). Their arguments cannot be discounted. In isolation, IQ scores mean little. Information about an individual's home environment, personality, socioeconomic status, and special abilities is crucial to understanding his or her intellectual functioning. The same argument must be made about the Scholastic Aptitude Test (SAT). The SAT has been widely criticized as a predictor of success in college (Nairn, 1980), but other researchers claim that, in combination with high school grades, the SAT is a good predictor of success in college for different ethnic groups and income levels (R. M. Kaplan, 1982). Interpretation of test scores by knowledgeable examiners is the key to the appropriate use of tests and testing.

Over the years, psychologists have tried to eliminate bias from testing by creating better tests and to establish better norms for comparison. Hundreds of studies continue to scrutinize IQ tests for potential bias, inaccuracies, and poor questions. IQ tests have been developed to allow psychologists to make predictions about performance, not to measure innate ability, and tests such as the WISC–R are excellent predictors of academic success. Of course, no test is perfect and no test will predict future performance exactly. Factors such as motivation and family orientation to problem solving certainly affect test scores (for example, Moore, 1986). Research continues into test construction, test validation, and the causes of differences among individuals' scores. Overall, experts see tests as adequately measuring the most important elements of intelligence, despite the tests' flaws or potential flaws (Snyderman & Rothman, 1987).

INTELLIGENCE: NATURE VERSUS NURTURE

Can intelligence be increased with special training? Are we born with all the intelligence we will ever have? Are programs designed to boost scholastic achievement among minorities and the culturally disadvantaged doomed to failure or are they the avenues to a successful society?

If you believe that intelligence is fixed at birth and not subject to much change due to experience, you subscribe to the genetic or nature point of view. Proponents of this view generally assert that intelligence tests accurately portray intelligence. But if you believe that intelligence is subject to experience and training and is a fluid, ever-changing concept, then you believe in the environmental or nurture point of view. You thus believe that intelligence tests as they are presently constructed are inadequate—they do not measure a person's adaptation to a constantly changing environment.

The Debate Continues

Learning Objective 9.15 The issue of nature versus nurture was first put under the microscope of research in 1969 in an article in the *Harvard Educational Review* by Arthur Jensen. This article generated an enormous amount of debate, concern, and, later,

scientific inquiry. Jensen asked this question: How much can you boost scholastic achievement? He wanted to know if intelligence could be increased, or if
it was fixed at birth. One issue he addressed in answering these questions was
the difference in measured IQ scores between blacks and whites. In a study of
1,200 California schoolchildren, he found that on the average blacks scored 16
points lower than whites on IQ tests.

Psychologists have long recognized that biological capacities established
even before birth, as well as people's life experiences, play an important role in
intelligence. They have observed how changes in an organism's environment
and biological functioning can affect its performance. As in other areas of psychology, researchers have debated the relative importance of nature and nurture in the development of intelligence. Jensen entered the debate on the side
of nature. Since 1969, he has continued to maintain that genetic heritage contributes significantly more than environmental factors do to the development of
intelligence (Jensen, 1976, 1977, 1980). The scientific community's response to
Jensen's claim was immediate. Psychologists criticized his logic and challenged
the accuracy of the studies he cited and the validity of IQ tests in general.
Jensen and those who adopted similar positions became targets of political and
personal abuse (see also Jensen & Inouye, 1980).

Adoption Studies

*Learning
Objective* 9.16

Researchers have tried to determine the relative influences of environment and
heredity by comparing the intellectual abilities of adopted children with the
abilities of their adoptive parents (J. M. Horn, 1983). Many of these studies have
used twins who were separated at birth. Identical (monozygotic) twins share
the same genetic heritage; therefore, any differences in their IQs must be the
result of environmental influences. Fraternal (dizygotic) twins have no more or
less genetic similarity than any other siblings. Loehlin, Lindzey, and Spuhler
(1975) analyzed many twin studies of both black and white children and concluded that the data were insufficient to confirm whether differences in the
measured IQs of blacks and whites are due to genetic or environmental causes.
One research team at the University of Southern California (Longstreath et al.,
1981) has tried to separate home intellectual environment and maternal IQ.
Their data strongly suggest that home environment has a much smaller effect
than the genetic influence of the mother's IQ. Other studies have found some
evidence in support of genetic differences (Scarr & Weinberg, 1983; Thompson,
Plomin, & DeFries, 1985), particularly at young ages but others have found
evidence that supports the influence of environment (for example, Plomin &
DeFries, 1980, 1983). If genetics were the sole factor in determining IQ, the
correlation for identical twins should be 1.0 whether they were raised together
or apart. Furthermore, the correlation decreases when any two siblings (twins
or not) are brought up apart from one another. These two findings lend strong
support to the idea that environment must play a role, if not the more important role, in determining IQ scores.

Many studies show that environment and lack of cultural opportunities or
experiences affect IQ scores. Adoption studies show clearly that environment
can augment intellectual achievement. One French adoption study showed a
14-point increase in IQ in children whose biological parents were unskilled
workers but whose adoptive parents were in a higher socioeconomic class

(Schiff, Duyme, Dumaret, & Tomkiewicz, 1982). In the same way, motivational changes induced by federal intervention programs such as Head Start have resulted in a 10-point IQ advantage (Zigler, Abelson, Trickett, & Seitz, 1982). Studies have also shown that where a person is raised affects IQ. Several studies have administered IQ tests to children reared in several communities in the Blue Ridge Mountains, an isolated area 100 miles west of Washington, D.C. Each community was composed of a few families in scattered, mud-plastered log huts. Most of the adults were illiterate, and communication with the outside world was limited. The investigators concluded that lack of language training and school experience accounted for the children's poor scores on standardized tests, particularly on tests that involved calculation and problem solving. The examiner often was unclear as to whether the child had correctly understood the directions. Because the IQs of the children were highest in communities with the fullest social development and lowest in communities with the least social development, the researchers concluded that the IQs of the children developed only as their environment demanded development. Sherman and Key (1932) also concluded from their studies that a person's IQ depends on the information-gathering opportunities available to that person. Of course, critics of IQ tests argue that if an IQ test is to measure differences in intellectual ability, it should do so regardless of social development. The issue has become even more complicated because some of the early studies on the role of genetics in IQ have been shown to have serious scientific flaws. Worse, some of the data were actually faked (see Hearnshaw, 1979; Kamin, 1974).

Other Factors in the Environment

Some researchers claim that current theorizing will never resolve the issue of nature versus nurture in intelligence testing (Mackenzie, 1984; Vroon, de Leeuw, & Meester, 1986). Factors such as family structure, number of children in the family, and other variables may be important (Rodgers & Rowe, 1985). For example, an inspiring English teacher, a stimulating television series, or a neighbor with a chemistry set may be variables that affect differences between the IQ of siblings (McCall, 1983). If such variables affect differences between brothers and sisters, it may be very difficult to estimate how they may affect differences between racial or ethnic groups.

Black–white differences in IQ, SAT scores, and other measures of achievement or ability are narrowing. The reasons for this narrowing of differences may be due to a generation of desegregation, more equal opportunities under the law, federal intervention programs for the culturally disadvantaged, socioeconomic factors that affect home environments, or to other factors (L. V. Jones, 1984). A gap in scores still exists. Even though blacks as a group score lower than whites on IQ tests, no systematic or convincing data exist to show that genetics affects the IQ of blacks, whites, or different ethnic minorities more than environment (Mackintosh, 1986). Recent research has shown that observed differences can be minimized with certain specialized training in problem-solving skills (for example, Borkowski & Krause, 1983). As Moore (1986) suggests,

> The use of a single standard to estimate the cognitive functioning of all children places those socialized in different cultural traditions at a significant disadvantage because they are not given credit for knowledge and behavioral styles derived from

their particular experience. Therefore, the average lower performance of black children on such measures is possibly an artifact of test content and procedures. (p. 317)

The interpretation of tests scores remains critical, but the relative importance of three factors has yet to be established: first, a genetic component may be involved; second, blacks in the United States are disproportionately represented among those who live in culturally impoverished areas; and third, IQ tests may contain a built-in bias against blacks. Perhaps more important than disputing the role of genetics, environment, or test bias is the recognition that within any racial or ethnic group, the differences among individuals are greater than the differences among the groups.

Finally, the fact remains that, to a great extent, rather than measuring innate intellectual capacity, IQ tests measure the degree to which people have adapted to the culture in which they live. All individuals have special capabilities, and how those capabilities are regarded is socially dependent. Being a genius in Africa may mean being a fine hunter or a good storyteller; in the United States, it may mean being an astute and aggressive salesperson. Too often, the concept of giftedness is attached to high academic achievement alone. This limited conception of intelligence is one reason educators in some settings are placing less emphasis on IQ test scores.

Researchers today are asserting that typical tests of intelligence are too limited because they do not take into account the many forms of intelligent behavior that occur outside the testing room (Frederiksen, 1986). Frederiksen suggests that realistic real-life problem situations might be used to supplement the usual psychological tests. This view is consistent with the idea of Robert Sternberg (1985) that intelligence must be evaluated on many levels, including the environment in which a person lives and works. This means examining how people solve problems in their world, how they deal with novel situations, and real-life problem-solving situations.

Your intelligence...   can expand...   or be shaped.

Family Size and Intelligence

Learning $\underline{9.17}$
Objective

The number of brothers or sisters you have may also influence your intelligence. Children from large families score lower on intelligence tests than those from smaller families. Some psychologists argue that family size may be one of the important environmental factors that determine a person's intelligence. University of Michigan psychologists Robert Zajonc and Gregory Markus (1975) found that when family size increases, scores on intelligence and achievement tests decrease. Furthermore, they suggest that the third and fourth child has a less optimal intellectual environment than a first or second child. These researchers believe that within a family, the intellectual growth of every member depends on the other members of the family. For example, when two mature adults have a child, the intellectual climate at home is that of two mature adults and a child. If we assign each adult 30 units and the child 0 units, the average level of intellectual ability in the home is 20 (60 ÷ 3). With a second child, the intellectual average decreases further. Even if we assign 2 units to the first child instead of 0, the average level of intellectual functioning in the family is only 15.5 (62 ÷ 4). With a third child, the average decreases to 13.2 (30 + 30 + 4 + 2 + 0 = 66 ÷ 5) (If you assume that the first child has matured to 4 units). See Table 9.3.

Zajonc and Markus suggest that the overall level of intellectual performance is likely to decrease for each new member of a family. Their model also suggests that children born earlier in a family perform better than children who are born later. Some research supports these claims (Munroe & Munroe, 1983); other research has tested them but failed to confirm them (for example, Brackbill & Nichols, 1982; Galbraith, 1982, 1983). Researchers like Richard Galbraith (1983) suggest that the focus of the model is invalid and that it should be reconceptualized. Zajonc maintains that his critics' analyses are wrong (Berbam, Moreland and Zajonc, 1986; Zajonc, 1983). He also asserts the effects of birth order on intelligence are most evident in teenagers.

TABLE 9.3: The Zajonc-Markus Model of Intellectual Climate in the Home

Year of Birth of Child	Number of Children	Value of Intellectual Climate	Average No. of Units
		Formula	
1970	1	Mother (30) + Father (30) + Baby (0) / Number in family (3)	=20.0
1972	2	Mother (30) + Father (30) + First child (2) + Baby (0) / Number in family (4)	=15.5
1974	3	66 ÷ 5	13.2
1976	4	72 ÷ 6	12.0
1978	5	80 ÷ 7	11.4
1980	6	90 ÷ 8	11.3
1982	7	102 ÷ 9	11.3
1984	8	116 ÷ 10	11.6
1986	9	132 ÷ 11	12.0
1988	10	150 ÷ 12	12.5

Note: This example assumes that for each 2 years of life, a child is credited with 2 units toward the intellectual climate in the home.

Zajonc and Markus's model of intelligence, birth order, and family size is a statistical one; the researchers acknowledge that it will not hold true for all individuals and all families. Even when it does apply, the effects are small. Furthermore, the researchers point out that other important factors, such as increased spacing between the birth of children, can cancel the negative effects. Large families also may contribute to the growth of individual members in areas other than intelligence by nurturing feelings of social competence, moral responsibility, and ego strength.

Because family size has decreased in the last two decades, and the spacing between children has increased, Zajonc and Markus predict that the declining trend in Scholastic Aptitude Test (SAT) scores, which began in the late 1960s, will be reversed in the late 1980s and early 1990s. The direction the trend actually takes will be the real test of their model (Zajonc, 1976, 1983; Zajonc & Bargh, 1980).

PROGRESS CHECK 9.4

1. Complete each of the following sentences with one of the options provided.

Learning Objective 9.13
A. Psychologists _____ intelligence tests actually measure intelligence.
(are convinced that : debate whether)

Learning Objective 9.13
B. Critics of intelligence tests who argue that a teacher's preconceived attitudes about a child will influence the evaluation of that child are concerned with _____.
(face validity : halo effects : the influences of motivation)

Learning Objective 9.13
C. Critics of the validity of IQ tests are concerned mainly with the _____.
(complexity of the tests : interpretation of scores)

Learning Objective 9.14
D. An intelligence test item is considered culturally biased if, because of _____ , it is more difficult for members of one group of people than for those of another group.
(innate abilities : life experiences : motivation and desire to succeed)

Learning Objective 9.14
E. To date, scientific studies examining the concern over cultural biases on intelligence tests suggest that most of the tests _____ culturally biased.
(are : are not)

Learning Objective 9.14
F. Most psychologists believe that an IQ score _____.
(can be taken at face value : has little meaning in isolation)

Learning Objective 9.15
G. An enormous amount of debate and scientific inquiry was prompted by Jensen's claim that _____ is the most significant factor contributing to intellectual ability.
(nature : nurture)

Learning Objective 9.16
H. Most of the twin and adoption studies investigating the relative contribution of nature and nurture to intellectual abilities suggest that _____ genetic heritage.
(IQ is determined by : nurture contributes equally or more than)

Learning Objective 9.16
I. The differences between the IQ and SAT scores of blacks and whites are _____.
(broadening : narrowing)

Learning Objective 9.16   J.   The differences in IQ scores among people within a particular racial or ethnic group are _____ than the differences between racial and ethnic groups.
(smaller : greater)

Learning Objective 9.17   K.   According to Zajonc and Markus, as family size increases, the intelligence scores of the children in the family _____ .
(also increase : decrease)

THE GIFTED

Learning Objective 9.18

If you were told that a child had an exceptionally high score on an intelligence test, you might be able to make some reasonable inferences about the child. You would be able to tell the parents that the child should do well in school. One thing psychologists know about IQ tests is that they are good predictors of academic achievement. It is not surprising, then, that IQ tests are a principal method (but not the only method) of determining who is a gifted child. Remember Rachel, who opened this chapter. She might be called gifted because of her high IQ, but she might not be so classified.

Gifted children are carefully defined by psychologists and educators. Gifted individuals represent one end of the continuum of intelligent and talented behavior. But exceptional ability is not limited to cognitive skills. Some children and adults are exceptional athletes or artists. Most six-year-olds enrolled in a ballet class will probably show average ability; dance teachers report that only an occasional child has a natural ability for dance. In the same way, many children and adults learn to play the piano, but few excel. Over a wide range of behaviors, some people excel in a particular area far beyond normal expectations but in other areas are rather average. Many gifted artists, musicians, and dancers would have only average scores on standardized IQ tests.

The phenomenon of gifted children has been recognized and discussed for centuries. Some, like Mozart, display their genius musically. Others display it in science; many great scientists made their most important theoretical discoveries very early in their careers. Although there is no universally accepted definition of giftedness (just as there is no universally agreed-on definition of intelligence), one definition has been in fairly wide use since 1972. It was given by then Commissioner of Education S. P. Marland in a report to the U. S. Congress.

> Gifted and talented children are those identifiable by professionally qualified persons and who by virtue of their outstanding abilities are capable of high performance. These are children who require education programs and services beyond those normally provided by the regular school program. . . .
>
> Children capable of high performance include those with demonstrated achievements and/or potential in any of the following areas: (a) general intellectual ability, (b) specific academic aptitude, (c) creative or productive thinking, (d) leadership ability, (e) visual and performing arts, or (f) psychomotor ability. (Marland, 1972, p. i-3)

The gifted child has a unique set of abilities. They may be superior cognitive abilities, leadership abilities, or abilities in the performing arts. As defined by Marland, gifted individuals require special education that goes beyond normal classroom activities. Without such special schooling, gifted individuals may not realize their full potential.

The United States has a special love-hate relationship with gifted individuals (Gallagher, 1979). Everyone wants the gifted to succeed; their successes

Gifted children, such as Olympic skater Jill Frost, show exceptional ability in particular areas.

represent future breakthroughs in both science and the arts. Yet public schools are designed for the average child. In some school systems, the special student, often the gifted one, is relegated to the back of the classroom or isolated in other ways from the other children simply because he or she is different. Such settings not only do not foster the gifted child's uniqueness, but they also sometimes even promote ridicule of that uniqueness.

The federal government has acknowledged the need for special education for gifted individuals, but states and communities bear the major financial burden for education (about 92 percent). In any year, states such as California, Pennsylvania, and Illinois spend more than the federal government on educating gifted and talented students. Some school systems have no programs; others allocate special instruction only in brief periods or to small groups. Schools in large cities are more likely to offer special programs that allow children to leave their regular classrooms for a certain period of each day, week, or month. Some school systems provide schools specifically for children with superior cognitive abilities—schools for the performing arts, or schools of science.

When a child expresses a desire to play a musical instrument or displays outstanding athletic abilities, most parents encourage that interest. Because formal education generally takes place in schools, educators should likewise foster children's exceptional intellectual abilities, using tests and teacher input to identify gifted and talented students and developing programs that encourage them to develop their potential. Society has an obligation to itself and to the gifted to nurture and foster their intellectual and talented gifts. The intelligence measured on an IQ test is indicative of a child's reasoning powers, and such reasoning powers can be expanded and enriched rather than left dormant.

MENTAL RETARDATION

Learning Objective 9.19

All parents want their children to grow, prosper, and make the most of their lives. Exceptional children like Rachel have the capacity to achieve great things. The term *exceptional*, however, refers not only to gifted children like Rachel but also to the learning disabled, the physically handicapped, and the mentally retarded. Mental retardation covers a wide range of behaviors from slow learning to severe mental and physical impairment. Many mentally retarded people are able to cope with their environment. Most of them learn to walk, to feed themselves, and to dress themselves; many work. Like other people, the mentally retarded hug those they love, ask for their parents and siblings, and get angry when things do not go well.

Mental retardation ═══
Below-average intellectual functioning as measured on an IQ test, accompanied by an impairment in adaptive behavior originating during childhood.

A diagnosis of **mental retardation** involves three criteria: a lower-than-normal IQ, as measured on a standardized test such as the WISC–R or the WAIS–R; difficulty adapting to the environment; and the presence of such problems before age eighteen. A score below 70 on a standardized IQ test is considered below normal. If the normal distribution curve is valid, about 3 percent of the population—or about 7 million people of the 241 million in the United States—are potentially retarded.

Levels of Retardation

There are four basic levels of mental retardation, each corresponding to a different range of scores on a standardized test of intelligence (see Table 9.4).

TABLE 9.4 Types and Distribution of Mental Retardation as Measured on the Stanford-Binet and Wechsler Tests

Classification	Stanford-Binet IQ	Wechsler IQ	Percentage of the Mentally Retarded
Mild	52–68	55–69	90
Moderate	36–51	40–54	6
Severe	20–35	25–39	3
Profound	Below 20	Below 25	1

Mild Retardation. The mildly mentally retarded (Wechsler IQs of 55 to 69) account for approximately 90 percent of people classified as retarded. Most can cope successfully with their environments with some help from family and friends. They usually require some degree of supervision in their work, but they can acquire certain academic and occupational skills (see, for example, Allington, 1981). As adults, they function intellectually at the level of a ten-year-old. There are many special programs that train the mildly retarded to work and teach them how to get along in the community. Few need to be institutionalized or exhibit severe behavior problems, although they sometimes display mild behavior problems in regular classrooms and the community.

Moderate Retardation. Moderate mental retardation (Wechsler IQs of 40 to 54) accounts for approximately 6 percent of those classified as retarded. Most live in an institution or as dependents on their families. Those who are not institutionalized need special classes and can hold simple jobs, though few are employed. The moderately retarded are able to speak, write, and interact with friends, but their motor coordination, posture, and social skills are clumsy. Their intellectual level is equivalent to that of a five- to six-year-old.

Severe Retardation. Only about 3 percent of retarded people display severe retardation (Wechsler IQs of 25 to 39). The severely retarded show severe motor, speech, and intellectual impairment and are dependent in various degrees on the staff of the institutions in which they live. They engage in little verbal activity. Most are unable to perform personal hygiene tasks and can perform simple tasks only with training. Severe retardation often results from birth disorders or traumatic injury to the brain.

Profound Retardation. One percent of the mentally retarded are classified as profoundly retarded (IQ below 25). These people are unable to master even simple tasks and require total supervision and constant care in an institution. Both their motor and intellectual development are minimal. Many are physically underdeveloped. Physical deformities and other congenital defects (such as deafness, blindness, and seizures) often accompany profound mental retardation.

Causes of Retardation

Learning Objective 9.20

In mental retardation, as in other areas of intellectual functioning, both nature and nurture are involved. Most researchers agree that organic factors are the

TABLE 9.5 : Biological Causes of Mental Retardation

Type of Event	Example
Systemic disease	Down's syndrome (mongolism) Phenylketonuria (PKU)
Infectious disease	Rubella (German measles) Encephalitis Syphilis
Physical trauma	Malnutrition Poisoning Hypoxia (oxygen deprivation)

primary causes of moderate, severe, and profound retardation. In cases of mild retardation, however, many psychologists cite such environmental factors as stress, culture, and family relationships as the principal causes.

Biological. An injury or disease before birth or in early childhood can cause brain damage or physical deformities that result in severe or profound retardation. Three types of organic events can cause retardation before birth (see Table 9.5). *Systemic diseases* include chromosomal aberrations (such as Down's syndrome) and genetically related metabolic disorders (such as phenylketonuria, PKU). *Infectious diseases* include rubella (German measles) and syphilis. *Physical trauma* includes poison, hormonal deficiency, malnutrition, and hypoxia, or a lack of oxygen in the mother's bloodstream. Pregnant women who smoke a great deal have a lower-than-normal level of oxygen in their bloodstreams; a direct causal relation between heavy smoking and mental retardation has not yet been firmly established, however.

Environmental. Individuals in whom no physiological basis for retardation can be identified and who remain mentally retarded are referred to as *socioculturally mentally retarded.* These individuals often have at least one relative, (usually a parent or sibling) who is also retarded. Most of them are classified as mildly retarded. Many come from lower socioeconomic classes and have been raised in environments that do not provide intellectual stimulation, require large amounts of intellectual activity, or otherwise foster intellectual growth. Because the mildly retarded can get along with others, are able to speak, and do not show severe motor disturbances, they often do not show signs of retardation until they begin school. Generally, the socioculturally retarded have better chances for development and growth than do people whose retardation stems from organic causes.

Education: Mainstreaming

Learning Objective 9.21

Along with other handicapped people, the mentally retarded are guaranteed a right to appropriate testing, evaluation, and education. In the last two decades, individuals have appealed to the courts to ensure proper education for the physically and mentally handicapped. They have argued that the constitutional rights of the handicapped are actively violated when they are tested and evaluated in inappropriate ways, and the courts have agreed. Under Public Law

Many mentally retarded individuals are able to complete their education and hold steady jobs.

94-142 (the Education for All Handicapped Children Act, 1975), the rights of minorities and the handicapped have been given special protection. Sattler has summarized this complicated law as follows:

> It mandates, for example, (a) that consideration be given to the child's native language, (b) that only valid tests be used for the assessment, (c) that more than one assessment technique be used, (d) that the child's physical handicaps be considered, (e) that all relevant factors be considered in the evaluation, (f) that a team approach be used, (g) that the assessment procedures not be racially or culturally discriminatory, (h) that an individualized educational program be designed, (i) that parents have the right to an independent evaluation, (j) that reevaluations be performed at least every three years, (k) that parents have the right to examine their child's records, and (l) that the child be placed in the least restrictive educational environment. (Sattler, 1982, p. 532)

This law is still being tested in the courts. The next decade may bring further changes in it, and psychologists may play an even more important role in determining the educational placement of the mentally retarded.

Traditionally, mildly retarded children have been sent to special schools. Over the past twenty years, however, there has been a shift toward mainstreaming in the public schools. **Mainstreaming** is the integration of mentally retarded children (and all children with special needs) into regular classroom settings. Its purpose is to help make life as normal as possible for the retarded child. In mainstreaming, children are assigned to a regular class for at least half of their school day. Consultants and teachers with special skills help with classroom instruction. Regular classroom procedures are modified only when necessary. Finally, each child's educational needs are assessed on the basis of

Mainstreaming
The administrative practice of placing exceptional children in regular classroom settings with the support of special education services.

actual performance in the classroom rather than on the basis of arbitrarily assigned labels (see Birch, 1974).

Various research studies of mainstreaming have produced conflicting data on its effectiveness. However, psychologists and educators in the field generally support mainstreaming. As a result, schools are rapidly placing children in new environments and replacing old methods as educators develop new ways of helping the retarded. It is likely that the next decade will bring further changes in the education of the retarded to allow each child, teenager, and adult to develop as fully as he or she can.

The Mentally Retarded and Employment

Increasingly, employers are coming to the aid of mentally retarded individuals for their mutual benefit. Many companies are hiring retarded workers once thought unemployable. Companies are realizing that if the retarded are placed in the right job, properly trained, and effectively motivated, they can be counted on to be good workers.

One drawback to hiring the mentally retarded is that training them often requires extra patience. However, once the workers are trained, they have few problems adjusting to the routine of a nine-to-five job. Another drawback is that mentally retarded workers sometimes need prompts from supervisors, or a check list to help keep them focused on their job. In addition, they often work more slowly than do nonretarded individuals in the same position.

On the positive side, retarded workers are likely to stay on a job of which others grow tired. In addition, the federal government provides tax benefits to employers of the retarded or physically handicapped. In balance, mentally retarded workers can benefit some employers in some industries. Those industries have to give these individuals a chance to prove their worth.

PROGRESS CHECK 9.5

1. Complete each of the following sentences with one of the options provided.

Learning Objective 9.18

A. Psychologists feel fairly confident that intelligence tests are good predictors of _____.
   (how flexible an individual can be : academic achievement)

Learning Objective 9.18

B. To be classified as gifted, an individual _____ exhibit above average intelligence.
   (must : does not have to)

Learning Objective 9.18

C. Gifted children _____ in at least one area.
   (are capable of high performance : do not require formal schooling)

Learning Objective 9.19

D. The term *exceptional* is used to describe _____ individuals.
   (only gifted : gifted, mentally retarded, and other)

Learning Objective 9.19

E. A person whose measured IQ is lower than _____ will probably be classified as mentally retarded.
   (70 : 85 : 100)

Learning Objective 9.20

F. Moderate, severe, and profound cases of mental retardation are generally the result of _____ causes.
   (organic : environmental)

Learning Objective 9.20   G. If a child is born mentally retarded because the mother was malnourished during her pregnancy, the mental retardation is the result of _____.
(a systemic disease : an infectious disease : physical trauma)

Learning Objective 9.20   H. Socioculturally mentally retarded children often _____.
(improve by age three : have one relative who is also retarded)

Learning Objective 9.21   I. The focus of mainstreaming is to help _____ the lives of mentally retarded children.
(shelter : normalize : determine goals in)

Learning Objective 9.21   J. In a mainstreaming educational program, _____ the criteria used to place children in a particular classroom.
(actual performance is : diagnostic labels are)

Learning Objective 9.21   K. Mentally retarded individuals _____ good employees.
(are seldom : can be)

Keeping Pace with Chapter 9

Applying Principles

9.1 Identify the type of mental retardation involved in each of the following situations.

mild retardation   severe retardation   moderate retardation   profound retardation

_____   A. Marceil has an IQ of 27. She lives on a ward in a state home for the mentally retarded and is very dependent on the staff to take care of her personal hygiene and to teach her very simple and basic skills. She talks a little, but not well or frequently.

_____   B. Ivan has an IQ of 67. He works eight hours a day in a warehouse under close supervision. He lives with a friend in an apartment near his family. He is able to live a fairly normal life although sometimes he gets confused and needs help to cope successfully with normal responsibilities and tasks involved in living.

_____   C. Blake is able to interact with friends, and he can write some words and sentences. He can pour a glass of milk and make a peanut butter sandwich by himself and can understand instructions on where to find a can of green beans in the grocery store. He is dependent on his family, but he earns a little money sweeping the floor at a nearby gas station. He frequently annoys people because he tends to interrupt conversations. Blake's IQ score is 45.

_____   D. Paul lives in an institution and cannot feed himself, walk, or talk, although he sometimes communicates with strange gestures and noises. His head is small and narrow in comparison to the rest of his body, and he was born with other congenital problems. Paul requires constant supervision and care. His IQ is estimated to be around 19.

Self-Test

Before proceeding to the Self-Test, REVIEW the Learning Objectives listed at the chapter opening and RECITE from memory everything you can remember in support of them. Then, take this Self-Test as if it were to be graded by your teacher. Use the Learning Objective numbers in the Answer Section as a reference to restudy the corresponding text pages and Progress Checks for any incorrectly answered questions.

1. For language to develop normally, a child must have a caregiver who

   A. speaks the language of the surrounding culture.
   B. plays sound games to teach phonemes.
   C. permits at least some exchange of language.
   D. understands how language develops.

2. A person who examines the meaning of the word *love* in the sentence "I love roses" is concerned with

   A. grammar.
   B. semantics.
   C. syntax.
   D. phonology.

3. Which of the following sentences is a transformation of the deep structure of the sentence "Clowns make me laugh"?

   A. "Clowns have funny faces."
   B. "I laugh when I watch clowns."
   C. "Clowns make me laugh."
   D. "Some clowns frown."

4. After being taken away from her isolated existence at age thirteen, Genie was unable to develop normal language because

   A. she had not received proper stimulation during her biological readiness stage.
   B. her vocal cords were underdeveloped.
   C. a systemic disease had left her mentally retarded.
   D. she was easily distracted by external stimuli and could not attend to verbal stimuli.

5. Although learning theories do account for some aspects of language acquisition, one thing they do *not* adequately explain is

   A. how regional dialects develop.
   B. how language acquisition becomes reinforcing in and of itself.
   C. the role that environmental influences have on the development of language.
   D. why certain behaviors such as language tend to develop in all children at about the same age.

6. Although chimpanzees have been taught languagelike abilities, they have not been able to

   A. attach meaning to symbols.
   B. combine symbols in meaningful ways in order to create sentences.
   C. generate novel and alternative ways of expressing an idea.
   D. learn a style of communication that can be understood by human beings.

7. Which of the following is usually *not* included in Wechsler's definition of intelligence?

   A. The idea that intelligence can be observed in behavior.
   B. A statement concerning a person's perceptual abilities.
   C. Reference to a person's ability to learn and use previously learned information.
   D. An idea concerning one's ability to adapt to the environment.

8. The Minnesota Multiphasic Personality Inventory (MMPI)

   A. measures intelligence.
   B. is an achievement test.
   C. cannot be standardized.
   D. accurately indicates the presence of psychological disturbances.

9. Chuck's teacher informed him that 92 percent of his classmates scored lower than he did on an intelligence test. The number 92 represents

   A. an intelligence quotient.
   B. a standard deviation.
   C. a percentile score.
   D. a raw score.

10. Which of the following is *not* a way of determining whether a test is reliable?

   A. Give the same test to the same person two or more times.
   B. Give the same person several alternate forms of the same test.
   C. Give a person one-half of a test and then the other half and compare the scores of both halves.
   D. Give a person the same test in two completely different testing environments.

11. Joy achieves an IQ score of 121 on an intelligence test she has just taken. The psychologist tells her he feels confident that her real IQ score falls somewhere between 116 and 126. This indicates that the test must

   A. not be reliable.
   B. not be valid.
   C. have a standard error of measurement of five points.
   D. make use of deviation IQs.

12. Wechsler argued that intelligence tests

   A. must be restricted to measures of spatial relations and verbal comprehension.
   B. provide a direct measure of intelligence.
   C. measure ideas that are equivalent to learned facts and nothing more.
   D. provide information about a person's intellectual functioning and resourcefulness.

13. Which of the following aspects of the Wechsler Intelligence Scales *differs* among the three tests?

   A. The content.
   B. How the tests are administered.
   C. How the tests are scored.
   D. The type of tasks (verbal or performance) that are involved.

14. Which of the following arguments is given in support of the validity of intelligence testing as a way of assessing a person's intellectual ability?

   A. IQ tests reflect the quality of a child's education.
   B. In Anglo-American society, IQ scores based on standardized tests are considered appropriate.
   C. Halo effects from evaluating IQ scores help some students.
   D. Practice in test taking helps students achieve better scores.

15. The concern that intelligence tests may be culturally biased

   A. is ignored by most psychologists.
   B. must be considered with sensitivity by people who interpret test scores.
   C. is one of Arthur Jensen's main criticisms of intelligence testing.
   D. is validated more often than not by scientific studies.

16. Jensen's claim that genetic heritage contributes significantly more than environmental factors to the development of intelligence

   A. is supported by data gathered from twin studies.
   B. is supported by Shimberg's study.
   C. made him a target of political and personal abuse.
   D. B and C

17. One explanation for why blacks as a group tend to score lower than whites on IQ tests is that

    A. IQ tests may contain a built-in cultural bias.
    B. blacks are disproportionately represented among those who live in culturally impoverished areas.
    C. a genetic component may be involved.
    D. all of the above are possible explanations, and research needs to continue in these areas.

18. Zajonc and Markus argue that the most important determinant(s) of an individual's level of intellectual functioning

    A. are family size and birth order.
    B. involves brain organization.
    C. is reading speed.
    D. is the intelligence level of the person's mother and father.

19. Intelligence tests are often used to determine whether a child is gifted because

    A. to be classified as gifted, a person must have an IQ score above 130.
    B. giftedness cannot be determined in any other way.
    C. gifted people will complete an intelligence test in less time than nongifted people.
    D. they are good predictors of academic achievement.

20. A gifted person will demonstrate a high level of performance in his or her

    A. creative or productive thinking abilities.
    B. leadership abilities.
    C. visual, performing arts, or psychomotor abilities.
    D. abilities in all or one of the above areas or in some other area.

21. A mildly retarded person can

    A. achieve an intellectual level comparable to a sixteen-year-old.
    B. work in skill areas with some supervision.
    C. care for himself in basic hygiene areas but cannot do much more on his own.
    D. achieve an IQ score above 70 on an intelligence test.

22. Individuals who are mentally retarded because of _____ have the best chance for developing some academic and occupational skills.

    A. organic causes
    B. sociocultural conditions
    C. physical trauma
    D. infectious diseases

23. When a child is placed in a mainstreaming educational system, the child typically

    A. stays in a regular classroom setting for at least half of the school day.
    B. learns from teaching other children who are mentally retarded.
    C. is assessed according to his or her mental age level and type of retardation.
    D. has only one teacher and learns on a one-to-one tutorial basis.

10

Social
Psychology

10

Learning Objectives

When you have mastered the material in this chapter, you will be able to:

1. Define *socialization* and briefly describe the field of social psychology. (p. 372)

2. Define *attitude*, describe the three basic components of an attitude, and describe three theories that offer ideas about how attitudes are formed. (p. 373)

3. Discuss how advertisements and interpersonal sources influence attitudes and attitude change. (p. 373)

4. Define *dissonance* and describe Leon Festinger's cognitive dissonance theory. (p. 377)

5. Describe Daryl Bem's self-perception model and also the balance and reactance theories of attitude and behavior change. (p. 377)

6. Discuss some of the ways we express ourselves by means of nonverbal communication and explain what psychologists know about the effects of having eye contact with other people. (p. 380)

7. Explain how we make decisions concerning the character of other people through the process of attribution. (p. 382)

8. Describe some ways in which we make errors when attributing motives to our own behaviors and the behaviors of other people. (p. 384)

9. Explain how self-perceptions develop and how they affect our psychological health. (p. 385)

10. Describe what is meant by self-serving biases and explain why people develop them. (p. 387)

11. Explain how learned helplessness develops. (p. 388)

12. Define *aggression* and describe three major approaches that attempt to explain why people are aggressive. (p. 390)

13. Discuss the influence television has on behavior and attitudes. (p. 391)

14. Describe Solomon Asch's classic experiment on conformity, identify some characteristics of a group that influence the probability of whether an individual will conform, and give three explanations for why people conform. (p. 396)

15. Discuss Stanley Milgram's studies on obedience to authority and identify some experimental problems and ethical issues that arise with research of this type. (p. 397)

16. Explain how social facilitation influences performance and identify some factors that cause social facilitation to occur. (p. 402)

17. Describe social loafing, group polarization, groupthink, and deindividuation and identify some nonproductive behavioral effects that these social phenomena have on individuals. (p. 403)

BEFORE YOU READ ON, take time to **SURVEY** the chapter, form an idea of what is to be learned (from margin Learning Objective numbers), and set goals for your study time. Then, ask yourself **QUESTIONS** about the material as you **READ,** seeking help for any sections you do not understand.

The school guidance counselor said, "Denise has an attitude problem." Denise had always been a good student and usually got along well with the other seventh-grade children. Her grades were good, and she had always been well behaved. According to the school guidance counselor, however, something was wrong. Denise was answering back, defiant, and impolite in class.

She had recently written an essay for English class entitled "How Not To Be an English Teacher"; she had refused to participate in a debate in her social studies class. In science, she failed to turn in homework assignments. In response to these teachers' reports, the counselor had called Denise's parents to arrange a meeting. Only Denise's mother showed up. Herein lay part of the problem—Denise's parents were in the beginnings of what looked to be a nasty divorce. Her parents argued loudly about money and both were fighting for custody of Denise and her younger brother.

At home, Denise went about her daily routine apparently unaffected by her parents' battles. Piano lessons, dancing classes, and Sunday school were all proceeding normally. Inside, however, she was angry with both parents and the situation in which she anticipated finding herself. She was frustrated at her inability to change the situation and angry at her parents for creating it. She also wondered how much she contributed to their problems. She felt powerless. She did not want to fight with her parents—too much of that was going on already. She thus was taking out her fears and frustrations in school, with the result that the guidance counselor said she had an "attitude problem."

DENISE DID NOT REALLY have an attitude problem: however she was angry, hurt, and most of all, frustrated. Like many children of the 1980s, Denise was about to become a pawn in her parents' divorce. She would be fought over, bargained over, and shared. Her change in behavior arose because of her frustration and inability to affect the outcome.

Denise's guidance counselor soon realized that her school behaviors were responses to her home environment. Even though Denise's behavior in class had gone astray, her basic attitudes about life, school, and her parents, which had been determined long ago, were relatively stable. Her so-called "attitude problem" really had nothing to do with attitudes. A person's attitudes to life in general are established early in life, are difficult to modify, and usually do not change on a day-to-day basis. However, people's specific attitudes and day-to-day behaviors are affected by the situations in which they find themselves. In Denise's case, her attitudes were stable, but her responses to her increasingly difficult home environment were aggressive responses.

Learning Objective 10.1 In studying individuals like Denise, psychologists have recognized the tie between people's attitudes and their day-to-day responses. Our values and behaviors are determined by our childhood experiences and by what other people do and say throughout our lives. Our attitudes in general, and especially those about ourselves, are determined not only by how other people see us, but also by how we *think* others see us. In some cases, we use other people's standards to measure our own behavior and self-worth. How the behavior and attitudes of other people influence individual behavior is the special concern of social psychologists.

Many of a person's basic attitudes are established through socialization. Socialization is the process by which people learn the behaviors, attitudes, and beliefs that allow them to function appropriately in society. Socialization begins early in life and has its greatest impact during the developmental years, although it is a lifelong process. Parents are the first and most important agents of socialization. They shape most of children's basic beliefs about the world: Is it a good place? How can they expect to be treated? How should they treat other people? Parents shape how children initially view the world and their own place in it. Other people and events also shape social behavior. Relatives, friends, clergy, teachers, politicians, and society itself all help modify individuals' attitudes and behavior.

Social psychology is the study of the causes of behavior as it is affected by social situations and other people. Individual behavior is affected by the context or surroundings in which people find themselves and it is also affected by the people with whom individuals associate. It is affected by the feelings they have developed over the years about themselves, other people, and the cultural variables. This chapter discusses the effects of social situations and stimuli and how they affect behavior. It discusses how people perceive, interact with, and respond to other people and the world.

Social psychologists focus on individual behavior. Consider Denise, whose behavior was affected by her home situation. Social psychologists have focused heavily on how individuals like Denise form attitudes and feelings about themselves and about other people. You will see that the field of social cognition— the way people interpret information that comes from other people—has grown in importance. Let us start with basic attitudes about the world, then discuss attitudes about other people, and then about ourselves.

Social psychology ══════
The study of how individual behavior is affected by the behaviors or characteristics of other people.

ATTITUDES

What do you think Denise would say if you asked her which situation she would prefer: (1) Her parents stay together; they do not divorce, but are unhappy; or (2) her parents divorce but have a chance of being happier. You might argue that Denise would be mature enough to put her parents' happiness first. You might also argue that Denise would assert that the family integrity was more important than individual happiness. We know that Denise would not be given the choice of her parents' future, but she will have choices of her own. She will have to choose whether to go to college, and if she does, which one. She will have to choose a career, whether to marry, and a life-style.

Whatever choices Denise, or you, make in life, it is likely that once you made your choices, you would find many reasons your choices were the correct ones. Stanford University psychologist Leon Festinger (1962) has asked whether some special psychological processes color a person's decisions once those decisions have been made. Festinger believes that an attitude process called *cognitive dissonance* is at work. For example, show two similar toys to a child and tell the child she can keep one but the other has to be returned to the store. Then ask the child which toy she likes better. Her response is likely to be the choice that she has made. Both Denise and our hypothetical child would make choices affected by their basic attitudes and, Festinger believes, by the special attitude process of cognitive dissonance. We examine cognitive dissonance further, in this chapter; first, let us examine some basics about attitudes.

Learning
Objective 10.2

Attitude ═══════════

A pattern of relatively enduring feelings, beliefs, and behavior tendencies toward other people, ideas, or objects.

You do not have to be a psychologist to recognize that much of a person's everyday behavior is shaped by attitudes. Our attitudes shape our responses to people and situations. An **attitude** is a lasting pattern of feelings, beliefs, and behavior tendencies toward other people, ideas, or objects.

An attitude has three basic components. Its *cognitive component* is belief, such as the belief that democracy is a system of government devised to provide freedom, liberty, and justice. Attached to the cognitive component is an *emotional component,* which involves feelings of like or dislike. As citizens of the United States, for example, people may feel that their government is the best one. They may take pride in the flag and feel joyous when singing the national anthem. Often linked with the cognitive and emotional components is a *behavioral component.* For example, people may display their beliefs and feelings about the United States through acts of patriotism or service. A family may display the flag on a national holiday to express a feeling of patriotism and a belief in democracy as a system.

Behavior is usually determined by a person's attitudes and how strongly those attitudes are held. However, individuals do not always display their attitudes publicly. Attitudes that are not firmly established are less likely to be displayed in overt behavior. A person's attitudes, experiences, and current behavior are interrelated. Attitudes are determined by experience; but attitudes, along with perceptions of the environment, also determine behavior.

Attitude Formation

Attitudes are established through learning, often early in life. People learn certain beliefs and learn to have certain feelings and reactions and to vote Republican or to root for the Miami Dolphins. Why do people have favorite colors? What are the learning processes that help establish a predisposition to like or dislike certain other people, objects, or situations? Three basic learning approaches attempt to explain the formation of attitudes. These approaches, discussed in detail in Chapter 2, are classical conditioning, instrumental conditioning, and social or observational learning.

Classical Conditioning. In classical conditioning, a formerly neutral stimulus comes to elicit a conditioned response. For example, each time a child overhears a parent make a negative comment about a political figure, neighbor, or relative, the process of classical conditioning pairs the formerly neutral stimulus (neighbor) with a comment (a negative one). If the child overhears such remarks repeatedly, the neighbor eventually evokes a negative response in the child. The pairing of attitudes with people, events, and ideologies is so effortless it often goes unnoticed, but it can shape a child's views and emotional responses to the world. It often forms the basis of the affective (or emotional) component of an attitude.

Instrumental Conditioning. One basic principle of instrumental conditioning states that a behavior that is performed and then reinforced is likely to recur. In socializing a child, parents help the child to develop "right" or "proper" attitudes by selectively reinforcing ideas and behaviors consistent with their own "correct" view of the world. Similarly, teachers shape their students' attitudes about competing theories by reinforcing them with grades for the "correct" responses, and therapists reinforce a client's adaptive thoughts. In-

Parents exert a strong influence on children's attitudes about religion.

strumental conditioning is often the basis of the behavioral component of an attitude.

Social Learning. According to social or observational learning theorists, people learn by watching other people and then imitating their behavior. When children watch a parent interact with someone, perhaps a grandparent or teacher, it is likely that when they next have to speak with that other person their attitudes will reflect the attitudes expressed by their model, the parent. Many people establish attitudes by watching the behavior of someone they consider significant and then imitating it. Children learn to imitate their parents' attitudes about politics, religion, and the economy. By watching and imitating the behavior of significant others, people learn new attitudes that eventually become their own. Like instrumental conditioning, social learning is often the basis of the behavioral component of an attitude.

Regardless of how attitudes are learned, it is clear that parents exert the most direct influence on children's early attitudes. Over time, as children go through school and interact with other people, new influences affect their attitudes and behaviors. Usually the first group of "new" people are playmates and teachers at nursery school or day care. In elementary school, the influence of nonfamily events increases; by high school, friends exert a major influence on teenagers' thinking about issues, themselves, and their behavior. Friends' views on politics, religion, sex, and marriage, on religious upbringing, on the type of school attended, and on the mass media—all influence a young person's developing attitudes.

Attitude Change

Learning Objective 10.3

Denise, who opened this chapter, was showing attitudes and behaviors in school that seemed inconsistent with those she previously exhibited. It is important to remember that people's attitudes do not have to be shown in their behavior, and that people can change behaviors and can change attitudes. Since people learn attitudes, they can unlearn them and learn new ones, although the process is usually difficult. You can see examples of people trying to change other people's attitudes all around you. Perhaps the most common way in which attitude change is attempted is in the mass media, particularly in television commercials. Television commercials try to get people to change their attitudes and ultimately their behavior: Use brand X rather than brand Y. Their appeal may be cognitive (X has more widgets per square inch than Y) or emotional (X will make you feel proud); whatever their appeal, they attempt ultimately to influence behavior: Buy X! Television has become the most influential medium of attitude change in the Western world. Private enterprise uses it; political candidates use it; health groups, fund-raising groups, and presidents use it.

Several important factors determine the likelihood and extent of attitude change. One factor is the characteristics of the person trying to affect the change. Another is the characteristics of the communication itself.

The Communicator.   Social psychologists have shown that to change an attitude, a person must believe in the integrity, credibility, and trustworthiness of the person trying to influence that change. For example, someone listening to a local conservationist discussing wildlife preservation might not be as convinced as she would if the speaker were nationally known. Similarly, a person told by his mother that he needs to lose ten pounds will not be as influenced by her opinion as by the family doctor's. When researchers have varied the perceived power, prestige, and degree of attractiveness of the person trying to change an attitude, they have found those variables extremely important (for example, Chaiken & Eagly, 1983).

The Communication.   Powerful and logical arguments are the most effective tools for changing attitudes, particularly when the targeted attitude is not too different from an already existing one (Nemeth & Endicott, 1976). Change is also more likely if a lack of change has unpleasant consequences (Evans, Rozelle, Noblitt, & Williams, 1975).

Fear is often an effective device in motivating attitude change. Social psychologist Ronald Rogers (1975) has suggested that fear is most effective in changing people's attitudes when (1) the magnitude of the fear-producing event or consequence is sufficiently great, (2) the event or consequence is likely if no adaptive behavior is performed, and (3) the behavior suggested is reasonable and has a reasonable chance of averting the danger (Hass, Bagley, & Rogers, 1975; Rogers & Mewborn, 1976). A study examining attitudes about the petroleum shortage in the mid-1970s found people who perceived the consequences as serious changed their attitudes about energy consumption, whereas those who perceived the negative consequences as minimal changed their attitudes only a little (Hass et al., 1975).

Several other variables affect people's willingness to change their attitudes. Some people are generally more easily persuaded than others. Some situations make people unreceptive no matter how good the arguments are. Face-to-face communications are often more effective than written ones. Another clearly identified variable is repetition. Researchers find that if people hear an argument, commercial, or political view often enough, they begin to believe it, regardless of its value. Repeated exposure to situations can change attitudes; repeated exposure to ideas, such as through television, can be an effective method of selling products, of changing stereotypes (Flerx, Fidler, & Rogers, 1976), or promoting political candidates. A consequence of television advertising for politicians is that voters rarely meet candidates for public office face-to-

The opinions of our friends can have a direct influence on our styles of dress and our behavior.

face. Candidates rely on television advertising because of its potent effects. Nobody denies that television can shape a campaign, but television is impersonal and many voters become indifferent about campaigns because they have never actually seen or met the candidates.

Changing people's attitudes about energy conservation is an example of a large-scale attitude change that various organizations have worked to accomplish. The technique used most often has been information campaigns focused on creating favorable attitudes toward conservation and on saving money through conservation. Such campaigns are not always effective, however, (Costanzo, Archer, Aronson, & Pettigrew, 1986). Sometimes people do not hear the advertisements or they do not understand or remember them. Sometimes people do not control the variable under discussion; for example, they may not control the heating system in their home. Some individuals do not have the money to invest in energy conservation devices.

Attitude changes also can be facilitated in other ways. Information received from friends and acquaintances is very important. Friends are more trusted than the media. Friends can show how energy conservation can be accomplished and how it can save money. Research has shown that modeling of energy conservation has a greater impact than merely presenting information (Aronson & O'Leary, 1983; Ester & Winett, 1982). For example, Leonard-Barton (1981) showed that the best predictor of a person's intention to purchase solar equipment is the number of acquaintances who currently own it. As Costanzo et al. (1986) suggest, "media sources are effective in creating awareness of a new technology, but interpersonal sources exert a far greater influence on the decision to adopt a new technology" (p. 528).

The Search for Consistency

Family summer vacations are generally fun trips the entire family eagerly anticipates. You may be able to remember a summer when you were a teenager in which you rebelled. Perhaps you announced you were not going on the annual trip. Teenagers often say that such family trips are boring and too much of a hassle and that teenagers have more important things to do. During teenage years, an adolescent's developing ideas about what is fun often do not include family affairs. Although most basic ideas about life and morals are established early in life, research has shown that new experiences continue to affect people as they mature. Psychologists' research has shown that attitudes develop and change throughout life as a result of many factors. Some people seek change throughout their lives, trying to keep pace with friends or relatives; other people try to maintain consistency and the status quo. Most people try to maintain some type of balance, a consistency between their attitudes and behavior.

Learning Objective 10.4

Cognitive Dissonance. Whenever people face a situation in which their attitudes conflict with their behavior, they feel uncomfortable. For example, you may believe you should be saving a portion of your income toward tuition; you do not want to get caught with a big tuition bill in four months! However, you spend every dime of your weekly check. Because your attitudes and your behavior are in conflict, you may feel uncomfortable, or even very upset. Leon Festinger (1957) referred to this feeling as dissonance—the feeling that results when a discrepancy exists between a person's beliefs, feelings, and overt behavior. In situations in which people feel dissonance, they usually feel motivated to try to reduce it. **Cognitive dissonance** theory suggests that people in situations in which their attitudes conflict either with their behavior or other attitudes must change either their attitudes or their behavior. For example, a person who holds deep religious beliefs might feel that for him, work on the Sabbath is inappropriate; he believes he should rest and become closer to God. But that man might realize that if he does not go to the office to catch up on paperwork he might lose his job. According to cognitive dissonance theory, such an individual has to change his attitudes about working on the Sabbath, or change his behavior and find a job that will allow him to stay home and study the Bible. Whether the change involves beliefs or behavior, it represents an attempt to increase consistency. Sometimes the search for consistency produces highly irrational attitudes.

Cognitive dissonance A state in which individuals feel uncomfortable because they hold two or more thoughts, attitudes, or behaviors that are inconsistent with one another.

Festinger's original claim was that for an attitude or behavior to change, negative consequences (dissonance) had to be associated with maintaining existing attitudes or behaviors. Thus, a person stops smoking because the dissonance associated with continued smoking (a behavior) and a belief that smoking causes lung cancer (a belief) is too great. Today cognitive dissonance theory is considered as much a motivation theory as it is a theory about attitude change: people are motivated to reduce cognitive dissonance through attitude and behavior change. Because motives stimulate behavior, cognitive dissonance can be used to change people's behavior. Furthermore, researchers have found that just as people who become highly motivated tend to show physiological arousal, so people experiencing cognitive dissonance show evidence of physiological arousal (Croyle & Cooper, 1983).

Learning Objective 10.5

One reason cognitive dissonance theory is so widely researched and accepted is that it can be used to explain many phenomena. Yet its wide scope is also one of its drawbacks—it attempts to explain too much. Social psychologist Daryl Bem (1972) claims that people do not change their attitudes because of an internal state such as dissonance; instead, in the absence of strong attitudes, people observe their own behavior in a situation and then infer their

When people experience cognitive dissonance, they often change either their beliefs or their behavior.

attitudes about the situation from their behavior. According to this view, people seldom understand the causes of their own attitudes and behavior. They are able to perceive their behavior only after the fact and in the context in which it occurred.

Bem's self-perception model is a distinct theoretical alternative to dissonance theory and to traditional attitude formation theories in general. Which theory better explains attitude formation and attitude change remains to be seen. Considerable research supports dissonance theory, but self-perception theory has great intuitive appeal. Social psychologists have yet to place their collective support behind either.

Balance theory ══════
An attitude theory stating that people prefer to hold consistent beliefs with one another and try to avoid incompatible beliefs.

Balance Theory.   **Balance theory** is an even more general theory of cognitive consistency. It states simply that a satisfying and harmonious relationship exists between two people who hold similar views. Research studies on balance theory show that friendships are based in part on the extent of agreement between two friends regarding which of their other acquaintances are acceptable and which are not. Suppose you like both Mary and Jeff, but Mary does not like Jeff. The relationship between you and Mary is imbalanced. In such a relationship, you experience an unpleasant state of tension and either try to change Mary's attitude or change your own. If you can change Mary's attitude about Jeff or decide that you do not like Jeff either, an imbalance no longer exists. According to balance theory, people who wish to maintain stable, balanced relationships have to agree so that unpleasant situations do not occur. Like cognitive dissonance theory, balance theory is considered a motivation theory because the unpleasant tension state that results from disagreement motivates people to change. Also, like cognitive dissonance theory, it assumes that people are decision makers whose thoughts ultimately determine their behavior.

Reactance Theory.   People's attitudes about situations or other people change when someone or something tries to restrict their freedom of choice. According to social psychologist Jack W. Brehm (1966), whenever people feel their freedom of choice is unjustly restricted, they are motivated to reestablish that freedom. Brehm calls this form of negative influence *reactance.* Thus, if an adolescent is told he cannot be friends with members of a minority group (thereby limiting his freedom of choice), he might seek out members of that group more often. Reactance theory is derived from the old notion of forbidden fruit: whenever people are forbidden to do something, that activity often becomes more attractive. Choosing the forbidden fruit may provide an individual with a sense of autonomy.

According to reactance theory, the extent of reactance is usually directly related to the extent of the restrictions on behavior. If the person does not consider the behavior in question to be very important and the restriction is slight, little reactance develops. The wording or delivery of the restriction also affects the extent of reactance. A person told that she *must* respond in a certain way is more likely to react negatively than if she merely receives a suggestion, or is given a free choice in responding. Think of television commercials: announcers often leave the choice up to you. Instead of telling you that you must choose brand X or brand Y, they present evidence for preferring their product but leave the "choice" to you and your logical thought processes. If they told you how you *had* to respond, you would probably show some reactance and not buy their product. The advertiser appeals directly to your need for balance and autonomy, and by giving you "independent" judgment avoids setting up reactance—even though the evidence presented is often lopsided. Similarly, when you convince a friend how to handle a situation, you usually do not tell her how she has to do it, but rather suggest alternatives. Clever advertisers and clever friends know that telling people how to behave restricts their sense of freedom. This domineering approach can result in no change or even in contrary behavior.

PROGRESS CHECK 10.1

1. Complete each of the following sentences with one of the options provided.

Learning Objective 10.1
A. The process by which people learn the behaviors, attitudes, and beliefs that allow them to function appropriately in society is called _____.
(social psychology : socialization : attitude formation)

Learning Objective 10.1
B. Socialization is _____ .
(complete around the age of eighteen : a lifelong process)

Learning Objective 10.1
C. Social psychologists study _____ behavior.
(individual : group)

Learning Objective 10.2
D. Sending a donation to your favorite charity represents the _____ component of an attitude that it is good to help those who are less fortunate.
(cognitive : emotional : behavioral)

Learning Objective 10.2
E. Attitudes are established through learning, are relatively enduring, and _____ .
(can be modified by new experiences : are not likely to change)

Learning Objective 10.2
F. The emotional or affective component of an attitude is probably established through _____ .
(classical conditioning : instrumental conditioning : social learning)

Learning Objective 10.3
G.   When trying to persuade other people, fear approaches _____ _____ .

(almost always make people unreceptive : work if a lack of change has unpleasant consequences)

Learning Objective 10.3
H.   If people repeatedly hear a particular argument, commercial, or political view, they begin to believe it _____ value.

(only if they find it to have : regardless of its)

Learning Objective 10.3
I.   People are more likely to be persuaded to buy a new product if they learn about it through _____ .

(television commercials : models provided by interpersonal sources)

Learning Objective 10.4
J.   Belief and behavior changes that are made in an attempt to reduce cognitive dissonance represent _____ one's life.

(an attempt to increase consistence in : irrational attitudes about)

Learning Objective 10.4
K.   Festinger's theory stresses that people are often _____ to reduce dissonance through attitude change.

(motivated : hesitant : unwilling)

Learning Objective 10.5
L.   Bem's self-perception model suggests that when a person does not have a strong attitude about something, that person will _____ .

(experience cognitive dissonance : infer an attitude from a behavior)

Learning Objective 10.5
M.   According to self-perception theory, people _____ understand the causes of their own attitudes and behavior.

(seldom : almost always)

Learning Objective 10.5
N.   Balance theory would suggest that the saying _____ best describes the condition that will lead to a satisfying and harmonious relationship.

("birds of a feather flock together" : "opposites attract")

Learning Objective 10.4 and 10.5
O.   Cognitive dissonance theory and balance theory can both be considered _____ theories.

(mechanistic : motivational : reinforcement)

Learning Objective 10.5
P.   According to reactance theory, when people behave in a manner contrary to what someone else has requested of them, they probably do so because they are motivated to _____ .

(rebel : establish a sense of autonomy : punish domineering people)

PERCEIVING OTHER PEOPLE AND OURSELVES

If you are standing on a street corner and a member of the opposite sex turns to you and asks for the time, this may not seem surprising—but if the individual is conspicuously wearing a watch, you might wonder about the action. Furthermore, if the person smiles, makes lengthy eye contact, and is extraordinarily thankful for your help, you might suspect that the person has more in mind than just learning the time. Sometimes people provide information about themselves directly, through words. At other times, they provide information nonverbally, through gazes, gestures, and other subtle means of expression. We have developed quite complex systems for inferring the causes of other people's behavior. These systems include the ways in which we present ourselves as well as the way we perceive others.

Nonverbal Communication

Learning Objective 10.6
Many of the conclusions people make about the content of other people's communications are based on facial expression: smiling usually expresses happi-

ness; furrowed brows and eye twitching suggest anger, disgust, or fear. Researchers have found that both children and adults are good interpreters of nonverbal messages, especially facial expressions. Most people are able to distinguish six emotions—happiness, sadness, surprise, fear, anger, and disgust—in the facial expressions of other people. Some people are better than others at interpreting these expressions. Individuals also differ greatly in their ability to convey information through nonverbal mechanisms (Buck, 1979; Buck, Baron, Goodman, & Shapiro, 1980).

Body language is the communication of information such as mood and attitude through body position and gestures. Both experimental studies and clinical reports have found a dramatic correlation between body movement and the emotional content of verbal messages. For example, if a person's body is relaxed, her conversation is unlikely to have aggressive content. Similarly, when the pitch of a person's voice is high, the aggressive content in the conversation is also likely to be high. Simple changes such as a tilt of the head, a nod, or eye contact can communicate positive attitudes to other people (Chaiken, Sigler, & Derlega, 1974). Research shows that women are often better than men at communicating and interpreting nonverbal messages, especially facial expressions (J. A. Hall, 1979). Women are also more likely than men to send nonverbal facial messages, but they are more cautious in the interpretation of nonverbal messages sent to them by men (Rosenthal & DePaulo, 1979). Children are also sensitive to nonverbal communications, and their reactions often affect their teachers' responses to them (Halberstadt & Hall, 1980).

Argyle (1972) has distinguished several other ways in which individuals convey information nonverbally. One is physical contact, such as hitting, striking, embracing, and kissing. Another is proximity, or the physical distance maintained during interactions with other people. In the next chapter, you see that in any given culture, the amount of space between two individuals conversing varies, depending on the nature of the conversation. Other methods of conveying information involve orientation and posture—the angle at which a person sits or stands (for example, leaning forward or relaxing backward). The more cues available (such as eye contact, proximity, and posture), the greater the amount of information conveyed (Schwarz, Foa, & Foa, 1983).

Body language
The communication of information through body positions and gestures.

Avoiding eye contact is one way in which we maintain our distance from strangers.

A person's eyes are one critical feature that conveys information about feelings. Several studies have investigated people's interpretative ability by presenting pictures in which only the pupils of people's eyes have been retouched. One such study showed subjects a photograph of a man looking off into space. The pupils of his eyes were small. In another photograph, the pupils of the man's eyes were retouched and made slightly larger. Subjects attributed distinctly different emotions (such as fear and joy) to the person in each photograph, even though all other aspects of the picture remained the same.

The eyes are perhaps one of the most potent nonverbal ways in which people convey information about themselves to other people. When a person looks at you, it may be a brief gaze or a stare. You might gaze back. Psychologists call this process *making eye contact.* You might avoid eye contact with some people, or, alternatively, you might gaze tenderly at someone you find attractive.

In an excellent review of eye-contact research, Kleinke (1986) suggests that psychologists have learned that they can gain a lot of information by analyzing peoples' eye contact. For example, people's gazes influence other people's evaluations of them. When people are looked at, they accept this as a sign of being liked. Men and women have come to understand than when eye contact is frequent, they may have some sexual attraction between them. People rate other people they meet as more pleasant if they have a moderate degree of eye contact rather than none.

We tend to judge people by the eye contact they make with us. Job applicants are rated more favorably when they make moderate amounts of eye contact. Speakers are rated more favorably when they make more rather than less eye contact. Therapists report that a lack of eye contact in therapy suggests a lack of involvement. Witnesses in a court trial are perceived as more credible when they make eye contact with the attorney. Eye contact also expresses the intensity of a person's feelings. Generally speaking, people prefer modest amounts of eye contact rather than constant or no eye contact.

Researchers are aware that people make eye contact more frequently in some situations than in others. In addition, people will gaze more frequently at other people who are in positions of authority. Physiological changes may occur with eye contact; gaze and eye contact research is continuing to grow because they are useful indicators of human emotions and relationships. They are powerful, nonverbal mechanisms by which people communicate.

Understanding the Causes of Behavior: Attribution Theory

Learning Objective 10.7

Attribution ═══════
The process by which a person infers another person's motives and intentions by observing his or her behavior.

If it is noon and you see someone eating a hamburger and French fries, you can be fairly certain the person is hungry because it is lunch time. Similarly, if you see a student working a crossword puzzle, you might infer that she enjoys doing crossword puzzles and that this is her way of passing the time. In getting to know other people, a person often infers the causes of their behavior. **Attribution** is the process by which someone infers or decides about other people's motives and intentions from observing their behavior. The process of attribution enables people to decide how they will behave toward other people. If you perceive another person as hostile, you might prepare to deal with the hostility or choose to avoid that person.

Attribution seems like a fairly straightforward process based on common sense. However, it must take into account internal as well as external causes of

Psychology and You: Can Dan Rather's Smile Elect a President?

Your vote in the next presidential election may be determined by Dan Rather's smile, Tom Brokaw's wink, or Peter Jennings' head nod. Are the newscasters biased? Do the newscasters' facial expressions affect your voting behavior? Do people who report the news consciously attempt to change your behavior?

Many news anchorpeople will state that they have no pretense of being objective; others will say that objectivity is their goal. Regardless, the content and style of delivery of a newscaster can have a potent effect on a television observer.

Brian Mullen of Syracuse University and ten colleagues (Mullen et al., 1986) examined the facial expressions of national network newscasters during the 1984 presidential election, looking to see if the newscasters exhibited biased facial expressions. They then conducted a telephone survey of television viewers to determine if voting behavior seemed to be influenced by the newscasters' facial expressions.

The researchers asked college students to rate videotaped segments of newscasters while they were referring to candidates. There was no sound from the television monitors. The subjects rated the newscasters' facial expressions on a series of scales from *extremely negative* to *extremely positive*. The results showed that Peter Jennings,

more than Tom Brokaw or Dan Rather, had a bias in favor of candidate Ronald Reagan. The other two newscasters showed no bias—they remained scrupulously neutral.

Did voters who watched Peter Jennings vote more often for Ronald Reagan than Brokaw's or Rather's audiences? The researchers called people randomly in several communities and asked them whom they watched on the evening news and for whom they voted. It was found that voters who regularly watched Peter Jennings were more likely to have voted for Ronald Reagan than were voters who watched the other newscasters.

The effects of this experiment were small. Also, other variables can affect voting behavior and who watches each news show. But by using a scientific method, these researchers were able to show a bias and to show that the bias affected behavior. It is not clear from the study whether viewers' political views influenced their decision to watch Jennings or Brokaw in the first place. Further, a voter's behavior in the next election is probably going to be based on the candidate, not on the newscaster who talks about the candidate. However, some small portion of voting behavior may be affected by the nonverbal gestures not only of the candidate but also of a television newscaster.

---

behavior. If internal causes seem to predominate, you will attribute a person's behavior to his or her personality; if external causes seem to play the larger role, you will attribute the person's behavior to the specific situation. Suppose our hypothetical student working the crossword puzzle really despises crossword puzzles and is completing one simply as part of an assignment? People can be mistaken when they infer the causes of another person's behavior.

Shaver (1977) has outlined three basic stages in the attribution process, each involving a question. Stage 1 asks: "Was the action observed?" Stage 2 asks: "Was the action intended?" Stage 3 asks: "Was the action coerced?"

Shaver is only one of a number of researchers who have tried to conceptualize the processes of attributions. Kelley's popular theory of attribution (1972) posits three criteria to help determine whether the causes of a behavior are internal or external: *consensus, consistency,* and *distinctiveness* (see Table 10.1). To infer that someone's internal characteristics are the cause of his or her

TABLE 10.1: Kelley's Criteria for Internal versus External Attributions

Internal	External

Low consensus:
  Few others act the same way.
	High consensus:
	  Others act the same way.

High consistency:
  Person acts in the same way in other similar situations.
	High consistency:
	  Person acts in the same way in other similar situations.

Low distinctiveness:
  Person acts in the same way on other occasions.
	High distinctiveness:
	  Person acts differently in other situations.

behavior, you must believe that (1) few other people in the same situation would act in the same way (low consensus), (2) this individual acts in the same way in other, similar situations (high consistency), and (3) this individual acts in the same way in different situations (low distinctiveness).

By contrast, you might infer that the person's behaviors were caused by external factors; such an individual was caused to do something not because of internal, long-lasting personal characteristics. In this case, you would believe that (1) most people would act this way in this sort of situation (high consensus), (2) the person acts this way in similar situations (high consistency), and (3) the person acts differently in other, different situations (high distinctiveness) (Jackson & Larrance, 1979; Kelley, 1972, 1973).

Suppose that someone you know is often rude to other people. You observe that other people in the same situation do not usually act this way (low consensus); that the person acts this way on other, similar occasions (high consistency); and that the person acts this way most of the time (low distinctiveness). You therefore attribute her rudeness to her personality—you think she is a rude person. But you would be much more likely to attribute her rudeness to situational factors if (1) most people would have acted rudely in the same situation (high consensus), (2) this person acts rudely in other, similar situations (high consistency), and (3) she acts differently in different situations (high distinctiveness).

Learning Objective 10.8

Errors in Attribution. People tend to perceive their own behavior as caused largely by situational factors, and the behavior of other people as stemming from personal characteristics (Fiske & Taylor, 1984; Jones & Nisbett, 1972). People often adopt views of events that obscure the real causes of other people's behavior, as well as of their own. When a person loses his temper, we often see him as a violent person. When a customer is hostile to a waiter or waitress in a restaurant, we see the customer as lacking patience and good judgment. We stereotype people and ignore situational factors that cause behavior—this behavior is called the *fundamental attribution error*. We assume that the person's behavior is caused by internal dispositions—which may or may not be true. The waiter or waitress may have provoked the restaurant patron by being slow or spilling the soup, for example. Another kind of error in attribution is called the *actor-observer effect*. For example, young children are often heard to say, "You made me hurt myself"; but when a friend hurts himself or herself, that friend will say, "You're clumsy."

A Just World. According to Melvin Lerner (1970), most people believe an appropriate relationship exists between what they do and what happens to them. In other words, they believe that the world is "just," that people get what they deserve, that luck and circumstance are less important than hard work and diligence in determining a person's fate. One consequence of such a belief is that victims of crime, poverty, or other misfortune are treated as if they had brought these events on themselves. Realizing that bad things can happen to good people threatens our belief that the world is just. Such errors in attribution help people maintain a sense of their own worth and a feeling of control. On the other hand, the ability to see that someone else has been injured unfairly can upset an individual's belief in a just world and perhaps motivate him or her to eliminate some causes of unjust suffering.

Implications.   Attribution has an important influence on people's judgments about other people. Juries must decide the innocence or guilt of defendants. Was the defendant's behavior observed and did it result from personal characteristics or was it coerced? In trials concerning war crimes, it is common for individuals to argue that they were simply following orders in a time of national emergency. This type of defense was prevalent in the Nuremberg trials at the end of World War II and in the trial of Lt. William Calley concerning his involvement in the Mai Lai massacre during the Vietnam War. The defense attorneys argued that their clients' behavior was coerced by threats from superior officers and by the prevailing attitudes of the times. A later section in this chapter discusses people's willingness to comply with the orders of people in positions of authority.

Self-Perception

Learning Objective 10.9

Whenever you examine your own behavior and personal characteristics, you are doing so in part through the eyes of other people. Our perceptions of ourselves are greatly affected by those of other people. Thus, when social psychologists study self-perception, they are examining how other people and social situations affect how we see ourselves, which can influence our everyday behaviors.

Self-perception ═══
Attitude toward and belief about oneself, largely formed during childhood and adolescence and often a reflection of others' perceived attitudes.

Self-perceptions are individuals' attitudes toward and beliefs about themselves. A number of factors determine a person's self-perception—physical appearance, work habits, athletic abilities, or abilities as a parent or mate. People develop a sense of themselves by combining aspects of their family, marital, occupational, recreational, sexual, and gender roles.

Self-perceptions develop over time and through experience. Even though attitudes about oneself are established early in life, they are reevaluated frequently and can have dramatic effects on behavior. Children ask, "Mommy, am I pretty?" or "Mommy, do you like me?" During adolescence, young people reassess earlier self-concepts and try to establish a firm identity consistent with previous attitudes and new values. Successful completion of this phase, which Erikson calls the "identity crisis" (see Chapter 8), results in a person's ability to adapt to new situations while retaining a firm understanding of self and of personal values.

To understand themselves fully, individuals need to understand the origins of their personal beliefs, to decide whether these beliefs should be maintained, and to examine their own behavior and realize its implications. If beliefs are inconsistent with behavior, cognitive dissonance may require a reexamination of both and a change in self-perception.

People's attitudes about themselves determine to a great extent how they evaluate the behavior of other people and the extent to which other people influence their behavior. Self-perception and the perceptions of other people are interactive. Individuals perceive other people in relation to their own value systems and ideas (Webster & Driskell, 1978). A very assertive person may view other assertive people as expressing normal, appropriate behavior. A relatively quiet, shy, and passive person may view assertive people as inappropriate, loud, or even aggressive. People usually develop self-perceptions by comparing themselves with other people. People with strong self-concepts generally know the type of behavior, people, politicians, and religious ideologies with which they are most comfortable.

Physical attractiveness and the attitudes of others are important variables that affect how we see ourselves.

Studies of social perception show that self-concepts are important to psychological health. Several important variables affect people's self-concepts: parental attitudes, social interactions with friends, and even biological predisposition. An impressive body of literature suggests that people's physical appearance affects other people's attitudes toward them; those attitudes, expressed in behavior, influence how individuals will subsequently perceive themselves (Horvath, 1981; Phillips & Zigler, 1980). Unfortunately, people's self-concepts may be determined largely by such superficial characteristics as physical attractiveness (Kellerman & Laird, 1982; Zweigenhaft, Hayes, & Haagen, 1980). For example, attractive schoolchildren are thought to get higher marks and to misbehave less and are predicted to have more successful careers than unattractive schoolchildren (Clifford & Walster, 1973; Dion, Berscheid, & Walster, 1972; Lerner & Lerner, 1977). Adults perceived as attractive are granted more freedom and liberties by other people than are unattractive adults (Cash & Kehr, 1978; Kleinke, Staneski, & Berger, 1975). These positive responses reinforce people's feelings about themselves and their abilities (Reis, Nezlek, & Wheeler, 1980). In addition, attractive adults are judged to have more positive traits and characteristics than are unattractive adults, especially when appearance is the first information provided (Benassi, 1982). People's physical characteristics or perceptions about those characteristics can set them up for a lifelong pattern of reinforcement or punishment. Adults with immature and childlike facial qualities are perceived as having childlike attributes. Adults with facial qualities characterized as babyfaced are perceived to have more warmth, submissiveness, honesty, and naïveté and less physical strength than adults with mature faces (Berry & McArthur, 1986). Physically unattractive and different people tend to be isolated, to be ignored by members of both sexes, and to have negative traits attributed to them (Krebs & Adinolfi, 1975). People who perceive themselves as physically less attractive are more likely to have anxiety problems in dealing with members of the opposite sex (Mitchell & Orr, 1976). (See Figure 10.1.)

FIGURE 10.1 : People's self-concepts are determined by many other people. Some individuals provide positive experiences; others provide negative ones. The development of a self-concept represents the sum of the positive and negative influences provided by other people. (From Albrecht, Thomas, & Chadwick, 1980)

Learning Objective 10.10

People are often not realistic in evaluating themselves, their capabilities, or their behavior. Social psychologists have demonstrated that people have what is called a *self-serving bias:* they tend to evaluate their own behavior as worthwhile, regardless of the situation. Most people consider themselves more charitable, more giving, more intelligent, more considerate, more sensitive, more likely to succeed, and possessing more leadership qualities than are most other people (see, for example, Felson, 1981). No matter how many car accidents they may have had, most people feel they are better-than-average drivers.

Attempts to understand the development and role of self-serving biases have focused on two possible explanations: self-esteem and self-presentation. Developing a self-serving bias bolsters an individual's self-esteem and need to feel good about self in comparison to others. It can be seen as an adaptive response that helps people deal with their limitations and gives them the courage to venture into areas they might normally not explore. Another view is that self-serving biases develop to allow people to present themselves to other people in a positive light (Weary et al., 1982). Self-serving biases do exist, but not in all people at all times. Individuals who suffer from depression and loneliness often have low levels of self-esteem and do not seem to develop a self-serving bias. Instead, these individuals may develop and exhibit maladjusted or abnormal behaviors.

Errors in attribution contribute to self-serving biases. People tend to accept credit for their successes and blame other people for their failures. Have you known someone who assumes that good things happen to her because she deserves them and that bad things happen to other people because (in a just world), they deserve them? When something bad happens to this person, she blames the event on bad luck or circumstances. This combination of attribution errors and a self-serving bias helps such an individual maintain self-esteem and appear competent to other people. However, this attitude can set up a person for disappointment if she is unable to set realistic goals.

Learned Helplessness

Learning Objective 10.11

What happens when you find yourself in a situation over which you have little control? Remember Denise's situation? She was caught in the middle of her parents' impending divorce. The divorce was going to affect her life in many important ways, but she had little control over the outcome of her parents' situation and her subsequent living arrangements. She responded with displaced anger, letting her frustrations out at school.

Among the other responses Denise could have made, some are adaptive and some less adaptive. Researchers have investigated similar situations in the laboratory. Consider this situation. Assume you are a subject in an experiment that requires you to solve puzzles. The puzzles are relatively simple, and there are only a few ways to solve them. Yet no matter what you do, you seem unable to find the correct sequence. Real life situations can (and do) also create frustration. For example, a university instructor trying to increase educational effectiveness through audiovisual presentations may find that the university's bureaucracy prevents her from obtaining the money to purchase a bulb for her projector. In such situations, most people feel frustrated by their lack of control over events.

Learned helplessness
The behavior of giving up or not responding, exhibited by subjects exposed to negative consequences or punishment over which they have no control.

Placed in situations in which they have no control over the negative things happening to them, both people and animals often stop responding. This failure to act is well documented. Seligman termed this behavior **learned helplessness.** Seligman (1975) and his colleagues have shown that dogs exposed to a series of inescapable shocks and then given a chance to escape further punishment fail to learn the escape response.

Researchers have studied the phenomenon of learned helplessness in human beings. A typical experiment presents different groups of subjects with a task. The first group receives reinforcement for correct responses. The second group receives reinforcement not dependent, or contingent, on performance. The third group (a control group) is never provided reinforcement. These studies have found that learned helplessness occurs whenever the group receiving consequences unrelated to performance shows deficits in learning compared to the other groups.

Learned helplessness has been shown to be a factor that interferes with human problem solving (Eisenberger, Park, & Frank, 1976) and that affects emotions (Gatchel & Proctor, 1976), especially depression (McCarron, 1973; Seligman, 1975). Seligman believes the major cause of learned helplessness is the organism's belief that its responses will not affect what happens to it in the future. Thus, when people feel their responses do not change what happens to them, anxiety, depression, and particularly nonresponsiveness result. These people learn they cannot control their environment and consequently develop a sense of hopelessness.

PROGRESS CHECK 10.2

1. Complete each of the following sentences with one of the options provided.

Learning Objective 10.6
A. Most people are able to distinguish _____ basic emotions through facial expressions.
(three • six • nine)

Learning Objective 10.6
B. Nonverbal information about feelings is communicated quite distinctly _____ .
(through the eyes • by the mouth • by forehead muscle movements)

Learning Objective 10.6
C. When men and women are compared, it had been found that _____ are better at communicating and interpreting nonverbal messages.
(women • men)

Learning Objective 10.6
D. Most people prefer _____ eye contact with other people.
(little or no • modest amounts of • almost constant)

Learning Objective 10.7
E. You will be more likely to attribute an individual's behavior to his or her personality if the causes of the behavior seem to be primarily _____ .
(internal • external)

Learning Objective 10.7
F. When attributing causes to our own behavior, we generally focus on _____ .
(situational factors • personal characteristics)

Learning Objective 10.7
G. The process by which we decide why someone was motivated to behave as he or she did is called _____ .
(consensus • attribution • actor-observer effect)

Learning Objective 10.8
H. When we categorize an individual into some group without paying attention to situational factors, we may be making an error in attribution called _____ .
(distinctiveness • fundamental attribution error • actor-observer effect)

Learning Objective 10.9
I. People usually develop self-perceptions by _____ .
(comparing themselves with other people • asking other people for an evaluation of their actions)

Learning Objective 10.9
J. Self-perception is strongly influenced by the feedback other people give us concerning _____ .
(person perception • our attractiveness • their innermost feelings)

Learning Objective 10.10
K. We would be *least* likely to observe a self-serving bias in people who _____ .
(are depressed or lonely • want to "look good" to others)

Learning Objective 10.11
L. When people are placed in situations in which they have no control over the negative things happening to them, they frequently _____ .
(attempt to escape • become violent • stop responding)

Learning Objective 10.11
M. Learned helplessness frequently leads to _____ .
(anxiety and depression • a reactance response • self-determination)

AGGRESSION

The reaction of Denise, who opened this chapter, to her parents' impending divorce was not uncommon. Like adults teenagers often become angry because they are frustrated, helpless, and have no control over a situation that greatly affects their lives. Of course, other responses are possible, but many adolescents have not yet learned a full set of coping skills. They are not yet fully mature and sometimes have a limited range of reactions to difficult situations. Anger and acting out, perhaps in the area of schoolwork and behavior in school, are ordinary and frequent responses.

Learning Objective 10.12

Hostile, aggressive responses are common in our society. You have seen such behaviors on television and probably know someone you think is hostile. For some reason, whenever you see this person, he or she is hostile and ugly. Are such individuals mean and nasty all the time? Are they constantly seeking to offend and hurt other people? Did they learn to become offensive as children, as teenagers, or is their behavior something new? Research has shown that under certain circumstances, many people act aggressively.

Aggression
Any behavior whose goal is to harm or injure another person or thing.

For social psychologists, **aggression** is any behavior whose goal is to harm or injure another person or thing. Most aggressive acts are not physical. A person may attempt to harm someone verbally, through gossip, rumor, or innuendo, or through a gesture. Aggression abounds in everyday life, on an international level in acts of war, and on an intimate level between friends. Psychologists study aggression to determine what behaviors people are capable of and why these behaviors occur. Three major approaches attempt to explain why people are aggressive: *instincts, acquired drives,* and *social learning.*

Instincts

Some psychologists, called *nativists,* believe that many aspects of behavior, including aggression, are inborn. Nativists believe that people are genetically predisposed toward aggression. Freud, for example, suggested that people have a death instinct, a destructive release of aggression against themselves. This concept is not widely accepted today, however.

Another nativistic view is that of ethologist and Nobel laureate Konrad Lorenz. Lorenz has investigated aggressive behavior through naturalistic observation. He has noted that most animals do not attempt to kill members of their own species: animals fight, but they have signals that indicate to the contestants when to stop fighting, at a point before death might occur. Human beings, however, attack and kill their own species through war and develop new technologies to attack their own species with ever greater ferocity. According to Lorenz (1964), people's aggression is instinctive and spontaneous and will continue to be expressed, often as a fighting instinct. Instinct serves to maximize the use of food, space, and resources in general. Lorenz believes aggression in human beings is inevitable: people will always be looking to express their aggressive (fighting) instincts. Lorenz stresses the possible social implications of people's aggressive instincts.

Frustration-aggression hypothesis
The view that frustration of goal-directed behavior leads to aggression.

Acquired Drives

A person's aggressive behavior results from the frustration of his or her goal-directed behavior. This is the **frustration-aggression hypothesis,** initially pro-

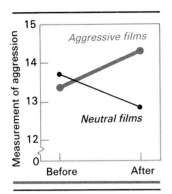

FIGURE 10.2 : A film with
aggressive content (*Clockwork
Orange*) or neutral content
(*Fiddler on the Roof*) was
shown to adult subjects. A
measure of aggressiveness was
made before and after viewing
the films. In a study by
Goldstein et al. (1975),
subjects were more hostile
after viewing an aggressive
film than before viewing the
film; those who saw the
neutral film became less
aggressive. (Adapted from
Goldstein et al., 1975)

posed by Dollard, Doob, Miller, Mowrer, and Sears (1939). This simple idea has
undergone a great deal of research, evaluation, and modification and continues to receive wide support (Bandura, 1973). Everyday experience demonstrates that people involved in goal-oriented tasks often become aggressive or
angry when frustrated. In one attempt to modify the theory, Berkowitz (1964)
examined the evidence for the frustration-aggression hypothesis and suggested that frustration creates a readiness for aggressive acts, rather than for
actual aggression. Even when frustration is present, Berkowitz claimed, certain
stimulus cues must be available before aggression occurs. Berkowitz's ideas
concerning the influence of stimulus cues on aggression generated much subsequent debate and research. Not all experiments attempting to repeat or extend Berkowitz's basic findings have obtained similar results (see Halderman &
Jackson, 1979; Tannenbaum & Zillman, 1975). Through this kind of research,
frustration-aggression theory has been refined to suggest that frustration may
cause a number of responses, one of which might be aggression. Aggression is
more likely to occur given the right circumstance and proper cues (Donnerstein, 1980). (See Figure 10.2.)

In many ways, psychologists find the frustration-aggression hypothesis too
simple. It is too sweeping in its assumptions; people do not always become
aggressive when frustrated. It also does not account for all the data. In important ways, however, the frustration-aggression hypothesis is an example of
good psychology. It has led to other research and other formulations that are
useful in describing behavior. No theory is perfect; no single theory can account for people's behavior all the time. But a good theory, such as Berkowitz's,
will generate new insights and more experimentation so that psychologists can
come closer to understanding and identifying the real causes of behavior.

Social Learning

Danny is watching a television rerun of *Star Wars*. On the screen, Darth Vader
and Obi-Wan Kenobi fight with thrilling seriousness. Almost without realizing
it, Danny reaches over and socks his sister, Sarah. Sarah screams, and the
children's mother comes into the room and insists they turn off that violence.
From a psychologist's viewpoint, Sarah and Danny's mother may have the right
idea. Children imitate characters seen in the movies or on television. Thrust
into situations for which a standard response has not yet been firmly established, children copy behavior. Just as a child presented with a new toy often
learns to use that toy by imitating another child, social psychologists argue that
if parents or teachers are aggressive, their children may learn to be aggressive
by imitating their behavior. Similarly, children who see someone being punished for aggressive behavior learn that aggressive behavior should not be
imitated.

According to Bandura, aggressive behavior can be established or eliminated through observational learning. Bandura argues that children are not
born with aggressive instincts but learn aggression by seeing other people (including parents) exhibiting aggressive behaviors; a person's family, subcul-
ture, and/or the mass media may provide aggressive models.

Bandura and several colleagues have investigated whether children are
likely to show aggression after they observe it in other people. In a classic
study, Bandura, Ross, and Ross (1963b) brought four-year-olds to a laboratory
where they saw adult actors exhibiting aggressive behaviors—kicking, hitting,

and otherwise acting aggressively toward a large inflated doll. A second group of subjects was shown a film in which the same actors exhibited similar aggressive behaviors. A third group of subjects saw a film depicting an aggressive cartoon character. After being shown the aggressive sequences, the subjects were observed in a different setting. The results showed that the subjects who had viewed aggression in any of these three forms were nearly twice as aggressive as the control group. The control group participated in all aspects of the experiment but were not exposed to aggressive models. The children imitated the previously seen aggressive behavior.

Many researchers have pointed out that certain aspects of experimental settings are inappropriate for drawing conclusions about the effect of social learning and violence in children. For example, the object of aggression in the Bandura studies was generally an inflated plastic toy, not a real person. Despite such problems, the results of these studies suggest that children exposed to aggressive situations imitate them in subsequent play.

Bandura believes that human beings exert strong cognitive control over their aggressive behavior: human awareness of the consequences of their actions guides their actions (for a review of cognitive control, see Chapter 5). Seeing a model rewarded for aggression promotes aggression in the observer (Bandura, 1971, 1973). Clearly, reinforcement and punishment are available mechanisms for teaching aggressive acts directly (Bandura & Walters, 1963), but in Bandura's view, simply viewing other people involved in aggressive acts is sufficient to establish, maintain, or eliminate aggressive behavior.

Aggressive Stimuli: Television

Learning Objective 10.13

Because people in our society watch so much television, that medium serves as a major source of models for imitative behavior. The fact that television portrays so much aggressive behavior has become a source of concern to parents and educators as well as to social psychologists. According to Gerbner and Gross (1976), half of all prime-time television characters are involved in violent activity of some kind, and about one-tenth in killing. To control on-screen lawlessness, about 20 percent of television males are engaged in law enforcement duties, whereas in the real world the figure is less than 1 percent. As a result, many researchers have investigated the effects of television watching on human behavior—especially on aggressive behavior.

A correlational study by McCarthy and her colleagues (1975) compared different kinds of television watching with the amount of violent behavior children showed in their day-to-day behavior. The variables measured were the numbers of hours of television watched, the kinds of programs watched, and behavior such as conflict with parents, fighting, and delinquency. The results supported the idea that children who watch a great deal of violence on television are more likely to be found in violent, aggressive activities than are children who watch less violence on television. The study also found that children who spent the most time in front of the television came from disadvantaged backgrounds. Because this study was correlational, we must be careful not to draw causal inferences or generalize from it.

Research by Bandura and his colleagues indicates that television is a major influence on aggressive behavior in both children and adults. One study found that aggressive children tend to watch more television, and television with more violent content, than do less aggressive children (Eron, 1982). Another study found that children exposed to many hours of television violence are more likely to be passive observers of real-life violence and less likely to intervene to help a victim of violence (Drabman & Thomas, 1975). Viewers of television violence are more likely to become fearful and to feel that they may become victims of violent acts. One study found that viewing violence at age eight predicted aggressive behavior at age nineteen (Eron & Huesmann, 1980). Another study showed that the imitative aggressive behaviors of second graders can be reversed with appropriate training and treatment (Huesmann et al., 1983). Television can also have positive effects. One study found that children exposed to "Sesame Street" and "Mr. Rogers' Neighborhood" were more likely than a control group to show good social behaviors and better personal behavior with other children (Coates, Pusser, & Goodman, 1976).

How does watching violence on television affect a viewer? Why does it operate on a person's, especially a child's, likelihood of committing violent acts? The impact of television violence occurs for several reasons. Baron & Byrne (1987) have suggested that there are four primary processes taking place. First, exposure to violence weakens inhibitions of viewers. Second, exposure to violence may suggest new ideas and techniques to the uninitiated. Third, viewing violence on television may prime or stimulate existing aggressive ideas. Fourth, viewing television violence may reduce a person's overall emotional sensitivity to violence (see Figure 10.3).

A large body of research exists on the effects of media violence, especially television, on children's attitudes, values, and aggressive behaviors. The results of most studies support the conclusion that television violence has a causal effect on aggressive behavior in children and adolescents (American Psychological Association, 1985; Pearl, Bouthilet, & Lazar, 1982; Surgeon General's Scientific Advisory Committee, 1972). But not all researchers agree however (Cook, Kendziersky, & Thomas, 1983; J. L. Freedman, 1984, 1986). Some claim that only laboratory studies show negative effects and that these studies are

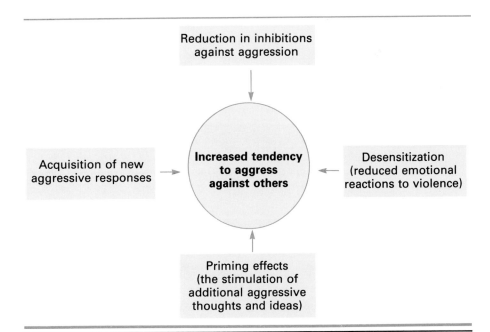

FIGURE 10.3 : The impact of media violence seems to stem primarily from four processes.

Many studies have shown that violent toys can have a direct effect on children's aggressive behavior.

biased. Friedrich-Cofer & Huston (1986) have evaluated both laboratory studies such as Bandura's and field-based naturalistic observation-type experiments. They find that laboratory studies on the whole show the negative effects of violence on television and that field studies, while less clear, also show similar deleterious effects of violence.

The findings have important social implications. Most children spend many hours viewing television (Liebert, Sprafkin, & Davidson, 1982). Children under the age of five believe what they see on television to be "the truth." Although television violence does not necessarily produce overt violent behavior, psychologists should be concerned about how it changes people's overall views about life (see Doob & MacDonald, 1979). Researchers today are particularly concerned about television violence because of the widespread availability of cable television, which displays both more violence and more explicit violence.

PROGRESS CHECK   10.3

1. Complete each of the following sentences with one of the options provided.

Learning Objective 10.12

A. Most aggressive acts _____ .
(occur unintentionally : are not physical)

Learning Objective 10.12

B. A nativistic view of aggression argues that people _____ aggressive behavior.
(learn : are predisposed toward)

Learning Objective 10.12

C. Although not widely accepted by contemporary psychologists, Freud established the idea that people may have a death instinct that is a destructive release of aggression toward _____ .
(others : themselves)

Learning Objective 10.12   D. Konrad Lorenz suggested that _____ most animals, human beings attack and kill members of their own species.
(like : unlike)

Learning Objective 10.12   E. Lorenz argues that human aggression is _____ .
(instinctive and inevitable : no longer necessary for survival)

Learning Objective 10.12   F. Berkowitz modified the traditional frustration-aggression hypothesis by suggesting that frustration _____ aggression.
(will be followed by : creates a readiness for)

Learning Objective 10.12   G. The refined frustration-aggression hypothesis suggests frustration is more likely to lead to aggression if _____ .
(anger can be justified : certain cues are available)

Learning Objective 10.12   H. According to the social learning approach, if children _____ _____ punished for aggressive behavior, they will be less likely to imitate aggressive behavior.
(are : see someone)

Learning Objective 10.12   I. In a study conducted by Bandura, Ross, and Ross, children who viewed aggressive films were _____ aggressive than (as) children who were not exposed to the films.
(no more : nearly twice as : about four times as)

Learning Objective 10.12   J. Bandura suggests that human aggression is learned through observational learning and that people exert a strong sense of _____ their aggressive behavior.
(emotion with : cognitive control over : territoriality with)

Learning Objective 10.13   K. Baron and Byrne believe that television violence _____ actual, real-world violent behavior.
(has little or no impact on : has at least four ways of influencing)

SOCIAL INFLUENCE

For decades, social psychologists have been studying the behavior of teenagers. Teenagers and preteens are at very vulnerable points in their lives—they are forming new attitudes and are emerging as adults. Consider the case of Bobbie. Bobbie knew how to get along with the girls who were older than she was. At eleven years of age, Bobbie was not especially mature physically. She was neither especially pretty nor especially talented. But Bobbie had learned what people like and what they do not like. She seemed attuned to what the older girls were talking about and who were their current idols. She convinced her mother that wearing make-up and tight jeans and shopping at the mall was the best way to spend a Saturday afternoon.

Unlike most of the other girls in her sixth-grade middle-school class, Bobbie worried about her make-up. She wouldn't swim in the neighborhood pool lest her hair get wet and she would have to blow dry it again. Watching videos on television was more important than homework; cute boys became an obsession. The latest way to roll one's jeans or wear a sweat shirt was a constant focus in her life. The good movies, the good singers, and the good places to eat, buy clothes, or go to camp all seemed to have been established by Bobbie's friends. Bobbie learned that by going along with her friends' suggestions, she quickly became one of the "in" crowd.

Bobbie was being heavily influenced by her peers. In order to gain their approval, Bobbie went along with their ideas. Social psychologists have learned that people are great conformists. Individuals can be affected by the behavior or mere presence of other people. Sometimes people imitate the behavior of people whom they respect and value; at other times, they conform to standards set up by organized groups. Conforming to group standards may mean something as simple as wearing a necktie to a funeral or refraining from speaking during a public address. People often "go along" or comply with the behavior of their peer or family group. Even though you wanted to eat lunch at McDonald's, if most of your group is eating at Burger King you will probably go along with them in order to enjoy their company. Similarly, people sometimes find themselves doing things they might never have imagined, simply because of peer pressure or in response to the direction of a generally respected leader. These behaviors can include positive prosocial behaviors as well as counterproductive ones. In their need to be liked, accepted, and respected, people sometimes allow their behavior to be influenced by the opinions and behaviors of other people.

Conformity

Learning Objective 10.14

Studies show that individuals often conform to group norms even when not pressured to do so. For example, an instructor may ask a class of 250 students to answer a relatively simple question, but no one volunteers. When asked, most students will report that they did not raise their hands because no one else did. Similarly, on formal occasions, individuals generally dress appropriately: at weddings, brides wear white; at funerals, people generally wear dark colors.

In an experiment on conformity in 1951, Solomon Asch used what has become a classic methodology. A group of subjects is brought into a room and told that the experiment involves line discrimination. However, only one member of the group is a naïve subject; the others are collaborators with the investigator and know the real purpose of the study. The subjects are told as a group that they will be shown two lines and asked to indicate which line is longer. The lines are then shown to the group. The discriminations are generally easy to make, but the subject-collaborators consistently make the wrong choice. Research has shown that when there are ten collaborators and one naïve subject, the naïve subject will generally go along with the group, even though the majority answer is obviously wrong. The naïve subject conforms, even though the group exerts no explicit or directly observable pressure to conform.

Of course, not all naïve subjects conform. Enough do, however, so that psychologists have been encouraged to investigate this phenomenon further. They have found that one critical variable is the number of collaborators involved. When one or two individuals collaborate, the pressure to conform is considerably less than if ten do. Another important variable is the number of dissenting votes. If even only one of fifteen collaborators agrees with the naïve subject, the naïve subject will choose the appropriate line. Furthermore, the one dissenting vote need not agree with the subject's; the mere presence of another dissenter from the majority viewpoint seems to be enough.

Both everyday experience and research show that dissenting opinion helps to counteract group influence. For example, when group decision-making takes place, a consistent minority can exert substantial influence, even when it

Although some people may not conform to society's expectations, they still conform to the attitudes of their own particular group.

is devoid of power, status, or competence (Moscovici, 1976; Moscovici, Lage, & Naffrechoux, 1969). The influence of a small minority on the decision making of a larger group has been found to be measurable in many contexts (Wolf & Latané, 1983). Even two people in a large group can seriously influence decision making. A flexible minority exerts a stronger influence (Mungy, 1982).

Several different theories hint at why people conform. The *social conformity* approach states that people conform to avoid the stigma of being wrong, deviant, out of line, or different from other people. When people find that their position is dramatically different from that of others in a group, they begin to question their own views. According to the social conformity view, people want to do the "right" thing, and they define "right" as whatever is generally accepted.

Another explanation for the presence or absence of conformity in a group relies on *attribution*. When a person is able to identify causes for other people's behavior in a group, conformity disappears (Ross, Bierbrauer, & Hoffman, 1976).

Another explanation for conformity (or the lack of it) is the importance of *independence* to the individuals involved. Although people in a group would like to be independent, they have to face the consequences of their independence. They risk serious disapproval and face peer pressure to conform. If they choose not to go along with the group, they may be seen as deviant and become less powerful. People often conform because being independent is so difficult.

Probably all three variables—social conformity, attribution, and the risks of independence—are partly responsible for the conformity effect. As psychologists try to sort out the variables and examine different theories, they approach understanding how groups manipulate and influence individual behavior.

Obedience

Learning Objective $\underline{10.15}$ Parents work hard to teach their children obedience. Obedience to parents is an appropriate behavior in our culture; but should people obey everyone whom they perceive as being in a position of power? The armed services demand

Obedience is an integral part of military training.

Stanley Milgram conducted important experiments on obedience, which revealed much about the effects of social influence.

obedience, and any job that requires team effort, particularly athletics, requires it. Obedience has a valid role. However, people must be able to draw a distinction between an appropriate authority and an individual who merely assumes a position of authority.

Much to his surprise, in a now famous study on obedience Stanley Milgram (1933–1984) found that ordinary people were remarkably willing to comply with the wishes of other people, especially if the other person or persons are seen as in some way important. The extent to which an individual goes along with a significant person reveals a great deal about social influence in general and obedience in particular. It may also reveal something about an individual's self-perception and values.

In his classic experiment, Milgram (1963) brought two subjects into a laboratory and told them they were participating in an experiment to investigate paired-associate learning. The subjects drew lots to determine who would be the teacher and who would be the learner. The learner was to indicate which of four words was associated with a pair of words previously presented. But the drawing was rigged. One subject was collaborating with the experimenter. The naïve subject was always the teacher; the collaborator was always the learner. The collaborator-learner was placed in a booth, and electrodes were attached to his arm. The naïve subject was shown a shock generator box containing thirty switches, each labeled with a different shock intensity. The intensity labels indicated low shock, moderate shock, very strong shock, extreme intensity shock, and danger—severe shock. The shock generator was not actually attached to the learner, but the naïve subject did not know this.

The collaborator-learner made many wrong responses, and the naïve subject was told to punish him with a shock every time he made an error. In addition, a social psychologist and a lab assistant wearing a white lab coat encouraged the naïve subject to increase the shock voltage one level each time the learner made a mistake. As the shock level increased, the collaborator-learner produced appropriate sounds of pain. When the shock intensity reached the point of severe shock, the learner pounded on the walls of the

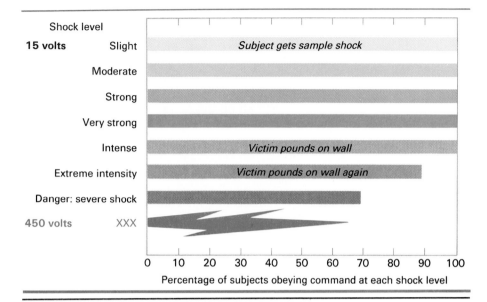

Shock level

15 volts Slight *Subject gets sample shock*

Moderate

Strong

Very strong

Intense *Victim pounds on wall*

Extreme intensity *Victim pounds on wall again*

Danger: severe shock

450 volts XXX

0 10 20 30 40 50 60 70 80 90 100

Percentage of subjects obeying command at each shock level

FIGURE 10.4 : In a study by Milgram, 65 percent of the subjects were willing to use the highest levels of shock intensity. Virtually all subjects were willing to provide shocks they thought to be of moderate or strong intensity. (Data from Milgram, 1963)

experimental booth and no longer made vocal responses to the paired-associate stimulus. The psychologist directed the subject to treat the learner's lack of response as an error and to continue to administer increasing levels of shock. As Figure 10.4 shows, 65 percent of the subjects continued to shock the learner until the completion of the shock series.

Milgram (1965a) has suggested that his experiment involved a particular type of experimental bias. He conducted his experiment at Yale University, an institution generally regarded with respect. In postexperimental interviews, several subjects remarked that the location and sponsor of the study gave them confidence in the integrity, competence, and benign purposes of the experimenters. Many subjects indicated that they would not have shocked the learner had the experiment been conducted elsewhere.

The issue of background authority is important in interpreting the results of Milgram's experiment. Consider how closely compliance is tied to institutions in day-to-day activities. People expose their throats on request to a razor blade in the barber shop but would not do so in a shoe store. In the latter setting, they willingly follow the clerk's request to stand in their stocking feet but would resist the suggestion in a bank. Similarly, in the laboratory of a positively regarded university, subjects may comply with a set of commands that would be resisted if given elsewhere. "One must always question the relationship of obedience to a person's sense of the context in which he is operating . . . " (Milgram, 1965a, p. 69).

To investigate this problem further, Milgram conducted a second study in an office building in Bridgeport, Connecticut. Subjects were contacted by mail and had no knowledge that Milgram or his associates were from Yale. Forty-eight percent of these subjects delivered the maximum level of shock, compared with 65 percent at Yale. Milgram concluded that the perceived function of an institution can induce compliance in subjects: an institution's qualitative position within a category (such as a "good" university) may be less important than the type of institution it is (a university, for instance, and not a factory).

In many other studies, scientists have repeated Milgram's methods and results. In one study, students enrolled in psychology classes at the University of Jordan were asked to deliver shocks. As in the original Milgram study, about 65 percent were willing to give shocks to other students. These results suggest that obedience to authority is not specific to Western culture (Shanab & Yahya, 1978).

Not all of Milgram's subjects were obedient. Some refused to deliver intense shocks. Furthermore, the presence of other subjects who refused to participate reduced the probability of obedience to as little as 10 percent (Milgram, 1965b; Powers & Geen, 1972). These data suggest that behavior is sensitive to both authority and peer behavior. An individual's ability to resist coercion in the presence of an ally who also refuses to participate indicates the importance of social influences on behavior. The subjects in the Milgram experiments simply found themselves in situations that powerfully influenced them.

As soon as Milgram studies were published, they raised ethical questions. Milgram's work was carefully scrutinized, and ultimately it has been judged to be ethical. The issue is deception and its potential harm to the subjects who participated in the research. It is often necessary in psychological testing to use naïve subjects (subjects who do not know what the experiment really is testing) in order to obtain unbiased responses. **Debriefing** is the procedure of explaining to subjects, after completion of an experiment, the true nature or purpose of the experiment. Debriefing preserves the validity of responses and is consistent with ethical considerations. Milgram's subjects were fully debriefed and shown that in fact they had not harmed the other person in the experiment. Nevertheless, these subjects now realized they were capable of inflicting severe pain on other people. Milgram had a psychiatrist interview a sample of his obedient subjects one year after their participation in the study, and no evidence was found of psychological trauma or injury. Another study reported that subjects viewed participation in an obedience experiment as a positive experience; they did not regret having participated, nor did they report even any short-term negative psychological effects (Ring, Wallston, & Corey, 1970). The ethics committee of the American Psychological Association actively and constantly scrutinizes research involving this kind of experimentation.

Milgram's study has important implications for social psychologists. His studies show how powerful people in positions of authority can change the course of events, and indeed potentially influence history; people in positions of power are obeyed. Milgram's studies challenge social psychologists to know why.

Debriefing
The procedure of explaining to subjects, after an experiment, the real purpose of the experiment.

PROGRESS CHECK 10.4

1. Complete each of the following sentences with one of the options provided.

Learning Objective 10.14

A. Studies that have used Solomon Asch's classic methodology have shown that an individual tends to conform to the group even when _____.

(the majority opinion is wrong : one person gives a dissenting vote)

Learning Objective 10.14

B. A small minority _____ influence on the decision-making processes of a large group.

(generally has little : can have substantial)

Learning Objective 10.14 C. A _____ minority exerts the strongest influence on group decision-making.
(consistent : flexible)

Learning Objective 10.14 D. The social conformity approach to why people conform suggests that _____ .
(being independent is difficult : people want to be "right")

Learning Objective 10.14 E. According to the attribution approach to conformity, if a person can attribute causes for the behavior of people in a group, the tendency to conform _____ .
(disappears : increases)

Learning Objective 10.15 F. In Milgram's obedience to authority study, _____ of the subjects delivered the most intense "danger—severe shock" to the collaborator-learner.
(10 percent : 48 percent : 65 percent)

Learning Objective 10.15 G. The fact that Milgram's study was conducted at Yale University brings up the issue that the study may have been affected by an experimental bias caused by _____ .
(intelligent subjects : background authority : misunderstood power)

Learning Objective 10.15 H. Milgram has suggested that in order to understand obedience to authority, we must question the relationship of obedience to a person's sense of _____ .
(morality : autonomy : the situational context)

Learning Objective 10.15 I. Research suggests that obedience to authority _____ specific to Western culture.
(is : is not)

Learning Objective 10.15 J. Milgram found that the probability of obedience dropped significantly when the _____ .
(subjects truly believed the shocks were real : subjects' peers refused to participate)

Learning Objective 10.15 K. _____ , after an experiment in which deception has been used, is important to preserve the validity of the subject's responses and to safeguard the ethical considerations that arise when using human subjects.
(Psychotherapy : Assessment : Debriefing)

BEHAVIOR IN GROUPS

A few pages ago, we met Bobbie, an eleven-year-old sixth grader. Bobbie seemed unusually preoccupied with looks, appearances, and other people's perceptions of her. In studying teenage behavior and individuals like Bobbie, psychologists have learned that our behavior is influenced by our childhood experiences, by other people, and especially by groups of other people. Consider how you feel when you first walk into a new class, a new dormitory, or a new social group. It is not surprising that you might feel somewhat shy or inhibited. Groups of people tend to alter individual behavior. Humans belong to all kinds of groups, both formal (such as the American Association of University Students) and informal (such as peers). Group membership helps satisfy the human desire to belong and gives people a sense of shared purpose. The nature of a group influences the kind and extent of social interactions that occur. By joining a group, people indicate they agree with or have a serious interest in its purposes. If a major function of the American Cancer Society is to raise money for cancer research, a person's membership indicates willingness to raise money for this purpose.

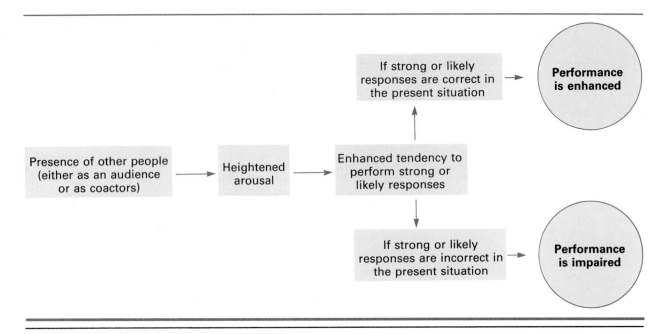

FIGURE 10.5 : According to the *drive theory* of social facilitation, the presence of other people increases our level of motivation or arousal, which, in turn, enhances the performance of our strongest or most likely responses in a given situation. If these responses are correct, performance is enhanced. If they are incorrect, performance is impaired.

Social Facilitation

Learning Objective 10.16

Social facilitation
The change in task performance that occurs when people are, or believe they are, in the presence of other people.

Individual behavior is affected not only by joining a group, but also by the presence of a group. One effect is called **social facilitation**—a change in performance, for either better or worse, due to the presence of other people. For example, a woman practicing a new game, sport, or other activity with some degree of success may do even better than before when other people enter the area, whereas another woman doing poorly may do even worse when she feels herself observed (see Figure 10.5).

Some researchers claim that the presence of other individuals produces a general increase in the anxiety and motivation levels of a learner or performer (Jackson & Latané, 1981; Zajonc, 1965). Many factors enter into social facilitation, including the number of individuals observing the subject, their gender, their relationship to the subject, and whether they are evaluating the subject, rather than simply watching.

Social facilitation is not seen in all group situations. On the other hand, it can be present even when there are no observers, if subjects *believe* they are being observed. Changes in performance due to social facilitation are relatively small. People may perform simple tasks more quickly in the presence of other people, but they do not necessarily perform them more accurately. Bond and Titus (1983) suggest that the effects of social facilitation are often overestimated, and the effect of merely believing oneself to be observed, underestimated. They caution that a model of social facilitation must take into account both the actual and believed presence of observers, as well as the perceived importance of the evaluation being performed.

Social Loafing

Learning Objective 10.17

Social loafing
The decrease in productivity that occurs when an individual works in a group instead of alone.

Whereas social facilitation generally produces improved performance, **social loafing** describes a decrease in an individual's effort and productivity as a result of working in a group. This phenomenon occurs when all members of a group are given the same task to perform. Early experiments on social loafing showed that when individuals had to pull on a rope alone, they exerted more effort than when other people helped. Similarly, when individuals were instructed to clap their hands and cheer, they clapped and cheered less loudly when they were part of a group (Latané, Williams, & Harkins, 1979). This is a disturbing result, because many decisions and work efforts are made in groups.

Research has shown that social loafing occurs among both males and females, in several cultures, and under a variety of conditions. A cross-cultural study (Gabrenya, Latané, & Wang, 1983) measured hand clapping and shouting behaviors in a group of 160 ninth-graders in Taiwan. The researchers discovered that the children exhibited social loafing with both behaviors.

Most psychologists claim that social loafing occurs because individual performance within a group cannot be evaluated; poor performance goes undetected and exceptional performance may go unrecognized. Consequently, people feel less pressure to work hard or efficiently. One study showed that as group size increased, individual members felt their own efforts were more dispensable—the group could function without their help. "Let George do it" became the prevailing attitude (Kerr & Bruun, 1983).

Social loafing is minimized when the task is attractive or rewarding and the group is committed to high task performance (Zaccaro, 1984). Social loafing is also less apparent when a group is small, when the members know each other well, or when a group leader calls on individuals by name or lets it be known that individual performance may be evaluated (Williams, Harkins, & Latané, 1981). Some cultural groups do not exhibit social loafing, and in fact exhibit the opposite (social striving) when in pairs. According to Gabrenya, Wang, and Latané (1985), members of cultures that are group oriented, as distinct from individualistic (like Americans), are more likely to show a complete lack of social loafing. People who deal with groups, such as fundraisers, teachers, or

According to the idea of social loafing, everyone in this game of tug-of-war is not pulling their hardest.

FIGURE 10.6 : After group discussions, people who hold mildly liberal or mildly conservative views tend to become even more liberal or more conservative. This tendency demonstrates part of the phenomenon of group polarization.

coaches, can improve group performance by remembering that individual performances need to be assessed if group performance is to equal the combined efforts of many individuals working alone.

Group Polarization

In groups, people are often willing to adopt views slightly more extreme than their individual views. They are willing to make decisions that are risky or even daring. A person who by himself is unwilling to invest money in a venture may change his mind on hearing that other members of the group are investing. A normally reserved individual may find himself swept away by the crowd at the end of a football game and surge onto the field with other fans to tear down the goalposts. Early formulations of such behavior focused on the willingness of individuals to behave in formerly unacceptable ways when other members of the group did so. Such formulations described individuals as making a *risky shift* in their behavior. More recent formulations of such behavior suggest that people in a group of like-minded individuals generally become more polarized in their attitudes. Thus, someone who holds conservative views, when placed in a group of conservatives, is likely to become even more conservative. Members of a group generally become more extreme in their initial direction of orientation. This phenomenon is known as **group polarization.** (See Figure 10.6.)

Group polarization occurs in a wide range of settings. Its effects are particularly evident in jury rooms. Jury members with an initially mild view toward a defendant tend to become even milder as a group; the initial view becomes the verdict. In general, after group discussion, a jury or other group is likely to take its initial view and argue for it more strongly (Kalven & Zeisel, 1966; Meyers & Kaplan, 1976).

One possible explanation for group polarization is **diffusion of responsibility,** the feeling of individual members that they cannot be held individually accountable for the group's actions. For example, if a group makes a decision to invest money, no one individual is responsible for that decision. This diffusion of responsibility allows for more extreme decisions than any individual would be willing to make alone.

Group polarization ====
The exaggeration of individuals' preexisting attitudes as a result of group discussion.

Diffusion of responsibility ====
The feeling of individuals in a group that they cannot be held individually responsible for the group's actions.

Although diffusion of responsibility may account for some aspects of group polarization, *social comparison* may also play a role. In a group, most individuals initially perceive themselves as being more extreme in their views than other members of the group—they feel more fair, more right-minded, more liberal, and so on. When they find that their positions are not far from those of other group members, they shift, or become polarized, to show that they are even more right-minded, fair, or liberal. They often become more assertive in expressing their views. Social comparison is an important factor accounting for group polarization.

The idea of *persuasive arguments* assert that people are persuaded to become more extreme in their views after hearing views similar to their own. After hearing persuasive, mildly liberal opinions, a person who is mildly liberal on an issue becomes even more liberal, more polarized. Furthermore, as more arguments favoring a particular view are presented in a group discussion, an individual becomes more likely to shift his or her view in that direction and become more extreme.

The data suggest that instead of becoming more reasonable, people within a group often retreat with greater frequency, and to a greater extent, to their initial view. If other people in a group hold similar views, this acts to reinforce those views and sometimes polarizes an individual to an even greater extent. Many important decisions made by families, churches, communities, and countries are made in groups. Yet from what psychologists have learned in the social psychology laboratory, we must question the value of group discussion when individuals often wind up maintaining their own views.

Groupthink

Group Think
The tendency of people in a group to seek concurrence among members when reaching a decision.

Closely related to group polarization is the phenomenon of **groupthink,** the tendency of people in a group to seek concurrence among members when reaching a decision. Rather than effectively evaluating alternative solutions to problems, group members tend to reinforce commonly held beliefs in the interests of getting along. Social psychologist Ivan Steiner (1982) suggests that groupthink occurs when members' overriding concern is to maintain group cohesiveness and harmony (see Figure 10.7).

FIGURE 10.7   The factors producing the development of *groupthink*.

Factors producing groupthink	Development of groupthink	
High level of group cohesiveness	Feelings of invulnerability	
Isolation of group from outside information or influence	Belief that group is completely right	**Very poor decisions**
Dynamic influential leader	Tendencies to ignore or discredit information contrary to group's position	(Decisions with low probability of success)
High stress from external threats	Strong pressures on group members to conform	
	Stereotyping of outgroup members	

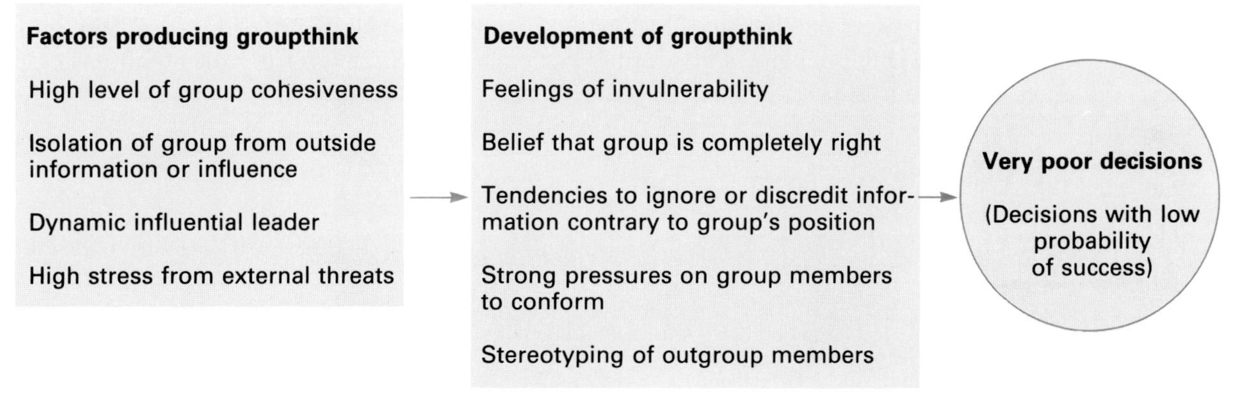

Groupthink also occurs when individuals in a groups feel a sense of cohesiveness and feel that the group cannot make mistakes. The group has a strong leader and a sense of purpose. Its members discredit information that does not agree with the group. When groupthink occurs, a group does not allow group members to disagree or take dissenting opinions. Groups engaged in groupthink tend to ignore information that the group does not have in common.

Irrational Group Behavior: Deindividuation

Deindividuation ══════
The process by which individuals in a group lose their sense of self-awareness and concern with evaluation.

When placed in a group, normally thoughtful people have been known to take part in irrational behaviors, such as college panty raids, a neighborhood brawl, a soccer game riot, or looting during a blackout. Many psychologists interpret irrational group behavior in terms of **deindividuation,** the process by which individuals lose their distinctive personalities in the context of a group. To people in a group, the consequences of individual behaviors may seem less clear than when they are confronted with a decision on their own.

Environmental conditions of anonymity and arousal can lead to shifts in people's perceptions of how their behavior will be viewed, and thus to less controlled or careful decisions about behavior (see Prentice-Dunn & Rogers, 1984). For example, in the early 1970s, the phenomenon of streaking became popular on college campuses. In streaking, a naked person darted out from behind a bush, ran across campus or through a crowded lobby, and disappeared. Soon streaking groups containing hundreds of students began to form. Within a large group, no single individual could be held responsible for the behavior of the group; the behavior was not considered a matter of individual responsibility, but a group decision. The individuals in the group became deindividuated.

The military uses the concept of deindividuation to advantage. During boot camp, recruits are made to feel that they are there to serve the group, not their individual conscience. Similarly, cults often used such group tactics to persuade other group members to go along, for the group's sake. In deindividuation, the attitude is that you do not have to be responsible yourself, that the group made the decision.

Deindividuation can account for many curious and irrational group behaviors. A key component of deindividuation is *anonymity*. Anonymity produces a lack of self-awareness and self-perception. A lack of self-awareness leads to decreased concern with social evaluation. When people have fewer concerns about being evaluated, they are more willing to engage in inappropriate or irrational behaviors. Without accurate self-perception, people can and do exhibit behaviors they would normally avoid except for the social influence of a group.

PROGRESS CHECK   10.5

1. Match each of the following key concepts and terms with the appropriate definition.

| social facilitation | groupthink | social loafing | deindividuation |
| group polarization | diffusion of responsibility | | |

Learning Objective 10.16   A. _____ A change in performance, generally for the better, although sometimes for the worse, that occurs when people are, or believe they are, in the presence of others.

Learning Objective 10.17   B. _____ Individuals lose their distinctive personalities and emit behavior they might never have shown before.

Learning Objective 10.17   C. _____ An individual's effort and productivity decrease as a result of performing the same task as other people in the group.

Learning Objective 10.17   D. _____ A phenomenon that takes place in group decision-making where the decisions that are made are more extreme than any one individual would make on his or her own because the members feel that they cannot be held individually accountable for the actions of the entire group.

Learning Objective 10.17   E. _____ The exaggeration of individual's preexisting attitudes as a result of group discussion.

Learning Objective 10.17   F. _____ A situation that occurs in group decision-making where the overriding concern of the members is to maintain group cohesiveness and harmony. As a result, commonly held beliefs are reinforced and alternative solutions are not effectively evaluated.

2. Complete each of the following sentences with one of the options provided.

Learning Objective 10.16   A. Social facilitation seems to influence behavior because _____ _____.
(other people provide encouragement : *we sense that our behavior is being evaluated)*

Learning Objective 10.17   B. Social loafing occurs because individual performance within a group _____.
(cannot be evaluated : *is easily replaced* : *is dispensable)*

Learning Objective 10.17   C. Social loafing can be stopped by making the performance of participants in the group _____.
(difficult : *moderately easy* : *identifiable* : *fun)*

Learning Objective 10.17   D. Social loafing is more likely to occur in cultures that have _____ orientation.
(an individualistic : *a group)*

Learning Objective 10.17   E. The social comparison explanation for why group polarization occurs suggests that individuals want to feel that their views on an issue are more _____ than the views of the other people in the group.
(flexible : *extreme* : *cautious)*

Learning Objective 10.17   F. If an individual with a mildly liberal view on a particular issue becomes even more liberal after hearing other people express opinions in support of that view, we would say that _____ led to the change.
(diffusion of responsibility : *risky shift* : *persuasive arguments)*

Learning Objective 10.17   G. Research shows that group discussions tend to lead the individual members of the group toward _____ opinions.
(adopting more reasonable : *retreating to their original)*

Learning Objective 10.17   H. Groupthink tends to occur when a group has a _____ _____ sense of purpose.
(weak leader and no : *a strong leader and a)*

Learning Objective 10.17   I. Deindividuation seems to occur because _____ can produce changes in an individual's self-awareness and concern over being evaluated.
(anonymity and arousal : *polarization and self-serving biases)*

Learning Objective 10.17   J. Deindividuation is used deliberately by groups such as _____ _____.
(professional athletic teams : *military boot camps)*

Keeping Pace with Chapter 10

*Applying
Principles*

10.1 Identify the learning process that is involved in forming attitudes in each of the following situations.

classical conditioning   instrumental conditioning   social learning

_____

A. Stanley's attitude about being on time is no secret to his friends; he has little hesitation in telling late arrivals "Everyone has the ability to be on time; therefore, you do too!" When Stanley was a child, his parents always hurried him. Each time he succeeded in being ready when they were, his parents would smile and show approval.

_____

B. Lacey grew up with an alcoholic father who frequently became physically abusive while consuming alcohol. Because the consumption of alcohol was so frequently paired with physical abuse, Lacey developed an attitude against alcohol and responds negatively whenever she observes one of her friends drinking.

_____

C. When driving through the metropolitan area of their city, Tom's mother repeatedly made elitest comments about their sophisticated urban life-style and criticized the life-style of people living in the suburbs. Having spent many hours listening to his mother, Tom acquired the same attitude and, as an adult, is very negative about getting together with acquaintances or going to a restaurant in suburban communities.

Identify the most prominent form of social influence that is taking place in each of the following situations.

social facilitation   group polarization   social loafing
groupthink   diffusion of responsibility   deindividuation

_____

A. As a new member of the community's most prestigious athletic club, Richard worried about looking like a real wimp around the other members who, most likely, had been exercising for some time. On his first day, he wore the most stylish exercise outfit he could buy and painfully overexerted himself in every activity.

_____

B. As the city council members gathered for their regular meeting, the prevailing group attitude was leaning toward raising the city's parking-meter fees. The council members listened to several reasonable, proven, and successful alternatives, as well as to a number of citizens who opposed the idea. They discussed the issue and reflected on their original reasons for raising the parking fees. The group ended up voting unanimously to raise the parking fees and later that evening released a very strong statement explaining why the action was their only reasonable alternative.

_____

C. Dean did not like the idea of expelling Scott. His feeling was to be lenient, and he knew other group members felt the same way. As the school psychologist assigned to the case, Dean knew that the child received no encouragement or support at home and that the school was Scott's only hope. In the end, the convenience of school personnel won. Even though they knew deep inside that Scott was being abandoned, all members in the group, including Dean, outwardly agreed to his expulsion.

_____

D. Kim works as a framer for a large housing development company. When he first started the job, he took the time to make accurate measurements and to make certain that all the joists were square. However, as the days went by, Kim noticed that the construction superintendent never recognized his careful efforts and never criticized other workers for sloppy workmanship. After several months on the job, Kim gradually gave up his need to do a good job and found himself spending more time joking around with the other framers.

_____

E. Harry was not especially thrilled by the idea of painting the complex a pale salmon color, but as he realized that the other people on the condominium association board of directors were leaning toward the pink tones, he went along with them, figuring it was not an important enough issue to "make waves" about.

_____

F. Cherlyn was bewildered as she sat in the city jail waiting for someone to post her bail and set her free. She, along with several team members and other cheerleaders, had been arrested for painting obscenities on their rival team's stadium. Cherlyn could not understand how she possibly could have done such a thing nor why she had not considered her own self-concept and values until after the police had arrived.

Self-Test

Before proceeding to the Self-Test, REVIEW the Learning Objectives listed at the chapter opening and RECITE from memory everything you can remember in support of them. Then, take this Self-Test as if it were to be graded by your teacher. Use the Learning Objective numbers in the Answer Section as a reference to restudy the corresponding text pages and Progress Checks for any incorrectly answered questions.

1. Social psychologists study

   A. how behavioral traditions develop in different cultures.
   B. the effects cultures have on group behavior.
   C. individual differences in life-style and opportunity.
   D. how social situations and other people influence individual behavior.

2. Which of the following is the cognitive component of the attitude that children should be respected as human beings?

   A. Believing that children are worthy of all the respect you would give to an adult.
   B. Feeling very upset if you see the rights of a child infringed on by an adult.
   C. Acknowledging a child for holding his or her own opinion about a social issue even if it differs from your own.
   D. Having a sense of elation when you read about a child who writes letters to politicians stating his or her concerns about human rights.

3. Attitude formation that occurs as a result of classical conditioning occurs

   A. because a person is reinforced for having a particular belief.
   B. with such little effort that the conditioning process frequently goes unnoticed.
   C. when someone watches the behavior of another person whom they hold in high esteem and then imitates it.
   D. if the person has the opportunity to practice the attitude with strangers.

4. An individual's attitude would be *least* likely to change if

   A. the individual perceives the speaker as being powerful and prestigious.
   B. the speaker presents new ideas that are quite different from the person's original opinion.
   C. the speaker shares ideas in a face-to-face communication.
   D. an attitude change would have positive consequences and avert danger.

5. Festinger claimed that in order for attitudes and behaviors to change when dissonance is present,

   A. the person must be fully aware of the dissonance.
   B. negative consequences must be associated with maintaining existing attitudes or behaviors.
   C. the reason for having certain attitudes or behaviors must be understood.
   D. A and C

6. According to the self-perception view put forth by Bem, the situations individuals find themselves in lead people to

   A. experience dissonance and make decisions that will influence their future behavior.
   B. make inferences concerning their emotions, attitudes, and the causes of their behaviors.
   C. pay attention to the reinforcements and punishments associated with change.
   D. establish friendships and business relationships that allow them to maintain a consistency in their belief systems.

7. If Mindy's father tells her she has to go to college and Mindy responds by moving out of the house, taking a full-time job at a fast-food restaurant, and spending her free time doing aerobics exercises, reactance theory would suggest that she

   A. has a rebellious attitude.
   B. found her father's ideas inconsistent with her long-term goals.
   C. behaved as she did in order to maintain a sense of autonomy.
   D. was not open to parental advice or suggestions.

8. Which of the following provides the best example of body language?

   A. Ollie's pupils contract when he walks out into the sunlight.
   B. Eve raises both of her hands above her head as she triumphs over being first to cross the finish line.
   C. Mark is bored, so he goes to bed.
   D. Lisa Beth stretches before beginning her aerobic exercises.

9. According to Kelley, we attribute behavior to internal causes when we evaluate a behavior and situation and find

   A. low consensus, consistency, and distinctiveness.
   B. high consensus, consistency, and distinctiveness.
   C. low consensus and distinctiveness, with high consistency.
   D. high consensus and distinctiveness, with low consistency.

10. People make errors when they attribute motives to someone's behavior because acknowledging the truth can threaten a person's

    A. belief that people get what they deserve.
    B. belief in a just world.
    C. sense of self-esteem and feelings of control.
    D. all of the above

11. An individual's physical characteristics and his or her perception of those characteristics

    A. can establish a lifelong pattern of reward or punishment.
    B. have very little to do with the person's ability to succeed.
    C. are studied by physiological psychologists, and social psychologists frequently draw on their findings.
    D. are the prevailing concerns of balance theory.

12. Which of the following is a good example of a self-serving bias?

    A. Bryant wants a better job so he looks for and finds one.

    B. Ted, who constantly struggles with his habit of procrastination, tells Sue how efficient he is with always getting his homework done ahead of schedule.

    C. Rayna sees Alex slip something under the bed and decides he is hiding something from her.

    D. Sheila buys a new outfit so she can look terrific on her first day at the university.

13. When a person believes he or she has no control because of the consistent noncontingent delivery of reinforcing or punishing consequences, the person is in a vulnerable position that could easily lead to

    A. trying harder to gain control.

    B. providing himself or herself with self-reward for achievements.

    C. behaving with a learned helplessness response pattern.

    D. escaping from the situation as soon as an opportunity arises.

14. The theories put forth by Lorenz and Freud concerning human aggression are considered _____ theories.

    A. nativistic

    B. social learning

    C. acquired drive

    D. behavioral

15. The most recent version of the frustration-aggression hypothesis suggests that

    A. when goal-directed behavior is interrupted, people will become aggressive.

    B. frustration may cause a variety of responses.

    C. aggressive people are more easily frustrated.

    D. A and C

16. Which of the following statements concerning the research that has investigated television's relationship to aggressive behavior is *false?*

    A. People who observe television violence are more likely to intervene and help victims of real violence.

    B. Most studies show that television violence increases the incidence of real-life violence.

    C. Aggressive children tend to watch more television than do nonaggressive children.

    D. Television can be beneficial in establishing positive social and personal behaviors.

17. Solomon Asch's conformity experiment

    A. made use of collaborators who actively pressured a naïve subject.

    B. involved a fairly difficult task of distinguishing between two lines of almost equal length.

    C. found that if one of the collaborators gave a dissenting vote, the naïve subject no longer went along with the majority.

    D. was designed to test the effects that attribution has on conformity.

18. Debriefing

    A. is used in experiments that involve deception.

    B. enables a researcher to conduct an experiment that might otherwise be considered unethical.

    C. enables a researcher to conduct an experiment that will provide valid, unbiased responses.

    D. all of the above

19. Social facilitation

    A. is observed in all group situations.

    B. can be observed in behavior even when there are no observers.

C. generally causes major changes in an individual's performance.

D. all of the above

20. Social loafing

A. occurs more frequently in large rather than small groups.

B. causes all other participants in the group to work more than their fair share.

C. is even more likely to occur if an individual feels his or her own efforts are rewarding and indispensible.

D. occurs after a person makes a risky shift.

21. Group polarization occurs because people

A. tend to change their opinion when provided with arguments that oppose their original opinion.

B. prefer to change their mind in order to maintain group cohesiveness and harmony.

C. tend to become more extreme in their opinions after hearing arguments that favor their initial views.

D. get into intense situations in which they lose their sense of self-awareness.

22. Deindividuation in a group is probably caused by

A. strong group leaders.

B. having values that differ from those of the group.

C. relying on one's own conscience.

D. anonymity.

11

Human
Relationships

11

Learning Objectives

When you have mastered the material in this chapter, you will be able to:

1. Explain what is meant by personal space, tell how the use of personal space varies among cultures, and describe the four spatial zones classified by Hall. (p. 416)

2. Define *crowding,* describe some variables that contribute to it, discuss how knowledge about crowding could improve some prison environments, and explain how people behave when they feel crowded. (p. 419)

3. Explain why privacy is important, discuss some ways people establish a sense of privacy, and describe the purpose of territorial behaviors. (p. 420)

4. Discuss bystander apathy, bystander involvement, and "unwillingness to ask for help" and explain why these behaviors occur. (p. 422)

5. Explain what is meant by interpersonal attraction and describe how proximity, reward and punishment, physical characteristics, and attitude similarity contribute to our feelings of attraction for another person. (p. 425)

6. Explain how people maintain friendships by establishing equity in the relationship and describe the similarities and differences between friendships and romantic relationships. (p. 428)

7. Describe what is meant by love according to several psychologists and discuss some behaviors that accompany love. (p. 428)

8. Give some reasons that public discussion of sexuality has become acceptable in recent years; define the terms *coitus, erogenous zones,* and *orgasm;* and explain how experiences of sexual behavior vary among individuals. (p. 431)

9. Discuss the development of sexual behavior in males and females and describe what researchers know about masturbation, premarital coitus, marital coitus, extramarital coitus, and attitudes about sex in males and females. (p. 433)

10. Describe current trends concerning marriage and state some reasons people marry. (p. 440)

11. Explain how married people define their roles, give some common reasons marriage partners typically must make adjustments in order to maintain a satisfying relationship, and discuss how different people measure the success of a marriage. (p. 441)

12. Make a distinction between internal conflict and external conflict, tell how people attempt to resolve conflict in marriage, and describe what happens when a couple fails to resolve conflict. (p. 445)

13. Describe four ineffective approaches to communications and explain how a couple can communicate effectively. (p. 447)

14. Discuss some variables that contribute to divorce or staying together and explain why people having difficulty with their marriage should consider therapy. (p. 448)

Alan and Alicia shared the first letter of their first names—but that was about all that seemed similar. Alan was a good student, career-oriented, and civic-minded. Alan had a plan for his life. He was an economics major, was planning on getting a Master's degree in international business, and intended to work for IBM, AT&T, or SONY. Alicia was an English major, an average student, and seldom thought about politics, her career, or the future—but she knew every top 40 or new wave hit and loved to dance. She came to college because she had nothing else to do, her parents were paying, and she did not want to get a nine-to-five job. She had no idea where she was heading and did not seem to understand the importance of setting long-term goals. Alicia was interested in more immediate pursuits, such as enjoying life, and establishing an identity different from her peers.

Alan and Alicia were an unlikely couple. However, by a strange set of circumstances, the two were paired up for a blind date. The evening was a disaster. He talked about school, economics, and the stock market. She talked about Julian Lennon, the academy awards, and the plumbing in her dormitory. The date ended mercifully early at 10:45.

It was a clear mismatch—but something kept Alan thinking about Alicia. He liked her eyes, and she had self-confidence. However, they had nothing in common. Alicia instantly forgot about Alan. He was not her type—too ambitious, self-centered, and dull. Three weeks later, Alan decided he needed some mindless entertainment. None of his friends were around, he had seen every movie in town, and he had no new female prospects. He ran through the list of all the people he had dated in the last year. Initially, he ruled out the idea of calling Alicia. But his roommate had just given him a strident lecture on being more flexible and open. So Alan decided to broaden his horizons and give pop culture a chance. Maybe she would turn out to be passionate!

Alicia found her phone conversation with Alan acceptable; he was even funny at one point. He acknowledged their initial difficulties and suggested that they give dating another try. Reluctantly, she decided to go out with him. Their second date went better. They went to a jazz club and listened to music they both liked. The conversation went more smoothly. The close confines of the club gave Alan an opportunity to smell a wonderful perfume Alicia wore. Alicia noticed that Alan's hands were strong and good looking. The chemistry was brewing.

ALAN AND ALICIA ARE LIKE thousands of people who date and begin a close, personal relationship. Sometimes people are introduced or fixed up. Other people meet at work, or perhaps they live in the same neighborhood; in all instances, they see each other, and even that brief contact allows them to be attracted to one another. That attraction is often established by a person's looks, demeanor, or perhaps the way he or she walks, talks, or conducts business. Outward physical appearances have a profound effect on people's perceptions of other people and on their willingness to open a relationship with them or to expand on an existing relationship.

Too often, however, people like Alan and Alicia do not get to know each other and never establish a relationship. Their differing life-styles and tastes keep them apart. They may remain at a distance, perhaps fearing the unknown, embarrassment, or rejection.

This chapter examines some issues of personal relationships. It examines some environmental factors in relationships, how and why people are attracted to one another, and why they sometimes stay away from strangers and strange situations. It also examines the nature of more intimate relationships involved in sexual behavior and marriage.

ENVIRONMENTAL FACTORS IN RELATIONSHIPS

Alan and Alicia were fixed up by mutual friends. However, they might have met in other ways. Many individuals begin a relationship by meeting in a dormitory, apartment building, or at work. A couple's relationship is often determined by where they meet. For example, people in their work environments often maintain a "business" relationship; this usually means that their interactions are relatively formal and that they keep personal ideas and feelings out of the relationship.

In an office environment, people often seek ways of maintaining their individuality and remaining separate from other people. Keeping to themselves helps some people feel more secure in an environment such as an office or a city that might bombard them with many confusing stimuli. One consequence of maintaining a sense of separateness, however, is that it often limits a person's ability to establish and maintain a close relationship with another person. Both environmental situations in which people find themselves and spaces and situations that people create (like fences around property or bookcases between office areas) establish a sense of separateness and individuality.

Everyone Has Personal Space

Learning Objective 11.1

A public environment often intrudes on a person's sense of self and individuality. People may walk arm in arm with a family member, but they avoid physical contact with a stranger. They may whisper in the ear of a friend, but they maintain their distance from an elevator operator. To help assert individuality and maintain a sense of personal control, human beings generally try to establish appropriate personal spaces. **Personal space** is the area or invisible boundary around an individual that he or she considers private. Encroachment on that space causes displeasure and often withdrawal. The size of this space can change, depending on the situation and the people who are with the individual. Linking arms may feel comfortable with a familiar date but uncomfortably close with a new date.

Personal space =====
The area around an individual that is considered private; the invisible boundary around a person.

The physical closeness between these two men indicates that they probably know each other well.

Some of the first views on personal space came from anthropologist Edward Hall. Hall (1966) suggested that personal space is a mechanism by which people communicate with other people. He observed that the use of personal space varies from culture to culture. In most cultures, people adhere to established norms of personal space that are learned in childhood. Western cultures insist on a fair amount of space between strangers, reserving proximity for intimacy and close friends. In contrast, Arab culture allows much smaller distances between strangers. An acceptable distance for strangers in Saudi Arabia might be unacceptable for suburbanites in San Diego (Watson & Graves, 1966). Similarly, in Japan much less space is available per person than in most Western countries. Accordingly, Japanese homes are designed to be small and provide little private space (Aiello & Thompson, 1980).

Research supports the idea that individuals maintain personal space. Consider the study by Barefoot, Hoople, and McClay (1972). One experimenter sat either close to or far from a prominently placed drinking fountain in the hall of an administration building and pretended to read a book. He or she recorded the number of people passing the fountain and the number who stopped to drink. The experimenter avoided looking at the subjects except for a brief glance. For half the subjects, the experimenter sat in a chair only one foot away from the drinking fountain; for the other half, five feet away. In a control condition, the experimenter sat on a bench opposite the fountain approximately ten feet away.

The experimenters reasoned that if the subjects cared strongly about not having their personal space violated, they would avoid drinking from the fountain in both the one-foot and five-foot conditions. As predicted, subjects tended to avoid a situation that would bring them into close physical proximity to another person. A smaller percentage of subjects drank from the fountain in the near condition than in the far and control conditions. These results support the general idea that an invasion of personal space is aversive.

Hall classified four spatial zones, or distances, that are used in social interactions with other people: *intimate, personal, social,* and *public.* At the distances associated with each zone, certain characteristic interactions are acceptable for Western cultures, and certain kinds of sensory events are associated with them.

An *intimate distance* (from zero to eighteen inches) is acceptable for comforting someone who is hurt, for lovers, and for contact sports. This closeness allows a person to hear another's breathing, smell the other person, and examine every detail of the person's skin, hair, and eyes. This distance is reserved for people who have great familiarity with one another.

A generally more acceptable distance for close friends and everyday interactions is *personal distance* (from one and a half to four feet). At one and a half to two feet, someone might tell a spicy story to a close friend. At two or three feet, that person might walk through the city streets and maintain a conversation. At two to four feet the individual can easily maintain good contact with a co-worker and yet not seem impersonal. Personal distances are those used for most social interactions.

Social distance (from four to twelve feet) is used for business and interactions with strangers. At four to six feet, people are close enough to communicate their ideas effectively while remaining separated. Sometimes, personal space in the social zone is controlled by the use of such physical barriers as a desk to separate a clerk, receptionist, or teacher from the people with whom he or she has to interact.

Public distance (from twelve to twenty-five feet) minimizes personal contact. When politicians speak to clubs, when teachers stand behind desks, when actors or musicians perform from a stage, the distance is sufficiently great to eliminate any personal communication between the individuals and their audience (see Figure 11.1).

Most researchers agree that individuals vary their personal space requirements as their overall and specific situations change (see, for example, Altman & Vinsel, 1977). As Altman has suggested, personal space is a privacy-regulating mechanism, and people make appropriate changes in their immediate environment to maintain a sense of privacy.

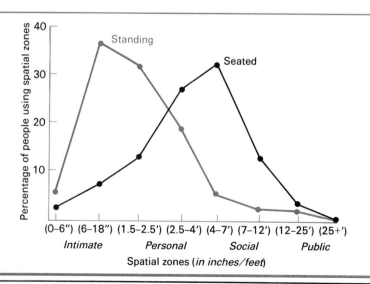

FIGURE 11.1 : While standing, people use primarily the personal and intimate zones. While seated, they use primarily the personal and social zones. (Altman & Vinsel, 1977)

Sometimes being in a crowd can be exhilarating. At other times, it can make us feel restricted and irritable.

People Like People, But No One Likes to Be Crowded

Learning Objective 11.2

In some situations where they are surrounded by dozens, hundreds, or even thousands of other people, individuals may feel closed in. At other times, the excitement of a crowd is exhilarating. It is not the size of a space or the absolute number of people within it that gives people a sense of being crowded. Density refers to the number of people in a specific space. Crowding, on the other hand, is a psychological state. **Crowding** is the perception that one's space has become too restricted, or limited. In an empty theater with a capacity of 400, a single person may experience a sense of loneliness, but as the theater fills up, he or she may begin to feel crowded. In the same way, early arrivals at a party often feel awkward and socially ill at ease in a nearly empty space. Yet within an hour, with perhaps only twenty people there, that space may feel too full of people, noise, and heat. Crowding refers to how individuals respond to a given density (Stokols, 1972, 1976).

Crowding
The perception that one's space is too restricted.

Crowding is affected by both social and spatial density. *Social density* refers to the number of people in a given space; *spatial density* refers to the size of a space with a given number of people in it. If both variables are manipulated at the same time, the actual effects of crowding are difficult or impossible to determine. Researchers must be careful to separate these variables.

The effects of crowding generally have deleterious effects on people and animals. Perhaps one place in which the effects of crowding are especially apparent is in a prison. The prison population has grown substantially in the last two decades, in part because of increases in the population and because of stricter sentencing laws. Prisons are so crowded that according to Cox, Paulus, and McCain (1984), a 1,000 square-foot apartment would have to house about 77 adults around the clock to approximate the level of crowding they observed in some prisons.

When these researchers studied prison populations, they found that crowded prisons, as compared to less crowded prisons, have increased rates of suicide, psychiatric problems, inmate-on-inmate assaults, and discipline problems. Their research shows that when inmates are kept apart from one another by being given small, private spaces, some of the negative effects can be reduced. In their private spaces, the inmates can avoid the feelings of crowding. If you calculate the amount of space per inmate, the researchers argue that even a very small amount of private space is better than a larger but shared open space. They conclude that open dormitories with more space have few if any redeeming values—rather, they argue that a smaller space with one or two inmates is desirable for the inmates' physical and psychological well-being.

The effects of crowding are not consistent across all situations or populations, but certain effects seem to be universal. In situations of high social density, people tend to feel alone or anonymous. They feel stressed, overloaded, and sometimes overaroused. They react by withdrawing, becoming apathetic and sometimes hostile. As social density increases, people begin to show adverse behavioral effects: they isolate themselves, feel stressed, and task performance is impaired.

Adding a few people to a room will not make a person withdraw. Similarly, shrinking living and working spaces by a few square feet will not produce dramatic behavioral changes. But shrink space, add a few people and a context of stress, and the ingredients for negative behavior are established. Altman (1975) explains the reaction of withdrawal in a context of privacy. People can help reestablish a sense of privacy by turning inward and tuning out the presence of others.

Privacy: Controlling Personal Space

Learning Objective 11.3

After being away from home for days, weeks, or months, people may begin to feel lonely for the comforts of home. They may yearn for the privacy of their own room, the familiarity of old books, and a sense of ownership. Most people grow up in homes that can provide them with a certain amount of privacy: they have their own place at the table, a shelf in the bathroom reserved for them, and, more generally, a certain territory that "belongs" to them. Their environment has consistency. In contrast, in dormitories, libraries, dining halls, and communal bathrooms, feelings of personalization are minimal or absent.

To a great extent, people try to control how the environment affects them. For example, individuals who are interrupted too many times when trying to study in their dorm room may lock their door, put out a "Do Not Disturb" sign, or perhaps go to the library. These responses can provide the feeling of control necessary for them to feel comfortable. Altman (1975) suggests that privacy is central to understanding the behavior of human beings in their environment, the key to understanding feelings of crowding and personal space. **Privacy** is the process of controlling boundaries between people so that access is limited. When a woman goes into a room and closes the door, she closes herself off from other people; she limits their access to her. She has set up a boundary—a closed door—behind which she can do what she wants as she wants. Similarly, two people may enter a room and close a door to control access, and groups of people who desire a sense of privacy (perhaps a therapy group or a family) may try to set themselves apart in order to engage in a particular activity.

Many people have difficulty finding privacy. Parents with many children often have little privacy. The president of the United States uses Camp David as

Privacy
The process of limiting access to people by controlling the boundaries between them.

a retreat where he can go to seek privacy. Sometimes a shower stall can provide a few minutes of time and inches of space that people can call their own.

At times, everyone needs quiet to reflect, study, or just relax. Privacy, in Altman's view (1975), allows people to develop and nurture a sense of self. Without privacy, people feel they have no control over who and what can intrude on them. This sense of helplessness can lead to lowered self-esteem and poor functioning. The idea that the self requires privacy is central to Altman's view of how the environment affects behavior. Although his view is not universally accepted, the fact remains that everyone seems to seek privacy, and it is in these private moments that people often determine the course of their lives.

Mechanisms of Control. People use various ways to control access to themselves. They can tell other people that they want to be alone. Indeed, they can insist on being alone; to some extent, all people use this device. The most common method is the use of nonverbal mechanisms: body position, head tilt, and duration of gaze are quick but clear ways of telling someone to "stay away." From an early age, children know their parents' nonverbal methods of telling someone they need some privacy: it might be a hand gesture, a nod of the head, or perhaps a stare over the top of a pair of glasses.

People also guard their privacy and ward off intruders in other ways. For example, the way someone dresses conveys a message to other people. Most people are more willing to approach someone who is dressed casually than someone who is attired more formally. However, people who are dressed too casually will scare some people off. People can also tell others how much privacy they desire by the shape and layout of their office spaces and homes. Architect Glenn Lym (1978) believes that one function of building design is to make evident the user's expectations about the kinds of space appropriate for different types of activities. These expectations are to a large extent determined by the individual's previous experiences with different types of space. According to Lym, a person's choice of floor plan in a house or layout in an office reflects his or her opinions about the proper relationships among people, activities, and space. The design of a living, work, or recreational space regulates interaction. For example, highly placed executives who want to avoid intrusions on their time and space by salespeople and the general public guard their privacy by locating their secretaries in outer offices.

Territoriality. Maintaining a sense of privacy is closely related to territoriality and is often an important goal in people's lives. In suburbia, the notion that, in poet Robert Frost's words, "good fences make good neighbors" is an axiom of living. People buy, furnish, and decorate houses and spend hours of back-breaking work weeding, trimming, and cutting lawns. They begin to exhibit clear signs of territorial behavior. **Territorial behavior** is behavior to establish, maintain, personalize, and defend a delimited space. Teenagers often mark their doors with signs that say "Keep Out" or "Private Property." Chainlink fences around a house tell a passerby something about the territorial sense of its owner.

Territorial behaviors help regulate privacy. Altman views territory as fixed in space. Personal space, in contrast, moves with a person as he or she moves about in the world. Many experts agree with Altman's view that a well-developed sense of self, including feelings of self-worth, status, and well-being, are tied to having a well-defined sense of privacy, personal space, and territory.

Territorial behavior
Behavior involved in establishing, maintaining, personalizing, and defending a delimited space.

Bystander apathy is a common and disturbing phenomenon of human behavior.

Bystander Apathy

*Learning
Objective*   11.4

Had Alan never called Alicia for their blind date, it might have been because he feared the embarrassment of being turned down. He might have felt it was not worth the risk of possible ridicule by Alicia. As research shows, people are often afraid to take such risks. Consider the situation wherein strangers might provide help to someone in trouble. If you are walking down the street with a bag of groceries and you drop them, what is the likelihood that someone will help you pick them up? If you approach someone for change to make a phone call, will he give it to you? What happens when a person observes a serious accident or crime? Will he or she do something to help?

In large cities, where many kinds of emergencies occur—accidents, thefts, even stabbings and killings—large numbers of people often watch and do nothing. Bibb Latané of Ohio State University and John Darley of Princeton (1970) investigated bystander apathy in a long series of studies. They found that in a situation that would require acting in a way that is uncomfortable for them, people must choose between helping or standing by apathetically; they must choose whether or not to introduce themselves into a situation.

Latané and Darley reasoned that people who felt anonymous in a situation might be more likely to help. To test this hypothesis, they brought college students to a laboratory and told them they were going to be involved in a study of persons who were having personal problems with college life. The researchers told the subjects that in the interests of preserving people's anonymity, a group discussion would be held over an intercom system rather than face to face, and that each person in the group would talk in turn. In fact, there was only one true subject in each experimental session. All the discussions heard were prerecorded and the tape recordings were turned on by informed subjects who worked for the researchers. During the group discussion, one subject appeared to have a serious nervous seizure. The dependent variable was the speed with which the naïve subject reported the emergency to the experimenter. The major independent variable was the number of people the naïve subject thought to be in the discussion group.

The naïve subjects were led to believe that their discussion group was one of three sizes. When the group consisted of only two subjects, 85 percent of the naïve subjects responded by helping before the end of the seizure. With three subjects in a group, 62 percent of the naïve subjects responded by the end of the seizure. When six were in the group, only 31 percent responded by the end of the seizure. All the subjects in the two-person groups eventually reported the emergency, compared with only 62 percent of the subjects in the six-person groups. Cast in the role of bystanders to an emergency, the naïve subjects were less likely to respond if they thought other people were present.

Despite their failure to respond, the subjects were not indifferent. Latané and Darley suggest that the subjects were in a state of indecision and conflict about whether to respond and were worried about the guilt and shame they would feel if they did not help. The subjects were also concerned about making fools of themselves by overreacting. If the other bystanders are strangers, helping someone may involve some personal risk—perhaps embarrassment or even punishment. Unfamiliarity with a specific situation or place also decreases willingness to act. Caught between two negative choices (letting the victim continue to suffer or rushing in but not knowing how to help), the subjects vacillated instead of choosing to intervene. As a result of their experimental studies, Latané and Darley suggested a five-step decision model to help understand the process influencing bystander intervention. These steps are (1) being aware of the situation, (2) defining the situation as an emergency, (3) accepting personal responsibility for helping, (4) deciding on the kind of help to give, and (5) acting.

The personality characteristics of the individual involved in a bystander situation are important. For example, Tice and Baumeister (1985) found that subjects who had a high degree of masculinity were less likely to respond. They argue that perhaps highly masculine subjects were too fearful of embarrassment or perhaps they were too willing to obey instructions to stay in the booth and finish the experiment. This bystander effect is in direct contrast to the general finding that men are more likely than women to help strangers (Eagly & Crowley, 1986), while women are generally seen as being more nurturing and caring. Differences between men and women in terms of their willingness to help are extremely complicated and must be interpreted cautiously. Men are not always more helpful in bystander situations and women are not always nurturant. The research into these gender differences continues.

Bystanders will help under some conditions. People's self-concepts and previous experiences affect their willingness to intercede. Bystanders who see themselves as especially competent in treating emergencies are likely to help a victim regardless of the number of other people present (Pantin & Carver, 1982). In general, Latané (1981) has found that speed of assistance decreases as the number of bystanders believed to be present increases (see Shotland & Heinhold, 1985). Latané asserts that the number of other people present also affects a variety of other social phenomena, such as tipping in restaurants (tip size decreases as party size increases) (see also Latané & Nida, 1981).

Everyone needs help from time to time. Research shows, however, that some of the same variables operating in bystander apathy are also involved in people's unwillingness to ask for help. People who need help even in such simple things as locating a street address often do not ask for it. The explanation may be embarrassment, or subjects may feel that acknowledging that they need help threatens their self-esteem (Fisher, Nadler, & Whitcher-Alagna, 1982). Threats to self-esteem and fears of embarrassment are part of the dynamics of helping or meeting strangers. Aware of these variables, psychologists are able to help people develop and maintain more intimate relationships.

PROGRESS CHECK 11.1

1. Complete each of the following sentences with one of the options provided.

Learning Objective 11.1   A.   Personal space refers to _____.
(a person's living quarters : a private, invisible area around a person)

Learning Objective 11.1   B.   The amount of personal space people require _____.
(is the same in all cultures : varies from culture to culture)

Learning Objective 11.1   C.   Invasions of personal space _____.
(are aversive and can cause withdrawal : seldom occur)

Learning Objective 11.1   D.   According to Hall, most social interactions occur at a_____ distance.
(personal : social : public)

Learning Objective 11.2   E.   Crowding is caused by _____ in a specific space.
(many people being : a person's reaction to the number of people)

Learning Objective 11.2   F.   According to Cox, Paulus, and McCain, prisons that provide inmates with _____ should have decreased rates of suicide, psychiatric problems, assaults, and discipline problems.
(spacious, open dormitories : small, private spaces)

Learning Objective 11.2   G.   In situations of high social density, people tend to feel_____.
(alone and anonymous : enthusiastic and involved)

Learning Objective 11.3   H.   The idea that _____ privacy is central to Altman's theory.
(the self requires : well-adjusted people do not need)

Learning Objective 11.3   I.   According to Altman, territory refers to a _____.
(fixed space : space that moves with a person)

Learning Objective 11.4   J.   Research conducted by Latané and Darley has shown that a bystander is more likely to help a person in need when _____ bystanders are present.
(few or no other : he or she feels anonymous because a number of)

Learning Objective 11.4   K.   Bystander apathy seems to occur because people _____.
(are indifferent to the problems of other people : experience indecision and conflict)

Learning Objective 11.4   L.   A person who _____ is most likely to help out in a bystander situation.
(feels competent to provide help : has strong masculine traits)

Learning Objective 11.4   M.   Often people who need help do not ask for it because_____.
(they do not realize they need help : to do so could threaten their self-esteem)

ATTRACTION

Alan and Alicia are typical of many people in Western culture. Most people like them will marry at least once before they die. Although people often seek privacy and want to maintain a sense of separateness, they also seek secure, warm, close human relationships. So, even though the divorce rate in the United States is very high, so is the number of new marriages. These facts substantiate what most people already know—people are attracted to one another; they derive from other people a sense of warmth, understanding, and emotional security. Social psychologists study the process of developing relationships to learn how one person's characteristics or behavior affect another person, positively or negatively. In particular, social psychologists study the process of interpersonal attraction—the tendency of one person to evaluate another person in a positive way.

Attraction refers to a positive attitude toward another person. Psychologists can measure these feelings and attitudes by using interviews and questionnaires and by observing subtle nonverbal indicators such as eye contact, helping behavior, and body distance between individuals. Research has shown that people are attracted to other people they consider good-looking. People are also generally attracted to members of the opposite sex. They are more likely to be attracted to people they spend time with and who share their attitudes. The process of attraction involves the characteristics of both the people involved and the situational variables.

Proximity

If you live in an apartment complex, you are more likely to be attracted to and develop a relationship with a neighbor in the building than with someone who lives several buildings away. Three decades of research show that the closer you live (and/or work) to someone, the more attracted you will be to that person. One reason is that you are likely to see that person often, and repeated exposure tends to lead to attraction (Moreland & Zajonc, 1979). Furthermore, the mere anticipation of being attracted to someone with whom you come in frequent contact leads to the development of attraction (Darley & Berscheid, 1967). Meeting people who are members of a group to which you belong (club, family, or work) facilitates your perception of them as sharing your beliefs, attitudes, and values, and that belief leads to attraction. Both everyday experience and scientific evidence show that the closer you live or work to someone, the more likely you are to be attracted to that person.

Rewards and Punishments

Learning theorists contend that people are attracted to other people who provide them with positive reinforcements. Similarly, they dislike people who punish them. The basic idea is simple: people like people who like them. If you like someone, you tend to assume (sometimes incorrectly) that he or she likes you.

*We are likely to become
friendly with people who live
close to us.*

When in need of social approval (for example, when self-esteem is low), people are even more likely to find themselves attracted to people who provide them with approval or other positive reinforcements (Jacobs, Berscheid, & Walster, 1971; Walster, 1965). In the absence of contradictory evidence, people assume that someone they like shares qualities similar to their own and returns their liking. They assume the other person both likes them and is like them.

Components of Attractiveness

Physical Characteristics.   People draw many kinds of conclusions based on a person's physical characteristics. As mentioned earlier, people's physical characteristics often set into motion a pattern of reinforcement or punishment over which they have little control. Human beings in all cultures pay particular attention to the way they appear to other people. Our own youth-oriented culture focuses heavily on physical appearance, especially facial appearance (Muesser, Grau, Sussman, & Rosen, 1984). Both men and women are attracted to individuals they consider physically attractive. Numerous experiments have shown that people ascribe more power, status, competence, and personal regard to such people than to people they consider less attractive (Webster & Driskell, 1978). In a typical experiment, subjects given two job résumés with two different pictures attached will evaluate the physically attractive individual more highly than the less attractive person. Similarly, high or low status labels associated with people have direct effects (Lipton & Hershaft, 1984).

Many studies have explored the components of physical attractiveness. Women like men of average height; men like women of medium size (for example, see Graziano, Brothen, & Berscheid, 1978; Kleinke & Staneski, 1980). Such characteristics as how often people smile and where and when they direct their gaze also influence people in deciding whether they find other people attractive.

Our understanding of physical attractiveness has practical applications. Remember, the basic finding in studies of attractiveness is that the more attractive the individual, the more positive characteristics people ascribe to the individual. Attractive people are preferred in the work place, for dates, and for friendships. Attractive people thus have an advantage. We all know, however, that most people can dress for success and make themselves more attractive. Men and women alike can find attractive ways to package their looks.

Attitude Similarity.   A real or perceived similarity in attitudes and opinions affects people's attraction to other people. If they perceive someone's attitudes as similar to their own, they will like that person. Similarly, if people like someone, it is also likely that they will perceive that person's attitudes as similar to their own. Both these phenomena have received considerable experimental support. Both grow out of cognitive consistency theory (discussed in Chapter 10), which suggests that sharing similar attitudes reduces cognitive dissonance. If a friend holds an idea contrary to yours, you experience cognitive dissonance. To avoid dissonance, people are motivated to feel attracted to people they believe share similar attitudes. Shared attitudes in turn lead to attraction and liking. As long as people believe the other person's attitudes are genuine, such liking will continue. However, if they feel that the person is

Millions of Americans are lonely. In fact, one survey found that one-quarter of Americans would report having felt lonely in the past few weeks. Of the 50 million people in the United States who currently are feeling lonely, 10 percent suffer from severe and persistent loneliness (Peplau & Goldston, 1984). Understanding the nature and causes of loneliness is important because loneliness appears to be a major contributing factor to premature death and also to many psychological disturbances. It can be linked to alcoholism, physical illness, depression, suicide, psychological paralysis, and intensified social isolation (Lynch, 1977; Price, 1985). Loneliness has no boundaries— it is experienced by men and women and people of all races, socioeconomic levels, and ages (Gordon, 1976; Perlman & Peplau, 1984).

Perlman & Peplau (1984) define *loneliness* as an unpleasant and distressing experience that occurs when a person's network of social relationships is significantly deficient in either quality or quantity. It occurs when there is a discrepancy between the person's needs and desire for social contact and the actual social contact. Loneliness is not synonymous with social isolation—people can be alone and content, or in a crowd and desperately alone. Loneliness is often accompanied by feelings of dissatisfaction, sadness, anxiety, hostility, emptiness, boredom, and restlessness. Feelings of loneliness can be painful but, in a positive light, they signal that something in our emotional or social environment is not as it should be and thus can prompt us to make some changes toward personal growth (Perlman & Peplau, 1984).

Two common types of loneliness are emotional loneliness and social loneliness. Emotional loneliness occurs when an individual does not have a personal, intimate relationship with at least one person whom he or she views as significant. Social loneliness occurs when an individual lacks adequate or expected connections with other people. Brief periods of feeling lonely are normal. When loneliness persists, however, it becomes a very painful and potentially life threatening problem (R. S. Weiss, 1984).

Everyone, at some time in life, feels lonely, but some people are more vulnerable to loneliness than are others. People who are shy and self-conscious, who have low self-esteem, or who lack effective social skills for making and keeping friends are more vulnerable to the experience of loneliness (Perlman & Peplau, 1984).

Because loneliness is affecting people in epidemic proportions, it cannot be explained only in terms of personality characteristics. It is an inherent problem of modern life, prompted by geographical mobility and the disintegration of the family (Gordon, 1976). The end of a marriage through divorce or death, the transition from adolescence to adulthood, moving to a new area for work or college, and retirement are some events that can lead to loneliness. Major life transitions (as described in Chapter 8) and modern life-patterns disrupt our ability to keep consistent intimate relationships. Gordon points out (p. 16) that because "personal identity seems to require the validation of another person's confirmation, many people feel faceless—empty, lonely."

Price (1985) suggests loneliness is a matter of self-perception—how loneliness is experienced is determined by how a person perceives and interprets the situation. He has found that a lonely person can find relief by becoming aware of lonely feelings, accepting that they exist, and taking action. Price says, "The element of choice is important in designing [your] own method for managing loneliness." (Price, 1985, p. 197) He acknowledges that breaking out of loneliness when you are perhaps feeling completely devoid of friends and at the bleakest point in your life is not easy, but it is a choice you have.

In his book *People of the Mirror: An Intimate Look at Loneliness* (1985), Price describes a Life/Loneliness Management Plan, a seven-step self-help approach to overcoming loneliness. Briefly, the steps are:

1. Consider yourself an instrument of change.
2. Resolve to do something.
3. Make a frank self-appraisal—strengths first, weaknesses second.
4. Develop a new plan to get to where you want to go.
5. Take charge of making things happen—appreciate what you have done thus far.
6. Reconstruct a sense of self by establishing a new kind of communication with other people.
7. Make a commitment to follow through.

---

ingratiating himself or herself solely for the purpose of gain, the initial attraction yields to feelings of disapproval (E. E. Jones, 1964).

The role of personality characteristics in attraction is less clear. Sometimes, people are attracted to other people with personalities similar to their own, and sometimes as in the case of Alan and Alicia, they are attracted to individuals with different personal characteristics. The most important variables seem to be reinforcement and similarity in attitudes, both of which are based on attributions or judgments about other people's characteristics and behavior.

Balance in Liking

*Learning
Objective*   11.6

We like people who like us, who have views similar to our own, and who are attractive. Equity in a relationship also plays an important role. *Equity theory* asserts that people attempt to maintain stable, consistent, interpersonal relationships in which the proportion of each member's contributions is equal to that of the other members of the group, so that all members are treated fairly. Sometimes, however, maintaining an evenly balanced relationship is difficult or impossible. People who feel they have been treated unfairly will usually try to get restitution. You may have been in an argument with someone and told how hurt you were by that person's behavior. The more you talked about the hurt, the bigger the hurt grew. Usually, the aim in such conversations is to get the person who hurt you to apologize or to make amends for the offending behavior. According to equity theory, one way people maintain a balanced relationship is to make restitution when it is demanded: if you harm me, then I need an apology. These apologies help restore a sense of autonomy to the injured individual. Similarly, people who do favors expect favors in return. When a politician responds to constituents' desires and has a playground or road built, he or she expects their votes on election day. Most people use the principles of equity theory unconsciously in day-to-day life. We may do a favor because we know we will need one in return sometime in the future.

Friendship and Close Relationships

Friendship is a two-way relationship between two people. Although by definition friendship does not involve romantic love, the same processes often imitate both. Psychologists Keith Davis and Michael Todd (1984) suggest that, ideally, friends:

> participate as equals
> enjoy each other's company
> have mutual trust
> provide mutual assistance
> accept each other as they are
> respect each other's judgment
> feel free to be themselves spontaneously
> understand each other in fundamental ways
> are intimate and share confidences

Although all friends talk about intimate topics, pairs of women speak more about family and personal matters and doubts and fears than do pairs of men (Aries & Johnson, 1983). Friendship does not involve the fascination and exclusiveness or the physical intimacy and intense attraction that usually accompany a romantic relationship. Friendships are generally less complicated relationships, but they satisfy many basic social needs.

What Is Love and To What Does It Lead?

*Learning
Objective*   11.7

People who become intimate often express behavior in unique ways. Flowers, moonlight walks, lengthy letters, and romance are all typical of a couple who are falling in love. Do sexual activities, especially intercourse, necessarily accompany an intimate relationship? Before marrying, some people stay abstinent. Other people have only a few partners until marriage. In the 1980s, many people were permissive about sex but required some degree of commitment from their partner.

Love may or may not be present in a premarital relationship; but people who marry usually share a sense of commitment and love, which helps to bind the marriage. Even though sex may occur without love, for most couples, the combination of love, sex, and emotional commitment binds them together and allows them to share a deep sense of intimacy.

Love is redefined by the poets of each generation; however, psychologists agree that several psychological, emotional, and social factors are part of the process of love. Before we consider some elements of love, let's look at what some psychologists have said about love. Noted psychoanalyst Erich Fromm focused on the idea that mature love is possible only if a person has achieved a secure sense of self-identity. Fromm wrote in 1956 that when people are in love, they become one and yet remain two individuals. Branden (1980) suggested that love is "a passionate spiritual-emotional-sexual attachment between a man and a woman that reflects a high regard for the value of each other's person." Heinlein (1961) wrote that love "is a condition in which the happiness of the other person is essential to your own." Social psychologist Keith Davis argued that love is characterized by exclusiveness, fascination, and sexual desire (Davis & Todd, 1982). Tennov (1981) asserted that the ultimate in romantic love is a state called *limerance;* this is a head-over-heels involvement and preoccupation with thoughts of the loved one.

Researchers identify some common elements in love relationships. Love usually involves the *idealization* of another person; we see our loved one in a positive light. Love usually involves *caring* for another person and often being *fascinated* with that person. In addition, love usually involves *respect, liking, companionship,* and *sexual attraction.* Love can be considered as a process. The process usually begins with infatuation, often based on physical characteristics. Over time, as people come to know one another, physical attraction leads the way toward shared interests, liking, companionship, and perhaps sexual intimacy. The process of love is constantly undergoing change. Many people have the mistaken idea that love is unidirectional and always grows stronger,

Companionship and sexual attraction are important elements in love relationships.

but most people recognize that we can fall out of love as quickly as we can fall into it.

Men and women seem to view love differently; for example, men report falling in love more quickly than women. Furthermore, people from different social backgrounds have various social, political, and even economic views about love. Because love is psychological, emotional, and social, it may or may not be shown in overt behavior. A person may love another yet not make this known; too often, one person loves another but is unable to express it in a meaningful way. This reluctance often leads to misunderstanding and the breakup of a relationship.

Distinguished psychologist David McClelland (1986) has noted that the mainstream view of love is that it is a state arising from people mutually reinforcing one another or providing benefits to one another. He says that when you talk to people who are in love, they tell you love involves much more than interdependence. People who are in love report that it includes intimacy, concern not rooted in guilt, a sense of enduring commitment in spite of separation, and a sense of harmony and true understanding of one another.

Regardless of how it occurs, love initiates a series of behaviors that are sustained because of it. Consider sexual behavior. The sexual behavior of both men and women is affected dramatically by the way they view love and its relationship to sex. The views people have of love, of sexual permissiveness, and of the nature of men and women shape—in many significant ways—the quantity *and particularly the quality* of their sexual relationships. A man and woman who are deeply in love and who share a sense of commitment, respect, and intimacy experience an emotional satisfaction from a sexual union that a couple engaging in sex on a first date cannot experience. It is the shared sense of love, commitment, and permanence that urges individuals on toward marriage, where companionship, lasting legal commitment, and sex are considered appropriate and necessary.

PROGRESS CHECK 11.2

1. Complete each of the following sentences with one of the options provided.

Learning Objective 11.5

A. The tendency of one person to evaluate another person in a positive way is a phenomenon that social psychologists refer to as _____.
(interpersonal attraction : love : aligning action)

Learning Objective 11.5

B. In the absence of contradictory evidence, we tend to assume that other people _____.
(like us and are like us : expect us to win their approval and liking)

Learning Objective 11.5

C. The behaviors of paying attention to personal physical appearance and caring about how we appear to other people are common in _____ cultures.
(all : modern but not primitive : modern Western)

Learning Objective 11.5

D. The most important variables in determining our attraction to other people are _____.
(ingratiating behaviors and attractiveness : reinforcement and similar opinions)

Learning Objective 11.6

E. Equity theory focuses on _____ a relationship.
(fairness and equality of contributions within : activities external to)

Learning Objective 11.6

F. A difference between a friendship and a romantic relationship is the
_____ the relationship.
(process that initiates : exclusiveness of : acceptance of intimate discussion in)

Learning Objective 11.7

G. Eric Fromm argued that a mature love can be achieved only when an individual
_____.
(acknowledges a state of limerance : has a secure sense of self-identity)

Learning Objective 11.7

H. _____ tend to report being in love earlier in a relationship.
(Men/Women)

SEXUAL BEHAVIOR

If the environmental variables are right, and if the attraction is there, people often become involved in an intimate relationship. Sometimes, such a relationship begins slowly with friendship; other times, it advances quickly toward romance. Alan and Alicia's first date was a disaster. Their second date went better, and some attraction was developing. If they were to continue to see each other, they would likely develop deeper feelings. They would probably become involved romantically, and perhaps sexually. Hopefully, Alan and Alicia would know how to express their feelings in positive ways.

Each of us has sexual feelings that we experience and express in different ways at different points in our lives. Not surprisingly, adolescents and college-age people are discovering, exploring, and learning how to manage their sexual feelings most effectively. Although seemingly simple ideas, these concepts were realized only recently; public discussion of sexuality has traditionally been considered taboo.

Learning Objective 11.8

Psychologists are among the professionals who have brought sexual behavior before the public for examination. They argue that sexual behavior is sometimes motivated by reasons that have little to do with sexuality. For example, some people seek sexual encounters to bolster their feelings of competence or to assert their authority. More often, people express through sexual behavior their feelings of intimacy, romance, and closeness. Psychologists seek the reasons for these expressions of sexual behavior and the situations most conducive to intimate sexual relationships.

In 1948, Alfred Kinsey, a biologist, published a report on the sexual behavior of the human male. The Kinsey report discussed masturbation, extramarital sex, and just about every other aspect of human sexual behavior. Much of the general public was shocked and outraged. Yet the report brought great relief to many people because it confirmed that they were normal. Kinsey found an astonishing lack of knowledge about sexuality within the population and introduced to the public topics that had never before been discussed in such an open form. In retrospect, the Kinsey report is not very astonishing. Sexual behavior is now very obvious and easily available for public scrutiny. Today, discussion of sex is not only open and popular, but has also become an American pastime. The media, press, and even school children are aware of different aspects of sexuality. The AIDS epidemic has created even closer scrutiny of sex and sexual behavior.

Two major studies on human sexual behavior were the pioneering work of Kinsey, Pomeroy, and Martin (1948) and Kinsey, Pomeroy, Martin, and Gebhard (1953). Their work has been substantiated and extended by contemporary researchers such as Morton Hunt (1974), DeLamter and MacCorquodale (1979), and Masters and Johnson (1966, 1970, 1979).

Virginia Johnson, along with her co-worker William Masters, was a pioneer in her research on human sexuality.

Sexual Intercourse

Couples usually experience deep feelings and a shared sense of intimacy as they engage in sexual activities. Romantic feelings, a sense of trust and love, and a sense of spirituality can accompany sexual intimacy. The most intense of these experiences is sexual intercourse. **Sexual intercourse** or **coitus** occurs when a man's penis is inserted into a woman's vagina. (We use the two terms, *sexual intercourse* and *coitus,* interchangeably.) Sexual intercourse may be a perfunctory activity that is performed routinely, or it may involve elaborate arrangements and emotional involvement. Each person who shares a sexual experience with someone else develops a personal set of techniques for bringing about sexual arousal, maintaining that sexual arousal, and achieving satisfaction.

When various parts of the body are touched, different feelings occur. The **erogenous zones** are parts of the body that can lead to sexual arousal when stimulated. There are a number of erogenous zones, and they are basically the same in men and women; individuals, however, are more or less sensitive to certain erogenous zones than to others. The most obvious ones are the genitals and the areas surrounding them. Other erogenous zones are the breasts, neck, armpits, mouth, and tongue. A common characteristic of all erogenous zones is that they all have billions of nerve endings; when these nerve endings are stimulated, the result is sexual arousal.

Sexual intercourse can be performed in many different ways. A couple typically develops a preference for one position or one approach to sexual intercourse over a period of time. The most common position for Americans is the face-to-face, man-on-top position; most women and men express a preference for it. In this position, the woman reclines on her back with her legs apart and her knees bent. The man inserts his erect penis into the woman's vaginal opening, and the sexual union is made easily. Variations of this face-to-face position include the woman taking a position above the man or both the man and the woman lying on their sides. None is "best" or "right," except what is comfortable and fulfilling for both sexual partners.

It must be recognized that sexual intercourse is not essential to the production of a fertilized egg. Sperm can, in fact, be artificially implanted in the woman (injected medically into the uterus by a physician). This procedure, called *artificial insemination,* is used frequently by couples when the male partner is sterile (incapable of producing sufficient amounts of sperm cells). For most couples, however, sexual intercourse is the normal means of producing children.

Orgasm: The Peak of the Sexual Experience

Sexual activity can take a variety of forms. It can be short-lived or lengthy. It can be simple or elaborate. It can be engaged in lovingly or with callousness. Sexual intercourse usually leads to an orgasm. An **orgasm** is the peak or climax of excitement during the sexual activity. An orgasm can occur during sexual intercourse, masturbation, or other kinds of sexual activity. An orgasm is a highly pleasurable, tension-relieving, seizure-like response that is the peak of physical gratification (see Masters & Johnson, 1966). A man can achieve an orgasm within two to five minutes from the beginning of sexual activity; a woman

---

Sexual intercourse ══
Sexual union of a male and female in which the penis is inserted into the vagina; also called *coitus.*

Erogenous zones ══
Areas of the body that are particularly sensitive to sexual excitement; these areas include the genitals as well as the mouth, neck, tongue, and breasts.

Orgasm ══
The peak of physical and emotional excitement in sexual activity; it is accompanied by involuntary muscular activity, intense pleasure, and, for the male, ejaculation.

usually requires from ten to twenty minutes to reach a state of arousal. A single orgasm lasts only from three to ten seconds and generally is extremely intense.

Women generally report two distinctly different kinds of orgasms, clitoral and vaginal. Clitoral orgasms are generally described as electrical, sharp, and intense, whereas vaginal orgasms are described as deep, diffuse, and throbbing. Even though women report these two distinct feelings, physiologically the two cannot be distinguished; in fact, good evidence suggests that all orgasms in women are mediated through the clitoris, even though the primary stimulation might be in the vagina (Eysenck & Wilson, 1979).

Sexual Behavior of the Male

Learning Objective $\underline{11.9}$ More than 99 percent of boys begin their regular sexual lives immediately after their first ejaculation; regular sexual behavior means a regularity of ejaculation. Kinsey reported that most boys experience ejaculation at approximately age thirteen and continue to have two or three orgasms a week for many years. Even though there is considerable variability, about 78 percent of men continue to have between one and seven orgasms per week throughout their lives; older males have fewer orgasms than younger ones, and married men have more orgasms than unmarried men (Brown, Kilmann, & Wanlass, 1982).

Men and women can engage in a wide range of sexual behaviors. Table 11.1 shows some of these behaviors and the ages by which they had first occurred in a large sample of male students (DeLamater & MacCorquodale, 1979). As would be expected, the more intimate and involved the sexual behavior, the older the men were when they first engaged in it. In this study, it is also

TABLE 11.1 Ages by Which Male College Students First Engaged in Different Sexual Behaviors (Expressed as Percentages)

Age*	Necking	French Kissing	Petting	Male Fondling of Female Genitals	Female Fondling of Male Genitals	Apposition	Intercourse	Male Active Oral-Genital Contact	Female Active Oral-Genital Contact
9	2.4	0.2	0.5	0.5	0.5		0.6		
10	4.7	0.2	0.5	0.5	0.5		0.6		
11	8.3	1.7	1.2	1.0	1.4	.6	1.2		0.3
12	20.1	5.2	3.5	1.8	1.9	1.5	1.5	0.7	0.7
13	35.2	17.4	8.3	4.3	4.2	3.5	2.7	1.1	1.5
14	52.7	33.6	20.6	8.8	8.1	4.7	3.7	1.9	2.2
15	74.0	54.7	41.0	23.2	18.9	13.1	8.3	3.4	4.5
16	88.9	75.3	67.4	47.2	39.5	33.8	23.7	12.2	12.9
17	95.4	87.8	84.8	69.6	65.2	60.4	49.3	32.1	33.1
18	98.9	96.0	94.4	89.1	85.3	82.9	76.2	63.9	60.6
19	99.4	98.0	97.9	96.4	95.1	93.7	88.2	81.9	80.9
20	99.7	98.7	98.9	98.0	98.3	97.2	95.9	94.2	93.8
21	100.0	100.0	99.4	99.1	100.0	99.6	99.0	98.4	98.0
22			99.7	99.4		99.6	99.6	99.6	99.6
23 or over			100.0	100.0		100.0	100.0	100.0	100.0
Number of individuals	418	402	397	370	354	334	324	261	262

Source: J. DeLamater and P. MacCorquodale, *Premarital Sexuality* (Madison: University of Wisconsin Press, 1979), p. 62.
* 19.49% of sample 18 or under, 41.07% under 19, 62.88% under 20, 83.99% under 21, and 92.11% under 22.

important to note that few subjects were engaged in heterosexual activity before the age of twelve. Striking, however, is the sharp increase in the percentage of men who engaged in intercourse and heterosexual oral-genital contact at ages seventeen and eighteen.

Masturbation ══════
Self-stimulation of the
genitals.

Masturbation. The most common form of ejaculatory experience for the adolescent boy is in self-stimulation; that is, **masturbation.** Most males have masturbated at one time or another and continue to do so on a regular basis. Frequency of masturbation is usually affected by education levels, age, and socioeconomic status. Males in their early adolescence masturbate about 2.4 times per week, although almost 20 percent may average four to seven times a week or more. Ninety-six percent of men who have attended college have masturbated; 90 percent of male students who have completed high school and 85 percent of those who have only attended grade school have masturbated. Almost 70 percent of males experience their first ejaculation through masturbation. The frequency of masturbation decreases as a man becomes older: men under age thirty-five, married or single, masturbate about seventy times per year, whereas men over age thirty-five masturbate about thirty-three to thirty-five times per year (see Athanasiou, 1976).

Premarital Coitus. Premarital heterosexual coitus refers to intercourse between two unmarried people; marital coitus refers to intercourse between marrieds; extramarital coition refers to intercourse between a man and a woman of whom at least one is married to someone else.

Most men have sexual intercourse before they marry, although the percentage varies with educational level. For example, 98 percent of the men who had attended only grade school experienced premarital coitus, compared to 84 percent of high school graduates and 67 percent of men with a college education. The percentage of males of college age who had experienced coitus was estimated to be about 50 percent in the 1930s; but more recent studies suggest 70 to 80 percent (Darling & Davidson, 1986; DeLamater & MacCorquodale, 1979). Hunt's data (1974) show significant increases in premarital coitus at all age and education levels.

Even though many college-age men report that they have engaged in premarital coitus with numerous partners, among college students 51 percent of male undergraduates in one major study reported having had three or fewer partners in their lifetime; for a similar age group of noncollege subjects, 37 percent reported having had three or fewer than three intercourse partners in their lifetime, and 50 percent, four or fewer than four partners (DeLamater & MacCorquodale, 1979).

Marital Coitus. For most men, marriage is the traditional framework within which intercourse takes place. Many factors, including age, work habits, health, and occupation, affect the frequency of marital intercourse among males. The frequency of intercourse among married men varies dramatically, depending on their age; early in a man's married life, he experiences intercourse considerably more often than later in his married life.

As with premarital coitus, there have been increases in frequency of marital coitus. Hunt (1974) found an increase of coitus at all age levels compared to a decade earlier. For example, Kinsey showed that males from ages sixteen to twenty-five were engaging in coitus 3.3 times per week; Hunt's data show an

TABLE 11.2: Frequency of Marital Intercourse, as
Reported in Kinsey (1948, 1953) and Hunt
(1974) Surveys

Kinsey (1948, 1953)		Hunt (1974)	
Age	Median*	Age	Median*
16–25	2.45	18–24	3.25
26–35	1.95	25–34	2.55
36–45	1.40	35–44	2.00
46–55	0.85	45–54	1.00
56–60	0.50	55 and over	1.00

*Median frequency means 50% of the married population have intercourse more frequently than the percentages expressed, while 50% have intercourse less frequently.

increase to 3.7 times per week. Of course, there is a great degree of variability from person to person in these data. (See Table 11.2.)

Extramarital Coitus. More than one-third of married males engage in extramarital sex. Again, educational level and age are related to the frequency of extramarital sex; college-educated men have less extramarital coitus during early marital years than in later years. By contrast, less-educated groups showed a tendency to decreased extramarital coitus over time. For most males, extramarital intercourse is usually sporadic and occurs on an occasion or two with different partners. Extramarital activity accounts for a fair proportion of sexual outlets for married males in certain segments of the population, but overall it accounts for only 5 to 10 percent of the orgasms of men in the United States. This pattern of sexual behavior remained relatively stable for the twenty years before the Hunt study (Hunt, 1974). The extent of a person's extramarital permissiveness is best predicted by the extent of a person's premarital attitudes and sexual behavior (Singh, Walton, & Williams, 1976).

Sexual Behavior of the Female

Perhaps due to cultural inhibitions, women show greater individual differences than do men in their sexual development. Many women are not fully sexually active until their twenties or mid-thirties. Indeed, some women enter marriage only to discover that their husbands wish to have sexual intercourse much more often than they do. Often, a couple is matched in terms of sexual drive in the early years of marriage; yet, as women enter their thirties and sometimes their forties, most find that their sexual needs increase while their spouses' desires often decrease. Consequently, the incidence of extramarital sex by women is greater among those in their late thirties than among those in their twenties.

Like men, women show that, as they grow older and mature, the nature of their sexual activities changes. Very few young girls engage in coital activity, but as they grow older, the percentage of women who are engaging in more complicated and intimate forms of sexual activity increases. Shown in Table 11.3 are the percentages of women from ages nine to twenty-three who are involved in various sexual activities. Much like the data presented for men in

TABLE 11.3 : Ages by Which Female College Students First Engaged in Different Sexual Behaviors (Expressed as Percentages)

Age*	Necking	French Kissing	Petting	Male Fondling of Female Genitals	Female Fondling of Male Genitals	Apposition	Intercourse	Male Active Oral-Genital Contact	Female Active Oral-Genital Contact
9	0.4								
10	0.9								
11	3.5	0.2							
12	11.2	1.4	0.2						
13	26.0	11.4	5.2	1.4	0.6	0.3	0.3		
14	44.6	24.3	11.5	4.8	2.9	3.2	1.5	1.1	0.8
15	65.6	45.9	24.2	15.3	10.6	10.5	5.4	1.9	1.7
16	82.5	68.8	50.2	32.3	26.3	23.7	14.3	11.3	12.4
17	90.7	81.2	71.2	57.9	51.1	46.4	35.3	30.0	29.1
18	98.0	93.4	88.0	80.6	77.2	74.6	66.9	62.8	63.0
19	99.7	97.5	97.5	93.4	92.9	91.3	87.1	85.5	83.2
20	100.0	98.2	98.2	97.7	96.7	97.1	96.0	94.9	96.5
21		99.5	99.5	99.4	98.8	99.6	99.1	98.8	97.8
22		99.7	99.7	99.7	99.7	100.0	99.5	100.0	100.0
23 or over		100.0	100.0	100.0	100.0		100.0		
Number of individuals	425	411	400	352	338	312	257	256	233

Source: J. DeLamater, and P. MacCorquodale, Premarital Sexuality (Madison: University of Wisconsin Press, 1979), p. 62.
* 18.65% of sample 18 or under, 46.86% under 19, 71.34% under 20, 88.36% under 21, and 96.52% under 22.

Table 11.1, there are fairly sharp increases in the percentages of women engaged in intercourse at ages sixteen, seventeen, and eighteen (DeLamater & MacCorquodale, 1979).

Masturbation. Masturbation is a common sexual activity for women. Even in the 1940s, we knew that approximately 62 percent of all women masturbate at one time or another during their lives. According to Kinsey, masturbation accounted for between 37 percent and 85 percent of total sexual outlet for unmarried females, compared to only about 10 percent for married females. Unmarried females of lower education levels depend more on premarital coitus than on masturbation. This disparity between educational levels is much smaller among older women. Kinsey's data were conservative; furthermore, more recent estimates show markedly more masturbation, particularly in single females (Hunt, 1974). Most women, between 50 percent and 90 percent, have masturbated at some time (Darling & Davidson, 1986). One popular but admittedly biased study has reported that 82 percent of women masturbate regularly (Hite, 1976).

Premarital Coitus. Coitus for women varies dramatically with their age and education; yet, nearly half the women in our society experience coitus prior to marriage, and at least 64 percent experience orgasm prior to marriage. According to the DeLamater and MacCorquodale (1979) study, premarital sexual intercourse for girls under the age of fifteen occurred in only 5 percent of the women; the percentage increased to 67 percent for age eighteen. Nearly 50 percent of fifteen- to nineteen-year-old girls have engaged in premarital coitus

(Zelnick & Kanter, 1980). As suggested, age and education are important varia-bles; for example, young college women are much more likely to experience premarital coitus with their future husbands than are women with a high school education (see, for example, Verner & Stewart, 1974).

Among college students, premarital sexual intercourse is on the increase. During the 1950s, 25 percent to 30 percent of female college students had premarital coitus, whereas studies in the early 1970s suggest a rate of between 41 percent and 44 percent (Kaats & Davis, 1970). According to one study, four out of five regularly dating college couples are engaging in coitus (Peplau, Rubin, & Hill, 1977). College age women are engaging in sexual activities and coitus with a greater frequency than ever before and with a frequency ap-proaching men (Darling & Davidson, 1986).

Data show that women are engaging in premarital coitus more often than ever before but that the number of partners with whom they share intimate sex lives is limited. For example, among a sample of college-age women (under age twenty-four), 55 percent of nonstudents and 65 percent of students had had three or fewer partners in their lifetime, and only 10 percent for either group had had more than ten partners (DeLamater & MacCorquodale, 1979).

The frequency of premarital sex in males has increased since 1948, but the increase for females is quite dramatic (see, for example, Levin, 1975). Accord-ing to Hunt (1974), two or three times as many unmarried females are having coitus in their late teens and early twenties as did a generation before. The nature of the relationship between a man and a woman who are experiencing sexual intercourse has also varied throughout the twentieth century. During the 1950s, most women experiencing premarital coitus were engaged to their partners; by 1968, however, most women were going steady with or just dating their partners (Bell & Chaskes, 1970).

Whereas in the 1950s, nearly half of the females confined their premarital coitus to the year before marriage, today this relationship is clearly changing (see, for example, Zelnick & Kanter, 1980). The so-called sexual revolution has occurred primarily among women, who have changed roles dramatically in the 1980s. They have entered the workforce in huge numbers and have taken on responsibilities heretofore reserved for men. As women's attitudes and behav-iors have changed in the boardroom, so, too, have they changed in the bed-room. As their behaviors have become more like those of men, the old double standard of relative restrictions for women has gradually become less noticea-ble.

Marital Coitus.   For married women, intercourse within marriage is the most frequent mode of sexual expression. The frequency of coitus in women shows a decrease as their age increases. For example, the average frequency for married women in their late teens is 2.8 times weekly; by the age of thirty, 2.2 times; at age forty, 1.5 times a week; and once weekly at fifty years of age. This finding is interesting and somewhat puzzling because research shows that women's sexual desires *increase* as they become older. The most likely reason for the decrease in frequency of coitus is that their male partners' sexual inter-est decreases as they become older. So, even though women may have an increased desire for sexual activity, their frequency of coitus in marriage de-creases as age increases. (See Figure 11.2 for the decline in frequency of inter-course for both men and women as they age.)

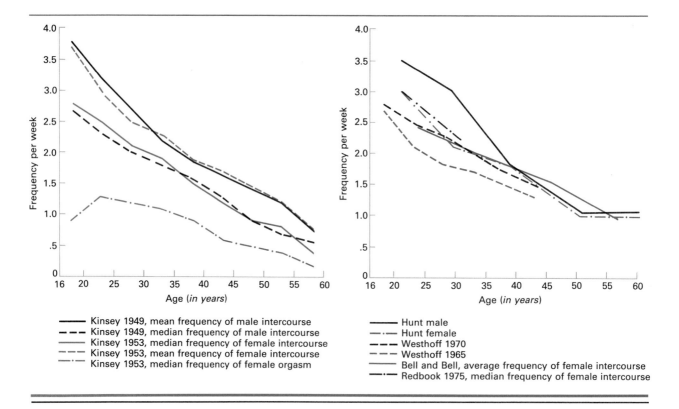

FIGURE 11.2   As people age, their frequency of intercourse per week declines over the years. Various studies have presented different data, yet all show the same basic trend. (After Gagnon, 1977, p. 195).

The percentage of women who reach orgasm during coitus varies with age; for example, 71 percent of women between the ages of sixteen and twenty-one reach orgasm during intercourse, whereas 90 percent of women between thirty-one and forty do so. Kinsey argued that 14 percent of women respond with multiple orgasms, but Masters and Johnson have concluded that the percentage is much higher and have indicated that women naturally respond with multiple orgasms.

Extramarital Coitus.   Even before the sexual revolution of the 1970s, the Kinsey studies showed that 26 percent of American married women had extramarital coitus before the age of forty; some recent estimates suggest 40 percent of married women have experienced extramarital sex. As in so many other areas of sexual behavior, age, education, and religious upbringing have a direct bearing on extramarital relationships. For example, college women had more extramarital intercourse before reaching the age of forty, as compared to women who had completed high school. Women born before 1900 had less extramarital intercourse before the age of forty than those born after 1900. Religiously inactive women had significantly more extramarital coition than religiously active women. At least 80 percent of women who had extramarital coitus had fewer than five partners; of this 80 percent, at least half had only one partner.

Do As I Say, Not As I Do: Attitudes and Behavior

Is there a difference between what people believe is proper sexual behavior and the behaviors in which they actually engage? Are people's perceptions of the sexual behavior of other people accurate? According to J. P. Roche (1986), both males and females tend to be more permissive in their own behavior than in what they define as a proper behavior. For example, among couples who were dating and reported to be in love, 58 percent reported that intercourse before marriage was proper, but among those same couples 66 percent were involved in sexual intercourse. Seventy-seven percent of these couples believed that other couples in the same situation were engaging in intercourse. Among engaged couples, the pattern of results was similar: 72 percent thought intercourse was proper, 78 percent were engaging in intercourse, and 90 percent of these couples believed that other couples were engaging in intercourse.

In the United States, college-age students despite the fear of AIDS, are engaging in sexual activity regularly. According to J. P. Roche (1986), more than 74 percent of the males and females reported in his study reported they had experienced intercourse before they were engaged to be married. Even though there are generally gender differences in that men are more permissive than women, this used to be especially true in the early stages of a dating relationship. In later stages of a relationship, differences between men and women seem to disappear. In the late 1980s, cultural, regional, and ethnic differences in sexual behaviors seemed to be disappearing. With the movement to equalize the sexes, a youth culture, improved transportation and communication and the spread of equal education, differences in sexual behaviors among groups, especially between men and women, are disappearing.

PROGRESS CHECK 11.3

1. Complete each of the following sentences with one of the options provided.

Learning Objective 11.8

A. The first study openly to discuss the nature of human sexual behavior was _____.
(conducted by Masters and Johnson : the Kinsey report)

Learning Objective 11.8

B. Coitus means the same thing as _____.
(sexual intercourse : an orgasm)

Learning Objective 11.8

C. A common characteristic of the body's erogenous zones is that they all _____.
(are covered by clothing in public : have many nerve endings)

Learning Objective 11.8

D. Research indicates that all female orgasms are mediated through the _____.
(clitoris : vagina)

Learning Objective 11.9

E. _____ show greater individual differences in sexual development when compared to others of their own sex.
(Men : Women)

Learning Objective 11.9

F. As men and women get older, they tend to experience_____ _____ in the degree of their sexual drives.
(harmony : a reversal)

Learning Objective 11.9

G. Since the Kinsey Report in 1948, the extent of premarital intercourse has increased for _____.
(women but not men : men but not women : men and women, but more for women)

Learning Objective 11.9

H. In their thirties or forties, women tend to have an increase in sexual desire and _____ in the frequency of coitus.
(an increase : a decrease)

Learning Objective 11.9

I. Males and females tend to be _____ permissive in their own behavior than in what they define as acceptable and proper sexual behavior.
(more : less)

MARRIAGE: AN INTIMATE RELATIONSHIP

Learning Objective **11.10**

Alan and Alicia might marry; the circumstances that surround their relationship might eventually move them close to intimacy, romance, and sexual involvement. People like Alan and Alicia pair off, become involved with one another, fall in love, develop a sense of shared commitment, and often marry. The situations in which people find themselves usually determine who, when, and why they will marry. Every person has his or her own needs and desires that will affect their urge and willingness to marry. Let us look at some recent trends in marriage patterns to see what types of social pressures and situations might operate on individuals like Alan and Alicia.

Most Americans marry. Nearly 95 percent of all Americans will marry at least once before they die; however, at the turn of the century, only about 70 percent of the population had been married at some time before they died. There also are other changing trends in marriage. One of the most obvious is that a young man and woman today are marrying for the first time at a later age. According to the U.S. Census Bureau, the average age of marriage is twenty-three for women and twenty-six for men. At the turn of the century,

One of the changing trends in marriage is that couples are marrying at a later age.

men were about four years older than their wives, but today the age span is half that. These statistics have far-ranging implications. Men and women are putting off marriage until they are older for a variety of reasons. One is the increased career opportunities for women. Another are the greater needs and opportunities for education and for establishing oneself in today's fast-paced economy. In addition, there is less of a push now from society to adjust to socially determined norms of when to marry and when to have children.

At any one time, about one-third of the adult population is single. According to the U.S. Census Bureau, many people are opting not to marry, (at least for a period of time). At least one out of every five households is maintained by a single person. Single people who eventually marry are doing so at a later age. Furthermore, more than two million couples living together are unmarried. It is important to realize that, even though the marriage rate is less now as compared to the 1970s, people are still marrying at a very high rate, even though their expectations of marriage differs from what they were in the 1950s.

Marriage is a legal term describing a committed relationship between two people with an expectation of permanence. Research shows that people marry for a number of reasons. A key reason for and function of marriage is to have a family. People also marry to fulfill material, sexual, and psychological needs. Often, people can fulfill their *material* needs by marrying and combining resources. People do not need to be married, however, to satisfy their *sexual needs*. Yet most people expect to fulfill their sexual desires through the institution of marriage.

By far the most important reason people marry is for their *psychological needs*. As we pointed out earlier, people want to form close, warm, intimate relationships with other persons. Marriage is generally seen as the most significant intimate relationship that can be achieved between two adults. It is a relationship in which certain trade-offs and role adjustments are normally expected; it is also a relationship that usually requires an understanding of each other's personal needs. To let such a relationship thrive, two individuals take on great responsibility for each other and provide each other with emotional support, romantic attachment, and security. People who are married normally try to support and understand each other's limitations and strengths. They try to provide unconditional, positive feelings for their mate and often become blind to his or her weaknesses. This means doing things they would not have to do if they were living alone and that are not particularly desirable at the time. The continuity of a marriage often necessitates being flexible and adjusting to one's spouse's needs as well as one's own.

Roles in Marriage

Every couple will have some adjustments to make when they marry. Alan and Alicia were both still in school. Would they interrupt their education for children? Would they seek a marriage in which they would share equally in housekeeping, banking, and shopping chores? Perhaps the most important thing every couple must do is to decide for themselves what they want from marriage. Many couples' goal is to achieve a sense of fulfillment and happiness that can be shared with another person.

Learning   11.11   Traditionally, in the United States, a woman's role has been to rear the
Objective   children and a man's, to support the family. Males typically are the ones who

After marriage, couples take on new roles and often share responsibilities.

protect the community and who work to guarantee a home and enough food for their family; also, males traditionally have been the ones to have the authority and the power. In today's society, however, many gender-based roles are changing. Families are no longer bound by the traditional roles of marriage.

Unlike the married couples of three decades ago, today's newly marrieds are asking for a great deal from their relationships. Today's youth insist on a marriage that fulfills all of the old needs (legal contract, financial security, sexual activity) plus some new ones. People are insisting on marriages that make them happy, fulfilled, and fully at ease.

Because people expect a great deal from marriage, they often find they must make a considerable readjustment when they set up a household. People who enter a marriage take on new roles. A *role* is the generally expected behavior of an individual who occupies a particular position. As children, most of us observed our parents' marriages and learned a great deal about roles in marriage from them. We know from social (observational) learning theory that people observe and imitate the behaviors of other people who are important to them. Newly married men and women take on new roles and therefore have new duties to fulfill that often require adjustments from a previous single life-style. Sometimes, however, the role that a man, for example, defines for himself is inconsistent with what his wife expects from him.

For some couples, *establishing* reasonable roles is apparently an easy task. *Implementing* those roles in a meaningful way, however, is the next task and may be a more difficult one. For example, if a husband sees himself as a good listener and defines that as part of his role, then he should implement that role by actually listening attentively to his wife's problems. Roles also need to be seen as *equivalent;* each member of a pair must see the role he or she has and the role the spouse has as being equivalent and fair. Both members need to see that each is contributing in equal ways to the relationship.

Roles established early in marriage often disappear as newly marrieds adjust to one another and settle in. Only after a couple begins to feel comfortable with one another can they commit themselves to developing a marriage and a relationship that is full and rich. According to Carl Rogers, people who are involved in a satisfying marriage should be able to dedicate themselves to each other and to the relationship. In a very human way, he suggests that people should be able to say:

> We each commit ourselves to working together on the changing process of our present relationship, because that relationship is currently enriching our life and we wish it to grow. (Rogers, 1978, p. 201)

By working to build a relationship, each person helps define his or her own roles and self-concept. This may cause the roles that society placed on them to fade somewhat; after dedicating themselves to a relationship, couples are better able to live by their own choice rather than by rules and roles other people have thrust on them (Rogers, 1978). For couples to reach this level of strength and love, their self-concepts must be well defined. (We discuss Carl Rogers and his theory more fully in Chapter 12.)

Adjustment in Marriage

Regardless of a couple's goals for marriage, it is likely that both partners will have to make some adjustments. No two marriages require the same adjustments, because no two marriages exhibit the same patterns of living; every couple forms their own unique style and mode of adjustment. Marriages almost by necessity are dynamic and constantly undergoing change. Most couples have two children; some have three, four, or more; and some decide to have no children. Each situation is unique and brings with it its own special problems and satisfactions. Each marriage has its own growth and conflict patterns.

The problems and adjustments in marriage are many. Couples must work out a division of labor, status, and money. In addition, each person in the relationship has psychological needs that must be fulfilled. As suggested, when two people enter into a marriage, they usually make certain adjustments to their previous day-to-day activities and move toward developing a satisfactory, shared life-style.

Sharing a life-style and being satisfied with it are important. Central to that satisfaction is finding a comfortable and balanced relationship with one's spouse; failing to do so affects one's performance in many areas of life.

Satisfaction in marriage is difficult to measure. In fact, there is no rigid scheme in the literature for classifying marriages as good or bad, or of high or low quality; too many variables can enter into the situation. For example, people currently rearing children are more likely to be dissatisfied with their marriages than are people who never had children or people whose children have left home. Parenthood is the primary time of stress in a marriage, and most partners who had been dissatisfied show more satisfaction as their children grow up and leave home. Many research studies support this view; for example, B. C. Miller (1976) found that, as the number of children in a family increases, companionship in marriage decreases.

People who are raising children have less time for their spouse. Most people are aware that, during these years, financial burdens are heavy and work-

loads are great; the result is a decrease in marital satisfaction. This U-shaped—
or curvilinear—relationship, is a well-accepted idea in the psychological literature. Most couples will tell you that their marital satisfaction decreases during
the childbearing years; there is still a significant question as to whether the
satisfaction levels then rise to the levels of earlier stages in the marriage.

The success of a relationship can be considered from the vantage point of
its satisfaction. A marital relationship is successful if each partner achieves
satisfaction. This means that the rewards to both partners are more important
than the challenges of the marriage. In the United States, most people consider
a good marital relationship to be one that shows stability, provides care and
affection for the children, and maintains a strong, efficient bond between partners. The mere continuance of a marriage is sometimes taken as a criterion of
its success. Even people who say their marriage is unsatisfactory often believe
that it is nevertheless "successful," since it has remained a legal entity for so
long.

Being satisfied in marriage does not mean that adjustment problems do
not exist. People often trade off one kind of need for another. For example,
some people want financial security. They will marry and perhaps be unsatis-
fied emotionally in order to attain financial status. Complete satisfaction in all
areas of marriage is usually not possible. Instead, people pair off and marry
people who satisfy the greatest number and most combinations of their relevant and important needs. This is an appropriate system of satisfying needs,
but there will be some adjustment problems; such problems, however, do not
necessarily rule out a chance for happiness.

For many people, being married is more pleasurable than being divorced
or single. As a group, married people report substantially greater global happiness than any category of unmarried people (Glenn, 1975); married people are
even physically healthier than other individuals (Verbrugge, 1979). Marital relationships might then be judged not in terms of the best *imaginable* conditions
but rather in terms of the best *possible* conditions, allowing for individual characteristics, the times, and other factors. If we judge all marriages by some
absolute scale of value, most would fail. By contrast, if we consider a marriage
in relation to other available living situations, the marriage is often comparatively pleasant and successful.

Parenthood after Age Thirty?

Marriage is difficult during the childbearing years. Today many individuals are
postponing marriage, and even after they marry they are postponing having
children. Plans for education, financial security, and careers often take precedence. Time flies by and individuals fast approach the age of thirty, thirty-five,
and forty, when the issue of parenthood becomes urgent.

Today, potential parents are asking, "Should we have children, and when?"
(J. B. Cohen, 1985). Women in their thirties have the most rapidly rising birth
rates. Women are waiting until they are older, and educated women are waiting even longer. Most people have children, although they are waiting longer
than their parents did.

Potential parents delay having children for several reasons even though
they recognize that as they grow older, especially beyond age thirty, medical
risks increase. According to Judith Cohen (1985), interpersonal reasons play an

Many couples are turning to day care so that they can maintain their careers while raising children.

important role in delaying parenthood. Potential parents are concerned about the impact a child will have on a relationship, knowing that as a couple with a child their relationships with friends and family are likely to change. These couples also are often concerned about the effects a child will have on their developing careers.

The impact on couples and their children is yet to be felt. But their concern about the conflict that a child might bring to their careers and their marriage is real, and the conflict they worry about can frequently be observed in couples who have had children.

Conflict in Marriage

Learning Objective 11.12

Couples must make some adjustments at each stage of their relationship; and almost inevitably conflicts arise. There are two basic sources of marital conflict—internal and external. *Internal conflict* is conflict felt by only one partner in a marriage but that ultimately affects both partners. For example, when a man wishes to change jobs and so must go back to school for a year, he is in a conflict situation. On one hand, he wants to go back to school and open up new opportunities for himself; on the other hand, he does not want to change his family's life-style, which would be inevitable for a year or so due to his lost income. *External conflict* is conflict that arises between two individuals over opposing needs or desires. One may want to go to the movies, the other to the opera. One partner may want to go to his mother's house, the other to her mother's house.

Internal conflict within a marriage is usually resolved when the principal partner reveals the conflict to the other partner. Usually, by sharing feelings in a fair and reasoned way, a choice can be made with which both partners can feel comfortable. External conflict can be resolved in any one of four ways. One way is for one partner to be the authority and to say, "*My* mother's house, and that's that!" Another way is for one partner to respond with passive acceptance: "Whatever you say, dear." The third possibility is to compromise, "One hour at your mother's, one hour at my mother's." But the most effective way is through creative problem solving; here, individuals choose options that are novel and acceptable to both members—"Let's skip going to the family's this weekend and go off to the beach and have a second honeymoon." This last option is the most appealing because it brings about a solution in which both partners feel that both their individual and their collective needs have been met.

Many marriages are heavily involved in conflict; communication between partners often seems to revolve around quarreling over small or sometimes major events in their lives. Quarrels may involve which program to watch on television, how vacations should be spent, or how money should be allocated. Many people avoid dealing directly with the conflict. They choose instead to express their feelings by pouting, withholding privileges, or remaining silent. Obviously, these behaviors do not resolve conflicts; eventually, most people try to resolve their disagreements more directly by arguing.

Arguments need not be vicious or destructive; they only become so when people allow their emotions to control their actions; they get mad and strike out at their partner (Bach & Wyden, 1970). People who want to resolve differences of opinion use creative problem-solving techniques. In creative problem-solving, there is no winner or loser; rather, a couple tries to agree on how to resolve a situation. Neither partner is declared a winner, neither is hurt, and both try to bring about greater understanding.

When people are unable to resolve their conflicts in ways that are not destructive, a power struggle develops. A power struggle occurs when two people battle for dominance in a conflict situation. A winner and a loser are bound to emerge, and someone is bound to feel hurt. Eventually, the partners are no longer trying to *solve* conflicts but to *win* conflicts and to demean one another. The conflict in the marriage becomes larger than the disagreement over the specific problem; in fact, the conflict can continue for conflict's sake.

Would listening help this couple's relationship?

When people lose sight of their goal to solve a specific situation and begin to play psychological games, they are no longer concerned with the original point or aim of the argument. Not dealing with the real problem leads such people astray and creates hurt feelings; intimacy and communication are lost.

Communication

Learning Objective 11.13

Being able to express one's needs, desires, feelings, and mood effectively is part of communication. People who communicate well with each other understand why they and their mate behave as they do. When people are having conflict in marriage, and when they are going through power struggles rather than solving problems, these situations are often due to a lack of communication. Most therapists assert that communication difficulty is the most common problem they encounter among couples who are looking to improve their relationship.

It is not hard to see that troubled relationships usually involve ineffective communication. Virginia Satir (1972) argues that these patterns can be devastating and that ineffective communicators can often be categorized as follows: distractors, computers, blamers, and placaters. *Distractors* never make a simple straightforward response to a question or a request; they often talk about irrelevant issues. Individuals characterized as *computers* are logical, cool, rational, and rarely recognize feelings and emotions; in being so cool and separate, they avoid the real issue. The *blamer* always blames other people and rides roughshod over the partner in an argument. The opposite of a blamer is a *placater,* who avoids conflict by trying to please, apologize, or in some way keep peace, regardless of whether his or her needs have been met.

Good communication when a conflict arises means not being a blamer or a distractor but rather effectively expressing needs and desires while listening attentively to one's partner's needs and desires. The aim of good conflict is a resolution of that conflict through a give-and-take that often involves trade offs. Winning and losing should not be the results of conflict; rather, conflict should result in a move toward successful sharing and mutual problem solving.

As Carl Rogers suggested, when people have good feelings about themselves and their partners, then whatever one member says or does can in some way affect the other. If a woman lets her spouse know she cares and is affected by what he says or does, she not only enhances her own self-worth, but also causes her partner to respond to her needs. To provide such an atmosphere, a person must not only hear the words but also be aware of the feelings of the person who is speaking. This kind of *active listening* enhances communication. Through mutual problem solving, people develop a more optimistic outlook and are better able to focus on specific problem areas.

When a couple is talking but neither partner fully listens to the other's feelings and thoughts, this is faulty communication. An opportunity to exchange ideas is missed, because the partners are not effectively listening to each other. Too often, faulty communication like this is reinforced by arguments and nasty sniping by a person we might characterize as a blamer or distractor.

Communicating ideas and feelings is no easy task. People take a risk when they express how they actually feel about a situation or each other; it is too easy to communicate destructive ideas in verbal exchanges rather than positive, enriching ideas. Too often, people want to avoid loser status, and so becoming a winner takes precedence over expressing feelings. When a man expresses his true feelings, he risks being ridiculed. Too often, that risk-taking is not reinforced; too often, it is punished. This is especially true when people are unfair in the way they respond; for example, the man's wife may blame him for his feelings or belittle those feelings. Carl Rogers (1978) tells us that this risk is difficult but potentially very fulfilling; speaking about someone in an ideal situation, he suggests that that person should be able to say:

> I will risk myself by endeavoring to communicate any persisting feeling, positive or negative, to my partner—to the full depth that I understand it in myself—as a living, present part of *me.* Then I will risk further by trying to understand, with all the empathy I can bring to bear, his or her response, whether it is accusatory and critical or sharing and self-revealing. (p. 204)

For Rogers, once a person presents his or her ideas honestly and with empathy, then positive change and development can occur. If the process is one-sided, prospects for growth become more dismal.

Failures in Adjustment

Learning Objective 11.14

People have just as many reasons for leaving a marriage as they do for entering into one. For some people, the cause of failure reflects unrealistic ideas and expectations about what marriage brings. Not surprisingly, divorce is too often the route of escape.

In recent years, there has been a large increase in the number of divorces. Today, the number exceeds one million divorces every year, and the divorce rate has more than doubled in the last twenty-five years. (There is some evidence that it is leveling off, however.) About one in three marriages ends in divorce. This does not mean that everyone has a 33 percent chance of being divorced. Divorce rates vary with age, socioeconomic status, and race. More divorces occur in a marriage's early and middle years than in its later years. Fewer divorces occur among people who have experienced solid premarital adjustment and a long engagement.

Psychologists are just beginning to grasp some of the profound implications of divorce. One problem is the readjustment that must take place. Divorced people are sadly unprepared for their new status. Often, they are lonely and alienated from family and friends—very much alone in a world in which they have not been alone for a long time. Given the readjustments that must be made, many people think long and hard before committing themselves to divorce. The decision is a difficult one because divorce has so many far-reaching implications. If a person believes he or she would be happier outside a marriage, then divorce may be the appropriate solution.

There is no single profile of an individual who is likely to stay married. The variables that enter into it are so diverse. However, researchers have found that if a person is of the middle class, engaged for a year before marriage, marries in his or her middle twenties, is a professional person and a college graduate, and comes from an unbroken home, his or her chances for divorce are significantly lower than the statistical averages (Spanier & Glick, 1981).

More often than not, people who have difficulty in marriage can be helped through marital counseling and psychotherapy. Sometimes one partner is willing to enter therapy but the other is not. The research literature clearly shows that people can be helped through counseling. You will see in Chapter 15 that psychotherapy and family counseling can help people rebuild lives and marriages that have been torn apart by discord and unhappiness. Too often, people wait too long, after too much damage has been done to the relationship to maintain the marriage. They commit themselves to divorce without trying to salvage their relationship through some type of counseling or therapy.

PROGRESS CHECK 11.4

1. Complete each of the following sentences with one of the options provided.

Learning Objective 11.10   A. Compared to marriage rates at the turn of the century, _____ _____ people today marry at least once during their lifetime.
(fewer : more)

Learning Objective 11.10   B. The primary reason that leads most people to marry is the desire to fulfill _____ needs.
sexual : material : psychological)

Learning Objective 11.11   C. When compared to marriages three decades ago, couples today expect _____ from the relationship.
(less : more)

Learning Objective 11.11   D. For a marriage to be satisfying, the roles a couple assumes must allow _____.
(one person to have the power : both partners to feel equivalency and fairness)

Learning Objective 11.11   E. Dissatisfaction in a marriage is most likely to be found in a marriage in which the couple _____ children.
(has never had : is currently raising their : has finished raising their)

Learning Objective 11.11   F. In recent years, potential parents have been postponing parenthood because of _____ reasons.
(biological : social : interpersonal)

Learning Objective 11.12   G. The resolution of internal marital conflict usually begins when one partner in the marriage _____.
(states his or her feelings : takes authority and makes a decision)

Learning Objective 11.12   H. Being satisfied in a marriage _____ that the couple has accomplished all necessary adjustments.
(indicates : does not necessarily indicate)

Learning Objective 11.12   I. Individuals who are involved in power struggles with their spouses try to _____.
(solve communication problems : win)

Learning Objective 11.13   J. _____ is the label Virginia Satir uses to describe a person who avoids conflict by trying to please, apologize, and keep the peace.
(Distractor : Computer : Placater)

Learning Objective 11.13   K. In order for healthy communications to take place in a marriage, _____.
(one person must be free of negative feelings : active listening must occur)

Learning Objective 11.13   L. Carl Rogers suggests that in order to have effective communications, an individual must be _____ how he or she feels.
(willing to risk sharing : fully aware of)

Learning Objective 11.14   M. The length of a couple's engagement to be married _____ related to the probability of divorce.
(appears to be : does not appear to be)

Keeping Pace with Chapter 11

Applying
Principles

11.2 Identify the type of communicator involved in each of the following situations.

distractor   placater   computer   blamer

_____

A. Sales have been down all year for Walt, and the family's financial status is showing his lack of success. At one point during the slow year, he considered changing his product line, and Lynn offered to help him financially with her time to get the new business started. However, Walt did not make the change because he did not have the personal motivation to carry the new plan through. *During an argument about money, Walt told Lynn that it was her fault and accused her of not giving support to his creative business plans.*

_____

B. Clay has been depressed and verbally abusive to everyone in the family for weeks. He has neglected his family responsibilities and avoided playful contact with the children. Teresa would like to help Clay but he won't tell her what is wrong, and at this point she is angry and fuming inside. *However, Teresa is afraid that if she says anything, the situation will get worse; so, instead of placing some constructive demands on Clay, she is just following his wishes the best she can.*

_____

C. Sheila is very worried about Erik, her thirteen-year-old son. He has been distant at home, and the school counselor has called several times in recent months reporting that Erik has caused trouble at school. Erik threatened to take his own life, and he frequently makes comments about hating people and killing people. *When Sheila talked to her husband Greg about wanting to seek help for Erik, Greg told her she was overreacting and that what Erik needed was some strong discipline and more duties around the house.*

_____

D. Juanita wants to stay home this summer, but she has not made her wishes known. It's only May but, nonetheless, José needs to make arrangements at work for time off so the family can have a summer vacation. *He asks Juanita how she feels about vacationing the last two weeks of July, and she replies, "Oh, I don't know, what do you think?" He asks her where she would like to go. She replies, "Mom and dad may need help moving." José asks Juanita if she wants to go on a vacation, and she says, "The kids will want to go." José cannot get any information about what Juanita wants so he makes his own decision and requests to have the last two weeks of July off.*

Self-Test

Before proceeding to the Self-Test, REVIEW the Learning Objectives listed at the chapter opening and RECITE from memory everything you can remember in support of them. Then, take this Self-Test as if it were to be graded by your teacher. Use the Learning Objective numbers in the Answer Section as a reference to restudy the corresponding text pages and Progress Checks for any incorrectly answered questions.

1. We learn about personal space needs

    A. through cultural norms during childhood.
    B. during adolescence as we are exposed to new spatial zones.
    C. generally during early adulthood as we gain insights into the needs of other people.
    D. none of the above; the personal space requirements of human beings appear to be inherited.

2. The spatial zone that Hall called *intimate distance*

   A. is commonly found in contact sports.
   B. would probably be observed quite frequently in an average friendship.
   C. is found only in romantic relationships.
   D. would be maintained while a person was telling a close friend a spicy story.

3. If a researcher observes 100 people in a 1,000 square foot room and then moves the people to a 10,000 square foot room and observes them there, the researcher is studying the effects of

   A. crowding.
   B. social density.
   C. spatial density.
   D. personal space.

4. _____ a privacy-regulating mechanism.

   A. Territorial behavior is
   B. The design and layout of an office or living space are
   C. Personal space is
   D. All of the above are privacy regulating mechanisms.

5. One explanation for bystander apathy is that

   A. bystanders may believe a risk of appearing foolish, feeling embarrassed, or being punished is present.
   B. people do not notice other people because they are preoccupied with their own problems.
   C. people tend not to help unless they are asked for help.
   D. people become so curious about the event that they are distracted from the fact that the person needs help.

6. A social psychologist would predict that you are most likely to be attracted to

   A. people you have only met once.
   B. your neighbors and work associates.
   C. people you have seen on television.
   D. people who have unique ideas that are quite different from your own.

7. According to equity theory, a person who has been treated unfairly in a friendship will usually

   A. do a favor to regain attention.
   B. demand restitution.
   C. forget the problem and go on as if nothing happened.
   D. discontinue the friendship.

8. Which of the following does *not* contribute to a description of romantic love?

   A. It is often accompanied by a state of limerance and involves idealization of another person.
   B. It has nothing to do with sexual attraction.
   C. It can be a condition in which the happiness of the other person is essential to your own happiness.
   D. It is an experience that is affected by social backgrounds and political and economic views.

9. Open discussions and scientific investigations about human sexual behavior are useful because

   A. they help clarify the factors that operate in intimate relationships.
   B. sexual behavior represents an activity present in the daily lives of people.
   C. they help people become aware of how their own sexual desires compare to those of other people.
   D. all of the above

10. Most males experience their first ejaculation

    A. before the age of twelve.
    B. through masturbation.
    C. during intercourse.
    D. the variations are so great there is no way to state norms.

11. Compared to trends at the turn of the century, marriage trends today show that

    A. the age difference between men and women who marry has decreased.
    B. fewer people marry.
    C. social norms are less prescriptive in terms of when people should marry and have children.
    D. the expectations marriage partners have for the relationship are less challenging.

12. For a marriage to be fulfilling and successful, the roles the couple adopt must

    A. allow for a division of labor based on biological characteristics.
    B. reflect traditional values.
    C. meet the couples expectations and be implemented in day-to-day interactions.
    D. all of the above

13. Satisfaction in marriage

    A. is determined by the number of children a couple has.
    B. means that a couple seldom argues.
    C. is impossible to achieve.
    D. is difficult to measure.

14. Potential parents are delaying parenthood because

    A. they are concerned about how a baby will affect their relationship and career.
    B. children are valued less in today's society.
    C. the medical community has made it clear that it is biologically safer for the mother to have a child in her thirties.
    D. compared to their parents' generation, changes in the economy have made it more difficult on young adults in recent generations to afford children.

15. Which of the following examples illustrates an external conflict?

    A. Lea has begun to feel insecure with some of Rob's behaviors and is beginning to distrust him.
    B. Although Linda contently does almost all of the housework and assumes she is pleasing Lou, Lou thinks she should do more.
    C. Mary wants to go skiing; Gregory wants to go shopping.
    D. Rhonda is afraid to tell Craig he is drinking too much.

16. Effective communications take place when

    A. one partner assumes a computer role and the other a placater role.
    B. one partner is willing to distract attention from the issue that has caused conflict.
    C. both partners find conflict undesirable.
    D. both partners are willing to express feelings and actively listen to the other.

17. Research shows that

    A. every person who marries has a 33 percent chance of getting divorced.
    B. the divorce rate is ten times higher today than it was twenty-five years ago.
    C. family counseling can help a couple regain strength and fulfillment from their marriage.
    D. A and C

12

Personality
and Its Assessment

12

Learning Objectives

When you have mastered the material in this chapter, you will be able to:

1. Describe what psychologists mean when they use the term *personality* and give definitions for the terms *trait* and *types*. (pp. 456)

2. Discuss Gordon Allport's theory of personality and explain what he meant by cardinal traits, central traits, and secondary traits. (p. 458)

3. Explain what Raymond Cattell means by surface traits and source traits and describe how factor analysis contributed to his theory. (p. 459)

4. Describe Eysenck's three personality types and discuss his views on biological determinants to personality. (p. 460)

5. Discuss how Cattell's and Eysenck's theories are similar and how they differ from Allport's theory; and, explain why many psychologists criticize trait theories and are interested in developing a more global theory of personality. (p. 460)

6. Explain how Sigmund Freud came to develop his theory of personality and discuss the impact his theory has had on modern psychology. (pp. 462)

7. Name the two basic human instincts and state the core tendency of personality, according to Freud; name Freud's theory and the therapeutic method based on his theory. (pp. 463)

8. Identify and describe the three levels of consciousness and the three structural components of personality as outlined by Freud. (pp. 463)

9. Describe the function of the libido and the nature and source of anxiety according to Freud. (pp. 464)

10. Describe five defense mechanisms that Freud identified and explain how and why people use them. (pp. 465)

11. Name and describe Freud's five psychosexual stages of personality development. (pp. 466)

12. Explain what is meant by a fixation and tell how fixations affect the outcome of personality development. (pp. 467)

13. State the basic assumptions that humanistic psychologists make about people. (pp. 472)

14. Give Carl Rogers's assumptions about people and personality development and explain what he meant by the *self* and the *ideal self.* (pp. 472)

15. Explain what a self-actualized person is like, describe how self-concepts develop, and discuss how people with healthy versus rigid self-concepts deal with new experiences. (p. 473)

16. Discuss Alfred Adler's view about personality development, tell how his fulfillment approach differs from Carl Rogers's approach, and explain how the concepts of birth order and life-styles fit into his theory. (pp. 475)

17. Explain how behavioral approaches differ from other theories of personality, identify the structural unit of personality, and explain how personality develops, according to behaviorists. (pp. 475)

18. Explain how personality is acquired through classical conditioning, instrumental conditioning, and observational learning; and explain how observational learning theories differ from traditional behavioral theories. (pp. 476)

19. Describe the cognitive approach to behavior and personality. (p. 483)

20. Make a distinction between global theories and microtheories; discuss Julian Rotter's locus of control microtheory. (pp. 483)

21. Explain Bandura's views on self-efficacy and explain how this quality affects other aspects of one's personality. (pp. 485)

22. Describe Mischel's cognitive social learning theory and explain, according to Mischel, how people interact with their environment in order to respond flexibly to various situations. (pp. 487)

23. Define *assessment* and explain why and how psychologists use assessment techniques; describe some of the common intelligence tests, objective personality tests, and projective tests psychologists use. (p. 488)

24. Name and describe three popular behavioral assessment techniques that psychologists use and discuss the future of personality and behavioral assessment. (p. 489)

BEFORE YOU READ ON, take time to **SURVEY** the chapter, form an idea of what is to be learned (from margin Learning Objective numbers), and set goals for your study time. Then, ask yourself **QUESTIONS** about the material as you **READ,** seeking help for any sections you do not understand.

Bud Ross's father was wealthy; he was also admired, respected, and sought after by most people who knew him. He played golf, tennis, and polo. He loved a party and had an endless supply of energy and enthusiasm. Bud was always amazed that he and his father were so different. Bud was soft-spoken, shy, and, by most people's standards, considered an introvert. When he found himself in a room full of strangers, he usually remained quiet, watched, and thought about what he might say or do.

Mr. Ross set a date for his retirement from the family business; Bud knew it would soon be time for him to take over. Bud was getting nervous; he wanted to spend some time thinking about himself and his future. He questioned his temperament, his ability to make difficult decisions, and his quiet nature.

Bud had not thought that the time for him to take over would come so soon. Faced with a big challenge, he questioned whether he was up to the task. Was he aggressive enough, assertive enough, decisive enough? When Bud tried to analyze himself, he noticed a silent yet potentially outspoken fellow inside his body, one who was witty, amiable, forthright, and decisive. Bud also knew that his outward behaviors hid his feelings. Bud's closest friends knew of his wit and amiable nature; but they also knew he had difficulty expressing the characteristics that came so easily to his father. When Bud confided his process of self-assessment to his closest friend, Len staunchly held that Bud had a terrific personality and would make a great manager. Len pointed out to Bud that his basic characteristics would stand him well in the business world—his careful and cautious nature, as well as his ability to think analytically would enable him to succeed.

Len's assessment of Bud's nature had a big impact. Bud began to think of himself not as a quiet, inwardly turned individual, but rather as a person who, through the strength of his character, could view business decisions cautiously and with care. Bud decided that his next meeting with his father would be preceded with a statement about how he viewed the qualities of a good businessman. He would assert that one need not be a carbon copy of "old Mr. Ross" to be an effective businessman or an effective person. He would open his meeting with his father by saying, "Dad, there are two Mr. Rosses who know how to run this business."

*Learning
Objective*   12.1

Personality ══════════
A set of relatively enduring behavioral characteristics that describe how a person reacts to the environment.

LIKE BUD, MOST PEOPLE can describe the characteristic way they respond to the world. Most people have fairly realistic impressions of themselves and often will use certain catchwords to describe their personalities—shy, sensitive, quiet, concerned, aggressive—all components of personality. Psychologists have tried systematically and scientifically to describe how individuals respond to the world, how they act in most situations. They call this *personality*. For most psychologists, **personality** is a set of relatively enduring, long-lasting behavioral responses that characterize how a person reacts to the environment. Personality is the way someone behaves in a variety of situations over a long period of time.

When we studied motivation, we looked at the *whys* of people's behavior and sought to understand its causes. When we examined social psychology, we looked at *how* people's basic attitudes were established and how they affected day-to-day behavior. In discussing personality, psychologists generally talk about enduring or long-lasting, stable characteristics of behavior. Psychologists who focus on personality recognize that any individual's behavior will not be consistent in every situation every day. It is difficult to assess a person's motives and attitudes from minute to minute. People's responses to the world vary for a variety of reasons. People like Bud are not always cautious, shy, or impulsive. Personality characterizes the way people respond in many or most circumstances.

If you assume that you know someone's personality, would you be good at predicting their behavior in different circumstances? You need not be a psychologist to recognize that a child who has feelings of inferiority needs to be treated somewhat differently than a child who is buoyantly self-confident. Parents and psychologists use their knowledge of a child's personality to help the child develop into the best kind of person he or she could be.

Each person's personality is unique, and no two people (even twins) in the same family are identical. Psychologists who study personality have sought to understand the process of personality development and the many influences that make a person unique. They have sought to understand why a person who is usually outgoing can sometimes be shy, or why a person who is generally cautious, like Bud Ross, might sometimes enter into a daring business venture.

Like the various personalities that people have, psychologists have found various ways to look at personality. Some have focused on the day-to-day traits that characterize people; other psychologists have focused on the inner conflicts that shape personality. This chapter explains that some psychologists assert that one's personality is to a great extent determined by genetics; other psychologists argue that stimuli in the environment are the determiners of behavior. Earlier chapters discussed that decision making and learning are often crucial determinants of behavior. At this point in our examination of psychology, you probably will not be surprised that many cognitive psychologists argue that human beings often make choices and cognitive decisions about the personality they want to portray and or feel most comfortable with.

These differing theoretical approaches often have markedly different assumptions about the causes of personality. Some approaches see a human being as an individual who reacts to the environment. Others focus on the internal, even genetic, influences that impel a person to action. Some of the earliest personality theories focused on the different traits people show—the varying elements of a person's day-to-day behaviors, such as shyness, impulsiveness, or aggressiveness. These trait theories make a lot of intuitive sense and thus have been very popular. Because they have intuitive appeal, are relatively limited in scope, and are easy to conceptualize, let us begin with them.

TRAIT AND TYPE THEORY

If you think back to when you realized that you were really going to go to college, you may remember questioning whether you felt capable. Like Bud Ross, you may have gone through a period of self-assessment. In this process, some people list their positive and negative qualities—such characteristics as outgoing, forthright, assertive, or sensitive. These people are trying to picture their unique qualities.

Every human being's behavior is different from everyone else's; we are different from our parents and siblings. But our own behavior tends to stay consistent—people who are cautious do not tend to invest in risky ventures. Assertive people are usually not shy at a party. Knowing a person's basic characteristics allows a psychologist, parent, or close friend to predict that person's behavior, at least to some extent.

Many psychologists who have studied personality can be characterized as trait theorists. These researchers have studied specific behaviors—traits—that might be guiding forces within the life of a specific individual. A **trait** is any readily identifiable behavior that characterizes the way an individual differs from other people. Bud Ross might have described his traits as cautious, shy, reserved, sober, and conservative. Such an individual is unlikely to characterize himself as excitable, outgoing, daring, or happy-go-lucky. This section examines the trait theories of two well-known trait psychologists, Gordon Allport

Trait
Any readily identifiable stable behavior that characterizes the way that an individual differs from other individuals.

According to trait theory, an angry, assertive attitude is viewed as a personal characteristic that influences behavior in many different situations.

and Raymond Cattell, and then examines the broader type theory of Hans Eysenck. **Types** are broad collections of traits tied together loosely and interrelated.

Allport's Trait Theory

Types ══════
Broad collections of traits that are tied together loosely and interrelated.

Learning ══ 12.2
Objective ══

One leading trait theorists was distinguished psychologist Gordon Allport (1897–1967). Allport's theory suggests that because each individual is unique, each person has a unique set of traits. If you know a person's traits, you know how he or she would respond to various environmental stimuli. But Allport was quick to find out that there are thousands of ways to characterize people's behavior. Among all of those traits some seemed more dominant than others.

Cardinal traits ════════
In Allport's theory, ideas and behaviors that determine the overall direction of a person's life.

Central traits ════════
In Allport's theory, behaviors that are reasonably easy to identify that characterize a person's day-to-day interactions.

Secondary traits ════════
In Allport's theory, specific behaviors that occur only in response to specific situations.

Allport eventually came to assert that people's behavior can be categorized as having traits that were either cardinal, central, or secondary. **Cardinal traits** are ideas and behaviors that determine the overall direction of a person's life. A clergyman may have certain cardinal traits, as might some philosophers or civil rights leaders; Allport noted that many people have no such overall guiding behaviors or ideas. More common, **Central traits** are reasonably easy to identify behaviors that characterize a person's day-to-day interactions. These central traits might be considered the basic units of personality. Allport felt that as few as ten central traits might adequately describe many individuals' personalities. *Controlled, apprehensive,* and *tense* are some terms for central traits; *self-assured, forthright,* and *practical* are other traits that might characterize a person. **Secondary traits** are specific behaviors that occur only in response to specific situations—a person may have a secondary trait of prejudice toward minorities, a deep desire to give donations to the homeless, or an indifferent reaction to Yuppies. Secondary traits are less characteristic of an individual's behavior, more easily modified, and not necessarily apparent on a day-to-day basis.

Since everyone has different combinations of traits, it is not surprising that from Allport's view everyone is unique. Knowing a person's traits should allow a psychologist to predict somewhat accurately how people will respond to their environment. Once you know a person's personality traits, behaviors should not be too surprising. To identify a person's traits, Allport recommended an in-depth study of that individual. Recently, other less time-consuming techniques to study the individual have been devised (Rosenzweig, 1986).

Factor Theory: Cattell

Learning Objective   12.3

Bud Ross was soft-spoken, shy, and perhaps introverted. Psychologists like Raymond B. Cattell (1905–   ) have argued that if you know even a few traits like this, you can tell a great deal about an individual like Bud. Cattell and many other theorists have done statistical analyses on both individuals and groups of individuals to see if groups of traits tend to occur together. Cattell used the technique of factor analysis. We discussed factor analysis in Chapter 9. Factor analysis is a statistical procedure in which groups of variables, or factors, are analyzed so a researcher can tell which factors are related to one another. When a factor analysis is done on intelligence, for example, verbal reasoning abilities and spatial abilities turn out to be separate but important factors in determining intelligence.

In trait theory, factor analysis shows that groups of traits tend to cluster together. Thus, people who describe themselves as warm and accepting also tend to rate themselves as high on the traits of nurturance and tenderness. Such individuals would not tend to rate themselves high on such traits as aggression, suspiciousness, and apprehensiveness. A researcher can see certain patterns and groups of traits within certain professions; for example, artists tend to see themselves as creative, sensitive, and open, whereas accountants

Personality traits cluster within certain professions; police officers are often seen as helpful, concerned individuals.

are more likely to have traits of carefulness, seriousness, conservativeness, and tough-mindedness. Factor analysis has shown that several groups of traits cluster together. From Cattell's view, many of the traits that can be factored out as representing a single cluster represent a higher-order trait. Cattell called obvious, day-to-day traits *surface traits.* The higher-order traits or clusters of traits he termed *source traits.* As the next section shows, Cattell's source traits come close to Eysenck's types. From Cattell's view, there were sixteen personality factors or source traits. He devised a measurement device called the *Sixteen Personality Factor Questionnaire,* or *16PF,* to describe personality profiles of individuals.

Eysenck's Type Theory

Learning Objective 12.4

You might classify Bud Ross as being a cautious person. There was no one specific trait that could characterize Bud, but taken together, he might be viewed as a careful and thoughtful type. Categorizing people as certain types who hold dominant motives or dominant personality characteristics was the focus of some personality theorists. So thought Hans Eysenck (1916–   ), another theorist who has made a strong mark on personality theory. Eysenck argued that there existed groups of interrelated traits. Whereas Allport and Cattell focused on the trait level, Eysenck focused on higher levels of trait organization—called *types.* He went a step beyond Cattell, arguing that all personality traits can be reduced to three types or basic dimensions: emotional stability or emotional instability, introversion or extroversion, and psychoticism.

Emotional stability refers to the extent to which people have control over their feelings. People can be spontaneous, genuine and warm, or they can be controlled, calm, flat, unresponsive, and stilted. *Introversion or extroversion* refers to the extent to which people are withdrawn and reserved; extroverts are socially outgoing and open. Eysenck's third dimension, *psychoticism,* is sometimes referred to as tough or tender mindedness; it measures the extent to which people isolate themselves from other people. At one extreme, individuals are troublesome, anti-authority, sensation-seeking, loners, insensitive, and risk takers; at the other end, people are characterized as less adventurous and bold, and more likely to have warm feelings toward other people, be gregarious and have tender feelings (see also Howarth, 1986).

Eysenck argues that personality has a biological basis but emphasizes that learning and experience shape an individual's specific behaviors. For example, he asserts that introverts and extroverts have different natural levels of arousal in the cortex of the brain. Accordingly, each type would seek more or less external stimulation to achieve a higher level of arousal—this is reflected in their outward behavior. A person with a high level of arousal may become a race-car driver or a politician; a person with lower arousal may become a security guard or an assembly line worker.

Learning Objective 12.5

Unlike Allport, who studied individual behavior, Eysenck used a technique favoring the study of groups of individuals and groups of traits. Allport focused on human uniqueness; Cattell and Eysenck asserted that we can characterize the way most people respond in various circumstances. Cattell argued that Allport's theory was too individualistic. The tight and simple nature of such factor analysis approaches is the strength of the Cattell and Eysenck theories. Furthermore, research has shown these factor analytic approaches to be good predictors of various behaviors.

Trait and Type Theory: Yesterday and Today

Trait and type theory are appealing because it is relatively easy to characterize individuals on a number of important dimensions. However, trait and type theory has been widely criticized—for example, which traits last for a lifetime? Second, people's behavior often depends on the situations or contexts in which they find themselves; traits cannot be expected to be excellent predictors of individual acts or behaviors (Epstein & O'Brien, 1985), although Allport's conceptions did allow for cross-situational behavior differences (Zuroff, 1986). This chapter later discusses some cognitive theorists like Walter Mischel who rely heavily on this notion. Third, these theories describe human behavior in terms of the traits that characterize people, but they do not explain why people develop those traits, or why those traits may or may not change over time.

Trait and type theories continue to evolve, but there has been another stream in the psychological study of personality. Many psychologists seek a theory of personality that is more all-encompassing and explains the causes of behavior. Of the theories just discussed, Eysenck's type approach comes closest to a global theory. However, psychologists especially want a theory of personality to explain why a person's behavior can be dramatically different in different situations. They want a theory that explains the development of personality and how personality theory can predict maladjustment. One such theory that has attempted to describe, explain, and predict behavior is the well-known and widely disputed theory of Freud. Freud's theory, which was one of the earliest personality theories, does overcome some of the shortcomings of trait theory but creates new dilemmas for psychological inquiry.

PROGRESS CHECK 12.1

1. Complete each of the following sentences with one of the options provided.

Learning Objective 12.1   A. Most psychologists think of personality as a set of _____ characteristics of behavioral responses that characterize how a person reacts to the environment.
(unique and idiosyncratic : relatively enduring and stable)

Learning Objective 12.1   B. A _____ is any readily identifiable behavior that characterizes the way one individual differs from other individuals.
(trait : type)

Learning Objective 12.2   C. Allport noted that some people, but not all people, have _____ _____ traits that determine the overall direction of their lives.
(central : cardinal : secondary)

Learning Objective 12.2   D. In Allport's theory, a central trait _____.
(occurs in response to specific situations : is the basic unit of personality)

Learning Objective 12.2   E. Bargaining for a lower price at places such as an antique shop or flea market would be considered a _____ trait by Allport.
(central : cardinal : secondary)

Learning Objective 12.2   F. From Allport's point of view, everyone has a unique personality because they develop _____.
(an individual cardinal trait : different combinations of traits)

Learning Objective 12.3

G. By using factor analysis, Cattell was able to determine that certain traits tend to _____.
(come and go over one's life span : cluster together)

Learning Objective 12.3

H. Cattell called higher-order traits _____ traits.
(surface : source)

Learning Objective 12.4

I. Hans Eysenck developed a _____ theory of personality.
(trait : clustered trait : type)

Learning Objective 12.4

J. Eysenck's third dimension of personality called _____ takes into account the degree to which people take risks, isolate themselves, and respond with feeling to other people.
(emotional stability : introversion-extroversion : psychoticism)

Learning Objective 12.4

K. From Eysenck's point of view, _____ account for the differences in personality types.
(cultural values : biological differences)

Learning Objective 12.5

L. Trait theories characterize the behavior of individuals _____ explain how the traits developed and why they do or do not change over time.
(and : but do not)

PSYCHOANALYTIC THEORY: SIGMUND FREUD

Learning Objective 12.6

Had Sigmund Freud analyzed our businessman Bud Ross, he would probably have focused on Bud's relationship with his parents, especially his father. Freud might have argued that Bud's spirit was dominated by an unresolved conflict that hampered his successful completion of important developmental stages.

Freud's theory is both controversial and complex, and his influence on psychological thought and on Western culture in general is very great. Freud's theory is so influential because it is a global theory providing general rules for predicting all behavior. Whereas most trait theories predict specific behaviors and are relatively easy to test experimentally, a global theory like Freud's is hard to put to an experimental test and makes few predictions about specific behaviors. As we discuss Freud's theory, you will see its complexity and why it is so difficult to test experimentally. Regardless of its testability, Freud's theory has shaped in important ways both psychologists' and nonpsychologists' thinking about personality.

Sigmund Freud (1856–1939) was an Austrian physician who worked as a neurologist. Early in his career, he used hypnosis to treat people with physical and emotional problems. Most of Freud's patients were from the middle and upper classes of Austrian society. Many were society matrons who, because they lived in a repressive society, had limited opportunities for the release of sexual tensions. Freud noticed that many of his patients needed to talk about their problems and that, having talked about them, they often felt better. From his work with these patients, Freud began to conceptualize a theory of behavior.

Learning Objective 12.7

Freud theorized that people have two basic instincts—sexual and aggressive. These instincts are not always socially acceptable. When people exhibit unacceptable behaviors, they often experience punishment, guilt, and anxiety. Freud's theory describes a conflict between a person's instinctual needs for gratification and the demands of society for socialization. For Freud, a person's core tendency is to maximize instinctual gratification while minimizing punishment and guilt (Maddi, 1976). Freud's approach to personality is called *psychoanalytic theory;* the method of therapy based on Freud's theory is called *psychoanalysis.*

Structure of Personality

Learning   12.8
Objective

Freud's theory is extraordinarily complex; it considers the sources and consequences of conflict and how people deal with it. For Freud, a person's source of energy is biologically determined and lies in the structure of consciousness.

Conscious behavior
Freud's first level of consciousness, which refers to behavior (feelings and actions) of which a person is aware.

Preconscious behavior
Freud's second level of consciousness, which refers to mental activity of which a person can become aware by attending to it.

Unconscious behavior
Freud's third level of consciousness, which refers to mental activity beyond a person's normal awareness. This material can be made available through psychoanalysis.

Id
In Freud's theory, the source of instinctual energy, which works on the pleasure principle.

Ego
In Freud's theory, the part of personality that seeks to satisfy the id and superego in accordance with reality.

Superego
In Freud's theory, the moral branch of mental functioning.

Sources of Conflict.   Freud stated that there are three levels of consciousness. The first is **conscious behavior,** the thoughts, feelings, and actions of which people are aware. The second, **preconscious behavior,** is mental activity of which people can become aware only if they attend to it closely. The third level, the **unconscious,** is mental activity of which people are unaware and cannot become aware except through certain techniques. Think of the levels of consciousness as layers of sand on a beach; the top layer is easy to sift through; the next layer, the preconscious, takes a bit more work to dig through; the deepest level, the unconscious, can be looked at only by means of special techniques.

According to Freud's theory, the primary structural elements of personality are the id, ego, and superego. These three forces reside in the unconscious. Each force accounts for a different aspect of functioning. Although these components may sound like real structures in the following discussion, the id, ego, and superego are concepts, not physical structures. The **id** is the source of a person's instinctual energy. It works on the *pleasure principle,* which assumes that people try to maximize immediate gratification. Freud considered much of a person's instinctual energy to be sexual, and the rest as aggressive. Deep within the unconscious, the demanding, irrational, and selfish id seeks only to maximize pleasure. It does not care about morals, society, or other individuals.

The second major component of functioning is the **ego.** Whereas the id seeks to maximize pleasure and to obtain gratification, the ego (which grows out of the id) seeks to satisfy the individual's instinctual needs in accordance with reality. The id is demanding, unrealistic, and works by the pleasure principle; the ego is patient, reasonable, and works by the reality principle. The id of a child who wants an ice cream cone tells her to grab the cone and eat it. Her ego tells her that if she grabs the cone without asking, she may be punished. Working on the *reality principle,* the child knows that the best way to achieve gratification is first to ask permission to eat the cone. Sometimes the ego stops the id from functioning, but more often it directs the id toward appropriate ways of behaving.

The third component in the structure of personality is the **superego.** The best way to characterize the superego is to think of it as the moral branch of mental functioning. The superego tells the id and the ego whether gratification in a particular instance is ethical. The superego helps control the id by internalizing parental authority through the process of socialization. If a child sees and wants an ice cream cone and asks her mother for it, her superego will indicate that her behavior is morally correct. This approach toward obtaining ice cream will not create guilt, fear, or anxiety in the child. In contrast, the child may see candy on the table and know her mother is out of the room. Her ego knows that taking the candy would be very simple and would satisfy her id. The superego,

According to Freud, maintaining a balance among the id, ego, and superego is crucial to normal personality development.

taking over the role of conscience and parental authority, restrains the child from taking the candy.

Thus, in terms of individual functioning Freud thought of the unconscious as being composed of three competing forces. In some people, the id is stronger than the superego; in others, the superego is strongest. The relative strengths of the id, ego, and superego determine each person's degree of adjustment.

Learning Objective 12.9

Libido
In Freud's theory, the instinctual life force that energizes the id. The libido works on the pleasure principle and seeks immediate gratification.

Sources of Energy. Freud assumed that the id is energized by two instinctual forces: the sexual life instinct and the aggressive or death instinct. He discussed the aggressive instinct only slightly and focused on the life (or sexual) instinct, the **libido.** The libido initially operates on the pleasure principle and seeks immediate gratification. The libido usually expresses itself through the id. An overly strong superego may try to control the id by producing guilt and shame. An overly strong ego may try to control the id by restraining sexual energy and allowing gratification only at certain times.

Anxiety
A generalized feeling of fear and apprehension that may or may not be connected to a particular event or object. Often accompanied by increased physiological arousal, these fears and apprehensions are generally attributed to unrealistic sources.

When the id, ego, and superego are not in a harmonious relationship or are out of balance, anxiety develops. **Anxiety** is a feeling of emotional discomfort. It is a state of tension characterized by fear and uneasiness and is often accompanied by increased physiological arousal. Anxiety can be mild (such as that before a quiz or a date), or it can be so powerful that it renders a person unable to perform even the simplest tasks. Anxiety need not be connected to a specific event. In fact, most of the fear and apprehension that characterize anxiety are unrealistic. Many of Freud's patients were so gripped by anxiety that they were unable to move their legs and were essentially paralyzed. Freud found that once they were able to discover the source of their anxiety and deal with it, their paralysis disappeared.

Learning Objective 12.10

Consequences of Conflict. Much behavior, according to Freud, reflects an attempt to deal with or escape from anxiety. Thus, how the ego deals with anxiety determines, to a great extent, how people behave. Freud believed that people avoid anxiety principally by developing defense mechanisms that try to

Defense mechanism ═══
A way of reducing anxiety by distorting reality.

Repression ═══════════
A defense mechanism by which people block anxiety-provoking feelings from conscious awareness and push them into the unconscious.

Projection ═══════════
A defense mechanism by which people attribute to other people their own undesirable traits.

Denial ═══════════
A defense mechanism by which people refuse to accept the true source of their anxiety.

Reaction formation ═══
A defense mechanism by which people behave in a manner opposite to their true but anxiety-provoking feelings.

Rationalization ═══════
A defense mechanism by which people reinterpret behavior in terms that render it acceptable.

defend the ego against the awareness of instinctual needs. A **defense mechanism** is a way of reducing anxiety by distorting reality. Although some defense against anxiety is normal and adaptive, people who use these mechanisms to such an extent that reality is truly distorted develop various forms of maladjustment.

Freud described many kinds of defense mechanisms. The most important is **repression,** in which anxiety-provoking behavior or thoughts are totally dismissed to the unconscious. When people repress a feeling or desire, they become totally unaware of that wish or desire. A young girl who has great ambition may repress it because she has been taught that ambition in women is inappropriate. Freud attributed many behavioral abnormalities and personality quirks to repressed feelings. Whenever a person responds to a situation by saying, "I don't know why I did that," Freud would argue that some repressed feeling or desire is expressing itself—the id is deviously getting around the ego and the superego.

The other major defense mechanisms are projection, denial, reaction formation, and rationalization. In **projection,** people attribute their own undesirable traits to other people. Thus, an individual who recognizes his own strong, aggressive tendencies may see other people as acting in an excessively aggressive way toward him. In **denial,** a person totally refuses to accept reality. Thus, someone with strong sexual urges may totally deny her interest in sex rather than deal with those urges. In **reaction formation,** a person defends against anxiety by adopting behaviors opposite to his or her true feelings. A classic example of reaction formation is the behavior of the person with strong sexual urges who channels his energy into religious fervor. Another is the censor of pornographic literature who has strong needs to view such literature. In **rationalization,** a person tries to reinterpret undesirable behavior to make it appear acceptable. Most people use rationalization at times. As they buy a fourth tennis racket, for example, they rationalize their extravagance by asserting, "I will play much better with this racket." When people rationalize, they try to make unreasonable feelings or behaviors seem reasonable.

People who use defense mechanisms are often unaware of doing so. Each mechanism is a way for the ego to deal with the uncomfortable feelings

A defense mechanism is a means of reducing anxiety by distorting reality.

that anxiety produces. Freud's conception of anxiety and how people deal with it is central to his theory of personality.

Freud's ideas about defense mechanisms have not gone unchallenged. For example, Holmes (1978) has closely examined the limited research on projection. Contrary to Freud's claim that projection reduces anxiety and stress, Holmes finds no reliable evidence that attributing one's own undesirable traits to others reduces stress. Holmes therefore questions whether projection is actually a defense mechanism. His analysis places at least part of Freud's theory in question.

Development of Personality

When people like Bud Ross look back on their life, they often try to seek some type of self-understanding. People believe that by looking at the developmental processes they underwent, they may gain insight into their current day-to-day behavior. Freud strongly believed this and developed an elaborate developmental stage theory of personality development.

According to Freud, the core aspects of personality are established early, remain stable throughout life, and can be changed only with great difficulty. A newborn's instincts are focused on the mouth. This is the infant's primary pleasure-seeking center. It is through the mouth that the infant obtains food, thereby reducing hunger. Thus, the first stage of development is called the **oral stage.** The infant achieves oral gratification through feeding, thumb sucking, and babbling. During these early months, people's basic feelings about the world are established. According to Freud, an adult who considers the world a bitter place probably had difficulty during the oral stage of development.

The second major stage of development is the **anal stage.** Around ages two and three, the child learns to respond to some of the demands of society. One principal demand parents make is that the child learn to control the bodily functions of urination and defecation. Most two- and three-year-olds experience pleasure in moving their bowels. Thus, the anal area of the body becomes the focus of certain pleasurable feelings. This stage established the basis for conflict between the id and the ego, between the desire for babyish pleasure and the demand for adult, controlled behavior. During the anal stage, Freud claimed, children develop certain lasting personality characteristics regarding control that reflect their toilet training.

Freud's third stage, the **phallic stage,** centers on the genitals. At around ages four and five, children begin to realize the difference between males and females. They become aware of sexuality. Males experience erections, and both males and females may masturbate. During this period, children want to know where babies come from. They also become increasingly aware of the sexual nature of the relationship between their parents. Freud claims that many feelings during this stage are repressed so deeply that neither children nor adults are aware of many of their own sexual urges. Nevertheless, sex role development begins during this period.

Had Freud analyzed Bud, it is likely he would have wanted to know about the events surrounding Bud's phallic stage, especially the Oedipal complex. In Freud's view, during the phallic stage, males develop the Oedipus complex, which involves fear of punishment and castration anxiety. The **Oedipus complex** is a boy's love for his mother, hostility toward his father, and the consequent fear of castration and/or punishment by the father. A major devel-

Oral stage Freud's first stage of personality development, from birth to about age two, during which infants obtain gratification primarily through the mouth.

Learning Objective 12.11

Anal stage Freud's second stage of personality development, from ages two to about three, during which children learn to control the immediate gratification obtained through defecation and become responsive to the demands of society.

Phallic stage Freud's third stage of personality development, from ages three to seven, during which children obtain gratification primarily from the genitals. During this stage, children pass through the Oedipus (or Electra) complex.

Oedipus complex Occurring during the phallic stage, feelings of rivalry with the parent of the same sex for love of the parent of the opposite sex, ultimately resolved through identification with the parent of the same sex.

According to Freud, a young boy has resolved the Oedipal complex when he begins to identify with and model the behavior of his father.

opmental achievement is the resolution of the Oedipus complex. A young boy eventually accepts his father's close relationship with his mother. Rather than feel excluded by it, he chooses to gratify his need for his mother's attention by identifying with his father. In this way, a young boy begins to model his behavior after that of his father.

For females, Freud argued that the Oedipus complex (sometimes called the Electra complex) follows a slightly different course. When a young girl realizes she has no penis, she develops what Freud called *penis envy.* By attaching her love to her father, she can thereby symbolically acquire a penis. A young girl may ask her father to marry her so they can raise a family together. When she realizes this is unlikely, she may identify with her mother and copy her mother's behavior as a means of obtaining (or sharing in) her father's affection. Like the young male, the young female identifies with the parent of the same sex in the hope of obtaining affection from the parent of the opposite sex. The critical component in resolving the Oedipus complex is the development of identification with the parent of the same sex. During this stage, the child selects role models based on securing the affection he or she desires. The existence of an Oedipus or Electra complex has been widely debated. At a minimum, these ideas have always been controversial, and many psychologists do not regard them as valid. Many feminists totally reject these ideas.

Freud's fourth stage of development, the **latency stage,** lasts from about age seven until puberty. During latency, the child continues to develop physically but sexual urges are relatively inactive. Much of a child's energy at this

Latency stage
Freud's fourth stage of personality development, from age seven until puberty, during which sexual urges are inactive.

STAGE	AGE (*in years*)
Oral The infant achieves gratification through oral activities, such as feeding, thumb sucking, and babbling.	 0–2
Anal The child learns to respond to some of the demands of society (such as bowel and bladder control).	 2–3
Phallic The child begins to realize the differences between males and females and becomes aware of sexuality.	 3–7
Latency The child continues his or her development, but sexual urges are relatively quiet.	 7–11
Genital The growing adolescent shakes off old dependencies and learns to deal maturely with the opposite sex.	 11–Adult

FIGURE 12.1 **:** Freud described five psychosexual stages of development.

time is channeled into social or achievement-related activities. According to Freud, no major changes occur during the latency period. However, on reaching the last stage of development, the **genital stage,** the sexuality, fears, and repressed feelings of earlier stages are once again exhibited. During the genital stage, the adolescent has to shake off dependence on parents and learn to deal with members of the opposite sex in socially and sexually mature ways. Many of an adolescent's repressed feelings of sexuality toward his or her mother and/or father resurface at this time. (See Figure 12.1.)

Genital stage ====
Freud's last stage of personality development, from the onset of puberty through adulthood, during which the sexual conflicts of childhood resurface in adolescents.

Day-to-Day Behavior

Learning ==== 12.12
Objective

According to Freud, a child's core tendencies interact with a child's learning experiences to shape the direction of his or her life. Negative experiences can affect profoundly development. For example, if a child cannot successfully resolve his Oedipal conflict because of an absent parent, appropriate sex roles may not develop.

TABLE 12.1: Conflict Approaches to Personality

Approach	Major Proponent	Core of Personality	Structure of Personality	Development	Peripheral Characteristics: Behavior Pathology Due to:
Conflict	Sigmund Freud	Maximizes gratification while minimizing punishment or guilt; instinctual urges direct behavior	Id, ego, superego	5 Stages: Oral, anal, phallic, latency, genital	Imbalances between the id, ego, and superego resulting in fixations

As children proceed from one stage to the next, they adjust their view of the world. If a child has not successfully passed through a stage, a fixation occurs. For example, a child who does not pass successfully through the phallic stage probably has not resolved the Oedipus complex and may still feel hostility toward the parent of the same sex. The child may suffer the consequences of this unresolved conflict throughout life. A boy may come to consider men generally hostile and wish to attach himself to females in a dependent relationship (the kind he might have had with his mother). (See Table 12.1.)

We have discussed the idea of fixation in relation to developmental psychology. In Chapter 8, Erikson's theory of social development allows for the possibility of fixation. Levinson uses a similar notion in analyzing the life cycle of adults. However, Freud was one of the first psychologists to use such a concept. No theorist claims that fixation at some stage prevents all further development—only that unless individuals master each stage successfully, they cannot fully deal with subsequent stages (see Figure 12.2 on the next page). Someone troubled by an unresolved conflict is vulnerable to maladjustment, because a partially unresolved conflict makes successful completion of later stages more difficult. Many of the stage theorists have used this idea.

According to Freud, good personality adjustment generally involves a balance among competing forces: the child, and later the adult, is neither too self-centered nor too moralistic. Restrictive, punitive, and overbearing parents produce emotionally disturbed children who have a difficult time coping with life. Fixations or partial fixations usually occur because of frustration or overindulgence that hinders the expression of sexual or aggressive energy at a particular psychological stage. As a result, the person develops defense mechanisms and sometimes maladjustment. Personality, then, reflects a continuous conflict between the individual's need for immediate gratification and the demands of society—two irrevocably opposed forces.

When it was first published around 1900, Freud's psychosexual theory of development received a lot of attention, both favorable and unfavorable. The notion that young children had sexual feelings toward their parents was considered absurd. Yet, as we watch young children and the way they identify with their parents, we can see that there are elements of truth to this conception of how development proceeds. However, Freud was not nearly as interested in the normal development of individuals as he was in the type of behavior pathology,

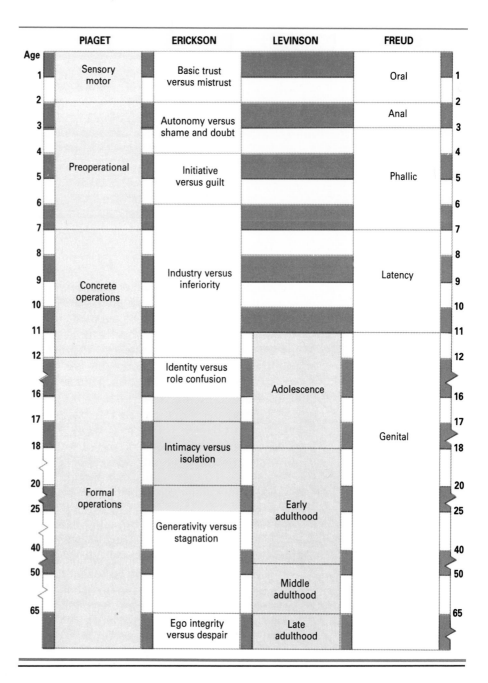

FIGURE 12.2 : The stage theories of Piaget, Erikson, Levinson, and Freud all suggest that individuals must master each stage before they can pass successfully through the next.

or disorder, that appeared as a result of imperfect development. In many senses, Freud's theory prepared the way for other stage theories of development, such as Piaget's, Levinson's, and Erikson's, although these later theories made more specific predictions about specific behaviors.

Freud's theories have been sharply criticized. Some psychologists object to his basic conception of human nature; others reject his predictions about the course of human behavior. Almost all agree that his theory makes specific predictions about individual behaviors almost impossible. We discuss global versus specific theories again later in this chapter.

PROGRESS CHECK 12.2

1. Match each of Freud's stages of psychosexual development with the appropriate description.

   latency   oral   genital   phallic   anal

Learning Objective 12.11   A.   _____ Stage 1: During this stage, the infant achieves gratification through feeding, thumb sucking, and babbling.

Learning Objective 12.11   B.   _____ Stage 2: During this stage, the two- to three-year-old begins to respond to society's demands. Pleasure is experienced through bodily functions, and controlled behavior is learned through such activities as toilet training.

Learning Objective 12.11   C.   _____ Stage 3: During this stage, four- and five-year-olds experience the Oedipus complex. Sex-role development begins, and children become aware of sexuality.

Learning Objective 12.11   D.   _____ Stage 4: During this stage, instinctual urges are channeled into social or achievement-related activities, sexual urges are relatively inactive, and no major changes in personality development occur. The stage begins around age seven and lasts until the onset of puberty.

Learning Objective 12.11   E.   _____ Stage 5: During this stage, the adolescent experiences the sexuality, fears, and repressed feelings from earlier stages and attempts to become independent from parents and to deal with members of the opposite sex in socially and sexually mature ways.

2. Complete each of the following sentences with one of the options provided.

Learning Objective 12.6   A.   Sigmund Freud's theory is called a _____ theory because it provides rules for predicting all behavior but makes few predictions concerning specific behaviors.
      (trait : type : microtheory : global)

Learning Objective 12.6   B.   One reason Freud's theory receives criticism is that it _____.
      (is difficult to test experimentally : is too specific)

Learning Objective 12.7   C.   Freud's theory describes a conflict between _____.
      (sexual and aggressive instincts : instinctual needs and social demands)

Learning Objective 12.7   D.   Freud's approach to personality development is called _____.
      (psychoanalysis : psychoanalytic theory)

Learning Objective 12.8   E.   Preconscious behavior involves mental activity that _____ a part of a person's awareness.
      (is : can become : cannot easily become)

Learning Objective 12.8   F.   The id, as described by Freud, is _____.
      (concerned about morals and ethics : selfish, irrational, and demanding)

Learning Objective 12.8   G.   The ego works on the _____ principle.
      (pleasure : reality)

Learning Objective 12.8   H.   The superego is _____.
      (the strongest component of personality : patient : a person's conscience)

Learning Objective 12.8   I.   The unconscious, according to Freud, is made up of three _____ _____ forces.
      (cooperative : competing)

Learning Objective 12.9   J.   The libido is the name Freud gave to the _____ instinct.
      (death : life)

Learning Objective 12.9

K. The libido usually expresses itself through the _____.
    (id : ego : superego)

Learning Objective 12.9

L. Once his patients discovered and dealt with the source of their _____, Freud found that their behavior disorders disappeared.
    (libido : consciousness : anxiety)

Learning Objective 12.10

M. Defense mechanisms protect people from uncomfortable emotional experiences by _____.
    (distorting reality : allowing the ego to recognize instinctual needs)

Learning Objective 12.10

N. If an individual adopts a behavior that is opposite of his or her true feelings, the person is using _____ as a defense mechanism.
    (rationalization : reaction formation : projection)

Learning Objective 12.10

O. Defense mechanisms are usually motivated by _____ thought.
    (conscious : unconscious)

Learning Objective 12.11

P. Children resolve the conflict that accompanies the Oedipus complex by identifying with the parent of the _____ sex.
    (same : opposite)

Learning Objective 12.12

Q. According to Freud, Erikson, Levinson, and other psychologists, a fixation at a particular stage _____.
    (prevents all future development : occurs because of unresolved conflicts)

Learning Objective 12.12

R. Fixations and partial fixations usually occur because a person _____.
    (is frustrated or overindulged : has a low level of libidinal energy)

HUMANISTIC APPROACHES: CARL ROGERS AND ALFRED ADLER

Learning Objective 12.13

While Freud might have tried to understand Bud Ross's relationship with his father, other theorists might have focused on Bud himself. Such well-known theorists as Carl Rogers and Alfred Adler would probably focus more intently on Bud's own conception of himself and what he would like to become. Both Adler and Rogers were humanists; they believed in the basic goodness of human beings and focused not on other people and environmental forces but on individuals and their own conceptions of themselves and what they would like to become. Adler was an optimist; he maintained that someone like Bud was in a lifelong search to better himself. Such humanistic theories assume that people are motivated by internal forces to achieve personal goals.

Humanistic theories that stressed fulfillment developed partly in response to Freud's theory, which stressed the conflict of inner forces. Unlike Freudian theory, humanistic fulfillment theories are generally less global and allow the theoretician and practitioner to make some predictions about specific behaviors. The two fulfillment theories discussed here are the general model developed by Carl Rogers and the more extreme version developed by Alfred Adler.

Carl Rogers

Learning Objective 12.14

Carl Rogers (1902–1987) believes that fulfillment is the motivating force of personality development. According to Rogers, people try to express their capabilities, potential, and talents to the fullest extent possible. Rogers suggests

Carl Roger's personality theory and client-centered therapy are structured around the concept of self.

Self ══════════
The main structural component of Roger's theory of personality. A group of perceptions that characterize an individual and his or her relationship to other people and to other aspects of his or her life.

Learning Objective *12.15*

Ideal self ══════════
That self a person would ideally like to be.

Self-actualization ══════════
For Rogers, the continuous growth of the self toward the ideal self.

that an inborn tendency in people directs them toward actualizing their inherited nature, and thus fulfilling their potential.

Rogers makes two basic assumptions about behavior. He assumes that behavior is goal-directed and worthwhile. He also assumes that because people are innately good, they will almost always choose adaptive, self-actualizing behaviors. These assumptions are also the foundation of his approach to the treatment of maladjustment (discussed in Chapter 15).

Structure of Personality.   Rogers's theory, like Freud's, developed out of his therapeutic interests and experiences. As a practicing clinical psychologist, Rogers listened to thousands of patients and was among the first to tape record and transcribe these interactions. He found that when patients were given the opportunity, they talked about their experiences and their thoughts about themselves.

Rogers's theory of personality is structured around the concept of self. The **self** is those perceptions individuals have of themselves and of their relationship to other people and to other aspects of life. The self is how people see their own behavior and internal characteristics. Rogers's theory assumes that individuals are constantly engaged in the process of fulfilling their potential, of actualizing the true self.

Rogers suggests that each person has a concept not only of self but also of an ideal self. An **ideal self** is the self that a person would like to be. When correspondence exists between the real self and the ideal self, a person is generally happy. In contrast, a great discrepancy between the real self and the ideal self often results in feelings of unhappiness and dissatisfaction.

Rogers's personality approach is unidirectional: it always moves in the direction of fulfillment. Rogers does not suggest that all people undergo growth at all times. During some periods, no growth is evident. For Rogers, a person's core tendency is to actualize, maintain, and enhance the experiencing organism. Rogers's basic principle is that people have a tendency to maximize self-concept through **self-actualization.** In this process, the self grows, expands, and becomes more social. People are self-actualized when they have expanded their self-concepts and developed their potential to approximate their ideal selves. Abraham Maslow, another humanistic psychologist, (whom we studied

Dodge Morgan, who tried to reach his full potential by sailing alone around the world, is a good example of a self-actualized individual.

in Chapter 5) listed the characteristics that he felt distinguished self-actualized people. In his view, self-actualized people:

are realistically oriented
accept themselves for what they are
have thoughts that are unconventional and spontaneous
are problem centered
have a need for privacy
are independent
have a fresh appreciation of people
have spiritual experiences
identify with people
have intimate relationships
are democratic
do not confuse the means with the end
have a good sense of humor
are creative and nonconformist
appreciate the environment

Although few people have all these traits, according to Maslow all people strive (and are directed) toward self-actualization. This self-actualization is generally continuous throughout life. When people's self-concepts are not what they would like them to be, anxiety develops. Like Freud, Rogers views anxiety as useful, but he views it as useful because it motivates people to try to actualize their best selves, to become all that they are capable of being.

Development of Personality.   Like many developmental theorists, Freud characterized development as a series of stages during which certain conflicts are more or less successfully resolved. Rogers suggests that development is not stage-like but continual. According to Rogers, personality development involves learning to evaluate oneself and mastering the process of self-actualization. Rogers was particularly aware that children develop basic feelings about themselves early in life. He understood the role of social influences in the development of self-concepts. When children are told that they are beautiful, intelligent, and clever, their ideas about themselves are very different from those of children who are told that they are bad, dirty, shameful, and a general nuisance.

Rogers does not claim that negative feelings toward children's behavior should not be expressed. Instead, he suggests that children must grow up in an atmosphere in which they can experience life fully. This involves their seeing the good sides of their behavior as well as the bad. Children need an environment in which they can explore different aspects of their personalities.

When children have been allowed to develop stable self-concepts, they respect themselves and other people. They are aware of themselves and of how other people see them. People with positive self-concepts and high self-esteem are generally flexible and open to new experiences, so that they can continue to grow and self-actualize. The development of a positive self-concept is crucial to Rogerian views of personality.

Day-to-Day Behavior.   Rogers suggests that people become unhappy when they are unable to fit new types of behavior into their self-concepts. People distort their perceptions of their behavior in order to make their behavior compatible with their self-concepts. For example, when a person whose self-concept includes high moral principles, strict religious observances, and strict self-control feels envy, he probably becomes anxious because such feelings are inconsistent with his self-concept. To avoid anxiety he denies or distorts what he is truly experiencing. He may deny that he feels envy, or he may insist that he is somehow entitled to the object or situation he covets. People with rigid self-concepts guard their self-concepts against potentially threatening feelings and experiences. In contrast, a healthy self-concept allows for new experiences and the acceptance or rejection of new experiences.

When people are moving in a positive direction, their lives have meaning. With each new experience, a person's self-concept becomes stronger and more defined, and the eventual goal of self-actualization is brought closer. Notice in the following exchange that Edith's self-concept is clearly defined.

> *Edith:* I've had a really good week. I did much better with my husband. I had a tough time with the children, though.
> *Therapist:* Oh?
> *Edith:* They kept attacking me.
> *Therapist:* How did their attacks make you feel?
> *Edith:* A little shaky—they said I was selfish and unfair. But I tried to keep *my* image of myself intact and remember that I am the parent. They can attack specific things I do or say, but I know I am basically doing the right thing by them.

Rogers's concept of personality shows an abiding concern for individual development. Rogers stresses that each person must evaluate his or her own situation from a personal (internal) frame of reference, not from the (external) framework of others. Unhappiness is the result of too great a discrepancy between the real and ideal selves, but the individual can reduce or eliminate that discrepancy. Thus, each person's happiness lies within his or her conception of self.

Freud's and Rogers's theories of personality make fundamentally different assumptions about human nature and about how it is expressed in behavior or personality. Freud saw this biologically driven human being in conflict; Rogers sees human beings as inherently good and trying to be everything that they might. Not surprisingly, the treatment procedures that have developed from their theories—psychoanalysis and nondirective therapy—are also different. We discuss these therapies in Chapter 15.

Alfred Adler (1870–1937) believed that social interaction is an important factor that influences personality development.

Learning Objective 12.16

Alfred Adler

Alfred Adler (1870–1937) was heavily influenced by Freud, and many psychologists generally consider his theory an extension of Freud's. Adler focused not simply on the self, but on the self as a member of society. Adler believed that people strive unceasingly to better themselves but, unlike Rogers, also believed that people also strive constantly for perfection and superiority. Rogers's theory has a less extreme view than Adler's; Rogers's theory was also developed twenty years later. In some ways, you can think of Adler's theory as the parent to Rogers's view.

Structure of Personality.   Adler believed that people are basically good and that their core tendency is to strive toward superiority or perfection. Whereas Rogers stressed fulfillment through self-actualization, Adler stressed fulfillment through striving toward specific goals. Some goals are fictional and unlikely to be reached. Adler spoke of *fictional finalism*—a goal state that is impossible to realize but acts as one of the energizers of behavior (Adler, 1969).

According to Adler, people are motivated, or energized, to strive for superiority and ultimately perfection by feelings of inferiority; when people experience a sense of imperfection, they seek to improve themselves. Thus, feelings of inferiority are not a negative factor; they compel people to strive for superiority and thereby express their core tendencies.

A crucial aspect of Adler's theory is the idea that people are inherently social beings. Unlike most other theorists, who assume that people are forced to be social, Adler believed that from birth on, people interact with parents, family, and society of their own free will. These innate social qualities temper people's drives for superiority.

One way people express their social approach to life is to adopt a unique style of life. An individual's style of life can express not only characteristics of personality, sentiments, and desires but also needs for superiority. Adler recognized that people do not try to achieve superiority in the same ways. Because they have different social goals, they seek to express their feelings and goals for superiority in different areas of life. Some people may seek to be superior artists; others may seek to be superior social advocates or homemakers. Each person develops a unique style of life in which attitudes and behaviors express a specific approach to achieving superiority. Because human beings are social beings, they will seek goals and values that are basically social in nature.

Development of Personality.   Like Rogers, Adler felt that children's social interactions are particularly important in determining eventual personality characteristics. But whereas Rogers stresses the role of social interaction in the development of self-concepts, Adler suggested that people are innately social. Thus, children's relationships with other people, particularly with parents, will largely determine their personalities. Conversely, relationships with other people in adulthood reflect early relationships with parents and other family members. For example, the firstborn child is likely to have a different relationship with people from a child who is born third. Firstborns tend to have high needs for achievement. They are pushed by their parents toward success, leadership, and independence. It is likely that a firstborn will develop a pattern of interaction and an eventual lifestyle that will reflect the high needs for achievement, encouraged during childhood years.

Day-to-Day Behavior.   Adler and his followers relied heavily on the idea that early relationships with siblings and family determine an individual's eventual choice of life-style. It therefore follows that birth order is important. In Adlerian theory, birth order largely determines the range of feelings children have about themselves and their family. For example, older children tend to have stronger needs for superiority than do younger children. However, a younger child who feels competitive with an older sibling may develop strong needs for success, mastery, and achievement.

Closely associated with birth order are feelings of inferiority. Each new child brings to the family new talents, strengths, and weaknesses, any of which may create feelings of inferiority or lack of worth in other family members. These feelings of inferiority, and the compensating need for perfection, determine the peripheral characteristics of behavior. If the family atmosphere stresses cooperation, respect, and love, then a child will probably express needs for superiority in positive, fulfilling, socially acceptable ways. But if the family atmosphere lacks love and harbors distrust or even neglect, then the child's need for superiority will probably express itself in antisocial, negative, and potentially destructive peripheral characteristics.

Adlerian psychology stresses social interaction. Normal behavior follows a course of socially acceptable striving and the development of an interesting and unique life-style. Although the need for superiority motivates all human development, this need finds unique expression in each individual. Adlerian psychologists typically assume that abnormal behavior has its roots in childhood—that poor social interactions, particularly with parents, have led to a misguided or faulty life-style. Adlerian therapists treat maladjusted behavior by helping the client achieve positive social interactions with other human beings, thus redirecting feelings of inferiority into ways of achieving feelings of accomplishment.

Both Adler and Rogers assume that human beings can and will fulfill themselves whenever possible. Rogers stresses self-actualization; Adler emphasizes an innate social need motivated by feelings of inferiority to strive toward perfection and superiority. To a great extent, psychologists see Adler as stressing an interpersonal route to fulfillment. Adler's ideas of an inferiority complex and of life-style have made their way into other popular theories of psychology (see Table 12.2.)

TABLE 12.2: Conflict and Fulfillment Approaches to Personality

Approach	Major Proponent	Core of Personality	Structure of Personality	Development	Peripheral Characteristics: Behavior Pathology Due to:
Conflict	Sigmund Freud	Maximizes gratification while minimizing punishment or guilt; instinctual urges direct behavior	Id, ego, superego	5 Stages: oral, anal, phallic, latency, genital	Imbalances between the id, ego, and superego resulting in fixations
Fulfillment	Carl Rogers	Actualizes, maintains, and enhances the experiences of life through the process of self-actualization	Self	Process of cumulative self-actualization	Wide discrepancy between real self and concept of ideal self
Fulfillment	Alfred Adler	Striving for superiority and perfection	None stated	Process of striving for superiority by overcoming feelings of inferiority	Inability to succeed; overwhelming feeling of inferiority

PROGRESS CHECK   12.3

1. Complete each of the following sentences with one of the options provided.

Learning Objective 12.13

A. Humanistic theories stress _____ internal forces.
(conflict among : fulfillment of personal goals motivated by)

Learning Objective 12.14

B. Carl Rogers believed that people _____ fulfilling their potential.
(must learn the importance of : have an inborn tendency that directs them toward)

Learning Objective 12.14

C. Rogers referred to the self that a person would like to be as the _____ self.
(total : real : ideal)

Learning Objective 12.15

D. Rogers's approach to personality is _____.
(unidirectional : supported by the saying "one step forward, five steps back")

Learning Objective 12.15

E. Carl Rogers and _____ agreed that people strive and are directed toward self-actualization.
(Sigmund Freud : Abraham Maslow)

Learning Objective 12.15

F. A self-actualized person _____ for privacy.
(has a need : has little need)

Learning Objective 12.15

G. According to Rogers, the happiness and stability a person is able to experience depend on the _____.
(person's self-concept : external forces that confront the person)

Learning Objective 12.16

H. According to Adler, the core tendency in personality development is to strive toward _____.
(cooperation and contentment : superiority and perfection)

Learning Objective 12.16

I. Adler focused on the self and also on the individual as a member of society because he believed that human beings are _____ social.
(forced to be : conditioned to be : inherently)

Learning Objective 12.16

J. Adler and his followers relied heavily on the idea that _____ determine(s) an individual's unique life-style.
(one's self-concept : early family relationships : inborn talents)

Learning Objective 12.16

K. According to Adler, one major factor contributing to a person's feeling of inferiority is _____.
(birth order : fictional finalism)

Learning Objective 12.16

L. Adler's theory of personality development _____.
(shows an abiding concern for the individual : stresses an interpersonal route to fulfillment)

BEHAVIORAL APPROACHES

Learning Objective 12.17

Behavioral personality theorists who considered Bud Ross's personality would probably say that Bud had been gradually shaped by his rewards and punishments into having a shy, quiet personality. Behavioral personality theorists suggest that personality develops as people learn from their environment. They assert that all behavior can be shaped and managed; they would say Bud had been taught to be quiet.

Many behavioral theorists today consider some ideas in conflict and fulfillment approaches to be old fashioned. They believe that to be practical in today's fast-paced society, people often need to change various aspects of their lives quickly and efficiently; many people do not have the time, money, or energy for a lengthy therapy or personality analysis. Behaviorists maintain that someone like Bud needs to be reinforced for any assertive decisions or behavior he is able to emit. They might urge Bud to ask his family and friends to praise him whenever they think he has shown improvement in being bold and firm; by being praised, he would learn to respond to himself and the world in new ways. The key word is *learn.*

Psychologists like Harvard University's B. F. Skinner assert that psychology needs a technology of behavior. Parts of that technology are an understanding of the contingencies of reinforcement, the defining of stimuli, and the measurement of responses. This technological approach means breaking down each behavior into its component parts of the learning process discussed in Chapter 2. Behaviorists such as Skinner reject such concepts as the id, ego, and superego in favor of data that they feel are definable, observable, and measurable: stimuli and responses. Skinner has written extensively on the nature of learning and the role of reinforcement. As a behaviorist, he believes that all behavior can be shaped and managed to achieve a potentially ideal individual in a potentially ideal society.

Unlike global theories, behavioral theories tend to center on precisely defined elements that can be tested in a laboratory or clinical setting. They avoid conceptualizing all of human nature and concentrate instead on predicting behavior in specific circumstances. As a result, their assertions are more easily tested. For Skinner and other behaviorists, personality is best understood as the response of an organism to the environment. For behaviorists, core characteristics of personality are less clear; they see the development of personality simply as a change in response characteristics—a person learns new behaviors in response to new environments and stimuli. Concerned mainly with the learning process, learning theorists see behavior as many fluctuating responses to changes in the environment.

For most behaviorists, the structural unit of personality is the response. Any behavior that is exhibited, regardless of the situation, is seen as a response to stimuli or as a response awaiting reinforcement (or punishment). Usually, behaviors (responses) are emitted to satisfy specific needs. For example,

Although many young children are shy, through repeated exposure to social situations they can develop outgoing personalities.

people generally eat because of hunger. Children may initially eat all their vegetables in the expectation of a positive response or reinforcement from parents, but continuous reinforcement eventually becomes unnecessary. Children eventually learn to eat vegetables because they taste good or are good for them, as well as because their parents are pleased with this behavior. For traditional behaviorists, the core tendency that organizes behavior is the reduction or satisfaction of social or biological needs that energize behavior. This result is accomplished through responses (behaviors) that are reinforced.

Using simple behavioral analysis, psychologists begin to see how people develop behavior patterns (such as eating their vegetables or being hostile) and why behavior is in constant flux. A behavioral approach suggests that learning is the process that shapes personality and that learning takes place through experience. Because new experiences happen all the time, a person is constantly learning about the world and changing response patterns accordingly. Thus, for a behaviorist, personality is always capable of change.

Just as there are several different learning principles involving the use of stimuli, responses, and reinforcement (for a review, see Chapter 2), there are behavioral personality theories based on classical conditioning, instrumental conditioning, or observational learning. These three approaches view the acquisition and maintenance of behavior from different angles. For example, the role of thought is extremely important in observational learning theories, but in classical or instrumental conditioning theories its role is nonexistent or minimal.

Classical Conditioning

Learning Objective 12.18

Most people are fearful or anxious at some time. Some people are fearful more often than not. How does an individual become a fearful person? What causes constant anxiety and apprehension? Many behavioral psychologists maintain that anxiety and fear are learned responses that can be learned through classical conditioning. As you probably remember from the discussion of classical conditioning in Chapter 2, in classical conditioning, a neutral stimulus is paired with another stimulus that elicits some response. The neutral stimulus might be a bell that, when paired with food, will elicit the response of salivation. Through careful pairing of the bell and the food, the bell alone can be made to elicit salivation.

Classical conditioning can account for a variety of behaviors. Some personality theorists claim that most emotional responses are classically conditioned. For example, many people are frightened of rats. Because rats are often encountered in dark cellars, dark cellars may themselves become fearful stimuli. Entering a dark cellar, an individual may experience fear because dark cellars are associated with rats and rats elicit fear. Such fears may later generalize to a fear of unknown places.

Many studies of personality have tried to classically condition behavior. Consider bedwetting, often a problem with children. Bedwetting occurs because a full bladder does not awaken the sleeping child. Mowrer and Mowrer (1938) conducted a study in which subjects slept on a special bed, equipped so that when urination occurred it sounded a bell that woke the child. The ringing of the bell became paired with increased bladder tension so that when the children felt an increase in bladder tension, they woke up and emptied their bladders in the toilet rather than in the bed.

Instrumental Conditioning

Instrumental behaviors are behaviors a person emits spontaneously. As each behavior is emitted, some consequences, such as reinforcement or punishment, occurs. These consequences are considered absolutely essential in instrumental conditioning, because behavior that is reinforced tends to recur. When people find that a certain behavior is reinforced, they tend to emit similar behaviors in similar situations. Much behavior can be explained as spontaneous behavior reinforced by the environment. For example, people who emit considerate or affectionate behavior are usually reinforced for this behavior and continue to be considerate and affectionate.

Behavioral psychologists often use the instrumental learning principles of reward and punishment to help children to control themselves. Consider the problem of discipline in school. Although psychology cannot provide all the answers, it can help. Here is what a group of behavioral psychologists did with a ten-year-old child in the Florida public school system who used obscenities very frequently. In an hour's time, he would often utter as many as 150 obscene words and phrases. Lahey, McNees, and McNees (1973) took the child out of the classroom for a minimum of five minutes each time he uttered an obscene word and placed him in a well-lit, empty room. The child was told he would be placed in the time-out room every time he made an obscene statement. In a few days, the number of obscenities uttered decreased dramatically, from two a minute to fewer than five an hour.

The time-out procedure is often used in learning situations in both the classroom and the laboratory. As with any kind of reinforcement or punishment procedure, the subject learns that the time-out procedure is contingent on behavior. In this case, time-out was punishing because the child found being in the classroom reinforcing. To avoid being put in the time-out room, the subject learns not to emit the behavior that results in his being placed there. In this case, he learns not to utter obscenities. Techniques such as the time-out procedure are used to shape behavior and personality, just as reinforcement is often used.

Observational Learning

Observational learning theories assume that people learn new behaviors by watching other people perform them. For example, children learn correct table manners by watching their parents use them. Similarly, a novice tennis player learns technique and strategy by watching a tennis pro. It is assumed that eventually the observer will imitate the behavior of the model. Parents often tell their older children to be good models for their younger siblings. They ask them to behave properly so that the younger children will do the same.

People do not exhibit all aspects of their personality at all times. Sometimes people are shy; at other times they may be outgoing. Many behaviors that have been learned through observational learning are not always expressed. Consider this one small element of personality—table manners. Many parents have noted that their children use excellent table manners only in the presence of company. Obviously, the children have learned the appropriate responses but choose to exhibit them only when they want to. Observational learning theorists explain this selective behavior in the following way. As children grow, their relationships with parents and other models change (Bandura, 1977a). A decreasing number of behaviors acquired by watching the behaviors of other people will be exhibited; as children grow older, they choose to exhibit certain behaviors and inhibit others.

Together, the imitative aspects of observational learning theory and the reinforcement properties of conditioned learning can account for most behaviors. However, observational learning approaches stress the importance of the relationship between the observer and the model in eliciting imitative behavior. For example, when children view the behavior of a parent or other important figure, their imitative behavior will be significantly more extensive than if they observe the actions of someone they consider less important. People can also learn abnormal behavior through imitation. Children who observe violent, aggressive behavior may, if reinforced, imitate that behavior rather than more socially desirable behaviors.

Unlike instrumental theories, in which reinforcement is considered central, observational learning theories assume that learning a new response can occur independently of reinforcement: personality develops as a function of imitating the behavior of other people. Later, however, reinforcement acts to maintain such behaviors once they are learned. For example, most people have observed aggressive, hostile behavior in other people but choose other ways to express emotions because they have been selectively reinforced for such behaviors.

PROGRESS CHECK   12.4

1. Complete each of the following sentences with one of the options provided.

Learning Objective 12.17

A. B. F. Skinner has asserted that psychology needs _____ behavior.
(to focus less on : a technology of : to personalize)

Learning Objective 12.17

B. Behaviorists have _____ concepts such as the id, ego, and superego.
(rejected : attempted to observe experimentally)

Learning Objective 12.17

C. For a behaviorist, the structural unit of personality is _____.
(reinforcement : the response : the self)

Learning Objective 12.17

D. According to behaviorists, people behave in specific ways in order to _____.
(satisfy specific needs : maintain consistency : feel in control)

Learning Objective 12.17

E. From a behavioral point of view, personality is _____.
(always capable of change : relatively permanent : unmeasureable)

Learning Objective 12.18

F. Classical conditioning is likely to occur when _____.
(two stimuli are paired : a consequence follows a behavior)

Learning Objective 12.18

G. The case in which behavioral psychologists gained control over a child's obscene language illustrates how an instrumental conditioning procedure called _____ can be used to shape personality.
(modeling : time-out : extinction)

Learning Objective 12.18

H. Observational learning theories suggest the primary factor leading to personality development is _____.
(reinforcement : imitation : practice)

Learning Objective 12.18

I. Observational learning theorists say that as children grow older, fewer observed behaviors are exhibited because the children _____.
(learn to choose which behaviors to exhibit or inhibit : observe less)

Learning Objective 12.18

J. _____ acts to maintain behaviors once they have been learned, according to observational learning theorists.
(The self : Society : Reinforcement)

COGNITIVE APPROACHES

Learning Objective $\overline{12.19}$

Cognitive approaches to personality appeared at first as a reaction to strict behavioral models. Cognitive views were soon influenced by the humanist view that people are basically good and strive to be better. Psychologists came to recognize that human thought exists and can be used to better a person's life. In important ways, cognitive theory grew out of and added new dimensions to behavioral theory. Many researchers now claim that people can change their behavior, their conceptions of themselves, and their personality in a relatively short period of time without long-term personality analysis if they are willing to change their thoughts. Cognitive psychologists share this idea with behavioral psychologists.

In some ways, cognitive theory is a natural extension of behavioral theory. For many theorists and practitioners, however, it goes beyond simple learning theory in that it allows psychologists to make predictions about behavior across a wider variety of situations. It brings in some of the uniqueness of human beings, especially their thought processes. According to cognitive theory, people choose to exhibit learned behavior according to the situation in which they find themselves and their own personal needs at a particular time. The cognitive emphasis is on the interaction of a person's thoughts and behavior.

If thought and behavior are closely intertwined, then affecting a person's thoughts should affect behavior. If, for example, a person with a strong need for recognition observes a technique that lends itself to gaining status, he or she may learn to think in terms of this technique, try it, practice it, and place value on it. Rotter (1964) developed a theory that focuses on the nature and sources of reinforcement that people acquire and can account for specific behaviors. Some psychologists classify Rotter's theory as a microtheory because it accounts for a limited range of behaviors, but does so very well. Other microtheories have focused on how different aspects of a person's thought processes shape behavior patterns. Bandura (1974, 1977a) has focused on human beings' ability and need to regulate their own behavior independently of externally delivered reinforcements. He emphasizes social learning and self-regulation. Mischel (1973) emphasizes the importance of people's interactions with their environment; people influence their environment as much as their environment (stimuli) influences them. This cognitive view suggests that personality development is innovative, adaptive, and constantly changing (Haan, Millsap, & Hartka, 1986).

Rotter's Locus of Control

Learning Objective $\overline{12.20}$

Many of the classic global theories have been criticized because they are not easy to study and, in many cases, impossible to examine. For example, in Freud's theory, the ego is not a physiological object or state that can be manipulated. In the same way, the concepts of self and of maximizing potential that appear in Rogers's theory are difficult to measure and assess. A global theory (like Freud's) is all encompassing. It attempts to account for all of personality and behavior. Smaller, well-researched theories, *microtheories,* account for specific behaviors in specific situations. Because of their smaller scope, they are easier to test.

One widely studied cognitive-behavioral microtheory is that of locus of control, developed by Julian Rotter (1964). Locus of control involves the extent to which individuals believe they or external factors control their lives. Rotter developed a test consisting of a series of statements about oneself and other people in general to assess whether individuals place their locus of control inside themselves (internal) or in their environment (external). The statements below are typical.

1. People's misfortunes result from the mistakes they make.   *vs.*   Many of the unhappy things in people's lives are partly due to bad luck.

2. With enough effort, we can wipe out political corruption.   *vs.*   It is difficult for people to have much control over the things politicians do in office.

3. There is a direct connection between how hard I study and the grades I get.   *vs.*   Sometimes I can't understand how teachers arrive at the grades they give.

4. What happens to me is my own doing.   *vs.*   Sometimes I feel that I don't have enough control over the direction my life is taking.

Locus of control has been researched extensively in relation to various types of therapy, need for achievement, and frustration. For example, people classified as internal are more likely to react negatively if their freedom of choice is restricted (Moyer, 1978). They are also more likely to report success falsely on an impossible task if the task has been rated as difficult and requiring skill (Karabenick & Srull, 1978). Such individuals feel they control their environment. They are more likely to engage in preventive health measures and are better at losing weight than are external persons (Balch & Ross, 1975). College students characterized as internal are more likely to profit from psychotherapy (Kilmann, Albert, & Sotile, 1975) and to show greater academic achievement (Findley & Cooper, 1983). Because individuals in therapy often blame their problems on other people, knowing an individual's locus of control can be an effective aid in therapy.

People develop expectancies based on their beliefs about the sources of reinforcement in their environment. These specific expectancies lead to specific behaviors (see Figure 12.3). Reinforcement of these behaviors then strengthens the expectancy and leads to increased belief in internal or external control (see, for example, Perlmuter, Scharff, Karsh, & Monty, 1980).

Locus of control describes several specific behaviors, but it is not comprehensive enough to explain all or even most of an individual's behavior. Furthermore, although internality-externality is treated as a single dimension, researchers have shown that locus of control may result from as many as four or five factors (Garza & Widlak, 1977; Zuckerman & Gerbasi, 1977a, 1977b). Smaller theories such as locus of control can be useful in helping psychologists understand the total picture that is human personality.

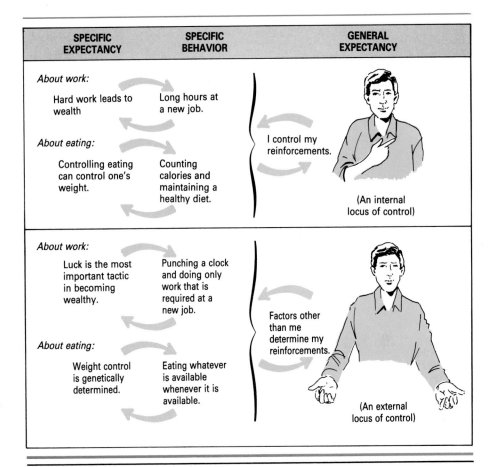

FIGURE 12.3 : A person's general expectations about life are determined in a three-stage process: specific expectancies lead to behaviors, which are reinforced. This cycle eventually leads to a general expectancy about life and then to an internal or external locus of control.

Bandura's Self-Efficacy

Learning ‾‾12.21‾‾
Objective

One of the most influential behavior theories of personality is that of Albert Bandura (1977a). Bandura has played a major role in reintroducing thought processes into learning and personality theory. His conception of personality began with observational learning theory and the idea that human beings observe, think about, and imitate behavior. His work in the 1960s, discussed earlier, showed that children and adults learn behavior by observing and imitating other people. Bandura's social learning theory was a crucial development in behavioral learning theory. In 1977, Bandura went a step farther; he argued that, in addition to observation and imitation, people's expectations of mastery and achievement, their convictions about their own effectiveness, determine both the types of behavior in which they will engage and the amount of risk they will undertake (Bandura, 1977a, 1977b). Judgments about self-efficacy or effectiveness determine how much effort people will expend and how long they will persist in the face of obstacles (Bandura, 1982a, 1982b). Bandura believes that people's emotional responses to situations are also partly determined by their expectations of success or failure; he argues (1982b) that a strong sense of self-efficacy allows people to feel free to select, influence, and even construct the circumstances of their own lives.

In attempting to find a cure for cancer, scientists must have a strong sense of self-efficacy-the belief that they can succeed in the face of obstacles.

Bandura's is an optimistic theory. It is a long way from the deterministic theory of Freud, who argued that biologically based forces locked in conflict determine human behavior. It is also a long way from a behavioral theory such as Skinner's, which suggests that environmental contingencies alone shape behavior. Bandura believes that human beings have choices, that they direct the course of their own lives (1982b). Society, parents, experiences, and luck help shape those lives. Bad luck or nonreinforcing experiences can damage a developing sense of self-efficacy. In contrast, observation of positive, prosocial models during the formative years can help people develop a strong sense of self-efficacy that will encourage them to direct their own lives. Bandura's theory allows for individual flexibility in behavior. People are not locked into specific responses to specific stimuli in a deterministic fashion. According to Bandura, people choose from among their models the behaviors they will imitate. Furthermore, they are free in any situation to adapt their behavior to the situation. By introducing thought processes into behavior, Bandura allows for different responses among people and within the same individual.

TABLE 12.3 : Conflict, Fulfillment, Behavioral, and Cognitive Approaches to Personality

Approach	Major Proponent	Core of Personality	Structure of Personality	Development	Peripheral Characteristics: Behavior Pathology Due to:
Conflict	Sigmund Freud	Maximizes gratification while minimizing punishment or guilt; instinctual urges direct behavior	Id, ego, superego	5 Stages: oral, anal, phallic, latency, genital	Imbalances between the id, ego, and superego resulting in fixations
Fulfillment	Carl Rogers	Actualizes, maintains, and enhances the experiences of life through the process of self-actualization	Self	Process of cumulative self-actualization	Wide discrepancy between real self and concept of ideal self
Fulfillment	Alfred Adler	Striving for superiority and perfection	None stated	Process of striving for superiority by overcoming feelings of inferiority	Inability to succeed; overwhelming feelings of inferiority
Behaviorism	B. F. Skinner	Reduction of social and biological needs that energize behavior through the emission of learned responses	Response	Process of learning new responses	Having learned faulty or inappropriate behaviors
Cognitive	Albert Bandura	Human beings are decision makers who shape their own destiny	Response	Process of observing other people and deciding what to do	Having chosen faulty or inappropriate behaviors

Mischel's Cognitive Social Learning

Learning Objective 12.22

Like Bandura, Walter Mischel claims that thought is crucial in determining human behavior. Like other social learning theorists, Mischel asserts that both past experiences and current reinforcement are important to behavior, but he stresses the importance of interaction between personal and situational variables.

Mischel (1973) focuses on the idea that individuals' behavior varies with time and situation. People who tend generally to be warm, caring, and attentive can, in some situations, become hostile and aggressive. People change their responses to suit the situation, based on their past experiences and their current assessment of the situation. For Mischel, day-to-day differences in personality merely reflect people's ability to adapt. Mischel often is characterized as an interactionist—he focuses on the interaction of people and the environment.

Mischel believes that several processes or variables determine people's response to a stimulus: *competencies,* what people know and can do; *encoding strategies,* the way people process, attend to, and select information; *expectancies,* people's anticipation of outcomes; *personal values,* the importance people attach to various situations; and *self-regulatory systems,* the system of rules people have established for themselves to guide their behavior (Mischel, 1979).

Mischel and other cognitive theorists argue that people can respond flexibly to various situations (for example, Cantor & Kihlstrom, 1982). People often make subtle adjustments in their tone of voice and overt behavior depending on the context in which they find themselves. This process of adjustment is called *self-regulation.* Mischel believes that individuals must be considered in relation to the environment, because they interpret their environments carefully and adjust their behavior accordingly (Mischel, 1983). Personal expectations, values, and previous experiences all affect behavior. Mischel (1984) and Epstein and O'Brien (1985) have now begun to explore cross-situational consistency of behavior and how individuals respond to the context in which they find themselves.

Microtheories Evolve

When behaviorists began formulating personality theories, they attempted to be scientific. They reacted against the Freudian concepts of unconscious mechanisms by suggesting that personality could be conceptualized in terms of scientifically measurable behaviors: stimuli, responses, and contingencies. Social learning theory was introduced in the 1950's; it was formalized and brought into the forefront in the 1960s. In the 1970s, thought entered the equation. Since then, behavioral theories have become more complex. Skinner's simple stimulus-response model was easy to conceptualize, but it failed to account for individual variability or flexibility on a daily or even minute-to-minute basis. In contrast, more recent theories using notions of social learning, thought, or self-efficacy, are not as easily tested experimentally but explain a wider range of phenomena (for example, Epstein, 1983). From the view of personality theorists such as Rotter, Bandura, and Mischel, human uniqueness is best explained by the idea that reinforcement, past experience, current feeling, future expectation, and subjective values all influence people's responses to their environment. Human beings have personalities that have characteristic ways of responding, but those personalities are subject to change depending on specific circumstances. (see Table 12.3.)

PROGRESS CHECK   12.5

1. Complete each of the following sentences with one of the options provided.

Learning Objective 12.19

A. Cognitive theory is based on the idea that people can change their behavior by changing their _____ .
    (external environment : thoughts)

Learning Objective 12.20

B. _____ concentrate on a limited range of behaviors, making predictions about specific behaviors that will occur in specific situations, and are relatively easy to test experimentally.
    (Global theories : Microtheories)

Learning Objective 12.20

C. A global theory like _____ is all-encompassing and attempts to account for all aspects of behavior and personality.
    (Freud's : Rotter's : Bandura's)

Learning Objective 12.20

D. People with an internal locus of control believe that they are _____ their environment and events in their lives.
    (in control of : controlled by)

Learning Objective 12.20

E. Research focusing on locus of control has shown that _____ lead to specific behaviors.
    (generalized needs : power needs : specific expectancies)

Learning Objective 12.21

F. People feel free to select, influence, and even construct the circumstances of their own lives if they have a strong _____ .
    (external locus of control : sense of self-efficacy)

Learning Objective 12.21

G. Self-efficacy refers to _____ .
    (one's effectiveness : self-pride : a superiority complex)

Learning Objective 12.21

H. Bandura's observational and self-efficacy theories promote the idea(s) of _____ .
    (predetermined behavior : choice and individual flexibility)

Learning Objective 12.22

I. Mischel's cognitive social learning theory suggests that day-to-day differences in personality reflect human beings' _____ .
    (ability to adapt : lack of consistency : vulnerability to consequences)

Learning Objective 12.22

J. Mischel is characterized as an interactionist because he focuses on the interaction between _____ variables.
    (personal and situational : psychodynamic and behavioral)

Learning Objective 12.22

K. Mischel suggests that people call on _____ when they adjust their behavior to be consistent with rules they have established to guide their behavior.
    (an encoding strategy : a self-regulation system : an expectancy process)

PSYCHOLOGICAL ASSESSMENT

Learning Objective 12.23

Assessment
The process of evaluating individual differences among human beings by using tests and direct observation of behavior. The role of the clinician is central in assessment techniques.

If you were a psychologist treating a child who was having difficulty in school, you might want to find out a lot about the child's personality in a short time. To assess a child's, or an adult's, personality is not easy. Over the years, psychologists have devised many tests and techniques to help them better understand both the normal and maladjusted person. **Assessment** is the process of evaluating the individual differences that occur among human beings. One principle assessment technique is to give a test like an intelligence test. Assessment can also include interviewing, observing people in natural settings, and, if the situation requires, recording certain physiological measures.

Psychologists use assessment techniques to understand human behavior, to learn more about normal personality development, and to help them diagnose and classify people who are maladjusted. They also use assessment techniques to identify causal factors in behavior and to help develop treatment plans for circumstances that need intervention (Haynes, 1984). This chapter shows that the theorists who developed ideas about personality have relied to various extents on one of these techniques. For example, Freud used projective tests, cognitive theorists such as Rotter have used scales of Internality and Externality, and Mischel and Bandura have observed people in natural settings.

As a theorist develops a theory of personality or a clinician develops a diagnosis of a client's problem, no single test will provide all the information necessary. To describe overall psychological functioning better, many psychologists administer a group or battery of tests that often includes the Minnesota Multiphasic Personality Inventory (MMPI), an intelligence test such as the WAIS-R (Wechsler Adult Intelligence Scale-Revised), and projective tests such as the Rorschach. Several other tests are used to assess more specific aspects of functioning. These include tests of vocational interests, special abilities, brain dysfunction, motor coordination, anxiety, and sexual functioning. More confidence can be placed in the data obtained from several tests than in data from a single test, and current levels of functioning are more easily characterized than are past levels of functioning.

This section examines some major assessment approaches that psychologists use. Various tests and approaches seek different information and approach that information gathering from different vantage points. An intelligence test, a projective test, and a test like the Minnesota Multiphasic Personality Inventory (MMPI) are very different from one another.

Intelligence Tests

Intelligence tests are often the first type of tests given in a psychological assessment, partly because they are excellent predictors of academic achievement. In examining intelligence tests in detail in Chapter 9, we saw that an intelligence test provides only a general indication of people's general behavior patterns. However, it does provide specific information about a person's level of intellectual functioning. Such tests often provide not only an overall IQ score but also often, like on the WISC-R, have scores that separate IQ into Verbal IQ and Performance IQ. These scores then have subscales that can examine specific components of Verbal IQ. These subscale scores can help a practitioner assess the reasons for a student's low grades. They may point to learning disabilities, or the overall IQ may be sufficiently low that a person may be classified as being on the borderline of retardation. You may want to go back to Chapter 9 to review some components of intelligence tests, particularly popular ones like the Wechsler tests.

Objective Personality Tests

Next to intelligence tests, the most widely given tests in assessment procedures are objective tests of personality. These tests, sometimes called *personality inventories,* generally consist of a series of true-false or check-the-best-answer questions. The aim of such tests vary. For example, Cattell's *16PF,* mentioned earlier, is most commonly used to screen job applicants or to examine individuals who fall within a normal range of functioning. The California Personality Inventory (CPI) is a widely used test of personality. Using a large sample of normal subjects as a reference group, the CPI examines such personality traits as sociability, self-control, and responsibility. The CPI is used primarily to identify and assess normal aspects of personality.

One of the most widely used and well-researched personality tests is the Minnesota Multiphasic Personality Inventory, or the MMPI. The MMPI consists of a series of 550 statements such as the ones below to which the examinee responds "true" or "false."

> I tire easily.
> I become very anxious before examinations.
> I worry about sex matters.
> I become bored easily.

The statements focus on attitudes, feelings, motor disturbances, and bodily complaints. The test contains ten subscales that describe various aspects of functioning and three additional scales to measure the truthfulness of the subject's responses.

Administered individually or to a group, the MMPI provides a profile that permits a psychologist to assess an individual's current level of functioning and characteristic way of dealing with the world. It also permits some reasonable predictions about the person's ability to function in specific situations. Together, a person's MMPI scores provide a description of his or her personality characteristics. The norms for the MMPI are based on the profiles of more than 700 normal people and a smaller group of psychiatric patients. A mean (or average) on each scale tells how most normal individuals score. A score above or below the mean is a deviant score. On the MMPI, a score significantly above the mean is considered evidence of maladjustment. Generally, the MMPI is used as a screening device for maladjustment.

Nearly 5,000 published studies have examined the MMPI, its validity (for example, Pollack & Shore, 1980), and its reliability (for example, Swenson, Pearson, & Osborne, 1973). Researchers have studied its predictive value over a wide number of variables, including disorders such as schizophrenia (Walters, 1983), racial differences (Bertelson, Marks, & May, 1982), age, characteristics such as education and socioeconomic status (Lanyon, 1968), family functioning (Bloomquist & Harris, 1984), and even the likelihood of death from cardiovascular disease (Gillum, Leon, Kamp, & Becerra-Aldama, 1980). For the most part, these studies support the MMPI as a valid and useful predictive tool.

Projective Tests

Projective test
A variety of different devices or instruments used to assess personality in which an examinee is shown a standard set of ambiguous stimuli and asked to respond in an unrestricted manner.

The aim of **projective tests** is to discover a person's unconscious motivations. The technique involves having an examinee provide unstructured responses to ambiguous stimuli, such as for pictures about which the examinee tells what he thinks might be occurring. The idea fundamental to projective tests is that a person's unconscious motives direct day-to-day thoughts and behavior. To uncover those unconscious ideas and motives, researchers ask examinees to provide responses that might reflect them. The examinee in a projective test reflects or "projects" his or her unconscious feelings, drives, and motives onto the ambiguous stimulus. In projective tests, a clinician supposedly can assess the deeper levels of a person's personality structure and detect motives of which the examinee is not aware.

Two widely used projective tests are the Rorschach Inkblot Test and the Thematic Apperception Test (TAT). These two tests do not restrict an examinee's responses, rather, each examinee responds in a unique way. Projective tests are used especially in cases in which it is particularly important to determine whether the examinee is responding truthfully or trying to hide something from the psychologist. Because these tests offer fewer guidelines for responding, examinees project their ideas and feelings into their responses.

In the Rorschach Test, ten inkblots are shown, one at a time, to an examinee—five black and white, two with some red ink, and the remaining three with various pastel colors. The inkblots are symmetrical in design with a specific shape or form (see Figure 12.4). Subjects are asked to tell the clinician what they see in the design. A detailed report of the response is made for later interpretation. After the ten inkblots have been shown, the examiner asks specific questions. Here is a typical response to a Rorschach inkblot:

> My first impression was a big bug, a fly maybe. I see in the background two facelike figures pointing toward each other as if they're talking. It also has a resemblance to a skeleton—the pelvis area. I see a cute little bat right in the middle. The upper half looks like a mouse. (Aiken, 1979, p. 261)

Good clinical judgment is necessary to place all of a subject's responses in a meaningful context. Although norms are available (Goldfried, Stricker, & Weiner, 1971) even for children (Levitt & Truumaa, 1972), skilled interpretation is particularly critical for this test, and long-term predictions can be formulated only with great caution (Exner, Thomas, & Mason, 1985).

Much more structured than the Rorschach is the Thematic Apperception Test, or TAT (discussed briefly in Chapter 5), The TAT consists of black-and-white pictures depicting one or more people in a variety of situations. Subjects are asked to tell a story describing the situation presented in each picture: what led up to the situation, what will happen in the future, and what the people are thinking and feeling. As part of a battery of personality tests, the TAT has been shown to be particularly useful in examining a person's characteristic way of dealing with other people and the needs that govern his or her interactions with the world.

FIGURE 12.4 : In a Rorschach test, the psychologist asks the subject to describe what he or she sees in an inkblot such as here. From these descriptions, the psychologist makes inferences about the subject's drives, motivations, and unconscious conflicts.

Psychology and You: Are Lie Detectors Without Merit?

As part of a personality evaluation to get a job, you may be asked to take a lie detector test. Lie detectors are widely used in criminal proceedings, personnel selection in industry, periodic honesty checks in business, and in ensuring national security. (Kleinmuntz & Szucko, 1984). To a great extent, various people have been acting as police by using the lie detector, but scientists have avoided studying the lie detector and its validity—until now.

The lie detector is a psychological assessment device of questionable merit based on simplistic assumptions; the validity of the test is not clear and its error rate is too high. If you were given a lie detector test for stealing, you might be accused of lying as much as 50 percent of the time—even when you told the truth!

Professionals refer to a lie detector test as a polygraph test. In a lie detector test, the subject's physiological responses are measured as he or she answers questions asked by a trained lie-detector expert. The measures are made on a polygraph machine, a machine that makes many *(poly–),* records *(–graphs)* of several physiological responses.

The essential assumptions of the lie detector test are that lying causes an involuntary uncontrollable physiological response, that this physiological response is measurable, and that people are aware of their lying. The fact is that lying is a complex response that does not always bring about a measurable physiological response; also people who lie often believe their lies. Liars often show no emotion when they lie, show no physiological response when tested, and even find lying emotionally satisfying. You thus can see that the basic ideas behind the lie detector test are misleading and false.

Both laboratory studies and field investigations of the polygraph test show that its error rate is very high. Even highly trained lie-detector experts make mistakes as much as 50 percent of the time. For example, in one study, trained experts read records from polygraph sessions in which they did not know the people from whom the tapes were gathered. Half of the polygraph records were from liars and half from innocent individuals. The experts misclassified innocent people and called them guilty 18 to 50 percent of the time (Horvath, 1977; Kleinmuntz & Szucko, 1984).

Psychologists who have reviewed the lie detector test and its assumptions conclude that the technique is easily faked, is flawed, and is based on untrue assumptions (Kleinmuntz & Szucko, 1984a; Saxe, Dougherty, & Cross, 1985). In spite of the evidence, many law enforcement personnel believe that the lie detector works. Private corporations like to use it, and even the federal government from time to time considers its use (Brooks, 1985; Katkin, 1985). Scientists place little to no belief in the polygraph test as presently constructed. They suggest it should not be considered true, should not be considered a psychological assessment device, should not be used, and certainly should not go unchallenged by the psychological community (Kleinmuntz & Szucko, 1984).

Behavioral Assessment

Learning Objective 12.24

Behavioral assessment
Procedures used for diagnosis, evaluation, and intervention in which direct observation, self-evaluation, and interviews are used. The technique avoids interpretation and indirect assessment.

A relative newcomer to assessment, **behavioral assessment** consists of a group of procedures that include naturalistic observation, self-monitoring, physiological measurement, and interviews. The focus of behavioral assessment has shifted over the years to include increasingly more techniques. Traditionally, behavioral assessment focused on overt behavior and behaviors that could be examined directly. Three of the most popular and widely used behavioral assessment techniques are behavioral assessment interviews, naturalistic observation, and self-monitoring.

Behavioral Assessment Interviews. If a person like Bud Ross, who opened this chapter, went to a psychologist for an assessment, it is likely the assessment would begin with an interview. Interviews have generally been considered an indispensable part of any assessment. Interviews allow a practitioner to hear from the client about himself or herself. In Bud's case, he might express some of his self-doubts and some of his strengths. Interviews are personal and give a client (and the client's family) an opportunity to express feelings, facts, and experiences that might not otherwise be available through traditional assessment procedures. Interviews allow the psychologist to evaluate a client's motivations and also give the psychologist a chance to tell the client about the assessment process.

The job interview is a good way to evaluate a candidate's personality and experience.

When conducted using a behavioral approach, interviews tend to be systematic and structured, focused on overt and current behaviors, and especially attentive to the situations in which behaviors occur (Haynes, 1984). Interviews can yield important information about a client's family situation, occupational stresses, and other events that might affect the behavior specifically being examined. For example, do the client's feelings of inferiority occur not at home but only at work? This fact could be important in both diagnosis and treatment. Interviews tend to be only part of a behavioral assessment; alone, they do not yield enough information, are subject to bias, and are sometimes not fully accurate. Taken together with other behavioral measures, however, the interview can be an important starting point.

Naturalistic Observation. Because behavioral assessment focuses on observable behavior, it is not surprising that one technique is naturalistic observation. We examined the basic process of naturalistic observation in Chapter 1. In behavioral assessment, the process of naturalistic observation involves two or more observers entering a client's natural environment and recording at certain predetermined intervals the occurrence of certain behaviors. For example, psychologists might observe the frequency of obscene verbalizations of a child in a classroom, or a hospitalized patient's frequency of references to his depressed state.

The focus of naturalistic observation as a behavioral assessment technique is to observe people without the interference or influence of the psychologist. The approach has great strengths because it can be an important source of information that would otherwise be unavailable or difficult to piece together. For example, it can help a psychologist realize the sequence of actions that may lead up to outburst, depressed feelings, or antisocial behaviors.

Naturalistic observation is not without problems, however. How does a researcher record behavior in a home setting without being observed? Are such samples of behavior representative of other interactions in other settings? In addition, the observers may come into the situation with some biases, make some inaccurate judgments, or not collect enough data. Naturalistic observation is not perfect, but as one technique of behavioral assessment, it has proved to be powerful.

Self-Monitoring.   Self-monitoring is the procedure wherein a person systematically records the occurrence of specific behaviors in himself or herself. The aim of this procedure is to have a person count and record the frequency and duration of specific events. For example, a woman might record the number and duration of migraine headaches, backaches, or feelings of panic she experiences. Clients have been asked to self-monitor eating patterns, sexual behaviors, smoking, and sleeping patterns, for example.

Self-monitoring is not expensive to conduct, is easy to do, and can be used for a variety of problems. It can bring to a practitioner a great deal of information that might otherwise be inaccessible. It allows the practitioner to probe into the events that may have preceded the monitored activity to see if some readily identifiable pattern exists.

Like naturalistic observation, self-monitoring is not without problems. The clients who are observing their own behavior have their own biases and may be inaccurate. Some behaviors are more difficult to monitor than others. In addition, once a person starts to monitor personal (and potentially deviant) behavior, the person may start to alter behavior because he or she is monitoring it.

Assessment: The Future

The history of personality assessment shows that it has grown from pencil-and-paper tests, often of intelligence or achievement within a specific discipline, to include a wide range of techniques. These techniques are continuing to evolve, especially in the area of behavioral assessment. Tests of brain functioning, although not part of a traditional assessment, are also part of the arsenal of psychological instruments. In every area of assessment, new research on new populations of people is helping personality theorists, practitioners, and researchers better understand human behavior and better predict the circumstances under which various behavioral patterns occur. In the 1980s, a special effort has been made to link assessment to treatment; researchers are arguing that diagnosing and classifying are not enough. A practitioner needs to judge what types of interventions and treatments follow from various diagnostic categories. Both researchers and practitioners also are seeking more direct information about behavioral patterns and maladjustment, often through behavioral assessment (Goldstein & Hersen, 1984).

PROGRESS CHECK 12.6

1. Complete each of the following sentences with one of the options provided.

Learning Objective 12.23

A.   If a psychologist wanted to describe a person's overall psychological functioning, he or she would probably administer _____.
(the MMPI : the TAT : a battery or several diagnostic tests)

Learning Objective 12.23

B.   The TAT and Rorschach Inkblot Test, which measure deeper levels of personality structure, such as a person's unconscious motivations, are called _____.
(personality inventories : projective tests)

Learning Objective 12.23

C.   Projective tests give important information because the respondents _____ and therefore project their own ideas and feelings into their responses.
(can respond anonymously : have fewer guidelines for how to respond)

Learning Objective 12.24   D.   Traditionally, behavioral assessment has focused on _____ behavior.
(overt and directly observable : abnormal : unconscious)

Learning Objective 12.24   E.   A behavioral assessment technique that is used to lessen any interference or influence that might occur simply because of the psychologist's presence is called _____.
(the interview : naturalistic observation : self-monitoring)

Learning Objective 12.24   F.   One problem that occurs with self-monitoring is that behavior may_____ simply because the client is monitoring it.
(change : solidify : be misdiagnosed)

Learning Objective 12.24   G.   In recent years, psychologists have made a special effort to link _____ with assessment results.
(diagnosis : classification : appropriate treatment)

Keeping Pace with Chapter 12

Applying Principles

Indicate which of the following defense mechanisms is being used by the person in each situation describe below.

repression   reaction formation   rationalization   projection   denial

_____   A.   A psychologist might classify Vince as a misogynist. He constantly belittles, restricts, blames, controls, and threatens his wife, treating her as if he hates her and wishes she would get out of his life; and yet, deep inside, he loves her and has a terrible fear she might leave him. His overbearing behaviors protect him from the anxiety he feels over being left alone and are unconsciously aimed at making her dependent on him so she will stay.

_____   B.   Lucy knew it was not in her best interest to go to Joe's party, thinking, "I should spend the evening studying for my psych final!" She quickly dismissed that idea, telling herself she could study for a few minutes in the morning and thinking the final probably would be an easy test. When Lucy found out she had flunked the final, she said to herself, "Oh well, no one's perfect!"

_____   C.   Carla was rather callous in telling her neighbor, Ted, that the garden he had joyfully tended all summer looked like a desert. Carla realized that she had hurt Ted's feelings but, unable to acknowledge that sometimes she is a rude person, she quickly and unconsciously rewrote the story. When she got home she told her husband, "Ted is all upset that he doesn't have the money to hire someone to get that garden of his in shape."

_____   D.   Gordon is a very manipulative and controlling kind of person. He has to have everything go his way and does all he can to ensure that it will. When Gordon is unsuccessful and senses he is not getting what he wants, he accuses the other person of being manipulative and controlling.

_____   E.   (In this case, a defense mechanism that normally protects Barry, fails. What is it?) Barry has always always been a reserved and shy person so, when he accidently blurted out, "Where's the sex-pack?" instead of, "Where's the six-pack?" everyone at the picnic laughed. Barry felt mortified, and his friend Don realized that he had just made what some people call a "Freudian slip." Because they cause Barry such embarrassment, thoughts about sex normally reside deep in his unconscious.

Before proceeding to the Self-Test, REVIEW the Learning Objectives listed at the chapter opening and RECITE from memory everything you can remember in support of them. Then, take this Self-Test as if it were to be graded by your teacher. Use the Learning Objective numbers in the Answer Section as a reference to restudy the corresponding text pages and Progress Checks for any incorrectly answered questions.

1. Personality theorists who focus on types study

   A. any readily identifiable stable behavior that characterizes the way an individual differs from other individuals.
   B. specific behaviors that occur only in response to specific situations.
   C. behaviors that are easy to identify and that characterize a person's day-to-day interactions.
   D. a broad collection of traits that are tied together loosely and are interrelated.

2. Allport believed that in many cases an individual's personality could be described by

   A. identifying his or her cardinal trait.
   B. identifying ten central traits.
   C. weighing secondary traits against central traits.
   D. comparing type sets to trait groups.

3. The 16PF personality measurement scale developed by Cattell

   A. is based on the assumption that groups of traits cluster together.
   B. provides an individual profile of surface traits.
   C. will probably be replaced by a factor analysis technique.
   D. all of the above

4. Eysenck asserts that the difference between introverts and extroverts is

   A. introverts are gregarious; extroverts are reserved.
   B. introverts are emotionally stable; extroverts are emotionally instable.
   C. that biologically different levels of arousal occur in the cortex of the brain.
   D. A and C

5. Cattell and Eysenck _____ to develop their theories of personality.

   A. studied individual behavior
   B. divided personality into sixteen important personality factors
   C. focused on small and specific clusters of traits
   D. used factor analysis approaches.

6. One reason Freud's theory of personality has had such a strong impact on psychology and Western culture in general is that the theory

   A. accurately described the psychological differences between men and women.
   B. has been tested extensively in experimental situations and shown to be valid.
   C. provided guidelines for explaining all aspects of personality and behavior.
   D. was based on case studies of people from a wide range of experiential and cultural backgrounds.

7. The core tendency of personality for all human beings, in Freud's psychoanalytic theory, is that people

   A. reduce needs by emitting learned responses.
   B. strive for superiority and perfection.
   C. enhance the experiences of life through self-actualization.
   D. maximize instinctual gratification while minimizing punishment or guilt.

8. The ego

   A. is the source of a person's instinctual energy.
   B. frequently directs the id toward appropriate and realistic behaviors.

C. controls the id by drawing on internalized rules and ethics.

D. works on the pleasure principle.

9. Which of the following is *not* true of anxiety? Anxiety

    A. develops when the id, ego, and superego are in conflict.

    B. is an uncomfortable feeling, usually accompanied by an *increase* in physiological arousal.

    C. is most frequently initiated by realistic fears and apprehensions.

    D. can be so powerful that it can psychologically or physiologically paralyze a person.

10. When people use the defense mechanism called rationalization they

    A. totally refuse to accept reality.

    B. make unreasonable feelings or behaviors seem reasonable.

    C. attribute to other people their own undesirable traits.

    D. adopt behaviors that are opposite of their true feelings.

11. When boys experience the Oedipus complex or girls, the Electra complex,

    A. boys develop castration anxiety and girls, penis envy.

    B. they are in the genital stage of psychosexual development.

    C. they struggle between babyish desires and the demand for controlled behavior.

    D. they channel most of their energy into social or achievement-related activities.

12. A fixation in one of the psychosexual stages

    A. prevents a person from any further development.

    B. can result in the development of defense mechanisms and maladjusted behavior.

    C. is a normal part of the developmental process.

    D. will occur even if parents place ordinary restraints on a child's instinctual urges.

13. Humanistic theories of personality assume that people

    A. are constantly questioning the meaning of life.

    B. have a basic goodness and are motivated by internal forces to achieve personal goals.

    C. are guided by a force that is omniscient, omnipresent, and omnipotent.

    D. insist on having things go their own way.

14. Carl Rogers believed that people experience unhappiness and dissatisfaction when

    A. they acknowledge the truth about their "real" self.

    B. there is a discrepancy between one's day-to-day self and the ideal self.

    C. the superego overpowers the ideal self.

    D. the id consumes the ideal self.

15. According to Rogers, a mature personality will develop if a person

    A. is protected from negative feelings.

    B. can learn to evaluate the good and bad sides of his or her behavior.

    C. is told what to think and how to behave.

    D. has strong role models.

16. *Fictional finalism* is the phrase Adler used to describe

    A. specific goals that motivated behavior but could never be attained.

    B. the process by which people failed to fulfill their true potentials.

    C. the dynamics and pervasive influence of a family atmosphere.

    D. the relationship between the individual and society.

17. For traditional behaviorists, the core tendency that organizes behavior and thus personality is

    A. the way an organism responds.

    B. best described as human nature.

C. the reduction or satisfaction of social or biological needs.

D. the ability to analyze one's self successfully.

18. Which of the following situations represents an instrumentally conditioned personality trait?

    A. Fred feels shy around strangers because he has associated strangers with being ridiculed.

    B. Brenda always has a joke to tell because when she does, people laugh.

    C. Craig is very assertive when trying to sell his product because he imitates the style of the best salesperson he ever met.

    D. Sharon is doing a super job in law school because she believes she can succeed.

19. Cognitive approaches to behavior and personality

    A. suggest that if a person's thoughts change, the person's behavior will also change.

    B. perceive personality as a menagerie of minute behaviors.

    C. seriously question the basic assumptions of behavioral psychology.

    D. encourage long-term therapy for people who experience confusion over who they are or what they want.

20. A person with an *external* locus of control would be more likely than a person with an internal locus of control to do all of the following *except*:

    A. falsely report doing well on a task that most people rate as being difficult and requiring skill.

    B. believe the environment will determine his or her fate.

    C. engage in behaviors such as preventive health measures.

    D. profit more from psychotherapy.

21. Self-efficacy determines

    A. the way people process, attend to, and select information.

    B. the importance that people attach to certain symbols.

    C. how much effort and how long a person will persist with a task in the face of obstacles.

    D. whether a person will be warm, caring, and attentive or hostile and aggressive.

22. Which of the following factors probably would *not* be considered important by Mischel in predicting how a person would respond to a particular stimulus?

    A. competency—what a person knows and can do.

    B. luck—being in the right place at the right time.

    C. encoding—how a person processes, attends to, and selects information.

    D. expectancy and values—anticipated outcomes and the importance a person places on the situation.

23. Which of the following statements concerning projective assessment tests is *false?*

    A. Projective tests consist of a series of true/false or multiple-choice questions.

    B. Skilled interpretation of a subject's responses is particularly critical when the Rorschach Inkblot Test is given.

    C. Projective tests are designed to discover a person's unconscious motivations.

    D. People taking the TAT are asked to tell stories about a series of black-and-white pictures of people shown in a variety of situations.

24. Behavioral assessment interviews

    A. are generally considered an indispensable part of any assessment.

    B. can provide biased and/or incomplete information.

    C. can provide important information that cannot easily be collected in other ways.

    D. all of the above

13

Stress and Maladjustment

13

Learning
Objectives

When you have mastered the material in this chapter, you will be able to:

1. Discuss the distinctions sometimes made between the terms *maladjustment* and *abnormal behavior* and explain why many contemporary psychologists prefer to use the term *maladjustment* for less serious disorders. (pp. 502, 506)

2. Define *model* and describe the statistical, medical, behavioral, and legal models of abnormal behavior. (p. 503)

3. Describe the biological, psychodynamic, humanistic, learning, and cognitive perspectives of maladjustment. (p. 506)

4. Describe the DSM-III-R, explain what it is used for, and discuss some of the controversies surrounding it. (p. 509)

5. Define stressor and characterize the stress response. (p. 512)

6. Describe the three stages in Hans Seyle's "general adaptation syndrome." (p. 514)

7. Describe the Holmes-Rahe Social Readjustment Scale and explain why some psychologists challenge its validity. (p. 514)

8. Characterize a Post-traumatic Stress Disorder, describe the kind of life experiences that can produce this disorder, and discuss how mental health practitioners have in the past and are now responding to traumatic stress. (p. 516)

9. Discuss some ways that work environment, time, life-cycle events, temperature changes, and noise can act as stressors and affect peoples' lives. (p. 517)

10. Discuss some ways people cope with and defend themselves against stress. (p. 520)

11. Discuss the relationships among stress, maladjustment, and psychotherapy. (p. 523)

12. Define anxiety and discuss its causes and effects according to Horney, Freud, May, and behavioral psychologists. (p. 525)

13. Explain why psychologists today feel that Freud's terms *neurosis* and *neurotic* are inappropriate and inefficient for describing maladjusted behaviors. (p. 526)

14. Identify the number of people in the United States who suffer from some type of anxiety disorder; characterize a Generalized Anxiety Disorder; and define free-floating anxiety. (p. 526)

15. Characterize Phobic Disorders, give some statistics concerning the number and type of people who have phobias, and describe Agoraphobia, Social Phobia, and Simple Phobia. (p. 527)

16. Characterize Obsessive-Compulsive Disorders and distinguish between psychodynamic and behavioral theories concerning the causes of this disorder. (p. 529)

17. Characterize a Psychoactive Substance Abuse Disorder and define the terms describing various aspects of this disorder. (p. 531)

18. Explain what is meant by a poly-drug abuser, tell why psychologists have trouble studying and treating drug abuse, and state some reasons drug abuse

is considered a problem by psychologists, physicians, law enforcement officials, and the public in general. (p. 532)

19. Give some statistics concerning the number of people who have alcohol-related problems, explain how alcohol affects behavior, and describe the conditions that can lead to alcohol intoxication. (p. 534)

20. Distinguish between problem drinking and alcoholism, describe two approaches to the treatment of alcoholism, and discuss the medical, psychological, and social problems that accompany alcohol abuse. (p. 536)

BEFORE YOU READ ON, take time to **SURVEY** the chapter, form an idea of what is to be learned (from margin Learning Objective numbers), and set goals for your study time. Then, ask yourself **QUESTIONS** about the material as you **READ,** seeking help for any sections you do not understand.

"**M**y son has flipped out," shouted an angry and upset Brenda Playman. She described her utter frustration with her twenty-one-year-old son, Gordon, who, with his girl friend of three weeks, had quit college to take to the highway on his motorcycle. His ultimate plan was to open up a Yamaha dealership and motorcycle repair shop. Brenda was sure Gordon had to be taking drugs and thought he might have fallen in with a religious cult. Was Gordon's girl friend leading him astray? Was he losing his mind?

Brenda Playman was certain that Gordon's decision was a serious mistake. When she questioned him, Gordon denied he was trying to escape from the pressure of college, denied being on drugs, and argued that the motorcycle life appealed to him and that this seemed like a good time to try new ventures. His mother, however, persisted in believing that this "motorcycle thing" was a symptom of something deeper. She thought he was trying to get even, reacting to a painful experience, or just running away. One afternoon, while having chest pains, she wondered whether there was something wrong with Gordon's hormonal system. Becoming more and more distressed, she began to fear that Gordon was undergoing a serious break with reality.

It was Brenda Playman herself, however, who was under strain. Brenda's questioning, fears, and speculations about her son were placing her under a lot of pressure. She was enraged, upset, and no longer in control of a part of her life. She had become nervous, critical of other people, and always irritable. Her tension caused her blood pressure to rise and she had migraine headaches. She was arguing with her husband and was short-tempered at work. She told herself she was "stressed out."

BRENDA PLAYMAN'S REACTION TO Gordon's decision to try a new life style was not surprising. Gordon had never been rebellious, nor had he intimated that he was unhappy at college. It was natural for her to be concerned by her son's uncharacteristic actions, but she was trying to take responsibility for his life. In doing so, Brenda placed herself under a lot of pressure. She felt stressed, angry, and helpless. Even though she might have considered Gordon's decision foolish, she should have realized that college students are growing, changing, and developing. Gordon's behavior was not bizarre nor at variance with the overall values of our society. A decision to leave school, re-evaluate one's options, and consider a career in business are not signs of maladjustment.

Everyone has a different way of responding to the environment and its stresses. Brenda Playman was responding to the changes in her son's life with headaches, chest pains, and shortness of breath, and she was feeling extremely stressed.

Learning Objective 13.1

Brenda Playman's reactions may be extreme, but they are not unusual. A human being's responses to stress vary greatly and depend on that person's biological state, genetic inheritance, and accumulated learning experiences. If Brenda's troubled feelings interfered with her ability to cope with day-to-day life, if she has exhibited bizarre symptoms, or if her behavior was in conflict with reality, we might say she was maladjusted. Sometimes there seems to be only a fine line between stress reactions, maladjustment, and abnormal behavior. Even mental health professionals sometime disagree on what constitutes abnormal behavior. Some practitioners claim that maladjustment and abnormality are the same. Others believe that maladjustment refers to less serious disorders and to failures in adjusting to day-to-day life; they reserve the term *abnormal behavior* for serious mental disorders, such as schizophrenia. To some extent, the argument is academic. People who are not coping with life suffer to the same extent whether their behavior is labeled maladjusted or abnormal. The formal diagnosis and treatment of their condition are not likely to differ in either case. For most psychologists, *maladjustment, abnormality,* and *mental disorder* refer to the same thing: a failure to cope effectively with the realities and demands of life. In this and the next two chapters, we use the terms interchangeably. Unfortunately, as recently estimated, nearly 20 percent of adults in the United States suffer from some type of maladjustment.

FIGURE 13.1 : The four major models of abnormal behavior.

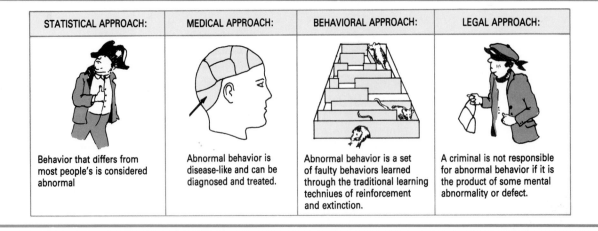

STATISTICAL APPROACH:	MEDICAL APPROACH:	BEHAVIORAL APPROACH:	LEGAL APPROACH:
Behavior that differs from most people's is considered abnormal	Abnormal behavior is disease-like and can be diagnosed and treated.	Abnormal behavior is a set of faulty behaviors learned through the traditional learning techniues of reinforcement and extinction.	A criminal is not responsible for abnormal behavior if it is the product of some mental abnormality or defect.

However, only 4 or 5 percent seek treatment. The range of their problems is staggering: some suffer from mild phobic disorders, others from disabling schizophrenia.

This chapter first discusses maladjustment and how psychologists define and classify abnormal behavior. We then discuss stress, a normal condition of everyday life, and explain its relationship with maladjustment. The discussion then moves on to how people who do not deal well with stress or with life in general show maladjusted behaviors. Maladjustment can be disruptive, or it can severely impair a person's day-to-day behavior. People's reactions to the difficulties in their lives fall along a continuum. We discuss how psychologists try to explain how anxiety develops and how substance abuse is related to stress and maladjustment. The next chapter considers some of the more extreme disorders that fall under the general topic of abnormal behavior.

DEFINING ABNORMAL BEHAVIOR

As Brenda Playman looked at her son and his behavior, she noticed Gordon's changing ideas and values. She found them peculiar and sometimes thought they were abnormal. To a psychologist, when a person changes attitudes, values, or ideas, this by itself is not a sign of maladjustment or abnormality. If Gordon had left school and also become depressed, lethargic, short-tempered, and aggressive, then a professional might be concerned. Alone, each characteristic—lethargy, short-temperedness, aggressiveness—is not descriptive of and does not characterize a maladjusted person. When these characteristics appear together and occur suddenly, however, a professional will become concerned—this may be a sign of maladjustment, or it may merely be a temporary reaction to stress at work or at home. Such changes may be due to a physical condition or might be just a temporary mood swing. These possibilities raise an important question for both Brenda Playman and psychologists: What is abnormal behavior?

Learning Objective 13.2

Like people in other areas of psychology, those in the field of abnormal psychology use several different approaches to try to define and understand the difference between normal and abnormal behavior. Four models of behavior—statistical, medical, behavioral, and legal—are commonly used to differentiate normal from abnormal behavior (see Figure 13.1). A **model** is an analogy that helps scientists discover relationships among data; it uses a structure from one field to help describe data in another. Models can help psychologists organize data and thus make predictions about behavior.

Model
A perspective or approach derived from data in one field, used to help describe data in another field.

Infrequent Behaviors: The Statistical Model

People's opinions about what is appropriate, from political and religious beliefs to hair lengths and dance styles, change with time. People watching movies from the 1930s and 1940s often notice how baggy and long the movie stars' clothes look. Of course, the reason the clothes look funny is that fashions have changed; when the movies were made, the clothes not only were appropriate but they also were the height of fashion.

Statistical model
An approach that specifies behavior deviating from the average as abnormal.

The **statistical model** defines abnormal behavior as behavior that differs significantly from the way most people do things. Just as a man who is significantly taller than the average person is said to be abnormally tall, a woman who spends all her time alone may be considered abnormal if the majority of people are more socially inclined.

The statistical model makes no assumptions about the causes of behavior or its origins. It simply compares the behavior of a single individual with that of other individuals in similar situations. The statistical approach to behavior suggests that most people function in the middle of the behavioral spectrum, with a few functioning at each end. When an individual exhibits a behavior not exhibited by a large portion of the population, his or her behavior is sometimes called maladjusted. Children who exhibit symptoms of hyperactivity, for example, are considered truly hyperactive only if they are well above the mean in terms of activity as determined by their teachers.

Although statistical models have proved useful, problems exist. For example, such models are particularly vulnerable to value changes over time. According to a statistical model, people are maladjusted if their behavior differs

Value changes over time make statistical models particularly vulnerable; fifty years ago these women would have been considered "indecent," though today their attire is considered acceptable and attractive.

significantly from that of their contemporaries. However, behaviors judged abnormal today may be judged quite differently in ten years. As new social movements occur, new definitions of maladjustment come about: these new definitions become the new standards of the statistical model. Furthermore, because the statistical approach is relative, it cannot specify the details of any behavior; deviance is expressed only in reference to a "social norm" based on averages; specific abnormal behavior itself is not described. Paradoxically, some of society's most valued abilities (such as artistic abilities) are not distributed normally. Should those behaviors be considered abnormal? Finally, the statistical model offers no suggestions for treating disorders.

A Physician's View: The Medical Model

Medical model ═══════
An approach that considers behavior to be the result of internal conditions or motivations.

Unlike the statistical model, the **medical model** is concerned with the causes of abnormal behavior, which are assumed to be internal. The medical model initially focused on the biological and physiological conditions that initiate abnormal behaviors. However, over time, the strict medical approach has given way to a medical analogy that now serves as the foundation for traditional psychology and psychiatry. The medical model assumes that some kind of internal motivation or cause exists for abnormal behavior and maladjustment.

The medical model has advantages over the statistical model. Its primary advantage is its assumption that abnormal behavior can be diagnosed, treated, and cured. The use of the medical model in the early part of this century led to more humane treatment of patients with mental health problems; it replaced their locked cages with a hospital setting.

The model also has disadvantages. Established by practitioners such as Freud, the medical model does not make good use of modern psychological insights, such as those of learning theory (Kazdin, 1978a, 1978b). It also uses varying and vaguely defined categories to describe behavior, and it bases treatment on these categories. It has emphasized hospitalization and drug treatment. Many of the terms and concepts used in psychology and psychiatry are borrowed from medicine, including *treatment, case, symptom, syndrome,* and also the term *mental illness* itself. More important, use of the medical model has placed the therapist in the role of a person who cures. Use of this model by professionals has created a tendency in lay persons to believe that association with someone who has behavior problems may induce behavior problems in them, much like exposure to infectious disease. Because of this contamination analogy, people tend to fear other people who have mental health problems, and this fear often hampers effective treatment programs.

Learning Is the Key: Behavioral Models

Behaviorists represent an important force in the field of abnormal psychology. They believe that abnormal behaviors—however defined—are caused by patterns of conditioning and learning. Behaviorists object to the medical model and its focus on underlying causes. Instead, they claim that abnormal behavior is the result of faulty learning. Rather than emphasize underlying thoughts and inner psychic forces, they focus on how people learn their behaviors. In the nature-versus-nurture controversy (discussed in Chapter 4), behaviorists take the environmental view. Thus, a woman who has learned to avoid certain people who produce feelings of anxiety in her may overgeneralize and become afraid of all people. Similarly, a boy who receives very few reinforcements for his efforts to be good may become pessimistic, introverted, and anxious. Behaviorally oriented psychologists try to help people modify their maladjusted behavior by using specific learning techniques to teach them new behaviors. Their decision to change a behavior is based not on the fact that other people label it abnormal, but on the fact that the behavior is distressing for the individual. Behaviorists may understand how a particular disorder came about, but they are more interested in changing it than in understanding its beginning.

Breaking the Law: The Legal Model

The legal model of abnormality centers on maintaining social norms. As long as an individual complies with society's demands for "normality," that individual is seen as well adjusted and sane. The terms *sane* and *insane* are legal terms, not psychological ones. There are three conditions under which people can be legally designated insane: (1) they are judged mentally incompetent to understand their responsibilities, (2) they are judged capable of harming either themselves or others, or (3) their crime is considered a consequence of mental abnormality. Attorneys often argue that people's behavior is abnormal if they are unable to distinguish right from wrong. In such cases, an individual is not considered responsible for a crime and is judged legally insane. The legal definition of abnormal behavior is too narrow to be clinically useful, and in many states is undergoing change. Many states are considering the use of verdicts such as "guilty, but mentally ill" and are taking such information into account at the time of sentencing.

Maladjustment by Any Other Name . . .

Most psychologists find it helpful to classify people's behavior and to be able to distinguish among different types of behavior disorders. In recent years, many psychologists have preferred to describe behavior in terms of *maladjustment* rather than in terms of *abnormality*. This is considered an important shift, because it implies that problem behaviors are treatable. A person's behavior may be maladaptive, but with treatment it can become adaptive and productive.

In addition to the approaches just discussed, some commonsense standards regarding abnormal behavior exist in every society. People whose behavior has lost touch with reality or who cannot distinguish right from wrong are often classified as abnormal. In most cases, definitions of abnormality are relative to a society's definition of what is normal. In the Soviet Union, for example, people are placed in mental institutions for a variety of reasons that often include political dissent (Farone, 1982). No one approach provides a definition of abnormal behavior that satisfies all theoreticians or practitioners.

EXPLAINING ABNORMAL BEHAVIOR

Learning Objective 13.3

If you were a practitioner talking to a person whose behavior is maladjusted, you would probably want to know why the person is having trouble. Many practitioners feel that understanding the causes of maladjustment is a necessary key to prescribing a course of treatment. But knowing that an individual is maladjusted is easier than knowing why. Over the years, psychologists have been developing theories about how and why people develop maladjusted

Maladjustment can be viewed from many different perspectives; the psychodynamic approach would explain this child's aggressive behavior quite differently than would a learning perspective.

behaviors. Theories of abnormal behavior attempt to explain the causes of abnormality by referring to the complex array of events that led up to, or predisposed, an individual to show maladjusted behaviors. Unlike the models of abnormality just discussed, which tend to describe what behavior is considered abnormal, these theories attempt to explain why the disorders exist. For example, the statistical model deals with abnormal as being different from current standards, and the medical model deals with maladjustment as "disease-like." Neither model suggests causes of specific disorders.

Psychologists have developed a full range of explanations and theories of abnormality from biological theories to learning theories. Behavioral theories are the newer theories and have recently received a good deal of attention. The following pages and the next chapters explore maladjustment and discuss different descriptions, explanations, and treatment programs.

There are five basic theoretical orientations to maladjusted behaviors. The *biological perspective* emphasizes the role of the body and its relationship to behavior. Genetic abnormalities, problems in the central nervous system, and hormonal changes are often the focus of people who adopt a biological perspective. Researchers and theoreticians who attempted to explain maladjustment through the biological perspective focus on the way one's body may influence or determine behavior. For example, research and theories on schizophrenia (discussed later in this chapter) have emphasized genetic heritage, nervous system malfunctions, and hormonal malfunctions. Researchers on all three fronts claim that schizophrenia is principally a biological problem, not a psychological one. Accordingly, they suggest treatments that often involve drugs to change biochemical and other bodily functions.

The *psychodynamic approach* is the orientation of Freud and his followers. Psychodynamic theories assume that maladjustment is a consequence of anxiety that results from unresolved conflicts and forces of which a person may not be aware. It asserts that maladjustment occurs when a person relies on too many defense mechanisms to avoid anxiety or when conflict within the mind reaches proportions that the person can no longer handle through defense mechanisms. For example, a woman may be guilt-ridden over emerging sexual feelings that she feels are inappropriate. Treatment usually involves helping a patient become aware of motivations, conflict, and desires, so that a more healthy life-style can emerge.

Growing out of the psychodynamic perspective is the *humanistic perspective.* The humanists also assume that inner psychic forces are important in establishing and maintaining a normal life-style. Unlike the psychodynamic theorists, they assert that human beings have much more control of their lives, and they focus on individual uniqueness and decision making. For example, humanists assert that a person who feels dependent and lacks self-confidence can learn to develop a sense of mastery and control. Such an individual needs to become more self-assured and feel more competent than at the current time. Humanistic theorists Carl Rogers and Alfred Adler, whom we discussed in the last chapter, assert that people seek to fulfill themselves and become everything that they might. Maladjustment occurs when people's expectations are very different from what they are currently achieving. Treatment usually involves helping people realize and accept their real self, adjust their ideas and expectations, and potentially strive toward becoming more like their ideal self.

The *learning perspective* focuses on how people learn from their environment to exhibit maladjustment and abnormal behaviors. Fundamental assumptions of learning theorists are that disordered behavior can be reshaped and that more appropriate, worthwhile behaviors can be substituted through traditional learning techniques, such as described in Chapter 2—classical conditioning, instrumental conditioning, and observational learning. Learning theorists assume that events in a person's environment reinforce and punish various behaviors selectively, and in doing so shape and create personality and maladjustment. For example, a man with low self-esteem may need to be reinforced for the positive characteristics of his behavior; he may need to create situations in which he can find such rewards. Treatment from the learning or behavioral perspective focuses on helping individuals shed their old maladaptive behaviors and helping them learn new, worthwhile coping strategies and prosocial behaviors.

The *cognitive perspective* asserts that human beings engage in behaviors, both prosocial and maladjusted, because of ideas and thoughts they have established. As thinking organisms, we decide how to behave, and many of our decisions are made on false assumptions or ideas that have little basis in reality. Maladjusted behavior occurs because people have irrational ideas. For example, if a person holds an irrational idea about his ability to achieve all A's in school, when he is really a poor student, this idea is going to cause him pain and probably subsequent maladjustment. To treat maladjustment, a practitioner helps an individual to develop new thought processes. By learning new values and ideas, the individual can replace maladjustment with new, worthwhile behaviors.

Each of these five orienting theories or perspectives—biological, psychodynamic, humanistic, learning, cognitive—explains maladjustment from a different view. None of them explain well all kinds of abnormal behavior; some of them explain very thoroughly certain types of disorders. You will see that for some disorders (such as phobias), learning theory explains the cause and prescribes a good course of treatment. For other disorders (such as schizophrenia), biological theories explain a significant part of the problem. Because this is so, many psychologists take an eclectic position, drawing on portions of all of these theoretical perspectives.

As we delve further into maladjustment and its treatment, these specific orienting theories will be discussed where appropriate. Before investigating maladjustment, however, it is important to understand the system that many clinical psychologists use to diagnose it. This system is called DSM-III-R.

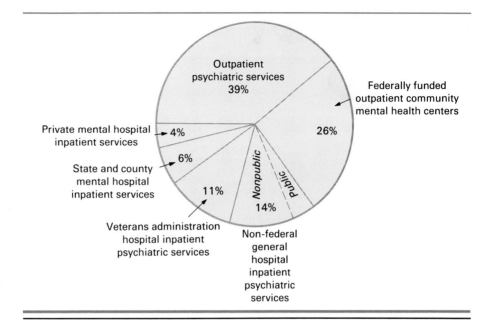

FIGURE 13.2 : Of the 3-1/2 million people who received treatment at mental health facilities, more than 75 percent were treated on an outpatient basis. (Data from Rosenstein & Milazzo-Sayre, 1981)

DIAGNOSIS: DSM-III-R

Learning Objective 13.4

If Brenda Playman had sought the help of a clinical psychologist, or if she had talked to a member of the clergy, would either of them have been sure whether Brenda was exhibiting some form of maladjustment? Would a practitioner be able to say that Brenda was merely experiencing a normal adaptive reaction to stress? Would such a diagnosis be accurate, or is it just a matter of opinion? In past years, there has been so much disagreement about diagnoses and maladjustment that few practitioners agree. Over the years, psychiatrists have developed some elaborate systems to classify various kinds of maladjustment. The most recent is the American Psychiatric Association's *Diagnostic and Statistical Manual of Mental Disorders-Revised (1987),* or *DSM-III-R;* it has undergone a great deal of study and development with the help of many mental health practitioners, including psychologists and social workers (see Figures 13.2 and 13.3).

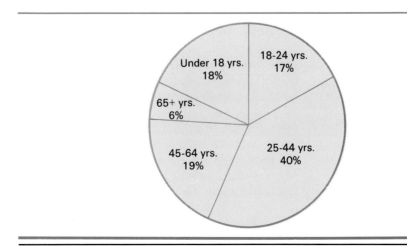

FIGURE 13.3 : The percentage of people in different age groups across the various types of centers that provide mental health treatment. (Data from Rosenstein & Milazzo-Sayre, 1981)

TABLE 13.1 : Major Classifications in DSM-III-R. Each
: Classification Is Further Broken Down into
: Subtypes (with Some Minor Modifications)

Disorder of Infancy, Childhood, and Adolescence	*Personality Disorders*
	Anxiety Disorders
Organic Mental disorders	*Somatoform Disorders*
Psychoactive Substance Use Disorders	*Dissociative Disorders*
	Sexual Disorders
Schizophrenia	*Sleep Disorders*
Delusional Disorders	*Factitious Disorders*
Psychotic Disorders	*Disorders of Impulse Control*
Mood (Affective) Disorders	*Adjustment Disorders*

Diagnostic categories used to lack precision. One hundred psychiatrists asked to diagnose a patient's problem would have shown a marked degree of variability in their diagnoses. Symptoms did not correspond to diagnoses. However, things changed for the better with the publication of DSM-III in 1980 and the revised edition in 1987. DSM-III-R designates major categories of maladjustment (see Table 13.1), with more than 200 subcategories. A practitioner must also make judgments about the severity of a disorder and how well the person is coping with it.

The new diagnostic manual has met with some resistance, some controversy, and, at a minimum, much interest (Millon, 1983). DSM-III and DSM-III-R's classification system differs dramatically from previous systems. Some psychologists applaud its increased recognition of social and environmental influences on behavior (Linn & Spitzer, 1982). However, many psychologists are unhappy with the continued use of psychiatric terms that perpetuate the use of a medical rather than behavioral model. Some psychologists feel that the manual has been influenced too much by politics (Schacht, 1985) and that it needs to go beyond mere diagnosis and include problem-oriented and problem-solving information rather than just symptoms (Longabaugh et al., 1986).

The DSM-III-R classification system will probably help the study of abnormal behavior because it permits more precise diagnoses. One study showed that diagnostic judgments using the new categories were quite uniform (Strober, Green, & Carlson, 1981). This increased precision does not change the fact that new labels cannot by themselves relieve the suffering of disturbed individuals or extend therapy to populations such as the disadvantaged and poor. DSM-III-R is not a cure-all, but most practitioners agree that proper diagnosis is a first step toward proper treatment. DSM-III-R is not the final word in diagnosing maladjustment. Many psychologists feel it needs considerable refinement, and they and psychiatrists are hard at work preparing DSM-IV.

Brenda Playman would probably not be diagnosed as suffering from a disorder described in the diagnostic manual. Her stress responses to the world seem reasonable and fall within normal ranges. But not everyone who goes through stressful family transitions, a career change, or a change of marriages can be said to adapt well. Many people become highly anxious when they are going through a period of transition. Some individuals put off dealing with certain conflicts in their lives, only to deal with them later. It would not be surprising for a psychologist to suggest that the stress of her relationship with her son might ultimately cause Brenda Playman a period of extreme stress or anxiety if she does not deal with it soon. Stress is often a component of maladjusted behavior, a symptom of inner conflict and turmoil. But does stress lead to maladjustment? Could Brenda Playman's stress cause her to become maladjusted? Let us take a closer look at stress and examine its relationship to maladjustment.

PROGRESS CHECK 13.1

1. Match each statement below with the model of abnormal behavior that supports the statement.

   statistical model   behavioral model   medical model   legal definition

Learning Objective 13.2   A. _____ Focuses primarily on changing problem behavior patterns rather than on trying to understand their underlying causes.

Learning Objective 13.2   B. _____ Suggests that most people function in the middle of the behavioral spectrum; people who function on either end of the spectrum are considered abnormal.

Learning Objective 13.2   C. _____ Considers a person abnormal if the person is unable to distinguish right from wrong.

Learning Objective 13.2   D. _____ Compares specific behavior patterns with current values and standards.

Learning Objective 13.2   E. _____ Suggests that internal motivations, inner psychic forces, and underlying thoughts cause abnormality and maladjustment.

Learning Objective 13.2   F. _____ Suggests that maladjusted behaviors are the result of a person's environment.

2. Complete each of the following sentences with one of the options provided.

Learning Objective 13.1   A. Psychologists who make a distinction between the terms *maladjustment* and *abnormal behavior* would refer to a serious behavior disorder like schizophrenia as _____.
   (a maladjustment : an abnormal behavior)

Learning Objective 13.1   B. In recent years, psychologists have preferred to use the term *maladjustment* when describing people who have difficulty coping because this term implies that the _____.
   (person is mentally ill : problem behavior can be treated)

Learning Objective 13.1   C. Nearly _____ of the adults in the United States suffer from some type of maladjustment.
   (5 percent : 20 percent : 33 percent)

Learning Objective 13.2   D. The statistical model describes abnormality in terms of _____ _____ and offers no suggestions for treating disorders.
   (specific behavioral details : social norms)

Learning Objective 13.2   E. The medical model places the _____ in the role of the person responsible for bringing about a cure.
   (patient : therapist)

Learning Objective 13.2   F. Behavioral psychologists are primarily interested in _____ maladjusted behaviors.
   (understanding the causes of : helping a person change)

Learning Objective 13.2
G. The terms *sane* and *insane* are _____ terms.
    (medical ⦂ legal ⦂ psychological)

Learning Objective 13.3
H. Theoretical perspectives toward maladjustment differ from models of malad-justment in that the theories focus more on _____ abnor-mal behavior.
    (describing what constitutes an ⦂ understanding the causes of)

Learning Objective 13.3
I. The _____ approach to abnormal behavior assumes that maladjustment is the result of genetic abnormalities, central nervous system problems, or hormonal imbalances.
    (biological ⦂ psychodynamic ⦂ cognitive)

Learning Objective 13.3
J. One major difference between the psychodynamic and humanistic perspectives of maladjustment is the degree _____.
    (of control they assign to the individual ⦂ to which they focus on external forces)

Learning Objective 13.3
K. The cognitive perspective to abnormal behavior focuses on faulty _____ as the cause of maladjusted patterns.
    (learning ⦂ thinking ⦂ self-concepts)

Learning Objective 13.4
L. DSM-III-R recognizes social and environmental influences on behavior _____ terms.
    (but perpetuates the use of medical ⦂ and has adopted behavioral)

Learning Objective 13.4
M. DSM-III-R _____ behavior disorders.
    (provides a list of cures for ⦂ is leading to more precise diagnoses of)

Learning Objective 13.4
N. One thing a number of psychologists would like to see included in DSM-IV, when it is published, is _____.
    (treatment and problem-solving information ⦂ more precise parameters for diagnoses)

STRESS

Learning Objective 13.5

Stressor
An environmental stimulus that affects an organism in ways that are either physically or psychologically injurious, usually producing anxiety, tension, and physiological arousal.

Stress
A nonspecific response by an organism to demands made on it.

Brenda Playman was not managing the pressures in her life very well. Her internal feelings were expressing themselves in her behavior toward other peo-ple. Because these pressures were bothering her, she was beginning to have difficulty coping. For some people, the pressures in their lives create serious maladjustment; other people cope effectively. A **stressor** is an environmental stimulus that acts on an organism in physically or psychologically injurious ways. Stressors usually produce anxiety, tension, and especially physiological arousal.

A stressor changes the way an organism responds: it induces a response of stress. **Stress** is a nonspecific response by the organism to demands made on it. Whenever forces in a situation affect someone either physically or psycho-logically, psychologists say the person is experiencing stress. This broad defini-tion of stress recognizes that at some time everyone experiences stress. Often, several stressors (such as money problems, work problems, or marital prob-lems) act together to affect behavior. These stressors may be quite dissimilar and still act together.

By itself, stress does not create maladjustment in the sense that DSM-III-R defines maladjustment. A person who experiences stress may develop some abnormal behaviors or even serious behavior disturbances, but usually stress is only one of many factors leading to maladjustment. People react to stress in a wide variety of ways. Some people show modest increases in physiological arousal. Others show significant physical symptoms and may exhibit anxiety. Their behavior may become less effective. In extreme cases, people become so aroused, anxious, and disorganized that psychologists say their behavior be-comes maladaptive or maladjusted.

Many common occurrences can act as stressors.

Arousal is a key characteristic of the stress response. When psychologists refer to arousal, they usually refer to changes in the autonomic nervous system. Autonomic nervous system changes characteristic of stress conditions include increased heart rate, breathing, and blood pressure, sweating of the palms, and dilation of the pupils. Arousal is the first change that occurs when a person feels stressed, and its effects on behavior can be dramatic. However, a specific stressor, such as a seemingly wayward son, does not produce the same amount of arousal in everyone. In each case, the resulting physiological and behavioral changes may be very different (see Table 13.2).

TABLE 13.2 : Physiological, Behavioral, and Cognitive
: Responses to Stress

Type of Response	Effect
Physiological	Increase in heart rate Elevation of blood pressure Muscular tension Slowdown of digestive system Release of adrenalin and noradrenalin
Behavioral	Decrease in performance level Avoidance of stressful situations Passivity/inertia
Cognitive	Distortions of thinking Decrease in intellectual functioning Unproductive, ruminative, anxiety- generating patterns of thought Indecisiveness

Source: Adapted from Beech, Burns, & Sheffield, 1982, p. 11.

*Learning
Objective* 13.6

Because stress is a *nonspecific* response, it is difficult to measure and study with precision. In the 1930s, Hans Selye (1907–1982) began a serious study of stressors and stress. He investigated the physiological changes in individuals experiencing various amounts of stress. Eventually, Selye conceptualized their responses to stress in terms of a *general adaptation syndrome* (1956, 1976). A *syndrome* is a set of responses. In the case of stress, it is a set of behaviorally defined physical symptoms. Selye's work set the stage for thousands of research works on stress and stress reactions. Selye himself published more than 1,600 articles on the topic.

According to Selye, people's response to a stressor can be divided into three stages: an initial phase of alarm, followed by a longer period of resistance, and a final stage of exhaustion. *Alarm* produces increased physiological arousal, and people become excited, anxious, or frightened. Metabolism speeds up dramatically; blood is shunted to the brain at the expense of the skin, resulting in a pale appearance. People may also experience such symptoms as loss of appetite, sleeplessness, headaches, ulcers, or hormone imbalances. All these symptoms are part of the initial short-term alarm reaction (see also Gottschalk, 1983).

People cannot stay highly aroused for long. The initial alarm response usually gives way to *resistance,* and physiological and behavioral responses become more moderate and sustained. People in the resistance stage often are irritable, impatient, and angry. They experience constant fatigue. The resistance stage can persist for a few hours, days, or even years.

The final stage of Selye's three-part syndrome is *exhaustion.* Because stress uses so much energy, it tends to affect both emotional and physical health. People under conditions of extreme stress show disorganized behavior. If their stress is not relieved, they become too exhausted to adapt. At this point, they again become extremely alarmed and then give up. The result is maladjustment, withdrawal, and (in some extreme cases) even death.

*Learning
Objective* 13.7

Selye made researchers aware of the impact of stress on day-to-day functioning. His work inspired other attempts to identify stressors. One result of this research was the development by Holmes and Rahe (1967) of the Social Readjustment Rating Scale, shown in Table 13.3. On the scale, an individual circles events pertinent to his or her life in recent months. Each event is rated for impact. Items such as the death of a spouse, divorce, and illness are rated as high stressors; other events, such as changes in eating habits, vacations, or Christmas, have lower ratings. The total points scored are an index of stress and of the likelihood of illness in the next two years. According to Holmes and Rahe, a score above 300 points makes physical symptoms likely. The researchers' basic assumption is that any stressful life event, and especially a combination of such events, will have damaging consequences for health.

Other studies have also found that the number and severity of stressful events in a person's life are good predictors of potential illness and maladjustment (for example, Justice, McBee, & Allen, 1977). How an individual perceives the stress is also important; when the source of stress is not under the person's control, the effect tends to be more serious (Hammen & Mayol, 1982). Although Holmes and Rahe's scale is used widely, some psychologists question its validity in predicting illness (Theorell et al., 1986), and others suggest that even "minor" life events can be used to predict maladjustment (Kanner, Coyne, Schaefer, & Lazarus, 1981).

TABLE 13.3 : The Social Readjustment Rating Scale

Rank	Life Event	Value
1	Death of spouse	100
2	Divorce	73
3	Marital separation	65
4	Jail term	63
5	Death of close family member	63
6	Personal injury or illness	53
7	Marriage	50
8	Fired at work	47
9	Marital reconciliation	45
10	Retirement	45
11	Change in health of family member	44
12	Pregnancy	40
13	Sex difficulties	39
14	Gain of new family member	39
15	Business readjustment	39
16	Change in financial state	38
17	Death of close friend	37
18	Change to different line of work	36
19	Change in number of arguments with spouse	35
20	Mortgage over $10,000	31
21	Foreclosure of mortgage or loan	30
22	Change in responsibilities at work	29
23	Son or daughter leaving home	29
24	Trouble with in-laws	29
25	Outstanding personal achievement	28
26	Wife begin or stop work	26
27	Begin or end school	26
28	Change in living conditions	25
29	Revision of personal habits	24
30	Trouble with boss	23
31	Change in work hours or conditions	20
32	Change in residence	20
33	Change in schools	20
34	Change in recreation	19
35	Change in church activities	19
36	Change in social activities	18
37	Mortgage or loan less than $10,000	17
38	Change in sleeping habits	16
39	Change in number of family get-togethers	15
40	Change in eating habits	15
41	Vacation	13
42	Christmas	12
43	Minor violations of the law	11

The Holmes-Rahe scale was devised based on the study of young male Navy personnel. This scale is obviously not applicable to older persons and other approaches and scales may be more appropriate for the general population (Dohrenwend & Shrout, 1985). It must also be remembered that no direct relationship exists between a stressful life event and illness; people have support systems, friends, and activities that affect how, when, and if stressful life events will affect them (Monroe & Steiner, 1986; Sarason, Sarason, Potter, & Antoni, 1985; Stretch, Vail & Tmaloney, 1985).

Stress is a complex term that refers to a whole series of interrelated variables and processes. It is not a simple variable that can be easily quantified, measured, and manipulated. When a researcher examines stress and stress reactions, the researcher has to consider both the person and the context in which the stressors are delivered (Lazarus, DeLongis, Folkman, & Gruen, 1985). As we continue our examination of stress, you will see that stress has many consequences as well as sources. (Flannery, 1986).

Consequences of Stress

Learning Objective 13.8

If someone told you that Brenda Playman, our stressed mother, had developed an ulcer, you probably would not be surprised. It is commonly recognized that people exposed to high levels of stress for long periods may develop stress-related disorders, including physical illness. Brenda was under a lot of stress, the cause of which was not very unusual. Sometimes, people experience catastrophic external events that engender a different kind of stress-related symptoms. Before the publication of the diagnostic manual DSM-III, people suffering from extreme stress, with frequently recurring dreams and reexperiences of traumatic situations, were commonly diagnosed as depressed or perhaps even schizophrenic. DSM-III-R designates one disorder as a Post-traumatic Stress Disorder. The common symptoms of Post-traumatic Stress Disorder are vivid, intrusive recollections or reexperiences of the traumatic event and occasional lapses of normal consciousness. People may develop anxiety, depression, or exceptionally aggressive behavior. They may avoid situations that resemble the traumatizing situation and develop a general mistrust of other people (Glover, 1984). Such behaviors eventually interfere with daily functioning, family interactions, and health.

Rape victims, hostages, and survivors of natural disasters (such as earthquakes) may suffer from this disorder (Davidson & Baum, 1986). Many of the 600,000 men and women in the United States who are veterans of the Vietnam War suffer from Post-traumatic Stress Disorder. At some time, perhaps months or years later (Tannant, Goulston & Dent, 1986), they are likely to show feelings of alienation, sleep disturbance, and difficulty concentrating. The Vietnam War was especially stressful for several reasons. Military personnel typically served only one year of duty in Vietnam; during that time, survival and not patriotism tended to be their primary concern. Combatants were aware that many people in the United States violently opposed the conflict. Drugs and alcohol were used widely to combat fear. Furthermore, many veterans were whisked home suddenly, without a chance to reacclimate gradually (Walker & Cavenar, 1982) they also were not given much social support (Keane et al., 1985). Any war takes a psychological toll on participants, but Walker and Cavenar (1982) argue that because of these unusual wartime conditions, veterans of the Vietnam War are especially likely to suffer from Post-traumatic Stress Disorder.

For a number of complicated psychological, political, and social reasons, mental health practitioners have tended to be unresponsive to individuals suffering from Post-traumatic Stress Disorder. Too often, clients have been held responsible for their responses to stress, and the prevalance of the disorder may be sharply underestimated (Laufer, Brett, & Gallops, 1985). Researchers are now recognizing that the children of people who suffer from Post-traumatic Stress Disorders are affected (Rosenheck, 1986) and that delayed reactions are common (Amen, 1985). Special help in the form of workshops or therapy is becoming available. Many Vietnam veterans, rape victims, and survivors of natural disasters are now being referred to appropriate treatment to help them cope more effectively.

Sources of Stress

Psychologists recognize that although individual situations differ, certain stressors are common to almost everyone. E. M. Gherman, a physician, has discussed several areas in which stress is present (1981). Some of the most common stressors identified are work, time, life events, and environmental functions such as temperature and noise.

Learning Objective 13.9

Work Environment. Stress at work usually occurs either because a workload is too burdensome or too light and understimulating. A person's perception of a job as either very important or trivial affects that person's behavior. Fears of retirement, of being passed over for promotion, and of organizational changes can also create pressure and anxiety. The physical setting itself can be overstimulating, with too many people around, or understimulating and too isolated (see, for example, Frankenhauser, Lundberg, & Forsman, 1980).

Stress at work, expressed as illness and absenteeism, costs both the worker and employer time and money in increased medical costs, disability payments, and physical suffering (Parkes, 1982). At a minimum, work-related pressure can cause headaches, migraines, and ulcers. Some studies (for example, Cook & Cashman, 1982) have related cardiovascular disease and heart attacks to stress (Rhodewalt, Hays, Chemers, & Wysocki, 1984). Many people who are unable to relieve stress and to cope effectively become further incapacitated through alcohol abuse.

Work-related stress can take many forms. Sometimes people in high-level decision-making positions face stress associated with the decision-making process. For example, what happens when an executive does not have all of the correct information, or has conflicting data that leave him or her unsure of what to decide? Janis (1982b, p. 70) quotes President Warren G. Harding, who was talking to a friend as he was struggling with a major domestic problem:

> John, I can't make a damn thing out of this tax problem. I listen to one side and they seem right, and then God! I talk to the other side and they seem just as right, and there I am where I started. I know somewhere there is a book that would give me the truth, but hell, I couldn't read the book. I know somewhere there is an economist who knows the truth, but I don't know where to find him and haven't the sense to know him and trust him when I did find him. God, what a job!

The three stages of Selye's general adaption syndrome (alarm, resistance, and exhaustion) are evident in the careers of individuals with especially high-stress jobs, particularly when stress is a constant factor. For example, air traffic controllers and surgeons experience considerable stress in their jobs. Responsible for the lives of other people every day, they must be alert and organized at all times. If they work too many hours without relief, they may make a mistake that could result in another person's death. Many air traffic controllers and surgeons display a deep exhaustion at home that eventually also shows at work. Responsibility, deadlines, and no chance to relax on the job can ultimately lead to decreased work efficiency (see Dirkin, 1983).

People who experience high levels of on-the-job stress often become exhausted and suffer from burnout.

A common stress reaction, especially for people with high standards, is burnout. People who face high levels of stress on a daily basis often lose energy and stop trying (Farber, 1983). Individuals who suffer burnout have feelings of hopelessness and emotional drain. Victims of burnout develop negative self-concepts due to their inability to maintain the high standards they have set for themselves. The stress of an individual with burnout often causes a loss of concern for other people, physical problems, and usually marital problems as well.

Time.   Some people's sense of urgency and competitiveness drives them to go faster and faster. Friedman and Rosenman (1974) have characterized such individuals as Type A personalities (see Chapter 5). They argue that Type A people are more likely to develop cardiovascular problems and heart attacks than are more relaxed or less competitive people. From the framework of Selye's stress theory, Type A individuals tolerate too much stress in the environment for too long; they have heart attacks because they have reached the stage of exhaustion.

Even people who are not aware of feeling stressed have only a limited number of hours each day in which to accomplish their tasks. When they have to complete several tasks in a short period of time, they may begin to feel overloaded. Most people manage time pressure by carefully allocating their time. They establish certain routines. People make lists, establish schedules, leave early, and even set aside leisure time in which to rid themselves of stressful feelings.

Life-Cycle Events.   Each stage of life offers people opportunities for learning more about themselves; life-cycle events also can engender stress. Marriage is both exciting and stressful; it is difficult for each partner to fulfill the others' needs at all times. For example, at times, one partner may not be fulfilling marital and/or role obligations, or one partner may make the spouse feel left out; both of these situations generally bring about stress (Ilfeld, 1982).

Similarly, parenting can be rewarding, but the rearrangement of schedules it requires and the added responsibilities can cause stress. An adolescent's problems in adjusting to adulthood can sometimes be stressful for both parents and teenager (Siddique & D'Arcy, 1984). Certainly, divorce is a stressful experience. Similarly, the death of a friend or loved one can be stressful, both at the time of the loss and in months following. Stress accompanies many of life's important events, even the enjoyable ones. Because stress is often unavoidable, proper management of stress is important.

Temperature.   Stress can come from complicated events in a person's environment, like the death of a relative. Stress can also come from simple, day-to-day variables, like temperature.

Temperature can be a stressor and can affect a number of behaviors, including academic performance (Pepler, 1972), efficiency in driving an automobile (Provins, 1958), and people's attraction to other people (Griffitt, 1970). Work performance is directly related to temperature. Performance under moderate and high temperatures shows dramatic differences. In a study of workers performing heavy labor, Wyndham (1969) found that under moderate temperatures, workers who performed better than others did so because of other situation variables such as the degree of supervision. But regardless of such variables, all workers showed poorer performance under high temperatures. Though not always straightforward, the results of temperature studies indicate that moderate temperatures allow for adaptive behaviors, whereas extreme temperatures produce decreases in work performance.

As mentioned in Chapter 5, extensions of the Yerkes-Dodson law suggest that performance on various tasks is optimal when a person's level of arousal is not extreme. Arousal can be defined in many ways; it is usually defined in terms of physiological measures such as heart rate, blood pressure, respiration, and the electrodermal response (the electrical conditions of the skin in the presence of sweat). As Figure 13.4 shows, the relation between arousal and performance depends on the task involved. When a person is engaged in an easy task, high levels of arousal can still yield good performance. In tasks that involve concentration and skill, high arousal often results in disorganized behavior. Changes in temperature directly affect levels of arousal: performance is optimal at moderate temperatures and becomes progressively worse at high or low temperatures.

FIGURE 13.4 : When arousal is low, a task performance is poor or nonexistent. Performance is usually best at moderate levels of arousal; at high levels of arousal, on complex tasks, performance usually deteriorates.

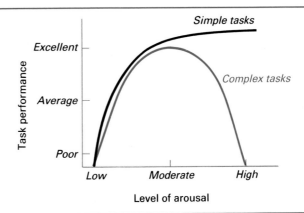

Noise. Another environmental variable that can greatly affect day-to-day behavior is noise. Defined as unwanted sound, noise is a stressor that can stimulate people to uncommonly high levels of arousal. A certain amount of noise is nearly always present in the environment, such as the sounds of typewriting, doors closing, and refrigerators opening. These noises are generally not stressors. They rarely raise levels of arousal or interfere with daily activities. A person listening to a favorite record has sought the sound and finds it pleasant. A noise that is continuous and not too loud (such as the buzzing of a fluorescent light) may be unwanted but is usually not too disruptive. However, loud, uncontrolled noise can impair human behavior, particularly behavior that involves concentration. A marching band practicing "The Stars and Stripes Forever" outside the window interrupts studying.

Noise can act as a moderate or severe stressor. As discussed in Chapter 6, high levels of sound can produce serious and long-lasting damage to the auditory system. Above 80 decibels, sound can produce hearing damage, and above 100 decibels, serious damage. Sound above 140 decibels is painfully loud and can damage the ear permanently, resulting in serious hearing loss. More important to environmental psychologists is how sound as a stressor influences day-to-day behavior.

A great deal of research has examined how noise affects human beings. The aim of this research is to apply this knowledge to practical situations in which noise is constant and at high levels—perhaps in cities or factories. Researchers have suggested that stressors such as noise can elicit aggression in human beings. But as with other aspects of behavior, no simple rule can equate a person's ability to work well or less well to a specific noise level. The type of task involved, the level of noise achieved, and personal characteristics such as gender, previous experience with noise, and attention span, must be considered. A relatively simple variable such as noise can influence day-to-day behavior in so many ways that environmental psychologists face a complex task.

The Yerkes-Dodson law predicts that low-level noise will not affect performance. For simple tasks, noise should have only minimal effects even at moderate levels; it might even facilitate performance. However, if it raises physiological arousal to very high levels, noise may impair performance. Glass and Singer (1972) confirmed these effects. At low levels of intensity, noise has only marginal effects on simple tasks. Even at fairly high levels of intensity, noise does not severely impair simple motor and cognitive tasks. However, unpredictable and intermittent noise of moderate intensity impairs performance on tasks that involve sustained attention or memory. Noise acts as a stressor when it interferes with communication, raises physiological arousal, or is so loud it causes pain and headaches. More commonly, noise simply interferes with a person's ability to concentrate.

Coping with Stress

Learning Objective 13.10

Many people need both medical and psychological therapy to relieve the physical ailments and feelings of anxiety resulting from stress. Both physicians and psychologists have tried to develop methods to help people cope. Coping refers to a person's efforts to manage environmental and internal demands that are causing or might cause stress.

Coping strategies should begin at the biological level. People's bodies respond to stress with specific reactions, including changes in hormone level,

TABLE 13.4 : Various Stress-Related Diseases and Conditions

System Affected	Resulting Condition
Cardiovascular system	Coronary artery disease Hypertension Strokes Rhythm disturbances of the heart
Muscular system	Tension headaches Muscle contraction backache
Locomotor system	Rheumatoid arthritis Related inflammatory disease of connective tissue
Respiratory and allergic disorders	Asthma Hay fever
Immunological disorders	Lowered resistance Autoimmune disease
Gastrointestinal disturbances	Ulcer Irritable bowel syndrome Diarrhea Nausea and vomiting Ulcerative colitis
Genito-urinary disturbances	Diuresis Erectile dysfunction Orgasmic dysfunction
Dermatological diseases	Eczema Neurodermatitis Acne
Other problems	Fatigue and lethargy

autonomic nervous system activity, and the amount of neurotransmitters in the brain. If responses stabilize at sustained high levels, physical illness may result, because high levels of physiological response cannot be maintained over long periods. Bleeding ulcers are one type of stress-induced ailment. Without relief from stress, such ulcers become worse (see Table 13.4).

In the view of psychologist Richard Lazarus (1982), people faced with constant stress tend to become either defense- or task-oriented. *Defense-oriented* coping strategies do not reduce stress but instead help people protect themselves from its effects. As discussed in Chapter 12, Freud and other personality theorists described various defense mechanisms by which people distort reality in order to defend themselves against pressures in the environment. For example, in rationalization, a person reinterprets reality to make it more palatable. Similarly, a man who expresses glee on accepting a new job but who is feeling a lot of stress and fear has developed a reaction formation; he has chosen to express a feeling opposite to the one he really feels. Many defense-oriented patterns described by personality theorists are unconscious processes over which people have little or no control. Often, they produce positive effects; defense-oriented coping strategies can ease distress and permit people to tolerate disturbances and deal with them. Some researchers claim that defense-oriented coping methods can be even more helpful than task-oriented ones (Mullen & Suls, 1982).

Most psychologists, however, especially behavioral psychologists, recommend *task-oriented* coping strategies. These strategies usually involve several

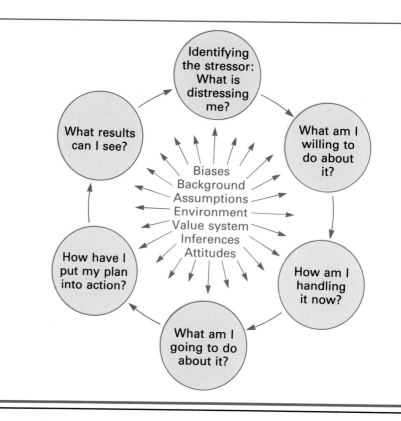

FIGURE 13.5 : The steps involved in developing a stress reduction program.

steps: (1) identifying the source of stress, (2) choosing an appropriate course of action for stress reduction, (3) implementing the plan, and (4) evaluating its success (see Figure 13.5).

Identifying the source of stress is often difficult. A woman experiencing work problems, financial problems, and problems with her teenage son must decide on which problem she wants to focus first. Even with their increased experience, older people seem to have as much difficulty as younger people in both identifying the sources of stress and controlling it (Lazarus & DeLongis, 1983; McCrae, 1982).

Once the problem is defined, people can choose from among several strategies. They can withdraw from a competitive, stress-inducing situation by quitting work, leaving a spouse, or declaring bankruptcy. More often, people turn to other people (Cohen & Hoberman, 1983) or other methods of coping. Because stress is usually accompanied by arousal and excitement, relaxation training is useful in reducing these effects. People can be taught to refocus their energies by using biofeedback, meditation, or other therapeutic relaxation methods such as systematic desensitization, discussed in Chapter 15.

Many people use cognitive coping strategies to manage stress. Either professionals or clients can conduct training sessions, or stress inoculations, to prepare for stress through gradual exposure to increasingly high stress levels (Janis, 1982b). Chapter 5 discussed a study in which subjects who viewed a film with painful scenes were able to control their emotional responses (Lazarus & Alfert, 1964). Such studies suggest that people can learn to manage their stress (to some extent) by using their thought processes. A major goal of these studies is to prepare people to react in constructive ways to early warning signs

Many therapists focus on helping their clients cope with stress.

of stress (Janis, 1982b). Other research has shown that people can also talk to themselves ("The sun will come out tomorrow") to help them cope more effectively (Turk, 1978). By talking to themselves, people gain control over their emotions, arousal, and stress reactions (Meichenbaum, 1975, 1977). The self-talk procedure, used widely, has been effective in helping people confront stressors and cope with pain (Turk, Meichenbaum, & Genest, 1983) and feelings of being overwhelmed (Mullen & Suls, 1982).

Helping other people cope with stress is a focus of many practitioners. Each of us also engages in coping strategies and in helping other people cope. Deborah Belle (1982) maintains that women are especially involved in providing social support and helping other people with coping. She cites Caplan, who painted a picture of mutual support system in families:

> In most families . . . shortly after members come home, they give detailed reports on their behavior at school, work, or in social situations, together with how others reacted to them, especially if these reactions were upsetting, surprising, or incomprehensible. In some families, such discussions take place regularly at mealtimes and have almost a ceremonial aspect. During these discussions, the other members of the group help the person evaluate not only his own reported behavior in the light of the family value system but also the meaning of the reactions of the people with whom he was involved. (Caplan, 1976, p. 23)

Stress: A Precursor to Maladjustment?

Learning Objective 13.11

"Staying cool" and "keeping a lid on it" are ways of describing how people use their cognitive self-help abilities to manage their emotional responses. Stress management is increasingly becoming a focus of highly stressed individuals as well as of psychologists. Researchers have realized that the effects of extended stress on physical and psychological well-being can be serious (Harder et al., 1980). People experiencing extended stress sometimes develop strokes, tension headaches, and sexual problems. They may show passivity and avoid other stressful situations. When they begin to exhibit psychological and physical fatigue, and when physical symptoms become increasingly evident, people often seek the help of mental health professionals.

Maladjustment is not a direct consequence of stress. A person may encounter many stressful forces without developing maladaptive behavior. However, when people under stress reach the point of exhaustion at which maladjustment seems likely, the help of a psychologist can be beneficial. Through therapy, a person troubled by stressful situations can help untangle personal feelings, understand the sources of the stress, and then do something about it. When people who are experiencing stress seek therapy, they are actively seeking to manage their lives in ways that allow worthwhile, effective behavior. For the many people who do not seek therapy, problems that might earlier have been handled with relative ease become complicated; treatment becomes more difficult. Some people resolve their problems and reduce stress. Those who fail to manage stress display maladaptive behavior, ideas, and feelings.

Progress Check 13.2

1. Complete each of the following sentences with one of the options provided.

Learning Objective 13.5

A. A stressor acts on an organism in a physically or psychologically _____ _____ way.
   (productive : injurious)

Learning Objective 13.5

B. Stress is a _____ response.
   (very specific : nonspecific)

Learning Objective 13.5

C. A key characteristic of the stress response is _____.
   (increased performance : physiological arousal)

Learning Objective 13.6

D. Metabolism speeds up dramatically and a person begins to look pale during the _____ stage of stress.
   (resistance : alarm : exhaustion)

Learning Objective 13.6

E. People experience constant fatigue that can last for days, or even years, during the _____ stage of stress.
   (resistance : alarm : exhaustion)

Learning Objective 13.7

F. The Holmes-Rahe Social Readjustment Scale was designed to help predict _____ stress.
   (how well a person can cope with : the likelihood of health problems resulting from)

Learning Objective 13.7

G. Stress has more serious effects on an individual when the stressor _____ his or her control.
   (is under : is not under)

Learning Objective 13.8

H. Vietnam veterans, rape victims, and survivors of natural disasters are among people who are likely to develop a _____.
   (general adaptation syndrome : Post-traumatic Stress Disorder)

Learning Objective 13.9

I. Boredom, caused by a work environment that is too isolated or a workload that is too light, frequently _____ stress.
   (protects people from the experience of : causes)

Learning Objective 13.9

J. The frequency of general adaptation syndrome is particularly apparent in people who have _____ jobs.
   (high-stress, lives-at-stake : irregularly scheduled : routine)

Learning Objective 13.9

K. When people are asked to perform in an environment that has a moderate temperature, they show _____ responses.
   (hostile : self-concern and a slowing in their : adaptive)

Learning Objective 13.9

L. Loud sounds tend to act as stressors _____.
   (when they cannot be controlled : whenever they occur)

Learning Objective 13.9

Learning Objective 13.10

Learning Objective 13.10

Learning Objective 13.10

Learning Objective 13.11

M. _____ behavior in human beings has been related to loud noise.
(Hyperactive : Aggressive : Lethargic)

N. Defense-oriented coping strategies _____ stressors.
(reduce : protect people from the effects of)

O. The first step in a task-oriented coping strategy involves _____
_____.
(identifying the stressor : learning to relax)

P. Stress inoculation uses _____ to help people cope with and reduce stress.
(relaxation training : gradual exposure to stress : meditation)

Q. Maladjustment _____ a direct consequence of stress.
(is : is not)

ANXIETY DISORDERS

Learning Objective 13.12

Brenda Playman, like many parents, was concerned about her son. It is not uncommon for such concern to overwhelm people. When individuals like Brenda become very concerned and stressed about family relationships, this reaction often gets in the way of their enjoyment of life in general. Sometimes, however, their anxiety and worry about a situation act as defense mechanisms to conceal more serious problems. In addition, family squabbles and the ensuing anxiety associated with them often initiate crises in other areas of a person's life.

Noted psychoanalyst Karen Horney asserted that anxiety is the central factor in both normal and abnormal behavior (Horney, 1937). She would have argued that if Brenda's apparent suffering due to concern for her son might really be due to other fears with which Brenda was not dealing. As a psychologist with a psychodynamic orientation, Horney believed that maladjustment occurs when too many defenses against anxiety pervade an individual's personality.

Anxiety is also a core concept in many other conceptions of maladjustment. For example, Freud viewed anxiety as the result of constant conflict among the id, ego, and superego. The defense mechanisms he described represented strategies for defending against anxiety. If people are unable to use these defense mechanisms, anxiety may pervade both the individual's daily activities and dreams (May, 1982).

Psychologists know that almost everyone experiences some anxiety. Some people feel anxious only before an unusual situation, such as an examination. However, the type of anxiety someone experiences before an examination is not the same as the constant anxiety of an individual who lives in its grip. People may or may not display their anxiety in their daily behavior. Although anxiety can be a positive, motivating force, its effects can also be debilitating. Left untreated, cases of severe anxiety may eventually lead to hospitalization. As Rollo May said, "Anxiety is characterized by feelings of powerlessness and helplessness, and when these are too strong to cope with, the anxiety paralyzes the person" (1982, p. 16).

Today, behavioral psychologists try to describe anxiety in a way that allows its effects on people to be measured. Anxiety is no longer regarded as a specific symptom. For most psychologists, **anxiety** refers to a wide range of symptoms, the most significant of which are fear, apprehension, inattention, palpitation,

Anxiety
A generalized feeling of fear and apprehension that may or may not be related to a particular event or object and often is accompanied by increased physiological arousal.

TABLE 13.5 : Percentage of Patients and Control Subjects
: Showing the Ten Most Common Symptoms
: of Anxiety Disoder

Symptom	Patients	Controls
Palpitations	97	9
Tires easily	95	19
Breathlessness	90	13
Nervousness	88	27
Chest pain	85	10
Sighing	79	16
Dizziness	78	16
Faintness	70	12
Apprehension	61	3
Headache	58	26

respiratory distress, dizziness, and fear of death (Marks & Lader, 1973) (see Table 13.5).

Many behaviorists view anxiety as a group of learned responses. For example, a child who sees a parent's hand raised to administer a spanking knows that pain will follow. The raised hand produces fear. After successive experiences with a sequence involving a raised hand followed by pain, the child comes to fear the hand raising itself. A troubled child will eventually show fear, generalized anxiety, and avoidance behaviors whenever he or she sees the parent raise a hand, even if the parent has no intention of administering a spanking. Such overgeneralized response patterns are common signs of psychological disorder.

Freud called nearly all forms of behavior associated with anxiety *neurotic.* Freud's term, *neurosis,* has made its way into everyday language, and nonpsychologists tend to describe any behavioral quirk as neurotic. However, psychologists today believe that using the term *neurosis* as a catchall is neither appropriate nor efficient. Precise and consistent diagnoses of maladjustment are essential to appropriate treatment.

What Freud characterized as neurotic disorders have markedly different symptoms. Each disorder represents a different pattern of behavior and maladjustment. Therefore, DSM-III-R classifies them under a variety of diagnostic categories. Those in which anxiety is the prominent feature are designated as Anxiety Disorders.

A study released in late 1984 by the National Institute of Mental Health showed that nearly 13 million citizens in the United States suffer from some form of Anxiety Disorder. Nearly all are anxious and have irrational fears about coping with life; rather than cope with their fears, they worsen their condition by avoiding confronting their problems. Whether these people have a Simple Phobic Disorder or an Obsessive-Compulsive Disorder, they tend to have difficulty functioning in everyday life. The symptoms of each Anxiety Disorder are somewhat different, and treatment depends on the type of disorder involved (see Chapter 15).

Generalized Anxiety Disorder

For a diagnosis of **Generalized Anxiety Disorder,** DSM-III-R states that a person must show persistent anxiety for at least six months. This chronic anxiety is

Free-floating anxiety ══
Persistent anxiety not
clearly related to any
specific object or situation,
accompanied by a sense of
impending doom.

called **free-floating anxiety** if it has no obvious source. Sometimes, however, the source of anxiety is obvious and specific. In extreme cases, symptoms of a Generalized Anxiety Disorder are the result of specific stressors in the environment, such as in prisoner-of-war camps, where specific anxieties become generalized. People diagnosed as having a Generalized Anxiety Disorder feel anxious almost constantly, and they often report especially intense anxiety. Other symptoms include sleep disturbances, excessive sweating, muscle tension, headaches, and insomnia. People with a Generalized Anxiety Disorder are tense and irritable, unable to concentrate, have difficulty making decisions, and often hyperventilate (Rapee, 1986).

Generally, psychologists describe three areas of functioning in which persons suffering from a Generalized Anxiety Disorder show impairment:

1. *Motor tension.* The person is unable to relax and exhibits jumpiness, restlessness, and tension.
2. *Autonomic hyperactivity.* The person sweats, has a dry mouth, high resting pulse rate, urinates frequently, and may also complain of a "lump" in the throat.
3. *Vigilance.* The person has difficulty concentrating and is irritable and impatient.

The following case study describes a person exhibiting symptoms of a Generalized Anxiety Disorder.

> After ten years of very successful practice, a 34-year-old dentist noted that his practice had declined slightly during the closing months of the year. Shortly after this he began to experience mild anxiety attacks and complained of continual worry, difficulty in sleeping, and a vague dread that he was "failing." As a result, he increased in hours of practice during the evenings from one to five nights and began driving himself beyond all reason in a desperate effort to "insure the success of his practice." Although his dental practice now increased beyond what is had been previously, he found himself still haunted by the vague fears and apprehensions of failure. These, in turn, became further augmented by frequent heart palpitations and pains that he erroneously diagnosed as at least an incapacitating if not fatal heart ailment. At this point his anxiety became so great that he voluntarily came to a clinic for assistance. (Coleman, Butcher, & Carson, 1980, p. 209).

Phobic Disorders

Learning $\overline{13.15}$
Objective

Phobic Disorder ══
A disorder characterized by
fear and subsequent
attempted avoidance of
specific objects or
situations, acknowledged
by the person as
unreasonable.

A **Phobic Disorder** is the fear of, and consequent attempt to avoid, specific objects or situations. A person who exhibits a phobia fears a specific situation and tends to avoid it even though he or she realizes that it represents no real danger. People suffering from Phobic Disorders exhibit avoidance and escape behaviors, show increased heart rate and breathing patterns, and report thoughts of disaster or severe embarrassment. Many psychologists agree that, once established, phobias are maintained by the relief derived from the escape or avoidance that they allow.

Diagnosis of a Phobic Disorder requires that fear experienced be disproportionate to the situation. For example, many people who fear heights would not avoid visiting a friend who happened to live on the top floor of a tall building. According to Agras, Sylvester, and Oliveau (1969), mild Phobic Disorders are found in about 7.5 percent of the population and severe disabling ones in less than 5.0 percent of the population. Mild Phobic Disorders are relatively common in well-adjusted people, but they occur even more frequently in patients with other disorders (Seif & Atkins, 1979). Phobias occur most frequently between the ages of thirty and sixty and about equally in men and women (Marks, 1977).

Fear of flying is a common simple phobia which many people struggle to overcome.

Agoraphobia
A disorder characterized by fear of being alone in public places from which escape might be difficult.

DSM-III-R classifies three basic kinds of phobias: Agoraphobia, Social Phobia, and Simple Phobia. **Agoraphobia** is a marked fear of being alone in public places from which escape might be difficult. It is accompanied by avoidance behaviors that eventually interfere with normal activities. The fear can become debilitating; some individuals avoid going into any open spaces, traveling in airplanes, or being in crowds. People with severe cases may decide never to leave their homes. Agoraphobia is often brought on by stress, particularly interpersonal stress. It is much more common in women than in men (I. G. Fodor, 1974) and is often accompanied by other disorders (Goldstein & Chambless, 1978; Marks, 1969).

Many individuals in our society now suffer from Agoraphobia. They find themselves in an environment that makes them feel alone and vulnerable (H. Lewis, 1981), and they attempt to avoid such situations. Eventually, they become fearful of all situations that might elicit feelings of vulnerability: open spaces, closed spaces, and crowds. Ultimately, they may become housebound and subsequently anxious and depressed. In one study, 93 percent of agoraphobics reported fear of heights and enclosed places, such as elevators (Buglass et al., 1977). The disorder brings about hyperventilation, extreme tension, and even cognitive disorganization (Zitrin, 1981). Agoraphobics feel weak and dizzy when they have an attack. Agoraphobics often are seriously depressed (Breier, Charney, & Heninger, 1984). Another study also showed that 95 percent of the agoraphobics studied also suffered from severe panic attacks—another related disorder characterized by both extreme fear and acute anxiety (Breier et al., 1986).

Agoraphobia is complicated, and incapacitating and is extraordinarily difficult to treat (Mathews, Gelder, & Johnston, 1981). Despite much research on treatment, no simple cause for the disorder has been found. The fear and avoidance of open places, crowds, and public transportation appear unrelated to any specific events. According to Freud and other psychoanalysts, traumatic childhood experiences may cause people to avoid objects, events, and situations that produce anxiety. Freudians speculate that agoraphobics may fear abandonment by a cold or nonnurturing mother, and that the fear has generalized to a fear of abandonment or helplessness. Most researchers today find

Freudian explanations of phobic behavior unconvincing. As an alternative, modern learning theory suggests that Agoraphobia may develop because people avoid situations they have found painful, or embarrassing. (Brehany & Geller, 1987)

A **Social Phobia** is an irrational fear of, and desire to avoid, one or more situations in which the individual may be exposed to the scrutiny of other people. A person with a Social Phobia fears behaving in an embarrassing or humiliating way. Social Phobias are in some ways easy to understand. Most people have been in situations in which they think they are being evaluated, and these thoughts create anxiety. The person with a Social Phobia avoids evaluation by refusing to deal with people or situations in which evaluation might occur. People who suffer from a Social Phobia fear eating in public and speaking before other people and would have great difficulty entering professions that require public performance and evaluation.

All specific phobias other than Agoraphobia and Social Phobia are classified as Simple Phobias. A person who exhibits a **Simple Phobia** shows an irrational and persistent fear of an object or situation, along with a compelling desire to avoid it. Most people are familiar with a variety of specific phobias that could be classified as Simple Phobias, such as *claustrophobia* (fear of closed spaces), *hematophobia* (fear of the sight of blood), and *acrophobia* (fear of heights).

Obsessive-Compulsive Disorders

Someone who washes his hands 100 times a day in order to avoid germs has an Obsessive-Compulsive Disorder. **Obsessive-Compulsive Disorders** are characterized by the presence of persistent unwanted thoughts, urges, and actions. Persons with Obsessive-Compulsive Disorders combat anxiety by carrying out ritual behaviors that reduce tension (see Pollak, 1979). Such compulsions are often strict routines. For example, a woman obsessed with the notion that germs are invading her immediate surroundings may have the compulsion to perform certain complex ritualistic cleaning acts. If she does not perform these compulsive acts, she may develop severe anxiety.

Persons with severe Obsessive-Compulsive Disorders may show seriously maladaptive behavior. Being orderly is not by itself a disorder, but when orderliness becomes the prime concern in a person's life, symptoms of Obsessive-Compulsive Disorder are apparent. Such people may live by a strict routine and become easily upset by changes in that routine. They may be overly meticulous and perfectionistic. They may become overly fond of indexing, tabulating, and organizing (Ingram, 1961).

Both psychodynamic and learning theorists have explanations for the Obsessive-Compulsive Disorder. Freud and other psychodynamic theoreticians considered the Obsessive-Compulsive Disorder to result largely from difficulties during the anal stage of development. As we saw in Chapter 12, parental approval or disapproval of toilet training is the hallmark of this Freudian stage of development. Freud suggests fixations or difficulties with establishing toilet training at this stage as the principal causes of the Obsessive-Compulsive Disorder.

The causes of this disorder are very straightforward for learning theorists. They argue that bringing order to a person's environment reduces uncertainty and risk and thus is reinforcing. Since reinforced behaviors tend to recur, these

Social Phobia
A disorder characterized by fear of, and desire to avoid, situations in which the person might be exposed to scrutiny by other people and might behave in an embarrassing or humiliating way.

Simple Phobia
A disorder characterized by irrational and persistent fear of an object or situation along with a compelling desire to avoid it.

Learning Objective 13.16

Obsessive-Compulsive Disorder
A disorder characterized by persistent and uncontrollable thoughts and irrational beliefs that cause an individual to perform compulsive rituals that interfere with daily life.

behaviors become exaggerated under times of stress, when people need to feel less threatened.

Neither explanation accounts for all of the data—Freud's explanation focusing on childhood events is ethically impossible to put to a controlled experimental test, and the learning accounts fail to explain fully how these behaviors actually reduce anxiety. Recently, even biological factors including chronic high levels of arousal have been implicated in the Obsessive-Compulsive Disorder (Turner, Beidel, & Nathan, 1985). Regardless of their orientation, practitioners report that Obsessive-Compulsive Disorders are relatively rare, although elements of the disorder appear in some other disorders. Treatment often includes relaxation exercises as well as helping people change their ideas about stress and the consequences of anxiety.

Although fewer people suffer from Obsessive-Compulsive Disorders than from Generalized Anxiety disorders, aspects of Obsessive-Compulsive Disorder are evident in many Anxiety Disorders. Even people without Anxiety Disorders sometimes exhibit ritualistic behaviors to help themselves cope with anxiety and adapt to their environments (Gottheil & Stone, 1974). Many people have small obsessions and compulsions that help them reduce anxiety. Sometimes, these take the form of supercleanliness, sometimes of job competitiveness. Aspects of the obsessive-compulsive personality are indigenous to Western civilization; it is not surprising that those behaviors become exaggerated in maladjustment (Pollack, 1979; Rachman & DeSilva, 1978).

PROGRESS CHECK 13.3

1. Match each of the following DSM-III-R diagnostic categories and terms with the appropriate diagnostic description.

Phobic Disorder	anxiety	Obsessive-Compulsive
free-floating anxiety	Generalized Anxiety Disorder	Disorder

Learning Objective 13.12

A. _____ Characterized by a wide range of symptoms including fear, apprehension, inattention, palpitation, respiratory distress, dizziness, and fear of death. When the symptoms become extreme, a person will become physically or psychologically paralyzed.

Learning Objective 13.14

B. _____ Characterized by chronic anxiety with no obvious source and frequently accompanied by a sense of impending doom.

Learning Objective 13.14

C. _____ Characterized by motor tension, autonomic hyperactivity, apprehension, irritability, and lack of concentration; anxiety persists for at least one month and its source usually is not obvious although, sometimes in extreme cases, a specific source can produce anxiety that becomes generalized.

Learning Objective 13.15

D. _____ Characterized by an unrealistic fear and behavior patterns that allow the person to avoid the feared object or situation.

Learning Objective 13.16

E. _____ Characterized by persistent, uncontrollable, and unwanted thoughts and urges that bring about feelings of anxiety; anxiety is reduced when the person can participate in ritual behaviors that accompany the thoughts.

2. Complete each of the following sentences with one of the options provided.

Learning Objective 13.12

A. Karen Horney suggests that maladjustment occurs when a person _____ _____ anxiety.
   (experiences : has too many defenses against)

Learning Objective 13.12   B. Behaviorists see anxiety as _____.
(intrapsychic urges : intrapsychic conflicts : overgeneralized response patterns)

Learning Objective 13.13   C. For psychologists, the term *neurosis* to describe a variety of behavioral oddities is _____.
(inappropriate and inefficient : descriptive and useful)

Learning Objective 13.14   D. The anxiety characteristic of Generalized Anxiety Disorder _____ _____ an obvious source.
(may or may not have : does not have : is diagnosed when there is)

Learning Objective 13.15   E. Phobias are most commonly found in both males and females and among people who are _____ years-old.
(three to eight : eighteen to twenty-seven : thirty to sixty)

Learning Objective 13.15   F. Mild Phobic Disorders _____.
(can be found in well-adjusted people : occur in response to real dangers)

Learning Objective 13.15   G. An extreme fear of being alone in public places from which escape may be difficult characterizes _____.
(a Social Phobia : Agoraphobia)

Learning Objective 13.15   H. Panic attacks are characterized by _____ and often accompany Agoraphobia.
(inappropriate laughing or crying : extreme fear and acute anxiety)

Learning Objective 13.15   I. All specific phobias other than Agoraphobia and Social Phobia are categorized as _____ in the DSM-III-R.
(Simple Phobia : Phobic Reactions : Acrophobia)

Learning Objective 13.16   J. Unavoidable thoughts, ideas, and urges are called _____.
(obsessions : compulsions)

Learning Objective 13.16   K. If a person who has an Obsessive-Compulsive Disorder is prevented from performing compulsive rituals, the _____.
(obsessions will cease : person will experience severe anxiety)

PSYCHOACTIVE SUBSTANCE ABUSE

Brenda Playman was so distressed with her son Gordon's new-found career path that, like many people, she may have turned to various substances to deal with her stress and anxiety. For a substance abuser, the substances vary; they may be tranquilizers, alcohol, cocaine, and marijuana, to name just a few.

It would be out of character for a woman like Brenda Playman to turn to a drug like alcohol to help relieve her stress. Brenda had always seen herself as conservative, at most a social drinker, and committed to groups like MADD (Mothers Against Drunk Driving). She belonged to MADD and had urged Gordon to join SADD, Students Against Drunk Driving. She could recite the statistics with ease: half of all the car deaths in the United States involved drinking in some way; auto accidents are the number one killer of teenagers in America. As an enlightened mother, Brenda could tell you about various state laws, how they affected *her* insurance rates, how alcohol abuse ruined a friend's family, and how her friend ultimately lost his life because of his substance abuse problems.

Learning Objective 13.17

Substance abuse is not confined to alcohol; in the late 1980s, psychologists are seeing more and more young people abusing a whole cabinet full of drugs as well as drugs that are illegal, such as cocaine, marijuana, and speed. According to the guidelines laid out in DSM-III-R, a person is said to have a Psychoactive Substance Abuse Disorder if (1) the substance has been used for at least one month, (2) the substance use has caused complications (such as legal difficulties or social or vocational problems), and (3) there is recurrent

I need the stuff...

Addiction

I'm trying to kick the stuff...

Withdrawal

I'm back on the stuff, but enjoying it less...

Tolerance

Addictive ══════
Causing a compulsive physiological need. Withholding an addictive drug produces withdrawal symptoms. Addictive drugs usually produce tolerance.

Dependence ══════
Reliance on regular use of a drug, without which the individual suffers a psychological, or physiological, reaction, or both.

use in hazardous situations (like driving a car). The substance abuse leads to psychological dependence or pathological use. *Psychological dependence* means a compelling desire to use the drug along with an inability to inhibit that desire; *pathological use* refers to out-of-control episodes.

Whenever a person exhibits substance abuse *and* shows evidence of withdrawal symptoms or tolerance, then we say the person is showing *substance dependence* (usually, but not always, to an addictive drug). An **addictive** drug is a drug that produces a physiological reaction in an individual when that drug is no longer administered. This reaction is called **dependence**. Without the drug, the user suffers from **withdrawal symptoms**—physical reactions that include headaches, nausea, dizziness, sneezing, stomach pain, and an intense craving for the withheld drug. Addictive drugs usually produce **tolerance**, a progressive insensitivity to repeated use of the drug in the same dosage. An addict must use increasingly greater amounts of the drug to achieve the desired high. Most addictive drugs produce both withdrawal symptoms and tolerance.

Trends in Substance Abuse

Learning Objective 13.18 ═══

Withdrawal symptoms ══════
A variety of physical states that occur when a drug is no longer administered to a person who has developed a physiological dependence on it.

Generally speaking, psychologists and nonpsychologists know when substance abuse is taking place. It occurs when people are using drugs for the purposes of mood-alteration and novel experiences and when these drugs are causing disturbances in a person's life. Patterns of drug use and abuse vary widely among individuals. It is not uncommon to find poly-drug abusers—individuals who are using drugs in combination with other drugs. For example, a heroin addict might also be taking amphetamines to experience unique effects. He then might switch to barbiturates when amphetamines become difficult to obtain. The consequence for psychologists is that studying drug abuse and treatment is exceedingly difficult. Few drug abusers have similar backgrounds, problems, and drug-abuse patterns. Their physiological health has often deteriorated, and effective treatment programs are hard to find and expensive (Blum, 1984). (See Table 13.6.)

TABLE 13.6: Drugs Commonly Involved in Drug Abuse

Type	Drug	Effect	Tolerance	Physiological Dependence
Sedatives	Alcohol	Reduces tension	yes	yes
	Barbiturates (e.g., Seconal)	Reduces tension and induces sleep	yes	yes
Stimulants	Amphetamines	Increased feelings feelings of alertness	yes	no
	Cocaine	Increased alertness decreased fatigue stimulate sex drive	no	no
Narcotics	Opium morphine heroin	Alleviate pain and tension; achieve a high	yes	yes
Psychedelics	Marijuana	Changes in mood and perception	no	no
Antianxiety	Librium Valium Tranxene	Alleviate tension induce relaxation	yes	yes

Note: Even though a drug may not produce physiological dependence, it may produce a psychological need that compels repeated use. Drugs such as cocaine, which do not produce a physiological dependence, are widely known to involve abuse and a psychological dependence.

Consider the wide range of drugs that are abused. First and foremost is alcohol. The past fifteen years have shown a dramatic increase in alcohol consumption, and its effects are devastating. Because of its widespread use, we focus on alcohol abuse in the next section.

Other drug substances also are widely abused. According to Blum (1984), more than 300,000 people die prematurely each year because of illness related to smoking. Despite efforts to curb smoking in youth, by age twelve, one in five children smoke cigarettes and ultimately become addicted. In the United States, nearly 50 million people are regular smokers. More than 20 million adults have used marijuana; nearly 10 percent of high school seniors use the drug daily. Heroin use has stabilized at approximately 500,000 individuals; prices have increased and drug potency has decreased, but the number of people who maintain themselves on this potent drug is very high. Barbiturates, tranquilizers, and amphetamines have been widely available and widely abused during the past two decades (see Figure 13.6). Levels of abuse have remained approximately constant during the 1980s.

Achieving wide use and abuse in the 1980s is cocaine, now being used at epidemic proportions. A central nervous system stimulant, cocaine use increases heartbeat, decreases appetite, and raises blood pressure. Smoked, sniffed, or injected, it produces a light-headed feeling, a sense of alertness, increased energy, and sometimes a sense of infallibility. Cocaine is classified by law as a drug with high abuse potential and little medical value; it is grouped with opiates, amphetamines, and barbiturates. Admissions to treatment centers for cocaine addiction have been sharply increasing, as have deaths associated with cocaine abuse. Associated with its high cost and abuse are often financial ruin, plus weight loss, depression, and other psychological disturbances.

Each drug mentioned here is capable of creating a dependence that can not only alter the course of a person's life but also dismantle a normal family

Tolerance
A progressive insensitivity to the effects of a specific drug and dosage when that drug is administered repeatedly.

534 CHAPTER THIRTEEN : *Stress and Maladjustment*

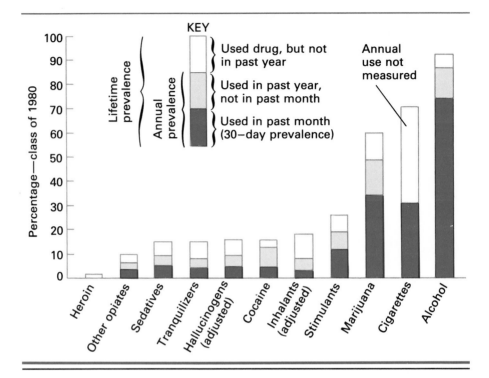

FIGURE 13.6 : Prevalence and recency of drug use of eleven types of drugs in graduating high school seniors in 1980. (From Highlights from student drug use in America 1975–1980, DHHS Publication No. ADM 81–1066, by L. D. Johnson, J. G. Bachman, and P. M. O'Malley. Washington, D.C.: U.S. Government Printing Office, 1980)

structure. Drug abuse in the 1980s has been under the critical eye of psychologists, physicians, and law enforcement officials. Education programs for young people are generally thought to be the most fruitful approach. Few drugs, however, no matter how widely abused, have achieved the status of abuse as alcohol, considered next.

Alcohol Use and Abuse

Learning Objective 13.19

Because alcohol is easily available, relatively inexpensive, and socially accepted, addiction is easy to establish and relatively easy to maintain. Most Americans consider some alcohol consumption appropriate. Some people consume alcoholic beverages before, during, and after dinner. Parties are often considered incomplete without it. The number of retail outlets for alcohol has increased. About 80 percent of urban American adults report having used alcohol at some time. Some changes are taking place in the types of alcoholic beverages consumed and their frequency and time of consumption. Even with these changes, alcohol consumption in the United States has been at an all-time high for more than a decade. It is estimated that 10 million people in the United States, or about 7 percent of the population over age eighteen, are problem drinkers or alcoholics (Chafetz, 1979).

Alcohol is a central nervous system depressant. It decreases inhibitions and thus increases some behaviors that are normally under tight control. Alcohol is absorbed into the bloodstream from the stomach and small intestines. It is absorbed rapidly if the stomach is empty. Mixing alcohol with water slows the absorption process; adding soda water or other carbonated beverages to alcohol speeds it up.

The effects of alcohol vary with the amount of alcohol in the bloodstream and with the weight and gender of the user (see Table 13.7). One ounce of

TABLE 13.7: Relationships between Alcohol Consumption and Blood Alcohol Level, by Gender and Weight

Absolute Alcohol (oz.)	Beverage Intake in 1 Hour	Blood Alcohol Levels (mg/100 ml)					
		Female (100 lbs.)	Male (100 lbs.)	Female (150 lbs.)	Male (150 lbs.)	Female (200 lbs.)	Male (200 lbs.)
1/2	1 oz. spirits* 1 glass wine 1 can beer	.045	.037	.03	.025	.022	.019
1	2 oz. spirits 2 glasses wine 2 cans beer	.090	.075	.06	.050	.045	.037
2	4 oz. spirits 4 glasses wine 4 cans beer	.180	.150	.12	.100	.090	.070
3	6 oz. spirits 6 glasses wine 6 cans beer	.270	.220	.18	.150	.130	.110
4	8 oz spirits 8 glasses wine 8 cans beer	.360	.300	.24	.200	.180	.150
5	10 oz. spirits 10 glasses wine 10 cans beer	.450	.370	.30	.250	.220	.180

*All spirits are assumed to be 100 proof.

alcohol will have less effect in a 200-pound man than on a 100-pound woman. One ounce of alcohol raises the blood alcohol level in a 200-pound man to .037 percent, which represents a low level of intoxication. The same amount of alcohol in a 100-pound woman has a more concentrated effect; it raises the blood alcohol level to .090 percent and will probably induce serious intoxication.

The behavior of individuals who have consumed alcohol is highly correlated to blood alcohol levels. Table 13.8 shows various blood alcohol levels and

TABLE 13.8: Behavioral Effects of Various Blood Alcohol Levels

Percentage of Blood Alcohol	Behavioral Effects
.05	Lowered alertness, impaired judgement, release of inhibitions, good feelings
.10	Slowed reaction times and impaired motor function, less caution
.15	Large, consistent increases in reaction time
.20	Marked depression in sensory and motor capability, decidedly intoxicated behavior
.25	Severe motor disturbance and impairment of sensory perceptions
.30	Stuporous but conscious—no comprehension of events in the environment
.35	Surgical anesthesia; lethal dose for about 1 percent of the population
.40	Lethal dose for about 50 percent of the population

the behaviors associated with them. A blood alcohol level below .10 percent may cause mild intoxication, with no dramatic behavioral effects. With increasing amounts of alcohol in the bloodstream, people typically exhibit progressively slowed behavior; often they show severe motor disturbances such as staggering. Blood alcohol levels greater than .10 percent usually indicate that the person has consumed too much alcohol to function responsibly. In most states a .10 percent blood alcohol level is used to define intoxication legally. People with a .10 percent or greater blood alcohol level are usually arrested and removed from the road if they are found driving (Langenbucher & Nathan, 1983).

People drink alcoholic beverages for a variety of reasons; most prevalent is a desire to relax. Many individuals have strong expectations of what alcohol will bring to their lives, which affects the amount they drink and their behavior after drinking (Critchlow, 1986). As a depressant, alcohol helps people rid themselves of anxiety. In doing so, they move from a state of active consciousness to one in which tension is relieved, but they are less alert and aware. After several drinks, they may behave in erratic, irrational ways. The altered alcoholic state is often dangerous both for the drinkers and for those around them.

Alcohol-related problems are medical, social, or psychological problems associated with alcohol use. A person who shows an alcohol-related problem is called a problem drinker and is said to be involved in **alcohol abuse**. **Alcoholism**, a physiological addiction to alcohol, is an alcohol-related problem. All alcoholics are problem drinkers, but not all problem drinkers are alcoholics (Wanberg & Horn, 1983).

Of Americans age eighteen and older who drink, 36 percent are potential problem drinkers. The percentage is higher for men (44 percent) than for women (27 percent), and higher for people age eighteen to twenty than for any other age group. Problem drinkers may have health or marital problems or trouble functioning socially because of drinking, but these problems alone do not constitute alcoholism. Alcoholism involves both a physiological and usually a psychological need to consume alcoholic products and to experience their effects.

Unlike heroin use, regular alcohol consumption does not necessarily lead to addiction. Many people are regular or semiregular social drinkers. They have no trouble controlling the amount of alcohol they consume, and they do not report cravings for alcohol. In contrast, alcoholics are addicted. Without alcohol, they develop physiological withdrawal symptoms. Alcoholics often develop tolerance; a single drink or even a few will not satisfy their cravings. Alcoholics are often unable to face the world without alcohol. Problem drinkers often begin drinking in order to escape from reality. Slowly, almost inperceptibly, alcohol becomes an addictive drug and the person is no longer just a problem drinker, but an alcoholic (Morey, Skinner, & Blashfield, 1984).

The causes of alcoholism are complex; societal pressures, heredity (Gabrielli et al., 1982), alcohol abuse in parents, and antisocial behavior are only some of the causes. Recent studies have carefully explored the complex relation among these variables (Vaillant & Milofsky, 1982) and are attempting to determine who is at risk for alcoholism (Schlusinger et al., 1986).

For some alcoholics, psychological and medical treatment is successful. The most widely known program of this type is Alcoholics Anonymous, which helps individuals abstain from alcohol by providing a therapeutic and emotionally warm environment. Its success rate is considerably better than that of

Learning Objective 13.20
_____

Alcohol-related problems ═══════
Medical, social, or psychological problems associated with alcohol use.

Alcohol abuse ═══════
Any situation in which a person shows problems related to alcohol use.

Alcoholism ═══════
Physiological addiction to alcohol, usually accompanied by psychological dependence.

treatment programs for heroin addicts. Programs such as Alcoholics Anonymous make abstinence their goal. This is also the goal endorsed by the National Institute of Alcohol Abuse and Alcoholism (Noble, 1978). The fundamental assumptions, based on past failures by alcoholics to control their drinking, are that 1) an alcoholic is an alcoholic forever, 2) that alcoholism should be considered disease-like in nature (Peele, 1984) and, 3) it is uncontrollable.

Some practitioners believe that limited, nonproblem drinking should or might be the goal of a treatment program (Vaillant & Milofsky, 1982). This view assumes that alcohol abuse is a learned behavior and can therefore be unlearned; it also assumes that for many problem drinkers abstinence is an unattainable goal. Those who prefer controlled use claim that alcohol abuse is merely a symptom of a larger underlying problem (see Marlatt, 1983; Sobell & Sobell, 1982). A clash exists between practitioners who claim that alcohol abuse is a disease that needs to be controlled and those who argue that is a learned, changeable behavior (Peele, 1984).

Few systematic, carefully controlled studies of alcoholism and procedures for its treatment exist. Owing to limited resources and social acceptance of alcohol consumption, most alcoholics go untreated (Noble, 1978). Some researchers are investigating the use of drugs and behavioral therapies to control alcohol intake (for example, Weins & Menustik, 1983). Others are studying detoxification centers and halfway houses as treatments for alcoholism. Researchers are becoming more sophisticated in evaluating personal, environmental, and treatment variables (Moos & Finney, 1983).

From both a medical and psychological standpoint, alcohol abuse is one of the greatest social problems in the United States. Prohibition in the 1920s and early 1930s brought even more crime, death, and sadness from bootleg alcohol than from legalized alcohol. Even now, drunkenness is the biggest law enforcement problem in the United States, accounting for millions of arrests each year. The Department of Transportation has estimated that alcohol is involved in

Although alcohol is considered socially acceptable, its use can lead to serious medical and psychological problems.

Substance abuse among youth is considered a serious health and mental health problem by medical doctors, psychologists, and the general public. Drug use, including the use of alcohol, impairs memory, alertness, and achievement. Children and teenagers are especially vulnerable. The principle place in which drug abuse begins is in the school environment. Drug use is found among students in all classes of society and in city, suburban, and urban settings. Student drug use disrupts the entire school system.

In the mid-1980s, a national campaign was begun to help rid school systems of drugs. Under the direction of Secretary of Education William J. Bennett, a plan was laid out for achieving drug-free schools. Most psychologists would agree with the steps outlined in this plan. The plan (Bennett, 1986) suggests the following steps for parents, school systems, students, and communities:

PARENTS

1. Teach standards of right and wrong and demonstrate these standards through personal example.
2. Help children to resist peer pressure to use drugs by supervising their activities.
3. Be knowledgeable about drugs and signs of drug use. When symptoms are observed, respond promptly.

SCHOOLS

4. Determine the extent and character of drug use and establish a means of monitoring that use regularly.
5. Establish clear and specific rules regarding drug use that include strong, corrective actions.
6. Enforce established policies against drug use fairly and consistently. Implement security measures to eliminate drugs on school premises.
7. Implement a comprehensive drug prevention curriculum from kindergarten through grade 12.
8. Reach out to the community for support and assistance in making the school's antidrug policy and program work by developing collaborative arrangements.

STUDENTS

9. Learn about the effects of drug use, the reasons drugs are harmful, and ways to resist pressures to try drugs.
10. Use an understanding of the danger posed by drugs to help other students avoid them.

COMMUNITIES

11. Help schools fight drugs by providing them with the expertise and financial resources of community groups and agencies.
12. Involve local law enforcement agencies in all aspects of drug prevention: assessment, enforcement, and education.

---

more than 28,000 automobile deaths and more than 80,000 automobile accidents each year. In addition, more often than not, people involved in violent crimes and suicides have been drinking.

In the 1980s, it is estimated that 45 percent of nineteen- to twenty-year-old drivers who were involved in fatal car crashes had been drinking (Fell, 1985). Forty-three percent of people convicted of homicide had been drinking before the crime. Alcohol also has been shown to be involved in child beating. It may cause chronic sexual impotence (Lemere & Smith, 1973), cognitive impairment (Goldman, 1983), increased risk of heart disease and cancer (Hennekens et al., 1979; Yano, Rhoads, & Kagan, 1977), and increased risk to the newborn infants of alcoholic mothers (Little, 1979; Warren, 1978). Yet, although alcoholism is widely recognized as a major health problem, and millions of federal dollars are spent on the treatment of alcoholism (Emrick & Hansen, 1983), very little money is spent on prevention (Nathan, 1983).

In summary, alcohol is a dangerous, potentially addictive drug. It alters a person's state of consciousness in dramatic ways; it affects a person's central nervous system and psychological stability, and its contribution to loss of life is enormous. The causes of alcoholism are exceedingly complex, because many reasons—physiological, genetic, and social—might explain any individual's addiction to alcohol. Although progress is being made in understanding the causes of alcohol addiction and in treating it, this consciousness-altering substance continues to affect millions of Americans each day. It alters their functioning, changes their view of themselves and the world, and affects their relationships with family and friends. Education and prevention among youth are considered the primary goals of many researchers who deal with alcohol use and abuse.

PROGRESS CHECK 13.4

1. Match each of the following key concepts and terms with the appropriate definition.

psychological dependence   dependence   pathological use
withdrawal symptoms   substance dependence   tolerance

Learning Objective 13.17   A. _____ The person has a compelling desire to use the drug and an inability to inhibit that desire.

Learning Objective 13.17   B. _____ The person has a psychoactive substance abuse disorder and shows signs of withdrawal symptoms or tolerance.

Learning Objective 13.17   C. _____ A progressive insensitivity to the effects of a specific drug when the drug has been used repeatedly. Larger doses become necessary to experience the desired effects.

Learning Objective 13.17   D. _____ The use of an addictive drug is necessary to prevent the physiological reaction that would occur if it was no longer administered.

Learning Objective 13.17   E. _____ A person experiences an intense craving for the drug, along with physical reactions that include headaches, nausea, dizziness, sneezing, and stomach pain when the drug is withheld.

Learning Objective 13.17   F. _____ A person has episodes when he or she is out of control with the use of a particular drug.

2. Complete each of the following sentences with one of the options provided.

Learning Objective 13.18   A. A poly-drug abuser is a person who abuses _____.
(drugs occasionally for fun or for stress reduction : various combinations of drugs)

Learning Objective 13.18   B. One out of every _____ twelve-year-olds smoke cigarettes.
(5 : 10 : 25 : 100)

Learning Objective 13.19   C. About _____ of the adult population in the United States is a problem drinker.
(7 percent : 20 percent : 36 percent)

Learning Objective 13.19   D. Alcohol is a central nervous system _____.
(stimulant : depressant)

Learning Objective 13.19   E. Carbonated beverages mixed with alcohol _____ the body's speed in absorbing the alcohol.
(slow : increase)

Learning Objective 13.19   F. A blood alcohol level of _____ is used as a legal definition of intoxication in most states.
(.10 percent : 1 percent : 10 percent)

Learning Objective 13.20   G. A person who is a problem drinker _____ an alcoholic.
(is also : is not : may or may not be)

Learning Objective 13.20   H. An alcoholic is _____.
(anyone who repeatedly becomes intoxicated : physically addicted to alcohol)

Learning Objective 13.20   I. Alcoholics Anonymous programs are based on the assumption that alcoholism is disease-like _____.
(but can be unlearned : and an alcoholic is an alcoholic forever)

Keeping Pace with Chapter 13

13.1 Identify the type of maladjustment illustrated in each of the following situations.

general adaptation syndrome	Simple Phobia	Generalized Anxiety Disorder
Social Phobia	Post-traumatic Stress Disorder	Obsessive-Compulsive Disorder
Agoraphobia	Psychoactive Substance Abuse Disorder	

_____

A. The earthquake struck and Maria lost her entire family. At first, there was much to do. Maria was worried, but she was strong. People needed help, and she desperately searched for her family members until there was no longer any hope of finding them alive. Eventually, things began to settle down, the city was cleaned up and rebuilding was beginning. Most people had been relocated to some kind of tolerable living shelter, and life was getting back to normal. At this time, Maria developed extreme anxiety and depression. She began losing her temper easily and occasionally she would relive the catastrophe and panic. She felt alienated from the people around her, avoided passing areas in the city that she had once considered her neighborhood, and had great difficulty coping with day-to-day living experiences.

_____

B. David, a young and aspiring lawyer, got involved in a bad deal with some friends and ended up being charged for the illegal sale of cocaine. David had been naïve and was not directly involved in the cocaine deals but, based on all that had happened, he was not sure that he would be able to prove his innocence. Initially, after his arrest, David experienced extreme anxiety and a loss of appetite. He looked pale, had trouble sleeping, and had frequent headaches. A few weeks later, he calmed down somewhat, but he was irritable, impatient, and easily became angry. Months later, when the trial finally convened, David seemed like a completely different person. He was exhausted and found it impossible to get excited about his job. His behavior was inconsistent and disorganized. He had withdrawn from almost all social activities. David had given up and had to rely on another lawyer to defend his case.

_____

C. Charles has been feeling upset with himself for months. He cannot seem to get control over his feelings, and yet, other than trying to make some career decisions, nothing is happening in his life that should be upsetting him to such an extreme degree. He finds himself constantly worrying that he will make a mistake, he is having trouble sleeping, and he feels a desperate fear that something bad is about to happen.

_____

D. May experiences severe heart palpatations and panic and feels she is suffocating if a dog comes near her. The anxiety she experiences is so great that she cannot visit friends who own dogs and must stay in or near the car if she goes on a family outing where people might be walking their dogs.

_____

E. Some people say Morris is a fanatic when it comes to keeping his garage neat and in order. The truth is, Morris experiences extreme anxiety if he does not do so. Morris hoses down the garage floor every morning and evening; the thought that some dust may have fallen on it causes him great discomfort. He has special compartments for nails and screws. He checks the drawers on these compartments several times each day to make sure they are closed just right. On several occasions, Morris has called into work, saying he had an emergency at home, because his concerns about dust left him needing to hose down the garage floor throughout the day.

_____

F. Lynn experiences her problem in a variety of different situations. For example, if a teacher asks the class a question, Lynn feels the spotlight is on her, as if the teacher and all of the students are looking at her and waiting for her to answer. Her face flushes, she starts breathing rapidly, and she feels embarrassed. Seconds seem like hours. Finally, when another student is called on for the answer, she feels some relief. Lynn's anxiety is so painful that she consistently ends up dropping classes in which the teachers tend to ask questions.

_____

G. Because of a serious back injury, Nick's doctor prescribed pills that relieved his physical pain. The pills had a second effect—they gave Nick a sense of euphoria. Normal work and life stresses did not seem to matter so much when he was taking the pills. Nick continued to complain about back pains and extended his ability to refill the prescription for as long as he could. Finally, when he was no longer able to convince his doctor that he still needed the pills, he began drinking alcohol more often than usual so he could keep his remaining pills for "emergency" stress days. After several months, Nick was out of pills, he was drinking alcohol throughout each day, his productivity level was at an all time low, he was depressed most of the time, and although he would tell himself to stay away from the alcohol, he continued to drink each day to avoid possible stress.

_____

H. Ginger is a prisoner to her home. She feels unsafe in open spaces. Rather than walking to visit her mother, Ginger insists on driving her car one block, from her garage to her mother's garage. She does this to avoid encountering and having to speak to anyone who might be walking down the street. Even the thought of passing a stranger while alone on the street causes Ginger to feel severe anxiety.

Self-Test

Before proceeding to the Self-Test, REVIEW the Learning Objectives listed at the chapter opening and RECITE from memory everything you can remember in support of them. Then, take this Self-Test as if it were to be graded by your teacher. Use the Learning Objective numbers in the Answer Section as a reference to restudy the corresponding text pages and Progress Checks for any incorrectly answered questions.

1. The terms *maladjustment, abnormal behavior,* and *mental disorder*

   A. are frequently used synonomously.
   B. are used for different purposes by some psychologists to distinguish between minor coping problems and serious behavior problems.
   C. refer to a failure to cope effectively with the realities and demands of life.
   D. all of the above

2. Two things that occurred as a direct result of the medical model were

   A. the development of IQ tests and the development of community mental health centers.
   B. more humane treatment for mental health patients and fears, held by lay people, of contamination.
   C. methods to measure the incidence of abnormal behavior and well-defined descriptions of behavior.
   D. a distinction between the terms *maladjustment* and *mental disorder;* and a definition of abnormal behavior.

3. Theorists who explain maladjusted behavior from a biological perspective would be most likely to suggest

   A. treatment that involves the use of drugs to change biochemical functions.
   B. that treatment will have little or no effect on the disorder.
   C. that people are unique individuals and behavioral disorders are purely the result of social labels.
   D. that inner psychic forces are the cause of the disorder.

4. Which of the following statements concerning the *Diagnostic and Statistical Manual of Mental Disorders* (DSM-III-R) is *false*? It

   A. was published by the American Psychological Association.
   B. designates 19 major categories of maladjustment and 200 subcategories.
   C. was developed to help mental health practioners make more precise diagnoses of mental health problems.
   D. gives more recognition to social and environmental influences than do DSM-I or DSM-II.

5. Stress is

   A. an environmental stimulus that acts on a person in physically or psychologically injurious ways.
   B. a response everybody experiences at some time in their life.
   C. characterized by a decline in autonomic nervous system activity.
   D. all of the above

6. In his description of a general adaptation syndrome, Seyle notes that the resistance stage occurs because

   A. a person has not yet recognized that a stressor is affecting his or her life.
   B. people cannot stay highly aroused for long periods of time.
   C. a person is fatigued.
   D. a person can no longer adapt to stress.

7. A number of psychologists have suggested that the number and severity of stressful events in a person's life are good predictors of

   A. how well adjusted the person is.
   B. how busy the person is.
   C. potential physical illness and/or maladjustment.
   D. how much control a person has over the environment.

8. Which of the following statements concerning a Post-traumatic Stress Disorder is *false*?

   A. Victims experience vivid recollections of the traumatic event.
   B. The disorder is frequently accompanied by anxiety, depression, or exceptionally aggressive behavior.
   C. Occasional lapses of normal consciousness can occur.
   D. The symptoms are always apparent within a few days after the traumatic event.

9. Which of the following does *not* describe a person who is experiencing burn out?

   A. a loss of energy, emotional drain, and resistance toward even trying.
   B. feelings of hopelessness, a negative self-concept, and a loss of concern for other people.
   C. a life-long history of neglecting to set high standards for self-achievement.
   D. physical and marital problems.

10. When temperatures or noise levels reach extremely high levels,

   A. performance becomes impaired.
   B. people become concerned with their own discomfort and may have trouble concentrating on anything else.

    C. people are more likely to exhibit disorganized or aggressive behaviors.

    D. all of the above

11. Bud is experiencing stress because he has overcommitted himself. Knowing that things will be better in a few weeks, when the semester ends, he copes with his current stress by saying, "Just a few more weeks. I can do it! I have the energy to succeed!" Bud is using a _____ coping strategy.

    A. defense-oriented

    B. stress inoculation

    C. self-talk

    D. relaxation

12. Coping strategies that make use of defense mechanisms

    A. involve an unconscious distortion of reality.

    B. eliminate environmental stressors.

    C. are not very effective.

    D. are frequently taught in stress-reduction training sessions.

13. Stress is likely to produce maladjusted behavior patterns

    A. whenever it occurs.

    B. if it occurs frequently.

    C. when it is accompanied by alarm responses.

    D. if it reaches the exhaustion stage.

14. Karen Horney believed that anxiety

    A. is a central factor in both normal and abnormal behavior.

    B. is the result of using too many defense mechanisms.

    C. should be classified as a stress disorder.

    D. A and C

15. Contemporary psychologists have abandoned the term *neurosis* to describe specific mental health problems, favoring instead,

    A. *neurotic* as a catch-all diagnosis.

    B. the concept of anxiety.

    C. a variety of diagnostic categories.

    D. the word *maladjustment.*

16. Free-floating anxiety

    A. is caused by a specific stressor that has become generalized.

    B. has no obvious source.

    C. is a symptom in most Phobic Disorders.

    D. is the kind of anxiety we feel momentarily just before doing something that causes us to feel a bit apprehensive.

17. Learning theorists have suggested that Agoraphobia develops when the agoraphobic

    A. loses control in a public place.

    B. is embarrassed by a stranger, or even a friend.

    C. is able to avoid painful or embarrassing situations.

    D. cannot find a safe place.

18. A person who fears embarrassing himself or herself and, as a result, literally cannot participate in an activity that most people consider normal and a part of every-day-life would be diagnosed as having _____.

    A. Agoraphobia

    B. a Specific Phobia

    C. a Simple Phobia

    D. a Social Phobia

19. Psychodynamic theorists believe that Obsessive-Compulsive Disorders are the result of

    A. genetic programming and the corresponding structure of the cortex.
    B. cultural-familial experiences.
    C. fear of abandonment.
    D. a fixation in the anal stage of development.

20. Which of the following is *not* one of the criteria used to diagnose a Psychoactive Substance Abuse Disorder? The substance

    A. has been used for at least one month.
    B. is an illegal drug.
    C. has caused major complications in the person's life.
    D. has caused a psychological dependence or is used pathologically.

21. Substance abuse has been closely associated with

    A. premature death.
    B. financial ruin, depression, and weight loss.
    C. dismantling normal family structures.
    D. all of the above

22. Alcohol

    A. slows down normal behavioral responses and interferes with motor movements.
    B. acts as a stimulant.
    C. can be harmful to one's health but is not a dangerous drug.
    D. produces a sense of alertness, increased energy, and a sense of infallibility.

23. People in alcohol treatment centers who believe that controlled drinking should be the goal of treatment

    A. realize that alcoholics can never learn abstinence.
    B. feel that alcohol abuse is merely a symptom of some other problem.
    C. assume that alcohol abuse is a learned disorder.
    D. B and C

Serious Behavior Disorders

14

Learning Objectives

When you have mastered the material in this chapter, you will be able to:

1. Discuss some characteristics of serious behavior disorders. (p. 547)

2. Characterize Attention-deficit Hyperactivity Disorder and Conduct Disorder and discuss the causes of these two childhood disorders. (p. 549)

3. Characterize Autism, a disorder diagnosed during infancy, and explain why it is considered a Pervasive Developmental Disorder. (p. 551)

4. Characterize Anorexia Nervosa and Bulimia Nervosa and discuss some possible causes of these two serious eating disorders. (p. 552)

5. Describe the main symptoms of Somatoform Disorders and Dissociative Disorders and characterize Somatization, Conversion, Psychogenic Amnesia, and Multiple Personality Disorders. (p. 555)

6. Describe some of the main symptoms of Personality Disorders and characterize the Paranoid, Dependent, Histrionic, and Narcissistic Personality Disorders. (p. 557)

7. Characterize an Antisocial Personality Disorder and discuss some possible biological and environmental causes of this disorder. (p. 557)

8. Describe the various subclassifications of Parphilias and discuss the probable causes of these sexual deviations. (p. 560)

9. Describe some of the main symptoms of Mood Disorders and characterize Bipolar Disorder and Major Depression. (p. 563)

10. Give some statistics concerning the number of people who have experienced Major Depressions, identify two criteria used to distinguish the severity of this disorder, and describe the thoughts and behaviors of a depressed person. (p. 565)

11. Discuss the biological and learning approaches concerning possible causes and the treatment of Major Depression. (p. 567)

12. Identify the five main symptoms necessary for a person to be diagnosed as having Schizophrenia and give some statistics concerning the number of people diagnosed as being schizophrenic. (p. 571)

13. Describe the thought, perceptual, and emotional disorders that commonly accompany schizophrenia. (p. 572)

14. Describe five types of Schizophrenic Disorders characterized in DSM-III-R. (p. 573)

15. Discuss some possible causes of Schizophrenia based on biological-genetic research and environmental theories. (p. 575)

BEFORE YOU READ ON, take time to **SURVEY** the chapter, form an idea of what is to be learned (from margin Learning Objective numbers), and set goals for your study time. Then, ask yourself **QUESTIONS** about the material as you **READ,** seeking help for any sections you do not understand.

Randy Bolland had invested eight years in his medical education. He had earned his undergraduate degree, then taken an extra year of chemistry and microbiology to get him into medical school, and three years of med school. He also had endured many sleepless nights, prep-courses, and pressures—the pressure of getting into medical school and then staying in. Randy found the work difficult, and his family noticed that his personality had become darker as he continued his studies. The days of carefree drinking with his college friends were gone. Randy had become serious, and intense and was considered by classmates as humorless. Medical school was exacting its toll.

All students about to enter their fourth and final year take a comprehensive examination, a major hurdle that was feared at Randy's school. Randy dreamed about it regularly. After a very anxious spring, in early summer Randy took the examination; two weeks later, he found out that he had not passed. Following an alcoholic binge, Randy returned to his apartment, only to settle into a deep depression. He kept saying over to himself, "I failed . . . I failed." From Randy's view, his life was all going down the drain.

His roommate, also a medical student (who had passed) tried to reason with him. He argued that Randy could spend the next semester preparing and retake the exam. His roommate correctly argued that it was only one test and that the test was subjective. There was no talking to Randy, however; he would not listen. He kept muttering about not being smart enough, about dragging his friends down with him, and about the utter uselessness of it all. Amidst his rambling, Randy reviewed his academic history and reinterpreted every success as a failure. He saw his eight-year investment in time, money, and learning as totally wasted.

Randy Bolland's setback turned out to be worse than anyone expected. His exam failure became to him a sign of his worthlessness. As the days and weeks passed, he felt more lonely, depressed, anxious, and sad. His humorlessness turned to moroseness. His energy dropped, he had sleepless nights, and he ended his three-month relationship with a female med student. He lost weight, lost interest in everything, and stayed in his apartment for days at a time. He spent the rest of the summer drinking and becoming increasingly depressed. His exam failure was the precipitating cause, and most third-year medical school students could diagnose that Randy Bolland may have been developing a full-scale Mood Disorder.

Learning Objective 14.1 RANDY BOLLAND'S REAL PROBLEM was not his exam failure, although this occurrence was the initiator of his depression. Many people like Randy are on the brink of a depressive disorder. An incident then occurs that pushes them over the top. Talking to a friend or roommate usually will not solve the problem; this is the time to talk with a professional.

Nearly 10 million Americans suffer from Mood or Affective Disorders such as depression. Sometimes people who suffer from such disorders become so hopeless, sad, and depressed that their problems obliterate the good things in their lives—their family, friends, and accomplishments. Some depressed or troubled individuals experience a distinct break with reality; they may begin to hallucinate, experience delusions, or develop bizarre ideas and behaviors. The behavior of a person who is seriously depressed is abnormal. The bizarre thought processes of a person with schizophrenia also result in maladjusted or abnormal behavior. [We discuss these serious behavior disorders and several others throughout this chapter.]

Everyday descriptions of maladjustment are usually exaggerated or inaccurate. For example, people may say that someone is "moody," "depressed," "paranoid," or "obsessive," but these terms have precise clinical meanings that most nonpsychologists do not know. Many people experience some symptoms of serious behavior disorders, but most of these people would not be diagnosed by a mental health practitioner as having a major disorder. Everyone experiences periods of depression or anxiety or periods in which they may act in a slightly paranoid manner, but such occasional lapses do not satisfy the DSM-III-R criteria. In the disorders discussed in this chapter, the individual's behavior is considered extreme. Most professionals agree that these behavior disorders require the special attention of mental health practitioners. They often have a complex origin and are difficult to treat.

Serious behavior disorders differ from the disorders discussed in Chapter 13, *Stress and Maladjustment,* in that they interfere much more drastically with the individual's ability to cope with normal, day-to-day living. The individual is less in touch with reality, the person's family is often unable to provide useful support, and professionals often have more difficulty finding a way to reach the person and provide effective treatment. With serious behavior disorders, behavior change through psychotherapy is less likely to occur than it is with the previously discussed disorders. Also, with serious disorders, medications are more commonly prescribed to help control erratic behavior patterns.

In this chapter, we consider six major DSM-III-R classifications of maladjustment—all of them serious behavior disorders. The first four include disorders of infancy, childhood, and adolescence; somatoform and dissociative disorders; personality disorders; and sexual disorders. These classifications tend to have more precise, focused symptoms than do depression and schizophrenia, the last two discussed here. Depression and schizophrenia are the most pervasive and devastating; they affect many areas of a person's day-to-day functioning. It is impossible to say that Schizophrenia is worse than a mood disorder such as Major Depression, or that a person's pain from an eating disorder is less severe than the pain from Schizophrenia. But it is often more difficult to trace the causes of Schizophrenia, and its symptoms often make treatment more difficult. The discussion begins with disorders of infancy, childhood, and adolescence.

DISORDERS OF INFANCY, CHILDHOOD, AND ADOLESCENCE

Randy Bolland was an adult who experienced a major stressor in his life that initiated a depression. If he were to seek the help of a psychologist, they probably would explore together many of the events that led up to medical school and how Randy interpreted them. They might have focused on the extent to which Randy valued his personal achievements and how Randy interpreted other people's evaluations of him. In Randy's case, the initiator of the depression, and perhaps its causes, may be clear. Depression is so well researched that psychologists know a great deal about it—even if they do not know a great deal about Randy Bolland himself.

However, this is not the case with disorders of childhood. Consider autism, for example. Autism is evident in the first two years of a child's life. It was widely recognized as a clinical disorder as far back as 1956; yet even today, relatively little progress is being made in understanding its cause and treatment.

DSM-III-R recognizes several disorders that occur in infancy, childhood, and adolescence. These disorders which are diagnosed only when the symptoms were evident before age nineteen, are categorized separately from adult disorders. They are: Attention-deficit Hyperactivity Disorders, Conduct Disorders, and Pervasive Developmental Disorders. Researchers are especially interested in these early years because during this time environmental experiences are relatively limited, and it is therefore easier to try to isolate the relative contributions of nature and nurture.

Attention-deficit Hyperactivity Disorder

When a five-year-old fails to complete tasks, is easily distracted, needs a lot of supervision, has difficulty sitting still, and generally acts before thinking, the child may be exhibiting symptoms of Attention-deficit Hyperactivity Disorder, also called *hyperkinetic syndrome*. A child with an **Attention-deficit Hyperactivity Disorder** (often called ADHD) shows inappropriate inattention, impulsiveness, and often hyperactivity.

Attention-deficit Hyperactivity Disorders must appear before age seven and are often evident before age three; they may disappear at puberty or continue into adolescence and adult life. The disorder appears in about 3 percent of children and is six to nine times more common in boys than in girls. Because a school setting requires children's attention and focused behavior, teachers are often the first to detect it. Children with an Attention-deficit Hyperactivity Disorder rarely seem able to stay seated or to pay attention in a classroom setting and make careless, impulsive errors on schoolwork and tests. They have limited attention for schoolwork or even play activities. In some school districts, as many as 25 percent of students have been classified as hyperactive—a percentage that many psychologists suggest means overdiagnosis (S. B. Campbell, 1985).

Labeling a child "hyperactive" or "minimally brain damaged" may itself be damaging. Even more than adults, children adopt the behavior characteristics attributed to them. Children who are told they are hyperactive are more likely to emit those behaviors; if expected to be inattentive, they are more likely to be inattentive. Once children are labeled, people often respond to them in ways that lead to further symptomatic behavior (R. A. Jones, 1977).

Many researchers feel that the influence of biology in Attention-deficit Hyperactivity Disorder is significant. They support their claims with the following findings: (1) children who exhibit these symptoms are likely to have another family member with the disorder, (2) symptoms of the disorder were usually evident early in the child's life, (3) parents of these children report that they were unusually active babies, (4) many of these children were born prematurely, (5) many exhibit perceptual and motor deficits, (6) some exhibit abnormalities in their electroencephalograms (Satterfield, Cantwell, Saul, & Yusin,

Learning Objective 14.2

Attention-deficit Hyperactivity Disorder A Disorder of Infancy, Childhood, and Adolescence beginning before age seven and characterized by restlessness, inattention, distractibility, and overactivity; also known as *hyperactive syndrome* or *hyperkinetic syndrome* or *hyperkinesis*.

TABLE 14.1 : DSM-III-R diagnostic criteria for Attention-deficit Hyperactivity Disorder. The disorder must have begun before the age of 7, have a duration of at least 6 months, and not be the result of Schizophrenia, Mood Disorder, or severe or profound mental retardation.

Note: Consider a criterion met only if the behavior is considerably more frequent than that of most people of the same mental age.

At least eight of the following must be present:

(1) often fidgets with hands or feet or squirms in seat (in adolescents, may be limited to subjective feelings of restlessness)

(2) has difficulty remaining seated when required to do so

(3) is easily distracted by extraneous stimuli

(4) has difficulty awaiting turn in games or group situations

(5) often blurts out answers to questions before they have been completed

(6) has difficulty following through on instructions from others (not due to oppositional behavior or failure of comprehension), e.g., fails to finish chores

(7) has difficulty sustaining attention in tasks or play activities

(8) often shifts from one uncompleted activity to another

(9) has difficulty playing quietly

(10) often talks excessively

(11) often interrupts or intrudes on others, e.g., butts into other children's games

(12) often does not seem to listen to what is being said to him or her

(13) often loses things necessary for tasks or activities at school or at home (e.g., toys, pencils, books, assignments)

(14) often engages in physically dangerous activities without considering possible consequences (not for the purpose of thrill-seeking), e.g., runs into street without looking

1974) and (7) children may not tolerate lower levels of arousal well (Zewtall, Falkengers, and Smith, 1985). Table 14.1 lists the criteria necessary for a clinical diagnosis of Attention-deficit Hyperactivity Disorder.

As discussed in Chapter 7, some treatments of the disorder focus on drugs (Cowart, 1982), others on diet, and still others on cognitive (thought) restructuring (Abikoff, 1985). Treatment often focuses on the use of physical agents to relieve symptoms (Cunningham, Siegel, & Offord, 1985). The success of these efforts suggests that the disorder may have a biological origin. Currently, the most effective treatment is a program of behavior modification at school and at home, together with medication. However, none of the approaches has been extremely successful in the long run (S. B. Campbell, 1985).

Conduct Disorders

Conduct Disorder ━━━━
A Disorder of Infancy, Childhood, and Adolescence usually beginning before age thirteen and characterized by persistent violation of the rights of other people or violation of major age-appropriate norms.

More serious than ordinary mischief and pranks, the acts of a child diagnosed as having a **Conduct Disorder** violate the basic rights of other people or the norms of society. Older children with a Conduct Disorder are sometimes involved in physical assault, mugging, and even rape (Stewart, DeBlois, Meardon, & Cummings, 1980). Those who are less aggressive persist in rule-breaking, truancy, or running away from home. Some children with Conduct

Disorders show attachment to other people but may be callous and manipulative in their dealings. Others have few friends and maintain very superficial relationships. They experience few feelings concerning the well-being of other people, and no feelings of guilt and remorse.

Conduct Disorders tend to be more common among boys. Often, children so diagnosed have problems at school. Research has shown that if a high frequency of such behaviors is established at an early age, they are likely to continue into adolescence (Loeber, 1982). With teenagers, associated problems often include unwanted pregnancies, fights, legal difficulties, and drug abuse; extreme antisocial behavior sometimes results in institutionalization.

The family backgrounds of children with symptoms of Conduct Disorder are less stable than the backgrounds of children with Attention-deficit Hyperactivity Disorders. The family environment often is one of strife and discord, frequently involving separations, divorces, and stepparents. Parents may exhibit symptoms of Antisocial Personality. Often, the discipline provided is harsh and inconsistent. Conduct Disorders are common among children who have been institutionalized at an early age. Robins (1970) suggests that such children are likely later to develop symptoms of the Antisocial Personality. Biological factors are probably involved and treatment sometimes involves drugs (M. Campbell et al., 1984), but the bulk of evidence suggests that a child's experiences in the home environment are more important in the development of a Conduct Disorder (Loeber & Dishion, 1983).

Autism: A Pervasive Developmental Disorder

Learning Objective 14.3

Autism is a Pervasive Developmental Disorder—that is, psychological development is severely affected in many areas simultaneously. Unlike those with Attention-deficit Hyperactivity Disorders or Conduct Disorders, children with Pervasive Developmental Disorders show gross distortions in development, language, perception, motor ability, and reality testing. Fairly rare (only 4 to 5 cases in 10,000 people), a child with an Autistic Disorder is said to be autistic. **Autism,** sometimes called *early infantile autism* or infantile autism, begins before age two and a half. As infants, children diagnosed as having an Autistic Disorder lack the responsiveness that normal babies show. They rarely if ever smile, are not cuddly, and rarely vocalize. As these infants mature physically, they communicate little or not at all and lack eye contact and social skills. They rarely seek comfort at times of distress. They make repetitive motions characterized as bizarre including unusual interest in and attachment to objects.

Autism
A Disorder of Infancy, Childhood, and Adolescence beginning before age two and a half and characterized by lack of responsiveness to other people, gross impairment in language skills, and bizarre responses to the environment; also known as *early infantile autism* or *autism.*

Children diagnosed as having an Autistic Disorder have low measured IQs; only 30 percent have a measured IQ greater than 70. Three or four times more common in boys than in girls, Autism leaves two-thirds of its children severely handicapped, unable to lead independent lives. Only 17 percent make adequate social adjustments and are able to do some type of work.

Gajzago and Prior describe a child with an Autistic Disorder:

A was described as a screaming, severely disturbed child who ran around in circles making high-pitched sounds for hours. He also liked to sit in boxes, under mats, and under blankets. He habitually piled up all furniture and bedding in the center of the room. At times he was thought deaf though he also showed extreme fear of loud noises. He refused all food except in a bottle, refused to wear clothes, chewed stones and paper, whirled himself, and spun objects. . . . He played repetitively with the same toys for months, lining things in rows, collected objects such as bottle

The problems of infantile autism were realistically portrayed in the popular TV series "St. Elsewhere" when Dr. Donald Westphall (actor Ed Flanders) refused to place his autistic son (Chad Allen) in an institution for handicapped children.

tops, and insisted on having two of everything, one in each hand. He became extremely upset if interrupted and if the order or arrangement of things were altered. (Gajzago & Prior, 1974, p. 264)

The causes of Autism are not well understood (see L. Wing, 1976). Since the first clinical description in the 1940s, evidence has not established either nature or nurture as its principal cause. Initially, researchers thought that cold, unresponsive parents were the cause (Kanner, 1943), but more recent research shows that the parents of these children are normal (McAdoo & DeMeyer, 1978). Kanner's early research suggested that autistic children come from higher socioeconomic classes; more recent research has disproved this claim (Keith et al., 1976; Ornitz & Ritvo, 1976). These issues remain unresolved (Cantwell, Baker, & Rutter, 1978). Some researchers have suggested that children with Autistic Disorders are not really withdrawn, but rather choose in an active way to manipulate the environment on their own terms—terms that exclude other people (Clancy & McBride, 1969; Tinbergen, 1974). Although there may be some biological predisposition to Infantile Autism, genetic studies have not shown one. The results of environmental studies are also equivocal. Only a few cases have been treated successfully, and these have required an intensive therapeutic environment. Behavioral techniques emphasizing reinforcement of prosocial behaviors have been effective in some cases (see Bartak, 1978; Lovaas, 1977; Ward, 1978).

Eating Disorders

Learning Objective 14.4

Like many adolescent girls, Marina worried about her weight. With Marina, however, the worry went beyond mere vanity; she seemed overly concerned and preoccupied with losing weight. Her concern began when she wanted to become a cheerleader; along with some friends, she went on a strict diet. When she reached her weightloss goal, she looked terrific. But she did not stop there. She continued to diet until she weighed only seventy-four pounds. Her eyes looked sunken and her arms and legs began to resemble sticks. Yet in spite of what her friends told her, Marina believed she still was too fat and continued to diet, exercise, and maintain a regimen aimed at bringing about further weight loss. Marina became a victim of Anorexia Nervosa, or "starvation disease."

One of the great joys in life, eating, has become the focus of a major diagnostic category in DSM-III-R. Eating disorders focus on the way individuals respond to food. Two of these disorders have received a great deal of attention in the news media: Anorexia Nervosa and Bulimia Nervosa.

Anorexia Nervosa is an eating disorder characterized by an obstinate and willful refusal to stop losing weight. Individuals with the disorder have an intense fear of being fat and a relentless pursuit of becoming thinner. The refusal to eat eventually brings about emaciation and sometimes malnutrition and even death. Victims can sustain permanent damage to their heart muscle tissue. This psychological disorder usually strikes young high school girls from well-educated families. As many as 40 out of every 10,000 young women may develop the disorder. These young people maintain a distorted picture of their appearance, seeing themselves as fat while in fact they are starving their bodies (Kalliopuska, 1982). Although many researchers continue to explore both the physiological and psychological origins of Anorexia Nervosa, many therapists believe the disease has strictly psychological origins.

Anorexia Nervosa usually affects adolescent girls who develop a distorted body image and an exaggerated fear of becoming fat.

Typically, Anorexia Nervosa patients are hospitalized and may need to be force-fed a liquid diet. In a structured hospital setting, weight gain with ano- rexic patients is usually successful. However, to achieve a weight gain, certain conditions seem necessary. There must be a reinforcing environment, staff members need to be present during meal times, and individual and family therapy are often key ingredients (Hsu, 1986). Forced to eat, and rewarded for eating by gaining privileges when they consume specified quantities of food, they may regain needed body weight and avoid permanent damage to their health. Psychotherapy is usually necessary to help these young women main- tain both a healthy self-image and body weight.

Unfortunately, however, as many as 50 percent of treated patients have relapses within one year. The causes of the disorder are still not totally clear, but researchers are convinced that such cultural factors as a preoccupation with weight and being thin are predisposing factors (Hsu, 1986).

Bulimia Nervosa, or Bulimia, is another eating disorder described in DSM- III-R; it involves binge eating (recognized by the person to be abnormal) and a consequent fear of not being able to stop eating voluntarily. Bulimia occurs in normal-weight women with no history of Anorexia Nervosa (see, for example, Garfinkel, Moldofsy, & Garner, 1980). Individuals who engage in binge eating experience pain (from a distended stomach) and become fearful of overeating. They thus often purge themselves of unwanted calories by vomiting and abuse of laxatives and diuretics. Bulimics have a distorted body image, perceiving themselves as much larger than they really are (Williamson, Kelley, Davis, Ruggiero, & Blouin, 1985). In addition, they have lower self-esteem than people who eat normally (Dykens & Gerrard, 1986), come from families they perceive as having poor relationships and a high level of conflict (Johnson & Flach, 1985), and often meet the criterion for having experienced some kind of clinical depression in the past (Walsh et al., 1985). Researchers believe that these purges reduce postbinge anguish. Although Bulimia is seldom incapacitating, various physical changes such as dehydration and electrolytic imbalances can occur, particularly if the woman is already underweight. Once begun, Bulimia has an average duration of five to six years (Johnson & Larson, 1982). The incidence of this binge-purge cycle increased alarmingly in the 1980s; eating disorders in general are being seen more frequently in hospitals and in psychi- atric and psychological settings (Schlesier-Stroop, 1984).

Most explanations of Bulimia have taken into account the mood swings and depressed attitudes of bulimic women (Robinson et al., 1983). One theory sug- gests that women who develop a binge-purge cycle of behavior are at risk for any kind of addictive behavior because of their mood fluctuations. According to Johnson and Larson (1982), such women may attach themselves to food as a means of lightening their mood swings and regulating tension. After binging, however, the women feel guilty and, to lessen their guilt and the potential consequence of gaining weight, they "get away with something" by purging themselves. Such women become entirely involved in food-related behaviors to the exclusion of contact with people.

DSM-III-R considers Anorexia Nervosa and Bulimia Nervosa clinically dis- tinct disorders. Many researchers have noted that frequently the disorders are looked at together (for example, Weiss & Ebert, 1983). Researchers who group the disorders argue that women who suffer from them often have the same background, are of the same age, and have similar life stresses. Until research- ers can show that these two disorders are more closely related, however, most professionals prefer to consider them separately. In any case, both disorders should be considered serious and potentially life-threatening forms of maladjustment. Treatment for these disorders seems most effective when behavioral therapy is the primary therapeutic technique (Schlesier-Stroop, 1984).

PROGRESS CHECK 14.1

1. Complete each of the following sentences with one of the options provided.

Learning Objective 14.1   A. People with serious behavior disorders show _____ of certain behavioral, emotional, and cognitive symptoms.
(extreme signs : occasional, temporary lapses)

Learning Objective 14.2   B. When symptoms of behavior or psychological disorders are evident before the age of _____, DSM-III-R categorizes the maladjustment as a Disorder of Infancy, Childhood, and Adolescence.
(17 : 18 : 19)

Learning Objective 14.2   C. Frequently, when a diagnostic label is attached to a child's behavior tendencies, _____ is observed in the symptoms of the disorder.
(an immediate decline : an increase)

Learning Objective 14.2   D. The most accepted explanations for the causes of an Attention-deficit Hyperactivity Disorder suggest that the disorder _____.
(has a biological origin : is the result of an unstable home environment)

Learning Objective 14.2   E. Children with _____ show attachments to people but often are callous and manipulative in their relationships.
(conduct disorders : autism)

Learning Objective 14.2   F. Children diagnosed as having a Conduct Disorder are likely to develop the symptoms of _____ Disorder later in life.
(a Schizophrenic : an Attention-deficit Hyperactivity : an Antisocial Personality)

Learning Objective 14.3   G. Children diagnosed as having a Pervasive Developmental Disorder _____ in development.
(are late : show gross distortions : show a regression)

Learning Objective 14.3   H. Autism begins before the age of _____.
(two and a half : five : eight)

Learning Objective 14.3   I. _____ characterize the behavior of autistic children.
(Immobility and muscular rigidity : Bizarre, repetitous motions)

Learning Objective 14.3   J. Children diagnosed as having Autism lack responsiveness to the _____ in their environment.
(objects : people)

Learning Objectives 14.2 and 14.3   K. Attention-deficit Hyperactivity Disorders, Conduct Disorders, and Autism are found more commonly in _____.
(girls : boys)

Learning Objective 14.4   L. Anorexia Nervosa is accompanied by _____.
(extreme mood swings : a false perception of being overweight)

Learning Objective 14.4   M. One factor that seems necessary for the successful treatment of Anorexia Nervosa is _____ during meal times.
(the anorexic needs privacy : staff members need to be present)

Learning Objective 14.4   N. Bulima Nervosa is characterized by _____.
(self-induced starvation : binge eating and purging)

SOMATOFORM AND DISSOCIATIVE DISORDERS

Learning Objective 14.5

Several kinds of maladjustments that used to be grouped together and called neuroses are today diagnosed as Somatoform or Dissociative Disorders. Clearly involving maladjustment, these disorders were previously assumed to have a large component of anxiety associated with them. Somatoform and Dissociative Disorders have been studied much less than many other disorders, probably because they are relatively rare. People beset with these disorders need attention and psychotherapy (see Chapter 15).

Somatoform Disorders

Somatoform Disorder
A disorder characterized by real physical symptoms not under voluntary control and for which no evident physical cause exists.

Somatization Disorder
A disorder characterized by recurrent and multiple complaints of several years' duration for which medical attention has been ineffective.

Conversion Disorder
A disorder characterized by the loss or alteration of physical functioning not due to a physiological disorder, but apparently due to internal psychological conflict.

Dissociative Disorder
A disorder characterized by a sudden, temporary alteration in consciousness, identity, or motor behavior.

Psychogenic Amnesia
A disorder characterized by the sudden inability, too extensive to be explained by ordinary forgetfulness, to recall important personal information.

Somatoform Disorders involve real physical symptoms not under voluntary control and for which no evident physical cause exists. The symptoms often include pain, but evidence suggests that the causes are psychological. Two Somatoform Disorders are the Somatization Disorder and the Conversion Disorder.

A **Somatization Disorder** involves recurrent and multiple complaints of several years' duration for which medical attention has not been effective, although individuals with the disorder tend to seek medical attention at least once a year. The disorder begins before age thirty, is rare in males, and is diagnosed in only about 1 percent of females. Patients report feeling sickly for a good part of their lives. Sometimes patients report muscle weakness, double vision, memory loss, deafness, or hallucinations. Gastrointestinal problems such as vomiting and diarrhea, painful menstrual periods with excessive bleeding, sexual indifference, and pains in the back, chest, and genitals are common. Patients are often beset by anxiety, as well as a depressed mood.

Although some countries such as India report a greater number of cases than others (Varma, Bouri, & Wig, 1981), Conversion Disorders are much rarer than most Anxiety Disorders (for a review, see M. M. Jones, 1980). A **Conversion Disorder** is a loss or alteration of physical functioning without the presence of physiological disorder, but apparently due to psychological conflict. Men and women are equally likely to develop a Conversion Disorder. People suffering from Conversion Disorders often report loss of the use of their arms, hands, or legs, loss of vision, or pain. They may develop multifaceted ailments. For example, a patient may become not only blind but also deaf, mute, or totally paralyzed. Although the patient may be unaware of the relationship, Conversion Disorders are generally thought to occur as a means of escaping or avoiding psychologically upsetting situations. Patients also sometimes receive a great deal of attention and support because of the symptoms accompanying this kind of disorder, and this reinforcement may help to maintain the disorder.

Dissociative Disorders

Dissociative Disorders and Psychogenic Amnesia used to be grouped together as hysterical neuroses. Today, psychologists recognize that the two disorders are fundamentally different. A **Dissociative Disorder** involves a sudden but temporary alteration in consciousness, identity, or memory. **Psychogenic Amnesia,** one Dissociative Disorder, is the sudden inability to recall important personal information, an inability that is too extensive to be explained by ordinary forgetfulness. Often, the amnesia is brought on by traumatic incidents

Psychologists at Work: Child Abuse

Child abuse involves the mistreatment of children, physically, emotionally, and sexually. It is estimated that more than 350,000 children are the victims of child abuse each year (National Center on Child Abuse and Neglect, 1981). Other researchers claim that the number of abused children is as high as 1.9 million. Child abuse has been implicated in the development of the Antisocial Personality Disorder (discussed next). According to Alfaro (1981), 50 percent of the families reported for abuse or neglect in New York State had at least one child who was later taken to court for delinquency or being ungovernable.

Child abuse is clearly an important psychological and social problem, but researchers have estimated that only about 5 percent of child abusers exhibit extreme symptoms of very disturbed behavior. The view of the typical child abuser as the deranged parent is an extreme exaggeration put forth by storytellers on television and in the movies (D. A. Wolfe, 1985).

Who are the child abusers? According to D. A. Wolfe (1985), abusive parents often display stress-related symptoms. Abusive parents often were abused themselves as children. Child abuse is often an attempt to gain control over a series of aversive events occurring in the environment.

In their marriages, abusive parents tend to argue a lot and disagree about many issues, which leads to debates about child-rearing practices and thus to additional family stress. Abusive parents often have unusually high expectations of their children and distorted perceptions of their behavior. The children of abusive parents often have more behavior problems than do nonabused children. For example, they are more likely to hit, kick, and grab (Lahey et al., 1984). Abusive parents are not necessarily more discipline-oriented, power-oriented, or authoritarian with their children than are nonabusing parents. However, they tend to rely on ineffective child-management techniques, including aversive control, blaming, scapegoating, threats, verbal degradations, and physical punishment. Their children, in return, often have low self-esteem, act out their fears and anger, and are often difficult to manage. In response, parents behave aggressively because they often do not know how to cope in any other way. They lack impulse control and feel helpless and frustrated. In many cases, this is how they were treated as children; they respond in kind.

Most psychologists consider child abuse as an interactive process involving parental competence, situational demands, and poor child management techniques. Prevention of child abuse is usually aimed at changing family patterns of interaction. Parents can be taught new coping skills, impulse control, and how to interact with their children in constructive rather than destructive ways. The aim of prevention is often altering children's behavior, reducing stress in the home, and especially teaching the parents effective child-management techniques, rather than aggressive and abusive ones.

---

involving threat of physical injury or death. The condition is relatively rare but is more common during wartime or a natural disaster. Recovery is usually complete.

Multiple Personality
A disorder characterized by the existence within an individual of two or more different personalities, each of which is dominant and directs the individual's behavior at distinct times.

Often associated with Psychogenic Amnesia but presenting a dramatically different kind of behavior is Multiple Personality. A diagnosis of **Multiple Personality** is appropriate when two or more distinct personalities, each of which is dominant at particular times, exist in a single person. Each personality has a unique style and its own memories and behavioral patterns. The switch from one personality to another is usually brought on by stress. The mass media and lay people often confuse Multiple Personality with schizophrenia, a much more common disorder. Each personality is usually unaware of any other, acknowledging (when active) that time has passed for which it cannot account although in some cases, one personality may eavesdrop on the other. Some people exhibit personalities of different gender. One personality may be adaptive and efficient at coping with life, whereas the other exhibits maladaptive behavior. Few cases are diagnosed before adolescence. Despite popular media accounts such as the movie *The Three Faces of Eve* and the book *Sybil,* Multiple Personality as a diagnosed disorder is *rare,* with actual recorded cases in history numbering fewer than 300. Psychologists have little data on or understanding of its causes (see Greaves, 1980) and still debate how it might best be classified (Benner and Joscelyne, 1984).

PERSONALITY DISORDERS

Learning Objective 14.6

People who are inflexible and have long-standing maladaptive ways of relating to the environment may be diagnosed as having a Personality Disorder. Often, these disorders are evident in childhood or adolescence and continue through adulthood. Individuals who exhibit Personality Disorders are easy to spot but difficult to treat. Some researchers suggest that Personality Disorders are really symptoms of a larger disorder waiting to show itself.

Personality Disorders are divided into three major types: (1) individuals whose behavior appears odd or eccentric, (2) individuals whose behavior appears fearful or anxious, and (3) individuals whose behavior appears dramatic, emotional, or erratic.

Individuals whose behavior is considered odd and eccentric include the *Paranoid Personality Disorder.* These individuals have unwarranted feelings of persecution and a mistrust of most everyone. They are hypersensitive to criticism and have a restricted range of emotional responses. Rarely seeking help for problems, they have strong fears of losing control and independence. They sometimes appear cold, humorless, and even scheming to other people. These behaviors rarely allow for a warm, close, intimate relationship with other people.

Fearful or anxious behaviors are characteristic of individuals who have a Dependent Personality Disorder. The Dependent Personality Disorder is characterized by individuals who allow other people to make all important decisions in their lives. They feel they can not function independently. To ensure that such dependency is maintained, they subordinate all of their personal needs to those of other people. Such individuals are self-effacing and try to make themselves appear pleasant and agreeable to other people. They act meek, subordinate, and affectionate to keep their protectors. When left to their own devices, however, they become anxious and unable to cope well. Battered wives often suffer from the Dependent Personality Disorder.

Antisocial Personality A disorder beginning before age fifteen and characterized by continuous and chronic behavior that violates the rights of other people through lying, theft, delinquency, and other violations of societal rules. The individual lacks feelings of guilt, cannot understand other people, behaves irresponsibly, does not fear punishment, and is often egocentric.

Dramatic emotional and erratic behaviors are characterized by the *Histrionic Personality Disorder,* in which people seek to get attention by exaggerating situations in their lives. They have stormy personal relationships and are attention-seeking, demanding, excessively emotional, and demand reassurance and praise. Closely related is the *Narcissistic Personality Disorder,* in which a person feels an extreme sense of self-importance, an expectation of special favors, a constant need for attention, a lack of caring for other people, and reaction to criticism with feelings of rage, shame, or humiliation.

Perhaps the most widely recognized personality disorder is the Antisocial Personality Disorder. Because it is common enough for most people to relate to its consequences, let us take a close look at it.

Learning Objective 14.7

A person who frequently changes jobs, does not take proper care of his or her children, has been arrested often, fails to pay bills, and is a constant liar displays behaviors described in the DSM-III-R as typical of an **Antisocial Personality Disorder**. People diagnosed as having an Antisocial Personality Disorder are relatively unsocialized adults whose behavior brings them into conflict with society. Incapable of loyalty to other people, selfish, callous, and irresponsible, they are seldom able to feel guilt or to learn from experience or punishment and may consistently blame other people for their behavior. People diagnosed as having an Antisocial Personality Disorder have deeply ingrained serious behavior problems. These individuals come into conflict with

John Hinckley, Jr., accused of an assassination attempt on President Ronald Reagan, exhibits many behavior characteristics of an anti-social personality.

society because they are unwilling to conform to and live by society's rules. They do not feel guilt or shame about not conforming; in fact, they do whatever they please. Some may brag about sexual exploits or have trouble maintaining steady employment. These individuals are characterized as smooth operators who have shallow relationships with other people (Schalling, 1978). Cleckley (1976) characterized the Antisocial Personality as lacking in social responsibility, insight, shame, and feelings for other people, yet socially engaging and even charming in a superficial way (see also V. W. Grant, 1977). Notorious individuals, often mass murders like Charles Manson, have been characterized as suffering from an Antisocial Personality Disorder.

As in so many areas of psychology, some psychologists believe that genetic and hereditary components determine the behavior of individuals diagnosed as having Antisocial Personality Disorders, others that the environment produces this behavior.

Adopted children separated at birth from antisocial parents are likely to show antisocial behavior later in life (Cadoret, 1978). This evidence is suggestive of a genetic contribution to the disorder. In addition, the brain waves of people diagnosed as having Antisocial Personality Disorders show abnormal activity. This fact has led some researchers to suggest that such individuals may have faulty brain mechanisms. One area that shows abnormal activity is the limbic system, which plays an important role in the regulation of fear-motivated behavior, including the avoidance of punishment (see Chapter 4). If the limbic system of such individuals is abnormal, their behavior may be due to some inherently faulty physiological mechanism.

It is also possible that the nervous systems of people diagnosed as having Antisocial Personality Disorders are different from those of normal people. When normal people do something wrong, they usually exhibit symptoms of anxiety such as fear, palpitations, sweating. However, if people's autonomic nervous systems function at sufficiently low levels, they will not experience the physiological symptoms of anxiety and thus will not learn to associate these symptoms with antisocial behavior. Evidence suggests that decreased autonomic arousal is present in individuals diagnosed as having Antisocial Personality Disorders (Waid, 1976).

People diagnosed as having Antisocial Personality Disorders can be made more aware of their environment (Lykken, 1957; Meyer, 1980; Schmauk, 1970). Schachter and Latané (1964) injected subjects diagnosed as having Antisocial Personality Disorders with either adrenalin (a hormone that increases autonomic nervous system activity) or a placebo. The subjects were not told what drug had been administered. Placed in a situation in which they could avoid receiving a shock, all the subjects learned to avoid the shock, but those injected with adrenalin learned more quickly. These results support the notion that such individuals are relatively anxiety free because of physiological underarousal. Schachter and Latané's work shows that such patients can learn to avoid punishment if their arousal level is raised. If such patients can be made more sensitive to their environments, they may develop greater social awareness.

Children's early experiences may significantly affect later personality development. This is true not only from a Freudian point of view, but also from a strictly behavioral standpoint. In a survey of subjects diagnosed as having Antisocial Personality Disorders, Greer (1964) found that 60 percent had lost one parent during childhood, at an earlier age than control subjects. Many other studies show that the early childhood experiences of such individuals differ significantly from those of control subjects. People diagnosed as having Antisocial Personality Disorders recall many more deviant events from their early years than do others, and their recollections generally are quite accurate.

Both Robins (1966) and Stott and Wilson (1977) found high correlations between antisocial behavior during childhood and adolescence and criminal behavior in adulthood. Some psychologists believe that child-rearing practices and unstable family situations render individuals diagnosed as having an Antisocial Personality Disorder unable to learn fear, guilt, and punishment avoidance. People diagnosed as having an Antisocial Personality Disorder seem to have learned faulty and maladaptive behaviors from their family situation, and consequently they themselves develop and display inappropriate behaviors. If the environmental viewpoint is correct, the Antisocial Personality Disorder may be a learned behavior.

SEXUAL DISORDERS

Learning Objective 14.8

Andy Marks had known for some time that his sexual desires and behaviors were unusual. Andy had told his wife about his sexual fantasies. Although she felt uncomfortable with some of the things Andy told her, his wife reasoned that as long as he relegated those ideas to his fantasy life, there would be no problem. However, when he was arrested for indecent exposure, his wife knew that Andy was acting out some of his sexual fantasies. Exhibitionism, the disorder in which a man exposes his genitals to unsuspecting members of the opposite sex, is against the law.

Few behaviors arouse more anxiety, fear, and superstition than those involving human sexuality. Many of Freud's notions about how personality develops involve sexuality. Many differences among people regarding desire for sex, problems with erectile or orgasmic dysfunction, and other types of sexual problems are temporary symptoms of some other type of problem that is not sexual in nature, such as anxiety or communication difficulty between partners.

Transvestites often make elaborate attempts to look like members of the opposite sex.

Sexual deviations ══════
Sexual practices directed toward objects rather than people, sexual encounters involving real or simulated suffering or humiliation, or sexual activity with a nonconsenting partner.

Fetishism ══════
A Sexual Disorder in which sexual arousal and gratification are brought about by objects such as shoes, underwear, or toilet articles.

Transvestic Fetishism ══
A Sexual Disorder characterized by recurrent and persistent cross-dressing for the purpose of achieving sexual excitement.

Sexual Deviations

Sexual deviations (called Paraphilias in DSM-III-R) are sexual practices directed toward objects rather than people, sexual encounters involving real or simulated suffering or humiliation, or sexual activities with nonconsenting partners. Many individuals involved in such behavior find it distasteful but are unable to involve themselves in normal sexual behavior. A sexual deviation is diagnosed as Sexual Disorder when the causes are psychological rather than physical. DSM-III-R classifies only a few disorders as true Paraphilias; however, some researchers maintain that there are many more (Money, 1984).

In **Fetishism**, sexual arousal and gratification are brought about primarily by objects, rather than by people. Instead of receiving sexual gratification with a woman, a man may have a fetish about her shoes. Instead of being aroused by a woman's sexuality, he may be aroused only by her gloves or underwear. Although Fetishism is found in both men and women, the incidence seems to be much higher in males. The disorder requires distress on the part of the individual and a minimum of six months duration.

In **Transvestic Fetishism** sometimes called Transvestism, or cross-dressing, an individual receives sexual gratification by dressing in the clothing of the opposite sex. Interference with this cross-dressing produces frustration. Transvestites consider themselves members of their own sex and are not necessarily homosexual in orientation.

Voyeurism ═══════════

A Sexual Disorder in which the preferred method of sexual gratification consists in repetitive observation of people in different states of undress or sexual activity.

Exhibitionism ═══════════

A Sexual Disorder in which the preferred method of sexual stimulation and gratification consists in repetitive acts of exposing the genitals to strangers.

Pedophilia ═══════════

A Sexual Disorder in which the preferred method of sexual stimulation and gratification consists in repetitive sexual activity with children.

Sexual Sadism ═══════════

A Sexual Disorder in which an individual inflicts physical or psychological pain on another person in order to achieve sexual excitement.

Sexual Masochism ═══════════

A Sexual Disorder in which an individual seeks physical or psychological pain, often including humiliation or being bound or beaten, in order to achieve sexual excitement.

Most normal people have a fairly wide range of sexual activities that they find gratifying. However, sexual activity that involves nonconsenting individuals is characterized as a sexual deviation. A person who practices **Voyeurism** achieves sexual satisfaction by watching other people in different states of undress or sexual activity. Most voyeurs or "peeping Toms" are men. Because voyeurs generally do no want to be seen, some researchers suggest that they enjoy the risk of discovery involved in watching other people. Voyeurism has to be exhibited for at least six months and the voyeur has to be distressed by his behaviors to be diagnosed as a voyeur.

Another unconventional sexual activity is **Exhibitionism**, in which adult males obtain sexual gratification primarily by exposing their genitals to unsuspecting observers, usually strangers. Most exhibitionists find the reactions of their victims sexually arousing. Like other sexual disorders the symptoms need to be present for at least six months and the person has to have acted on his urges or be distressed by them to be diagnosed as an exhibitionist.

Some men derive sexual satisfaction through sexual contact with children. Their disorder is called **Pedophilia**. A pedophile is a man who molests, fondles, or has sexual relations with a child. Most pedophiles are calm, quiet individuals who are well acquainted with the child; sometimes they are related to the child. Many are married and seemingly well adjusted, both sexually and socially. The personality profiles of pedophiles vary as a function of age. Younger pedophiles have little sexual experience. Older pedophiles generally suffer from loneliness, and some from schizophrenia (Regestein & Reich, 1978). One half of pedophiles were themselves sexually abused as children.

Two other major types of Paraphilias are **Sexual Sadism** and **Sexual Masochism**. A sadist achieves sexual gratification by inflicting pain on a sexual partner. A masochist achieves sexual gratification from experiencing pain inflicted by someone else. Sadists and masochists are often sexual partners; the sadist provides the pain for the masochists, and both achieve sexual satisfaction. The pain involved can be physical, mental, or emotional. Although some sadists inflict physical pain and may even mutilate their partners, most achieve sexual satisfaction through fantasies. Many normal males and females have sadomasochistic elements in their sexual relationships. Only when people's sexual gratification comes solely or principally from either sadism or masochism are they considered sexually deviant.

Causes of Sexual Disorders

Most psychologists agree that most sexual disorders are learned behaviors. For example, Freudians typically assert that problems during the Oedipal period create sexual problems later in life. Agreeing in part with Freud, most behavioral practitioners assert that early in a child's life, certain normal sex-role stereotyping goes haywire. They argue that a difficult adolescence and a poor emerging self-concept are important learning factors that may predispose an individual to psychosexual disorders. Often anger, hostility, shame, and doubt are present in people who suffer from such disorders. As adults, individuals who have had a difficult time with parents and peers may exhibit some of those problems through the sexual arena. Sexual disorders like those described in this chapter have not been studied as much as have disorders such as depression (considered next). Thus, psychologists know less than they would like

Psychologists at Work: The Violence of a Rapist

Rape is the forcible sexual assault with an unwilling partner, usually but not always a woman. It is a violent crime that has come under the critical eye of researchers who have sought to understand the motivation of the rapist.

More than 78,000 cases of rape were reported during 1983, according to the Uniform Crime Reports. Many experts assert that this figure is only one-fourth of the actual number that occur. Victims of rape can be young or old, attractive or unattractive. Victims are forced to engage in sexual intercourse and often other sexual activities as well. Unfortunately, psychologists' interest in violent behavior and victimization like rape has been sporadic, often after sensational incidents reported by the news media. Rape is not a DSM-III-R classification; rather, rape is a crime that often involves an individual who has some other disorder, such as Antisocial Personality Disorder.

Certain facts about rapists are coming into focus. Rapists tend to be young, often between fifteen and twenty-five years of age; sixty-one percent are under twenty-five years of age (Sadock, 1980). Often, they are poor, culturally disadvantaged, and uneducated. Many have willing sexual partners; indeed, half are married, although their high level of aggressiveness probably precludes a happy, stable marriage. Rapists often have some history of sexual dysfunctions, but this finding is not consistent across all studies. Rapists tend to be more responsive to violence than do other men (Quinsey et al., 1984).

According to Richard T. Rada (1983) of the University of New Mexico's school of medicine, researchers tend to agree about the following elements about rapists and the crime of rape:

1. There is no such thing as a typical rapist.
2. Rape is a violent assault that combines aggressive and sexual elements; the degree to which these two elements are combined varies among individuals.
3. Rape does not appear to be prompted by the absence of voluntary sexual partners.
4. Rape is not usually an impulsive act prompted by a spur-of-the-moment sexual or aggressive feeling; many rapes are planned, often in a meticulous manner.

According to experts, rape should be considered a crime of control, power, dominance, and brutality. Feminists object to rape's being referred to as a sexual assault because this definition obscures the violent, brutal nature of the crime and places the women in a posture often requiring her to be questioned—when *she* was the victim. According to Rada (1983), the rapist's primary motivation is to control his victim. A woman's sexual intimacy is an intensely personal act that she controls. By forcibly taking control through sex, he controls her.

Why does the rapist desire control? Rada contends that rapists have a need to be loved that is unmet by other people; instead of earning love and respect, the rapist tries to take it, brutally, by force. As Sadock (1980) has argued, rape is an act of violence and humiliation that happens to be expressed through sexual means. Probably few other social acts are viewed so negatively as rape. It is likely that the next decade will see more research into the rape act, the dynamics that leads up to rape, and especially more research into the rapist himself.

---

about biological contributions or about the families and early experiences of individuals with psychosexual disorders. Research is scanty, but most practitioners focus on behavioral treatments and on teaching people new, adaptive ways of expressing feelings, fears, and sexual urges.

PROGRESS CHECK 14.2

1. Complete each of the following sentences with one of the options provided.

Learning Objective 14.5

A. A disorder that is diagnosed before the age of thirty, is rare in males, is found in only about 1 percent of females, and is characterized by multiple physical complaints for which no medical cause can be found is called a _____ _____ Disorder.
(Hypochondriac : Somatization : Conversion)

Learning Objective 14.5

B. Psychogenic Amnesia is an example of a _____ Disorder.
(Somatoform : Dissociative)

　　C.　In Multiple Personality Disorder, the switch from one personality to another is _____.
(very unpredictable : usually brought on by stress : anxiety producing)

　　D.　In a Multiple Personality, each personality is usually _____ of the other personalities.
(aware and able to discuss the life : unaware)

　　E.　A person who has a _____ Personality Disorder gets attention by exaggerating events out of proportion.
(Paranoid : Histrionic)

　　F.　People diagnosed as having an Antisocial Personality Disorder tend to _____.
(experience extreme anxiety and guilt : be charming in a superficial way)

　　G.　One explanation for why people diagnosed as having Antisocial Personality Disorders do not learn through experience how to avoid punishment is that they have a faulty _____.
(cerebral cortex : limbic system : corpus callosum)

　　H.　By injecting _____ into subjects diagnosed as having Antisocial Personality Disorders, Schachter and Latané have shown that these people can learn to avoid punishment if their autonomic arousal is increased.
(adrenalin : dopamine : serotonin)

　　I.　In a survey of subjects diagnosed as having an Antisocial Personality Disorder, Greer found that _____ had lost one parent during early childhood.
(35 percent : 60 percent : 82 percent)

　　J.　A person who is a peeping Tom, achieving sexual satisfaction by watching other people in various states of undress or sexual activity, has a sexual deviation called _____.
(Fetishism : Voyeurism : Exhibitionism)

　　K.　Pedophilia refers to a sexual deviation in which the person achieves sexual gratification by having sexual contact with _____.
(objects : children)

　　L.　A sadist is an individual who achieves sexual gratification by _____ _____ someone else.
(inflicting pain on : experiencing pain inflicted by)

　　M.　People who cross-dress, wearing the clothes of the opposite sex because they believe themselves to be members of that sex, _____.
(have a Sexual Deviation : are transsexuals : are transvestites)

MOOD (AFFECTIVE) DISORDERS: DEPRESSION

Learning Objective **14.9**

Randy Bolland, who opened this chapter, became depressed because of a specific event—his failure on his comprehensive exams. Depression is considered by DSM-III-R to be Affective or Mood Disorder. Affective Disorders are debilitating disorders that affect emotion more than thought. They are often caused or at least initiated by an event, although for many individuals, the symptoms of Mood Disorders occur gradually.

There are two major types of Affective or Mood Disorders that each involves depression: Bipolar Disorders and Depressive Disorders. Some people still refer to Bipolar Disorders as *Manic/Depressive disorders,* but this term is outdated. The disorder is referred to as *bipolar* because patients' behavior vacillates between two extremes—from mania to depression. The Manic phase is characterized by rapid speech, inflated self-esteem, distractibility, impulsiveness, and

TABLE 14.2 : Manic and Depressive Behaviors

	Manic Behavior	Depressive Behavior
Emotional characteristics	Elated, euphoric	Gloomy, hopeless
	Very sociable, expansive	Socially withdrawn
	Impatient	Irritable, indecisive
Cognitive characteristics	Distractible	Slowness of thought
	Desire for action	Obsessive worrying about death
	Impulsive	Negative self-image
	Talkative	Delusions of guilt
	Grandiose	Difficulty concentrating
	Inflated self-esteem	
Motor characteristics	Hyperactive	Decreased motor activity
	Decreased need for sleep	Fatigue
	Sexual indiscretion	Difficulty in sleeping
	Fluctuating appetite	Decreased sex drive
		Decreased appetite

decreased need for sleep. Patients with a Bipolar Disorder are easily distracted, get angry when things do not go their way, and often seem to have boundless energy. A manic episode in these patients is sometimes followed by depression; the person becomes depressed, moody, sad, lacks energy, and feels hopeless. In between episodes of excitement and depression, patients can be relatively normal for a few days, weeks, or months; or they can rapidly vacillate between excitement and depression. Bipolar Disorders often begin in a person's late twenties. Bipolar Disorders seem to have a biological basis (Leber, Beckham, & Danker-Brown, 1985) and respond fairly well to drug treatment, especially Lithium.

The key component of Bipolar Disorders is a shift from mania or excited states to depressive states of sadness and hopelessness. People diagnosed as suffering from Depressive Disorders, especially Major Depression, show no such vacillation. (See Table 14.2). Major Depression is eight times more common than Bipolar Disorders. Whether brought on gradually or by a specific event, the symptoms of depression are often the same: sadness, a lack of energy, sometimes excessive drinking, or even use of tranquilizers. Many people feel depressed, out of sorts, and have difficulties with their spouse or employer. When such people are sad, anxious, and having personal problems, psychologists do not typically call this feeling depression. The feelings that accompany depression are much more severe. Depression or as it is more appropriately called in DSM-III-R, Major Depression, brings with it a much more serious, devastating, and all-encompassing set of problems. Because of the great frequency of Major Depression, we focus on it in the rest of this section.

The essential characteristics of **Major Depression** are a depressed, sad, hopeless mood and a loss of interest in all or almost all usual activities and pastimes. People experiencing a Major Depression show at least some impairment of social and occupational functioning, although their behavior is not necessarily overtly bizarre. Depressed individuals experience symptoms such as poor appetite, weight loss, insomnia, loss of energy, feelings of worthlessness, intense guilt feelings, inability to concentrate, difficulty sleeping, and

Major Depression ▬▬▬
A disorder characterized by loss of interest in almost all usual activities as evidenced by a sad, hopeless, or discouraged mood. Other symptoms include sleep disturbance, loss of appetite, loss of energy, and feelings of unworthiness and guilt.

Depression is characterized by extreme feelings of loneliness, hopelessness and loss of interest in everyday activity.

Learning ___14.10___
Objective

Affect ═══════════
A person's emotional
response.

sometimes even thoughts of death and suicide. They withdraw from social and physical contact with other people and may be slow in movement and speech. Every task seems to require a great effort, and few activities seem worthwhile.

Many people experience occasional stress and fatigue. Sometimes they have sleepless nights or feel that life has no real purpose. When people's **affect** or emotional response becomes so depressed or sad that a change occurs in their outlook and overt behavior, they may be suffering from depression. Often Major Depression represents an excessive or prolonged reaction to the loss of a loved one or to a failure in one's own life, such as the loss of a job or home. In the United States, about 9 to 26 percent of females and 5 to 12 percent of males have experienced a major depressive episode at some time. About 6 percent of females and 3 percent of males have experienced episodes sufficiently severe to require hospitalization.

There is little disagreement that children can become sad, but many researchers maintain that they can not become depressed in the adult sense of the word and that they do not exhibit adult depressive behaviors (Hodges & Siegel, 1985). This does not deny that children sometimes exhibit some forms of depression, but they do not generally meet the DSM-III-R criteria for it. Research on childhood depression has increased considerably in the last decade (Kazdin et al., 1985).

A major depressive episode can occur at any age although the age at which Major Depression first occurs is before age forty. Symptoms are usually rapidly apparent and last for a few weeks or months. The episode may occur once or many times. Sometimes depressive episodes are separated by years of normal functioning, followed by two or three brief episodes of depression a few weeks apart. In as many as 35 percent of cases, the depressive symptoms become chronic. Females are twice as likely as males to be diagnosed as depressed (H. B. Kaplan, 1977; Nolen-Hoeksma, 1987) and are more likely to express feelings of depression openly (Blumenthal, 1975).

Most people who exhibit symptoms of a Major Depression are able to describe their reasons for feeling sad and dejected, but they may be unable to explain why their response is so deep and so prolonged. Although their reactions may be appropriate at the time of the loss or failure, for example after a death or divorce (Menaghan & Lieberman, 1986), the continuation of the responses over an extended period leads to maladjustment and eventually prevents them from coping with life's demands.

Because so many different circumstances can bring about a depressive reaction, the extent of depression varies dramatically from individual to individual. One criterion used to distinguish among various types of depression is whether the depressed reaction stems from a single episode or is recurrent. Another is the presence or absence of **psychotic** behavior, indicating that the person is out of touch with reality. People with psychotic symptoms can no longer compare their personal view of the world with external cues to see how closely the two correspond. Psychologists say that people with psychotic symptoms are poor at reality testing. Reality testing is the person's ability to judge accurately the demands of the environment and his or her ability to deal with those demands. People with poor reality testing are unable to cope with the demands of life in rational and reasonable ways because their reasoning ability is grossly impaired. They generally need hospitalization and constant, regular therapy.

As in other disorders people who exhibit symptoms of Major Depression show a variety of behaviors. They have a gloomy outlook on life, especially slow thought processes, an extremely distorted view of current problems, and a tendency to blame themselves (Silberman, Weingartner, & Post, 1983). They may also have delusions or false beliefs that induce guilt, sin, and feelings of shame. Sometimes these distortions are consistent with their basic ideas concerning their own guilt and unworthiness. In other cases, the delusions have little apparent connection with the reasons for depression. In such circumstances, people often report delusions of persecution. Seriously disturbed patients show great disruption in thought and motor processes (Weingartner et al., 1981), a total lack of spontaneity and motivation (Cohen et al., 1982). Such patients typically report that they have no hope for themselves or the world. Nothing seems to interest them. Some feel responsible for severe world problems such as economic depression, disease, or hunger. They report strange diseases and may insist that their body is disintegrating or that their brain is being eaten from the inside out.

People who experience serious depressive episodes show extreme reactions, such as dramatic slowing of activities and loss of enthusiasm. They may sit unmoving for long periods, show no interest in the world about them, and abstain from eating and sex. Such patients report feelings of unworthiness, failure, and guilt. Many consider suicide (Pokorny, 1977). Beck reports a typical self-description:

> I am feeling depressed. I feel as though I'm dragging myself down as well as my family. I have caused my parents no end of aggravation. The best thing would be if I dug a hole and buried myself in it. If I would get rid of myself, everybody would be upset for a time but then they would get over it. They would be better off without me. (A. T. Beck, 1972, p. 81)

Not all people diagnosed as having a major depression exhibit psychotic symptoms or consider suicide. However, some people who are dramatically and profoundly depressed become totally unresponsive and must be confined to bed, fed and bathed, and even their personal hygiene attended to. Patients in

---

Psychotic
Describes a gross impairment of reality testing that interferes with an individual's ability to meet the ordinary demands of life.

this kind of psychotic depressive stupor have completely lost touch with reality. They hallucinate regularly and may believe the world is a strange place containing many strange animals. Totally confused, isolated, and withdrawn, these individuals accept the guilt for all that is wrong in the world and see themselves as total failures.

Theories of Depression

Learning
Objective 14.11

As in so many other areas of psychology, various theories have attempted to explain the nature of depression. Those that best explain and describe the nature of depression are the biological and learning approaches. Psychodynamic and humanistic approaches attempt to account for depressive behaviors, but the data convince most psychologists that depression is caused either by biological or learning factors.

Biological Theories   Evidence suggests that depression may be biologically or genetically based (Depue & Monroe, 1978; McNeal & Cimbolic, 1986). For example, neurotransmitters in the brain have received significant attention as possible causes of depression. As discussed in Chapter 4, neurotransmitters are chemicals released across the synapse when a neuron fires. One neurotransmitter—norepinephrine—seems particularly important in depression. The *norepinephrine hypothesis* states that an insufficient amount of norepinephrine at receptor sites causes depression. Research has shown that if the substance level at the site is increased, depression is alleviated (for example, Buchsbaum, Coursey, & Murphy, 1976; Buchsbaum et al., 1978). Because aversive stimuli are known to decrease norepinephrine levels, being in a stressful situation could decrease a person's level of norepinephrine and bring about depression. This idea has received some support (Turkington, 1982), although considerable disagreement exists concerning the specific chemicals and how they might work (J. M. Davis, 1977). The most recent research suggests that the norepinephrine hypothesis is not untrue, but that the biological underpinnings of depression are more complex. Depression may be caused because of many substances in the brain that have gone haywire in addition to norepinephrine levels (McNeal & Cimbolic, 1986; Thase, Frank, & Kupfer, 1985).

Most practicing psychologists know that antidepressant drugs (tricyclics) seem to help certain types of depressed patients. How these drugs work and how they affect neurotransmitters in the brain is not totally clear (Linnoila, Karoum, Rosenthal, & Potter, 1983). Brain mechanisms and neurochemical substances are difficult to investigate. Research has combined traditional treatment (such as psychotherapy) with drug treatment. In one study (DiMascio et al., 1979), severely depressed patients were given one of three treatments: psychotherapy alone, an antidepressant drug alone, or a combination of psychotherapy and drug therapy. The results were dramatic. When compared to a group of control subjects, psychotherapy and drug therapy were equally effective; both treatments reduced depressive symptoms. However, the combination of psychotherapy and drug therapy was found to help the most.

Learning Theories   In contrast to biological theorists, learning theorists argue that people who are depressed have learned depressed behaviors. A person who develops symptoms of depression may have few close relationships and get little social support from relationships that do exist. Social support in the form of family and friends often acts as a buffer to stress. Without such social supports, any stressor that occurs may have deleterious effects (Aneshensel & Stone, 1982). People with poor social skills, who never learn to express prosocial behaviors, and who are punished for the behaviors they do emit experience the world as aversive and depressing.

Peter Lewinsohn (1974) believes that depressed individuals have few positive reinforcements in their lives. Many depressed people live in nonreinforcing environments. They may be old, sickly, or unhealthy. According to Lewinsohn, once people become depressed, their depression will be maintained because other people will find them unpleasant and avoid them, thus creating a nonreinforcing environment (Lewinsohn & Talkington, 1979; Lewinsohn, Youngren, & Grosscup, 1979). Lewinsohn stresses that depressed persons often lack the social skills requisite to obtain reinforcement. Even though Lewinsohn's approach has been widely heralded as one of the best developed behavioral approaches to depression, the skills he refers to have never been precisely defined (Hammen & Krantz, 1985).

Psychiatrist Aaron Beck has proposed another influential learning theory. Beck suggests that depressed people already have negative views of themselves, the environment, and the future that cause them to magnify their errors. They compare themselves with other people, usually unfairly, and when they come up short, they see the difference as disastrous. Not only do they view themselves poorly, but they also see the human condition as universally

TABLE 14.3 : To assess the extent of a person's depression accurately, Beck (1972) developed an inventory or scale that can be administered. Shown are some of the items from the scale. People have to choose which statement best describes how they feel at the time they complete the inventory.

Feeling	Descriptive Statement
Sadness	I do not feel sad. I feel blue or sad. I am blue or sad all the time and I can't snap out of it. I am so sad or unhappy that it is quite painful. I am so sad or unhappy that I can't stand it.
Sense of failure	I do not feel like a failure. I feel I have failed more than the average person. I feel I have accomplished very little that is worthwhile or that means anything. As I look back on my life all I can see is a lot of failures. I feel I am a complete failure as a person (parent, husband, wife).
Guilt	I don't feel particularly guilty. I feel bad or unworthy a good part of the time. I feel quite guilty. I feel bad or unworthy practically all of the time now. I feel as though I am very bad or worthless.
Self-dislike	I don't feel disappointed in myself. I am disappointed in myself. I don't like myself. I am disgusted with myself. I hate myself.

Source: Adapted from A. T. Beck, 1972, pp. 333–334.

wretched and view the world as a place that defeats positive behavior. Their poor self-concept, along with negative hopes for the world, produces negative future expectations. Those negative feelings and expectations produce depression. Beck (1967, 1972, 1976) believes that depression does not cause negative feelings; instead, negative feelings and expectation *cause* depression. To assess the extent of a person's depression accurately, Beck (1972) developed an inventory of statements for people to choose among to describe their current feelings. Table 14.3 presents several items from this inventory.

Research supports Beck's assertion that depressed individuals are likely to hold negative views. People who consider themselves depressed select depressed ideas to describe the world. They are harsher on themselves than are nondepressed individuals, and they have particularly low levels of self-expectation (Space & Cromwell, 1980). Beck's theory has been influential among psychologists because it is consistent with the notion that depression stems from a lack of appropriate (positive) reinforcements in their environment and because it acknowledges both cognitive and environmental variables.

Learned helplessness
The behavior of giving up or not responding, exhibited by subjects exposed to negative consequences or punishment over which they have no control.

Another approach to depression that emphasizes learning is **learned helplessness.** As presented in Chapter 10, learned helplessness results when a person learns that rewards and punishments are not contingent on behavior. Faced with loss of control, some people may stop responding. In a version of this basic idea, Seligman (1976) incorporated a cognitive aspect based on attribution theory. Seligman suggests that people's beliefs about the cause of their successes or failures determine whether they become depressed. When they attribute the cause of their mistakes or failures to conditions in themselves, they come to regard themselves with low self-esteem (Raps et al., 1982). When they believe that eventual outcomes are unrelated to anything in their control, people develop a sense of learned helplessness. For example, a man who through his experiences believes that his efforts to manage his emotions never work, may stop trying to manage them. Eventually, such people choose not to respond to the environment because they have learned that their response makes no difference (see also Garber, Miller, & Seaman, 1979; Peterson & Seligman, 1984).

Despite slight differences, Lewinsohn's, Beck's, and Seligman's views all suggest that reinforcement—and where, how, and when it is obtained—determines the course and nature of depression. Some are more cognitive (thought-related) than others; yet all make the same basic assumption that depression is learned.

Nature and Nurture

At present, no clear-cut cause of depression has been identified. Treatment using drugs has shown that neurotransmitters are probably involved in depression, and reasonable evidence suggests that the level of neurotransmitters in the brain determines or causes depression, rather than that depression causes a lower level of neurotransmitters. At the same time, evidence for learning theories is compelling. People are depressed because they have developed negative views about the world. Often, such individuals held similar views before the onset of their depression. Reinforcements no longer have value to depressed patients, who often choose lethargy rather than responsiveness, regardless of the reinforcement (see Akiskal, 1979). Research from the field of psychoneuroimmunology (as discussed in Chapter 5) may also contribute to our understanding of how both nature and nurture contribute to the causes, and possibly the treatment, of serious disorders such as depression. Depression is a major maladjustment that affects millions of individuals and their families. As psychologists' knowledge about the relation between neurochemistry and behavior becomes more complete, the number of depressed people may decrease.

PROGRESS CHECK 14.3

1. Complete each of the following sentences with one of the options provided.

Learning Objective 14.9

A. Affective Disorders have a primary debilitating affect on _____

_____.

(emotions : thoughts)

Learning Objective 14.9

B. A person who suffers from Bipolar Disorder _____.
(vacillates between mania and depression : does not respond to drug treatment)

Learning Objective 14.10

C. _____ are more likely to be diagnosed as depressed and to express feelings of depression openly.
(Women : Men)

Learning Objective 14.10

D. The key differences between a normal experience of depression and a maladjusted one are the _____ the depression.
(events that trigger : duration and extent of)

Learning Objective 14.10

E. A person who exhibits psychotic symptoms is _____.
(depressed : bewildered by problems in life : out of touch with reality)

Learning Objective 14.10

F. Depressed people have slow thought processes, a distorted view of current problems, and a tendency to blame _____ _____.
(themselves or they may have delusions of persecution : other people)

Learning Objective 14.11

G. Although the most recent research suggests that an explanation for the causes of depression will be much more complex, one biological explanation offered suggests that stressful events decrease a person's _____ and this leads to depression.
(autonomic activity : arousal levels : norepinephrine levels)

Learning Objective 14.11

H. Lewinsohn, a learning theorist, suggests that depression occurs and is maintained by _____.
(punishment from other people : self-punishment : a lack of positive reinforcement)

Learning Objective 14.11

I. According to Beck, a cognitive learning theorist, _____.
(depression causes negative feelings : negative feelings cause depression)

Learning Objective 14.11

J. A nonresponsive behavioral pattern that develops when reinforcement and punishment are not contingent on behavior is called _____ _____ and, according to Seligman, can lead to depression.
(resistance : learned helplessness : uncommitted reaction)

SCHIZOPHRENIA

Randy Bolland's career was about to go down the drain. His depression had left him unable to cope with the pressures of medical school. His friends and relatives could tell him that another semester of study would put him over the top, but seriously depressed people like Randy are unlikely to listen to such rational ideas. Depression and its effects can be devastating. For many practitioners, however, depression seems easier to deal with than the disorder of Schizophrenia. Both physical and psychological treatments can be used to help depressed individuals—people suffering from depression often get back on their feet again. This is not always the case with Schizophrenia. The disorders share some common features, but there are distinct differences, and the disorder of Schizophrenia is generally considered more serious and devastating to a person's total functioning.

Learning Objective 14.12

Schizophrenia is truly a disabling disorder. It often begins slowly, with more symptoms developing as time passes. Consider this brief case history. Gene does not have many friends. He has trouble relating to his peers, and they have difficulty understanding him. One reason Gene is not well liked is that he is moody. Sometimes outgoing and friendly, at other times quite depressed and withdrawn, his behavior makes lasting friendships difficult. Sometimes Gene's behavior is bizarre, and he does and says strange things, almost as if he wanted to attract attention. Sometimes his conversation does not seem logical, and at times he appears lost in a dream world.

Unlike many other psychological disorders, Schizophrenia often incapacitates a person and hospitalization becomes necessary. Although Gene has not yet been hospitalized, his behavior presents many characteristics of a person diagnosed as having Schizophrenia. People with Schizophrenia display sudden changes in mood, thought, perception, and overall behavior. Those changes are often accompanied by distortions of reality and an inability to respond appropriately in thought or feeling.

The term *schizophrenia* has been used as a catchall for a number of different types of disorders. However, according to DSM-III-R, diagnosis of **Schizophrenia** requires the presence of the following features:

1. Lack of reality testing
2. Involvement of more than one area of psychological functioning
3. Deterioration in social and intellectual functioning
4. Onset of illness generally before age forty-five
5. Duration of illness of at least six months

Schizophrenia
A disorder characterized by lack of reality testing and deterioration of social and intellectual functioning, beginning before age forty-five and lasting at least six months. Individuals with this diagnosis often show serious personality disintegration with significant changes in thought, mood, perception, and behavior.

There are five types of Schizophrenia, each with different symptoms, diagnostic criteria, and causes. However, all meet the five criteria listed here.

About 1 percent of the United States population is diagnosed as having some kind of schizophrenic disorder, and almost 38 percent of the patients admitted to mental hospitals each year are diagnosed as schizophrenic (Mandersheid et al., 1986). Approximately 100,000 to 200,000 new cases of Schizophrenia are diagnosed each year; many other hundreds of thousands go untreated or undiagnosed. The diagnosis occurs more frequently among lower socioeconomic groups and nonwhites (Kramer, 1982) and more frequently among young people than among older individuals. The total cost of Schizophrenia in economic terms is at least $12 billion a year (Gunderson & Mosher, 1978). Its cost in human terms is inestimable. Curiously, European psychiatrists assign the diagnosis much less frequently then do American professionals. For example, in the United States the number of new cases each year is ten times as great as in Great Britain (after adjustment for population size) (J. K. Wing, 1978).

Essential Characteristics

Learning Objective 14.13

Patients diagnosed as having some form of Schizophrenia have problems with various aspects of behavior, particularly with attention, emotion, perception, and motor behavior. Some patients exhibit problems in all these areas; others have problems in only one area. The most common schizophrenic behaviors appear as severe disturbances in thought, perception, and emotion (affect).

Thought Disorders. One of the first signs that a person may be suffering from Schizophrenia is difficulty maintaining logical thought and coherent conversation. People with Schizophrenia show disordered thinking, and their

Many people who are seen on the streets talking to themselves and exhibiting disordered thought patterns are schizophrenic; yet often these cases go undiagnosed and untreated.

memory is often impaired (Sengel & Lovallo, 1983). The thought and conversation of people with Schizophrenia are characterized by random changes in topic and lack both meaning and order. Referring to his own thoughts, one patient reported:

> My thoughts get all jumbled up. I start thinking or talking about something but I never get there. Instead I wander off in the wrong direction and get caught up with all sorts of different things that may be connected with the things I want to say but in a way I can't explain. People listening to me get more lost than I do. (McGhie & Chapman, 1961, p. 108)

Delusion
A false belief, inconsistent with reality, held in spite of evidence to the contrary.

People with Schizophrenia often have delusions. A **delusion** is a false belief held even in the face of contrary evidence. Many schizophrenics have delusions of persecution and believe the world is a hostile place. They believe they are victims of plots and conspiracies. These delusions of persecution are often accompanied by delusions of grandeur: the patient believes he or she is a particularly important person. This importance becomes the reason for his or her persecution (see Zigler & Levine, 1983). Simetimes the patient takes on the role of an important character in history, such as General Douglas MacArthur, and deludes himself that people are conspiring to do him harm.

Perceptual Disorders. Another sign of Schizophrenia is the presence of aberrant perceptual experiences, or hallucinations. Hallucinations may be visual, tactile, or olfactory; most often they are auditory. The patient imagines hearing voices originating outside his or her head. The voices may comment on the patient's behavior; they may direct the patient to behave in certain ways. Hallucinations, probably have a biological basis and are caused by abnormal brain responses (Asaad & Shapiro, 1986).

Emotional Disorders. One of the most striking characteristics of Schizophrenia is the display of inappropriate emotional responses, or affect. For example, a patient with schizophrenia may become depressed and cry when her favorite food falls on the floor, yet the death of a close friend or relative may appear as hysterically funny. Some patients with Schizophrenia show no emotion (either appropriate or inappropriate) and seem incapable of experiencing a normal range of feeling. Their emotional range is constricted, or flat. They show blank, expressionless faces even when presented with a deliberately provocative remark or situation.

Types of Schizophrenia

Learning Objective 14.14

DSM-III-R provides explicit criteria for the diagnosis of five basic types of Schizophrenia: Disorganized, Paranoid, Catatonic, Residual, and Undifferentiated. As shown in Table 14.4, patients with Schizophrenia manifest a wide variety of symptoms. Ninety-seven percent show a lack of insight into their disorder; more than 70 percent report verbal and auditory hallucinations. More than 65 percent hear voices, are suspicious, and show a flattening of affect or emotional expression (Sartorious, Shapiro, & Jablewsky, 1974). Sometimes it is difficult to determine which category most appropriately describes a patient (Gift et al., 1980).

Disorganized Type. Possibly because of a change in diagnostic practices, the number of cases of Disorganized Type Schizophrenia has decreased

TABLE 14.4: Types and Symptoms of Schizophrenic Disorders as Described in DSM-III-R

Classification	Symptoms
Disorganized	Frequent incoherence, absence of systematized delusions, and blunted, inappropriate, or silly affect
Catatonic	Stupor in which there is a marked decrease in reactivity to environment; or an excited phase in which there is excited motor activity apparently purposeless and not influenced by external stimuli
Paranoid	Delusions and hallucinations of persecution or grandeur, and/or unfounded jealousy
Undifferentiated	Prominent delusions, hallucinations, incoherence, or grossly disorganized behavior and does not meet the criteria for any of the other types, or meets the criteria for more than one type
Residual	History of at least one previous episode of schizophrenia with prominent psychotic symptoms but has at present a clinical picture without any prominent psychotic symptoms, and there is continuing evidence of the illness such as inappropriate affect, illogical thinking, social withdrawal, or eccentric behavior

Disorganized Type
One of five major subtypes of Schizophrenia, characterized by frequent incoherence, absence of systematized delusions, and blunted, inappropriate, or silly affect.

Paranoid Type
One of five major subtypes of Schizophrenia, characterized by delusions, hallucinations of persecution and/or grandeur, and sometimes irrational jealousy.

dramatically in the twentieth century (J. R. Morrison, 1974), accounting for as few as 5 percent of diagnosed cases (Guggenheim & Babigian, 1974). The **Disorganized Type** of Schizophrenia is characterized by severely disturbed thought processes. Patients have hallucinations and delusions and are frequently incoherent. They may exhibit bizarre affect and experience periods of giggling, crying, and/or irritability for no apparent reason. Their behavior can be silly, inappropriate, or even obscene. Such patients often lack good personal hygiene. They exhibit a severe disintegration of normal personality, a loss of reality testing, and have a poor prognosis.

Paranoid Type. The Paranoid Type of Schizophrenia accounts for as many as 45 percent of diagnosed cases of Schizophrenia (Guggenheim & Babigian, 1974; Nathan, Zare, Simpson, & Andbert, 1969). **Paranoid Type** schizophrenics are among the most difficult to identify and study because their outward behavior often seems appropriate to their situation. Although Paranoid Types have bizarre delusions, hallucinations, and thought processes, their behavior is less fragmented and incoherent than that of the Disorganized Type. They often seek out other people and do not show extreme withdrawal from social interaction.

The degree of disturbance varies over time. Paranoid Type patients may be alert, intelligent, and responsive, but their delusions and hallucinations impair their ability to deal with reality (see Kendler, 1980), and their behavior is often unpredictable and sometimes hostile. Although they are able to take care of their own body functions and can get along well with other people, Paranoid Type individuals show a lack of reality testing. They have extreme delusions of persecution and, occasionally, of grandeur. They may be angry and argumentative. They may feel that certain events in the world have a particular significance to them. For example, if the president of the United States makes a

Catatonic Type

One of five major subtypes of Schizophrenia, characterized by stupor, in which the individual is mute, negative, and basically unresponsive, or by displays of excited or violent motor activity.

Catatonic Type schizophrenics sometimes show excessive activity—other times they are withdrawn, unresponsive, and inhibited.

Learning Objective — 14.15

Residual Type

One of the five major subtypes of Schizophrenia, characterized by inappropriate affect, illogical thinking, or eccentric behavior.

Undifferentiated Type

One of the five major subtypes of Schizophrenia characterized by all the essential features of Shizophrenia but do not fall into the catagories of Disorganized, Catatonic, or Paranoid Type.

speech deploring crime, a Paranoid Type patient may feel that the president is referring specifically to the patient's crimes. Patients diagnosed as Paranoid Types may see bizarre images and are likely to have auditory hallucinations. They may feel they are being chased by ghosts or intruders from another planet.

Catatonic Type.   Five percent of first admissions to mental hospitals are diagnosed as **Catatonic Type** schizophrenics (Guggenheim & Babigian, 1974). There are two subtypes: excited and withdrawn. Catatonic Type Schizophrenia is the type often portrayed in popular films because both subtypes involve extreme overt behavior. *Excited* catatonic patients show excessive activity. They may talk and shout continuously. They may engage in seemingly uninhibited, agitated, and aggressive motor activity. These episodes usually appear and disappear suddenly. *Withdrawn* catatonic patients tend to appear stuporous, mute, and negative; although they occasionally exhibit signs of the excited phase, they usually show a high degree of muscular rigidity. They are not immobile but have a decreased level of speaking, moving, and responding. Even though they may remain mute and unresponsive, such patients may be totally aware of events around them. Catatonic Type patients may use immobility and unresponsiveness to maintain control over their environment. Catatonia relieves them of the responsibility of responding to external stimuli.

Residual Type.   People who show symptoms attributable to Schizophrenia but who remain in touch with reality are characterized as **Residual Type.** Such patients show inappropriate affect, illogical thinking, or eccentric behavior and have a history of at least one previous schizophrenic episode.

Undifferentiated Type.   Some patients exhibit all the essential features of Schizophrenia—prominent delusions, hallucinations, incoherence, and grossly disorganized behavior—but do not fall into the categories of Disorganized, Catatonic, or Paranoid Type. These individuals are classified as **Undifferentiated Type.**

Causes of Schizophrenia

Schizophrenia is such a devastating disorder that understanding its causes has always been difficult. Research theories of Schizophrenia have taken markedly different positions about its origins. Biologically oriented psychologists have focused on chemicals in the brain and a person's genetic heritage. Learning theorists have argued that a person's environment and early experiences cause schizophrenia. Freudian psychologists have talked about fixations during the oral stage of development. The arguments for each approach are compelling, and data have been gathered to support the various theories.

Biological Factors.   If biological or genetic makeup were the determining factor in Schizophrenia, children of individuals diagnosed as having a Schizophrenic Disorder would also have the disorder. Researchers would be able to identify some chemical or gene present in persons with Schizophrenia and absent in the normal population.

The children and siblings of schizophrenic patients are more likely to exhibit maladjustment (Janes, Weeks, & Worland, 1983) and schizophrenic symptoms than are relatives of people in the normal population (Walker & Emory,

1983). Patients with Schizophrenia constitute about 1 percent of the United States population; yet if one parent has Schizophrenia, the probability that an offspring also will have Schizophrenia is significantly greater; various studies show results between 3 and 14 percent. If both parents have Schizophrenia, children have about a 35 percent probability of developing it (D. Rosenthal, 1970).

The probability that two individuals will show the same trait is called the **concordance rate.** Most family members do not have exactly the same genetic heritage. Only identical (monozygotic) twins have identical genes. If the basis of Schizophrenia were totally genetic, the concordance rate for Schizophrenia would be 100 percent in all cases of identical twins (for a review, see Kessler, 1980). However, this is not the case. Various studies of Schizophrenia in identical twins show concordance rates from zero to 86 percent, (Dalby, Morgan, & Lee, 1986; Gottesman & Shields, 1982).

Several researchers examined the concordance rates of identical twins reared in different adoptive homes (Heston, 1966; D. Rosenthal, 1970). A concordance rate for identical twins is greater than that for fraternal twins (or for brothers and sisters) would support the importance of genetics in Schizophrenia. The concordance rate for Schizophrenia in monozygotic (identical) twins is almost five times the rate in dizygotic (fraternal) twins. Furthermore, adoptive studies of monozygotic twins raised by nonbiological parents show a higher concordance rate than for the general population (Kety, 1979; Kety, Rosenthal, Wender, & Schulsinger, 1968; Rosenthal et al., 1968). Such results have led Kety and his co-workers (1979) to conclude that genetics must be the fundamental cause of Schizophrenia.

In addition to genetic studies, researchers have discovered that chemicals in the bloodstream may contribute to the development of Schizophrenia. Theories based on those studies generally argue that too much or too little of some type of brain substance, or the presence or absence of a particular type of chemical in the brain, occurs in cases of Schizophrenia. Several studies have supported the importance of the neurotransmitter dopamine. Dopamine pathways are considered one of the main sites of biochemical disturbance in the brain (Bowers, 1982; Kety, 1979). Drugs called *phenothiazines* appear to block receptor sites in the dopamine pathways. When patients with Schizophrenia take phenothiazines, many of their disturbed thought processes and hallucinations disappear. Conversely, drugs that stimulate the dopamine system (such as amphetamines) aggravate existing Schizophrenic Disorders. Although much of this evidence is controversial, it does suggest that dopamine may play an important role in Schizophrenia (Meltzer & Stahl, 1976; Snyder, 1974).

Evidence for the biological causes of Schizophrenia has come from a wide variety of sources. One relatively new hypothesis, called the *viral hypothesis,* states that schizophrenic symptoms may be produced by a unique virus acting on a genetic predisposition to Schizophrenia; according to this theory, people diagnosed as having Schizophrenia have contracted a virus, either before birth or at some time during their life (Crow et al., 1979; Kessler, 1980).

Research into the biological and genetic bases of Schizophrenia continues on all fronts. One interesting example is the use of dialysis. Physicians Herbert Wagemaker and Robert Cade (1977) used the medical procedure of dialysis to remove different chemicals from the blood of patients diagnosed as Schizophrenic. They have speculated that the cause of Schizophrenia might be a buildup of a specific substance in a patient's bloodstream—perhaps a virus.

Concordance rate
The percentage of occasions when two groups or individuals show the same trait.

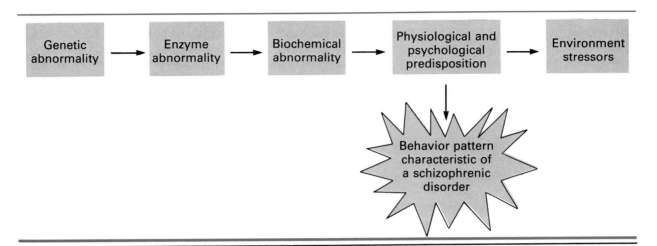

FIGURE 14.1   According to the biological view of schizophrenia, the environment triggers behaviors in people who are predisposed to it. Thus, for people who opt for the combined view of nature and nurture, genetic abnormalities lead to situations in which environmental stressors trigger the behavioral pattern of schizophrenia.

Not all research has supported Wagemaker and Cade's results, and some researchers feel the evidence is very weak (for example, Schulz et al., 1981; Wagemaker, Rogers, & Cade, 1984), but the idea has intrigued researchers.

Much evidence suggests the presence of some kind of biological determinant or predisposition to Schizophrenia (Bowers, 1982; Farone & Tsuang, 1985). People born with that predisposition have a greater probability of developing Schizophrenia at some point in life than do other people (Kety, 1979; Stone, 1980). Studies of brain dysfunction are examining the possible role of biological factors in Schizophrenia (Seidman, 1983). Initial results suggest that brain impairment is present in 20 percent of people diagnosed as Schizophrenic (see Figure 14.1 and Table 14.5).

Environmental Factors. Some psychologists believe that a person's interactions with the environment determine whether Schizophrenia will develop. Freudian psychologists suggest that early childhood relationships determine whether a person will become fixated at the oral stage and develop a disorder such as Schizophrenia. Such a person has not yet developed an ego and is still making judgments based on the id's pleasure principle. Lacking the

TABLE 14.5 Likelihood of Recovery from Schizophrenia

	Percentage Recovered	Percentage Improved	Percentage Unimproved
DSM-III-R Categories			
Disorganized Type	9	36	55
Paranoid Type	16	48	36
Catatonic Type	28	44	28
Alternative Dimensions			
Acute	39	57	4
Chronic	18	38	44

Source: Stephens, 1978, p. 38.

ego, which uses the reality principle in making judgments, the individual will seek immediate gratification and thus be unable to deal effectively with reality.

Freud's view of Schizophrenia is consistent with clinical observation. Schizophrenic patients are withdrawn and have few close social contacts. In addition, much of their language is self-centered. Both behaviors are evidence of egocentrism and self-centeredness, precisely those characteristics Freud attributed to the functioning of the id. Freud argued that a person who has successfully passed through the oral stage and has developed a strong ego is more likely to suffer from some other disorder than a Schizophrenic Disorder.

Behaviorists assert that faulty reinforcement and extinction schedules cause schizophrenia. Behavioral accounts rely on traditional learning principles such as those discussed in Chapter 2. This approach argues that reinforcement and extinction procedures, as well as social learning processes, can account for many of the behavior patterns of schizophrenic patients. Imagine a child brought up in a family with considerable marital discord, where the father is an alcoholic and neither parent can show much caring or affection for each other or for anyone else. Such a child, receiving no reinforcement for interest in events, people, and objects in the outside world, may become withdrawn and may begin to exhibit schizophrenic-like behavior. Other people may reinforce such behavior by catering to the child's inattention.

Theodore Lidz (1973) has suggested that the families of persons diagnosed as schizophrenic may show marital schism or marital skew. *Marital schism* is characterized by continuing overt conflict between spouses, with each undermining the worth of the other to their children. Competition for the loyalty of the children is often present. In *marital skew,* one parent shows abnormal (even schizophrenic-like) behavior that the other parent accepts without question. Lidz argues that children who grow up in homes with marital schism or skew adopt the family's faulty view of the world and relationships and thus are likely to expect reinforcement for abnormal behaviors. Growing up in such an emotionally fragmented environment may predispose individuals to emotional disorder and eventual Schizophrenia (Walker et al., 1983).

Even in families in which marital schism or marital skew is absent, parents sometimes confuse their children. In play, they may hold up a toy and say, "No, you may not have this," while at the same time smiling and giving other nonverbal assurances that the child may have the toy. A normally adjusted child understands that his parent is teasing. However, not all children understand this and not all situations are so clearly cued. Some parents chronically place their children in situations that offer two competing messages. A situation in which an individual is given two competing messages (take the toy or don't take the toy) is called a **double bind.** Double bind situations usually occur between individuals with a strong emotional attachment, such as parents and family members (Mishler & Waxler, 1968). Games such as this, if played consistently, may shape an environment of confusion conducive to the development of Schizophrenia (Reilly & Muzekari, 1979).

Both psychoanalytic and behavioral theories suggest that a person's relationship to the environment can bring about Schizophrenia. However, neither approach seems capable of fully accounting for schizophrenic behavior. It has been noted that patients with Schizophrenia have trouble concentrating and focusing their attention. Psychologists who favor an environmental view believe that a person who stops attending to appropriate cues may begin to act strangely and to develop a pattern of behavior that will eventually be diagnosed

Double bind ═══════
A situation in which an individual is given two different and inconsistent messages.

as schizophrenic (Nuechterlein, 1977; Shakow, 1977). Learning theory in particular suggests that people diagnosed as having a Schizophrenic Disorder are likely to develop and maintain that disorder because of faulty reinforcement patterns. A person who receives a great deal of attention for behaviors that other people see as bizarre is likely to continue those behaviors. Other reinforcement theories suggest that bizarre behavior and thoughts are themselves reinforcing because they allow the person to escape from acute anxiety and an overactive autonomic nervous system.

It is also possible that children and adults develop Schizophrenia because their home environments are not conducive to normal emotional growth. People who develop Schizophrenia tend to come from families in which there is considerable conflict. The parents of such patients are generally contentious, often alcoholics, and themselves have insecure emotional relationships.

Nature and Nurture Many variables determine whether an individual will develop Schizophrenia. Some people, either because of family environment, genetic history, or brain chemistry, are more vulnerable than others to a Schizophrenic Disorder. The more vulnerable the individual, the less necessary an environmental stress or other disorder (such as anxiety) is to initiate an episode of Schizophrenia (Zubin & Spring, 1977). Although the causes of Schizophrenia are still undetermined, research suggests:

1. A connection exists between genetics and Schizophrenia, although genetics alone cannot account for the development of Schizophrenia.
2. Specific types of chemical substances in the brain are associated with Schizophrenia.
3. Environmental factors (such as the presence of marital schism, marital skew, and double bind) contribute to the development of Schizophrenia. Among these factors, early childhood relationships may be especially important.
4. The most likely cause of Schizophrenia is a biological predisposition in the individual, aggravated by a climate of emotional immaturity, lack of communication, and emotional instability.

PROGRESS CHECK 14.4

1. Match each of the following types of Schizophrenic Disorder with the appropriate description.

Disorganized Type   Residual Type   Paranoid Type
Undifferentiated Type   Catatonic Type

Learning Objective 14.14

A. _____ Individuals in this category are among the most difficult to identify because they enjoy social interaction and may appear alert, intelligent, and responsive. However, they are psychotic and sometimes hostile; they experience bizarre visual and auditory hallucinations; and they have delusions of persecution and grandeur.

Learning Objective 14.14

B. _____ Individuals in this category are not exhibiting psychotic symptoms at the time of diagnosis. Although they remain in touch with reality, they do exhibit inappropriate affect, illogical thinking, or eccentric behavior and have a history of at least one previous schizophrenic episode in which psychotic symptoms were apparent.

Learning Objective 14.14   C. _____ Individuals in this category exhibit a severe disintegration of normal personality. They are psychotic; lack good personal hygiene; and are incoherent, exhibiting severely disturbed thoughts, delusions, hallucinations, and bizarre affect.

Learning Objective 14.14   D. _____ Individuals in this category maintain control over their environment by being withdrawn, remaining unresponsive and immobile for long periods of time; or by being excited, exhibiting seemingly uninhibited, agitated, and aggressive behaviors.

Learning Objective 14.14   E. _____ Individuals in this category exhibit all the essential features of a Schizophrenic Disorder but do not fall into any of the other categories.

2. Complete each of the following sentences with one of the options provided.

Learning Objective 14.12   A. In order for a diagnosis of Schizophrenia to be correctly assigned, the patient must show _____.
(a lack of reality testing : symptoms before the age of sixteen)

Learning Objective 14.13   B. Hearing voices or seeing things that are not being perceived by normal people is called a _____.
(delusion : hallucination)

Learning Objective 14.13   C. A schizophrenic who exhibits no emotion and seems to be incapable of experiencing a normal range of feelings is said to be exhibiting _____ affect.
(flat : inappropriate : ambivalent)

Learning Objective 14.14   D. Of those people who are classified as having Schizophrenia, nearly 45 percent are diagnosed as the _____ Type.
(Paranoid : Catatonic : Residual)

Learning Objective 14.15   E. If both parents have Schizophrenia, the probability of offspring developing the disorder is about _____.
(3 percent : 14 percent : 35 percent)

Learning Objective 14.15   F. Genetic research concerning the causes of Schizophrenia has shown that the concordance rate for identical twins is _____ than that for fraternal twins.
(no different : three times lower : five times higher)

Learning Objective 14.15   G. Evidence suggests that too much of the neurotransmitter _____ plays an influential role in the development of Schizophrenia.
(acetylcholine : dopamine : phenothiazine)

Learning Objective 14.15   H. A relatively new hypothesis suggests that schizophrenic symptoms may be produced by _____ acting on a genetic predisposition to Schizophrenia.
(chemical food additives : a virus : environmental stressors)

Learning Objective 14.15   I. According to Freud, Schizophrenia would be more likely to occur in a person who had a fixation in the _____ stage of development.
(oral : anal : phallic)

Learning Objective 14.15   J. A family situation in which parents undercut one another and compete for the loyalty of the children, creating an environment conducive for the development of Schizophrenia, is called a marital _____.
(schism : skew)

Learning Objective 14.15   K. When a parent gives a child two competing messages simultaneously, the child is put in a _____ situation, which can contribute to the development of Schizophrenia.
(dual expectation : double bind : variable-extinction)

Learning Objective 14.15   L.   A learning theorist might suggest that the bizarre thoughts and behaviors of a schizophrenic continue because they _____.
                                 (allow the person to escape from anxiety ⦂ are entertaining)

Learning Objective 14.15   M.   The most likely cause of Schizophrenia is a _____ that is aggravated by a climate of emotional immaturity, lack of communication, and emotional instability.
                                 (poor home environment ⦂ biological predisposition)

Keeping Pace with Chapter 14

Applying Principles

14.1   Identify the type of disorder illustrated in each of the following situations.

| Attention-deficit Hyperactivity Disorder | Personality Disorder (Histrionic) | Mood or Affective Disorder |
| Somatization Disorder | Schizophrenia | Antisocial Personality Disorder |

_____   A.   Cliff's behavior is psychotic, and he has lived in a psychiatric state hospital for seven years. He does not realize that there is anything unusual about his behavior, he sometimes hears voices, his emotional responses are frequently inappropriate, and his thought is illogical. For example, after hearing on television that the police were looking for a murder suspect, Cliff, who did not in any way resemble the description of the suspect, began attaching pieces of paper to his clothing with paper clips. Strange whisper-like voices told him that the police were after him, but he could disguise himself by wearing paper. When he had eye contact with someone in the hospital, Cliff either giggled or screamed in rage.

_____   B.   Derrick is in touch with reality although if you knew him well, you might wonder how this could be true. Derrick is a compulsive liar. He charms people into friendships by telling them about his large savings account and his rodeo trophies as well as a number of sad stories about how he has been framed by the law and fallen victim to self-serving people. After winning a friendship, Derrick's stories continue. He uses them to obtain loans from his new friend, promising to pay his debt back the next day. However, he always has a new story and money never comes. Eventually, Derrick's new acquaintance realizes that he has been lying all along, that he sees his behavior as normal and feels no guilt. Derrick cannot keep a job, has never had a real friend, and has taken advantage of dozens of people.

_____   C.   Jeremy has his parents and his first-grade teacher at the end of their wits. He talks incessantly and interrupts constantly. He fidgets with all kinds of small objects and is constantly moving about. He does not seem to know how to sit still. Jeremy does not pay attention when people talk to him; he will not even sit still and watch a cartoon. At school, he is disruptive to the class. He talks out, leaves his desk, and darts around the classroom. Jeremy has impulsively destroyed other children's personal possessions on several occasions. He once bent the lid on another child's lunch box and another time he tore up a classmate's artwork. Jeremy regrets his bad behavior and does not know why he does such things.

_____   D.   Lois is twenty-six-years old and experiences anxiety and depression most of the time. She has visited several physicians a number of times in the past year because after eating she experiences severe abdominal pains and vomiting. Lois has undergone numerous tests, but none of the physicians have been able to detect a physiological cause for her problem. Recently, her problem has been diagnosed as having a psychological origin.

E. Daryl's disorder comes and goes. Sometimes he goes for several years of normal functioning and then suddenly his symptoms become apparent, last a few weeks, subside, and then recur. Daryl's symptoms include an extreme loss of energy and interest, a sense of hopelessness and self-worth, sleep difficulties, a loss of appetite, withdrawal from people, and self-blame.

F. Melody lost her job as a secretary because she had created so many problems throughout the office. Little things seemed to upset her immensely, and when she became upset she took up everyone's time complaining. One afternoon, Melody's boss asked her to do a rush typing job on a short but important report for a meeting. Melody immediately complained to him. She then complained about the job to four other secretaries. She sought and demanded pity from other secretaries who were trying to work. Because Melody had spent so much time complaining about a relatively simple task, she was unable to finish it before the meeting. She was fired. Unless Melody gets professional help for her maladjusted behavior, she probably will always have trouble keeping a job or maintaining stable personal relationships.

Self-Test

Before proceeding to the Self-Test, REVIEW the Learning Objectives listed at the chapter opening and RECITE from memory everything you can remember in support of them. Then, take this Self-Test as if it were to be graded by your teacher. Use the Learning Objective numbers in the Answer Section as a reference to restudy the corresponding text pages and Progress Checks for any incorrectly answered questions.

1. Which of the following statements is *not* true of a serious behavior disorder? Serious behavior disorders

   A. generally have a complex origin.
   B. cause mild disruptions in a person's ability to cope with normal, day-to-day living.
   C. are frequently difficult to treat.
   D. generally require the attention of a mental health practitioner.

2. Attention-deficit Hyperactivity Disorder is characterized by

   A. breaking rules, truancy, and running away from home.
   B. callous and manipulative behaviors.
   C. little or no desire for affection or personal contact with other people.
   D. hyperactivity and is sometimes called hyperkinetic syndrome.

3. A child diagnosed as having a Conduct Disorder

   A. may be characterized as aggressive or nonaggressive, socialized or undersocialized.
   B. is likely to have come from a home that provided harsh, inconsistent discipline.
   C. is unlikely to experience guilt, remorse, or concern about the well-being of other people.
   D. all of the above

4. _____ is an example of a Pervasive Developmental Disorder.

   A. An Attention-deficit Hyperactivity Disorder
   B. A Conduct Disorder
   C. Autism
   D. Bulima

5. Anorexia Nervosa is typically found in

   A. women over age twenty-five.
   B. adolescent females from well-educated families.
   C. young women who have a history of physical ailments.
   D. men or women who have unsuccessfully tried to diet on a number of occasions.

6. Conversion Disorders are thought to occur because the individual

   A. can no longer cope with personal failure.
   B. can find no other way to escape or avoid a painful situation.
   C. is reinforced for bizarre behaviors.
   D. is unable to accommodate a rash of incoming stimuli.

7. Which of the following statements usually is *not* true of the personalities in a Multiple Personality Disorder? They

   A. confuse and fragment an individual's thoughts by simultaneously urging specific and opposing behaviors.
   B. sometimes "listen in" on the others.
   C. can exhibit different genders even though they all belong to the same person.
   D. each have a unique style, memories, and behavior patterns.

8. A person who has unwarranted feelings of persecution and mistrust and a restricted range of emotional response and who is hypersensitive to criticism and unlikely to seek help for problems would be classified as having a

   A. Paranoid Personality Disorder.
   B. Dependent Personality Disorder.
   C. Histrionic Personality Disorder.
   D. Narcissistic Personality Disorder.

9. Which of the following symptoms does *not* seem to contribute to the development of an Antisocial Personality?

   A. a faulty limbic system
   B. decreased autonomic arousal
   C. a slowing of the central nervous system
   D. unstable and/or abusive family environments during childhood.

10. A diagnosis of Transvestism implies that the individual

   A. achieves sexual gratification through cross-dressing.
   B. has a homosexual or lesbian orientation.
   C. feels trapped in the body of the wrong sex.
   D. has a Gender Identity Disorder.

11. A person who experiences sexual arousal solely or principally from objects rather than from another person

   A. is a Voyeur.
   B. is an Exhibitionist.
   C. is a Pedophile.
   D. has a fetish.

12. During the manic phase of Bipolar Disorder, the person

   A. shows few signs of the disorder and behaves relatively normally.
   B. is moody and sad, lacks energy, and feels hopeless.
   C. has rapid speech and an inflated sense of self-esteem and is distractible and impulsive.
   D. is deeply depressed.

13. People who exhibit symptoms of a Major Depression

   A. are usually unable to provide reasons for why they feel depressed.
   B. may need to be hospitalized.

C. almost always blame their loved ones for their problems.

D. are usually too depressed to consider suicide.

14. The most effective treatment for a Major Depression seems to be

    A. time itself.
    B. psychotherapy.
    C. antidepressant drugs.
    D. a combination of psychotherapy and drug therapy.

15. Based on the learning theories concerning the causes of Major Depression discussed in this book, which of the following reasons was *not* offered as an explanation? Depressed people

    A. have few close relationships, leaving them without a common buffer to stress.
    B. have negative views of themselves, the environment, and the future.
    C. do not get enough physical exercise.
    D. feel they have no control over the consequences of their behavior.

16. For a person to be diagnosed as having a Schizophrenic Disorder, the symptoms must

    A. be present for at least one month.
    B. be psychotic.
    C. affect only one area of psychological functioning.
    D. involve a flattening of affect.

17. A delusion is

    A. a false belief and is inconsistent with reality.
    B. a perceptual malfunction that causes a person to see things or hear voices of people who are not present.
    C. an incoherent and random pattern of thinking.
    D. an experience of feeling important followed by the feeling of being the target of a conspiracy.

18. _____ Type schizophrenics are among the most difficult to identify because their outward behavior frequently seems appropriate to their situation.

    A. Disorganized
    B. Paranoid
    C. Catatonic
    D. Undifferentiated

19. Wagemaker and Cade have shown that _____ can be an effective treatment because it decreases substances in the blood that seem to contribute to schizophrenic behavior.

    A. vitamin therapy
    B. injections of phenothiazine
    C. relaxation therapy
    D. dialysis

20. In a marital skew relationship,

    A. parents compete for a child's loyalty.
    B. one parent shows abnormal behaviors and the other parent accepts them without question.
    C. teasing games involving inconsistent and different messages leave a child confused.
    D. a love-hate atmosphere is apparent.

Psychotherapy

15

Learning Objectives

When you have mastered the material in this chapter, you will be able to:

1. Identify some of the ways that emotional and behavioral disorders are treated and define psychotherapy, insight therapy, and behavior therapy. (p. 588)

2. Discuss some variables that affect the outcome of psychotherapy and explain what is meant by a placebo effect. (p. 589)

3. Comment on the effectiveness of psychotherapy, why its effectiveness presents research difficulties, and how a psychotherapist and client can determine if progress is being made. (p. 590)

4. Give two basic assumptions about and the primary goal of insight therapies. (p. 591)

5. Explain the connection that many clinical psychologists have with Freudian theory and state some of the drawbacks of psychoanalysis. (p. 592)

6. Discuss the goals of psychoanalysis, some specific techniques a psychoanalyst uses, and two patient responses that commonly occur during the process. (p. 592)

7. Distinguish between ego-analysis and traditional psychoanalysis. (p. 594)

8. State the basic assumptions about people that led to the development of client-centered therapy and discuss the goals, techniques, and therapeutic attitudes associated with this type of therapy. (p. 594)

9. Describe the therapeutic goals and techniques of Gestalt therapy. (p. 596)

10. Describe some basic assumptions and goals of behavior therapy and discuss the views that insight therapists and behavior therapists have about symptom substitution. (p. 599)

11. List the basic three-step procedure and the four common techniques used in behavior therapy and explain when psychologists use a blend of therapeutic techniques. (p. 601)

12. Explain how positive reinforcement and token economies are used in instrumental conditioning to establish desired behaviors. (p. 601)

13. Explain how extinction, punishment, and time-out are used in instrumental conditioning to decrease undesired behaviors. (p. 604)

14. Describe two approaches to counterconditioning: systematic desensitization and aversive counterconditioning; and give some examples of the types of behaviors successfully treated with these approaches. (p. 604)

15. Explain how modeling is used as a therapeutic technique. (p. 607)

16. State the major goal of cognitive restructuring therapy and describe the approaches used by Ellis, Beck, and Meichenbaum. (p. 608)

17. Describe some ways psychologists use hypnosis and meditation as parts of psychotherapy. (p. 610)

18. Describe group therapy and explain why it is an important therapeutic technique. (p. 613)

19. Describe the basic approach to traditional group therapy and discuss how this type of therapy helps an individual group member. (p. 614)

20. State the basic goals of encounter group therapy. (p. 615)

21. Identify the goals of family therapy and discuss some techniques commonly used to improve family interactions. (p. 615)

22. Discuss the community psychology approach to mental health, explain the purpose of neighborhood clinics, and identify some unique populations on which community psychologists focus. (p. 617)

23. Describe the role played by paraprofessionals, discuss some services provided by crisis intervention centers, and explain why community psychologists are considered action-oriented and change-oriented. (p. 618)

BEFORE YOU READ ON, take time to **SURVEY** the chapter, form an idea of what is to be learned (from margin Learning Objective numbers), and set goals for your study time. Then, ask yourself **QUESTIONS** about the material as you **READ,** seeking help for any sections you do not understand.

At fifty-seven years of age, Tom Gredler was proud to say he was a self-made man. He was also proud to say that pulling oneself up by one's own bootstraps was the way to solve personal problems. But Tom Gredler's bootstraps had worn thin, his usual coping mechanisms were failing, and he was facing a crisis. Tom had been retired for six years; he had planned to make the most of his retirement, but he found that his free time was driving him into small bouts of depression. The plant at which he had made paper products had been his life. He had worked so hard for so many years that he had never developed any hobbies or outside activities. Now, six years into his retirement, he was bored, anxious for a challenge, and having anxiety attacks.

Tom Gredler had never heard of an anxiety attack. But the panic he felt, his fast heart beat, increased blood pressure, and the lump in his throat were classic symptoms of an acute anxiety attack. The first time he had an attack, he took a cold shower and lay down. The second time, he took a drink of bourbon. The third time, the attack occurred while he was driving, and he almost hit a truck. Tom went to his family doctor for help—he wondered if he was having a heart attack. His physician quickly recognized the symptoms and referred Tom to a clinical psychologist. It took Tom two additional attacks, one in the middle of the night, before he called the clinician.

Tom's therapist was about his age. He had seen many individuals who were facing similar crises in their retirement. His first task was to help Tom identify his problem. It took four sessions before Tom realized that he was feeling inadequate. He realized that no one relied on him any longer and that he missed the action of the plant. He missed the validation that his daily work gave to his life. He was stressed, and he had not realized that his stress occurred

: through a lack of work. The therapist tried to help Tom recognize his fears and
: to gain a realistic idea of what he could and could not expect from retirement,
: his friends, and his family.

TOM GREDLER WAS NOT UNUSUAL; many retirees experience feelings of
stress during a period in their life when they are supposed to be reaping the
benefits of years of hard work. Retirement for some people is a safe haven, a
time to catch up and enjoy. For other people, however, retirement can be a
time of crisis, of distress, of looking back and realizing mistakes as well as
successes. During retirement, many individuals ask themselves if their current
situation is or their past life has been meaningful.

Periodic questioning and self-doubt are normal. Many people use such
periods to identify what is important to them and to get organized before going
on to meet other challenges. Sometimes, however, self-doubt is overwhelming
and leads to anxiety, unhappiness, and maladjustment. In such cases, many
people make the adaptive response of seeking professional help. Tom chose
psychotherapy, although many types of treatment are available that do not
involve psychotherapy. Severely depressed individuals may need antidepressants or, in extreme cases, electroconvulsive shock therapy. People diagnosed
as having a Schizophrenic Disorder may need antipsychotic drugs. People
whose disorders are less severe may be involved in treatments that include
manipulations of their diet or physical exercise such as jogging. Psychologists
do not rule out such alternative forms of treatment. In fact, in many situations
such programs are the preferred method of treatment. However, psychotherapy is the approach most psychologists use in treating emotional disorders.
Psychotherapy is the treatment of maladjustments by psychological means. Its
goals are to help people cope better with life and achieve more emotionally
satisfying life-styles. Psychotherapy can help individuals like Tom adapt to new
and challenging situations as their lives continually change.

There are two general types of psychological treatment: insight therapy and
behavior therapy. **Insight therapy** tries to help patients understand the motivations underlying their behavior. Insight therapists assume that maladjustment
and abnormal behavior occur when people do not understand themselves
adequately. In contrast, **behavior therapy,** sometimes called behavior modification, is based on the assumption that most behaviors, whether normal or
abnormal, are learned. Behavior therapists try to change maladjusted or abnormal behaviors by using learning principles. The specific techniques used in
any psychotherapy vary with the therapist's view of how personality and abnormal behavior develop. In addition to various psychotherapies, this chapter discusses the factors involved in the choice of an appropriate psychotherapist—
one who is best suited to an individual's particular problem—and some of the
necessary conditions for effective therapy.

INGREDIENTS OF EFFECTIVE PSYCHOTHERAPY

Many individuals like Tom who seek psychotherapy wonder if this type of intervention will really help them. Some people question whether talking therapies

Learning Objective 15.1

Psychotherapy
The treatment of maladjustment by psychological means.

Insight therapy
A therapy that attempts to discover relationships between unconscious motivations and current behavior. Insight therapy assumes that abnormal behavior results from individuals' failure to understand their unconscious motivations and needs. Once people understand their motivations, behavior should change.

Behavior therapy
A therapy based on the application of learning principles to human behavior. Synonymous with behavior modification, behavior therapy focuses on changing overt behaviors rather than on understanding subjective feelings, unconscious processes, or motivations.

Learning Objective 15.2

If therapy is to be effective, the client must feel comfortable in expressing personal thoughts and feelings.

can really make a difference. The answer is simple: therapy is effective—but not all therapists, clients, and therapies are the same. Many factors can affect the outcome of psychotherapy. Among the most important are the therapist's gender, personality, level of experience, and empathy (see, for example, Gurman & Razin, 1977). No matter what type of therapy is involved, some ingredients must be present in both the therapist and the client for therapeutic change to occur. *First,* a good therapist communicates to the client interest, understanding, respect, tact, maturity, and ability to help. *Second,* a good therapist uses suggestion, encouragement, interpretation, example, and (perhaps) rewards to help the client change or rethink his or her situation. *Third,* the client must be willing to make some changes in his or her life-style and ideas; behavioral change does not occur just because a person wants to be happy. A therapist who is knowledgeable, accepting, and objective will facilitate behavior change, but the client is the one who makes the changes (Arieti, 1980; Garfield, 1973; Strupp, 1973).

Other variables, such as the client's social class, age, education, therapeutic expectations, and level of anxiety, are also important (see, for example, Berzins, Bednar, & Severy, 1975; Luborsky et al., 1980). Proper motivation is also important; it is difficult to treat or help a reluctant client. Helping a client to become motivated to change is often the first focus of therapy (W. R. Miller, 1985). Therapists need to be sensitive to all of these variables. For example, because women today experience unique life stresses, therapy must be nonsexist and sensitive to the psychology of women (Hare-Mustin, 1983). Similarly, therapy must address the special obstacles facing a client from a racial or other minority if other problems are to be resolved (Jones & Gray, 1983).

Often, people imply that many clients could have achieved relief from their symptoms without psychotherapy. This view involves a factor common to both insight and behavior therapies—the placebo effect. A **placebo effect** is a change in behavior that occurs as a result of an individual's expectation of change, rather than as a result of any specific treatment. Physicians have found that people prescribed harmless sugar pills and told the pills will help them

Placebo effect

A nonspecific therapeutic change that occurs as a result of a person's expectations of change rather than as a direct result of any specific treatment.

sometimes experience relief from symptoms. In much the same way, patients in psychotherapy may show relief from many symptoms simply because they have entered therapy and now expect change. Placebo effects in psychotherapy are likely to be transient; any long-lasting therapeutic effects are more likely due to the client's and therapist's efforts during therapy. Researchers are especially aware of potential placebo effects (Parloff, 1986).

Learning
Objective 15.3

There have been many challenges to the effectiveness of psychotherapy. Most research, however, indicates that psychotherapy is extremely effective. One of the most important research studies, by Smith and Glass (1977), used sophisticated statistical techniques to analyze volumes of data describing the outcome of different therapies (Smith, Glass, & Miller, 1980). Research analyzing the overall effect of psychotherapy in a wide variety of situations has also found positive effects (Nicholson & Berman, 1983; Shapiro & Shapiro, 1982, 1983). However, effectiveness varies with the type of disorder being treated (Shapiro & Shapiro, 1982). For example, psychotherapy has a high success rate for specific phobias, but it is less successful for Schizophrenic Disorders; long-term group therapy has been shown to be more effective than short-term individual therapy in some disorders (Piper, Debbane, Bienvenu, & Garant, 1984); and behavior therapy is usually the most effective approach with children (Casey & Berman, 1985).

Many researchers contend that most psychotherapies are equivalent; that is, regardless of the approach a therapist uses, the results are often the same. Not all researchers agree, however, (Stiles, Shapiro, & Elliott, 1986). Noted psychologist Alan Kazdin (1986) has asserted that research on the effects of psychotherapy is exceedingly difficult to conduct and interpret. He maintains that such research is often done with ideal conditions, using narrow approaches that do not replicate real-life therapeutic situations. For example, research is often done using clients solicited through newspaper advertisements (Krupnick, Shea, & Elkin, 1986). Are such studies generalizable to regular client populations (Forsyth & Strong, 1986)? Kazdin does not claim that such research should not be done, but rather that its narrow focus must be carefully evaluated and that new research methodologies need to be developed. To answer such question as "Which therapy is best?" may be fruitless—rather, a question such as "Which therapy will help which clients, with which problems, with which type therapist?" may be a more carefully phrased and better question. Not all clients, therapists, treatments, and amounts of time in therapy are equivalent. For these reasons, therapy research needs to address both theory and practice (Howard, Kopta, Krause, & Orlinsky, 1986; Morrow-Braddley & Elliott, 1986). Psychotherapy is effective, but the research done to investigate it often is not as thorough as practitioners would like. New psychotherapy research strategies are under development (Gendlin, 1986). As more research studies are completed, we will see a clearer picture of how certain approaches are best used to treat certain disorders with particular types of clients.

On the practical side, how does a therapist or client know that progress is being made in therapy? According to researchers Mahrer and Nadler (1986), there are eleven signs of good moments and good progress in therapy. They suggest a "good moment" and good progress is happening when:

1. The client is providing personally revealing and significant material.
2. The client is exploring the meaning of feelings and occurrences.
3. The client is exploring material avoided earlier in therapy.

4. The client is expressing significant insight into personal behavior.
5. The client's method of communicating is active, alive, and energetic.
6. There is a valued client-therapist working relationship.
7. Clients feel free to express strong feelings toward the therapist—either positive or negative.
8. The client is expressing strong feelings outside of therapy.
9. The client moves toward a different set of personality characteristics.
10. The client is showing improved functioning outside of therapy.
11. The client indicates a general state of well-being, good feelings, and positive attitudes.

PROGRESS CHECK   15.1

1. Complete each of the following sentences with one of the options provided.

Learning Objective 15.1

A. Behavior therapy is sometimes called _____.
(insight therapy : client-centered therapy : behavior modification)

Learning Objective 15.1

B. The specific therapeutic techniques used by a psychotherapist depend on his or her view of _____.
(how personality and abnormal behaviors develop : why the client entered therapy)

Learning Objective 15.2

C. Psychotherapy is effective when the _____.
(therapist tells the client how to change : client makes changes)

Learning Objective 15.2

D. Placebo effects occur in _____ therapy.
(insight : behavior : insight and behavior)

Learning Objective 15.2

E. Placebo effects are usually _____ changes in behavior.
(short-term : long-lasting)

Learning Objective 15.3

F. Although much research indicates that psychotherapy is effective and although most psychologists agree, more research is needed to determine _____
_____.

(specific information about what therapy is effective with what client : if it really is effective)

Learning Objective 15.3

G. One signal to therapist and client that therapy is successfully progressing is seen when the client _____.
(explores previously avoided material : lets the therapist do most of the talking)

INSIGHT THERAPY

Learning Objective __15.4__

When people go through changes in their lives, they sometimes alter the ways they normally behave. Some people become withdrawn, others become depressed, others seek out new relationships. Tom Gredler, who opened this chapter, had anxiety attacks. Tom sought the help of a therapist, and in doing so, took the first step in trying to understand his feelings. If Tom saw an insight therapist, he would probably spend a great deal of time exploring early relationships and feelings toward significant people in his life. Through such verbal explorations, Tom might become aware of important conflicts in his life and also of his true motivations.

The two basic assumptions of insight therapy are that becoming aware of one's motivations helps a person change and become more adaptive, and that unresolved conflicts, of which the patient remains unaware (and is therefore unable to deal with), are the causes of maladjustment. The goal of insight therapy is the treatment of the causes of abnormal behavior rather than the actual behaviors themselves. Insight therapies try to help individuals view life from a different perspective so they can choose more adaptive life-styles. This section discusses three representative insight therapies.

Psychoanalysis

Learning Objective 15.5

Psychoanalysis
A lengthy insight therapy developed by Freud that aims at uncovering conflicting unconscious impulses through special techniques that include free association, dream analysis, and transference.

Classical Freudian **psychoanalysis** focuses on helping a patient uncover the unconscious motivations that have led to psychological conflict and maladaptive behavior. Psychoanalysis is practiced by therapists specifically trained in its theory and practice. Most clinical psychologists, even those who are insight-oriented, are not psychoanalysts. However, many therapists use a therapy loosely connected to or rooted in Freudian theory. Psychologists say that such therapies are psychodynamically based.

Psychoanalysis is not suitable for everyone. Because of the difficult problems addressed in psychoanalysis, a patient must be highly motivated and articulate and able to grasp the complicated and subtle relationships explored. Many people who seek therapy are not sufficiently personally motivated, or financially able to undertake psychoanalysis. Traditional psychoanalysis involves meeting with the therapist for one hour five days a week for approximately five years; thus, a typical psychoanalysis might easily cost $100,000. Many people understandably are not prepared to invest the time, money, and energy required to complete a psychoanalysis.

Learning Objective 15.6

Goals of Therapy.   According to Freudian theory, conflicts among unconscious thoughts and processes produce maladjusted behavior. The result of an imbalance among the id, ego, and superego, these conflicts are seldom directly accessible to the individual (see Chapter 12). Many individuals who seek psychotherapy are not happy with their behavior but are unable to change. The goal of psychoanalysis is to help patients understand the unconscious motivations that keep them from changing. Only when patients become aware of the unconscious motivations that direct their behavior can they begin realistically and freely to choose behaviors that will enable them to lead more fulfilling lives (for a review, see Bellak, 1983; McGlashan & Miller, 1982). Because psychoanalysis is based on the development of a unique relationship between the therapist and patient, compatibility is critical; patient and therapist usually decide within the first few sessions if they feel comfortable working with one another.

Techniques.   Psychoanalysis uses several techniques designed to help the patient and therapist bring to light and examine the many conflicting demands of the patient's personality. Most of these techniques are specific to psychoanalysis. For example, a patient in traditional psychoanalysis lies on a couch, and the therapist sits out of view. This arrangement allows a patient to be more relaxed and feel less threatened by the presence of the therapist. Similarly, because Freud believed that current behaviors are the result of unconscious motivations that may have their basis in early childhood experiences or trauma, many techniques used in psychoanalysis involve the exploration of early experiences. Contemporary followers of Freud are somewhat less rigid in their use of the Freudian techniques. For example, psychoanalysts today more often use a face-to-face orientation than the couch. Other techniques discussed next are also often updated to meet both the analyst's and patient's needs.

In traditional Freudian psychoanalysis, the patient lies on a couch with the therapist sitting out of view.

Free association ═══════
A psychoanalytic technique in which a person reports to the therapist his or her thoughts and feelings as they occur, regardless of how illogical their order or content may appear.

Dream analysis ═══════
A psychoanalytic technique in which a patient's dreams are interpreted, used to gain insight into the individual's unconscious motivations.

Two major techniques used in psychoanalysis are free association and dream analysis. In **free association,** the patient is asked to report whatever comes to mind, regardless of how trivial or meaningless it might seem, regardless of how agreeable or disagreeable it might feel to disclose the thought. The purposes of free association are to help the patient learn to recognize connections and patterns among his or her thoughts and to allow the unconscious to express itself uncensored. Although patients may tend to censor thoughts, memories, or images that they feel are shameful, embarrassing, or difficult to talk about, an individual who is working hard at psychoanalysis will try not to withhold any information.

In **dream analysis,** a patient is asked to describe his or her dreams in detail to the therapist. The therapist may even encourage the patient to dream. Freud believed that dreams represent the unconscious trying to express itself consciously. Because dreams provide access to material in the unconscious, the goal of dream analysis is to discover, with the help of the therapist, the meaning of the patient's dreams and thereby to disclose his or her unconscious desires and motivations.

Dream analysis is often a part of psychoanalysis but is rarely used in nondirective, client-centered therapy.

Dream analysis — interpretation

Client-centered — nondirective

Both free association and dream analysis involve interpretation by the therapist. The analyst's beliefs may or may not be shared with the patient. An analyst tries to discern common threads in a patient's behavior and thoughts. For example, if a patient becomes jittery every time he speaks about women, the therapist may speculate that the patient's nervousness results from early difficulties with women, perhaps with his mother. As a result, the therapist may encourage the patient to explore his attitudes and feelings about women, and about his mother in particular.

Two other concepts central to psychoanalysis are resistance and transference. **Resistance** is a patient's unwillingness to cooperate with the therapist, sometimes to the point of becoming belligerent. Analysts usually interpret this behavior to mean that the patient wishes to avoid discussing a particular subject or that an especially difficult stage in therapy is being approached. To minimize resistance, therapists try to be accepting of their patient's behavior. When a therapist does not judge but merely listens, the patient is more likely to explain and describe his or her feelings thoroughly. The patient also learns to be more accepting of those feelings.

In **transference,** patients transfer feelings from earlier relationships to the therapist. By permitting transference, the therapist gives the patient an opportunity to understand those feelings better and can guide or direct the individual in the exploration of repressed or difficult material. The examination of thoughts or feelings previously considered unacceptable (and therefore often repressed) helps the patient understand and identify the underlying conflicts that direct his or her behavior.

Ego-analysts.   A group of psychoanalysts referred to as **ego-analysts** or ego-psychologists have modified some of Freud's basic ideas about psychoanalysis. Like Freud, ego-analysts assume that psychoanalysis is the appropriate method for treating patients with emotional problems. However, unlike Freud, they assume that people have voluntary control over when, whether, and in what way their biological urges will be expressed. Ego-analysts have adopted a therapy aimed at helping patients develop stronger control of the ego, the part of personality that operates on the reality principle and tries to control behavior by responding realistically to the demands of the environment. Traditional psychoanalysts focus primarily on unconscious material in the id and superego and only later try to increase the patient's ego control.

Effectiveness.   Because psychoanalysis is so costly and time-consuming, there is understandable concern about its effectiveness. The few studies that have made appropriate comparisons show that psychoanalysis can be as effective as other therapies (Luborsky & Spence, 1978) but is no more effective than other types of therapy (Fisher & Greenberg, 1977).

Client-Centered Therapy

Client-centered therapy, developed by Carl Rogers, is also an insight therapy, but unlike psychoanalysis it assumes that people have a considerable amount of choice, control, and free will in determining their behavior (Ford & Urban, 1963; Rogers, 1951, 1959, 1961). Freud saw human beings as inherently selfish and hedonistic, and problem behaviors as the result of conflicting impulses. Rogers, on the other hand, sees human beings as basically good, competent,

---

Resistance
In psychoanalysis, an unwillingness to cooperate by which a patient signals his or her reluctance to provide the therapist with information or to help the therapist understand or interpret a situation.

Transference
A psychoanalytic procedure in which a therapist becomes the object of a patient's emotional attitudes about an important person in his or her life, such as a parent.

Learning Objective 15.7

Ego-analysis
A psychoanalytic approach to therapy that assumes that the ego has greater control over behavior than Freud suggested and thus is more concerned with reality testing and control over the environment than with unconscious motivations and processes.

Learning Objective 15.8

Client-centered therapy
An insight therapy developed by Carl Rogers that seeks to help people evaluate the world and themselves from their own perspective by providing a nondirective environment and unconditional positive regard for the client.

and social beings who are moving forward and growing. For Rogerian therapists, problem behaviors occur when the environment prevents an individual from developing and expressing his or her innate potential. The following assumptions have helped shape Rogers's approach to treatment:

1. People are innately good and are effective in dealing with their environment.
2. Behavior is purposeful and goal-directed.
3. Healthy people are aware of all their behavior; they choose their behavior patterns.
4. A client's behavior can be understood only from his or her own point of view. Even if a client has misconstrued events in the world, the therapist must understand how the client sees those events.
5. Effective therapy occurs only when a client modifies his or her behavior, not when the therapist manipulates it.

Goals of Therapy. As noted in Chapter 12 Rogers conceives of personality as structured around the self. He believes that people have an innate tendency to actualize themselves and their potential. Throughout life, each person moves toward his or her ideal self, maturing into a fulfilled individual by the process of self-actualization. The understanding of self is also central to Rogerian therapy. The goal of Rogerian therapy is to help people make these changes—to release an already existing capacity in a potentially competent individual. According to Rogers, the client asks the therapist to help in the process of self-actualization and the formation of a strong self-concept. A Rogerian therapist does not provide a cure. Instead, the therapist helps the client gain a realistic perspective (a sense of self) from which to view the world.

Techniques. To help the client discover and actualize an as yet undiscovered self, Rogers's client-centered therapy is nondirective. In **nondirective therapy** the therapist does not direct the client, but instead facilitates the client's search for growth. The client learns to evaluate the world from his or her own vantage point, with little interpretation by the therapist. The therapist considers the client and his or her emotional health from the client's point of view. Even the use of the word *client* rather than *patient* is critical in Rogers's approach to therapy. In psychoanalysis, therapists direct patients' "cures" and help them understand their behavior. In Rogerian therapy, the therapist is not an omniscient source of authority.

One basic tenet of client-centered therapy is that the therapist must be a warm, accepting person who projects positive feelings toward the client. To counteract a client's negative experiences with people who may have been unaccepting and thus have taught the client that he or she is bad or unlikable, client-centered therapists try to show unconditional respect and positive regard. They try to communicate their acceptance and recognition of the full range of the client's emotions, and they encourage the client to discuss those feelings, whatever the client may say or do. This *empathic understanding* is an important part of the therapeutic relationship. The therapist accepts the client as is, with good and bad points, and with a respect for the client's worth as an individual.

In client-centered therapy, individuals learn to reevaluate the world by using a new frame of reference—themselves. In Rogerian therapy particularly, clients must learn to clarify and adopt their own point of view in order to feel worthwhile and fulfilled. Although client-centered therapists are nondirective,

Nondirective therapy ▬
A form of therapy in which the client determines the direction of therapy while the therapist remains permissive, almost passive, and totally accepts the client's feelings and behavior.

they are nevertheless highly trained. When they identify a faulty set of behaviors or attitudes, they can guide the client simply by asking the right questions or responding with an exclamation such as "Oh" or "Ah, hum." Even a small movement, such as a nod or gesture of the hand, can help the client stay on the right track.

In Rogerian therapy, the therapist and client face each other, generally sitting in chairs on either side of a desk. A concentrated work atmosphere rather than a relaxed atmosphere is maintained, and the client directs the conversation. Initially, the client tends to express attitudes and ideas adopted from other people. Thus, a woman who feels pressured to succeed might say, "I should get top grades in my courses," She implies: "because my parents count on my success." As therapy progresses and the client experiences the empathic understanding of the therapist, the client usually begins to use her own ideas when evaluating herself (Rogers, 1951). As a result, she begins to talk about herself in more positive ways and tries to behave as she wants to, rather than as she thinks other people want her to. She may now make a statement such as "I should make good grades in my courses only if they mean something to me." This statement reflects a new, more positive, more accepting attitude about herself. As the client feels better about herself, she will eventually suggest to the therapist that she knows how to deal with the world and may be ready to leave therapy.

Gestalt Therapy

Learning   15.9
Objective

Gestalt therapy ━━━━━
An insight therapy founded by Perls that emphasizes the importance of a person's being aware of his or her current feelings and situation.

Gestalt therapy differs significantly from both psychoanalysis and client-centered therapy. It moves away from traditional insight therapies like psychoanalysis by focusing on insight into current feelings and behaviors. It assumes that human beings are responsible for themselves and their lives and that individuals need to focus not on the past but on the present.

Fredrick S. Perls (1893–1970) was the founder and principal proponent of Gestalt therapy. A physician and psychoanalyst trained in Europe, he came to the United States but was generally treated as an outcast by the psychoanalytic community. Instead of stressing the "why" of past behavior, like Freudians and Rogerians, Perls stressed the "how" and the "what" of the present. Perls assumed that the best way to help patients come to terms with anxiety and other unpleasant feelings was to focus on the patient's current understanding and awareness of the world rather than on past situations and experiences.

Goals of Therapy.   Gestalt therapists believe that people who are not fully aware of events around them feel weak and divided, fraught with tension, and consumed by fears and anxiety that cloud their perceptions of reality. Only when individuals are aware of the here and now can they become sensitive to previous tensions and repressions that have made their behavior maladaptive. Once they have become aware of their current feelings and accepted themselves, patients can understand earlier behaviors and plan future appropriate behaviors. Thus, the goal of Gestalt therapy is to expand the patient's awareness of the here and now of current attitudes and feelings, so that natural adaptive functioning can resume.

From a Gestalt view, the healthy person is in touch with his or her feelings and reality. When a person has "unfinished business", or unresolved conflicts, these feelings must be dealt with (Perls would have called these conflicts "in-

Psychologist Fritz Perls (1893–1970) developed the Gestalt model of therapy.

complete Gestalts"). Thus, therapy for Gestalt psychologists focuses on reinstating and returning a person to his or her whole self.

Techniques. Gestalt therapy does not concentrate on uncovering past causes for current behaviors. It examines current feelings and behaviors of which a client may be unaware. Gestalt therapy should be considered an experiential therapy designed to help clients develop themselves fully so they can have more complete emotional responses to current situations. The therapist usually asks a client to concentrate on current feelings about a difficult past experience. The underlying assumption is that feelings expressed in the present can be understood and dealt with more easily than can remembered responses and events. Thus, a Gestalt therapist may ask a patient to relive a situation and discuss it as if it were happening in the present.

Many Gestalt techniques are designed to help patients become more alert to significant sensations in themselves and about their surroundings. One technique is to have patients change the way they talk about the world, to talk about feelings or emotions as if those feelings belonged to another person. Another technique is to ask patients to behave in a manner opposite to the way they feel. For example, a man who feels hostile or aggressive toward his boss might be asked to behave as if his relationship to his employer were warm and affectionate. The point of having patients use different types of language and deal with situations in different ways is to help them understand their true feelings and thus to enlarge their understanding of the world. Previously internalized anxiety is experienced in the present and channeled into more prosocial and productive behaviors.

The goals of therapy are to help people to resolve old conflicts and to enable them to resolve conflicts in the future. Therapy does not fix people; rather, it helps them make themselves whole and enables them to continue to live adaptive lives in the future. (Table 15.1 summarizes the goals and techniques of the three insight therapies just discussed.)

TABLE 15.1 Summary of Insight Therapies

Type of Therapy	Goal	Techniques
Psychoanalysis	To discover conflicts and repressed instinctual urges; to show how instinctual urges control current behavior	A directive therapy in which the analyst takes an active role in interpreting the patients' dreams and free associations.
Client-centered therapy	To help people gain perspective to adapt and self-actualize and fulfill their potential as individuals	A nondirective therapy in which the client analyzes his or her own behavior; the therapeutic environment is totally accepting, with the therapist providing unconditional positive regard.
Gestalt therapy	To expand awareness of the here and now to resume natural functioning	An electic therapy in which the client is asked to see the world from a different perspective and is encouraged to focus on current situations rather than past ones.

PROGRESS CHECK   15.2

1. Complete each of the following sentences with one of the options provided.

Learning Objective 15.4

A. Most insight therapists focus treatment on _____.
(unconscious and unresolved conflicts : teaching adaptive behaviors)

Learning Objective 15.5

B. Because pyschoanalysis involves understanding complicated and subtle relationships among thoughts, unresolved conflicts, and interactions with the therapist, a person who seeks this type of treatment must be _____ _____.
(greatly in need of help : highly motivated and articulate)

Learning Objective 15.6

C. Psychoanalysis is based on _____.
(the identification of life goals : a unique patient-therapist relationship)

Learning Objective 15.6

D. One goal of free association is to help the patient _____.
(relax : make connections among thoughts : become assertive)

Learning Objective 15.6

E. Freud believed that dreams occur when unconscious thought tries to _____ _____ conscious thought.
(understand : change : express itself in)

Learning Objective 15.6

F. A psychoanalyst tries to _____ in a patient's behavior and thoughts.
(find the good : detect common threads)

Learning Objective 15.6

G. Resistance can be minimized if the therapist _____ the patient's unwillingness to cooperate.
(makes interpretations concerning : accepts : ignores)

Learning Objective 15.6

H. Transference allows the _____ feelings.
(therapist to accept the patient's : patient to work through repressed)

Learning Objective 15.7

I. Ego-analysts differ from traditional psychoanalysts in that they focus on the part of personality that operates on _____.
(unconscious material : the pleasure principle : the reality principle)

Learning Objective 15.8

J. Client-centered therapy is based on the idea that problem behaviors are the result of _____.
(an inability to express innate potential : conflicting impulses)

Learning Objective 15.8

K. A primary goal of client-centered therapy is to help the client achieve an understanding of _____.
(the here-and-now : self : unconscious motives)

Learning Objective 15.8

L. Client-centered therapists use _____ to facilitate the client's search for growth.
(a nondirective approach : interpretation)

Learning Objective 15.8

M. An important part of client-centered therapy involves the therapist's ability to _____ the client's feelings and behaviors.
(direct the cure for : have an empathetic understanding of : change)

Learning Objective 15.9

N. In Gestalt therapy, the patient is asked to focus on _____ situations and problems.
(the relativity of : a hierarchy of : current)

Learning Objective 15.9

O. Perls used the phrase _____ to describe unresolved conflicts.
(hogwash : distracting issues : incomplete Gestalts)

Learning Objective 15.9

P. Gestalt therapy is considered _____ insight therapy.
(a nondirective : an experiential : an analytical)

BEHAVIOR THERAPY

Learning Objective 15.10

Some people do not want to discuss early childhood experiences, explore unconscious motivations, or seek the resolution of inner conflicts. Like Tom Gredler, they may just want to get on with their career or family life. Sometimes therapists agree that the problem that brings an individual to insight therapy does not warrant such an exploration. Behavior therapy is often the alternative.

But there are other reasons for behavior therapy. Had Tom sought a behavior therapist because of his anxiety, the therapist might have taught him how to deal with or reduce his anxiety. Exploration of inner conflicts and motivation might be held to a minimum or be nonexistent. Alternatively, the therapist would focus on teaching Tom more adaptive behaviors and on helping him unlearn old maladaptive ones that brought about anxiety.

Behavior therapy, or behavior modification as it is sometimes called, involves the systematic application of learning principles to help people replace maladaptive behaviors with new ones. Behavior therapists are not interested in discovering the origins of a behavior, only in altering it. Thus, the goal of therapy for a person who has a nervous twitch is to eliminate it. Because the focus of treatment is current behavior, even if the therapist does not reach a firm conclusion about the causes of a problem behavior, the absence of such information seldom affects the method of treatment. Behavior therapists treat people by having them first unlearn old, faulty behaviors and then learn new ones (Kazdin, 1978a). Insight is not considered necessary for behavior change, and concepts such as unconscious motivation are not used.

Behavior therapists assume that people display abnormal behavior because of problems in adjusting to their situation; if they are taught new ways of coping, the maladjustment will disappear.

Behavior therapists do not always focus on behavior problems that originally brought the client to therapy. Sometimes, in examining a client's problems, a therapist becomes aware that the client's current problem is caused by some other situation. In such a case, the therapist may decide to focus on altering the causal situation. For example, the therapist may discover that a client's marriage is faltering because of excessive arguments with his spouse, and that the arguments usually follow a period of heavy drinking. She may further discover that the drinking is brought about by a hard day at work, aggravated by the client's excessively high expectations for his own performance (Goldfried & Davison, 1976). In this situation, the therapist would probably focus on helping the client develop realistic standards that will ease the originating cause of his problem—the tension felt at work. The therapist might focus on helping the client develop realistic standards consistent with a client's known capabilities, past performance, and realistic future performance.

Clients in behavior therapy are not encouraged to take on the values of the therapist or to interpret past events to find their meaning. Although a behavior therapist may uncover a chain of events leading to a specific behavior, that discovery will not prompt a close examination of the client's early experiences. In fact, many behavior therapists consider the unnecessary exploration of a client's internal experiences an invasion of privacy.

Behavior therapy
Sometimes called *behavior modification,* a therapy based on the application of learning principles to human behavior and aimed at changing overt behaviors rather than subjective feelings, unconscious processes, or motivations.

Psychologists at Work: Helping the Compulsive Gambler

What is the most difficult case for a psychologist? Different psychologists will answer this question differently, depending on their orientation and training. However, there are some behavior maladjustments on which psychotherapists tend to agree; for example, most would say that the maladjustment of compulsive gambling is always difficult to treat. DSM-III-R calls it Pathological gambling.

If you spend most of your time, money, emotions, and thought on gambling, you would probably be considered a compulsive or pathological gambler. As a compulsive gambler, your problem might go unrecognized for many years. If you tried to get help, you might discover that professionals who knew about your disorder are difficult to find and that specialized treatment facilities are almost nonexistent. Compulsive gambling is an ingrained compulsion that has been practiced, rewarded, is legal, and difficult to change. A compulsive gambler is driven by overwhelming uncontrollable impulses to gamble (Peck, 1986).

According to expert Cecil Peck (1986), about 2 or 3 million individuals in the United States are involved in compulsive financial risk-taking behaviors—gambling. Compulsive gambling has devastating effects. Compulsive gamblers lose time from work, their families see less of them, and lying characterizes their relationships with their spouses. Such individuals borrow heavily and get into debt on a grand scale. Creditors then apply pressure to pay. After being bailed out by family and friends, compulsive gamblers often become even more consumed with gambling. They sometimes become involved with seeking illegal loans or writing bad checks. The high anxiety that often accompanies compulsive gambling takes its toll at gambling itself—sharp gamblers ultimately loose their skill, not to mention their assets.

For most people, gambling is not tied up with their self-worth; life has other rewards, and they have rarely had a big win. According to Peck (1986), the opposite is true for the compulsive gambler. For compulsive gamblers, the act of placing a bet has become a compulsion, an overwhelming urge which they cannot resist. The compulsive gambler lives with the illusion that with the next bet, the "big win" will come. When his world comes crashing down about him instead, the compulsive gambler often feels hopeless and is physically and psychologically exhausted. His marriage is often in shambles, his job is all but lost. He is distrusted by former friends. His options are running out—he faces imprisonment, running away or suicide; or, he can seek psychological help.

When compulsive gamblers enter therapy, most psychologists see a combination of factors that require a unique mix of therapeutic techniques. Treating compulsive gamblers is therefore often a multistage process (Peck, 1986). First, the high anxiety and down-and-out hopelessness of a gambler must be considered. Practical problems must be solved: legal counseling is often necessary, interpersonal relationships with spouse must be renewed, huge debts must be resolved. Gamblers Anonymous as a therapeutic help is considered a must. For especially difficult cases, short-term intense structured environments are often considered. This sometimes means a controlled, live-in arrangement offering support and a structured place in which gambling is not allowed and activities are monitored.

The second stage of therapy often involves a mix of psychotherapy and also family therapy to help rebuild old relationships. Psychotherapy may involve an examination of early life relationships as well as behavior modification for the gambler and his or her traumatized family. Learning new ways for living, new behaviors to replace gambling, and finding self-worth are often primary goals.

The compulsive, pathological gambler presents a difficult case for a psychologist. A therapist has to take a very caring approach, and has to be willing to use a variety of approaches and techniques. The therapist has to be knowledgeable in family therapy, learning theory, reinforcement methods, and traditional therapy techniques. In many ways, treating the compulsive gambler requires a practitioner to be flexible, resourceful, and clever.

Goals of Therapy

The goal of behavior modification is to influence current behavior by using basic learning principles to restructure an individual's responses. Using an educational rather than a medical model, a behavior therapist teaches skills rather than treating an illness. Behavior therapists assume that people's behavior is influenced by changes in their environment, in the way they respond to that environment, and in the way they interact with other people (Stolz, Wienckowski, & Brown, 1975). Of course, when people enter a therapeutic relationship, many aspects of their behavior may change, not just those specifically treated. Thus, a person being treated for a nervous tic might find that not only had the frequency of tics decreased, but also that he could now engage more easily in discussions about emotional topics and perform better on the job. Furthermore, behaviorists argue, once a person's behavior has changed, many attitudes, fears, and intrapsychic conflicts may become easier to modify.

Most insight therapists assume that if only the overt behavior is treated, symptom substitution may occur. **Symptom substitution** is the appearance of one behavior to replace another that has been eliminated by treatment. Thus, insight therapists argue that if a therapist eliminates a nervous tic without examining the underlying causes of that tic, the client may express his disorder by developing some other symptom, such as a speech impediment. In contrast, behaviorists predict no symptom substitution.

Several studies support the behaviorists' view: if treatment involves proper use of behavioral principles, symptom substitution does not occur (for example, Kazdin, 1975). The data show unquestionably that behavior therapy is at least as effective as insight therapy and, in some cases, more effective (Miller & Berman, 1983; Shapiro & Shapiro, 1982, 1983).

Basic Techniques

Learning Objective 15.11

All the variables that are important in insight therapy are also important in behavior therapy; the atmosphere of both types of session might seem the same to a client or an observer. However, the techniques used generally differ greatly.

Behavior therapy usually involves three general procedures: (1) identification of the problem behavior and its frequency; (2) the treatment itself, perhaps including reeducation, communication training, or some type of counterconditioning; and (3) subsequent observation to assess whether there has been a lasting behavior change. If the client still exhibits the new behavior, the therapist knows that treatment has been effective.

Behavior therapy uses four general techniques to help people change their behavior: instrumental conditioning, counterconditioning, modeling, and cognitive restructuring. Before describing the techniques, let us emphasize that therapy often involves the combination of one, two, three, or more techniques. The more complicated a disorder, the more likely a practitioner is to integrate, combine, and use a mix of therapeutic approaches (see for example, Chambless, Goldstein, Gallagher, & Bright, 1986).

A therapist may use several different behavioral techniques or a combination of insight and behavioral techniques. A good psychotherapist will use whatever combination of techniques is necessary to help the client efficiently and effectively. When a therapist combines approaches, this is using an *eclectic* approach.

Instrumental (Operant) Conditioning

Learning Objective 15.12

Instrumental conditioning involves the delivery of positive reinforcers or rewards for correct responses. As explained in Chapter 2, a reinforcer is any event that increases the probability that a previous response will recur. Positive reinforcement can be used to develop and maintain useful behaviors. In addition, the removal of positive reinforcement can be used to decrease the frequency of antisocial behavior. Positive reinforcement techniques have been used in such places as classrooms, mental institutions, prisons, and restaurants. They have

Symptom substitution

The appearance of one symptom to replace another that has been eliminated.

Rewarding inmates with leisure activities has proven effective in maintaining good behavior in prisons.

been used to help people who want to lose weight, stop smoking, or make new friends.

Operant conditioning procedures are used in a variety of settings to bring about a wide range of desirable behaviors, including increased reading speed, improved classroom behaviors, proper toilet use, and the maintenance of personal hygiene. One of their most effective uses has been with children who are antisocial, slow learners, or in some way maladjusted (Drabman, 1976; Kazdin, 1975). Other researchers have found them to be effective with patients in mental hospitals. For example, Ayllon and Haughton (1964) instructed staff members to reinforce hospitalized patients for psychotic verbalizations during one period and for neutral verbalizations during another. As expected, the frequency of psychotic verbalizations increased when reinforced and decreased when not reinforced (see Figure 15.1). Regardless of the desired behaviors, the

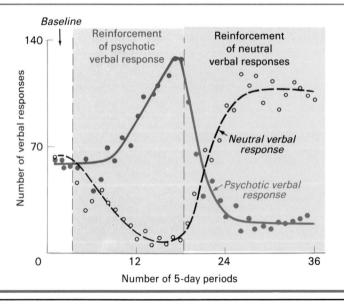

FIGURE 15.1 : A study by Ayllon and Haughton (1964) found that reinforcement affected the frequency of psychotic and neutral verbal behavior in hospitalized patients.

approach is generally the same: because a behavior that is reinforced tends to recur, therapists reinforce only desirable behaviors.

Token Economy.   In a **token economy,** participants receive tokens when they engage in appropriate behavior. Later, they exchange the tokens for other positively reinforcing items or activities, such as candy, new clothes, or games. A token is used in a token economy in much the same way that money is used in general society. The more tokens people earn, the more reinforcing events they can receive in exchange.

Token economies are used to modify behavior in social settings, usually with groups of people. Their purpose is to strengthen behaviors compatible with social norms. For example, a patient in a hospital might receive tokens for cleaning tables, helping in the hospital laundry, and/or maintaining personal hygiene and appearance. The number of tokens delivered for each behavior is determined by the level of difficulty of the behavior or job and how long the person has performed it. Thus, a patient might receive three tokens for brushing her teeth, but forty for engaging in prosocial helping behaviors. At the end of a week, the patient could redeem the tokens for special toilet articles, reading and writing materials, or special passes to walk around the hospital grounds.

Ayllon and Azrin (1965) monitored the performance of a group of patients over a forty-five-day period. They found that when tokens (reinforcement) were contingent on performance, the group of patients produced about forty-six hours of work per day; when tokens were not delivered, performance dropped to about ten hours per day (see Figure 15.2).

One advantage of a token economy is that it can be administered by a paraprofessional, such as a ward nurse, or by anyone else; partents, aides, correctional officers, and friends all can be involved in a token economy (Ayllon

Token economy
An instrumental conditioning procedure in which tokens are given to the patient to reinforce socially acceptable behavior. The tokens are later exchanged for desirable items or privileges.

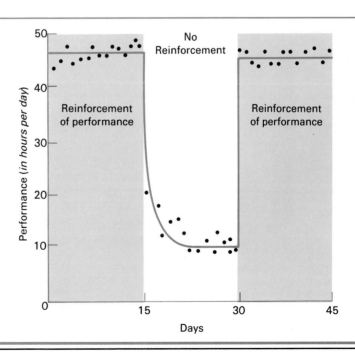

FIGURE 15.2 : Ayllon and Azrin found that tokens increased the number of hours worked by patients.

& Azrin, 1965, 1968; Stolz, Wienckowski, & Brown, 1975). Not only do token economies help patients learn and maintain specific task behaviors such as housekeeping and self-care (Gershone, Erickson, Mitchell, & Paulson, 1977), but the expression of such behaviors is also often accompanied by a decrease in depression and hallucination (O'Brien & Azrin, 1972).

Learning Objective 15.13

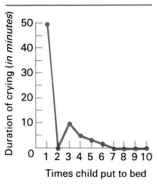

FIGURE 15.3 : If a child cries when put to bed, extinction procedures (the removal of reinforcement) can dramatically decrease the duration of crying. Shown is the duration of crying over several bedtimes when the crying is consistently ignored.

Time-out
A punishment procedure in which a person is removed from a desired or reinforcing situation to decrease the likelihood that an undesired behavior will recur.

Counterconditioning
A process of reconditioning in which a person learns a new response to a familiar stimulus.

Learning Objective 15.14

Extinction and Punishment.   Extinction and/or punishment can be used to decrease the frequency of an undesired behavior. As explained in Chaper 2, extinction can be used to decrease the likelihood that a person will exhibit a behavior by withholding reinforcers. Suppose a three-year-old is raising havoc in the house by demanding to be read an extraordinary number of stories. If no one reads the stories to him, he screams violently until he gets what he wants; by reading him the stories when he cries, his parents reinforce his crying behavior: he cries, they read. One way to eliminate his crying behavior is to stop reinforcing it. The reinforcement is reading, so the reading must be discontinued. Now when the child cries, the parents do not read him a story. Chances are that the child will cry loudly and violently, perhaps for two or three nights, trying to get the parent to read. However, if the parents fail to reinforce the child's behavior, that behavior will eventually extinguish (C. D. Williams, 1959). Figure 15.3 shows similar results obtained through extinction procedures to reduce bedtime crying.

A second way to decrease the frequency of undesired behavior is to punish it. Punishment often involves the presentation of an aversive stimulus. For example, if a child continues to play with fragile objects on a table, parents sometimes say "No!" and slap his hands (Koegal & Covert, 1972). In the laboratory with adult subjects, a researcher might provide a stronger type of aversive stimulus, perhaps an electric shock. Usually, punishment for undesired behaviors is combined with positive reinforcement for prosocial and desired behaviors.

Time-out.   As mentioned in Chapter 2, **time-out** or physical removal from sources of reinforcement (more properly called the time-out from reinforcement procedure) is a widely used technique that involves many basic principles of learning theory. Time-out acts as a punishment because it decreases specific undesired behaviors. Suppose a child regularly throws temper tantrums each time she wants a piece of candy, an ice-cream cone, or her little brother's toys. Out of frustration and embarrassment, her parents often give in. In the time-out procedure, however, when the child misbehaves, she is removed and placed in a room without toys, television, or other people; she might be placed in a "thinking chair" away from the rest of the family. In time-out, not only does the child not get what she wants, but she is also removed from any potential source of reinforcement. The child is kept in the chair or the time-out room for a set period of time. If she refuses to stay, more time is added. When time-out is combined with positive reinforcers for appropriate behavior, children with behavior problems often make dramatic gains (Wahler, 1976).

Counterconditioning

The second major approach to behavior therapy, **counterconditioning,** aims at teaching a person a new, adaptive response to a familiar stimulus. Usually a

In counterconditioning techniques people are encouraged to learn new responses to previously fearful stimuli.

specific stimulus (S_1) elicits a specific response (R_1). It is hoped that after an individual has undergone counterconditioning, or reconditioning, the same stimulus (S_1) will elicit a new response (R_2). There are two basic approaches to counterconditioning: systematic desensitization and aversive counterconditioning.

Systematic desensitization

A counterconditioning procedure in which a person first learns deep relaxation and then imagines a series of progressively fearful situations. With each successive experience, the person learns relaxation rather than fear as a new response to a formerly fearful stimulus.

Systematic Desensitization.   In **systematic desensitization,** people are taught to relax when presented with stimuli that formerly elicited anxiety. For example, driving alone in an automobile is a stimulus situation (S_1) that sometimes brings about an overly dramatic and inappropriate fear response (R_1). Eventaully, with therapy, the idea of driving alone (S_1) might instead elicit a response of curiosity or even relaxation (R_2) (Wolpe, 1958).

Systematic desensitization is a three-stage process. *First,* the subject learns how to relax. *Second,* the subject describes the specific situations that arouse anxiety. *Third,* while deeply relaxed, the subject imagines the scenes that elicit anxiety. The subject is exposed gradually to the source of anxiety, usually by imagining a series of progressively fearful or anxiety-provoking situations developed by the client and therapist together. For example, the psychologist might first ask a client who fears driving alone to imagine a car at a great distance. Further imagining might move the car closer. Eventually, the client would begin to imagine getting in the car. As the client realizes he will not be hurt or isolated by merely imagining this scene, he becomes able to tolerate more stressful imagery and may eventually perform the imagined behavior.

Much controversy exists about how systematic desensitization works. Research continues to examine systematic desensitization both as a therapeutic tool and as a process. Regardless of how it works, systematic desensitization has been a successful form of treatment for thousands of people (Berman, Miller, & Massman, 1985).

Systematic desensitization involves the development and use of imagery.

Aversive counterconditioning ▬▬▬

A counterconditioning technique that pairs an aversive or noxious stimulus with a stimulus that elicits undesirable behavior so that the subject will adopt new behaviors in response to the original stimulus.

Aversive Counterconditioning. The second major type of counterconditioning is aversive counterconditioning. In **aversive counterconditioning,** a noxious or aversive stimulus is paired with a stimulus that elicits undesirable behavior. As with systematic desensitization, the objective is to teach the individual a different response to the original stimulus. For example, alcoholics generally find alcohol rewarding even though they may realize that alcohol is destructive to physical health and personal relationships. A behavior therapist would concentrate on teaching an alcoholic a new response to alcohol. The first step might be to teach the person to associate alcohol with nausea. If verbal instruction is not enough, the therapist might arrange to administer a drug that causes nausea whenever alcohol is consumed. The goal would be to make alcohol or the consequences of drinking unpleasant. Eventually with such treatment, just the thought of alcohol would produce nausea and thus avoidance behavior (Davidson, 1974). In general, counterconditioning techniques are most effective when combined with other contingencies that promote adaptive behavior patterns. In many cases, aversive counterconditioning is combined with positive reinforcement for prosocial behaviors (e.g., Foxx, McMorrow, Bittle, & Bechtel, 1986).

PROGRESS CHECK 15.3

1. Complete each of the following sentences with one of the options provided.

Learning Objective 15.10

A. The goal(s) of behavior therapy is (are) to _____.
   (reshape personality : *modify maladaptive behaviors and teach adaptive behaviors)*

Learning Objective 15.10

B. Many behavior therapists consider the exploration of a client's internal experiences _____.
   (an invasion of privacy : *to be essential to the therapeutic process)*

Learning Objective 15.10

C. Behavior therapists assume that fears, attitudes, and intrapsychic conflicts can be more easily changed when a _____.
(person's behavior changes : person is aware of what causes certain feelings)

Learning Objective 15.10

D. Symptom substitution _____ behavior therapy.
(is the primary drawback of : does not seem to occur in)

Learning Objective 15.11

E. The first step(s) in a behavior modification treatment plan is (are) to _____ the problem behavior.
(identify and measure : discover the person's feelings concerning)

Learning Objective 15.11

F. The more complicated a disorder, the more likely it is that a psychotherapist will _____.
(use a behavioral approach : combine and integrate several approaches)

Learning Objective 15.12

G. In a token economy, a person receives objects that _____.
(are intrinsically reinforcing : can be traded for privileges)

Learning Objective 15.12

H. The goal of a token economy is to increase behaviors that are compatible with _____.
(social norms : a person's self-image)

Learning Objective 15.12

I. One advantage of a token economy is that the treatment plan can be administered _____.
(by a paraprofessional : on an intermittent basis)

Learning Objective 15.13

J. When extinction, punishment, or time-out are used to decrease undesirable behaviors, _____ is provided to strengthen desireable behaviors.
(stimulus control : counterconditioning : positive reinforcement)

Learning Objective 15.13

K. A technique used in behavior therapy that involves physically removing the person (usually a child) from the source of reinforcement is called _____.
(response cost : extinction : time-out)

Learning Objective 15.14

L. The primary goal of counterconditioning is to change the way a person responds to _____ stimuli.
(unconditioned : previously conditioned : abnormal)

Modeling

Learning Objective 15.15

Imitation is the highest form of flattery. If the president wears a sweater, the sweater industry assumes correctly that many men are likely to begin wearing them. People imitate musical tastes and commitment to social causes as well as dress styles. Children are particularly sensitive to the behavior of other people, especially that of their parents. They often learn toilet training, table manners, and responses to animals by observing and imitating parents or other models.

Adults also learn new responses by watching and observing models. Albert Bandura and colleagues (1969) have shown that people can benefit from therapy in which **modeling** is the principal therapeutic technique. Bandura, Blanchard, and Ritter (1969) asked people with snake phobias to watch live and filmed displays of other people handling snakes. In both cases, the subjects' fears were reduced. The same technique has been effective in treating fear of dogs (Hill, Liebert, & Mott, 1968) and other animals (Bandura & Barab, 1973), test anxiety (Jaffe & Carlson, 1972), and sexual dysfunction (Wincze & Caird, 1976).

A therapist who uses the modeling approach tries to teach a client to observe and imitate the behavior of purposeful, worthwhile, goal-directed people.

Modeling
Learning by observing and imitating the behavior of other people.

One problem with modeling is that people often observe the behavior of inappropriate models. For example, although parents generally are appropriate role models, they may also unconsciously teach some maladaptive behaviors by example. The modeling approach to behavior assumes that people who exhibit abnormal behavior have been exposed to and have copied inappropriate behaviors. This is the reason many people want television and movie violence curtailed. People who oppose television and movie violence argue that people imitate the behaviors they see on the screen. As parents, friends, teachers, older brothers and sisters, people must realize that other people not only observe their behavior, but they also think about it and often imitate it.

Cognitive Restructuring (Cognitive Behavior Therapy)

Learning Objective 15.16

Although most behavior therapies deal only with overt behavior, an increasing number of behavior therapists are also taking thought processes into account. Cognitive therapists are interested in modifying the maladaptive or faulty thought patterns of disturbed individuals (Mahoney, 1977). Like other forms of behavior therapy, cognitive restructuring therapy focuses on current behavior and is unconcerned with childhood experiences. Cognitive behavior therapy is at least as effective as other behavior therapies (Miller & Berman, 1983) and, in some cases, more effective (Shapiro & Shapiro, 1982).

Rational-emotive therapy
A cognitive behavior therapy originated by Albert Ellis that emphasizes the importance of logical, rational thought processes.

Rational-Emotive Therapy. The best-known cognitive therapy is **rational-emotive therapy,** developed by Albert Ellis. Most behavior therapies assume that abnormal behavior is caused by faulty or irrational behavior patterns. Ellis and his colleagues assume that abnormal behavior results from faulty and irrational patterns of thinking (Ellis, 1962, 1970; Ellis & Harper, 1961). If faulty thought processes can be replaced with rational ideas about the world, maladjustment and abnormal behavior will disappear.

Ellis believes that psychological disturbance is the result of events in a person's life that give rise to irrational beliefs. Three mistaken beliefs, which may concern the individual, other people, or the world in general, lead to negative emotions and behaviors. Thus, the first goal of rational-emotive therapy is to help the person examine past events that have produced irrational beliefs. The therapist's tasks are to uncover the client's thought patterns and to help the client recognize that his or her way of thinking is faulty; the therapist tries to alter irrational beliefs and thought patterns. If rational-emotive therapy is successful, the client will adopt new behaviors based on new and rational thought processes.

Ellis presents several basic irrational assumptions that he feels are the cause of many emotional problems and maladaptive behaviors (Ellis & Harper, 1961). These irrational assumptions include the following:

Irrational Idea: It is a dire necessity for an adult to be loved and approved by almost everyone for virtually everything he or she does.

Irrational Idea: A person must be thoroughly competent, adequate, and successful in all possible respects.

Irrational Idea: Certain people are bad, wicked, or villainous and should be punished for their sins.

Irrational Idea: It is catastrophic when things are not going the way you would like.

Irrational Idea: Human unhappiness is externally caused. People have little or no ability to control their sorrows or to rid themselves of negative feelings.

These irrational assumptions are based on a common truth: people have needs to be liked, to be competent, and to be loved and made to feel secure. Only when people place *irrational* or exaggerated value on them do these needs become maladaptive and lead to emotional disturbance, anxiety, and abnormal behavior. People who are experiencing anxiety, depression, and maladjustment in general are unhappy because they have adopted too many "shoulds" and "musts." As Ellis says, "Once a human being believes the kind of nonsense included in these notions, he will inevitably tend to become inhibited, hostile, defensive, guilty, ineffective, inert, uncontrolled, unhappy" (1962, p. 89). Rational-emotive therapy tries to place a person's cognitive assumptions about the world into a reasonable framework. It tries to balance an individual's needs with the demands of a complex and changing environment. Ellis (1987) has strong feelings about mental health and worries about people maintaining consistently good mental health. In his own words:

> All people are born with very strong tendencies to think crookedly about their important desires and preferences and to self-defeatingly escalate them into dogmatic, absolutistic shoulds, musts, oughts, demands, and commands. . . . Because of their upbringing and their genetic tendencies, some people are significantly more prone than are others to think, emote, and behave self-defeatingly. . . . I hypothesize that virtually all humans often hold blatant irrational beliefs and therefore are far from being consistently sane and self-helping. But I also hypothesize that just about all people—and especially those we label as severely neurotic, borderline, or psychotic—frequently hold several subtle or tricky irrationalities—and therefore are even less likely to eradicate them (Ellis, 1987, p. 373).

Research shows that children, adolescents, adults, and even aged populations often maintain irrational ideas (Hyer, Jacobsen, & Harrison, 1985) and that cognitive therapy is often especially effective. Cognitive behavior therapy has been effectively used in the treatment of depression (Murphy et al., 1984), Bulimia (Kirkley, et al., 1985; Ordman & Kirschenbaum, 1985) weight loss (Jordan, Canavan, & Steer, 1985), and phobias (Heimberg et al., 1985). It continues to be a widely used therapeutic technique. (Table 15.2 summarizes the goals and techniques of the behavior therapies just discussed.)

Other Cognitive Methods.   Another cognitive restructuring therapy, which also focuses on irrational ideas, is the cognitive therapy of Aaron Beck (1963). Described earlier in the discussion of depression in Chapter 14, Beck's theory assumes that depression is caused by people's negative views about the world, themselves, and the future. From Beck's point of view, a client needs to be helped to identify unrealistic thinking and to learn new ways to formulate personal experiences. Clients need to be helped to use the same problem-solving techniques that they use in the rest of their lives. Individuals who expect to improve in therapy and who develop positive ideas about their future in fact improve the most (Steinmetz, Lewinsohn, & Antonuccio, 1983).

Some researchers feel that what people might say to themselves will determine the things they will do. If you took this view, as does Donald Meichenbaum, you would argue that a goal of therapy would be to change the things people say to themselves. Meichenbaum's view is extremely cognitive; he asserts that a therapist has to change individuals' self-instructions, so that his or

TABLE 15.2 : Summary of Behavior Therapies

Type of Therapy	Goal	Technique
Operant conditioning	To teach subjects new responses to old stimuli	Subjects learn new responses; reinforcement and punishment are used to establish new behaviors and eliminate "faulty" or undesirable ones.
Counterconditioning: Systematic desensitization	To teach subjects new, adaptive responses	Subjects learn new responses (such as relaxation) by imagining fearful stimuli while deeply relaxed.
Aversive counterconditioning	To teach subjects new adaptive responses	Subjects learn new responses by associating a noxious stimulus with the stimulus that elicited the undesirable behavior.
Modeling	To teach subjects to observe and imitate useful behaviors	Subjects observe models and try to imitate their behavior.
Cognitive Methods: Rational-emotive therapy	To change the way subjects think about themselves and the world	Subjects learn to think situations through logically and to reconsider many of the irrational assumptions that have guided their lives.

her behavior will change. Meichenbaum has developed self-help techniques that use adaptive thinking and training procedures to teach individuals to think in ways that ameliorate their problem behaviors. These self-help techniques have benefited people with problems as diverse as shyness, speech impediments, impulsivity, and even schizophrenia (Glass, Gottman, & Shmurak, 1976; Meichenbaum, 1974; Meichenbaum & Cameron, 1973). Rather than reform irrational beliefs, clients learn a repertoire of possible activities that they can use to help make their behavior more adaptive. For example, Meichenbaum's subjects might conduct private monologues in which they work through adaptive ways of thinking and coping with situations. The use of such statements, in combination with relaxation training and reinforcement for adaptive behavior, makes this kind of self-instructional procedure very effective. Research on such self-therapy has shown that it is very effective as a cognitive behavior therapy (Dush, Hirt, & Schroeder, 1983). Table 15.3 presents a summary of the major approaches to therapy and provides an analysis of important issues.

Hypnosis and Meditation

Learning Objective 15.17   Many therapists, both insight therapists and behavior modification therapists, use as an adjunct to their therapy the techniques of hypnosis and meditation.

TABLE 15.3: Comparison of Psychoanalytic, Client-centered and Gestalt, and Behavioral Approaches to Psychotherapy

Issue	Psychoanalysis	Client-Centered and Gestalt	Behavior Therapy
Nature of psychopathology	Maladjustment reflects inadequate conflict resolution and fixation in early development, which leave overly weak ego controls or strong impulses or both.	Pathology reflects an incongruity between the depreciated self and the potential, desired self. The person is overly dependent on other people for gratification and self-esteem.	Symptomatic behavior derives from faulty learning or learning of maladaptive behaviors. The symptom is the problem; there is no "underlying disease."
Goal of therapy	Attainment of psychosexual maturity, strengthened ego functions, and reduced control by unconscious and repressed impulses.	Fostering self-determination, authenticity, and integration by releasing human potential and expanding awareness.	Relieving symptomatic behavior by suppressing or replacing maladaptive behaviors.
Role of therapist	An investigator, uncovering conflicts and resistances.	An authentic person in true encounter with patient, sharing experience. Facilitates patient's growth potential.	A trainer, helping subject unlearn old behaviors and learn new ones.
Role of unconscious material	Primary in classical psychoanalysis, less emphasis in ego-analysis.	Emphasis is primarily on conscious experience.	No concern with unconscious processes.
Role of insight	Central, though conceived as coming not solely from intellectual understanding but also from "corrective emotional experiences."	Used by many people, but there is more emphasis on awareness and on how and what questions rather than on why questions.	Irrelevant and unnecessary.

Source: Adapted from Korchin, 1976, table 14-2.

Hypnosis
An altered state of consciousness brought about by trance-induction procedures. Subjects' responsiveness to a hypnotist's suggestions increases as they become more deeply hypnotized.

Most people are familiar with **hypnosis.** They have seen it demonstrated at night clubs, in the movies, or perhaps even in a dentist's office. Hypnotized subjects are aware of their surroundings and are clearly conscious, but their level of awareness and their willingness to follow instructions are altered. Psychologists are interested in possible uses of hypnosis as a therapeutic tool.

Although hypnosis has been used as a therapeutic technique for 150 years, some researchers still question its validity and reliability. Research has shown that simply indicating to subjects that they will be participating in an hypnosis experiment can affect their behavior (Barber & Calverley, 1965; Hilgard, 1965). The skeptics remain in the minority, however, and hypnosis as a procedure is still widely used, particularly in therapy (for example, Porter, 1978; Sanders, 1978). Active research to determine its therapeutic value continues (for example, Wagstaff, 1983).

Evidence suggests that a subject's hypnotic susceptibility can affect the outcome of some therapeutic intervention techniques (Mott, 1979). Sometimes, therapists use hypnosis to help patients relax, remember, reduce anxiety, or even lose weight. In such studies, groups of obese patients were hypnotized during several therapy sessions. The subjects were given posthypnotic suggestions that successfully decreased their desire to eat (Hershman, 1955; Mann, 1959). Other studies have shown that hypnosis can help relieve test anxiety (Boutin, 1978), but that it does not increase academic skill learning

(R. D. Cole, 1979) or verbal comprehension (Brabender & Dickhaus, 1978). Hypnosis has also proved a successful method in the treatment of medical problems such as psoriasis (Frankel & Misch, 1973), warts (Johnson & Barber, 1978), vaginismus (involuntary spasms of the vaginal muscles) (Gottesfeld, 1978), and reducing nausea after chemotherapy (Hendler & Redd, 1986).

Clinical reports suggest that hypnosis also can be helpful in reducing smoking, although there is little sound evidence to indicate that it can actually eliminate smoking (Johnston & Donoghue, 1971; see also MacHovec & Man, 1978). After hypnotizing smokers in a single session, H. E. Stanton (1978) found that 60 percent of the subjects stopped smoking after a single hypnotic session; in a follow-up six months later, 45 percent were still nonsmokers. Other psychologists, however, doubt the effectiveness of hypnosis in stopping smoking (Athanasou, 1974; Hunt & Bespalec, 1974).

To achieve therapeutic changes, many therapists have their clients become involved with a related technique, meditation. **Meditation** is a technique for achieving a feeling of detachment from the world through intense concentration, restriction of incoming stimuli, and deep relaxation.

Meditation has been compared with biofeedback, because subjects are taught to relax deeply and to concentrate in order to bring their bodies under voluntary control for long periods (see Shapiro, 1977; Wallace & Benson, 1972). Meditation has also been compared with hypnosis because of the trancelike state it induces.

Many of the physiological changes that occur during meditation can also be induced by other techniques, such as hypnosis, systematic desensitization, or even psychotherapy. Deikman (1976) sees meditation as one of several techniques that individuals can use to achieve a state of calmness so that information can enter the receptive modes of functioning. Deikman believes that two modes of consciousness exist—one active and one receptive. According to Deikman, meditation allows the receptive mode to function. With practice, meditators can learn to switch to their receptive mode to permit "the operation of capacities that are nonfunctional in the action mode" (1976, p. 83).

Meditation ══════
A state of consciousness induced by a variety of techniques and characterized by concentration, restriction of sensory stimuli, and deep relaxation.

Deep muscle relaxation and meditation are useful in helping students overcome anxiety.

PROGRESS CHECK 15.4

1. Complete each of the following sentences with one of the options provided.

Learning Objective 15.15

A. _____ encourages psychotherapists to use modeling as a therapeutic technique.
(Perls • Ellis • Bandura)

Learning Objective 15.15

B. A therapist who uses the modeling approach encourages clients to _____ people who have purposeful, worthwhile, and goal-directed behaviors.
(talk to and ask questions of • observe and imitate)

Learning Objective 15.16

C. Rational-emotive therapists assume that maladjusted emotions and behaviors are the result of _____.
(irrational thinking • intrapsychic conflict • faulty conditioning)

Learning Objective 15.16

D. Ellis argues that people become unhappy and have other negative feelings if they have too many _____.
("shoulds" and "musts" in their thinking • responsibilities in life)

Learning Objective 15.16

E. Individuals who _____ actually improve the most in therapy.
(want to improve • want to be happy • expect to improve)

Learning Objective 15.16

F. Meichenbaum's cognitive restructuring approach makes use of _____ techniques.
(extinction • shaping • self-help)

Learning Objective 15.17

G. Hypnosis and meditation are two techniques that are sometimes used by _____ therapists.
(insight • behavior • insight and behavior)

Learning Objective 15.17

H. Hypnosis, as a therapeutic technique to help people stop smoking, _____ concerning its effectiveness.
(has strong research support • is under scientific debate)

Learning Objective 15.17

I. Many of the _____ that occur during meditation can also be induced by other techniques, such as hypnosis, systematic desensitization, biofeedback, and even psychotherapy.
(physiological changes • "aha" experiences)

GROUP THERAPY

Learning Objective 15.18

People who experience loneliness often feel that they are the only ones in the world who feel the way they do. In attempting to achieve some balance in their lives, Tom, who opened this chapter, and others like him may feel isolated, noncommunicative, and very much apart from other people. One aim of group therapy is to show people like Tom that they are not alone that other people share similar problems and frustrations. Most important, through group discussions people can cope better with their lives.

When a group of people meet together for the purpose of receiving psychological help, that treatment is called **group therapy.** Introduced around the turn of the century, group therapy became formalized as a technique in the 1930s and has been increasingly popular as a therapy technique since World War II.

Group therapy is popular among therapists because so many more people can be treated at once. It is popular with clients because it is less expensive than individual therapy. A therapist who sees clients only in individual therapy

Group therapy ════
A method in which several people meet as a group with a therapist for the treatment of emotional and behavioral problems.

can see at most forty clients a week, or one an hour. But in a single hour with a group, a therapist might help eight to ten clients; in five hours of group therapy, a psychologist can help as many as forty clients. Because the therapist's fee can be split among the members of the group, therapy is less expensive for the individual members.

Group therapy is an important technique not only because more patients can be treated and because it is less expensive, but also because it is more effective than individual therapy in the treatment of many problems (Spiegel & Bloom, 1983). Some therapy groups are formal; others consider themselves simply as helping organizations. Groups such as Weight Watchers and Alcoholics Anonymous have been successful not only in the treatment of overeating and alcohol addiction, but also in helping people with problems such as smoking or gambling. The social pressures that operate in a group can be very powerful in shaping behavior. The other people in a group can also provide useful models for behavior.

Group therapy can involve a variety of techniques. Each group has its own type of clients, therapist, and approach. Whether it is a psychoanalytic, client-centered, Gestalt, or behavior therapy group, each group confronts its members and their problems in a different way; no two groups are the same, and no two groups deal with an individual member in the same way. The way a group handles certain problems is determined largely by the type of group it is and the orientation of its therapist.

Learning <u>15.19</u>
Objective

In traditional group therapy, a number of clients, usually fewer than ten, meet on a regular basis with a therapist at a clinic, hospital, or the therapist's office. Usually the therapist controls the composition of the group, selecting members on the basis of what they can gain from and offer to the group. The goal is to construct a group whose members are compatible in terms of age, needs, and problems.

The format of traditional group psychotherapy varies, but generally each member describes his or her problems to the other members, who in turn relate their experiences with similar problems and how they have coped with them. This procedure is helpful in a number of ways. *First,* an individual has a chance to express his or her fears and anxieties to other people who are warm and accepting; each member eventually realizes that every person has emotional problems. *Second,* the members of the group help one another by giving advice about a particular problem. *Third,* by watching others cope with difficult problems, each group member can learn how to handle personal anxieties and problems. *Fourth,* a group member can role play or otherwise "try out" new behaviors in a safe, nonpunitive yet evaluative environment. *Fifth,* the group can exert pressure on a member to behave in more appropriate ways.

Groups are not necessarily sedate and quiet. A group may pressure a member into confronting his wife or mother and may require him to report on his confrontation at the next session. Intense expressions of emotion may occur as members interact. As a group develops cohesiveness and the members learn to understand themselves and each other, members are able to provide mutual help when difficult problems arise during therapy. Sometimes the therapist may be directive in helping the group cope with a specific problem. At other times, the therapist may allow the group to work through its problems independently. Most group therapists feel that members benefit from participating in the group learning process. (R. H. Klein, 1983), although the technique has its critics (for example, Kanas et al., 1980).

Single parents can band together in support groups; that is one form of specialized group therapy.

In traditional group therapy, the therapist (or therapists—sometimes a group has two) allows the group to determine its own structure and ways of functioning. As members feel better able to cope with life and problems, they may leave the group. They are replaced by new members who must establish relations with the other members and find a way to fit into the group's continuing social structure.

Learning Objective 15.20

Encounter group therapy
A group of people who meet together to learn more about their feelings, behavior, and interactions.

Encounter group therapy has developed in recent years as an outgrowth of the sensitivity training movement. Most encounter and sensitivity groups are designed to help people self-actualize and develop better interpersonal relationships. Self-actualization (discussed in Chapter 12) is the process by which people move toward fulfilling their potential. It is at the pinnacle of Abraham Maslow's pyramid of needs (see Chapter 5). Encounter groups bring together people who want to increase their awareness and effectiveness as individuals.

Each encounter group is unique. Some groups are very much like regular therapy groups in terms of format and goals. Other groups are specialized for blacks, female athletes, drug addicts, alcoholics, homosexuals, singles or anorexics. An encounter group may have minimal leader participation or it may follow a formal procedure. Some encounter groups have been held in the nude, in swimming pools, and at mountain retreats.

Learning Objective 15.21

A specialized form of group therapy called *family therapy* has emerged during the last thirty years. Treating the entire family at once is the key to family therapy. Little used before the 1950s, family therapy recently has received a great deal of attention. The aim in family therapy is to change the ways a family interacts. One member of a family, perhaps a delinquent child, is sometimes identified as the "problem." Family therapists believe that whoever is identified in this way may also be used as a scapegoat by the family. The individual labeled as the problem diverts the family's attention from other, more important problems that may be more difficult to confront. From a family therapist's point of view, the real patients in family therapy are the family's structure and organization (Jacobson & Bussob, 1983).

Family therapists attempt to change family systems. A family system is the way family members interact (M. D. Stanton, 1981). One common intervention technique used in family therapy is *reframing*. In reframing, a therapist reinterprets or reframes a behavior (or set of behaviors) so that behavior can be

Psychologists at Work: Brief Intermittent Therapy

In an award-winning address to the American Psychological Association, Nicholas Cummings (1985, 1986) described a new model for psychotherapy. He calls it *brief intermittent therapy* throughout the life cycle. The model is based on blending all psychotherapeutic orientations and skills into one approach. The brief therapy approach focuses on identifying the client's current problem and treating that problem with the most effective treatment as quickly as possible.

Brief therapy differs from other psychotherapeutic approaches because it rejects such ideas as (1) the concept of an ideal therapist, a person who can do all things for all people; (2) that one specific therapeutic approach can efficiently help all people with any behavior or emotional problem; (3) that the unconscious or the person's life history must be understood fully before the client can terminate therapy without the risk of maybe having to return for help with the same problem or some other problem in the future; and, (4) that the therapist and client only get one chance to resolve any past or future psychological difficulties.

The basic goal of brief therapy is to give the client what he or she needs. To achieve this goal, brief therapy focuses on treating the client's problem efficiently and getting the client back on his or her own as quickly as possible. Brief therapy believes it is important to save the client time and money, knowing the client can and will return to therapy if help is needed in the future.

A therapist who uses the brief therapy throughout the life-cycle approach begins treatment wanting to end it. However, there are no limits to how many sessions will take place. In other words, the client is free to stay in therapy as long as it is needed.

In the first session of brief therapy, the therapist makes sure that treatment begins. He or she does not waste time taking a case history or allowing the client to say things that go unheard. The therapist strives to perform an "operational diagnosis" in the first session. An operational diagnosis is not a DSM-III-R diagnosis that labels a person, but rather it is an answer to the question, "Why is the client here today instead of last week or last month, last year, or next year?" Cummings says that by answering this question, the therapist knows the specific problem for which the client is seeking help.

Also in the first session, the therapist creates a therapeutic contract with the client. Cummings says, "Every client makes a therapeutic contract with every therapist in the first session, every time. But in 99 percent of the cases the therapist misses it (1986, p. 430)." If the therapist misses the client's contract, the client, wanting to be a good client, will adopt the therapist's contract. When this happens, the client's needs are not being directly addressed. Cummings cites an example, saying, "If a client comes in to the office and says, 'Doctor, I'm glad you have this comfortable chair because I'm going to be here awhile,' and the therapist does not respond to that, the therapist has just made a contract for long-term therapy." By recognizing the client-stated therapeutic contract, the goals for brief therapy can be established.

The brief therapist also gives homework to the client during the first session and in each session thereafter. The homework is tailored to the client's goals and the therapeutic contract. Homework allows the client to take responsibility for his or her own therapy.

Cummings has challenged psychotherapists to give up their notions that the particular therapeutic approach they have learned and used is the best approach. He recommends that they go back to school to learn a variety of approaches. He also encourages them to practice in groups, so they can consult with one another and share their skills. In this way, they can give the clients what is needed and provide them with brief therapy.

In American Biodyne Centers, founded by Cummings and his colleagues, psychotherapists who as a team are able to use more than 50 therapeutic approaches and work together. Cummings has thirty years experience with the brief therapy approach and says this about client success: "In tracking them for ten, twenty, or twenty-five years, we have found that it takes less time in psychotherapy overall than it would if we kept a client in therapy twice a week for a year or a year and a half or even eight months. And I could report on case after case that demonstrates this (p. 429)."

Unfortunately, much of the published research on the effectiveness of brief psychotherapy is inadequate (Koss, Butcher, & Strupp, 1986). However, when treatment goals are tailored to meet a client's needs and to fit the time available, researchers have found it to be effective. So far, the research on brief psychotherapy has been limited to a narrow range of clients with a narrow range of problems, but the research is continuing.

---

viewed less critically by other family members. For example, a therapist might reframe or redescribe the behavior of a parent whom the family sees as uninvolved; the parent may be redescribed as "fearful of closeness because he fears his own inadequacy and loves his family so much." By describing the behavior more positively, the therapist tries to lessen the amount of blaming taking place that might obscure other problems. Other techniques used in family therapy involve restructuring the family's interactions. For example, if a son is responding too submissively to his domineering mother, the therapist may suggest that the son be assigned household chores only by his father.

Researchers know that teaching parents specific behavior skills helps them control their children. They also know that training family members in communication skills improves the psychological environment in a home. However, the effects of treating families as units, and of the specific techniques described here, remain poorly documented (Garrigan & Bambrick, 1979). Although family therapy is now common in the United States and Canada, its procedures are difficult to use with families that are disorganized or that lack home involvement. While recognizing that not all families profit equally from behavioral interventions (O'Leary & Carr, 1982), many psychologists, social workers, and psychiatrists use family therapy to help individuals and families change. Little carefully conducted research exists on family therapy, but what does exist suggests that it is beneficial and better than many alternative treatments (Hazelrigg, Cooper, & Borduin, 1987).

COMMUNITY PSYCHOLOGY

Learning Objective 15.22

Community psychology
An approach to the treatment of mental health problems that provides local services on a continuous basis in order to reach people who might not otherwise seek them out.

In 1963, President John F. Kennedy sent a message to Congress calling for "a bold new approach" to mental illness. His message was followed by legislation and funding for community mental health centers. As the concept of community mental health developed, so did a new branch of psychology: **community psychology.**

Some community psychologists focus heavily on mental health issues in the community. They recognize that ideally all people who need mental health services would seek out a practitioner. But Community psychologists try to reach out through community mental health centers to people who might not otherwise seek needed services.

Community mental health centers provide services on a continuous basis. They may offer partial hospitalization programs for people who require hospitalization during the day but who can return home to their families at night, or short-term hospitalization or outpatient care for people who live at home while receiving therapy. Community mental health centers also offer consultation and education programs. They provide lectures, forums, and literature to the community on a variety of topics, including therapy, family planning, and drug rehabilitation.

Community psychology has a focus much broader than just community mental health. It focuses on prevention, intervention, and planning. Community psychologists are involved in school, planning commissions, and prison settings. They coordinate, plan, and help set up programs by which psychological skills, techniques, and knowledge are brought into the community.

One special focus of community psychology is primary prevention. Primary prevention has as its goal lowering the rate of new cases of a disorder or counteracting harmful circumstances that might lead to maladjustment or a disorder. Primary prevention usually does not work on specific individuals but whole populations. Sometimes, primary prevention programs focus on the entire community, other times on people with some mild risk, such as on children of low socioeconomic status, and other times on high-risk groups, such as on children of schizophrenic parents (Forgays, 1983).

An outreach group for war veterans organized with the help of a psychologist is an example of community psychology at work.

Special Programs: The Neighborhood Clinic and Crisis Intervention

In response to growing public awareness of mental health problems, a special kind of service agency—the neighborhood clinic—has developed. Neighborhood clinics try to help communities cope with the problems of mental health, unemployment, and lack of education. Many larger communities have special treatment facilities that protect the anonymity of both juvenile and adult clients while providing free treatment for a variety of problems, including drug addiction, alcoholism, and emotional or psychological disorders. Information on clients is not given out to authorities, parents, or friends. Many neighborhood clinics have been established by members of the community and are supported by local donations and benefactors. Some receive government money.

One aim of community psychology is to encourage people in the community to become involved with local therapy and intervention programs as paraprofessionals. **Paraprofessionals** are people with specific mental health skills that allow them to undertake many important and necessary tasks that professional psychologists do not have time to handle. Many paraprofessionals are housewives, high school teachers, or college students. They do not probe past experiences, interpret dreams, or engage in lengthy therapy (McGee, 1983). Although paraprofessionals can never fully replace highly trained psychologists or psychiatrists, they can help improve mental health conditions in the community. They can be empathic, attentive listeners who help individuals assess their problems and suggest appropriate available community resources (McGee, 1983).

One area in which psychologists and paraprofessionals have been particularly successful is crisis intervention. Crisis intervention centers attempt to help people deal with short-term, stressful situations requiring immediate therapeutic attention. The paraprofessional, psychologist, or psychiatrist provides direct, immediate, and supportive therapy aimed at helping individuals cope with problems resulting from rape, delinquency, drug use, illness, marital problems, poverty, and aging (Auerbach & Kilmann, 1977). The crisis often involves a specific event; for example, a man may have lost his job, a child may be seriously ill, or a woman may have been raped. Crisis intervention involves no specific set of techniques or procedures. Generally, only brief contact occurs between the crisis workers and the person needing help, but the level of activity is high. The crisis worker uses any therapeutic technique or activity that seems

Learning Objective 15.23

Paraprofessional
A person who works alongside professional psychologists and aids them in providing psychological services.

helpful, ranging from telephone contacts to working with the entire family. The focus is on the immediate circumstances, not on childhood experiences.

Crisis intervention has a series of recognizable stages (McGee, 1983). First, an event occurs that upsets an individual. If the usual resources available to that person fail to help, anxiety and depression may result. At that point, the individual is open to suggestions of alternative ways to handle the situation. Crisis intervention offers the individual the opportunity to learn these new ways of coping as well as new ways of behaving. Without crisis intervention, further psychological deterioration may follow.

In recognizing that everyone has crises at some time, and that successful resolution (using crisis intervention, if necessary) is important to psychological health and growth, crisis intervention centers have introduced the use of hotlines. Hotlines are telephones that are staffed twenty-four hours a day to answer calls from people who need immediate help. On a hotline, crisis workers try to deliver immediate, directive therapy. A person who is contemplating suicide might call a therapist on a hotline to receive immediate support and encouragement plus a referral for further help. Hotline therapy does not take the place of systematic psychotherapy, but it can be an important mode of intervention for a person who suddenly has become panicked or dramatically disturbed.

How does a practitioner help? What does he or she say? In a now classic paper, Cadden (1964) suggests the following techniques:

1. Help the client confront the crisis.
2. Help the client confront difficulties in manageable doses.
3. Help the client obtain necessary information from reliable sources.
4. Help with everyday tasks if necessary, for example, transportation.
5. Help the client avoid placing blame.
6. Avoid giving false assurances that may not come true. Be realistic.
7. Help the client accept help.

Some studies show that crisis intervention therapy is more effective than traditional therapy; others show little or no difference. One problem in evaluating crisis therapy is the variety of techniques therapists use (Slaikeu, 1984). This flexibility of approach permits the delivery of situation-specific therapy, but it also makes controlled comparisons difficult (see Slaikeu, 1979).

Psychology as a Community Activity: Action and Change

One aim of community psychology is to provide service to the community, including people who might not otherwise be able to afford the services of a psychotherapist or counselor. Although a need will always exist for psychotherapists who see patients on a private basis, there is a growing need for general community psychological services. Because the aims of community psychology are to identify and deal with potential mental health problems within a community before they arise, community psychologists are action-oriented. They deliver a variety of services, including staffing mental health centers, twenty-four-hour hotlines, and suicide prevention centers. They also provide psychological services to groups of alcoholics or drug addicts and establish prevention programs to identify high-risk individuals and provide them with appropriate services before a need for crisis intervention and/or hospitalization arises.

Rather than wait for the community to seek out psychological help, community psychologists provide programs that reach out to the community. To deliver mental health services, they often rely on social support networks made up of family, friends, religious and social organizations, and "self-help" groups with common interests and needs. A key element in all these helping groups is community involvement. The general aims of community psychology have been to strengthen existing social support networks and stimulate the formation of new networks to meet new challenges (Gonzales et al., 1983). Though lacking professional training, members of the community can help extend care to special populations and can also help each other.

Community psychologists are also change-oriented. Because many community psychologists believe that some social conditions and organizational procedures can make existing maladjustments worse (and sometimes create a new maladjustment), they often advocate change in community institutions and organizations. Their aim is to improve the health of the community through preventive as well as therapeutic means.

PROGRESS CHECK 15.5

1. Complete each of the following sentences with one of the options provided.

Learning Objective 15.18

A. Group therapy has gained popularity among clients because it is _____ _____ individual therapy.
(not as confrontive as : less expensive than : more exciting than)

Learning Objective 15.18

B. The _____ in a group can be very powerful in shaping new behaviors.
(specific techniques used : social pressures that operate)

Learning Objective 15.19

C. In traditional group therapy, the therapist _____ structure and methods of group functioning.
(determines the therapeutic : allows the group to determine its own)

Learning Objective 15.20

D. The general goal of encounter groups is to help people _____ _____.
(overcome fears : become more aware : manage stress)

Learning Objective 15.21

E. The key to family therapy is _____.
(detecting the scapegoat : treating the entire family)

Learning Objective 15.21

F. A technique used in family therapy in which the therapist describes a behavior so it can be viewed less critically by other family members is called _____.
(interaction restructuring : paradoxical intervention : reframing)

Learning Objective 15.22

G. _____ extend services to people who might not otherwise seek help.
(Family therapists : Group therapists : Community psychologists)

Learning Objective 15.22

H. Neighborhood clinics are a product of _____.
(family therapy : community psychology)

Learning Objective 15.22

I. Community psychologists focus on problems found _____ settings.
(primarily in urban : in a variety of populations and)

Learning Objective 15.23

J. When a therapist or paraprofessional talks with someone on a crises intervention hotline, he or she will use _____ therapeutic techniques.
(self-help : immediate, directive : written scripts that outline a variety of)

Learning Objective 15.23   K.   Because they focus on _____, community psychologists
                                  are considered action-oriented and change-oriented.
                                  (prevention : *group behavior* : *quick cures)*

Keeping Pace with Chapter 15

Applying
Principles

15.1 Identify the type of psychotherapy being used in each of the following situations.

psychoanalysis   family therapy   rational-emotive therapy
group therapy   behavior modification   crisis intervention
client-centered therapy brief intermittent therapy

_____   A.   Because Perry has repeatedly behaved with hostility and aggression toward
                         people around him, he has been placed in a juvenile detention center. His
                         therapist gives him tokens for prosocial behaviors, puts him in a "thinking
                         room" for aggressive behaviors, and withholds reinforcement for less
                         complicated undesirable behaviors.

_____   B.   Bob and Marge Miller and their three children, Tommi, Pete, and Sandi, are
                         meeting together with a psychotherapist. Arguing had become a major
                         pastime around their household. When they entered therapy, Bob and
                         Marge reported that Sandi was starting the arguments and they wanted her
                         to get help so that they could have some peace again. As therapy
                         progressed, it became apparent that everyone in the family was
                         argumentative and that Sandi was being blamed unfairly. The therapist
                         used a variety of techniques to help the Millers improve their interactions
                         with one another.

_____   C.   Angie becomes very anxious whenever she feels secrets are being kept from
                         her. Her anxiety starts when she has a thought like, "He isn't telling me
                         about the party because he had a lot of fun without me." Angie's therapist
                         is attempting to teach her that just because someone does not tell
                         everything does not mean that the person has lost interest in her.

_____   D.   Cindy's teenage daughter left the house in a huff, suggesting that she
                         "Might just run away." Cindy called the police, but still in an emotional
                         turmoil and at her wits' end about what else to do, she then called FOR–
                         HELP, the community hotline. After talking a while with the hotline worker,
                         Cindy feels comforted, and together they came to the conclusion that based
                         on her daughter's style she will probably be home by midnight. If not,
                         Cindy is to call again.

_____   E.   Nick describes a recent dream to his therapist. In the dream, Nick's pet cat
                         was in a paper bag and kept trying to escape, but Nick would not let it out.
                         His therapist interpreted this dream to mean that Nick did not want to "let
                         the cat out of the bag" and suggested that he must have some deep
                         feelings that he does not trust admitting to himself or other people.

_____   F.   Lai meets once a week with other displaced homemakers to discuss her
                         fears, successes, and needs. With the help of her therapist and the other
                         people who meet with her, she comes to feel comfortable with herself and
                         her life-style.

_____   G.   Stephan visits with his therapist once a week and talks about events in his
                         life that are causing him concern. His therapist frequently restates the
                         feelings that Stephan expresses, allowing Stephan the opportunity to
                         evaluate the world from his own vantage point.

Self-Test

Before proceeding to the Self-Test, REVIEW the Learning Objectives listed at the chapter opening and RECITE from memory everything you can remember in support of them. Then, take this Self-Test as if it were to be graded by your teacher. Use the Learning Objective numbers in the Answer Section as a reference to restudy the corresponding text pages and Progress Checks for any incorrectly answered questions.

1. Psychotherapy is
   A. the use of electroconvulsive shock, tranquilizers, and antipsychotic drugs as a way of treating emotional disorders.
   B. the manipulation of diet and physical exercise to promote general health.
   C. the treatment of emotional and behavioral disorders by using psychological methods.
   D. all of the above

2. The results of psychotherapy are influenced by
   A. whether a placebo effect occurs.
   B. the color scheme used to decorate the therapist's office.
   C. the therapist's sensitivity to such things as the client's age, sex, race, and expectations of therapy.
   D. the client's wish to be happy.

3. Kazdin argues that researchers are not detecting differences in the effectiveness of various therapeutic approaches because
   A. the focus of research is too narrow.
   B. change comes from inside the client, not from outside therapeutic applications.
   C. results based on therapist reports concerning success rather than client reports.
   D. although they appear different on the surface, the various approaches are really quite similar when applied in therapy.

4. Insight therapies believe that behavior will become more adaptive when the client
   A. admits that his or her current behaviors are counterproductive.
   B. becomes aware of unresolved conflicts.
   C. is able to describe situations in life that cause anxiety.
   D. understands the therapist's interpretation of the problem behavior.

5. Clinical psychologists who use therapeutic techniques that are rooted in Freudian theories
   A. usually have been specifically trained in psychoanalysis.
   B. refer to their therapies as psychodynamic therapy.
   C. focus on the treatment of actual behavior problems rather than on the causes of the behavior problem.
   D. are considered behavior therapists.

6. Sharon's therapist is empathetic, understanding, and very attentive, and yet, Sharon continues to respond to him as if he is not going to hear, care about, or accept what she has to say. After many months of therapy, Sharon becomes more spontaneous and realizes that as a child her parents subtlely but powerfully transmitted the attitude, "children should be seen and not heard." Sharon's early behavior toward the therapist illustrates
   A. free assocation.   C. transference.
   B. resistance.   D. reaction formation.

7. Ego-analysts assume that
   A. because it is such a lengthy process, psychoanalysis is not the most appropriate method for treatment.

B. uprooting unconscious material in the id and superego should be the focus of treatment.

C. increasing the patient's ego control should be the final stage of therapy.

D. therapy should focus on developing the part of the personality that responds realistically to the demands of the environment.

8. Client-centered therapy is based on Rogers's assumption that

A. some people are born selfish and hedonistic.

B. even healthy people cannot be fully aware of their behaviors.

C. people have a considerable amount of free will and thus can determine their own behavior.

D. an effective therapist can intervene and change situations that are too troublesome for the patient.

9. Gestalt therapists focus on

A. past experiences; they ask "why" questions about problem behaviors.

B. present feelings and behaviors; they ask "how" and "what" questions.

C. future goals and probable outcomes; they ask "when" questions.

D. who owns the problem; they ask "who" questions.

10. Behavior therapists use _____ model in therapy.

A. a medical

B. a legal

C. a client-centered

D. an educational

11. A behavior therapist knows that treatment has been effective when

A. insight is achieved.

B. the patient describes a new coping skill.

C. follow-up observations show that the new behavior is still occurring.

D. the patient is able to identify reinforcers in his or her life.

12. In instrumental conditioning, positive reinforcement is used in all of the following ways *except:* It is not

A. used as a consequence for desired behaviors.

B. removed to decrease the frequency of undesired behaviors.

C. used in combination with extinction and punishment procedures.

D. used to bribe children into acceptable behavior before implementing a behavior modification treatment plan.

13. An extinction procedure involves

A. withholding the reinforcers that normally follow an undesired behavior.

B. removing a person from an environment that is reinforcing.

C. taking a privilege or special possession away from a person when he or she misbehaves.

D. the presentation of an aversive stimulus.

14. When aversive counterconditioning is used, the patient

A. is exposed to the fear-producing stimulus until he or she recognizes the unreasonableness of the phobic feelings.

B. gradually becomes less emotional.

C. learns a new behavior in response to a stimulus that brings pleasure but needs to be avoided.

D. learns to challenge fear-producing stimuli.

15. A therapeutic technique that allows a child's fear of dogs to diminish simply because the child observes other children playing with dogs is called

A. operant conditioning.

B. modeling.

C. cognitive restructuring.

D. play therapy.

16. Rational-emotive therapy

    A. tries to place people's cognitive assumptions about their experiences in a reasonable framework.
    B. encourages people to put a high value on the things they think they need to remain happy.
    C. is based on the idea that abnormal behaviors cause irrational thoughts.
    D. is best described as a self-help technique.

17. With practice, meditation makes it easier for a person to

    A. switch into the active mode of consciousness.
    B. enter the receptive mode of conciousness.
    C. hear therapeutic instructions.
    D. A and C

18. A primary goal of group therapy is to provide people with an environment that allows them to

    A. talk about a behavior problem without having to face pressures to change.
    B. see that other people experience similar problems.
    C. find friends who will accept behaviors that are unacceptable to the general population.
    D. discover that the way they are is acceptable to everyone except themselves.

19. The people who meet as a group in traditional group therapy

    A. usually are compatible with regard to age, needs, and problems.
    B. are required to complete at least three months of individual therapy before entering the group.
    C. are asked not to give advice to other members of the group.
    D. generally have minor behavioral quirks but do not have any significant emotional problems.

20. Encounter groups are an outgrowth of

    A. behavior therapy.
    B. people who have met in group therapy and want to interact again.
    C. human resource development in business and industry.
    D. the sensitivity training movement.

21. From a family therapist's point of view, the patient in family therapy is

    A. the family member who is used as a scapegoat.
    B. the family member or members who do the scapegoating.
    C. the person who actually causes the problem.
    D. the family structure and organization.

22. Community mental health centers

    A. offer partial hospitalization programs for people who need to be cared for while their families are at work.
    B. provide consultation and therapy for individuals with emotional problems.
    C. focus on prevention, intervention, and planning.
    D. all of the above

23. A community psychologist might be found doing all of the following *except*:

    A. identifying potential problems, such as the spread of AIDS, and implementing programs to prevent them from occurring.
    B. organizing and relying on social support networks.
    C. giving elementary school children intelligence tests.
    D. advocating changes in relationships between social service agencies and unemployed or homeless citizens.

Appendix

Scientific and Statistical Methods

Appendix

Learning Objectives

When you have mastered the material in the Appendix, you will be able to:

1. Distinguish between correlational studies and experiments and describe how psychologists design experiments. (p. 627)

2. Define descriptive statistics and describe three ways in which researchers organize raw data. (p. 628)

3. Define mean, mode, and median and explain why researchers use measures of central tendency. (p. 631)

4. Describe two measures of variability and explain what they tell researchers about individual subjects within a group. (p. 631)

5. Describe a normal curve and explain how standard deviations help clarify the data represented in a normal curve. (p. 633)

6. Explain how researchers use correlation coefficients to describe data. (p. 635)

7. Describe inferential statistics and explain what is meant by a significant difference. (p. 637)

BEFORE YOU READ ON, take time to **SURVEY** the Appendix, form an idea of what is to be learned (from margin Learning Objective numbers), and set goals for your study time. Then, ask yourself **QUESTIONS** about the material as you **READ,** seeking help for any sections you do not understand.

A RESEARCH ILLUSTRATION: SMOKING STUDIES

*Learning
Objective* A.1

In 1964, the U.S. surgeon general issued a report showing that the frequency of heart disease and lung cancer was higher in people who smoked cigarettes than in those who did not. This report was based in part on questionnaires investigating the relationship between cigarette smoking and health. The questionnaires typically asked individuals if they smoked, how much they smoked, and the condition of their health. Many studies asked relatives of people dying of cancer or heart conditions about those individuals' past smoking habits. The results of these surveys were dramatic: people who smoked had a shorter life expectancy than nonsmokers. A twenty-five-year-old man who smoked a pack of cigarettes a day could expect to die six years sooner than a nonsmoker the same age.

These early smoking studies showed a correlation between smoking and a shorter life span. A *correlation* is a number that describes the extent to which two or more factors are related: if one factor or variable changes, a correlation will describe how the other variable will change. These early studies did not argue that cigarette smoking itself caused a shorter life span—a correlational study cannot argue cause and effect. However, they did claim that people who smoke more die at younger ages.

Hypothesis
A tentative idea adopted to account for some facts. More important, it guides the investigation of others.

The results of these early studies led scientists to **hypothesize**—or develop a tentative idea—that cigarette smoking was detrimental to an organism's health. New experiments were conducted to assess directly the effects of cigarette smoking. In these experiments, animals were rewarded for smoking cigarettes. The experiments used a smoking machine that allowed researchers to control the amount of cigarette smoke inhaled. A typical experiment might involve four groups of monkeys. The first group of monkeys would serve as a control group against which all the other monkeys would later be compared to see if smoking produced any measurable effect; this control group would smoke no cigarettes. The second, third, and fourth groups might smoke the equivalent of three, ten, and thirty cigarettes a day, respectively. Every day for several months, the monkeys in the three experimental groups would smoke in the machine for the allotted time periods. At the end of each week, and at periodic intervals after the conclusion of the experiment, the health of all the animals would be assessed. Veterinarians would examine the animals thoroughly, including their blood pressure, pulse, and blood analysis. In these checkups, the animals in the control group would probably appear as healthy as ever, whereas the monkeys who inhaled cigarette smoke would probably show a variety of ailments, including increased blood pressure and heart rate and a reduced ability to transfer oxygen into the bloodstream.

In this hypothetical (yet typical) experimental setup, the nonsmoking group of monkeys would have remained healthy, whereas the other three groups would have developed cardiovascular and lung disorders. A researcher conducting such an experiment must be sure that all monkeys in the experiment come from the same colony, are nearly the same age, and provide a balanced sample with regard to sex and other characteristics. As discussed in Chapter 1, good experimentation requires careful assignment of subjects to groups. To ensure the validity of inferences from sample data, the experimenter should draw both the control group and the experimental groups from essentially the same larger population. Any differences found among subjects should be due to experimental manipulation rather than to differences among the subjects themselves. The assignment of subjects to their respective groups often requires that they be matched with regard to such important variables as age, weight, sex, and (if appropriate) socioeconomic class. Every good experiment will have a control group against which to compare the experimental group. A control group provides a standard. Reliable data (data that can be repeated) can be obtained only if the control and experimental groups have been drawn from the same initial population. If other health-affecting variables in this hypothetical study are properly controlled (held constant), a researcher can conclude that any difference in the animals' physical condition at the conclusion of the experiment is the result of cigarette smoking.

GOOD EXPERIMENTATION

As mentioned in Chapter 1, a good experiment requires an experimental group, a control group, and a sufficient number of carefully selected subjects in each group. Researchers must make enough observations of these groups to ensure that the behaviors observed are representative.

Proper selection of subjects is a key element of good research. Sometimes subjects are selected randomly; at other times, they are chosen with respect to a specific variable (such as gender or age). In either case, experimental subjects must be representative of the population to which they will be compared. The proper selection of subjects permits meaningful generalizations of the data to the population.

Equally important is the description of the independent and dependent variables. If the independent variable manipulates drug dosage, that dosage must be specified carefully—for example, rats might receive 10 milligrams of a drug for each kilogram of body weight. Thus, regardless of individual weight, each rat would receive a proper amount of the drug to make comparisons possible. The variable being measured, the dependent variable, must likewise be carefully specified. A dependent variable such as running speed is easily specified; however, a variable such as arousal, anxiety, or depression is more difficult to define precisely. In such cases, a researcher must carefully describe the behavior that will be measured. Such variables are operationally defined. An *operational definition* is a concrete description of how the variable being studied will be measured. For example, if the behavior being measured is anxiety, anxiety might be defined operationally as a change in the electrodermal response (a measure of nervous system arousal) or as a ten-point change on a specified anxiety scale.

After the variables have been specified carefully and the subjects chosen properly, the researcher conducts the experiment, hoping it will yield interpretable, meaningful results. However, if irrelevant factors or variables affect the results, such interpretations become difficult.

In summary, a good experiment has carefully selected sample populations and defined variables. It minimizes extraneous variables as much as possible. Finally, it produces results that can be repeated and are meaningful.

DESCRIPTIVE STATISTICS

Learning Objective $\overline{A.2}$ Statistics is a branch of mathematics. Researchers use statistics to evaluate and organize the way they think about experimental data. To make experimental

Descriptive statistics ═══
A method of describing, summarizing, and condensing data.

results interpretable, researchers use **descriptive statistics**—statistics that summarize, condense, and describe data.

Organizing Data

When psychologists conduct experiments, they often produce large amounts of data that must be assessed. Suppose a social psychologist asks parents to monitor the number of hours their children watch television. The parents might report between zero and twenty hours of television watching a week. The following list shows the actual number of hours of television watched by 100 children.

11	18	5	9	6	20	2	5
9	7	15	3	6	11	9	14
6	1	10	3	4	4	10	4
8	8	9	10	13	12	9	8
16	1	15	9	4	3	7	10
10	5	6	12	8	2	13	8
14	12	6	9	8	12	5	17
10	7	3	14	13	7	9	2
10	17	11	13	16	7	5	4
15	11	9	11	16	8	15	17
14	7	10	10	12	8	10	11
11	1	12	7	6	0	5	13
19	18	9	8				

The first step in making these numbers meaningful is to organize them into a frequency distribution. A **frequency distribution** records the number of times each score occurs. As the frequency distribution in Table A.1 shows,

Frequency
distribution ═══
A chart or array, usually arranged from the highest to lowest score, showing the number of instances of each obtained score.

TABLE A.1 ⋮ A frequency distribution for the number of hours of TV watched by 100 children. Few individuals score very high or very low; most individuals have scores in the middle range.

Number of Hours of TV Watching	Number of Individuals Watching	Total Number of Individuals
0	1	1
1	1 1 1	3
2	1 1 1	3
3	1 1 1 1	4
4	1 1 1 1 1	5
5	1 1 1 1 1 1	6
6	1 1 1 1 1 1 1	7
7	1 1 1 1 1 1 1	7
8	1 1 1 1 1 1 1 1 1	9
9	1 1 1 1 1 1 1 1 1 1	10
10	1 1 1 1 1 1 1 1 1	9
11	1 1 1 1 1 1 1	7
12	1 1 1 1 1 1	6
13	1 1 1 1 1	5
14	1 1 1 1	4
15	1 1 1 1	4
16	1 1 1	3
17	1 1 1	3
18	1 1	2
19	1	1
20	1	1

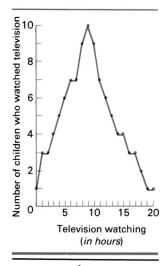

FIGURE A.1 ⋮ This frequency polygon shows the number of hours of TV watched by 100 children. Frequency, or the number of children who watched for each duration, is shown on the ordinate or vertical axis; the actual scores occur on the abscissa or horizontal axis.

Frequency polygon ===
A graph of a frequency distribution that shows the number of instances of obtained scores; usually data points are connected by straight lines.

Normal distribution ===
A bell-shaped distribution of scores, usually obtained only for large sample populations, in which most scores tend to cluster around the mean, with a few scores occurring much higher and a few much lower.

Learning Objective $\overline{A.3}$

more children watched nine hours of television weekly than any other number of hours. That number occurs more frequently than any other among the data.

A **frequency polygon** is a graph constructed from a frequency distribution; it shows the different possible scores on the horizontal axis (known as the *abscissa*) and the frequency of each score on the vertical axis (known as the *ordinate*). Figure A.1 on the previous page shows data from the frequency distribution in Table A.1 graphed in a frequency polygon. Straight lines connect the data points.

When a large number of scores is involved, a frequency polygon often takes the shape of a bell. This bell-shaped curve is called a **normal distribution,** or normal curve. Normal distributions usually show a few individual scores at each extreme of the scale and many scores at the center. Normal distributions are quite common for many naturally occurring phenomena, such as height, weight, and intelligence.

Measures of Central Tendency

A measure of central tendency is a descriptive statistic that tells what single score best represents an entire set of scores. It is a way of summarizing and condensing data. Consider the following statement: "Men are taller than women." Because people know that some women are taller than some men, they assume that the statement means: *"on the average,* men are taller than women"; in other words, if a person takes all the men and women in the world and compares their heights, *on the average* men will be taller. Almost every group has members who score higher or lower than the group as a whole. To

TABLE A.2 : Calculation of Mean Height for Men and Women, in Inches

Men	Height in Inches	Women	Height in Inches
Arnold	62	Ruth	58
Stephen	62	Harriet	59
Louis	64	Marcy	61
Jason	67	Mickey	64
Joshua	68	Sharon	64
Storm	68	Rozzy	66
Mallett	69	Bonnie	66
Evan	70	Golde	66
Michael	70	Cheryl	66
Dave	70	Leona	67
Steven	70	Iris	67
Morry	70	Nancy	67
Alan	70	Theresa	67
Bernie	70	Sylvia	67
Lester	70	Jay	68
Al	70	Linda	68
Corey	73	Elizabeth	71
Michael	79	Jesse	75
Andrew	79	Gabrielle	76
Scott	79	Sarah	77
Total height	1400	Total height	1340
Mean: $\dfrac{\Sigma S}{N} = \dfrac{1400}{20} = 70$ in.		Mean: $\dfrac{\Sigma S}{N} = \dfrac{1340}{20} = 67$ in.	

Mean height (*in inches*)

70
66
62
58
54

Men　　Women

FIGURE A.2 : These mean heights for men and women reflect an average computed for thousands of people in each group.

Mean ═══════

A measure of central tendency calculated by dividing the sum of the scores by the number of scores; the arithmetic average.

```
58 |
59 |
60
61 |
62 | |
63
64 | |
65
66 | | | |
67 | | | | |
68 | | | |
69 |
70 | | | | | | | | |   Mode
71 |
72
73 |
74
75 |
76 |
77 |
78
79 | | |
```

FIGURE A.3 **:** The mode is the data point that occurs with the greatest frequency.

Mode ═══════

A measure of central tendency; the most frequent observation.

Median ═══════

A measure of central tendency; the point at which 50 percent of all observations occur either above or below.

Learning Objective $\underline{A.4}$

Variability ═══════

A measure of the extent to which scores in a distribution differ from one another.

describe the group *as a whole,* researchers often use a measure of central tendency. The most frequently used measure of central tendency is the mean.

Mean. "Men are taller than women." How might someone go about investigating the truth of this statement? One way would be to measure the height of a large number of men, taking a careful sample from each country, race, and age group, and then repeat the procedure for women. After measuring the height of many thousands of men and women, a person might then calculate the average heights of the samples (see Table A.2) and plot the results on a bar graph, as in Figure A.2. This is in fact the way the data in Figure A.2 were computed. For each group, the heights of the subjects were measured, added together, and divided by the number of subjects in the group. The resulting number, the **mean,** represents the arithmetic average in terms of height for a person in that group. Mathematically, this formula is written as

$$\frac{\Sigma S}{N}$$

where Σ means to sum up; S stands for each individual score, and N stands for the number of scores available.

Mode. Another way of describing the central tendency of a set of data is the mode. The **mode** is the most frequent observed data point. Figure A.3 shows the same data presented in Table A.2, but this time the frequency of different scores is plotted. Table A.2 indicates that only one person is 58 inches tall and only three are 79 inches tall. Figure A.3 reflects that information. The mode occurs at 70 inches because more people are 70 inches tall than any other height. Thus, the mode of that group of data is 70 inches.

Median. The **median** is the 50 percent point: half the observations fall above the median and the other half fall below. Figure A.4 on the next page shows the same data as Table A.2. When the scores are arranged from lowest to highest, half the data fall above 68 and half below. The median of the data set is therefore 68.

Very often, the mean, mode, and median are the same number. All three descriptive statistics are measures of central tendency and tell the researcher something about the average (or typical) subject. If you had to guess the height of a person you had never met, your best guess would place a male at about 70 inches and a female at about 67 inches because these are the average heights for males and females.

Measures of Variability: The Range and Standard Deviation

A measure of central tendency is a single number that describes a hypothetical "average" subject. In real life, however, some people score above the mean and others score below. Knowing how an average subject might score is not as useful as knowing the full range of scores in a group.

A statistic that describes the extent to which scores differ from one another in a distribution is called a measure of **variability.** In a group of forty subjects taking a test, some will score high and some will score low. If all the subjects score the same, no variability exists. However, such an outcome is very unlikely. Many personal and situational characteristics affect the scores obtained

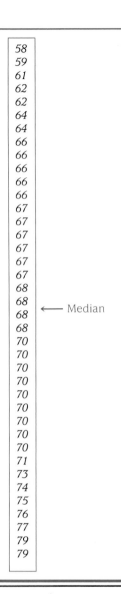

58	
59	
61	
62	
62	
64	
64	
66	
66	
66	
66	
66	
66	
67	
67	
67	
67	
67	
67	
68	
68	← Median
68	
68	
70	
70	
70	
70	
70	
70	
70	
70	
70	
71	
73	
74	
75	
76	
77	
79	
79	

FIGURE A.4 : The median is the 50 percent point. It is the point at which half the points fall above and half the points fall below.

Range
A measure of variability that describes the spread of scores within a group, calculated by subtracting the lowest score from the highest.

Standard deviation
A descriptive statistic that provides a measure of variability in a set of data.

by individuals. If they know the extent of that variability, researchers can estimate how much subjects differ from the mean or "average" subject. One such measure of variability is the range. The **range** indicates the spread of scores in a distribution. The range is calculated by subtracting the lowest score from the highest score. If the lowest score on a test is 20 and the highest is 85, the range is 65 points. The mean might be 45, 65, or 74 points. Regardless of the mean, the range remains 65; there was a 65-point spread from the lowest to the highest score.

The range provides a relatively crude measure of how subjects within a group vary. In a group of 100 students, nearly all may have scored within 10 points of the average or mean score of 65 points. Yet one score of 20 and another of 95 produces a range of 75. More precise measures of the spread of scores within a group are available. These indicate not only the mean and the spread of a group of scores, but also how the scores are distributed.

Suppose a group of thirty tenth-graders chosen at random is involved in a reaction time study that measures how fast the subjects press a button when a light is flashed. The list below shows the number of milliseconds it took each student to press the button. Clearly, the reaction times vary.

450	490	500
610	520	470
480	492	585
462	600	490
740	700	595
500	493	495
498	455	510
470	480	540
710	722	575
490	495	570

The mean is 540. A person told only the mean reaction time must assume that is the best estimate of how long it takes a tenth-grade student to respond to the light. But for information about how the average response time is related to response times that were above and below the average, the person would need a measure of variability such as standard deviation.

A **standard deviation** is a descriptive statistic that tells a researcher about the variability of data. Table A.3 shows the reaction times of two groups of subjects responding to a light. Although the mean is the same for both groups, the first group shows a large degree of variability and the second group shows little. The standard deviation (the estimate of variability) for Group 1 subjects will therefore be substantially higher than that for Group 2 subjects.

Knowing the variability associated with each mean (knowing more about the performance of persons who make up the group) allows a researcher to guess more accurately how long it would take a person in that group to respond to a light. A standard deviation gives information about all the members in a group, not just about an average member. A researcher can predict more confidently that a subject in Group 2 will respond in 555 milliseconds because subjects in that group showed only a small standard deviation. In contrast, the standard deviation (the variability of scores) in the first group was high. Even though the best guess for both groups is exactly the same (555 milliseconds), a researcher could be more confident guessing for Group 2 than for Group 1 because the deviation in Group 2 is less.

TABLE A.3: Reaction times in milliseconds, mean reaction times, and standard deviations for two groups of subjects. Group 1 shows a wider range of scores and thus greater variability. Group 2, by contrast, shows a narrow range of scores and little variability.

Group 1	Group 2
380	530
400	535
410	540
420	545
470	550
480	560
500	565
720	570
840	575
930	580
Mean = 555	Mean = 555
Standard deviation = 197	Standard deviation = 17

The Normal Curve

Normal curve
A bell-shaped graph in which the mean, mode, and median are assumed to be equal. Normal curves are symmetrical around the mean and occur only when a large sample of scores is taken.

The description of many events follows the pattern of a normal curve. A **normal curve** is a graph representing a distribution of scores. In a normal curve, the mean, mode, and median are generally assumed to be the same, and the distribution of scores is symmetrical around that central point. Height, for example, is normally distributed. There are more people of average height than people who are either very tall or very short. As Figure A.5 shows, many more people are 69 inches tall than are 78 inches tall. Height, weight, shoe size, intelligence, and scores on tests in introductory psychology are very often normally distributed.

Standard deviations help describe the characteristics of a normal curve. In a normal curve, the bulk of the data occur within eight standard deviations (four on either side) of the mean. As shown in Figure A.6 on the next page, each standard deviation on either side of the mean accounts for a different proportion of the population.

In Figure A.7, also on the next page, the mean is 50 and the standard deviation is 10. Each increment of 10 points above or below the mean accounts for fewer and fewer individuals. Scores between 50 and 60 account for

FIGURE A.5: In a normal distribution, or a normal curve, many more people are of average height, weight, or intelligence than are at the extremes.

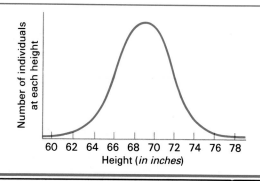

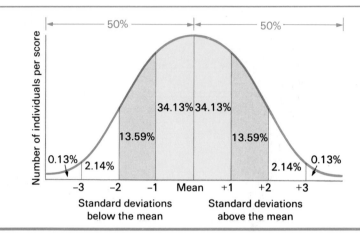

34.13 percent of individuals tested; scores of 60 to 70 account for only 13.59 percent. A score above 70 accounts for only about 3 percent of the individuals tested. The sum of these percentages represents 50 percent of the scores (34.13 + 13.59 +2.14 + .13). The normal curve can be used to describe any characteristic of a number of subjects in which the results are normally distributed. Figure A.8 shows a normal curve for height, with a mean of 70 inches and a standard deviation of 4 inches.

Knowing the mean and a standard deviation of a set of data, a person can estimate where an individual in the sample population stands relative to others. For example, if Dennis is 74 inches tall, his height is one standard deviation above the mean; he is taller than 84 percent of the population

(.13 + 2.14 + 13.59 + 34.13 + 34.13 = 84.12%),

whereas at 66 inches Rob is taller than only 16 percent of the population.

The results of tests used by colleges to help decide whom to admit are generally normally distributed. For example, the Scholastic Aptitude Test (SAT) is designed to have a mean of 500 and a standard deviation of 100.

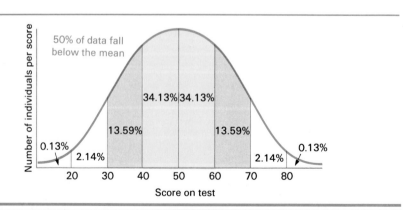

FIGURE A.7 : In this normal curve, the standard deviation is 10 points.

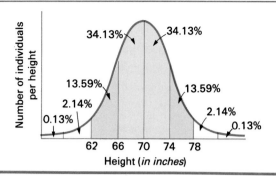

FIGURE A.8 : When the mean distribution of height is 70 and the standard deviation is 4, Dennis, who is 74 inches tall, is taller than 84 percent of the sample population (.13 + 2.14 + 13.59 + 34.13 + 34.13 = 84.12), whereas Rob, who is 66 inches tall, is taller than only 16 percent of the population (.13 + 2.14 + 13.59 = 15.86).

Correlation

Learning Objective *A.6*

Correlation
A measure of the degree to which two variables are related, expressed in terms of a correlation coefficient that varies from −1 to +1. These coefficients express how changes in one variable are associated with changes in another.

To compare data gathered in various surveys and questionnaires, a researcher performs a correlation study. A **correlation** study is a study that demonstrates a relationship between two variables. A correlation implies that an increase in the value of one variable will be accompanied by a corresponding increase or decrease in the value of a second variable. The degree of relationship between two variables is expressed by a numerical value called the *correlation coefficient.* The correlation coefficient ranges from −1 to +1. It is never greater than 1.0.

When two variables are perfectly correlated, they are said to have a correlation of 1. Two variables are perfectly correlated if knowing the value of one enables a person to predict *precisely* the value of the second. For example, in Figure A.9 knowing the speed at which a car is traveling will allow someone to predict precisely the distance it will travel in one hour: there is a perfect relationship between the speed of the automobile and the distance traveled. But consider two variables that are not perfectly related, such as height and weight. Although tall people generally weigh more than short people, this relationship is not perfect. Some tall people weigh less than some short people. This imperfect relationship is shown in Figure A.10, which indicates that knowing a person's height does not allow someone to predict his or her weight exactly. These two variables, height and weight, show a relationship, or correlation, of .65.

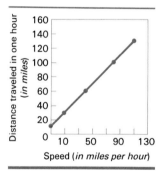

FIGURE A.9 : When two variables are perfectly correlated, they have a correlation of 1. With a correlation of 1, knowing the value of one variable allows a person to predict precisely the value of the second variable.

FIGURE A.10 : When two variables are related, knowing the value of one helps a person predict the value of the second. A perfect prediction is not available unless the correlation is a correlation of 1.

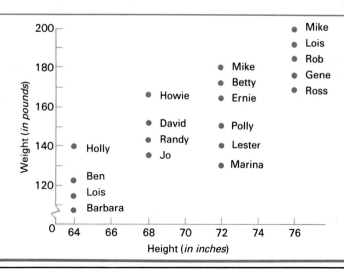

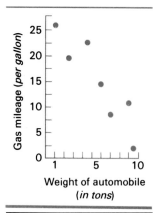

FIGURE A.11 : An increase in one variable does not always mean an increase in the other. In a negative correlation, an increase in one variable has associated with it a decrease in the other.

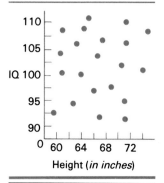

FIGURE A.12 : When two variables show no relationship, they have a correlation of 0 (zero). Weight and height are correlated, but IQ and height have a correlation of 0.

FIGURE A.13 : The left panel shows a positive correlation: an increase in one variable has associated with it an increase in the other. The right panel shows a negative correlation; an increase in one variable has associated with it a decrease in the other. The middle panel shows a 0 (zero) correlation, with one variable not related to the other.

When one variable shows an increase in value and a second also shows an increase, the two variables are positively related. Such a relationship is called a positive correlation. Height and weight show a positive correlation: generally, as height increases, so does weight. All variables are not related in this manner. Consider the relationship between automobile weight and gas mileage. As automobile weight increases, gas mileage decreases. Figure A.11 shows the relationship (though not a perfect one) between weight and gas mileage. These variables have a correlation of about −.6 or −.7. This is a *negative* correlation: as one variable increases, the other decreases. The correlation between the two variables is just as strong as in the height and weight example, but the direction of the correlation is changed: it is negative.

Another example of negative correlation is that between the loudness of a sound and an observer's distance from the sound. People who live close to an airport report that aircraft noise is painfully loud; those who live farther away report less noise. The loudness of the aircraft noise is directly related to the distance from the airport. The two variables have a negative correlation: as distance from the airport increases, loudness decreases. It is important to remember that a relationship of +.7 is no stronger than a relationship of −.7. Both show a correlation of .7. Only the *direction* of the relationship is changed by the plus or minus sign.

Some variables (such as eye color and weight) show no relationship. A total lack of correlation is expressed by a correlation coefficient of 0 (zero). Figure A.12 plots some data for height and IQ data. The results show no systematic relationship between IQ and height. The two variables show a correlation of 0.

Correlations can vary from −1 through 0 to +1. A correlation of 0 implies no relationship. Any correlation greater or less than 0, regardless of its sign, indicates that the variables are related. If the sign is positive, the variables are positively related; if the sign is negative, the variables are negatively related (see Figure A.13). The larger the number, the greater the correlation. A correlation of −.8 is greater than a correlation of +.7; a correlation of +.6 is greater than a correlation of −.5. The strength of the relationship between the variables is determined by the size of the number, not by its sign.

As discussed in Chapter 1, correlation studies make no statements regarding cause and effect. They do not tell a researcher that one event causes another. Correlations simply show that, if there is an increase in one variable, a researcher is likely to find an increase (or decrease) in another.

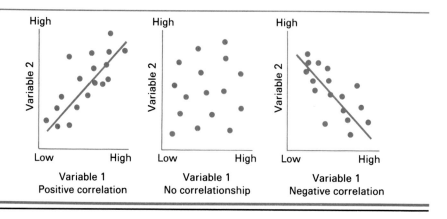

INFERENTIAL STATISTICS

To help make decisions about data, a branch of statistics called inferential statistics has been developed. **Inferential statistics** is used to decide whether two or more groups differ from one another and whether this difference is the result of chance. When psychologists refer to **significant difference,** they mean that the obtained difference in performance of two groups can be repeated experimentally and is not the result of chance variations among the scores. A significant difference means that a persistent, similar pattern of scores will be observed if the test or task is repeated using another, similar group of subjects. As a general rule, psychologists assume that a difference is statistically significant if the likelihood of its occurring by chance alone is less than 5 out of 100. Many researchers will accept a difference as significant only if the likelihood of its occurring by chance is less than 1 out of 100.

Generally, psychologists compare differences between two or more groups of subjects; for example, they may compare subjects receiving a treatment to subjects in a control group, which does not receive the treatment. Inferential statistics uses formulas that take into consideration means, individual subject scores, and overall variability. A mean tells what the average subject in a group does. A measure of variability describes how a group's set of scores is distributed. The smaller the variability, the greater the likelihood that the two groups differ significantly. It is sometimes difficult to decide what is a significant difference. Suppose the hypothetical reaction-time study described earlier was altered and the students were given injections of caffeine (experimental group) or saltwater (control group) before the experiment. The results might now show the experimental group responded to the flashing light 20 milliseconds faster than the control group. In this case, the 20-millisecond difference in reaction times is probably due to the presence of caffeine. On the other hand, if the difference between response times was 5 milliseconds and the variability within the groups is very small, the 5-millisecond difference may represent a significant difference. If the variability is very large, a difference of 30 milliseconds between two groups may not be considered significant (see Figure A.14).

Table A.4 on the next page presents data from two groups of subjects who also responded to a light. In this sample, the first group took 10 milliseconds less to respond than the second group. However, much variability exists within both groups. In the presence of such high variability, a researcher would probably be unwilling to believe those two groups really differ.

Even if statistically significant differences are obtained, most researchers require that an experiment be repeated and produce the same results a second

FIGURE A.14 : To determine whether a difference between two groups is significant, researchers try to decide if the difference could be due to mere chance or is really due to manipulation of the independent variable.

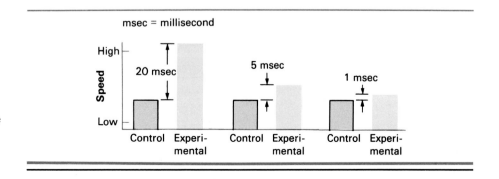

TABLE A.4 : Mean reaction times, and standard deviations
: for two groups of subjects. The two groups of
: subjects show a 10 millisecond difference in
: reaction time, but the wide degree of
: variability in each group decreases the
: likelihood that a researcher would accept this
: difference as significant.

Group 1	Group 2
390	380
400	400
410	410
420	420
460	470
480	480
510	500
600	720
870	840
910	930
Mean = 545	Mean = 555
Standard deviation = 192	Standard deviation = 197

time. Repeating an experiment for the purpose of verifying a result is called
replicating the experiment. If, after replicating an experiment, the same results
are obtained and the probability that these results are due to chance is less
than 5 percent, a researcher will generally say that the observed difference
between the two groups is significant.

Keeping Pace with the Appendix

Applying Principles

New knowledge becomes more meaningful when you can relate it to actual life
experiences. Here, you have an opportunity to think more deeply about some of the
concepts discussed in the Appendix and to practice applying them. The exercise will
contribute to your learning whether it is done before or after the Self-Test. So,
whenever you feel prepared, try applying your new knowledge to these situations
and to your own life experiences.

Use the information given on pages 630–631 to solve the following problems: The
mean shoe size for women is size 8 and there is a standard deviation of 1; indicate
the percentage of women who would wear the following shoe sizes.

A. size 4 $\frac{1}{2}$ _____   E. size 8 $\frac{1}{2}$ _____
B. size 5 $\frac{1}{2}$ _____   F. size 9 $\frac{1}{2}$ _____
C. size 6 $\frac{1}{2}$ _____   G. size 10 $\frac{1}{2}$ _____
D. size 7 $\frac{1}{2}$ _____   H. size 11 $\frac{1}{2}$ _____

I. Judy wears a size 6 shoe. Give the percentage of women who have a shoe size
larger than Judy. _____

Self-Test

Before proceeding to the Self-Test, REVIEW the Learning Objectives listed at the Appendix opening and RECITE from memory everything you can remember in support of them. Then, take this Self-Test as if it were to be graded by your teacher. Use the Learning Objective numbers in the Answer Section as a reference to restudy the corresponding text pages and Progress Checks for any incorrectly answered questions.

1. When a researcher conducts an experiment, he or she wants to be sure that any differences between the control and experimental groups are due to

   A. the hypothesis.
   B. the experimental manipulation.
   C. differences among the subjects.
   D. the operational definition.

2. In an experiment, the dependent variable

   A. provides a standard on which group differences can be measured.
   B. is the aspect of the experiment that is controlled and manipulated by the experimenter.
   C. represents the effect and is measured by the experimenter.
   D. is an extraneous variable.

3. A normal distribution is represented

   A. by the median.
   B. in a frequency distribution.
   C. on a bell-shaped curve.
   D. on the abscissa.

4. Which of the following is a measure of central tendency?

   A. the mean
   B. a correlation coefficient
   C. a standard deviation
   D. all of the above

5. By subtracting the lowest score from the highest score, researchers are able to determine the

   A. median score.
   B. mode.
   C. range of scores.
   D. standard deviations.

6. By using standard deviations to understand data, researchers can describe

   A. the group as a whole.
   B. how much individual subjects differ from the group as a whole.
   C. the most frequently observed data point.
   D. the half-way point in a set of data.

7. A normal curve is divided

   A. into segments based on the experimenter's preference.
   B. by the number of subjects tested.
   C. to determine correlation coefficients.
   D. into eight standard deviations.

8. Of the choices below, the correlation coefficient of _____ shows the strongest relationship between two variables.

   A. −.1
   B. −.9

C. +.5
D. +32

9. A zero correlation represents

   A. no relationship between variables.
   B. a positive correlation.
   C. a negative correlation.
   D. a perfect relationship between two variables.

10. When researchers refer to a significant difference, they mean that the

    A. scores of two groups showed great variability.
    B. experimental results have social importance.
    C. results of a study occurred by chance.
    D. results of a study can be replicated by another similar study.

Study Guide Answers

Chapter One

Progress Check Answers

1.1 **1.** A. heart beat, thinking, talking, and swimming B. solve problems by changing C. is not D. psychologist E. psychologist F. medical doctors G. psychoanalyst H. are often similarities

1.2 **1.** A. school B. community C. counseling D. clinical E. experimental F. developmental G. educational H. industrial/organizational I. social **2.** A. and experts expect them to be even better B. human services C. clinical D. may be converging E. prevention F. ask questions about the therapeutic approach G. animals H. nonclinical I. a fast clock J. withhold rewards

1.3 **1.** A. psychoanalytic approach B. structuralism C. Gestalt psychology D. eclecticism E. functionalism F. behaviorism **2.** A. 1879 B. William James C. private contents of consciousness D. stimuli and responses E. behaviorism F. thought G. an eclectic H. biological and environmental influences I. have achieved

1.4 **1.** A. correlation B. variable C. independent variable D. dependent variable **2.** A. unique to psychology B. sometimes discover things almost by accident C. a significant difference D. influence the results E. control F. larger G. ask additional questions H. the target behavior may not be exhibited I. correlations J. an evolving

Applying Principles Answers

1.1 **1.** A. breakfast B. academic performance **2.** A. reward B. cooperation **3.** A. alcohol B. number of dreams

Self-Test Answers

Answer	Learning Objective		Answer	Learning Objective
1. B	1.1		8. A	1.8
2. C	1.2		9. B	1.9
3. B	1.3		10. C	1.10
4. C	1.4		11. B	1.11
5. D	1.5		12. A	1.12
6. D	1.6		13. B	1.13
7. A	1.7			

Chapter Two

Progress Check Answers

2.1 **1.** A. conditioning B. learning C. classical conditioning D. higher-order conditioning **2.** A. similar B. changes in behavior C. involuntarily D. unlearned E. weaker F. elicit G. a chain of H. the unconditioned stimulus I. unconditioned J. timing K. withheld L. spontaneous recovery M. discrimination N. limited

2.2 **1.** A. shaping B. negative reinforcement C. reinforcer D. secondary reinforcer or punisher E. primary reinforcer or punisher F. punishment **2.** A. voluntary B. an organism "operates" on the environment C. cumulative recorder D. superstitious E. need it F. escape G. often return to H. an interval I. variable-ratio J. generalization K. extinction L. eventually disappears M. follows

2.3 **1.** A. hold in high esteem B. be aggressive and violent C. by observing such responses D. thinking E. rehearse

Applying Principles Answers

2.1 **A.** 1. USC—electrical shock 2. UCR—pain and increased arousal 3. NS/CS—light switch 4. CR—arousal (heart) and apprehension **B.** 1. UCS—food 2. UCR—salivation 3. NS/CS—can opener 4. CR—signs of anticipation

2.2 A. fixed-ratio B. variable-ratio C. variable-interval D. fixed-interval

Self-Test Answers

Answer	Learning Objective		Answer	Learning Objective
1. B	2.1		11. C	2.10
2. B	2.2		12. B	2.11
3. C	2.3		13. C	2.12
4. C	2.4		14. B	2.15
5. C	2.4		15. D	2.16
6. C	2.5		16. A	2.17
7. A	2.6		17. A	2.18
8. A	2.7		18. B	2.18
9. C	2.8		19. D	2.19
10. D	2.9		20. A	2.20

Chapter Three

Progress Check Answers

3.1 **1.** A. different but dependent   B. could relearn   C. difficult   D. von Restorff effect   E. recall   F. Serial-recall   G. amazingly accurate   H. memory enhancement

3.2 **1.** A. memory trace   B. is not   C. crowding of information   D. Proactive inhibition   E. repression   F. Anterograde   G. new   H. rare   I. coding, storage, and retrieval of

3.3 **1.** A. semantic memory   B. sensory register   C. icon   D. long-term memory   E. short-term memory   F. episodic memory   **2.** A. is under debate   B. decays and is forgotten   C. acoustically   D. subsystems operate in a temporary way   E. importance   F. give full attention to   G. long-term

3.4 **1.** A. organizing your thoughts   B. mediation   C. consolidation   D. is an   E. hormones   F. placing proteins into the brains of naïve rats   G. precise locations in the brain

Applying Principles Answers

3.1 A. anterograde amnesia   B. recency effect   C. retroactive inhibition   D. decay   E. proactive inhibition   F. primacy effect   G. retrograde amnesia   H. motivated forgetting

Self-Test Answers

Answer	Learning Objective	:	Answer	Learning Objective
1. C	3.1	:	8. B	3.8
2. A	3.2	:	9. B	3.8
3. D	3.3	:	10. B	3.8
4. A	3.4	:	11. C	3.8
5. B	3.5	:	12. B	3.9
6. A	3.6	:		
7. A	3.7	:		

Chapter Four

Progress Check Answers

4.1 **1.** A. an intimate interplay   B. can seldom   C. nature   D. nurture   E. only if the environment encourages them   F. chromosome   G. 23   H. a recessive gene   I. fraternal   J. the relative contributions of nature and nurture   K. biological states and brain are

4.2 **1.** A. pituitary gland   B. pancreas gland   C. thyroid gland   D. adrenal gland   **2.** A. directly into the blood system   B. pituitary gland   C. islets of Langerhans   D. hypoglycemia   E. managing one's diet   F. learned   G. absence of

4.3 **1.** A. all-or-none   B. synapse   C. refractory period   D. action potential   E. neurotransmitter   **2.** A. how brain damage affects behavior   B. an axon   C. negatively   D. a spike discharge   E. dopamine   F. corpus callosum   G. forebrain   H. limbic system   I. amygdala   J. language and speech   K. peripheral   L. sympathetic

4.4 **1.** A. electroencephalography   B. brain disorders   C. alpha   D. involuntary   E. reinforcing   F. a variety of

4.5 **1.** A. Weil   B. Tart   C. Jaynes   D. Ornstein   **2.** A. affected by biological and environmental factors   B. levels   C. receptive   D. focused attention   E. receptive   F. independently   G. interact   H. may be misleading   I. right   J. inhibited

4.6 **1.** A. do not necessarily need   B. eye movements   C. four   D. stage 2   E. 90 minutes   F. NREM   G. an active, almost paradoxical   H. catch up on REM and stage 4   I. become anxious and irritable   J. visual imagery   K. unorganized, spontaneous brain stimulation   L. 37 percent   M. cannot learn much   N. consolidated in memory

Applying Principles Answers

4.1 A. somatic   B. sympathetic   C. central   D. parasympathetic

Self-Test Answers

Answer	Learning Objective	:	Answer	Learning Objective
1. B	4.3	:	13. C	4.12
2. B	4.4	:	14. A	4.12
3. A	4.5	:	15. B	4.13
4. B	4.6	:	16. A	4.14
5. D	4.7	:	17. C	4.16
6. D	4.8	:	18. B	4.18
7. A	4.8	:	19. D	4.19
8. B	4.9	:	20. D	4.19, 4.20
9. D	4.10	:	21. C	4.20
10. B	4.10	:	22. C	4.21
11. C	4.11	:	23. A	4.22
12. C	4.12	:		

Chapter Five

Progress Check Answers

5.1 **1.** A. cognitive theory   B. drive theory   C. humanistic theory   D. expectancy theory   **2.** A. need   B. mechanistic   C. Humanistic   D. brain detects low blood-sugar   E. amount and type   F. ventromedial   G. size   H. of a variety of external factors   I. voluntary   J. even though it is not caused

5.2 **1.** A. Imprinting   B. inconclusive   C. moderate   D. its internal response to a stimulus   E. mechanistic   F. has competing needs or goals   G. stronger

5.3 **1.** A. learned motives   B. have a physiological origin   C. self, others, and relationships   D. sleep   E. firstborn children   F. no new methods for   G. Type B   H. Type A   I. control

5.4 **1.** A. one's own thoughts   B. denial orientation   C. the internal pleasures derived from the activity   D. receives extrinsic rewards   E. unhealthy thought patterns   F. innate   G. achieves his or her true nature   H. physiological   I. tied to middle-class cultural experiences

5.5 **1.** A. subjective   B. to observe and measure
C. is a sensitive period for healthy   D. engaged in self-
destructive behaviors   E. have an inborn need for
social stimulation   F. Crying   G. autonomic   H. skin
conductance
   5.6 **1.** A. Cannon   B. Schachter-Singer   C. James-
Lange   **2.** A. self-regulation plays   B. Health
psychology   C. immune   D. can influence   E. cortex
and thalamus   F. external cues   G. makes it unlikely
that

Applying Principles Answers

   5.1 **1.** A. approach-avoidance   B. approach-
approach   C. no conflict exists   D. avoidance-
avoidance

Self-Test Answers

Answer	Learning Objective		Answer	Learning Objective
1. B	5.1		12. A	5.12
2. B	5.2		13. B	5.13
3. C	5.3		14. D	5.14
4. B	5.4		15. A	5.15
5. A	5.5		16. D	5.16
6. C	5.6		17. D	5.17
7. C	5.7		18. D	5.18
8. D	5.8		19. B	5.20
9. A	5.9		20. B	5.21
10. D	5.10		21. A	5.21
11. D	5.11		22. B	5.22

6.5 **1.** A. pitch   B. loudness   C. sound
2. A. visual   B. middle   C. hair cells in the inner ear
are   D. cochlea   E. nerve   F. frequencies   G. sweet
H. rods   I. olfactory   J. space travel   K. insensitive
L. gates   M. An endorphin called enkephalin   N. it is
safer than drugs   O. telepathy

Application Answers

   6.1   A. monocular depth cue   B. monocular
depth cue   C. binocular depth cue   D. Gestalt laws of
organization   E. Gestalt laws of organization
F. monocular depth cue   G. illusion

Self-Test Answers

Answer	Learning Objective		Answer	Learning Objective
1. C	6.1		14. C	6.15
2. A	6.2		15. C	6.15
3. C	6.3		16. A	6.16
4. A	6.4		17. B	6.17
5. B	6.5		18. B	6.18
6. B	6.7		19. A	6.18
7. D	6.8		20. D	6.19
8. D	6.9		21. C	6.20
9. C	6.10		22. A	6.21
10. B	6.11		23. C	6.22
11. C	6.12		24. D	6.23
12. B	6.13		25. A	6.24
13. D	6.14			

Chapter Six

Progress Check Answers

   6.1 **1.** A. feel it is unnecessary to make
B. interact with   C. varied sensory experience
D. during critical periods   E. bored and irritable
F. improves
   6.2 **1.** A. retina   B. cornea   C. pupil   D. iris
E. crystalline lens   F. photoreceptors   G. cones   H.
rods   I. fovea   J. receptive fields   **2.** A. many types
B. wavelengths ranging from 400 to 750 nanometers
C. improves   D. rods than cones   E. convergence
F. Duplicity   G. cones   H. more   I. optic chiasm
J. single-unit recording   K. more   L. sensitive   to
experience
   6.3 **1.** A. brightness   B. hue   C. saturation
2. A. do not possess   B. brighter   C. wide   D. fire,
but not as often   E. retina   F. are different, but
compatible   G. Monochromats   H. lack specific color-
absorbing pigments   I. gender-linked   J. develops with
experience   K. binocular depth   L. texture
M. Accommodation   N. very little   O. convergence
P. Ponzo   Q. continuity   R. Law of Prägnanz
   6.4 **1.** A. one-quarter of a   B. and conducting a
visual search   C. different   D. attenuation theory
E. limited capacity   F. a limited image space
G. photographlike   H. nonperceptual variables

Chapter Seven

Progress Check Answers

   7.1 **1.** A. embryo   B. zygote   C. placenta
D. fetus   **2.** A. a Fallopian tube   B. 266   C. is formed
D. during the second trimester   E. fifth   F. second
trimester   G. drugs of any kind   H. how the mother
responds to the child   I. different   J. active labor
K. within two hours after   L. cognitive and motor
development
   7.2 **1.** A. complex   B. timetable   C. visual cliff
D. can behave according to   E. Babinski   F. rooting
G. Moro   H. nine
   7.3 **1.** A. biological   B. eighteen   C. three days
or less   D. six to seven   E. has developed   F. takes
place immediately   G. eat and sleep better   H. infant
I. genetic and environmental factors   J. the potential
emotional climate   K. Self-demand   L. should not be
thought of as being
   7.4 **1.** A. concrete operations   B. sensory-
motor   C. preoperations   D. formal operations
2. A. how   B. a stage   C. assimilated
D. Intentionality   E. decentration   F. make
appearance-reality distinctions   G. formal operations
H. recognizing and providing stimuli for   I. ask
different questions   J. acquires language
   7.5 **1.** A. twelve   B. alone or alongside   C. enter

nursery school or kindergarten   D. type of toys
E. quality of attention   F. should not try   G. does not
reduce   H. relatives or friends   I. negative and
positive   J. care for themselves when parents are not
home   K. follow a special diet

Application Answers

7.1   A. appearance-reality distinction
B. egocentrism   C. accommodation   D. assimilation
E. object permanence   F. conservation
G. decentration   H. intentionality

Self-Test Answer

Answer	Learning Objective		Answer	Learning Objective
1. B	7.1		13. C	7.13
2. C	7.2		14. A	7.13
3. C	7.3		15. B	7.13
4. D	7.4		16. D	7.15
5. B	7.5		17. D	7.17
6. A	7.6		18. C	7.18
7. A	7.7		19. C	7.19
8. C	7.8		20. D	7.20
9. D	7.8		21. B	7.21
10. A	7.9		22. C	7.22
11. D	7.10		23. B	7.22
12. C	7.12			

Chapter Eight

Progress Check Answers

8.1   **1.** A. basic trust vs. mistrust   B. autonomy
vs. shame and doubt   C. initiative vs. guilt
D. industry vs. inferiority   E. identity vs. role confusion
F. intimacy vs. isolation   G. generativity vs. stagnation
H. ego integrity vs. despair   **2.** A. growth   B. must
be considered in a cultural context   C. Puberty
D. just before   E. by both sexes   F. moderately strict
G. a normal part of intimate relationships   H. 20
percent   I. reached epidemic proportions   J. failed to
resolve his or her   K. a full life span   L. on a
continuum of doing one's best
8.2   **1.** A. rigid and rule bound   B. allows a
person to be flexible   C. justice   D. reward and
punishment   E. conscience   F. how reasoning
develops   G. higher or lower   H. opportunities for role
playing
8.3   **1.** A. 1970s   B. can take years   C. unique
patterns of interacting with life events   D. early
adulthood   E. early   F. middle   G. Both men and
women   H. thirty   I. high-frequency   J. change as
people face new challenges
8.4   **1.** A. 74.7   B. limited   C. a prejudice
against   D. according to negative stereotypes
E. homeostasis   F. autoimmunity   G. chronic brain
disorders   H. little   I. health   J. a decline in
intellectual functioning   K. the tests are timed   L. are
not certain about whether   M. more
8.5   **1.** A. mid-life   B. is a natural process   C. as
a temporary defense   D. denial   E. find the

acceptance stage easier   F. give up hope for a cure
G. an insightful discussion of feeling shared by dying
people   H. of a terminal disease   I. make difficult
decisions

Applying Principles Answers

8.1   A. Level 3, Part 1   B. Level 1   C. Level 3,
Part 2   D. Level 2

Self-Test Answers

Answer	Learning Objective		Answer	Learning Objective
1. D	8.2		12. C	8.10
2. C	8.3		13. D	8.11
3. B	8.4		14. D	8.12
4. D	8.5		15. C	8.13
5. D	8.6		16. D	8.14
6. A	8.7		17. A	8.15
7. B	8.7		18. C	8.17
8. C	8.8		19. A	8.18
9. D	8.8		20. D	8.19
10. D	8.9		21. A	8.19
11. B	8.10		22. B	8.20

Chapter Nine

Progress Check Answers

9.1   **1.** A. morpheme   B. syntax   C. grammar
D. psycholinguistics   E. phonology   F. phonemes
G. semantics   H. transformational grammar   **2.** A. do
not necessarily mature   B. quality   C. forty-five
D. To   E. is not   F. are born with the ability
G. surface   H. developed constrained and rule-
governed   I. being reinforced by parents and their own
words   J. the generation of infinite numbers of
sentences   K. lateralization   L. simply mirror teacher
responses   M. spontaneity and effort
9.2   **1.** A. percentile score   B. representative
sample   C. norms   D. deviation IQ   E. raw score
F. standard score   G. reliability   H. validity
2. A. behaviorally   B. adapt to the environment   C. a
battery of tests   D. an achievement   E. standardized
F. a representative sample of the population
G. standard deviation   H. 34.13 percent   I. of
imperfect reliability   J. only
9.3   **1.** A. cognitive developmental stages
B. indirect   C. some underlying attribute
D. cognitive   E. verbal fluency   F. children ages four
to six and a half   G. verbal and nonverbal   H. solve
novel problems   I. environmental background
J. mental processing abilities
9.4   **1.** A. debate whether   B. halo effects
C. interpretation of scores   D. life experiences   E. are
not   F. has little meaning in isolation   G. nature
H. nurture contributes equally or more than
I. narrowing   J. greater   K. decrease
9.5   **1.** A. academic achievement   B. does not
have to   C. are capable of high performance
D. gifted, mentally retarded, and other   E. 70
F. organic   G. physical trauma   H. have one relative

who is also retarded   I. normalize   J. actual performance is   K. can be

Applying Principles Answers
9.1   A. severe   B. mild   C. moderate
D. profound

Self-Test Answers

Answer	Learning Objective		Answer	Learning Objective
1. C	9.1		13. A	9.12
2. B	9.2		14. B	9.13
3. B	9.3		15. B	9.14
4. A	9.4		16. C	9.15
5. D	9.5		17. D	9.16
6. C	9.6		18. A	9.17
7. B	9.7		19. D	9.18
8. D	9.8		20. D	9.18
9. C	9.9		21. B	9.19
10. D	9.10		22. B	9.20
11. C	9.10		23. A	9.21
12. D	9.11			

Chapter Ten

Progress Check Answers
10.1   1. A. socialization   B. a lifelong process
C. individual   D. behavioral   E. can be modified by
new experiences   F. classical conditioning   G. work
if a lack of change has unpleasant consequences
H. regardless of its   I. models provided by
interpersonal sources   J. an attempt to increase
consistency in   K. motivated   L. infer an attitude from
a behavior   M. seldom   N. "birds of a feather flock
together"   O. motivational   P. establish a sense of
autonomy
10.2   1. A. six   B. through the eyes   C. women
D. modest amounts of   E. internal   F. situational
factors   G. attribution   H. fundamental attribution
error   I. comparing themselves with other people
J. our attractiveness   K. are depressed or lonely
L. stop responding   M. anxiety and depression
10.3   1. A. are not physical   B. are predisposed
toward   C. themselves   D. unlike   E. instinctive and
inevitable   F. creates a readiness for   G. certain cues
are available   H. see someone   I. nearly twice as
J. cognitive control over   K. has at least four ways of
influencing   L. believe television to be "the truth"
10.4   1. A. the majority opinion is wrong   B. can
have substantial   C. flexible   D. people want to be
"right"   E. disappears   F. 65 percent   G. background
authority   H. the situational context   I. is not
J. subjects' peers refused to participate   K. Debriefing
10.5   1. A. social facilitation   B. deindividuation
C. social loafing   D. diffusion of responsibility
E. group polarization   F. groupthink   **2.** A. we sense
that our behavior is being evaluated   B. cannot be
evaluated   C. identifiable   D. an individualistic
E. extreme   F. persuasive arguments   G. retreating
to their original   H. a strong leader and a
I. anonymity and arousal   J. military boot camps

Applying Principles Answers
10.1   A. instrumental conditioning   B. classical
conditioning   C. social learning
10.2   A. social facilitation   B. group polarization
C. diffusion of responsibility   D. social loafing
E. groupthink   F. deindividuation

Self-Test Answers

Answer	Learning Objective		Answer	Learning Objective
1. D	10.1		12. B	10.10
2. A	10.2		13. C	10.11
3. B	10.2		14. A	10.12
4. B	10.3		15. B	10.12
5. B	10.4		16. A	10.13
6. B	10.5		17. C	10.14
7. C	10.5		18. D	10.15
8. B	10.6		19. B	10.16
9. C	10.7		20. A	10.17
10. D	10.8		21. C	10.17
11. A	10.9		22. D	10.17

Chapter Eleven

Progress Check Answers
11.1   1. A. a private, invisible area around a
person   B. varies from culture to culture   C. are
aversive and can cause withdrawal   D. personal   E. a
person's reaction to the number of people   F. small,
private spaces   G. alone and anonymous   H. the self
requires   I. fixed space   J. few or no other
K. experience indecision and conflict   L. feels
competent to provide help   M. to do so could threaten
their self-esteem
11.2   1. A. interpersonal attraction   B. like us
and are like us   C. all   D. reinforcement and similar
opinions   E. fairness and equality of contributions
within   F. exclusiveness of   G. has a secure sense of
self-identity   H. Men
11.3   1. A. the Kinsey report   B. sexual
intercourse   C. have many nerve endings   D. clitoris
E. Women   F. a reversal   G. men and women, but
more for women   H. a decrease   I. more
11.4   1. A. more   B. psychological   C. more
D. both partners to feel equivalency and fairness   E. is
currently raising their   F. interpersonal   G. states his
or her feelings   H. does not necessarily indicate
I. win   J. Placater   K. active listening must occur
L. willing to risk sharing   M. appears to be

Applying Principles Answers
11.1   A. blamer   B. placater   C. computer
D. distractor

Self-Test Answers

Answer	Learning Objective		Answer	Learning Objective
1. A	11.1		4. D	11.1 & 11.3
2. A	11.1		5. A	11.4
3. C	11.2		6. B	11.5

Answer	Learning Objective		Answer	Learning Objective
7. B	11.6	:	13. D	11.11
8. B	11.8	:	14. A	11.11
9. D	11.8	:	15. C	11.12
10. B	11.9	:	16. D	11.13
11. C	11.10	:	17. C	11.14
12. C	11.11	:		

Answer	Learning Objective		Answer	Learning Objective
7. D	12.7	:	16. A	12.16
8. B	12.8	:	17. C	12.17
9. C	12.9	:	18. B	12.18
10. B	12.10	:	19. A	12.19
11. A	12.11	:	20. B	12.20
12. B	12.12	:	21. C	12.21
13. B	12.13	:	22. B	12.22
14. B	12.14	:	23. A	12.23
15. B	12.15	:	24. D	12.24

Chapter Twelve

Progress Check Answers

12.1 **1.** A. relatively enduring and stable B. trait C. cardinal D. is the basic unit of personality E. secondary F. different combinations of traits G. cluster together H. source I. type J. psychoticism K. biological differences L. but do not

12.2 **1.** A. oral B. anal C. phallic D. latency E. genital **2.** A. global B. is difficult to test experimentally C. instinctual needs and social demands D. psychoanalytic theory E. can become F. selfish, irrational, and demanding G. reality H. a person's conscience I. competing J. life K. id L. anxiety M. distorting reality N. reaction formation O. unconscious P. same Q. occurs because of unresolved conflicts R. is frustrated or overindulged

12.3 **1.** A. fulfillment of personal goals motivated by B. have an inborn tendency that directs them toward C. ideal D. unidirectional E. Abraham Maslow F. has a need G. person's self-concept H. superiority and perfection I. inherently j. early family relationships K. birth order L. stresses an interpersonal route to fulfillment

12.4 **1.** A. a technology of B. rejected C. the response D. satisfy specific needs E. always capable of change F. two stimuli are paired G. time-out H. imitation I. learn to choose which behaviors to exhibit or inhibit J. Reinforcement

12.5 **1.** A. thoughts B. Microtheories C. Freud's D. in control of E. specific expectancies F. sense of self-efficacy G. one's effectiveness H. choice and individual flexibility I. ability to adapt J. personal and situational K. a self-regulation system

12.6 **1.** A. a battery or several diagnostic tests B. projective tests C. have fewer guidelines for how to respond D. overt and directly observable E. naturalistic observation F. change G. appropriate treatment

Applying Principles Answers

12.1 A. reaction formation B. rationalization C. denial D. projection E. repression

Self-Test Answers

Answer	Learning Objective		Answer	Learning Objective
1. D	12.1	:	4. C	12.4
2. B	12.2	:	5. D	12.5
3. A	12.3	:	6. C	12.6

Chapter Thirteen

Progress Check Answers

13.1 **1.** A. behavioral model B. statistical model C. legal definition D. statistical model E. medical model F. behavioral model **2.** A. an abnormal behavior B. problem behavior can be treated C. 20 percent D. social norms E. therapist F. helping a person change G. legal H. understanding the causes of I. biological J. of control they assign to the individual K. thinking L. but perpetuates the use of medical M. is leading to more precise diagnoses of N. treatment and problem-solving information

13.2 **1.** A. injurious B. nonspecific C. physiological arousal D. alarm E. resistance F. the likelihood of health problems resulting from G. is not under H. Post-traumatic Stress Disorder I. causes J. high-stress, lives-at-stake K. adaptive L. when they cannot be controlled M. Aggressive N. protect people from the effects of O. identifying the stressor P. gradual exposure to stress Q. is not

13.3 **1.** A. anxiety B. free-floating anxiety C. Generalized Anxiety Disorder D. Phobic Disorder E. Obsessive-Compulsive Disorder **2.** A. has too many defenses against B. overgeneralized response patterns C. inappropriate and inefficient D. may or may not have E. thirty to sixty F. can be found in well-adjusted people G. Agoraphobia H. extreme fear and acute anxiety I. Simple Phobia J. obsessions K. person will experience severe anxiety

13.4 **1.** A. psychological dependence B. substance dependence C. tolerance D. dependence E. withdrawal symptoms F. pathological use **2.** A. various combinations of drugs B. 5 C. 7 percent D. depressant E. increase F. .10 percent G. may or may not be H. physically addicted to alcohol I. an alcoholic is an alcoholic forever

Applying Principles Answers

13.1 A. Post-traumatic Stress Disorder B. general adaptation syndrome C. Generalized Anxiety Disorder D. Simple Phobia E. Obsessive-Compulsive Disorder F. Social Phobia G. Psychoactive Substance Abuse Disorder H. Agoraphobia

Self-Test Answers

Answer	Learning Objective		Answer	Learning Objective
1. D	13.1		13. D	13.11
2. B	13.2		14. D	13.12
3. A	13.3		15. C	13.13
4. A	13.4		16. B	13.14
5. B	13.5		17. C	13.15
6. B	13.6		18. D	13.15
7. C	13.7		19. D	13.16
8. D	13.8		20. B	13.17
9. C	13.9		21. D	13.18
10. D	13.9		22. A	13.19
11. C	13.10		23. D	13.20
12. A	13.10			

Answer	Learning Objective		Answer	Learning Objective
7. A	14.5		14. D	14.11
8. A	14.6		15. C	14.11
9. C	14.7		16. B	14.12
10. A	14.8		17. A	14.13
11. D	14.8		18. B	14.14
12. C	14.9		19. D	14.15
13. B	14.10		20. B	14.15

Chapter Fifteen

Progress Check Answers

15.1 **1.** A. behavior modification   B. how personality and abnormal behaviors develop   C. client makes changes   D. insight and behavior   E. short-term   F. specific information about what therapy is effective with what client   G. explores previously avoided material

15.2 **1.** A. unconscious and unresolved conflicts B. highly motivated and articulate   C. a unique patient-therapist relationship   D. make connections among thoughts   E. express itself in   F. detect common threads   G. accepts   H. patient to work through repressed   I. the reality principle   J. an inability to express innate potential   K. self   L. a nondirective approach   M. have an empathetic understanding of N. current   O. incomplete gestalts   P. an experiential

15.3 **1.** A. modify maladaptive behaviors and teach adaptive behavior   B. an invasion of privacy C. person's behavior changes   D. does not seem to occur in   E. identify and measure   F. combine and integrate several approaches   G. can be traded for privileges   H. social norms   I. by a paraprofessional J. positive reinforcement   K. time-out   L. previously conditioned

15.4 **1.** A. Bandura   B. observe and imitate C. irrational thinking   D. "shoulds" and "musts" in their thinking   E. expect to improve   F. self-help G. insight and behavior   H. is under scientific debate I. physiological changes

15.5 **1.** A. less expensive than   B. social pressures that operate   C. allows the group to determine its own   D. become more aware E. treating the entire family   F. reframing G. Community psychologists   H. community psychology   I. in a variety of populations and J. immediate, directive   K. prevention

Applying Principles Answers

15.1   A. behavior modification   B. family therapy C. rational-emotive therapy   D. crisis intervention E. psychoanalysis   F. group therapy   G. client-centered therapy

Self-Test Answers

Answer	Learning Objective		Answer	Learning Objective
1. C	15.1		3. A	15.3
2. C	15.2		4. B	15.4

Chapter Fourteen

Progress Check Answers

14.1 **1.** A. extreme signs   B. nineteen   C. an increase   D. has a biological origin   E. conduct disorders   F. an Antisocial Personality   G. show gross distortions   H. two and a half   I. Bizarre, repetitious motions   J. people   K. boys   L. a false perception of being overweight   M. staff members need to be present   N. binge eating and purging

14.2 **1.** A. Somatization   B. Dissociative C. usually brought on by stress   D. unaware E. Histrionic   F. be charming in a superficial way G. limbic system   H. adrenalin   I. 60 percent J. Voyeurism   K. children   L. inflicting pain on M. are transsexuals

14.3 **1.** A. emotions   B. vacillates between mania and depression   C. Women   D. duration and extent of   E. out of touch with reality   F. themselves or they may have delusions of persecution G. norepinephrine levels   H. a lack of positive reinforcement   I. negative feelings cause depression J. learned helplessness

14.4 **1.** A. Paranoid Type   B. Residual Type C. Disorganized Type   D. Catatonic Type E. Undifferentiated Type   **2.** A. a lack of reality testing B. hallucination   C. flat   D. Paranoid   E. 35 percent F. five times higher   G. dopamine   H. a virus   I. oral J. schism   K. double bind   L. allow the person to escape from anxiety   M. biological predispostion

Applying Principles Answers

14.1   A. Schizophrenia   B. Personality Disorder (Antisocial)   C. Attention-deficit Hyperactivity Disorder D. Somatization Disorder   E. Affective Disorder F. Personality Disorder (Histrionic)

Self-Test Answers

Answer	Learning Objective		Answer	Learning Objective
1. B	14.1		4. C	14.3
2. D	14.2		5. B	14.4
3. D	14.2		6. B	14.5

Answer	Learning Objective		Answer	Learning Objective
5. B	15.5	:	15. B	15.15
6. C	15.6	:	16. A	15.16
7. D	15.7	:	17. B	15.17
8. C	15.8	:	18. B	15.18
9. B	15.9	:	19. A	15.19
10. D	15.10	:	20. D	15.20
11. C	15.11	:	21. D	15.21
12. D	15.12	:	22. D	15.22
13. A	15.13	:	23. C	15.23
14. C	15.14	:		

Appendix ═══════════════

Applying Principles Answers

A. .13%   B. 2.14%   C. 13.59%   D. 34.13%
E. 34.13%   F. 13.59%   G. 2.14%   H. .13%   I. 97%

Self-Test Answers

Answer	Learning Objective		Answer	Learning Objective
1. B	A.1	:	6. B	A.4
2. C	A.1	:	7. D	A.5
3. C	A.2	:	8. B	A.6
4. A	A.3	:	9. A	A.6
5. C	A.4	:	10. D	A.7

References

Aarons, L. (1976). Sleep assisted instruction. *Psychological Bulletin, 83,* 1–40.

Abikoff, H. (1985). Efficacy of cognitive training interventions in hyperactive children: A critical review. *Clinical Psychology Review, 5,* 479–512.

Abramowitz, S. I., & Bell, N. W. (1985). Biofeedback, self-control and tension headache. *Journal of Psychosomatic Research, 29,* 95–99.

Acredolo, L. P., & Hake, J. L. (1982). Infant perception. In B. B. Wolman (Ed.), *Developmental psychology handbook.* Englewood Cliffs, NJ: Prentice-Hall.

Adams, H. E., Feuerstein, M., & Fowler, J. L. (1980). Migraine headaches: review of parameters, etiology, and intervention. *Psychological Bulletin, 87,* 217–237.

Ader, R. (Ed.). (1981). *Psychoneuroimmunology.* New York: Academic Press.

Adler, A. (1969). *The science of living.* Garden City, NY: Anchor Books. (Original work published 1929)

Agnew, H. W., Jr., & Webb, W. B. (1973). The influence of time course variable on REM sleep. *Bulletin of the Psychonomic Society, 2,* 131–133.

Agras, S., Sylvester, D., & Oliveau, D. (1969). The epidemiology of common fears and phobias. Unpublished manuscript, as cited in G. C. Davison & J. M. Neale, (1978), *Abnormal psychology: An experimental clinical approach* (2nd ed.). New York: John Wiley & Sons.

Aguilera, D. C., & Messick, J. M. (1982). *Crisis Intervention: Theory and methodology* (4th ed.). St. Louis: Mosby.

Aiello, J. R., & Thompson, D. E. (1980). Personal space, crowding, and spatial behavior in a cultural context. In I. Altman, A. Rapoport, & J. F. Wohlwill (Eds.), *Human behavior and environment: Vol. 2. Advances in theory and research.* New York: Plenum Press.

Aiken, L. R. (1979). *Psychological testing and assessment* (3rd ed.). Boston: Allyn and Bacon.

Aiken, L. R. (1985). *Dying, death, and bereavement.* Boston: Allyn and Bacon.

Ainsworth, M. D. S. (1979). Infant-mother attachment. *American Psychologist, 34,* 932–937.

Akiskal, H. S. (1979). The biobehavioral approach to depression. In R. A. DePue (Ed.), *Psychobiology of the depressive disorders.* New York: Academic Press.

Albert, I. B. (1975). REM sleep deprivation. *Biological Psychiatry, 19,* 341–351.

Albert, M. S., Butters, N., & Levin, J. (1979). Temporal gradients in the retrograde amnesia of patients with alcoholic Korsakoff's disease. *Archives of Neurology, 36,* 211–216.

Albrecht, S. L., Thomas, D. L., & Chadwick, B. A. (1980). *Social psychology.* Englewood Cliffs, NJ: Prentice-Hall.

Alder, E. M., & Cox, J. L. (1983). Breast feeding and post-natal depression. *Journal of Psychosomatic Research, 27,* 139–144.

Alfaro, J. D. (1981). Report on the relationship between child abuse and neglect and later socially deviant behavior. In R. J. Hunner & Y. E. Walker (Eds.), *Exploring the relationship between child abuse and delinquency* (pp. 175–219). Montclair, NJ: Allanheld, Osmun.

Alheid, G. F., McDermott, L. J., Kelly, J., Halaris, A., Grossman, S. P. (1977). Deficits in food and water intake after knife cuts that deplete striatal DA or hypothalamic NE in rats. *Pharmacological Biochemistry of Behavior, 6,* 273–287.

Allen, K. E., Turner, K. D., & Everett, P. M. (1970). A behavior modification classroom for head start children with problem behaviors. *Exceptional Children, 37,* 119–127.

Allen, M. (1983). Models of hemispheric specialization. *Psychological Bulletin, 93,* 73–104.

Allen, M. G. (1976). Twin studies of affective illness. *Archives of General Psychiatry, 33,* 1476–1478.

Allen, R. P. (1986). The sleepy patient: Evaluation and management. *Clinical Psychology Review, 6,* 51–66.

Allington, R. L. (1981). Sensitivity to orthographic structure in educable mentally retarded children. *Contemporary Educational Psychology, 6,* 135–139.

Altman, I. (1975). *The environment and social behavior.* Monterey, CA: Brooks/Cole.

Altman, I., & Vinsel, A. M. (1977). Personal space: An analysis of E. T. Hall's proxemics framework. In I. Altman, A. Rapoport, & J. F. Wohlwill (Eds.), *Human behavior and environment: Vol. 2. Advances in theory and research.* New York: Plenum Press.

Amen, D. G. (1985). Post-Vietnam stress disorder: A metaphor for current and past life events. *American Journal of Psychotherapy, 39,* 580–582.

American Psychiatric Association (1980). *Diagnostic and statistical manual of mental disorders* (3rd ed.). Washington, DC: Author.

American Psychiatric Association (1987). *Diagnostic and statistical manual of mental disorders* (Third Edition-Revised). Washington, D.C.

American Psychological Association. (1985). *Violence on TV. A social issue release from the Board of Social and Ethical Responsibility for Psychology.* Washington, DC: Author.

Ames, L. D., Gillespie, C., Haines, J., Ilg, F. L. (1979). *The Gesell Institute's child from one to six.* New York: Harper & Row.

Anastasi, A. (1981). Coaching, test sophistication, and developed abilities. *American Psychologist, 36,* 1086–1093.

Anderson, R., Manoogian, S., & Reznick, J. (1976). Undermining and enhancing of intrinsic motivation in pre-school children. *Journal of Personality and Social Psychology, 34,* 915–922.

Aneshensel, C. S., & Stone, J. D. (1982). Stress and depression: A test of the buffering model of social support. *Archives of General Psychiatry, 39,* 1392–1396.

Appel, J. B., & Peterson, N. J. (1965). What's wrong with punishment? *Journal of Criminal Law, Criminology, and Police Science, 156,* 450–453.

Arenberg, D. (1978). Differences and changes with age in the Benton visual retention test. *Journal of Gerontology, 33,* 534–540.

Argyle, M. (1972). Nonverbal communication in human social interaction. In R. Hinte (Ed.), *Nonverbal communication.* New York: Cambridge University Press.

Aries, E. J., & Johnson, F. L. (1983). Close friendship in adulthood: Conversational content between same-sex friends. *Sex Roles, 9,* 1183–1196.

Arieti, S. (1980). Psychotherapy of schizophrenia: New and revised procedures. *American Journal of Psychotherapy, 34,* 464–476.

Aronson, E., & O'Leary, M. (1983). The relative effects of models and prompts on energy conservation. *Journal of Environmental Systems, 12,* 219–224.

Aronson, M. K., Levin, G., & Lipkowitz, R. (1984). A community-based family/patient group program for Alzheimer's disease. *The Gerontologist, 24,* 339–342.

Asaad, G., & Shapiro, B. (1986). Hallucinations: Theoretical and clinical overview. *American Journal of Psychiatry, 143,* 1088–1097.

Aslin, R. N., & Jackson, R. W. (1979). Accommodative-convergence in young infants: Development of a synergistic sensory-motor system. *Canadian Journal of Psychology, 33,* 222–231.

Athanasiou, R. (1976). Frequency of masturbation in adult men and women. *Medical Aspects of Human Sexuality,* Feb., 121.

Athanasou, J. A. (1974). Smoking behavior and its modification through hypnosis: A review and evaluation. *Terpnos Logos, 2*(2), 4–15.

Atkinson, J. W. (1964). *An introduction to motivation.* Princeton, NJ: Van Nostrand.

Auerbach, S. M., & Kilmann, P. R. (1977). Crisis intervention: A review of outcome research. *Psychological Bulletin, 84,* 1189–1217.

Ayllon, T., & Azrin, N. H. (1965). The measurement and reinforcement behavior of psychotics. *Journal of the Experimental Analysis of Behavior, 8,* 357–383.

Ayllon, T., & Azrin, N. H. (1968). *The token economy: A motivational system for therapy and rehabilitation.* New York: Appleton-Century-Crofts.

Ayllon, T., & Haughton, E. (1964). Modification of symptomatic verbal behavior of mental patients. *Behavior Research and Therapy, 2,* 87–97.

Bach, G., & Wyden, P. (1970). *The intimate caring: How to fight fair in love and marriage.* New York: Avon Press.

Baddeley, A. D. & Hitch, G. (1974). Working memory. In G. Bower (Ed.), *Recent advances in learning and motivating.* (Vol. 8). New York: Academic Press.

Baddeley, A. D., & Longman, D. J. A. (1966). The influence of length and frequency of training session on rate of learning to type. (Unpublished manuscript, Medical Research Council Applied Psychology Unit, Cambridge.) In A. D. Baddeley (Ed.), *The Psychology of Memory.* New York: Basic Books.

Baddeley, A. D., & Warrington, E. K. (1970). Amnesia and the distinction between long- and short-term memory. *Journal of Verbal Learning and Verbal Behavior, 9,* 176–189.

Bahrick, L. E., Walker, A. S., & Neisser, U. (1981). Selective looking by infants. *Cognitive Psychology, 13,* 377–390.

Balch, P., & Ross, A. W. (1975). Predicting success in weight reduction as a function of locus of control: A unidimensional and multi-dimensional approach. *Journal of Consulting and Clinical Psychology, 43,* 119.

Balick, L., Elfner, L., May, J. (1982). Biofeedback treatment of dysmenorrhea. *Biofeedback and Self-Regulation, 7,* 499–520.

Ball, G. G. (1972). Self-stimulation in the ventromedial hypothala-

mus. *Science, 178,* 72–73.

Bandura, A. (1964). The stormy decade: Fact or fiction? *Psychology in the Schools, 1,* 224–231.

Bandura, A. (1969). *Principles of behavior modification.* New York: Holt, Rinehart and Winston.

Bandura, A. (1971). Analysis of modeling processes. In A. Bandura (Ed.), *Psychological modeling—conflicting theories.* Chicago: Aldine-Atherton.

Bandura, A. (1973). *Aggression: A social learning analysis.* Englewood Cliffs, NJ: Prentice-Hall.

Bandura, A. (1974). Behavior theory and the models of man. *American Psychologist, 29,* 859–869.

Bandura, A. (1977a). Self-efficacy: Toward a unifying theory of behavioral change. *Psychological Review, 84,* 191–215.

Bandura, A. (1977b). *Social learning theory.* Englewood Cliffs, NJ: Prentice-Hall.

Bandura, A. (1982a). Self-efficacy: Mechanism in human agency. *American Psychologist, 37,* 122–147.

Bandura, A. (1982b). The psychology of chance encounters and life paths. *American Psychologist, 37,* 747–755.

Bandura, A. (1983). Self-efficacy determinants of anticipated fears and calamities. *Journal of Personality and Social Psychology, 45,* 464–469.

Bandura, A., & Barab, P. G. (1973). Processes governing disinhibitory effects through symbolic modeling. *Journal of Abnormal Psychology, 82,* 1–9.

Bandura, A., Blanchard, E. B., Ritter, B. (1969). Relative efficacy of desensitization and modeling approaches for inducing behavioral, affective, and attitudinal changes. *Journal of Personality and Social Psychology, 13,* 173–199.

Bandura, A., Jeffery, R. W., & Gagdos, E. (1975). Generalized change through participant modeling with self-directed mastery. *Behavior Research and Therapy, 13,* 141–152.

Bandura, A., & Menlove, F. L. (1968). Factors determining vicarious extinction of avoidance through symbolic modeling. *Journal of Personality and Social Psychology, 8,* 99–108.

Bandura, A., Ross, D., & Ross, S. A. (1963a). Imitation of film-mediated aggressive models. *Journal of Abnormal and Social Psychology, 66,* 3–11.

Bandura, A., Ross, D., & Ross, S. A. (1963b). Vicarious reinforcement of imitative learning. *Journal of Abnormal and Social Psychology, 67,* 601–607.

Bandura, A., Ross, D., & Ross, S. A. (1963c). A comparative test of the status envy, social power, and secondary reinforcement theories of identificatory learning. *Journal of Abnormal and Social Psychology, 67,* 527–534.

Bandura, A., & Walters, R. (1963). *Social learning and personality development.* New York: Holt, Rinehart and Winston.

Barber, T. X., & Calverley, D. S. (1965). Toward a theory of hypnotic behavior: Effects on suggestibility of defining the situation as hypnosis and defining response in suggestions, it's easy. *Journal of Abnormal and Social Psychology, 29,* 98–107.

Barclay, C. R., & Wellman, H. M. (1986). Accuracies and inaccuracies in autobiographical memories. *Journal of Memory and Language, 25,* 93–103.

Bardon, J. I. (1982). The role and function of the school psychologist. In A. Reynolds & T. B. Gutkin (Eds.), *The handbook of school psychology.* New York: John Wiley & Sons.

Bardon, J. I. (1983). Psychology applied to education: A specialty in search of an identity. *American Psychologist, 38,* 185–196.

Barefoot, J. C., Hoople, H., & McClay, D. (1972). Avoidance of an act which would violate personal space. *Psychonomic Science, 28,* 205–206.

Baron, R. A., & Byrne, D. (1987). *Social Psychology: Understanding human interaction* (5th ed.). Boston: Allyn and Bacon.

Bartak, L. (1978). Educational approaches. In M. Rutter & E. Schopler (Eds.), *Autism: A reappraisal of concepts and treatment.* New York: Plenum Press.

Bartlett, F. C. (1932). *Remembering: A study in experimental and social psychology.* New York: Macmillan.

Baruth, L. G. (1979). *A single parent's survival guide: How to raise the children.* Dubuque, IA: Kendall/Hunt.

Bauer, R. H. (1977). Memory processes in children with learning disabilities: Evidence for deficient rehearsal. *Journal of Experimental Child Psychology, 24,* 415–430.

Bauer, R. H. (1979). Memory, acquisition, and category clustering in learning-disabled children. *Journal of Experimental Child Psychology, 27,* 365–383.

Baumeister, R. F., & Tice, D. M. (1985). Self-esteem and responses to success and failure: Subsequent performance and intrinsic motivation. *Journal of Personality, 53,* 450–467.

Beach, F. A. (1983). Hormones and psychological processes (Daniel Berlyne Memorial Lecture). *Canadian Journal of Psychology, 37,* 193–210.

Beck, A. T. (1963). Thinking and depression: 1. Idiosyncratic content in cognitive distortions. *Archives of General Psychiatry, 9,* 324–333.

Beck, A. T. (1967). *Depression: Clinical, experimental, and the theoretical aspects.* New York: Hober.

Beck, A. T. (1972). *Depression: Causes and treatment.* Philadelphia: University of Pennsylvania Press.

Beck, A. T. (1976). *Cognitive therapy and emotional disorders.* New York: International Universities Press.

Beck, J. (1966). Effects of orientation and of shape similarity on perceptual grouping. *Perception and Psychophysics, 1,* 311–312.

Bee, H. L. (1987). *The journey of adulthood.* New York: Macmillan.

Beech, H. R., Burns, L. E., & Sheffield, B. F. (1982). *A behavioral approach to the management of stress: A practical guide to techniques.* New York: John Wiley & Sons.

Bekerian, D. A., & Bowers, J. M. (1983). Eyewitness testimony: Were we misled? *Journal of Experimental Psychology: Learning, Memory, and Cognition, 9,* 139–145.

Bell, P. A., & Baron, R. A. (1976). Aggression and heat: The mediating negative effect. *Journal of Applied Social Psychology, 6,* 18–30.

Bell, R. B., & Chaskes, J. B. (1970). Premarital sexual experience among coeds, 1958 and 1968. *Journal of Marriage and the Family, 32,* 81–84.

Bellak, L. (1983). Psychoanalysis in the 1980s. *American Journal of Psychotherapy, 37,* 476–482.

Belle, D. (1982). The stress of caring: Women as providers of social support. In L. Goldberger & S. Breznitz (Eds.), *Handbook of stress: Theoretical and clinical aspects.* New York: The Free Press, a division of Macmillan.

Belsky, J., & Steinberg, L. D. (1978). The effects of day care: A critical review. *Child Development, 49,* 929–949.

Bem, D. J. (1972). Self-perception theory. In L. Berkowitz (Ed.), *Advances in experimental social psychology.* New York: Academic Press.

Bem, S. L. (1975). Sex-role adaptability: One consequence of psychological androgyny. *Journal of Personality and Social Psychology, 31,* 634–643.

Benassi, M. A. (1982). Effects of order of presentation, primacy, and attractiveness on attributions of ability. *Journal of Personality and Social Psychology, 43,* 48–58.

Benner, D. G., & Joscelyne, B. (1984). Multiple personality as a borderline disorder. *Journal of Nervous and Mental Diseases, 172,* 98–105.

Bennett, W. J. (Secretary). (1986). *What works. Schools without drugs.* Washington, D.C.: United States Department of Education.

Benson, K., & Feinberg, I. (1977). The beneficial effect of sleep in a Jenkins and Dallenbach paradigm. *Psychophysiology, 14,* 375–384.

Berbaum, M. L., Moreland, R. L., and Zajonc, R. B. (1986). Contentions over the confluence model: A reply to Price, Walsh, and Vilburg. *Psychological Bulletin, 100,* 270–274.

Berg, M. (1986). Toward a diagnostic alliance between psychiatrist and psychologist. *American Psychologist, 41,* 52–59.

Berkowitz, L. (1964). The effects of observing violence. *Scientific American, 210*(2), San Francisco: W. H. Freeman.

Berkowitz, L., & Donnerstein, E. (1982). External validity is more than skin deep: Some answers to criticisms of laboratory experiments. *American Psychologist, 37,* 245–257.

Berman, J. S., Miller, R. C., & Massman, P. J. (1985). Cognitive therapy versus systematic desensitization: Is one treatment superior? *Psychological Bulletin, 97,* 451–461.

Bernal, G., & Berger, S. M. (1976). Vicarious eyelid conditioning. *Journal of Personality and Social Psychology, 34,* 62–68.

Berry, D. S., & McArthur, L. Z. (1986). Perceiving character in faces: The impact of age-related craniofacial changes on social perception. *Psychological Bulletin, 100,* 3–18.

Berry, E. M., Hirsch, J., Most, J., & Thornton, J. (1986). The role of dietary fat in human obesity. *International Journal of Obesity, 10,* 123–131.

Bersoff, D. N. (1981). Testing and the law. *American Psychologist, 36,* 1047–1056.

Bertelson, A. D., Marks, P. A., & May, G. D. (1982). MMPI and race: A controlled study. *Journal of Consulting and Clinical Psychology, 50,* 316–318.

Berzins, J. I., Bednar, R. L., & Severy, L. J. (1975). The problem of intersource consensus in measuring therapeutic outcomes: New data and multi-variate perspectives. *Journal of Abnormal Psychology, 84,* 10–19.

Bexton, W. H., Heron, W., & Scott, T. H. (1954). Effects of decreased variation in the sensory environment. *Canadian Journal of Psychology, 8,* 70–76.

Bigham, J. (1894). Memory: Studies from Harvard (II). *Psychological Review, 1,* 453–461.

Birch, J. W. (1974). *Mainstreaming.* Reston, VA: Council for Exceptional Children.

Bird, E. D., Spokes, E. G. S., & Iversen, L. L. (1979). Increased dopamine concentration in limbic areas of brain from patients dying with schizophrenia. *Brain, 102,* 347–360.

Bishop, J. E. (1986). Technology. Researchers track pain's path, develop new kind of reliever. *The Wall Street Journal,* p. 23.

Blakemore, C. (1978). Maturation and modification in the developing visual system. In R. Held, H. W. Leibowitz, & H.-L. Teuber (Eds.), *Handbook of sensory physiology: Vol. 8. Perception.* New York: Springer-Verlag.

Blakemore, C., & Cooper, G. F. (1970). Development of the brain depends on the visual environment. *Nature, 228,* 477–478.

Blanchard, E. B., Andrasik, F., Neff, D. F., Arena, J. G., Ahles, T. A., Jurish, S. E., Pallmeyer, T. P., Saunders, N. L., Teders, S. J., Barron, K. D., & Rodichok, L. D. (1982). Biofeedback and relaxation training with three kinds of headache: Treatment effects and their prediction. *Journal of Consulting and Clinical Psychology, 50,* 562–575.

Blanchard, R., Steiner, B. W., & Clemmensen, L. H. (1985). Gender dysphoria, gender reorientation, and the clinical management of transsexualism. *Journal of Consulting and Clinical Psychology, 53,* 295–304.

Bloom, F. E. (1981). Neuropeptides. *Scientific American* (10), 148–168.

Bloom, F. E., Lazerson, A., & Hofstadter, L. (1985). *Brain, mind, and behavior.* New York: W. H. Freeman.

Bloomquist, M. L., & Harris, W. G. (1984). Measuring family functioning with the MMPI: A reliability and concurrent validity study of three MMPI family scales. *Journal of Clinical Psychology, 40,* 1209–1214.

Blum, K. (1984). *Handbook of abusable drugs.* New York: Gardner Press.

Blumenthal, M. D. (1975). Measuring depressive symptomatology in a general population. *Archives of General Psychiatry, 32,* 971–978.

Bond, C. F., Jr., & Titus, L. J. (1983). Social facilitation: A meta-analysis of 241 studies. *Psychological Bulletin, 94,* 265–292.

Bonnet, M. H. (1980). Sleep, performance, and mood after the energy-expenditure equivalent of 40 hours of sleep deprivation. *Psychophysiology, 17,* 56–63.

Booth, A., & Edwards, J. N. (1980). Fathers: The invisible parent. *Sex Roles, 6,* 445–456.

Borkowski, J. G., & Krause, A. (1983). Racial differences in intelligence: The importance of the executive system. *Intelligence, 7,* 379–395.

Botwinick, J. (1973). *Aging and behavior.* New York: Springer.

Botwinick, J. (1984). *Aging and behavior: A comprehensive integration of research findings* (3rd ed.). New York: Springer.

Boutin, G. E. (1978). Treatment of test anxiety by rational stage directed hypnotherapy: A case study. *American Journal of Clinical Hypnosis, 21,* 52–57.

Bower, G. H. (1972). Stimulus sampling theory of encoding variability. In A. W. Melton & E. Martin (Eds.), *Coding processes in human memory.* Washington, DC: V. H. Winston.

Bower, G. H. (1981). Mood and memory. *American Psychologist, 36,* 126–148.

Bower, T. G. R. (1966). The visual world of infants. *Scientific American, 215,* 80–92.

Bower, T. G. R. (1976). Repetitive processes in child development. *Scientific American, 235,* 38–47.

Bowerman, M. F. (1973). Structural relationships in children's utterances: Syntactic or semantic? In T. E. Moore (Ed.), *Cognitive development and the acquisition of language.* New York: Academic Press.

Bowers, M. B., Jr. (1982). Biochemical processes in schizophrenia: An update. *Schizophrenia Bulletin, 6,* 393–403.

Bowlby, J. (1958). The nature of the child's tie to his mother. *International Journal of Psychoanalysis, 39,* 350–373.

Bowlby, J. (1973). *Attachment and loss: Vol. 2. Separation: Anxiety and anger.* New York: Basic Books.

Bowlby, J. (1977). The making and breaking of affectional bonds: Etiology and psychopathology in the light of attachment theory. *British Journal of Psychiatry, 130,* 201–210.

Brabender, V., & Dickhaus, R. C. (1978). Effect of hypnosis on comprehension of complex verbal material. *Perceptual and Motor Skills, 47,* 1322.

Brackbill, Y. (1979). Obstetrical medication and infant behavior. In J. D. Osofsky (Ed.), *Handbook of infant development.* New York: John Wiley & Sons.

Brackbill, Y., & Nichols, P. L. (1982). A test of the confluence model of intellectual development. *Developmental Psychology, 18,* 192–198.

Bradley, R. H., & Caldwell, B. M. (1976). The relation of infants' home environments to mental test performance at fifty-four months: A follow-up study. *Child Development, 47,* 1172–1174.

Braine, M. D. S. (1963). On learning the grammatical order of words. *Psychological Review, 70,* 323–348.

Branden, N. (1980). *The psychology of romantic love.* Los Angeles: J. P. Tarcher.

Bregman, N. J., & McAllister, H. A. (1982). Motivation and skin temperature biofeedback: Yerkes-Dodson revisited. *Psychophysiology, 19,* 282–285.

Brehm, J. W. (1966). *A theory of psychological reactance.* New York: Academic Press.

Brehony, K. A., & Geller, E. S. (1981). Agoraphobia: Appraisal of research and a proposal for an integrativemodel. In M. Her-

sen, R. M. Eisler, & P. M. Miller (Eds.), *Progress in behavior modification* (Vol. *12*). New York: Academic Press.

Breier, A., Charney, D. S., & Heninger, G. R. (1984). Major depression in patients with agoraphobia and panic disorder. *Archives of General Psychiatry, 41,* 1129–1135.

Breier, A., Charney, D. S., & Heninger, G. R. (1986). Agoraphobia with panic attacks. Development, diagnostic stability, and course of illness. *Archives of General Psychiatry, 43,* 1029–1036.

Brody, H. (1978). Cell counts in cerebral cortex and brainstem. In R. Katzman, R. D. Terry, & K. L. Bick (Eds.), *Aging: Vol. 7. Alzheimer's disease: Senile dementil and related disorders.* New York: Raven Press.

Brook, J. S., Whiteman, M., & Gordon, A. S. (1983). Stages of drug use in adolescence: Personality, peer, and family correlates. *Developmental Psychology, 19,* 269–277.

Brooks, J. (1985). Polygraph testing. Thoughts of a sceptical legislator. *American Psychologist, 40,* 348–354.

Brown, D. T., & Minke, K. M. (1986). School psychology graduate training. A comprehensive analysis. *American Psychologist, 41,* 1328–1338.

Brown, G. E., Jr., Kilmann, P. R., & Wanlass, R. L. (1982). Characteristics of male and female masturbation. Paper presented at the Southeastern Psychological Association, New Orleans.

Brown, H. B. (1935). An experience in identification testimony. *Journal of the American Institute of Criminal Law, 25,* 621–622.

Brown, J. (1958). Some tests of the decay theory of immediate memory. *Quarterly Journal of Experimental Psychology, 10,* 12–21.

Brown, R. (1970). The first sentences of child and chimpanzee. In R. Brown (Ed.), *Psycholinguistics: Selected papers.* New York: Free Press.

Brownell, K. D. (1982). Obesity: Understanding and treating a serious, prevalent, and refractory disorder. *Journal of Consulting and Clinical Psychology, 50,* 820–840.

Bryant, L. E., & Budd, K. S. (1984). Teaching behaviorally handicapped preschool children to share. *Journal of Applied Behavior Analysis, 17,* 45–56.

Buchsbaum, M. S., Coursey, R. D., & Murphy, D. L. (1976). The biochemical high-risk paradigm: Behavioral and familial correlates of low platelet monoamine oxidase activity. *Science, 194,* 339–341.

Buck, R. (1979). Individual differences in nonverbal sending accuracy and electrodermal responding: The externalizing-internalizing dimension. In R. Rosenthal (Ed.), *Skill in nonverbal communication.* Cambridge, MA: Oelgeschlager, Gunn, & Hain.

Buck, R. (1980). Nonverbal behavior and the theory of emotion: The facial feedback hypothesis. *Journal of Personality and Social Psychology, 38,* 811–824.

Buck, R., Baron, R., Goodman, N., & Shapiro, B. (1980). Unitization of spontaneous nonverbal behavior in the study of emotion communication. *Journal of Personality and Social Psychology, 39,* 522–529.

Buckhour, R., Figueroa, D., Hoff, E. (1974). *Eyewitness identifications: Effects of suggestion and bias in identifications from photographs* (Report No. Cr-11). Brooklyn: Brooklyn College Center for Responsive Psychology.

Buglass, D., Clarke, J., Henderson, A. S., Kreitman, N., & Presley, A. S. (1977). A study of agoraphobic housewives. *Psychological Medicine, 7,* 73–86.

Burdi, A. R., Poissonnet, C-M., Garn, S. M., Lavalle, M., Sabet, M. D., & Bridges, P. (1985). Adipose tissue growth patterns during human gestation: A histometric comparison of buccal and gluteal fat depots. *International Journal of Obesity, 9,* 247–256.

Burnam, M. A., Pennebaker, J. W., & Glass, D. C. (1975). Time consciousness, achievement striving, and the Type A coronary-prone behavior pattern. *Journal of Abnormal Psychology, 84,* 76–79.

Butterfield-Picard, H., & Magno, J. B. (1982). Hospice the adjective, not the noun: The future of a national priority. *American Psychologist, 37,* 1254–1259.

Cabanac, M. (1986). Money versus pain: Experimental study of a conflict in humans. *Journal of the Experimental Analysis of Behavior, 46,* 37–44.

Cadden, V. (1964). Crisis in the family. Appendix B. In G. Caplan (Ed.), *Principles of preventive psychiatry.* New York: Basic Books.

Cadoret, R. J. (1978). Psychopathology in adopted-away offspring of biologic parents with antisocial behavior. *Archives of General Psychiatry, 35,* 176–184.

Callaway, E., Halliday, R., & Naylor, H. (1983). Hyperactive children's event-related potentials fail to support underarousal and maturational-lag theories. *Archives of General Psychiatry, 40,* 1243–1248.

Campagna, A. F., & Harter, S. (1975). Moral judgment in sociopathic and normal children. *Journal of Personality and Social Psychology, 31,* 199–205.

Campbell, M., Small, A. M., Green, W. H., Jennings, S. J., Perry, R., Bennett, W. G., & Anderson, L. (1984). Behavioral efficacy of haloperidol and lithium carbonate. A comparison in hospitalized aggressive children with conduct disorder. *Archives of General Psychiatry, 41,* 650–656.

Campbell, S. B. (1985). Hyperactivity in preschoolers: Correlates and prognostic implications. *Clinical Psychology Review, 5,* 405–428.

Cannon, W. B. (1927). The James-Lange theory of emotion: A critical examination and an alternative theory. *American Journal of Psychology, 39,* 106–124.

Cantor, N., & Kihlstrom, J. F. (1982). Cognitive and social processes in personality. In G. T. Wilson & C. M. Franks (Eds.), *Contemporary behavior therapy.* New York: Guilford Press.

Cantwell, D. P., Baker, L., & Rutter, M. (1978). Family factors. In M. Rutter & E. Schopler (Eds.), *Autism: A reappraisal of concepts and treatment.* New York: Plenum Press.

Caplan, G. (1976). The family as a support system. In G. Caplan & M. Killilea (Eds.), *Support systems and mutual help: Multidisciplinary explorations.* New York: Grune & Stratton.

Carlson, C. R., Gantz, F. P., & Masters, J. C. (1983). Adults' emotional states and recognition of emotion in young children. *Motivation and Emotion, 7,* 81–102.

Caron, R. F., Caron, A. J., Carlson, V. R., & Cobb, L. S. (1979). Perception of shape-at-a-slant in the young infant. *Bulletin of the Psychonomic Society, 1,* 229–243.

Cartwright, G. F., & Derevensky, J. L. (1977–1978). Interactive computer-assisted testing: A feasibility study. *Journal of Educational Technology Systems, 6,* 219–228.

Carver, C. S., & Glass, D. C. (1978). Coronary-prone behavior pattern and interpersonal aggression. *Journal of Personality and Social Psychology, 36,* 361–366.

Casey, R. J., & Berman, J. S. (1985). The outcome of psychotherapy with children. *Psychological Bulletin, 98,* 388–400.

Cash, T. F., & Kehr, J. (1978). Influence of nonprofessional counselors' physical attractiveness and sex on perceptions of counselor behavior. *Journal of Counseling Psychology, 25,* 336–342.

Cermak, L. S. (1972). *Human memory.* New York: Ronald Press.

Chafetz, M. E. (1979). Alcohol and alcoholism: The complexities of alcohol abuse require multiple research approaches toward effective treatment and prevention. *American Scientist,*

67, 293–299.

Chaiken, A. L., Sigler, E., & Derlega, V. J. (1974). Nonverbal mediators of teacher expectancy effects. *Journal of Personality and Social Psychology, 30,* 144–149.

Chaiken, S., & Eagly, A. H. (1983). Communication modality as a determinant of persuasion: The role of communicator salience. *Journal of Personality and Social Psychology, 45,* 241–256.

Chambless, D. L., Goldstein, A. J., Gallagher, R., & Bright, P. (1986). Integrating behavior therapy and psychotherapy in the treatment of agoraphobia. *Psychotherapy, 23,* 150–159.

Child, I. L. (1985). Psychology and anomalous observations. The question of ESP in dreams. *American Psychologist, 40,* 1219–1230.

Chomsky, N. (1957). *Syntactic structures.* The Hague, Netherlands: Mouton.

Chomsky, N. (1972). *Language and mind* (rev. ed.). New York: Harcourt Brace Jovanovich.

Chomsky, N. (1975). *Reflections on language.* New York: Pantheon Books.

Chumlea, W. C. (1982). Physical growth in adolescence. In B. B. Wolman (Ed.), *Handbook of developmental psychology.* Englewood Cliffs, NJ: Prentice-Hall.

Clancy, H. & McBride, G. (1969). The autistic process and its treatment. *Journal of Child Psychology and Psychiatry, 10,* 233–244.

Clarizio, H., & Veres, V. (1984). A short-form version of the WISC-R for the learning disabled. *Psychology in the Schools, 21,* 154–157.

Clarke-Stewart, A. (1978). And Daddy makes three: The father's impact on mother and young child. *Child Development, 49,* 466–478.

Cleckley, H. (1976). *The mask of sanity* (5th ed.). St. Louis, C. V. Mosby.

Clifford, M. M., & Walster, E. (1973). Research note: The effect of physical attractiveness on teacher expectation. *Sociology of Education, 46,* 248–258.

Coates, B., Pusser, H. E., & Goodman, I. (1976). The influence of "Sesame Street" and "Mister Rogers' Neighborhood" on children's social behavior in the preschool. *Child Development, 47,* 138–144.

Cohen, D. B. (1979). Dysphoric affect and REM sleep. *Journal of Abnormal Psychology, 88,* 73–77.

Cohen, J. B. (1985). *Parenthood after 30: A guide to personal choice.* Lexington, MA: D. C. Heath.

Cohen, J. F., & Tronick, E. Z. (1983). Three-month-old infants' reaction to simulated maternal depression. *Child Development, 54,* 185–193.

Cohen, R. M., Weingartner, H., Smallberg, S., Pickar, D., & Murphy, D. L. (1982). Effort and cognition in depression. *Archives of General Psychiatry, 39,* 593–597.

Cohen, S., & Hoberman, H. M. (1983). Positive events and social supports as buffers of life change stress. *Journal of Applied Social Psychology, 13,* 99–125.

Cole, N. S. (1981). Bias in testing. *American Psychologist, 36,* 1067–1077.

Cole, R. D. (1979). The use of hypnosis in a course to increase academic and test-taking skills. *International Journal of Clinical and Experimental Hypnosis, 27,* 21–28.

Coleman, J. C., Butcher, J. N., & Carson, R. C. (1980). *Abnormal psychology and modern life* (6th ed.). Glenview, IL: Scott, Foresman.

Collins, A., & Adams, M. J. (1977). Comparison of two teaching strategies in computer-assisted instruction. *Contemporary Educational Psychology, 2,* 133–148.

Collins, A. M., & Quillan, M. R. (1972). Experiments on semantic memory and language comprehension. In L. W. Gregg (Ed.),

Cognition in learning and memory. New York: John Wiley & Sons.

Condry, J. (1977). Enemies of exploration: Self-initiated versus other-initiated learning. *Journal of Personality and Social Psychology, 35,* 459–477.

Conrad, R., & Hull, A. J. (1964). Information, acoustic confusion, and memory span. *British Journal of Psychology, 55,* 429–432.

Cook, T. C., & Cashman, P. M. M. (1982). Stress and ectopic beats in ships' pilots. *Journal of Psychosomatic Research, 26,* 559–569.

Cook, T. D., Kendziersky, D. A., & Thomas, S. V. (1983). The implicit assumptions of television: An analysis of the 1982 NIMH Report on Television and Behavior. *Public Opinion Quarterly, 47,* 161–201.

Cooper, R. A., Bloom, F. E., & Roth, R. H. (1982). *The biochemical basis of neuropharmacology.* New York: Oxford University Press.

Costanzo, M., Archer, D., Aronson, E., & Pettigrew, T. (1986). Energy conservation behavior. The difficult path from information to action. *American Psychologist, 41,* 521–528.

Coverman, S., & Sheley, J. F. (1986). Change in men's housework and child-care time, 1965–1975. *Journal of Marriage and the Family, 48,* 413–422.

Covin, T. M., & Sattler, J. M. (1985). A longitudinal study of the Stanford-Binet and WISC-R with special education students. *Psychology in the Schools, 22,* 274–276.

Cowart, V. S. (1982). Stimulant therapy for attention disorders. *Journal of the American Medical Association, 248,* 279–287.

Cox, V. C., Paulus, P. B., & McCain, G. (1984). Prison crowding research. The relevance for prison housing standards and a general approach regarding crowding phenomena. *American Psychologist, 39,* 1148–1160.

Craik, F. I. M. (1977). Age difference in human memory. In J. E. Biren & K. W. Schaie (Eds.), *Handbook of the psychology of aging.* New York: Van Nostrand Reinhold.

Craik, F. I. M., & Byrd, M. (1981). Aging and cognitive deficits: The role of attentional resources. In F. I. M. Craik & S. E. Trehub (Eds.), *Aging and cognitive processes.* New York: Plenum Press.

Crawford, M. P. (1985). Psychology, technology, and professional service. *American Psychologist, 40,* 415–422.

Critchlow, B. (1986). The powers of John Barleycorn. Beliefs about the effects of alcohol on social behavior. *American Psychologist, 41,* 751–764.

Crook, C. K. (1979). The organization and control of infant sucking. *Advances in Child Development and Behavior, 14,* 209–252.

Crook, T. H., & Miller, N. E. (1985). The challenge of Alzheimer's disease. *American Psychologist, 40,* 1245–1250.

Crow, T. J., Johnstone, E. C., Owens, D. G. C., Ferrier, I. N., MacMillan, J. F., Parry, R. P., & Tyrrell, D. A. J. (1979). Characteristics of patients with schizophrenia or neurological disorder and virus-like agent in cerebro-spinal fluid. *Lancet, 1,* 842–844.

Crowl, R. K., & MacGinitie, W. H. (1974). The influence of students' speech characteristics on teacher's evaluations of oral answers. *Journal of Educational Psychology, 66,* 304–308.

Croyle, R. T., & Cooper, J. (1983). Dissonance arousal: Physiological evidence. *Journal of Personality and Social Psychology, 45,* 782–791.

Cummings, N. A. (1986). The dismantling of our health system: Strategies for the survival of psychological practice. *American Psychologist, 41,* 426–431.

Cunningham, C. E., Siegel, L. S., & Offord, D. R. (1985). A developmental dose-response analysis of the effects of methylphenidate on the peer interactions of attention deficit disordered boys. *Journal of Child Psychology, 26,* 955–971.

Cunningham, M. R. (1977). Personality and the structure of the nonverbal communication of emotion. *Journal of Personality, 45,* 564–584.

Cuperfain, R., & Clarke, T. K. (1985). A new perspective of subliminal perception. *Journal of Advertising, 14,* 36–41.

Curtiss, S. (1977). *Genie: A psycholinguistic study of a modern-day "wild child."* New York: Academic Press.

Cutler, N. N., et al. (19xx).

Cutler, W. B., Preti, G., Krieger, A., Huggins, G. R., Garcia, C. R., & Lawley, H. J. (1986). Human axillary secretions influence women's menstrual cycles: The role of donor extract from men. *Hormones & Behavior, 20,* 463–473.

Dalby, J. T., Morgan, D., & Lee, M. L. (1986). Single case study. Schizophrenia and mania in identical twin brothers. *The Journal of Nervous and Mental Disease, 174,* 304–308.

Damon, W. (1980). Structural-development theory and the study of moral development. In M. Windmiller, N. Lambert, & E. Turiel (Eds.), *Moral development and socialization.* Boston: Allyn and Bacon.

Daniels, D., & Plomin, R. (1985). Origins of individual differences in infant shyness. *Developmental Psychology, 21,* 118–121.

Darley, J. M., & Berscheid, E. (1967). Increased liking as a result of the anticipation of personal contact. *Human Relations, 20,* 29–40.

Darling, C. A., & Davidson, Sr., J. K. (1986). Coitally active university students: Sexual behaviors, concerns, and challenges. *Adolescence, 21,* 403–419.

Davidson, L. M., & Baum, A. (1986). Chronic stress and posttraumatic stress disorders. *Journal of Consulting and Clinical Psychology, 54,* 303–308.

Davidson, W. S. (1974). Studies of aversive conditioning for alcoholics: A critical review of theory and research methodology. *Psychological Bulletin, 81,* 571–581.

Davis, J. M. (1977). Central biogenic amines and theories of depression and mania. In W. E. Fann, I. Karacan, A. D. Pokorny, & R. L. Williams (Eds.), *Phenomenology and treatment of depression.* New York: Spectrum Publications.

Davis, K., & Todd, M. J. (1984). Prototypes, paradigm cases, and relationship assessment: The case of friendship. In S. Duck & D. Perlman (Eds.), *Sage series in personal relationships* (Vol. 1). Beverly Hills, CA: Sage Publications.

Davis, K. E., & Todd, M. J. (1982). Friendship and love relationships. In K. E. Davis & M. J. Todd (Eds.), *Advances in Descriptive Psychology,* vol. 2, Greenwich, CT.: JAI Press.

Davis, S. M., & Drichta, C. E. (1980). Biofeedback theory and application in allied health speech pathology. *Biofeedback and Self-Regulation, 5,* 159–174.

Dawson, E. E., Jr. (1981). The hospice: An educational-service model providing counseling opportunities and indirect benefits for older widows. *Death Education, 5,* 107–119.

Day, R. H., & McKenzie, B. E. (1977). Constancies in the perceptual world of the infant. In W. Epstein (Ed.), *Stability and constancy in visual perception.* New York: John Wiley & Sons.

Day, R. L., Kitahata, L. M., Kao, F. F., Motoyama, E. K., & Hardy, J. D. (1975). Evaluation of acupuncture aneshesia: A psychophysical study. *Anesthesiology, 43,* 501–517.

Dechateau, P. (1977). The importance of the neonatal period for the development of synchrony in the mother-infant dyad—a review. *Birth and the Family Journal, 4,* 10–24.

Deci, E. L. (1971). Effects of externally mediated rewards on intrinsic motivation. *Journal of Personality and Social Psychology, 18,* 105–115.

Deci, E. L. (1972). Effects of contingent and non-contingent rewards and controls on intrinsic motivation. *Organizational Behavior and Human Performance, 8,* 217–229.

Deci, E. L. (1975). *Intrinsic motivation.* New York: Plenum Press.

DeGregorio, E., & Carver, C. S. (1980). Type A behavior pattern, sex role orientation, and psychological adjustment. *Journal of Personality and Social Psychology, 39,* 286–293.

Deikman, A. (1976). Bimodal consciousness and the mystic experience. In P. R. Lee, R. E. Ornstein, D. Galin, A. Deikman, & C. T. Tart (Eds.), *Symposium on consciousness, San Francisco, 1974.* New York: Viking Press.

DeLamater, J., & MacCorquodale, P. (1979). *Premarital sexuality.* Madison: University of Wisconsin Press.

Delk, J. L. (1977). Use of EMG through biofeedback and behavioral treatment of an obsessive-phobic-depressive syndrome. *Diseases of the Nervous System, 38,* 938–939.

Dembroski, T. M., & McDougall, J. M. (1978). Stress effects on affiliation preferences among subjects possessing the Type A coronary-prone behavior pattern. *Journal of Personality and Social Psychology, 36,* 23–33.

Dembroski, T. M., McDougall, J. M., & Shields, J. L. (1977). Physiologic reactions to social challenge in persons evidencing the Type A coronary-prone behavior pattern. *Journal of Human Stress, 3,* 2–9.

Dement, W. C., Greenberg, S., & Klein, R. (1966). The effect of partial REM sleep deprivation and delayed recovery. *Journal of Psychiatric Research, 4,* 141–152.

Dement, W. C., & Kleitman, N. (1957). The relation of eye movements during sleep to dream activity: An objective method for the study of dreaming. *Journal of Experimental Psychology, 53,* 339–346.

Dement, W. C. (1960). The effect of dream deprivation. *Science, 131,* 1705–1707.

Dement, W. C., & Kleitman, N. (1957). The relation of eye movements during sleep to dream activity: An objective method for the study of dreaming. *Journal of Experimental Psychology, 53,* 339–346.

Denny, N. W. (1982). Aging and cognitive changes. In B. B. Wolman (Ed.), *Handbook of developmental psychology.* Englewood Cliffs, NJ: Prentice-Hall.

DePue, R. A., & Monroe, S. M. (1978). The unipolar-bipolar distinction in the depressive disorders. *Psychological Bulletin, 85,* 1001–1029.

Derogatis, L. R., Meyer, J. K., & Vasquez, N. (1978). A psychological profile of the transsexual. *Journal of Nervous and Mental Disease, 166,* 234–254.

Derr, A. M. (1986). How learning disabled adolescent boys make moral judgments. *Journal of Learning Disabilities, 19,* 160–163.

Dershowitz, A. M. (1986). *Reversal of fortune inside the Von Bulow case.* New York: Random House.

DeValois, R. L., & Jacobs, G. H. (1968). Primate color vision. *Science, 162,* 533–540.

De Vries, B., & Walker, L. J. (1986). Moral reasoning and attitudes toward capital punishment. *Developmental Psychology, 22,* 509–513.

Dietvorst, T. F. (1978). Biofeedback assisted relaxation training with patients recovering from myocardial infarction. *Dissertation Abstracts International, 38* (7-B), 3389.

DiMascio, A., Weissman, M. M., Prusoff, B. A., Neu, C., Zwilling, M., & Klerman, G. L. (1979). Differential symptom reduction by drugs and psychotherapy in acute depression. *Archives of General Psychiatry, 36,* 1450–1456.

Dion, K., Berscheid, E., & Walster, E. (1972). What is beautiful is good. *Journal of Personality and Social Psychology, 24,* 285–290.

Dipietro, J. A. (1981). Rough and tumble play: A function of gender. *Developmental Psychology, 17,* 50–58.

Dirkin, G. R. (1983). Cognitive tunneling: Use of visual information under stress. *Perceptual and Motor Skills, 56,* 191–198.

Dixon, N. F. (1981). *Preconscious processing.* New York: John Wiley & Sons.

Dohrenwend, B. P., & Shrout, P. E. (1985). "Hassles" in the conceptualization and measurement of life stress variables. *American Psychologist, 40,* 780–785.

Dollard, J., Doob, L. W., Miller, N. E., Mowrer, O. H., & Sears, R. R. (1939). *Frustration and aggression.* New Haven: Yale University Press.

Donnerstein, E. (1980). Pornography and violence against women: Experimental studies. *Annals of the New York Academy of Sciences, 347,* 277–288.

Doob, A. N., & MacDonald, G. E. (1979). Television viewing and fear of victimization: Is the relationship causal? *Journal of Personality and Social Psychology, 37,* 170–179.

Dowling, J. E., & Boycott, B. B. (1966). Organization of the primate retina: Electron microscopy. *Proceedings of the Royal Society (London),* Series B, *166,* 80–111.

Drabman, R. S. (1976). Behavior modification in the classroom. In W. E. Craighead, A. E. Kazdin, & M. H. Mahoney (Eds.), *Behavior modification: Principles, issues and applications.* Boston: Houghton Mifflin.

Drabman, R. S., & Thomas, M. H. (1975). The effects of television on children and adolescents: Does TV violence breed indifference? *Journal of Communication, 25,* 86–89.

Drachman, D. A., & Arbit, J. (1966). Memory and the hippocampal complex, 2. *Archives of Neurology, 15,* 52–61.

Drennen, W. T., & Holden, E. W. (1984). Trait/set interactions in EMG biofeedback. *Psychological Reports, 54,* 843–849.

Dreyer, P. H. (1982). Sexuality during adolescence. In B. B. Wolman (Ed.), *Handbook of developmental psychology.* Englewood Cliffs, NJ: Prentice-Hall.

Drumm, P., Gardner, B. T., & Gardner, R. A. (1986). Vocal and gestural responses of cross-fostered chimpanzees. *American Journal of Psychology, 99,* 1–29.

Duffy, E., & Lacey, O. L. (1946). Adaptation in energy mobilization: Changes in general level of palmer conductants. *Journal of Experimental Psychology, 36,* 437–452.

Dunant, Y., & Israël, M. (1985). The release of acetylcholine. *Scientific American, 252,* 58–85.

Duncan, J. (1980). The locus of interference in the perception of simultaneous stimuli. *Psychological Review, 87,* 272–300.

Dush, D. M., Hirt, M. L., & Schroeder, H. (1983). Self-statement modification with adults: A meta-analysis. *Psychological Bulletin, 94, 3,* 408–422.

Dykens, E. M., & Gerrard, M. (1986). Psychological profiles of purging bulimics, repeat dieters, and controls. *Journal of Consulting and Clinical Psychology, 54,* 283–288.

Eagly, A. H., & Crowley, M. (1986). Gender and helping behavior: A meta-analytic review of the social psychological literature. *Psychological Bulletin, 100,* 283–308.

Easterbrooks, M. A., & Goldberg, W. A. (1985). Effects of early maternal employment on toddlers, mothers, and fathers. *Developmental Psychology, 21,* 774–783.

Ebbinghaus, H. (1885). *Uber die gedachtnis.* Leipzig, Germany: Duncker & Humbolt.

Eisdorfer, C. (1983). Conceptual models of aging. *American Psychologist, 2,* 197–202.

Eisdorfer, C., & Wilkie, F. (1977). Stress, disease, aging, and behavior. In J. E. Birren & K. W. Schaie (Eds.), *Handbook of the psychology of aging.* New York: Van Nostrand Reinhold.

Eisenberg, L. (1980). Adolescent suicide: On taking arms against a sea of troubles. *Pediatrics, 66,* 315–320.

Eisenberger, R., Park, D. C., & Frank, M. (1976). Learned industriousness and social reinforcement. *Journal of Personality and Social Psychology, 33,* 327–332.

Elkind, D. (1981a). Giant in the nursery—Jean Piaget. In E. M.

Hetherington & R. D. Parke (Eds.), *Contemporary readings in child psychology* (2nd ed.). New York: McGraw-Hill.

Elkind, D. (1981b). *The hurried child.* Reading, MA: Addison-Wesley.

Ellingson, R. J. (1975). Ontogenesis of sleep in the human. In C. G. Lairy & P. Salzarulo (Eds.), *The experimental study of human sleep: Methodological problems.* Amsterdam: Elsevier Press.

Ellis, A. (1962). *Reason and emotion in psychotherapy.* New York: Stuart Press.

Ellis, A. (1970). *The essence of rational psychotherapy: A comprehensive approach to treatment.* New York: Institute for Rational Living.

Ellis, A., & Harper, R. A. (1961). *A guide to rational living.* North Hollywood, CA: Wilshire Book.

Emery, P. E. (1983). Adolescent depression and suicide. *Adolescence, 18,* 245–258.

Emrick, C. D., & Hansen, J. (1983). Assertions regarding effectiveness of treatment for alcoholism: Fact or fancy? *American Psychologist, 38,* 1078–1088.

Epstein, S. (1983). Aggregation and beyond: Some basic issues on the prediction of behavior. *Journal of Personality, 51,* 360–392.

Epstein, S., & O'Brien, E. J. (1985). The person-situation debate in historical and current perspective. *Psychological Bulletin, 98,* 513–537.

Ericsson, K. A. (1985). Memory skill. *Canadian Journal of Psychology, 39,* 188–231.

Erikson, E. H. (1959). Identity and the life cycle: Selected papers. *Psychological Issues, 1,* 1–171.

Erikson, E. H. (1963). *Childhood and society* (2nd ed.). New York: W. W. Norton.

Erikson, E. H. (1968). *Identity: Youth and crisis.* New York: W. W. Norton.

Erlenmeyer-Kimling, L., & Jarvik, L. F. (1963). Genetics and intelligence: A review. *Science, 142,* 1477–1479.

Eron, L. D. (1982). Parent-child interaction, television violence, and aggression of children. *American Psychologist, 37,* 197–211.

Eron, L. D., & Huesmann, L. R. (1980). Adolescent aggression and television. *Annals of the New York Academy of Sciences, 347,* 319–331.

Ester, P., & Winett, R. A. (1982). Toward more effective antecedent strategies for environmental programs. *Journal of Environmental Systems, 11,* 201–221.

Etaugh, C. (1980). Effects of nonmaternal care on children. *American Psychologist, 35,* 309–319.

Evans, R. I., Rozelle, R. M., Noblitt, R., & Williams, D. L. (1975). Explicit and implicit persuasive communications over time to initiate and maintain behavior change: New perspectives utilizing a real-life dental hygiene situation. *Journal of Applied Social Psychology, 5,* 150–156.

Exner, Jr., J. E., Thomas, E. A., & Mason, B. (1985). Children's Rorschachs: Description and prediction. *Journal of Personality Assessment, 49,* 13–14.

Eysenck, H. J., & Wilson, G. (1979). *The psychology of sex.* London: J. M. Dent & Sons, Ltd.

Fallon, A. E., & Rozin, P. (1985). Sex differences in perceptions of body shape. *Journal of Abnormal Psychology, 94,* 102–105.

Fantz, R. L. (1961). The origin of form perception. *Scientific American, 204,* 66–72.

Fantz, R. L., & Miranda, S. B. (1975). Newborn infant attention to form of contour. *Child Development, 46,* 224–228.

Farber, B. A. (1983). Introduction: A critical perspective on burnout. In A. P. Goldstein & L. Krasner (Eds.), *Stress and burnout in the human service professions.* New York: Pergamon Press.

Farber, E. A., & Egeland, B. (1982). Developmental consequences of out-of-home care for infants in low-income population. In E. F. Zigler & E. W. Gordon (Eds.), *Day care: Scientific and social policy issues.* Boston: Auburn House.

Farone, S. (1982). Psychiatry and political repression in the Soviet Union. *American Psychologist, 37,* 1105–1112.

Farone, S. V., & Tsuang, M. T. (1985). Quantitative models of the genetic transmission of schizophrenia. *Psychological Bulletin, 98,* 41–66.

Feingold, B. F. (1975a). Hyperkinesis and learning disabilities linked to artificial food flavors and colors. *American Journal of Nursing, 75,* 797–803.

Feingold, B. F. (1975b). *Why is your child hyperactive?* New York: Random House.

Feingold, B. F. (1976). Hyperkinesis and learning disabilities linked to the ingestion of artificial food colors and flavors. *Journal of Learning Disabilities, 9*(9), 19–27.

Feldman, S. S., Nash, S. C., & Aschenbrenner, B. G. (1983). Antecedents of fathering. *Child Development, 54,* 1628–1636.

Fell, J. C. (1985). *Alcohol involvement in fatal accidents 1980–1984.* Washington, DC: National Center for Statistics and Analysis, United States Department of Transportation, National Highway Traffic Safety Administration.

Felson, R. B. (1981). Ambiguity and bias in the self-concept. *Social Psychology Quarterly, 44,* 64–69.

Fenno, R. F. (1959). *The president's cabinet.* Cambridge: Harvard University Press.

Festinger, L. (1954). A theory of social comparison processes. *Human Relations, 7,* 117–140.

Festinger, L. (1957). *A theory of cognitive dissonance.* Evanston, IL: Row, Petersen.

Festinger, L. (1962). Cognitive dissonance. *Scientific American, 207*(4), 93–107.

Filinson, R. (1984). Diagnosis of senile dementia Alzheimer's type: The state of the art. *Clinical Gerontologist, 2,* 3–23.

Findley, M. J., & Cooper, H. M. (1983). Locus of control and academic achievement: A literature review. *Journal of Personality and Social Psychology, 44,* 419–427.

Fischer, J., & Gochros, H. L. (1975). *Planned behavior change: Behavior modification in social work.* New York: Free Press.

Fishbein, D. (1985). Biofeedback applications to psychiatric disorders. *The Psychological Record, 35,* 3–21.

Fisher, C. D. (1978). The effects of personal control, competence, and extrinsic reward systems on intrinsic motivation. *Organizational Behavior and Human Performance, 21,* 273–288.

Fisher, D. F., Jarombek, J. J., & Karsh, R. (1974). *Short-term memory (1958–1973): An annotated bibliography.* Aberdeen Proving Ground, MD: U.S. Army Human Engineering Laboratory.

Fisher, D. F., & Karsh, R. (1971). Modality effects and storage in sequential short-term memory. *Journal of Experimental Psychology, 87,* 410–414.

Fisher, E. B., Jr., DeLamater, A. M., Bertelson, A. D., & Kirkley, B. G. (1982). Psychological factors in diabetes and its treatment. *Journal of Consulting and Clinical Psychology, 50,* 993–1003.

Fisher, J. D., Nadler, A., & Whitcher-Alagna, S. (1982). Recipient reactions to aid. *Psychological Bulletin, 91,* 27–54.

Fisher, S., & Greenberg, R. P. (1977). *Scientific credibility of Freud's theory and therapy.* New York: Basic Books.

Fiske, S. T., & Taylor, S. E. (1984). *Social cognition.* Reading, MA: Addison-Wesley.

Fitzgerald, L. F., & Osipow, S. H. (1986). An occupational analysis of counseling psychology. *American Psychologist, 41,* 535–544.

Flanagan, G. (1962). *The first nine months of life.* New York: Simon & Schuster.

Flannery, R. B., Jr. (1986). Major life events and daily hassles in predicting health status: Methodological inquiry. *Journal of Clinical Psychology, 42,* 485–487.

Flavell, J. H. (1963). *The developmental psychology of Jean Piaget.* New York: Van Nostrand Reinhold.

Flavell, J. H. (1986). The development of children's knowledge about the appearance-reality distinction. *American Psychologist, 41,* 418–425.

Flerx, V. C., Fidler, D. S., & Rogers, R. W. (1976). Sex-role stereotypes: Developmental aspects and early intervention. *Child Development, 47,* 998–1007.

Floge, L. (1985). The dynamics of child-care use and some implications for women's employment. *Journal of Marriage and the Family,* 143–154.

Flynn, J. R. (1984). The mean IQ of Americans: massive gains 1932 to 1978. *Psychological Bulletin, 95,* 29–51.

Fodor, I. G. (1974). The phobic syndrome in women: Implications for treatment. In V. Franks & V. Burtle (Eds.), *Women in therapy.* New York: Brunner/Mazel.

Fodor, J. A. (1981). The mind-body problem. *Scientific American, 244*(1), 114–124.

Ford, D. H., & Urban, H. B. (1963). *Systems of psychotherapy: A comparative study.* New York: John Wiley & Sons.

Ford, M. E. (1979). The construct validity of egocentrism. *Psychological Bulletin, 86,* 1169–1188.

Ford, M. R. (1982). Biofeedback treatment for headaches, Raynaud's disease, essential hypertension, and irritable bowel syndrome: A review of the long-term follow-up literature. *Biofeedback and Self-Regulation, 7,* 521–536.

Forgays, D. G. (1983). Primary prevention of psychopathology. In M. Hersen, A. E. Kazdin, & A. S. Bellack (Eds.), *The clinical psychology handbook.* New York: Pergamon Press.

Forsyth, D. R., & Strong, S. R. (1986). The scientific study of counseling and psychotherapy. A unificationist view. *American Psychologist, 41,* 113–119.

Foulkes, W. D. (1962). Dream report from different stages of sleep. *Journal of Abnormal and Social Psychology, 65,* 14–25.

Fowler, M. J., Sullivan, M. J., & Ekstrand, B. R. (1973). Sleep and memory. *Science, 179,* 302–304.

Fox, N., Kagan, J., & Weiskopf, S. (1979). The growth of memory during infancy. *Genetic Psychology Monographs, 99,* 91–130.

Fox, R., Aslin, R. N., Shea, S. L., & Dumais, S. T. (1980). Stereopsis in human infants. *Science, 207,* 323–324.

Foxx, R. M., McMorrow, M. J., Bittle, R. G., & Bechtel, D. R. (1986). The successful treatment of a dually-diagnosed deaf man's aggression with a program that included contingent electric shock. *Behavior Therapy, 17,* 170–186.

Frank, R. A., & Cohen, D. J. (1979). Psychosocial concomitants of biological maturation in preadolescence. *American Journal of Psychiatry, 136,* 1518–1524.

Frankel, F. H., & Misch, R. C. (1973). Hypnosis in a case of long-standing psoriasis in a person with character problems. *International Journal of Clinical and Experimental Hypnosis, 21,* 121–130.

Frankenhauser, M., Lundberg, U., & Forsman, L. (1980). Note on arousing Type A persons by depriving them of work. *Journal of Psychosomatic Research, 24,* 45–47.

Frederiksen, N. (1986). Toward a broader conception of human intelligence. *American Psychologist, 41,* 445–452.

Freedman, D. X., & Glass, R. M. (1982). Psychiatry: Molecular and receptor studies. *Journal of the American Medical Association, 247,* 2975–2977.

Freedman, J. L. (1984). Effect of television violence on aggressiveness. *Psychological Bulletin, 96,* 227–246.

Freedman, J. L. (1986). Television violence and aggression: A rejoinder. *Psychological Bulletin, 100,* 372–378.

French, J. L. (1984). On the conception, birth, and early development of school psychology. With special reference to Penn-sylvania. *American Psychologist, 39,* 976–987.

French, S. N. (1980). Electromyographic biofeedback for tension control during fine motor skill acquisition. *Biofeedback and Self-Regulation, 5,* 221–228.

Freud, A. (1965). *Normality and pathology in childhood: Assessment of development.* New York: International Universities Press.

Freud, S. (1933). *New introductory lectures on psycho-analysis.* New York: W. W. Norton.

Friedman, M., & Rosenman, R. H. (1974). *Type A behavior and your heart.* Greenwich, CT: Fawcett.

Friedrich-Cofer, L., & Huston, A. C. (1986). Television violence and aggression: The debate continues. *Psychological Bulletin, 100,* 364–371.

Fromm, E. (1956). *The art of loving.* New York: Harper & Row.

Furumoto, L., & Scarborough, E. (1986). Placing women in the history of psychology. The first American women psychologists. *American Psychologist, 41,* 35–42.

Gabrenya, W. K., Latané, B., & Wang, Y. (1983). Social loafing in cross-cultural perspective. *Journal of Cross-Cultural Psychology, 14,* 368–384.

Gabrenya, W. K., Jr., Wang, Y., & Latané, B. (1985). Social loafing on an optimizing task: Cross-cultural differences among Chinese and Americans. *Journal of Cross-Cultural Psychology, 16,* 223–242.

Gabrielli, W. F., Jr., Mednick, S. A., Volavka, J., Pollock, V. E., Schulsinger, F., & Turan, M. I. (1982). Electroencephalograms in children of alcoholic fathers. *Psychophysiology, 19,* 404–407.

Gagnon, G. H. (1977). *Human sexualities.* Glenview, IL: Scott, Foresman & Company.

Gajzago, C., & Prior, M. (1974). Two cases of "recovery" in Kanner syndrome. *Archives of General Psychiatry, 31,* 264–268.

Galbraith, R. C. (1982). Sibling spacing and intellectual development: A closer look at the confluence models. *Developmental Psychology, 18,* 181–191.

Galbraith, R. C. (1983). Individual differences in intelligence: A reappraisal of the confluence model. *Intelligence, 7,* 185–194.

Galin, D. (1974). Implications for psychiatry of left and right cerebral specialization: A neurophysiological context for unconscious processes. *Archives of General Psychiatry, 31,* 572–583.

Gallagher, J. J. (1979). Issues and education for the gifted. In A. H. Passow (Ed.), *The gifted and the talented: Their education and development* [78th Yearbook for the National Society for the Study of Education]. Chicago: University of Chicago Press.

Gallup, G. G., Jr., & Suarez, S. D. (1985). Alternatives to the use of animals in psychological research. *American Psychologist, 40,* 1104–1111.

Ganz, L. (1978). Sensory deprivation and visual discrimination. In R. Held, H. W. Leibowitz, & H.-L. Teuber (Eds.), *Handbook of sensory physiology: Vol. 8. Perception.* New York: Springer-Verlag.

Garber, J., Miller, W. R., & Seaman, S. F. (1979). Learned helplessness, stress, and the depressive disorders. In R. A. DePue (Ed.), *The psychobiology of the depressive disorders.* New York: Academic Press.

Garfield, S. L. (1973). Basic ingredients or common factors in psychotherapy? *Journal of Consulting and Clinical Psychology, 41,* 9–12.

Garfinkel, P. E., Moldofsy, H., & Garner, D. M. (1980). The heterogeneity of anorexia nervosa: Bulimia as a distinct subgroup. *Archives of General Psychiatry, 37,* 1036–1040.

Garrigan, J. J., & Bambrick, A. F. (1979). New findings in research on go-between process. *International Journal of Family Therapy, 1,* 76–85.

Garza, R. T., & Widlak, F. W. (1977). The validity of locus of control dimensions for Chicano populations. *Journal of Personality Assessment, 41,* 635–643.

Gastorf, J. W., Suls, J., & Sanders, G. S. (1980). Type A coronary-prone behavior pattern and social facilitation. *Journal of Personality and Social Psychology, 38,* 773–780.

Gatchel, R. J., & Proctor, J. D. (1976). Physiological correlates of learned helplessness in man. *Journal of Abnormal Psychology, 85,* 27–34.

Gazzaniga, M. S. (1967). The split brain in man. *Scientific American, 8,* 24–29.

Gazzaniga, M. S. (1983). Right hemisphere language following brain bisection: A 20-year perspective. *American Psychologist, 38,* 525–537.

Geiger, D. L. (1978). "Note: How future professionals view the elderly: A comparative analysis of social work, law, and medical students' perceptions." *The Gerontologist, 18,* 591–594.

Gelman, R. (1981). Preschool thought. In E. M. Hetherington & R. D. Parke (Eds.), *Contemporary readings in child psychology* (2nd ed.). New York: McGraw-Hill.

Gendlin, E. T. (1986). What comes after traditional psychotherapy research? *American Psychologist, 41,* 131–136.

George, A. (1974). Adaptation to stress in political decision making: The individual, small group, and organizational contexts. In G. V. Coelho, D. A. Hamburg, & J. E. Adams (Eds.), *Coping and adaptation.* New York: Basic Books.

Gerbner, G., & Gross, L. (1976) The scary world of TV's heavy viewer. *Psychology Today, Sept.,* 41–45.

German, D. (1983). Analysis of word-finding disorders on the Kaufman Assessment Battery for Children. (K-ABC). *Journal of Psychoeducational Assessment, 1,* 121–134.

Gershone, J. R., Erickson, E. A., Mitchell, J. E., & Paulson, D. A. (1977). Behavioral comparison of a token economy and a standard psychiatric treatment ward. *Journal of Behavior Therapy and Experimental Psychiatry, 8,* 381–385.

Geschwind, N. (1972). Language and the brain. *Scientific American, 226,* (4) 76–83.

Gherman, E. M. (1981). *Stress & the bottom line: A guide to personal well-being and corporate health.* New York: AMACOM.

Gibson, C. J., Logue, M., & Growdon, J. H. (1985). CSF monoamine metabolite levels in Alzheimer's and Parkinson's disease. *Archives of Neurology, 42,* 489–492.

Gibson, J. J. (1950). *The perception of the visual world.* Boston: Houghton Mifflin.

Gift, T. E., Strauss, J. S., Ritzler, B. A., Kokes, R. F., & Harder, D. W. (1980). How diagnostic concepts of schizophrenia differ. *Journal of Nervous and Mental Disease, 168,* 3–8.

Gillum, R., Leon, G. R., Kamp, J., & Becerra-Aldama, J. (1980). Prediction of cardiovascular and other disease onset and mortality from 30-year longitudinal MMPI data. *Journal of Consulting and Clinical Psychology, 48,* 405–406.

Glass, C. R., Gottman, J. M., & Shmurak, S. H. (1976). Response-acquisition and cognitive self-statement modification approaches to dating-skills training. *Journal of Counseling Psychology, 23,* 520–526.

Glass, D. C. (1977). *Behavior patterns, stress, and coronary disease.* Hillsdale, NJ: Lawrence Erlbaum Associates.

Glass, D. C., & Singer, J. E. (1972). *Urban stress.* New York: Academic Press.

Glass, D. C., Snyder, M. L., & Hollis, J. F. (1974). Time urgency and the Type A coronary-prone behavior pattern. *Journal of Applied Social Psychology, 4,* 125–140.

Glenn, N. D. (1975). Psychological well-being in the post-parental stage. *Journal of Marriage and the Family, 37,* 105–110.

Glover, H. (1984). Themes of mistrust and the posttraumatic stress disorder in Vietnam veterans. *American Journal of Psychotherapy, 37,* 445–452.

Golden, M., Rosenbluth, L., Grossi, M., Policare, H., Freeman, H., & Brownlee, E. (1978). *The New York City infant day care study.* New York: Medical and Health Research Association of New York City.

Goldfried, M. R., & Davison, G. C. (1976). *Clinical behavior therapy.* New York: Holt, Rinehart and Winston.

Goldfried, M. R., Stricker, G., & Weiner, I. R. (1971). *Rorschach handbook of clinical and research applications.* Englewood Cliffs, NJ: Prentice-Hall.

Goldman, M. S. (1983). Cognitive impairment in chronic alcoholics: Some cause for optimism. *American Psychologist, 38,* 1045–1054.

Goldstein, A. J., & Chambless, D. L. (1978). A reanalysis of agoraphobia. *Behavior Therapy, 9,* 47–57.

Goldstein, G., & Hersen, M. (1984). Historical perspectives. In G. Goldstein & M. Hersen (Eds.), *Handbook of Psychological Assessment.* New York: Pergamon Press.

Goldstein, J. H., Rosnow, R. L., Raday, T., Silverman, I., & Gaskell, G. D. (1975). Punitiveness in response to films varying in content: A cross-national field study of aggression. *European Journal of Social Psychology, 5,* 149–165.

Goleman, D. (1985). *Vital lies, simple truths.* New York: Simon & Schuster.

Gonzales, L. R., Hays, R. B., Bond, M. A., & Kelly, J. G. (1983). Community mental health. In M. Hersen, A. E. Kazdin, & A. S. Bellack (Eds.), *The clinical psychology handbook.* New York: Pergamon Press.

Gordon, S. (1976). *Lonely in America.* New York: Simon & Schuster.

Gorney, R., Loye, D., & Steele, G. (1977). Impact of dramatized television entertainment on adult males. *American Journal of Psychiatry, 134,* 170–174.

Gottsfeld, M. L. (1978). Treatment of vaginismus by psychotherapy with adjunctive hypnosis. *American Journal of Clinical Hypnosis, 20,* 272–277.

Gottesman, I., & Shields, J. (1982). *Schizophrenia: the epigenetic puzzle.* Cambridge: Cambridge University Press.

Gottheil, E., & Stone, G. C. (1974). Psychosomatic aspects of orality and anality. *Journal of Nervous and Mental Disease, 159,* 182–190.

Gottschalk, L. A. (1983). Vulnerability to "stress." *American Journal of Psychotherapy, 37,* 5–23.

Graham, C. H., Sperling, H. G., Hsia, Y., & Coulson, A. H. (1961). The determination of some visual functions of a unilaterally color-blind subject: Methods and results. *Journal of Psychology, 51,* 3–32.

Grant, B. W. (1975). *Schizophrenia: A source of social insight.* Philadelphia: Westminster Press.

Grant, V. W. (1977). *The menacing stranger.* Oceanside, NY: Dabor Science Publications.

Graziano, W., Brothen, T., & Berscheid, E. (1978). Height and attraction: Do men and women see eye-to-eye? *Journal of Personality, 46,* 128–145.

Greaves, G. B. (1980). Multiple personality: 165 years after Mary Reynolds. *Journal of Nervous and Mental Disease, 168,* 577–596.

Greenberg, M., & Morris, N. (1974). Engrossment: The newborn's impact upon the father. *American Journal of Orthopsychiatry, 44,* 520–531.

Greer, S. (1964). Study of parental loss in neurotics and sociopaths. *Archives of General Psychiatry, 11,* 177–180.

Greif, G. L. (1985). Single fathers rearing children. *Journal of Marriage and the Family,* 185–191.

Griffitt, W. (1970). Environmental effects on interpersonal affective behavior: Ambient affective temperature and attraction. *Journal of Personality and Sexual Psychology, 15*(3), 240–244.

Gross, A. M. (1984). Behavioral interviewing. In T. H. Ollendick & M. Hersen (Eds.), *Child behavioral assessment: Principles and procedures.* New York: Pergamon Press.

Grossman, F. M. (1983). Percentage of WAIS-R standardization sample obtaining verbal-performance discrepancies. *Journal of Consulting and Clinical Psychology, 51,* 641–642.

Grossman, S. P., & Grossman, L. (1977). Food and water intake in rats after transections of fibers en passage in the tegmentum. *Physiological Behavior, 18,* 647–658.

Guggenheim, F. G., & Babigian, H. M. (1974). Catatonic schizophrenia: Epidemiology and clinical course. *Journal of Nervous and Mental Disease, 158,* 291–305.

Guilford, J. P. (1959). Three faces of intellect. *American Psychologist, 14,* 469–479.

Guilford, J. P. (1967). *The nature of human intelligence.* New York: McGraw-Hill.

Guilford, J. P. (1980). Fluid and crystallized intelligence: Two fanciful concepts. *Psychological Bulletin, 88,* 406–412.

Guilford, J. P. (1982). Cognitive psychology's abnormalities: Some suggested remedies. *Psychological Review, 89,* 48–59.

Gunderson, J. G., & Mosher, L. R. (1978). The cost of schizophrenia. In R. Cancro (Ed.), *Annual review of the schizophrenic syndrome (1976–7).* New York: Brunner/Mazel.

Gurman, A. S., & Razin, A. M. (1977). *Effective psychotherapy: A handbook of research.* New York: Pergamon Press.

Haaf, R. A., Smith, P. H., & Smitley, S. (1983). Infant response to facelike patterns under fixed-trial and infant-control procedures. *Child Development, 54,* 172–177.

Haan, N., Langer, J., & Kohlberg, L. (1976). Family patterns of moral reasoning. *Child Development, 47,* 1204–1206.

Haan, N., Millsap, R., & Hartka, E. (1986). As time goes by: Change and stability in personality over fifty years. *Psychology and Aging, 1,* 220–232.

Haber, R. N. (1969). Eidetic images. *Scientific American, 220*(4), 36–44.

Haber, R. N. (1979). Twenty years of haunting eidetic imagery: Where's the ghost? *Behavioral and Brain Sciences, 2,* 583–629.

Haber, R. N. (1983). The impending demise of the icon: A critique of the concept of iconic storage in visual information processing. *The Behavioral and Brain Sciences, 6,* 1–54.

Haber, R. N. (1985). An icon can have no worth in the real world: Comments on Loftus, Johnson, and Shimamura's "How much is an icon worth?" *Journal of Experimental Psychology: Human Perception and Performance, 11,* 374–378.

Halberstadt, A. G., & Hall, J. A. (1980). Who's getting the message? Children's nonverbal skills and their evaluation by teachers. *Developmental Psychology, 6,* 564–573.

Halderman, B. I., & Jackson, T. T. (1979). Naturalistic study of aggression: Aggressive stimuli and horn-honking: A replication. *Psychological Reports, 45,* 880–882.

Haley, J. (1976). *Problem solving therapy.* New York: W. W. Norton.

Hall, E. T. (1966). *The hidden dimension.* Garden City, NY: Doubleday.

Hall, J. A. (1979). Gender, gender roles, and nonverbal communication skills. In R. Rosenthal (Ed.), *Skill in nonverbal communication.* Cambridge, MA: Oelgeschlager, Gunn & Hain.

Hall, J. F. (1982). *An invitation to learning and memory.* Boston: Allyn and Bacon.

Hall, V. C., & Turner, R. R. (1974). The validity of the "different languages explanation" for poor scholastic performance by black students. *Review of Educational Research, 44,* 69–81.

Hammen, C., & Krantz, S. E. (1985). Measures of psychological processes in depression. In E. E. Beckham & W. R. Leber (Eds.), *Handbook of depression. Treatment, assessment, and research.* Homewood, IL: Dorsey Press.

Hammen, C., & Mayol, A. (1982). Depression and cognitive characteristics of stressful life-event types. *Journal of Abnormal Psychology, 91,* 165–174.

Hampstead, W. J. (1977). The effects of EMG assisted relaxation training with hyperkinetic children: An alternative to medication. *Dissertation Abstracts International, 38,* (10-B), 5017.

Hanks, R. (1985). Moral reasoning in adolescents: A feature of intelligence or social adjustment? *Journal of Moral Education, 14,* 43–55.

Harder, D. W., Strauss, J. S., Kokes, R. F., Ritzler, B. A., & Gift, T. E. (1980). Life events and psychopathology severity among first psychiatric admissions. *Journal of Abnormal Psychology, 89,* 165–180.

Haré-Mustin, R. D. (1983). An appraisal of the relationship between women and psychotherapy. *American Psychologist, 38,* 593–601.

Harlow, H. F. (1959). Love in infant monkeys. *Scientific American, 200,* 68–86.

Harlow, H. F. (1962). The heterosexual affectional system in monkeys. *American Psychologist, 17,* 1–9.

Harlow, H. F., & Zimmerman, R. R. (1958). The development of affectional responses in infant monkeys. *Proceedings of the American Philosophic Society, 102,* 501–509.

Harris, E. L., Noyes, R., Jr., Crowe, R. R., & Chaudhry, D. R. (1983). Family study of agoraphobia: Report of a pilot study. *Archives of General Psychiatry, 40,* 1061–1064.

Hartnagel, T. F., Teevan, J. R., Jr., & McIntyre, J. J. (1975). Television violence and violent behavior. *Social Forces, 54,* 341–351.

Hass, J. W., Bagley, G. S., & Rogers, R. W. (1975). Coping with the energy crisis: Effects of fear appeals upon attitudes toward energy consumption. *Journal of Applied Psychology, 60,* 754–756.

Hatch, J. P. (1981). Voluntary control of sexual responding in men and women: Implications for the etiology and treatment of sexual dysfunctions. *Biofeedback and Self-Regulation, 6,* 191–206.

Haynes, S. N. (1984). Behavioral assessment of adults. In G. Goldstein & M. Hersen (Eds.), *Handbook of psychological assessment.* New York: Pergamon Press.

Hearnshaw, L. S. (1979). *Cyril Burt, psychologist.* Ithaca, NY: Cornell University Press.

Hebb, D. O. (1949). *Organization of behavior.* New York: John Wiley & Sons.

Hebb, D. O. (1972). *Textbook of psychology* (3rd ed.). Philadelphia: W. B. Saunders.

Heckler, M. M. (1985). Psychology in the public forum. The fight against Alzheimer's disease. *American Psychologist, 40,* 1240–1244.

Heffler, A. J. (1978). Hearing loss due to noise exposure. *Otolaryngological Clinics of North America, 11,* 723–740.

Heimberg, R. G., Becker, R. E., Goldfinger, K., & Vermilyea, J. A. (1985). Treatment of social phobia by exposure, cognitive restructuring, and homework assignments. *The Journal of Nervous and Mental Disease, 173,* 236–245.

Heinlein, R. (1961). *Stranger in a strange land.* New York: Putnam.

Held, R., & Hein, A. (1963). Movement produced stimulation in the development of visually guided behavior. *Journal of Comparative and Physiological Psychology, 56,* 872–876.

Hellige, J. B., & Wong, T. M. (1983). Hemisphere-specific interference in dichotic listening: Task variables and individual differences. *Journal of Experimental Psychology: General, 112,* 218–239.

Hemshorn, A. (1985). They call it Alzheimer's disease. *Journal of Gerontological Nursing, 11,* 36–38.

Hendler, C. S., & Redd, W. H. (1986). Fear of hypnosis: The role of labeling in patients' acceptance of behavior interventions. *Behavior Therapy, 17,* 2–13.

Hennekens, S. H., Willett, W., Rosner, B., Cole, D. S., Mayrent, S. L. (1979). Effects of beer, wine, and liquor in coronary deaths. *Journal of the American Medical Association, 242,* 1973–1974.

Henry, K. R. (1984). Cochlear damage resulting from exposure to four different octave bands of noise at three ages. *Behavioral Neuroscience, 98,* 107–117.

Herman, C. P., Olmsted, M. P., & Polivy, J. (1983). Obesity, externality, and susceptibility to social influence: An integrated analysis. *Journal of Personality and Social Psychology, 45,* 926–934.

Herman, C. P., & Polivy, J. (1975). Anxiety, restraint, and eating behavior. *Journal of Abnormal Psychology, 84,* 666–672.

Hermann, D. J., & Harwood, J. R. (1980). More evidence for the existence of separate semantic and episodic stores in long-term memory. *Journal of Experimental Psychology: Human Learning and Memory, 6,* 467–478.

Heron, W. (1957). The pathology of boredom. *Scientific American, 196*(1), 52–56.

Hershenson, M. (1982). Moon illusion and spiral aftereffect: Illusions are due to the loom-zoom system? *Journal of Experimental Psychology: General, 111,* 423–440.

Hershman, S. (1955). Hypnosis in the treatment of obesity. *International Journal of Clinical and Experimental Hypnosis, 3,* 136–140.

Hertzog, C., Schaie, K. W., & Gribbin, K. (1978). Cardiovascular disease and changes in intellectual functioning from middle to old age. *Journal of Gerontology, 33,* 872–883.

Heston, L. L. (1966). Psychiatric disorders in foster home reared children of schizophrenic mothers. *British Journal of Psychiatry, 11,* 819–825.

Hilgard, E. R. (1965). *Hypnotic susceptibility.* New York: Harcourt, Brace, & World.

Hilgard, E. R., & Morgan, A. H. (1975). Heart rate and blood pressure in the study of laboratory pain in man under normal conditions and as influenced by hypnosis. *Acta Neurobiologiae Experimentalis, 35,* 501–513.

Hill, F. (1982). *Principles of learning: A handbook of applications.* Palo Alto, CA: Mayfield.

Hill, J. H., Liebert, R. M., & Mott, D. E. W. (1968). Vicarious extinction of avoidance behavior through films: An initial test. *Psychological Reports, 22,* 192.

Hintzman, D. L. (1978). *The psychology of learning and memory.* San Francisco: W. H. Freeman.

Hirsch, H. V. B., & Spinelli, D. N. (1971). Modification of the distribution of receptive field orientation in cats by selective exposure during development. *Experimental Brain Research, 13,* 509–527.

Hite, S. (1976). *The Hite report.* New York: Dell Publishing Company.

Hobson, J. A. (1983). Sleep mechanisms and pathophysiology: Some clinical implications of the reciprocal interaction hypothesis of sleep cycle control. *Psychosomatic Medicine, 45,* 123–140.

Hobson, J. A., & McCarley, R. W. (1977). The brain as a dream state generator: An activation-synthesis of the dream process. *American Journal of Psychiatry, 134,* 1335–1348.

Hochberg, J. E. (1974). Organization and the Gestalt tradition. In E. C. Carterette & M. P. Friedman (Eds.), *Handbook of perception.* New York: Academic Press.

Hochberg, J. E. (1979). Sensation and perception. In E. Hearst (Ed.), *The first century of experimental psychology.* New York: John Wiley & Sons.

Hodges, K. K., & Siegel, L. J. (1985). Depression in children and adolescents. In E. E. Beckham & W. R. Leber (Eds.), *Handbook of depression. Treatment, assessment, and research.* Homewood, IL: Dorsey Press.

Hoffman, D. D. (1983). The interpretation of visual illusions. *Scientific American, 249,* 154–162.

Holder, M. D., & Roberts, S. (1985). Comparison of timing and classical conditioning. *Journal of Experimental Psychology: Animal Behavior Processes, 11,* 172–193.

Holloway, F. A. (1977). State-dependent retrieval based on time of day. In B. Ho, D. Chute, & D. Richards (Eds.), *Drug discrimination and state-dependent learning.* New York: Academic Press.

Holmes, D. S. (1978). Projection as a defense mechanism. *Psychological Bulletin, 85,* 677–688.

Holmes, T. H., & Rahe, R. H. (1967). The social readjustment rating scale. *Journal of Psychosomatic Research, 11,* 213–218.

Hoon, E. F. (1980). Biofeedback-assisted arousal in females: A comparison of visual and auditory modalities. *Biofeedback and Self-Regulation, 5,* 175–191.

Hoon, P. W., Bruce, K., & Kinchloe, B. (1982). Does the menstrual cycle play a role in sexual arousal? *Psychophysiology, 19,* 21–26.

Horn, J. L. (1982). The aging of human abilities. In B. B. Wolman (Ed.), *Handbook of developmental psychology.* Englewood Cliffs, NJ: Prentice-Hall.

Horn, J. M. (1983). The Texas adoption project: Adopted children and their intellectual resemblance to biological and adoptive parents. *Child Development, 54,* 268–275.

Horney, K. (1937). *The neurotic personality of our time.* New York: W. W. Norton.

Horvath, F. S. (1977). The effects of selected variables on the interpretation of polygraph records. *Journal of Applied Psychology, 62,* 127–136.

Horvath, T. (1981). Physical attractiveness: The influence of selected torso parameters. *Archives of Sexual Behavior, 10,* 21–24.

Hovland, C. I. (1937). The generalization of conditioned responses: 1. The sensory generalization of conditioned responses with varying frequencies of tone. *Journal of General Psychology, 17,* 125–148.

Howard, A., Pion, G. M., Gottfredson, G. D., Flattau, P. E., Oskamp, S., Pfafflin, S. M., Bray, D. W., & Burstein, A. G. (1986). Human Resources in Psychology. The changing face of American psychology. A report from the committee on employment and human resources. *American Psychologist, 41,* 1311–1327.

Howard, K. I., Kopta, S. M., Krause, M. S., & Orlinsky, D. E. (1986). The dose-effect relationships in psychotherapy. *American Psychologist, 41,* 159–164.

Howarth, E. (1986). What does Eysenck's psychoticism scale really measure? *British Journal of Psychology, 77,* 223–227.

Hsu, L. K. G. (1986). The treatment of anorexia nervosa. *American Journal of Psychiatry, 143,* 573–581.

Hubel, D. H. (1979). The brain. In *The brain* [Scientific American book]. San Francisco: W. H. Freeman.

Hubel, D. H., & Wiesel, T. N. (1962). Receptive fields, binocular interaction, and functional architecture in the cat's visual cortex. *Journal of Physiology, 160,* 106–154.

Hubel, D. H., & Wiesel, T. N. (1979). Brain mechanisms of vision. In *The brain* [Scientific American book]. San Francisco: W. H. Freeman.

Hudspeth, A. J. (1983). The hair cells of the inner ear. *Scientific American, 248,* 54–73.

Huesmann, L. R., Eron, L. D., Klein, R., Brice, P., & Fischer, P. (1983). Mitigating the imitation of aggressive behaviors by changing children's attitudes about media violence. *Journal of Personality and Social Psychology, 44,* 899–910.

Hunt, M. (1974). *Sexual behavior in the 1970s.* New York: Dell Publishing Company.

Hunt, W. A., & Bespalec, B. A. (1974). An evaluation of current methods of modifying smoking behavior. *Journal of Clinical Psychology, 30,* 431–438.

Hurvich, L., & Jameson, D. (1974). Opponent processes as a model of neural organization. *American Psychologist, 30,* 88–102.

Hyer, L. A., Jacobsen, R., & Harrison, W. R. (1985). Irrational ideas. Older vs. younger inpatients. *The Journal of Nervous and Mental Disease, 173,* 232–235.

Ilfeld, F. W., Jr. (1982). Marital stressors, coping styles, and symptoms on depression. In L. Goldberger & S. Breznitz (Eds.), *Handbook of stress: Theoretical and clinical aspects.* New York: The Free Press, a division of Macmillan.

Ingbar, D. H., & Gee, J. B. L. (1985). Pathophysiology and treatment of sleep apnea. *Annual Review of Medicine, 36,* 369–395.

Ingram, I. M. (1961). Obsessional personality and anal-erotic character. *Journal of Mental Science, 107,* 1035–1042.

Inhelder, B., & Piaget, J. (1958). *The growth of logical thinking from childhood to adolescence.* New York: Basic Books.

Insua, A. M. (1983). WAIS-R factor structures in two cultures. *Journal of Cross-Cultural Psychology, 14,* 427–438.

Intraub, H. (1980). Presentation rate and the representation of briefly glimpsed pictures in memory. *Journal of Experimental Psychology: Human Learning and Memory, 6,* 1–12.

Intraub, H., & Nicklos, S. (1985). Levels of processing and picture memory: The physical superiority effect. *Journal of Experimental Psychology: Learning, Memory, and Cognition, 11,* 284–298.

Israely, Y. (1985). The moral development of mentally retarded children: Review of the literature. *Journal of Moral Education, 14,* 33–42.

Jackson, J. M., & Latané, B. (1981). All alone in front of all those people: Stage fright as a function of number and type of co-performers and audience. *Journal of Personality and Social Psychology, 40,* 73–85.

Jackson, L. A., & Larrance, D. T. (1979). Is a "refinement" of attribution theory necessary to accommodate the learned helplessness reformulation? A critique of the reformulation of Abramson, Seligman, and Teasdale. *Journal of Abnormal Psychology, 88,* 681–682.

Jacobs, L., Berscheid, E., & Walster, E. (1971). Self-esteem and attraction. *Journal of Personality and Social Psychology, 17,* 84–91.

Jacobson, N. S., & Bussob, N. (1983). Marital and family therapy. In M. Herson, A. E. Kazdin, and A. S. Bellack, *The clinical psychology handbook.* New York: Pergamon Press.

Jaffe, P. G., & Carlson, P. M. (1972). Modeling therapy for test anxiety: The role of model affect and consequences. *Behavior Research and Therapy, 10,* 329–339.

James, W. (1884). What is an emotion? *Mind, 9,* 188–205.

Janes, C. L., Weeks, D. G., & Worland, J. (1983). School behavior in adolescent children of parents with mental disorder. *Journal of Nervous and Mental Disease, 171,* 234–240.

Janis, I. L. (1982a). Decisionmaking under stress. In L. Goldberger, & S. Breznitz (Eds.), *Handbook of stress. Theoretical and Clinical aspects.* New York: The Free Press, a division of Macmillan.

Janis, I. L. (1982b). Stress inoculation in health care: Theory and research. In D. Beichenbaum & M. Jaremko (Eds.), *Stress prevention and management: A cognitive behavioral approach.* New York: Plenum Press.

Jaynes, J. (1976). *The origin of consciousness in the breakdown of the bicameral mind.* Boston: Houghton Mifflin.

Jenkins, H. M., & Harrison, R. H. (1960). Effect of discrimination training on auditory generalization. *Journal of Experimental Psychology, 59,* 244–253.

Jenkins, J. G., & Dallenbach, K. M. (1924). Oblivescence during sleep and waking. *American Journal of Psychology, 35,* 605–612.

Jensen, A. R. (1969). How much can we boost IQ and scholastic achievement? *Harvard Educational Review, 39,* 1–123.

Jensen, A. R. (1970). Can we and should we study race differences? In J. Hellmuth (Ed.), *Disadvantaged child* (Vol. 3). New York: Brunner/Mazel.

Jensen, A. R. (1976). Test bias and construct validity. *Phi Delta Kappan, 58,* 340–346.

Jensen, A. R. (1977). Cumulative deficit in IQ of blacks in the rural south. *Developmental Psychology, 3,* 184–191.

Jensen, A. R. (1980). Can we be neutral about bias? *Contemporary Psychology, 25,* 868–871.

Jensen, A. R. (1984). The black-white difference on the K-ABC: Implications for future tests. *The Journal of Special Education, 18,* 377–408.

Jensen, A. R., & Inouye, A. R. (1980). Level I and Level II abilities in Asian, white, and black children. *Intelligence, 4,* 41–49.

Joffe, L. S. (1980). *The relation between mother-infant attachment and compliance with maternal commands and prohibitions.* Unpublished doctoral dissertation, University of Minnesota, Minneapolis.

John, E. R., Chester, P., Bartlett, F., & Victor, I. (1968). Observational learning in cats. *Science, 159,* 1489–1491.

Johnson, C., & Flach, A. (1985). Family characteristics of 105 patients with bulimia. *American Journal of Psychiatry, 142,* 1321–1324.

Johnson, C., & Larson, R. (1982). Bulimia: An analysis of moods and behavior. *Psychosomatic Medicine, 44,* 341–351.

Johnson, R. F. Q., & Barber, T. X. (1978). Hypnosis, suggestions, and warts: An experimental investigation implicating the importance of "believed in efficacy." *American Journal of Clinical Hypnosis, 20,* 165–174.

Johnston, E., & Donoghue, J. R. (1971). Hypnosis and smoking: A review of the literature. *American Journal of Clinical Hypnosis, 13,* 265–272.

Johnston, L. D., Bachman, J. G., & O'Malley, P. M. (1980). *Highlights from student drug use in America 1915–1980* (DHHS Publication No. ADM 81–1066). Washington, DC: U.S. Government Printing Office.

Jones, B. (1983). Measuring degree of cerebral lateralization in children as a function of age. *Developmental Psychology, 19,* 237–242.

Jones, B. E., & Gray, B. A. (1983). Black males and psychotherapy: Theoretical issues. *American Journal of Psychotherapy, 37,* 77–85.

Jones, E. E. (1964). *Ingratiation: A social psychological analysis.* New York: Appleton-Century-Crofts.

Jones, E. E., & Nisbett, R. E. (1972). The actor and the observer: Divergent perceptions of causes of behavior. In E. E. Jones et al. (Eds.), *Attribution: Perceiving the causes of behavior.* Morristown, NJ: General Learning Press.

Jones, L. V. (1984). White-black achievement differences. The narrowing gap. *American Psychologist, 39,* 1207–1213.

Jones, M. M. (1980). Conversion reaction: Anachronism or evolutionary form? A review of the neurologic, behavioral, and psychoanalytic literature. *Psychological Bulletin, 87,* 427–441.

Jones, R. A. (1977). *Self-fulfilling prophecies: Social, psychological, and physiological effects of expectancies.* Hillsdale, NJ: Lawrence Erlbaum Associates.

Jordan, H. A., Canavan, A. J., & Steer, R. A. (1985). Patterns of weight change: The interval 6 to 10 years after initial weight loss in a cognitive-behavioral treatment program. *Psychological Reports, 57,* 195–203.

Just, M. A., & Carpenter, P. A. (1980). A theory of reading: From eye fixations to comprehension. *Psychological Review, 87,* 329–354.

Justice, B., McBee, G. W., & Allen, R. H. (1977). Live events, psychological distress, and social functioning. *Psychological Reports, 40,* 467–473.

Kaats, G. R., & Davis, K. E. (1970). The dynamics of sexual behavior of college students. *Journal of Marriage and the Family, 32,* 390–399.

Kagan, J. (1979). Family experience and the child's development. *American Psychologist, 34,* 886–891.

Kagan, J., Kearsley, R. B., & Zelazo, P. R. (1980). *Infancy: Its place in human development.* Cambridge, MA: Harvard University Press.

Kahn, J. P., Kornfield, D. S., Blood, D. K., Lynn, R. B., Heller, S. S., & Frank, K. A. (1982). Type A behavior and the thallium stress test. *Psychosomatic Medicine, 44,* 431–436.

Kahn, S. (1975). *Why and how we laugh.* New York: Philosophical Library.

Kales, A., Tan, T. L., Kollar, E. J., Naithoh, P., Preson, T. A., & Malmstrom, E. J. (1970). Sleep patterns following 205 hours of sleep deprivation. *Psychosomatic Medicine, 32,* 189–200.

Kalliopuska, M. (1982). Body-image disturbances in patients with anorexia nervosa. *Psychological Reports, 51,* 715–722.

Kalven, H. G., Jr., & Zeisel, H. (1966). *The American jury.* Boston: Little, Brown.

Kamin, L. J. (1974). *The science and politics of IQ.* Hillsdale, NJ: Lawrence Erlbaum Associates.

Kanas, N., Rogers, M., Kreth, E., Patterson, L., & Campbell, R. (1980). The effectiveness of group psychotherapy during the first three weeks of hospitalization: A controlled study. *Journal of Nervous and Mental Disease, 168,* 487–492.

Kanfer, F., & Marston, A. R. (1963). Human reinforcement: Vicarious and direct. *Journal of Experimental Psychology, 65,* 292–296.

Kanner, A. D., Coyne, J. C., Schaefer, C., & Lazarus, R. S. (1981). Comparison of two modes of stress measurement: Daily hassles and uplifts versus major life events. *Journal of Behavioral Medicine, 4,* 1–39.

Kanner, L. (1943). Autistic disturbances of affective content. *Nervous Child, 2,* 217–240.

Kaplan, H. B. (1977). Gender and depression: A sociological analysis of a conditional relationship. In W. E. Fann, I. Karacan, A. D. Pokorny, & R. L. Williams (Eds.), *Phenomenology and treatment of depression.* New York: Spectrum Publications.

Kaplan, L. J. (1978). *Oneness and separateness: From infant to individual.* New York: Simon & Schuster.

Kaplan, R. M. (1982). Nader's raid on the testing industry. Is it in the best interest of the consumer? *American Psychologist, 37,* 15–23.

Kaplan, R. M., & Singer, R. D. (1976). Television violence and viewer aggression: A reexamination of the evidence. *Journal of Social Issues, 32,* 35–70.

Karabenick, S. A., & Srull, T. K. (1978). Effects of personality and situational variation in locus of control on cheating. Determinants of the "congruence effect." *Journal of Personality, 46,* 72–95.

Karlsson, J. L. (1966). *The biologic base of schizophrenia.* Springfield, IL: Thomas Press.

Katkin, E. S. (1985). Psychology in the public forum. Polygraph testing, psychological research, and public policy. An introductory note. *American Psychologist, 40,* 346–347.

Kaufman, A. S. (1982). The impact of WISC-R research for school psychologists. In C. R. Reynolds & T. B. Gutkin (Eds.), *The handbook of school psychology.* New York: John Wiley & Sons.

Kaufman, A. S. (1983). Some questions and answers about the Kaufman Assessment Battery for Children (K-ABC). *Journal of Psychoeducational Assessment, 1,* 205–218.

Kaufman, A. S. (1984). K-ABC and controversy. *The Journal of Special Education, 18,* 409–444.

Kaufman, A. S., & Kaufman, N. L. (1983). *K-ABC: Kaufman assessment battery for children. Interpretive manual.* Circle Pines, MN: American Guidance Service.

Kazdin, A. E. (1975). *Behavior modification in applied settings.* Homewood, IL: Dorsey Press.

Kazdin, A. E. (1978a). Behavior therapy: Evolution, and expansion. *Counseling Psychologist, 7,* 34–37.

Kazdin, A. E. (1978b). *History of behavior modification. Experimental foundations of contemporary research.* Baltimore: University Park Press.

Kazdin, A. E. (1986). Comparative outcome studies of psychotherapy: Methodological issues and strategies. *Journal of Consulting and Clinical Psychology, 54,* 95–105.

Kazdin, A. E., Esbeldt-Dawson, K., Sherick, R. B., & Colbus, D. (1985). Assessment of overt behavior and childhood depression among psychiatrically disturbed children. *Journal of Consulting and Clinical Psychology, 53,* 201–210.

Keane, T. M., Scott, W. O., Chavoya, G. A., Lamparski, D. M., & Fairbank, J. A. (1985). Social support in Vietnam veterans with posttraumatic stress disorder: A comparative analysis. *Journal of Consulting and Clinical Psychology, 53,* 95–102.

Keesey, R. E. (1980). A set-point analysis of the regulation of body weight. In A. J. Stunkard (Ed.), *Obesity.* Philadelphia: W. B. Saunders.

Keith, S. J., Gunderson, J. G., Reifman, A., Bucksbaum, S., & Mosher, L. R. (1976). Special report: Schizophrenia 1976. *Schizophrenia Bulletin, 2,* 509–565.

Keller, H., & Schölmerich, A. (1987). Infant vocalizations and parental reactions during the first 4 months of life. *Developmental Psychology, 23,* 62–67.

Kellerman, J. M., & Laird, J. D. (1982). The effect of appearance on self-perceptions. *Journal of Personality, 50,* 296–315.

Kelley, H. H. (1972). Attribution in social interaction. In E. E. Jones et al. (Eds.), *Attribution: Perceiving the causes of behavior.* Morristown, NJ: General Learning Press.

Kelley, H. H. (1973). Process of causal attribution. *American Psychologist, 28,* 107–128.

Kellogg, W. N. (1968). Communication and language in the home-raised chimpanzee. *Science, 162,* 423–427.

Kelly, C., & Goodwin, G. C. (1983). Adolescents' perception of three styles of parental control. *Adolescence, 18,* 567–571.

Kendler, K. S. (1980). The nosologic validity of paranoia (simple delusional disorder): A review. *Archives of General Psychiatry, 37,* 699–706.

Kennell, J. H., Voos, D. K., & Klaus, M. H. (1979) Parent-infant bonding. In J. D. Osofsky (Ed.), *Handbook of infant development.* New York: John Wiley & Sons.

Kent, M. A., & Peters, M. A. (1973). Effects of ventromedial hypothalamic lesions on hunger-motivated behavior in rats. *Journal of Comparative and Physiological Psychology, 83,* 92–97.

Keppel, G., & Underwood, B. J. (1962). Proactive inhibition in short-term retention of single items. *Journal of Verbal Learning and Verbal Behavior, 1,* 153–161.

Kerr, N., & Bruun, S. E. (1983). Dispensability of member effort and group motivation losses: Free-rider effects. Journal of

Personality and Social Psychology, 44, 78–94.

Kessler, S. (1980). The genetics of schizophrenia: A review. Schizophrenia Bulletin, 6, 404–416.

Kety, S. S. (1979). The biological substrates of schizophrenia. In T. Fukuda & H. Mitsuda (Eds.), Schizophrenic psychoses. New York: Igaku-Shoin.

Kety, S. S., Rosenthal, D., Wender, P. H., & Schulsinger, F. (1968). Mental illness in the biological and adoptive families of adopted schizophrenics. In D. Rosenthal & S. Kety (Eds.), Transmission of schizophrenia. Oxford: Pergamon Press.

Khachaturian, Z. S. (1985). Progress of research on Alzheimer's disease. Research opportunities for behavioral scientists. American Psychologist, 40, 1251–1255.

Kilbourne, W. E., Painton, S., & Ridley, D. (1985). The effect of sexual embedding on responses to magazine advertisements. Journal of Advertising, 14, 48–56.

Kilmann, P. R., Albert, B. M., & Sotile, W. M. (1975). Relationship between locus of control, structure of therapy, and outcome. Journal of Consulting Psychology, 43, 588.

Kimball, C. P. (1982). Stress and psychosomatic illness. Journal of Psychosomatic Research, 26, 63–67.

Kimmel, D. C. (1980). Adulthood and aging: An interdisciplinary view (2nd ed.). New York: John Wiley & Sons.

Kingsbury, S. J. (1987). Cognitive differences between clinical psychologists and psychiatrists. American Psychologist, 42, 152–156.

Kinsbourne, M. (1982). Hemispheric specialization and the growth of human understanding. American Psychologist, 37, 411–420.

Kinsey, A. C., Pomeroy, W. B., & Martin, C. E. (1948). Sexual behavior in the human male. Philadelphia, Penn.: W. B. Saunders Company.

Kinsey, A. C., Pomeroy, W. B., Martin, C. E., & Gebhard, P. H. (1953). Sexual behavior in the human female. Philadelphia, Penn.: W. B. Saunders Company.

Kirkley, B. G., Schneider, J. A., Agras, W. S., & Bachman, J. A. (1985). Comparison of two group treatments for bulimia. Journal of Consulting and Clinical Psychology, 53, 43–48.

Klagsbrun, S. C. (1982). Ethics in hospice care. American Psychologist, 37, 1263–1265.

Klaus, M. H., & Kennell, J. H. (1976). Maternal-infant bonding. St. Louis: C. V. Mosby.

Klaus, M. H., & Kennell, J. H. (1983). Bonding: The beginnings of parent-infant attachment (rev. ed.), Antonia W. Hamilton (Ed.). New York: New American Library.

Klein, R. H. (1983). Group treatment approaches. In M. Hersen, A. E. Kazdin, & A. S. Bellack (Eds.), The clinical psychology handbook. New York: Pergamon Press.

Klein, R. P. (1985). Caregiving arrangements by employed women with children under 1 year of age. Developmental Psychology, 21, 403–406.

Kleinginna, P. R., Jr., & Kleinginna, A. M. (1981). A categorized list of definitions, with suggestions for a consensual definition. Motivation and Emotion, 5, 345–380.

Kleinke, C. L. (1986). Gaze and eye contact: A research review. Psychological Bulletin, 100, 78–100.

Kleinke, C. L., & Staneski, R. A. (1980). First impressions of female bust size. Journal of Social Psychology, 110, 123–134.

Kleinke, C. L., Staneski, R. A., & Berger, D. E. (1975). Evaluation of an interviewer as a function of the interviewer gaze, reinforcement of subject gaze, and interviewer attractiveness. Journal of Personality and Social Psychology, 31, 115–122.

Kleinmuntz, B., & Szucko, J. J. (1984). Lie detection in ancient and modern times. A call for contemporary scientific study. American Psychologist, 39, 766–776.

Kleitman, N., & Englemann, T. G. (1953). Sleep characteristics. Journal of Applied Physiology, 6, 269–282.

Klinnert, M. D., Campos, J., Sorce, J., Emde, R. N., & Svejda, M. (1982). The development of social referencing in infancy. In R. Plutchik & H. Kellerman (Eds.), Emotion: Theory, research, and experience, Vol. 2: Emotion in early development. New York: Academic Press.

Knesper, D., Pagnucco, D. J., & Wheeler, J. R. C. (1985). Similarities and differences across mental health service providers and practice settings in the United States. American Psychologist, 40, 1352–1369.

Koegel, R. I., & Covert, A. (1972). The relationship of self-stimulation to learning in autistic children. Journal of Applied Behavior Analysis, 5, 381–387.

Kohlberg, L. (1963). The development of children's orientation toward a moral order: Sequence in the development of moral thought. Vita Humana, 6, 11–33.

Kohlberg, L. (1969). The cognitive-developmental approach to socialization. In D. A. Goslin (Ed.), Handbook of socialization theory and research. Chicago: Rand McNally.

Kohlberg, L. (1971). From is to ought: How to commit the naturalistic fallacy and get away with it in the study of moral development. In T. Mischel (Ed.), Cognitive development and epistemology. New York: Academic Press.

Kohlberg, L. (1976). Moral stages and moralization: The cognitive-developmental approach. In T. Likcona (Ed.), Moral development and behavior. New York: Holt, Rinehart and Winston.

Korchin, S. J. (1976). Modern clinical psychology: Principles in intervention in the clinic and community. New York: Basic Books.

Koss, M. P., Butcher, J. N., & Strupp, H. H. (1986). Brief psychotherapy methods in clinical research. Journal of Consulting & Clinical Psychology, 54, 60–67.

Kosslyn, S. M. (1975). Information representation in visual images. Cognitive Psychology, 7, 341–370.

Kosslyn, S. M. (1978). Measuring the visual angle of the mind's eye. Cognitive Psychology, 7, 356–389.

Kotelchuck, M. (1976). The infant's relationship to the father: Experimental evidence. In M. E. Lamb (Ed.), The role of the father in child development. New York: John Wiley & Sons.

Kramer, M. (1982). The continuing challenge: The rising prevalence of mental disorders, associated chronic diseases, and disabling conditions. In M. O. Wagenfeld, P. V. Lemkau, & B. Justice (Eds.), Public mental health: Perspectives and prospects. Beverly Hills, CA: Sage Publications.

Krebs, D., & Adinolfi, A. A. (1975). Physical attractiveness, social relations, and personality style. Journal of Personality and Social Psychology, 31, 245–253.

Krogh, S. L., & Lamme, L. L. (1985). "But what about sharing?" Children's literature and moral development. Young Children, 48–51.

Krump, M. A., Chatton, M. J., & Tierney, L. M. (Eds.). (1986). Current medical diagnosis and treatment. Los Altos, CA: Lange Medical Publications.

Krupnick, J., Shea, T., & Elkin, I. (1986). Generalizability of treatment studies utilizing solicited patients. Journal of Consulting and Clinical Psychology, 54, 68–78.

Kübler-Ross, E. (1969). On death and dying. New York: Macmillan.

Kübler-Ross, E. (1975). Death: The final stage of growth. Englewood Cliffs, NJ: Prentice-Hall.

Kübler-Ross, E. (1981). Living with death and dying. New York: Macmillan.

Kundel, H. L., & Nodine, C. F. (1978). Studies of eye movements and visual search in radiology. In J. W. Senders, D. G. Fisher, & R. A. Monty (Eds.), Eye movements and the higher psychological processes. Hillsdale, NJ: Lawrence Erlbaum Associates.

Labov, W. (1970). The logic of nonstandard English. In F. Williams (Ed.), *Language and poverty.* Chicago: Rand McNally.

Lachman, S. J. (1983). The concept of learning: Connectioning and selectioning. *Academic Psychology Bulletin, 5,* 155–168.

Lahey, B. B., Conger, R. D., Atkeson, B. M., & Treiber, F. A. (1984). Parenting behavior and emotional status of physically abusive mothers. *Journal of Consulting and Clinical Psychology, 52,* 1062–1071.

Lahey, B. B., Green, K. D., & Forehand, R. (1980). On the independence of ratings of hyperactivity, conduct problems, and attention deficits in children: A multiple regression analysis. *Journal of Consulting and Clinical Psychology, 48,* 566–574.

Lahey, B. B., McNees, M. P., & McNees, M. C. (1973). Control of an obscene "verbal tic" through timeout in an elementary school classroom. *Journal of Applied Behavior Analysis, 6,* 101–104.

Lamb, M. E. (1979). Paternal influences and the father's role. *American Psychologist, 34,* 938–943.

Lancy, D. F., & Goldstein, G. I. (1982). The use of nonverbal Piagetian tasks to assess the cognitive development of autistic children. *Child Development, 53,* 1233–1241.

Lange, C. G. (1922). *The emotions* (English translation). Baltimore: Williams & Wilkins. (Original work published 1885).

Langenbucher, J. W., & Nathan, P. E. (1983). Psychology, public policy, and the evidence for alcohol intoxication. *American Psychologist, 38,* 1070–1077.

Langford, G. W., Meddis, R., & Pearson, A. J. D. (1974). Awakening latency from sleep from meaningful and nonmeaningful stimuli. *Psychophysiology, 11,* 1–5.

Langman, B., & Cockburn, A. (1975). Sirhan's gun. *Harper's. 250*(1496), 16–27.

Lanyon, R. I. (1968). *A handbook of MMPI group profiles.* Minneapolis: University of Minnesota Press.

Largeman, R. R. (1976). *The social-emotional effects of age of entry into full-time group care.* Unpublished doctoral dissertation, University of California, Berkeley.

LaRue, A., & Jarvik, L. F. (1982). Old age and biobehavioral changes. In B. B. Wolman (Ed.), *Handbook of developmental psychology.* Englewood Cliffs, NJ: Prentice-Hall.

Latané, B. (1981). The psychology of social impact. *American Psychologist, 36,* 343–356.

Latané, B., & Darley, J. M. (1970). *The unresponsive bystander: Why doesn't he help?* New York: Meredith.

Latané, B., & Nida, S. (1981). Ten years of research on group size and helping. *Psychological Bulletin, 89,* 307–324.

Latané, B., Williams, K., & Harkins, S. (1979). Many hands make light work: The causes and consequences of social loafing. *Journal of Personality and Social Psychology, 37,* 822–832.

Laufer, R. S., Brett, E., & Gallops, M. S. (1985). Symptom patterns associated with posttraumatic street disorder among Vietnam veterans exposed to war trauma. *American Journal of Psychiatry, 142,* 1304–1307.

Lawrence, F. C., Tasker, G. E., Daly, C. T., Orhiel, A. L., & Wozniak, P. H. (1986). Adolescents' time spent viewing television. *Adolescence, 21,* 431–434.

Lazarus, R. S. (1974). Cognitive and coping processes in emotion. In B. Weiner (Ed.), *Cognitive views of human motivation.* New York: Academic Press.

Lazarus, R. S. (1982). The psychology of stress and coping, with particular reference to Israel. In C. D. Spielberger, I. G. Sarason, & N. A. Milgram (Eds.), *Stress and anxiety* (Vol. 8). Washington, DC: Hemisphere Publishing.

Lazarus, R. S., & Alfert, E. (1964). Short-circuiting of threat by experimentally altering cognitive appraisal. *Journal of Abnormal and Social Psychology, 69,* 195–205.

Lazarus, R. S., & DeLongis, A. (1983). Psychological stress and coping in aging. *American Psychologist, 38,* 245–254.

Lazarus, R. S., DeLongis, A., Folkman, S., & Gruen, R. (1985). Stress and adaptational outcomes. *American Psychologist, 40,* 770–779.

Leber, W. R., Beckham, E. E., & Danker-Brown, P. (1985). Diagnositc criteria for depression. In E. E. Beckham & W. R. Leber (Eds.), *Handbook of depression. Treatment, assessment, and research.* Homewood, IL: Dorsey Press.

Lee, P. K., Andersen, T. W., Modell, J. H., & Saga, S. A. (1975). Treatment of chronic pain with acupuncture. *Journal of the American Medical Association, 232,* 1133–1135.

Leiner, H. C., Leiner, A. L., & Dow, R. S. (1986). Does the cerebellum contribute to mental skills? *Behavioral Neuroscience, 100,* 443–454.

Lemere, F., & Smith, J. W. (1973). Alcohol-induced sexual impotence. *American Journal of Psychiatry, 130,* 212–213.

Lemere, F., & Voegtlin, W. (1950). An evaluation of the aversive treatment of alcoholism. *Quarterly Journal of Studies on Alcohol, 11,* 199–204.

Lempers, J. O., Flavell, E. H., & Flavell, J. H. (1977). The development in very young children of tacit knowledge concerning visual perception. *Genetic Psychology Monographs, 95,* 3–53.

Leonard-Barton, D. (1981). The diffusion of active residential solar energy equipment in California. In A. Shama (Ed.), *Marketing solar energy innovations* (pp. 243–257). New York: Praeger.

Lepper, M. R. (1985). Microcomputers in education. Motivational and social issues. *American Psychologist, 40,* 1–18.

Lepper, M. R., & Greene, D. (1978). Overjustification research and beyond: Toward a means-end analysis of intrinsic motivation. In M. R. Lepper & D. Greene (Eds.), *The hidden cost of reward.* Hillsdale, NJ: Lawrence Erlbaum Associates.

Lepper, M. R., Greene, D., & Nisbett, R. E. (1973). Undermining children's intrinsic interest with extrinsic reward: A test of the overjustification hypothesis. *Journal of Personality and Social Psychology, 28,* 129–137.

Lerner, M. J. (1970). The desire for justice and reactions to victims. In J. Macaulay & L. Berkowitz (Eds.), *Altruism and helping behavior: Social psychological studies of some antecedents and consequences.* New York: Academic Press.

Lerner, R. M., Karson, M., Meisels, M., & Knapp, J. R. (1975). Actual and perceived attitudes of late adolescents and their parents: The phenomenon of the generation gaps. *Journal of Genetic Psychology, 126,* 195–207.

Lerner, R. M., & Lerner, J. V. (1977). Effects of age, sex, and physical attractiveness on child-peer relations, academic performance, and elementary school adjustment. *Developmental Psychology, 13,* 585–590.

Lerner, R. M., & Shea, J. A. (1982). Social behavior in adolescence. In B. B. Wolman (Ed.), *Handbook of development psychology.* Englewood Cliffs, NJ: Prentice-Hall.

Levander, S., & Sachs, C. (1985). Vigilance performance and autonomic function in narcolepsy: Effects of central stimulants. *Psychophysiology, 22,* 24–31.

Levere, T. E., Morlock, G. W., Thomas, L. P., & Hart, F. D. (1974). Arousal from sleep: The differential effect of frequencies equated from loudness. *Physiology and Behavior, 12,* 573–582.

Levin, R. J. (1975). The *Redbook* report on premarital and extramarital sex: The end of the double standard? *Redbook,* Oct., 38–44, 190–192.

Levinson, D. J. (1978). *The seasons of a man's life.* New York: Alfred A. Knopf.

Levinson, D. J. (1980). Toward a conception of the adult life course. In N. J. Smelser & E. H. Erikson (Eds.), *Themes of work and love in adulthood.* Cambridge: Harvard University Press.

Levitt, E. E., & Truumaa, A. (1972). *The Rorschach technique with children and adolescents: Application and norms.* New York: Grune & Stratton.

Levitt, M. J., Weber, R. A., Clark, M. C., & McDonnell, P. (1985). Reciprocity of exchange in toddler sharing behavior. *Developmental Psychology, 21,* 122–123.

Levy, J. (1983). Language, cognition, and the right hemisphere: A response to Gazzaniga. *American Psychologist, 38,* 538–541.

Levy, L. H. (1984). The metamorphosis of clinical psychology. Toward a new charter as human services psychology. *American Psychologist, 39,* 486–494.

Lewinsohn, P. M. (1974). Classical and theoretical aspects of depression. In I. S. Calhoun, H. E. Adams, & K. M. Mitchell (Eds.), *Innovative treatment methods in psychopathology.* New York: Wiley Interscience.

Lewinsohn, P. M., & Talkington, J. (1979). Studies on the measurement of unpleasant events and relations with depression. *Applied Psychological Measurement, 3,* 83–101.

Lewinsohn, P. M., Youngren, M. A., & Grosscup, J. (1979). Reinforcement and depression. In R. A. DePue (Ed.), *The psychobiology of the depressive disorders.* New York: Academic Press.

Lewis, H. (1981). *Freud and modern psychology.* New York: Plenum Press.

Lewis, M., & Weinraub, M. (1976). The father's role in the infant's social network. In M. E. Lamb (Ed.), *The role of the father in child development.* New York: John Wiley & Sons.

Lewis, T. L., & Maurer, D. (1980). Central vision in the newborn. *Journal of Experimental Child Psychology, 29,* 475–480.

Lidz, T. (1973). *The origin and treatment of schizophrenic disorders.* New York: Basic Books.

Liebert, R. M., Sprafkin, J. M., & Davidson, E. S. (1982). *The early window: Effects of television on children and youth.* (2nd ed.). New York: Pergamon Press.

Lilly, J. C. (1956). Mental effects of reduction of ordinary levels of physical stimuli in intact, healthy persons. *Psychiatric Research Reports, 5,* 1–28.

Linn, L., & Spitzer, R. L. (1982). DSM-III: Implications for liaison psychiatry and psychosomatic medicine. *Journal of the American Medical Association, 247,* 3207–3209.

Linn, S., Reznick, J. S., Kagan, J., & Hans, S. (1982). Salience of visual patterns in the human infant. *Developmental Psychology, 5,* 651–657.

Linnoila, M., Karoum, F., Rosenthal, N., & Potter, W. Z. (1983). Electroconvulsive treatment and lithium carbonate: Their effects on norepinephrine metabolism in patients with primary, major depressions. *Archives of General Psychiatry, 40,* 677–680.

Lipsky, M., Kassinove, H., & Miller, N. (1980). Effects of rational-emotive therapy, rational role reversal, and rational-emotive imagery on the emotional adjustment of community mental health center patients. *Journal of Consulting and Clinical Psychology, 48,* 366–374.

Lipton, J. P., & Hershaft, A. M. (1984). "Girl," "woman," "guy," "man": The effects of sexist labeling. *Sex Roles, 10,* 183–197.

Littig, L. W., & Williams, C. E. (1978). Need for affiliation, self-esteem, and social distance of black Americans. *Motivation and Emotion, 2,* 369–374.

Little, R. E. (1979, Fall). Drinking during pregnancy: Implications for public health. *Alcohol Health and Research World* [NIAA, Public Health Service Alcohol, Drug Abuse, and Mental Health Administration, DHEW], *4.*

Lloyd, R. W., Jr., & Salzberg, H. C. (1975). Controlled social drinking: An alternative to abstinence as a treatment goal for some alcohol abusers. *Psychological Bulletin, 82,* 815–842.

Loeber, R. (1982). The stability of antisocial and delinquent child behavior: A review. *Child Development, 53,* 1431–1446.

Loeber, R., & Dishion, T. (1983). Early predictors of male delinquency: A review. *Psychological Bulletin, 94,* 68–99.

Loehlin, J. C., Lindzey, G., & Spuhler, J. N. (1975). *Race differences in intelligence.* San Francisco: W. H. Freeman.

Loftus, E. F. (1974). Reconstructing memory: The incredible eyewitness. *Psychology Today,* pp. 116–119.

Loftus, E. F. (1979). The malleability of human memory. *American Scientist, 67,* 310–320.

Loftus, E. F., & Burns, T. E. (1982). Mental shock can produce retrograde amnesia. *Memory and Cognition, 10,* 318–323.

Loftus, E. F., & Palmer, J. C. (1974). Reconstruction of automobile destruction: An example of the interaction between language and memory. *Journal of Verbal Learning and Verbal Behavior, 11,* 585–589.

Loftus, G. R. (1985). On worthwhile icons: Reply to Di Lollo and Haber. *Journal of Experimental Psychology: Human Perception and Performance, 11,* 384–388.

Loftus, G. R., & Loftus, E. F. (1976). *Human memory: The processing of information.* Hillsdale, NJ: Lawrence Erlbaum Associates.

Loftus, G. R., Shimamura, A. P., & Johnson, C. (1985). How much is an icon worth? *Journal of Experimental Psychology: Human Perception and Performance, 11,* 1–13.

Loh, H. H., & Colleagues. (1976). Beta-endorphin is a potent analagesic agent. *Proceedings of the National Academy of Science, 73,* 2895–2898.

Longabaugh, R., Stout, R., Kriebel, G. W., Jr., McCullough, L., & Bishop, D. (1986). DSM-III and clinically identified problems as a guide to treatment. *Archives of General Psychiatry, 43,* 1097–1103.

Longstreath, L. E., Davis, B., Carter, L., Flint, D., Owen, J., Rickert, M., & Taylor, E. (1981). Separation of home intellectual environment and maternal IQ as determinants of child IQ. *Developmental Psychology, 17,* 532–541.

Lorenz, K. (1964). Ritualized fighting. In J. D. Carthy & F. J. Ebling (Eds.), *The natural history of aggression.* New York: Academic Press.

Lothstein, L. M. (1978). The psychological management and treatment of hospitalized transsexuals. *Journal of Nervous and Mental Disease, 166,* 255–262.

Lovaas, O. I. (1977). *The autistic child: Language development through behavior modification.* New York: Irvington.

Lovallo, W. R., & Pishkin, V. (1980). A psychological comparison of Type A and B men exposed to failure and uncontrollable noise. *Psychophysiology, 17,* 29–36.

Lovatt, F. J., & Warr, P. B. (1968). Recall after sleep. *American Journal of Psychology, 81,* 523–527.

Lowell, E. L. (1952). The effect of need for achievement on learning and speed of performance. *Journal of Psychology, 33,* 31–40.

Lowell, S. H., & Paparella, M. M. (1977). Presbycusis: What is it? *Annals of Otology, Rhinology, and Laryngology, 85,* 1710–1717.

Luborsky, L., Mintz, J., Auerbach, A., Christoph, P., Bachrach, H., Todd, T., Johnson, M., Cohen, M., & O'Brien, C. P. (1980). Predicting the outcome of psychotherapy. *Archives of General Psychiatry, 37,* 471–481.

Luborsky, L., & Spence, D. P. (1978). Quantitative research on psychoanalytic therapy. In S. L. Garfield & A. E. Bergin (Eds.), *Handbook of psychotherapy and behavior change: An empirical analysis* (2nd ed.). New York: John Wiley & Sons.

Luger, G. F., Bower, T. G. R., & Wishart, J. G.(1983). A model of the development of the early infant object concept. *Perception, 12,* 21–34.

Lundin, R. W. (1961). *Personality: An experimental approach.* New York: Macmillan.

Lutkenhaus, P., Grossman, K. E., & Grossman, K. (1985). Infant-mother attachment at twelve months and style of interaction with a stranger at the age of three years. *Child Development, 56,* 1538–1542.

Lykken, D. T. (1957). A study of anxiety in the sociopathic personality. *Journal of Abnormal and Social Psychology, 55,* 6–10.

Lym, G. R. (1978). *A psychology of building.* Englewood Cliffs, NJ: Prentice-Hall.

Lynch, J. J. (1977). *The broken heart: The medical consequences of loneliness.* New York: Basic Books.

MacHovec, F. J., & Man, S. C. (1978). Acupuncture and hypnosis compared: Fifty-eight cases. *American Journal of Clinical Hypnosis, 21,* 45–47.

Mackay, A. V. P., Bird, E. D., Spokes, E. G., Rossor, J., Iversen, L. L., Creese, I., & Snyder, S. H. (1980). Dopamine receptors and schizophrenia: Drug effect or illness? *Lancet, 11,* 915–916.

Mackenzie, B. (1984). Explaining race differences in IQ. The logic, the methodology, and the evidence. *American Psychologist, 39,* 1214–1233.

Mackintosh, N. J. (1986). The biology of intelligence? *British Journal of Psychology, 77,* 1–18.

MacNichol, E. F. (1964). Three-pigment color vision. *Scientific American, 211,* 48–56.

Macrae, J. W., & Herbert-Jackson, E. (1976). Are behavioral effects of infant day care programs specific? *Developmental Psychology, 12,* 269–270.

Maddi, S. R. (1976). *Personality theories: A comparative analysis* (3rd ed.). Homewood, IL: Dorsey Press.

Mahoney, M. J. (1977). Reflections on the cognitive-learning trend in psychotherapy. *American Psychologist, 32,* 5–13.

Mahrer, A. R., & Nadler, W. P. (1986). Good moments in psychotherapy: A preliminary review, a list, and some promising research avenues. *Journal of Consulting & Clinical Psychology, 54,* 10–15.

Maier, N. R. F., & Klee, J. B. (1941). Studies of abnormal behavior in the rat: 17. Guidance versus trial and error and their relation to convulsive tendencies. *Journal of Experimental Psychology, 29,* 380–389.

Mann, H. (1959). Group hypnosis in the treatment of obesity. *American Journal of Clinical Hypnosis, 1,* 114–116.

Manstead, A. S. R. (1979). Role-playing replication of Schacter and Singer's (1962) study of the cognitive and physiological determinates of emotional state. *Motivation and Emotion, 3,* 251–264.

Marks, I. M. (1969). *Fears and phobias.* New York: Academic Press.

Marks, I. M. (1977). Clinical phenomena in search of laboratory models. In J. D. Maser & M. E. P. Seligman (Eds.), *Psychopathology experimental models.* San Francisco: W. H. Freeman.

Marks, I. M., & Lader, M. (1973). Anxiety states (anxiety neurosis): A review. *Journal of Nervous and Mental Disease, 156,* 3–18.

Marks, W. B., Dobell, W. H., & MacNichol, J. R. (1964). The visual pigments of single primate cones. *Science, 143,* 1181–1183.

Marland, S. P., Jr. (1972). *Education of the gifted and talented* (Vol. 1). Washington, DC: U.S. Government Printing Office.

Marlatt, G. A. (1983). The controlled-drinking controversy: A commentary. *American Psychologist, 38,* 1097–1110.

Marquis, D. P. (1931). Can conditioned responses be established in the newborn infant? *Journal of Genetic Psychology, 39,* 479–492.

Marshall, W. A., & Tanner, J. M. (1969). Variations in the pattern of pubertal changes in girls. *Archives of Disease in Childhood, 44,* 291–303.

Marslen-Wilson, W. D., & Teuber, H. L. (1975). Memory for remote events in anterograde amnesia: Recognition of public figures from newsphotographs. *Neuropsychologia, 13,* 353–364.

Martin, R., & Haroldson, S. (1977). Effect of vicarious punishment on stuttering frequency. *Journal of Speech and Hearing Research, 20,* 21–26.

Massaro, D. W., & Warner, D. S. (1977). Dividing attention between auditory and visual perception. *Perception and Psychophysics, 21,* 569–574.

Masters, W. H., & Johnson, V. E. (1966). *Human sexual response.* Boston: Little, Brown.

Masters, W. H., & Johnson, V. E. (1970). *Human sexual inadequacies.* Boston: Little, Brown.

Masters, W. H., & Johnson, V. E. (1979). *Homosexuality in perspective.* Boston: Little, Brown.

Mathews, A. M., Gelder, M. G., & Johnston, D. W. (1981). *Agoraphobia: Nature and treatment.* London, Guilford Press.

Mauer, D., & Salapatek, P. (1976). Development changes in the scanning of faces by young infants. *Child Development, 47,* 523–527.

May, R. (1982). Anxiety and values. In C. D. Spielberger & I. G. Sarason (Eds.), *Stress and anxiety* (Vol. 8). Washington, DC: Hemisphere Publishing.

McAdoo, W. G., & DeMeyer, M. K. (1978). Personality characteristics of parents. In M. Rutter & E. Schopler (Eds.), *Autism: A reappraisal of concepts and treatment.* New York: Plenum Press.

McCall, R. B. (1983). Environmental effects on intelligence: The forgotten realm of discontinuous nonshared within-family factors. *Child Development, 54,* 408–415.

McCarron, L. T. (1973). Psychophysiological discriminants of reactive depression. *Psychophysiology, 10,* 223–230.

McCarthy, E. D., Langner, T. S., Gersten, J. C., Eisenberg, J. G., & Orzeck, L. (1975). The effects of television on children and adolescents: Violence and behavior disorders. *Journal of Communication, 25,* 71–85.

McClelland, D. C. (1961). *The achieving society.* Princeton, NJ: Van Nostrand.

McClelland, D. C. (1975). *Power: The inner experience.* New York: Irvington.

McClelland, D. C. (1986). Some reflections on the two psychologies of love. *Journal of Personality, 54,* 334–353.

McClelland, D. C., Atkinson, J. W., Clark, R. W., & Lowell, E. L. (1953). *The achievement motive.* New York: Appleton-Century-Crofts.

McClintock, M. K. (1971). Menstrual synchrony and suppression. *Nature, 229,* 244–245.

McCormick, D. A., & Thompson, R. F. (1984). Cerebellum: Essential involvement in the classically conditioned eyelid response. *Science, 223,* 296–299.

McGaugh, J. L. (1983). Preserving the presence of the past. Hormonal influences on memory storage. *American Psychologist, 38,* 161–174.

McGaugh, J. L., & Herz, M. J. (Eds.) (1970). *Controversial issues in consolidation of the memory trace.* New York: Atherton Press.

McGee, R. K. (1983). Crisis intervention and brief psychotherapy. In M. Hersen, A. E. Kazdin, & A. S. Bellack (Eds.), *The clinical psychology handbook.* New York: Pergamon Press.

McGhie, A., & Chapman, J. (1961). Disorders of attention and perception in early schizophrenia. *British Journal of Medical Psychology, 34,* 103–116.

McGlashan, T. H., & Miller, G. H. (1982). The goals of psychoanalysis and psychoanalytic psychotherapy. *Archives of General Psychiatry, 39,* 377–388.

McGrath, M. J., & Cohen, D. B. (1978). REM sleep facilitation of adaptive waking behavior: A review of the literature. *Psychological Bulletin, 85,* 24–57.

McGraw, K. O., & Fiala, J. (1982). Undermining the Zeigarnik effect: Another hidden cost of reward. *Journal of Personality, 50,* 58–66.

McKenzie, B. E., Tootell, H. E., & Day, R. H. (1980). Development of visual size constancy during the 1st year of human infancy. *Developmental Psychology, 16,* 163–174.

McNeal, E. T., & Cimbolic, P. (1986). Antidepressants and biochemical theories of depression. *Psychological Bulletin, 99,* 361–374.

McNeill, D. (1970). Explaining linguistic universals. In J. Morton (Ed.), *Biological and social factors in psycholinguistics.* London: Logos Press.

Meddis, R., Pearson, A. J. D., & Langford, G. N. (1973). An extreme case of healthy insomnia. *EEG in Clinical Neurophysiology, 35,* 213–224.

Mehrabian, A. (1980). The effects of emotional state on approach-avoidance behaviors. In A. Mehrabian (Ed.), *Basic dimensions for general psychological theory.* Cambridge, MA: Oelgeschlager, Gunn & Hain.

Meichenbaum, D. (1974). *Cognitive behavior modification.* Morristown, NJ: General Learning Press.

Meichenbaum, D. (1975). Self-instructional methods. In F. H. Kanfer & A. P. Goldstein (Eds.), *Helping people change.* New York: Pergamon Press.

Meichenbaum, D. (1977). *Cognitive behavior modification.* New York: Plenum Press.

Meichenbaum, D., & Cameron, R. (1973). Training schizophrenics to talk to themselves: A means of developing attentional controls. *Behavior Therapy, 4,* 515–534.

Melamed, L. E., Haley, M., & Gildrow, W. (1973). An examination of the role of task-oriented attention in the use of active and passive movement in visual adaption. *Journal of Experimental Psychology, 98,* 125–201.

Melton, G. B. (1983). Toward "personhood" for adolescents: Autonomy and privacy as values in public policy. *American Psychologist, 38,* 99–103.

Meltzer, H. Y., & Stahl, S. M. (1976). The dopamine hypothesis of schizophrenia: A review. *Schizophrenia Bulletin, 2,* 19–76.

Meltzoff, A. N., & Moore, K. (1983). Newborn infants imitate adult facial gestures. *Child development, 54,* 702–709.

Melville, J. (1977). *Phobias and compulsions.* New York: Penguin Books.

Melzack, R., & Loeser, J. D. (1978). Phantom body pain in paraplegics: Evidence for a central "pattern generating mechanism" for pain. *Pain, 4,* 195–210.

Melzack, R., & Wall, P. D. (1965). Pain mechanisms: A new theory. *Science, 150,* 971–979.

Melzack, R., & Wall, P. D. (1970). Psychophysiology of pain. *International Anesthesiology Clinics, 8,* 3–34.

Menaghan, E. G., & Lieberman, M. A. (1986). Changes in depression following divorce: A panel study. *Journal of Marriage and the Family, 48,* 319–328.

Mercer, J. R. (1977). The struggle for children's rights: Critical juncture for school psychology. *School Psychology Digest, 6,* 4–19.

Meyer, R. (1980). The antisocial personality. In R. Woody (Ed.), *The encyclopedia of mental assessment.* San Francisco: Jossey-Bass.

Meyers, D. G., & Kaplan, M. F. (1976). Group induced polarization in simulated juries. *Personality and Social Psychology Bulletin, 2,* 63–66.

Milgram, S. (1963). Behavioral study of obedience. *Journal of Abnormal and Social Psychology, 67,* 371–378.

Milgram, S. (1965a). Some conditions of obedience and disobedience to authority. *Human Relations, 18,* 57–75.

Milgram, S. (1965b). Liberating effects of group pressure. *Journal of Personality and Social Psychology, 1,* 127–134.

Miller, B. C. (1976). A multivariate developmental model of marital satisfaction. *Journal of Marriage and the Family, 4,* 643–657.

Miller, B. C., McCoy, J. K., Olson, T. D., & Wallace, C. M. (1986).

Parental discipline and control attempts in relation to adolescent sexual attitudes and behavior. *Journal of Marriage and the Family, 48,* 503–512.

Miller, G. A. (1956). The magic number seven, plus or minus two: Some limits on our capacity for processing information. *Psychological Review, 63,* 81–97.

Miller, N. E. (1944). Experimental studies of conflict. In J. McV. Hunt (Ed.), *Personality and behavioral disorders* (Vol. 1). New York: Ronald Press.

Miller, N. E. (1959). Liberalization of basic S-R concepts: Extensions to conflict behavior, motivation, and social learning. In S. Koch (Ed.), *Psychology: A study of a science* (Vol. 2). New York: McGraw-Hill.

Miller, N. E. (1969). Learning of visceral and glandular responses. *Science, 163,* 434–445.

Miller, N. E. (1985). The value of behavioral research on animals. *American Psychologist, 40,* 423–440.

Miller, R. C., & Berman, J. S. (1983). The efficacy of cognitive behavior therapies: A quantitative review of the research evidence. *Psychological Bulletin, 94,* 39–53.

Miller, S. A. (1986). Certainty and necessity in the understanding of Piagetian concepts. *Developmental Psychology, 22,* 3–18.

Miller, W. R. (1985). Motivation for treatment: A review with special emphasis on alcoholism. *Psychological Bulletin, 98,* 84–107.

Millman, J., Bishop, C., & Ebel, R. (1965). An analysis of testwiseness. *Educational and Psychological Measurement, 25,* 707–726.

Millon, T. (1983). The DSM-III: An insider's perspective. *American Psychologist, 38,* 804–814.

Milner, B. (1966). Amnesia following operation on the temporal lobes. In C. W. M. Whitty & O. L. Zangwill (Eds.), *Amnesia.* London: Butterworth.

Milner, B., Corkin, S., & Teuber, H. L. (1968). Further analysis of hippocampal amnesic syndrome: 14-year follow-up study of H. M. *Neuropsychologia, 6,* 215–234.

Milner, B., & Kolb, B. (1985). Performance of complex arm movements and facial-movement sequences after cerebral commissurotomy. *Neuropsychologia, 23,* 791–799.

Mischel, W. (1973). Toward a cognitive social learning reconceptualization of personality. *Psychology Review, 80,* 252–283.

Mischel, W. (1979). On the interface of cognition and personality: Beyond the person-situation debate. *American Psychologist, 34,* 740–754.

Mischel, W. (1983). Alternatives in the pursuit of the predictability and consistency of persons: Stable data that yield unstable interpretations. *Journal of Personality, 51,* 578–604.

Mischel, W. (1984). Convergences and challenges in the search for consistency. *American Psychologist, 39,* No. 4, 351–364.

Mishler, E. G., & Waxler, N. E. (1968). Family interaction processes and schizophrenia: A review of current theories. In E. G. Mishler & N. E. Waxler (Eds.), *Family processes and schizophrenia.* New York: Science House.

Mitchell, K. R., & Orr, F. E. (1976). Heterosexual social competence, anxiety, avoidance, and self-judged physical attractiveness. *Perceptual and Motor Skills, 43,* 553–554.

Money, J. (1984). Paraphilias: Phenomenology and classification. *American Journal of Psychotherapy, 38,* 164–168.

Monroe, S. M., & Steiner, S. C. (1986). Social support and psychopathology: Interrelations with preexisting disorder, stress, and personality. *Journal of Abnormal Psychology, 95,* 29–39.

Mook, D. G. (1983). In defense of external invalidity. *American Psychologist, 38,* 379–388.

Moore, E. G. J. (1986). Family socialization and the IQ test performance of traditionally and transracially adopted black children. *Developmental Psychology, 22,* 317–326.

Moos, R. H., & Finney, J. W. (1983). The expanding scope of alcoholism: Treatment evaluation. *American Psychologist, 1036–1044.*

Moran, J. D. III, & Jennings, M. S. (1983). Moral judgments in parochial schools and public school second graders. *Psychological Reports, 52,* 579–585.

Moreland, R. L., & Zajonc, R. B. (1979). Exposure effects may not depend on stimulus recognition. *Journal of Personality and Social Psychology, 37,* 1085–1089.

Morey, L. C., Skinner, H. A., & Blashfield, R. K. (1984). A typology of alcohol abusers: Correlates and implications. *Journal of Abnormal Psychology, 93,* 408–417.

Morgan, M. (1983). Decrements in intrinsic motivation among rewarded and observer subjects. *Child Development, 54,* 636–644.

Morrison, D. M. (1985). Adolescent contraceptive behavior: A review. *Psychological Bulletin, 98,* 538–568.

Morrison, J. R. (1974). Changes in subtype diagnosis of schizophrenia: 1920–1966. *American Journal of Psychiatry, 131,* 674–677.

Moscovici, S. (1976). *Social influence and social change.* London: Academic Press.

Moscovici, S., Lage, E., & Naffrechoux, M. (1969). Influence of a consistent minority and the responses of a majority in a color perception task. *Sociometry, 32,* 365–380.

Moskowitz, B. A. (1978). The acquisition of language. *Scientific American, 239*(5), 92–108.

Mott, T., Jr. (1979). The clinical importance of hypnotizability. *American Journal of Clinical Hypnosis, 21,* 263–269.

Mowrer, O. H., & Mowrer, W. A. (1938). Enuresis: A method for its study and treatment. *American Journal of Orthopsychiatry, 8,* 436–459.

Moyer, W. W. (1978). Effects of loss of freedom on subjects with internal or external locus of control. *Journal of Research and Personality, 12,* 253–261.

Muesser, K. T., Grau, B. W., Sussman, S., & Rosen, A. J. (1984). You're only as pretty as you feel: Facial expression as a determinant of physical attractiveness. *Journal of Personality and Social Psychology, 46,* 469–478.

Mullen, B., & Suls, J. (1982). The effectiveness of attention and rejection as coping styles: A meta-analysis of temporal differences. *Journal of Psychosomatic Research, 26,* 43–49.

Mullen, B., Tice, D. M., Baumeister, R. F., Dawson, K. E., Riordan, C. A., Radloff, C. E., Goethals, G. R., Kennedy, J. G., & Rosenfeld, P. (1986). Newscasters' facial expressions and voting behavior of viewers: Can a smile elect a president? *Journal of Personality and Social Psychology, 51,* 291–295.

Mungy, G. (1982). The power of minorities. In H. Tajfel (Ed.), *European monographs in social psychology* (Vol. 31). London: Academic Press.

Munroe, R. L., & Munroe, R. H. (1983). Birth order and intellectual performance in East Africa. *Journal of Cross-Cultural Psychology, 14,* 3–16.

Murphy, E. H. (1985). Effects of pattern deprivation on visual cortical cells in the rabbit: A reevaluation. *Journal of Neurophysiology, 53,* 1535–1550.

Murphy, G. E., Simons, A. D., Wetzel, R. D., & Lustman, P. J. (1984). Cognitive therapy and pharmacotherapy. *Archives of General Psychiatry, 41,* 33–36.

Murphy, J. K., Sperr, E. V., & Sperr, S. J. (1986). Chronic pain: An investigation of assessment instruments. *Journal of Psychosomatic Research, 30,* 289–296.

Murray, E. J., & Berkun, M. M. (1955). Displacement as a function of conflict. *Journal of Abnormal and Social Psychology, 51,* 47–56.

Muuss, R. E. (1986). Adolescent eating disorder: Bulimia. *Adolescence, 21,* 257–267.

Nairn, A., & Associates (1980). *The reign of ETS: The corporation that makes up minds.* Washington, DC: Nader.

Nassau, K. (1980). The causes of color. *Scientific American, 243*(4), 124–156.

Nathan, P. E. (1983). Failures in prevention: Why we can't prevent the devastating effect of alcoholism and drug abuse. *American Psychologist, 38,* 459–467.

Nathan, P. E., Zare, N., Simpson, H. F., & Andbert, M. M. (1969). A systems analytic model of diagnosis: 1. The diagnostic validity of abnormal psychomotor behavior. *Journal of Clinical Psychology, 25,* 3–9.

National Center on Child Abuse and Neglect. (1981). *Executive summary: National study of the incidence and severity of child abuse and neglect* (DHHS Publication No. OHDS 81-30329. Washington, DC: U.S. Government Printing Office.

National Center for Health Statistics. (1983). Eye care visits and use of eyeglasses or contact lenses: United States 1979–1980. *Vital and Health Statistics, 10,* No. 145.

Natsoulas, T. (1978). Consciousness. *American Psychologist, 33,* 906–914.

Nelson, C., & Horowitz, F. D. (1983). The perception of facial expressions and stimulus motion by two- and five-month-old infants using holographic stimuli. *Child Development, 54,* 868–877.

Nelson, K. (1973). Structure and strategy in learning to talk. *Monographs of the Society for Research in Child Development, 38* (Serial No. 149).

Nelson, S. D., & Stapp, J. (1983). Research activities in psychology: An update. *American Psychologist, 38,* 1321–1329.

Nemeth, C., & Endicott, J. (1976). The midpoint as an anchor: Another look at discrepancy of position and attitude change. *Sociometry, 39,* 11–18.

Neustatler, P. (1982). Aluminum tie to Alzheimer's? Intake of metal now an issue. *Medical Tribune, 23,* 1.

Newcomer, S. F., Udry, J. R., & Cameron, F. (1983). Adolescent sexual behavior and popularity. *Adolescence, 18,* 515–522.

Newman, B. M. (1982). Mid-life development. In B. B. Wolman (Ed.), *Handbook of developmental psychology.* Englewood Cliffs, NJ: Prentice-Hall.

Newman, P. R. (1982). The peer group. In B. B. Wolman (Ed.), *Handbook of developmental psychology.* Englewood Cliffs, NJ: Prentice-Hall.

Nicholson, R. S., & Berman, J. S. (1983). Is follow up necessary in evaluating Psychotherapy? *Psychological Bulletin, 93,* 261–278.

Nisbett, R. E. (1972). Hunger, obesity, and the ventromedial hypothalamus. *Psychological Review, 79,* 433–453.

Noble, E. P. (Ed.) (1978). *Alcohol and health* (Third Special Report to the U.S. Congress from the Secretary of DHEW). Washington, DC: U.S. Government Printing Office.

Nolen-Hoeksma, S. (1987). Sex differences in unipolar depression: Evidence and theory. *Psychological Bulletin, 101,* 259–282.

Nuechterlein, K. H. (1977). Reaction time and attention in schizophrenia: A critical evaluation of the data theories. *Schizophrenia Bulletin, 3,* 373–428.

Nuechterlein, K. H., & Holroyd, J. C. (1980). Biofeedback in the treatment of tension headache: Current status. *Archives of General Psychiatry, 37,* 866–873.

O'Brien, F., & Azrin, N. H. (1972). Symptom reduction by functional displacement in a token economy: A case study. *Journal of Behavior Therapy and Experimental Psychiatry, 3,* 205–207.

Olds, J., & Milner, P. (1954). Positive reinforcement produced by electrical stimulation of septal area and other regions of rat

brain. *Journal of Comparative and Physiological Psychology,
47,* 419–427.

O'Leary, K. D., & Carr, E. G. (1982). Childhood disorders. In G. T.
Wilson & C. M. Franks (Eds.), *Contemporary behavior therapy.* New York: Guilford Press.

Olson, G. A., Olson, R. D., Kastin, A. J., & Coy, D. H. (1979). Endogenous opiates: Through 1978. *Neuroscience and
Biobehavioral Review, 3,* 285–299.

Omizo, M. M., & Williams, R. E. (1982). Biofeedback-induced
training as an alternative for the elementary school learning-
disabled child. *Biofeedback and Self-Regulation, 7,* 139–148.

Omura, Y. (1976). Patho-physiology of acupuncture effects, ACTH
and morphine-like substances, pain, phantom sensations
(phantom pain, itch, and coldness), brain micro-circulation,
and memory. *Acupuncture & Electro-Therapeutic Research
Institute Journal, 2,* 1–31.

Omura, Y. (1977). Critical evaluation of the methods of measurement of "tingling threshold," "pain threshold," and "pain
tolerance" by electrical stimulation. *Acupuncture & Electro-
Therapeutic Research International Journal, 2,* 161–236.

Ordman, A. M., & Kirschenbaum, D. S. (1985). Cognitive-behavioral therapy for bulimia: An initial outcome study. *Journal
of Consulting and Clinical Psychology, 53,* 305–313.

O'Regan, K. (1979). Saccade size control in reading: Evidence for
the linguistic control hypothesis. *Perception and Psychophysics, 25,* 501–509.

Ornitz, E. M., & Ritvo, E. R. (1976). The syndrome of autism: A
critical review. *American Journal of Psychiatry, 133,* 609–
621.

Ornstein, R. E. (1976). A science of consciousness. In P. R. Lee,
R. E. Ornstein, D. Galin, A. Deikman, & C. T. Tart (Eds.),
Symposium of consciousness, San Francisco, 1974. New York:
Viking Press.

Ornstein, R. E. (1977). *The psychology of consciousness* (2nd ed.).
New York: Harcourt Brace Jovanovich.

Osterberg, O. (1973). Circadian rhythms of food intake in oral
temperature in "morning" and "evening" groups of individuals. *Ergonomics, 16,* 203–209.

Paivio, A. (1971). *Imagery and verbal processes.* New York: Holt,
Rinehart and Winston.

Palmore, E. B. (1982). Predictors of the longevity difference: A
25-year follow-up. *The Gerontologist, 22,* 513–518.

Pantin, H. M., & Carver, C. S. (1982). Induced competence and the
bystander effect. *Journal of Applied Social Psychology, 12,*
100–111.

Pardine, P., Dytell, R., & Napoli, A. (1981). Transfer benefits of
biofeedback: A research note. *Perceptual and Motor Skills,
52,* 373–374.

Parke, R. D. (1979). Perspectives on father-infant interaction. In
J. D. Osofsky (Ed.), *Handbook of infant development.* New
York: John Wiley & Sons.

Parke, R. D., & O'Leary, S. E. (1976). Father-mother-infant interaction in the newborn period: Some findings, some observations, and some unresolved issues. In K. Riegel &
J. Meacham (Eds.), *The developing individual in a changing
world: Vol. 2. Social and environmental issues.* The Hague,
Netherlands: Mouton.

Parker, D. E. (1980). The vestibular apparatus. *Scientific American, 243*(5), 118–135.

Parloff, M. B. (1986). Placebo controls in psychotherapy research:
A sine qua non or a placebo for research problems? *Journal
of Consulting and Clinical Psychology, 54,* 79–87.

Parmelee, A. H., & Stern, E. (1972). Development of states in in-
fants. In C. D. Clemente, T. P. Purpara, & F. E. Meyer (Eds.),
Sleep and the maturing nervous system. New York: Academic
Press.

Pavlov, I. P. (1927). *Conditioned reflexes.* London: Oxford University Press.

Pearl, D., Bouthilet, L., & Lazar, J. (Eds.) (1982). *Television and
behavior: Ten years of scientific progress and implications for
the eighties:* Vols. 1 & 2. Washington, DC: U.S. Government
Printing Office.

Peck, C. P. (1986). A public mental health issue. Risk-taking behavior and compulsive gambling. *American Psychologist, 41,*
461–465.

Peele, S. (1984). The cultural context of psychological approaches
to alcoholism. Can we control the effects of alcohol? *American Psychologist, 39,* 1337–1351.

Pelham, W. E., Schendler, R. W., Bologna, N. C., & Contreras, J. A.
(1980). Behavioral and stimulant treatment of hyperactive
children: A therapy study with methylphenidate probes in a
within-subject design. *Journal of Applied Behavior Analysis,
13,* 221–236.

Peplau, L. A., Rubin, Z., & Hill, C. T. (1977). Sexual intimacy in
dating relationships. *Journal of Social Issues, 33,* 86–109.

Pepler, R. (1972). The thermal comfort of students in climate controlled and non-climate controlled schools. *ASHRAE Trans-
actions, 78,* 97–109.

Perlman, D., & Peplau, L. A. (1984). Loneliness research: A survey
of empirical findings (pp. 13–46). In L. A. Peplau & S. E.
Goldston (Eds.), *Preventing the harmful consequences of se-
vere and persistent loneliness* (DHHS Publication No.
ADM 84-1312). Washington, DC: U.S. Government Printing
Office.

Perlmuter, L. C., Scharff, K., Karsh, R., & Monty, R. A. (1980).
Perceived control: A generalized state of motivation. *Motivation and Emotion, 4,* 35–45.

Perret-Clermont, A.–N. (1980). *Social interaction and cognitive
development in children.* (H. Tajfel, Ed.; C. Sherrard, Trans.).
London: Academic Press.

Peters, R. H., Luttmers, L. L., Gunion, M. W., & Wellman, P. J.
(1978). Ventromedial hypothalamic syndrome: Finickiness?
Physiology and Behavior, 20, 279–285.

Peterson, C., & Seligman, M. E. P. (1984). Causal explanations as
a risk factor for depression: Theory and evidence. *Psychological Review, 91,* 347–374.

Peterson, L. R., & Peterson, M. J. (1959). Short-term retention of
individual verbal items. *Journal of Experimental Psychology,
58,* 193–198.

Phillips, D. A., & Zigler, E. (1980). Children's self-image disparity:
Effects of age, socioeconomic status, ethnicity, and gender.
Journal of Personality and Social Psychology, 39, 689–700.

Piaget, J. (1932). *The moral judgment of the child.* London: Rout-
ledge & Kegan Paul.

Piper, W. E., Debbane, E. G., Bienvenu, J. P., & Garant, J. (1984). A
comparative study of four forms of psychotherapy. *Journal
of Consulting and Clinical Psychology, 52,* 268–279.

Pirenne, M. H. (1967). *Vision and the eye.* London: Science Paperbacks.

Pirolli, P. L., & Anderson, J. R. (1985). The role of practice in fact
retrieval. *Journal of Experimental Psychology: Learning,
Memory, and Cognition, 11,* 136–153.

Plomin, R., & DeFries, J. C. (1980). Genetics and intelligence: Recent data. *Intelligence, 4,* 15–24.

Pokorny, A. D. (1977). Suicide in depression. In W. E. Fann,
I. Karacan, A. D. Pokorny, & R. L. Williams (Eds.), *Phenome-
nology and treatment of depression.* New York: Spectrum
Publications.

Pollack, D., & Shore, J. H. (1980). Validity of the MMPI with naive
Americans. *American Journal of Psychiatry, 137,* 946–950.

Pollak, J. M. (1979). Obsessive-compulsive personality: A review.
Psychological Bulletin, 86, 225–241.

Porter, J. (1978). Suggestions and success imagery for study problems. *International Journal of Clinical and Experimental Hypnosis, 26,* 63–75.

Portnoy, F. C., & Simmons, C. H. (1978). Day care and attachment. *Child Development, 49,* 239–242.

Powell, D. A., Milligan, W. L., & Furchtgott, E. (1980). Peripheral autonomic changes accompanying learning and reaction time performance in older people. *Journal of Gerontology, 35,* 57–65.

Power, T. G., & Chapieski, M. L. (1986). Childrearing and impulse control in toddlers: A naturalistic investigation. *Developmental Psychology, 22,* 271–275.

Powers, P. C., & Geen, R. G. (1972). Effects of the behavior and the perceived arousal of a model on instrumental aggression. *Journal of Personality and Social Psychology, 23,* 175–184.

Powley, T. L. (1977). The ventromedial hypothalamic syndrome, satiety, and a cephalic phase hypothesis. *Psychological Review, 84,* 89–126.

Prentice-Dunn, S., & Rogers, R. W. (1984). Effects of deindividuating situational cues and aggressive models on subjective deindividuation and aggression. *Journal of Personality and Social Psychology, 39,* 104–113.

Preti, G., Cutler, W. B., Garcia, C. R., Huggins, G. R., & Lawley, H. J. (1986). Human axillary secretions influence women's menstrual cycles: The role of donor extract of females. *Hormones and Behavior, 20,* 474–482.

Price, R. (1985). *People of the mirror: An intimate look at loneliness.* Far Hills, NJ: New Horizon Press.

Prinz, R. J., Roberts, W. A., & Hantman, E. (1980). Dietary correlates of hyperactive behavior in children. *Journal of Consulting and Clinical Psychology, 48,* 760–769.

Provins, K. A. (1958). Environmental conditions and driving efficiency: A review. *Economics, 2,* 63–88.

Quilitch, H. R., & Risley, T. R. (1973). The effects of play materials on social play. *Journal of Applied Behavior Analysis, 6,* 573–578.

Quinsey, V. L., Chaplin, T. C., & Upfold, D. (1984). Sexual arousal to nonsexual violence and sadomasochism themes among rapist and non-sex-offenders. *Journal of Consulting and Clinical Psychology, 52,* 651.

Rachman, S., & DeSilva, P. (1978). Abnormal and normal obsessions. *Behavior Research and Therapy, 16,* 223–248.

Rada, R. T. (1983). Rape. In W. E. Fann, I. Karacan, A. D. Pokorny, & R. L. Williams (Eds.), *Phenomenology and treatment of psychosexual disorders.* New York: SP Medical & Scientific Books.

Rader, N., Bausano, M., & Richards, J. E. (1980). On the nature of the visual-cliff-avoidance response in human infants. *Child Development, 51,* 61–68.

Rapee, R. (1986). Differential response to hyperventilation in panic disorder and generalized anxiety disorder. *Journal of Abnormal Psychology, 95,* 24–28.

Raps, C. S., Reinhard, K. E., Peterson, C., Abramson, L. Y., & Seligman, M. E. P. (1982). Attributional style among depressed patients. *Journal of Abnormal Psychology, 91,* 102–108.

Raskin, M., Bali, L. R., & Peeke, H. V. (1980). Muscle biofeedback and transcendental meditation. *Archives of General Psychiatry, 37,* 93–97.

Regestein, Q. R., & Reich, P. (1978). Pedophilia occurring after onset of cognitive impairment. *Journal of Nervous and Mental Disease, 166,* 794–798.

Reilly, S., & Muzekari, L. (1979). Responses of normal and disturbed adults and children to mixed messages. *Journal of Abnormal Psychology, 88,* 203–208.

Reis, H. T., Nezlek, J., & Wheeler, L. (1980). Physical attractiveness in social interaction. *Journal of Personality and Social Psychology, 38,* 604–617.

Reisenzein, R. (1983). The Schachter theory of emotion: Two decades later. *Psychological Bulletin, 94,* 239–264.

Rescorla, R. A. (1977). Pavlovian 2nd-order conditioning: Some implications for instrumental behavior. In H. Davis & H. Herwit (Eds.), *Pavlovian-operant interactions.* Hillsdale, NJ: Lawrence Erlbaum Associates.

Restle, F. (1970). Moon illusion explained on the basis of relative size. *Science, 167,* 1092–1096.

Rhodewalt, F., Hays, R. B., Chemers, M. M., & Wysocki, J. (1984). Type A behavior, perceived stress, and illness: A person-situation analysis. *Personality and Social Psychology Bulletin, 10,* 1, 149–159.

Richards, J. E., & Rader, N. (1983). Affective, behavioral, and avoidance responses on the visual cliff: Effects of crawling onset age, crawling experience, and testing age. *Psychophysiology, 20,* 633–642.

Ring, K., Wallston, K., & Corey, M. (1970). Mode of debriefing as a factor affecting subjective reaction to a Milgram-type obedience experiment: An ethical inquiry. *Representative Research in Social Psychology, 1,* 67–88.

Roballey, T. C., McGreevy, C., Rongo, R. R., Schwantes, M. L., Steger, P. J., Wininger, M. A., & Gardner, E. B. (1985). The effect of music on eating behavior. *Bulletin of the Psychonomic Society, 23,* 221–222.

Robbins, M., & Meyer, D. (1970). Motivational control of retrograde amnesia. *Journal of Experimental Psychology, 84,* 220–225.

Roberts, A. H. (1985). Biofeedback. Research, training, and clinical roles. *American Psychologist, 40,* 938–948.

Robins, L. N. (1966). *Deviant children grown up.* Baltimore: Williams & Wilkins.

Robins, L. N. (1970). The adult development of the antisocial child. *Seminars in Psychiatry, 2,* 420–434.

Robinson, R. G., Tortosa, M., Sullivan, J., Buchanan, E., Andersen, A. E., & Folstein, M. F. (1983). Qualitative assessment of psychologic state of patients with anorexia nervosa or bulimia: Response to caloric stimulus. *Psychosomatic Medicine, 45,* 283–292.

Roche, A. F., Wainer, H., & Thissen, D. (1975). *Skeletal maturity, the knee joint as a biological indicator.* New York: Plenum Press.

Roche, J. P. (1986). Premarital sex: Attitudes and behavior by dating stage. *Adolescence, 21,* 107–121.

Rockstein, M., & Sussman, M. (1979). *Biology of aging.* Belmont, CA: Wadsworth.

Rodgers, J. L., & Rowe, D. C. (1985). Does contiguity breed similarity? A within-family analysis of nonshared sources of IQ differences between siblings. *Developmental Psychology, 21,* 743–746.

Rodin, J. (1979). *Obesity theory and treatment: An uneasy couple?* Paper presented at the meeting of the Association for the Advancement of Behavior Therapy, San Francisco.

Rodman, H., Pratto, D. J., & Nelson, R. S. (1985). Child care arrangements and children's functioning: A comparison of self-care and adult-care children. *Developmental Psychology, 21,* 413–418.

Rogers, C. R. (1951). *Client-centered therapy.* Boston: Houghton Mifflin.

Rogers, C. R. (1959). A theory of therapy, personality, and interpersonal relationships, as developed in the client-centered framework. In S. Koch (Ed.), *Psychology: A study of a science* (Vol. 3). New York: McGraw-Hill.

Rogers, C. R. (1961). *On becoming a person: A therapist's view of psychotherapy.* Boston: Houghton Mifflin.

Rogers, C. R. (1978). *Psychotherapy and personality change.* Chicago: University of Chicago Press.

Rogers, R. W. (1975). Protection motivation theory of fear appeals and attitude change. *Journal of Psychology, 91,* 93–114.

Rogers, R. W., & Mewborn, C. R. (1976). Fear appeals on attitude change: Effects of a threat's noxiousness, probability of occurrence, and efficacy of coping responses. *Journal of Personality and Social Psychology, 34,* 54–61.

Rosenheck, R. (1986). Impact of posttraumatic stress disorder of World War II on the next generation. *The Journal of Nervous and Mental Disease, 174,* 319–322.

Rosenstein, M. J., & Milazzo-Sayre, L. J. (1981). Characteristics of admissions to selected mental-health facilities, 1975. Rochville, Maryland: U.S. Dept. of Health and Human Services.

Rosenthal, D. (1970). *Genetic theory in abnormal behavior.* New York: McGraw-Hill.

Rosenthal, D., Wender, P. H., Kety, S. S., Schulsinger, F., Welner, J., & Ostergaard, L. (1968). Schizophrenic's offspring reared in adoptive homes. In D. Rosenthal and S. S. Key (Eds.), *The transmission of schizophrenia.* Oxford: Pergamon Press.

Rosenthal, R., & DePaulo, B. M. (1979). Sex differences in accommodation in nonverbal communication. In R. Rosenthal (Ed.), *Skill in nonverbal communication.* Cambridge, MA: Oelgeschlager, Gunn & Hain.

Rosenzweig, M. R. (1984). Experience, memory and the brain. *American Psychologist, 39,* 365–376.

Rosenzweig, S. (1986). Idiodynamics vis-a-vis psychology. *American Psychologist, 41,* 241–245.

Ross, L., Bierbrauer, G., & Hoffman, S. (1976). The role of attribution processes in conformity and dissent. *American Psychologist, 31,* 148–157.

Roth, M. (1978). Diagnosis of senile and related forms of dementia. In R. Katzman, R. D. Terry, & K. L. Bick (Eds.), *Alzheimer's disease: Senile dementia and related disorders.* New York: Raven Press.

Rothman, G. R. (1980). The relationship between moral judgment and moral behavior. In M. Windmiller, N. Lambert, & E. Turiel (Eds.), *Moral development and socialization.* Boston: Allyn and Bacon.

Rotter, J. B. (1964). *Clinical psychology* (2nd ed.). Englewood Cliffs, NJ: Prentice-Hall.

Rowland, K. F. (1977). Environmental events predicting death for the elderly. *Psychological Bulletin, 84,* 349–372.

Ruderman, A. J. (1986). Dietary restraint: A theoretical and empirical review. *Psychological Bulletin, 99,* 247–262.

Rudman, H. C. (1977). The standardized test flap. *Phi Delta Kappan, 59,* 179–185.

Rumbaugh, D. M., & Savage-Rumbaugh, S. (1978). Chimpanzee language research: Status and potential. *Behavior Research Methods and Instrumentation, 10,* 119–131.

Russell, M. J. (1976). Human olfactory communication. *Nature, 260,* 520–522.

Rutter, M. (1982). Social-emotional consequences of day care for preschool children. In E. F. Zigler & E. W. Gordon (Eds.), *Day care: Scientific and social policy issues.* Boston: Auburn House.

Ryan, R. M., Mims, V., & Koestner, R. (1983). Relation of reward contingency and interpersonal context to intrinsic motivation: A review and test using cognitive evaluation theory. *Journal of Personality and Social Psychology, 45,* 736–750.

Sadock, V. (1980). Special areas of interest. In H. Kaplan, A. Freedman, & B. Sadock (Eds.), *Comprehensive textbook of psychiatry/III.* Baltimore: Williams & Wilkins.

Sakitt, B., & Long, G. M. (1979). Cones determine subjective offset of a stimulus but rods determine total persistence. *Vision Research, 19,* 1439–1443.

Sampson, E. E. (1981). Cognitive psychology as ideology. *American Psychologist, 36,* 730–743.

Samuels, S. J. (1970). Interaction of list length and low stimulus similarity on the Von Restorff effect. *Journal of Educational Psychology, 61,* 57–58.

Sanders, R. J. (1985). Teaching apes to ape language: Explaining the imitative and nonimitative signing of a chimpanzee (Pan troglodytes). *Journal of Comparative Psychology, 99,* 197–210.

Sanders, R. W. (1978). Systematic desensitization in the treatment of child abuse. *American Journal of Psychiatry, 135,* 483–484.

Sarason, I. G., Sarason, B. R., Potter III, E. H., & Antoni, M. H. (1985). Life events, social support, and illness. *Psychosomatic Medicine, 47,* 156–163.

Sartorious, N. (1982). Epidemiology and mental health policy. In M. O. Wagenfeld, P. V. Lemkau, & B. Justice (Eds.), *Public mental health: Perspectives and prospects.* Beverly Hills, CA: Sage Publications.

Sartorious, N., Shapiro, R., & Jablewsky, N. (1974). The international pilot study of schizophrenia. *Schizophrenia Bulletin, 1,* 24–34. (Experimental Issue No. 11)

Satir, V. (1972). *Peoplemaking.* California: Science and Behavioral Books, Inc.

Satterfield, J. H., Cantwell, D. P., Saul, R. E., & Yusin, A. (1974). Intelligence, academic achievement, and EEG abnormalities in hyperactive children. *American Journal of Psychiatry, 131,* 391–395.

Sattler, J. M. (1982). *Assessment of children's intelligence and special abilities* (2nd ed.). Boston: Allyn and Bacon.

Savage-Rumbaugh, E. S., Pate, J. L., Lawson, J., Smith, S. T., & Rosenbaum, S. (1983). Can a chimpanzee make a statement? *Journal of Experimental Psychology: General, 112,* 457–492.

Saxe, L., Doughtery, D., & Cross, T. (1985). The validity of polygraph testing. *American Psychologist, 40,* 355–366.

Scarr, S., & Weinberg, R. A. (1983). The Minnesota adoption studies: Genetic differences and malleability. *Child Development, 54,* 260–267.

Schacht, T. E. (1985). DSM-III and the politics of truth. *American Psychologist, 40,* 513–521.

Schachter, F. F. (1979). *Everyday mother talk to toddlers.* New York: Academic Press.

Schachter, S. (1971). Some extraordinary facts about obese humans and rats. *American Psychologist, 26,* 129–144.

Schachter, S., Goldman, R., & Gordon, A. (1968). Effects of fear, food deprivation, and obesity on eating. *Journal of Personality and Social Psychology, 10,* 91–97.

Schachter, S., & Latané, B. (1964). Crime, cognition, and the autonomic nervous system. *Nebraska Symposium on Motivation, 12,* 221–275.

Schachter, S., & Singer, J. E. (1962). Cognitive, social, and physiological determinants of emotional state. *Psychological Review, 69,* 379–399.

Schaie, K. W., & Willis, S. L. (1986). *Adult development and aging* (2nd ed.). Boston: Little, Brown.

Schalling, D. (1978). Psychopathy—related personality variables and the psychophysiology of socialization. In R. D. Hare & D. Shalling (Eds.), *Psychopathic behavior: Approaches to research.* Chichester, England: John Wiley.

Schiff, M., Duyme, M., Dumaret, A., & Tomkiewicz, S. (1982). How much *could* we boost scholastic achievement and IQ scores? A direct answer from a French adoption study. *Cognition, 12,* 165–196.

Schlesier-Stroop, B. (1984). Bulimia: A review of the literature. *Psychological Bulletin, 95, 2,* 247–257.

Schmauk, F. J. (1970). Punishment, arousal, and avoidance learning in sociopaths. *Journal of Abnormal Psychology, 76,* 443–453.

Schoggen, M., & Schoggen, P. (1976). Environmental forces in the home lives of three-year-old children in three population subgroups. *JSAS Catalog of Selected Documents in Psychology, 6*(1, Ms. No. 1178).

Schulz, S. C., Van Kammen, D. P., Balow, J. E., Flye, M. W., & Bunney, W. E., Jr. (1981). Dialysis in schizophrenia: A double-blind evaluation. *Science, 211,* 1066–1068.

Schwartz, B., & Reilly, M. (1985). Long-term retention of a complex operant in pigeons. *Journal of Experimental Psychology: Animal Behavior Processes, 11,* 337–355.

Schwartz, P. (1983). Length of day-care attendance and attachment behavior in eighteen-month-old infants. *Child Development, 54,* 1073–1078.

Schwarz, L. M., Foa, U. G., & Foa, E. B. (1983). Multichannel nonverbal communication: Evidence for combinatory rules. *Journal of Personality and Social Psychology, 45,* 274–281.

Schweickert, R., & Boruff, B. (1986). Short-term memory capacity: Magic number or magic spell? *Journal of Experimental Psychology: Learning, Memory, and Cognition, 12,* 419–425.

Scriver, C. R., & Clow, C. L. (1980). Phenylketonuria: Epitome of human biochemical genetics. *New England Journal of Medicine, 303,* 1336–1342.

Sears, R. R. (1982). Obituary: Harry Fredrick Harlow (1905–1981). *American Psychologist, 37,* 1280–1281.

Seidman, L. J. (1983). Schizophrenia and brain dysfunction: An integration of recent neurodiagnostic findings. *Psychological Bulletin, 94,* 195–238.

Seif, M. N., & Atkins, A. L. (1979). Some defensive and cognitive aspects of phobias. *Journal of Abnormal Psychology, 88,* 42–51.

Seligman, M. E. P. (1975). *Helplessness.* San Francisco: W. H. Freeman.

Seligman, M. E. P. (1976). *Learned helplessness and depression in animals and humans.* Morristown, NJ: General Learning Press.

Selye, H. (1956). *The stress of life.* New York: McGraw-Hill.

Selye, H. (1976). *Stress in health and disease.* London: Butterworth.

Sengel, R. A., & Lovallo, W. R. (1983). Effects of cueing on immediate and recent memory in schizophrenics. *Journal of Nervous and Mental Disease, 171,* 426–430.

Shakow, D. (1977). Segmental set: The adaptive process in schizophrenia. *American Psychologist, 32,* 129–139.

Shanab, M. E., & Yahya, K. A. (1978). A cross-cultural study of obedience. *Bulletin of the Psychonomic Society, 11,* 267–269.

Shapiro, D. (1977). A biofeedback strategy in the study of consciousness. In N. Zinberg (Ed.), *Alternate states of consciousness.* New York: Macmillan.

Shapiro, D. A., & Shapiro, D. (1983). Comparative therapy outcome research: Methodological implications of meta-analysis. *Journal of Consulting and Clinical Psychology, 51,* 42–53.

Shapiro, P. N., & Penrod, S. (1986). Meta-analysis of facial identification studies. *Psychological Bulletin, 100,* 139–156.

Shaver, K. G. (1977). *Principles of social psychology.* Cambridge, MA: Winthrop.

Shaywitz, S. E., Cohen, D. J., & Shaywitz, B. A. (1980). Behavior and learning difficulties in children of normal intelligence born to alcoholic mothers. *Journal of Pediatrics, 96,* 978–982.

Sheridan, M. S. (1985). Things that go beep in the night: Home monitoring for apnea. *Health and Social Work,* 63–70.

Sherman, M., & Key, C. B. (1932). The intelligence of isolated mountain children. *Child Development, 3,* 279–290.

Shimamura, A. P., & Squire, L. R. (1986). Korsakoff's syndrome: A study of the relation between anterograde amnesia and remote memory impairment. *Behavioral Neuroscience, 100,* 165–170.

Shimberg, M. E. (1929). An investigation into the validity of norms with special reference to urban and rural groups. *Archives of Psychology, 104,* 1–62.

Shneidman, E. S. (1976). Death work and stages of dying. In E. S. Shneidman (Ed.), *Death: Current perspectives.* Palo Alto, CA: Mayfield.

Shock, N. W. (1977). Biological theories of aging. In J. E. Birren & K. W. Schaie (Eds.), *Handbook of the psychology of aging.* New York: Van Nostrand Reinhold.

Shotland, R. L., & Heinold, W. D. (1985). Interpersonal relations and group processes. Bystander response to arterial bleeding: Helping skills, the decision-making process, and differentiating the helping response. *Journal of Personality and Social Psychology, 49,* 347–456.

Siddique, C. M., & D'Arcy, C. (1984). Adolescence, stress, and psychological well-being. *Journal of Youth and Adolescence, 13,* 459–471.

Siegel, O. (1982). Personality development in adolescence. In B. B. Wolman & G. Stricker (Eds.), *Handbook of developmental psychology.* Englewood Cliffs, NJ: Prentice-Hall.

Silberman, E., K., Weingartner, H., & Post, R. M. (1983). Thinking disorder in depression. Logic and strategy in an abstract reasoning task. *Archives of General Psychiatry, 40,* 775–780.

Simkins, L. (1982). Biofeedback: Clinically valid or oversold? *Psychological Record, 32,* 3–17.

Singer, L. M., Brodzinsky, D. M., Ramsay, D., Steir, M., & Waters, E. (1985). Mother-infant attachment in adoptive families. *Child Development, 56,* 1543–1551.

Singh, B. K., Walton, B. L., & Williams, J. S. (1976). Extramarital sexual permissiveness: Conditions and contingencies. *Journal of Marriage and the Family, 38,* 701–712.

Skinner, B. F. (1937). Two types of conditioned reflex: A reply to Konorski and Miller, *Journal of General Psychology, 16,* 272–279.

Skinner, B. F. (1938). *The behavior of organisms.* New York: Appleton-Century-Crofts.

Skinner, B. F. (1948). Superstition in the pigeon. *Journal of Experimental Psychology, 38,* 168–172.

Skinner, B. F. (1956). A case history in scientific method. *American Psychologist, 11,* 221–233.

Slaikeu, K. A. (1979). Temporal variable in telephone crisis intervention: Their relationship to selected process and outcome variables. *Journal of Consulting and Clinical Psychology, 47,* 193–195.

Slaikeu, K. A. (1984). *Crisis intervention.* Boston: Allyn and Bacon.

Smith, L. K., & Fowler, S. A. (1984). Positive peer pressure: The effects of peer monitoring on children's disruptive behavior. *Journal of Applied Behavior Analysis, 17,* 213–227.

Smith, M. E. (1976). Ophthalmic aspects. In F. U. Steinberg (Ed.), *Cowdry's: The care of the geriatric patient.* St. Louis: C. V. Mosby.

Smith, M. L., & Glass, G. V. (1977). Meta-analysis of psychotherapy outcome studies. *American Psychologist, 32,* 752–760.

Smith, M. L., Glass, G. V., & Miller, T. I. (1980). *The benefits of psychotherapy.* Baltimore: Johns Hopkins University Press.

Smolak, L. (1986). Language. In L. Smolak (Ed.), *Infancy* (pp. 180–287). Englewood Cliffs, NJ: Prentice-Hall.

Smyser, A. A. (1982). Hospices: Their humanistic and economic value. *American Psychologist, 37,* 1260–1262.

Snyder, S. H. (1974). *Madness and the brain.* New York: McGraw-Hill.

Snyder, S. H. (1980). Brain peptides as neurotransmitters. *Science, 209,* 976–983.

Snyder, S. H. (1982). What is schizophrenia? *Schizophrenia Bulletin, 8,* 595–597.

Sobell, M. B., & Sobell, L. C. (1982). Controlled drinking: A concept coming of age. In K. R. Blanstein & J. Polivy (Eds.), *Self-control and self-modification of emotional behavior.* New York: Plenum Press.

Solso, R. L. (1979). *Cognitive psychology.* New York: Harcourt Brace Jovanovich.

Sorce, J. F., & Emde, R. N. (1981). Mother's presence is not enough: Effect of emotional availability on infant exploration. *Developmental Psychology, 17,* 737–745.

Sorce, J. F., Emde, R. N., Campos, J., & Klinnert, M. D. (1985). Maternal emotional signaling: Its effect on the visual cliff behavior of 1-year-olds. *Developmental Psychology, 21,* 195–200.

Space, L. G., & Cromwell, R. L. (1980). Personal constructs among depressed patients. *Journal of Nervous and Mental Disease, 168,* 150–158.

Spanier, G. B., & Glick, P. C. (1981). Marital instability in the United States: Some correlates and recent changes. *Family Relations, 30,* 329–338.

Spencer, J. A., & Fremouw, W. J. (1979). Binge eating as a function of restraint and weight classification. *Journal of Abnormal Psychology, 88,* 262–267.

Sperling, G. (1960). The information available in brief visual presentations. *Psychological Monographs, 15,* 201–293.

Sperry, R. W. (1968). Mental unity following surgical disconnection of the cerebral hemispheres. In *Harvey Lectures.* New York: Academic Press.

Spiegel, D., & Bloom, J. R. (1983). Group therapy and hypnosis reduce metastatic breast carcinoma pain. *Psychosomatic Medicine, 45,* 333–340.

Spitz, R. (1945). Hospitalism: An inquiry into the genesis of psychiatric conditions in early childhood. *Psychoanalytic Study of the Child, 1,* 53–74.

Sroufe, L. A., & Waters, E. (1977). Attachment as an organizational construct. *Child Development, 48,* 1184–1199.

Staats, A. W., & Staats, C. K. (1963). *Complex human behavior: A systematic extension of learning principles.* New York: Holt, Rinehart and Winston.

Stagner, R. (1985). Aging in industry. In J. E. Birren and K. W. Schaie (Eds.), *Handbook of the psychology of aging* (2nd ed.). New York: Van Nostrand Reinhold.

Standing, L. (1973). Learning 10,000 pictures. *Quarterly Journal of Experimental Psychology, 25,* 207–222.

Standing, L., Conezio, J., & Haber, R. N. (1970). Perception and memory for pictures: Single trial learning of 2500 visual stimuli. *Psychonomic Science, 19,* 73–74.

Stanton, H. E. (1978). A one-session hypnotic approach to modifying smoking behavior. *International Journal of Clinical and Experimental Hypnosis, 26,* 22–29.

Stanton, M. D. (1981). Strategic approaches to family therapy. In A. S. Gurmon & D. P. Kiniskenn (Eds.), *Handbook of family therapy.* New York: Brunner/Mazel.

Stapp, J., & Fulcher, R. (1983). The employment of APA members: 1982. *American Psychologist, 38,* 1298–1320.

Stapp, J., Fulcher, R., & Wicherski, M. (1984). Human resources in psychology. The employment of 1981 and 1982 doctorate recipients in psychology. *American Psychologist, 39,* 1408–1423.

Stapp, J., Tucker, A. M., & VandenBos, G. R. (1985). Human resources in psychology. Census of psychological personnel: 1983. *American Psychologist, 40,* 1317–1351.

St. Claire-Smith, R., & MacLaren, D. (1983). Response preconditioning effects. *Journal of Experimental Psychology: Animal Behavior Processes, 9,* 41–48.

Steinberg, L. (1986). Latchkey children and susceptibility to peer pressure: An ecological analysis. *Developmental Psychology, 22,* 433–439.

Steiner, I. D. (1982). Heuristic models of groupthink. In M. Brandstatter, J. H. Davis, & G. Stocker-Kreichgauer (Eds.), *Group decision making.* New York: Academic Press.

Steinmetz, J. L., Lewinsohn, P. M., & Antonuccio, D. O. (1983). Prediction of individual outcome in a group intervention for depression. *Journal of Consulting and Clinical Psychology, 51,* 331–337.

Stephens, J. H. (1978). Long-term prognosis and follow-up in schizophrenia. *Schizophrenia Bulletin, 4,* 25–47.

Sternbach, R. A. (1968). *Pain: A psychophysiological analysis.* New York: Academic Press.

Sternbach, R. A. (1974). *Pain patients: Traits and treatment.* New York: Academic Press.

Sternbach, R. A. (1975). Psychophysiology of pain. *International Journal of Psychiatry in Medicine, 6,* 63–73.

Sternberg, R. J. (1984). The Kaufman Assessment Battery for Children: An information-processing analysis and critique. *The Journal of Special Education, 18,* 269–279.

Sternberg, R. J. (1985). Beyond IQ. A triarchic theory of human intelligence. Cambridge: Cambridge University Press.

Stevens, C. F. (1979). The neuron. In *The brain* [Scientific American book]. San Francisco: W. H. Freeman.

Stewart, M. A., DeBlois, C. S., Meardon, J., & Cummings, C. (1980). Aggressive conduct disorder in children. *Journal of Nervous and Mental Disease, 168,* 604–610.

St. George-Hyslop, P. H., Tanzi, R. E., Polinsky, R. J., et al. (1987). The genetic defect causing familial Alzheimer's disease maps on chromosome 21. *Science, 235,* 821–944.

Stiles, W. B., Shapiro, D. A., & Elliott, R. (1986). "Are all psychotherapies equivalent?" *American Psychologist, 41,* 165–180.

Stokols, D. (1972). On the distinction between density and crowding: Some implications for future research. *Psychological Review, 79,* 275–277.

Stokols, D. (1976). The experience of crowding in primary and secondary environments. *Environment & Behavior, 8,* 49–86.

Stolz, S. B., Wienckowski, L. A., & Brown, B. S. (1975). Behavior modification: A perspective on critical issues. *American Psychologist, 30,* 1027–1048.

Stone, M. H. (1980). *The borderline syndromes.* New York: McGraw-Hill.

Stott, D. H., & Wilson, D. M. (1977). The adult criminal as a juvenile. *British Journal of Criminology, 17,* 47–57.

Streissguth, A. P., Barr, H. M., & Martin, D. C. (1983). Maternal alcohol use and neonatal habituation assessed with the Brazelton Scale. *Child Development, 54,* 1109–1118.

Stretch, R. H., Vail, J. D., & Maloney, J. P. (1985). Posttraumatic stress disorder among army nurse corps Vietnam veterans. *Journal of Consulting and Clinical Psychology, 53,* 704–708.

Striegel-Moore, R. H., Silberstein, L. R., & Rodin, J. (1986). Toward an understanding of risk factors for bulimia. *American Psychologist, 41,* 246–263.

Strober, M., Green, J., & Carlson, G. (1981). Reliability of psychiatric diagnosis in hospitalized adolescents. *Archives of General Psychiatry, 38,* 141–145.

Strupp, H. H. (1973). On the basic ingredients of psychotherapy. *Journal of Consulting and Clinical Psychology, 41,* 1–8.

Stunkard, A. J. (1980). *Obesity.* Philadelphia: W. B. Saunders.

Suedfeld, P. and Kristeller, J. L. (1982). Stimulus reduction as a technique in health psychology. *Health Psychology* Vol. 1, p. 337–357.

Sugarman, S. (1983). Why talk? Comment on Savage-Rumbaugh et al. *Journal of Experimental Psychology: General, 112,* 493–497.

Suinn, R. M. (1982). Intervention with Type A behaviors. *Journal of Consulting and Clinical Psychology, 50,* 933–949.

Surgeon General's Scientific Advisory Committee on Television and Social Behavior. (1972). *Television and growing up: The impact of televised violence.* Washington, DC: U.S. Government Printing Office.

Surwit, R. S., Feinglos, M. N., & Scovern, A. W. (1983). Diabetes and behavior: A paradigm for health psychology. *American Psychologists, 38,* 255–262.

Surwit, R. S., & Keefe, F. J. (1978). Fontalis EMG feedback training: An electronic panacea? *Behavior Therapy, 9,* 779–792.

Svejda, M. J., Campos, J. J., & Emde, R. N. (1980). Mother-infant "bonding": Failure to generalize. *Child Development, 51,* 775–779.

Swanson, J. M., & Kinsbourne, M. (1979). State-dependent learning and retrieval: Methodological cautions and theoretical considerations. In J. F. Kihlstrom & F. J. Evans (Eds.), *Functional disorders of memory.* Hillsdale, NJ: Lawrence Erlbaum Associates.

Swenson, W. M., Pearson, J. S., & Osborne, D. (1973). *An MMPI source book: Basic item, scale, and pattern data on 50,000 medical patients.* Minneapolis: University of Minnesota Press.

Snyderman, M., & Rothman, S. (1987). Survey of expert opinion on intelligence and aptitude testing. *American Psychologist, 42,* 137–144.

Szucko, J. J., & Kleinmuntz, B. (1981). Statistical versus clinical lie detection. *American Psychologist, 36,* 488–496.

Tallent, N. (1985). Why do they call them "IQ tests"? *Psychological Reports, 57,* 665–666.

Tannenbaum, P. H., & Zillman, D. (1975). Emotional arousal in the facilitation of aggression through communication. In L. Berkowitz (Ed.), *Advances in experimental social psychology* (Vol. 8). New York: Academic Press.

Tanner, J. M., Whitehouse, R. H., & Takaishi, M. (1966). Standards from birth to maturity for height, weight, height velocity, and weight velocity: British children 1965. *Archives of the Diseases of Childhood, 41,* 455–471.

Tart, C. T. (1972). States of consciousness and state-specific sciences. *Science, 176,* 1203–1210.

Tart, C. T. (1977). Putting the pieces together: A conceptual framework for understanding discrete states of consciousness. In N. E. Zinberg (Ed.), *Alternate states of consciousness.* New York: Macmillan.

Tate, D. F., Glavan, L., & Ungar, G. (1976). Isolation and identification of two learning-induced brain peptides. *Pharmacology, Biochemistry, and Behavior, 5,* 441–448.

Teevan, R. C., & McGhee, P. E. (1972). Childhood development of fear of failure motivation. *Journal of Personality and Social Psychology, 21,* 345–348.

Tennant, C. C., Goulston, K. J., & Dent, O. F. (1986). The psychological effects of being a prisoner of war: Forty years after release. *American Journal of Psychiatry, 143,* 620–622.

Tennov, D. (1981). *Love and limerance.* Briarcliffe Manor, NY: Stein and Day.

Terrace, H. S. (1979). How Nim Chimpski changed my mind. *Psychology Today, 13,* 65–76.

Terrace, H. S. (1980). *Nim.* New York: Alfred A. Knopf.

Terrace, H. S. (1985). In the beginning was the "name." *American Psychologist, 40,* 1011–1028.

Thase, M. E., Frank, E., & Kupfer, D. J. (1985). Biological processes in major depression. In E. E. Beckham & W. R. Leber (Eds.), *Handbook of depression. Treatment, assessment, and research.* Homewood, IL: Dorsey Press.

Theorell, T., Svensson, J., Knox, S., Waller, D., & Alvarez, M. (1986). Young men with high blood pressure report *few* recent life events. *Journal of Psychosomatic Research, 30,* 243–249.

Thompson, L. A., Plomin, R., & DeFries, J. C. (1985). Parent-infant resemblance for general and specific cognitive abilities in the Colorado Adoption Project. *Intelligence, 9,* 1–13.

Tice, D. M., & Baumeister, R. F. (1985). Masculinity inhibits helping in emergencies: Personality does predict the bystander effect. *Journal of Personality and Social Psychology, 49,* 420–428.

Tilley, A., & Warren, P. (1983). Retrieval from semantic memory at different times of day. *Journal of Experimental Psychology: Learning Memory and Cognition, 9,* 718–724.

Tinbergen, N. (1974). Etiology and stress disease. *Science, 185,* 20–27.

Titchener, E. B. (1898). *A primer of psychology.* New York: Macmillan.

Tomarken, A. J., & Kirschenbaum, D. S. (1984). Effects of plans for future meals on counterregulatory eating by restrained and unrestrained eaters. *Journal of Abnormal Psychology, 93,* 458–472.

Trachtman, G. M. (1981). On such a full sea. *School Psychology Review, 10,* 138–181.

Tronick, E., Als, H., Adamson, L., Wise, S., & Brazelton, T. B. (1978). The infant's responses to entrapment between contradictory messages in face-to-face interaction. *Journal of the American Academy of Child Psychiatry, 17,* 1–13.

Tulving, E. (1972). Episodic and semantic memory. In E. Tulving & W. Donaldson (Eds.), *Organization and memory.* New York: Academic Press.

Tulving, E., & Pearlstone, Z. (1966). Availability versus accessibility of information for words. *Journal of Verbal Learning and Verbal Behavior, 5,* 381–391.

Tune, G. S. (1969). Sleep and wakefulness in 509 normal human adults. *British Journal of Medical Psychology, 42,* 75–79.

Turk, D. C. (1978). Cognitive behavioral techniques on the management of pain. In J. P. Foreyt & D. J. Rathgen (Eds.), *Cognitive behavior therapy: Research and application.* New York: Plenum Press.

Turk, D. C., Meichenbaum, D., & Genest, M. (1983). *Pain and behavioral medicine. A cognitive-behavioral perspective.* New York: Guilford Press.

Turkington, C. (1982). Depression seen induced by decline in NE levels. *APA Monitor, 13*(11), 6.

Turnbull, C. M. (1961). Notes and discussions: Some observations regarding the experiences and behavior of the Bambute Pygmies. *American Journal of Psychology, 7,* 304–308.

Turner, S. M., Beidel, D. C., & Nathan, R. S. (1985). Biological factors in obsessive-compulsive disorders. *Psychological Bulletin, 97,* 430–450.

Underwood, B. J. (1957). Interference and forgetting. *Psychological Review, 64,* 49–60.

U.S. Bureau of the Census, *Census of population: Characteristics of the population* (selected years). Washington, DC: U.S. Government Printing Office.

U.S. Department of Health and Human Services. (1984). *Long-term care financing and delivery systems: Exploring some alternatives* (HCFA Publication No. 03174). Washington, DC: U.S. Government Printing Office.

Uzgiris, I. C. (1972). Patterns of cognitive development in infancy. Feb., *Merrill-Palmer Institute Conference on Infant Development,* Detroit.

Vaillant, G. E., & Milofsky, E. S. (1982). The etiology of alcoholism: A prospective view. *American Psychologist, 37,* 494–503.

Valian, V. (1986). Syntactic categories in the speech of young children. *Developmental Psychology, 22,* 562–579.

Valins, S. (1966). Cognitive effects of false heart-rate feedback. *Journal of Personality and Social Psychology, 4,* 400–408.

Van Praag, H. M. (1978). Neuralendocrine disorders in depression and their significance for the monoamine hypothesis of depression. *Acta Psychiatrica Scandinavica, 57,* 389–404.

Varma, V. K., Bouri, M., & Wig, N. N. (1981). Multiple personality in India: Comparison with hysterical possession state. *American Journal of Psychotherapy, 35,* 113–120.

Verner, A. M., & Stewart, C. S. (1974). Adolescent sexual behavior in middle America revisited: 1970–1973. *Journal of Marriage and the Family, 36,* 728–735.

Verbrugge, L. M. (1979). Marital status and health. *Journal of Marriage and the Family, 41,* 267–285.

Vernon, P. E. (1979). *Intelligence: Heredity and environment.* San Francisco: W. H. Freeman.

Villee, M. S. (1975). *Human endocrinology, a developmental approach.* Springfield, IL: Chas. C Thomas.

Vogel, G. W. (1975). A review of REM sleep deprivation. *Archives of General Psychiatry, 32,* 749–760.

Von Senden, M. (1932). *Raum- und Gaestaltauffassung bei operierten. Blindgeborernin vor und nach der Operation.* Leipzig, Germany: Barth.

Vroon, P. A., de Leeuw, J., & Meester, A. C. (1986). Distribution of intelligence and educational level in fathers and sons. *British Journal of Psychology, 77,* 137–142.

Wagemaker, H., & Cade, R. (1977). The use of hemodialysis in chronic schizophrenia. *American Journal of Psychiatry, 134,* 684–685.

Wagemaker, H., Rogers, J. L., & Cade, R. (1984). Schizophrenia, hemodialysis, and the placebo effect. *Archives of General Psychiatry, 41,* 805–808.

Wagstaff, G. F. (1983). Suggested improvement of visual acuity: A statistical reevaluation. *International Journal of Clinical and Experimental Hypnosis, 36,* 239–240.

Wahler, R. G. (1976). Deviant child behavior within the family: Developmental speculation in behavior change strategies. In H. Leitenberg (Ed.), *Handbook of behavior modification and behavior therapy.* Englewood Cliffs, NJ: Prentice-Hall.

Waid, W. M. (1976). Skin conductance response to both signaled and unsignaled noxious stimulation predicts level of socialization. *Journal of Personality and Social Psychology, 34,* 923–929.

Walk, R. D., & Gibson, E. J. (1961). A comparative and analytical study of visual depth reception. *Psychological Monographs, 75* (Whole No. 15).

Walker, B. A., & Mehr, M. (1983). Adolescent suicide—a family crisis: A model for effective intervention by family therapists. *Adolescence, 18,* 285–292.

Walker, E., & Emory, E. (1983). Infants at risk for psychopathology: Offspring of schizophrenic parents. *Child Development, 54,* 1269–1285.

Walker, E., Hoppes, E., Mednick, S., Emory, E., Schulsinger, F. (1983). Environmental factors related to schizophrenia in psychophysiologically labile high-risk males. *Journal of Abnormal Psychology, 90,* 313–320.

Walker, J. I., & Cavenar, J. O. (1982). Vietnam veterans: Their problems continue. *Journal of Nervous and Mental Disease, 170,* 174–180.

Walker-Andrews, A. S. (1986). Intermodal perception of expressive behaviors: Relation of eye and voice? *Developmental Psychology, 22,* 373–377.

Wallace, R. K., & Benson, H. (1972). The physiology of meditation. In *Altered states of awareness: Readings from Scientific American.* San Francisco: W. H. Freeman.

Walsh, B. T., Roose, S. P., Glassman, A. H., Gladis, M., & Sadik, C. (1985). Bulimia and depression. *Psychosomatic Medicine, 47,* 123–131.

Walster, E. (1965). The effect of self-esteem on romantic liking.

Journal of Experimental Psychology, 1, 184–197.

Walters, G. D. (1983). The MMPI and schizophrenia: A review. *Schizophrenia Bulletin, 9,* 226–246.

Wanberg, K. W., & Horn, J. L. (1983). Assessment of alcohol use with multidimensional concepts and measures. *American Psychologist, 38,* 1055–1069.

Wandersman, L. P. (1981). Ecological relationships in family day care. *Child Care Quarterly, 10,* 89–102.

Ward, A. J. (1978). Early childhood autism and structural therapy: Outcome after 3 years. *Journal of Consulting and Clinical Psychology, 46,* 586–587.

Warren, K. R. (1978). Fetal alcohol syndrome: New perspectives. *Alcohol Health and Research World* [NIAAA, Public Health Service Alcohol, Drug Abuse, and Mental Health Administration, DHEW], *4.*

Watson, O. M., & Graves, T. D. (1966). Quantitative research in proxemic behavior. *American Anthropologist, 68,* 971–985.

Weary, G., Harvey, J. H., Schwieger, P., Olson, C. T., Perloff, E., & Pritchard, S. (1982). Self-presentation and the moderation of self-serving biases. *Social Cognition, 1,* 140–159.

Webb, W. B., & Agnew, H. W., Jr. (1974). Sleep and waking in a time-free environment. *Aerospace Medicine, 45,* 617–622.

Webb, W. B., & Agnew, H. W., Jr. (1975). The effects on subsequent sleep of an acute restriction of sleep length. *Psychophysiology, 12,* 367–370.

Webb, W. B., & Agnew, H. W., Jr. (1977). Analysis of the sleep stages in sleep-wakefulness regimens of varied length. *Psychophysiology, 14,* 445–450.

Webb, W. B., & Kersey, J. (1967). Recall of dreams and the probability of stage 1-REM sleep. *Perceptual and Motor Skills, 24,* 627–630.

Webster, M., & Driskell, J. E. (1978). Status generalization: A review and some new data. *American Sociological Review, 43,* 230–236.

Wechsler, D. (1958). *The measurement and appraisal of adult intelligence* (4th ed.). Baltimore: Williams & Wilkins.

Wechsler, D. (1975). Intelligence defined and undefined: A relativistic appraisal. *American Psychologist, 30,* 135–139.

Weil, A. T. (1972). *The natural mind: A new way of looking at drugs and the higher consciousness.* Boston: Houghton Mifflin.

Weil, A. T. (1977). The marriage of the sun and the moon. In N. E. Zinberg (Ed.), *Alternate states of consciousness.* New York: Macmillan.

Weiner, M. A. (1986). *Maximum immunity.* Boston: Houghton Mifflin.

Weingartner, H. (1977). Human state-dependent learning. In B. T. Ho, D. Richards, & D. L. Chute (Eds.), *Drug discrimination and state-dependent learning.* New York: Academic Press.

Weingartner, H., Cohen, R. M., Murphy, D. L., Martello, J., & Gerdt, C. (1981). Cognitive processes in depression. *Archives of General Psychiatry, 38,* 42–47.

Weingartner, H., Rapaport, J. L., Buchsbaum, M. S., Bunney, W. E., Jr., Ebert, M. H., Mikkelsen, E. J., & Caine, E. D. (1980). Cognitive processes in normal and hyperactive children and their response to amphetamine treatment. *Journal of Abnormal Psychology, 89,* 25–37.

Weinman, M. L., Mathew, R. J., & Claghorn, J. L. (1982). A study of physician attitude on biofeedback. *Biofeedback and Self-Regulation, 7,* 89–98.

Weinraub, M., & Wolf, B. (1983). Effects of stress and social supports on mother-child interactions in single- and two-parent families. *Child Development, 54,* 1297–1311.

Weins, A. N., & Menustik, C. E. (1983). Treatment outcome and patient characteristics in an aversion therapy program for alcoholism. *American Psychologist, 38,* 1089–1096.

Weisenberg, M. (1977). Pain and pain control. *Psychological Bulletin, 84,* 1008–1044.

Weiss, R. S. (1984). Loneliness: What we know about it and what we might do about it (pp. 3–12). In L. A. Peplau and S. E. Goldston (Eds.), *Preventing the harmful consequences of severe and persistent loneliness* (DHHS Publication No. ADM No. 84-1312). Washington, DC: U.S. Government Printing Office.

Weiss, S. R., & Ebert, M. H. (1983). Psychological and behavioral characteristics of normal-weight bulimics and normal-weight controls. *Psychosomatic Medicine, 45,* 293–304.

Wells, G. L., & Loftus, E. F. (Eds.). (1984). *Eyewitness testimony: Psychological perspectives.* Cambridge: Cambridge University Press.

Wells, G. L., & Murray, D. M. (1983). What can psychology say about the *Neil v. Biggers* criteria for judging eyewitness accuracy? *Journal of Applied Psychology, 68,* 347–362.

Whissell, C. M. (1985). The role of the face in human emotion: First system or one of many? *Perceptual and Motor Skills, 61,* 3–12.

White, B. L. (1978). *Experience and environment* (Vol. 2). Englewood Cliffs, NJ: Prentice-Hall.

White, S. H., Day, M. C., Freeman, P. K., Hantmann, S. A., & Messenger, K. P. (1973). *Federal programs for young children: Review and recommendations* (3 vols). Washington, DC: U.S. Government Printing Office.

Whitmer, P. O. (1978). EMG biofeedback manipulation of arousal and the test of the overarousal and underarousal areas of childhood hyperactivity. *Dissertation Abstracts International, 38,* (7-B), 3423.

Wideman, M. V., & Singer, J. E. (1984). The role of psychological mechanisms in preparation for childbirth. *American Psychologist, 39,* 1357–1371.

Willerman, L. (1979). Effects of families on intellectual development. *American Psychologist, 34,* 923–929.

Williams, C. D. (1959). Case report: The elimination of tantrum behavior by extinction procedures. *Journal of Abnormal and Social Psychology, 59,* 269.

Williams, J. I., & Cram, D. M. (1978). Diet in the management of hyperkinesis: A review of the tests of Feingold's hypothesis. *Canadian Psychiatric Association Journal, 23,* 241–248.

Williams, K., Harkins, S., & Latané, B. (1981). Identifiability as a deterrent to social loafing: Two cheering experiments. *Journal of Personality and Social Psychology, 40,* 303–311.

Williams, R. L. (1970). Black pride, academic relevance, and individual achievement. *Counseling Psychologist, 2,* 18–22.

Williams, R., Karacan, I., & Hursch, C. (1974). *EEG of human sleep.* New York: John Wiley & Sons.

Williamson, D. A., Kelley, M. L., Davis, C. J., Ruggiero, L., & Blouin, D. C. (1985). Psychopathology of eating disorders: A controlled comparison of bulimic, obese, and normal subjects. *Journal of Consulting and Clinical Psychology, 53,* 161–166.

Willis, F. N. (1966). Initial speaking distance as a function of the speaker's relationships. *Psychonomic Science, 5,* 221–222.

Wilson, E. O. (1975). *Sociobiology: A new synthesis.* Cambridge: Harvard University Press.

Wilson, G. T., & Davison, C. G. (1971). Processes of fear reduction in systematic desensitization: Animal studies. *Psychological Bulletin, 76,* 1–14.

Wincze, J. P., & Caird, W. K. (1976). The effects of systematic desensitization and video desensitization in the treatment of essential sexual dysfunction in women. *Behavior Therapy, 7,* 335–342.

Windmiller, M. (1980). Introduction. In M. Windmiller, N. Lambert, & E. Turiel (Eds.), *Moral development and socialization.* Boston: Allyn and Bacon.

Wing, J. K. (1978). *Reasoning about madness.* Oxford: Oxford University Press.

Wing, L. (Ed.) (1976). *Early childhood autism* (2nd ed.). New York: Pergamon Press.

Wolberg, L. R. (1980). *Handbook of short-term psychotherapy.* New York: Grune & Stratton.

Wolf, S., & Latané, B. (1983). Majority and minority influence on restaurant preferences. *Journal of Personality and Social Psychology, 45,* 282–292.

Wolfe, D. A. (1985). Child-abusive parents: An empirical review and analysis. *Psychological Review, 97,* 462–482.

Wolkind, S. N. (1974). The components of "affectionless psychopathy" in institutionalized children. *Journal of Child Psychology and Psychiatry, 15,* 215–220.

Wolpe, J. (1958). *Psychotherapy by reciprocal inhibition.* Stanford, CA: Stanford Univ. Press.

Woodrow, K. M., Friedman, G. D., Siegelaub, A. B., & Collen, M. F. (1972). Pain tolerance: Differences according to age, sex, and race. *Psychosomatic Medicine, 34,* 548–556.

Woodward, W. R. (1982). The "discovery" of social behaviorism and social learning theory, 1870–1980. *American Psychologist, 37,* 396–410.

Worell, J. (1978). Sex roles and psychological well-being: Perspectives on methodology. *Journal of Consulting and Clinical Psychology, 46,* 777–791.

Wozniak, P. R. (1984). Making sociobiological sense out of sociology. *The Sociological Quarterly, 25,* 191–204.

Wyndham, C. H. (1969). Adaptation to heat and cold. *Environmental Research, 7,* 442–469.

Wyszecki, G., & Stiles, W. S. (1967). *Color science: Concepts and methods, quantitative data and formulas.* New York: John Wiley & Sons.

Yano, K., Rhoads, G. G., & Kagan, A. (1977). Coffee, alcohol, and risk of coronary heart disease among Japanese men living in Hawaii. *New England Journal of Medicine, 297,* 405–409.

Yogman, M., Dixon, S., Tronick, E., Als, H., & Brazelton, T. B. (1977). *The goals and structure of face-to-face interaction between infants and fathers.* Paper presented at the biennial meeting of SRCD, New Orleans.

Yonas, A., Granrud, C. E., & Petersen, L. (1985). Infants' sensitivity to relative size information for distance. *Developmental Psychology, 21,* 161–167.

Yuille, J. C., & Cutshall, J. L. (1986). A case study of eyewitness memory of a crime. *Journal of Applied Psychology, 71,* 291–301.

Yussen, S. R. (1977). Characteristics of moral dilemmas written by adolescents. *Developmental Psychology, 13,* 162–163.

Zaccaro, S. J. (1984). Social loafing: The role of task attractiveness. *Personality and Social Psychology Bulletin, 10,* 99–106.

Zaidel, E. (1983). A response to Gazzaniga: Language in the right hemisphere, convergent perspectives. *American Psychologist, 38,* 542–546.

Zajonc, R. B. (1965). Social facilitation. *Science, 149,* 269–274.

Zajonc, R. B. (1976). Family configuration and intelligence. *Science, 192,* 227–236.

Zajonc, R. B. (1983). Validating the confluence model. *Psychological Bulletin, 93,* 457–480.

Zajonc, R. B., & Bargh, J. (1980). The confluence model: Parameter estimation for six divergent data sets on family factors and intelligence. *Intelligence, 4,* 349–361.

Zajonc, R. B., & Markus, G. B. (1975). Birth order and intellectual development. *Psychological Review, 82,* 74–88.

Zelnick, M., & Kanter, J. F. (1980). Sexual activity, contraceptive use and pregnancy among metropolitan-area teenagers: 1971–1979. *Family Planning Perspectives, 12,* 230–237.

Zentall, S. S. (1980). Behavioral comparisons of hyperactive and normally active children in natural settings. *Journal of Abnormal Child Psychology, 8, 93–109.

Zentall, S. S., Falkenberg, S. D., & Smith, L. B. (1985). Effects of color stimulation and information on the copying performance of attention-problem adolescents. *Journal of Abnormal Child Psychology, 13,* 501–511.

Zepelin, H. (1986). REM sleep and the timing of self-awakenings. *Bulletin of the Psychonomic Society, 24,* 254–256.

Zigler, A., Abelson, W. D., Trickett, P. K., & Seitz, V. (1982). Is an intervention program necessary in order to improve economically disadvantaged children's IQ scores? *Child Development, 53,* 340–348.

Zigler, E., & Levine, J. (1983). Hallucinations vs. delusions. A developmental approach. *Journal of Nervous and Mental Disease, 171,* 141–146.

Zigler, E., & Muenchow, S. (1983). Infant day care and infant-care leaves: A policy vacuum. *American Psychologist, 38,* 91–94.

Zins, J. E., & Barnett, D. W. (1983). The Kaufman Assessment Battery for Children and school achievement: A validity study. *Journal of Psychoeducational Assessment, 1,* 235–241.

Zitrin, C. M. (1981). Combined pharmacological and psychological treatment of phobias. In M. Mavissakalian & D. H. Barlow (Eds.), *Phobias: Psychological and pharmacological treat-* ments. New York: Guilford Press.

Zola-Morgan, S., Cohen, N. J., & Squire, L. R. (1983). Recall of remote episodic memory in amnesia. *Neuropsychologia, 21,* 487–500.

Zubin, J., & Spring, B. (1977). Vulnerability—a new view of schizophrenia. *Journal of Abnormal Psychology, 86,* 103–126.

Zuckerman, M. (1969). Variables affecting deprivation results and hallucinations, reported sensations, and images. In J. P. Zubek (Ed.), *Sensory deprivation.* New York: Appleton-Century-Crofts.

Zuckerman, M., & Gerbasi, K. C. (1977a). Belief in internal control or belief in a just world: The use and misuse of the I-E scale in prediction of attitudes and behavior. *Journal of Personality, 45,* 356–378.

Zuckerman, M., & Gerbasi, K. C. (1977b). Dimensions of the I-E scale and their relationship to other personality measures. *Educational and Psychological Measurements, 37,* 159–175.

Zuroff, D. C. (1986). Was Gordon Allport a trait theorist? *Journal of Personality and Social Psychology, 51,* 993–1000.

Zweigenhaft, R. L., Hayes, K. N., & Haagen, C. H. (1980). The psychological impact of names. *Journal of Social Psychology, 110,* 203–210.

Name Index

Geschwind, N., 332-333
Gherman, E. M.,
Gibson, C. J., 312
Gibson, E. J., 245
Gibson, J. J., 189
Gift, T. E., 523, 573
Gildrow, W., 190
Gillespie, C., 263-264
Gillum, R., 490
Gladdis, M., 553
Glass, C. R., 610
Glass, D. C., 163, 520
Glass, G. V., 590
Glass, R. M., 117
Glassman, A. H., 553
Glavan, L., 95
Glenn, N. D., 444
Glick, P. C., 448
Glover, H., 516
Gochros, H. L., 51
Goethals, G. R., 383
Goldberg, W. A., 267
Golden, M., 269
Goldfinger, K., 609
Goldfried, M. R., 491, 599
Goldman, M. S., 538
Goldman, R., 153
Goldstein, A. J., 528, 601
Goldstein, G., 494
Goldstein, G. I., 261
Goldstein, J. H., 391
Goleman, D., 218
Gonzales, L. R., 620
Goodall, J. vanL., 27-28
Goodman, I., 393
Goodman, N., 381
Goodwin, G. G., 282
Gordon, A., 153
Gordon, A. S., 286
Gordon, S., 427
Gottesfeld, M. L., 612
Gottesman, I., 576
Gottfredson, G. D., 10
Gottheil, E., 530
Gottschalk, L. A., 514
Gottman, J. M., 610
Goulston, K. J., 516
Graham, C. H., 204
Granrud, C. E., 246
Grant, V. W., 558
Grau, B. W., 426
Graves, T. D., 417
Gray, B. A., 589
Graziano, W., 426
Greaves, 556
Green, J., 510
Green, K. D., 271
Green, W. H., 551
Greenberg, M., 266
Greenberg, R. P., 594
Greenberg, S., 136
Greene, D., 107
Greer, S., 559
Greif, G. L., 268
Gribbin, K., 309
Griffitt, W., 519
Gross, L., 392

Grosscup, J., 568
Grossi, M., 269
Grossman, F. M., 347
Grossman, K., 251
Grossman, K. E., 251
Grossman, L., 151
Grossman, S. P., 151
Growdon, J. H., 312
Guggenheim, F. G., 574, 575
Guilford, J. P., 345
Gunderson, J. G., 552, 572
Gunnion, M. W., 150
Gurman, A. S., 589

Haaf, R. A., 245
Haagen, C. H., 386
Haan, N., 301, 483
Haber, R. N., 79, 87, 217
Haines, J., 263-264
Hake, J. L., 246
Halaris, A., 151
Halberstadt, A. G., 381
Halderman, B. I., 391
Haley, M., 190
Hall, E. T., 417
Hall, J. A., 381
Hall, V. C., 351
Hammen, C., 514, 568
Hampstead, W. J., 127
Hanks, R., 295
Hans, S., 246
Hansen, J., 538
Hantman, E., 272
Hantmann, S. A., 326
Harder, D. W., 523, 573
Harding, W. G., 517
Haré-Mustin, R. D., 589
Harkins, S., 403
Harlow, H. F., 21-22, 174, 241
Haroldson, S., 67
Harper, R. A., 608
Harris, W. G., 490
Harrison, W. R., 609
Hart, F. D., 133
Hartka, E., 301, 483
Harvey, J. H., 387
Hass, J. W., 375
Hatch, J. P., 127
Haughton, E., 602
Hayes, K. N., 386
Haynes, S. N., 490, 493
Hays, R. B., 517, 620
Hearnshaw, L. S., 355
Hebb, D. O., 192
Heckler, M. M., 312
Heimberg, R. G., 609
Hein, A., 190
Heinlein, R., 429
Heinold, W. D., 423
Held, R., 190
Heller, S. S., 163
Hellige, J. B., 122
Hemshorn, A., 312
Heninger, G. R., 528
Hennekens, S. H., 538
Henry, K. R., 222
Herbert-Jackson, E., 269

Herman, C. P., 151
Heron, W., 191, 192
Herring, E., 203
Hersen, M., 494
Hershaft, A. M., 426
Hershenson, M., 210
Hershman, S., 610
Hertzog, C., 309
Herz, M., 84
Heston, L. L., 576
Hilgard, E. R., 228, 611
Hill, C. T., 437
Hill, J. H., 607
Hill, W. F., 41
Hinckley, J., Jr., 558
Hirsch, H. V. B., 199
Hirsch, J., 151
Hirt, M. L., 616
Hitch, G., 89
Hite, S., 436
Hoberman, H. M., 522
Hobson, J. A., 138-139
Hochberg, J. E., 211-212
Hodges, K. K., 565
Hoff, E., 80
Hoffman, D. D., 210
Hoffman, S., 397
Hofstadter, L., 312
Holden, E. W., 127
Holder, M. E., 43
Hollis, J. F., 163
Holloway, F. A., 85
Holmes, D. S., 466
Holmes, T. H., 514
Holroyd, J. C., 228
Hoon, E. F., 127
Hoople, H., 417
Hoppes, E., 578
Horn, J. L., 354, 536
Horney, K., 525
Horowitz, F. D., 245
Horvath, F. S., 492
Hovland, C. I., 58
Howard, A., 10
Howard, K. I., 590
Howarth, E., 460
Hsia, Y., 204
Hsu, L. K. G., 553
Hubel, D. H., 115, 198
Hudspeth, A. J., 221
Huesmann, L. R., 392, 393
Hull, A. J., 88
Hunt, E., 431, 434, 435, 436, 437
Hunt, W. A., 612
Hurvich, L., 203
Huston, A. C., 394
Hyer, L. A., 609

Ilfield, F. W., Jr., 518
Ilg, F. L., 263-264
Ingbar, D. H., 137
Ingram, I. M., 529
Inhelder, B., 259
Inouye, A. R., 354
Insua, A. M., 347
Intraub, H., 79
Israël, M., 116

Subject Index

Figure and Table Credits:

Table 2.1, p. 41—Hill, W. F. *Principles of Learning: A handbook of applications.* Palo Alto: Mayfield Publishing Co., 1982

Fig. 2.6, p. 45—Pavlov, I. P. *Conditioned Reflexes.* London: Oxford University Press, 1927, p. 58.

Fig. 2.7, p. 45—Jenkins, H. M. & Harrison, R. H. Effect of discrimination training of auditory generalization, *Journal of Experimental Psychology,* 1960, 59, 244—253. Copyright 1960 by the American Psychological Association. Reprinted by permission of the publisher and author.

Fig. 2.8, p. 46—Adapted from *Psychology of learning and behavior* by Barry Schwartz, by permission of W. W. Norton & Company, Inc. Copyright ©1978 by W. W. Norton & Company, Inc.

Fig. 2.14, p. 60—Williams, C. D. Case report: The elimination of tantrum behavior by extinction procedures, *Journal of Abnormal and Social Psychology,* 1959, 59, p. 269. Copyright 1959 by the American Psychological Association. Reprinted by permission of the publisher and author.

Table 3.1, p. 78—Hall, J. F. *An invitation to learning and memory.* Boston, MA: Allyn & Bacon, 1982, p. 153.

Fig. 3.2, p. 87—Peterson, L. R., & Peterson, M. J. Short-term retention of individual verbal items, *Journal of Experimental Psychology,* 1959, 58, p. 195. Copyright 1959 by the American Psychological Association. Reprinted by permission of the publisher and author.

Fig. 4.1, p. 107—Erienmeyer-Kimling, L. & Jarvik, L. F. Genetics and Intelligence: A review. *Science,* 1963, 142, 1477—1479. Copyright 1963 by the AAAS.

Fig. 4.13, p. 132—© Michael Heron 1986/Woodfin Camp & Associates.

Fig. 4.14, p. 133 and Fig. 4.15, p. 134—Reproduced from *Some Must Watch While Some Must Sleep* by William C. Dement, by permission of W. W. Norton & Company, Inc. Copyright ©1972, 1974, 1976 by William C. Dement.

Fig. 4.16, p. 135—Reprinted by permission of *The New England Journal of Medicine,* 290, 487—499, 1974.

Fig. 5.1, p. 153—From Schacter, S. Some extraordinary facts about obese humans and rats. *American Psychologist,* 1971, 26, p. 130. Copyright 1971 by the American Psychological Association. Reprinted by permission of the publisher and author.

Fig. 5.3, p. 162—From Murray, H. A. *Thematic Apperception Test.* Cambridge, Mass.: Harvard University Press. Copyright 1943 by the President and Fellows of Harvard College, copyright 1971 by H. A. Murray.

Fig. 5.4, p. 165—From Lazarus, R. S., & Alfert, E. Shortcircuiting of threat by experimentally altering cognitive appraisal, *Journal of Abnormal and Social Psychology,* 1964, 69, 195—205. Copyright 1964 by the American Psychological Association. Reprinted by permission of the publisher and author.

Fig. 5.6, p. 173—Harlow Primate Lab, University of Wisconsin.

Fig. 5.2, p. 157—From *Textbook of Psychology* by D. O. Hebb. Copyright ©1972 by W. B. Saunders Company. Reprinted by permission of CBS College Publishing.

Fig. 6.1, p. 190—Held, R. & Hein, A. Movement produced stimulation in the development of visually guided behavior, *Journal of Comparative and Psysiological Psychology,* 1963, 66, 372—376.

Fig. 6.2, p. 191—Heron, W. The pathology of boredom, *Scientific American,* January, 1957, pp. 52—53.

Fig. 6.4, p. 194—Dowling, J. E., & Boycott, B. B. Organization of the primate retina: Electron Microscopy, *Proceeding of the Royal Society,* 1966, 166, 80—111.

Fig. 6.5, p. 195—From Pirenne, M. H. *Vision and the eye.* London: Science Paperbacks, Chapman & Hall, Ltd., 1967, p. 32.

Fig. 6.9, p. 198—Redrawn, with permission, from Neil R. Carlson, *Physiology of Behavior,* 2nd edition (Boston: Allyn and Bacon, 1981), p. 179.

Fig. 6.10, p. 199—Hubel, D. H. The visual cortex of the brain, *Scientific American,* 1963, 207, 54—62.

Fig. 6.12, p. 202—Reprinted with permission from *Vision Research, 4,* MacNichol, E. F., Jr., Retinal mechanisms of color vision. Copyright 1964, Pergamon Press, Ltd.

Fig. 6.14, p. 204—Reproduced from *The Journal of General Physiology,* 1960, 43, 115—128. By copyright permission of the Rockefeller University Press.

Fig. 6.20, p. 211—Beck, J. Effects of orientation and of shape similarity on perceptual grouping. *Perception and Psychophysics,* 1966, 300—302.

Fig. 6.22, p. 216—From S. M. Kosslyn, Information representation in visual images, in *Cognitive Psychology,* 1975, 7, 341—370.

Fig. 7.1, p. 244—Fantz, R. L., The origin of form perception, *Scientific American,* May 1961. Photo by David Linton.

Fig. 7.2, p. 245—Permission from the photographer, William Vandivert. Prior publication in *Scientific American* April 1960, 65.

Fig. 7.4, p. 250—Tanner, J. M. Standards from birth to maturity for height, weight, height velocity and weight velocity: British children, 1965, *Archives of the Diseases of Childhood,* 1966, 41, 455—471.

Fig. 7.6, p. 256—Fox, N., Kagan, J., & Weiskopf, S. The growth of memory during infancy, *Genetic Psychology Monographs,* 1979, 99, 91—130, a publication of the Helen Dwight Reid Educational Foundation.

Table 7.2, p. 247—Papilla, D. E. & Olds, S. W. *A child's world: Infancy through Adolescence* (3rd ed.) New York: McGraw Hill, 1982.

Fig. 8.1, p. 293—Kohlberg, L. The development of children's orientation toward a moral order: Sequence in the development of moral thought. *Vita Humana,* 1963, 6, 11—33.

Fig. 8.2, p. 298—From *The Seasons of a Man's Life,* by Daniel J. Levinson. Copyright © 1978 by Daniel J. Levinson. Reprinted by permission of Alfred A. Knopf, Inc.

Tables 8.2, p. 308; 8.3, p. 310; and 8.4, p. 313—From Bee, H. L. *The Journey of Adulthood.* New York: Macmillan Pub. Co. 1987.

Fig. 9.1, p. 329—Moskowitz, B. A. The acquisition of language, *Scientific American,* 1978, 239 (5), 92—108.

Fig. 9.2, p. 330—Free Press, a division of Macmillan, Inc., from Psycholinguistics, selected papers (Chapter 8, The first sentences of child and chimpanzee), by Brown, R. (Ed.). Copyright © 1970 by The Free Press.

Fig. 9.6, p. 345—Guilford, J. P. Three faces of intellect, *American Psychologist,* 1959, 14, 469—479. Copyright 1959 by the American Psychological Association. Reprinted by permission of the publisher and author.

Table 9.4, p. 361—Adapted from Jerome M. Sattler, *Assessment of Children's Intelligence and Special Abilities,* Second Edition. Copyright © 1982 by Allyn & Bacon, Inc. Used with permission.

Table 9.5, p. 362—Loehlin, J. C., Lindzey, G., & Spuhler, J. N. Race differences in intelligence. New York: W. H. Freeman Co., 1975.

Fig. 10.2, p. 391—Goldstein, J. H., Rosnow, R. L., Raday, T. Silverman, I. & Gaskell, G. D. Punitiveness in response to films varying in content: A cross-national field study of aggression. *European Journal of Social Psychology,* 1975, 5, 149—165. Copyright 1975. Reprinted by permission of John Wiley & Sons, Ltd.

Fig. 10.3, p. 393; Fig. 10.5, p. 402 and Fig. 10.7, p. 405—Baron, R. A. & Byrne, D. *Social Psychology: Understanding Human Interaction,* 5th Edition, Boston: Allyn & Bacon, Inc., 1987.

Fig. 10.4, p. 399—Milgram, S. Behavioral study of obedience, *Journal of Abnormal and Social Psychology,* 1963, 67, 371—378. Copyright 1963 by the American Psychological Association. Reprinted by permission of the publisher and author.

Fig. 11.1, p. 418—Altman, I. & Vinsel, A. M. Personal space: An analysis of E. T. Hall's proxemics framework. In Altman & J. F. Wohlwill (Eds.), *Human behavior and environment: Advances in theory and research* (Vol. 2), New York: Plenum Press, 1977.

Table 11.1, p. 433—Delamater, J. & MacCorquodale, P. *Premarital Sexuality,* 1979, Madison: University of Wisconsin Press.

Table 11.3, p. 436—Delamater, J. & MacCorquodale, P. *Premarital Sexuality,* Madison: University of Wisconsin Press, 1979.

Fig. 11.2, p. 438—From *Human Sexualities* by J. H. Gagnon. Copyright ©1977 by Scott, Foresman and Company. Reprinted by permission.